Canadian

Eighth

Edition

AUDITING
and Other
Assurance
Services

Alvin J. Arens
Price Waterhouse Auditing Professor
Michigan State University

James K. Loebbecke
Kenneth A. Sorensen Peat Marwick Professor of Auditing
University of Utah

W. Morley Lemon
PricewaterhouseCoopers Professor of Auditing
University of Waterloo

Ingrid B. Splettstoesser
York University

Prentice Hall Canada Inc.
Scarborough, Ontario

Canadian Cataloguing in Publication Data

Auditing and other assurance services

Canadian 8th ed.
Seventh edition by W. Morley Lemon, Alvin J. Arens, James K. Loebbecke.
Previously published under title: Auditing: an integrated approach.
ISBN 0-13-084192-7

1. Auditing. I. Arens, Alvin J. II. Title: Auditing: an integrated approach.

HF5667.A69 2000   657'.45   C99-932115-3

© 2000, 1997, 1993, 1987, 1984 Prentice-Hall Canada Inc., Scarborough, Ontario
Pearson Education

Prentice-Hall, Inc., Upper Saddle River, New Jersey
Prentice-Hall International (UK) Limited, London
Prentice-Hall of Australia, Pty. Limited, Sydney
Prentice-Hall Hispanoamericana, S.A., Mexico City
Prentice-Hall of India Private Limited, New Delhi
Prentice-Hall of Japan, Inc., Tokyo
Simon & Schuster Southeast Asia Private Limited, Singapore
Editora Prentice-Hall do Brasil, Ltda., Rio de Janeiro

ISBN 0-13-084192-7

Acquisitions Editor: Samantha Scully
Developmental Editor: Anita Smale, C.A.
Production Editor: Mary Ann McCutcheon
Copy Editor: Karen Kligman
Production Coordinator: Deborah Starks
Cover Design: David Chung
Cover Image: Eye Wire
Page Layout: Nelson Gonzalez

2 3 4 5   04 03 02 01 00

Printed and bound in USA

Visit the Prentice Hall Canada Web site! Send us your comments, browse our catalogues, and more at **www.phcanada.com**. Or reach us through e-mail at **phcinfo_pubcanada@prenhall.com**.

CONTENTS

PREFACE

The Canadian Eighth Edition of *Auditing and Other Assurance Services* contains many changes, two new chapters and numerous revisions, but the objectives and emphasis remain essentially the same.

The book is an introduction to auditing for students who have not had significant experience in auditing. It is intended for a one-semester course at the undergraduate or graduate level. The book is also appropriate for introductory professional development courses for public accounting firms, internal auditors, and government auditors.

The primary emphasis in this text is on the auditor's decision-making process. We believe the most fundamental concepts in auditing concern determining the nature and amount of evidence the auditor should accumulate after considering the unique circumstances of each engagement. If a student of auditing understands the objectives to be accomplished in a given audit area, the circumstances of the engagement, and the decisions to be made, he or she should be able to determine the appropriate evidence to gather and how to evaluate the evidence obtained.

The title of the book reflects the expansion of auditing beyond financial statement auditing to other assurance services. Our primary purpose is to integrate the most important concepts of financial statement auditing and the general assurance engagement framework. Integrated cases are used to emphasize practical aspects in a logical manner to assist students in understanding financial statement audit decision making and evidence accumulation. For example, internal control and fraud awareness is integrated into each of the chapters dealing with a particular functional area and is related to tests of controls; tests of controls are, in turn, related to the tests of details of financial statement balances for the area; and audit sampling is applied to the accumulation of audit evidence rather than treated as a separate topic. Since most organizations use automated information systems to some extent, issues related to auditing such systems are addressed in every chapter; no longer is there a separate "computer audit" chapter.

ORGANIZATION

The text is divided into six parts.

Part 1, The Auditing Profession (Chapters 1–4) The book begins with a description of the nature of auditing, of assurance engagements, and of firms that complete the engagements. Public accounting and the accounting bodies in Canada and professional associations are examined. International accounting standards are also discussed. In Chapter 2 there is a detailed discussion of auditor's reports. It emphasizes the conditions that affect the type of report the auditor must issue and the type of auditor's report applicable to each condition under varying levels of materiality. Chapter 3 explains ethical dilemmas, professional ethics, and the rules of conduct governing the professional activities of public accountants in Canada. Chapter 4 ends this part with an investigation of the auditor's legal liability.

Part 2, The Financial Statement Auditing Process (Chapters 5–10) The first two of these chapters discuss the auditor's and management's responsibilities, audit objectives, and general concepts of evidence accumulation. In addition, Chapter 6 emphasizes analytical procedures as an audit tool. The remaining chapters deal with planning the engagement and the decision process the auditor goes through. Chapter 8 introduces materiality and risk, and shows their effect on the audit. Understanding internal control and assessing control risk are discussed in Chapter 9, which emphasizes a proper methodology for understanding the two elements of internal control. Chapter 10 summarizes Chapters 5 through 9 and integrates them with the remainder of the text.

Part 3, Application of the Auditing Process to the Sales and Collection Cycle (Chapters 11–14) These chapters apply the concepts from Part 2 to the audit of sales, cash receipts, and the related income statement and balance sheet accounts. The first chapter explains sampling, combining the two chapters of the previous edition into a fourteen-step process that can be used for different forms of sampling. Then, the appropriate audit procedures for sales and cash receipts are related to internal control and audit objectives for tests of controls. The content in Chapter 13 is new and explains how analytical review can be used to achieve low, moderate, or high levels of assurance during the audit of the sales cycle. Chapter 14 uses audit objectives and the results of internal controls tests to formulate tests of details of balances. Students learn to apply audit sampling to the audit of sales, cash receipts, and accounts receivable by incorporating sampling into the appropriate test, and showing the design, conduct, and evaluation of the sample.

Part 4, Application of the Auditing Process to Other Cycles (Chapter 15–20) Each of these chapters deals with a specific transaction cycle or part of a transaction cycle in much the same manner as Chapters 12 through 14 deal with the sales and collection cycle. Each chapter in Part 4 is meant to demonstrate the relationship of internal control and tests of controls for each broad category of transactions to the related balance sheet and income statement accounts. Cash in the bank is studied late in the text to demonstrate how the audit of cash balances is related to most other audit areas.

Part 5, Completing the Audit and Offering Other Services (Chapters 21–25) This set of chapters begins by summarizing all financial statement audit tests, reviewing working papers, and looking at other aspects of completing the audit. Chapter 22 begins by reviewing the audit process in the context of automated information systems, explaining how the audit process expands, and how the basic-level topics have been incorporated into the text:

- Chapter 7 explains the importance of competence regarding information systems and how knowledge of business is affected.
- Chapter 8 has an appendix that describes the difference between centralized, decentralized, and distributed systems, and how this affects the type of information that needs to be collected during the development of knowledge of the business and assessment of risks during the audit process.
- Chapter 9 notes that control evaluation includes the control environment, general computer controls, and application controls. Categories of general controls are briefly explained using Hillsburg Hardware (an example business that is used throughout the text). Application controls include manual controls, controls performed by the computer, and controls that require both manual and computerized components.
- In Chapter 12, the chapter on the sales and collection cycle, the difference between the master file (semi-permanent data) and transaction data is shown. Tables are used to compare manual controls to simple batch system controls and to simple online system controls by audit assertion. Subsequent cycle chapters rely on the descriptions in this chapter. Subsequent cycles are not affected as much as the sales and collection cycle since this chapter includes a point-of-sale system. Audit tests and audit procedures have been updated to enable testing of all three types of controls (manual, automated, and combined). The appendix to this chapter explains the test data approach and generalized audit software.
- Chapter 16 includes a section on the conversion audit of an accounts payable system, i.e. audit tests needed when a computer system is implemented. It is handled in terms of audit assertions.
- Chapter 20, the cash chapter, reflects the increased use of electronic commerce and explains how to audit cash when it is transmitted electronically for debit cards, payroll payments, and automatic monthly payments (such as mortgages).

Special topics, such as data communications (including internet and hacking), disaster recovery planning, computer fraud, and automation in small businesses, complete Chapter 22.

Chapters 23 to 25 focus on assurance engagements and business advisory services. Chapter 23 examines various types of engagements and reports, other than the audit of financial statements, using generally accepted accounting principles. Topics covered include special engagements, reviews and compilations, the auditor's involvement with prospectuses, reports on the application of accounting principles, examinations of future-oriented financial information, and the auditor's involvement with pensions. Chapter 24 is new, and provides an overview of a variety of special topics, such as ISO-14000 audits (environmental management systems audits), forensic audits, and WebTrust. It is deliberately light reading, since its purpose is to tell students about all of the wonderful opportunities available to qualified accountants. (You may consider having students read chapter this chapter right after Chapter 1.) Chapter 25 focuses on operational auditing and comprehensive auditing.

SUPPLEMENTS

Several supplements are available for faculty and/or students' use.

Instructor's Manual with Media Guide This integrated resource assists the instructor in teaching the course. The features include instructions for assignments as well as helpful suggestions on how to effectively teach each chapter. To enhance and simplify course planning, chapter Learning Objectives are integrated throughout the problem material. This manual includes descriptions, questions, and solutions for the CBC videos that have been chosen to accompany this text. This manual also includes enlarged Transparency Masters of key text tables and exhibits.

Solutions Manual This comprehensive resource provides detailed solutions to all the end-of-chapter review questions, multiple choice questions, problems, and cases. The *Solutions Manual* includes answers to more than 600 review questions, more than 200 discussion questions, and more than 50 cases and integrated cases.

Test Item File The Test Item File contains over 3300 items, including the following question types: true/false, multiple choice, exercises/problems, critical thinking/essay, fill-in-the-blanks, and short answer. There are also questions adapted from professional exams, and questions on the chapter opening vignettes. Each test item in this effective testing tool includes the correct answer (or suggested answers for essay questions), and indicates the level of difficulty.

PH Test Manager (Windows CD-ROM), Prentice Hall's computerized test files, by Engineering Software Associates (ESA), Inc., uses a state-of-the-art software program that allows you to create tests and exams, then evaluate and track student results.

PowerPoint Electronic Transparencies A variety of PowerPoint slides are available for each chapter of the text. This computerized supplement provides the instructor with an interactive presentation that outlines the chapter material and reinforces text concepts using colourful graphics and charts. Instructors have the flexibility to customize the existing slides to meet their course needs. The supplement includes more than 900 slides, allowing instructors to click each key point on screen for an accumulating presentation of information.

Practice Set: The Lakeside Company—Case Studies in the Life-Cycle of an Audit
This updated and revised version of the efficient and effective Practice Set guides the student through the life cycle of an audit from beginning to end. Lakeside now uses more modern information systems, including a point-of-sale system that accepts debit cards and credit cards. In keeping with current audit practices, a greater emphasis on a risk-based audit approach is used. The cases are designed to create a realistic view of how an auditor organizes and carries out an audit examination. A *Solutions Manual* is also available.

Companion Website Learn more about this exciting resource on pages xvi and xvii.

ACKNOWLEDG-MENTS FOR THE CANADIAN EIGHTH EDITION

I am very pleased to welcome Ingrid Splettstoesser as a co-author on this edition. I believe that her ideas and contribution have made a great text even better.

I would like to thank my wife Sandra for her work and support for me; I dedicate this book to her.

W. Morley Lemon

I would like to thank my many colleagues at York University and at other institutions for their suggestions and comments. Thank you also for the assistance received from public accounting practitioners and legal professionals. In particular, I have benefitted from the very helpful reviews and assistance of John Beech, Chair of the Assurance Services Development Board; David Rozee, Deloitte & Touche; James Brown, Institute of Chartered Accountants of Ontario; Mark Davies, Maury Budin, and Sandy Law, KPMG; L. Denise Esdon, Ernst & Young; Neil McFadgen and Alan Bottomley, PricewaterhouseCoopers; Mindy Paskell-Mede, Nicholl, Paskell-Mede; Erik Peters, Ontario Provincial Auditor General, and staff members Paul Amodeo, Maureen Buckley, David Chan, John McDowell, and Larry Yarmolinsky; Ken Valallee, Arthur Andersen; Richard Wood, Richard Farrar, Don Sheehy, and Karla Tays-Dunphy, Grant Thornton; and Lynn Worthington and Mike Jones, BDO Dunwoody.

Thanks are also due to the following reviewers for their valuable feedback: Louise Hayes, York University; Bruce MacLean, Dalhousie University; Michael Maingot, University of Ottawa; Michael Perretta, Sheridan College; Sandra Robinson, Concordia University; and Scott Sinclair, British Columbia Institute of Technology.

Morley Lemon was a great sounding board for the ideas and changes that have been implemented in this edition. In addition, I would like to thank Morley for helping to usher this book through the latter stages of the production process while I dealt with a medical emergency. Patrick Ferrier and Anita Smale of Prentice Hall have been wonderfully supportive and helpful; their contributions are much appreciated.

Finally, I would like to thank my family for their love and support; I dedicate this book to them.

Ingrid B. Splettstoesser

The Prentice Hall Canada

companion **Website...**

Your Internet companion to the most exciting, state-of-the-art educational tools on the Web!

The Prentice Hall Canada Companion Website is easy to navigate and is organized to correspond to the chapters in this textbook. The Companion Website is comprised of four distinct, functional features:

1) **Customized Online Resources**

2) **Online Study Guide**

3) **Reference Material**

4) **Communication**

Explore the four areas in this Companion Website. Students and distance learners will discover resources for indepth study, research and communication, empowering them in their quest for greater knowledge and maximizing their potential for success in the course.

A NEW WAY TO DELIVER EDUCATIONAL CONTENT

1) Customized Online Resources

Our Companion Websites provide instructors and students with a range of options to access, view, and exchange content.

- **Syllabus Builder** provides *instructors* with the option to create online classes and construct an online syllabus linked to specific modules in the Companion Website.

- **Mailing lists** enable *instructors* and *students* to receive customized promotional literature.

- **Preferences** enable *students* to customize the sending of results to various recipients, and also to customize how the material is sent, e.g., as html, text, or as an attachment.

- **Help** includes an evaluation of the user's system and a tune-up area that makes updating browsers and plug-ins easier. This new feature will enhance the user's experience with Companion Websites.

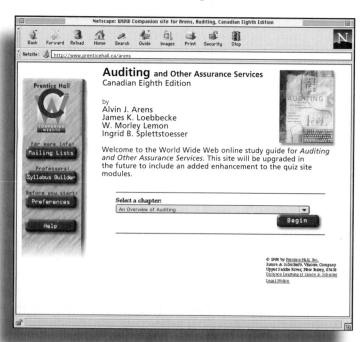

Prentice Hall

COMPANION WEBSITE

2) Online Study Guide

Interactive Study Guide modules form the core of the student learning experience in the Companion Website. These modules are categorized according to their functionality:

• Multiple Choice   • Problems   • Fill in the Blanks   • Essay Questions
The Fill in the Blanks and Multiple Choice modules provide students with the ability to send answers to our grader and receive instant feedback on their progress through our Results Reporter. Students can check suggested answers after submitting their problems.

3) Reference Material

Reference material broadens text coverage with up-to-date resources for learning. **Accounting's Greatest Hits** supplies links to hundreds of accounting and auditing websites. **Web Destinations** provides a directory of websites relevant to the subject matter in each chapter. **Net News (Internet Newsgroups)** are a fundamental source of information about a discipline, containing a wealth of brief, opinionated postings. **Net Search** simplifies key term search using Internet search engines.

4) Communication

Companion Websites contain the communication tools necessary to deliver courses in a **Distance Learning** environment. **Message Board** allows users to post messages and check back periodically for responses. **Live Chat** allows users to discuss course topics in real time, and enables professors to host on-line classes.

Communication facilities of Companion Websites provide a key element for distributed learning environments. There are two types of communication facilities currently in use in Companion Websites:

• **Message Board** – this module takes advantage of browser technology providing the users of each Companion Website with a national newsgroup to post and reply to relevant course topics.

• **Live Chat** – enables instructor-led group activities in real time. Using our chat client, instructors can display Website content while students participate in the discussion.

Companion Websites are currently available for:
• Horngren: Accounting
• Horngren: Introduction to Financial Accounting
• Horngren: Cost Accounting
• Horngren: Management Accounting
• Starke: Contemporary Mangement in Canada
• Kotler: Principles of Marketing
• Evans: Marketing Essentials
Note: CW content will vary slightly from site to site depending on discipline requirements.

The Companion Website can be found at:

www.prenticehall.ca/arens

PRENTICE HALL CANADA

26 Prince Andrew Place,
Don Mills, Ontario M3C 2T8

To order:
Call: 1-800-567-3800
Fax: 1-800-263-7733

For samples:
Call: 1-800-850-5813
Fax: (416) 299-2539
E-mail: phcinfo_pubcanada@prenhall.com

1

AN OVERVIEW OF AUDITING AND ASSURANCE SERVICES

ALL THAT GLITTERS ISN'T GOLD

Gold! Just as the discovery of gold in the Klondike started the 1890s gold rush in the Yukon, the announcement of a major gold discovery in Indonesia in 1993 sent Bre-X Minerals, Ltd. shares soaring on the Toronto Stock Exchange. The discovery had been billed as the "gold discovery of the century," and fights emerged over who had the rights to mine the gold.

There was plenty of intrigue surrounding the gold find. Fire destroyed all the geologists' records of the find, and the exploration manager mysteriously plunged from a helicopter in an alleged suicide just before the announcement that the gold discovery appeared to be a fraud. Allegedly, the gold samples on which the original discovery was based had been "salted" with gold, and the samples had been destroyed, preventing independent verification. However, a separate, independent analysis of the discovery by another company indicated insignificant amounts of gold, resulting in a 90 percent decline in the value of Bre-X shares.[1]

Source: William C. Symonds and Michael Shari, "After Bre-X, the Glow is Gone," *Business Week*, April 14, 1997, pp. 38–39.

---

[1]Each chapter's opening vignette illustrates important auditing principles.

Auditing provides many economic benefits to society. Most companies incorporated under federal or provincial legislation and meeting a size test must have an annual financial statement audit. This includes companies that obtain funds through securities markets or that obtain financing from banks and other financial institutions. In most cases, the borrowing company can obtain a lower rate by having a financial statement audit performed annually. Therefore, audited financial statements reduce the cost of capital.

Auditors, including public accountants, government auditors, and internal auditors, also assist companies in improving operations and internal controls. Auditors often make suggestions to management that ultimately reduce costs by promoting operational efficiency and reducing errors and fraud. Finally, when management and other employees are aware that an audit is being performed, they are often more careful in their work and are less likely to make errors or commit fraud.

This chapter presents background information about the nature of auditing and the major influences affecting auditing activities. Since audits are a subset of assurance engagements, this chapter also describes general assurance engagements. The first part of the chapter discusses professional accounting organizations in Canada. This is followed by a discussion of auditing in a broad sense. It describes what auditing is, why it is needed, the various types of audits and auditors, and the economics of financial statement auditing. Assurance engagements are defined and examples provided. The remainder of the chapter focuses on audits performed for purposes of external reporting by independent public accountants. It describes the nature of public accounting firms, the influence of the professional accounting organizations, the nature of generally accepted auditing standards and the Canadian Institute of Chartered Accountants' (CICA's) Assurance Recommendations and Guidelines. Quality control and the role of Canadian and U.S. securities commissions are the final topics in the chapter.

PROFESSIONAL ACCOUNTING/ AUDITING ORGANIZATIONS

OBJECTIVE 1-1

Describe the professional accounting organizations in Canada and how the professional designations CA, CGA, and CMA are obtained.

Canadian Institute of Chartered Accountants
www.cica.ca

Certified General Accountant's Association of Canada
www.cga-canada.org

Society of Management Accountants of Canada
www.cma-canada.org

Before beginning a discussion of auditing, it is appropriate to disclose who performs the auditing function — external and internal — in Canada. There are five major organizations in Canada or represented in Canada that provide a professional designation relating to accounting and/or auditing. The organizations, the designation awarded, and the manner of qualifying for the designation are discussed below. All organizations require that individuals have a university degree and obtain relevant work experience.

The senior body is the Canadian Institute of Chartered Accountants whose members are chartered accountants or CAs. The use of the title "chartered accountant" (CA) is regulated by provincial law. The educational requirements for becoming a CA vary among provinces, with a common experience requirement of 30 months. All provinces require that an individual, to qualify as a CA, pass a national uniform examination administered by the CICA.

The use of the title "certified general accountant" (CGA), awarded by the Certified General Accountants Association of Canada (CGAAC), is also regulated by provincial law. Experience requirements are set at a minimum of two years in a combination of intermediate and senior positions in accounting or finance. Individuals, depending upon educational background, must pass a variety of subject-based examinations, with a capstone national examination.

The Society of Management Accountants of Canada (SMAC) administers the Certified Management Accountant (CMA) program, leading to the CMA designation. The use of this title is also restricted by provincial law to those persons earning the right to use it. Students must also pass exams in required subject areas as well as uniform national exams after completing an SMAC course of study. It is possible to gain exemption from subject area exams by taking appropriate university courses. Students, furthermore, must meet experience requirements.

Institute of Internal Auditors
www.theiia.org

Information Systems Audit
and Control Association
www.isaca.org

Internal auditors have a professional organization, the Institute of Internal Auditors (IIA), and a professional designation, "certified internal auditor" (CIA). The designation is earned by passing a set of exams that are administered worldwide by the IIA and by meeting experience requirements. Unlike the other professional organizations discussed above, the IIA membership includes persons not having a CIA.

The Information Systems Audit and Control Association (ISACA) awards the CISA (Certified Information Systems Auditor) designation to individuals passing an international examination and meeting experience requirements. Persons not having the CISA designation can join ISACA as associate members, much like persons not having a CIA can join the IIA.

With the continuous changes in business environments, each of these organizations offers continuing education programs, providing the opportunity for members to go on to become specialists in particular areas such as taxation, information systems, management consulting, or business valuations. Professional organizations in many of these specialized areas offer specific programs of study leading to further specialist designations.

NATURE OF AUDITING

Auditing is the accumulation and evaluation of evidence about information to determine and report on the degree of correspondence between the information and established criteria. Auditing should be done by a competent, independent person.

OBJECTIVE 1-2
Define and explain auditing.

This description includes several key words and phrases. Each is discussed in this section and analyzed more extensively in later chapters. For ease of understanding, the terms are discussed in a different order than they occur in the description.

INFORMATION AND ESTABLISHED CRITERIA

To do an audit, there must be information in a *verifiable form* and some standards (*criteria*) by which the auditor can evaluate the information. Information can and does take many forms. Auditors routinely perform audits of quantifiable information, including companies' financial statements and individuals' federal income tax returns. Auditors also perform audits of more subjective information, such as the effectiveness of computer systems and the efficiency of manufacturing operations.

The criteria against which information is evaluated vary depending on the information being audited. For example, in the audit of historical financial statements by public accounting firms, the criteria are generally accepted accounting principles. To illustrate, this means that in the audit of Magna International Inc.'s financial statements, Ernst & Young, the CA firm, determines whether Magna International Inc.'s financial statements have been prepared in accordance with generally accepted accounting principles. For the audit of tax returns by Revenue Canada, the criteria are the provisions of the *Income Tax Act*. In the audit of Magna's corporate tax return by Revenue Canada, the *Income Tax Act*, rather than generally accepted accounting principles, would provide the criteria for assessment.

For more subjective information, such as auditing the effectiveness of computer operations, it is more difficult to establish criteria. Typically, auditors and the entities being audited agree on the criteria well before the audit starts. For a computer application, the criteria might, for example, include the absence of input, output, or programming errors.

Magna International Inc.
www.magna.ca

Ernst & Young
www.eyi.com

ACCUMULATING AND EVALUATING EVIDENCE

Evidence is defined as any information used by the auditor to determine whether the information being audited is stated in accordance with the established criteria. Evidence takes many different forms, including oral testimony of the auditee (client), written communication with outsiders, and observations by the auditor. It is important to obtain a sufficient quality and volume of evidence to satisfy the audit objectives. The process of determining the amount of evidence necessary and evaluating whether the information corresponds to the established criteria is a critical part of every audit. It is the primary subject of this book.

COMPETENT, INDEPENDENT PERSON

The auditor must be *qualified* to understand the criteria used and *competent* to know the types and amount of evidence to accumulate to reach the proper conclusion after the evidence has been examined. The auditor also must have an *independent mental attitude*. It does little good to have a competent person who is biased performing the evidence accumulation when unbiased information and objective thinking are needed for the judgments and decisions to be made.

Independence cannot be absolute, but it must be a goal that is worked toward, and it can be achieved to a certain degree. For example, even though an auditor of published financial statements is paid the audit fee by a company, he or she may still be sufficiently independent to conduct audits that can be relied upon by users. Auditors may or may not be sufficiently independent if they are also company employees. They would normally not be sufficiently independent for auditing published financial statements, but would be for auditing the efficiency of a company's computer operations.

REPORTING

The final stage in the audit process is the *auditor's report* — the communication of the findings to users. Reports differ in nature, but in all cases they must inform readers of the degree of correspondence between information and established criteria. Reports also differ in form and can vary from the highly technical types usually associated with financial statements to a simple oral report in the case of an audit of a small department's effectiveness.

Figure 1-1 summarizes the important ideas in the description of auditing by illustrating an audit of an individual's tax return by a Revenue Canada auditor. The objective is to determine whether the tax return was prepared in a manner consistent with the requirements of the *Income Tax Act*. To accomplish this objective, the auditor examines supporting records provided by the taxpayer and from other sources, such as the taxpayer's employer. After completing the audit, the Revenue Canada auditor will issue a report to the taxpayer assessing additional taxes, advising that a refund is due, or stating that there is no change in the status of his or her return.

Revenue Canada
www.rc.gc.ca

FIGURE 1-1
Audit of a Tax Return

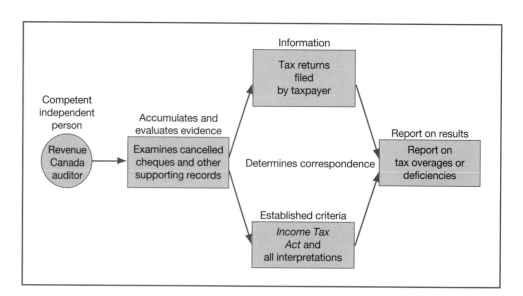

DISTINCTION BETWEEN AUDITING AND ACCOUNTING

OBJECTIVE 1-3

Distinguish between auditing and accounting.

Many financial statement users and members of the general public confuse *auditing* and *accounting*. The confusion occurs because most auditing is usually concerned with accounting information, and many auditors have considerable expertise in accounting matters. The confusion is increased by giving the title "public accountant" to individuals who perform the external audit function. The term "public accountant" is discussed on page 7.

Accounting is the recording, classifying, and summarizing of economic events in a logical manner for the purpose of providing financial information for decision making. The function of accounting, both to an entity and to society as a whole, is to provide certain types of quantitative information that management and others can use to make decisions. To provide relevant information, accountants must have a thorough understanding of the principles and rules that provide the basis for preparing the accounting information. In addition, accountants must develop a system to make sure that the entity's economic events are properly recorded on a timely basis and at a reasonable cost.

In *auditing* accounting data, the concern is with determining whether recorded information properly reflects the economic events that occurred during the accounting period. Since the accounting rules are the criteria for evaluating whether the accounting information is properly recorded, any auditor involved with these data must also thoroughly understand the rules. In the context of the audit of financial statements, these are generally accepted accounting principles. Throughout this text, the assumption is made that the reader has already studied generally accepted accounting principles.

In addition to understanding accounting, the auditor must also possess expertise in the accumulation and interpretation of audit evidence. It is this expertise that distinguishes auditors from accountants. Determining the proper audit procedures and the number and types of items to test, and evaluating the results are tasks that are unique to the auditor.

TYPES OF AUDITS

Four types of audits are discussed in this section: financial statement audits, operational audits, compliance audits, and comprehensive audits.

FINANCIAL STATEMENT AUDITS

OBJECTIVE 1-4

Describe the four primary types of audits.

An *audit of financial statements* is conducted to determine whether the *overall* financial statements — the information being verified — are stated in accordance with specified criteria. Normally, the criteria are generally accepted accounting principles, although it is also possible to conduct audits of financial statements prepared using the cash basis or some other basis of accounting appropriate for the organization. The financial statements most commonly included are the balance sheet, income statement, and cash flow statement, including accompanying footnotes.

COMPLIANCE AUDITS

The purpose of a *compliance audit* is to determine whether the auditee is following specific procedures or rules set down by some higher authority. A compliance audit for a private business could include determining whether accounting personnel are following the procedures prescribed by the company controller, reviewing wage rates for compliance with minimum wage laws, or examining contractual agreements with bankers and other lenders to be sure the company is complying with legal requirements. In the audit of governmental units such as school boards, there is increased compliance auditing due to extensive regulation by higher government authorities. In virtually every private and not-for-profit organization, there are prescribed policies, contractual agreements, and legal requirements that may call for compliance auditing.

Results of compliance audits are generally reported to someone within the organizational unit being audited rather than to a broad spectrum of users. Management, as opposed to outside users, is the primary group concerned with the extent of compliance with certain prescribed procedures and regulations. Hence, a significant portion of work of this type is done by auditors employed by the organizational units themselves. There are exceptions. When an organization wants to determine whether individuals or organizations that are obliged to follow its requirements are actually complying, the auditor is employed by the organization issuing the requirements. An example is the auditing of taxpayers for compliance with the *Income Tax Act* — the auditor is employed by the government to audit the taxpayers' tax returns.

OPERATIONAL AUDITS

Canada Post
www.canadapost.ca

An *operational audit* is a review of any part of an organization's operating procedures and methods for the purpose of evaluating *efficiency* and *effectiveness*. At the completion of an operational audit, recommendations to management for improving operations are normally expected. An example of an operational audit is evaluating the efficiency and accuracy of processing payroll transactions by a newly installed computer system. Another example, for which most accountants would feel less qualified, is evaluating the efficiency, accuracy, and customer satisfaction in processing the distribution of letters and packages by a company such as Canada Post.

Because of the many different areas in which operational effectiveness can be evaluated, it is impossible to characterize the conduct of a typical operational audit. In one organization, the auditor might evaluate the relevancy and sufficiency of the information used by management in making decisions to acquire new capital assets, while in a different organization the auditor might evaluate the efficiency of the paper flow in processing sales. In operational auditing, the reviews are not limited to accounting. They can include the evaluation of organization structure, computer operations, production methods, marketing, and any other area in which the auditor is qualified.

The conduct of an operational audit and the reported results are less easily defined than either a financial statement audit or a compliance audit. Efficiency and effectiveness of operations are far more difficult to evaluate objectively than compliance or the presentation of financial statements in accordance with generally accepted accounting principles, and establishing criteria for evaluating the information in an operational audit is an extremely subjective matter. In this sense, operational auditing is more similar to management consulting than to what is generally regarded as auditing. Operational auditing has increased in importance in the past decade. It is studied in greater depth in Chapter 25.

COMPREHENSIVE AUDITS

The term *comprehensive audit* was coined by James J. Macdonnell, a former Auditor General of Canada, to describe the auditing process carried out by his office. A comprehensive audit has three components:

1. a financial statement audit,
2. a compliance audit, and
3. a value-for-money audit, which is a form of operational audit. A value-for-money audit considers economy, efficiency, and effectiveness.

Comprehensive audits will be considered further in the following discussion of government auditors and in Chapter 25.

Table 1-1 summarizes the four types of audits and includes an example of each type and an illustration of three of the key parts of the definitions of auditing applied to each type of audit.

TABLE 1-1

EXAMPLES OF THE FOUR TYPES OF AUDITS

TYPE OF AUDIT	EXAMPLE	INFORMATION	ESTABLISHED CRITERIA	AVAILABLE EVIDENCE
Financial Statement Audit	Annual audit of TransCanada PipeLines financial statements	TransCanada PipeLines financial statements	Generally accepted accounting principles	Documents, records, and outside sources of evidence
Operational Audit	Evaluate whether the computerized payroll processing for subsidiary H is operating efficiently and effectively	Number of payroll records processed in a month, costs of the department, and number of errors made	Company standards for efficiency and effectiveness in payroll department	Error reports, payroll records, and payroll processing costs
Compliance Audit	Determine if bank requirements for loan continuation have been met	Company records	Loan agreement provisions	Financial statements and calculations by the auditor
Comprehensive Audit	Audit by the Auditor General of Canada Mortgage and Housing Corp. (CMHC)	CMHC financial statements and company records	Public sector accounting standards	CMHC documents, records, outside sources, and CMHC financial statements

TYPES OF AUDITORS

OBJECTIVE 1-5

Describe the primary types of auditors.

In this section, the four most widely known types of auditors are discussed briefly. They are public accountants, government auditors, Revenue Canada auditors, and internal auditors.

PUBLIC ACCOUNTANTS

Public accounting firms have as a primary responsibility the performance of the audit function on published financial statements of all publicly traded companies and most other reasonably large companies. Such an audit is known as an *attestation* engagement because the auditor attests to the fair presentation in the financial statements. If the shareholders appoint the auditors, the audit is a statutory audit. Because of the widespread use of audited financial statements in the Canadian economy, as well as businesses' and other users' familiarity with these statements, it is common to use the terms *auditor* and *public accounting firm* synonymously even though there are several types of auditors. Another term frequently used to describe a public accounting firm is *independent auditor*.

A number of Canadian provinces restrict the audit attest function to chartered accountants licensed in that province. Other provinces also license certified general accountants to perform the audit attest function, while still other provinces do not require a licence to perform an attest audit. The two bodies whose members perform most of the attest audits in Canada are the Canadian Institute of Chartered Accountants (CICA) and the Certified General Accountants Association of Canada (CGAAC). The term *public accountant* is used frequently throughout this book to describe an individual who is licensed to perform the audit attest function.

Most young professionals who want to become public accountants start their careers working for a public accounting firm. After they become public accountants, many leave the firm to work in industry, government, or education. These people may continue to be members of a professional body but may lose their right to practise as independent auditors. CAs and CGAs must meet licensing requirements to maintain their right to practise in most provinces. It is common, therefore, to find people who are CAs or CGAs but who have not practised as independent auditors for a time.

The Government of Canada and the various provincial governments have Auditors General who are responsible for auditing the ministries, departments, and agencies who report to that government. These government auditors may be appointed by a bipartisan committee or by the government or party in power in that jurisdiction. They report to their respective legislatures and are responsible to the body appointing them. The primary responsibility of the government audit staff is to perform the audit function for government. The extent and scope of the audits performed are determined by legislation in the various jurisdictions. For example, in 1977, the federal parliament made a revision to existing legislation in passing the *Auditor General Act* that required the Auditor General to report to the House of Commons on the *efficiency* and *economy* of expenditures or whether *value for money* had been received.

In 1984, the House of Commons passed *Bill C-24* which amended the *Financial Administration Act* with respect to Crown corporations.[2] The implications are significant for auditors in public practice and in the government. Included among its stipulations are the following:

1. Internal audits that look at financial matters or compliance with regulations, and audits that look at whether or not the operations are conducted in an efficient, effective, and economic manner are required.
2. External audits of the financial statements are required.
3. Special examinations of efficiency, effectiveness, and economy must be carried out every five years.

The audit responsibilities of these government auditors are much like those of a public accounting firm. Most of the financial information prepared by various government agencies and, in some cases, by Crown corporations is audited by these government auditors before the information is submitted to the various legislatures. Since the authority for expenditures and receipts of governmental agencies is defined by law, there is considerable emphasis on compliance in these audits.

James J. Macdonnell defined comprehensive auditing as being

> broader than the traditional financial audit. It assesses the adequacy of management control systems to ensure due regard to economy and efficiency, as well as the procedures employed to measure and report on the effectiveness of the programs on which the funds are spent. It calls for a combination of audit concepts and methods and integrates a variety of disciplines ranging well beyond the traditional financial accounting orientation. Comprehensive auditing at the federal level in Canada has introduced a new dimension of public disclosure: whether public funds have been providing value for money. This new dimension is . . . one of the key elements of comprehensive auditing.[3]

He was instrumental in organizing the Canadian Comprehensive Auditing Foundation in 1980. The foundation is made up of governmental auditors from the federal and provincial governments, accountants from the private sector, including public accounting firms, and academics. The goal of the foundation is to develop comprehensive auditing techniques to improve the work of the public sector auditor.

The Canadian Comprehensive Auditing Foundation defines a comprehensive audit as follows:

> An examination that provides an objective and constructive assessment of the extent to which:
>
> • financial, human, and physical resources are managed with regard to economy, efficiency, and effectiveness; and

---

[2]The interested reader is referred to *A Director's Introduction to the Audit and Special Examination Provisions of the Financial Administration Act* (as amended by Bill C-24) published by the Canadian Comprehensive Auditing Foundation from which this material is taken.

[3]From an unpublished speech given by James J. Macdonnell on May 14, 1980, to the second seminar of Senior Government Audit Institutions in Mexico City.

- accountability relationships are reasonably served.

The comprehensive audit examines both financial and management controls, including information systems and reporting practices, and recommends improvements where appropriate.[4]

An example of audit work in the public sector is the evaluation of the computer operations of a particular governmental unit. The auditor can review and evaluate any aspect of the computer system, but he or she is likely to emphasize the adequacy of the equipment, the efficiency of the operations, the adequacy and usefulness of the output, and similar matters with the objective of identifying means of providing the same services for less cost.

In many provinces, experience as a government auditor fulfills the experience requirement for a professional designation. In those provinces, if an individual passes the professional examination and fulfills the experience stipulations of the particular professional organization, he or she may then obtain the professional certification.

As a result of their great responsibility for auditing the expenditures of the various governments, their use of advanced auditing concepts, their eligibility to be professional accountants, and their opportunities for performing comprehensive audits, government auditors are highly regarded in the auditing profession.

REVENUE CANADA AUDITORS

Revenue Canada Taxation, under the direction of the Minister of National Revenue, has as its responsibility the enforcement of the federal tax laws as they have been defined by Parliament and interpreted by the courts. A major responsibility of Revenue Canada is to audit the returns of taxpayers to determine whether they have complied with the tax laws. The auditors who perform these examinations are referred to as Revenue Canada auditors. These audits can be regarded as solely compliance audits.

It might seem that the audit of returns for compliance with the federal tax laws would be a simple and straightforward problem, but nothing could be further from the truth. The tax laws are highly complicated, and there are hundreds of volumes of court interpretations. The tax returns being audited vary from the simple returns of individuals who work for only one employer and take the standard tax deductions to the highly complex returns of multinational corporations. There are taxation problems involving individual taxpayers, sales taxes, goods and services tax, corporate taxes, trusts, and so forth. An auditor involved in any of these areas must have considerable knowledge to conduct an audit.

INTERNAL AUDITORS

Internal auditors, many of whom are members of the IIA, are employed by individual companies to audit for management, much as the Auditor General does for Parliament. The internal audit group in some large firms can include over a hundred persons and typically reports directly to the president, another high executive officer, or even the audit committee of the board of directors.

Internal auditors' responsibilities vary considerably, depending upon the employer. Some internal audit staffs consist of only one or two employees who may spend most of their time doing routine compliance auditing. Other internal audit staffs consist of numerous employees who have diverse responsibilities, including many outside the accounting area. In recent years, many internal auditors have become involved in operational auditing or have developed expertise in evaluating computer systems.

---

[4]*Comprehensive Auditing: Concepts, Components and Characteristics*, Ottawa: Canadian Comprehensive Auditing Foundation.

To operate effectively, an internal auditor must be independent of the line functions in an organization, but will not be independent of the entity as long as an employer-employee relationship exists. Internal auditors provide management with valuable information for making decisions concerning the efficient and effective operation of its business. Users from outside the entity, however, are unlikely to want to rely on information verified by internal auditors because of their lack of independence. This lack of independence is the major difference between internal auditors and public accounting firms.

ECONOMIC DEMAND FOR AUDITING

OBJECTIVE 1-6

Discuss why reducing information risk is a prime economic reason behind the demand for financial statement audits.

Auditing services are used extensively by businesses, governments, and not-for-profit organizations. A brief study of the economic reasons for auditing is useful for understanding why auditing is so necessary, as well as some of the legal problems auditors face.

To illustrate the need for auditing, consider the decision of a bank manager in making a loan to a business. That decision will be based on such factors as previous financial relations with the business and the financial condition of the business as reflected by its financial statements. Assuming the bank makes the loan, it will charge a rate of interest determined primarily by three factors:

1. *Risk-free interest rate.* This is approximately the rate the bank could earn by investing in Canada Treasury Bills for the same length of time as the business loan.
2. *Business risk for the customer.* This risk reflects the possibility that the business will not be able to repay its loan because of economic or business conditions such as a recession, poor management decisions, or unexpected competition in the industry.
3. *Information risk.* This risk reflects the possibility that the information upon which the business decision was made was inaccurate. A likely cause of the information risk is the possibility of inaccurate financial statements.

Auditing has no effect on either the risk-free interest rate or business risk. It can have a significant effect on information risk. If the bank manager is satisfied that there is no information risk, the risk is eliminated and the overall interest rate to the borrower can be reduced. Even if information risk cannot be totally eliminated, its reduction can have a significant effect on the borrower's ability to obtain capital at a reasonable cost. For example, assume a large company has total interest-bearing debt of approximately $1 billion. If the interest rate on that debt is reduced by only 1 percent, the annual savings in interest is $10 million.

CAUSES OF INFORMATION RISK

As society becomes more complex, there is an increased likelihood that unreliable information will be provided to decision makers. There are several reasons for this: remoteness of information, bias and motives of provider, voluminous data, and the existence of complex exchange transactions.

Remoteness of information In the modern world, it is virtually impossible for a decision maker to have much firsthand knowledge about the organization with which he or she does business. Information provided by others must be relied upon. Whenever information is obtained from others, the likelihood of its being intentionally or unintentionally misstated increases.

Bias and motives of provider If information is provided by someone whose goals are inconsistent with those of the decision maker, the information may be *biased* in favour of the provider. The reason could be an honest optimism about future events or an intentional emphasis designed to influence users in a certain manner. In either case, the result is a misstatement of information. For example, in a lending decision in which the borrower provides financial statements to the lender, there is considerable likelihood that the statements will be biased in favour of the borrower to enhance the chance of obtaining a loan. The misstatement could be in the form of outright incorrect dollar amounts or inadequate or incomplete disclosures of information.

Voluminous data   As organizations become larger, so does the volume of their exchange transactions. This increases the likelihood that improperly recorded information will be included in the records — perhaps buried in a large amount of other information. For example, if a cheque issued by a large government agency in payment of a vendor's invoice is overstated by $200, there is a fairly good chance it will not be uncovered unless the agency has instituted reasonably complex procedures to find this type of misstatement. If large numbers of minor misstatements remain undiscovered, the combined total could be significant.

Complex exchange transactions   In the past few decades, exchange transactions between organizations have become increasingly complex and hence more difficult to record properly. For example, the correct accounting treatment of pension costs and obligations or the proper way to account for foreign operations pose relatively difficult and important problems. Other examples include the proper combining and disclosing of the results of operations of subsidiaries in different industries and the proper disclosure of derivatives under Section 3860 of the *CICA Handbook*.

REDUCING INFORMATION RISK

Managements of businesses and the users of their financial statements may conclude that the best way to deal with information risk is simply to have it remain reasonably high. A small company may find it less expensive to pay higher interest costs than to increase the costs of reducing information risk.

For larger businesses, it is usually practical to incur such costs to reduce information risk. There are three main ways to do so.

User verifies information   The user may go to the business premises to examine records and obtain information about the reliability of the statements. Normally, that is impractical because of costs. In addition, it would be economically inefficient for all users to verify the information individually. Nevertheless, some users perform their own verification. For example, Revenue Canada does considerable verification of businesses and individuals to determine whether tax returns filed reflect the actual tax due the government.

User shares information risk with management   There is considerable legal precedent indicating that management is responsible for providing reliable information to users. If users rely on inaccurate financial statements and as a result incur a financial loss, there is a basis for a lawsuit against management.

A difficulty with sharing information risk with management is that users may not be able to collect on losses. If a company is unable to repay a loan because of bankruptcy, it is unlikely that management will have sufficient funds to repay users. Nevertheless, users do evaluate the likelihood of being able to share their information risk loss with management.

Audited financial statements are provided   The most common way for users to obtain reliable information is to have an independent audit performed. The audited information is then used in the decision-making process on the assumption that it is reasonably complete, accurate, and unbiased.

Whenever more than one decision maker uses a particular type of information, it is usually less expensive to have someone perform the audit for all the users than to have each user verify the information individually. Since the financial statements of most companies have many users, there is considerable demand for auditing.

Typically, management engages the auditor to provide assurances to users that the financial statements are reliable. If the financial statements are ultimately determined to be materially incorrect, the auditor can be sued by both the users and management. Users sue on the basis that the auditor had a professional responsibility to make sure the financial information was reliable. Users are also likely to sue management. Management sues the auditor as an agent who had a responsibility to management to make sure the information was reliable. Auditors obviously have considerable legal responsibility for their work.

Summary   In business practice, all three methods are used to reduce information risk. As society becomes more complex, reliance on auditors to reduce information risk increases. In many cases, federal or provincial regulations have been passed requiring an annual audit by a public accounting firm. For example, all companies filing annually with the various provincial securities commissions, such as the Alberta Securities Commission, are required to have an annual audit. Similarly, governmental units such as Crown corporations and municipalities must be periodically audited. Although not required by specific regulations, many lenders such as banks require annual audits for companies having loans outstanding to their bank over a specific amount.

KPMG International
www.kpmg.com

CAPITAL COSTS TO SHRINK

According to a recent article in *Accounting Today*, corporations are paying too much for new capital and independent auditors are part of the solution. Robert Elliott, a senior partner with KPMG, believes that the cost of capital could shrink significantly in the next five years due to advances in technology, streamlined regulations, and broader audit coverage.

Elliott uses a hypothetical example to illustrate his prediction. Assuming a cost of capital of 13 percent, he estimates that this rate is comprised of the following:

- 5.5 percent risk-free interest rate
- 3.5 percent economic risk premium (*business risk*)
- 4 percent information cost (*information risk*)

According to Elliott's example, information risk comprises approximately 30 percent of the cost of capital. Elliott believes that the following factors will drastically reduce information risk in the next five to ten years:

- Technological advances, including reduction in silicon-based memory costs, will drastically decrease the cost of providing relevant and timely information to investors.
- As more companies go "on-line," the risk of investors obtaining outdated information decreases.
- New accounting and auditing standards already require better disclosures about segment operations, risks, and uncertainties. New rules may require data on nonfinancial performance and forward-looking information.
- Auditors will find more efficient ways to audit, which may provide new levels of assurance.

Elliott predicts that when and if all of the above factors materialize, the cost of capital in his hypothetical example could be reduced from 13 percent to 11.5 percent. The entire reduction would result from reduced information risk.

Source: Adapted from *Accounting Today*, December 11, 1995, p. 16.

ASSURANCE ENGAGEMENTS

OBJECTIVE 1-7

Define and provide examples of assurance engagements.

A financial statement audit is an example of a broader category of engagements called assurance engagements. Section 5025 of the *CICA Handbook* defines an assurance engagement as

> an engagement where, pursuant to an accountability relationship between two or more parties, a practitioner is engaged to issue a written communication expressing a conclusion concerning a subject matter for which the accountable party is responsible.

For a financial statement audit, one example of an accountability relationship is between management and shareholders. The practitioner (CA or CGA) would issue an audit report (the written communication) which expresses a conclusion regarding the financial statements (the subject matter for which the accountable party is responsible). Another example of an assurance engagement would be the practitioner attesting to the accuracy of data used in advertising.

Assurance engagements are discussed further in Chapter 23. Since the term "assurance" is broader than simply "audit," many public accounting firms are using the term "general assurance services" to include their financial statement related engagements rather than the term "audit."

PUBLIC ACCOUNTING FIRMS

OBJECTIVE 1-8

Describe the nature of public accounting firms, what they do, and their structure.

There are currently more than a thousand public accounting firms in Canada. These firms range in size from a sole practitioner to the more than 4,900 professional staff employed by Canada's largest CA firm, PricewaterhouseCoopers. Four size categories can be used to describe public accounting firms: "Big Five" international firms, national firms, large local and regional firms, and small local firms.

INTERNATIONAL FIRMS

PricewaterhouseCoopers
www.pwcglobal.com

Deloitte & Touche
www.deloitte.com

Arthur Andersen
www.arthurandersen.com

Grant Thornton
www.grantthornton.com

BDO Dunwoody
www.bdo.ca

The five largest accounting firms in the world, referred to as the "Big Five," include PricewaterhouseCoopers, KPMG, Deloitte&Touche, Ernst&Young, and Arthur Andersen. In Canada, the seven largest firms include the Big Five plus Grant Thornton and BDO Dunwoody.[5] They audit most of the 1,000 largest companies in Canada. Their gross revenues ranged from $148.5 million to over $685 million for 1999;[6] international revenues are more than $5 billion for the largest of these firms. These firms range in size from a staff of several hundred professionals in Toronto to smaller offices with fewer than twenty people.

These international firms are so large because they need to be able to serve all major international cities as the globalization of businesses increases. For example, if a Canadian company has branches in the United States, Brazil, and Spain, the public accounting firm doing the audit needs auditors in each of those countries. Each of the Big Five now has the capability to serve all major international markets.

NATIONAL FIRMS

Several other firms in Canada are referred to as national firms because they have offices in most major cities. Their revenues range from $11 million to more than $145 million.[7] These firms perform the same services as international firms and compete directly with them for clients. In addition, each is affiliated with firms in other countries and therefore has an international capability.

---

[5]*The Bottom Line* (April, 1999), p. 12.

[6]Ibid, p. 12.

[7]Ibid, p. 12.

LARGE LOCAL AND REGIONAL FIRMS

There are fewer than 50 public accounting firms with professional staffs of more than 50 people. Some have only one office and serve clients primarily within commuting distance. Others have several offices in a province or region and service a larger radius of clients. These firms compete with other public accounting firms, including the Big Five, for clients. Many of them become affiliated with associations of public accounting firms to share resources for such matters as technical information and continuing education. Firms in this category have revenues that range upwards to $7 million.

SMALL LOCAL FIRMS

Most of these public accounting firms have fewer than 25 professionals in their single-office firm. They perform audits and related services primarily for smaller businesses and not-for-profit entities, although some do have one or two clients with public ownership.

ACTIVITIES OF PUBLIC ACCOUNTING FIRMS

Public accounting firms perform seven broad categories of services: audits, reviews, compilations, special reports, tax services, management advisory services, and accounting and bookkeeping services. Audits, reviews, and many special reports are also assurance engagements (see Chapter 23).

AUDITS

Audits of historical cost financial statements are a major service provided by many of the larger public accounting firms. In the audit of financial statements, the responsible other party is the client who is making various assertions in the form of its published financial statements. The auditor's report expresses an opinion on whether those financial statements are in conformity with generally accepted accounting principles or another appropriate disclosed basis of accounting. External users of financial statements look to the auditor's report as an indication of the reliability of the statements for their decision-making purposes.

REVIEWS

Many smaller, non-public companies wish to issue financial statements to various users, but do not wish to incur the cost of an auditor's report to accompany them. A review, which provides a much lower degree of assurance than an audit, is usually provided to the company in such a situation. The amount of work done by the public accountant is considerably less than in an audit and so the cost to the client is less.

COMPILATIONS

A compilation involves the preparation by the public accountant of financial statements from the client's records or from information provided to the public accountant. The work done by the public accountant is much less extensive than in a review, and the cost is correspondingly much less. No assurance is provided by a compilation.

SPECIAL REPORTS

Public accountants may also prepare special reports for clients where the public accountant audits and provides an opinion on financial information other than financial statements or on compliance with an agreement or regulations, or where the public accountant performs specified audit procedures on financial information other than financial statements. For example, an auditor might provide an opinion on the sales at a Shoppers Drug Mart in a Saskatoon shopping mall because the store's rent is based on sales and the owner of the mall requires an audit opinion. (Reviews, compilations, and special reports are discussed in Chapter 23.)

TAX SERVICES

Public accounting firms prepare corporate and individual tax returns for both audit and non-audit clients. In addition, sales tax, tax planning, and other aspects of tax services are provided by most firms. Tax services are now performed by almost every public accounting firm, and for many small firms such services are far more important to their practice than auditing.

MANAGEMENT ADVISORY SERVICES

Most public accounting firms provide certain services that enable their clients to operate their businesses more effectively. These range from simple suggestions for improving the client's accounting system to aids in marketing strategies, computer installations, and pension benefit consulting. Many large firms now have departments involved exclusively in management advisory services with little interaction with the audit or tax staff. Examples of such services, also called *business advisory services*, are discussed in Chapter 24.

ACCOUNTING AND BOOKKEEPING SERVICES

Some small clients lack the personnel or expertise to prepare even their own journals and ledgers. Many small public accounting firms spend much of their time performing this type of work, termed *write-up* work. Many firms have used accounting software packages to provide bookkeeping services to clients. In some instances, the public accounting firm also conducts a review or even an audit after the bookkeeping services have been provided; in other instances, financial statements are compiled by the public accounting firm.

STRUCTURE OF PUBLIC ACCOUNTING FIRMS

Because of their responsibility for the audit of financial statements, it is essential that professionals working for public accounting firms have a high level of *independence* and *competence*. Independence permits the auditors to remain unbiased in drawing conclusions about the financial statements. Competence permits auditors to conduct the audit efficiently and effectively. Confidence in an auditor's independence and competence enables users to rely upon the statements. The large number of public accounting firms in Canada makes it impossible for users to evaluate the independence and competence of individual firms. Consequently, an organizational structure for public accounting firms has emerged that encourages, but certainly does not guarantee, these qualities.

The organizational form used by most public accounting firms is that of a *sole proprietorship* or a *partnership,* although some provinces allow special purpose limited liability partnerships. In a typical firm, several CAs or CGAs join together to practise as partners, offering auditing and other services to interested parties. The partners normally hire professional staff to assist them in their work. Most of these assistants for the assurance engagements are, or aspire to become, CAs or CGAs.

The existence of a separate entity to perform audits encourages independence by avoiding an employee–employer relationship between public accounting firms and their clients. A separate entity also enables a public accounting firm to become sufficiently large so that it is rare for any one client to represent a significant portion of a partner's total income, thereby endangering the firm's independence. Competence is encouraged by having a large number of professionals with related interests associated in one firm, which facilitates a professional attitude and continuing professional education.

The organizational hierarchy in a typical public accounting firm includes partners, managers, supervisors, seniors or in-charge auditors, and assistants, with a new employee usually starting as an assistant and spending two or three years in each classification before achieving partner status. The titles of the positions vary from firm to firm, but the structure is basically the same in all. When we refer in this text to the *auditor*, we mean the particular person performing some aspect of a financial statement audit. It is common to have one or more auditors from each level on larger engagements.

PROFESSIONAL ACCOUNTING ORGANIZATIONS

These organizations serve as umbrella organizations to which all certified members belong by virtue of their membership in a provincial institute/*ordre* or have joined as associate members (IIA and ISACA only). Depending upon the organization, they coordinate the examination processes, provide for continuing education activities, fund research projects, produce relevant publications, and engage in standard setting and peer review processes.

RESEARCH AND PUBLICATIONS

CAmagazine
www.camagazine.com

Each association has some form of monthly newsletter or national magazine. For example, in its role as representative of the CAs in Canada, the CICA publishes a wide range of materials. These include the monthly *CAmagazine*, accounting and auditing research studies, and the bi-annual *Financial Reporting in Canada*. It coordinates the Uniform Final [CA] Exam and publishes the Board of Examiners' Report on each year's exam. It also coordinates the common activities of the provincial institutes and *ordre*.

CONTINUING EDUCATION

CGA Magazine
www.cgacanada.org/
index.html

CMA Management Magazine
www.managementmag.com

The CICA is very active in continuing professional education, sponsoring seminars, and developing and providing material to the provincial institutes and *ordre* for use by their membership.

The Certified General Accountants Association of Canada plays a similar role in the professional lives of CGAs, as does the Society of Management Accountants of Canada in the lives of CMAs and the Institute of Internal Auditors in the lives of CIAs. For example, CGAAC publishes *CGA Magazine* and SMAC publishes *CMA*. In addition, CGAAC and SMAC administer exams and provide professional guidance and continuing professional education. They also conduct research and publish materials of interest to their members and students.

ESTABLISHING STANDARDS AND RULES

The CICA has been given the authority by the *Canada Business Corporations Act* and the various provincial incorporating acts to set accounting and auditing standards which must be followed by public accountants doing audits of companies chartered under one of those acts. This is done by stating that the financial statements should be prepared in accordance with the standards as set out in the *CICA Handbook*.

In its role as standard setter, the CICA supports research by its own research staff and, through grants, by others. It also sets the standards, which are called "Recommendations" and are codified in the *CICA Handbook*, and proposes guidelines and rules for members and other public accountants to follow.

You learned in an earlier accounting course about the accounting standards or Recommendations (Sections 1000 to 4999 of the *CICA Handbook*) issued by the Accounting Standards Board and about the Accounting Guidelines also issued by the Accounting Standards Board of the CICA. You also learned about the Emerging Issues Committee (EIC) of the CICA which issues Abstracts on contemporary accounting issues.

This text will focus on standards or Recommendations, issued by another body of the CICA, the Assurance Standards Board (ASB). It will also focus on Assurance and Related Services Guidelines and EDP Auditing Guidelines issued by the ASB.

Assurance and Related Services Recommendations are issued by the Assurance Standards Board and are the rules underlying the audits, assurance engagements, and related services activities carried on by the public accountants. Assurance and Related Services Recommendations are the italicized portions of Sections 5000 to 9200 of the *CICA Handbook.* These are considered to be authoritative rules.

Assurance and Related Services Guidelines also are issued by the Assurance Standards Board. They do not have the authority of Assurance and Related Services Recommendations and are either interpretations of existing Recommendations or the views of the ASB on a particular matter of concern. An example is Auditing Guideline 25 (AuG-25) issued in June 1998 entitled "Auditor's Report on Summarized Financial Statements."

EDP Auditing Guidelines also are issued by the Assurance Standards Board and have an emphasis on either auditing in an EDP environment or auditing using EDP. The EDP Guidelines do not have the authority of Assurance and Related Services Recommendations. An example is EDP Auditing Guideline 2 (EDP-2) "Computer-assisted Audit Techniques."

The Public Sector Accounting and Auditing Standards Board (PSAAB) was established by the CICA to issue standards and guidelines relating to accounting and auditing in the "public sector." In March 1999, auditing activities were transferred to the Assurance Standards Board (ASB), and PSAAB became PSAB (Public Sector Accounting Standards Board). The public sector is defined as federal, provincial, territorial, and local governments and government entities such as Crown corporations.

WAYS PUBLIC ACCOUNTANTS ARE ENCOURAGED TO PERFORM EFFECTIVELY

Because public accounting firms play an important social role, it is essential for the management of those firms and their professional staff to conduct themselves appropriately and do high-quality audits and other services. The various professional organizations (CICA and CGAAC) and other outside organizational influences have developed several mechanisms to increase the likelihood of appropriate audit quality and professional conduct. These are summarized in Figure 1-2 and discussed in the remainder of this and subsequent chapters. For example, the ability of individuals to sue public accounting firms exerts considerable influence on the way practitioners perform audits. Legal liability is studied in Chapter 4. The codes of professional conduct of the various accounting bodies also have a significant influence on members. The codes are meant to provide a standard of conduct for members who are in public practice. The codes and related issues of professional conduct are examined in Chapter 3. Shaded circles indicate items discussed in this chapter.

FIGURE 1-2
Ways the Profession and Society Encourage Public Accountants to Conduct Themselves at a High Level

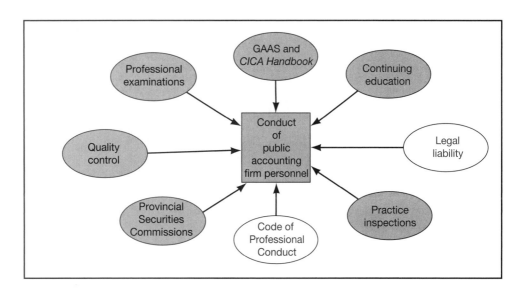

GENERALLY ACCEPTED AUDITING STANDARDS

OBJECTIVE 1-11

Use generally accepted auditing standards as a basis for further study.

Auditing standards are general guidelines to aid auditors in fulfilling their professional responsibilities in the audit of historical financial statements. They include consideration of professional qualities such as competence and independence, reporting requirements, and evidence.

The broadest guidelines available are the eight *generally accepted auditing standards* (GAAS) detailed in Section 5100. Developed by the CICA in 1975, they, with the exception of the changes to Examination Standards 1 and 2 which were amended in 1996 and 1992 and changes to the reporting standards which were substantially changed in 1990, have been little changed since their conception. These standards are not sufficiently specific to provide any meaningful guide to practitioners, but they do represent a framework upon which the CICA can provide Recommendations. These eight standards, summarized in Figure 1-3, are stated in their entirety as follows:

General Standard

The examination should be performed and the report prepared by a person or persons having adequate technical training and proficiency in auditing, with due care and with an objective state of mind.

Examination Standards

(i) The work should be adequately planned and properly executed using sufficient knowledge of the entity's business as a basis. If assistants are employed, they should be properly supervised.

(ii) A sufficient understanding of internal control should be obtained to plan the audit. When control risk is assessed below maximum, sufficient appropriate audit evidence should be obtained through tests of controls to support the assessment.

(iii) Sufficient appropriate audit evidence should be obtained, by such means as inspection, observation, enquiry, confirmation, computation, and analysis, to afford a reasonable basis to support the content of the report.

Reporting Standards

(i) The report should identify the financial statements and distinguish between the responsibilities of management and of the auditor.

(ii) The report should describe the scope of the auditor's examination.

(iii) The report should contain either an expression of opinion on the financial statements or an assertion that an opinion cannot be expressed. In the latter case, the reasons therefore should be stated.

(iv) Where an opinion is expressed, it should indicate whether the financial statements present fairly, in all material respects, the financial position, results of operations and changes in financial position in

FIGURE 1-3
Summary of Eight Generally Accepted Auditing Standards

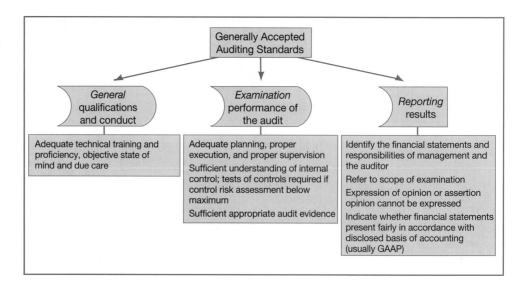

accordance with an appropriate disclosed basis of accounting, which except in special circumstances should be generally accepted accounting principles. The report should provide adequate explanation with respect to any reservation contained in such opinion.

AUDITING RECOMMENDATIONS

American Institute of Certified Public Accountants
www.aicpa.org

As was previously indicated, the Recommendations in the *CICA Handbook* are the most authoritative references available to public accountants performing audits of the financial statements of companies incorporated under the various federal or provincial incorporating acts or listed on one of the Canadian stock exchanges. In addition, CAs are required by their rules of professional conduct to follow the Recommendations of the *CICA Handbook*. The Recommendations are a framework for the auditor to use to assist him or her in the conduct of the audit engagement. The framework is built upon the eight generally accepted auditing standards. Frequently, these Recommendations are referred to as auditing standards or GAAS, even though they are not one of the eight generally accepted auditing standards.

Auditing standards in the United States are issued by the American Institute of Certified Public Accountants (AICPA). They are called Statements on Auditing Standards (SASs) and are numbered 1 to 85 (at time of writing). In certain areas, the CICA or AICPA will not have issued a Recommendation or will have different levels of detail. For example, SAS No. 85, "Management Representations," provides specific lists of representations to be obtained from management, whereas the *CICA Handbook* provides more general guidance. Another authoritative source would be International Standards on Auditing (ISAs) discussed on page 21.

The Assurance and Related Services Recommendations are classified as

5000	General Assurance and Auditing
6000	Specific Items
7000	Specialized Areas
8000	Review Engagements
9000	Related Services

New Recommendations are assigned a number within an appropriate series. For example, "Communication of matters identified during the financial statement audit" was assigned Section 5750 when it was issued in 1997.

Although GAAS and the Assurance and Related Services Recommendations are the authoritative auditing pronouncements for members of the profession, they provide less direction to auditors than might be assumed. There are almost no specific audit procedures required by the standards; and there are no specific requirements for auditors' decisions, such as determining sample size, selecting sample items from the population for testing, or evaluating results. Some practitioners believe the standards should provide more clearly defined guidelines for determining the extent of evidence to be accumulated. Such specificity would eliminate some difficult audit decisions and provide a line of defence for a public accounting firm charged with conducting an inadequate audit. However, highly specific requirements could turn auditing into mechanistic evidence gathering, devoid of professional judgment. From the point of view of both the profession and the users of auditing services, there is probably greater harm in defining authoritative guidelines too specifically than too broadly.

GAAS and the Assurance and Related Services Recommendations should be looked upon by practitioners as *minimum standards* of performance, rather than as maximum standards or ideals. Any professional auditor constantly seeking means of reducing the scope of the audit by relying only on the standards, rather than evaluating the substance of the situation, fails to satisfy the spirit of the standards. At the same time, the existence of auditing standards does not mean the auditor must always follow them blindly. If the requirement of a Recommendation is impossible to perform, the auditor might adopt some other course of action that allows adherence to the spirit of the Recommendation. Similarly, if the amount involved is not material, it is also unnecessary to follow the standard. It is important to note, however, that the burden of justifying departures from the standards falls upon the practitioner.

When the *CICA Handbook* is silent on an issue, the auditor must turn to other authoritative sources. These include the SASs issued by the AICPA, the ISAs issued by the International Federation of Accountants, textbooks, journals, and technical publications. Materials published by the CICA, mentioned earlier in the chapter, such as *CAmagazine* and audit technique studies, are particularly useful in furnishing assistance on specific questions.

In the remainder of this section, GAAS are discussed briefly. There is further study of the standards and frequent reference to General Assurance and Auditing Recommendations throughout the text.

ADEQUATE TECHNICAL TRAINING AND PROFICIENCY

The *general standard* stresses the important qualities the auditor should possess. The general standard is normally interpreted as requiring the auditor to have formal education in auditing and accounting, adequate practical experience for the work being performed, and continuing professional education. Recent court cases clearly demonstrate that the auditor must be technically qualified and experienced in those industries in which the auditor has clients.

In any case in which the public accountant or the accountant's assistants are not qualified to perform the work, a professional obligation exists to acquire the requisite knowledge and skills, suggest someone else who is qualified to perform the work, or decline the engagement.

OBJECTIVE STATE OF MIND

The importance of an objective state of mind or independence was stressed earlier in the definition of auditing. The *Rules of Professional Conduct* of the various provincial institutes of CAs and the *ordres* as well as the GAAS in the *CICA Handbook* stress the need for independence. The rules of conduct of CGAAC also stress the need for independence for CGAs engaged in public accounting. The *Canada Business Corporations Act* (*CBCA*), which is similar to several of the provincial incorporating acts, also requires the auditor to be independent. Public accounting firms are required to follow several practices to increase the likelihood of independence of all personnel. For example, there are established procedures for larger audits that usually utilize an audit committee whenever there is a dispute between management and the auditors.[8] Specific methods to ensure that auditors maintain their independence are studied in Chapter 3.

To assist the auditor, the CBCA specifies the auditor's qualifications in Section 161 but also provides the auditor with statutory rights and responsibilities. These give the auditor the right to attend shareholder meetings and the right to have access to the necessary records, information, and explanations necessary to conduct the audit. These rights afford the auditor the necessary access for completion of the audit.

DUE CARE

The general standard involves *due care* in the performance of all aspects of auditing. Simply stated, this means that the auditor is a professional responsible for fulfilling his or her duties diligently and carefully. As an illustration, due care includes consideration of the completeness of the working papers, the sufficiency of the audit evidence, and the appropriateness of the auditor's report. As a professional, the auditor

---

[8]An audit committee is a subcommittee of the board of directors of a company. The majority of the audit committee members should be composed of directors not belonging to management. The internal and external auditors usually report to the audit committee.

must not be guilty of negligence or bad faith, but he or she is not expected to make perfect judgments in every instance.

ADEQUATE PLANNING, PROPER EXECUTION, AND PROPER SUPERVISION

The *examination standards* concern evidence accumulation and other activities during the actual conduct of the audit in the field. The first standard deals with ascertaining that the engagement is sufficiently well planned and executed to ensure an adequate audit and that there is proper supervision of assistants. Supervision is essential in auditing because a considerable portion of the field work or examination is done by inexperienced staff members.

SUFFICIENT UNDERSTANDING OF INTERNAL CONTROL

One of the most widely accepted points in the theory and practice of auditing is the importance of the client's accounting systems and whether internal controls are sufficient to generate reliable financial information. If the auditor is convinced the client has excellent controls that provide reliable data and safeguard assets and records, the amount of audit evidence to be accumulated can be significantly less than for a system that is not adequate. In some instances, the controls may be so inadequate as to preclude reliance on the data in the records and an audit may not be possible.

SUFFICIENT APPROPRIATE AUDIT EVIDENCE

The decision as to how much evidence and of what quality to accumulate for a given set of circumstances is one requiring professional judgment. A major portion of this book is concerned with the study of evidence accumulation and the circumstances affecting the amount needed.

FOUR REPORTING STANDARDS

The four reporting standards require the auditor to prepare a report on the financial statements identifying the financial statements and the responsibilities of management and the auditors and indicating the scope of the auditor's examination. The report must contain either an expression of opinion or explain why no opinion can be expressed. The opinion should indicate whether or not the statements are in accordance with an appropriate disclosed basis of accounting (usually GAAP). Section 5400 of the *CICA Handbook*, which deals more specifically with the auditor's report, is discussed in Chapter 2.

INTERNATIONAL AUDITING STANDARDS

The CICA, the CGAAC, and the SMAC are members of the International Federation of Accountants (IFAC), a body that seeks to harmonize auditing standards on a worldwide basis. IFAC, through the International Auditing Practices Committee (IAPC), issues International Standards on Auditing (ISAs) and International Auditing Practice Statements (IAPS) for the guidance of accountants in member countries. ISAs are standards and are authoritative while IAPS provide guidance and are not authoritative.

In addition, the provincial securities commissions are members of the International Organization of Securities Commissions (IOSCO). IOSCO members are concerned with securities which are issued by a company in one country and sold in a second country. For example, shares of Inco, a Canadian company, are traded on the Toronto Stock Exchange (under the jurisdiction of the Ontario Securities Commission [OSC]) and on the New York Stock Exchange (under the jurisdiction of the U.S. Securities and Exchange Commission [SEC]); Inco's shares are said to be "cross-listed." Both the OSC and the SEC are members of IOSCO. IOSCO members are concerned about International Auditing Standards as they have to decide on the quality, sufficiency, and appropriateness of evidence collected and the report issued for audits of financial statements submitted to them for cross-listing.

Section 5101 of the *CICA Handbook* is entitled "International Standards on Auditing." It describes the CICA's role in IFAC and IAPC. It also describes the comparison process the Assurance Standards Board goes through when a new ISA is issued or when the *Handbook* is changed in order to provide guidance to Canadian auditors as to significant differences between Canadian and IAPC standards and thus GAAS. Finally, the ISAs are compared to the *CICA Handbook* and the differences noted.

A Canadian auditor must conduct an audit of a Canadian or foreign company in accordance with Canadian GAAS (i.e., follow the *Handbook*) and may, in addition, conduct the audit in accordance with international GAAS (i.e., the ISAs or the GAAS of another country such as the U.S.). In such a case, the auditor may report that the audit was conducted using Canadian and foreign GAAS. It is important to note that Canadian GAAS would be the floor in this case.

Where there are reporting differences between Canadian GAAS and the ISAs or foreign GAAS, the auditor should follow Canadian reporting standards. An example is the Auditing Guideline 21 "Canadian–United States Reporting Conflicts." AuG-21 requires the auditor to issue an auditor's report in compliance with Canadian GAAS and to also issue a separate comment explaining the conflict between the reporting standards.

The *Handbook* takes precedence over the ISAs when there is a conflict. For example, if the auditor discovers a material misstatement, paragraph 5135.22 of the *CICA Handbook* requires the auditor to communicate the fact of the misstatement to the audit committee. ISA 240, "Fraud and Error" is silent on the matter. If a Canadian auditor discovered a material misstatement in the conduct of a statutory audit, he or she would be obliged to follow paragraph 5135.22 and not ISA 240.

A Canadian auditor who is engaged to conduct an examination in accordance with International Standards on Auditing should not just rely on Section 5101 of the *Handbook* as a source for his or her knowledge of the ISAs but rather should consult the most current version of the *IFAC Handbook* for the ISAs themselves.

There are two broad areas where the *IFAC Handbook* differs from the *CICA Handbook*. The *IFAC Handbook* generally provides more detailed procedural guidance in certain areas, and it includes guidance on issues that are covered in Canada by the rules of conduct of the provincial institutes and *ordre* of CAs.

QUALITY CONTROL

OBJECTIVE 1-14

Identify quality control standards and practices within the accounting profession.

For a public accounting firm, quality control comprises the methods used to make sure that the firm meets its professional responsibilities to clients. These methods include the organizational structure of the public accounting firm and the procedures the firm sets up. For example, a public accounting firm might have an organizational structure that assures the technical review of every engagement by a partner who has expertise in the client's industry.

Quality control is closely related to, but distinct from, GAAS. A public accounting firm must make sure that generally accepted auditing standards are followed on every audit. Quality controls are the methods used by the firm that help it meet those standards consistently on every engagement. Quality controls are therefore established for the entire public accounting firm and all the activities in which the firm is involved; GAAS, on the other hand, are applied to each engagement on an individual basis.

While Canada does not have explicit quality control standards, in the United States SAS 25 requires a CPA firm to establish quality control policies and procedures. The standard recognizes that a quality control system can only provide reasonable assurance, rather than a guarantee, that GAAS are followed.

While neither the CICA nor the AICPA has set out specific quality control procedures for public accounting firms, both have provided guidance to practitioners in public practice. In 1993, the CICA published a monograph, *Guide for Development of Quality Control Systems in Public Accounting*. Don MacLean, the study's author, suggests that public accounting firms should consider clients, personnel, professional engagement management, practice management, and quality control assessment as part of quality control. The Assurance Standards Board suggested five elements of quality control that public accounting firms should consider in setting up their own policies and procedures. The elements are described in Table 1-2.

TABLE 1-2

FIVE ELEMENTS OF
QUALITY CONTROL

ELEMENT	SUMMARY OF REQUIREMENTS	EXAMPLE OF A PROCEDURE
Independence, integrity, and objectivity	All personnel on engagements should maintain independence in fact and in appearance, perform all professional responsibilities with integrity, and maintain objectivity in performing their professional responsibilities.	Each partner and employee must answer an "independence questionnaire" annually, dealing with such things as stock ownership and membership on boards of directors.
Personnel management	Policies and procedures should be established to provide the firm with reasonable assurance that: • All new personnel should be qualified to perform their work competently. • Work is assigned to personnel who have adequate technical training and proficiency. • All personnel should participate in continuing professional education and professional development activities that enable them to fulfill their assigned responsibilities. • Personnel selected for advancement have the qualifications necessary for fulfillment of their assigned responsibilities.	Each professional must be evaluated on every engagement using the firm's individual engagement evaluation report.
Acceptance and continuation of clients and engagements	Policies and procedures should be established for deciding whether to accept or continue a client relationship. These policies and procedures should minimize the risk of associating with a client whose management lacks integrity. The firm should also only undertake engagements that can be completed with professional competence.	A client evaluation form, dealing with such matters as predecessor auditor comments and evaluation of management, must be prepared for every new client before acceptance.
Engagement performance	Policies and procedures should exist to make sure that the work performed by engagement personnel meets applicable professional standards, regulatory requirements, and the firm's standards of quality.	The firm's director of accounting and auditing is available for consultation and must approve all engagements before their completion.
Monitoring	Policies and procedures should exist to make sure that the other four quality control elements are being effectively applied.	The quality control partner must test the quality control procedures at least annually to make sure the firm is in compliance.

The quality control procedures that a public accounting firm employs will depend on the size of the firm, the number of practice offices, and the nature of the practice. The quality control procedures of a 150-office international firm with many complex multinational clients would vary considerably from those of a 5-person firm specializing in small audits in one or two industries.

One of the ways in which the CA profession in Canada has dealt with quality control is through the establishment of *practice inspection* by the provincial institutes and *ordre*. Practice inspection is administered by the provincial institute or *ordre* and is usually mandatory for CAs in public practice. A practice inspection of each practice unit (usually an office but it could be each partner in the office) is normally completed every four years but could be yearly if the practice unit is not found to be maintaining the level of practice standards set forth by the provincial practice inspection committee.

In essence, practice inspection involves a review, by full-time or part-time practice inspectors hired by the provincial practice inspection committee, of the practice unit's quality control procedures over its auditing and review engagements and the unit's compliance with the *CICA Handbook*. Practice inspection in Ontario is representative of that carried out by other provincial institutes and is used to illustrate practice inspection generally. The practice procedures to be reviewed have been determined by the Institute of Chartered Accountants of Ontario to include

- File and statement preparation including the use of appropriate forms, documentation, and second-person review
- Objectivity
- Maintenance of professional skills and standards through professional development, review of periodicals, self-study, and other aids
- Staff recruiting, advancement, and supervision including planning and budgeting of time, assigning of personnel, on-the-job training, and staff progress reviews
- Outside consultation as necessary, including the use of practice advisers, the CICA technical advisory bureau, other practitioners, and non-CA specialists
- Office administration in relation to supervision of internal quality control, liability insurance, file retention, professional conduct, and acceptance and continuation of engagements

The amount of work done by the practice inspector depends on the degree of documentation the practice unit has on its quality control procedures. If the controls are well documented and the practice inspector finds that the controls are being complied with, the inspection will be much briefer than if there is no documentation or if the controls are not being complied with.

While the purpose of practice inspection in Ontario is educational, the Practice Inspection Committee does have sanctions it can impose. These include re-inspection the following year and referral to the Professional Conduct Committee, whose powers include the power to require the member to take courses, the power to remove the practice unit's right to train students, and the power to expel the member from the Institute and forfeit the member's right to use the appellation Chartered Accountant.

Practice inspection can be beneficial to the profession and individual firms. The profession gains if reviews result in practitioners doing higher quality audits. A firm can also gain if the practice inspection improves the firm's practices and thereby enhances its reputation and effectiveness and reduces the likelihood of lawsuits. Of course, practice inspection is costly. There is always a trade-off between costs and benefits.

Another form of quality control is continuing professional education or professional development. As mentioned earlier, each of the three professional accounting bodies have professional development programs created to assist its members in maintaining their professional skills. It behooves the member, whether in practice or in industry, government, or education, to avail himself or herself of professional development opportunities.

PROVINCIAL SECURITIES COMMISSIONS

OBJECTIVE 1-15

Summarize the role of securities commissions in Canada and the U.S.

Securities regulation in Canada is a provincial matter; therefore, companies that issue securities in Canada must abide by rules promulgated by the provincial securities commission. There is an umbrella organization, the Canadian Securities Administrators, made up of members of the securities commissions of British Columbia, Alberta, Saskatchewan, Manitoba, Ontario, and Quebec, which sets policies to which the member commissions agree to adhere. For example, *National Policy Statement No. 27*, issued in 1972, established the *CICA Handbook* as GAAP for securities issued under the authority of the members of the Canadian Securities Administrators.

The provincial securities commissions are responsible for administering the purchase and sale of securities within their jurisdictions. For example, the British Columbia Securities Commission includes the Vancouver Stock Exchange in its jurisdiction. While the *CICA Handbook* sets GAAP for prospectuses in Section 4000, the securities commissions must approve each actual prospectus. Prospectuses are discussed further in Chapter 23.

SECURITIES AND EXCHANGE COMMISSION

Since many Canadian companies sell their stocks and borrow money in the United States, they must meet the requirements of the Securities and Exchange Commission (SEC). It is therefore appropriate to review the functions and operations of that body.

The overall purpose of the Securities and Exchange Commission an agency of the U.S. federal government, is to assist in providing investors with reliable information upon which to make investment decisions. To this end, the *Securities Act of 1933* requires most companies planning to issue new securities to the public to submit a registration statement to the SEC for approval. The *Securities Act of 1934* provides additional protection by requiring the same companies and others to file detailed annual reports with the commission. The commission examines these statements for completeness and adequacy before permitting a company to sell its securities through the securities exchanges.

Although the SEC requires considerable information that is not of direct interest to CPAs, the securities acts of 1933 and 1934 require financial statements, accompanied by the opinion of an independent certified public accountant, as part of a registration statement and subsequent reports.

Of special interest to auditors are several specific reports that are subject to the reporting provisions of the securities acts. The most important of these are the following:

- *Forms S-1 to S-16.* These forms must be completed and registered with the SEC whenever a company plans to issue new securities to the public. The S-1 form is the general form when there is no specifically prescribed form. The others are specialized forms. For example, S-10 is for restrictions of landholders' royalty interests in gas and oil. All S forms apply to the *Securities Act of 1933*.
- *Form 8-K.* This report is filed at the end of any month in which significant events have occurred that are of interest to public investors. Such events include the acquisition or sale of a subsidiary, a change in officers or directors, an addition of a new product line, or a change in auditors.
- *Form 10-K.* This report must be filed annually within 90 days after the close of each fiscal year. Extensive detailed financial information is contained in this report, including audited financial statements.
- *Form 10-Q.* This report must be filed quarterly for all publicly held companies. It contains certain financial information and requires audit involvement whenever there is a change in accounting principles.

Since large CPA firms usually have clients that must file one or more of these reports each year, and the rules and regulations affecting filings with the SEC are extremely complex, most CPA firms have specialists who spend a large portion of their time making sure their clients satisfy all SEC requirements.

The SEC has considerable influence in setting generally accepted accounting principles and disclosure requirements for financial statements as a result of its authority for specifying reporting requirements considered necessary for fair disclosure to investors. The AICPA's Accounting Principles Board followed the practice of working closely with the SEC, and the successor Financial Accounting Standards Board (FASB) has continued that tradition. In addition, the SEC has power to establish rules for any CPA associated with audited financial statements submitted to the commission. Even though the commission has taken the position that accounting principles and auditing standards should be set by the profession, the SEC's attitude is generally considered in any major change proposed by the FASB or the AICPA or the Auditing Standards Board.

The SEC requirements of greatest interest to CPAs are set forth in the commission's *Regulation S-X* and Accounting Series Releases. These publications constitute important basic regulations, as well as decisions and opinions on accounting and auditing issues affecting any CPA dealing with publicly held companies.

ESSENTIAL TERMS

Accounting — the recording, classifying, and summarizing of economic events in a logical manner for the purpose of providing financial information for decision making (p. 5).

Assurance and Related Services Guidelines — interpretations of Assurance and Related Services Recommendations or views of the Assurance Standards Board on particular matters of concern; less authoritative than Assurance and Related Services Recommendations (p. 17).

Assurance and Related Services Recommendations — a framework for the auditor to use to assist him or her in the conduct of an audit engagement; the rules underlying the audits and related services activities carried on by public accountants; the italicized portions of Volume II of the *CICA Handbook*. They are issued by the Assurance Standards Board (p. 17).

Assurance engagement — issuance of a written communication expressing a conclusion on a subject matter where an accountable party is responsible as part of an accountability relationship (p. 13).

Attestation — a written communication regarding the reliability of another party's written assertion (p. 7).

Auditing — the accumulation and evaluation of evidence about information to determine and report on the degree of correspondence between the information and established criteria (p. 3).

Assurance Standards Board — a committee of the CICA that has the responsibility for issuing Assurance and Related Services Recommendations and Assurance and Related Services Guidelines (p. 17).

Auditor General — responsible for auditing federal and provincial ministries, departments, and agencies, including Crown corporations (p. 8).

Auditor's report — the communication of audit findings to users (p. 4).

Canadian Comprehensive Auditing Foundation (CCAF) — develops comprehensive auditing techniques to assist the work of public sector auditors (p. 8).

Canadian Institute of Chartered Accountants (CICA) — sets the accounting and auditing standards in the private and public sectors which must be followed by public accountants in Canada; one of the three major accounting organizations in Canada providing a professional designation relating to accounting and auditing; umbrella organization of the provincial institutes and *ordre* that regulates the CA profession in Canada (p. 2).

Certified General Accountant (CGA) — one of three professional designations in Canada relating to accounting and auditing (p. 2).

Certified General Accountants Association of Canada (CGAAC) — one of the three major accounting organizations in Canada providing a professional designation relating to accounting and auditing; umbrella organization of the provincial associations that regulates the CGA profession in Canada (p. 2).

Certified Management Accountant (CMA) — one of three professional designations in Canada relating to accounting and auditing (p. 2).

Chartered Accountant (CA) — one of three professional designations in Canada relating to accounting and auditing (p. 2).

Compliance audit — (1) a review of an organization's financial records performed to determine whether the organization is following specific procedures, rules, or regulations set down by some higher authority; (2) an audit performed to determine whether an entity that receives financial assistance from a federal or provincial government has complied with specific laws and regulations (p. 5).

Comprehensive audit — audit in the public sector consisting of three components: (1) financial statement audit; (2) compliance audit; (3) value-for-money audit (p. 6).

Evidence — any information used by the auditor to determine whether the information being audited is stated in accordance with established criteria (p. 3).

Financial statement audit — an audit conducted to determine whether the overall financial statements of an entity are stated in accordance with specified criteria (usually GAAP) (p. 5).

Generally accepted auditing standards (GAAS) — eight auditing standards, developed by the CICA, consisting of the general standard, examination standards, and reporting standards; often called auditing standards (p. 18).

Independent auditor — a public accountant or accounting firm that performs audits of commercial and noncommercial entities (p. 7).

Information risk — the risk that information upon which a business decision is made is inaccurate (p. 10).

Internal auditor — an auditor employed by a company to audit for the company's board of directors and management (p. 9).

Operational audit — a review of any part of an organization's operating procedures and methods for the purpose of evaluating efficiency and effectiveness (p. 6).

Provincial securities commissions — provincial organizations with quasi-legal status which administer securities regulations within their jurisdictions (p. 25).

Public Sector Accounting Board (PSAB) — a committee of the CICA that has responsibility for establishing accounting standards for entities in the public sector (p. 17).

Quality control — methods used by a public accounting firm to make sure that the firm meets its professional responsibilities (p. 22).

Revenue Canada auditor — an auditor who works for Revenue Canada and conducts examinations of taxpayers' returns (p. 9).

Securities and Exchange Commission (SEC) — a U.S. federal agency that oversees the orderly conduct of the securities markets; the SEC assists in providing investors in public corporations with reliable information upon which to make investment decisions (p. 25).

Society of Management Accountants of Canada (SMAC) — one of the three major accounting organizations in Canada providing a professional designation relating to accounting and auditing; umbrella organization of the provincial societies that regulates the CMA profession in Canada (p. 2).

Statements on Auditing Standards — pronouncements issued by the American Institute of CPAs to interpret generally accepted auditing standards (p. 19).

Value-for-money audit — an audit that considers the economy, efficiency, and effectiveness with which operations are conducted (p. 6).

REVIEW QUESTIONS

1-1 Briefly describe the accounting organizations that exist in Canada and identify the professional designations they award.

1-2 Explain what is meant by determining the degree of correspondence between information and established criteria. What are the information and established criteria for the audit of Jones Ltd.'s tax return by a Revenue Canada auditor? What are they for the audit of Jones Ltd.'s financial statements by a public accounting firm?

1-3 Describe the nature of evidence the Revenue Canada auditor will use in the audit of Jones Ltd.'s tax return.

1-4 In the conduct of audits of financial statements, it would be a serious breach of responsibility if the auditor did not thoroughly understand accounting. However, many competent accountants do not have an understanding of the auditing process. What causes this difference?

1-5 What are the differences and similarities among audits of financial statements, compliance audits, and operational audits?

1-6 List five examples of specific operational audits that could be conducted by an internal auditor in a manufacturing company.

1-7 What are the major differences in the scope of the audit responsibilities for public accountants, auditors from the Auditor General's office, Revenue Canada auditors, and internal auditors?

1-8 What is comprehensive auditing?

1-9 Discuss the major factors in today's society that have made the need for independent audits much greater than it was 50 years ago.

1-10 Distinguish the following three risks: risk-free interest rate, business risk, and information risk. Which one or ones does the auditor reduce by performing an audit?

1-11 Identify the major causes of information risk, and identify the three main ways information risk can be reduced. What are the advantages and disadvantages of each?

1-12 Although the *CICA Handbook* standards provide general guidance, the application of these standards is dependent upon particular circumstances. In practice, a professional accountant may encounter situations where *CICA Handbook* standards do not exist or may not apply. Since there is no substitute for the exercise of professional judgment in the determination of what constitutes fair presentation and good practice, it has been suggested that too much effort is being directed towards the development of standards. Discuss the issues raised in the above statements.

(CICA adapted)

1-13 What major characteristics of the organization and conduct of public accounting firms permit them to fulfill their social function competently and independently?

1-14 What roles are played by the CICA, the CGAAC, and the SMAC for their members?

1-15 What role does the *CICA Handbook* have in the professional activities of public accountants in Canada?

1-16 Distinguish between generally accepted auditing standards and generally accepted accounting principles, and give two examples of each.

1-17 Differentiate between the authority of Assurance and Related Services Recommendations and Assurance and Related Services Guidelines.

1-18 The first examination standard requires the performance of the examination by a person or persons having adequate technical training and proficiency as an auditor or auditors. What are the various ways auditors can fulfill the requirement of the standard?

1-19 Generally accepted auditing standards have been criticized by different sources for failing to provide useful guidelines for conducting an audit. The critics believe the standards should be more specific to enable practitioners to improve the quality of their performance; as the standards are now stated they provide little more than an excuse to conduct inadequate audits. Evaluate this criticism of the eight generally accepted auditing standards.

1-20 Which is more authoritative for a Canadian auditor: the *CICA Handbook* or the *IFAC Handbook*? Explain the differences between them.

1-21 What is meant by the term "quality control" as it relates to a public accounting firm?

1-22 The following is an example of a public accounting firm's quality control procedure requirement: "Any person being considered for employment by the firm must have completed a basic auditing course and have been interviewed and approved by an audit partner of the firm before he or she can be hired as a full-time member of the audit staff." Which element of quality control does this procedure affect, and what is the purpose of the requirement?

1-23 State what is meant by the term "practice inspection"? What are the implications of the term for the CA profession?

MULTIPLE CHOICE QUESTIONS

1-24 The following questions deal with audits by public accounting firms. Select the best response for each question.

a. Which of the following *best* describes why an independent auditor is asked to express an opinion on the fair presentation of financial statements?
   (1) It is a customary courtesy for all shareholders of a company to receive an independent report on management's stewardship of the affairs of the business.
   (2) It is management's responsibility to seek available independent aid in the appraisal of the financial information shown in its financial statements.
   (3) The opinion of an independent party is needed because a company may *not* be objective with respect to its own financial statements.
   (4) It is difficult to prepare financial statements that fairly present a company's financial position and changes in financial position and operations without the expertise of an independent auditor.

b. The policies of Rogers & Co., public accountants, require that all members of the audit staff submit weekly time reports to the audit manager, who then prepares a weekly summary report for Rogers' review on any variance from the budget. This practice is evidence of Rogers & Co.'s professional concern about compliance with which of the following generally accepted auditing standards?
   (1) Quality control.
   (2) Due professional care.
   (3) Adequate review.
   (4) Adequate planning.

(AICPA adapted)

1-25 The following questions deal with types of audits and auditors. Select the best response for each question.

a. Operational audits generally have been conducted by internal auditors and governmental audit agencies but may be performed by public accountants. A primary purpose of an operational audit is to provide
   (1) a means of assurance that internal accounting controls are functioning as planned.
   (2) aid to the independent auditor, who is conducting the examination of the financial statements.

   (3) the results of internal examinations of financial and accounting matters to a company's top-level management.
   (4) a measure of management performance in meeting organizational goals.

b. Which of the following *best* describes the operational audit?
   (1) It concentrates on implementing financial and accounting control in a newly organized company.
   (2) It requires the constant review by internal auditors of the administrative controls as they relate to the operations of the company.
   (3) It attempts and is designed to verify the fair presentation of the results of a company's operations.
   (4) It concentrates on seeking aspects of the operations in which waste could be reduced by the introduction of controls.

c. Comprehensive auditing extends beyond examinations leading to the expression of opinion on the fairness of financial presentation and includes audits of efficiency, economy, and effectiveness, as well as
   (1) accuracy.
   (2) evaluation.
   (3) internal control.
   (4) adherence to specific rules or procedures.

(AICPA adapted)

1-26 The following questions deal with generally accepted auditing standards (GAAS) and quality control procedures. Select the one response that is best for each question.

a. The general standard, which states in part that the examination is to be performed by a person or persons having adequate technical training, requires that an auditor have
   (1) proficiency in business and financial matters.
   (2) ability in planning and supervision of the audit work.
   (3) education and experience in the field of auditing.
   (4) knowledge in the areas of financial accounting.

b. Which of the following *best* describes what is meant by generally accepted auditing standards?

(1) Measures of the quality of the auditor's performance.

(2) Acts to be performed by the auditor.

(3) Procedures to be used to gather evidence to support financial statements.

(4) Audit objectives generally determined on audit engagements.

c. The general standard of the generally accepted auditing standards includes a requirement that

(1) field work be adequately planned and supervised.

(2) informative disclosures in the financial statements be reasonably adequate.

(3) due professional care be exercised by the auditor.

(4) the auditor's report state whether or not the financial statements conform to generally accepted accounting principles.

d. What is the common concern or character of the three generally accepted auditing standards classified as examination standards?

(1) The competence, independence, and professional care of persons performing the audit.

(2) The criteria of audit planning and evidence gathering.

(3) Criteria for the content of the auditor's report on financial statements and related footnote disclosures.

(4) The need to maintain an independence in mental attitude in all matters relating to the audit.

(AICPA adapted)

DISCUSSION QUESTIONS AND PROBLEMS

1-27 Daniel Charon is the loan officer of the Georgian Bay Bank. Georgian Bay Bank has a loan of $260,000 outstanding from Regional Delivery Service Ltd., a company specializing in the delivery of products of all types on behalf of smaller companies. Georgian Bay's collateral on the loan consists of 20 small delivery trucks with an average original cost of $25,000.

Charon is concerned about the collectibility of the outstanding loan and whether the trucks still exist. He therefore engages Susan Virms, public accountant, to count the trucks, using registration information held by Charon. She is engaged because she spends most of her time auditing used automobile and truck dealerships and has extensive specialized knowledge about used trucks. Charon requests that Virms issue a report stating

1. which of the 20 trucks is parked in Regional's parking lot on the night of June 30.

2. the condition of each truck, using the categories of poor, good, and excellent.

3. the fair market value of each truck using the current "blue book" for trucks, which states the approximate wholesale prices of all used truck models, and the conditions of the trucks using the poor, good, and excellent categories.

Required

a. Identify which aspects of this narrative fit each of the following parts of the definition of auditing:

(1) information.

(2) established criteria.

(3) accumulates and evaluates evidence.

(4) competent, independent person.

(5) report of results.

b. Identify the greatest difficulties Virms is likely to have doing this assurance engagement.

1-28 Five undergraduates with majors in accounting are discussing alternative career plans. The first student plans to become a Revenue Canada auditor because his primary interest is income taxes. He believes a background in tax auditing will provide him with a better exposure to income taxes than will any other available career choice. The second undergraduate has decided to go to work for a public accounting firm for at least five years, possibly as a permanent career. She feels a wide variety of experience in auditing and related fields offers a better alternative than any other option. The third student has decided upon a career in internal auditing with a large industrial company because of the many different aspects of the organization with which internal auditors become involved. The fourth student plans to become an auditor with the Auditor General because she believes that this career will provide excellent experience in computer auditing techniques. A fifth student plans to pursue some aspect of auditing as a career but has not decided upon the particular type of organization to enter. He is especially interested in an opportunity to continue to grow professionally, but meaningful and interesting employment is also an important consideration.

Required

a. What are the major advantages and disadvantages of each of the four types of auditing careers?

b. What other types of auditing careers are available to those who are qualified?

1-29 In the normal course of performing their responsibilities, auditors frequently conduct examinations or reviews of the following:

1. Federal income tax returns of an officer of a corporation to determine whether he or she has included all taxable income in the return

2. Disbursements of a branch of the Canadian government for a special research project to determine whether the project was conducted effectively and efficiently

3. Computer operations of a corporation to evaluate whether the computer centre is being operated as efficiently as possible

4. Annual statements for the use of management

5. Operations of Revenue Canada to determine whether Revenue Canada auditors are using their time efficiently in conducting audits

6. Statements for bankers and other creditors when the client is too small to have an accounting staff

7. Financial statements of a branch of the Canadian government to make sure the statements present fairly the actual disbursements made during a certain period

8. Federal income tax returns of a corporation to determine whether the tax laws have been followed

9. Financial statements for the use of shareholders when there is an internal audit staff

10. A bond indenture agreement to make sure a company is following all requirements of the contract

11. The computer operations of a large corporation to evaluate whether the internal controls are likely to prevent misstatements in accounting and operating data

12. Disbursements of a branch of the Canadian government for a special research project to determine whether the expenditures were consistent with the legislative bill that authorized the project

Required

For each of the examples above, state the type of auditor (public accountant, Auditor General, Revenue Canada, or internal) that would most likely be used and the type of audit (audit of financial statements, compliance audit, operational/value-for-money audit, or comprehensive audit) that would take place.

1-30 A large conglomerate is considering acquiring a medium-sized manufacturing company in a closely related industry. A major consideration for the management of the conglomerate in deciding whether to pursue the merger is the operational efficiency of the company. Management has decided to obtain a detailed report, based on an intensive investigation, of the operational efficiency of the sales, production, and research and development departments.

Required

a. Whom should the conglomerate engage to conduct the operational audit?

b. What major problems are the auditors likely to encounter in conducting the investigation and writing the report?

1-31 The Consumers' Union is a nonprofit organization that provides information and counsel on consumer goods and services. A major part of its function is testing different brands of consumer products that are bought on the open market and reporting the results of the tests in *Consumer Canada*, a monthly publication. Examples of the types of products it tests are mid-sized automobiles, residential dehumidifiers, canned tuna, and children's jeans.

Required

a. Compare the concept of information risk introduced in this chapter with the information risk problem faced by a buyer of an automobile.

b. Compare the four causes of information risk faced by users of financial statements that were discussed in the chapter with those faced by a buyer of an automobile.

c. Compare the three ways users of financial statements can reduce information risk with those available to a buyer of an automobile.

d. In what ways is the service provided by Consumers' Union similar to audit services, and in what ways does it differ?

1-32 The following comments summarize the beliefs of some practitioners about quality control and practice inspection:

> Quality control and practice inspection are quasi-governmental methods of regulating the profession. There are two effects of such regulation. First, it gives a competitive advantage to national CA firms because they already need formal structures to administer their complex organizations. Quality control requirements do not significantly affect their structure. Smaller firms now need a more costly organizational structure, which has proven unnecessary because of existing partner involvement on engagements. The major advantage smaller CA firms have traditionally had is a simple and efficient organizational structure. Now that advantage has been eliminated because of quality control requirements. Second, quality control and practice inspection are not needed to regulate the profession. The first four elements of quality control have always existed, at least informally, for quality firms. Three things already provide sufficient assurance that informal quality control elements are followed without practice inspection. They are competitive pressures to do quality work, legal liability for inadequate performance, and a code of professional ethics requiring that CAs follow generally accepted auditing standards.

Required

a. State the pros and cons of these comments.

b. Evaluate whether control requirements and practice inspection are worth their cost.

1-33 For each of the following quality control procedures taken from the quality control manual of a medium-sized regional public accounting firm, identify the applicable element of quality control from Table 1-2 (p. 23).

a. Appropriate accounting and auditing research requires adequate technical reference library facilities. Each practice office must maintain minimal facilities including a list of individuals within the firm who have specialized knowledge of various industries to help ensure an awareness of problems unique to specific industries. In addition, an extensive library of industry auditing material is maintained in the office of the director of accounting and auditing.

b. Each audit engagement of the firm is directed by a partner and, in most instances, a manager of the firm. On every engagement, an attempt is made to maintain a continuity of personnel on a year-to-year basis.

c. When prospective employees are interviewed by campus recruiters and are deemed to possess the potential for employment, they will be further screened by a practice office interview pursuant to the firm's procedure for practice office visitation. Practice office partners make the final hiring decisions pursuant to the guidelines established by the director of personnel.

d. At all stages of any engagement, effort is made to involve professional staff at appropriate levels in the accounting and auditing decisions. Various approvals of the manager or senior accountant are obtained throughout the audit.

e. No employee will have any direct or indirect financial interest, association, or relationship (e.g., a close relative serving a client in a decision-making capacity) not disclosed that might be adverse to the firm's best interest.

f. Each office of the firm shall be visited on at least an annual basis by review persons selected by the director of accounting and auditing. The procedures to be undertaken by the reviewers are illustrated in the office review program.

g. A closing conference including all staff will be held and those in attendance shall sign the checklist indicating they have reviewed certain points with the director of accounting and auditing.

h. Existing clients of the firm are reviewed on a continuing basis by the engagement partner. Termination may result if circumstances indicate there is a reason to question the integrity of management or our independence, or if accounting and auditing differences of opinion cannot be reconciled. Doubts concerning whether the client–auditor relationship should be continued must be promptly discussed with the director of accounting and auditing.

i. Individual partners submit the nominations of those persons whom they wish to be considered for partners. To become a partner, an individual must have exhibited a high degree of technical competence, possess integrity, motivation, judgment, and a desire to help the firm progress through the efficient dispatch of the job responsibilities to which he or she is assigned.

j. Through our continuing employee evaluation and counselling program, and through the quality control review procedures as established by the firm, educational needs are reviewed and formal staff training programs modified to accommodate changing needs. At the conclusion of practice office reviews, apparent accounting and auditing deficiencies are summarized and reported to the firm's director of personnel.

1-34 In light of recent business failures, the public has expressed concern about the usefulness of the financial statement audit and the auditor's report. Because of these concerns, the accounting faculty at a local university has organized a panel to discuss the function of the auditor's report and the possible expansion of the auditor's responsibilities.

The faculty has invited a representative from industry, the investment community, and the banking community and you, a professional accountant in public practice, to sit on the panel.

You have noted the following excerpts from presentations by the other participants.

Mr. Don Bogart, Vice-President, Finance, Casablanca Industries: Our audit fees, in my opinion, are already far too high. I believe you should reconsider the need for increased auditor involvement and perhaps even the need for an annual audit, which has become an unnecessary evil. If the auditor's role is to be expanded, something must be done to reduce the costs and maximize the benefits.

Ms. Elizabeth Ashton, Financial Analyst: I would be more comfortable if the independent auditor attested to business viability, management credibility and future-oriented data. We question the relevance of audited financial statements to the decisions we have to make.

Mr. Richard Shivas, Senior Corporate Loan Officer: I agree with Elizabeth. In addition to historical-cost financial statements, we need current value and prospective information on which to base our decision. We would like more assurance from the auditor than is presently conveyed with the financial statement audit that the company will be able to turn its assets into profits. We are tired of hearing about problems when it is too late.

Required

Present your comments.

(CICA adapted)

1-35 Raymonde, the owner of a small company, asked Holmes, public accountant, to conduct an audit of the company's records. Raymonde told Holmes that an audit is to be completed in time to submit audited financial statements to a bank as part of a loan application. Holmes immediately accepted the engagement and agreed to provide an auditor's report within three weeks. Raymonde agreed to pay Holmes a fixed fee plus a bonus if the loan was granted.

Holmes hired two accounting students to conduct the audit and spent several hours telling them exactly what to do. Holmes told the students not to spend time reviewing the controls but instead to concentrate on proving the mathematical accuracy of the ledger accounts, and summarizing the data in the accounting records that support Raymonde's financial statements. The students followed Holmes' instructions and after two weeks gave Holmes the financial statements, which did not include footnotes. Holmes reviewed the statements and prepared an unqualified auditor's report. The report did not refer to generally accepted accounting principles.

Required

Briefly describe each of the generally accepted auditing standards and indicate how the actions of Holmes resulted in a failure to comply with each standard.

Organize your answer as follows:

Brief Description of GAAS	Holmes' Actions Resulting in Failure to Comply with GAAS

(AICPA adapted)

1-36 Four years ago, the European Exchange Club (EEC) was formed in an effort to create a united social group out of several separate regional clubs in the vicinity of the city of Decker, located in central Canada. The purpose of the group is to combine resources to meet the recreational, cultural, and social needs of its collective members. EEC was formed through the collaboration of 10 clubs including Russians, Italians, Portuguese, Greeks, Germans, and others.

It is now December. EEC's executives have spent the last four years planning and preparing for its operation. The club's community centre is expected to be fully completed next year. The facilities of the club will include a multipurpose building to house banquets, meetings, and arts activities; hiking trails; indoor/outdoor tennis facilities; bicycle trails; baseball diamonds; an indoor/outdoor pool, and a soccer field.

The multi-purpose building is 75 percent complete, and EEC's executives have stated that it is "approximately within budget" of the total $3.5 million cost. The two hectares of land on which the facility is built were provided by the provincial government by way of a five-year lease at $1 a year. The adjacent land of 24 ha was contributed to the club by The Italian Clubs of Canada. Previously, this land had been leased to a farmer for $54,000 a year. The 26 ha will be used for the previously mentioned activities, incurring estimated annual operating costs of $1.8 million. Estimated additional operating and administrative costs are $750,000.

John Mendez-Smith, the newly elected president of the club, has approached your firm to prepare a report that provides recommendations on accounting, finance, and internal control issues. He has also asked you to identify the merits of an audit and potential problems that might exist.

Required

a. What are the advantages to EEC of having an audit conducted?

b. Why would EEC approach a public accounting firm to provide recommendations on accounting, finance, and internal control issues?

(CICA adapted)

2

THE AUDITOR'S REPORT

THE AUDITOR'S REPORT WAS TIMELY, BUT AT WHAT COST?

Halvorson & Co., public accountants, was hired as the auditor for Machinetron, Inc., a company that manufactured high-precision, computer-operated lathes. Machinetron had been started by Al Trent, a man considered a fine engineer as well as an astute businessperson. The owners of the company felt that he was ready to take Machinetron public, and they engaged Halvorson to conduct their upcoming audit and assist in the preparation of a prospectus for a securities offering.

Because Machinetron's machines were large and complex, they were expensive. Although the number of sales per year were few, the high sales prices resulted in large revenue. In addition, individual sales often transpired over a long period of time and Trent negotiated many of the sales personally. Due to these facts, improper recording of just one or two systems could represent a material misstatement of the financial statements. The engagement partner in charge of the Machinetron audit was Susan Lehman, who had significant experience in auditing manufacturing companies. She realized the risks associated with a growing company, including testing the existence of recorded sales at year end. For that reason, she insisted that the staff obtain confirmations of the receivables associated with all sales occurring during the months just before year end.

In addition to her responsibilities on the Machinetron engagement, Lehman was overburdened with work for two other clients. She conducted her review of the working papers on the same day that Trent wanted to make the prospectus effective. In reviewing the confirmation working papers, she saw that a major receivable for a sale occurring at year end was supported by an electronic mail message rather than by a conventional confirmation reply. Apparently, relations were "touchy" with this customer, and Trent discouraged the staff from talking directly with the customer about the confirmation. Finally, this E-mail arrived. Given that the machine had been shipped (although not yet paid for), the staff felt the sale was supported.

At the end of the day, a meeting was called at Machinetron's office. It was attended by Lehman, Trent, a representative of Machinetron's underwriting firm, and the company's lawyer. When Trent asked Lehman if there were any problems with the audit, Lehman mentioned the E-mail confirmation. She said she felt her firm needed to obtain a better form of confirmation. At this news, Trent blew his stack. After a few moments, Machinetron's lawyer stepped in and got Trent to calm down. He offered to write Halvorson & Co. a letter stating that in his opinion, an E-mail had legal substance as a valid confirmation reply. Lehman, feeling under tremendous pressure, accepted this proposal and the registration went ahead.

Six months later, Machinetron issued a public statement indicating that its revenues reported for the previous fiscal year and the first two quarters of the current fiscal year were overstated due to improperly recorded sales, including the sale supported by the E-mail confirmation. An Ontario Securities Commission investigation followed, during which it was discovered that the subject E-mail was sent by Trent, not the customer. Halvorson & Co. suffered significant damages. Susan Lehman ultimately left public accounting.

OBJECTIVE 2-1

Describe the nature of and need for the auditor's report.

Reports are essential to the audit or other attestation process because they inform users of the attested-to information, what the auditor did, and the conclusions reached. From the user's perspective, the report is considered the primary product of the attestation process. Paragraph 5020.10 of the *CICA Handbook* requires that a public accountant who "associates himself or herself with information by performing services in respect of that information [communicate] the nature and extent of his or her involvement with the information . . . ." *Association* arises when the public accountant performs services with respect to the information or permits his or her name to be used in connection with the information. The term "services" includes audits, review engagements, and compilations. An example of an auditor "consenting to the use of his or her name" would be when the client prepares condensed financial information from the audited financial statements and indicates that the information came from financial statements audited and reported on by the public accountant, and the auditor has knowledge of the client's action and consents to it.

Section 5020 refers to "information" and is not limited to financial statements. You will learn in Chapter 23 that the public accountant performs a range of services for clients of which audits of financial statements are only a part; the communication provided by the public accountant ranges from an auditor's report in the case of an audit engagement to a notice to reader in the case of a compilation engagement. An auditor's report is the appropriate and required communication only when an audit is conducted.

As indicated in Chapter 1, the focus of this text will be on the audit of financial statements and thus on the auditor's report; the other forms of communication, however, will be discussed in Chapters 23 to 25.

The requirements for issuing auditor's reports are derived from the four generally accepted auditing standards of reporting, included on pages 18 and 19. The first standard requires the identification of the financial statements and a clear differentiation between the responsibilities of management and those of the auditor. The second standard requires a clear-cut statement from the auditor on the nature of his or her examination. The third standard is especially important because it requires an expression of opinion about the overall financial statements or an explicit statement that an opinion is not possible, along with the reasons it is not possible. The fourth standard states that when an opinion is expressed by the auditor, "it should indicate whether the financial statements present fairly, in all material respects, the financial position, results of operations, and changes in financial position in accordance with an appropriate disclosed basis of accounting." The appropriate disclosed basis normally would be generally accepted accounting principles (GAAP); however, in some situations, it might not be. Paragraph 5100.05 suggests financial statements prepared in accordance with regulatory legislation as an example of a situation in which financial statements would not be prepared in accordance with GAAP. A significant portion of the Auditing Recommendations in the *Handbook* concerns reporting requirements. Given the importance of auditor's reports as a communication device, that is not surprising.

The accounting profession recognizes the need for uniformity in reporting as a means of avoiding confusion. Users would have considerable difficulty interpreting the meaning of an auditor's report if each were an original creation. The professional standards, therefore, have defined and enumerated the types of auditor's report that should be included with financial statements. The wording of auditor's reports is reasonably uniform, but different auditor's reports are appropriate for different circumstances. The auditor must use judgment to determine which report and, thus, what wording is appropriate.

The auditor's report is the final step in the entire audit process. The reason for studying it now, rather than later, is to permit reference to different auditor's reports as evidence accumulation is studied throughout the text. Once the form and content of the final product of the audit is understood, evidence accumulation concepts become more meaningful.

STANDARD UNQUALIFIED AUDITOR'S REPORT

CONDITIONS FOR STANDARD UNQUALIFIED REPORT

> **OBJECTIVE 2-2**
>
> **Specify the conditions that justify issuing the standard unqualified auditor's report, and describe the report.**

The most common type of audit report is the *standard unqualified auditor's report*. It is also often referred to as the *auditor's standard report*. It is used when the following conditions have been met:

1. An audit engagement has been undertaken to express an opinion on financial statements.
2. The general standard has been followed by the auditor in all respects on the engagement.
3. Sufficient appropriate audit evidence has been accumulated, and the auditor has conducted the engagement in a manner that allows him or her to conclude that the three examination standards have been met.
4. The financial statements, which include the balance sheet, the income statement, the statement of retained earnings, the cash flow statement, and the notes to the financial statements, are fairly presented in accordance with an appropriate disclosed basis of accounting, which usually is generally accepted accounting principles.
5. There are no circumstances which, in the opinion of the auditor, would require him or her to modify the wording of the report or to add an additional explanatory paragraph.

When these conditions are met, the standard unqualified auditor's report on the financial statements, as shown in Figure 2-1, is issued. Different auditors may vary the wording slightly in the standard report, but the meaning will be the same.

PARTS OF STANDARD UNQUALIFIED AUDITOR'S REPORT

Each standard unqualified auditor's report includes eight distinct parts. These parts are labelled in bold letters in Figure 2-1.

1. *Report Title.* Paragraph 5400.07 states that the auditor's report should be titled.
2. *Addressee.* Paragraph 5400.31 requires that the addressee of the auditor's report be disclosed. In most cases, the addressees are the shareholders since it is usually they who appoint the auditor. If the auditor is appointed by some other person or group, the report should be addressed to that body. When the shareholders appoint the auditor, the audit is a *statutory audit*.
3. *Introductory Paragraph.* The first paragraph of the auditor's report does three things. First, it makes the simple statement that the public accounting firm has done an *audit*. The scope paragraph clarifies what is meant by an audit.

Second, it lists the financial statements that were audited, including the balance sheet date and the period for the income statement, the statement of retained earnings, and the cash flow statement. While the notes to the financial statements are not mentioned specifically, they are an integral part of the financial statements and their inclusion is implicit. It should be noted that the failure to follow GAAP *cannot* be remedied by disclosure of such failure in the notes to the financial statements. For example, failing to record amortization expense on the income statement cannot be remedied by disclosing the failure in the notes. The terms used to describe the financial statements in the auditor's report should be identical to those used by management on the financial statements.

Third, the introductory paragraph states that the financial statements are the responsibility of management and that the auditor's responsibility is to express an opinion on the financial statements. In this way, the introductory paragraph (a) communicates that management is responsible for selecting the appropriate generally accepted accounting principles and for making the measurement decisions and disclosures in applying those principles, and (b) clarifies the respective roles of management and the auditor.

4. *Scope Paragraph.* The scope paragraph is a factual statement about what the auditor did in the audit. This paragraph first states that the auditor followed generally accepted auditing standards. The remainder briefly describes important aspects of an audit.

The scope paragraph states that the audit is designed to obtain *reasonable assurance* about whether the statements are free of *material* misstatement. The inclusion of the word "material" conveys the meaning that auditors search for significant misstatements, not minor errors that do not affect users' decisions.

FIGURE 2-1
The Standard Auditor's Report

REPORT TITLE	**AUDITOR'S REPORT**
ADDRESSEE	To the Shareholders of Far West Industries Ltd.
INTRODUCTORY PARAGRAPH (factual statement)	We have audited the balance sheet of Far West Industries Ltd. as at June 30, 2000, and the statements of income, retained earnings, and cash flows for the year then ended. These financial statements are the responsibility of the company's management. Our responsibility is to express an opinion on these financial statements based on our audit.
SCOPE PARAGRAPH (factual statement)	We conducted our audit in accordance with generally accepted auditing standards. Those standards require that we plan and perform an audit to obtain reasonable assurance whether the financial statements are free of material misstatement. An audit includes examining, on a test basis, evidence supporting the amounts and disclosures in the financial statements. An audit also includes assessing the accounting principles used and significant estimates made by management, as well as evaluating the overall financial statement presentation.
OPINION PARAGRAPH (conclusions)	In our opinion, these financial statements present fairly, in all material respects, the financial position of the company as at June 30, 2000, and the results of its operations and cash flows for the year then ended in accordance with generally accepted accounting principles.
NAME OF PUBLIC ACCOUNTING FIRM	*Zalkey White & Co.* Chartered Accountants
PLACE OF ISSUE **AUDITOR'S REPORT DATE**	Red Deer, Alberta October 15, 2000

The use of the term "reasonable assurance" is intended to indicate that an audit cannot be expected to eliminate completely the possibility that a material error or fraud or other irregularity will exist in the financial statements. In other words, an audit provides a high level of assurance, but it is not a guarantee.

The remainder of the scope paragraph discusses the audit evidence accumulated and states that the auditor believes the evidence accumulated was appropriate for the circumstances to express the opinion presented. The words "test basis" indicate that sampling was used rather than an audit of every transaction and amount on the statements. Whereas the introductory paragraph of the report states that management is responsible for the preparation and content of the financial statements, the scope paragraph states that the auditor has the responsibility to evaluate the appropriateness of those accounting principles, estimates, and financial statement disclosures and presentations given. The auditor cannot simply accept management's representations about appropriateness.

5. *Opinion Paragraph.* The third paragraph in the standard auditor's report states the auditor's conclusions based on the results of audit evidence accumulated during the audit. This part of the auditor's report is so important that frequently the entire report is referred to as simply the *auditor's opinion.* The opinion paragraph is stated as an opinion rather than as a statement of absolute fact or a guarantee. The intent is to indicate that the conclusions are based on professional judgment. Using the terminology of Chapter 1, the phrase "in our opinion" indicates that there may be some information risk associated with the financial statements, even though the statements have been audited.

   The opinion paragraph is directly related to the four generally accepted auditing reporting standards listed on pages 18 and 19. The auditor is required to state an opinion about the financial statements taken as a whole, including a conclusion about whether the company followed an appropriate disclosed basis of accounting, usually generally accepted accounting principles.

   One of the most controversial parts of the auditor's report is the meaning of the term *presents fairly.* The auditor means that the financial statements are fairly presented in accordance with the accounting principles described in the opinion paragraph. A lay person may mistake "presents fairly" to mean that the values in the financial statements represent the realizable values of the assets. It is important that lay people understand the auditor's message.

   GAAP normally results in the most appropriate disclosure; if GAAP does not provide the most appropriate disclosure, the auditor will suggest management utilize another form of disclosure that does provide the most appropriate disclosure. The auditor who permits management to deviate from GAAP must be able to explain the deviation if called upon to do so. Occasionally the courts have concluded that auditors are responsible to look beyond generally accepted accounting principles to determine whether users might be misled if those principles are followed. It is also necessary to examine the substance of transactions and balances for possible misinformation. For example, the rules of professional conduct promulgated by the professional accounting bodies in Canada state that a member of that body shall not be associated with financial information that is false or misleading or fail to reveal any material fact or misstatement of which the member is aware that makes the financial statement false or misleading.

6. *Name of Public Accounting Firm.* The name identifies the public accounting firm or practitioner that has performed the audit. Typically, the firm's name is used, since the entire firm has the legal and professional responsibility to make certain the quality of the audit meets professional standards.

7. *Place of Issue.* Paragraph 5400.32 suggests that the place of issue may be identified in the letterhead on which the auditor's report is printed or at the foot of the report as is illustrated in Figure 2-1.

8. *Auditor's Report Date.* The appropriate date for the report is the one on which the auditor has completed the most important auditing procedures in the field. Section 5405 refers to ". . . substantial completion of examination . . . ." This date is important to users because it indicates the last day of the auditor's responsibility for the review of significant events that occurred after the date of the financial statements. For example, if the balance sheet is dated December 31, 1999, and the audit report is dated March 6, 2000, the implication is that the auditor has searched for material, unrecorded transactions, and events that occurred up to March 6, 2000, that may have had an effect on 1999 statements.

Section 5405 discusses, among other things, double dating of the auditor's report. Double dating is done when a material event occurs after the completion of field work and thus after the date of the auditor's report and before the date the report is issued. If the event is material, the auditor will review the amended financial statements for the inclusion of a note about the event and any related adjustments that are required. The auditor will then double date the report as follows:

> March 6, 2000
> except for Note 17 which is
> as of April 2, 2000

If the effect of the event was so material as to change the 1999 financial statements significantly, the auditor would probably extend the audit for the financial statements as a whole and date the report with the revised date for completion of field work. In the example provided, the new date of the auditor's report would be April 2, 2000.

CATEGORIES OF AUDITOR'S REPORTS

OBJECTIVE 2-3

Identify the four categories of audit reports.

Most knowledgeable users of financial statements read the auditor's report. When they observe that the report consists of three standard paragraphs, they conclude that the five conditions listed on page 35 have been met. Such a report provides users comfort that information risk has been reduced to a reasonable level.

A deviation from the standard unqualified report will cause knowledgeable users of financial statements to recognize that the auditor intends to communicate additional or limiting information. In extreme cases, the auditor may conclude that the financial statements are materially misstated, but usually the cause of the deviation is less significant. Nevertheless, the information must have potential relevance to users or the auditor wouldn't include it.

The categorization of audit reports in Figure 2-2 is used throughout the remainder of the chapter. The departures from a standard unqualified report are considered increasingly severe as one goes down the figure. Stated differently, a denial or

FIGURE 2-2
Four Categories of
Audit Reports

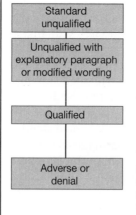

Standard unqualified	The five conditions stated on page 35 have been met.
Unqualified with explanatory paragraph or modified wording	A complete audit took place and financial statements are fairly presented in accordance with disclosed accounting principles, but the auditor believes that it is important or required to provide additional information.
Qualified	The auditor concludes that the financial statements are fairly presented, but the scope of the auditor's examination has been restricted or there has been failure to comply with GAAP.
Adverse or denial	The auditor concludes that the scope limitation is so significant that the auditor is unable to form an opinion as to whether the financial statements are fairly presented (denial) or that the deviation from GAAP is so significant that the financial statements are not fairly presented (adverse).

adverse opinion is normally far more important to users than an unqualified report with an explanatory paragraph or modified wording.

UNQUALIFIED AUDITOR'S REPORT WITH EXPLANATORY PARAGRAPH OR MODIFIED WORDING

OBJECTIVE 2-4

Describe the circumstances when an unqualified report with an explanatory paragraph or modified wording is appropriate.

In certain situations, an unqualified auditor's report is issued, but the wording deviates from the standard unqualified report. It is important to distinguish between these reports and the qualified, adverse and denial reports. The *unqualified report with explanatory paragraph or modified wording* meets the criteria of a complete audit with satisfactory results and financial statements that are fairly presented, but the auditor believes it is important, or is required, to provide additional information. In a *qualified, adverse, or denial report*, the auditor either has not performed a complete audit or is not satisfied that the financial statements are fairly presented.

The reasons for the addition of an explanatory paragraph or a modification in the wording of the unqualified standard report are:

- The appropriate disclosed basis of accounting is not generally accepted accounting principles; or
- The auditor wishes to provide additional explanatory information.

Both of these situations are discussed in turn below.

UNQUALIFIED AUDITOR'S REPORT WHEN THE APPROPRIATE DISCLOSED BASIS OF ACCOUNTING IS NOT GAAP

In certain situations, an unqualified auditor's report is issued when the disclosed basis of accounting is not generally accepted accounting principles.

Paragraph 5400.22 permits a departure from the *CICA Handbook* Recommendations when "the auditor concludes that following the Recommendations would result in misleading financial statements." An unqualified opinion is appropriate if the auditor is satisfied that the disclosure related to the departure is adequate.

Reporting standard (iv) requires the auditor's report to state "whether the financial statements present fairly, in all material respects, the financial position, results of operations, and changes in financial position in accordance with an appropriate disclosed basis of accounting, which except in special circumstances should be generally accepted accounting principles." Paragraph 5100.05 suggests that such situations might include financial statements prepared in accordance with regulatory legislation or with contractual requirements. In such circumstances, the auditor would express the opinion that the financial statements presented fairly the financial position, results of operations, and cash flows in accordance with the disclosed basis of accounting.

MODIFICATIONS IN THE STANDARD UNQUALIFIED AUDITOR'S REPORT

The auditor may be reporting under the requirements of a statute that requires the auditor to include information in addition to that provided in the auditor's report. Normally, such explanatory information, if it is lengthy, should be included in a separate paragraph after the opinion paragraph. For example, Auditing Guideline 14 (AuG-14), "Auditor's Report on the Financial Statements of Federally Regulated Financial Institutions," provides guidance on the wording of the auditor's report of a financial institution governed by a federal statute such as the *Bank Act* or the *Insurance Companies Act*. Similarly, AuG-10, "Legislative Requirements to Report on the Consistent Application of Generally Accepted Accounting Principles," allows the auditor to state that accounting principles have been applied on a basis consistent with the preceding year.

Paragraph 5701.05 also suggests that if the auditor wishes to expand his or her report to include other information and explanations, such information should also be included in a paragraph following the opinion paragraph. For example, when comparative financial statements are presented that were not audited or were audited by another auditor, that information would be disclosed in a paragraph following the opinion paragraph.

FINANCIAL STATEMENTS PREPARED USING A BASIS OF ACCOUNTING OTHER THAN GAAP

The Auditing Standards Board issued a Re-Exposure Draft "Auditor's Report on Financial Statements Prepared Using a Basis of Accounting Other than Generally Accepted Accounting Principles " in 1997. The proposed *Handbook* material will deal with the special circumstances when it is appropriate for the auditor's report on financial statements to refer to a basis of accounting other than generally accepted accounting principles and the wording of the auditor's report.

REPORTING ON COMPARATIVE FINANCIAL STATEMENTS

AuG-8, "Auditor's Report on Comparative Financial Statements," affects those companies filing financial statements with the Ontario Securities Commission (OSC). The *CICA Handbook* normally requires the auditor to report only on the current year's financial statements. The OSC Staff Accounting Communique No. 3 requires that audit reports dated after December 31, 1989, refer to both periods under audit. AuG-8 provides examples of wording that would be used for the standard unqualified report, and examples of opinions with reservations.

CANADA–UNITED STATES REPORTING DIFFERENCES

In Chapter 1, we described the existence of cross-listed organizations, those companies that are listed on multiple stock exchanges. AuG-21, "Canada-United States Reporting Differences," provides guidance to the auditor on report preparation for Canadian companies where the audit report would differ under Canadian and U.S. GAAP. This arises due to treatment differences for disclosures of going concern problems and of changes in generally accepted accounting principles between periods.

The guideline requires that the report be prepared in accordance with Canadian GAAS and that any additional comments required be attached, but be distinct from the auditor's report.

CHANGES IN GAAP OR THE APPLICATION THEREOF

Paragraph 5400.17 requires the auditor to evaluate a change in accounting principle or in the application of an accounting principle in the financial statements being reported on and to assess whether or not the new principle, or the application, is in accordance with generally accepted accounting principles. In addition, the auditor must assess whether the method of accounting for the change, which may be retroactive or prospective, and the disclosure of the change are also in accordance with GAAP.

If the change, its application, and its disclosure are in accordance with GAAP, the auditor should express an unqualified opinion. On the other hand, if the change or its application or its disclosure in the financial statements is not in accordance with GAAP, the auditor should issue a qualified or adverse opinion.

Recall that the financial statements must be in accordance with generally accepted accounting principles or an appropriate disclosed basis of accounting. Accordingly, paragraph 5400.17 applies only in the case of a change when the basis of accounting is an appropriate disclosed basis and not GAAP.

Certain changes in the financial statements may not be changes in a principle or in its application. Examples of such changes include:

1. Changes in an estimate, such as a decrease in the life of an asset for amortization purposes.
2. Error corrections not involving principles, such as a previous year's mathematical error.
3. Variations in format and presentation of financial information.
4. Changes because of substantially different transactions or events, such as new endeavours in research and development or the sale of a subsidiary.

A change in estimate need not be disclosed in the notes although disclosure may be desirable. An error correction, on the other hand, must be fully disclosed.

UNUSUAL UNCERTAINTIES AFFECTING THE FINANCIAL STATEMENTS

A number of estimates are customarily made by management in the preparation of financial statements, including the useful lives of amortizable assets, the collectibility of receivables, and the realizability of inventory and other assets. There is usually enough evidence to permit reasonable estimation of these items. Sometimes, however, the auditor encounters a situation in which the outcome of a matter cannot be reasonably estimated at the time the statements are being issued. These matters are defined as contingencies. Examples include threats of the expropriation of assets, income tax or litigation contingencies (collectible or payable) and guarantees of the indebtedness of others.

There are also less specific situations in which the ability of the company to continue to operate as a going concern is open to question.[1] Paragraphs 5510.51–53 of the *CICA Handbook* address this problem. For instance, the existence of one or more of the following factors causes uncertainty about the ability of a company to continue to operate:

- Recurring operating losses
- Serious deficiencies in working capital
- An inability to obtain financing sufficient for continued operations
- An inability to comply with terms of existing loan agreements
- The possibility of an adverse outcome of one or more contingencies
- Insufficient funds to meet liabilities
- A plan to significantly curtail or liquidate operations
- External factors that could force an otherwise solvent enterprise to cease operations

The auditor's concern in such situations is the possibility that recorded assets will not be recoverable at their recorded value. For example, capital assets recorded at cost may be worth far less if the company is forced to liquidate because of bankruptcy.

The appropriate type of opinion to issue when either specific or general uncertainties exist depends on the materiality of the items in question and on the disclosure of the items by management in the notes. An unqualified opinion is appropriate if the uncertainty is not disclosed but is immaterial. If the amount involved is material but the accounting treatment, disclosure, and presentation of either a contingency or going concern problem are in accordance with GAAP, the auditor would not refer to the uncertainty in the auditor's report. The auditor must be very sure that the disclosure is such that it draws attention to the uncertainty.

Canadian practice prior to August 1980, and present American practice, required the auditor to draw the reader's attention to going concern problems by mention in the auditor's report. The topic was well researched by the Auditing Standards Committee of the CICA, and that body concluded that disclosure of going concern problems was management's responsibility. Therefore, if the going concern problem is adequately disclosed, the auditor makes no mention of it in the auditor's report.

CONDITIONS REQUIRING A DEPARTURE FROM AN UNQUALIFIED AUDITOR'S REPORT

It is essential that auditors and readers of auditor's reports understand the circumstances when a standard unqualified report is not appropriate (there is a reservation of opinion) and the type of auditor's report issued in each circumstance. In the study of auditor's reports that depart from an unqualified report, there are three closely related topics: the conditions requiring a departure from an unqualified opinion, the types of opinions other than unqualified, and materiality.

OBJECTIVE 2-5

List the two conditions requiring a departure from an unqualified auditor's report.

---

[1]For a thorough and interesting discussion of this topic see Boritz, J. E., *The "Going Concern" Assumption: Accounting and Auditing Implications,* Toronto: CICA, 1991 and CICA Exposure Draft, *"Auditor's Responsibility to Evaluate the Going Concern Assumption,"* 1995.

First, the two conditions requiring a departure are briefly summarized. Each is discussed in greater depth later in the chapter.

1. Scope Restriction: The scope of the auditor's examination has been restricted
When the auditor has not accumulated sufficient evidence to determine if financial statements are stated in accordance with GAAP, a scope restriction exists. There are two major causes of scope restrictions: restrictions imposed by the client and those caused by circumstances beyond either the client's or auditor's control. An example of a client restriction is management's refusal to permit the auditor to confirm material receivables or to physically examine inventory. An example of a restriction caused by circumstances is when the engagement is not agreed upon until after the client's year end. It may not be possible to physically observe inventories, confirm receivables, or perform other important procedures after the balance sheet date.

2. GAAP Departure: The financial statements have not been prepared in accordance with GAAP   Paragraph 5510.06 lists three examples of departures from generally accepted accounting principles:

1. An inappropriate accounting treatment; for example, failure to capitalize a capital lease.
2. An inappropriate valuation of an item in the financial statements; for example, failure to provide an adequate allowance for doubtful accounts.
3. A failure to disclose essential information in an informative manner; for example, failure to adequately disclose a going concern problem.

AUDITOR'S REPORTS OTHER THAN UNQUALIFIED

Whenever any of the two conditions requiring a departure from an unqualified report exists and is material, a report other than an unqualified report must be issued. Three main types of auditor's reports are issued under these conditions: *qualified opinion*, *adverse opinion*, and *denial of opinion*.

QUALIFIED OPINION

As described, a qualified or reservation of opinion can result from a limitation on the scope of the audit or failure to follow generally accepted accounting principles.
A qualified opinion can be used only:

OBJECTIVE 2-6

Identify the three types of auditor's reports that can be issued when an unqualified opinion is not justified.

1. For a scope limitation: The auditor's field work has been restricted, but the restriction is confined to a specific area such as opening inventory.
2. For a GAAP departure: The financial statements are fairly presented except for failure to comply with GAAP and the effect can be quantified or isolated.

An adverse opinion or a denial must be used if the auditor believes the condition being reported upon is extremely material. For this reason, the qualified opinion is considered a less severe type of report for disclosing departures than an adverse opinion or a denial.

A qualified opinion can take the form of a *qualification of both the scope and the opinion or of the opinion alone*. It is possible to have more than one qualification in the same report. A scope and opinion qualification can be issued only when the auditor has not been able to accumulate all the evidence required by generally accepted standards. Therefore, this type of qualification is used when the auditor's scope has been restricted by the client or when circumstances exist that prevent the auditor from conducting a complete audit.

The use of a qualification of the opinion alone is normally restricted to those situations in which a GAAP departure exists.

Whenever an auditor issues a qualified opinion, he or she must use either the term *except for* or, less frequently, *except that* and *except as* in the opinion paragraph. The implication is that the auditor is satisfied that the overall financial statements are correctly stated "except for" a particular part. Examples of qualifications are given later in the chapter. It is unacceptable to use these phrases with any type of audit opinion other than a qualified one.

It is worth noting that qualified opinions are fairly rare in practice. The provincial securities commissions will accept qualified statements from a public company only in rare circumstances. Lenders or creditors may not accept qualified statements from private companies. Consequently the conditions giving rise to the qualifications are often corrected.

ADVERSE OPINION

An adverse opinion is used only when the auditor concludes the overall financial statements are so *materially misstated or misleading* that they do not present fairly the financial position or results of operations and changes in financial position in conformity with generally accepted accounting principles because of a GAAP departure.

DENIAL OF OPINION

A denial is issued whenever the auditor has been *unable to satisfy himself or herself* that the overall financial statements are fairly presented. The necessity for denying an opinion may arise because of a *severe limitation on the scope* of the audit examination, which would prevent the auditor from expressing an opinion on the financial statements as a whole.

The denial is distinguished from an adverse opinion in that it can arise only from a *lack of knowledge* by the auditor, whereas to express an adverse opinion, the auditor must have knowledge that the financial statements are not fairly stated. Both denials and adverse opinions are used only when the extent of the scope limitation or the effects of noncompliance with GAAP are material and pervasive.

MATERIALITY

OBJECTIVE 2-7

Explain how materiality affects audit reporting decisions.

Materiality is an essential consideration in determining the appropriate type of report for a given set of circumstances. For example, if a misstatement is immaterial relative to the financial statements of the entity for the current period and is not expected to have a material effect in future periods, it is appropriate to issue an unqualified report. A common instance is the immediate expensing of office supplies rather than carrying the unused portion in inventory because the amount is insignificant.

Another consideration is the pervasiveness or significance of the scope limitation or the departure from GAAP. If the scope limitation is pervasive, a denial is appropriate; if the departure from GAAP is pervasive, an adverse opinion is appropriate. If the limitation or non-GAAP conditions are material but not significant or pervasive, a qualified opinion is appropriate.

DEFINITION

The common definition of materiality as it applies to accounting and, therefore, to audit reporting is provided in paragraph 5130.05 and is

> A misstatement in financial statements is considered to be material if knowledge of the misstatement would affect a decision of a reasonable user of the statements.

In applying this definition, three levels of materiality are used for determining the type of opinion to issue. The relationship of level of materiality to type of opinion and the significance in terms of a reasonable user's decision are presented in Table 2-1.

Amounts are immaterial When a misstatement in the financial statements exists but is unlikely to affect the decisions of a reasonable user, it is considered to be immaterial. An unqualified opinion is therefore appropriate. For example, assume management recorded unexpired insurance as an asset in the previous year and decides to expense it in the current year to reduce record-keeping costs. Management has

TABLE 2-1

RELATIONSHIP OF MATERIALITY TO TYPE OF OPINION AND SIGNIFICANCE IN TERMS OF REASONABLE USER'S DECISION

MATERIALITY LEVEL	SIGNIFICANCE IN TERMS OF REASONABLE USER'S DECISIONS	TYPE OF AUDIT REPORT	
		AUDITING RELATED Scope restricted by client or conditions	**ACCOUNTING RELATED** Financial statements not prepared in accordance with GAAP*
Immaterial	Decisions are unlikely to be affected.	Unqualified: Standard report	Unqualified: Standard report
Material	Decisions are likely to be affected only if the information in question is important to the specific decisions being made. The overall financial statements are considered fairly stated. Thus, there is a material error, but it does not overshadow the financial statements as a whole.	Qualified: Additional paragraph and qualified opinion (*except for*)	Qualified: Qualified scope, additional paragraph, and qualified opinion (*except for*)
Material and pervasive	Most or all decisions based on the financial statements are likely to be significantly affected. It is so material that the overall fairness of the financial statements is in question.	Denial of opinion	Adverse opinion

*or an appropriate disclosed basis of accounting

failed to follow GAAP, but if the amounts are small, the misstatement would be immaterial, and a standard unqualified auditor's report would be appropriate.

Amounts are material but do not overshadow the financial statements as a whole The second level of materiality exists when a misstatement in the financial statements would affect a user's decision, but the overall statements are still useful. For example, knowledge of a large misstatement in capital assets might affect a user's willingness to loan money to a company if the assets were the collateral. A misstatement of inventory does not mean that cash, accounts receivable, and other elements of the financial statements, or the financial statements as a whole, are materially incorrect.

To make materiality decisions when a condition requiring a departure from an unqualified report exists, the auditor must evaluate all effects on the financial statements. Assume the auditor is unable to satisfy himself or herself whether inventory is fairly stated (scope limitation) in deciding on the appropriate type of opinion. Because of the effect of a misstatement in inventory on other accounts and on totals in the statements, the auditor needs to consider the materiality of the combined effect on inventory, total current assets, total working capital, total assets, income taxes, income taxes payable, total current liabilities, cost of goods sold, net income before taxes, and net income after taxes.

When the auditor concludes that a misstatement is material but does not overshadow the financial statements as a whole, a qualified opinion (using "except for") is appropriate.

Amounts are so material or so pervasive that overall fairness of statements is in question The highest level of misstatement exists when users are likely to make incorrect decisions if they rely on the overall financial statements. To return to the previous example of inventory, a large misstatement could be so material to the financial statements as a whole that the auditor's report should indicate the financial statements taken as a whole cannot be considered fairly stated. When the highest level of misstatement exists, the auditor must issue either a denial of opinion or an adverse opinion.

When determining whether an exception is material and pervasive, the extent to which the exception affects different parts of the financial statements must be considered. This is referred to as *pervasiveness*. A misclassification between cash and accounts receivable affects only those two accounts and is therefore not pervasive. On the other hand, failure to record a material sale could be pervasive because it affects sales, accounts receivable, income tax expense, accrued income taxes, and retained earnings, which in turn affect current assets, total assets, current liabilities, total liabilities, owners' equity, gross margin, and operating income.

As misstatements become more pervasive, the likelihood of issuing an adverse opinion rather than a qualified opinion is increased. For example, suppose the auditor decides a misclassification between cash and accounts receivable should result in a qualified opinion because it is material; the failure to record a sale of the same dollar amount may result in an adverse opinion because of pervasiveness.

MATERIALITY DECISIONS

In concept, the effect of materiality on the type of opinion to issue is straightforward. In application, deciding upon actual materiality in a given situation is a difficult judgment. There are no simple, well-defined guidelines that enable auditors to decide when something is immaterial, material, or material and pervasive.

There are differences in applying materiality for deciding whether failure to follow GAAP is material compared to deciding whether a scope limitation is material. A discussion follows for making materiality decisions in these two situations.

Materiality decisions — GAAP departure When a client has failed to follow GAAP, the audit report will be unqualified, qualified opinion only, or adverse, depending on the materiality and pervasiveness of the departure. Several aspects of materiality must be considered.

Dollar amounts compared with a base. The primary concern in measuring materiality when a client has failed to follow GAAP is usually the total dollar misstatement in the accounts involved, compared to some base. A $10,000 misstatement might be material for a small company, but not for a larger one. Misstatements must, therefore, be compared with some measurement base before a decision can be made about the materiality of the failure to follow GAAP. Common bases include net income before taxes, total assets, current assets, and working capital.

For example, assume the auditor believes there is a $100,000 overstatement of inventory because of the client's failure to follow GAAP. Also assume recorded inventory of $1,000,000, current assets of $3,000,000, and net income before taxes of $2,000,000. In this case, the auditor must evaluate the materiality of a misstatement of inventory of 10 percent, current assets of 3.3 percent, and net income before taxes of 5 percent.

To evaluate overall materiality, the auditor must also combine all unadjusted errors and judge whether there may be individually immaterial errors that, when combined, significantly affect the statements. In the inventory example above, assume the auditor believes there is also an overstatement of $150,000 in accounts receivable. The total effect on current assets is now 8.3 percent ($250,000 divided by $3,000,000) and on net income before taxes is 12.5 percent ($250,000 divided by $2,000,000).

When comparing potential misstatements with a base, the auditor must carefully consider all accounts affected by a misstatement (pervasiveness). It is, for example, important not to overlook the effect of an understatement of ending inventory on cost of goods sold, income before taxes, income tax expense, and accrued income taxes payable.

Measurability. The dollar error of some misstatements cannot be accurately measured. For example, a client's unwillingness to disclose an existing lawsuit or the acquisition of a new company subsequent to the balance sheet date is difficult, if not impossible, to measure in terms of dollar amounts. The materiality question the auditor must evaluate in such a situation is the effect on statement users of the failure to make the disclosure.

Nature of the item. The decision of a user may also be affected by the kind of misstatement in the financial statements. The following may affect the user's decision and, therefore, the auditor's opinion in a different way than most misstatements.
1. Transactions are illegal or fraudulent.
2. An item may materially affect some future period even though it is immaterial when only the current period is considered.
3. An item has a "psychic" effect (e.g., small profit versus small loss or cash balance versus overdraft).
4. An item may be important in terms of possible consequences arising from contractual obligations (e.g., the effect of failure to comply with a debt restriction may result in a material loan being called).

Materiality decisions — scope limitations   When there is a scope limitation in an audit, the audit report will be unqualified, qualified scope and opinion, or denial, depending on the materiality and pervasiveness of the scope limitation. The auditor will consider the same three factors included in the previous discussion, but they will be considered differently. The size of *potential misstatements,* where there are scope limitations, is important in determining whether an unqualified report, a qualified report, or a denial of opinion is appropriate. For example, if recorded accounts payable of $400,000 was not audited, the auditor must evaluate the potential misstatement in accounts payable and decide how materially the financial statements could be affected. The pervasiveness of these potential misstatements must also be considered.

It is typically more difficult to evaluate the materiality of potential misstatements resulting from scope limitations than for failure to follow GAAP. Misstatements resulting from failure to follow GAAP are known. Those resulting from scope limitations must usually be subjectively measured in terms of potential or likely misstatements. For example, the recorded accounts payable of $400,000 might be understated by more than a million dollars, which may affect several totals including gross margin, net earnings, and total liabilities.

DISCUSSION OF CONDITIONS REQUIRING A DEPARTURE	You should now understand the relationship among the conditions requiring a departure from an unqualified report, the major types of reports other than unqualified, and the three levels of materiality. This part of the chapter examines the conditions requiring a departure from an unqualified report in greater detail and shows examples of reports.

AUDITOR'S SCOPE HAS BEEN RESTRICTED

OBJECTIVE 2-8
Draft appropriately modified auditor's reports under a variety of circumstances.

There are two major categories of scope restrictions: those caused by a client and those caused by conditions beyond the control of either the client or the auditor. The effect on the auditor's report is the same for either, but the interpretation of materiality is likely to be different. Whenever there is a scope restriction, the appropriate response is to issue an unqualified report, a qualification of scope and opinion, or a denial of opinion, depending on materiality and pervasiveness.

For client-imposed restrictions, the auditor should be concerned about the possibility that management is trying to prevent discovery of misstated information. In such cases, it would probably be appropriate to issue a denial of opinion whenever materiality and pervasiveness are in question. When restrictions are due to conditions beyond the client's control, a qualification of scope and opinion is more likely.

Two restrictions occasionally imposed by clients on the auditor's scope relate to the observation of physical inventory and the confirmation of accounts receivable, but other restrictions may also occur. Reasons for client-imposed scope restrictions may be a desire to save audit fees and, in the case of confirming receivables, to prevent possible conflicts between the client and customer when amounts differ. A qualified report or denial of opinion resulting from a client restriction requires a reservation paragraph to describe the restriction; the reservation paragraph is located between the scope and opinion paragraph. In addition, the opinion paragraph must be modified.

The most common case in which conditions beyond the client's and auditor's control cause a scope restriction is an engagement agreed upon after the client's balance sheet date. The confirmation of accounts receivable, physical examination of inventory, and other important procedures may not be possible under those circumstances. When the auditor cannot perform procedures he or she considers desirable but can be satisfied with alternative procedures that the information being verified is fairly stated, an unqualified report is appropriate. If alternative procedures cannot be performed, a scope qualification and, depending on the materiality and pervasiveness, either an opinion qualification or a denial of opinion is necessary. A reservation paragraph would describe the restriction.

For example, the report in Figure 2-3 would be appropriate for an audit in which the amounts were material but not pervasive, and the auditor had been unable to audit the financial statements of a company's foreign affiliate and could not satisfy himself or herself by alternative procedures. The first paragraph is omitted from the example because it contains standard wording.

When the amounts are so material that a denial of opinion is required, the introductory, scope, and middle paragraphs could remain the same, but the opinion paragraph might be as shown in Figure 2-4.

STATEMENTS ARE NOT IN CONFORMITY WITH GAAP

When the auditor knows that the financial statements may be misleading because they were not prepared in conformity with generally accepted accounting principles, he or she must issue a qualified or an adverse opinion, depending on the materiality and pervasiveness of the item in question. The opinion must clearly state the nature of the deviation from accepted principles and the amount of the misstatement, if it is known. Figure 2-5 shows an example of a qualified opinion when a client did not capitalize leases as required by GAAP. The first and second paragraphs in the example are omitted because they include standard wording.

FIGURE 2-3
Qualified Scope and Opinion Report Due to Scope Restriction

INTRODUCTORY PARAGRAPH	**AUDITOR'S REPORT**
	(Same introductory paragraph as standard report)
SCOPE PARAGRAPH — QUALIFIED	Except as explained in the following paragraph, we conducted our audit . . . (remainder is the same as the scope paragraph in the standard report).
THIRD PARAGRAPH — ADDED	We were unable to obtain audited financial statements supporting the Company's investment in a foreign affiliate stated at $475,000, or its equity in earnings of that affiliate of $365,000, which is included in net income, as described in Note X to the financial statements. Because of the nature of the Company's records, we were unable to satisfy ourselves as to the carrying value of the investment or the equity in its earnings by means of other auditing procedures.
OPINION PARAGRAPH — QUALIFIED	In our opinion, except for the effects of such adjustments, if any, as might have been determined to be necessary had we been able to examine evidence regarding the foreign affiliate investment and earnings, these financial statements present fairly, in all material respects, the financial position of Laughlin Corporation as of December 31, 2000, and the results of its operations and cash flows for the year then ended in accordance with generally accepted accounting principles.

FIGURE 2-4
Denial of Opinion Due to Scope Restriction

	AUDITOR'S REPORT
INTRODUCTORY PARAGRAPH	(Same introductory paragraph as standard report)
SCOPE PARAGRAPH — QUALIFIED	(Same scope paragraph as Figure 2-3)
THIRD PARAGRAPH — ADDED	(Same third paragraph as Figure 2-3)
OPINION PARAGRAPH — DENIAL	In view of the possible material effects on the financial statements of the matters described in the preceding paragraph, we are unable to express an opinion as to whether these financial statements are presented fairly in accordance with generally accepted accounting principles.

FIGURE 2-5
Qualified Opinion Report Due to Non-GAAP

	AUDITOR'S REPORT
INTRODUCTORY AND SCOPE PARAGRAPHS	(Same introductory and scope paragraphs as standard report)
THIRD PARAGRAPH — ADDED	The Company has excluded from property and debt in the accompanying balance sheet certain lease obligations that, in our opinion, should be capitalized in order to conform with generally accepted accounting principles. If these lease obligations were capitalized, property would be increased by $4,600,000, long-term debt by $4,200,000, and retained earnings by $400,000 as of December 31, 2000, and net income and earnings per share would be increased by $400,000 and $1.75, respectively, for the year then ended.
OPINION PARAGRAPH — QUALIFIED	In our opinion, except for the effects of not capitalizing lease obligations, as discussed in the preceding paragraph, these financial statements present fairly, in all material respects, the financial position of Ajax, Inc., as of December 31, 2000, and the results of its operations and cash flows for the year then ended in accordance with generally accepted accounting principles.

When the amounts are so material and pervasive that an adverse opinion is required, the scope would still be unqualified, the reservation paragraph could remain the same, but the opinion paragraph might be as shown in Figure 2-6.

When the client fails to include information that is necessary for the fair presentation of financial statements in the body of the statements or in the related footnotes, it is the responsibility of the auditor to present information in the auditor's report and to issue a qualified or an adverse opinion. It is common to put this type of qualification in an added paragraph (the scope paragraph will remain unqualified) and to refer to the added paragraph in the opinion paragraph. Figure 2-7 shows an example of an auditor's report in which the auditor considered the financial statement disclosure inadequate.

FIGURE 2-6
Adverse Opinion Due to Non-GAAP

	AUDITOR'S REPORT
INTRODUCTORY AND SCOPE PARAGRAPHS	(Same introductory and scope paragraphs as standard report)
THIRD PARAGRAPH — ADDED	(Same third paragraph as that used for the third paragraph in Figure 2-5)
OPINION PARAGRAPH — ADVERSE	In our opinion, because of the effects of the matters discussed in the preceding paragraph, these financial statements do not present fairly, in accordance with generally accepted accounting principles, the financial position of Ajax, Inc. as of December 31, 2000, or the results of its operations and cash flows for the year then ended.

FIGURE 2-7

Qualified Opinion Due to Inadequate Disclosure

INTRODUCTORY AND SCOPE PARAGRAPHS

THIRD PARAGRAPH — ADDED

OPINION PARAGRAPH — QUALIFIED

AUDITOR'S REPORT

(Same introductory and scope paragraphs as standard report)

On January 15, 2000, the company issued debentures in the amount of $3,600,000 for the purpose of financing plant expansion. The debenture agreement restricts the payment of future cash dividends to earnings after December 31, 1999. In our opinion, disclosure of this information is required to conform with generally accepted accounting principles.

In our opinion, except for the omission of the information discussed in the preceding paragraph, these financial statements present fairly . . . (remainder is the same as the opinion in the standard report).

EXISTENCE OF MORE THAN ONE CONDITION REQUIRING A QUALIFICATION

Auditors may encounter situations involving more than one of the conditions requiring modification of the unqualified report. In these circumstances, the auditor should qualify his or her opinion for each condition. Paragraph 5510.33 states that "[it] is essential that all reservations be disclosed because the reader of an auditor's report should be able to assume that the financial statements, except with respect to matters on which the auditor has expressed a reservation of opinion, are presented fairly in accordance with generally accepted accounting principles." An example is presented in Figure 2-8.

FIGURE 2-8

Qualified Opinion (Departure from GAAP and a Scope Limitation)

INTRODUCTORY PARAGRAPH

SCOPE PARAGRAPH — MODIFIED WORDING

THIRD PARAGRAPH — ADDED

OPINION PARAGRAPH — MODIFIED WORDING

AUDITOR'S REPORT

(Same introductory paragraph as standard report)

Except as explained in the following paragraph, we conducted our audit . . . (remainder is the same as the scope paragraph in the standard report).

Management has advised us that the company may become liable with respect to guarantees given for indebtedness of a subsidiary located in another country. However, management has declined to provide us with further information and will not permit us to contact the subsidiary as management believes disclosure is not in the company's best interests. As a result, we have been unable to obtain sufficient audit evidence to form an opinion with respect to the possible liability. Furthermore, the matter has not been disclosed in the notes to the financial statements. In our opinion, such disclosure is required under generally accepted accounting principles.

In our opinion, except that disclosure has not been made with respect to the contingent liability referred to in the preceding paragraph and except for the effect of adjustments, if any, which we may have determined to be necessary had we been able to obtain sufficient information regarding this matter, these financial statements present fairly, in all material respects, . . . (remainder is the same as the opinion in the standard report).

REPORTS INVOLVING RELIANCE ON ANOTHER AUDITOR OR A SPECIALIST

In Canada, although the main or primary auditor may rely on another auditor or a specialist in determining the appropriate opinion to issue on the financial statements, the primary auditor takes responsibility for that opinion, and only the name of the primary auditor appears on the auditor's report. *CICA Handbook* Sections 6930 and 5360 deal with the (primary) auditor's reliance on another auditor and on a specialist respectively.

The auditor may rely on another auditor because the client's business is either too complex or widespread and the primary auditor either does not have the personnel or the proximity to all the client locations to do the audits with his or her own personnel. For example, the primary auditor, a public accounting firm located in Halifax, may rely on another public accounting firm located in Regina as the secondary auditor to audit the Halifax client's subsidiary located in Regina.

Section 6930 requires the primary auditor to assess the secondary auditor's professional qualifications, competence, and integrity in determining whether or not to rely on the secondary auditor. As you will discover in Chapter 4, the primary auditor who does rely on a secondary auditor is responsible for any deficiencies in the secondary auditor's work. The decision on whether or not to rely on that work is based on the primary auditor's judgment.

As was mentioned above, if the primary auditor decides that an unqualified opinion is appropriate, the name of the secondary auditor is not mentioned. If however, the primary auditor decides that a qualified or denial of opinion is appropriate *and the qualification arises because of inability to rely on the work of the secondary auditor*, the explanation of the qualification in the third paragraph could mention the name of the secondary auditor in explaining the reason for the qualification.

The auditor may have to rely on a specialist, such as an actuary, in completing the audit. Normally the auditor would not mention the specialist or reliance on the specialist. However, if the auditor believes that a qualified or denial of opinion is appropriate *and the qualification arises because of inability to rely on the work of the specialist*, the explanation of the qualification in the third paragraph would mention the name of the specialist in explaining the reason for the qualification.

NEGATIVE ASSURANCE

It is inappropriate to include in the auditor's report any additional comments that counterbalance the auditor's opinion. For example, the use of such terminology as "However, nothing came to our attention that would lead us to question the fairness of the presentations" as a part of a denial of opinion is inappropriate and a violation of the standards of reporting. A statement of this kind, which is referred to as *negative assurance*, tends to confuse readers about the nature of the auditor's examination and the degree of responsibility he or she is assuming.

The use of negative assurance is considered appropriate only in the case of review engagements (Section 8000) and prospectuses (Section 7100). These are considered in Chapter 23.

AUDITOR'S DECISION PROCESS FOR AUDITOR'S REPORTS

OBJECTIVE 2-9

Describe the process for deciding the appropriate auditor's report.

Auditors use a well-defined process for deciding the appropriate auditor's report in a given set of circumstances. There are four steps to the process.

1. *Determine whether any condition exists requiring a departure from a standard unqualified report.* The most important of these conditions were identified in Table 2-1. Auditors identify these conditions as they perform the audit and include information about any condition in the working papers as discussion items for audit reporting. If none of these conditions exist, which is the case in the great majority of all audits, the auditor issues a standard unqualified auditor's report.

2. *Decide the materiality and pervasiveness of each condition.* When a condition requiring a departure from a standard unqualified opinion exists, the auditor evaluates the potential effect on the financial statements. For departures from generally accepted accounting principles or scope restrictions, the auditor must decide among immaterial, material, and material and pervasive. All other conditions require only a distinction between immaterial and material. The materiality decision is a difficult one, requiring considerable judgment. For example, assume that there is a scope limitation in auditing inventory. It is difficult to assess the potential misstatement of an account that the auditor does not audit.

3. *Decide the appropriate type of report for the condition, given the materiality and pervasiveness level.* After making the first two decisions, it is easy to decide the appro-

priate type of opinion by using a decision aid. An example of such an aid is Table 2-1. For example, assume that the auditor concludes that there is a departure from generally accepted accounting principles and it is material, but not material and pervasive. Table 2-1 shows that the appropriate audit report is a qualified opinion with an additional paragraph discussing the departure. The introductory and scope paragraphs will be included using the standard wording.

4. *Write the auditor's report.* Most public accounting firms have auditor's report manuals that include precise wording for different circumstances to help the auditor write the auditor's report. Also, one or more partners in most public accounting firms have special expertise in writing auditor's reports. These partners typically write or review all auditor's reports before they are issued.

ESSENTIAL TERMS

Adverse opinion — a report issued when the auditor believes the financial statements are materially misstated or misleading as a whole so that they do not present fairly the entity's financial position or the results of its operations and cash flows in conformity with generally accepted accounting principles (p. 43).

Denial of opinion — a report issued when the auditor has not been able to become satisfied that the overall financial statements are fairly presented (p. 43).

Material misstatement — a misstatement in the financial statements, knowledge of which would affect a decision of a reasonable user of the statements (p. 43).

Qualified opinion — a report issued when the auditor believes that financial statements are fairly stated but that either there was a material, but not pervasive, limitation in scope of the audit, or there was a failure to follow GAAP that resulted in a material, but not pervasive, misstatement in the financial statements. (p. 42).

Standard unqualified auditor's report — the report a public accountant issues when all auditing conditions have been met, no significant misstatements have been discovered and left uncorrected, and it is the auditor's opinion that the financial statements are fairly stated in accordance with generally accepted accounting principles (p. 35).

REVIEW QUESTIONS

2-1 Explain why auditor's reports are important to users of financial statements.

2-2 What five circumstances are required for a standard unqualified report to be issued?

2-3 List the eight parts of an unqualified auditor's report and explain the meaning of each part. How do the parts compare with those found in a qualified report?

2-4 What are the purposes of the introductory paragraph in the auditor's report? Identify the most important information included in the introductory paragraph.

2-5 What are the purposes of the scope paragraph in the auditor's report? Identify the most important information included in the scope paragraph.

2-6 What are the purposes of the opinion paragraph in the auditor's report? Identify the most important information included in the opinion paragraph.

2-7 What is meant by the term "appropriate disclosed basis of accounting"? How does such a basis differ from GAAP? When is such a basis acceptable?

2-8 On February 17, 2000, a public accountant completed the examination of the financial statements for the Buckheizer Corporation for the year ended December 31, 1999. The audit is satisfactory in all respects. On February 26, the auditor completed the tax return and the pencil draft of the financial statements. The final auditor's report was completed, attached to the financial statements, and delivered to the client on March 7. What is the appropriate date on the auditor's report?

2-9 Explain what action an auditor should take when a client tells the auditor that the company has changed from straight-line to accelerated amortization. Explain what action an auditor should take when a client tells the auditor that the company has decided that the useful life of a significant capital asset should be increased from five to ten years.

2-10 Explain what is meant by "contingencies." Give an example of a contingency and discuss its appropriate disclosure in the financial statements.

2-11 What is meant by "going concern consideration"? Provide an example of such a condition and describe how it might be appropriately disclosed in the financial statements.

2-12 List the conditions requiring a departure from an unqualified opinion, and give one specific example of each of those conditions.

2-13 Distinguish between a qualified opinion, an adverse opinion, and a denial of opinion, and explain the circumstances under which each is appropriate.

2-14 Define "materiality" as it is used in audit reporting. What conditions will affect the auditor's determination of materiality?

2-15 Distinguish between the three levels of materiality an auditor considers when assessing how to deal with a non-GAAP condition in the financial statements.

2-16 How does an auditor's opinion differ between scope limitations caused by client restrictions and limitations resulting from conditions beyond the client's control? What is the effect of each on the auditor's work?

2-17   Munroe Corp. had a bad year financially and the president, Jan de Boer, instructed the controller not to amortize the capital assets so that the company would show a small profit. The controller argued that GAAP required Munroe to amortize the capital assets on a regular basis and a qualified auditor's report would likely result. De Boer told the controller to disclose the failure to record amortization in the notes to the financial statements. You are the in-charge auditor on the Munroe audit. Write a memo to de Boer in response to the controller's suggestion.

2-18   Identify the three alternative opinions that may be appropriate when the client's financial statements are not in accordance with GAAP. Under what circumstance is each appropriate?

2-19   When an auditor discovers more than one condition that requires modification of the unqualified report, what should the auditor's report include?

2-20   At times, for a variety of reasons, an auditor must rely on another firm of auditors to perform part of an audit. What reference does the primary auditor make to the secondary auditor in the auditor's report?

MULTIPLE CHOICE QUESTIONS

2-21   The following questions concern unqualified auditor's reports. Choose the best response.

a.   An auditor's unqualified standard report
(1)   implies only that items disclosed in the financial statements and footnotes are properly presented and takes no position on the adequacy of disclosure.
(2)   implies that disclosure is adequate in the financial statements and footnotes.
(3)   explicitly states that all material items have been disclosed in conformity with generally accepted accounting principles.
(4)   explicitly states that disclosure is adequate in the financial statements and footnotes.

b.   The date of a public accountant's opinion on the financial statements of a client should be the date of the
(1)   receipt of the client's letter of representation.
(2)   completion of all important audit procedures.
(3)   submission of the report to the client.
(4)   closing of the client's books.

c.   A primary auditor would refer in the auditor's report to the examination of another auditor because
(1)   the other auditor is not the primary auditor's agent.
(2)   the work of the other auditor was material in relation to the primary auditor's work.
(3)   the principle auditor was unable to express an opinion without reservation because of an inability to rely on the work of the other auditor.
(4)   the primary auditor had doubts as to the competence of the secondary auditor.

(AICPA adapted)

2-22   The following question concerns auditor's reports other than unqualified reports. Choose the best response.

a.   If an auditor issues an adverse auditor's report when there is a very material contingency, the reader of the auditor's report should conclude that
(1)   the auditor was not able to form an opinion on the outcome of the contingency.
(2)   the auditor became aware of the contingency after the balance sheet date but prior to the audit report date.
(3)   there were no audit procedures available to the auditor by which he or she could obtain satisfaction concerning the outcome of uncertainty.
(4)   the note disclosure with respect to the contingency was not adequate.

b.   A public accountant will issue an adverse auditor's opinion if
(1)   the scope of his or her examination is limited by the client.
(2)   his or her exception to the fairness of presentation is so material and pervasive such that an "except for" opinion is not justified.
(3)   he or she did not perform sufficient auditing procedures to form an opinion on the financial statements taken as a whole.
(4)   major uncertainties exist concerning the company's future such that an "except for" opinion is not justified.

c.   An auditor will express an "except for" opinion if
(1)   the client refuses to provide for a probable income tax liability that is very material.
(2)   there is a high degree of uncertainty associated with the client company's future.
(3)   he or she did not perform procedures sufficient to form an opinion on the valuation of accounts receivable which are material.
(4)   the auditor is basing his or her opinion in part upon work done by another auditor.

d.   Under which of the following circumstances should an auditor issue a qualified or adverse opinion?
(1)   The financial statements contain a departure from generally accepted accounting principles, the effect of which is material.
(2)   The primary auditor decides to make reference to the report of another auditor who audited a subsidiary.
(3)   There has been a material change between periods in the method of the application of accounting principles.
(4)   Note disclosure describing significant uncertainties affecting the financial statements is not adequate.

(AICPA adapted)

2-23 A careful reading of a standard unqualified auditor's report indicates several important phrases. Explain why each of the following phrases or clauses is used rather than the alternative provided.

a. "In our opinion, these financial statements present fairly" rather than "These financial statements present fairly."

b. "We conducted our audit in accordance with generally accepted auditing standards" rather than "Our audit was performed to detect material misstatements in the financial statements."

c. "These financial statements present fairly, in all material respects, the financial position" rather than "These financial statements are correctly stated."

d. "In accordance with generally accepted accounting principles" rather than "are properly stated to represent the true economic conditions."

e. "Brown & Phillips, CAs (firm name)," rather than "James E. Brown, CA (individual partner's name)."

2-24 Roscoe, public accountant, has completed the examination of the financial statements of Excelsior Corporation as of and for the year ended December 31, 1999. Roscoe also examined and reported on the Excelsior financial statements for the prior year. Roscoe drafted the following report for 1999:

> We have audited the balance sheet and statements of income and retained earnings of Excelsior Corporation as of December 31, 1999. We conducted our audit in accordance with generally accepted accounting standards. Those standards require that we plan and perform the audit to obtain reasonable assurance about whether the financial statements are free of misstatement.
>
> We believe that our audits provide a reasonable basis for our opinion.
>
> In our opinion, the financial statements referred to above present fairly the financial position of Excelsior Corporation as of December 31, 1999, and the results of its operations for the year then ended in conformity with generally accepted auditing standards, applied on a basis consistent with those of the preceding year.
>
> (Signed)
>
> Roscoe, Public Accountant

Other Information:

- Excelsior is presenting comparative financial statements.
- Excelsior does not wish to present a cash flow statement for either year.
- During 1999, Excelsior changed its method of accounting for long-term construction contracts, properly reflected the effect of the change in the current year's financial statements, and restated the prior year's statements. Roscoe is satisfied with Excelsior's justification for making the change. The change is discussed in footnote 12.
- Roscoe was unable to perform normal accounts receivable confirmation procedures, but alternate procedures were used to satisfy Roscoe as to the existence of the receivables.
- Excelsior Corporation is the defendant in a lawsuit, the outcome of which is highly uncertain. If the case is settled in favour of the plaintiff, Excelsior will be required to pay a substantial amount of cash which might require the sale of certain capital assets. The litigation and the possible effects have been properly disclosed in footnote 11.
- Excelsior issued debentures on January 31, 1997, in the amount of $10,000,000. The funds obtained from the issuance were used to finance the expansion of plant facilities. The debenture agreement restricts the payment of future cash dividends to earnings after December 31, 1998. Excelsior declined to disclose this essential data in the footnotes to the financial statements.

Required

a. Identify and explain any items included in "Other Information" that need not be part of the auditor's report.

b. Explain the deficiencies in Roscoe's auditor's report as drafted.

(AICPA adapted)

2-25 For the following independent situations, assume you are the audit partner on the engagement.

1. During your examination of Debold Batteries Ltd., you conclude there is a possibility that inventory is materially overstated. The client refuses to allow you to expand the scope of your examination sufficiently to verify whether the balance is actually misstated.

2. You are auditing Woodcolt Linen Services, Inc., for the first time. Woodcolt has been in business for several years but has never had an audit before. After the audit is completed, you conclude that the current year balance sheet is stated correctly in accordance with GAAP. The client did not authorize you to do test work for any of the previous years.

3. You were engaged to examine the Cutter Steel Corp.'s financial statements after the close of the corporation's fiscal year. Because you were not engaged until after the balance sheet date, you were not able to physically observe inventory, which is very material. On the completion of your audit, you are satisfied that Cutter's financial statements are presented fairly, including inventory about which you were able to satisfy yourself by the use of alternative audit procedures.

4. Four weeks after the year-end date, a major customer of Prince Construction Ltd. declared bankruptcy. Because the customer had confirmed the balance due to Prince at the balance sheet date, management refuses to charge off the account or otherwise disclose the information. The receivable represents approximately 10 percent of accounts receivable and 20 percent of net earnings before taxes.

5. You complete the audit of Johnson Department Store Ltd., and, in your opinion, the financial statements are fairly presented. On the last day of the examination, you discover that one of your supervisors assigned to the audit had a material investment in Johnson. If you decide no auditor's report can be issued, explain your decision.

6. Auto Delivery Company Ltd. has a fleet of several delivery trucks. In the past, Auto Delivery had followed the policy of purchasing all equipment. In the current year, they decided to lease the trucks. This change in policy is fully disclosed in footnotes.

Required

For each situation, state the type of auditor's report that should be issued. If your decision depends on additional information, state the alternative reports you are considering and the additional information you need to make the decision.

2-26 For the following independent situations, assume you are the audit partner on the engagement.

1. Kieko Corporation has prepared financial statements but has decided to exclude the statement cash flow. Management explains to you that the users of their financial statements find that particular statement confusing and prefer not to have it included.

2. Jet Stream Airlines, Inc., has been audited by your firm for ten years. In the past three years their financial condition has steadily declined. In the current year, for the first time, the current ratio is below 2:1, which is the minimum requirement specified in Jet Stream's major loan agreement. You now have reservations about the ability of Jet Stream to continue in operation for the next year.

3. Approximately 20 percent of the audit for Furtney Farms, Inc., was performed by a different public accounting firm, selected by you. You have reviewed its working papers and believe it did an excellent job on its portion of the audit. Nevertheless, you are unwilling to take complete responsibility for its work.

4. The controller of Fair City Hotels Co. Ltd. will not allow you to confirm the receivable balance from two of its major customers. The amount of the receivable is material in relation to Fair City's financial statements. You are unable to satisfy yourself as to the receivable balance by alternative procedures.

5. In the last three months of the current year, Oil Refining Corp. decided to change direction and go significantly into the oil-drilling business. Management recognizes that this business is exceptionally risky and could jeopardize the success of its existing refining business, but there are significant potential rewards. During the short period of operation in drilling, the company has had three dry wells and no successes. The facts are adequately disclosed in footnotes.

6. Your client, Auto Rental Corporation, has changed from straight-line to accelerated depreciation. The effect on this year's income is immaterial, but the effect in future years is likely to be material. The facts are adequately disclosed in footnotes.

Required

a. For each situation, identify which of the conditions requiring modification of or a deviation from an unqualified standard report is applicable.

b. State the level of materiality as immaterial, material, or material and pervasive. If you cannot decide the level of materiality, state the additional information needed to make a decision.

c. Given your answers in parts (a) and (b), identify the appropriate auditor's report from the following choices:
  1. Unqualified — standard wording
  2. Qualified opinion only — except for
  3. Scope and opinion qualified
  4. Denial
  5. Adverse

2-27 The following are independent situations for which you will recommend an appropriate auditor's report:

1. Subsequent to the date of the financial statements as part of the post-balance sheet date audit procedures, a public accountant learned of heavy damage to one of a client's two plants due to a recent fire; the loss will not be reimbursed by insurance. The newspapers described the event in detail. The financial statements and appended notes as prepared by the client did not disclose the loss caused by the fire.

2. A public accountant is engaged in the examination of the financial statements of a large manufacturing company with branch offices in many widely separate cities. The public accountant was not able to count the substantial undeposited cash receipts at the close of business on the last day of the fiscal year at all branch offices.

   As an alternative to this auditing procedure used to verify the accurate cutoff of cash receipts, the public accountant observed that deposits in transit as shown on the year-end bank reconciliation appeared as credits on the bank statement on the first business day of the new year. The public accountant was satisfied as to the cutoff of cash receipts by the use of the alternative procedure.

3. On January 2, 2000, the Retail Auto Parts Company Limited received a notice from its primary supplier that, effective immediately, all wholesale prices would be increased by 10 percent. On the basis of the notice, Retail Auto Parts revalued its December 31, 1999, inventory to reflect the higher costs. The inventory constituted a material proportion of total assets; however, the effect of the revaluation was material to current assets but not to total assets or net income. The increase in valuation is adequately disclosed in the footnotes.

4. During 1999, the research staff of Scientific Research Corporation devoted its entire efforts toward developing a new pollution-control device. All costs that could be attributed directly to the project were accounted for as deferred charges and classified on the balance sheet at December 31, 1999, as a noncurrent asset. In the course of her audit of the corporation's 1999 financial statements, Marika Vlasic, public accountant, found persuasive evidence that the research conducted to date would

probably result in a marketable product. The deferred research charges are significantly material in relation to both income and total assets.

5. For the past five years, a public accountant has audited the financial statements of a manufacturing company. During this period, the examination scope was limited by the client as to the observation of the annual physical inventory. Since the public accountant considered the inventories to be of material amount and he was not able to satisfy himself by other auditing procedures, he was not able to express an unqualified opinion on the financial statements in each of the five years.

    The public accountant was allowed to observe physical inventories for the current year ended December 31, 1999, because the client's banker would no longer accept the qualified auditor's reports. In the interest of economy, the client requested that the public accountant not extend his audit procedures to the inventory as of January 1, 1999.

6. During the course of the examination of the financial statements of a corporation for the purpose of expressing an opinion on the statements, a public accountant is refused permission to inspect the minute books. The corporation secretary instead offers to give the public accountant a certified copy of all resolutions and actions relating to accounting matters.

7. A public accountant has completed her examination of the financial statements of a bus company for the year ended December 31, 1999. Prior to 1999, the company had been amortizing its buses over a 10-year period. During 1999, the company determined that a more realistic estimated life for its buses was 12 years and computed the 1999 amortization on the basis of the revised estimate. The public accountant has satisfied herself that the 12-year life is reasonable.

    The company has adequately disclosed the change in estimated useful lives of its buses and the effect of the change on 1999 income in a note to the financial statements.

Required

a. For each situation, identify which of the conditions requiring a deviation from or modification of an unqualified standard report is applicable.

b. State the level of materiality as immaterial, material, or material and pervasive. If you cannot decide the level of materiality, state the additional information needed to make a decision.

c. Given your answers in parts (a) and (b), identify the appropriate auditor's report from the following alternatives:
   (1) Unqualified — standard wording
   (2) Qualified opinion only — except for
   (3) Qualified scope and opinion
   (4) Denial
   (5) Adverse

(AICPA adapted)

2-28 GAAP (*CICA Handbook*, paragraph 1000.23) suggests that accounting principles need to be consistently applied if the financial statements of an entity are to be comparable over time. Users of audited financial statements are entitled to assume, therefore, that accounting principles have been consistently applied unless the footnotes and/or the auditor's report provide information to the contrary.

Assume that the following list describes changes that have a material effect on a client's financial statements for the current year.

1. A change from the FIFO method of inventory pricing to the LIFO method of inventory pricing.

2. A change from the completed-contract method to the percentage-of-completion method of accounting for long-term construction contracts.

3. A change in the estimated useful life of previously recorded fixed assets based on newly acquired information.

4. Correction of a mathematical error in inventory pricing made in a prior period.

5. A change from direct costing to full absorption costing for inventory valuation.

6. A change from presentation of statements of individual companies to presentation of consolidated statements.

7. A change from deferring and amortizing preproduction costs to recording such costs as an expense when incurred because future benefits of the costs have become doubtful. The new accounting method was adopted in recognition of the change in estimated future benefits.

8. A change in the percentages applied to aged accounts receivable in determining the appropriate allowance for doubtful accounts. The new percentages are based on a change in the company's credit policy.

Required

Identify the type of change described in each item above, and indicate how the change would be disclosed to users of the financial statements. Organize your answer sheet as shown below. For example, the change from the FIFO method of inventory pricing to the LIFO method of inventory pricing described in (1) above would appear as shown. (Assume that each item is material.)

ITEM NO.	TYPE OF CHANGE	DESCRIPTION OF DISCLOSURE
1.	A change from one generally accepted method of cost determination of inventory for another generally accepted method of cost determination of inventory.	The change should be applied retroactively with restatement of all prior periods presented. The notes to the financial statements should describe the change and the effect of the change as well as the fact that the change was applied retroactively.

(AICPA adapted)

2-29 You are the senior on the audit of Kootenay Real Estate Holdings Ltd., a company listed on the Vancouver Stock Exchange whose year end is December 31. As you complete your audit and prepare your auditor's report, you learn that a U.S. subsidiary, Kootenay (U.S.), Inc., whose year end is September 30, has been subjected to a series of foreclosures over the past four months on properties located in Texas. Although you are concerned that the continued viability of Kootenay (U.S.) may be threatened, the management of the Canadian parent does not want to delay the issue of the consolidated financial statements. Management will not permit you to request the auditors of the U.S. firm to follow up on your discovery.

Required

Draft the auditor's report you deem to be appropriate for the year ended December 31, 1999. Consider Kootenay (U.S.), Inc., to be material to the Canadian parent. The audit was completed March 9, 2000.

2-30 You are the in-charge on the audit of Saskatoon Building Products Limited (SBP), a company listed on the Alberta Stock Exchange. In the course of your audit, you discover that SBP's working capital ratio is below 2:1 and that, therefore, the company is in default on a substantial loan from Prairie Bank. Management announces to you its intention to sell a large block of provincial bonds, which were included in long-term investments, and some land that had been purchased for expansion, which was included in capital assets. Management proposes including the bonds and land as current assets pending disposition. Such inclusion would increase the current ratio to 2.2:1.

Prairie Bank and your client have not enjoyed cordial relations of late, and you have been advised by Avril Chui, the manager of the Saskatoon branch, that they "are looking forward to receiving the audited statements because they are concerned that SBP has been having problems."

Required

a. Draft the memo to your partner outlining the problem.

b. Draft the auditor's report.

2-31 The following are two unrelated situations:

1. You are the auditor of Xact Ltd., a company which at December 31, 1999, had working capital of $200,000, total assets of $2,500,000, and total liabilities of $2,200,000. During the three years ended December 31, 1999, the company has sustained operating losses totalling $700,000.

   Management has been informed that Butler Inc. will not renew a debenture they hold issued by Xact in the amount of $500,000 and maturing September 30, 2000. The debenture is presently classed as a long-term liability. Although preliminary discussions have already been held with various commercial lenders, it presently appears uncertain as to whether Xact will be able to refinance this debt. In addition, it appears doubtful that Xact will be able to obtain short-term borrowing to finance the debt.

2. Your client, Bat Ltd., owns 15 percent of the shares of Bird Ltd. The 1999 pre-tax net income of Bat is $1,000,000 and its shareholder's equity is $3,000,000.

   The investment in Bird is carried on Bat's balance sheet (as of December 31, 1999) at $250,000, which represents original cost. Bird has incurred significant losses in the past few years. A current appraisal by a qualified business valuator indicates that the current market value of 100 percent of the issued and outstanding shares of Bird is $1,000,000. You are also aware that an investor who held 20 percent of the shares of Bird recently sold those shares for $180,000.

   Your client, Bat Ltd., insists that the shares be shown at their original cost of $250,000 but is willing to expand note disclosure.

Required

a. Outline possible deviations (if any) from a standard auditor's report that may be necessary, and give reasons. State your assumptions.

b. Outline the minimum note disclosure you would consider adequate in the circumstances. What additional disclosure would be desirable?

(CICA adapted)

2-32 The following is an auditor's report, except for the opinion paragraph, of Tri-Nation Corp.

AUDITOR'S REPORT

To the Shareholders of Tri-Nation Corp.

We have audited the accompanying consolidated balance sheet of Tri-Nation Corp. and subsidiaries as of July 31, 1999, and the related statements of income, shareholders' equity, and cash flow for the year then ended. These financial statements are the responsibility of the company's management. Our responsibility is to express an opinion on these financial statements based on our audit.

Except as explained in the following paragraph, we conducted our audit in accordance with generally accepted auditing standards. Those standards require that we plan and perform an audit to obtain reasonable assurance as to whether the financial statements are free of material misstatement. An audit includes examining, on a test basis, evidence supporting the amounts and disclosures in the financial statements. An audit also includes assessing the accounting principles used and significant estimates made by management, as well as evaluating the overall financial statement presentation.

The company had significant deficiencies in internal control, including the lack of detailed records and certain supporting data which were not available for our examination. Therefore, we were not able to obtain sufficient evidence in order to form an opinion on the accompanying financial statements, including whether the inventory at July 31, 1999, ($670,490) was stated at lower of cost or market, or whether the deferred subscription revenue ($90,260) is an adequate estimate for the applicable liability, as discussed in notes 5 and 12, respectively.

Required

Write the opinion paragraph for this auditor's report. State any assumptions you have made.

2-33 The following tentative auditor's report was drafted by a staff accountant and submitted to a partner in the public accounting firm of Bettrioni & Bee.

AUDITOR'S REPORT

To the Audit Committee of Athabaska Widgets, Inc.

We have examined the consolidated balance sheet of Athabaska Widgets, Inc., and subsidiaries as of December 31, 1999, and the related consolidated statement of income, retained earnings, and cash flow for the year then ended. These financial statements are the responsibility of the company's management. Our responsibility is to express an opinion on these financial statements based on our audit.

Our examinations were made in accordance with generally accepted auditing standards as we considered necessary in the circumstances. Other auditors examined the financial statements of certain subsidiaries and have furnished us with reports thereon containing no exceptions. Our opinion expressed herein, insofar as it relates to the amounts included for those subsidiaries, is based solely upon the reports of the other auditors.

As discussed in note 4 to the financial statements, on January 8, 2000, the company halted the production of certain medical equipment as a result of inquiries by the Alberta Medical Association, which raised questions as to the adequacy of some of the company's sterilization equipment and related procedures. Management is not in a position to evaluate the effect of this production halt and the ensuing litigation, which may have an adverse effect on the financial position of Athabaska Widgets, Inc.

As fully discussed in note 7 to the financial statements, in 1999 the company extended the use of the average cost method of accounting to include all inventories. In examining inventories, we engaged Dr. Irwin Same (Nobel Prize winner, 1992) to test check the technical requirements and specifications of certain items of equipment manufactured by the company.

In our opinion, except for the effects, if any, on the financial statements of the ultimate resolution of the matter discussed in the second preceding paragraph, the financial statements referred to above present fairly the financial position of Athabaska Widgets, Inc., as of December 31, 1999, the results of operations for the year then ended, in conformity with generally accepted accounting principles.

> To be signed by
> Bettrioni & Bee

> March 1, 2000, except for note 4 for
> which the date is January 8, 2000

Required

Identify deficiencies in the staff accountant's tentative report that constitute departures from the generally accepted standards of reporting.

(AICPA adapted)

2-34 Following are the complete financial statements of the Yu Manufacturing Corporation and the auditor's report of the examination for the year ended January 31, 1999. The examination was conducted by John Smith, sole practitioner, who has examined the corporation's financial statements and has reported on them for many years.

YU MANUFACTURING CORPORATION
Statements of Condition January 31, 1999 and 1998

	1999	1998
Assets		
Current assets:		
Cash	$ 43,822	$ 51,862
Accounts receivable, pledged — less allowance for doubtful accounts of $3,800 in 1999 and $3,000 in 1998 (see note)	65,298	46,922
Inventories, pledged — at average cost, not in excess of replacement cost	148,910	118,264
Other current assets	6,280	5,192
Total current assets	$264,310	$222,240
Capital assets:		
Land — at cost	38,900	62,300
Buildings — at cost, less accumulated amortization of $50,800 in 1999 and $53,400 in 1998	174,400	150,200
Machinery and equipment — at cost, less accumulated amortization of $30,500 in 1999 and $25,640 in 1998	98,540	78,560
Total capital assets	$311,840	$291,060
Total assets	$576,150	$513,300
Liabilities and Shareholders' Equity		
Current liabilities:		
Accounts payable	$ 27,926	$ 48,161
Other liabilities	68,743	64,513
Current portion of long-term mortgage payable	3,600	3,600
Income taxes payable	46,840	30,866
Total current liabilities	$147,109	$147,140
Long-term liabilities:		
Mortgage payable	90,400	94,000
Total liabilities	$237,509	$241,140
Shareholders' equity:		
Capital stock, no par value, 1,000 shares authorized, issued and outstanding	$100,000	$100,000
Retained earnings	236,641	172,160
Total shareholders' equity	$338,641	$272,160
Total liabilities and shareholders' equity	$576,150	$513,300

YU MANUFACTURING CORPORATION
Income Statements for the Year Ended January 31, 1999 and 1998

	1999	1998
Income:		
Sales	$884,932	$682,131
Other income	3,872	2,851
Total	$888,804	$684,982
Costs and expenses:		
Costs of goods sold	$452,013	$353,842
Selling expenses	241,698	201,986
Administrative expenses	72,154	66,582
Provision for income taxes	45,876	19,940
Other expenses	12,582	13,649
Total	$824,323	$655,999
Net income	$ 64,481	$ 28,983

January 31, 1999
To: Mr. Paul Yu, President

Yu Manufacturing Corporation

I have examined the balance sheet of the Yu Manufacturing Corporation and the related statements of income and retained earnings.

These statements present fairly the financial position and results of operations in conformity with generally accepted principles of accounting applied on a consistent basis. My examination was made in accordance with generally accepted auditing standards and, accordingly, included such tests of the accounting records and such other auditing procedures as I considered necessary in the circumstances.

(Signed)

John Smith

Required

List and discuss the deficiencies of the auditor's report prepared by John Smith. Your discussion should include justification that the matters you cited are deficiencies. (Do not check the additions in the statements. Assume that the additions are correct.)

(AICPA adapted)

2-35 Grogus Limited (GL) is a private company, incorporated in 1995 under federal legislation. GL was audited for the first time for the year ended July 31, 1999, by a CA who issued a qualified audit opinion because GL did not record amortization. According to the CA's estimate, the amount not recorded last year was $125,000 or approximately 20 percent of last year's income. During the current year, the vice-president of finance approached the CA indicating that he wanted an unqualified opinion for the year ending July 31, 2000, as he anticipates that the company will become a public company in the near future.

The vice-president of finance has presented the CA with the following contentious accounting issues facing the company:

1. GL has not in the past recorded amortization on its fixed assets. The president's feelings about this subject were noted in last year's report to the shareholders as follows: "Our capital assets are increasing, not decreasing in value. In my opinion, the recording of this fictitious expense (amortization) will make our financial statements misleading."

    The Board of Directors, however, has agreed that amortization will be recorded this year in order to obtain an unqualified opinion. The computation of the amortization expense would take into consideration residual value of the capital assets and a remaining asset life of 12 years, which the CA agrees is the maximum remaining life of the assets. According to the Board of Directors, residual values have been estimated after giving effect to expected increases of $1,000,000 in those values over the next 12 years.

2. During 1999, GL was sued by a customer who used one of GL's products to manufacture items that were returned by its customers due to failure of the GL component. The amount in dispute is $250,000. It is estimated that the legal fees will amount to $50,000.

    Correspondence this year indicates that an out-of-court settlement for $100,000 would be acceptable to the customer. GL wants to accrue no more than $74,000 because GL officials feel that the customer will eventually accept this amount or less.

3. During the year, the company has incurred expenditures of $400,000 related to the development of a refinement on one of its existing products. The large majority of the costs were related to the design, construction, and testing of pre-production prototypes. The technical feasibility of the refinement has been clearly established and management is now optimistic that it will be a profitable product for the company.

    Similar expenditures of $200,000 had been written off last year, as at that time it was management's opinion that they would not continue with the project. Management has reinstated the $200,000 of expenditures incurred last year by a credit to miscellaneous income and intends to write off the total development costs incurred of $600,000 over a period of five years.

4. In connection with the installation of a new computer system during the year, software costs of $270,000 were incurred and capitalized. GL is willing to amortize such costs over this year and the next five years to the end of the computer lease.

5. During the year, the company sold a building for a gain of $200,000 which has been included in miscellaneous income. The related income taxes of $75,000 were included in the provision for income taxes.

6. Last year GL capitalized $60,000 of interest on debt during the period of construction of one of its manufacturing buildings. The $60,000 was expensed for income tax purposes, but no future income tax liability was recorded. GL is willing to amortize the capitalized sums over a period of 20 years, commencing in the current year.

7. In both this and the previous year, GL has received approximately 40 percent of its revenue from one customer. The loss of this customer would result in significant excess capacity for the company.

    GL's net income for the current year was $1,500,000 prior to recording any adjustment(s) required to resolve the contentious accounting issues.

Required

a. Discuss the audit report considerations for each issue presented. Describe the alternative methods available for resolving each contentious issue.

b. Assume management has agreed with all your recommendations. Draft your auditor's report, omitting the scope paragraph.

(CICA adapted)

2-36 Raven Limited is a Canadian company engaged in a wholesaling business and currently distributes three major product lines. Over the years, the company has distributed several other product lines, only to discontinue them when the competition became too intense. During the past three years, one of its product lines, the carbon filtering systems, has suffered a continual decline in sales volume and has had a negative effect on the company's operating profits. At December 31, 1998, a significant portion of the inventory of carbon filtering systems was about two years old.

In October 1998, management decided to discontinue distribution of carbon filtering systems, and notified the company's customers that it would continue to sell the inventory on hand but would no longer accept orders for items that would have to be purchased from a manufacturer. After this notice was sent to the company's customers, the sales volume of carbon filtering systems declined even further. Therefore, management decided in early 1999 to sell this inventory in bulk to one of the company's competitors.

Management informs you in Feburary 1999 that it is currently negotiating the sale with one competitor and that the asking price is $1,100,000, which it is confident it will get. It is unwilling to permit you to review any documentation supporting the current negotiations because of a commitment made not to disclose the purchaser's identity. It also informs you that the only firm written offer received so far is from a second competitor and the amount of this offer is $800,000. It is prepared to provide you with a copy of this offer.

Based on these facts, management concludes that a write-down of $500,000 (i.e., to the amount of $1,100,000 currently being negotiated) is all that is required. Management believes that this should be treated as an extraordinary item and will make any disclosure you request, but will not change its position on this item.

Required

Discuss the effect of this issue on the auditor's report.

(CICA adapted)

3

PROFESSIONAL ETHICS

PROFESSIONAL ACCOUNTANTS ARE HELD TO THE HIGHEST ETHICAL STANDARDS

Steve Smith stared blankly at the empty chair across from him at staff training school. Yesterday, that chair had been occupied by Bruce Tucker. Steve had gone to school with Bruce and had been a little surprised when Bruce received an offer from the firm. Bruce was a nice enough guy, but he hadn't been an ace in the classroom. The buzz at coffee break that morning was that the firm discovered that Bruce had lied about his grade point average on his résumé, and that there were other inconsistencies on his résumé as well. The word was that Bruce had been summarily dismissed from the firm.

Wow! thought Steve. He had known students who cheated and others who padded expense reports from their interview trips. He felt that these actions were wrong but hadn't given them much thought. His thoughts were interrupted by the voice of Tom Conigliaro, the training session leader. "We'll start this morning with a discussion of the firm's ethical requirements. The public depends on us, and we are held to the highest ethical standards of any profession."

Ethics is a topic that is receiving a great deal of attention throughout our society today. This attention is an indication of both the importance of ethical behaviour in maintaining a civil society, and a significant number of notable instances of unethical behaviour. The authors believe that ethical behaviour is the backbone of the practice of public accounting and deserving of serious study by all accounting students. This chapter is intended to motivate such study. It begins with a definition and discussion of ethics at a general level, continues with a consideration of ethical dilemmas and how they can be approached, and ends with a discussion of ethics in the accounting profession focused on certain of the more important rules of conduct of chartered accountants and certified general accountants, who make up the bulk of practising public accountants in Canada. Certified management accountants and certified internal auditors also have rules of conduct promulgated by their respective organizations, but their rules tend to focus more on their dealings with their employers than on their relationship with the public.

While certain of the rules to be discussed, such as integrity and due care, are common to CAs, CGAs, CMAs, and CIAs, others, such as independence, relate more to public accountants performing the attest function and engaged in internal auditing. The focus of this chapter will be on, primarily, those rules of conduct that apply to public accounting; many of those rules, such as independence, also apply to internal auditing. The references to public accountants or professional public accountants in this chapter are to CAs, CGAs, or CMAs who serve the public in a variety of ways through the firms to which they belong; the references are not to firms made up of individuals who may also provide services to the public but who do not have a professional designation.

WHAT ARE ETHICS?

OBJECTIVE 3-1

Distinguish ethical behaviour from unethical behaviour in personal, professional, and business contexts.

Ethics can be defined broadly as a set of moral principles or values. Each of us has such a set of values, although we may or may not have considered them explicitly. Philosophers, religious organizations, and other groups have defined in various ways ideal sets of moral principles or values. Examples of prescribed sets of moral principles or values at the implementation level include laws and regulations, church doctrine, codes of business ethics for professional groups such as CAs, CGAs, CMAs, and CIAs, and codes of conduct within individual organizations such as accounting firms, corporations, and universities.

An example of a prescribed set of principles is that developed by the Josephson Institute for the Advancement of Ethics, included in Figure 3-1. The Josephson Institute was established as a not-for-profit foundation to encourage ethical conduct of professionals in the fields of government, law, medicine, business, accounting, and journalism.

It is common for people to differ in their moral principles or values. For example, a person might examine the Josephson Institute's ethical principles and conclude that several principles should not be included. Even if two people agree on the ethical principles that determine ethical behaviour, it is unlikely that they will agree on the relative importance of each principle. These differences result from all of our life experiences. Parents, teachers, friends, and employers are known to influence our values, but so do television, team sports, life successes and failures, and thousands of other experiences.

NEED FOR ETHICS

Ethical behaviour is necessary for a society to function in an orderly manner. It can be argued that ethics is the glue that holds a society together. Imagine, for example, what would happen if we couldn't depend on the people we deal with to be honest. If parents, teachers, employers, siblings, coworkers, and friends all consistently lied, it would be almost impossible for effective communication to occur.

The need for ethics in society is sufficiently important that many commonly held ethical values are incorporated into laws. For example, laws dealing with driving while intoxicated and selling drugs concern responsible citizenship and respect for others. Similarly, if a company sells a defective product, it can be held accountable if harmed parties choose to sue through the legal system.

A considerable portion of the ethical values of a society cannot be incorporated into law due to the judgmental nature of certain values. Looking again at Figure 3-1 at the honesty principle, it is practical to have laws that deal with cheating, stealing, lying, or deceiving others. It is far more difficult to establish meaningful laws that deal with many aspects of principles such as integrity, loyalty, and pursuit of excellence. That does not imply that these principles are less important for an orderly society.

FIGURE 3-1
Illustrative Prescribed
Ethical Principles

The following list of ethical principles incorporates the characteristics and values that most people associate with ethical behaviour.

Honesty Be *truthful, sincere, forthright, straightforward, frank, candid*; do not *cheat, steal, lie, deceive*, or act *deviously*.

Integrity Be *principled, honourable, upright, courageous*, and *act on convictions*; do not be *two-faced*, or *unscrupulous*, or adopt an *end-justifies-the-means* philosophy that ignores principle.

Promise Keeping Be *worthy of trust, keep promises, fulfill commitments, abide by the spirit as well as the letter of an agreement*; do not interpret agreements in an *unreasonably technical or legalistic manner* in order to rationalize noncompliance or create excuses and justifications for breaking commitments.

Loyalty (Fidelity) Be *faithful* and *loyal* to family, friends, employers, clients, and country; do not *use or disclose information learned in confidence*; in a professional context, *safeguard the ability to make independent professional judgments* by scrupulously *avoiding undue influence and conflicts of interest*.

Fairness Be *fair* and *open-minded*, be willing to admit error and, where appropriate, change positions and beliefs, demonstrate a commitment to *justice*, the *equal treatment* of individuals, *tolerance for and acceptance of diversity*, do not *overreach* or *take undue advantage of another's mistakes or adversities*.

Caring for Others Be *caring, kind*, and *compassionate; share*, be *giving*, be of *service to others; help those in need* and *avoid harming others*.

Respect for Others Demonstrate *respect for human dignity, privacy*, and *the right to self-determination* of all people; be *courteous, prompt*, and *decent; provide others with the information they need to make informed decisions about their own lives*; do not *patronize, embarrass*, or *demean*.

Responsible Citizenship *Obey just laws*; if a law is unjust, openly protest it; *exercise all democratic rights and privileges responsibly* by *participation* (voting and expressing informed views), *social consciousness*, and *public service*; when in a position of leadership or authority, *openly respect* and *honour democratic processes of decision making, avoid unnecessary secrecy or concealment of information*, and *assure that others have all the information they need to make intelligent choices and exercise their rights*.

Pursuit of Excellence *Pursue excellence* in all matters; in meeting your personal and professional responsibilities, be *diligent, reliable, industrious*, and *committed*; perform all tasks to the *best of your ability*, develop and maintain a *high degree of competence*, be *well informed* and *well prepared*; do not be *content with mediocrity*; do not *"win at any cost."*

Accountability Be *accountable, accept responsibility for decisions*, for the *foreseeable consequences of actions and inactions*, and for *setting an example for others*. Parents, teachers, employers, many professionals, and public officials have a special obligation to *lead by example*, to *safeguard and advance the integrity and reputation of their families, companies, professions, and the government itself*; an ethically sensitive individual *avoids even the appearance of impropriety*, and *takes whatever actions are necessary to correct or prevent inappropriate conduct of others*.

Most people define unethical behaviour as conduct that differs from what they believe would have been appropriate given the circumstances. Each of us decides what constitutes ethical behaviour. It is important to understand what causes people to act in a manner that we decide is unethical.

There are two primary reasons why people act unethically: the person's ethical standards are different from those of society as a whole, or the person chooses to act selfishly. In many instances, both reasons exist.

Person's ethical standards differ from general society Extreme examples of people whose behaviour violates almost everyone's ethical standards are drug dealers, bank robbers, and larcenists. Most people who commit such acts feel no remorse when they are apprehended because their ethical standards differ from those of society as a whole.

There are also many far less extreme examples where others violate our ethical values. When people cheat on their tax returns, treat other people with hostility, lie on employment applications, or perform below their competence level as employees, most of us regard that as unethical behaviour. If the other person has decided that this behaviour is ethical and acceptable, there is a conflict of ethical values that is unlikely to be resolved.

The person chooses to act selfishly   The difference between ethical standards that differ from general society's and acting selfishly is illustrated in the following example. Person A finds a briefcase in an airport containing important papers and $1,000. He tosses the briefcase and keeps the money. He brags to his family and friends about his good fortune. Person A's values probably differ from most of society's. Person B faces the same situation but responds differently. He keeps the money but leaves the briefcase in a conspicuous place. He tells nobody and spends the money on a new wardrobe. It is likely that Person B has violated his own ethical standards, but he has decided that the money was too important to pass up. He has chosen to act selfishly.

A considerable portion of unethical behaviour results from selfish behaviour. Political scandals result from the desire for political power; cheating on tax returns and expense reports is motivated by financial greed; performing below one's competence and cheating on tests are typically due to laziness. In each case, the person knows that the behaviour is inappropriate but chooses to do it anyway because of the personal sacrifice needed to act ethically.

ETHICS IN BUSINESS

There have been many well-publicized cases of failures by business persons to conduct their affairs consistently with society's ethical values. For example, recently a well-known food manufacturer admitted to intentionally mislabelling a food product for the purpose of reducing product costs. Similarly, management of several financial institutions over the past decade has been charged with misusing company assets for personal gain and in some cases converting company assets to personal use.

There are several potential effects of these types of cases and the frequent criticisms of business in movies, television, and other media. One is to create the impression that unethical business behaviour is normal behaviour. Another is to conclude that management cannot conduct itself ethically and also have its business succeed financially. Finally and perhaps most important is to conclude that actions must be extreme to constitute unethical behaviour. There is considerable evidence that none of these conclusions about business ethics is correct. A large number of highly successful businesses follow ethical business practices because management believes that it has a social responsibility to conduct itself ethically, but also because it is good business to do so. For example, it is socially responsible to treat employees, customers, and vendors honestly and fairly, but in the long run such actions also result in business success.

The decision of management to operate its business ethically is not a new business philosophy. For example, in the 1930s, Rotary International developed its code of ethics that is still used extensively by millions of businesspeople. It uses four questions that are called the *Four Way Test* of ethical behaviour for any ethical issue a business faces:

- Is it the truth?
- Is it fair to all concerned?
- Will it build goodwill and better friendships?
- Will it be beneficial to all concerned?

Many companies have established their own formal ethical codes of conduct for management and employees. These codes are intended to encourage all personnel to act ethically and to provide guidance as to what constitutes ethical behaviour. For example, the third paragraph of "Management's Responsibilities for Financial Statements" provided by Canadian Tire Corporation, Limited (Figure 5-4 on page 130) discusses management's responsibility for its employees and internal policies.

Canadian Tire Corporation, Limited
www.canadiantire.ca

ETHICAL DILEMMAS

OBJECTIVE 3-2

Identify ethical dilemmas and describe how they can be addressed.

An ethical dilemma is a situation a person faces in which a decision must be made about the appropriate behaviour. A simple example of an ethical dilemma is finding a diamond ring, which necessitates deciding whether to attempt to find the owner or to keep it. A far more difficult ethical dilemma to resolve is the following one; it is the type of case that might be used in an ethics course:

> Qin Zhang is the in-charge on the September 30, 1999, audit of Paquette Forest Products Inc., a forest products company that produces lumber and paper products in northern Manitoba. The company employs 375 people and is the main employer in the remote town of Duck Lake, Manitoba; the other businesses in Duck Lake provide goods and services to Paquette Forest Products and its employees.
>
> In the course of the audit, Qin discovers that the company has had a number of failures of the equipment that removes the sulphuric acid from the paper production process, and as a result, thousands of litres of untreated water have been dumped into the Loon River and Duck Lake. Qin learns that the cost of replacing the equipment so that no further spills are likely is much more than the company can afford and that if ordered to replace the equipment by the environment ministry, the company would be forced to cease operations. What should Qin do?

Auditors, accountants, and other businesspeople face many ethical dilemmas in their business careers. Dealing with a client who threatens to seek a new auditor unless an unqualified opinion is issued presents a serious ethical dilemma if an unqualified opinion is inappropriate. Deciding whether to confront a supervisor who has materially overstated departmental revenues as a means of receiving a larger bonus is a difficult ethical dilemma. Continuing to be a part of the management of a company that harasses and mistreats employees or treats customers dishonestly is a moral dilemma, especially if the person has a family to support and the job market is tight. Deciding whether or not to report negligence of a supervisor to a partner is a problem young staff accountants may face.

RATIONALIZING UNETHICAL BEHAVIOUR

There are alternative ways to resolve ethical dilemmas, but care must be taken to avoid methods that are rationalizations of unethical behaviour. The following are rationalization methods commonly employed that can easily result in unethical conduct:

1. *Everybody does it.* The argument that it is acceptable to falsify tax returns, cheat on exams, or sell defective products is commonly based on the rationalization that everyone else is doing it and therefore it is acceptable.
2. *If it's legal, it's ethical.* Using the argument that all legal behaviour is ethical relies heavily on the perfection of laws. Under this philosophy, one would have no obligation to return a lost object unless the other person could prove that it was his or hers.

3. *Likelihood of discovery and consequences.* This philosophy relies on evaluating the likelihood that someone else will discover the behaviour. Typically, the person also assesses the severity of the penalty (consequences) if there is a discovery. An example is deciding whether to correct an unintentional overbilling to a customer when the customer has already paid the full billing. If the seller believes the customer will detect the error and respond by not buying in the future, the seller will inform the customer now; otherwise the seller will wait to see if the customer complains.

RESOLVING ETHICAL DILEMMAS

In recent years, formal frameworks have been developed to help people resolve ethical dilemmas. The purpose of such a framework is in identifying the ethical issues and deciding on an appropriate course of action using the person's own values. The six-step approach that follows is intended to be a relatively simple approach to resolving ethical dilemmas:

1. Obtain the relevant facts. Care must be taken that assumptions are not taken as fact.
2. Identify the ethical issues from the facts.
3. Determine the stakeholders who are affected by the outcome of the dilemma and how each stakeholder is affected. (A stakeholder is a person or group who has a stake in an organization's or an individual's activities. A partial list of stakeholders of a company would include shareholders, creditors, managers and employees, customers, suppliers, the community, the government, and so on.)
4. Identify the alternatives available to the person who must resolve the dilemma.
5. Identify the likely consequence of each alternative.
6. Decide the appropriate action.

An illustration is used to demonstrate how a person might use this six-step approach to resolve an ethical dilemma.

ETHICAL DILEMMA

Bryan Longview has been working six months as a staff assistant for De Souza & Shah, public accountants. Currently he is assigned to the audit of Reyon Manufacturing Corp. under the supervision of Karen Van Staveren, an experienced audit senior. There are three auditors assigned to the audit, including Karen, Bryan, and a more experienced assistant, Martha Mills. During lunch on the first day, Karen says, "It will be necessary for us to work a few extra hours on our own time to make sure we come in on budget. This audit isn't very profitable anyway, and we don't want to hurt our firm by going over budget. We can accomplish this easily by coming in a half hour early, taking a short lunch break, and working an hour or so after normal quitting time. We just won't write that time down on our time report." Bryan recalls reading in the firm's policy manual that working hours and not charging for them on the time report is a violation of De Souza & Shah's employment policy. He also knows that seniors are paid bonuses, instead of overtime, whereas staff are paid for overtime but get no bonuses. Later, when discussing the issue with Martha, she says, "Karen does this on all of her jobs. She is likely to be our firm's next audit manager. The partners think she's great because her jobs always come in under budget. She rewards us by giving us good engagement evaluations, especially under the cooperative attitude category. Several of the other audit seniors follow the same practice."

RESOLVING THE ETHICAL DILEMMA USING THE SIX-STEP APPROACH

Relevant facts   There are three key facts in this situation that deal with the ethical issue and how the issue will likely be resolved:

- The staff person has been informed he will work hours without recording them as hours worked.

- Firm policy prohibits this practice.
- Another staff person has stated that this practice is common practice for Karen and also for other seniors in the firm.

Ethical issue   The ethical issue in this situation is not difficult to identify.

- Is it ethical for Bryan to work hours and not record them as hours worked in this situation?

Who are the stakeholders and how is each affected?   There are typically more stakeholders affected in situations where ethical dilemmas occur than would normally be expected. The following are the key stakeholders involved in this situation:

WHO	HOW AFFECTED
Bryan	Being asked to violate firm policy. Hours of work will be affected. Pay will be affected. Performance evaluations may be affected. Attitude about firm may be affected.
Martha	Same as Bryan.
Karen	Success on engagement and in firm may be affected. Hours of work will be affected.
De Souza & Shah	Stated firm policy is being violated. May result in underbilling clients in current and future engagements. May affect firm's ability to realistically budget engagements and bill clients. May affect the firm's ability to motivate and retain employees.
Audit staff assigned to Reyon Manufacturing in the future	May result in unrealistic time budgets. May result in unfavourable time performance evaluations. May result in pressures to continue practice of not charging for hours worked.
Other staff in De Souza & Shah	Following the practice on this engagement may motivate others to follow the same practice on other engagements.

Bryan's available alternatives

- Refuse to work the additional hours.
- Perform in the manner requested.
- Inform Karen that he will work the additional hours and will charge the additional hours to the engagement.
- Talk to a manager or partner about Karen's request.
- Refuse to work on the engagement.
- Quit working for the firm.

Each of these options includes a potential consequence, the worst likely one being termination by the firm.

Consequences of each alternative   In deciding the consequences of each alternative, it is essential to evaluate both the short- and long-term effects. There is a natural tendency to emphasize the short term because those consequences will occur quickly, even when the long-term consequences may be more important. For example, consider the potential consequences if Bryan decides to work the additional hours and not report them. In the short term, he will likely get good evaluations for cooperation and perhaps a salary increase. In the longer term, what will be the effect of not reporting the hours this time when other ethical conflicts arise? Consider the following similar ethical dilemmas Bryan might face in his career as he advances:

- An audit firm supervisor asks Bryan to work three unreported hours daily and 15 each weekend.
- An audit firm supervisor asks Bryan to initial certain audit procedures as having been performed when they were not.

- Bryan concludes that he cannot be promoted to manager unless he persuades assistants to work hours that they do not record.
- Management of a client informs Bryan, who is now a partner, that either the company gets an unqualified opinion for a $40,000 audit fee or the company will change auditors.
- Management of a client informs Bryan that the audit fee will be increased by $25,000 if Bryan can find a plausible way to increase earnings by $1 million.

Notice how each dilemma is more serious than the one preceding it; the penalty that Bryan would face if he were to be caught grows more severe as the dilemma grows more serious. In short, if Bryan agrees to work the additional hours and not report them, he has put himself on a slippery slope that grows ever steeper.

Appropriate action   Only Bryan can decide the appropriate option to select in the circumstances after considering his ethical values and the likely consequences of each option. At one extreme, Bryan could decide that the only relevant consequence is the potential impact on his career. Most of us would conclude that Bryan is an unethical person if he follows that course. At the other extreme, Bryan can decide to refuse to work for a firm that permits even one supervisor to violate firm policies. Many people would consider such an extreme reaction naive.

SPECIAL NEED FOR ETHICAL CONDUCT IN PROFESSIONS

Our society has attached a special meaning to the term "professional." A professional is expected to conduct himself or herself at a higher level than most other members of society. For example, when the press reports that a physician, clergyperson, member of Parliament, or CA, CGA, or CMA has been indicted for a crime, most people feel more disappointment than when the same thing happens to people who are not labelled as professionals.

The term "professional" means a responsibility for conduct that extends beyond satisfying the person's responsibilities to himself or herself and beyond the requirements of our society's laws and regulations. A CA, CGA, or CMA in public practice, as a professional, recognizes a responsibility to the public, to the client, and to fellow practitioners, including honourable behaviour, even if that means personal sacrifice.

The underlying reason for a high level of professional conduct by any profession is the need for *public confidence* in the quality of service by the profession, regardless of the individual providing it. For the professional public accountant, it is essential that the client and external financial statement users have confidence in the quality of audits and other services. If users of services do not have confidence in physicians, judges, or public accountants, the ability of those professionals to serve clients and the public effectively is diminished.

It is not practical for users to evaluate the performance of professional services because of their *complexity*. A patient cannot be expected to evaluate whether an operation was properly performed. A financial statement user cannot be expected to evaluate audit performance. Most users have neither the competence nor the time for such an evaluation. Public confidence in the quality of professional services is enhanced when the profession encourages high standards of performance and conduct on the part of all practitioners.

In recent years, increased competition has made it more difficult for professional public accountants and many other professionals to conduct themselves in a professional manner. Increased competition sometimes has the effect of making public accounting firms more concerned about keeping clients and maintaining a reasonable profit. Because of the increased competition, many public accounting firms have implemented philosophies and practices that are frequently referred to as *improved business practices*. These include such things as improved recruiting and personnel practices, better office management, and more effective advertising and other promotional methods. Public accounting firms are also attempting to become more efficlient in doing audits in a variety of ways. For example, they are obtaining efficiency through the use of computers, effective audit planning, and careful assignment of staff.

Most people, including the authors, believe these changes in practice are desirable for our society's benefit as long as they do not interfere with the conduct of CAs, CGAs, or CMAs as professionals. A public accounting firm can implement effective business practices and still conduct itself in a highly professional manner.

DIFFERENCE BETWEEN PUBLIC ACCOUNTING FIRMS AND OTHER PROFESSIONALS

Public accounting firms who provide attestation services have a different relationship with users of financial statements than most other professionals have with the users of their services. Lawyers, for example, are typically engaged and paid by a client and have primary responsibility to be an advocate for that client. Public accounting firms providing attestation services are engaged and paid by the company issuing the financial statements, but the primary beneficiaries of the audit are statement users. Frequently the auditor doesn't know or have contact with the statement users, but has frequent meetings and ongoing relationships with client personnel.

It is essential that users regard such public accounting firms as competent and unbiased. If users were to believe that such public accounting firms do not perform a valuable service (reduce information risk), the value of those firms' audit and other assurance services would be reduced, and the demand for audits would thereby also be reduced. There is, therefore, considerable incentive for such public accounting firms to conduct themselves at a high professional level.

WAYS PROFESSIONAL ACCOUNTANTS IN PUBLIC PRACTICE ARE ENCOURAGED TO CONDUCT THEMSELVES PROFESSIONALLY

There are several ways in which society and the accounting bodies whose respective members are in public practice conducting audits (e.g., CAs and CGAs) encourage those in public practice to conduct themselves appropriately and to do high-quality audits and related services. Figure 3-2 shows the most important ways. Several of these were discussed in Chapter 1, including GAAS requirements and the Recommendations of the *CICA Handbook*, professional examinations, quality control, the provincial securities commissions, practice inspection, and continuing education. The ability of individuals to sue public accounting firms also exerts considerable influence on the way practitioners conduct themselves and audits. Legal liability is studied in Chapter 4. The *code of professional conduct* of the public accountant's respective accounting body also has a significant influence on the practitioner. It is meant to provide a standard of conduct for members of that body. These codes, some of their more important tenets, and related issues of professional conduct are the content of the remainder of this chapter.

FIGURE 3-2

Ways the Profession and Society Encourage Public Accountants to Conduct Themselves at a High Level

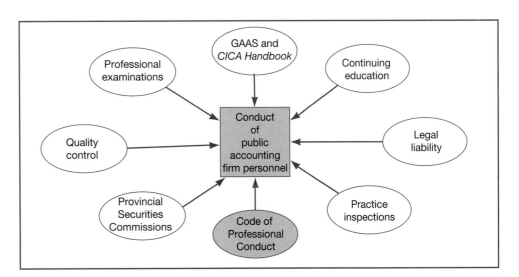

CODE OF PROFESSIONAL CONDUCT

OBJECTIVE 3-4

Explain the purpose and general content of a typical professional accounting code of ethics.

A code of conduct can consist of *general statements* of ideal conduct or *specific rules* that define unacceptable behaviour. The advantage of general statements is the emphasis on positive activities that encourage a high level of performance. The disadvantage is the difficulty of enforcing general ideals because there are no minimum standards of behaviour. The advantage of carefully defined specific rules is the enforceability of minimum behaviour and performance standards. The disadvantage is the tendency of some practitioners to define the rules as maximum rather than minimum standards. A second disadvantage is that some practitioners may view the code as the law and conclude that if some action is not prohibited, it must be ethical. A practitioner must consider the intent of the code in addressing whether a particular action is acceptable or not.

A professional code of conduct serves both the members of the body promulgating the code and the public. It serves members by setting standards the members must meet and providing a benchmark against which the members will be measured by their peers. The public is served because the code provides them with a list of the standards to which the members of the body should adhere and helps them determine their expectations of members' behaviour.

The provincial institutes and Quebec *ordre* of chartered accountants determine the rules of professional conduct for members and students of that provincial institute or *ordre*. The provincial institutes and *ordre* have harmonized their rules of professional conduct so that, generally, the same set of rules applies to all CAs in Canada. Certain rules (e.g., confidentiality, which is discussed below) apply to students as well as to members. All of the rules apply to members in public practice, while a smaller number of them also apply to members who are not engaged in the practice of public accounting. The profession is moving to have the rules of conduct apply to public accounting firms as well as to individual members. Several years previously, only individual members of a firm could face charges before the Discipline Committee. This change had been suggested by the Commission to Study the Public's Expectation of Audits[1] as well as by members of the chartered accountancy profession over the past several years.

The rules of conduct for certified general accountants are determined by the CGAAC and apply to all CGAs in Canada; the provincial associations are charged with administering the code and have the power to amend and add to this national code of conduct. The rules do not apply to students. While all the rules apply to members in public practice, certain of the rules apply also to "accountants in employment"; that is, members not in public practice.

The rules of conduct for certified management accountants are a provincial matter. They do not apply to students who are aspiring to become members. The provincial societies do not differentiate between members in public practice and other members, although certain rules do apply to members in public practice.

Generally the codes of conduct of the three professional accounting bodies, the CICA, the CGAAC, and the SMAC, have attempted to accomplish both the objectives of general statements of ideal conduct and of specific rules. For example, there are three parts to the *Rules of Professional Conduct* of the Institute of Chartered Accountants of Ontario: principles which are stated in broad terms, the rules themselves, and interpretation of the rules. Figure 3-3 is illustrative. The parts are listed in order of increasing specificity: the principles provide ideal standards of conduct, whereas ethical rulings are more specific, and the interpretations are very specific.

PRINCIPLES OF PROFESSIONAL CONDUCT

The principles generally are characteristics that the professional body deems desirable in its members. An organization is judged by the behaviour of its members; therefore, one principle would be that members behave in a way that enhances and

---

[1]See Recommendation 26, "50 Ways to Change Our Ways," *CAmagazine* (July 1988), pp. 37 and 44.

FIGURE 3-3
Code of Professional
Conduct

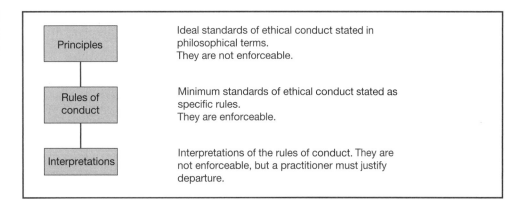

Principles	Ideal standards of ethical conduct stated in philosophical terms. They are not enforceable.
Rules of conduct	Minimum standards of ethical conduct stated as specific rules. They are enforceable.
Interpretations	Interpretations of the rules of conduct. They are not enforceable, but a practitioner must justify departure.

does not detract from the reputation of all the members. Members should act *ethically* and act in a way that will serve the *public interest*. When a member of a profession is disciplined by the courts, the profession's reputation suffers along with that of the member. It is a mistake to think that only the member loses his or her reputation in such a situation.

Other common principles are that members act with *integrity and due care* in the performance of their professional activities, that they maintain (i.e., keep current) their professional competence, that they do not undertake work for which they lack the necessary competence, and that they behave in a professional way towards colleagues. The accountant must maintain *confidentiality* with respect to the affairs and business of the client. There is one principle that relates more specifically to public accountants: the accountant should ensure that he or she maintains an *independent or objective state of mind* when providing assurance services (e.g., audits or reviews) for clients.

A careful examination of these principles will likely lead to the conclusion that most are applicable to any professional, not just professional accountants. For example, physicians should behave in a way that is not discreditable to their profession, they should act ethically and in a way that serves the public interest, and they should exercise integrity and due care. Physicians should maintain their professional competence and behave in a professional way towards their colleagues. They should not breach their clients' confidentiality. One difference between auditors and other professionals, as discussed earlier, is that most professionals need not be concerned about remaining independent.

These principles will be explored more fully in the balance of this chapter.

RULES OF CONDUCT

The discussion that follows will consider some of the more important rules of conduct followed by public accountants in Canada. A student interested in obtaining a particular professional designation (e.g., CA, CGA, CMA, or CIA) should refer to and become familiar with the specific rules of conduct of the body to which he or she seeks admission.

As was mentioned previously, while all the rules discussed below apply to members of the professional accounting bodies in public practice, some of the rules discussed do not apply to members who are not engaged in the practice of public accounting. The difference will be apparent in the ensuing discussion.

Figure 3-3 indicated that while principles are not enforceable, the rules of conduct are. For that reason, the rules of conduct of the accounting bodies are stated in more precise language than the principles can be. Because of their enforceability, the rules are often called *Rules* or *Code of Professional Conduct*.

The difference between the standards of conduct set by the *principles* and those set by the *rules of conduct* is shown in Figure 3-4. When practitioners conduct themselves at a minimum level, as shown in Figure 3-4, that does not imply unsatisfactory con-

FIGURE 3-4
Standards of Conduct

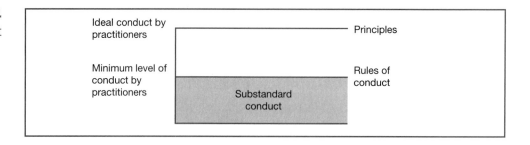

duct. The profession has presumably set the standards sufficiently high to make the minimum conduct satisfactory.

At what level do practitioners conduct themselves in practice? As in any profession, the level varies among practitioners. Some operate at high levels, whereas others operate as close to the minimum level as possible. Unfortunately, some also conduct themselves below the minimum level set by the profession. It is hoped that there are few of those.

INTERPRETATIONS OF RULES OF CONDUCT

The need for published interpretations of the rules of conduct arises when there are frequent questions from practitioners about a particular rule. The various institutes and *ordre* of chartered accountants issue interpretations of certain rules of conduct together with the rules themselves. Interpretations are not officially enforceable, but a departure from the interpretations would be difficult, if not impossible, for a practitioner to justify in a disciplinary hearing.

APPLICABILITY OF THE RULES OF CONDUCT

As was mentioned previously, the rules of conduct for CAs and CGAs specifically state that while the rules are for all CAs and CGAs respectively, certain rules, because of their nature, may not apply to members who are not in public practice.

It would be a violation of the rules if someone did something on behalf of a member that would have been a violation if the member had done it. An example is a banker who states in a newsletter that Johnson and Able, public accountants, have the best tax department in the province and consistently get large refunds for their tax clients. That is likely to create false or unjustified expectations and is a violation of both the CA and CGA rules of conduct.

A member is also responsible for compliance with the rules by employees and partners.

DEFINITIONS

A few definitions must be understood to minimize misinterpretation of the rules to be discussed below.

- *Client* — the person(s) or entity which retains a member or his or her firm, engaged in the practice of public accounting, for the performance of professional services.
- *Firm* — a proprietorship or partnership engaged in the practice of public accounting, including individual partners thereof.
- *Member* — a member of the Canadian Institute of Chartered Accountants (and a provincial institute or *ordre*) or of the Certified General Accountants Association of Canada (and a provincial association).
- *Practice of public accounting* — holding out to be a public accountant and at the same time performing for a client one or more types of services rendered by public accountants.

The intent of this section is to discuss several rules of conduct that are fundamental to the practice of public accounting. As such, they are found in differing forms and to differing degrees in the rules of professional conduct of CAs, CGAs, CMAs and CIAs. It must be pointed out that the rules of conduct governing the behaviour of these four groups of professionals are much more extensive and detailed than the ensuing discussion.

INDEPENDENCE

OBJECTIVE 3-5

Discuss independence as it applies to a public accountant.

Generally, the rules of conduct promulgated by the accounting bodies require their members who are engaged in the practice of public accounting to be independent when they perform certain functions. For example, the rules require that auditors of historical financial statements be independent. Independence is usually required for other types of attestation engagements such as review engagements. However the rules usually permit a public accounting firm to do tax returns and provide management services without being independent.

As you learned in Chapter 1, independence is also very important for internal auditors if they are to properly carry out their jobs. *Standards for the Professional Practice of Internal Auditing* published by the Institute of Internal Auditors provides guidance to persons engaged in internal auditing, not just to members of the IIA. The first standard in the publication states that "Internal auditors should be independent of the activities they audit." It is possible for internal auditors to be independent even though they are employees of their client; this can be accomplished through the internal auditor's organizational status and by the internal auditor having an independent mental attitude. The ensuing discussion will focus on attest audits but applies equally to internal audits.

Independence is one of the most important rules of conduct and it tends to be thoroughly discussed. This is as it should be. Without independence, the attest function has no relevance in society.

Independence in auditing means taking an *unbiased viewpoint* in the performance of audit tests, the evaluation of the results, and the issuance of the auditor's report. If the auditor is an advocate for the client, a particular banker, or anyone else, he or she cannot be considered independent. Independence must certainly be regarded as the auditor's most critical characteristic. The reason that many diverse users are willing to rely upon the professional public accountant's reports as to the fairness of financial statements is their expectation of an unbiased viewpoint.

Not only is it essential that professional public accountants maintain an independent attitude in fulfilling their responsibilities, but it is also important that the users of financial statements have confidence in that independence. These two objectives are frequently identified as *independence in fact* and *independence in appearance*. Independence in fact exists when the auditor is actually able to maintain an unbiased attitude throughout the audit, whereas independence in appearance is the result of others' interpretation of this independence. If auditors are independent in fact but users believe them to be advocates for the client, most of the benefit of the audit function will be lost.

Although it is possible to take the extreme position that anything affecting either independence in fact or in appearance must be eliminated to ensure a high level of respect in the community, it is doubtful whether this would solve as many problems as it would create. The difficulty with this position is that it is likely to restrict significantly the services offered to clients, the freedom of public accountants to practise in the traditional manner, and the ability of public accounting firms to hire competent staff. At this point it will be helpful to examine some conflicts of independence that have arisen, evaluate their significance, and determine how the profession has resolved them.

Independence may be broadly thought of as having four facets:

- financial independence
- independence of mental attitude
- investigative independence
- reporting independence

The four facets essential to independence are discussed in turn below.

Financial independence   Financial independence relates to not having a financial interest in the client and may be manifested by not

- owning stock in the client.
- owing money to or being owed money by a client (considerations such as banking at a client bank or being owed an audit fee by the client [but not past due fees] would be excluded).
- having a single client whose fee(s) represents a major portion of the public accountant's total revenue.
- being engaged and paid by management. In some audit situations, while the shareholders appoint the auditors at their annual meeting, in fact the shareholders are voting on a public accounting firm suggested by management, the very people whose work the auditor will be reviewing. One way to improve the situation is to have the audit committee of the board of directors nominate the auditors. Independence is also enhanced if the audit committee, which is discussed in more detail below, sets the audit fee and determines the scope of the audit in consultation with the auditors.
- performing management advisory services for the client. This point has been contentious for a number of years. One group believes that an auditor can become so beholden to a client that the auditor will fail to have the appropriate scepticism; for example, the consulting fee may exceed the audit fee. Another group believes that the public accountant's professionalism will result in a proper audit and that there are synergistic effects for both the audit and the management advisory services flowing from the same firm doing both. The issue is not resolved; there are no specific prohibitions to performing management consulting for an audit client in the various rules of professional conduct.

Rules of conduct of the CAs, CGAs, and CMAs deal with financial independence because lack of independence is likely to affect the users' perception of the auditors' independence. It is the authors' experience that individual public accounting firms often have rules with respect to financial independence that are more stringent than those of the professional association. Some public accounting firms do not permit any ownership by staff of a client's stock regardless of which office of the firm serves the client. These firms have decided to have higher requirements than the minimums set by the rules of conduct of the various professional associations.

Independence of mental attitude   An independent mental attitude is essential to achieving independence in fact. Paragraph 5090.04 of the *CICA Handbook* states that "The auditor performs the audit with an attitude of professional scepticism" while assuming management's good faith. Paragraph 5090.04 captures the spirit of independence of mental attitude. The auditor should not allow long association or friendship to colour his or her evaluation, nor should the auditor approach an audit with the view that management and the employees are dishonest.

An auditor's professionalism dictates that the auditor be unbiased; however, there is no yardstick, as there is with financial independence, to measure whether or not the auditor has an independent mental attitude. This is an issue that the auditor must decide for himself or herself.

Investigative independence   Investigative independence means that the auditor has the time and resources (i.e., the fee is adequate for the job and staffing is appropriate for the job) to obtain sufficient appropriate audit evidence and that the auditor has access to all evidence needed to reach the proper opinion as to the fairness of the financial statements. Investigative independence would be impaired if there was a deadline so that the job was rushed, if the fee was too low so that the auditor cut back on testing, or if the auditor was denied access to evidence (e.g., if the auditor were not permitted to count inventory).

Reporting independence   Reporting independence means reporting at a sufficiently high level that the report will be acted on. For example, an auditor who reported to management when the auditor believed management to be guilty of fraud would not have reporting independence. On the other hand, if the auditor reported to an audit committee (discussed below) made up of independent (i.e., non-management) members of the board of directors, the auditor would have reporting independence.

Summary   Independence is broader than not owning shares in a client. The four facets of independence discussed above take the broadest view of independence; all four must be present if the auditor is to be truly independent.

AUDIT COMMITTEE

An audit committee is a selected number of members of a company's board of directors who provide a forum that is independent of management for both the external and internal auditors. Most audit committees are made up of three to five or sometimes as many as seven directors. Incorporating acts generally require that the majority of the committee must be outside directors (i.e., not part of company management).

A typical audit committee decides such things as which public accounting firm to retain and the scope of services the public accounting firm is to perform. The audit committee also meets with the public accounting firm to discuss the progress and findings of the audit and helps resolve conflicts between the public accounting firm and management. Many of the same comments could be made about the audit committee and the internal auditors. While audit committees are looked upon with favour by most auditors, users, and management, they exist mainly on the boards of directors of larger companies.

Section 165(1) of the *Canada Business Corporations Act* states that an audit committee is required for all companies incorporated under the Act that distribute their securities to the public. Section 165(2) permits the director who administrates the *Canada Business Corporations Act* to waive this requirement if he or she thinks such a waiver is appropriate. The sole duty required of a member of the audit committee by the Act, in Section 165(3), is to review the financial statements before they are issued. Other incorporating acts also require corporations to have audit committees; the responsibilities assigned to the committee vary.

The auditor has the right to attend meetings of the audit committee and to call meetings if he or she feels they are necessary. Directors who become aware of *any* misstatements in issued financial statements must notify the auditor and the audit committee of the misstatements.

The audit committee may do the minimum required by statute or may be more active. Among other activities, some audit committees

- Review the entire annual report
- Review the scope and cost of the audit with the external auditors
- Act as a liaison between the external auditors and management
- Adjudicate disputes between the external auditors and management
- Act as a liaison between the internal auditors and management
- Adjudicate disputes between the internal auditors and management

Needless to say, the audit committee can add significantly to the external auditor's independence.

If a public accountant records transactions in the journals for the client, posts monthly totals to the general ledger, makes adjusting entries, and subsequently does an audit, there is some question as to whether the public accountant can be independent in his or her audit role. Generally, the rules of conduct permit a public accounting firm to do both bookkeeping and auditing for the same client. This conclusion is presumably based on a comparison of the effect on independence of having both bookkeeping and auditing services performed by the same public accounting firm with the additional cost of having a different public accounting firm do the audit. There are three important requirements that the auditor should satisfy before it is acceptable to do bookkeeping and auditing for the client:

1. The client must accept full responsibility for the financial statements. The client must be sufficiently knowledgeable about the enterprise's activities and financial condition and the applicable accounting principles so that the client can reasonably accept such responsibility, including the fairness of valuation and presentation and the adequacy of disclosure. When necessary, the public accountant should discuss accounting matters with the client to be sure that the client has the required degree of understanding.
2. The public accountant must not assume the role of employee or of management conducting the operations of an enterprise. For example, the public accountant should not consummate transactions, have custody of assets, or exercise authority on behalf of the client. The client must prepare the source documents on all transactions in sufficient detail to identify clearly the nature and amount of such transactions and maintain accounting control over data processed by the public accountant, such as control totals and document counts.
3. The public accountant, in making an examination of financial statements prepared from books and records that the public accountant has maintained completely or in part, must conform to generally accepted auditing standards. The fact that the public accountant has processed or maintained certain records does not eliminate the need to perform sufficient audit tests.

The first two requirements are often difficult to satisfy for smaller clients where the owner may have little knowledge of or interest in accounting or processing transactions.

The accounting profession and society, especially in the past decade, have been concerned about ensuring that (1) auditors maintain an unbiased attitude in performing their work (independence in fact) and (2) users perceive auditors as being independent (independence in appearance). Many of the elements shown in Figure 3-2 and other requirements or inducements encourage public accountants to maintain independence in fact and appearance. These are now briefly summarized. The most important have already been discussed in Chapter 1 and early in Chapter 2.

Legal liability   The penalty involved when a court concludes that a practitioner is not independent can be severe, including criminal action. The courts have certainly provided major incentives for auditors to remain independent. Legal liability is studied in Chapter 4.

Rules of professional conduct   The existing rules of conduct restrict public accountants in their financial and business relationships with clients. They are a considerable aid in maintaining independence.

Generally accepted auditing standards   The general standards require the auditor to maintain an objective state of mind in all matters related to the assignment.

Public accounting firm quality control standards   Most public accounting firms establish policies and procedures to provide reasonable assurance that all personnel are independent.

Audit committee An audit committee, as was recently discussed, can help auditors remain independent of management.

Shopping for accounting principles Management may consult with other accountants on the application of accounting principles. Although consultation with other accountants is an appropriate practice, it can lead to a loss of independence in certain circumstances. For example, suppose one public accounting firm replaces the existing auditors on the strength of accounting advice offered but later finds facts and circumstances that require the public accounting firm to change its stance. It may be difficult for the new public accounting firm to remain independent in such a situation. The Auditing Standards Board issued Section 7600, "Reports on the Application of Accounting Principles, Auditing Standards or Review Standards," setting out requirements that must be met when a public accounting firm is requested to provide a written opinion on the application of accounting principles or auditing standards by a party other than the client (also discussed in Chapter 23). Such an opinion would be issued for specific circumstances or transactions relating to an audit, review, or compilation client of another public accounting firm. It applies if the public accountant is asked to provide a generic or hypothetical opinion on the application of accounting principles or auditing standards.

The purpose of Section 7600 is to minimize the likelihood of management following the practice commonly called "opinion shopping" and the potential threat to independence of the kind described above. Primary among the requirements is that the consulted or "reporting" accounting firm should communicate with the entity's incumbent accountant to ascertain all the available facts relevant to forming a professional judgment on the matters the firm has been requested to report on.

Approval of auditor by shareholders The *Canada Business Corporations Act* and other incorporating acts require shareholders to approve the selection of a new auditor or continuation of the existing one. Shareholders are usually a more objective group than management. It is questionable, however, whether they are in a position to evaluate the performance of previous or potential auditors.

Conclusion Regardless of the rules set forth by the rules of conduct of the various accounting bodies, it is essential that the public accountant maintain an unbiased relationship with management and all other parties affected by the performance of the public accountant's responsibilities. In every engagement, including those involving management advisory and tax services, the public accountant must not subordinate his or her professional judgment to that of others. Even though pressures on the public accountant's objectivity and integrity are frequent, the long-run standing of the profession in the financial community demands resisting those pressures. If the conflicts are sufficiently great to compromise the public accountant's independence, it may be necessary for the public accounting firm to resign from the engagement.

CONFIDENTIALITY

Discuss confidentiality as it applies to a public accountant.

The rules of conduct for CAs, CGAs, and CMAs state that members shall not disclose any confidential client or employer information without the specific consent of the client or employer. In general, the rules also prohibit using confidential or inside information to earn profits or benefits.

The rule against disclosure does not apply if the member is called upon to disclose the information by the courts. Communication between an auditor and client is not privileged as it is between lawyer and client; a court can require a public accountant to produce all files and documents held by the public accountant including confidential advice provided to the client by the public accountant. For this reason, the auditor must be careful what information is put into the file, recognizing that the file could appear as a court document. The rule against disclosure also does not apply if the member's professional body requires the confidentiality rule to be waived in connection with the body's exercise of its duties (e.g., when an auditor is called upon to produce working papers in connection with the disciplinary process, or when an auditor is required to produce files as part of practice inspection).

While the rules of professional conduct with respect to confidentiality are quite clear, as you will discover in Chapter 4, the auditor may be confronted with a situation where he or she must choose between confidentiality and other rules of conduct or another course of action. For example, Objective 4-7 in Chapter 4 discusses the auditor's legal responsibilities for client confidentiality. A situation is described where an auditor has two clients who deal with each other; the auditor must choose between violating the rule respecting confidentiality or the rule respecting association with false or misleading financial information. Chapter 4, in the two legal cases reviewed on page 112, also illustrates the conflict that arises when an auditor has information about one client that could be beneficial to a second client. The situation described and the two legal cases mentioned demonstrate how auditors face ethical dilemmas where they cannot rely on the rules of conduct to provide a solution.

NEED FOR CONFIDENTIALITY

During an audit or other type of engagement, practitioners obtain a considerable amount of information of a confidential nature, including officers' salaries, product pricing and advertising plans, and product cost data. If auditors divulged this information to outsiders or to client employees who have been denied access to the information, their relationship with management would be seriously strained and, in extreme cases, would cause the client harm. The confidentiality requirement applies to all services provided by public accounting firms, including tax and management services.

Ordinarily, the public accounting firm's working papers can be provided to someone else only with the express permission of the client. This is the case even if a public accountant sells his or her practice to another public accounting firm or is willing to permit a successor auditor to examine the working papers prepared for a former client. Permission is not required from the client, however, if the working papers are subpoenaed by a court or are used as part of practice inspection. If the working papers are subpoenaed, the client should be informed immediately. The client and the client's lawyer may wish to challenge the subpoena.

MAINTENANCE OF THE REPUTATION OF THE PROFESSION

OBJECTIVE 3-7

Discuss the standard of behaviour required of a public accountant.

The rules of all three accounting bodies in Canada require their members to behave in the best interest of their profession and the public. This means accountants should not take advantage of the trust placed in them by their profession and by the public. It means that an accountant should not be publicly critical of a colleague (i.e., by making a complaint about the colleague's behaviour to their professional body or by being critical, as a successor auditor, to the new client) without giving the colleague a chance to explain his or her actions first.

Actions by a member of a professional body — in law, medicine, or any other profession — reflect on the member but also on the body itself. For example, a lawyer who steals trust monies sullies not only his or her own reputation but also that of the law profession; the theft brings all lawyers into disrepute. Reputation is affected by anti-social behaviour such as harassment and discrimination, since such behaviour is considered abhorrent, resulting in professional disciplinary actions. Therefore, it is essential that an accountant behave in an exemplary manner as a member of the professional body.

INTEGRITY AND DUE CARE

OBJECTIVE 3-8
Discuss integrity and due care as they apply to a public accountant.

The rules of conduct for CAs, CGAs, and CMAs require their members to act with integrity and due care. Integrity is one of the hallmarks of the profession. One of a professional accountant's most important assets is his or her reputation for honesty and fair dealing; if users of financial statements audited by or prepared by an accountant do not believe in the practitioner's honesty or fairness, the value of the financial statements or the audit is diminished. The professional accountant's behaviour with clients, colleagues, employers, and employees must be above reproach.

Due care in the performance of his or her duties is also a hallmark of a professional. The public accountant has a legal duty of care to certain users of financial statements, as will be seen in Chapter 4. Due care means the application by a professional of a level of care and skill in accordance with what would reasonably be expected of a person of his or her rank and training. Note that due care is mentioned in the general standard of GAAS in Section 5100 of the *CICA Handbook*.

COMPETENCE

OBJECTIVE 3-9
Discuss the responsibility of a public accountant to maintain professional competence.

As a professional, a CA, CGA, or CMA has a responsibility to maintain his or her professional competence. The rules of conduct of the three professional bodies require practitioners to maintain competence; similarly the GAAS state the necessity of "adequate technical training and proficiency." The public expects that all professionals will strive to keep abreast of the latest techniques and methodologies.

The accounting associations offer continuing professional education courses in a variety of subject areas to assist their members in maintaining their competence. In addition, there are a number of other organizations which provide courses.

Members are encouraged to keep current in a variety of ways. The various institutes and the *ordre* of chartered accountants have practice inspections (discussed in Chapter 1) over a four-year period of all public practice units. Certified general accountants are required to attend a certain number of continuing professional education courses a year. Primarily, however, it is a professional accountant's professionalism that dictates that he or she keep current.

The general standard, of GAAS explicitly and of the rules of conduct of the various professional accounting bodies implicitly, requires the auditor to have the necessary technical knowledge and competence to conduct the audit. This is especially true as businesses — and accounting for them — increase in complexity. An auditor should not undertake an audit of a client unless that auditor has both knowledge of that client's business and industry and of the technical aspects of the audit itself. For example, the audit of an insurance company requires knowledge of auditing the policy reserves that form a significant part of the insurance company's liabilities. Many of the larger accounting firms are forming industry specialization groups within the firm that are responsible for all audits within their specialty.

An audit firm should decline a new audit if the firm either lacks or does not have access to the technical knowledge required to complete the audit. Similarly, an auditor within a firm should ensure that he or she has or has access to the technical knowledge required to complete the audit.

ADHERENCE TO GAAP AND GAAS

All three professional accounting bodies require their members in practice as public accountants and working in industry not to associate themselves with false or misleading information or to fail to reveal material omissions from financial statements. Users of financial statements prepared by or audited by professional accountants are entitled to believe that the financial statements are complete and fairly present the financial position of the company. They are entitled to believe that the financial statements are not false and misleading. They are entitled to rely on the integrity of the accountants involved.

Given that public trust of professional accountants does exist, if an accountant were to betray this trust and provide a clean opinion on financial statements he or she knows to be misleading, users would accept the statements as correct and would suffer a loss. Objective 3-8 discusses integrity and its importance to a public accountant; discovery that the public accountant was associated with false and misleading financial information or failed to reveal a material fact would destroy the accountant's reputation for integrity.

CAs, CGAs, and CMAs are required to comply with professional standards when preparing and auditing financial statements. These standards would include the standards of the professional body but, more importantly, GAAP and GAAS as set out in the *CICA Handbook*. As you learned in Chapter 1, the *Canada Business Corporations Act* and the incorporating acts of many of the provinces require financial statements to be prepared according to GAAP as specified by the *CICA Handbook* and also require the auditor's report to be in accordance with the standards of the *Handbook*. The Canadian Securities Administrators, who set policy for the securities commissions and stock exchanges in Canada, also specify the *Handbook* as the source of GAAP.

ADVERTISING AND SOLICITATION

A profession's reputation is not enhanced if the members openly solicit one another's clients or engage in advertising that is overly aggressive, self-laudatory, or critical of other members of the profession, or that makes claims that cannot be substantiated. As a consequence, the three professional accounting bodies in Canada either explicitly or implicitly prohibit solicitation of another public accountant's client and advertising that is not in keeping with the profession's high standards.

Responding to a request for information from a client of another public accounting firm is not solicitation, nor is responding to an invitation to tender from another firm's client. Rather, solicitation is approaching the client of another public accounting firm to convince him or her to switch to one's own firm. It is a targeted act of seeking a specific professional engagement.

Advertising that is in good taste is acceptable. It may include complimentary material about the accounting firm but should not claim any superior skills or make promises that can't be kept (e.g., a promise that certain favourable results will be achieved). Advertising is a general process of informing potential users of the availability of services.

There has been a gradual change over the past few years as the rules regarding solicitation and advertising have been made less stringent. As a consequence, the public accounting firms are competing much more strenuously than before. Advertising in the various media is much more common. There is an increased emphasis on marketing and more competitive pricing of services. Many public accounting firms have developed sophisticated advertising for national journals read by businesspeople and for local newspapers. It is common for public accounting firms to make formal and informal presentations at the request of management in order to convince them to change public accounting firms. Price bidding for audits and other services is now common and often highly competitive. As a result of these changes, some companies now change auditors more often than they did previously to reduce audit cost.

Has the quality of audits become endangered by these changes? The existing legal exposure of public accountants, the disciplinary processes of the professional accounting bodies, practice inspection requirements, and the potential for interference by the securities commissions and government has kept audit quality high. In the opinion of the authors, the changes in the rules have caused greater competition in the profession, but not so much that high-quality, efficiently run public accounting firms have been significantly harmed. However, for this to continue to be so, public accounting firms need to be on guard so that increasing competitive pressures do not cause auditors to reduce quality below an acceptable level.

OTHER RULES

OBJECTIVE 3-12

Discuss other rules of conduct, including those dealing with contingent fees and with reporting breaches of the rules.

Breaches of the rules   The rules of conduct of the professional accounting bodies require members who are aware of a breach of the rules by another member to report that member to the profession's discipline committee after first advising the member of the intent to make a report. The three bodies are self-regulating and therefore must police themselves. It is important that the member be notified of the intent to report the breach in case there are mitigating circumstances of which the reporting member is not aware.

Contingent fees   The charging of a fee based on the outcome of an audit, such as the granting of a loan by a bank, could easily impair the auditor's independence. Contingent fees are prohibited for audits, reviews, and any other engagements (such as assurance engagements) that require the auditor to be objective.

Communication with predecessor auditor   The rules of conduct of the CAs and CGAs and incorporating acts such as the *Canada Business Corporations Act* require a (potential) successor auditor, prior to accepting an appointment as auditor, to communicate with the incumbent auditor to inquire if there are any circumstances of which the incumbent is aware that might preclude the successor from accepting the appointment. The successor would ask the potential client to authorize the incumbent to provide the information requested. If the client refuses to do so, the successor should be reluctant to accept the appointment because it is likely that the client is hiding something.

Professionalism dictates that the incumbent *should* respond to the successor's request and be candid in responding. However, the incumbent may not respond or may not be as frank as he or she could be.

The communication between the incumbent and the successor is important because it prevents a successor from unknowingly accepting an appointment that might, if all the facts were known, be rejected. For example, if the incumbent resigned after finding that management of the client was dishonest and was engaged in fraud, it is unlikely any public accounting firm would accept the client if the incumbent had passed on that knowledge. In short, the required communication protects prospective successors, and thus the profession, from getting involved with undesirable clients. The client acceptance decision is discussed in Chapter 7.

Professional liability insurance   In several provinces, members practising public accounting are required to carry professional liability insurance. Two issues arise that can cause confusion: defining what is public accounting, and the extent of work being done for no remuneration.

For example, during tax season, individuals may prepare tax returns for family and friends at no charge. Since basic advice such as maximization of RRSP contributions is often included, this process is considered to be practising public accounting. However, if only a limited number of returns are being prepared for no remuneration, a public practice is not being carried on. If more than a handful of returns are being prepared and fees are being charged, either on a full- or part-time basis, then professional liability insurance would be required.

Other rules   The rules of conduct of the professional accounting bodies include many more rules than have been described here; an aspiring professional accountant should make himself or herself aware of the rules of conduct of the professional body to which membership is sought. The rules not covered, and those described above, may be categorized as general rules, rules that deal with protection of the public, rules that deal with relations with other accountants, and rules that relate to the conduct of a professional practice.

ENFORCEMENT

OBJECTIVE 3-13

Describe the enforcement mechanisms for the rules of conduct

The rules of conduct for chartered accountants are established and administered provincially. The rules of conduct for certified general accountants are promulgated by CGA-Canada. The provincial CGA associations have the power to add rules and have the responsibility for enforcing the rules. The rules of conduct for certified management accountants are promulgated and administered by the provincial societies.

The various professional bodies have the power to impose penalties ranging from public censure in the body's newsletter, or requiring courses to be taken to upgrade skills, to levying fines or expulsion. As pointed out earlier, the three professional accounting bodies are self-regulating; that is, they have the responsibility for developing their own rules of conduct and for disciplining members who violate the rules. There is a danger that the public will perceive the disciplinary process as not being as stringent as it should be and that there is a reluctance to punish members who break the rules. One way this issue is being dealt with is by including laypersons on the disciplinary committees. A second approach is to make information available to the public about findings of the discipline committees and punishments meted out by them.

IT'S ALL A MATTER OF TRUST

Today's business environment clearly is different from that of 20 years ago. [Public accountants have] found themselves in a far more competitive business climate than ever before.

Public practitioners today must be particularly concerned with the efficiency and the effectiveness of their work. One can't cut corners and hope to prosper; one can't act unprofessionally and expect to survive. Maintaining skills throughout a career, exercising due professional care, following the promulgated standards for whatever kind of work is being done, and acting professionally in all endeavours are a practitioner's keys to success.

The bottom line is dedication to professional excellence. The [AICPA's rules of conduct] call for members to "observe the profession's technical and ethical standards, strive continually to improve competence and the quality of services, and discharge professional responsibility to the best of the member's ability." That's not a lofty ideal; it's what is needed to ensure public trust in the profession.

Source: Adapted from Michael A. Pearson, "Doing the Right Thing," *Journal of Accountancy*, (June 1995), p. 86

Journal of Accountancy
www.aicpa.org/pubs/jofa/index.htm

ESSENTIAL TERMS

Audit committee — selected members of a client's board of directors, who provide a forum for the auditors to remain independent of management (p. 75).

Client information — information communicated by a client to a professional (p. 77).

Confidential client information — client information that may not be disclosed without the specific consent of the client except under authoritative professional or legal investigation (p. 77).

Ethical dilemma — a situation in which a decision must be made about the appropriate behaviour (p. 65).

Ethics — a set of moral principles or values (p. 62).

Financial independence — not having a financial interest in the client (p. 74).

Independence — impartiality in performing professional services (p. 73).

Independence in appearance — the auditor's ability to maintain an unbiased viewpoint *in the eyes of others* (p. 73).

Independence in fact — the auditor's ability to take an unbiased viewpoint in the performance of professional services (p. 73).

Independence of mental attitude — an impartial mental attitude; an unbiased view of the client (p. 74).

Investigative independence — having the time and resources to obtain sufficient appropriate audit evidence (p. 74).

Reporting independence — reporting at a sufficiently high level that the report will be acted upon (p. 75).

Stakeholder — a person or group who has a stake in an organization's or an individual's activities (p. 66).

3-1 Explain the need for a code of professional ethics for public accountants. In which ways should the public accountants' code of ethics be similar to and different from that of other professional groups, such as lawyers or dentists?

3-2 List the three parts which normally comprise a code of professional conduct, and state the purpose of each.

3-3 What is meant by the statement, "The rules of professional conduct of a professional accounting organization should be regarded as a minimum standard"?

3-4 Distinguish between independence in fact and independence in appearance. State three activities that may not affect independence in fact but are likely to affect independence in appearance.

3-5 Why is an auditor's independence so essential?

3-6 What are the four facets of independence discussed in the chapter? Explain why each is a necessary component of a public accountant's independence.

3-7 Some observers object to public accounting firms providing management advisory services for an audit client. Why do they object? Are they correct in objecting?

3-8 Many people believe that a public accountant cannot be truly independent when payment of fees is dependent on the management of the client. Explain a way of reducing this appearance of lack of independence.

3-9 The auditor's working papers usually can be provided to someone else only with the permission of the client. What is the rationale for such a rule?

3-10 The rules of conduct of CAs, CGAs, and CMAs require them to report a breach of the rules of conduct by a member to their profession's disciplinary body. What should they do before making such a report?

3-11 After accepting an engagement, a public accountant discovers that the client's industry is more technical than at first realized and that he or she (i.e., the accountant) is not competent in certain areas of the operation. What should the public accountant do in this situation?

3-12 Define what is meant by solicitation, and explain why you think the accounting professions have rules against solicitation.

3-13 Identify and explain factors that should keep the quality of audits high even though advertising and tendering are allowed.

3-14 What do you think are the reasons that the rules of conduct of the professional accounting bodies contain restrictions on advertising by public accounting firms?

3-15 Why do you think the rules of conduct of the professional accounting bodies which pertain to public accounting ban contingent fees for audits?

3-16 Assume an auditor makes an agreement with a client that the audit fee will be contingent upon the number of days required to complete the engagement. Is this likely to be a violation of the auditor's rules of conduct? What is the essence of the rule of professional ethics dealing with contingent fees for audits, and what are the reasons for the rule?

3-17 Why is it so important that a successor auditor communicate with the incumbent before accepting an appointment as auditor? What should the successor do if the incumbent doesn't reply?

3-18 The following questions concern independence and the rules of professional conduct or GAAS. Choose the best response.

a. What is the meaning of the generally accepted auditing standard that requires the auditor to be independent?
   (1) The auditor must be without bias with respect to the client under audit.
   (2) The auditor's sole obligation is to third parties.
   (3) The auditor may have a direct ownership interest in his or her client's business if it is not material.
   (4) The auditor must adopt a critical attitude during the audit.

b. The independent audit is important to readers of financial statements because it
   (1) measures and communicates financial and business data included in financial statements.
   (2) determines the future stewardship of the management of the company whose financial statements are audited.
   (3) involves the objective examination of and reporting on management-prepared statements.
   (4) reports on the accuracy of all information in the financial statements.

(AICPA adapted)

3-19 The following questions concern possible violations of the rules of conduct discussed in the chapter. Choose the best response.

a. In which one of the following situations would a public accountant be in violation of the rules of conduct in determining his or her audit fee?
   (1) A fee equal to last year's fee plus 10 percent.
   (2) A fee based on the nature of the service rendered and the public accountant's particular expertise instead of the actual time spent on the engagement.
   (3) A fee based on whether the public accountant's report on the client's financial statements results in the approval of a bank loan.
   (4) A fee based on the fee charged by the prior auditor.

b. The rules of conduct state that a public accountant shall not disclose any confidential information obtained in the course of a professional engagement except with the consent of his or her client. In which one of the situations given below would disclosure by a public accountant be in violation of the rules?
   (1) Disclosing confidential information in compliance with a subpoena issued by a court.
   (2) Disclosing confidential information to another accountant interested in purchasing the public accountant's practice.

(3) Disclosing confidential information in connection with a disciplinary hearing by the public accountant's professional conduct committee.

(4) Disclosing confidential information in order to properly discharge the public accountant's responsibilities in accordance with his or her profession's standards.

(AICPA adapted)

DISCUSSION QUESTIONS AND PROBLEMS

3-20   Mary Frost, an audit senior in your office, states that members of her public accounting firm should not have any social interaction with a client's staff because such interaction threatens independence. Norman Amey, another senior, disagrees, saying social interaction makes for a smoother audit.

Required

What do you think is the correct view and why?

3-21   Trish Mulcahy, a new junior in your office, says that she doesn't understand why she can't work on the audit of a company that is a client of your firm and that is owned by her uncle. Trish says she knows she must have an independent attitude and she will; her relationship to the owner is not important.

Required

What would you say in answer to her question? Would you let her work on the audit?

3-22   Each of the following scenarios involves a possible violation of the rules of conduct discussed in the chapter. Indicate whether each is a violation and explain why if you think it is.

a. John Brown is a public accountant, but not a partner, with three years of professional experience with Lyle and Lyle, Public Accountants, a one-office public accounting firm. He owns 25 shares of stock in an audit client of the firm, but he does not take part in the audit of the client and the amount of stock is not material in relation to his total wealth.

b. In preparing the corporate tax returns for a client, Phyllis Allen, public accountant, observed that the deductions for contributions and interest were unusually large. When she asked the client for backup information to support the deductions, she was told, "Ask me no questions, and I will tell you no lies." Allen completed the return on the basis of the information acquired from the client.

c. A client requested assistance of Kim Tanabe, public accountant, in the installation of a computer system for maintaining production records. Tanabe had no experience in this type of work and no knowledge of the client's production records, so he obtained assistance from a computer consultant. The consultant is not in the practice of public accounting, but Tanabe is confident of her professional skills. Because of the highly technical nature of the work, Tanabe is not able to review the consultant's work.

d. Five small Moncton public accounting firms have become involved in an information project by taking part in an interfirm working paper review program. Under the program, each firm designates two partners to review the working papers, including the tax returns and the financial statements, of another public accounting firm taking part in the program. At the end of each review, the auditors who prepared the working papers and the reviewers have a conference to discuss the strengths and weaknesses of the audit. They do not obtain the authorization from the audit client before the review takes place.

e. James Thurgood, public accountant, stayed longer than he should have at the annual Christmas party of Thurgood and Thurgood, Public Accountants. On his way home, he drove through a red light and was stopped by a police officer, who observed that he was intoxicated. In a jury trial, Thurgood was found guilty of driving under the influence of alcohol. Since this was not his first offence, he was sentenced to 30 days in jail and his driver's licence was revoked for one year.

f. Bill Wendal, public accountant, set up a casualty and fire insurance agency to complement his auditing and tax services. He does not use his own name on anything pertaining to the insurance agency and has a highly competent manager, Renate Jones, who runs it. Wendal frequently requests Jones to review with the management of an audit client the adequacy of the client's insurance if it seems underinsured. He feels that he provides a valuable service to clients by informing them when they are underinsured.

g. Michelle Rankin, public accountant, provides tax services, management advisory services, and bookkeeping services and conducts audits for the same client. Since her firm is small, the same person frequently provides all the services.

3-23   Each of the following situations involves possible violations of the rules of conduct that apply to professional accountants discussed in the chapter. For each situation, state whether it is a violation of the rules as described. In those cases in which it is a violation, explain the nature of the violation and the rationale for the existing rule.

a. Mario Danielli is the partner on the audit of a charitable organization. He is also a member of the board of directors, but this position is honorary and does not involve performing a management function.

b. Fenn and Company, Public Accountants, has time available on a computer that it uses primarily for its own record keeping. Aware that the computer facilities of Delta Equipment Corp., one of Fenn's audit clients, are inadequate for company needs, Fenn maintains on its computer certain routine accounting records for Delta.

c. Marie Godette, CA, has a law practice. Godette has recommended one of her clients to Sean O'Doyle, public accountant. O'Doyle has agreed to pay Godette 10 percent of the fee O'Doyle receives from Godette's client.

d. Theresa Barnes, CA, has an audit client, Choi, Inc., which uses another public accounting firm for management services work. Barnes sends her firm's literature covering its management services capabilities to Choi on a monthly basis unsolicited.

e. A bank issued a notice to its depositors that it was being audited and requested them to comply with the public accounting firm's effort to obtain a confirmation on the deposit balances. The bank printed the name and address of the public accounting firm in the notice. The public accounting firm has knowledge of the notice.

f. Wally Gutowski, a practicing public accountant, has written a tax article that is being published in a professional publication. The publication wishes to inform its readers about Gutowski's background. The information, which Gutowski has approved, includes his academic degrees, other articles he has had published in professional journals, and a statement that he is a tax expert.

g. Marcel Poust, public accountant, has sold his public accounting practice, which includes bookkeeping, tax services, and auditing, to Sheila Lyons, public accountant. Poust obtained permission from all audit clients for audit-related working papers before making them available to Lyons. He did not get permission before releasing tax- and management services-related working papers.

h. Murphy and Company, Public Accountants, is the principle auditor of the consolidated financial statements of Cranbrook, Inc., and subsidiaries. Cranbrook accounts for approximately 98 percent of consolidated assets and consolidated net income. The two subsidiaries are audited by Trotman and Company, Public Accountants, a firm with an excellent professional reputation. Murphy insists on auditing the two subsidiaries because he deems this necessary to warrant the expression of an opinion.

3-24 The *Canada Business Corporations Act* requires all companies incorporated under it to have audit committees.

Required

a. Describe an audit committee.

b. What are the typical functions performed by an audit committee?

c. Explain how an audit committee can help an auditor be more independent.

d. Your friend's mother, who is chair of an audit committee of a large publicly traded company, knows that you are studying auditing and has asked you for advice on how she can make the audit committee she chairs more effective. Your response should consider both sides of each recommendation you make.

3-25 Diane Harris, public accountant, is the auditor of Fine Deal Furniture, Inc. In the course of her audit for the year ended December 31, 1999, she discovered that Fine Deal had serious going concern problems. Henri Fine, the owner of Fine Deal, asked Harris to delay completing her audit.

Harris is also the auditor of Master Furniture Builders Ltd., whose year end is January 31. The largest receivable on Master Furniture's list of receivables is Fine Deal Furniture; the amount owing represents about 45 percent of Master Furniture's total receivables, which in turn are 60 percent of Master Furniture's net assets. The management of Master Furniture is not aware of Fine Deal's problems and is certain the amount will be collected in full.

Master Furniture is in a hurry to get the January 31, 2000, audit finished because the company has made an application for a sizable loan from their bank to expand their operations. The bank has informally agreed to advance the funds based on draft financial statements submitted by Master Furniture just after the year end.

Required

What action should Harris take and why?

3-26 The following relate to auditors' independence.

Required

a. Why is independence so essential for auditors?

b. Compare the importance of independence of professional public accountants with that of other professionals, such as lawyers.

c. Explain the difference between independence in appearance and in fact.

d. Describe the four facets of independence. Can any one of the four be ignored?

e. Discuss how each of the following could affect independence in fact and independence in appearance, and evaluate the social consequence of prohibiting auditors from doing each one.
  (1) Ownership of stock in a client company.
  (2) Having bookkeeping services for an audit client performed by the same person who does the audit.
  (3) Recommending adjusting entries to the client's financial statements and preparing financial statements, including footnotes, for the client.
  (4) Having management services for an audit client performed by individuals in a department that is separate from the audit department.

(5) Having the annual audit performed by the same audit team, except for assistants, for five years in a row.

(6) Having the annual audit performed by the same public accounting firm for 10 years in a row.

(7) Having management select the public accounting firm.

3-27 Marie Janes encounters the following situations in doing the audit of a large auto dealership. Janes is not a partner.

1. The sales manager tells her that there is a sale on new cars (at a substantial discount) that is limited to long-established customers of the dealership. Because her firm has been doing the audit for several years, the sales manager has decided that Janes should also be eligible for the discount.

2. The auto dealership has an executive lunchroom that is available free to employees above a certain level. The controller informs Janes that she can also eat there any time.

3. Janes is invited to and attends the company's annual Christmas party. When presents are handed out, she is surprised to find herself included. The present has a value of approximately $200.

Required

a. Assuming Janes accepts the offer or gift in each situation, has she violated the rules of conduct?

b. Discuss what Janes should do in each situation.

3-28 The following are situations that may violate the general rules of conduct of professional accountants discussed in the chapter. Assume in each case that the public accountant is a partner.

1. Simone Able, public accountant, owns a substantial limited partnership interest in an apartment building. Juan Rodriquez is a 100 percent owner in Rodriquez Marine Ltd. Rodriquez also owns a substantial interest in the same limited partnership as Able. Able does the audit of Rodriquez Marine Ltd.

2. Horst Baker, public accountant, approaches a new audit client and tells the president that he has an idea that could result in a substantial tax refund in the prior year's tax return by application of a technical provision in a tax law that the client had overlooked. Baker adds that the fee will be 50 percent of the tax refund after it has been resolved by Revenue Canada. The client agrees to the proposal.

3. Chantal Contel, public accountant, advertises in the local paper that her firm does the audit of 14 of the 36 largest drugstores in the city. The advertisement also states that the average audit fee, as a percentage of total assets for the drugstores she audits, is lower than any other public accounting firm's in the city.

4. Olaf Gustafson, public accountant, sets up a small loan company specializing in loans to business executives and small companies. Gustafson does not spend much time in the business because he works full time with his public accounting practice. No employees of Gustafson's public accounting firm are involved in the small loan company.

5. Louise Elbert, public accountant, owns a material amount of stock in a mutual fund investment company, which in turn owns stock in Elbert's largest audit client. Reading the investment company's most recent financial report, Elbert is surprised to learn that the company's ownership in her client has increased dramatically.

6. Kerry Finigan, public accountant, does the audit, tax return, bookkeeping, and management services work for Gilligan Construction Company Limited. Before she makes any major business decision, Mildred Gilligan follows the practice of calling Finigan to determine the effect on her company's taxes and the financial statements. Finigan attends continuing education courses in the construction industry to make sure she is technically competent and knowledgeable about the industry. Finigan normally attends board of directors' meetings and accompanies Gilligan when she is seeking loans. Mildred Gilligan often jokingly introduces Finigan with this statement, "I have my three business partners — my banker, the government, and my public accountant, but Finny's the only one that is on my side."

Required

Discuss whether the facts in any of the situations indicate violations of the rules of conduct for professional accountants discussed in the chapter. If so, identify the nature of the violation(s).

3-29 Gilbert and Bradley formed a corporation called Financial Services, Inc., each man taking 50 percent of the authorized common stock. Gilbert is a public accountant and a member of one of the professional accounting bodies in Canada. Bradley is a CPCU (Chartered Property Casualty Underwriter). The corporation performs auditing and tax services under Gilbert's direction and insurance services under Bradley's supervision. The opening of the corporation's office was announced by an 8 cm, two-column "card" in the local newspaper.

One of the corporation's first audit clients was the Grandtime Corp. Grandtime had total assets of $600,000 and total liabilities of $270,000. In the course of his examination, Gilbert found that Grandtime's building, with a book value of $240,000, was pledged as security for a 10-year term note in the amount of $200,000. The client's statements did not mention that the building was pledged as security for the note. However, as the failure to disclose the lien did not affect either the value of the assets or the amount of the liabilities and his examination was satisfactory in all other respects, Gilbert rendered an unqualified opinion on Grandtime's financial statements. About two months after the date of his opinion, Gilbert learned that an insurance company was planning to loan Grandtime $150,000 in the form of a first mortgage note on the building. Realizing that the insurance company was unaware of the existing lien on the building, Gilbert had Bradley notify the insurance company of the fact that Grandtime's building was pledged as security for the term note.

Shortly after the events just described, Gilbert was charged with a violation of professional ethics.

Required

Identify and discuss the ethical implications of those acts by Gilbert that were in violation of the rules of conduct discussed in the chapter.

3-30 Barbara Whitley had great expectations about her future as she sat at her graduation ceremony in May 1998. She was about to receive her Masters of Accountancy degree, and the following week she would begin her career on the audit staff of Green, Thresher & Co., a public accounting firm. Things looked a little different to Barbara in February 1999. She was working on the audit of Delancey Fabrics Ltd., a textile manufacturer with a calendar year end. The pressure was enormous. Everyone on the audit team was putting in 70-hour weeks, and it still looked as if the audit wouldn't be done on time. Barbara was doing work in the property area, vouching additions for the year. The audit program indicated that a sample of all items over $10,000 should be selected, plus a judgmental sample of smaller items. When Barbara went to take the sample, Jack Bean, the senior, had left the client's office and couldn't answer her questions about the appropriate size of the judgmental sample. Barbara forged ahead with her own judgment and selected 50 smaller items. Her basis for doing this was that there were about 250 such items, so 50 was a reasonably good proportion of such additions.

Barbara audited the additions with the following results: the items over $10,000 contained no errors; however, the 50 small items contained a large number of errors. In fact, when Barbara projected them to all such additions, the amount seemed quite significant.

A couple of days later, Jack Bean returned to the client's office. Barbara brought her work to Jack in order to apprise him of the problems she found, and got the following response: "My God, Barbara, why did you do this? You were only supposed to look at the items over $10,000 plus 5 or 10 little ones. You've wasted a whole day on that work, and we can't afford to spend any more time on it. I want you to throw the schedules where you tested the last 40 small items away and forget you ever did them."

When Barbara asked about the possible audit adjustment regarding the small items, none of which arose from the first 10 items, Jack responded, "Don't worry, it's not material anyway. You just forget it; it's my concern, not yours."

Required

a. In what way is this an ethical dilemma for Barbara?

b. Use the six-step approach discussed in the book to resolve the ethical dilemma.

3-31 In 1993, Giles Nadeau was a bright, upcoming audit manager in the Winnipeg office of a national public accounting firm. He was an excellent technician and a good "people person." Giles also was able to bring new business into the firm as the result of his contacts in the francophone business community.

Giles was assigned a new client in 1994, XYZ Securities, Inc., a privately held broker-dealer in the secondary market for Canadian government securities. Neither Giles nor anyone else in the Winnipeg office had broker-dealer audit experience. However, Giles was able to obtain audit aids for the industry from his firm's national office, which he used to get started.

Giles was promoted to partner in 1995. Although this was a great step forward for him (he was a new staff assistant in 1985), Giles was also under a great deal of pressure. Upon making partner, he was required to contribute capital to the firm. He also felt he must maintain a special image with his firm, his clients, and within the francophone community. To accomplish this, Giles maintained an impressive wardrobe, bought a Cadillac Seville and a small speedboat, and traded up to a nicer house. He also entertained freely. Giles financed much of this higher living with credit cards. He had American Express, Diners Club, en Route, and Visa cards and ran up a balance of about $40,000.

After the audit was completed and before the 1996 audit was to begin, Giles contacted Lynda Oakes, the CFO of XYZ Securities, with a question. Giles had noticed an anomaly in the financial statements that he couldn't understand and asked Oakes for an explanation. Lynda's reply was as follows: "Giles, the 1995 financial statements were materially misstated and you guys just blew it. I thought you might realize this and call me, so here's my advice to you. Keep your mouth shut. We'll make up this year the loss we covered up last year, and nobody will ever know the difference. If you blow the whistle on us, your firm will know you screwed up, and your career as the star in the office will be down the tubes."

Giles said he'd think about this and get back to Lynda the next day. When Giles called Lynda, he had decided to go along with her. After all, it would only be a "shift" of a loss between two adjacent years. XYZ is a private company and no one would be hurt or know the difference. In reality, he was the only person exposed to any harm in this situation, and he had to protect himself, didn't he?

When Giles went to XYZ to plan for the 1996 audit, he asked Lynda how things were going and she assured him they were fine. He then said to Oakes, "Lynda, you guys are in the money business. Maybe you can give me some advice. I've run up some debts and I need to refinance them. How should I go about it?"

After some discussions, Lynda volunteered a "plan." She would give Giles a cheque for $15,000. XYZ would request its bank to put $60,000 in an account in Giles's name and guarantee the loan security on it. Giles would pay back the $15,000 and have $45,000 of refinancing. Giles thought the plan was great and obtained Lynda's cheque for $15,000.

During 1996 through 1998, three things happened. First, Giles incurred more debts and went back to the well at XYZ. By the end of 1998, he had "borrowed" a total of $125,000. Second, the company continued to lose money in various "off-the-books" investment schemes. These losses were covered up by falsifying the results of normal operations. Third, the audit team, under Giles's leadership, "failed to find" the frauds and issued unqualified opinions.

In 1997, Lynda had a tax audit of her personal 1997 return. She asked Giles's firm to handle it, and the job was assigned to Bob Smith, a tax manager. In reviewing Lynda's records, Smith found a $15,000 cheque payable from Oakes to Nadeau. Smith asked to see Nadeau and inquired about the cheque. Giles somewhat broke down and confided in Smith about his problems. Smith responded by saying, "Don't worry Giles, I understand. And believe me, I'll never tell a soul."

In 1999, XYZ's continuing losses caused it to be unable to deliver nonexistent securities when requested by a customer. This led to an investigation and bankruptcy by XYZ. Losses totalled in the millions. Giles's firm was held liable, and Giles was found guilty of conspiracy to defraud. He is still in prison today.

Required

a. Try and put yourself in Giles Nadeau's shoes. What would you have done (be honest with yourself) when told of the material misstatement in mid-1995?

b. What do you think of Bob Smith's actions to help Giles?

c. Where does one draw the line between ethical and unethical behaviour in the situations described in this case study?

3-32 CA was employed by Potvin and Associates (Potvin), Chartered Accountants, as an audit manager, until approximately five months ago. During his employment with Potvin, CA was involved in the audit engagement of Yonge Investments Limited (YIL) for the year ended December 31, 1997. The audit engagement was completed by February 1998, and the financial statements were issued soon thereafter. In September 1998, CA was hired as the chief financial officer of YIL.

The common voting shares of YIL are owned by three persons. The two major shareholders, who own 41 percent of the voting shares, interviewed CA several times before YIL hired him. CA replaced a son of one of the owner-interviewers; the son had decided to return to university to study international marketing.

Share ownership of YIL is as follows:

Preferred shares, 5 percent dividend rate, all owned by the founder of the company: $5,600,000

Common shares

Son of the founder (Joe)	$410,000
Daughter of the founder (Marianne)	$410,000
First wife of the founder	$180,000

The second wife of the founder sold her common shares to their children, Joe and Marianne.

CA reports to the "Management team," which consists of Joe and Marianne. YIL has three divisions:

Division AL - manufactures various aluminum products such as storm doors, storm windows, aluminum containers, and similar products.

Division TM - performs telephone marketing, including the selling of a variety of products imported from Asia.

Division RE - has real-estate holdings, short-term securities investments, and head-office assets.

The founder retired several years ago. Marianne is responsible for Division AL, and Joe is in charge of Division TM. Division RE is managed jointly by Joe and Marianne. The first wife of the founder is not active in the business, and she receives only the annual financial statements and a dividend cheque.

Potvin has audited the financial statements of YIL for the past five years. The firm was engaged by Marianne, with the agreement of Joe. The audited financial statements are sent to all shareholders and to the company's banker, and they are used for income tax purposes. CA has been instructed that all contacts with the auditors are to be handled by Marianne. Otherwise, CA is responsible for all financial reporting and control matters.

CA has recently become aware of the following matters:

1. The telephone marketing division uses high-pressure selling tactics, and it processes the vast majority of its telephone sales through customers' credit card numbers. Salespersons are paid by commission only. No invoice is rendered to customers, most of whom do not ask for a telephone number or an address of Division TM. Shipments are made from a warehouse, which lists only a postal box number on its shipping form. To date, no provision has been made for returns, but CA is aware of some customer dissatisfaction with some relatively new products.

2. Joe is the 100 percent owner of ABC Company (ABC), a sales and distribution company in another province. During the past year, approximately 14 percent of the imported goods purchased by Division TM have been sold to ABC. In order to save handling costs, the goods are shipped directly to ABC from YIL's supplier. CA believes that, on average, Division TM sells these goods to ABC for about 20 percent less than their cost. Periodically, ABC sells goods to Division TM. YIL's audited financial statements do not include any notes about these matters.

3. Division AL generates scrap aluminum as a result of its manufacturing process. A perpetual inventory of scrap aluminum has never been maintained, primarily because it is picked up twice a week by a scrap dealer friend of Marianne's, under a long standing arrangement. Scrap aluminum is not shown in the cost records because all material drawn from inventory stores is fully charged to the cost of a product, using job order costing. The auditors seem to be satisfied with this approach, presumably because the proceeds from disposal are negligible.

4. For the past several years, Division AL has had to make a material writedown at each year end to show the results of the physical count of raw materials. CA is satisfied that the procedures are more than adequate for the physical count and that all jobs include the full cost for material that is being drawn from inventory storage. The inventory is enclosed in a secure area. The inventory adjustments have been included in cost of goods sold on the financial statements.

5. YIL has guaranteed personal bank loans to both Joe and Marianne, according to the minutes of a directors' meeting of two years ago. The guarantees are considered to be part of the "compensation package" and are not disclosed in the financial statements.

6. The unstated policy of YIL is to lend money to the owners at the prime rate of interest of one of the Canadian chartered banks. The amounts loaned are included in trade accounts receivable on the company's financial statements, and write-offs are included with cost of goods sold.

7. CA was given a file of copies of some of the auditors' working papers that affect other portions of the company's or owners' affairs. One working paper shows that YIL sold some paintings to Joe and Marianne for $50,000 each, which the working paper notes as "approximately fair market value." The working paper also notes that Joe and Marianne donated these paintings to a public art gallery and received receipts, for income tax purposes, for $205,000 each. The $205,000 was based on an appraisal by a local art dealer. A copy of the appraisal, which is included in the working papers, states the total value of the paintings as $410,000. CA will be responsible for preparing the income tax returns of several company employees including Joe and Marianne.

8. YIL's investment broker also maintains trading accounts for several company officials. The broker has agreed to pool purchases and sales of securities so that savings on brokerage fees are obtained whenever the company and one or more officials buy and sell the same security. The auditors' working papers show that broker's fees are allocated on the basis of dollars belonging to each participant. The broker also allows the officials and YIL to buy from and sell to each other at no fee, through their respective brokerage accounts. YIL guarantees the accounts of only Joe and Marianne. The financial statements do not contain a note concerning the arrangement with the investment broker.

It is now February 1999, and the auditors have completed the audit and have presented the standard management representation letter to Marianne, Joe, and CA for signature. Marianne and Joe have signed the letter and have passed it on to CA to sign.

Required

Assuming the role of CA, what would you do and why?

(CICA adapted)

4

LEGAL LIABILITY

IT TAKES THE NET PROFIT FROM MANY AUDITS TO OFFSET THE COST OF ONE LAWSUIT

Orange & Rankle, a CPA firm in San José, California, audited a small high-tech client that developed software. A significant portion of the client's capital was provided by a syndicate of 40 limited partners. The owners of these interests were knowledgeable business and professional people, including several lawyers.

Orange & Rankle audited the company for four consecutive years, from its inception, for an average annual fee of approximately U.S.$13,000. The audits were well done by competent auditors. It was clear to the firm and to others who subsequently reviewed the audits that they complied with generally accepted auditing standards in every way.

In the middle of the fifth year of the company's existence, it became apparent that the marketing plan it had developed was overly optimistic, and the company was going to require additional capital or make a significant strategy change. The limited partners were polled and refused to provide the capital. The company folded its tent, and filed for bankruptcy. The limited partners lost their investment in the company. They subsequently filed a lawsuit against all parties involved in the enterprise, including the auditors.

Over the next several years the auditors proceeded through the process of preparing to defend themselves in the lawsuit. They went through complete discovery, hired an expert witness on auditing-related issues, filed motions and so forth. They attempted a settlement at various times, but the plaintiffs would not agree to a reasonable amount. Finally, during the second day of trial, the plaintiffs settled for a nominal amount.

It was clear that the plaintiffs knew the auditors bore no fault, but kept them in the suit anyway. The total *out-of-pocket* cost to the audit firm was U.S.$1 million, not to mention personnel time, possible damage to its reputation, and general stress and strain. Thus, the cost of this suit, where the auditors were completely innocent, was more than 75 times the average annual audit fee earned from this client.

This chapter-opening vignette describes a U.S. case, but the total cost relative to the audit fee is instructive. Legal liability and its consequent effects are considered by many of the leaders of the public accounting profession in Canada, as in the United States, to be the profession's most important problem. While the U.S. environment is considered to be more litigious than the Canadian environment, litigation is a problem for public accountants in Canada.

The following discussion helps put the problem in perspective. (Remember that some of the data are U.S. figures.)

It was reported that in 1991, the six largest auditing firms in the U.S. incurred a combined U.S.$447 million in direct costs in the settlement and defence of lawsuits. This represented 9 percent of their accounting and auditing revenues. This was an increase from 7.7 percent in 1990, and it has since been estimated that these costs have risen to as high as 11.9 percent of comparable 1994 revenues. Further, it is estimated that the profession's aggregate liability exposure exceeds U.S.$30 billion. While comparable figures for Canada are not available, that litigation is a problem in Canada is supported by the fact that there are, at time of writing, several lawsuits outstanding against Canadian public accounting firms with damages claimed in those suits alone of more than $2.4 billion.[1]

Although firms have insurance to help alleviate the impact of assessed damages, the premiums are high and the policies available to the firm have large deductible amounts. The deductibles are such that the large firms are essentially self-insured for losses of many millions of dollars.

The problem of liability in the U.S. became more visible in 1990 when the seventh largest CPA firm, Laventhol & Horwath, filed for bankruptcy. A primary cause was the large number of suits alleging malpractice with large amounts of damages claimed that were facing the firm. A plan to liquidate the firm was approved by the court in 1992, requiring the partners of the firm to pay $48 million to avoid personal bankruptcy. A second large firm, Panell Kerr Forster, closed or sold about 90 percent of its offices and reorganized its offices as individual professional corporations in 1992. A former partner of that firm was quoted as saying that the liability was one of the reasons for this massive restructuring.

Accountants' liability also affects the profession in human terms. For example, evidence suggests that a number of partners and managers leaving the six largest public accounting firms in recent years were influenced by the effect of ongoing litigation costs on future profits.

While Mindy Paskell-Mede, editor of the Law column in *CAmagazine*,[2] does not believe the damage claims in Canada against auditors are likely to reach U.S. proportions, she does suggest that she believes that a bankruptcy like that of Laventhol & Horwath could occur in Canada. Paskell-Mede goes on to describe differences between the Canadian and U.S. legal systems that she believes will mitigate against auditors' legal problems in Canada becoming the legal crisis that exists for auditors in the United States. The principal differences are:

- Jury trials for civil suits involving auditors are rare in Canada, while almost every U.S. auditor liability suit is decided by a jury. In addition, in Ontario, special commercial judges hear more business civil cases. The judges who do hear auditor-related cases in Canada tend to be more knowledgeable than the juries who decide U.S. cases.
- Punitive damages tend to be much smaller or nonexistent in Canada. In the U.S., punitive damages are often many times the value of compensatory damages.

---

[1]It should be noted that the final settlements are often considerably less than the amounts claimed.

[2]This material is taken from Paskell-Mede, Mindy, "What Liability Crisis?" *CAmagazine* (May 1994), pp. 42–43.

- Costs sanctions (i.e., the loser pays part of the winner's court costs) are "more effective" in Canada. In the United States, the unsuccessful plaintiff often incurs no costs as the lawyer's costs and fee are contingent on a successful lawsuit. As a consequence, frivolous lawsuits are less common in Canada. In February 1997, in *Mele et al. v. Thorne Riddel et al.*, defendant accountants obtained solicitor-and-client costs (a set tariff that provides a significant saving on out-of-pocket costs). In this case, the plaintiff charged "reckless" behaviour and "secret commissions" without any evidence. The judge felt that plaintiffs should be discouraged from such actions.
- Class action suits against auditors are less common in Canada.[3]
- The regulatory environment (legislative and regulatory systems) is less aggressive towards auditors in Canada than in the U.S.

These factors should be kept in mind in the study of auditor's liability later in the chapter.

This chapter discusses the nature of legal liability of public accountants. First, the reasons for increased litigation against public accountants are discussed. This is followed by a detailed examination of the nature of the lawsuits and the sources of potential liability. Significant lawsuits involving public accountants that relate to the various issues are presented in summary form. You will note that the cases discussed come from the United States, the United Kingdom, and Canada; the legal systems in all three countries (except in Quebec, whose private law is based on French civil law[4]) are based on English common law; as a consequence, when judges in all three countries hand down decisions, while they have no obligation to follow decisions in the other countries, they will often refer to those decisions in the course of giving their own judgment. The chapter ends with a discussion of the options available to the profession and individual practitioners to minimize liability while meeting society's needs.

CHANGED LEGAL ENVIRONMENT

Professionals have always had a duty to provide a reasonable level of care while performing work for those they serve. Audit professionals have a responsibility under common law to fulfill implied or expressed contracts with clients. They are liable to their clients for negligence and/or breach of contract should they fail to provide the services or should they fail to exercise due care in their performance. Auditors may also be held liable under the tort of negligence or due to provincial securities acts to parties other than their clients in certain circumstances. Although the precise legal definition of the auditor's *third party* (people who do not have a contract with the auditor) liability continues to evolve, the position of the Supreme Court of Canada, at this time, remains that the auditor owes a duty of care to third parties who are part of a limited group of persons whom the auditor knows will use and rely on the audit, and that the auditor's knowledge extends to the purpose or transaction for which the financial statements would be used.

Note the use of the term "evolve" here; in Canada, as in other countries, lower courts are presenting other definitions. You will see further discussion of this shortly. Finally, in rare cases auditors have also been held liable for criminal acts. A criminal conviction against an auditor can result only when it is demonstrated that the auditor acted with criminal intent.

---

[3]The interested reader is directed to Grossman, Barbara J., "Class Rules," in the Law column, *CAmagazine* (March 1996), pp. 31–33 and 43.

[4]Smyth, J. E., D. A Soberman, and A. J. Easson, *The Law and Business Administration in Canada*, Seventh Edition, Scarborough, Ontario: Prentice Hall Canada Inc., 1995, pp. 46–47.

A relatively new area of liability is fiduciary duty. Fiduciary duty is a confused and growing body of Canadian law that has affected accountants and may also affect auditors. The Supreme Court of Canada case of *Robert L. Hodgkinson v. David L. Sims and Jerry S. Waldman* (File No. 23033, 1997) summarized many of the then current definitions of a fiduciary. On page 385 of the case, the court indicates that "the hallmark of a fiduciary relationship is that one party is dependent upon or in the power of the other." It then looks to three conditions: (1) the fiduciary has the ability to exercise discretion or power, (2) discretion or power can be unilaterally exercised, and (3) the beneficiary is peculiarly vulnerable. The court then goes on to say that this is not an absolute test. This is a new and difficult legal area. It is not further discussed in this text since in an ordinary auditor–client relationship, no fiduciary duty would arise. However, the law is developing very rapidly in this area, with uncertain results.

The five sources of auditor's legal liability identified in the previous paragraphs are the main focus of this chapter. They are summarized in Table 4-1, with an example of a potential claim from each source.

In recent years, both the number of lawsuits and size of awards to plaintiffs have significantly increased in both Canada and the United States, although the increase in the United States has been more significant because of a number of factors, including the more litigious climate in that country. Many of the lawsuits brought against auditors are brought by third parties. There are no simple reasons for this increase, but the following are major factors:

- The growing awareness of the responsibilities of public accountants by users of financial statements.
- An increased consciousness on the part of the provincial securities commissions regarding their responsibility for protecting investors' interests.
- Increased market volatility, resulting in losses to third parties such as shareholders and institutional investors.
- The greater complexity of auditing and accounting due to such factors as the increasing size of business, the sophistication of computer-based systems, and the intricacies of business operations.
- Society's increasing acceptance of lawsuits by injured parties against anyone who might be able to provide compensation and who appears to be at least partially responsible for the loss. This is frequently called the "deep-pocket" concept of liability.
- The willingness of public accounting firms to settle their legal problems out of court in an attempt to avoid costly legal fees and adverse publicity rather than resolving them through the judicial process.
- The difficulty courts have in understanding and interpreting technical accounting and auditing matters.

TABLE 4-1

FIVE MAJOR SOURCES OF AUDITOR'S LEGAL LIABILITY

SOURCE OF LIABILITY	EXAMPLE OF POTENTIAL CLAIM
Client — liability to client under common law	Client sues auditor for not discovering a defalcation during the audit.
Third party — liability to third parties under common law	Bank sues auditor for not discovering materially misstated financial statements.
Liability under provincial securities acts	A purchaser of stock issued by a company sues the auditor for not discovering materially misstated financial statements in a prospectus.
Criminal liability	Court prosecutes auditor under the *Criminal Code of Canada* for knowingly issuing an incorrect auditor's report.
Fiduciary duty — one party has an obligation to act for the benefit of another, and that obligation includes discretionary power	An accountant acting as trustee for a client invests in inappropriate investment vehicles and otherwise squanders the assets of the trust.

DISTINCTION AMONG BUSINESS FAILURE, AUDIT FAILURE, AND AUDIT RISK

Many accounting and legal professionals believe that a major cause of lawsuits against public accounting firms is the lack of understanding by financial statement users of the difference between a *business failure* and an *audit failure* and between an *audit failure* and *audit risk*. These terms are first defined then followed by a discussion of how misunderstanding in the differences between the terms often results in lawsuits against auditors.

OBJECTIVE 4-2

Explain why the failure of financial statement users to differentiate among business failure, audit failure, and audit risk has led to lawsuits.

Business failure This occurs when a business is unable to repay its lenders or meet the expectations of its investors, due to economic or business conditions such as a recession, poor management decisions, or unexpected competition in the industry. The extreme case of business failure is filing for bankruptcy. As stated in Chapter 1, there is always some risk that a business will fail.

Audit failure This occurs when the auditor issues an erroneous audit opinion as the result of an underlying failure to comply with the requirements of generally accepted auditing standards. For example, the auditor may have assigned unqualified assistants to perform audit tasks, and because of their lack of competence, they failed to find material misstatements that qualified auditors would have discovered.

Audit risk This is the risk that the auditor will conclude that the financial statements are fairly stated and an unqualified opinion can therefore be issued when, in fact, they are materially misstated. As will be shown in subsequent chapters, auditing cannot be expected to uncover all material financial statement misstatements. Auditing is limited by sampling, and certain misstatements and well-concealed frauds are extremely difficult to detect; therefore, there is always some risk that the audit will not uncover a material financial statement misstatement even when the auditor has complied with generally accepted auditing standards.

Most accounting professionals agree that in most cases when an audit has failed to uncover material misstatements, and the wrong type of audit opinion is issued, a legitimate question may be raised as to whether the auditor followed due care. If the auditor failed to use due care in the conduct of the audit, then there is an audit failure. In such cases, the law often allows parties who suffered losses as a result of the auditor's breach of duty of care owed to them to recover some or all of the losses proximately caused by the audit failure. It is difficult in practice to determine when the auditor has failed to follow due care because of the complexity of auditing. It is also not always clear who has a right to expect the benefits of an audit because of the evolving nature of the law. Nevertheless, an auditor's failure to follow due care can be expected to result in a claim of negligence and, where appropriate, damages against the public accounting firm.

The difficulty arises when there has been a business failure, but not an audit failure. For example, when a company goes bankrupt or cannot pay its debts, it is common for statement users to claim there was an audit failure, particularly when the most recently issued auditor's opinion indicates the financial statements were fairly stated. This conflict between statement users and auditors often arises because of what is referred to as the *expectation gap between users and auditors*. Most auditors believe that conducting an audit in accordance with generally accepted auditing standards is all that can be expected of auditors. Many users believe auditors guarantee the accuracy of financial statements, and some users even believe the auditor guarantees the financial viability of the business. Fortunately for the profession, the courts continue to support the auditor's view. Unfortunately, the expectation gap often results in unwarranted lawsuits. Perhaps the profession has a responsibility to educate financial statement users about the role of auditors and the difference between business failure, audit failure, and audit risk. Realistically, however, auditors must recognize that, in part, the claims of audit failure may also result from the hope of those who suffer a business loss to recover damages from any source, regardless of who is at fault.

LEGAL CONCEPTS AFFECTING LIABILITY

OBJECTIVE 4-3

Define the primary legal concepts and terms concerning accountant's liability.

The public accountant is responsible for every aspect of his or her public accounting work, including auditing, taxes, management advisory services, and accounting and bookkeeping services. For example, if a public accountant negligently failed to properly prepare and file a client's tax return, the public accountant can be held liable for any penalties and interest the client was required to pay plus the tax preparation fee charged.

Most of the major lawsuits against public accounting firms have dealt with audited or unaudited financial statements. The discussion in this chapter deals primarily with these two aspects of public accounting. The areas of liability in auditing can be classified as (1) liability to clients, (2) liability to third parties under common law and statute law, and (3) criminal liability. Several legal concepts apply to all of these types of lawsuits against public accountants. These are the *prudent person concept*, *liability for the acts of others*, and the *lack of privileged communication*.

PRUDENT PERSON CONCEPT

There is agreement within the profession and the courts that the auditor is not a guarantor or insurer of financial statements. The auditor is only expected to conduct the audit with due care. Even then, the auditor cannot be expected to be perfect.

The standard of due care to which the auditor is expected to be held is often referred to as the *prudent person concept*. It is expressed in *Cooley on Torts* as follows:

> Every man who offers his service to another and is employed assumes the duty to exercise in the employment such skill as he possesses with reasonable care and diligence. In all these employments where peculiar skill is prerequisite, if one offers his service, he is understood as holding himself out to the public as possessing the degree of skill commonly possessed by others in the same employment, and, if his pretensions are unfounded, he commits a species of fraud upon every man who employs him in reliance on his public profession. But no man, whether skilled or unskilled, undertakes that the task he assumes shall be performed successfully, and without fault or error. *He undertakes for good faith and integrity, but not for infallibility*, and he is liable to his employer for negligence, bad faith, or dishonesty, but not for losses consequent upon pure errors of judgment.

LIABILITY FOR ACTS OF OTHERS

The partners of a public accounting firm may have *joint and several liability* if a suit for tort or negligence is brought against the partnership. In other words, each partner may be held liable in a civil action for the tort or negligent actions of each of the other partners and employees in the partnership. Ontario provincial legislation has given accounting firms the ability to reduce their liability by forming *limited liability partnerships* (LLPs). Under this organizational form, individual partners who had nothing to do with the engagement or with the supervision of the staff who carried out the engagement would not be liable on their personal assets. In the absence of fraud or actual knowledge, only the person who did the work and those who supervised that person, as well as the firm itself, would be liable.

The partners may also be liable for the work of others on whom they rely under the laws of agency. The two groups an auditor is most likely to rely on are *other public accounting firms* engaged to do part of the work and *specialists* called upon to provide technical information. Where a primary–secondary auditor relationship exists, the primary auditor would be entitled to rely upon the work of the secondary auditor, assuming that the primary auditor had conducted sufficient quality control work with respect to that secondary auditor. If the auditor proved that there was appropriate reliance on the work of a specialist, there would be an extremely strong defence that the auditor was not negligent and would not be liable to the plaintiff.

LACK OF PRIVILEGED COMMUNICATION

Public accountants do not have the right under common law to withhold information from the courts on the grounds that the information is privileged. As stated in Chapter 3, information in an auditor's working papers can be subpoenaed by a court.

Confidential discussions between the client and auditor cannot be withheld from the courts. In the very specific situation where an accountant prepares documentation as a result of a lawyer's request to be used in existing or potential litigation, only that documentation could be considered privileged (e.g., *Cineplex Odeon v. MNR* [Ministry of National Revenue], 1994).

DEFINITIONS OF LEGAL TERMS

The material in the rest of the chapter can be covered more effectively if the most common legal terms affecting public accountant's liability are understood.

NEGLIGENCE AND FRAUD

The first four terms deal with the auditor's negligence or fraud. The distinctions are useful for discussing the application of the law to various types of lawsuits against auditors because they affect the outcome of many suits.

Negligence   Absence of reasonable care that can be expected of a person in a set of circumstances. When negligence of an auditor is being evaluated, it is in terms of what other competent auditors would have done in the same situation.

Tort action for negligence   Failure of a party to meet its social or professional obligations, contractual or otherwise, thereby causing injury to another party to whom a duty was owed. A typical negligence action against a public accountant is a bank's claim that an auditor had a duty to uncover material errors in financial statements that had been relied on in making a loan.

A plaintiff in a tort action (i.e., a case brought by a plaintiff for an alleged wrong suffered at the hands of the defendant) for negligence against a public accountant must prove all of the following to succeed:

1. The accountant (defendant) must owe a duty of care to the plaintiff.
2. The defendant must have been negligent in the performance of that duty (i.e., did not act in accordance with the prudent person concept).
3. The plaintiff must have suffered a loss.
4. There must be a connection between the defendant's negligence and the plaintiff's loss. For example, the plaintiff relied on financial statements audited by the defendant, who was negligent in the performance of the audit, and the plaintiff suffered a loss because of that reliance.

Fraud   A false assertion that has been made knowingly, or without belief in its truth, or recklessly without caring whether or not it is true. The plaintiff must also be able to prove that the accountant intended the plaintiff to act on the assertion, that the plaintiff did act on it, and that, as a consequence, the plaintiff suffered a loss. An example is an auditor giving a standard (unqualified) opinion on financial statements that will be used to obtain a loan when the auditor *knows* the financial statements contain a material misstatement.

Constructive fraud   Existence of such recklessness that, even though there was no actual intent to defraud, a court will impute or construe fraud to the action. For example, if a public accountant failed to follow most of the generally accepted auditing standards, he or she may be found to have committed constructive fraud even though no intent to deceive statement users has been proved. This concept has been used in foreign court cases, but has not been used in Canadian cases. It is therefore not discussed further in this chapter. We will focus instead on negligence and fraud.

CONTRACT LAW

Breach of contract   Failure of one or both parties in a contract to fulfill the requirements of the contract. An example is the failure of a public accounting firm to deliver a tax return on the agreed-upon date. Parties who have a relationship that is established by a contract are said to have *privity of contract*.

Typically, public accounting firms and clients sign an *engagement letter* to formalize their agreement about the services to be provided, fees, and timing. There can be privity of contract without a written agreement, but an engagement letter defines the contract more clearly.

Third-party beneficiary A third party who does not have privity of contract but is known to the contracting parties and is intended to have certain rights and benefits under the contract. A common example is a bank that has a large loan outstanding at the balance sheet date and requires an audit as a part of its loan agreement. The naming of a third party in an engagement letter often establishes that party as a third-party beneficiary. The third party would claim negligence.

COMMON AND STATUTORY LAW

Common law, judge-made law, or case law Law that has been developed through court decisions rather than through government statutes. The bulk of the law of negligence has been created in this fashion. An example is an auditor's liability to a bank related to the auditor's failure to discover material misstatements in financial statements that were relied on in issuing a loan. This law is continually evolving as new decisions are handed down by the courts; what might be used as a successful defence by an auditor today may not be successful tomorrow, while a defence that was not successful in the past might now be successful. The thing to remember is that common law is always evolving as new precedents are set by the courts.

Statutory law Laws and regulations that have been passed by a Canadian government body, either federal or provincial. The *Canada Business Corporations Act* is an important statutory law affecting auditors of companies incorporated under its jurisdiction.

OTHER TERMS

Civil action An action between individuals such as those that may be brought for breach of contract or tort.

Criminal action An action brought under a provision of criminal statute law, for example, the *Criminal Code of Canada*.

Contributory negligence When a person injured by a public accountant's negligence has also been negligent, and this negligence has also caused or contributed to the person's loss or injuries, this is known as contributory negligence. A common example of such negligence is failure to give a public accountant information requested during the preparation of a tax return. The client later sues the accountant for improper preparation of the return. The court may hold that there was contributory negligence by the client, and any damages that the client is awarded would be reduced in proportion to the amount that the client's own negligence was responsible for the loss.

LIABILITY TO CLIENTS

> **OBJECTIVE 4-4**
>
> **Describe accountants' liability to clients, the related defences, and some significant legal cases.**

The term *client* refers to the entity being audited and not to its owners or shareholders. Although the shareholders vote to appoint the auditors, the contract is between the enterprise and the auditors. In effect, shareholders are third parties and are discussed further, together with liability to other third parties, on page 103.

Lawsuits against public accountants from clients vary widely, including such claims as failure to complete an audit engagement on the agreed-upon date, inappropriate withdrawal from an audit, failure to discover a defalcation, and breach of the confidentiality requirements of public accountants. Typically, these lawsuits are relatively rare, and they do not receive the publicity often given to third party suits. *Transamerica Commercial Finance*, Figure 4-15 on page 112, is a Canadian case in this area.

A typical lawsuit involves a claim that the auditor did not discover an employee defalcation (theft of assets) as a result of negligence in the conduct of the audit. The lawsuit can be for breach of contract, a tort action for negligence, or both. Tort actions can be based on ordinary negligence or fraud. Note that, while it might sound odd for plaintiffs to claim under both breach of contract and negligence, the way each is proven and the amount of damages available under each might be different. By claiming under both, the plaintiff is thus covering all bases. The plaintiff cannot, however, be awarded damages twice for one event or loss.

The principal issue in cases involving alleged negligence is usually the level of care required. Although it is generally agreed that nobody is perfect, not even a professional, in most instances any significant misstatement will create a doubt regarding competence. In the auditing environment, failure to meet generally accepted auditing standards is often strong evidence of negligence. An example of an audit case raising the question of negligent performance by a public accounting firm is the case of *Haig v. Bamford* (see Figure 4-9 on page 105). The reader should remember from the study of generally accepted auditing standards in Chapter 1 that determining due care and the amount and type of evidence to be obtained on an audit are subjective decisions. In a suit where negligence by an auditor was alleged, the court would hear evidence from one or more expert (auditing) witnesses as to the decision they would have reached in similar circumstances. From this evidence, a judge or jury would decide what the average public accountant would do and, therefore, what the accountant being sued should have done. In this way, the determination of negligence occurs.

The question of level of care becomes more difficult in the environment of unaudited financial statements (i.e., a review or compilation) in which there are few accepted standards to evaluate performance. Examples of lawsuits dealing with the failure to uncover fraud in unaudited financial statements are the U.S. *1136 Tenants* case, summarized in Figure 4-1, and the Canadian *Multi Graphics* case, summarized in Figure 4-2.

FIGURE 4-1

1136 Tenants v. Max Rothenberg and Company (1967)

The *1136 Tenants* case was a civil case concerning a CPA's failure to uncover fraud as a part of unaudited financial statements. The tenants recovered approximately $235,000.

A CPA firm was engaged by a real estate managing agent for $600 per year to prepare financial statements, a tax return, and a schedule showing the apportionment of real estate taxes for the 1136 Tenants Corporation, a cooperative apartment house. The statements were sent periodically to the tenants. The statements included the word "unaudited," and there was a cover letter stating that "The statement was prepared from the books and records of the corporation and no independent verifications were taken thereon."

During the period of the engagement, from 1963 to 1965, the manager of the management firm embezzled significant funds from the tenants of the cooperative. The tenants sued the CPA firm for negligence and breach of contract for failure to find the fraud. There were two central issues in the case. Was the CPA firm engaged to do an audit instead of only write-up work, and was there negligence on the part of the CPA firm? The court answered yes on both counts. The reasoning for the court's conclusion that an audit had taken place was the performance of "some audit procedures" by the CPA firm, including the preparation of a worksheet entitled "missing invoices." Had the CPA followed up on these, the fraud would likely have been uncovered. Most important, the court concluded that even if the engagement had not been considered an audit, the CPA had a duty to follow up on any potential significant exceptions uncovered during an engagement.

The case has two implications for public accountants:

1. Engagement letters that detail what the client and auditor expect to be done are very important so that both know exactly what is to be done.
2. All unexplained and unusual items should be followed to their conclusion unless they are not material. However, the public accountant should be very careful to ensure that the item that is not material is not part of a larger material item or a symptom of a serious (and possibly material) problem.
3. Once an audit procedure has been undertaken on a review or non-audit engagement, it must be completed. Even though the procedure is not required, it should be followed through to completion.

FIGURE 4-2

*466715 Ontario
Limited operating as
Multi Graphics Print &
Litho v. Helen Proulx
and Doane Raymond
(1998)*

Doane Raymond (now Grant Thornton), carried out review engagements between 1985 and 1993 for Multi Graphics Print and Litho for an annual fee of about $1,500. Helen Proulx, the sole bookkeeper, commenced fraudulent activity in 1988, when she was given signing authority. Shortly afterwards, a computerized ACCPAC Bedford system was installed. The fraud involved Proulx preparing cheques to herself, signing and cashing them (the cheques were recorded as payable to suppliers or to reimbursement of petty cash), pocketing money for C.O.D. orders and issuing fictitious invoices, and having a differential between the amount deposited and the amount recorded and pocketing the difference. Over $100,000 was stolen. The owners signed cheques over $1,000 and did not handle mail or review source documents or bank statements.

When the fraud was discovered, Multi Graphics sued the accountants, claiming that the accountants ought to have known of the control problems at Multi Graphics and should have alerted the owners to the related dangers. The accountants countered by saying that they were retained to provide review services. The engagement letter explicitly described a review engagement, stating that there was no responsibility to consider internal controls or to detect fraud. The accountants were not consulted on issues of internal controls, the change in the computerized accounting system or the change in signing authority.

The court ruled in favour of Doane Raymond, finding that the accountants had fulfilled their professional and contractual obligations, and that the agreement between the parties specifically excluded responsibility to detect fraud and error. The court added that the duty of care in a review engagement would not create the obligation to go any further than the accountants did.[5]

AUDITOR'S DEFENCES AGAINST CLIENT SUITS FOR NEGLIGENCE

The public accounting firm normally uses one of or a combination of six defences when there are legal claims of negligence by clients: lack of duty to perform the service, absence of misstatement, absence of negligence, contributory negligence, no damages, and absence of causal connection.

Lack of duty   The lack of duty to perform the service means that the public accounting firm claims there was no duty owed to the client to perform the task that is now said to have been negligently performed. For example, the public accounting firm might claim that errors were not uncovered because the firm did a review engagement, not an audit. A common way for a public accounting firm to demonstrate a lack of duty to perform is by use of an *engagement letter*.[6] Many litigation experts believe well-written engagement letters are one of the most important ways public accounting firms can reduce the likelihood of adverse legal actions.

Harry Kuziw et al v. James W. Abbott et al. (Figure 4-3) illustrates reliance and a lack of duty.

Absence of misstatement   Prior to addressing negligence, the defendant accountants could provide evidence that the financial statements were in accordance with GAAP, that is, that there were no material errors. Thus, even if the auditors had been negligent, the appropriate financial statements would not have differed from those on which the plaintiff relied. Therefore, no grounds exist for suing the auditors, since the financial statements appropriately portray the financial situation of the organization.

The Bottom Line
www.butterworths.ca/
tbl.htm

---

[5]Kulig, P., "Doane Raymond Absolved of Wrongdoing," *The Bottom Line* (November 1, 1998), p. 14, and trial judgment, Ontario Court (General Division), 95-CU-87608, August 20, 1998.

[6]Two types of letters that are commonly used by auditors to reduce potential liability to clients are an engagement letter and a representation letter. An engagement letter is a signed agreement between the public accounting firm and the client identifying such items as whether an audit is to be done, other services to be provided, the date by which the work is to be completed, and the fees. The representation letter documents oral communication between auditors and management, and states management's responsibilities for fair presentation in the financial statements. See also Chapters 7 and 21.

FIGURE 4-3
*Kuziw et al. v. Abbott
et al.* (1984)

Abbott *et al.* provided accounting services to Graf-Tech Publication Services Ltd. for several years. William J. Hemenway, a member of the firm of Abbott *et al.*, who had done work for Harry Kuziw in connection with other investments that Kuziw had made, introduced Kuziw to Graf-Tech in early 1980 in response to Kuziw's request for information about "business opportunities."

Graf-Tech was suffering from cash shortages and was being pressed by Revenue Canada for overdue payroll deductions. It was also suffering from managerial weaknesses. Hemenway explained both the positive and negative aspects of Graf-Tech to Kuziw and provided him with statements with "Accountant's Comments" dated June 30, 1979, and with statements for January and February 1980 that had each been prepared with a "Notice to Reader." Kuziw knew that no audit had been done and appeared to understand the implications of work done under then Section 8100 (now Section 9200) of the *CICA Handbook*. The court found that Kuziw had conducted an extensive investigation on his own including discussions with the senior management of Graf-Tech and with the manager of the bank where Graf-Tech banked. Kuziw's lawyer suggested outside accounting advice but Kuziw demurred.

Kuziw made two investments and gave guarantees totalling $235,000 over the next several months. In addition, he became active in Graf-Tech's management. Despite this assistance, the company went into receivership in late 1980. Among the reasons for the receivership was the fact that Graf-Tech's principal contract was much less profitable than had been believed and than had been indicated by the financial statements prepared by Hemenway's firm some months earlier.

The Court of the Queen's Bench of Manitoba, upheld on appeal by the Court of Appeal of Manitoba, found that while Hemenway had known that Kuziw planned to rely on the financial statements he had prepared, Kuziw had not relied to any significant degree on the information. Accordingly, Kuziw could not succeed. The court went on to state that it believed that Hemenway had "discharged his professional responsibility."

This case is of interest, in addition to its finding, because the judgment discusses at some length the difference between an audit and a compilation, as well as the responsibility of the accountant under the latter.

Absence of negligence Evidence to refute a claim would be that the audit was performed in accordance with generally accepted auditing standards. Even if there were undiscovered unintentional misstatements (errors) or intentional misstatements or misrepresentations (fraud and other irregularities), the auditors will argue that they are not responsible if the audit was properly conducted. The public accounting firm is not expected to be infallible. Similarly, Sections 5090, 5135, and 5136 of the *CICA Handbook* make it clear that an audit in accordance with GAAS is subject to limitations and cannot be relied upon for complete assurance that all errors, fraud and other irregularities, and illegal acts will be found.

Section 5090 states, in part:

> The objective of an audit of financial statements is to express an opinion whether the financial statements present fairly . . . . Such an opinion is not an assurance as to the future viability of the enterprise nor an opinion as to the effectiveness with which its operations, including internal control, have been conducted.
>
> The operations of an enterprise are under the control of management, which has the responsibility for the accurate recording of transactions and the preparation of financial statements. . . . The financial statements [are] the representations of management.[7]

The section goes on to explain that "The auditor . . . seeks reasonable assurance whether the financial statements are free of material misstatement [i.e., material error or fraud]." It also states that "Absolute assurance in auditing is not attainable" and lists the reasons. These include the need for judgment, the use of testing (i.e., sampling rather than examining the entire population), the inherent limitations of internal control, and the fact that the evidence an auditor examines is persuasive, not conclusive. These factors should be remembered when reading about risk in Chapter 8.

---

[7]The judge, in the 1933 decision by the Manitoba Court of Appeal in the case of *International Laboratories Limited v. Dewar et al.*, put the onus on management for the detection of fraud.

Paragraph 5135.15 states, in part:

> In an audit conducted in accordance with generally accepted auditing standards, the auditor's professional responsibility is fulfilled by complying with those standards. . . . An audit does not guarantee all material misstatements will be detected. . . . A material misstatement may subsequently be discovered in the financial statements even though the auditor has adhered to generally accepted auditing standards. . . .

It is likely that the courts will accept the *CICA Handbook* as evidence of appropriate standards of behaviour for the auditor, but it is possible that the courts could decide that an auditor who complied with the *Handbook* had been negligent. Such circumstances would be rare, but could occur if the court thought the auditor had complied with the letter and not the spirit of the rules, or if GAAP was not sufficiently informative. Figure 4-4, *Kripps v. Touche Ross & Co.* (1997), describes a suit in which investors succeeded in arguing that financial statements, although prepared according to GAAP, were misleading since they did not adequately disclose the fact that a large portion of its investments held by a mortgage company was "non-performing," (i.e. in default).

The courts recognize that it is possible to make a valid exercise of judgment that, nonetheless, has an unfavourable outcome. In that case, the auditor would not be found negligent. The auditor would want expert testimony that he or she had made a valid exercise of judgment. For example, the auditor might have selected a sample from a population for testing that was not representative of that population and, hence, had not found a material misstatement that was present in the population. The courts would likely determine that the auditor had not been negligent since the auditor had made a valid exercise in judgment in selecting the sample.

Requiring auditors to discover all material misstatements would, in essence, make them insurers or guarantors of the accuracy of the financial statements. The courts do not require that. *Cameron v. Piers, Conrod & Allen* (Figure 4-5) is an example of a case

FIGURE 4-4

Kripps v. Touche Ross (1997)[8]

Stephen Kripps and five other individuals sued Touche Ross & Co. (now Deloitte & Touche) in 1986 over the losses they incurred when Victoria Mortgage Corporation Ltd. (VMCL) failed in 1985. Touche Ross was VMCL's auditor from 1980 to 1984. During 1984, VMCL's financial statements were included in a prospectus issued by the company in 1984. The plaintiffs argued that they relied on the financial statements in the prospectus for their investment decisions, and that the financial statements were misleading.

The plaintiffs contended that loans of $3.5 million in default over 90 days, equivalent to one-quarter of the value of VMCL's portfolio, should have been disclosed. Also, the financial statements did not make adequate provision for losses on the portfolio.

Eleven years later, the courts have finally laid this case to rest. The first trial judge dismissed the case, saying that the plaintiffs had relied on attractive interest rates when making their investment. The B.C. Court of Appeals reversed this decision in April 1997 in a 2:1 decision. The plaintiffs argued that they placed reliance on the prospectus, a document that encouraged people to invest in a company.

Two judges agreed that although GAAP did not require disclosure of the loans, the phrase "present fairly" should have overridden the specific rules of GAAP, and that GAAP was a tool to achieve fair presentation. Deloitte & Touche sought leave to appeal at the Supreme Court of Canada, but in November 1997 that was denied.

This ruling is important for auditors for several reasons:

1. It reaffirms that auditors who have given consent to inclusion of financial statements in a prospectus owe a duty of care to investors who relied on the prospectus.
2. It is consistent with paragraph 1000.61 of the *CICA Handbook* which indicates that where following *Handbook* recommendations would result in misleading financial statements, alternative disclosures would be desirable. These standards were in place prior to the court decision.
3. Auditors should view GAAP as a floor.

---

[8]From Daisley, Brad, "Professional's Liability Law Overhauled," *The Lawyer's Weekly*, Vol. 17, No. 4 (May 30, 1998), pp. 1, 12; and Chigbo, Okey, "GAAP Under Fire," *CAmagazine* (January/February 1998), pp. 22–30.

FIGURE 4-5

Cameron v. Piers, Conrod & Allen (1985)[9]

Piers, Conrod & Allen (PCA) were the auditors for Cameron Limited and its subsidiary, Kentville Publishing Company Limited. The year end of the latter company was October 31, while that of the former company was December 31. Kentville was run by a competent accountant who was in frequent contact with and highly regarded by the owner of Cameron Limited.

PCA normally began the audit of Kentville early in the new year but was unable to gain access to the books for the year ended October 31, 1979, at that time. Kentville's manager continued to delay the Kentville audit through March and April 1980. In the meantime PCA had begun the audit of Cameron and in that connection needed to verify the valuation of Kentville on the Cameron books.

The auditor from PCA received reassurances from the Kentville manager that the owner of Cameron Limited was being kept abreast of the situation at Kentville. In addition, the auditor had talked to the owner's son, who was himself an accountant, and had made him aware of the delay.

The auditor from PCA and his staff went to the offices of Kentville and did what work was considered necessary to complete the audit of Cameron. At that time, there was no indication of any serious problems at Kentville. The Cameron December 31, 1979, financial statements were issued with an unqualified opinion. The notes to the financial statements indicated that the accounts of Kentville and other subsidiaries were not consolidated but were carried at cost.

Subsequently, the manager of Kentville was hospitalized. The records and financial affairs of Kentville were found to be in disarray. PCA was hired to go into Kentville and straighten the records out. It was discovered that the reports that the manager had been giving to the owner of Cameron and to the auditor were not accurate.

Cameron Limited sued PCA on the grounds that PCA had been negligent in evaluating Cameron's investment in Kentville as at December 31, 1979. The court found (sustained on appeal) that the auditor had not been negligent in that he had exercised reasonable care and skill in attempting to evaluate Cameron's investment in Kentville. It was not inappropriate for the auditor to rely on the manager of Kentville, a trusted employee of the owner of Cameron; the auditor did his best to ascertain the facts.

where the public accountant was not negligent; the court ruled that the auditor had satisfied the prudent person concept.

Contributory negligence A defence of contributory negligence means that the public accounting firm claims that part or all of the loss arose because of the claimant's own negligence. For example, suppose the client is the claimant and argues that the public accounting firm was negligent in not uncovering an employee theft of cash. A likely contributory negligence defence is the auditor's claim that the public accounting firm informed management of a weakness in the internal controls that enhanced the likelihood of the fraud, but management did not correct it. Management often does not correct internal control weaknesses because of cost considerations, attitudes about employee honesty, or procrastination. In the event of a lawsuit of the nature described, the auditor is unlikely to lose the suit, assuming a strong contributory negligence defence, if the client was informed in writing of internal control weaknesses. An example of contributory negligence as a partial defence is the case *of H. E. Kane Agencies Ltd. v. Coopers & Lybrand* summarized in Figure 4-6.

In a Canadian case, *Breau v. Touchie* (1992), the accountant prepared false financial statements for a franchisee indicating that the franchisee had invested loan proceeds in his franchise. When the franchise failed, the franchisee sued his accountant for breach of contract and negligence. The accountant was found liable on both counts, but the plaintiff/franchisee's mismanagement contributed to the failure of the business, so liability was apportioned 50 percent to the accountant and 50 percent to the franchisor.

No damages (or reduced damages) It is possible that the financial statements were misstated and that the audit was negligently performed but that the plaintiff did not suffer any damages. This was one of the issues addressed by the Supreme Court of Canada in the *Hercules Management v. Ernst & Young* (Figure 4-11). Damages were

---

[9]Rowan, Hugh, Q.C., "Stymied by Management: A Case of Negligence?"
CAmagazine (April 1986), pp. 80–87.

FIGURE 4-6

H.E. Kane Agencies Ltd.
v. Coopers & Lybrand
(1983)[10]

Coopers & Lybrand had been the auditors of H.E. Kane Agencies Ltd. for a number of years. The president of Kane Agencies was Harold Kane, and he ran the operation; his son Charles was an employee. In 1967 Charles persuaded his father to expand into the travel business, and Kane Agencies became an agent for Air Canada.

An invoice was prepared whenever an airline ticket was sold, but the sale was not recorded until payment was received from the customer. Kane Senior did not like credit, so very little credit was extended. Reports were submitted twice monthly to Air Canada indicating ticket sales with the net cost of the tickets enclosed. Initially, sales were for a relatively small amount to a wide variety of customers.

In 1974, Kane Agencies changed the thrust of its travel business when it started doing business with Trade Resources (International) Limited. Now Kane Agencies did have a dominant customer. The accounting for ticket sales was changed for this new customer; an invoice was prepared when payment was received and not, as previously, when the ticket was sold. As a result, Charles Kane knew about the size of the outstanding receivable from Trade Resources, but his father did not. Charles would report the sale to Air Canada at the time the ticket was paid for and not when it was issued, so that there was a delay in recording the liability.

Trade Resources went bankrupt in 1976 owing Kane Agencies in excess of $250,000. Kane sued Coopers & Lybrand claiming that the accounting firm had been negligent in not discovering the deception that Charles was perpetrating on his father and Air Canada. Coopers & Lybrand claimed that Harold Kane had not supervised the travel division and that Charles Kane had willfully concealed the unreported ticket sales from them.

The judge assessed Kane Agencies damages at $87,599 but found that the company had contributed to the loss through the conduct of Harold in not supervising the travel business and not noticing the Trade Resources receivable and the conduct of Charles in setting up the arrangement that caused the loss. Accordingly, the damages payable by Coopers & Lybrand to Kane Agencies were reduced by 50 percent.

claimed by a third party, the shareholders, but the Supreme Court stated that the damages were suffered by the corporate entity itself rather than by the shareholders. Thus, those plaintiffs (the shareholders) had no standing in law to claim the damages.

Absence of causal connection   To succeed in an action against the auditor, the client must be able to show that there is a close causal connection between the auditor's breach of the standard of due care and the damages suffered by the client. For example, assume an auditor failed to complete an audit on the agreed-upon date. The client alleges that this caused a bank not to renew an outstanding loan, which caused damages. A potential auditor defence is that the bank refused to renew the loan for other reasons, such as the weakening financial condition of the client. The case of *Toromont Industrial Holdings v. Thorne et al.*, discussed in Figure 4-10 on page 106, illustrates absence of causal connection; the court ruled that the purchaser, Toromont, did not rely on an incorrect auditor's report but rather had decided to purchase Cimco Ltd. prior to receiving the audited financial statements.[11]

LIABILITY TO THIRD PARTIES UNDER COMMON LAW

OBJECTIVE 4-5

**Describe accountants'
liability to third
parties under
common law, the
related defences, and
some significant legal
cases.**

A public accounting firm may be potentially liable to third parties if a loss was incurred by the claimant due to reliance on misleading financial statements. Third parties are any people with whom the auditor did *not* enter into a contract and include actual and potential shareholders, vendors, bankers and other creditors or investors, employees, and customers. A typical suit might occur when a bank is unable to collect a major loan from an insolvent customer. The bank will claim that

[10]See Rowan, Hugh, Q.C., "Giving Credit Where Credit's Not Due, Part 1," *CAmazagine* (June 1983), pp. 69–71; Rowan, "Giving Credit Where Credit's Not Due, Part 2," *CAmazagine* (August 1983), pp. 97–102; and Rowan, "When Fault Is Divided," *CAmazagine* (August 1986), pp. 84–87

[11]Smyth, J. E., D. A. Soberman,. and A. J. Easson, *The Law and Business Administration in Canada*, Seventh Edition, Scarborough, Ontario: Prentice Hall Canada Inc., 1995, pp. 112–114.

misleading audited financial statements were relied upon in making the loan, and that the public accounting firm should be held responsible because it failed to perform the audit with due care. Understanding when the auditor will be held liable calls for an understanding of the continuing evolution of this area of the law.

EVOLUTION OF LIABILITY

The leading precedent-setting auditing case in third party liability was a 1931 U.S. case, *Ultramares Corporation v. Touche*. It established the traditional common law approach known as the *Ultramares* doctrine. The case has been cited many times in England and Canada. It is summarized in Figure 4-7.

FIGURE 4-7
Ultramares Corporation v. Touche (1931)

The creditors of an insolvent corporation (Ultramares) relied on the audited financials and subsequently sued the accountants, alleging that they were guilty of negligence and fraudulent misrepresentation. The accounts receivable had been falsified by adding to approximately $650,000 in accounts receivable another item of over $700,000. The creditors alleged that careful investigation would have shown the $700,000 to be fraudulent. The accounts payable contained similar discrepancies. The court held that the accountants had been negligent but ruled that accountants would not be liable to third parties for honest blunders beyond the bounds of the original contract unless they were third-party beneficiaries. The court held that only one who enters into a contract with an accountant for services can sue if those services are rendered negligently.

The court went on, however, to order a new trial on the issue of fraudulent misstatement. The form of certificate then used said, "We further certify that subject to provisions for federal taxes on income the said statement in our opinion presents a true and correct view of the financial condition." The court pointed out that to make such a representation if one did not have an honest belief in its truth would be fraudulent misrepresentation.

The key aspect of the *Ultramares* doctrine is that ordinary negligence is insufficient for liability to third parties because of the lack of privity of contract between the third party and the auditor. The judge commented that it would be inappropriate to hold the auditors liable to third parties in the circumstances, since this would open the doors to indeterminate liability of an indeterminate amount to an indeterminate number of people. The case was followed by other jurisdictions on the basis of the policy considerations underlying this judgment. In addition, *Ultramares* also held that if there had been fraud or constructive fraud, the auditor could be held liable to more general third parties.

Traditionally, third parties in Canada were in a similar position to those in the United States: they were effectively prevented from suing successfully for negligent misstatements if they had no contract with the auditor. The situation began to change in 1963 with an English case, *Hedley Byrne & Co. Ltd. v. Heller & Partners Ltd.* (Figure 4-8). This case too was a landmark case. Although the case was British, not Canadian, and did not deal specifically with accountants, it contained very real implications for them. In the United Kingdom it was viewed as the long-awaited statement about the law of negligent misstatement and it came from the most senior court of that country, the House of Lords. All common law countries were naturally interested in its outcome. The defence of lack of privity enunciated in *Ultramares* was said by the House of Lords to be no longer relevant. The various opinions of the law lords on the

FIGURE 4-8
Hedley Byrne v. Heller & Partners (1963)

Hedley Byrne was an advertising agency that was about to incur a liability for advertising for a client. They asked their bankers to find out from the client's bankers, Heller & Partners, if the client was credit-worthy. Heller replied in the affirmative to the banker, who passed the information on to Hedley Byrne, and so Hedley Byrne, a third party, incurred the liability. Subsequently, the client was unable to pay its accounts, and Hedley Byrne sued Heller for negligence.

Heller & Partners had issued a disclaimer together with their opinion and thus the House of Lords ruled in their favour. However, with respect to the lack of privity, the Lords found that not to be a bar to success by the plaintiff, Hedley Byrne. Some of the law lords argued that despite the lack of privity, Heller owed a duty of care to Hedley Byrne and that Heller should have foreseen that Hedley Byrne would rely on their statement about the client.

FIGURE 4-9

Haig v. Bamford et al.
(1976)[12]

Scholler Furniture & Fixtures Ltd. needed additional working capital and approached Saskatchewan Economic Development Corporation (SEDCO) for further advances. SEDCO agreed to grant the advances providing Scholler would produce satisfactory audited financial statements for the fiscal period ended March 31, 1965, and gain the infusion of additional equity capital in the amount of $20,000.

Scholler told his accountants, Bamford *et al.*, that he needed audited financial statements for SEDCO, his bank, and a potential but then unknown investor. The statements were prepared, with an auditor's report appended and shown to Haig who invested the required $20,000.

Subsequently, the company again foundered, and investigation revealed that the financial statements included $28,000 of revenue received in advance as earned revenue; the corrected statements showed that the company had lost money and not earned a sizable profit as shown by the earlier statements. Subsequently, it was discovered that Bamford *et al.*, although they were told an audit was required and although they appended an auditor's report, had not done an audit.

Later Haig advanced additional funds but the company went into receivership. Haig sued the accountants for negligence and sought to recover both his original investment and later advance.

The Supreme Court, in their decision, concurred with lower courts that Bamford *et al.* had been negligent. Insofar as the extent of the duty of care on the part of the accountants to third parties, the court said there were three possible tests:

1. Foreseeability of the use of audited financial statements by the plaintiff
2. Actual knowledge of the limited class who will rely on the audited statements
3. Actual knowledge of the person who will rely on the audited statements

The appropriate test was deemed to be 2. The court decided that Haig was entitled to recover his original investment from the auditors because he had relied on the financial statements that had been negligently prepared. He was not entitled to recover subsequent investments because he made them based on his own information.

case did not make it clear to whom those providing opinions on statements would owe a duty of care. The notion of foreseeable third parties was introduced as a possible test of the extent of duty. The law lords said that those uttering negligent misstatements may be liable to third parties but did not make it clear precisely under what circumstances. Courts in a number of countries have been grappling with the issue ever since.

The next case of importance on this issue was decided by the Supreme Court of Canada in 1976. The case was *Gordon T. Haig v. Ralph L. Bamford et al.*; see Figure 4-9.

This case confirms the finding in *Hedley Byrne v. Heller* that lack of privity is not necessarily a valid defence. However, the Supreme Court decided it should not consider the foreseeability test (i.e., test 1) as it was not relevant to the particular circumstances. Instead, the narrower test of actual knowledge of the limited class was deemed to be appropriate; that is, in Canada, persons making negligent misstatements (in this case, auditors) are potentially liable to all those third parties who were members of a limited group of whom the auditors had knowledge at the time the audit was performed and the audited financial statements were issued. For example, the test of actual knowledge would apply if an auditor was asked to give an opinion on financial statements to be shown to several local banks for purposes of obtaining a loan. The narrowest of the three tests, that the auditor must know the actual individual, was rejected as being too narrow.

At about the same time, another case of interest was unfolding; it was *Toromont Industrial Holdings Limited v. Thorne, Gunn, Helliwell & Christenson*. This case, summarized in Figure 4-10, reached its final resolution in the High Court of Justice in Ontario.

The *Toromont* case raises several interesting issues. The judgment, which referred both to *Hedley Byrne* and a lower court decision on *Haig v. Bamford*, confirmed the broadening of an auditor's liability to third parties known to be using the audited

---

[12]The *Haig v. Bamford* case first decided in a lower court in 1972 for the plaintiff. That decision was appealed and reversed by the Saskatchewan Court of Appeal in 1974. Haig appealed that decision and was successful in the Supreme Court of Canada in 1976.

Toromont proposed to acquire all of the shares of Cimco Ltd. for cash and Toromont shares. The purchase price was based on Cimco's assets, liabilities, and financial position at that date. Prior to purchase, a partner from the accounting firm that did Toromont's audit talked to a partner of Thorne, Cimco's auditors, about the work the latter had done with regard to the December 31, 1968, financial statements. Cimco's financial statements at this point were in draft form. In other words, Thorne *et al.* were aware of Toromont's interest in the financial statements prior to their being issued.

The court decided that the financial statements did present fairly the financial position at December 31, 1968, but that the auditors, Thorne *et al.*, had been negligent in their performance of the 1968 audit. The reasons given were as follows:

1. They did not obtain sufficient evidence about certain contracts.
2. They relied too heavily on oral evidence from management.
3. They did not adequately check the system of internal control in force although they relied on it.
4. The accounts included goodwill with respect to a company sold two years previously.

In addition a senior partner of Thorne, although not connected with the audit, was very involved with Cimco's senior management.

The court concluded that Thorne *et al.* had been negligent and that Toromont did have a right of action as Thorne knew Toromont would be relying on the financial statements. The court, however, also concluded that Toromont did not suffer any loss from the negligence, and so the case was dismissed.

financial statements. In the case of *Toromont v. Thorne*, Toromont was able to prove that Thorne et al. owed a duty of care to Toromont and that Thorne et al. had been negligent in the performance of that duty, but Toromont was not able to prove that it suffered a loss. As a consequence, Toromont did not succeed.

The next discussion flows from two English decisions made in 1989: *Caparo Industries PLC v. Dickmans* and *Al Saudi Banque et al. v. Clark Pixley*. Prior to the decision in these cases, the consensus among commentators was that the duty of care expected of auditors was expanding. These cases, therefore, came as something of a surprise as they appear to restrict the auditor's liability.

In *Caparo*,[13] the law lords determined that an auditor would not be liable to investors who made a decision to invest in a company after the audited financial statements had been published or to shareholders at the time the audit was conducted who made an investment decision (e.g., to hold or sell shares already owned or to buy additional shares) after the statements had been published. The court held that the persons uttering the statements should only be liable if the third parties used them for the purpose for which they were prepared. In this case, the law lords held that the audit was provided to evaluate management. In *Al Saudi Banque*, the courts found that auditors were not liable to creditors who relied on financial statements on which the auditors had opined.

In November 1989, the B.C. Supreme Court, in the case of *Dixon v. Deacon, Morgan, McEwan, Easson et al.*, handed down a decision in which it concluded that, while it was foreseeable that Dixon would rely on the audited financial statements, the requirement of proximity was lacking. In addition, the court decided after weighing "the relationship of the parties, the nature of the risk and the public interest in the proposed solution"[14] that it would not be fair to impose a duty of care on the auditors because this would give Dixon a cause of action which was not included in securities acts.

---

[13]The ensuing material comes from Rowan, Hugh, "A Fair Share of Care," *CAmagazine* (December 1989), pp. 63–68; Paskell-Mede, Mindy, "Duty's Not in the Eye of the Beholder," *CAmagazine* (April 1990), pp. 29–31; Pound, Richard W., "Duty in Question," *CGA Magazine* (August 1990), pp. 14–15; and DuPlessis, Dorothy and Barbara Trenholm, "Limiting Auditor Liability," *CGA Magazine* (November 1991), pp. 30–35.

[14]Pound, Richard W., "Duty in Question," *CGA Magazine* (August 1990), p. 14.

In 1991, in *Calvert v. Spencer*,[15] Judge Van Camp also cited *Caparo*. She ruled that while Spencer did not have a duty of care to Calvert when the 1979 statements for Superior Restaurant and Hotel Supplies Limited were prepared, he did have a duty of care once he became aware that Calvert, as a potential purchaser of Superior, had asked for and received the statements. In her judgment, Judge Van Camp awarded damages to Calvert and held that Calvert was two-thirds responsible. In 1997, in *Hercules Management v. Ernst & Young*,[16] as mentioned earlier, the court ruled that the auditors had no special knowledge that the shareholders planned to use the financial statements for investment decisions and that there was no privity of contract. The auditors relied on *Caparo* in their defence that they owed no duty of care to the shareholders. Figure 4-11 describes this case further, and shows that the Supreme Court of Canada agreed with the lower court.

FIGURE 4-11
Hercules Managements Ltd. v. Ernst & Young (1997)[17]

Hercules Managements Ltd. and other shareholders of Northguard Acceptance Ltd. (NGA) and of Northguard Holdings Ltd. (NGH) sued Ernst and Young in 1988 after both NGA and NGH went into receivership in 1984. The plaintiffs argued that the audit reports for the years 1980, 1981, and 1982 were negligently prepared and that the shareholders suffered financial losses due to reliance on these reports.

This action was dismissed both by the Manitoba Court of Queen's Bench and by the Manitoba Appeal Court on the grounds that (1) the defendants did not owe the plaintiffs a duty of care and (2) the claims should be brought by the corporations and not by the shareholders individually, since a shareholder cannot succeed for a reduction in value of equity, even if a duty of care was owed, because the loss of equity is really the loss suffered by the company.

In May 1997, the Supreme Court of Canada generally agreed. The court said audited financial reports call for "a duty of care" by auditors when they are used "as a guide for the shareholders, as a group, in supervising or overseeing management." Thus, there appears to be no direct liability to the shareholders for any reduction in the value of their equity.

This case has entrenched the principle of no general auditor liability where this might give rise to an indeterminate amount of such liability in the absence of any evidence that the auditor knew of a specific purpose, other than corporate governance, to which the financial statements would be put. However, Brenda Eprile, the then executive director of the Ontario Securities Commission (OSC), was said to state that provincial regulators were working on a legal framework that would re-establish the legal liabilities of auditors to investors. Although she is no longer the executive director of the OSC, the OSC continues to push for this legislation, which would need to be passed by the provincial legislature.

The current status of the duty of care issue in Canada is far from clear. *Hercules* is a binding case in Canada that clearly limits auditor liability; however, *Kripps* (Figure 4-4) goes the other way by expanding legal liability to potential investors.

AUDITOR DEFENCES AGAINST THIRD-PARTY SUITS

The defences available to auditors in suits by clients are also available in third-party lawsuits.

The previous section outlined the lack of duty of care defence. As the preceding discussion has suggested, the court, in *Ultramares*, limited the auditor's liability for negligence to parties being in privity with the auditor. *Hedley Byrne* introduced the

---

[15]Jeffrey, Gundi, "Ruling Clarifies in Duty of Care Suit," *The Bottom Line* (October 1991), pp. 1 and 2.

[16]Paskell-Mede, Mindy, "What Liability Crisis?" *CAmagazine* (May 1996), pp. 47–48.

[17]From Mathias, Philip, "Auditors Not Legally Liable to Investors, Top Court Rules," *The Financial Post* (May 24, 1997), p. 3; and Paskell-Mede, Mindy and Don Selman, "Point, Counterpoint," *CAmagazine* (September 1997), pp. 39–40.

notion of the auditor having a duty of care to foreseeable third parties; *Haig v. Bamford* narrowed the responsibility for duty of care by the auditor to the limited class whom the auditor actually knew would use and rely on the financial statements. The more recent cases in both the United Kingdom and Canada suggest that we now know that the limited class is to be defined in relation to the known purpose of the financial statements and that, therefore, each case should be decided on its own factual context.

The second defence in third-party suits, absence of misstatement, is also known as "no error" in the financial statements. Thus, a plaintiff's damages would be inappropriately calculated because the financial statements on which they relied would have been accurate.

Next is non-negligent performance. If the auditor conducted the audit in accordance with GAAS, there is a strong inference of no negligence. Recognize, however, that non-negligent performance is difficult to demonstrate to a court. Proving lack of negligence normally involves a debate between experts hired by both sides. The judge, who is a layperson with respect to accounting and auditing, then assesses the credibility of the experts from both sides in order to make an independent decision based upon legal, accounting, and auditing concepts.

Absence of causal connection in third-party suits has two variations. The first occurs when there is a material misstatement in the financial statements, the second when there is a defalcation at the client or plaintiff's place of business. When there is a misstatement in the financial statements, it usually means nonreliance on the financial statements by the user. For example, assume the auditor can demonstrate that a lender relied upon an ongoing banking relationship with a customer, rather than the financial statements, in making a loan. The fact that the auditor was negligent in the conduct of the audit would not be relevant in that situation. In the case of a defalcation, the auditors would not be liable for the entire loss caused by the culprit (e.g., if there had been a certain amount of defalcation that had already taken place before the auditors could have been expected to detect it). Normally, the auditor is only held liable for additional fraud committed after the first date on which the whistle could have been blown. Another good example of "no causal connection" arises in tax cases. Sometimes misfired tax planning results in the client paying additional taxes. The accountant would not be liable to reimburse the client for taxes paid, but only for the interest and penalties, since nothing could have been done legitimately to avoid payment of the taxes.

Finally, it is possible to find contributory negligence if it could be said the claimants were themselves negligent, say, by ignoring other relevant information. It would be more common, however, for the auditor to defend on one of the other bases outlined above.

CRIMINAL LIABILITY

OBJECTIVE 4-6

Specify what constitutes criminal liability for accountants, and describe an important legal case.

Fraud by anyone can be a criminal act and the perpetrator can be subject to criminal prosecution.[18] The criminal action would be brought by the Attorney-General; conviction of a professional accountant would likely result in a charge of criminal misconduct by the professional accountant's institute (or *ordre*) in the case of CAs, his or her association in the case of CGAs, or society in the case of CMAs. In addition, a civil action for damages could be brought by the person(s) suffering a loss from the fraudulent act.

Fraud may include an auditor's association with financial statements he or she knows are materially misstated or false. For example, if the auditor of a company gave an unqualified auditor's report on the company's financial statements knowing that inventory was grossly overvalued, it is possible the auditor would be found guilty of criminal fraud and could be sued in a civil action.

---

[18]Section 338 of the *Criminal Code of Canada*.

Suppose in this case that inventory was to be valued at the lower of cost or market but the auditor deliberately did not include drastic decreases in market value which occurred in the second month following the balance sheet date. Failure to reflect all the information in the auditor's possession in the financial statements would make them misleading *despite their being in accordance with GAAP*. This occurs when there are multiple alternatives under GAAP or where GAAP requires limited disclosure. The auditor could be judged guilty of fraud.

While there are almost no Canadian cases involving fraud, there have been several U.S. cases. Fraud, however, is interpreted more liberally in the U.S. There the term "fraud" is used more liberally in civil cases, where errors in financial statement disclosures occur, which benefit management or others. Although not great in absolute number, these U.S. fraud cases damage the integrity of the profession, both in Canada and the U.S., due to their high profile, and reduce the profession's ability to attract and retain outstanding people. On the positive side, these court actions encourage practitioners to use extreme care and exercise good faith in their activities.

The leading case of criminal action against CPAs is *United States v. Simon*, which occurred in 1969. That case is summarized in Figure 4-12. Simon has been followed by three additional major criminal cases. In *United States v. Natelli* (1975), two auditors were convicted of criminal liability for certifying the financial statements of National Student Marketing Corporation that contained inadequate disclosures pertaining to accounts receivable.

In *United States v. Weiner* (1975), three auditors were convicted of securities fraud in connection with their audit of Equity Funding Corporation of America. Equity Funding was a financial conglomerate whose financial statements had been overstated through a massive fraud by management. The fraud was so extensive and the audit work so poor that the court concluded the auditors must have been aware of the fraud and were therefore guilty of complicity. In Canada, these auditors would likely have been found guilty of negligence.

In *ESM Government Securities v. Alexander Grant & Co.* (1986), it was revealed by management to the partner in charge of the audit of ESM that the previous year's audited financial statements contained a material misstatement. Rather than complying with professional and firm standards in such circumstances, the partner agreed to say nothing in the hope that management would work its way out of the problem during the current year. Instead, the situation worsened, eventually to the point where losses exceeded $300 million. The partner was convicted of criminal charges for his role in sustaining the fraud and is now serving a 12-year prison term. In this case, the partner personally benefited from the fraud and would likely also have been found guilty of fraud in Canada.

Several practical lessons can be learned from these four cases:

- An investigation of the integrity of management is an important part of deciding on the acceptability of clients and the extent of work to perform.
- Financial independence in appearance and fact by all individuals on the engagement is essential, especially in a defence involving criminal actions.
- Transactions with related parties require special scrutiny because of the potential for misstatement.
- Generally accepted accounting principles cannot be relied upon exclusively in deciding whether financial statements are fairly presented. In *Kripps*, Figure 4-4, the auditors were found to have complied with GAAP but yet to have provided inadequate disclosure. There is disagreement about the extent to which this ruling affects the profession, but the auditor needs to ensure that the substance of the statements provides sufficient disclosure within the context of materiality.
- Good documentation may be just as important in the auditor's defence of criminal charges as in a civil suit.
- The potential consequences of the auditor knowingly committing a wrongful act are so severe that it is unlikely that the potential benefits could ever justify the actions.

FIGURE 4-12

United States v. Simon
(1969)

The case was a criminal one concerning three auditors prosecuted for filing false statements with a government agency and violation of the 1934 *Securities Exchange Act*. The CPA firm had already settled out of court for civil liability for over $2 million after the audit client, Continental Vending Corporation, filed for bankruptcy.

The main issue of the trial was the reporting of transactions between Continental and its affiliate, Valley Commercial Corporation. Before the audit was complete, the auditors had learned that Valley was not in a position to repay its debt, and it was accordingly arranged that collateral would be posted. The president of Continental Vending, Harold Roth, and members of his family transferred their equity in certain securities to Continental's counsel, as trustee to secure Roth's debt to Valley and Valley's debt to Continental. Note 2 included with the financial statements read as follows:

> The amount receivable from Valley Commercial Corp. (an affiliated company of which Mr. Harold Roth is an officer, director, and stockholder) bears interest at 12 percent a year. Such amount, less the balance of the notes payable to that company, is secured by the assignment to the Company of Valley's equity in certain marketable securities. As of February 15, 1963, the amount of such equity at current market quotations exceeded the net amount receivable.

The government contended that this note was inadequate and should have disclosed that the amount receivable from Valley was uncollectible at September 30, 1962, since Valley had loaned approximately the same amount to Roth, who was unable to pay. The note should also have stated that approximately 80 percent of the securities Roth had pledged was stock and convertible debentures of Continental Vending. The defendants called eight expert independent accountants as witnesses. They testified generally that, except for the error with respect to netting, the treatment of the Valley receivable in Note 2 was in no way inconsistent with generally accepted accounting principles or generally accepted auditing standards. Specifically, they testified that neither generally accepted accounting principles nor generally accepted auditing standards required disclosure of the makeup of the collateral or of the increase in the receivables after the closing date of the balance sheet, although three of the eight stated that in light of hindsight they would have preferred that the makeup of the collateral be disclosed. The witnesses also testified that the disclosure of the Roth borrowings from Valley was not required, and seven of the eight were of the opinion that such disclosure would be inappropriate.

The defendants asked for two instructions which, in substance, would have told the jury that a defendant could be found guilty only if, according to generally accepted accounting principles, the statements as a whole did not fairly present the financial condition of Continental at September 30, 1962, and then only if this departure from accepted standards was due to willful disregard of those standards with knowledge of the falsity of the statements and an intent to deceive.

The judge declined to give those instructions and instead said that the critical test was whether the *statements were fairly presented and, if not, whether the defendants had acted in good faith*. Proof of compliance with generally accepted standards was "evidence which may be very persuasive but not necessarily conclusive that he acted in good faith, and that the facts as certified were not materially false or misleading."

The appeals court upheld the earlier conviction of the three auditors with the comment that even without satisfactory showing of motive, "the government produced sufficient evidence of criminal intent. Its burden was not to show that the defendants were wicked men . . . but rather that they had certified a statement knowing it to be false."

The effect on the three men was significant. The total fine was $17,000, but far more important, they lost their CPA certificates and were forced to leave the profession. They were ultimately pardoned by President Nixon.

MONEY LAUNDERING

Part XII.2 of the *Criminal Code*, Bill C-61, is known informally as the "proceeds of crime" legislation. In *R. v. Loewen* (1996), an accountant was convicted of laundering $125,000 of money. The accountant stated that he had a "few companies" through which he could move money to an undercover police officer. He then transferred the money through various accounts, retaining a commission. If this accountant was a professionally designated accountant, actions by the accountant's professional organization would have followed, likely expelling the accountant from the organization.

This case clearly demonstrates the accountant undertaking a criminal act. However, the legislation also applies to individuals who accept property (including fees), should they know or be willfully blind to the fact that the property was obtained illegally. Such individuals could be charged with possession or laundering. This is an additional incentive for accountants to be cautious when they have any doubts regarding management integrity.

CONFLICT BETWEEN CONFIDENTIALITY AND ASSOCIATION WITH FALSE AND MISLEADING INFORMATION

OBJECTIVE 4-7

Discuss the auditor's responsibilities when confidentiality conflicts with other rules of professional conduct.

The issue here is whether a public accountant has greater responsibility for the rule of professional conduct regarding confidentiality or for the rule regarding association with false and misleading financial information.

Consider the following scenario which could easily occur in a public accounting firm. PA & Co., public accountants, are the auditor for both BG Construction Inc. (BG) and Carter Building Supplies Ltd. (CBS). BG, whose year end is January 31, 1998, owes a large amount of money to CBS, whose year end is February 28, 1998. Suppose an audit of BG is completed but the statements have not been issued. As BG's auditor, you are concerned about whether the company will be able to continue to operate or will become insolvent.

As auditor of BG, you are aware during your audit of CBS that a material asset of CBS (the receivable from BG) may be worthless. How do you ensure that CBS's February 28, 1998, financial statements are not misleading? There is a conflict between the confidentiality due BG and the association with CBS's financial statements (potentially false and misleading if the receivable from BG is not reserved) if you provide a clean opinion. If the auditor cannot persuade BG to disclose the problem to CBS either directly or through the issue of BG's financial statements, the auditor should probably resign from the CBS audit. The BG confidentiality issue is a common problem because a public accounting firm often has clients who conduct business with one another.

Two U.S. cases in the early 1980s addressed the question of public accounting firms' responsibility to inform users when they have information normally considered confidential under the public accounting profession's rules of conduct. They are *Consolidata Services, Inc.* and *Fund of Funds*. Both are included as illustrative cases in Figures 4-13 and 4-14, respectively. A recent Canadian case, *Transamerica Commercial*

FIGURE 4-13

Consolidata Services, Inc. v. Alexander Grant & Company (1981)

Consolidata Services Inc. was a payroll services company that prepared payroll cheques and disbursed payroll moneys to clients, employees, and taxing authorities. The CPA firm's relationship with Consolidata involved tax work rather than auditing or accounting services. In addition, the CPA firm recommended the payroll services to existing clients, and Consolidata, in return, recommended the CPA firm to its clients.

In a meeting between representatives of the CPA firm and Consolidata, it was determined that Consolidata was insolvent. After discussion with its legal counsel, the CPA firm requested that Consolidata notify its customers about the insolvency, but management refused to do so. The president then informed the CPA firm that he had resigned. The CPA firm informed management of its intent to inform its customers of Consolidata's insolvency. Consolidata requested the CPA firm to wait ten days to enable them to borrow money to correct their solvency problem.

The CPA firm partners decided to call all twelve of its clients that used Consolidata's payroll services to advise them not to send in any more money. No one informed Consolidata's other 24 customers.

The client sued for negligence and breach of contract for breaking an obligation of confidentiality. The court found in favour of Consolidata Services, Inc., in the amount of $1.3 million.

FIGURE 4-14

The Fund of Funds Limited v. Arthur Andersen & Co. (1982)

Fund of Funds was a mutual investment company specializing in buying other mutual funds. In the late 1970s, management decided to diversify by making large investments in oil and gas properties. Approximately $90 million was paid for more than 400 natural resource properties under an agreement with King Resources Company. An agreement was signed between Fund of Funds and King Resources that all properties were to be sold on an arm's-length basis at prices no less favourable to Fund of Funds than King Resources ordinarily received. An important fact in the case was that the CPA firm audited both Fund of Funds and King Resources and the same key audit personnel were involved in both audits under separate contracts. During the audit of King Resources, it came to the CPA firm's attention that profits on oil and gas property sales to Fund of Funds were actually much higher than comparable sales to other customers of King Resources. The CPA firm did not report that information to Fund of Funds' management and Fund of Funds' management did not determine the facts until considerably later. Fund of Funds' management contended that the CPA firm had a duty either to inform them of the violation of the agreement or resign from one of the audits. The CPA firm contended it had a responsibility under the rules of conduct of the *AICPA Code of Professional Ethics* to keep the information confidential.

The court awarded damages to Fund of Funds' shareholders in the amount of $80 million, the largest judgment ever made against a CPA firm at that time. The amount was reduced on appeal.

Finance Corporation, addressed this issue in the context of an auditor's responsibility to disclose normally confidential information to a major creditor, when the financial statements are not misstated. This case is outlined in Figure 4-15.

In the two U.S. cases, the information had or would have had a significant effect on the plaintiff client or other clients of the same CPA firm. In the *Consolidata Services* case, the CPA firm informed other clients of confidential information that was obtained during a conference with Consolidata Services. The CPA firm did so on the advice of legal counsel and contended it had a professional duty to inform other clients and help them avoid losses. In the *Fund of Funds* case, the CPA firm obtained confidential information during the course of another audit that would have been beneficial to Fund of Funds. On the advice of legal counsel, the CPA firm did not use the confidential information to help Fund of Funds avoid losses. In both cases, the CPA firm lost the court case to the client. These cases are apparently contradictory but, as in every case, the facts are not identical. This points to a dilemma facing public accounting firms in both Canada and the U.S. It is difficult to do the "right thing" even when there are good intentions. Cases such as these make public accounting firms critical of the legal system. These two cases also point out the need for the auditing profession to examine the rules of conduct for confidentiality and attempt to clarify the requirements consistent with common law.

The *Transamerica* case illustrates how accountants could be in possession of information that would be important for creditors in lending decisions. In this particular

FIGURE 4-15

Transamerica Commercial Finance Corporation, Canada v. Dunwoody & Company and F. S. Hirtle (1996)[19]

Dunwoody and Company was the auditor for the years ended January 31,1984 to 1987 for a Toyota car dealership called Robin Hood Holdings Ltd. The partner responsible for the engagement was F. S. Hirtle, named as a co-defendant. Transamerica financed the Toyota dealership by providing a credit line of $1.1 million, $500,000 of which was for used vehicle inventory and $200,000 for a capital loan.

Because of decreasing liquidity, Robin Hood Holdings Ltd. engaged in dubious financial practices. For the year ending January 31, 1986, the company used inter-company financial transfers to obtain unauthorized borrowing from the bank (known as "kiting"). The auditors detected this, advised the client in writing to discontinue this practice, and ensured that the financial statements accurately reflected cash balances. In January 1997, Transamerica conducted a surprise vehicle inventory and found several used vehicles missing. The vehicles had already been sold.

This resulted in a credit review, and a representative of Transamerica held a meeting with the auditors on March 1997 while the audit was in progress. During this meeting, Mr. Hirtle discussed financial reorganization issues with Transamerica but did not disclose the kiting (which continued) or the fact that, during the audit, two fictitious vehicles were discovered in inventory. The auditors again warned Robin Hood Holdings Ltd. to discontinue the kiting.

Transamerica concluded that credit should continue to be extended but that Robin Hood required careful monitoring (which Transamerica did not do). In January 1998, the auditors discovered 15 to 20 fictitious vehicles, and continuing financial irregularities. After consulting with legal counsel, Dunwoody advised that it would not be providing Robin Hood with an auditor's opinion.

Transamerica put Robin Hood into receivership, operated the dealership in an attempt to reduce its losses, and eventually sold it as a going concern. Transamerica calculated its losses at over $1 million and sued Dunwoody to recover these losses on the basis that Dunwoody should have disclosed the financial irregularities and the fictitious inventory in March 1997.

Both the Supreme Court of British Columbia in 1994 and the Court of Appeal for British Columbia dismissed the plaintiff's action, awarding the defendant some costs. The courts found that the defendant owed a professional duty of confidentiality to its client. They also found that the plaintiff did not rely on the defendants and that its losses arose solely from its own business and management decisions made during the course of its dealings with Robin Hood.

[19]Trial judgment, Supreme Court of British Columbia, No. C902491 (February 18, 1994), and trial judgment, Court of Appeal for British Columbia, CA018550 (April 18, 1996).

case, it supports the view that the auditor is justified in maintaining client information as confidential when the financial statements are not misleading.

Although there have not been cases like *Consolidata Services* and *Fund of Funds* in Canada, the cases are interesting because they illustrate a conflict Canadian public accountants may face.

THE PROFESSION'S RESPONSE TO LEGAL LIABILITY

OBJECTIVE 4-8
Describe what the profession and the individual public accountant can do to reduce the threat of litigation.

There are a number of things the CICA, the CGAAC, the SMAC, and the public accounting profession as a whole can do to reduce the practitioner's exposure to lawsuits. The instituting of practice inspection by the provincial institutes and *ordre* of members in public practice (discussed in Chapter 1) is one positive step in recognizing additional responsibility that the public demands of professionals. Some of the others are discussed briefly.

1. *Conduct research in auditing.* Continued research is important in finding better ways to do such things as uncover unintentional material misstatements or management and employee fraud, communicate audit results to statement users, and make sure that auditors are independent. Significant research already takes place through the CICA, the CGAAC, the SMAC, public accounting firms, and universities. For example, one public accounting firm has funded a series of auditing symposia at the University of Waterloo at which auditing research and issues are discussed by an audience of academics and practitioners.
2. *Set standards and rules.* The CICA must constantly set standards and revise them to meet the changing needs of auditing. New Assurance and Related Services Recommendations, Assurance and Related Services Guidelines, revisions of the rules of conduct of the various professional accounting bodies, and other pronouncements must be issued as society's needs change and as new technology arises from experience and research.
3. *Set requirements to protect auditors.* The CICA can help protect public accountants by setting certain requirements that better practitioners already follow. Naturally, these requirements should not be in conflict with meeting users' needs. An example of a practice that presently does not exist as a standard, but that many auditors follow, is procuring a written letter of representation from management in all audits.
4. *Establish practice inspection requirements.* The periodic examination of a firm's practices and procedures is a way to educate practitioners and identify firms not meeting the standards of the profession.
5. *Defend unjustified lawsuits.* It is important that public accounting firms continue to oppose unwarranted lawsuits even if, in the short run, the costs of winning are greater than the costs of settling.
6. *Educate users.* It is important to educate investors and others who read financial statements as to the meaning of the auditor's opinion and the extent and nature of the auditor's work. Users must be educated to understand that auditors do not test 100 percent of all records and do not guarantee the accuracy of the financial records or the future prosperity of the company. It is also important to educate users to understand that accounting and auditing are arts, not sciences, and that perfection and precision are unachievable. For example, the present auditor's report is much more informative to users than the previous report.
7. *Sanction members for improper conduct and performance.* One characteristic of a profession is its responsibility for policing its own membership. The three professional accounting bodies have disciplinary procedures that are designed to deal with the problems of inadequate performance by members, but more rigorous review of alleged failures is still needed.
8. *Lobby for changes in laws.* If the risk exposure of auditors to legal liability becomes too high, insurance will either be prohibitively expensive or unobtainable, and self-insurance is not an option. If the risk exposure does start to approach an

unacceptable level, governments should be lobbied at least to ensure viable insurance coverage exists. Lobbying can produce results such as the June 1998 law permitting limited liability partnerships (LLPs) in Ontario.

THE INDIVIDUAL PROFESSIONAL ACCOUNTANT'S RESPONSE TO LEGAL LIABILITY

Practising auditors may also take specific action to minimize their liability. Most of this book deals with that subject. A summary of several of these practices is included at this point.

1. *Deal only with clients possessing integrity.* There is an increased likelihood of having legal problems when a client lacks integrity in dealing with customers, employees, units of government, and others. A public accounting firm needs procedures to evaluate the integrity of clients and should dissociate itself from clients found lacking.

2. *Hire qualified personnel and train and supervise them properly.* A considerable portion of most audits is done by young professionals with relatively little experience. Given the high degree of risk public accounting firms have in doing audits, it is important that these young professionals be qualified and well trained. Supervision of their work by experienced and qualified professionals is also essential.

3. *Follow the standards of the profession.* A firm must implement procedures to make sure that all firm members understand and follow the Recommendations of the *CICA Handbook* and other authoritative sources of GAAP and GAAS, their profession's rules of conduct, and other professional guidelines.

4. *Maintain independence.* Independence is more than merely financial. Independence, in fact, requires an attitude of responsibility separate from the client's interest. Much litigation has arisen from a too willing acceptance by an auditor of a client's representation or of a client's pressures. The auditor must maintain an attitude of *healthy scepticism.*

5. *Understand the client's business.* The lack of knowledge of industry practices and client operations has been a major factor in auditors failing to uncover errors in several cases. It is important that the audit team be educated in these areas.

6. *Perform quality audits.* Quality audits require that appropriate evidence be obtained and appropriate judgments be made about the evidence. It is essential, for example, that the auditor evaluate a client's internal controls and modify the quantity and quality of evidence obtained to reflect the findings. Improved auditing reduces the likelihood of misstatements and the likelihood of lawsuits.

7. *Document the work properly.* The preparation of good working papers helps in organizing and performing quality audits. Quality working papers are essential if an auditor has to defend an audit in court.

8. *Obtain an engagement letter and a representation letter.* These two letters are essential in defining the respective obligations of client and auditor. They are helpful especially in lawsuits between the client and auditor, but also in third-party lawsuits.

9. *Maintain confidential relations.* Auditors are under an ethical and sometimes legal obligation not to disclose client matters to outsiders.

10. *Carry adequate insurance.* It is essential for a public accounting firm to have adequate insurance protection in the event of a lawsuit. Although insurance rates have risen considerably in the past few years as a result of increasing litigation, professional liability insurance is still available for all public accountants.

11. *Seek legal counsel.* Whenever serious problems occur during an audit, a public accountant would be wise to consult experienced counsel. In the event of a potential or actual lawsuit, the auditor should immediately seek an experienced lawyer.

CONCLUSION

The auditing profession has been under a great deal of attack in recent years not only in court but also by politicians and the media. Demands for increased regulation and increased legal liability are heard frequently. The profession is struggling to respond constructively to these pressures.

The determination of the extent to which auditors should be legally responsible for the reliability of financial statements is relevant to both the profession and society. Clearly, the existence of legal responsibility is an important deterrent to the inadequate and even dishonest activities of some auditors.

No reasonable public accountant would want the profession's legal responsibility for fraudulent or incompetent performance eliminated. It is certainly in the profession's self-interest to maintain public trust in the competent performance of the auditing function.

However, it is unreasonable for auditors to be held legally responsible for every misstatement in financial statements. The auditor cannot serve as the insurer or guarantor of financial statement accuracy or business health. The audit costs to society that would be required to achieve such high levels of assurance would exceed the benefits. Moreover, even with increased audit costs, well-planned frauds would not necessarily be discovered, nor errors of judgment eliminated.

It is necessary for the profession and society to determine a reasonable trade-off between the degree of responsibility the auditor should take for fair presentation and the audit cost to society. Public accountants, the various provincial securities commissions, and the courts will all have a major influence in shaping the final solution.

LESSONS LEARNED FROM AUDITOR LITIGATION

In considering the advisability of the laws being considered in reform of accountants' liability, it is useful to consider actual experiences with past accountants' litigation. Accordingly, a review was conducted of 23 cases of alleged audit failure with which I have been involved as a litigation consultant and expert witness. Of these 23 cases, six were clearly without merit and should not have been brought on equitable grounds. Of the 17 that were with merit, 13 did, in fact, represent a real audit failure. In considering the nature of the failure in each case, it was observed that the evidence that would lead the auditor to identify the error or irregularity that existed was usually there. In other words, the problem was not any inadequacy in the audit process as presented by professional standards; it was a *lack of professional scepticism* on the part of the auditor. The auditor had evidence in his or her possession that indicated the problem, but did not see it as such.

Source: Presentation by James K. Loebbecke at the Forum on Responsibilities and Liabilities of Accountants and Auditors, United Nations Conference on Trade and Development, March 16, 1995.

APPENDIX A   SECURITIES LEGISLATION

In Chapter 1 it was pointed out that a number of Canadian companies were listed on American stock exchanges or sold securities in the United States or both, and that these companies were therefore subject to the requirements of the *Securities Act of 1933* and the *Securities Exchange Act of 1934*. The following discussion pertains to the civil liability of accountants under a typical Canadian Securities Act, the *Ontario Securities Act*, and relevant U.S. acts.

ONTARIO SECURITIES ACT

Part XXIII, Civil Liability, deals with liability for misrepresentation in a prospectus. It applies not only to auditors, but issuers, those selling securities, underwriters, and directors. Auditors are not referred to directly but are described in Section 130(1) as those "whose consent has been filed pursuant to a requirement of the regulations but only with respect to reports, opinions or statements that have been made by them." The section states that the purchaser who purchases the security based on the prospectus is deemed to be relying on representations with respect to that prospectus. Thus, the issue of privity would be automatically dealt with in the event that the purchaser sued the auditor or others.

Section 130(8) goes on to state that all persons or companies specified in the first section are jointly and severally liable, but that the amount recoverable (specified in the next paragraph of the Act) would not exceed the price at which the securities were offered to the public.

Section 131 specifies the same deemed reliance, liability, and amount recoverable in the context of a take-over bid circular.

U.S. LAWS

Securities Act of 1933 This act deals with the information in registration statements and prospectuses. It concerns only the reporting requirements for companies issuing new securities. The only parties that can recover from auditors under the 1933 act are original purchasers of securities. The amount of the potential recovery is the original purchase price less the value of the securities at the time of the suit. If the securities have been sold, users can recover the amount of the loss incurred.

The Securities Act of 1933 imposes an unusual burden on the auditor. Section 11 of the 1933 act defines the rights of third parties and auditors. These are summarized as follows:

- Any third party who purchased securities described in the registration statement may sue the auditor for material misrepresentations or omissions in audited financial statements included in the registration statement.
- The third-party user does not have the burden of proof that he or she relied on the financial statements or that the auditor was negligent or fraudulent in doing the audit. The user must prove only that the audited financial statements contained a material misrepresentation or omission.
- The auditor has the burden of demonstrating as a defence that (1) an adequate audit was conducted in the circumstances or (2) all or a portion of the plaintiff's loss was caused by factors other than the misleading financial statements. The 1933 act is the only common or statutory law where the burden of proof is on the defendant.
- The auditor has responsibility for making sure the financial statements were fairly stated beyond the date of issuance, up to the date the registration statement became effective, which could be several months later. For example, assume the audit report date for December 31, 1998, financial statements is February 10, 1999, but the registration statement is dated November 1, 1999. In a typical audit, the auditor must review transactions through the audit report date, February 10, 1999. In statements filed under the 1933 act, the auditor is responsible to review transactions through the registration statement date, November 1, 1999.

Although the burden may appear harsh to auditors, there have been few cases tried under the 1933 act.

Securities Exchange Act of 1934 The liability of auditors under the *Securities Exchange Act of 1934* frequently centres on the audited financial statements issued to the public in annual reports or submitted to the SEC as a part of annual 10-K reports.

Every company with securities traded on national and over-the-counter exchanges is required to submit audited statements annually. There are obviously a much larger number of statements falling under the 1934 act than under the 1933 act.

In addition to annual audited financial statements, there is potential legal exposure to auditors for quarterly (10-Q), monthly (8-K), or other reporting information. The auditor is frequently involved in reviewing the information in these other reports; therefore, there may be legal responsibility. However, few cases have involved auditors for reports other than auditor's reports.

SEC Sanctions   Closely related to auditor's liability is the Security and Exchange Commisssion's (SEC's) authority to sanction. The SEC has the power in certain circumstances to sanction or suspend practitioners from doing audits for SEC companies. Rule 2(e) of the SEC's *Rules of Practice* says:

> The commission may deny, temporarily or permanently, the privilege of appearing or practising before it in any way to any person who is found by the commission . . . (1) not to possess the requisite qualifications to represent others, or (2) to be lacking in character or integrity or to have engaged in unethical or improper professional conduct.

The SEC has temporarily suspended a number of individual CPAs from doing any audits of SEC clients in recent years. It has similarly prohibited a number of CPA firms from accepting any new SEC clients for a period, such as six months. At times, the SEC has required an extensive review of a major CPA firm's practices by another CPA firm. In some cases, individual CPAs and their firms have been required to participate in continuing education programs and to make changes in their practice. Sanctions such as these are published by the SEC and are often reported in the business press, making them a significant embarrassment to those involved.

Foreign Corrupt Practices Act of 1977   Another significant congressional action affecting both CPA firms and their clients was the passage of the *Foreign Corrupt Practices Act of 1977*. The act makes it illegal to offer a bribe to an official of a foreign country for the purpose of exerting influence and obtaining or retaining business. The prohibition against payments to foreign officials is applicable to all U.S. domestic firms, regardless of whether they are publicly or privately held, and to foreign companies filing with the SEC.

Apart from the bribery provisions that affect all companies, the law also requires SEC registrants under the *Securities Exchange Act of 1934* to meet additional requirements. These include the maintenance of reasonably complete and accurate records and an adequate system of internal control. The law significantly affects all SEC companies, but the unanswered question to the profession at this time is, How does it affect auditors?

The act may affect auditors through their responsibility to review and evaluate systems of internal control as a part of doing the audit. Most auditors believe that they are not currently required to do a review of internal control thorough enough to judge whether their clients meet the requirements of the *Foreign Corrupt Practices Act*. To date, there have been no legal cases affecting auditors' legal responsibilities under the *Foreign Corrupt Practices Act*. However, there is considerable disagreement about auditors' responsibilities under the law. There is likely to be ongoing discussion and litigation to resolve the issue.

Absence of causal connection — a legal defence under which the professional contends that the damages claimed by the client were not brought about by any act of the professional (p. 103).

Absence of negligence — a legal defence under which the professional claims that the disputed service was properly performed; an auditor would claim that the audit was performed according to generally accepted auditing standards (p. 100).

Audit failure — a situation in which the auditor issues an erroneous audit opinion as the result of an underlying failure to comply with the requirements of generally accepted auditing standards (p. 94).

Audit risk — the risk that the auditor will conclude that the financial statements are fairly stated and an unqualified opinion can therefore be issued when in fact they are materially misstated (p. 94).

Business failure — the situation when a business is unable to repay its lenders, or meet the expectations of its investors because of economic or business conditions (p. 94).

Common law — laws developed through court decisions rather than through government statutes; also called *judge-made law* or *case law* (p. 97).

Constructive fraud — conduct that the law construes as fraud even though there was no actual intent to deceive; considered to be so reckless that the courts decide it is tantamount to fraud (p. 96).

Contributory negligence — a legal defence under which the professional claims that the client failed to perform certain obligations and that it is the client's failure to perform those obligations that brought about the claimed damages (p. 97).

Criminal liability for auditors — the possibility of being found guilty under criminal law; defrauding a person through knowing involvement with false financial statements (p. 108).

Defalcation — theft of assets (p. 97).

Expectations gap — the conflict between what some users expect from an auditor's report and what the auditor's report is designed to deliver; some users believe that an auditor's report is a guarantee as to the accuracy of the financial statements, although the report is in fact an opinion based on an audit conducted according to generally accepted auditing standards (p. 94).

Fiduciary duty — a party (such as an accountant) has an obligation to act for the benefit of another, and that obligation includes discretionary power (p. 93).

Fraud — a false assertion that has been made knowingly, without belief in its truth, or recklessly without caring whether it's true or not (p. 96).

Lack of duty to perform — a legal defence under which the professional claims that no contract existed with the plaintiff; therefore no duty existed to perform the disputed service (p. 99).

Legal liability — the professional's obligation under the law to provide a reasonable level of care while performing work for those he or she serves (p. 92).

Limited liability partnership (LLP) — an organizational structure whereby only the person who does the work, those who supervise that person, and the firm itself are liable, but not other individual partners within the firm (p. 95).

Negligence — failure to exercise reasonable care in the performance of one's obligations to another (p. 96).

Prudent person concept — the legal concept that a person has a duty to exercise reasonable care and diligence in the performance of his or her obligations to another (p. 95).

Tort action for negligence — a legal action taken by an injured party against the party whose negligence resulted in the injury (p. 96).

4-1   The legal environment in which a public accountant in Canada operates is changing. Discuss some of the reasons for the changes.

4-2   What effect do you think litigation against a public accountant has on other public accountants and on society as a whole?

4-3   Distinguish between business risk and audit risk. Why is business risk a concern to auditors?

4-4   How does the *prudent person concept* affect the liability of the auditor?

4-5   A partner in a public accounting firm may be held liable for errors in the work of others. Identify at least two groups of such others and explain why the partner might be liable.

4-6   Differentiate between a "criminal action" and a "civil action."

4-7   A common type of lawsuit against public accountants is for the failure to detect a defalcation. State the auditor's responsibility for such discovery. Give authoritative support for your answer.

4-8   What is meant by "contributory negligence"? Under what conditions will this likely be a successful defence?

4-9   What are the purposes of an engagement letter and a letter of representation?

4-10   Discuss auditor's liability to third-party users in common law, describing how it has changed over time.

4-11   Is the auditor's liability affected if the third party was unknown rather than known? Explain.

4-12   The *Caparo* case decision in England was enthusiastically received by auditors in Canada. What effect did it have on Canadian common law? Will *Caparo* solve the auditor–third party liability problem? Explain.

4-13   Distinguish between the auditor's potential liability to the client, liability to third parties under common law, and criminal liability. Describe one situation for each type of liability in which the auditor could be held legally responsible.

4-14   In what ways can the profession positively respond and reduce liability in auditing?

4-15   In what ways can an individual public accountant positively respond and reduce liability in auditing?

MULTIPLE CHOICE QUESTIONS

4-16 The following questions concern public accounting firms' liability under common law. Choose the best response.

a. Natasha Sharp, a public accountant, was engaged by Peters & Sons, a partnership, to give an opinion on the financial statements that were to be submitted to several prospective partners as part of a planned expansion of the firm. Sharp's fee was fixed on a *per diem* basis. After a period of intensive work, Sharp completed about half of the necessary field work. Then, due to unanticipated demands upon her time by other clients, Sharp was forced to abandon the work. The planned expansion of the firm failed to materialize because the prospective partners lost interest when the auditor's report was not promptly available. Sharp offered to complete the task at a later date. This offer was refused. Peters & Sons suffered damages of $4,000 as a result. Under the circumstances, what is the probable outcome of a lawsuit between Sharp and Peters & Sons?
   (1) Peters & Sons will recover damages for breach of contract.
   (2) Sharp will recover damages for breach of contract.
   (3) Sharp will be compensated for the reasonable value of the services actually performed.
   (4) Neither Sharp nor Peters & Sons will recover against the other.

b. Magnus Enterprises Inc. engaged a public accounting firm to perform the annual examination of its financial statements. Which of the following is a correct statement with respect to the public accounting firm's liability to Magnus for negligence?
   (1) Such liability cannot be varied by agreement of the parties.
   (2) The public accounting firm will not be liable if it can show that it exercised the ordinary care and skill of a reasonable person in the conduct of its own affairs.
   (3) The public accounting firm must not only exercise reasonable care in what it does, but also must possess at least that degree of accounting knowledge and skill expected of a public accountant.

(4) The public accounting firm will be liable for any fraudulent scheme it does not detect.

c. Wilhelm Corporation orally engaged Humm & Dawson to audit its year-end financial statements. The engagement was to be completed within two months after the close of Wilhelm's fiscal year for a fixed fee of $22,500. Under these circumstances, what obligation is assumed by Humm & Dawson?
   (1) None, because the contract is unenforceable since it is not in writing.
   (2) An implied obligation to take extraordinary steps to discover all defalcations.
   (3) The obligation of an insurer of its work, which is liability without fault.
   (4) An implied promise to exercise reasonable standards of competence and care.

4-17 The following questions deal with important concepts with respect to auditor's legal liability. Choose the best response.

a. The most significant aspect of the *Haig v. Bamford* case was that it
   (1) defined the auditor's responsibilities in tort law to third parties.
   (2) extended the auditor's responsibility for events after the end of the audit period.
   (3) defined foreseeable third parties.
   (4) created a more general awareness of the auditor's responsibility for discovering misstatements.

b. If a public accounting firm is being sued for civil fraud by a third party based upon materially false financial statements, which of the following is the best defence the accountants could assert?
   (1) Lack of privity.
   (2) Lack of reliance.
   (3) Contributory negligence on the part of the client.
   (4) A disclaimer contained in the engagement letter.

(AICPA adapted)

DISCUSSION QUESTIONS AND PROBLEMS

4-18 Helmut & Co., a public accounting firm, was the new auditor of Mountain Ltd., a private company in the farm equipment and supply business. The previous auditor, Lopez and Williams, had been Mountain's auditor for the previous 10 years, ending with the December 31, 1997, statements.

In early February, 1999, Helmut & Co. began the audit for the year ended December 31, 1998. The audit was to be run by Frost, a senior who had just joined Helmut from another firm. Frost was to be assisted by two juniors.

Sara Mountain, the president of Mountain Ltd., approached Frost and said that the Bank of Trail was prepared to increase their loan to Mountain upon receipt of the

1998 financial statements so there was some urgency in finishing the audit.

The juniors were assigned the accounts receivable and inventory sections, both of which were significant in relation to total assets, while Frost concentrated on the income statement and the remaining balance sheet accounts. The audit was finished quickly, and after a cursory review of the file and statements by Martin Helmut, senior partner of Helmut & Co., the signed auditor's report was appended to the financial statements, which were delivered to Mountain, who in turn sent them to the bank.

The bank increased the bank loan significantly based principally on the very successful year the company had enjoyed, despite the fact that the farm supply business was depressed. Several months later, Mountain Ltd. made an assignment in bankruptcy. The trustee found that many accounts receivable were still outstanding from the balance sheet date and that inventory on hand included substantial quantities of obsolete and damaged goods that had been included in the year-end inventory at cost. In addition, the year-end inventory amount included inventory that had been sold prior to the year end.

Bank of Trail sued Helmut & Co. for negligence. Helmut's lawyers argued they were not in privity and had not been negligent in any event.

Required

Discuss Helmut & Co.'s defence. Is lack of privity a defence in this case? Was Helmut & Co. negligent? Explain your answer fully.

4-19 Brown Cosden & Co., a medium-sized public accounting firm, was engaged to audit Joslin Supply Inc. Several staff were involved in the audit, all of whom had attended the firm's in-house training program in effective auditing methods. Throughout the audit, Verna Cosden spent most of her time in the field, planning the audit, supervising the staff, and reviewing their work.

A significant part of the audit entailed verifying the physical count, cost, and summarization of inventory. Inventory was highly significant to the financial statements and Cosden knew that the inventory was pledged as collateral for a large loan to Maritimes Eastern Bank. In reviewing Joslin's inventory count procedures, Cosden told the president that she believed the method of counting inventory at different locations on different days was highly undesirable. The president stated that it was impractical to count all inventory on the same day because of personnel shortages and customer preference. After considerable discussion, Cosden agreed to permit the practice if the president would sign a statement that no other method was practical. The public accounting firm had at least one person at each site to audit the inventory count procedures and actual count. There were more than 40 locations.

Eighteen months later Cosden found out that the worst had happened. Management below the president's level had conspired to materially overstate inventory as a means of covering up obsolete inventory and inventory losses due to mismanagement. The misstatement had occurred by physically transporting inventory at night to other locations after it had been counted in a given location. The accounting records were inadequate to uncover these illegal transfers.

Both Joslin Supply Inc. and Maritimes Eastern Bank sued Brown Cosden & Co.

Required

Answer the following questions, setting forth reasons for any conclusions stated.

a. What defence should Brown Cosden & Co. use in the suit by Joslin?

b. What defence should Brown Cosden & Co. use in the suit by Maritimes Eastern Bank?

c. Is Brown Cosden & Co. likely to be successful in its defences?

d. Would the issues or outcome be significantly different if Joslin Supply Inc. was a public company?

4-20 The public accounting firm of André, Mathieu & Paquette (AMP) was expanding very rapidly. Consequently, it hired several junior accountants, including Jim Small. The partners of the firm eventually became dissatisfied with Small's production and warned him that they would be forced to discharge him unless his output increased significantly.

At that time, Small was engaged in audits of several clients. He decided that to avoid being fired, he would reduce or omit entirely some of the standard auditing procedures listed in audit programs prepared by the partners. One of the public accounting firm's clients, Newell Corporation, was in serious financial difficulty and had adjusted several of the accounts being examined by Small to appear financially sound. Small prepared fictitious working papers in his home at night to support purported completion of auditing procedures assigned to him, although he in fact did not examine the adjusting entries. The public accounting firm rendered an unqualified opinion on Newell's financial statements, which were grossly misstated. Several creditors, relying on the audited financial statements, subsequently extended large sums of money to Newell Corporation.

Required

Would the public accounting firm be liable to the creditors who extended the money because of their reliance on the erroneous financial statements if Newell Corporation should fail to pay them? Explain.

(AICPA adapted)

4-21 Chang and Williams, a firm of public accountants, audited the accounts of Sampson Jewellery, Inc., a corporation that imports and deals in fine jewellery. Upon completion of the examination, the auditors supplied Sampson Jewellery with 20 copies of the audited financial statements. The firm knew in a general way that Sampson Jewellery wanted that number of copies of the auditor's report to furnish to banks and other potential lenders.

The balance sheet was in error by approximately $800,000. Instead of having a $600,000 net worth, the corporation was insolvent. The management of Sampson Jewellery had doctored the books to avoid bankruptcy. The assets had been overstated by $500,000 of fictitious and nonexisting accounts receivable and $300,000 of nonexisting jewellery listed as inventory, when in fact Sampson Jewellery had only empty boxes. The audit failed to detect these fraudulent entries. Martinson, relying on the audited financial statements, loaned Sampson Jewellery $200,000. He seeks to recover his loss from Chang and Williams.

Required

State whether each of the following is true or false and give your reasons.

a. If Martinson alleges and proves negligence on the part of Chang and Williams, he will be able to recover his loss.

b. If Martinson alleges and proves fraud on the part of Chang and Williams, he will be able to recover his loss.

c. Martinson does not have a contract with Chang and Williams.

d. Martinson is a third-party beneficiary of the contract Chang and Williams made with Sampson Jewellery, Inc.

(AICPA adapted)

4-22   Jan Sharpe recently joined the public accounting firm of Spark, Watts, and Wilcox. She quickly established a reputation for thoroughness and a steadfast dedication to following prescribed auditing procedures to the letter. On her third audit for the firm, Sharpe examined the underlying documentation of 200 disbursements as a test of purchasing, receiving, vouchers payable, and cash disbursement procedures. In the process, she found 12 disbursements for the purchase of materials with no receiving reports in the documentation. She noted the exceptions in her working papers and called them to the attention of the in-charge accountant. Relying on prior experience with the client, the in-charge accountant disregarded Sharpe's comments, and nothing further was done about the exceptions.

Subsequently, it was learned that one of the client's purchasing agents and a member of its accounting department were engaged in a fraudulent scheme whereby they diverted the receipt of materials to a public warehouse while sending the invoices to the client. When the client discovered the fraud, the conspirators had obtained approximately $70,000, $50,000 of which was recovered after the completion of the audit.

Required

Discuss the legal implications and liabilities to Spark, Watts, and Wilcox as a result of the facts just described.

(AICPA adapted)

4-23   In confirming accounts receivable on December 31, 1998, the auditor found 15 discrepancies between the customer's records and the recorded amounts in the subsidiary ledger. A copy of all confirmations that had exceptions was turned over to the company controller to investigate the reason for the difference. He, in turn, had the bookkeeper perform the analysis. The bookkeeper analyzed each exception, determined its cause, and prepared an elaborate working paper explaining each difference. Most of the differences in the bookkeeper's report indicated that the errors were caused by timing differences in the client's and customer's records. The auditor reviewed the working paper and concluded that there were no material exceptions in accounts receivable.

Two years subsequent to the audit, it was determined that the bookkeeper had stolen thousands of dollars in the previous three years by taking cash and overstating accounts receivable. In a lawsuit by the client against the public accountant, an examination of the auditor's December 31, 1998, accounts receivable working papers, which were subpoenaed by the court, indicated that one of the explanations in the bookkeeper's analysis of the exceptions was fictitious. The analysis stated the error was caused by a sales allowance granted to the customer for defective merchandise the day before the end of the year. The difference was actually caused by the bookkeeper's theft.

Required

a. What are the legal issues involved in this situation? What should the auditor use as a defence in the event that she is sued?

b. What was the public accountant's deficiency in conducting the audit of accounts receivable?

4-24   Ann Abbass, a public accountant, is the auditor for Juniper Manufacturing Corporation, a privately owned company that has a June 30 fiscal year end. Juniper arranged for a substantial bank loan that was dependent on the bank receiving, by September 30, audited financial statements which showed a current ratio of at least 2:1. On September 25, just before the audit report was to be issued, Abbass received an anonymous letter on Juniper's stationery indicating that a five-year lease by Juniper, as lessee, of a factory building accounted for in the financial statements as an operating lease was, in fact, a capital lease. The letter stated that there was a secret written agreement with the lessor modifying the lease and creating a capital lease.

Abbass confronted the president of Juniper, who admitted that a secret agreement existed but said it was necessary to treat the lease as an operating lease to meet the current ratio requirement of the pending loan and that nobody would ever discover the secret agreement with the lessor. The president said that if Abbass did not issue her report by September 30, Juniper would sue Abbass for substantial damages that would result from not getting the loan. Under this pressure and because the working papers contained a copy of the five-year lease agreement that supported the operating lease treatment, Abbass issued her report with an unqualified opinion on September 29.

In spite of the fact that the loan was received, Juniper went bankrupt within two years. The bank is suing Abbass to recover its losses on the loan, and the lessor is suing Abbass to recover uncollected rents.

Required

Answer the following questions, setting forth reasons for any conclusion stated.

a. Is Abbass liable to the bank?

b. Is Abbass liable to the lessor?

c. Is there potential for criminal action against Abbass?

(AICPA adapted)

4-25   Baerg & Vetzel, a public accounting firm, were the auditors of South-Western Development, Inc., a real estate company that owned several shopping centres in southwestern Ontario. It was South-Western's practice to let each shopping centre manager negotiate that centre's leases; they felt that such an arrangement resulted in much better leases because a local person did the negotiating.

Two of the centre managers were killed in a plane accident returning home from a company meeting at the head office in Windsor. In both cases, the new managers appointed to take their places discovered kickback schemes in operation; the manager had negotiated lower rents than normal in return for kickbacks from the tenants.

South-Western brought in a new public accounting firm, Jasper & Co., to investigate the extent of the fraud at those two locations and the possibility of similar frauds at other centres. Jasper & Co. completed their investigation and found that four locations were involved quite independently of one another and that the total loss over five years was over $1,000,000.

South-Western sued Baerg & Vetzel for negligence for $1,000,000 plus interest.

Required

What defence would Baerg & Vetzel use? What would they have to prove?

4-26   In 1998, the Board of Directors of Lively Plays Inc., fired George Drewerson, the co- founder and another senior management representative of the company, claiming that they had engaged in fraudulent financial activities and had defrauded the company of $4 million. Payley and Karson, Chartered Accountants, have been the auditors of Lively Plays Inc. for many years, and have also been the personal tax advisers of Mr. Drewerson during that time.

Lively Plays Inc. engaged personnel from another office of Payley and Karson to conduct a forensic audit (a special investigation of the fraud). Mr. Drewerson obtained a court injunction delaying the release of the report on the grounds that Payley and Karson owed him a fiduciary duty. Thus, Mr. Drewerson should have had the right to review the special report before it was released to determine whether any confidential information should be released.

Required

a. Describe the role of Payley and Karson, and discuss the apparent conflict of interest in this situation.

b. If Mr. Drewerson were found to be guilty of fraud, and had declared the income from the fraud on his income tax return, what would be the potential liability of Payley and Karson?

4-27   Marino Rossi, a public accountant, audited the financial statements of Newfoundland Rugs Ltd. Cooke, the president of Newfoundland Rugs, told Rossi that the company was planning a private placement of company bonds to raise $500,000 of needed capital. The audit proceeded smoothly, and the audited financial statements were issued.

Unbeknownst to Rossi, several significant receivables represented consignment accounts and not receivables, but Cooke had persuaded the companies involved to sign the receivable confirmations Rossi had sent out, indicating they agreed that they owed the balances reported at the balance sheet date. In addition, a large number of rolls of low quality interior carpeting had been classed as first quality. The effect of these two fraudulent acts resulted in a profit of $150,000 (instead of a loss of $480,000) and a positive net worth

(instead of a negative net worth).

Newfoundland Rugs borrowed the money on the private placement and then went bankrupt several months later.

Required

a. Could the lenders on the private placement succeed in a suit against Rossi? If so, what must they prove?

b. What defence would Rossi use?

4-28   Sarah Robertson, a public accountant, was the auditor of Majestic Ltd. and had been for several years. As she and her staff prepared for the audit for the year ended December 31, 1998, Herb Majestic told her that he needed a large bank loan to "tide him over" until sales picked up as expected in late 1999.

In the course of the audit, Robertson discovered that the financial situation at Majestic was worse than Majestic had revealed and that the company was technically bankrupt. She discussed the situation with Herb Majestic, who pointed out that the bank loan would "be his solution" — he was sure he would get it as long as the financial statements didn't look too bad.

Robertson stated that she believed the statements would have to include a going concern note. Majestic said that such a note really wasn't needed because the bank loan was so certain and that inclusion of such a note would certainly cause the management of the bank to change its mind about the loan.

Robertson finally acquiesced, and the audited statements were issued without the note. The company received the loan but things didn't improve as Majestic thought they would, and the company filed for bankruptcy in August 1999.

The bank sued Sarah Robertson for fraud.

Required

Indicate whether or not you think the bank would succeed in its lawsuit. Support your answer.

4-29   A fundamental purpose of the external audit is to allow users to place reliance on the financial statements to which the auditor's report is attached. As a result, the auditor may be responsible to a variety of users of financial statements.

Required

Discuss the external auditor's potential liability to third parties for negligence and the effect this potential liability has on the conduct of the audit.

(CICA adapted)

4-30   A partner in your public accounting firm has asked you to explain to a group of juniors the importance of engagement letters and the importance of following up unusual or unexplained items discovered during the audit or review.

Required

Provide the explanation your partner has requested using material from the chapter.

4-31   In late 1998 and early 1999, Your Best Magnets Inc. (YBM) offices in New York and Toronto were raided by the U.S. Organized Strike Force and the Royal Canadian Mounted Police. Records were seized, and the public company and its officers were charged with money laundering. The company has since been delisted and investigations continue. One newspaper article showed the flow of a single YBM transaction of $2.3 million being split into different amounts, moving between 10 different banks and as many different companies. Connections were shown with Russian organized crime.

The auditors of YBM, Delskiny and Lather, CPAs, were subpoenaed to appear before a grand jury in the United States. Assume that the auditors conducted their audit in accordance with GAAS.

Required

a. What are the auditor's normal responsibilities during an audit engagement with respect to assessing management integrity?

b. How does the assessment of management integrity tie in to the nature of evidence to be collected during the audit?

c. Assume that one of the directors of YBM was a member of Russian organized crime, known to local and international police forces but not publicly known. What is the auditor's normal responsibility regarding detection of criminal affiliations of directors?

d. How does crime affiliation by directors or other management affect the fair presentation of financial statements?

e. The company's financial statements in 1996 showed $13.6 million worth of North American magnet sales — a figure that exceeded total magnet imports to the continent that year. YBM officials created fictitious sales lists and destroyed banking records. Auditors identified questionable transactions, demanded explanations from management, and received supporting evidence. A clean auditor's report was issued in 1996. Discuss the potential legal liability of the auditors should it be discovered that several sales on the sales lists were for fictitious companies.

4-32   Western Leasing Incorporated (WLI) was a leasing company headquartered in Burnaby, B.C., that leased equipment to construction companies, restaurants, gas stations, and medical and dental practices. WLI grew rapidly during the 1980s and by the mid-1990s had a portfolio of over $100 million of gross lease receivables. WLI obtained its financing from its primary banker, Western Bank. The line of credit obtained by Western was secured by WLI's lease receivables. In order to maintain its credit line, WLI was required to maintain positive earnings and a positive net worth, and to provide Western with annual audited financial statements. WLI engaged the accounting firm of Lau Lewis & Co. as its auditors. Through the year ended December 31, 1997, Lau Lewis & Co. had audited WLI for 10 consecutive years. Each audit had resulted in an unqualified opinion.

In June of 1998, WLI's president, Wally Vernon, became seriously ill and was forced to take sudden retirement. The Maxwell family, who owned all of the stock of WLI but were not actively involved in management other than holding two seats on the board, hired a consultant to consider Vernon's replacement. The consultant advised the Maxwells that an outsider should be brought in as the new CEO and that he perceived that there were serious problems at WLI.

As its next step, the Maxwells hired Carol Riddell as WLI's new CEO. Riddell promptly informed the Maxwells that she believed there were a number of serious problems at WLI, including the quality of the lease portfolio. She requested that Lau Lewis & Co. be brought in to do a June 30 special audit. This was done and, to Lau Lewis and the Maxwells' unpleasant surprise, it was discovered that WLI's lease receivable loss reserves were understated by approximately $16 million. This amount resulted in a violation of the company's lending agreement. This default eventually resulted in WLI's filing for bankruptcy, with eventual losses to the Maxwells in excess of $10 million. The Maxwells sued Lau Lewis & Co. for breach of contract, claiming that it failed to properly conduct its audits of WLI, for at least the period 1990 through 1997, the period during which, the Maxwells and Riddell concluded, Vernon and other management personnel made misrepresentations to Lau Lewis & Co. about the condition of many leases, misrepresentations that Lau Lewis failed to find.

During the discovery portion of the litigation, the Maxwells' attorney deposed Harold Raines, the Lau Lewis manager on the WLI audit. The following questions and answers are excerpted from that deposition.

Q. How long were you associated with the WLI audit, Mr. Raines?

A. Ever since we did it. I started as staff auditor on the job and worked my way up to manager.

Q. Have you ever been to a training program on auditing leasing companies?

A. No, sir. WLI was so small, I guess the partners in our firm didn't think it was necessary. Besides, when you get right down to it, all audits are about the same. I don't think there is anything special about a leasing company audit.

Q. Have you ever read an industry audit guide for commercial finance companies?

A. I may have; I don't recall.

Q.   What were the higher risk areas in the audit?

A. I'm not sure I looked at it that way. We have a standard audit program where we try to do the appropriate things in all areas of the audit. Saying that one area is riskier than another doesn't make sense.

Q. How did you audit the lease loss reserve account?

A. We did several things:
   • We asked for and received a delinquency list that showed all leases past due.
   • We tested the completeness of the list by pulling a sample of lease cards and seeing that those we selected were on the delinquency list if they were overdue.

- We discussed the large delinquent leases with Mr. Vernon and obtained his estimate of the potential losses. We added those up and compared them to the loss reserve balance to judge its reasonableness.

Q. When you added the potential losses for December 31, 1995, what did they total in relation to the balance in the loss reserve account?

A. They were significantly less than the reserve account balance. As I recall, the reserve account balance was about $3 million and the sum of the potential losses was only about $2.7 million.

Q. And you believe that indicates that the overall loss reserve was adequate to cover all losses?

A. Well, yes. But more important, WLI thought it was. They said so in their representation letter to us which we obtained at the end of the audit.

Q. As I understand it, in the closing conference for the audit, Mr. Vernon told you that ABC Manufacturing Corp., one of their largest customers, had filed bankruptcy at about year end, yet that lease wasn't on the delinquency list. Didn't that cause you concern that the delinquency list might not be complete?

A. No, not really. After all, Mr. Vernon volunteered the information. Also, when I weighed 10 years of good experience with Mr. Vernon against that one incident, I certainly felt he was as trustworthy as ever.

Required

a. Analyze Raines's responses to the questions posed in terms of possible violations by Lau Lewis & Co. of generally accepted auditing standards.

b. Assuming Lau Lewis & Co. did fail to comply with generally accepted auditing standards in its audit of WLI, what should its responsibility be for damages relative to the responsibility of the other parties involved?

5

AUDIT RESPONSIBILITIES AND OBJECTIVES

WHERE WERE THE AUDITORS?

Barry Minkow was a true "whiz kid." He started ZZZZ Best Company, a high-flying carpet cleaning company that specialized in insurance restoration contracts, at the age of sixteen. In 1982, when Minkow started the business, it was run out of his garage, but a mere five years later he had taken the company public and it had sales of $U.S. 50 million and earnings of over $U.S. 5 million. The market value of Minkow's stock in ZZZZ Best exceeded $U.S. 100 million.

As it turned out, Minkow's genius lay not in business but in deception. Instead of being a solid operating company, ZZZZ Best was an illusion. There were no large restoration jobs and no real revenues and profits. They were only on paper and supported by an effective network of methods to deceive shareholders, the securities regulators, and the reputable professionals who served the company, including its auditors. Many asked, "How could this happen? Where were the auditors?"

When ZZZZ Best first started to grow, Minkow ran into the common problem of needing credit. He devised a scheme with an insurance adjuster to validate nonexistent jobs to potential creditors. Minkow could then get large sums of cash or credit without doing any real work. The scam was broadened when ZZZZ Best started needing audits. To fool the auditors, the co-conspirator insurance adjuster was kept busy running a company that generated false contracts for ZZZZ Best. When the auditors tried to check on those contracts, the adjuster confirmed them. Minkow even went so far as to take auditors to real work sites, sites that weren't actually his. He even leased a partially completed building and hired subcontractors to perform work on the site, all for the sake of a visit by the auditors.

As incredible as the ZZZZ Best story may seem, when asked about it, most knowledgeable observers would answer, It's not the first time, and it won't be the last. It is also not the last time people will ask, Where were the auditors?

The study of evidence accumulation begins with this chapter. It is necessary first to understand the objectives of an audit and the way the auditor approaches accumulating evidence. Those are the most important topics covered in this chapter. Figure 5-1 summarizes the five topics that provide keys to understanding evidence accumulation; these are the steps used to develop audit objectives.

FIGURE 5-1
Steps to Develop Audit Objectives

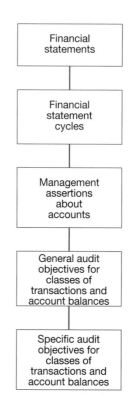

Figure 5-2 presents the December 31, 1998, financial statements of Hillsburg Hardware Ltd., which is incorporated under the *Canada Business Corporations Act*. The adjusted trial balance from which the financial statements were prepared is included in Figure 5-3 on page 129. These financial statements will be used as a frame of reference for subsequent discussion. Footnotes and the cash flow statement have been excluded to keep the discussion as simple as possible. Assume Ross and Co., CAs, audited the December 31, 1997, financial statements and are also doing the 1998 audit.

OBJECTIVE OF CONDUCTING AN AUDIT OF FINANCIAL STATEMENTS

Paragraph 5090.01 of the *CICA Handbook* states (in part):

> The objective of an audit of financial statements is to express an opinion whether the financial statements present fairly, in all material respects, the financial position, results of operations and changes in financial position in accordance with generally accepted accounting principles. . . .

OBJECTIVE 5-1

Know the objective of conducting an audit of financial statements.

Paragraph 5090.01 appropriately emphasizes the expression of an opinion on *financial statements*. The only reason auditors accumulate evidence is to enable them to reach conclusions about whether financial statements are fairly stated in all material respects and to issue an appropriate auditor's report.

When, on the basis of adequate evidence, the auditor concludes that the financial statements are unlikely to mislead a prudent user, the auditor gives an audit opinion on their fair presentation and associates his or her name with the statements. If facts

FIGURE 5-2
Hillsburg Hardware Ltd.
Financial Statements

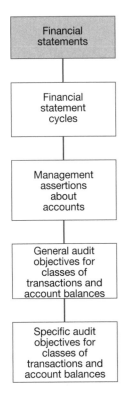

HILLSBURG HARDWARE LTD.

BALANCE SHEET
December 31, 1998
(in thousands)

Assets

Current assets

Cash	$ 41	
Trade accounts receivable (net)	948	
Other accounts receivable	47	
Inventories	1,493	
Prepaid expenses	21	
Total current assets		$2,550

Capital assets

Land	$ 173	
Buildings	1,625	
Delivery equipment	188	
Furniture and fixtures	127	
Less: Accumulated amortization	(1,596)	
Net book value of capital assets		517
Total assets		$3,067

Liabilities and Shareholders' Equity

Current liabilities

Trade accounts payable	$ 236	
Notes payable	167	
Accrued payroll	67	
Accrued payroll benefits	6	
Accrued interest and dividends payable	102	
Estimated income tax	39	
Goods and services tax payable	42	
Total current liabilities		$ 659

Long-term liabilities

Notes payable	$1,206	
Future income tax, liability	37	
Other accrued payables	41	
Total long-term liabilities		1,284

Shareholders' equity

Capital stock	$ 250	
Retained earnings	874	
Total shareholders' equity		1,124
Total liabilities and shareholders' equity		$3,067

HILLSBURG HARDWARE LTD.

COMBINED STATEMENT OF INCOME AND

RETAINED EARNINGS
for Year Ending December 31, 1998
(in thousands)

Sales		$7,721	
Less: Goods and services tax	$ 505		
Returns and allowances	62	567	
Net sales			$7,154
Cost of goods sold			5,162
Gross profit			$1,992

Selling expense

Salaries and commissions	$ 387	
Advertising	131	
Sales payroll benefits	71	
Travel and entertainment	56	
Sales meetings and training	46	
Miscellaneous sales expense	34	
Sales and promotional literature	15	
Total selling expense		$ 741

Administrative expense

Executive and office salaries	$ 276
Bad debt expense	166
Amortization — office building and equipment	73
Office repairs and maintenance	57
Miscellaneous office expense	47
Insurance	44

FIGURE 5-2
(Continued)

Stationery and supplies	38	
Telephone and fax	36	
Administrative payroll benefits	34	
Travel and entertainment	28	
Miscellaneous general expense	26	
Rent	16	
Legal fees and retainers	14	
Auditing	12	
Postage	12	
Dues and memberships	3	
Total administrative expense	882	
Total selling and administrative expense		1,623
Earnings from operations		369
Other income and expense		
Interest expense	$120	
Gain on sale of assets	(36)	84
Earnings before income taxes		$ 285
Income taxes		87
Net income		$ 198
Retained earnings at January 1, 1998		771
		$ 969
Dividends		(95)
Retained earnings at December 31, 1998		$ 874

FIGURE 5-3
Hillsburg Hardware Ltd.
Adjusted Trial Balance

HILLSBURG HARDWARE LTD.
TRIAL BALANCE
December 31, 1998

TRANSACTION CYCLE		DEBIT	CREDIT
S, A, P, C	Cash in bank	$41,378	
S	Trade accounts receivable	1,009,800	
S	Allowance for uncollectible accounts		$62,000
S	Other accounts receivable	47,251	
A, I	Inventories	1,493,231	
A	Prepaid expenses	21,578	
A	Land	172,821	
A	Buildings	1,625,200	
A	Delivery equipment	187,917	
A	Furniture and fixtures	127,321	
A	Accumulated amortization		1,596,006
A	Trade accounts payable		235,999
C	Notes payable		166,700
P	Accrued payroll		67,489
P	Accrued payroll benefits		5,983
C	Accrued interest		7,478
C	Dividends payable		95,000
A	Income tax payable		39,772
A	Goods and services tax payable		42,281
C	Long-term notes payable		1,206,000
A	Future income tax, liability		36,912
A	Other accrued payables		41,499
C	Capital stock		250,000
C	Retained earnings		771,354
S	Sales		7,721,389
A	Goods and services tax	505,000	
S	Sales returns and allowances	62,083	
I	Cost of goods sold	5,162,038	
P	Salaries and commissions	386,900	
P	Sales payroll benefits	71,100	
A	Travel and entertainment — selling	55,517	
A	Advertising	130,563	
A	Sales and promotional literature	16,081	
A	Sales meetings and training	46,224	
A	Miscellaneous sales expense	34,052	
P	Executive and office salaries	276,198	
P	Administrative payroll benefits	34,115	
A	Travel and entertainment — administrative	28,080	
A	Stationery and supplies	38,128	
A	Postage	12,221	

FIGURE 5-3
(Continued)

A	Telephone and fax	36,115	
A	Dues and memberships	3,013	
A	Rent	15,607	
A	Legal fees and retainers	14,153	
A	Auditing	12,142	
A	Amortization — office building and equipment	72,604	
S	Bad debt expense	166,154	
A	Insurance	44,134	
A	Office repairs and maintenance	57,196	
A	Miscellaneous office expense	46,980	
A	Miscellaneous general expense	26,192	
A	Gain on sale of assets		35,987
A	Income taxes	87,330	
C	Interest expense	120,432	
C	Dividends	95,000	
		$12,381,849	$12,381,849

Note: Letters in the left-hand column refer to the following transaction cycles, which are discussed later.

S = Sales and collection   I = Inventory and warehousing
A = Acquisition and payment   C = Capital acquisition and repayment
P = Payroll and personnel

or evidence discovered subsequent to their issuance indicate that the statements were actually not fairly presented, the auditor is likely to have to demonstrate to the courts or regulatory agencies that he or she conducted the audit in a proper manner and drew reasonable conclusions. Although not an insurer or a guarantor of the fairness of the presentations in the statements, the auditor has considerable responsibility for notifying users as to whether or not the statements are properly stated. If the auditor believes the statements are not fairly presented or is unable to reach a conclusion because of insufficient evidence or prevailing conditions, the auditor has the responsibility for notifying the users through the auditor's report.

MANAGEMENT'S RESPONSIBILITY

OBJECTIVE 5-2

Describe management's responsibilities in preparing financial statements.

Canadian Tire Corporation, Limited
www.canadiantire.ca

The professional literature makes it clear that the responsibility for adopting sound accounting policies, maintaining adequate internal control, and making fair representations in the financial statements *rests with management* rather than with the auditor. The primary responsibility for internal control and the financial statements appropriately rests with management given that the entity's transactions and related assets, liabilities, and equity are within the direct knowledge and control of management throughout the year. In contrast, the auditor's knowledge of these matters and internal control is limited to that acquired during the audit.

In recent years, the annual reports of many public companies have included a statement about management's responsibilities and relationship with the public accounting firm. Figure 5-4 presents a report of management's responsibility by the management of Canadian Tire Corporation, one of Canada's largest retail hardware distributors. It is taken from Canadian Tire Corporation's January 3, 1998, annual report. The first paragraph states management's responsibilities for the fair presentation of the financial statements, while the second paragraph discusses management's responsibilities with respect to internal control. The third paragraph comments on the Audit Committee, the Board of Directors, and their role with respect to the financial statements..

Management's responsibility for the fairness of the representations (assertions) in the financial statements carries with it the privilege of determining which disclosures it considers necessary. Although management has the responsibility for the preparation of the financial statements and the accompanying footnotes, it is acceptable for an auditor to draft this material for the client or to offer suggestions for clarification. In the event that management insists on financial statement disclosure that the audi-

FIGURE 5-4
Canadian Tire
Corporation
Management Report

The management of Canadian Tire Corporation, Limited is responsible for the integrity of the accompanying Consolidated Financial Statements and all other information in the annual report. The financial statements have been prepared by management in accordance with generally accepted accounting principles, which recognize the necessity of relying on some best estimates and informed judgments. All financial information in the annual report is consistent with the Consolidated Financial Statements.

To discharge its responsibilities for financial reporting and safeguarding of assets, management depends on the Corporation's systems of internal accounting control. These systems are designed to provide reasonable assurance that the financial records are reliable and form a proper basis for the timely and accurate preparation of financial statements. Management meets the objectives of internal accounting control on a cost-effective basis through: the prudent selection and training of personnel, adoption and communication of appropriate policies, and employment of an internal audit program.

The Board of Directors oversees management's responsibilities for financial statements primarily through the activities of its Audit Committee, which is composed solely of Directors who are neither officers nor employees of the Corporation. This Committee meets with management and the Corporation's independent auditors, Deloitte & Touche, to review the financial statements and recommend approval by the Board of Directors. The Audit Committee is also responsible for making recommendations with respect to the appointment and remuneration of the Corporation's auditors. The Audit Committee also meets with the auditors, without the presence of management, to discuss the results of their audit, their opinion on internal accounting controls, and the quality of financial reporting.

The financial statements have been audited by Deloitte & Touche, whose appointment was ratified by shareholder vote at the annual shareholders' meeting. Their report is presented below.*

Stephen E. Bachand
President and
Chief Executive Officer
March 12, 1998

Gerald S. Kishner
Executive Vice-President, Finance and Administration
and Chief Financial Officer

*Note: The auditor's report is not shown. It was a standard auditor's report.

tor finds unacceptable, the auditor can either issue an adverse or qualified opinion or, as a last resort, withdraw from the engagement.

AUDITOR'S RESPONSIBILITIES

OBJECTIVE 5-3

Describe the auditor's responsibilities to verify financial statements and discover material misstatements (errors or fraud and other irregularities) and illegal acts.

Paragraph 5090.04 of the *CICA Handbook* states that "The auditor performs the audit with an attitude of professional scepticism, and seeks reasonable assurance whether the financial statements are free of material misstatement." Section 5090 goes on to suggest that the auditor should assume good faith on the part of management in conducting the audit.

The requirement for an attitude of scepticism does not mean that the auditor should conduct the audit with an attitude of disbelief or of distrust in management. Rather, it means that the auditor should not be blind to evidence that suggests that documents, books, or records have been altered or are incorrect. The auditor should not assume that management is dishonest, but the possibility of dishonesty must be considered. The concept of reasonable assurance indicates that the auditor is not an insurer or guarantor of the correctness of the financial statements.

There are several reasons why the auditor is responsible for reasonable but not absolute assurance. First, most audit evidence results from testing a sample of a population such as accounts receivable or inventory. Sampling inevitably includes some risk of not uncovering a material misstatement. Also, the areas to be tested; the type, extent, and timing of those tests; and the evaluation of test results require significant judgment on the part of the auditor. Even with good faith and integrity, auditors can make mistakes and errors in judgment. Second, accounting presentations contain complex estimates, which inherently involve uncertainty and can be affected by future events. As a result, the auditor has to rely on evidence that is persuasive but not convincing. Third, fraudulently prepared financial statements are often extremely difficult, if not impossible, for the auditor to detect, especially when there is collusion among management. If the auditor were responsible for making certain that all the assertions in the statements were correct, evidence requirements and the resulting cost of the audit function would increase to such an extent that audits would not be economically feasible. The auditor's best defence when subsequently discovered material misstatements are not uncovered in the audit is that the audit was conducted in accordance with generally accepted auditing standards.

Paragraph 5090.05 points out that "The assumption of management's good faith is a fundamental auditing postulate." If the auditor were to assume the contrary, he or she could not accept evidence supplied by management since the auditor would believe that evidence to be false. Instead, the auditor accepts evidence believing it to be true unless his or her testing of the evidence indicates otherwise.

The *CICA Handbook*, in Section 5135 "The Auditor's Responsibility to Detect and Communicate Misstatements," details how the auditor should utilize professional scepticism when considering the risk of the financial statements containing material error or fraud and other irregularities. Section 5135 distinguishes between two types of misstatements, *errors* and *fraud and other irregularities*. An error is an *unintentional* misstatement of the financial statements, whereas fraud and other irregularities are *intentional*. Two examples of errors are a mistake in extending price times quantity on a sales invoice and overlooking older raw materials in determining lower of cost or market for inventory.

For fraud and other irregularities, a distinction can be drawn between *theft of assets*, often called "defalcation" or "employee fraud," and *fraudulent financial reporting*, often called "management fraud." Another way of characterizing the difference is that employee fraud is perpetrated against the company while management fraud is perpetrated for the company (i.e., for the company's benefit). An example of theft of assets is a clerk taking cash at the time a sale is made and not entering the sale in the cash register. An example of fraudulent financial reporting is the intentional overstatement of sales near the balance sheet date to increase reported earnings. In the case of the former, the company loses the money stolen; in the case of the latter, the company appears more profitable and, presumably, its stock rises in price.

It is usually more difficult for auditors to uncover fraud and other irregularities than errors. This is because of the intended deception associated with fraud and other irregularities. The auditor's responsibility for uncovering fraud and other irregularities deserves special attention.

MANAGEMENT FRAUD

Management fraud is inherently difficult to uncover because (1) it is possible for one or more members of management to override internal controls, and (2) there is typically an effort to conceal the misstatement. Instances of management fraud may include omission of transactions or disclosures, fraudulent amounts, or misstatements of recorded amounts.

Audits cannot be expected to provide the same degree of assurance for the detection of material management fraud as is provided for an equally material error. Concealment by management makes fraud more difficult for auditors to find. The cost of providing equally high assurance for management fraud and for errors is economically impractical for both auditors and society.

Unfortunately, there have been several instances of highly material management fraud discovered after audited financial statements have been issued. Typically, these cases are widely discussed in the financial press and among regulatory bodies because the consequences to creditors and investors are often extremely harmful. The auditor of a company in these circumstances is normally sued even if the audit was prudently conducted following generally accepted auditing standards. The outcome of such a case is decided in the courts.

Factors indicating potential management fraud Due to criticism of the profession resulting from auditors' nondiscovery of several large management frauds, auditors now have greater responsibility for discovering management fraud than they did previously. The most important change has been increased emphasis on auditors' responsibility to evaluate factors that may indicate an increased likelihood of management fraud. For example, assume that management is dominated by a president who makes most of the major operating and business decisions. He has a reputation in the business community for making optimistic projections about future earnings and then putting considerable pressure on operating and accounting staff to make sure those projections are met. He has also been associated with other companies in the past that have gone bankrupt. These factors, considered together, may cause the auditor to conclude that the likelihood of management fraud is fairly high. In such a circumstance, the auditor should put increased emphasis on searching for material management fraud.

The auditor may also uncover circumstances during the audit examination that may cause suspicions of management fraud. For example, the auditor may find that management has lied about the age of certain inventory items. When such circumstances are uncovered, the auditor must evaluate their implications and consider the need to modify planned audit evidence requirements.

EMPLOYEE FRAUD

The profession has also been emphatic that the auditor has less responsibility for the discovery of employee fraud than for errors. If auditors were responsible for the discovery of all employee fraud, auditing tests would have to be greatly expanded, because many types of employee fraud are extremely difficult if not impossible to detect. The procedures that would be necessary to uncover all cases of fraud would certainly be more expensive than the benefits would justify. For example, if there is fraud involving the collusion of several employees that includes the falsification of documents, it is unlikely that such a fraud would be uncovered in a normal audit.

As the auditor assessed the likelihood of material management fraud, he or she should also evaluate the likelihood of material employee fraud. That is normally done initially as a part of understanding the entity's internal control and assessing control risk. Audit evidence should be expanded when the auditor finds an absence of adequate controls or failure to follow prescribed procedures, if he or she believes material employee fraud could exist.

COMPUTER FRAUD

Computer fraud consists of fraud conducted with the assistance of computer software or hardware. This could include deliberately programming functions into a computer program so that it incorrectly calculates interest, placing unauthorized employees ("horses") on a computerized payroll system, falsifying an electronic mail message, or obtaining "free" long distance telephone services.

These forms of fraud could be conducted by management, other employees, or by parties external to the company. They may be difficult to detect or may be obvious. For example, "salami fraud" whereby an employee takes a small amount of interest from each customer and then places this fraction of a penny into the employee's account is extremely difficult to detect if the employee uses multiple bank accounts. Telephone fraud could be detectable by looking for telephone calls outside normal business hours and by running analytical tests on monthly telephone services used.

As with other forms of error or fraud, the auditor cannot be expected to always detect immaterial fraud but should investigate unusual relationships or patterns. Good internal controls spanning the development, acquisition, or use of automated systems help to prevent computer fraud.

HELPING AUDITORS UNCOVER MANAGEMENT FRAUD

Researchers studying management fraud concluded that for management fraud to exist, three factors must be present. For each factor, they identified several red flags to help auditors predict whether the factor indicated a high, moderate, or low assessed likelihood of management fraud. The three factors and a few of the red flags for each factor follow.

FACTOR 1
Conditions Allow Management Fraud to Take Place

- Weak internal control.
- Dominant management, where operating and financial decisions are being made by one or a few persons acting together.
- Difficult-to-audit situations, such as where there are frequent and significant difficult-to-audit transactions or balances.
- Significant judgment is needed to determine the total of an account balance or class of transactions.
- New client, particularly where there is no prior audit history or sufficient information from the predecessor auditor.
- Inexperienced or improperly trained accounting personnel.

FACTOR 2
Management Is Motivated to Commit Fraud

- Rapid growth of the company, such that many changes are taking place within the company and its environment.
- Adverse legal circumstances, such as regulatory allegations or a major litigation.
- The client's profitability is inadequate or inconsistent compared to its industry.
- There is a risk that the company will not be able to meet its financial obligations.
- Management makes unduly aggressive accounting decisions, especially for current year earnings.
- Management and client personnel display significant disrespect and resentment toward regulatory bodies.

FACTOR 3
Those in a Position to Commit the Fraud Have a Receptive Attitude

- Weak internal control.
- A decentralized organization, where there is inadequate monitoring.
- Management places undue emphasis on meeting earnings projections or other quantitative targets.
- Dishonesty, lies, or evasiveness, where managers have lied to the auditors, have been overly evasive in responses to audit inquiries, or have shown some other indication of dishonesty.
- Apparent illegal acts have occurred and may have been covered up.
- Management appears to be willing to take risks that don't seem prudent under the circumstances.

The authors recommend one or more of the following actions when there is a moderate or high risk of management fraud:

- **Critically challenging the client's choice of accounting principles.**
- **Assigning more experienced personnel to the engagement.**
- **Doing more audit work at year end instead of at interim dates.**
- **Closely supervising assistants.**
- **Performing additional or more effective audit procedures.**
- **In extreme circumstances, withdrawing from the engagement.**

Source: Loebbecke, Eining and Willingham, "Auditors' Experience with Material Irregularities, Frequency, Nature, and Detectability," *Auditing: A Journal of Practice & Theory*, Vol. 9, No. 1, Fall 1989, p. 1.

Accounting Today
www.faulknergray.com/
account/acttoday.htm

ILLEGAL ACTS

Illegal acts are defined in Section 5136 as "a violation of a domestic or foreign statutory law or government regulation attributable to the entity under audit, or to employees acting on the entity's behalf." Two examples of illegal acts are a violation of income tax laws and a violation of an environmental protection law. Section 5136 points out that an auditor's responsibility is to comply with GAAS and, as a result, that the auditor may not detect an illegal act or become aware that an illegal act has occurred.

The performance of an illegal act by management or an employee of a company may affect the company (and the financial statements) in a variety of ways. For example, the payment of a bribe by a subsidiary in a foreign country could lead to expulsion of the company and/or expropriation of the company's assets; the balance sheet could be affected. Failing to dispose properly of untreated waste products could make the company liable for fines and penalties; the income statement could be affected. Even if the magnitude of the illegal act itself is not material, the consequences could well be so. As such, the auditor must be interested in illegal acts so that their potential impact may be properly evaluated.

When an illegal act is discovered, the auditor must consider whether such an act is a reflection of the company's corporate culture. Are such acts condoned or encouraged by management? If management does not promote ethical behaviour, the auditor should question management's good faith and consider whether continued association with the client is desirable.

Section 5136 suggests that the auditor should inquire of management about its policies designed to prevent illegal acts and "obtain written representations from management [that there are no] violations or possible violations of laws and government regulations" that would affect the financial statements or notes thereto. The section goes on to say that, other than inquiry of management, the auditor should not search for illegal acts unless there is reason to believe they may exist.

Direct-effect illegal acts Certain violations of laws and regulations have a direct financial effect on specific account balances in the financial statements. For example, a violation of income tax laws directly affects income tax expense and income taxes payable. The auditor's responsibilities under Section 5136 for these direct-effect illegal acts are the same as for errors or fraud and other irregularities. On each audit, the auditor will, therefore, normally evaluate whether there is evidence available to indicate material violations of federal or provincial tax laws. This might be done by discussions with client personnel and examination of reports issued by Revenue Canada after it has completed an examination of the client's tax return.

Indirect-effect illegal acts Most illegal acts affect the financial statements only indirectly. For example, if a company violates environmental protection laws, there is an effect on the financial statements only if there is a fine or sanction. Potential material fines and sanctions indirectly affect financial statements by creating the need to disclose a contingent liability for the potential amount that might ultimately be paid. This is called an *indirect-effect illegal act*. Other examples of illegal acts that are likely to have only an indirect effect are violations of insider securities trading regulations, employment equity laws and employee safety requirements.

Auditing standards clearly state that the auditor provides *no assurance* that indirect-effect illegal acts will be detected. Auditors lack legal expertise, and the frequent indirect relationship between illegal acts and the financial statements makes it impractical for auditors to assume responsibility for discovering those illegal acts.

There are three levels of responsibility that the auditor has for finding and reporting illegal acts.

- *Evidence accumulation when there is no reason to believe indirect-effect illegal acts exist.* Many audit procedures normally performed on audits to search for errors or fraud and other irregularities may also uncover illegal acts. Examples include reading the minutes of the board of directors and inquiring of the client's lawyers about litigation. The auditor should also inquire of management about policies it has established to prevent illegal acts and whether management knows of any laws or regulations that the company has violated. Other than these procedures, the auditor should not search for indirect-effect illegal acts unless there is reason to believe they may exist.

- *Evidence accumulation and other actions when there is reason to believe direct- or indirect-effect illegal acts may exist.* The auditor may find indications of possible illegal acts in a variety of ways. For example, the minutes may indicate that an investigation by a government agency is in progress, or the auditor may identify unusually large payments to consultants or government officials.

    When the auditor believes an illegal act may have occurred, it is necessary to take several actions. First, the auditor should inquire of management at a level above those likely to be involved in the potential illegal act. Second, the auditor should consult with the client's lawyers or another specialist who is knowledgeable about the potential illegal act. Third, the auditor should consider accumulating additional evidence to determine if there actually is an illegal act. All three of these actions are intended to provide the auditor information about whether the suspected illegal act actually exists.

- *Actions when the auditor knows of an illegal act.* The first course of action when an illegal act has been identified is to consider the effects on the financial statements, including the adequacy of disclosures. These effects may be complex and difficult to resolve. For example, a violation of equal opportunity laws could involve significant fines, but it could also result in the loss of customers or key employees which could materially affect future revenues and expenses. If the auditor concludes that the disclosures relative to an illegal act are inadequate, the auditor should modify the auditor's report accordingly.

The auditor should also consider the effect of such illegal acts on his or her relationship with management. If management knew of the illegal act and failed to inform the auditor, it is questionable whether management can be believed in other discussions.

The auditor should communicate with the audit committee or others of equivalent authority to make sure they know of the illegal act. The communication can be oral or written. If it is oral, the nature of the communication and discussion should be documented in the working papers. If the client either refuses to accept the auditor's modified report or fails to take appropriate remedial action concerning the illegal act, the auditor may find it necessary to withdraw from the engagement. Such decisions are complex and normally involve consultation by the auditor with the auditor's lawyers.

FINANCIAL STATEMENT CYCLES

OBJECTIVE 5-4

Describe the financial-statement-cycles approach to segmenting the audit.

Audits are performed by dividing the financial statements into smaller segments or components. The division makes the audit more manageable and aids in the assignment of tasks to different members of the audit team. For example, most auditors treat capital assets and notes payable as different segments. Each segment is audited separately but not completely independently (e.g., the audit of capital assets may reveal an unrecorded note payable.) After the audit of each segment is completed, including interrelationships with other segments, the results are combined. A conclusion can then be reached about the financial statements taken as a whole.

There are different ways of segmenting an audit. Referring to the financial statements in Figure 5-2, one obvious approach would be to treat every account balance on the statements as a separate segment. Segmenting that way is usually inefficient. It would result in the independent audit of such closely related accounts as inventory and cost of goods sold.

THE CYCLE APPROACH TO SEGMENTING AN AUDIT

A more common way to divide an audit is to keep closely related types (or classes) of transactions and account balances in the same segment. This is called the *cycle approach*. For example, sales, sales returns, cash receipts, and charge-offs of uncollectible accounts are four classes of transactions that cause accounts receivable to increase and decrease. They are therefore all part of the sales and collection cycle. Similarly, payroll transactions and accrued payroll are a part of the payroll and personnel cycle.

The logic of using the cycle approach can be seen by thinking about the way transactions are recorded in journals, data files, or data bases and summarized in the general ledger and financial statements. Figure 5-5A shows that flow for manual, paper-based systems. Transactions are written into journals, the totals posted to the general ledger, and financial statements prepared from the general ledger. Figure 5-5B shows the flow for batch processing systems. Transactions are entered into subsystems, resulting in transactions being retained in history files for each subsystem. The transactions are used to update the appropriate master files. Each subsystem is used to print a report summarizing the transactions entered (called a "history report," or often still a "journal"). The general ledger subsystem is used to prepare the financial statements. Figure 5-5C, which depicts data base processing, looks deceptively simple, since all transactions are updated against a single data base containing all company data. Such systems are normally more complex than batch processing systems, however.

To the extent that it is practical, the cycle approach combines transactions recorded in different journals or subsystems with the general ledger balances that result from those transactions.

FIGURE 5-5A

Transaction Flow from Journals to Financial Statements for Manual Systems

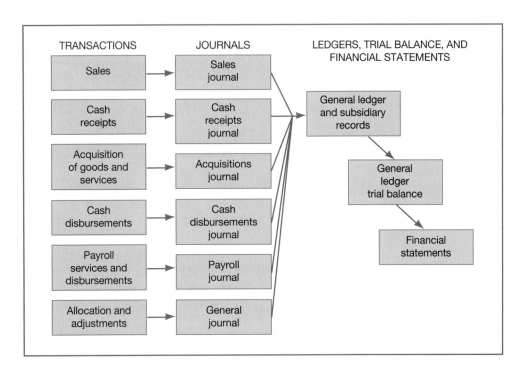

FIGURE 5-5B

Transaction Flow from Data Entry to Financial Statements for Batch Processing Systems

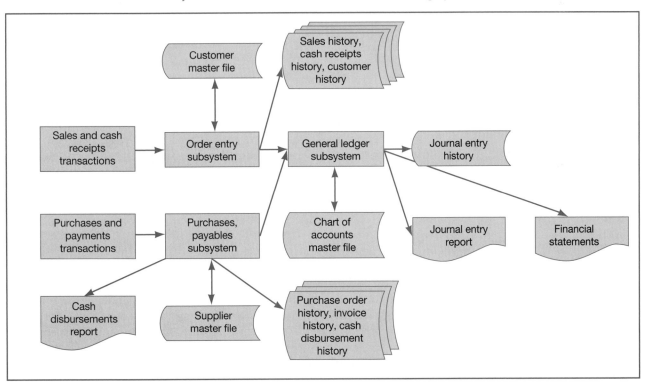

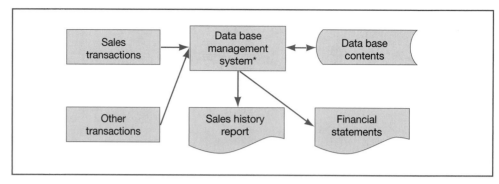

*The structure and complexity depend upon the type of data base used.

The cycles used in this text are shown in Table 5-1. The transaction types associated with each cycle for Hillsburg Hardware Ltd., as well as the 1998 financial statement accounts, are included.

The following observations expand the information contained in Table 5-1.

- All general ledger accounts and transaction types for Hillsburg Hardware Ltd. are included at least once. For a different company, the number and types of transactions and general ledger accounts would differ, but all would be included.
- Some transaction types and general ledger accounts are included in more than one cycle. When that occurs, it means the transaction type is used to record transactions from more than one cycle and indicates a tie-in between the cycles. The most important general ledger account included in and affecting several cycles is the general cash (cash in bank). General cash connects most cycles.
- The capital acquisition and repayment cycle is closely related to the acquisition and payment cycle. The acquisition of goods and services includes the purchase of inventory, supplies, and general services in performing the main business operations. Transactions in the capital acquisitions cycle are related to financing the business, such as issuing stock or debt, paying dividends, and repaying of debt. The same transaction type is used to record transactions for both cycles, and the transactions are similar. There are two reasons for treating capital acquisition and repayment separately from the acquisition of goods and services. First, the transactions are related to financing a company rather than to its operations. Second, most capital acquisition and repayment cycle accounts involve few transactions, but each is often highly material and therefore should be audited extensively. Considering both reasons, it is more convenient to separate the two cycles.
- The inventory and warehousing cycle is closely related to all other cycles, especially for a manufacturing company. The cost of inventory includes raw materials (acquisition and payment cycle), direct labour (payroll and personnel cycle), and manufacturing overhead (acquisition and payment and payroll and personnel cycles). The sale of finished goods involves the sales and collection cycle. Because inventory is material for most manufacturing companies, it is common to borrow money using inventory as security. In those cases, the capital acquisition and repayment cycle is also related to inventory and warehousing.

RELATIONSHIPS AMONG CYCLES

Figure 5-6 on page 140 illustrates the relationship of the cycles to one another. In addition to the five cycles, general cash is also shown. Each cycle is studied in detail in later chapters.

Figure 5-6 shows that cycles have no beginning or end except at the origin and final disposition of a company. A company begins by obtaining capital, usually in the form of cash. In a manufacturing company, cash is used to acquire raw materials, cap-

TABLE 5-1

CYCLES APPLIED TO HILLSBURG HARDWARE LTD.

| CYCLE | TRANSACTION TYPES INCLUDED IN THE CYCLE (See Figures 5-5A, B, C) | GENERAL LEDGER ACCOUNT INCLUDED IN THE CYCLE (See Figure 5-3) | |
		Balance Sheet	Income Statement
Sales and collection	Sales Cash receipts Journal entries	Cash in bank Trade accounts receivable Other accounts receivable Allowance for uncollectible accounts	Sales Sales returns and allowances Bad debt expense
Acquisition and payment	Acquisitions Cash disbursements Journal entries	Cash in bank Inventories Prepaid expenses Land Buildings Delivery equipment Furniture and fixtures Accumulated amortization Trade accounts payable Other accrued payables Income tax payable Future income tax, liability Goods and services tax payable	Advertising[S] Amortization — office building and equipment[A] Auditing[A] Dues and memberships[A] Gain on sale of assets Goods and services tax Income taxes Insurance[A] Legal fees and retainers[A] Miscellaneous general expense[A] Miscellaneous office expense[A] Miscellaneous sales expense[S] Office repairs and maintenance expense[A] Postage[A] Rent[A] Sales and promotional literature[S] Sales meetings and training[S] Stationery and supplies[A] Taxes[A] Telephone and fax[A] Travel and entertainment —selling[A] Travel and entertainment —general[S]
Payroll and personnel	Payroll Journal entries	Cash in bank Accrued payroll Accrued payroll benefits	Salaries and commissions[S] Sales payroll benefits[S] Executive and office salaries[A] Administrative payroll benefits[A]
Inventory and warehousing	Acquisitions Sales Journal entries	Inventories	Cost of goods sold
Capital acquisition and repayment	Acquisitions Cash disbursements Journal entries	Cash in bank Notes payable Long-term notes payable Accrued interest Capital stock Retained earnings Dividends Dividends payable	Interest expense

S = Selling expense
A = General and administrative expense

ital assets, and related goods and services to produce inventory (acquisition and payment cycle). Cash is also used to acquire labour for the same reason (payroll and personnel cycle). Acquisition and payment and payroll and personnel are similar in nature, but the functions are sufficiently different to justify separate cycles. The combined result of these two cycles is inventory (inventory and warehousing cycle). At a

FIGURE 5-6

Relationships Among
Transaction Cycles

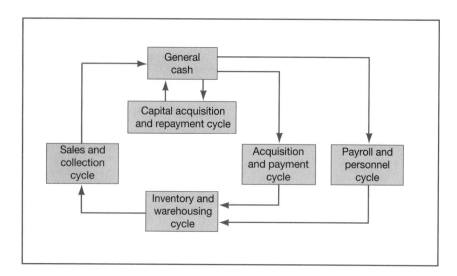

subsequent point, the inventory is sold and billings and collections result (sales and collection cycle). The cash generated is used to pay dividends and interest and to start the cycles again. The cycles interrelate in much the same way in a service company, where there will be no inventory but there may be unbilled receivables.

Transaction cycles are of major importance in the conduct of the audit. For the most part, auditors treat each cycle separately during the audit. Although auditors should take care to interrelate different cycles at different times and be aware of the interrelationships among the cycles, they must treat the cycles somewhat independently in order to manage complex audits effectively.

SETTING AUDIT OBJECTIVES

OBJECTIVE 5-5

Describe why the auditor obtains assurance by auditing classes of transactions and ending balances in accounts.

Auditors conduct audits consistently with the cycle approach by performing audit tests of the transactions making up ending balances and also by performing audit tests of the account balances themselves. Figure 5-7 illustrates this important concept by showing the four classes of transactions that determine the ending balance in accounts receivable. Assume that the beginning balance of $96 was audited in the prior year and is therefore considered reliable. If the auditor could be completely sure that each of the four classes of transactions was correctly stated, the auditor could also be sure that the ending balance of $166 was correctly stated. But it may be impractical for the auditor to obtain complete assurance about the correctness of each class of transactions resulting in less than complete assurance about the ending balance in accounts receivable. In such a case, overall assurance can be increased by auditing the ending balance of accounts receivable. Auditors have found that, generally, the most efficient way to conduct audits is to *obtain some combination of assurance for each class of transactions and for the ending balance in the related account.*

For any given class of transactions, there are several audit objectives that must be met before the auditor can conclude that the transactions are properly recorded. They are called *transaction-related audit objectives* in the remainder of this book. For example, there are specific sales transaction-related audit objectives and specific sales returns and allowances transaction-related audit objectives.

Similarly, there are several audit objectives that must be met for each account balance. They are called *balance-related audit objectives*. For example, there are specific accounts receivable balance-related audit objectives and specific accounts payable balance-related audit objectives. It will be shown later that the transaction-related and balance-related audit objectives are somewhat different but closely related. Throughout the remainder of this text, the term "audit objectives" refers to both transaction-related and balance-related audit objectives.

Before examining audit objectives in more detail, it is necessary to understand management assertions. These are studied next.

FIGURE 5-7
Balances and
Transactions Affecting
Those Balances for
Accounts Receivable

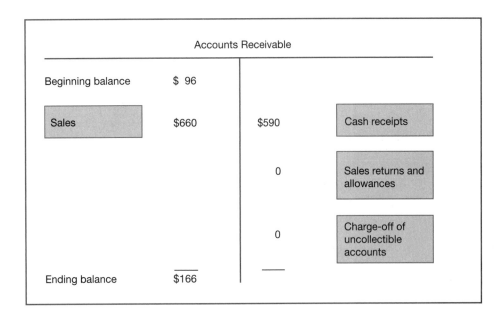

MANAGEMENT ASSERTIONS

OBJECTIVE 5-6

Identify the five categories of management assertions about financial information.

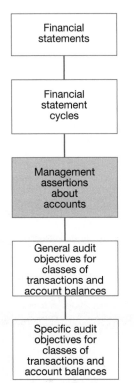

Assertions are implied or expressed representations by management about classes of transactions and the related accounts in the financial statements. As an illustration, the management of Hillsburg Hardware Ltd. asserts that cash of $41,000 (see Figure 5-2) was present in the company's bank accounts or on the premises as of the balance sheet date. Unless otherwise disclosed in the financial statements, management also asserts that the cash was unrestricted and available for normal use. Similar assertions exist for each asset, liability, equity, revenue, and expense item in the financial statements. These assertions apply to both classes of transactions and account balances.

Management assertions are directly related to generally accepted accounting principles. These assertions are part of the *criteria management uses to record and disclose accounting information in financial statements*. Return to the definition of auditing in Chapter 1, on page 3. It states, in part, that auditing is a comparison of information (financial statements) to established criteria (assertions established according to generally accepted accounting principles). Auditors must therefore understand the assertions to do adequate audits.

Paragraph 5300.17 of the *CICA Handbook* lists and describes seven assertions that management makes with respect to items in the financial statements. This text generally uses these same assertions, except that "ownership" has been extended to "rights and obligations," affecting both assets and liabilities, as described below.

Assertions about existence Assertions about existence deal with whether assets, obligations, and equities included in the balance sheet actually existed on the balance sheet date. For example, management asserts that merchandise inventory included in the balance sheet exists and is available for sale at the balance sheet date.

Assertions about occurrence Assertions about occurrence concern whether recorded transactions included in the financial statements actually occurred during the accounting period. Management asserts that sales in the income statement represent exchanges of goods or services that actually took place.

Assertions about completeness These management assertions state that all transactions and accounts that should be presented in the financial statements are included. For example, management asserts that all sales of goods and services are recorded and included in the financial statements. Similarly, management asserts that notes payable in the balance sheet include all such obligations of the entity.

The completeness assertion deals with matters opposite from those of the existence or occurrence assertions. The completeness assertion is concerned with the possibility of omitting items from the financial statements that should have been included, whereas the existence or occurrence assertions are concerned with inclusion of amounts that should not have been included.

Thus, recording a sale that did not take place would be a violation of the occurrence assertion, whereas the failure to record a sale that did occur would be a violation of the completeness assertion.

Assertions about valuation An asset or liability is asserted as being recorded at an appropriate carrying value. This involves the use of management judgment to determine whether the value is accurately recorded originally (normally at cost) and whether the current carrying value is appropriate. For fixed assets, this includes determining the amount of amortization that should be written off against the asset, and whether the asset value has been impaired or not, thus requiring a writedown. Inventory should be examined for potential obsolescence, and accounts receivable should be assessed for collectibility. Management asserts that its estimates and conclusions on valuation are those that should be used for the financial statements.

Assertions about measurement or allocation These assertions deal with whether the asset, liability, equity, revenue, and expense accounts have been included in the financial statements at appropriate amounts and in the proper period. For example, management asserts that property is recorded at historical cost equal to the invoice amount and that such cost is accurately allocated to appropriate accounting periods using the amortization rate that has been determined. Similarly, management states that the correct quantities and prices were used to calculate ending inventory amounts, and that only the inventory on hand at the end of the year was included in inventory.

Assertions about ownership: rights and obligations These management assertions deal with whether assets are the rights of the entity and liabilities are the obligations of the entity at a given date. For example, management asserts that assets are owned by the company or amounts capitalized for leases in the balance sheet represent the cost of the entity's rights to leased property, and that the corresponding lease liability represents an obligation of the entity.

Assertions about statement presentation (and disclosure) These assertions deal with whether components of the financial statements are properly combined or separated, described, and disclosed. For example, management asserts that obligations classified as long-term liabilities on the balance sheet will not mature within one year. Similarly, management asserts that amounts presented as extraordinary items in the income statement are properly classified and described.

TRANSACTION-RELATED AUDIT OBJECTIVES

OBJECTIVE 5-7

Identify the six general transaction-related audit objectives, explain their purpose, and relate them to management assertions.

The auditor's transaction-related audit objectives follow and are closely related to management assertions. That is not surprising since the auditor's primary responsibility is to determine whether management assertions about financial statements are justified.

These transaction-related audit objectives are intended to provide a *framework* to help the auditor accumulate sufficient competent audit evidence required by the third examination standard and decide the proper evidence to accumulate for classes of transactions given the circumstances of the engagement. The objectives remain the same from audit to audit, but the evidence varies depending on the circumstances.

A distinction must be made between *general transaction-related audit objectives* and *specific transaction-related audit objectives* for each class of transactions. The general transaction-related audit objectives discussed here are applicable to every class of transactions but are stated in broad terms. Specific transaction-related audit objectives are also applied to each class of transactions but are stated in terms tailored to a class of transactions, such as sales transactions. Once you know the general transaction-related audit objectives, they can be used to develop specific transaction-related audit objectives for each class of transactions being audited. The six general transaction-related audit objectives are discussed next.

GENERAL TRANSACTION-RELATED AUDIT OBJECTIVES

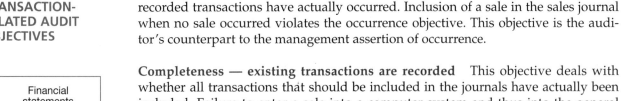

Occurrence — recorded transactions occurred   This objective deals with whether recorded transactions have actually occurred. Inclusion of a sale in the sales journal when no sale occurred violates the occurrence objective. This objective is the auditor's counterpart to the management assertion of occurrence.

Completeness — existing transactions are recorded   This objective deals with whether all transactions that should be included in the journals have actually been included. Failure to enter a sale into a computer system and thus into the general ledger when a sale occurred violates the completeness objective. The objective is the counterpart to the management assertion of completeness.

The occurrence and completeness objectives emphasize opposite audit concerns; occurrence deals with potential overstatement and completeness with unrecorded transactions (understatement).

Accuracy — recorded transactions are stated at the correct amounts   This objective deals with the accuracy of information for accounting transactions. For sales transactions, there would be a violation of the accuracy objective if the quantity of goods shipped was different from the quantity billed, the wrong selling price was used for billing, extension or adding errors (perhaps due to program errors) occurred in billing, or the wrong amount was updated to the master file. Accuracy is one part of the measurement assertion.

Classification — transactions included in the client's records are properly classified   Examples of misclassifications for sales are including cash sales as credit sales, recording a sale of operating capital assets as revenue, and misclassifying commercial sales as residential sales. Classification is also a part of the measurement assertion.

Timing — transactions are recorded on the correct dates   A timing error occurs if transactions are not recorded on the dates the transactions took place. A sales transaction, for example, should be recorded on the date of shipment. Timing is also a part of the measurement assertion.

Posting and summarization — recorded transactions are updated to the master files and are correctly summarized   This objective deals with the accuracy of the transfer of information from recorded transactions to subsidiary records (or master files) and summarization to the general ledger. For example, if a sales transaction is recorded in the wrong customer's record and thus to the wrong customer in the master file, it is a violation of this objective. Posting and summarization is also a part of the measurement assertion.

Since the posting of transactions to subsidiary records, the general ledger, and other related master files is typically accomplished automatically by computerized accounting systems, the risk of random human error in posting is minimal. Once the auditor has established that the computer is functioning properly, there is a reduced concern about posting or summarization errors.

The general transaction-related audit objectives must be applied to each material type (class) of transaction in the audit. Such transactions typically include sales, cash receipts, acquisitions of goods and services, payroll, and so on. Table 5-2 summarizes the six transaction-related audit objectives. It includes the general form of the objectives, the application of the objectives to sales transactions, and the assertions. Notice that only three general assertions are associated with transaction-related audit objectives. This shows that four of the assertions are not satisfied by performing tests of controls, but instead are satisfied by substantive tests of transactions.

TABLE 5-2

MANAGEMENT ASSERTIONS, GENERAL AUDIT OBJECTIVES, AND SPECIFIC AUDIT OBJECTIVES

MANAGEMENT ASSERTION	GENERAL TRANSACTION-RELATED AUDIT OBJECTIVES	SPECIFIC SALES TRANSACTION-RELATED AUDIT OBJECTIVES	GENERAL BALANCE-RELATED AUDIT OBJECTIVES	SPECIFIC BALANCE-RELATED AUDIT OBJECTIVES APPLIED TO INVENTORY
Existence	N/A	N/A	Existence	All recorded inventory exist at the balance sheet date.
Occurrence	Occurrence	Recorded sales are for shipments made to nonfictitious customers.	N/A	N/A
Completeness	Completeness	Existing sales transactions are recorded.	Completeness	All existing inventory has been counted and included in inventory.
Valuation	N/A	N/A	Valuation	Inventories have been written down where net realizable value is less than book value.
Measurement	Accuracy	Recorded sales are for the amount of goods shipped and are correctly billed and recorded.	Accuracy	Inventory quantities agree with items physically on hand. Prices used to extend inventory cost are materially correct. Extensions of price times quantity are correct and details are correctly added.
Measurement	Classification	Sales transactions are classified to the correct account.	Classification	Inventory items are properly classified as raw materials, work in process, or finished goods.
Allocation	Timing	Sales are recorded on the correct dates.	Cutoff	Purchases at year end are recorded in the correct period. Sales at year end are recorded in the correct period.
Measurement	Posting and summarization	Sales transactions are updated correctly to the customer master file, and the posting to the general ledger summed these transactions correctly.	Detail tie-in	Total of inventory items agrees with general ledger.
Rights and obligations	N/A	N/A	Rights and obligations	The company has title to all inventory items listed. Inventories are not pledged as collateral.
Presentation and disclosure	N/A	N/A	Presentation and disclosure	Major categories of inventories and their bases of valuation are disclosed. The pledge of assignment of any inventories is disclosed.

BALANCE-RELATED AUDIT OBJECTIVES

Identify the nine general balance-related audit objectives, explain their purpose, and relate them to management assertions.

Balance-related audit objectives are similar to the transaction-related audit objectives just discussed. They also follow from management assertions, and they provide a framework to help the auditor accumulate sufficient appropriate evidence. There are also both general and specific balance-related audit objectives.

There are two differences between balance-related and transaction-related audit objectives. First, as the terms imply, balance-related audit objectives are applied to account balances, whereas transaction-related audit objectives are applied to classes of transactions such as sales transactions and cash disbursements transactions. Second, there are more audit objectives for account balances than for classes of transactions. There are nine balance-related audit objectives compared to six transaction-related audit objectives. These are also shown on Table 5-2.

Because of the way audits are done, balance-related audit objectives are almost *always* applied to the ending balance in balance sheet accounts, such as accounts receivable, inventory, and notes payable. Balance-related objectives are also applied to certain income statement accounts. These usually involve non-routine transactions and unpredictable expenses, such as legal expense or repairs and maintenance. Other income statement accounts are closely related to balance sheet accounts and are tested simultaneously (e.g., amortization expense with accumulated amortization, interest expense with notes payable).

When using the balance-related audit objectives as a framework for auditing balance sheet account balances, the auditor accumulates evidence to verify detail that supports the account balance, rather than verifying the account balance itself. For example, in auditing accounts receivable, the auditor obtains a listing of the aged accounts receivable balances from the client that agrees to the general ledger balance (see page 468 for an illustration). The accounts receivable balance-related audit objectives are applied to the customer accounts in that listing.

Following is a brief discussion of the nine general balance-related audit objectives. Throughout the discussion, there is reference to a supporting schedule, which refers to client-provided working papers or reports such as the accounts receivable listing just described.

GENERAL BALANCE-RELATED AUDIT OBJECTIVES

Existence — amounts included exist This objective deals with whether the amounts included in the financial statements should actually be included. For example, inclusion of an account receivable from a customer in the accounts receivable trial balance when there is no receivable from that customer violates the existence objective. Similarly, if the same inventory is accidentally counted twice and thus inventory is inflated, the existence objective has been violated. This objective is the auditor's counterpart to the management assertion of existence or occurrence.

Completeness — existing amounts are included This objective deals with whether all amounts that should be included have actually been included. Failure to include an account receivable from a customer when the receivable exists violates the completeness objective. Forgetting to count and include certain types of inventory does the same. This objective is the counterpart to the management assertion of completeness.

The existence and completeness objectives emphasize opposite audit concerns; existence deals with potential overstatement and completeness with unrecorded transactions and amounts (understatement).

Valuation (realizable value) — assets are included at the amounts estimated to be realized This objective concerns whether an account balance has been reduced for declines from historical cost to net realizable value. Examples when this objective applies are considering the adequacy of the allowance for uncollectible accounts receivable and writedowns of inventory for obsolescence. The objective applies only to asset accounts and is part of the valuation assertion.

Accuracy — amounts included are stated at the correct amounts The accuracy objective refers to amounts being included at the correct arithmetic amount. An inventory item on a client's inventory listing could be wrong because the number of units of inventory on hand was misstated, the unit price was wrong, or the total was incorrectly extended due to a programming error. Each of these violates the accuracy objective. Accuracy is one part of the measurement assertion.

Classification — amounts included in the client's listing are properly classified Classification involves determining whether items on a client's listing are included in the correct accounts. For example, on the accounts receivable listing, receivables must be separated into short-term and long-term, and amounts due from affiliates, officers, and directors must be classified separately from amounts due from customers. Inventory should be correctly classified by type. Classification is also a part of the measurement assertion.

Cutoff — transactions near the balance sheet date are recorded in the proper period In testing for cutoff, the objective is to determine whether transactions are recorded in the proper period. The transactions that are most likely to be misstated are those recorded near the end of the accounting period. It is proper to think of cutoff tests as a part of verifying either the balance sheet accounts or the related transactions, but for convenience, auditors usually perform them as a part of auditing balance sheet accounts. Cutoff is also part of the measurement assertion.

Detail tie-in — transaction details sum to the master files amounts, and subsidiary records (manual or automated) agree with the total in the account balance in the general ledger Account balances on financial statements are supported by details in data files and schedules prepared by clients. The detail tie-in objective is concerned that the details are accurately prepared, correctly added, and agree with the general ledger. For example, individual accounts receivable on a listing of accounts receivable should agree to the customer master file and the total should equal the general ledger control account. Detail tie-in is also a part of the measurement assertion.

Rights and obligations In addition to existing, most assets must be owned before they can be included in the financial statements. Similarly, liabilities must belong to the entity. Rights are always associated with assets and obligations with liabilities. This objective is the auditor's counterpart to the management assertion of rights and obligations (ownership).

Presentation and disclosure — account balances and related disclosure requirements are properly presented in the financial statements In fulfilling the presentation and disclosure objective, the auditor tests to make certain that all balance sheet and income statement accounts and related information are correctly set forth in the financial statements and properly described in the body and footnotes of the statements. This objective has its counterpart in the management assertion of presentation and disclosure.

Presentation and disclosure is closely related to, but distinct from, classification. Accounting information for balance-related audit objectives is correctly classified if all information on a report or in a data file supporting an account balance is summarized in the appropriate accounts. The information is correctly disclosed if those account balances and related footnote information are properly combined, described, and presented in the financial statements. For example, if a long-term note receivable is included on an accounts receivable listing, there is a violation of the classification objective. If the long-term note receivable is correctly classified but combined with accounts receivable on the financial statements, there is a violation of the presentation and disclosure objective.

SPECIFIC BALANCE-RELATED AUDIT OBJECTIVES

After the general balance-related audit objectives are understood, specific balance-related audit objectives for each account balance on the financial statements can be developed. There should be at least one specific balance-related audit objective for each general balance-related audit objective unless the auditor believes that the general balance-related audit objective is not relevant or is unimportant in the circumstances. There may be more than one specific balance-related audit objective for a general balance-related audit objective. For example, specific balance-related audit objectives for rights and obligations of the inventory of Hillsburg Hardware Ltd. could include that (1) the company has title to all inventory items listed and (2) inventories are not pledged as collateral unless it is disclosed.

RELATIONSHIPS AMONG MANAGEMENT ASSERTIONS AND BALANCE-RELATED AUDIT OBJECTIVES

The reason there are more general balance-related audit objectives than management assertions is to provide additional guidance to auditors in deciding what evidence to accumulate. Table 5-2 illustrates this by showing the relationships among management assertions, the general balance-related audit objectives, and specific balance-related audit objectives as applied to inventory for a company such as Hillsburg Hardware Ltd.

HOW AUDIT OBJECTIVES ARE MET

OBJECTIVE 5-9

Describe the process by which audit objectives are met, and use it as a basis for further study.

The auditor must obtain sufficient appropriate audit evidence to support all management assertions in the financial statements. As stated earlier, this is done by accumulating evidence in support of some appropriate combination of transaction-related audit objectives and balance-related audit objectives. Table 5-2 shows a significant overlap between the two types of audit objectives. The only assertions that must be addressed through balance-related audit objectives, rather than some combination of balance- and transaction-related audit objectives, are rights and obligations and presentation and disclosure.

The auditor plans the appropriate combination of audit objectives and the evidence that must be accumulated to meet them by following an audit process. An audit process is a well-defined methodology for organizing an audit to ensure that the evidence gathered is both sufficient and appropriate, and that all required audit objectives are both specified and met. The audit process described in this text has four specific phases. These are shown in Figure 5-8. An expanded summary of the audit

FIGURE 5-8
Four Phases of an Audit

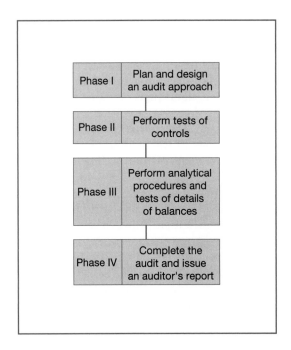

process is presented in Figure 10-10 on page 328. The remainder of this chapter provides a brief introduction to each of the four phases.

PLAN AND DESIGN AN AUDIT APPROACH (PHASE I)

For any given audit, there are many ways an auditor can accumulate evidence to meet the overall audit objectives. Two overriding considerations affect the approach the auditor selects: *sufficient appropriate audit evidence must be accumulated to meet the auditor's professional responsibility*, and *the cost of accumulating the evidence should be minimized*. The first consideration is the more important, but cost minimization is necessary if public accounting firms are to be competitive and profitable. If there were no concern for controlling costs, decision making about the types and amounts of evidence to select would be easy. Auditors would keep adding evidence, without concern for efficiency, until they were sufficiently certain there were no material misstatements.

Concern for sufficient appropriate audit evidence and cost control necessitates planning the engagement. The plan should result in an effective audit approach at reasonable cost. Planning and designing an audit approach can be broken down into several parts. Two are addressed briefly here. Others are discussed in later chapters.

Obtaining knowledge of the client's business To interpret adequately the meaning of information obtained throughout the audit, an *understanding of the client's business and industry* is essential. Unique aspects of different businesses are reflected in the financial statements. An audit of a life insurance company could not be performed with due care without an understanding of the unique characteristics of that business. Imagine attempting to audit a client in the bridge construction industry without understanding the construction business and the percentage-of-completion method of accounting. Neither audit could be effectively conducted without an awareness of the business environment or regulatory environment within which these businesses function. Examination Standard (i) of generally accepted auditing standards in paragraph 5100.02 *requires* the auditor to use "sufficient knowledge of the entity's business" as a basis for planning the audit.

Understanding the client's internal control and assessing control risk It was pointed out in Chapter 1 that the ability of the client's internal controls to generate reliable financial information and safeguard assets and records is one of the most important and widely accepted concepts in the theory and practice of auditing. If the client has excellent internal controls, *control risk* will be low and the amount of audit evidence to be accumulated can be significantly less than when internal controls are inadequate.

Examination Standard (ii) of generally accepted auditing standards in paragraph 5100.02 *requires* the auditor to gain a sufficient understanding of internal control to plan the audit. This understanding is obtained by reviewing organization charts and procedural manuals, by discussions with client personnel, by completing internal control questionnaires and flowcharts, and by observing client activities. Many firms have software that assists in the evaluation process by prompting the auditor to answer specific questions and then providing a summary of the likely effects of the responses on control risk.

After the auditor gains an understanding of internal control, he or she is in a position to evaluate how effective controls should be in preventing and detecting errors or fraud and other irregularities. This evaluation involves identifying specific controls that reduce the likelihood that errors or fraud and other irregularities will occur and not be detected and corrected on a timely basis. Supervisory, managing, or monitoring controls are specifically identified as having important effects. This process is referred to as *assessing control risk*.

PERFORM TESTS OF CONTROLS (PHASE II)

Where the auditor has assessed control risk at a level below maximum based on the identification of controls, he or she may then reduce the extent to which the accuracy of the financial statement information related directly to those controls must be validated through the accumulation of evidence. However, to justify using a control risk assessment below maximum, the auditor must test the effectiveness of the controls. The procedures involved in this type of testing are commonly referred to as *tests of controls*. For example, assume that the client's order entry software requires that all amounts over $10,000 must be entered twice. This control is directly related to the accuracy transaction-related audit objective for sales. One possible test of the effectiveness of this control is for the auditor to enter a transaction over $10,000 and observe whether the system requests a second entry.

Auditors also evaluate the client's recording of transactions by verifying the dollar amounts of transactions. An example is for the auditor to compare the unit selling price on a duplicate sales invoice with the approved sales price in the inventory master file as a test of the accuracy objective for sales transactions. Like the test of control in the previous paragraph, this test satisfies the accuracy transaction-related audit objective for sales.

DO ANALYTICAL PROCEDURES AND TESTS OF DETAILS OF BALANCES (PHASE III)

Phase III procedures are described as substantive procedures; there are two general categories of phase III procedures: analytical procedures and tests of details of balances. Analytical procedures are those that assess the overall reasonableness of transactions and balances. An example of an analytical procedure that would provide some assurance for the accuracy objective for both sales transactions (transaction-related audit objective) and accounts receivable (balance-related audit objective) is to have the auditor run an exception report (using audit software) of sales transactions for unusually large amounts and compare total monthly sales to prior years. If a company is consistently using incorrect sales prices, significant differences are likely.

Tests of details of balances are specific procedures intended to test for monetary misstatements in the balances in the financial statements. An example related to the accuracy objective for accounts receivable (balance-related audit objective) is direct written communication with the client's customers. Tests of ending balances are essential to the conduct of the audit because most of the evidence is obtained from a source independent of the client and therefore considered to be of high quality.

There is a close relationship among the general review of the client's circumstances, results of understanding internal control and assessing control risk, analytical procedures, and the tests of details of the financial statement account balances. If the auditor has obtained a reasonable level of assurance for any given audit objective by performing tests of controls and analytical procedures, the tests of details for that objective can be significantly reduced. In most instances, however, some tests of details of significant financial statement account balances are necessary.

COMPLETE THE AUDIT AND ISSUE AN AUDITOR'S REPORT (PHASE IV)

After the auditor has completed all the procedures for each audit objective and for each financial statement account, it is necessary to combine the information obtained to reach an *overall conclusion* as to whether the financial statements are fairly presented. This is a highly subjective process that relies heavily on the auditor's professional judgment. In practice, the auditor continuously combines the information obtained as he or she proceeds through the audit. The final combination is a summation at the completion of the engagement. When the audit is completed, the public accountant must issue an auditor's report to accompany the client's published financial statements. The report must meet well-defined technical requirements which are affected by the scope of the audit and the nature of the findings. These reports have already been studied in Chapter 2.

SUMMARY

This chapter discusses the objectives of the audit and the way the auditor subdivides an audit to result in specific audit objectives. The auditor then accumulates evidence to obtain assurance that each objective has been satisfied.

The illustration on meeting the accuracy objectives for sales transactions and accounts receivable shows that the auditor can obtain assurance by accumulating evidence using tests of controls, analytical procedures, and tests of details of balances. In some audits, there is more emphasis on certain of these tests such as analytical procedures and tests of controls, whereas on others there is emphasis on tests of details of balances. We will study the circumstances under which it is appropriate to emphasize each of these three types of tests in later chapters.

ESSENTIAL TERMS

Analytical procedures — use of comparisons and relationships to determine whether account balances or other data appear reasonable (p. 149).

Balance-related audit objectives — nine audit objectives that must be met before the auditor can conclude that any given account balance is fairly stated. The general balance-related audit objectives are existence, completeness, valuation, accuracy, classification, cutoff, detail tie-in, rights and obligations, and presentation and disclosure (p. 145).

Cycle approach — a method of dividing an audit by keeping closely related types of transactions and account balances in the same segment (p. 136).

Error — an unintentional misstatement of the financial statements (p. 131).

Fraud or other irregularity — an intentional misstatement of the financial statements (p. 131).

Illegal acts — violations of laws or government regulations other than irregularities (p. 134).

Management assertions — implied or expressed representations by management about classes of transactions and related accounts in the financial statements (p. 141).

Management fraud — a fraud or other irregularity resulting in fraudulent financial reporting (p. 131).

Specific audit objectives — transaction-related or balance-related audit objectives for each class of transactions and account balance (p. 140).

Tests of controls — audit procedures to test the effectiveness of control policies and procedures in support of a reduced assessed control risk (p. 149).

Tests of details of balances — an auditor's tests for monetary errors or fraud and other irregularities in the details of balance sheet and income statement accounts (p. 149).

Transaction-related audit objectives — six audit objectives that must be met before the auditor can conclude that the total for any given class of transactions is fairly stated. The general transaction-related audit objectives are occurrence, completeness, accuracy, classification, timing, and posting and summarization (p. 142).

REVIEW QUESTIONS

5-1 State the objective of the audit of financial statements. In general terms, how do auditors meet that objective?

5-2 Distinguish between management's and the auditor's responsibility for the financial statements being audited.

5-3 Distinguish between the terms "errors" and "fraud and other irregularities." What is the auditor's responsibility for finding each?

5-4 Distinguish between management fraud and employee fraud. Discuss the likely difference between these two types of fraud on the fair presentation of financial statements.

5-5 "It is well accepted in auditing that throughout the conduct of the ordinary examination, it is essential to obtain large amounts of information from management and to rely heavily on management's judgments. After all, the financial statements are management's representations, and the primary responsibility for their fair presentation rests with management, not the auditor. For example, it is extremely difficult, if not impossible, for the auditor to evaluate the obsolescence of inventory as well as management can in a highly complex business. Similarly, the collectibility of accounts receivable and the continued usefulness of machinery and equipment is heavily dependent on management's willingness to provide truthful responses to questions." Reconcile the auditor's responsibility for discovering material misrepresentations by management with these comments.

5-6 List three major considerations that are useful in predicting the likelihood of management fraud in an audit. For each of the considerations, state two actions the auditor can take to evaluate its significance in the engagement.

5-7 Define the term "illegal act." What is the auditor's responsibility with respect to illegal acts by clients?

5-8 Describe what is meant by the cycle approach to auditing. What are the advantages of dividing the audit into different cycles?

5-9 Identify the cycle to which each of the following general ledger accounts would ordinarily be assigned: sales, accounts payable, retained earnings, accounts receivable, inventory, and repairs and maintenance.

5-10 Why are sales, sales returns and allowances, bad debts, cash discounts, accounts receivable, and allowance for uncollectible accounts all included in the same cycle?

5-11 Define what is meant by a management assertion about financial statements. Identify the seven categories of management assertions described in the text.

5-12 Distinguish between the general audit objectives and management assertions. Why are the general audit objectives more useful to auditors?

5-13 An acquisition of equipment repairs by a construction company is recorded in the wrong accounting period. Which transaction-related audit objective has been violated? Which transaction-related objective has been violated if the acquisition has been capitalized as a capital asset rather than expensed?

5-14 Distinguish between the existence and completeness

balance-related audit objectives. State the effect on the financial statements (overstatement or understatement) of a violation of each in the audit of accounts receivable.

5-15 What are specific audit objectives? Explain their relationship to the general audit objectives.

5-16 Identify the management assertion and general balance-related audit objective for the specific balance-related audit objective: All recorded capital assets exist at the balance sheet date.

5-17 Explain how management assertions, general balance-related audit objectives, and specific balance-related audit objectives are developed for an account balance such as accounts receivable.

5-18 Identify the four phases of the audit. What is the relationship of the four phases to the objective of the audit of financial statements?

MULTIPLE CHOICE QUESTIONS

5-19 The following questions concern the reasons auditors do audits, or responsibilities during audits. Choose the best response.

a. Which of the following *best* describes the reason why an independent auditor reports on financial statements?
   (1) A management fraud may exist, and it is more likely to be detected by independent auditors.
   (2) Poorly designed internal controls may be in existence.
   (3) Different interests may exist between the company preparing the statements and the persons using the statements.
   (4) A misstatement of account balances may exist and is generally corrected as the result of the independent auditor's work.

b. An independent audit aids in the communication of economic data because the audit
   (1) guarantees that financial data are fairly presented.
   (2) confirms the accuracy of management's financial representations.
   (3) lends credibility to the financial statements.
   (4) assures the readers of financial statements that any fraudulent activity has been corrected.

c. The major reason an independent auditor gathers audit evidence is to
   (1) form an opinion on the financial statements.
   (2) detect fraud.
   (3) assess control risk.
   (4) evaluate management.

(AICPA adapted)

d. The primary responsibility for the adequacy of disclosure in the financial statements and footnotes rests with the
   (1) partner assigned to the engagement.
   (2) staff member who drafts the statements and footnotes.

   (3) auditor in charge of field work.
   (4) client.

(AICPA adapted)

5-20 The following questions deal with errors or fraud and other irregularities. Choose the best response.

a. An independent auditor has the responsibility to design the audit examination to provide reasonable assurance of detecting errors or fraud and other irregularities that might have a material effect on the financial statements. Which of the following, if material, would be a *fraud* as defined in the *CICA Handbook*?
   (1) Misinterpretation of facts that existed when the financial statements were prepared.
   (2) Misappropriation of an asset or groups of assets.
   (3) Clerical mistakes in the accounting data underlying the financial statements.
   (4) Mistakes in the application of accounting principles.

b. Although the discovery of fraud is not the objective of the public accountant's ordinary audit engagement, the public accountant would be responsible for the detection of fraud if it is material and the public accountant failed to detect it due to
   (1) management's failure to disclose an unrecorded transaction. The documents pertaining to the transaction are kept in a confidential file.
   (2) management's description of internal control.
   (3) management's misstatement of the value of an inventory of precious gems.
   (4) the amount of fidelity bond coverage for certain employees not being compatible with the amount of potential defalcation that might be committed.

c. If an independent auditor's examination leading to an opinion on financial statements causes the auditor to believe that material misstatements exist, the auditor should
   (1) consider the implications and discuss the matter with appropriate levels of management.

(2) make the investigation necessary to determine whether the errors or fraud and other irregularities have in fact occurred.

(3) request that management investigate to determine whether the errors or fraud and other irregularities have in fact occurred.

(4) consider whether the errors or fraud and other irregularities were the result of a failure by employees to comply with existing internal controls.

(AICPA adapted)

DISCUSSION QUESTIONS AND PROBLEMS

5-21 The reports below are taken from the same page of a published annual report.

COREL CORPORATION

MANAGEMENT'S REPORT

Management is responsible for the preparation of the Company's consolidated financial statements. Management believes that the consolidated financial statements fairly reflect the form and substance of transactions and that the consolidated financial statements reasonably present the Company's financial condition and results of operations in conformity with generally accepted accounting principles. Management has included in the Company's consolidated financial statements amounts based on estimates and judgments that it believes are reasonable under the circumstances.

KPMG, the independent auditors appointed by the shareholders of the Company, have audited the Company's consolidated financial statements in accordance with generally accepted auditing standards and they provide an objective, independent review of the fairness of reported operating results and financial position.

The Board of Directors of the Company has an Audit Committee which meets with financial management and the independent auditors to review accounting, auditing, internal accounting controls, and financial reporting matters.

Dr. Michael C.J. Cowpland
Chairman, President and CEO

Michael P.O'Reilly
Vice-President of Finance, CFO
and Treasurer

AUDITOR'S REPORT

We have audited the consolidated balance sheets of Corel Corporation as at November 30, 1997 and November 30, 1996 and the consolidated statements of operations and retained earnings (deficit) and changes in financial position for the years ended November 30, 1997, 1996, and 1995. These financial statements are the responsibility of the Company's management. Our responsibility is to express an opinion on these financial statements based on our audit.

We conducted our audit in accordance with generally accepted auditing standards. Those standards require that we plan and perform an audit to obtain reasonable assurance whether the financial statements are free of material misstatement. An audit includes examining, on a test basis, evidence supporting the amounts and disclosures in the financial statements. An audit also includes assessing the accounting principles used and significant estimates made by management, as well as evaluating the overall financial statement presentation.

In our opinion, these consolidated financial statements present fairly, in all material respects, the financial position of the Company as at November 30, 1997, and 1996, and the results of operations and the changes in financial position for the years ended November 30, 1997, 1996 and 1995 in accordance with generally accepted accounting principles.

Generally accepted accounting principles in Canada differ in some respects from those applicable in the United States (note 10).

KPMG

KPMG
Chartered Accountants
Ottawa, Canada
January 16, 1998
(except for Note 12 which
is at February 23, 1998)

Required

a. What are the purposes of the two reports and who was responsible for writing each?

b. What information does the management's report provide to users of financial statements?

c. Explain the purpose of the audit committee as described in the third paragraph of management's report.

d. Is the auditor's report a standard unqualified report or is it different? Explain your answer.

e. How long after the balance sheet date did the CA firm complete the audit field work?

5-22 Frequently, questions have been raised regarding the responsibility of the independent auditor for the discovery of fraud (including defalcations and other similar irregularities), and concerning the proper course of conduct of the independent auditor when his or her examination discloses specific circumstances that arouse suspicion as to the existence of fraud.

Required

a. What are (1) the function and (2) the responsibilities of the independent auditor in the examination of financial statements? Discuss fully, but in this part do not include fraud in the discussion.

b. What are the responsibilities of the independent auditor for the detection of fraud and other irregularities? Discuss fully.

c. What is the independent auditor's proper course of conduct when his or her examination discloses specific circumstances that arouse his or her suspicion as to the existence of fraud and other irregularities?

(AICPA adapted)

5-23 A competent auditor has done a conscientious job of conducting an audit, but because of a clever fraud by management, a material misstatement is included in the financial statements. The fraud, which is an overstatement of inventory, took place over several years, and it covered up the fact that the company's financial position was rapidly declining. The fraud was accidentally discovered in the latest audit by an unusually capable audit senior, and the audit committee was immediately informed. Subsequent investigation indicated that the company was near bankruptcy, and the value of the stock dropped from $26 per share to $1 per share in less than one month. Among the losing shareholders were pension funds, university endowment funds, retired couples, and widows. The individuals responsible for perpetrating the fraud were bankrupt.

After making an extensive investigation of the audit performance in previous years, the audit committee was satisfied that the auditor had done a high-quality audit and had followed generally accepted auditing standards in every respect. The audit committee concluded that it would be unreasonable to expect auditors to uncover this type of fraud.

Required

State your opinion as to who should bear the loss of the management fraud. Include in your discussion a list of potential bearers of the loss, and state why you believe they should or should not bear the loss.

5-24 The classes of transactions and the titles of the journals used for Phillips Equipment Rental Co. Ltd. are shown at the top of the right-hand column.

Required

a. Identify one financial statement balance that is likely to be affected by each of the nine classes of transactions.

b. For each class of transactions, identify the journal that is likely to be used to record the transactions.

CLASSES OF TRANSACTIONS	TITLES OF JOURNALS
Purchase returns	Cash receipts register
Rental revenue	Cash disbursements journal
Charge-off of uncollectible accounts	Acquisitions journal
Acquisitions of goods and services (except payroll)	Revenue history
Collection of goods and services tax	Payroll journal
Adjusting entries (for payroll)	Adjustments history
Payroll service and payments	
Cash disbursements (except payroll)	
Cash receipts	

c. Identify the transaction cycle that is likely to be affected by each of the nine classes of transactions.

d. Explain how total rental revenue, as cited on the financial statements of Phillips Equipment Rental Co. Ltd., is accumulated in journals and summarized on the financial statements. Assume there are several adjusting entries for rental revenue at the balance sheet date.

5-25 The following general ledger accounts are included in the trial balance for an audit client, Singh Wholesale Stationery Store Inc.:

Accounts payable
Accounts receivable
Accrued sales salaries
Accumulated amortization of furniture and equipment
Advertising expense
Allowance for doubtful accounts
Amortization expense — furniture and equipment
Bad-debt expense
Bonds payable
Cash
Common stock
Furniture and equipment
Goods and services tax payable
Income tax expense
Income tax payable
Insurance expense
Interest expense
Interest income
Interest receivable
Inventory
Notes payable
Notes receivable — trade
Prepaid interest expense
Property tax expense
Property tax payable
Purchases
Rent expense
Retained earnings
Salaries, office and general
Sales
Sales salaries expense
Telephone and fax expense
Travelling expense
Unexpired insurance

Required

a. Identify the accounts in the trial balance that are likely to be included in each transaction cycle. Some accounts will be included in more than one cycle. Use the format shown below.

CYCLE	BALANCE SHEET ACCOUNTS	INCOME STATEMENT ACCOUNTS
Sales and collection		
Acquisition and payment		
Payroll and personnel		
Inventory and warehousing		
Capital acquisition and repayment		

b. How would the general ledger accounts in the trial balance probably differ if the company were a retail store rather than a wholesale company? How would they differ for a hospital or a government unit?

5-26 The following is the detailed chart of accounts for Atlantic Metal Specialties Ltd.

BALANCE SHEET ACCOUNTS (100–299)

Assets (100–199)

Current Assets (100–129)

101	Cash in bank
102	Payroll cash
103	Petty cash
106	Notes receivable — trade
109	Accounts receivable
109.1	Allowance for doubtful accounts
115	Finished goods
116	Work in process
117	Materials
120	Prepaid property tax
121	Prepaid insurance
122	Miscellaneous prepaid items

Capital Assets (130–159)

130	Land
132	Buildings
132.1	Accumulated amortization — buildings
135	Machinery and equipment — factory
135.1	Accumulated amortization — machinery and equipment — factory
143	Automobiles
143.1	Accumulated amortization — automobiles
146	Office furniture and fixtures
146.1	Accumulated amortization — office furniture and fixtures

Intangible Assets (170–179)

170	Goodwill
171	Patents
172	Franchises, licences, and other privileges

Liabilities and Capital (200–299)

Current Liabilities (200–219)

201	Notes payable
203	Accounts payable
206	Accrued payroll
207	Accrued interest payable
208	Accrued sales tax
200	Other accrued liabilities
210	Goods and services tax payable
211	Employees income tax payable
212	Employee benefits payable
214	Estimated federal income tax payable
216	Long-term debt (due within one year)
218	Dividends payable

Long-Term Liabilities (220–229)

220	Bonds payable
222	Mortgage payable
224	Other long-term debt
226	Future income tax liability

Capital (250–299)

250	Common stock
260	Retained earnings

INCOME STATEMENT ACCOUNTS (300–899)

Sales (300–349)

301	Sales
301.1	Sales returns
301.2	Sales allowances
301.3	Sales discounts
301.4	Goods and services tax

Cost of Goods Sold (350–399)

351	Cost of goods sold
353	Purchases
353.1	Purchase returns
353.2	Purchase allowances
356	Materials price variance
357	Materials quantity variance
358	Purchases discounts
366	Labour rate variance
367	Labour efficiency variance
372	Applied factory overhead
376	Factory overhead spending variance
377	Factory overhead idle capacity variance
378	Factory overhead efficiency variance
379	Over- or underapplied factory overhead

Factory Overhead (400–499)

400	Factory overhead control
401	Salaries — factory
411	Indirect materials
412	Indirect labour
414	Freight in
417	Training
420	Overtime premium
422	Employee benefits
425	Vacation pay
427	Worker's compensation
434	Fuel — factory
436	Light and power
438	Telephone and fax
440	Tools
442	Defective work
450	Insurance expense
460	Amortization expense — buildings
461	Amortization expense — machinery and equipment
462	Repairs and maintenance of buildings
463	Repairs and maintenance of roads
464	Repairs and maintenance of transportation facilities
465	Repairs and maintenance of machinery and equipment
480	Rent of equipment
485	Property tax
486	Amortization of patents

Marketing Expenses (500–599)

500	Marketing expenses control
501	Salaries — sales supervision
503	Salaries — salespeople
504	Salaries — clerical help
507	Sales commissions
515	Freight out
522	Employee benefits
530	Supplies
534	Fuel
536	Light and power
538	Telephone and fax
546	Postage
548	Travel expenses
550	Insurance expense
560	Amortization expense — buildings
561	Amortization expense — automobiles
562	Repairs and maintenance of buildings
565	Advertising
567	Display materials
568	Conventions and exhibits
580	Rent of equipment
585	Property tax

Administrative Expenses (600–699)

600	Administrative expenses control
601	Salaries — administrative
604	Salaries — administrative clerical help
620	Overtime premium
622	Employee benefits
630	Supplies
634	Fuel
636	Light and power
638	Telephone and fax
646	Postage
648	Travel expenses
650	Insurance expense
660	Amortization expense — buildings
661	Amortization expense — furniture and fixtures
662	Repairs and maintenance of buildings
670	Legal and accounting fees
680	Rent of equipment
685	Property tax
691	Donations
693	Uncollectible accounts expense

Other Expenses (700–749)

701	Interest paid on notes payable
703	Interest paid on mortgage
707	Interest paid on bonds
708	Goods and services tax

Other Income (800–849)

801	Income from investments
816	Interest earned
817	Rental income
818	Miscellaneous income

Income Deductions (890–899)

890	Federal income tax expense

c. For each account in the chart of accounts, identify the transaction cycle to which the account pertains. Some accounts belong to more than one cycle.

5-27 Following are the detailed financial statement titles for Podilchak Electronics Ltd. The business primarily involves repairing and selling parts for televisions, VCRs, CD players, and video games.

PODILCHAK ELECTRONICS LTD. BALANCE SHEET December 31, 1997

Assets
Current assets
  Cash
  Accounts receivable
  Less: Allowance for doubtful accounts
  Notes receivable
  Inventories — at average cost
  Supplies on hand
  Prepaid expenses
    Total current assets
Long-term investments
  Securities at cost (market value $62,000)
Capital assets
  Land — at cost
  Buildings — at cost
  Less: Accumulated amortization
    Total capital assets
Intangible assets
  Goodwill
    Total assets

Liabilities and Shareholders' Equity
Current liabilities
  Notes payable to banks
  Accounts payable
  Goods and services tax payable
  Accrued interest on notes payable
  Accrued federal income taxes
  Accrued salaries, wages, and other expenses
  Deposits received from customers
    Total current liabilities
Long-term debt
  Twenty-year 8 percent debentures, due July 1, 1999
    Total liabilities
Shareholders' equity
  Preferred stock, $1.80, cumulative
  Authorized and outstanding, 10,000 shares
  Common
  Authorized, 200,000 shares; issued and outstanding, 100,000 shares
Earnings retained in the business
  Appropriated
  Unappropriated
    Total shareholders' equity
      Total liabilities and shareholders' equity

Required

a. Explain the differences among a chart of accounts, a general ledger trial balance, and financial statements. What are the relationships among them?

b. What are the reasons for and benefits of associating general ledger trial balance accounts with transaction cycles?

PODILCHAK ELECTRONICS LTD.
INCOME STATEMENT
for the year ended December 31, 1997

Sales
  Revenues
    Less: Sales discounts
      Sales returns and allowances
      Goods and services tax
    Net sales

Cost of goods sold
  Parts inventory, January 1, 1997
  Purchases of parts
  Less: Purchase discounts
    Net purchases

  Freight and transportation-in
  Total parts available for sale
  Less: Merchandise inventory, December 31, 1997
    Cost of goods sold
    Gross profit on sales

Operating expenses
  Selling expenses
    Sales salaries and commissions
    Sales office salaries
    Travel and entertainment
    Advertising expense
    Freight and transportation-out
    Shipping supplies and expense
    Postage and stationery
    Amortization of sales equipment
    Telephone and fax
  Administrative expenses
    Officers' salaries
    Office salaries
    Legal and professional services
    Utilities expense
    Insurance expense
    Amortization of building
    Amortization of office equipment
    Stationery, supplies, and postage
    Miscellaneous office expenses
      Income from operations

Other income
  Rental income

Other expense
  Interest on bonds and notes
    Income before taxes
Income taxes
    Net income for the year
    Earnings per share

Required

Identify the accounts in the detailed financial statements that are likely to be included in each transaction cycle. Some accounts will be included in more than one cycle. Use the format shown below.

CYCLE	BALANCE SHEET ACCOUNTS	INCOME STATEMENT ACCOUNTS
Sales and collection		
Acquisition and payment		
Payroll and personnel		
Inventory and warehousing		
Capital acquisition and repayment		

5-28 The following are specific balance-related audit objectives applied to the audit of accounts receivable (a through h) and management assertions (1 through 5). The list referred to in the specific balance-related audit objectives is the list of the accounts receivable from each customer at the balance sheet date.

SPECIFIC BALANCE-RELATED AUDIT OBJECTIVE

a. There are no unrecorded receivables.
b. Receivables have not been sold or discounted.
c. Uncollectible accounts have been provided for.
d. Receivables that have become uncollectible have been written off.
e. All accounts on the list are expected to be collected within one year.
f. Any agreement or condition that restricts the nature of trade receivables is known and disclosed.
g. All accounts on the list arose from the normal course of business and are not due from related parties.
h. Sales cutoff at year end is proper.

MANAGEMENT ASSERTION

1. Existence
2. Occurrence
3. Completeness
4. Valuation
5. Measurement
6. Rights and obligations
7. Presentation and disclosure

Required

For each specific balance-related audit objective, identify the appropriate management assertion.

5-29 The following are specific transaction-related audit objectives applied to the audit of cash disbursements (a through f), management assertions (1 through 7), and general transaction-related audit objectives (8 through 13).

SPECIFIC AUDIT OBJECTIVE

a. Recorded cash disbursement transactions are for the amount of goods or services received and are correctly recorded. 4.
b. Cash disbursement transactions are properly included in the accounts payable master file and are correctly summarized. 2
c. Recorded cash disbursements are for goods and services actually received. 1
d. Cash disbursement transactions are properly classified. 7
e. Existing cash disbursement transactions are recorded. 3
f. Cash disbursement transactions are recorded on the correct dates. 5

MANAGEMENT ASSERTION

1. Existence
2. Occurrence
3. Completeness
4. Valuation
5. Measurement
6. Rights and obligations
7. Presentation and disclosure

GENERAL TRANSACTION-RELATED AUDIT OBJECTIVE

Occurence
8. Existence *c*
9. Completeness *e*
10. Accuracy *a*
11. Classification *d*
12. Timing *f*
13. Posting and summarization *b*

GENERAL BALANCE-RELATED AUDIT OBJECTIVE

1. Existence
2. Completeness
3. Valuation
4. Accuracy
5. Classification
6. Cutoff
7. Detail tie-in
8. Rights and obligations
9. Presentation and disclosure

Required

a. Explain the differences among management assertions, general transaction-related audit objectives, and specific transaction-related audit objectives and their relationships to one another.

b. For each specific transaction-related audit objective, identify the appropriate management assertion.

c. For each specific transaction-related audit objective, identify the appropriate general transaction-related audit objective.

5-30 The following are two specific balance-related audit objectives in the audit of accounts payable. The list referred to in the objectives is the aged accounts payable trial balance produced using the supplier master file. The total of the list equals the accounts payable balance on the general ledger.

1. All accounts payable included on the list represent amounts due to valid vendors.

2. There are no unrecorded accounts payable.

Required

a. Explain the difference between these two specific balance-related audit objectives.

b. Which of these two objectives applies to the general balance-related audit objective existence, and which one applies to completeness?

c. For the audit of accounts payable, which of these two specific balance-related audit objectives would usually be more important? Explain.

5-31 The following are nine general balance-related audit objectives for the audit of any balance sheet account (1 through 9) and eleven specific balance-related audit objectives for the audit of property, plant, and equipment (a through k).

SPECIFIC BALANCE-RELATED AUDIT OBJECTIVE

a. There are no unrecorded capital assets in use.
b. The company has valid title to the assets owned.
c. Details of property, plant, and equipment agree with the general ledger.
d. Capital assets physically exist and are being used for the purpose intended.
e. Property, plant, and equipment are recorded at the correct amount.
f. The company has a contractual right for use of assets leased.
g. Liens or other encumbrances on property, plant, and equipment items are known and disclosed.
h. Cash disbursements and/or accrual cutoff for property, plant, and equipment items are proper.
i. Expense accounts do not contain amounts that should have been capitalized.
j. Amortization is determined in accordance with an acceptable method and is materially correct as computed.
k. Capital asset accounts have been properly adjusted for declines in historical cost.

Required

a. What are the purposes of the general balance-related audit objectives and the specific balance-related audit objectives? Explain the relationship between these two sets of objectives.

b. For each general balance-related objective, identify one or more specific balance-related audit objectives. No letter can be used for more than one general balance-related audit objective.

CASES

5-32 Leslie Donald is the audit manager responsible for the annual audit of ABC Electronics Ltd. (ABC), a Canadian public company involved in the manufacture and distribution of highly competitive electronic products. He has completed his review of the audit files and has discussed a number of issues with the audit senior. Since the partner in charge of the engagement has arranged to meet with the chairman of ABC's audit committee three days from now, Leslie has decided to write a memo to the partner to outline a number of matters that bother him. These concerns arise as

a result of the following information that has come to his attention:

1. Based on results for the first three quarters of the year, ABC management estimated annual net income of $1,000,000. Primarily as a result of audit adjustments to provide for obsolete inventory, net income has been reduced to slightly more than $300,000. Consequently, management will not be receptive to proposals for any adjustments that further reduce earnings.

2. The senior had written short audit notes throughout the files, including the following:

> Testing of controls over disbursements showed that, out of a sample of 150 cheques tested, 24 cases of incomplete supporting documentation were discovered.

> Twelve of the 24 exceptions found in our disbursement tests were payments totalling $50,000 to some freelance management consultants who traditionally have been paid without an invoice. These payments have been satisfactorily verified by telephone conversations. The other 12 cheques were issued to Sales Promotion Enterprises Ltd., and, although not supported by invoices, were approved by Bill Rogerson, the general manager. These cheques total $85,000 and all bear a second endorsement by I. B. Graten. They have been charged to account 809, Inventory on Consignment, and the inventory has been confirmed by Sales Promotion Enterprises Ltd. as being on hand at year end. Sales Promotion Enterprises Ltd. is properly included in the master vendor files. Therefore, there appears to be no weakness in computer controls relating to these payments.

> Our tests of sales invoices disclosed no errors or unusual conditions except that invoices to Global Galaxy Stores (Global) are priced at 5 percent over the approved price list. By industry standards, it appears that such conditions are not justified. The invoicing clerk's explanation was that this policy was established verbally by Bill Rogerson, and Global was the only customer to which this price applied. This explanation appears to be satisfactory since Global has always paid its account within 30 days. Since Global is also our client, I have agreed the year end balance to our Global audit files.

3. Leslie asked Bill Rogerson for an explanation for payments to Sales Promotion Enterprises Ltd. Bill claimed that he could not remember the transaction well but, in view of the immaterial amount involved and his approval for each payment, suggested that the payments were of no audit significance. Later, Leslie and Bill had lunch together, and Bill offered some additional information on a confidential basis. He said that Sales Promotion Enterprises Ltd. was owned by a buyer for one of ABC's largest customers, Global. The payments guaranteed orders from Global at prices favourable to ABC, and orders in the past year had exceeded $8,000,000. Bill explained that the arrangements were made by ABC's president and, for obvious reasons, were to be considered highly confidential.

Since Bill seemed to be in a talkative mood, Leslie asked him about the other unsupported payments. Bill claimed to have no knowledge of the management consultants.

Required

Assume the role of Leslie Donald, the audit manager, and prepare the memo to the audit partner. Identify potential problems. For each problem, indicate the parties affected by the problem, alternative methods of dealing with the problem, reporting responsibilities, and a recommended course of action.

(CICA adapted)

5-33 CA has been the auditor for several years of Widget Limited, a widely owned public company which operates a wholesaling business. During the last few years, the company's net income has been declining steadily and its management has been criticized severely by some influential shareholders.

At the commencement of the current year's audit, CA was given draft financial statements that showed a large increase in net income over the previous year. Suspecting that income may have been overstated for the current year's audit, CA has determined that
- The company's method of operation and level of efficiency are unchanged.
- Sales volume was the same this year as for the past several years.
- Unit selling prices and purchasing costs have not changed.
- The company's nonwholesaling revenues have remained at the same low level.

Required

List the methods that could have been used to overstate net income for the year.

(CICA adapted)

6

AUDIT EVIDENCE

SOMETIMES THE MOST IMPORTANT EVIDENCE ISN'T FOUND IN THE ACCOUNTING RECORDS

Crenshaw Properties Inc. (CPI) was a real-estate developer that specialized in self-storage facilities that it sold to limited partner investors. CPI's role was to identify projects, serve as general partner with a small investment, and raise capital from pension funds. CPI had an extensive network of people who marketed these investments on a commission basis. As managing partner, CPI earned significant fees for related activities, including promotional fees, investment management fees, and real-estate commissions.

As long as the investments were successful, CPI prospered. Because the investments were reasonably long-term, the underlying investors did not pay careful attention to them. However, in the mid-1980s, the market for self-storage units in many parts of the country became oversaturated. Occupancy rates, rental rates, and market values declined.

Ralph Smalley, of Hambusch, Robinson & Co., did the annual audit of CPI. As part of the audit, Smalley obtained financial statements for all of the partnerships in which CPI was the general partner. He traced amounts back to the original partnership documents and determined that amounts agreed with partnership records. Smalley also determined that they were mathematically accurate. The purpose of doing these tests was to determine that the partnership assets, at original cost, exceeded liabilities, including the mortgage on the poperty and loans from investors. Under the agreements, CPI as a general partner was liable for any deficiency.

Every year, Smalley concluded that there were no significant deficiencies in partnership net assets for which CPI would be liable. What Smalley failed to recognize in the late 1980s, however, was that current market prices had declined significantly due to cash flows that were lower than those projected in the original partnership offering

This chapter begins by describing audit evidence and the four major evidence decisions. It also discusses the meaning of *sufficient appropriate audit evidence*. The seven types of evidence available to satisfy the third examination standard are then defined and discussed. The chapter ends with a more detailed discussion of analytical procedures.

NATURE OF EVIDENCE

OBJECTIVE 6-1

Explain the nature of audit evidence.

Evidence was defined in Chapter 1 as *any information used by the auditor* to determine whether the information being audited is stated in accordance with the established criterion. The information varies widely in the extent to which it persuades the auditor whether financial statements are stated in accordance with generally accepted accounting principles. Evidence includes persuasive information, such as the auditor's count of marketable securities, and less persuasive information, such as responses to questions by the client's employees.

AUDIT EVIDENCE CONTRASTED WITH LEGAL AND SCIENTIFIC EVIDENCE

The use of evidence is not unique to auditors. Evidence is also used extensively by scientists, lawyers, and historians.

Through television, most people are familiar with the use of evidence in legal cases dealing with the guilt or innocence of a party charged with a crime such as robbery. In legal cases, there are well-defined rules of evidence enforced by a judge for the protection of the innocent. It is common, for example, for legal evidence to be judged inadmissible on the grounds that it is irrelevant, prejudicial, or based on hearsay.

Similarly, in scientific experiments the scientist obtains evidence to draw conclusions about a theory. Assume, for example, a medical scientist is evaluating a new medicine that may provide relief for asthma sufferers. The scientist will gather evidence from a large number of controlled experiments over an extended period of time to determine the effectiveness of the medicine.

The auditor also gathers evidence to draw conclusions. Different evidence is used by auditors than by scientists or lawyers, and it is used in different ways, but in all three cases, evidence is used to reach conclusions. Table 6-1 illustrates key characteristics of evidence from the perspective of a scientist doing an experiment, a legal case involving an accused thief, and an auditor of financial statements. There are six bases of comparison. Note the similarities and differences among the three professions.

AUDIT EVIDENCE DECISIONS

OBJECTIVE 6-2

Describe the four audit evidence decisions that the auditor must make to create an audit program.

A major decision facing every auditor is determining the appropriate types and *amount of evidence* to accumulate to be satisfied that the components of the client's financial statements and the overall statements are fairly stated. This judgment is important because of the prohibitive cost of examining and evaluating all available evidence. For example, in an audit of financial statements of most organizations, it is impossible for the public accountant to examine the contents of all computer files or available evidence such as cancelled cheques, vendors' invoices, customer orders, payroll time cards, and the many other types of documents and records.

The auditor's *decisions* on evidence accumulation can be broken into the following four subdecisions:

TABLE 6-1

CHARACTERISTICS OF
EVIDENCE FOR A
SCIENTIFIC
EXPERIMENT, A LEGAL
CASE, AND AN AUDIT
OF FINANCIAL
STATEMENTS

BASIS OF COMPARISON	SCIENTIFIC EXPERIMENT INVOLVING TESTING A MEDICINE	LEGAL CASE INVOLVING AN ACCUSED THIEF	AUDIT OF FINANCIAL STATEMENTS
Use of the evidence	Determine effects of using the medicine	Decide guilt or innocence of accused	Determine if statements are fairly presented
Nature of evidence	Results of repeated experiments	Direct evidence and testimony by witnesses and party involved	Various types of audit evidence generated by the auditor, third parties, and the client
Party or parties evaluating evidence	Scientist	Jury and judge	Auditor
Certainty of conclusions from evidence	Vary from uncertain to near certainty	Requires guilt beyond a reasonable doubt	High level of assurance
Nature of conclusions	Recommend or not recommend use of medicine	Innocence or guilt of party	Issue one of several alternative types of auditor's reports
Typical consequences of incorrect conclusions from evidence	Society uses ineffective or harmful medicine	Guilty party is not penalized or innocent party found guilty	Statement users make incorrect decisions and auditor may be sued

1. Which audit procedures to use
2. What sample size to select for a given procedure
3. Which particular items to select from the population
4. When to perform the procedures

AUDIT PROCEDURES

An *audit procedure* is the detailed instruction for the collection of a particular type of audit evidence that is to be obtained at some time during the audit. For example, evidence such as physical inventory counts, comparisons of cancelled cheques with cash disbursements, journal entries, and shipping document details is collected using audit procedures.

In designing audit procedures, it is common to spell them out in sufficiently specific terms to permit their use as instructions during the audit. For example, the following is an audit procedure for the verification of cash disbursements:

- Obtain the cash disbursements report and compare the payee name, amount, and date on the cancelled cheque with the cash disbursement report.

Several commonly used audit procedure terms are defined and illustrated with examples later in this chapter.

SAMPLE SIZE

Once an audit procedure is selected, it is possible to vary the sample size from one to all the items in the population being tested. In the audit procedure above, suppose there are 6,600 cheques recorded in the cash disbursements report. The auditor might select a sample size of 40 cheques for comparison with the cash disbursements report. The decision of how many items to test must be made by the auditor for each audit procedure. The sample size for any given procedure is likely to vary from audit to audit.

ITEMS TO SELECT

After the sample size has been determined for a particular audit procedure, it is still necessary to decide the particular items to test. If the auditor decides, for example, to select 40 cancelled cheques from a population of 6,600 for comparison with the cash disbursements journal, several different methods can be used to select the specific cheques to be examined. The auditor could (1) select a week and examine the first 40 cheques, (2) select the 40 cheques with the largest amounts (also known as "key items"), (3) select the cheques randomly, or (4) select those cheques the auditor thinks are most likely to be in error. Or a combination of these methods could be used.

TIMING

An audit of financial statements usually covers a period such as a year, and an audit is usually not completed until several weeks or months after the end of the period. The timing of audit procedures can therefore vary from early in the accounting period to long after it has ended. In the audit of financial statements, the client normally wants the audit completed one to three months after year end.

Audit procedures often incorporate sample size, items to select, and timing into the procedure. The following is a modification of the audit procedure previously used to include all four audit evidence decisions. (Italics identify the timing, items to select, and sample size decisions).

- Obtain the *October* cash disbursements report and compare the payee name, amount, and date on the cancelled cheque with the cash disbursements report for a *randomly selected sample of 40* cheque numbers.

AUDIT PROGRAM

The detailed instructions for the entire collection of evidence for an audit area is called an *audit program*. The audit program always includes a list of the audit procedures. It usually also includes the sample sizes, items to select, and the timing of the tests. Normally, there is an audit program for each component of the audit. Therefore, there will be an audit program for accounts receivable, for sales, and so on. An example of an audit program that includes audit procedures, sample size, items to select, and timing is given on page 325 in Table 10-4. The right side of the audit program also includes the audit objectives for each procedure, as studied in Chapter 5.

Most auditors use computers to facilitate the preparation of audit programs. The simplest application of computers is the inputting of the audit program to facilitate changes and updating from one year to the next. A more sophisticated application is the use of a special software program that helps the auditor during the planning considerations of the audit to select appropriate procedures from an audit procedures data base.

PERSUASIVENESS OF EVIDENCE

OBJECTIVE 6-3

Explain the third examination standard and discuss its relationship to the three determinants of the persuasiveness of evidence.

The third examination standard requires the auditor to accumulate *sufficient appropriate audit evidence to support the opinion issued*. Because of the nature of audit evidence and the cost considerations of doing an audit, it is unlikely that the auditor will be completely convinced that the opinion is correct. However, the auditor must be persuaded that his or her opinion is correct with a high level of assurance. By combining all evidence from the entire audit, the auditor is able to decide when he or she is sufficiently persuaded to issue an auditor's report.

The three determinants of the persuasiveness of evidence are *sufficiency*, *appropriateness*, and *timeliness*. Notice that the first two are taken directly from the third examination standard.

SUFFICIENCY

The *quantity* of evidence obtained determines its sufficiency. Quantity is measured primarily by the sample size the auditor selects. For a given audit procedure, the evidence obtained from a sample of 50 would ordinarily be more sufficient than from a sample of 25.

There are several factors that determine the appropriate sample size in audits. The two most important ones are the auditor's expectation of errors and the effectiveness of the client's internal controls. To illustrate, assume that during the audit of Lau Computer Parts Inc., the auditor concludes that there is a high likelihood of obsolete inventory due to the nature of the client's industry. The auditor would sample more inventory items for obsolescence in an audit such as this than in one where the likelihood of obsolescence was low. Similarly, if the auditor concludes that a client has effective rather than ineffective internal controls over recording capital assets, a smaller sample size in the audit of purchases of capital assets is warranted. Expectation of errors and internal controls and their effect on sample size are critical topics in this book and are studied in depth in subsequent chapters, starting with Chapter 8.

In addition to affecting sample size, the particular items tested affect the sufficiency of evidence. Samples containing population items with large dollar values, items with a high likelihood of error, and items that are representative of the population are usually considered sufficient. In contrast, most auditors would usually consider samples insufficient that contain only the largest dollar items from the population, unless these items make up a large portion of the total population.

APPROPRIATENESS

Appropriateness or *competence* refers to the quality of evidence, to the degree to which the evidence can be considered believable or worthy of trust. If evidence is considered to be highly competent, it is a great help in persuading the auditor that the financial statements are fairly stated. For example, if an auditor counted inventory, that evidence would be more appropriate than if management gave the auditor its own figures. Generally, the more appropriate the evidence, the less evidence is needed. Auditors, as well as the authors of this text, also use the term *reliability of evidence* as a synonym for appropriateness.

Appropriateness of evidence deals only with the audit procedures selected. Appropriateness cannot be improved by selecting a larger sample size or different population items. It can only be improved by selecting audit procedures that contain a higher quality of one or more of the following six characteristics of appropriate evidence.

Relevance Evidence must *pertain to or be relevant to the objective* the auditor is testing before it can be persuasive. For example, assume the auditor is concerned that a client is failing to bill customers for shipments (completeness transaction-related audit objective). If the auditor selected a sample of duplicate sales invoices and traced each to related shipping documents, the evidence would *not be relevant* for the completeness objective. A relevant procedure would be to compare a sample of shipping documents with related duplicate sales invoices to determine if each shipping document had been billed. The reason the second audit procedure is relevant and the first is not is because the shipment of goods is the normal criteria used for determining whether a sale has occurred and should have been billed. By tracing from shipping documents to duplicate sales invoices, the auditor can determine if shipments have been billed to customers. When the auditor traces from duplicate sales invoices to shipping documents, it is impossible to find unbilled shipments.

Relevance can only be considered in terms of specific audit objectives. Evidence may be relevant to one objective but not to a different one. In the previous example, when the auditor traced from the duplicate sales invoices to related shipping documents, the evidence was relevant to the existence transaction-related audit objective. Most evidence is relevant to more than one, but not all, objectives.

Auditor's direct knowledge   Evidence obtained directly by the auditor through physical examination, observation, computation, and inspection is more appropriate than information obtained indirectly. For example, if the auditor calculates the gross margin as a percentage of sales and compares it with previous periods using an audit software program, the evidence would be more reliable than if the auditor relied on the calculations of the controller.

Independence of provider   Evidence obtained from a source outside the entity is more reliable than that obtained from within. For example, external evidence such as communications from banks, lawyers, or customers is generally regarded as more reliable than answers obtained from inquiries of the client. Similarly, documents that originate from outside the client's organization are considered more reliable than those that originate within the company and have never left the client's organization. An example of external evidence is an insurance policy, while a purchase requisition is internal evidence.

Effectiveness of client's internal controls   When a client's internal controls are effective, evidence obtained therefrom is more reliable than when they are weak. For example, if internal controls over sales and billing are effective, the auditor can obtain more appropriate evidence from sales invoices and shipping documents than if the controls are inadequate.

Qualifications of individuals providing the information   Although the source of information is independent, the evidence will not be reliable unless the individual providing it is qualified to do so. For this reason, communications from law firms and bank confirmations are typically more highly regarded than accounts receivable confirmations from persons not familiar with the business world. Also, evidence obtained directly by the auditor may not be reliable if he or she lacks the qualifications to evaluate the evidence. For example, examination of an inventory of diamonds by an auditor who is not trained to distinguish between diamonds and glass would not provide reliable evidence of the existence of diamonds.

Degree of objectivity   Objective evidence is more reliable than evidence that requires considerable judgment to determine whether it is correct. Examples of objective evidence include confirmation of accounts receivable and bank balances, the physical count of securities and cash, and the adding (footing) of a list of accounts payable to determine if it is the same as the balance in the general ledger. Examples of subjective evidence include communication from a client's lawyers as to the likely outcome of outstanding lawsuits against the client, observation of obsolescence of inventory during physical examination, and inquiries of the credit manager about the collectibility of noncurrent accounts receivable. In evaluating the reliability of subjective evidence, the qualifications of the person providing the evidence is important.

TIMELINESS

The timeliness of audit evidence can refer either to when it was accumulated or to the period covered by the audit. Evidence is usually more persuasive for balance sheet accounts when it is obtained as close to the balance sheet date as possible. For example, the auditor's count of marketable securities on the balance sheet date would be more persuasive than a count two months earlier. For income statement accounts, evidence is more persuasive if there is a sample from the entire period under audit rather than from only a part of the period. For example, a random sample of sales transactions for the entire year would be more persuasive than a sample from only the first six months.

COMBINED EFFECT

The persuasiveness of evidence can be evaluated only after considering the combination of sufficiency, appropriateness, and timeliness. A large sample of evidence is not persuasive unless it is relevant to the audit objective being tested. A large sample of evidence that is neither appropriate nor timely is also not persuasive. Similarly, a small sample of only one or two pieces of appropriate and timely evidence also lacks persuasiveness. The auditor must evaluate the degree to which all three qualities have been met in deciding persuasiveness.

There are direct relationships among the four evidence decisions and the three qualities that determine the persuasiveness of evidence. Table 6-2 shows those relationships.

To illustrate the relationships shown in Table 6-2, assume an auditor is verifying inventory that is a major item in the financial statements. Generally accepted auditing standards require that the auditor be reasonably persuaded that inventory is not materially misstated. The auditor must therefore obtain a sufficient amount of appropriate and timely evidence about inventory. This means deciding which procedures to use for auditing inventory to satisfy the appropriateness requirement, as well as determining the proper sample size and items to select from the population to satisfy the sufficiency requirement. Finally, the auditor must determine timing of these procedures. The combination of these four evidence decisions must result in sufficiently persuasive evidence to satisfy the auditor that inventory is materially correct. The audit program for inventory will reflect these decisions. In practice, the auditor applies the four evidence decisions to specific audit objectives in deciding sufficient appropriate evidence.

TABLE 6-2

RELATIONSHIPS AMONG EVIDENCE DECISIONS AND PERSUASIVENESS

AUDIT EVIDENCE DECISIONS	QUALITIES AFFECTING PERSUASIVENESS OF EVIDENCE
Audit procedures	Appropriateness Relevance Auditor's direct knowledge Independence of provider Effectiveness of internal controls Qualifications of provider Objectivity of evidence
Sample size and items to select	Sufficiency Adequate sample size Selecting appropriate population items
Timing	Timeliness When procedures are performed Portion of period audited

PERSUASIVENESS AND COST

In making decisions about evidence for a given audit, both persuasiveness and cost must be considered. It is rare when only one type of evidence is available for verifying information. The persuasiveness and cost of all alternatives should be considered before selecting the best type or types. The auditor's goal is to obtain a sufficient amount of timely, reliable evidence that is relevant to the information being verified, and to do so at the lowest possible total cost. However, cost is never an adequate justification for omitting a necessary procedure.

TYPES OF AUDIT EVIDENCE

OBJECTIVE 6-4

List and describe the seven types of evidence used in auditing.

The *CICA Handbook*, in the third examination standard, specifies that audit evidence may be obtained through the methods of inspection, observation, inquiry, confirmation, computation, and analysis and then defines and explains the terms in Section 5300. These methods can be combined, divided, and renamed into seven broad categories or *types of evidence* as follows:

EVIDENCE METHODS IN *CICA HANDBOOK*	SEVEN TYPES OF EVIDENCE
• Inspection	• Physical examination
• Observation	• Documentation
• Inquiry	• Observation
• Confirmation	• Inquiries of the client
• Computation	• Confirmation
• Analysis	• Reperformance
	• Analytical procedures

The seven broad categories are defined and discussed shortly. The order in which the categories are listed and discussed should not be interpreted as signifying the relative strengths of the types or categories of evidence. In other words, the fact that "physical examination" appears at the top of the list does not mean that any evidence belonging to that category is automatically stronger than evidence belonging to another category. The quality of each piece of evidence, regardless of type, must be evaluated according to the criteria of its type.

Before beginning the study of types of evidence, it is useful to show the relationships among auditing standards, which were studied in Chapter 1, types of evidence, and the four evidence decisions discussed earlier in this chapter. These relationships are shown in Figure 6-1. Notice that the standards are general, whereas audit procedures are specific. Types of evidence are broader than procedures and narrower than the standards. Every audit procedure obtains one or more types of evidence.

PHYSICAL EXAMINATION

Physical examination is the inspection or count by the auditor of a *tangible asset*. This type of evidence is most often associated with inventory and cash, but it is also applicable to the verification of securities, notes receivable, and tangible capital assets. The distinction between the physical examination of assets, such as marketable securities and cash, and the examination of documents, such as cancelled cheques and sales documents, is important for auditing purposes. If the object being examined, such as a sales invoice, has no inherent value, the evidence is called *documentation*. For example, before a cheque is signed, it is a document; after it is signed, it becomes an asset; and when it is cancelled, it becomes a document again. Technically, physical examination of the cheque can only occur while the cheque is an asset.

Physical examination, which is a direct means of verifying that an asset actually exists (existence objective), is regarded as one of the most reliable and useful types of audit evidence. Generally, physical examination is an objective means of ascertaining both the quantity and the description of the asset. In some cases, it is also a useful method for evaluating an asset's condition or quality. However, physical examination is not sufficient evidence to verify that existing assets are owned by the client (rights and obligations objective), and in many cases the auditor is not qualified to judge such qualitative factors as obsolescence or authenticity (net realizable value for the valuation objective). Proper valuation for financial statement purposes usually cannot be determined by physical examination.

FIGURE 6-1

Relationships Among
Auditing Standards,
Types of Evidence, and
the Four Audit
Evidence Decisions

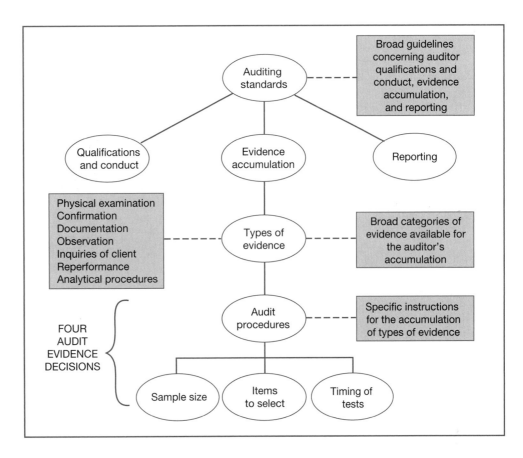

CONFIRMATION

Confirmation describes the *receipt* of a *written or oral response* from an *independent third party* verifying the accuracy of information that was *requested by the auditor*. The request is made to the client, and the client asks the independent third party to respond directly to the auditor. Since confirmations come from sources who are independent of the client, they are a highly regarded and often used type of evidence. However, confirmations are relatively costly to obtain and may cause some inconvenience to those asked to supply them. Therefore, they are not used in every instance in which they are applicable. Because of the high reliability of confirmations, auditors typically obtain written responses rather than oral ones whenever it is practical. Written confirmations are easier for supervisors to review and provide more support if it is necessary to demonstrate that a confirmation was received.

Whether or not confirmations should be used depends on the reliability needs of the situation as well as the alternative evidence available. Traditionally, confirmations are not used to verify individual transactions between organizations, such as sales transactions, because the auditor can use documents for that purpose. Similarly, confirmations are seldom used in the audit of capital-asset additions because these can be verified adequately by documentation and physical examination. While confirmations are generally a very reliable form of evidence, the auditor must be aware that the third party providing the confirmation may be careless or may not have the correct information; the auditor should not automatically assume the confirmation is correct, especially if the response is unexpected or contradicts other evidence. In addition, the third party may not be independent of the client.

The *CICA Handbook* requires confirmation of accounts receivable except: when combined inherent risk and control risk (defined on pages 240–241) and other substantive procedures would provide sufficient appropriate evidence; or when confirmation would be ineffective in providing reliable audit evidence. This requirement exists because accounts receivable usually represent a significant balance on the financial statements, and confirmations are a highly reliable type of evidence about them.

Although confirmation is not required for any account other than accounts receivable, this type of evidence is useful in verifying many types of information. The major types of information that are frequently confirmed, along with the source of the confirmation, are indicated in Table 6-3.

TABLE 6-3

INFORMATION
FREQUENTLY
CONFIRMED

INFORMATION	SOURCE
Assets	
Cash in bank	Bank
Accounts receivable	Customer
Notes receivable	Maker
Owned inventory out on consignment	Consignee
Inventory held in public warehouses	Public warehouse
Cash surrender value of life insurance	Insurance company
Liabilities	
Accounts payable	Creditor
Notes payable	Lender
Advances from customers	Customer
Mortgages payable	Mortgagor
Bonds payable	Bondholder
Owners' Equity	
Shares outstanding	Registrar and transfer agent
Other Information	
Insurance coverage	Insurance company
Contingent liabilities	Company law firm(s), bank and others
Bond indenture agreements	Bondholder
Collateral held by creditors	Creditor

To be considered reliable evidence, confirmations must be controlled by the auditor from the time they are prepared until they are returned. If the client controls the preparation of the confirmation, performs the mailing, or receives the responses, the auditor has lost control and with it independence; thus the reliability of the evidence is reduced.

DOCUMENTATION

Documentation is the auditor's examination of the *client's documents and records* to substantiate the information that is or should be included in the financial statements. The documents examined by the auditor are the records used by the client to provide information for conducting its business in an organized manner. Since each transaction in the client's organization is normally supported by at least one document, there is a large volume of this type of evidence available. For example, the client often retains a customer order, a shipping document, and a duplicate sales invoice for each sales transaction. These same documents are useful evidence for verification by the auditor of the accuracy of the client's records for sales transactions. Documentation is a form of evidence widely used in every audit because it is usually readily available to the auditor at a relatively low cost. Sometimes it is the only reasonable type of evidence available.

Documents can be conveniently classified as internal and external. An *internal document* is one that has been prepared and used within the client's organization and is retained without ever going to an outside party such as a customer or a vendor. Examples of internal documents include duplicate sales invoices, employees' time reports, exception reports, and inventory receiving reports. An *external document* is one that has been in the hands of someone outside the client's organization who is a party to the transaction being documented, but that is either currently in the hands of the client or readily accessible. In some cases, external documents originate outside the client's organization and end up in the hands of the client. Examples of this type of external document are vendors' invoices, cancelled notes payable, and insurance policies. Other documents, such as cancelled cheques, originate with the client, go to an outsider, and are finally returned to the client.

The primary determinant of the auditor's willingness to accept a document as reliable evidence is whether it is internal or external, and when internal, whether it was created and processed under conditions of good internal control. Internal documents created and processed under conditions of weak internal control may not constitute reliable evidence.

Since external documents have been in the hands of both the client and another party to the transaction, there is some indication that both members are in agreement about the information and the conditions stated on the document. Therefore, external documents are regarded as more reliable evidence than internal ones. Some external documents have exceptional reliability because they are prepared with considerable care and, frequently, have been reviewed by lawyers or other qualified experts. Examples include title papers to property such as land, insurance policies, indenture agreements, and contracts.

When auditors use documentation to support recorded transactions or amounts, it is often referred to as *vouching*. To vouch recorded acquisition transactions, the auditor might, for example, trace from the acquisitions report to supporting vendors' invoices and receiving reports and thereby satisfy the existence objective. If the auditor traces from receiving reports to the acquisitions report to satisfy the completeness objective, it would not be appropriate to call it vouching.

Audit Implications of EDI, an audit technique study published jointly by the CICA and the AICPA in 1996, provides an indication of how the auditing profession's view of documentation is changing. First, EDI is described (Electronic Data Interchange — the electronic exchange of standardized business transactions), and then the study goes on to indicate that EDI has grown significantly in the past decade, quoting surveys that state that EDI will grow in Canada at 25 to 30 percent a year for the next several years. This change in business practices increases the dependence of organizations on computer-based information systems. Purchase, shipping, billing, cash receipt, and cash disbursement transactions may be available only in electronic form. Financial statement assertions indicated as being most affected by EDI are completeness, accuracy, and authorization of transactions, resulting in a need for new audit techniques.

Other forms of automation, such as image processing systems, where documents are scanned and converted into electronic images rather than being stored in paper format, also require changes in audit techniques. Auditors need to assess the strength of such electronic evidence based upon controls in place over changes to such documents, just as they would assess the strength of internal paper documentation.

OBSERVATION

Observation is the use of the senses to assess certain activities. Throughout the audit, there are many opportunities to exercise sight, hearing, touch, and smell to evaluate a wide range of things. For example, the auditor may tour a plant to obtain a general impression of a client's facilities, observe whether equipment is rusty to evaluate whether it is obsolete, and watch individuals perform accounting tasks to determine whether the person assigned a responsibility is performing it. Observation is rarely sufficient by itself because there is the risk that the client's personnel involved in accounting activities are aware of the auditor's presence. They may, therefore, perform their responsibilities in accordance with company policy but resume normal activities once the auditor is out of sight. It is necessary to follow up initial impressions with other kinds of corroborative evidence. Nevertheless, observation is useful in most parts of the audit.

INQUIRIES OF THE CLIENT

Inquiry is the obtaining of *written* or *oral information* from the client in response to questions from the auditor. Although considerable evidence is obtained from the client through inquiry, it usually cannot be regarded as conclusive because it is not from an independent source and may be biased in the client's favour. Therefore, when the auditor obtains evidence through inquiry, it is normally necessary to obtain further corroborating evidence through other procedures. As an illustration, when the auditor wants to obtain information about the client's method of recording and controlling accounting transactions, he or she usually begins by asking the client how internal controls operate. Later, the auditor performs tests of controls to determine if the transactions are recorded (completeness objective) and authorized in the manner stated.

REPERFORMANCE

As the word implies, *reperformance* involves rechecking the computations and transfers of information made by the client during the period under audit. Rechecking of computations consists of testing the client's arithmetical accuracy. It includes such procedures as extending sales invoices and inventory, adding reports and subsidiary ledgers, and checking the calculation of amortization expense and prepaid expenses. Rechecking of transfers of information consists of tracing amounts to be confident that when the same information is included in more than one place, it is recorded at the same amount each time. For example, the auditor normally makes limited tests to ascertain that the information in the sales history report has been included for the proper customer and at the correct amount in the subsidiary accounts receivable files and is accurately summarized in the general ledger.

When done manually, reperformance involves selecting a sample of transactions. However, many auditors use computer-assisted audit techniques so that reperformance can occur for a whole class of transactions. For example, in the inventory file, quantity on hand times unit price can be extended, added, and agreed to the general ledger control total.

ANALYTICAL PROCEDURES

Analytical procedures use comparisons and relationships between financial and nonfinancial information to determine whether account balances appear reasonable. An example is comparing the gross margin percent in the current year with the preceding year's. For certain audit objectives or small account balances, analytical procedures may be the only evidence needed. For other accounts, other types of evidence may be reduced when analytical procedures indicate that an account balance appears reasonable. In some cases, analytical procedures are also used to isolate accounts or transactions that should be investigated more extensively to help in deciding whether additional verification is needed. An example is comparison of the current period's total repair expense with previous years' and investigation of the difference, if it is significant, to determine the cause of the increase or decrease.

Section 5301 of the *CICA Handbook* states that analytical procedures should be used *during the planning and completion phases on all audits*. For certain audit objectives or small account balances, analytical procedures alone may be sufficient evidence. In most cases, however, additional evidence beyond analytical procedures is also necessary to satisfy the requirement for sufficient competent evidence.

Because analytical procedures are an important part of planning audits, performing tests of each cycle, and completing audits, their use is studied more extensively at the end of this chapter, in Chapter 13, and in most remaining chapters of this book. Normally, specialized software or spreadsheet templates are used to perform analytical procedures.

RELIABILITY OF TYPES OF EVIDENCE

The criteria discussed earlier in the chapter for determining the reliability of evidence are related to the seven types of evidence in Table 6-4. Several observations are apparent from a study of Table 6-4.

First, the effectiveness of the client's internal controls has a significant effect on the reliability of most types of evidence. For example, internal documentation from a company with effective internal controls is more reliable because the documents are more likely to be accurate. Similarly, analytical procedures will not be appropriate evidence if the internal controls that produced the data provide information of questionable accuracy.

Second, both physical examination and reperformance are likely to be highly reliable if internal controls are effective, but their use differs considerably. These two types of evidence effectively illustrate that equally reliable evidence may be completely different.

Third, a specific type of evidence is rarely sufficient by itself to provide competent evidence to satisfy any objective. It is apparent from examining Table 6-4 that observation, inquiries of the client, and analytical procedures are examples of this.

TABLE 6-4

RELIABILITY OF TYPES OF EVIDENCE

	CRITERIA TO DETERMINE RELIABILITY				
TYPE OF EVIDENCE	Independence of Provider	Effectiveness of Client's Internal Control	Auditor's Direct Knowledge	Qualifications of Provider	Objectivity of Evidence
Physical examination	High (auditor does)	Varies	High	Normally high (auditor does)	High
Confirmation	High	Not applicable	Low	Varies — usually high	High
Documentation	Varies — external more independent than internal	Varies	Low	Varies	High
Observation	High (auditor does)	Varies	High	Normally high (auditor does)	Medium
Inquiries of client	Low (client provides)	Not applicable	Low	Varies	Varies — low to high
Reperformance	High (auditor does)	Varies	High	High (auditor does)	High
Analytical procedures	High/low (auditor does/client responds)	Varies	High	Not applicable	Low

COST OF TYPES OF EVIDENCE

The two most expensive types of evidence are physical examination and confirmation. Physical examination is costly because it normally requires the auditor's presence when the client is counting the asset, often on the balance sheet date. For example, physical examination of inventory can result in several auditors travelling to widely separated geographical locations. Confirmation is costly because the auditor must follow careful procedures in the confirmation preparation, mailing, and receipt, and in the follow-up of nonresponses and exceptions.

Documentation and analytical procedures are moderately costly. If client personnel locate documents for the auditor and organize them for convenient use, documentation usually has a fairly low cost. When auditors must find those documents themselves, documentation can be extremely costly. Even under ideal circumstances, information and data on documents are sometimes complex and require interpretation and analysis. For example, it is usually time-consuming to read and evaluate a client's contracts, lease agreements, and minutes of the board of directors' meetings. Analytical procedures require the auditor to decide which analytical procedures to use, enter data to make the calculations, and evaluate the results. Doing so may take considerable time.

The three least expensive types of evidence are observation, inquiries of the client, and reperformance. Observation is normally done concurrently with other audit procedures. An auditor can easily observe whether client personnel are following appropriate inventory counting procedures at the same time he or she counts a sample of inventory (physical examination). Inquiries of clients are done extensively on every audit and normally have a low cost. Certain inquiries may be costly, such as obtaining written statements from the client documenting discussions throughout the audit.

Reperformance can vary in cost. It can be low when it involves simple calculations and tracing that can be done at the auditor's convenience. Costs per transaction are reduced when the auditor's computer software is used to perform these tests after obtaining a copy of the client data files.

APPLICATION OF TYPES OF EVIDENCE TO EVIDENCE DECISIONS

Finally, an application of three types of evidence to the four evidence decisions for one audit objective is shown in Table 6-5. First, examine column 5 in Table 5-2 on page 144. These are the specific objectives of the audit of inventory for Hillsburg Hardware Ltd. The overall objective is to obtain persuasive evidence (sufficient, appropriate, and timely), at minimum cost, that inventory is materially correct. The auditor must therefore decide which audit procedures to use to satisfy each objective, what the sample size should be for each procedure, which items from the population to include in the sample, and when to perform each procedure.

TABLE 6-5

TYPES OF EVIDENCE AND DECISIONS FOR A SPECIFIC AUDIT OBJECTIVE*

| TYPE OF EVIDENCE | EVIDENCE DECISIONS | | | |
	Audit Procedure	*Sample Size*	*Items to Select*	*Timing*
Observation	Observe client's personnel counting inventory to determine whether they are properly following instructions	All count teams	Not applicable	Balance sheet date
Physical examination	Count a sample of inventory and compare quality and description to client's counts	120 items	40 items with large dollar value, plus 80 randomly selected	Balance sheet date
Documentation	Compare quantity on client's perpetual records to quantity on client's counts	70 items	30 items with large dollar value, plus 40 randomly selected	Balance sheet date

*Balance-related audit objective: Inventory quantities agree with items physically on hand.

One objective from Table 5-2 is selected for further study: inventory quantities agree with items physically on hand. Several types of evidence are available to satisfy this objective. Table 6-5 lists three types of evidence and gives examples of the four evidence decisions for each type.

SPECIAL TERMS

OBJECTIVE 6-5

Define terms commonly used in auditing.

Audit procedures are the detailed steps, usually written in the form of instructions, for the accumulation of the seven types of audit evidence. They should be sufficiently clear to enable members of the audit team to understand what is to be done.

Several different terms are commonly used to describe audit procedures. These are presented and defined in Table 6-6. To help you understand the terms, an illustrative audit procedure and the type of evidence with which it is associated are shown.

ANALYTICAL PROCEDURES

OBJECTIVE 6-6

Discuss the purposes of analytical procedures.

The Assurance Standards Board in paragraphs 5300.30 and 5301.01 define *analysis* as including (1) the process of identifying elements or components of financial statement amounts, including transactions that are included in the amount that might result in the amount being materially misstated; and (2) the process of performing analytical procedures. Auditors utilize *analytical procedures*, which use financial and nonfinancial data in meaningful comparisons and relationships to determine whether account balances or other data appear reasonable. The results of the analytical procedures can be used to help in designing the nature, timing, and extent of other audit procedures so that sufficient appropriate audit evidence may be obtained and the appropriate opinion given in the auditor's report.

For example, the auditor might compare current year recorded commissions expense to total recorded sales multiplied by the average commission rate as a test of the overall reasonableness of recorded commissions. For this analytical procedure to be relevant, the auditor has likely concluded that recorded sales are correctly stated, all sales earn a commission, and there is an average actual commission rate that is readily determined.

As will be discussed below, the Assurance Standards Board, in Section 5301, suggests that the auditor should use analysis in planning the audit and may use analysis as a substantive procedure. The section concludes by suggesting that the auditor should use analytical procedures in his or her overall evaluation of the financial statements.

PURPOSES AND TIMING OF ANALYTICAL PROCEDURES

The most important reasons for utilizing analytical procedures are discussed in this section. As a part of that discussion, the appropriate timing is also examined.

UNDERSTANDING THE CLIENT'S BUSINESS

In the next chapter, there is a discussion of the need to obtain knowledge about the client's industry and business. Analytical procedures are one of the techniques commonly used in obtaining that knowledge.

Generally, an auditor considers knowledge and experience about a client company obtained in prior years as a starting point for planning the examination for the current year. By conducting analytical procedures where the current year's unaudited information is compared to prior years' audited information, changes are highlighted. These changes can represent important trends or specific events, all of which will influence audit planning. For example, a decline in gross margin percentages over time may indicate increasing competition in the company's market area and the

TABLE 6-6

TERMS, AUDIT
PROCEDURES, AND
TYPES OF EVIDENCE

TERM AND DEFINITION	ILLUSTRATIVE AUDIT PROCEDURE	TYPE OF EVIDENCE
Examine — A reasonably detailed study of a document or record to determine specific facts about it.	*Examine* a sample of vendors' invoices to determine whether the goods or services received are reasonable and of the type normally used by the client's business.	Documentation
Scan — A less detailed examination of a document or record to determine if there is something unusual warranting further investigation.	*Scan* the sales report, looking for large and unusual transactions. For large sales history files, run an exception report using audit software of large amounts.	Analytical procedures
Read — An examination of written information to determine facts pertinent to the audit and the recording of those facts in a working paper.	*Read* the minutes of a board of directors' meeting and summarize all information that is pertinent to the financial statements in a working paper.	Documentation
Compute — A calculation done by the auditor independent of the client.	*Compute* the inventory turnover ratios and compare to previous years as a test of inventory.	Analytical procedures
Recompute — A calculation done to determine whether a client's calculation is correct.	*Recompute* the unit sales price times the number of units for a sample of duplicate sales invoices and compare the totals to the client's calculations.	Reperformance
Foot — Addition of a column of numbers to determine if the total is the same as the client's.	*Foot* the sales history files using audit software and compare all totals to the general ledger.	Reperformance
Trace — An instruction normally associated with documentation or reperformance. The instruction should state what the auditor is tracing and where it is being traced from and to. Frequently, an audit procedure that includes the term *trace* will also include a second instruction, such as *compare* or *recompute*.	*Trace* a sample of sales transactions from the sales reports to sales invoices and *compare* customer name, date, and the total dollar value of the sale.	Documentation
	Trace postings from the sales reports to the general ledger accounts.	Reperformance
Compare — A comparison of information in two different locations. The instruction should state which information is being compared in as much detail as practical.	Select a sample of sales invoices and *compare* the unit selling price as stated on the invoice to the master files of unit selling prices authorized by management.	Documentation
Count — A determination of assets on hand at a given time. This term should only be associated with the type of evidence defined as physical examination.	*Count* petty cash on hand at the balance sheet date.	Physical examination
Observe — The act of observation should be associated with the type of evidence defined as observation.	*Observe* whether the two inventory count teams independently count and record inventory quantities.	Observation
Inquire — The act of inquiry should be associated with the type of evidence defined as inquiry.	*Inquire* of management whether there is an obsolete inventory on hand at the balance sheet date.	Inquiries of client

need to consider inventory pricing more carefully during the audit. Similarly, an increase in the balance in capital assets may indicate a significant acquisition that must be reviewed.

ASSESSMENT OF THE ENTITY'S ABILITY TO CONTINUE AS A GOING CONCERN

Analytical procedures are often useful as an indication that the client company is encountering severe financial difficulty. The likelihood of financial failure must be considered by the auditor in the assessment of audit-related risks (discussed further in Chapter 8) as well as in connection with management's use of the going concern assumption in preparing the financial statements.[1] Certain analytical procedures can be helpful in that regard. For example, if a higher than normal ratio of long-term debt to net worth is combined with a lower than average ratio of profits to total assets, a relatively high risk of financial failure may be indicated. Not only would such conditions affect the audit plan, they may indicate that substantial doubt exists about the entity's ability to continue as a going concern, which would require disclosure in the notes to the financial statements.

INDICATION OF THE PRESENCE OF POSSIBLE MISSTATEMENTS IN THE FINANCIAL STATEMENTS

Significant unexpected differences between the current year's unaudited financial data and other data used in comparisons are commonly referred to as *unusual fluctuations*. Unusual fluctuations occur when significant differences are not expected but do exist, or when significant differences are expected but do not exist. In either case, one of the possible reasons for an unusual fluctuation is the presence of an accounting error or fraud and other irregularities. Thus, if the unusual fluctuation is large, the auditor must determine the reason for it and satisfy himself or herself that the cause is a valid economic event and not an error or fraud. For example, in comparing the ratio of the allowance for uncollectible accounts receivable to gross accounts receivable with that of the previous year, suppose the ratio had decreased while, at the same time, accounts receivable turnover also decreased. The combination of these two pieces of information would indicate a possible understatement of the allowance. This aspect of analytical procedures is often referred to as *attention directing* because it results in the performance of more detailed procedures by the auditor in the specific audit areas where errors or fraud and other irregularities might be found.

REDUCTION OF DETAILED AUDIT TESTS

When an analytical procedure reveals no unusual fluctuations, the implication is that the possibility of a material misstatement is minimized. In that case, the analytical procedure constitutes substantive evidence in support of the fair statement of the related account balances, and it is possible to perform fewer detailed tests in connection with those accounts. For example, if analytical procedure results of a small account balance such as prepaid insurance are favourable, no detailed tests may be necessary. In other cases, certain audit procedures can be eliminated, sample sizes can be reduced, or the timing of the procedures can be moved farther away from the balance sheet date.

Analytical procedures are usually inexpensive compared with tests of details, since in many cases they can be automated. Most auditors therefore prefer to reduce tests of details with analytical procedures whenever possible. To illustrate, it may be far less expensive to calculate and review sales and accounts receivable ratios than to confirm accounts receivable. If it is possible to reduce confirmations by doing analytical procedures, considerable cost savings can occur.

The extent to which analytical procedures provide useful substantive evidence depends on their reliability in the circumstances. For some audit objectives and in some circumstances, they may be the most effective procedure to apply. These objectives might include proper classification of transactions, completeness of recording transactions, and accuracy of management's judgments and estimates in certain areas, such as the allowance for uncollectible accounts. For other audit objectives and

---

[1]For an interesting and thorough coverage of this topic, see Boritz, J. E., *The Going Concern Assumption: Accounting and Implications*, Toronto: CICA, 1991. Current standards are described in the CICA exposure draft *Auditor's Responsibility to Evaluate the Going Concern Assumption*, 1995.

circumstances, analytical procedures may be considered attention directing at best, and not relied on for gathering substantive evidence. An example is determining the validity of sales transactions. The factors that determine when analytical procedures are effective are discussed in a later section of the chapter.

TIMING

Analytical procedures are performed principally at any of three times during an engagement. Paragraph 5301.08 states that analysis should be used in the *planning phase* to assist in determining the nature, extent, and timing of other auditing procedures to be performed. Performance of analytical procedures during planning helps the auditor identify significant matters requiring special consideration later in the engagement. For example, the calculation of inventory turnover before inventory price tests are done may indicate the need for special care during those tests.

Analytical procedures are often done *during the testing phase* of the examination in conjunction with other audit procedures. For example, the prepaid portion of each insurance policy might be compared with the same policy for the previous year as a part of doing tests of prepaid insurance.

Paragraph 5301.23 states that analytical procedures should be used *during the completion phase* of the audit. Such tests are useful at that point as a final review for material misstatements or financial problems, and to help the auditor take a final "objective look" at the financial statements that have been audited. It is common for a partner to do a detailed review of the analytical procedures during the final review of working papers and financial statements. Typically, a partner has a good understanding of the client and its business because of ongoing relationships. Knowledge about the client's business combined with effective analytical procedures is a way to identify possible oversights in an audit.

The purposes of analytical procedures for each of the three different times they are performed is shown in Figure 6-2. The shaded boxes in the matrix indicate that certain purposes are applicable to a certain phase. Notice that purposes vary for different phases of the audit. Analytical procedures are performed during the planning phase for all four purposes, whereas the other two phases are used primarily to determine appropriate audit evidence and to reach conclusions about the fair presentation of financial statements.

FIGURE 6-2
Timing and Purposes of
Analytical Procedures

	PHASE		
PURPOSE	**(Required)** **Planning** **Phase**	**Testing** **Phase**	**(Required)** **Completion** **Phase**
Understand client's industry and business	Primary purpose		
Assess going concern			
Indicate possible misstatements (attention directing)	Primary purpose		Primary purpose
Reduce detailed tests		Primary purpose	

FIVE TYPES OF ANALYTICAL PROCEDURES

An important part of using analytical procedures is selecting the most appropriate procedures. There are five major types of analytical procedures:

1. Compare client and industry data.
2. Compare client data with similar prior-period data.
3. Compare client data with client-determined expected results.
4. Compare client data with auditor-determined expected results.
5. Compare client data with expected results using nonfinancial data.

These procedures are facilitated by many of the firm's software tools which provide direct linkages to client data.

COMPARE CLIENT AND INDUSTRY DATA

Suppose you are doing an audit and obtain the following information about the client and the average company in the client's industry:

	CLIENT		INDUSTRY	
	1999	1998	1999	1998
Inventory turnover	3.4	3.5	3.9	3.4
Gross margin percent	26.3%	26.4%	27.3%	26.2%

If we look only at client information for the two ratios shown, the company appears to be stable with no apparent indication of difficulties. However, compared with the industry, the client's position has worsened. In 1998, the client did slightly better than the industry in both ratios. In 1999, it did not do nearly as well. Although these two ratios by themselves may not indicate significant problems, the example illustrates how comparison of client data with industry data may provide useful information about the client's performance. For example, the company may have lost market share, its pricing may not be competitive, it may have incurred abnormal costs, or it may have obsolete items in inventory.

The Financial Post Company, Dun & Bradstreet Canada Limited, Robert Morris Associates, and other publishers accumulate financial information for thousands of larger companies and compile the data for different lines of business; local credit bureaus compile data for companies in their community. Many public accounting firms purchase these publications for use as a basis for industry comparisons in their audits.

The most important benefits of industry comparisons are as an aid to understanding the client's business and as an indication of the likelihood of financial failure. The ratios in Dun & Bradstreet Canada, for example, are primarily of a type that bankers and other credit executives use in evaluating whether a company will be able to repay a loan. That same information is useful to auditors in assessing the relative strength of the client's capital structure, its borrowing capacity, and its likelihood of financial failure.

A major weakness in using industry ratios for auditing is the difference between the nature of the client's financial information and that of the firms making up the industry totals. Since the industry data are broad averages, the comparisons may not be meaningful. Frequently, the client's line of business is not the same as the industry standards. In addition, different companies follow different accounting methods, and this affects the comparability of data. If most companies in the industry use FIFO inventory valuation and straight-line amortization, and the audit client uses LIFO and accelerated amortization, comparisons may not be meaningful. This does not mean that industry comparisons should not be made. Rather, it is an indication of the need for care in interpreting the results.

The Financial Post
www.canoe.ca/fp

Dun & Bradstreet Canada
  Limited
  www.dnb.ca

Robert Morris Associates
  www.rmahq.org

USING ANALYTICAL PROCEDURES EFFECTIVELY

According to an article in the *Journal of Accountancy*, auditors can obtain more relevant information and provide a valuable service to their clients by comparing the results of analytical procedures with similar companies in the same geographical area. The author of the article, Michael D. Chase, CPA, President of Professional Development Training Corp., writes:

> The knowledge we acquire about audit clients' businesses and their industries helps us design more effective and efficient analytical procedures. However, such procedures are useless unless we can compare test results with prior-year balances, budgeted amounts, or industry averages. A far more effective and reliable approach is to compare a client's business "vital signs" (for example, current assets, current liabilities, net sales, direct job costs, number of employees, and so on) with benchmarks — industry averages for companies in the same geographic area.

Source: Michael D. Chase, CPA, "Local Area Statistics: A Practice Development Tool," *Journal of Accountancy* (June 1994), p. 100.

COMPARE CLIENT DATA WITH SIMILAR PRIOR-PERIOD DATA

Suppose the gross margin percentage for a company has been between 26 and 27 percent for each of the past four years but is 23 percent in the current year. This decline in gross margin should be a concern to the auditor. The cause of the decline could be a change in economic conditions. However, it could also be caused by misstatements in the financial statements, such as sales or purchase cutoff errors, unrecorded sales, overstated accounts payable, or inventory costing errors. The auditor should determine the cause of the decline in gross margin and consider the effect, if any, on evidence accumulation.

There are a wide variety of analytical procedures where client data are compared with similar data from one or more prior periods. The following are common examples.

Compare the current year's balance with that for the preceding year One of the easiest ways to make this test is to include the preceding year's adjusted trial balance results in a separate column of the current year's trial balance spreadsheet. The auditor can easily compare the current year's and previous year's balance to decide early in the audit whether a particular account should receive more than the normal amount of attention because of a significant change in the balance. For example, if the auditor observes a substantial increase in supplies expense, the auditor should determine whether the cause was an increased use of supplies, a misstatement in the account due to a misclassification, or a misstatement in supplies inventory.

Compare the detail of a total balance with similar detail for the preceding year If there have been no significant changes in the client's operations in the current year, much of the detail making up the totals in the financial statements should also remain unchanged. By briefly comparing the detail of the current period with similar detail of the preceding period, it is often possible to isolate information that needs further examination. Comparison of details may take the form of details over time or details at a point in time. A common example of the former is comparing the monthly totals for the current and preceding year for sales, repairs, and other accounts. An example of the latter is comparing the details of loans payable at the end of the current year with those at the end of the preceding year.

Compute ratios and percentage relationships for comparison with previous years The comparison of totals or details with previous years as described in the two pre-

TABLE 6-7

INTERNAL
COMPARISONS AND
RELATIONSHIPS

RATIO OR COMPARISON	POSSIBLE MISSTATEMENT
Raw material turnover for a manufacturing company.	Misstatement of inventory or cost of goods sold or obsolescence of raw material inventory.
Sales commissions divided by net sales.	Misstatement of sales commissions.
Sales returns and allowances divided by gross sales.	Misclassified sales returns and allowances or unrecorded returns or allowances subsequent to year end.
Goods and services tax payable (current year) divided by goods and services tax payable (preceding year).	Failure to accrue properly the goods and services tax owing at year end.
Each of the individual manufacturing expenses as a percentage of total manufacturing expense.	Significant misstatement of individual expenses within a total.

ceding paragraphs has two shortcomings. First, it fails to consider growth or decline in business activity. Second, relationships of data to other data, such as sales to cost of goods sold, are ignored. Ratio and percentage relationships overcome both shortcomings. The example discussed earlier about the decline in gross margin is a common percentage relationship used by auditors.

A few types of ratios and internal comparisons are included in Table 6-7 to show the widespread use of ratio analysis. In all cases, the comparisons should be with calculations made in previous years for the same client. There are many potential ratios and comparisons available for use by an auditor. Subsequent chapters dealing with specific audit areas describe other examples. Normally, the auditor will arrange to have trial balance information entered annually into audit software that calculates a range of ratios and comparisons automatically.

Many of the ratios and percentages used for comparison with previous years are the same ones used for comparison with industry data. For example, it is useful to compare current year gross margin with industry averages and previous years. The same can be said for most of the ratios described in Appendix A at the end of this chapter.

There are also numerous potential comparisons of current- and prior-period data beyond those normally available from industry data. For example, the percent of each expense category to total sales can be compared with that of previous years. Similarly, in a multiunit operation (e.g., a retail chain), internal comparisons for each unit can be made with previous periods (e.g., the revenue and expenses for individual retail outlets in a chain of stores can be compared).

COMPARE CLIENT DATA WITH CLIENT-DETERMINED EXPECTED RESULTS

Most companies prepare *budgets* for various aspects of their operations and financial results. Since budgets represent the client's expectations for the period, an investigation of the most significant areas in which differences exist between budgeted and actual results may indicate potential misstatements. The absence of differences may also indicate that misstatements are unlikely. It is common, for example, in the audit of local, provincial, and federal governmental units to use this type of analytical procedure.

Whenever client data are compared with budgets, there are two special concerns. First, the auditor must evaluate whether the budgets were realistic plans. In some organizations, budgets are prepared with little thought or care and therefore are not realistic expectations. Such information has little value as audit evidence. The second concern is the possibility that current financial information was changed by client personnel to conform to the budget. If that has occurred, the auditor will find no differences in comparing actual data with the budget even if there are misstatements in the financial statements. Discussing budget procedures with client personnel is used to satisfy the first concern. Assessment of control risk and detailed audit tests of actual data are usually done to minimize the likelihood of the latter concern.

A second common type of comparison of client data with expected results occurs when the *auditor calculates the expected balance for comparison with the actual balance*. In this type of analytical procedure, the auditor makes an estimate of what an account balance should be by relating it to some other balance sheet or income statement account or accounts, or by making a projection based on some historical trend. An example of calculating an expected value based on relationships of accounts is the independent calculation of interest expense on long-term notes payable by multiplying the ending monthly balance in notes payable by the average monthly interest rate (see Figure 6-3). An example of using a historical trend would be where the moving average of the allowance for uncollectible accounts receivable as a percent of gross accounts receivable is applied to the balance of gross accounts receivable at the end of the audit year to determine an expected value for the current allowance.

FIGURE 6-3

Hillsburg Hardware
Overall Tests of
Interest Expense
December 31, 1999

Hillsburg Hardware Ltd. Overall Test of Interest Expense 31/12/98	Schedule _N-3_ Date Prepared by _9M_ _6/3/99_ Approved by _MW_ _12/3/99_

Interest expense per general ledger   120,432 [1]

Computation of estimate:

Short-term loans:

Balance outstanding at month-end: [2]

Jan.	147,500
Feb.	159,200
Mar.	170,600
Apr.	170,800
May	130,200
June	93,700
July	70,000
Aug.	– 0 –
Sept.	– 0 –
Oct.	42,700
Nov.	126,300
Dec.	209,000
Total	1,320,000

Average ($\div$12) 110,000 @ 12.5% [3] 13,750

Long-term loans:

Beginning balance 1,326,000 [2]
Ending balance   1,206,000 [2]
           2,532,000

Average ($\div$2) 1,266,000 @ 8.5% [4] 107,610

Estimated total interest expense   121,360

Differences   (928)[5]

Legend and Comments
[1] Agrees with general ledger and working trial balance.
[2] Obtained from general ledger.
[3] Estimated, based on examination of several notes throughout the year with rates ranging from 12% to 13%.
[4] Agrees with permanent file schedule of long-term debt.
[5] Difference not significant. Indicates that interest expense per books is reasonable.

COMPARE CLIENT DATA WITH EXPECTED RESULTS UTILIZING NONFINANCIAL DATA

Suppose that in auditing a hotel, you can determine the number of rooms, room rate for each room, and occupancy rate. Using those data, it is relatively easy to estimate total revenue from rooms to compare with recorded revenue. The same approach can sometimes be used to estimate such accounts as tuition revenue at universities (average tuition times enrollment), factory payroll (total hours worked times wage rate), and cost of materials sold (units times materials cost per unit).

The major concern in using nonfinancial data is the accuracy of the data. In the previous illustration, it is appropriate to use an estimated calculation of hotel revenue as audit evidence unless the auditor is not satisfied with the reasonableness of the count of the number of rooms, room rate, and occupancy rate. It would be more difficult for the auditor to evaluate the accuracy of the occupancy rate than the other two items.

USING STATISTICAL TECHNIQUES AND COMPUTER SOFTWARE

The use of statistical techniques is desirable to make analytical procedures more relevant. Many auditors use computer software to make statistical and nonstatistical calculations easier. These two auditors' tools are discussed briefly.

STATISTICAL TECHNIQUES

Several statistical techniques that aid in interpreting results can be applied to analytical procedures. The advantages of using statistical techniques are the ability to make more sophisticated calculations and their objectivity.

The most common statistical technique for analytical procedures is regression analysis. Regression analysis is used to evaluate the reasonableness of a recorded balance by relating (regressing) the total to other relevant information. For example, the auditor might conclude that total selling expenses should be related to total sales, the previous year's selling expenses, and the number of salespeople. The auditor would then use regression analysis to statistically determine an estimated value of selling expenses for comparison with recorded values, or to assess the profitability of different product lines. Regression and other statistical methods commonly used for analytical procedures can be found in several advanced auditing texts dealing with statistical sampling techniques for auditing. An example is provided in Chapter 13.

> **OBJECTIVE 6-8**
>
> **Explain the benefits of using statistical techniques and computer software for analytical procedures.**

AUDITOR'S COMPUTER SOFTWARE

Computer-based audit software can be used to do extensive analytical procedures as a byproduct of other audit testing. In the past several years, most public accounting firms have implemented a variety of computer software as tools for doing more efficient and effective audits. One feature common to all such software is the ability to input or import the client's general ledger into the auditor's computer system. Adjusting entries and financial statements are thereby computerized to save time. These are linked to working papers and cross-referenced, saving many hours of tedious working-paper referencing. Some systems also link directly to client data.

The general ledger information for the client is saved and carried forward in the auditor's computerized data file year after year. The existence of current and previous years' general ledger information on the auditor's computer files permits extensive and inexpensive computerized analytical calculations. The analytical information can also be shown in different forms such as graphs and charts to help interpret the data.

A major benefit of computerized analytical procedures is the ease of updating the calculations when adjusting entries to the client's statements are made. If there are several adjusting entries to the clients' records, the analytical procedures calculations can be quickly revised. For example, a change in inventory and cost of goods sold affects a large number of ratios. All affected ratios can be recalculated immediately.

APPENDIX A   COMMON FINANCIAL RATIOS

Auditors' analytical procedures often include the use of general financial ratios during planning and final review of the audited financial statements. These are useful for understanding the most recent events and financial status of the business, and for viewing the statements from the perspective of a user. The general financial analysis may be effective for identifying possible problem areas for additional analysis and audit testing, as well as business problem areas for which the auditor can provide other assistance. This appendix presents a number of widely used general financial ratios.

SHORT-TERM DEBT-PAYING ABILITY

$$\text{Current ratio} = \frac{\text{current assets}}{\text{current liabilities}}$$

$$\text{Quick ratio} = \frac{\text{cash + marketable securities + net accounts receivable}}{\text{current liabilities}}$$

$$\text{Cash ratio} = \frac{\text{cash + marketable securities}}{\text{current liabilities}}$$

Many companies follow an operating cycle whereby production inputs are obtained and converted into finished goods, and then sold and converted into cash. This requires an investment in working capital; that is, funds are needed to finance inventories and accounts receivable. A majority of these funds come from trade creditors and the balance comes from initial capitalization, bank borrowings, and positive net cash flow from operations.

At any given time, a company can attain a net working capital position. This is the excess of current assets over current liabilities, and is also measured by the current ratio. Presumably, if net working capital is positive (i.e., the current ratio is greater than 1.0), the company has sufficient available assets to pay its immediate debts; and the greater the excess (the larger the ratio), the better off the company is in this regard. Thus, companies with a comfortable net working capital position are considered preferred customers by their bankers and trade creditors and are given favourable treatment. Companies with inadequate net working capital are in danger of not being able to obtain credit.

However, this is a somewhat simplistic view. The current assets of companies will differ in terms of both valuation and liquidity, and these aspects will affect a company's ability to meet its current obligations. One way to examine this problem is to restrict the analysis to the most available and objective current assets. Thus, the quick ratio eliminates inventories from the computation, and the cash ratio further eliminates accounts receivable. Usually, if the cash ratio is greater than 1.0, the company has excellent short-term debt-paying ability. In some cases, it is appropriate to state marketable securities at market value rather than cost in computing these ratios.

SHORT-TERM LIQUIDITY

If a company does not have sufficient cash and cash-like items to meet its obligations, the key to its debt-paying ability will be the length of time it takes the company to convert less liquid current assets into cash. This is measured by the short-term liquidity ratios.

The two turnover ratios — accounts receivable and inventory — are very useful to auditors. Trends in the accounts receivable turnover ratio are frequently used in assessing the reasonableness of the allowance for uncollectible accounts. Trends in the inventory turnover ratio are used in identifying a potential inventory obsolescence problem.

$$\text{Average accounts receivable turnover} = \frac{\text{gross credit sales net of returns}}{\text{average gross receivables}}$$

$$\text{Average days to collect (or number of days' sales in accounts receivable)} = \frac{\text{average gross receivables} \times 365}{\text{gross credit sales net of returns}}$$

$$\text{Average inventory turnover} = \frac{\text{cost of goods sold}}{\text{average inventory}}$$

$$\text{Average days to sell (or average day sales in inventory)} = \frac{\text{average inventory} \times 365}{\text{cost of goods sold}}$$

$$\text{Average days to convert inventory to cash} = \text{average days to sell} + \text{average days to collect}$$

When the short-term liquidity ratios (and the current ratio) are used to examine a company's performance over time or to compare performance among companies, differences in inventory accounting methods, fiscal year ends, and cash-credit sales mix can have a significant effect. With regard to inventories, a few companies have adopted the LIFO method. This can cause inventory values to differ significantly from FIFO values. When companies with different valuation methods are being compared, the company's LIFO value inventory can be adjusted to FIFO to obtain a better comparison.

When two companies have different fiscal year ends, such that one is on a natural business year and the other is not, the simple average gross receivables and inventory figures for the former will be lower. This will tend to cause the natural business year company to appear more liquid than it really is. If this is a problem, an averaging computation with quarterly data can be used.

Finally, the use of net sales per the financial statements in the receivables liquidity ratios can be a problem when a significant portion of sales is for cash. This will be somewhat mitigated when the proportions are fairly constant among periods or companies for which comparisons are being made.

ABILITY TO MEET LONG-TERM DEBT OBLIGATIONS AND PREFERRED DIVIDENDS

$$\text{Debt to equity ratio} = \frac{\text{total liabilities}}{\text{total equity}}$$

$$\text{Tangible net assets to equity ratio} = \frac{\text{total equity} - \text{intangible assets}}{\text{total equity}}$$

$$\text{Times interest earned} = \frac{\text{operating income}}{\text{interest expense}}$$

$$\text{Times interest and preferred dividends earned} = \frac{\text{operating income}}{\text{interest expense} + (\text{preferred dividends}/1 - \text{tax rate})}$$

A company's long-run solvency depends on the success of its operations and on its ability to raise capital for expansion or even survival over periods of temporary difficulty. From another point of view, common shareholders will benefit from the leverage obtained from borrowed capital that earns a positive net return.

A key measure in evaluating this long-term structure and capacity is the debt-to-equity ratio. If this ratio is too high, it may indicate the company has used up its borrowing capacity and has no cushion for future events. If it is too low, it may mean available leverage is not being used to the owner's benefit. If the ratio is trending up, it may mean earnings are too low to support the needs of the enterprise. And, if it is trending down, it may mean the company is doing well and setting the stage for future expansion.

The tangible net assets-to-equity ratio indicates the current quality of the company's equity by removing those assets whose realization is wholly dependent on future operations such as goodwill. This ratio can be used to interpret better the debt-to-equity ratio.

Lenders are generally concerned about a company's ability to meet interest payments as well as its ability to repay principal amounts. The latter will be appraised by evaluating the company's long-term prospects as well as its net asset position. The realizable value of assets will be important in this regard and may involve specific assets that collateralize the debt.

The ability to make interest payments is more a function of the company's ability to generate positive cash flows from operations in the short run, as well as over time. Thus, times interest earned shows how comfortably the company should be able to make interest (and preferred dividend) payments, assuming earnings trends are stable.

OPERATING AND PERFORMANCE RATIOS

The key to remedying many financial ills is to improve operations. All creditors and investors, therefore, are interested in the results of operations of a business enterprise, and it is not surprising that a number of operating and performance ratios are in use. The most widely used operating and performance ratio is earnings per share, which is an integral part of the basic financial statements for most companies. Several additional ratios can be calculated and will give further insights into operations.

The first of these is the efficiency ratio. This shows the relative volume of business generated from the company's operating asset base. In other words, it shows whether sufficient revenues are being generated to justify the assets employed. When the efficiency ratio is low, there is an indication that additional volume should be sought

$$\text{Earnings per share} = \frac{\text{earnings} - \text{preferred dividends}}{\text{common shares}}$$

$$\text{Efficiency ratio} = \frac{\text{gross sales net of returns}}{\text{tangible operating assets}}$$

$$\text{Profit margin ratio} = \frac{\text{operating income}}{\text{gross sales net of returns}}$$

$$\text{Profitability ratio} = \frac{\text{operating income}}{\text{tangible operating assets}}$$

$$\text{Return on total assets ratio} = \frac{\text{income before interest} + \text{taxes}}{\text{total assets}}$$

$$\text{Return on common equity ratio} = \frac{\text{income before taxes} - (\text{preferred dividends}/1 - \text{tax rate})}{\text{common equity}}$$

Leverage ratios (computed separately for each source of capital other than common equity, for example, short-term debt, long-term debt, deferred taxes) =

$$\frac{(\text{return on total assets} \times \text{amount of source}) - \text{cost attributable to source}}{\text{common equity}}$$

$$\text{Book value per common share} = \frac{\text{common equity}}{\text{number of common shares}}$$

before more assets are obtained. When the ratio is high, it may be an indication that assets are being fully utilized (i.e., there is little excess capacity) and an investment in additional assets will soon be necessary.

The second ratio is the profit margin ratio. This shows the portion of sales that exceeds cost (both variable and fixed). When there is weakness in this ratio, it is generally an indication that either (1) gross margins (revenues in excess of variable costs) are too low or (2) volume is too low with respect to fixed costs.

Two ratios that indicate the adequacy of earnings relative to the asset base are the profitability ratio and the return on total assets ratio. In effect, these ratios show the efficiency and profit margin ratios combined.

An important perspective on the earnings of the company is what kind of return is provided to the owners. This is reflected in the return (before taxes) on common equity. If this ratio is below prevailing long-term interest rates or returns on alternative investments, owners will perceive that they should convert the company's assets to some other use, or perhaps liquidate, unless return can be improved.

An interesting supplemental analysis is provided through leverage analysis. Here, the proportionate share of assets for each source of capital is multiplied by the company's return on total assets. This determines the return on each source of capital. The result is compared to the cost of each source of capital (e.g., interest expense), and a net contribution by capital source is derived. If this amount is positive for a capital source, it may be an indication that additional capital should be sought. If the leverage is negative from a capital source, recapitalization alternatives and/or earnings improvements should be investigated. It is also helpful to use this leverage analysis when considering the debt-to-equity ratio.

The final operating and performance ratio is book value per common share. This shows the combined effect of equity transactions over time.

The use of operating and performance ratios is subject to the same accounting inconsistencies mentioned for the liquidity ratios previously identified. The usefulness of these ratios in making comparisons over time or among companies may be affected by the classification of operating versus nonoperating items, inventory methods, amortization methods, amortization of goodwill, research and development costs, and off-balance-sheet financing.

ILLUSTRATION

Computation of the various ratios is illustrated using the financial statements of Hillsburg Hardware Ltd. introduced in Chapter 5 (pp. 127–129).

Simplifying assumptions:

1. Assumes average receivables and inventories for the year are not significantly different from the year-end balances.
2. Assumes there is no preferred stock and the tax rate is 48 percent.
3. Assumes there are 250,000 common shares with a market value of $26 per share.

$$\text{Earnings per share} = \frac{198 - 0}{250} = 0.79$$

$$\text{Current ratio} = \frac{2,550}{659} = 3.87$$

$$\text{Quick ratio} = \frac{41 + 948 + 47}{659} = 1.57$$

$$\text{Cash ratio} = \frac{41}{659} = 0.06$$

$$\text{Accounts receivable turnover} = \frac{7{,}721 - 62}{948} = 8.08$$

$$\text{Days to collect} = \frac{948 \times 365}{7{,}721 - 62} = 45.18$$

$$\text{Inventory turnover} = \frac{5{,}162}{1{,}493} = 3.46$$

$$\text{Days to sell} = \frac{1{,}493 \times 365}{5{,}162} = 105.57 \text{ days}$$

$$\text{Days to convert to cash} = 45.18 + 105.57 = 150.75 \text{ days}$$

$$\text{Debt to equity} = \frac{659 + 1{,}284}{1{,}124} = 1.73$$

$$\text{Tangible net assets to equity} = \frac{1{,}124}{1{,}124} = 1.00$$

$$\text{Times interest earned} = \frac{369}{120} = 3.08$$

$$\text{Times interest and preferred dividends earned} = \frac{369}{120 + 0/(1 - 0.48)} = 3.08$$

$$\text{Efficiency ratio} = \frac{7{,}721 - 62}{3{,}067} = 2.50$$

$$\text{Profit margin ratio} = \frac{369}{7{,}721 - 62} = 0.05$$

$$\text{Profitability ratio} = \frac{369}{3{,}067} = 0.12$$

$$\text{Return on total assets} = \frac{369 + 36}{3{,}067} = 0.13$$

$$\text{Return on common equity} = \frac{285 - 0/(1 - 0.48)}{1{,}124} = 0.25$$

Leverage ratios:

$$\text{Current liabilities} = \frac{(0.13 \times 659) - 0}{1{,}124} = 0.08$$

$$\text{Long-term notes payable} = \frac{(0.13 \times 1{,}206) - 120}{1{,}124} = 0.03$$

$$\text{Book value per common share} = \frac{1{,}124}{250} = 4.50$$

ESSENTIAL TERMS

Analysis — identification of components of financial statements and analytical procedures (p. 173).

Analytical procedures — use of comparisons and relationships to determine whether account balances or other data appear reasonable (p. 170).

Appropriateness of evidence — the degree to which evidence can be considered believable or worthy of trust; evidence is appropriate when it is obtained from (1) an independent provider, (2) a client with effective internal controls, (3) the auditor's direct knowledge, (4) qualified providers such as law firms and banks, or (5) objective sources (p. 163).

Audit procedure — detailed instruction for the collection of a type of audit evidence (p. 161).

Audit program — detailed instructions for the entire collection of evidence for an audit area or an entire audit; always includes audit procedures and may also include sample sizes, items to select, and timing of the tests (p. 162).

Audit software — software used to automate preparation of audit working papers or the analysis of client data files (p. 181).

Budgets — written records of the client's expectations for the period; a comparison of budgets with actual results may indicate whether or not misstatements are likely (p. 179).

Confirmation — the auditor's receipt of a written or oral response from an independent third party verifying the accuracy of information requested (p. 167).

Documentation — the auditor's examination of the client's documents and records to substantiate the information that is or should be included in the financial statements (p. 168).

External document — a document, such as a vendor's invoice, that has been used by an outside party to the transaction being documented, and that the client now has or can easily obtain (p. 168).

Inquiry of the client — the obtaining of written or oral information from the client in response to questions during the audit (p. 170).

Internal document — a document, such as an employee time report, that is prepared and used within the client's organization (p. 168).

Observation — the use of the senses to assess certain activities (p. 169).

Persuasiveness of evidence — the degree to which the auditor is convinced that the evidence supports the audit opinion; the three determinants of persuasiveness are the sufficiency, appropriateness, and timeliness of the evidence (p. 162).

Physical examination — the auditor's inspection or count of a tangible asset (p. 166).

Relevance of evidence — the pertinence of the evidence to the audit objective being tested (p. 163).

Reliability — see *appropriateness of evidence.*

Reperformance — the rechecking of the computations and transfers of information made by the client during the period under audit (p. 170).

Sufficiency of evidence — the quantity of evidence; appropriate sample size (p. 164).

Timeliness — the timing of audit evidence in relation to the period covered by the audit (p. 165).

Unusual fluctuations — significant unexpected differences indicated by analytical procedures between the current year's unaudited financial data and other data used in comparisons (p. 175).

Vouching — the use of documentation to support recorded transactions or amounts (p. 169).

REVIEW QUESTIONS

6-1 Discuss the similarities and differences between evidence in a legal case and evidence in the audit of financial statements.

6-2 List the four major evidence decisions that must be made on every audit.

6-3 Describe what is meant by an audit procedure. Why is it important for audit procedures to be carefully worded?

6-4 Describe what is meant by an audit program for accounts receivable. What four things should be included in an audit program?

6-5 State the third examination standard. Explain the meaning of each of the major phrases of the standard.

6-6 Explain why the auditor can only be persuaded with a reasonable level of assurance, rather than convinced, that the financial statements are correct.

6-7 Identify the three factors that determine the persuasiveness of evidence. How are these three factors related to audit procedures, sample size, items to select, and timing?

6-8 Identify the six characteristics that determine the appropriateness of evidence. For each characteristic, provide one example of a type of evidence that is likely to be appropriate.

6-9 List the seven types of audit evidence included in this chapter, and give two examples of each.

6-10 What are the four characteristics of the definition of a confirmation? Distinguish between a confirmation and external documentation.

6-11 Distinguish between internal documentation and external documentation as audit evidence and give three examples of each.

6-12 Explain the importance of analytical procedures as evidence in determining the fair presentation of the financial statements.

6-13 Identify the most important reasons for performing analytical procedures.

6-14 Your client, Harper Ltd., has a contractual commitment as a part of a bond indenture to maintain a current ratio of 2.0. If the ratio falls below that level on the balance sheet date, the entire bond becomes payable immediately. In the current year, the client's financial statements show that the ratio has dropped from 2.6:1 or 2.6 to 2.05:1 or 2.05 over the past year. How should this situation affect your audit plan?

6-15 Distinguish between attention-directing analytical procedures and those intended to reduce detailed substantive procedures.

6-16 "Analytical procedures are essential in every part of an audit, but these tests are rarely sufficient by themselves for any audit area." Explain why this statement is correct or incorrect.

6-17 Gail Gordon, a public accountant, has found ratio and trend analysis relatively useless as a tool in conducting audits. For several engagements, she computed the industry ratios included in publications by The Financial Post Company and compared them with client ratios. For most engagements, the client's business was significantly different from the industry data in the publication, and the client would automatically explain away any discrepancies by attributing them to the unique nature of its operations. In cases in which the client had more than one branch in different industries, Gordon found the ratio analysis no help at all.

How could Gordon improve the quality of her analytical procedures?

6-18 At the completion of every audit, Roger Morris, public accountant, calculates a large number of ratios and trends for comparison with industry averages and prior-year calculations. He believes the calculations are worth the relatively small cost of doing them because they provide him with an excellent overview of the client's operations. If the ratios are out of line, Morris discusses the reasons with the client and frequently makes suggestions on how to bring the ratio back in line in the future. In some cases, these discussions with management have been the basis for management services engagements. Discuss the major strengths and shortcomings in Morris's use of ratio and trend analysis.

6-19 It is imperative that the auditor follow up on all material differences discovered through analytical procedures. What factors affect such investigations?

MULTIPLE CHOICE QUESTIONS

6-20 The following questions concern the appropriateness and persuasiveness of evidence. Choose the best response.

a. Which of the following types of documentary evidence should the auditor consider to be the most reliable?
  (1) A sales invoice issued by the client and supported by a delivery receipt from an outside trucker.
  (2) A cheque, issued by the company and bearing the payee's endorsement, that is included with the bank statements mailed directly to the auditor.
  (3) A working paper prepared by the client's controller and reviewed by the client's treasurer.
  (4) Confirmation of an account payable balance mailed by and returned directly to the auditor.

b. The most reliable type of documentary audit evidence that an auditor can obtain is
  (1) calculations by the auditor from company records.
  (2) confirmations received directly from third parties.
  (3) physical examination by the auditor.
  (4) external documents.

c. Audit evidence can come in different forms with different degrees of persuasiveness. Which of the following is the *least* persuasive type of evidence?
  (1) Vendor's invoice.
  (2) Bank statement obtained from the client.
  (3) Computations made by the auditor.
  (4) Prenumbered sales invoices.

d. Which of the following is the least persuasive documentation in support of an auditor's opinion?
  (1) Schedules of details of physical inventory counts conducted by the client.
  (2) Notation of inferences drawn from ratios and trends.
  (3) Notation of appraisers' conclusions documented in the auditor's working papers.
  (4) Lists of negative confirmation requests for which no response was received by the auditor.

(AICPA adapted)

6-21 The following questions deal with analytical procedures. Choose the best response.

a. Analytical procedures are
  (1) statistical tests of financial information designed to identify areas requiring intensive investigation.
  (2) analytical procedures of financial information made by a computer.
  (3) substantive tests of financial information made by a study and comparison of relationships among data.
  (4) diagnostic tests of financial information that may not be classified as evidential matter.

b. Significant unexpected fluctuations identified by analytical procedures will usually necessitate a(n)
  (1) consistency qualification.
  (2) understanding of the client's internal controls.
  (3) explanation in the representation letter.
  (4) auditor investigation.

c. Which of the following situations has the best chance of being detected when a public accountant compares revenues and expenses with the prior year and investigates all changes exceeding a fixed percentage?
  (1) The company changed its capitalization policy for small tools in the current year.
  (2) An increase in property tax rates has not been recognized in the company's current accrual.
  (3) The cashier began lapping accounts receivable in the current year.
  (4) Because of worsening economic conditions, the current provision for uncollectible accounts was inadequate.

d. Your analytical procedures and other tests of the Dey Corp. reveal that the firm's poor financial condition makes it unlikely that it will survive as a going concern. Assuming that the financial statements have otherwise been prepared in accordance with generally accepted accounting principles, what disclosure should you make of the company's precarious financial position?

(1) You should issue an unqualified opinion and, in a paragraph between the scope and opinion paragraphs of your report, direct the reader's attention to the poor financial condition of the company.

(2) You should insist that a note to the financial statements clearly indicates that the company appears to be on the verge of bankruptcy.

(3) You need not insist on any particular disclosure, since the company's poor financial condition is clearly indicated by the financial statements themselves.

(4) You should insist that the management indicate on each of the statements that the company has a going concern problem.

(AICPA adapted)

DISCUSSION QUESTIONS AND PROBLEMS

6-22　The following are examples of documentation typically obtained by auditors:

1. Vendors' invoices
2. General ledgers
3. Bank statements
4. Cancelled payroll cheques
5. Payroll time cards
6. Purchase requisitions
7. Receiving reports (documents prepared when merchandise is received)
8. Minutes of the board of directors
9. Remittance advices
10. Signed TD-1s (Employees' Income Tax Withholding Exemption Certificates)
11. Signed lease agreements
12. Duplicate copies of bills of lading
13. Subsidiary accounts receivable records
14. Cancelled notes payable
15. Duplicate sales invoices
16. Articles of incorporation
17. Notes receivable

Required

a. Classify each of the preceding items according to type of documentation: (1) internal or (2) external.

b. Explain why external evidence is more reliable than internal evidence.

6-23　The following are examples of audit procedures:

1. Review the accounts receivable with the credit manager to evaluate their collectibility.
2. Stand by the payroll time clock to determine whether any employee "punches in" more than one time.
3. Count inventory items and record the amount in the audit working papers.
4. Obtain a letter from the client's law firm addressed to the public accounting firm stating that the law firm is not aware of any existing lawsuits.
5. Extend the cost of inventory times the quantity on an inventory listing to test whether it is accurate.

6. Obtain a letter from an insurance company to the public accounting firm stating the amount of the fire insurance coverage on building and equipment.
7. Examine an insurance policy stating the amount of the fire insurance coverage on buildings and equipment.
8. Calculate the ratio of cost of goods sold to sales as a test of overall reasonableness of gross margin relative to the preceding year.
9. Obtain information about the system of internal controls by asking the client to fill out a questionnaire.
10. Trace the total on the cash disbursements journal to the general ledger.
11. Watch employees count inventory to determine whether company procedures are being followed.
12. Examine a piece of equipment to make sure a major acquisition was actually received and is in operation.
13. Calculate the ratio of sales commissions expense to sales as a test of sales commissions.
14. Examine corporate minutes of directors' meetings to determine the authorization of the issue of bonds.
15. Obtain a letter from management stating there are no unrecorded liabilities.
16. Review the total of repairs and maintenance for each month to determine whether any month's total was unusually large.
17. Compare a duplicate sales invoice with the sales journal for customer name and amount.
18. Add the sales journal entries to determine whether they were correctly totalled.
19. Make a petty cash count to make sure the amount of the petty cash fund is intact.
20. Obtain a written statement from a bank stating the client has $15,671 on deposit and liabilities of $50,000 on a demand note.

Required

Classify each of the preceding items according to the seven types of audit evidence: (1) physical examination, (2) confirmation, (3) documentation, (4) observation, (5) inquiries of the client, (6) reperformance, and (7) analytical procedures.

6-24 List two examples of audit evidence the auditor can use in support of each of the following:

a. Recorded amount of entries in the purchase journal

b. Physical existence of inventory

c. Accuracy of accounts receivable

d. Ownership of capital assets

e. Liability for accounts payable

f. Obsolescence of inventory

g. Existence of petty cash.

6-25 Seven different types of evidence were discussed. The following questions concern the reliability of that evidence.

a. Explain why confirmations are normally more reliable evidence than inquiries of the client.

b. Describe a situation in which confirmation would be considered highly reliable and another in which it would not be reliable.

c. Under what circumstances is the physical observation of inventory considered relatively unreliable evidence?

d. Explain why reperformance tests are highly reliable but of relatively limited use.

e. Give three examples of relatively reliable documentation and three examples of less reliable documentation. What characteristics distinguish the two?

f. Give several examples in which the qualifications of the respondent or the qualifications of the auditor affect the reliability of the evidence.

g. Explain why analytical procedures are important evidence even though they are relatively unreliable by themselves.

6-26 In an examination of financial statements, an auditor must judge the appropriateness of the audit evidence obtained.

a. In the course of his or her examination, the auditor asks many questions of the client's officers and employees.
   (1) Describe the factors the auditor should consider in evaluating oral evidence provided by the client's officers and employees.
   (2) Discuss the competence and limitations of oral evidence.

b. An auditor's examination may include computation of various balance sheet and operating ratios for comparison with previous years and industry averages. Discuss the appropriateness and limitations of ratio analysis.

(AICPA adapted)

6-27 As auditor of the Star Manufacturing Corp., you have obtained a trial balance taken from the books of Star one month prior to year end:

	DR. (CR.)
Cash in bank	$87,000
Trade accounts receivable	345,000
Notes receivable	125,000
Inventories	317,000
Land	66,000
Buildings, net	350,000
Furniture, fixtures, and equipment, net	325,000
Trade accounts payable	(213,000)
Goods and services tax payable	(22,000)
Mortgages payable	(400,000)
Capital stock	(300,000)
Retained earnings	(510,000)
Sales (net)	(3,130,000)
Cost of sales	2,300,000
General administrative expenses	622,000
Legal and professional fees	3,000
Interest expense	35,000

Notes:
There are no inventories consigned either in or out.
All notes receivable are due from outsiders and held by Star.

Required

Which accounts should be confirmed with outside sources? Briefly describe from whom they should be confirmed and the information that should be confirmed. Organize your answer in the following format:

ACCOUNT NAME	FROM WHOM CONFIRMED	INFORMATION TO BE CONFIRMED

(AICPA adapted)

6-28 The following audit procedures were performed in the audit of inventory to satisfy specific balance-related audit objectives as discussed in Chapter 5. The audit procedures assume the auditor has obtained the inventory count records that list the client's inventory. The general balance-related audit objectives from Chapter 5 are also included.

AUDIT PROCEDURES

1. Using audit software, extend unit prices times quantity, foot the extensions, and compare the total to the general ledger.

2. Trace selected quantities from the inventory listing to the physical inventory to make sure the items exist and the quantities are the same.

3. Question operating personnel about the possibility of obsolete or slow-moving inventory.

4. Select a sample of quantities of inventory in the factory warehouse, and trace each item to the inventory count sheets to determine if it has been included and if the quantity and description are correct.

5. Using both this year's and last year's inventory data files, compare quantities on hand and unit prices, print-

ing any with greater than a 30 percent or $15,000 variation from one year to the next.

6. Examine sales invoices and contracts with customers to determine if any goods are out on consignment with customers. Similarly, examine vendors' invoices and contracts with vendors to determine if any goods on the inventory listing are owned by vendors.

7. Send letters directly to third parties who hold the client's inventory and request that they respond directly to us.

GENERAL BALANCE-RELATED AUDIT OBJECTIVES

Existence
Completeness
Valuation
Accuracy
Classification
Cutoff
Detail tie-in
Rights and obligations
Presentation and disclosure

Required

a. Identify the type of audit evidence used for each audit procedure.

b. Identify the general balance-related audit objective or objectives satisfied by each audit procedure.

6-29 Audit procedures differ from, but are related to, types of evidence. The following questions relate to types of evidence and audit procedures.

Required

a. What is an audit procedure?

b. Why should audit procedures be specific and carefully written?

c. For each of the following types of evidence, carefully write one audit procedure for the audit of accounts receivable.

TYPE OF EVIDENCE	AUDIT PROCEDURE
(1) Confirmation	
(2) Documentation	
(3) Inquiries of the client	
(4) Reperformance	
(5) Analytical procedures	

6-30 The following are nine situations, each containing two means of accumulating evidence.

1. Confirm accounts receivable with business organizations versus confirming receivables with consumers.

2. Physically examine 8-cm steel plates versus examining electronic parts.

3. Examine duplicate sales invoices when several competent people are checking one another's work versus examining documents prepared by a competent person in a one-person staff.

4. Physically examine inventory of parts for the number of units on hand versus examining them for the likelihood of inventory being obsolete.

5. Discuss the likelihood and amount of loss in a lawsuit against the client with client's in-house legal counsel versus discussion with the public accounting firm's own legal counsel.

6. Confirm a bank balance versus confirming the oil and gas reserves with a geologist specializing in oil and gas.

7. Confirm a bank balance versus examining the client's bank statements.

8. Physically count the client's inventory held by an independent party versus confirming the count with an independent party.

9. Physically count the client's inventory versus obtaining a count from the company president.

Required

a. Identify the six factors that determine the appropriateness of evidence.

b. For each of the nine situations, state whether the first or second type of evidence is more reliable.

c. For each situation, state which of the six factors discussed in the chapter affect the appropriateness of the evidence.

6-31 Following are 10 audit procedures with words missing and a list of several terms commonly used in audit procedures.

AUDIT PROCEDURES

1. _____ whether the accounts receivable bookkeeper is prohibited from handling cash.

2. _____ ratio of cost of goods sold to sales and compare the ratio to previous years.

3. _____ the sales journal and _____ the total to the general ledger.

4. _____ the sales journal, looking for large and unusual transactions requiring investigation.

5. _____ of management whether all accounting employees are required to take annual vacations.

6. _____ the balance in the bank account directly with the Crowchild Bank.

7. _____ all marketable securities as of the balance sheet date to determine whether they equal the total on the client's list.

8. _____ a sample of duplicate sales invoices to determine if the controller's approval is included and _____ each duplicate sales invoice to the sales journal for comparison of name and amount.

9. _____ the unit selling price times quantity on the duplicate sales invoice and compare the total to the amount on the duplicate sales invoice.

10. _____ the agreement between Rimouski Wholesale Inc. and the client to determine if the shipment is a sale or a consignment.

TERMS

Examine
Scan
Read
Compute
Extend
Recompute
Foot
Trace
Compare
Count
Observe
Inquire
Confirm

Required

a. For each of the 12 blanks in procedures 1 through 10, identify the most appropriate term.

b. For each of procedures 1 through 10, identify the type of evidence that is being used.

6-32   In auditing the financial statements of a manufacturing company, the public accountant has found that the traditional audit trail has been replaced by an electronic one. As a result, the public accountant may place increased emphasis on analytical procedures of the data under audit. These tests, which are also applied in auditing visibly posted accounting records, include the computation of ratios that are compared with prior-year ratios or with industry-wide norms. Examples of analytical procedures are the computation of the rate of inventory turnover and the computation of the number of days in receivables.

Required

a. Discuss the advantages to the public accountant of the use of analytical procedures in an audit.

b. In addition to the computations given, list five ratios that an auditor may compute during an audit on balance sheet accounts and related income accounts. For each ratio listed, name the two (or more) accounts used in its computation.

c. When an auditor discovers that there has been a significant change in a ratio when compared with the preceding year's, he or she considers the possible reasons for the change. Give the possible reasons for the following significant changes in ratios:
   (1) The rate of inventory turnover (ratio of cost of sales to average inventory) has decreased from the preceding year's rate.
   (2) The number of days' sales in receivables (ratio of average daily accounts receivable to sales) has increased over the prior year.

(AICPA adapted)

6-33   Your comparison of the gross margin percentage for Singh Drugs Ltd. for the years 1996 through 1999 indicates a significant decline. This is shown by the following information:

	1999	1998	1997	1996
Sales (thousands)	$14,211	$12,916	$11,462	$10,351
COGS (thousands)	9,223	8,266	7,313	6,573
Gross margin	$4,988	$4,650	$4,149	$3,778
Percentage	35.1	36.0	36.2	36.5

A discussion with Marilyn Adams, the controller, brings to light two possible explanations. She informs you that the industry gross profit percentage in the retail drug industry declined fairly steadily for three years, which accounts for part of the decline. A second factor was the declining percentage of the total volume resulting from the pharmacy part of the business. The pharmacy sales represent the most profitable portion of the business, yet the competition from discount drugstores prevents these sales from expanding as fast

	SINGH DRUGS LTD.				INDUSTRY GROSS PROFIT PERCENTAGE FOR RETAILERS OF DRUGS AND RELATED PRODUCTS
	Drug Sales	Non-Drug Sales	Drug Cost of Goods Sold	Non-Drug Cost of Goods Sold	
1999	$5,126	$9,085	$3,045	$6,178	32.7
1998	$5,051	$7,865	$2,919	$5,347	32.9
1997	$4,821	$6,641	$2,791	$4,522	33.0
1996	$4,619	$5,732	$2,665	$3,908	33.2

as the non-drug items such as magazines, candy, and many other items sold. Adams feels strongly that these two factors are the cause of the decline.

The additional information at the bottom of the previous page is obtained from independent sources and the client's records as a means of investigating the controller's explanations.

Required

a. Evaluate the explanation provided by Adams. Show calculations to support your conclusions.

b. Which specific aspects of the client's financial statements require intensive investigation in this audit?

6-34 In the audit of Worldwide Wholesale Inc., you performed extensive ratio and trend analysis. No material exceptions were discovered except for the following:

1. Commission expense as a percentage of sales had stayed constant for several years but has increased significantly in the current year. Commission rates have not changed.
2. The rate of inventory turnover has steadily decreased for four years.
3. Inventory as a percentage of current assets had steadily increased for four years.
4. The number of days' sales in accounts receivable has steadily increased for three years.
5. Allowance for uncollectible accounts as a percentage of accounts receivable has steadily decreased for three years.
6. The absolute amounts of amortization expense and amortization expense as a percentage of gross fixed assets are significantly smaller than in the preceding year.

Required

a. Evaluate the potential significance of each of the exceptions above for the fair presentation of financial statements.

b. State the follow-up procedures you would use to determine the possibility of material misstatements.

6-35 As part of the analytical procedures of Mahogany Products, Inc., you perform calculations of the following ratios:

RATIO	INDUSTRY AVERAGES		MAHOGANY PRODUCTS, INC.	
	1999	1998	1999	1998
1. Current ratio	3.30	3.80	2.20	2.60
2. Days to collect receivables	87.00	93.00	67.00	60.00
3. Days to sell inventory	126.00	121.00	93.00	89.00
4. Purchases divided by accounts payable	11.70	11.60	8.50	8.60
5. Inventory divided by current assets	0.56	0.51	0.49	0.48
6. Operating earnings divided by tangible assets	0.08	0.06	0.14	0.12
7. Operating earnings divided by net sales	0.06	0.06	0.04	0.04
8. Gross margin percentage	0.21	0.27	0.21	0.19
9. Earnings per share	$14.27	$13.91	$2.09	$1.93

Required

For each of the preceding ratios:

a. State whether there is a need to investigate the results further and, if so, the reason for further investigation.

b. State the approach you would use in the investigation.

c. Explain how the operations of Mahogany Products, Inc., appear to differ from those of the industry.

6-36 Following are the auditor's calculations of several key ratios for Cragston Star Products Ltd. The primary purpose of this information is to assess the risk of financial failure, but any other relevant conclusions are also desirable.

RATIO	1999	1998	1997	1996	1995
Current ratio	2.08	2.26	2.51	2.43	2.50
Quick ratio	0.97	1.34	1.82	1.76	1.64
Earnings before taxes divided by interest expense	3.50	3.20	4.10	5.30	7.10
Accounts receivable turnover	4.20	5.50	4.10	5.40	5.60
Days to collect receivables	108.20	83.10	105.20	80.60	71.60
Inventory turnover	2.03	1.84	2.68	3.34	3.36
Days to sell inventory	172.60	195.10	133.90	107.80	108.30
Net sales divided by tangible assets	0.68	0.64	0.73	0.69	0.67
Operating income divided by net sales	0.13	0.14	0.16	0.15	0.14

Operating income divided by tangible assets	0.09	0.09	0.12	0.10	0.09
Net income divided by common equity	0.05	0.06	0.10	0.10	0.11
Earnings per share	$4.30	$4.26	$4.49	$4.26	$4.14

Required

a. What major conclusions can be drawn from this information about the company's future?

b. What additional information would be helpful in your assessment of this company's financial condition?

c. Based on the ratios above, which particular aspects of the company do you believe should receive special emphasis in the audit?

CASE

6-37   Solomon Corp. is a highly successful, closely held Vancouver, British Columbia, company that manufactures and assembles specialty parts for automobiles that are sold in auto parts stores in the West. Sales and profits have expanded rapidly in the past few years, and the prospects for future years are every bit as encouraging. In fact, the Solomon brothers are currently considering either selling out to a large company or going public to obtain additional capital.

The company originated in 1960 when Frank Solomon decided to manufacture tooled parts. In 1975, the company changed over to the auto parts business. Fortunately, it has never been necessary to expand the facilities, but space problems have recently become severe and expanded facilities will be necessary. Land and building costs in Vancouver are currently extremely inflated.

Management has always relied on you for help in its problems inasmuch as the treasurer is sales-oriented and has little background in the controllership function. Salaries of all officers have been fairly modest in order to reinvest earnings in future growth. In fact, the company is oriented toward long-run wealth of the brothers more than toward short-run profit. The brothers have all of their personal wealth invested in the firm.

A major reason for the success of Solomon has been the small but excellent sales force. The sales policy is to sell to small auto shops at high prices. This policy is responsible for fairly high credit losses, but the profit margin is high and the results have been highly successful. The firm has every intention of continuing this policy in the future.

Your firm has been auditing Solomon Corp. since 1970, and you have been on the job for the past three years. The client has excellent internal control and has always been very cooperative. In recent years, the client has attempted to keep net income at a high level because of borrowing needs and future sellout possibilities. Overall, the client has always been pleasant to deal with and willing to help in any way possible. There have never been any major audit adjustments, and an unqualified opinion has always been issued.

In the current year, you have completed the tests of the sales and collection area. The tests of controls for sales and sales returns and allowances were excellent, and an extensive confirmation yielded no material errors. You have carefully reviewed the cutoff for sales and for sales returns and allowances and find these to be excellent. All recorded bad debts appear reasonable, and a review of the aged trial balance indicates that conditions seem about the same as in past years.

	31-12-98 (CURRENT YEAR)	31-12-97	31-12-96	31-12-95
Balance Sheet				
Cash	$ 49,615	$ 39,453	$ 51,811	$ 48,291
Accounts receivable	2,366,938	2,094,052	1,756,321	1,351,470
Allowance for doubtful accounts	(250,000)	(240,000)	(220,000)	(200,000)
Inventory	2,771,833	2,585,820	2,146,389	1,650,959
Current assets	$4,938,386	$4,479,325	$3,734,521	$2,850,720
Capital assets	3,760,531	3,744,590	3,498,930	3,132,133
Total assets	$8,698,917	$8,223,915	$7,233,451	$5,982,853
Current liabilities	$2,253,422	$2,286,433	$1,951,830	$1,625,811
Long-term liabilities	4,711,073	4,525,310	4,191,699	3,550,481
Owners' equity	1,734,422	1,412,172	1,089,922	806,561
Total liabilities and owners' equity	$8,698,917	$8,223,915	$7,233,451	$5,982,853
Income Statement				
Sales (net of G.S.T.)	$6,740,652	$6,165,411	$5,313,752	$4,251,837
Sales returns and allowances	(207,831)	(186,354)	(158,367)	(121,821)
Sales discounts allowed	(74,147)	(63,655)	(52,183)	(42,451)
Bad debts expense	(248,839)	(245,625)	(216,151)	(196,521)
Net sales	$6,209,835	$5,669,777	$4,887,051	$3,891,044
Gross margin	$1,415,926	$1,360,911	$1,230,640	$1,062,543
Net income after taxes	$ 335,166	$ 322,250	$ 283,361	$ 257,829
Aged Accounts Receivable				
0–30 days	$ 942,086	$ 881,232	$ 808,569	$ 674,014
31–60 days	792,742	697,308	561,429	407,271
61–120 days	452,258	368,929	280,962	202,634
>120 days	179,852	146,583	105,361	67,551
Total	$2,366,938	$2,094,052	$1,756,321	$1,351,470

Required

a. Evaluate the information in the case to provide assistance to management for improved operation of its business. Prepare the supporting analysis using an electronic spreadsheet program. (Instructor's option)

b. Do you agree that sales, accounts receivable, and allowance for doubtful accounts are probably correctly stated? Show calculations to support your conclusion.

6-38 A lawyer you know is working on a case for one of his clients who has commenced legal proceedings against an industrial company and its auditor in connection with the company's failure. The auditor, ironically, had precipitated the failure by refusing to issue an unqualified auditor's opinion on the most recent annual financial statements. The CA's professional judgment is being questioned, not because of this refusal and its consequences, but because the lawyer's client claims that the financial statements for prior years should not have received unqualified auditor's opinions.

The lawyer will be reviewing the audit files before the case goes to court. He will also have the opportunity to cross-examine the company's auditor in court.

The lawyer has come to you, Janet Brown, CA, for assistance in the preparation of his case. He has asked you to describe the general characteristics of good professional judgment and, in particular, the steps you would expect the CA to have taken to ensure that he was exercising good professional judgment in this situation.

Required

a. Assume the role of Janet Brown and draft a response to the lawyer.

b. What are the characteristics of working papers that should be present in the defendant CA's working papers?

(CICA adapted)

6-39 You, CA, have been engaged by your provincial institute to perform a practice inspection of Dow and Harder, Chartered Accountants (DH). This inspection involves a review of audit files for a DH client to determine whether generally accepted auditing standards (GAAS) were appropriately applied. If, in your opinion, GAAS were not applied, you are to state the procedures that would have been more appropriate in the circumstances. A report detailing the results of your review will be presented to the senior partner of DH and the institute's practice inspection committee.

You select for inspection the completed audit files of Geriatric Supply Limited (GSL), DH's largest client. GSL has been in business for over 30 years and has been an audit client of DH for much of this time. A private company, GSL had sales of $8 million for the year ended June 30, 1998. GSL paid DH approximately $50,000 in fees for the audit, income tax, and consulting services for the year.

Until December 31, 1997, GSL was a manufacturing and distribution company that manufactured products to order using labour-intensive methods. Under its contract with a provincial government, GSL shipped all its products to hospitals and government-owned nursing homes in the province as soon as the products were completed. GSL demanded a deposit equal to 30 to 40 percent of the selling price of a product before it would commence manufacturing that product. It required full payment in advance for products requiring extra design work.

On December 31, 1997, the contract with the provincial government expired. GSL had anticipated the nonrenewal of the contract and during 1997 began to acquire the machinery needed for mass production.

In order to compete in its newly targeted markets, GSL now maintains a finished-goods inventory in different sizes and colours. A one-year warranty had to be provided, and dealers in the newly arranged dealer network had to be allowed to return unsold products. Some dealers were granted extended credit terms of 120 days.

GSL's sales for made-to-order products were $4,750,000 for the six months ended December 31, 1997. This amount was collected by March 31, 1998. These sales resulted in $45,000 of minor repair work in fiscal 1998.

Your review of DH's 1998 working papers for GSL reveals the following:

1. Compliance audit procedures were completed in December 1997. Substantive audit procedures were completed in August 1998.

2. According to the working papers, DH did not circularize receivable confirmations "because the government institutions rarely responded in prior years."

3. DH's staff attended the June 30, 1998, inventory count and performed test counts of finished-goods inventory. The working papers state: "There was a significant amount of in-process, machine-produced inventory. The valuation of this inventory was discussed with management."

4. The working papers state: "The overhead application method and rate are consistent with those of prior years. Both fixed and variable manufacturing overhead are applied as a percentage of the direct labour cost."

5. Throughout fiscal 1998, GSL used job-order costing. Products that were being machine-manufactured for inventory were produced in batches of 50 or more and were then placed in finished-goods storage until sold. Actual costs of material and labour were charged to the applicable job number. At year end, DH relied on the compliance work performed in December 1997.

6. The auditors included the following comments in their working papers: "No accruals for warranty costs are required, as these have not been material in prior years. It is not clear what effect the design changes for the new products will have. During July and early August 1998, only $50,000 was incurred for repairs on products sold prior to year end."

7. The financial statements at June 30, 1998, show deferred costs of $162,800 for developing GSL's dealer network. The audit working papers state: "We were able to substantiate 80 percent of these items by checking to invoices. The remaining amount was discretionary and was discussed with management."

8. The new products being inventoried for shipment to dealers were developed over several years, and design costs incurred before January 1998 were expensed. In the six months ended June 30, 1998, design costs of $122,000 were incurred and were included with work-in-process inventory. The audit working papers state: "We looked at purchase invoices and payroll records and discussed these items with management. Appears reasonable."

9. Per the working papers: "The client is financing the current assets with a demand bank loan, secured by receivables, inventory, and a second mortgage on the building and machinery. The loan cannot exceed the aggregate of 65 percent of receivables and 40 percent of finished goods inventory. We have to report on compliance with these limits annually to the bank."

10. According to the working papers: "Commencing January 1, 1998, manufacturing overhead variances are being charged to inventory. The calculation was checked, and the treatment was discussed with the bookkeeper."

11. The working papers contain the following note: "The company decided to adopt the following policy regarding the interest on the bank loan and the financing required for machinery purchase: one-half of the interest is to be expensed, and one-half is to be allocated to manufacturing overhead. This is appropriate because a 1:1 debt-to-equity ratio seems reasonable in this business."

12. According to the working papers: "All cash receipts for the period from July 1 to August 10, 1998, were traced back to the receivables ledger at June 30, 1998, and to other documents. No discrepancies were found."

13. A review note in the working papers states: "A standard-form audit report is appropriate. A consistency qualification is not required because all accounting changes can be considered changes in practices rather than policies."

14. Another review note states: "I phoned the owners, and they agreed to accrue their standard yearly bonuses of 20 percent of income before income tax and not to withdraw the cash for several months. This will assist liquidity but will not help the bank's covenant with respect to maintaining a minimum retained-earnings balance. We should invoice this client monthly."

15. The working papers state: "The income statements for the years ended June 30, 1998, and June 30, 1997, were compared. Management explained that the differences were caused by volume changes."

16. The working papers state: "We traced journal entries to shipping records around the June 30, 1998, cutoff and found no problems."

Required

a. List all examples of evidence examined in the DH file of GSL. For each item of evidence, provide an example of the evidence appropriateness. Organize your answer in two columns as follows:

DH EVIDENCE	EVIDENCE APPROPRIATENESS

b. Identify any other problems associated with the GSL audit, for each of the following phases of the audit:
  (1) Knowledge of business
  (2) Planning
  (3) Testing
  (4) Reporting

c. Did DH violate GAAS during the audit of GSL? Support your answer.

(CICA adapted)

7

AUDIT PLANNING AND DOCUMENTATION

AN AUDITOR WHO DOESN'T UNDERSTAND A CLIENT'S BUSINESS TAKES A GREAT RISK

Art Myers, of Myers & Co., public accountants, got an opportunity to break into the health care market when his dentist, Dr. Gary Nettles, approached him about auditing Prairie Dental Associates, a new dental health maintenance organization (DHMO) that Gary and his associates had started. Prairie's main business was to market dental care plans to commercial entities, charge a monthly membership fee per employee, and provide dental services to those members.

When Prairie was formed, its owners hired Maureen O'Sullivan to be the chief financial officer even though she had no DHMO experience. Just prior to the end of Prairie's first fiscal year, Art met with Maureen to plan Prairie's initial audit. Neither Art nor Maureen had any direct experience with a health maintenance organization (nor did anyone else in Myers & Co.), but they both read articles and other literature about the subject including the *AICPA Health Care Audit Guide.*

A specific area of focus at the planning meeting was how to estimate the liability for medical services rendered but not yet billed to the DHMO. This liability is called "incurred but not recorded" (IBNR) and was new to both Art and Maureen. Art agreed to investigate how to calculate this and get back to Maureen.

Art's approach was to contact a friend of his who audited a DHMO in the U.S. His friend, who only had one DHMO client, sent Art a copy of some working papers that included a formula for estimating the IBNR liability. The formula was based on historical data and made sense to Art. He gave the formula to Maureen, who applied it using the twelve months of data available from the initial year of operations. During the audit, Myers & Co. determined the formula was applied accurately.

Shortly after the completion of Prairie's second year of operations, Maureen O'Sullivan had some personal problems that required her to move to another city. Prairie replaced Maureen with Bart Chemers, primarily because Bart had previously worked for a DHMO in the U.S.

When Bart saw how IBNR was estimated, he questioned the formula used and made an in-depth investigation of the situation. He determined that the formula was significantly underestimating the IBNR liability, that the liability was materially understated in the previously audited financial statements, and that, as a result, the rates negotiated in contracts with participants were much lower than they should have been. This finding led to a change in auditors and a sizable monetary settlement by Myers & Co.

This chapter introduces the topic of planning an audit and designing an audit approach, and discusses four major parts of the planning process. You can see how planning fits into the overall audit by examining Figure 5-8 on page 147. This chapter also deals with the study of auditor's working papers to document what the auditor did and the auditor's conclusions.

PLANNING

OBJECTIVE 7-1

Discuss why adequate audit planning is essential.

The first generally accepted auditing examination standard in Section 5100 requires adequate planning.

> The work is to be adequately planned and properly executed using sufficient knowledge of the entity's business as a basis. If assistants are employed, they should be properly supervised.

Section 5150 of the *CICA Handbook* defines audit planning as "developing a general strategy and a detailed approach for the expected nature, extent, and timing of the examination."

There are three main reasons why the auditor should properly plan engagements: to enable the auditor to obtain sufficient appropriate audit evidence for the circumstances, to help keep audit costs reasonable, and to avoid misunderstandings with the client. Obtaining sufficient appropriate audit evidence is essential if the public accounting firm is to minimize legal liability and maintain a good reputation in the professional community. Keeping costs reasonable helps the firm remain competitive and thereby retain its clients, assuming the firm has a reputation for doing quality work. Avoiding misunderstandings with the client is important for good client relations and for facilitating quality work at reasonable costs. For example, suppose the auditor informs the client that the audit will be completed before June 30 but is unable to finish it until August because of inadequate scheduling of staff. The client is likely to be upset with the public accounting firm and may even sue for breach of contract.

Figure 7-1 presents the seven major parts of audit planning: preplan, obtain background information about the client, obtain information about the client's legal obligations, perform preliminary analytical procedures, assess materiality and risk, understand internal control and assess control risk, and develop an overall audit plan and audit program. Each of the first six parts is intended to help the auditor develop the last part, an effective and efficient overall audit plan and audit program. The first four parts of the planning phase of an audit are studied in this chapter. The last three are studied separately in each of the next three chapters.

FIGURE 7-1

Planning an Audit and
Designing an Audit
Approach

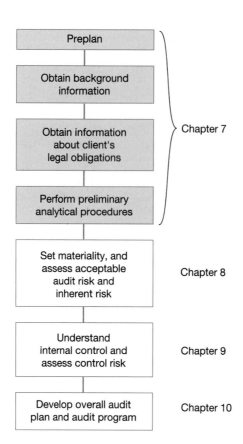

Before beginning the discussion of the first four parts of the planning phase, it is useful to briefly introduce two risk terms that are discussed in depth in the next chapter: acceptable audit risk and inherent risk. These two risks have a significant effect on the conduct and cost of audits. Much of the early planning on audits deals with obtaining information to help auditors assess these risks.

Acceptable audit risk is a measure of how willing the auditor is to accept that the financial statements may be materially misstated after the audit is completed and an unqualified opinion has been issued. When the auditor decides on a lower acceptable audit risk, it means that the auditor wants to be more certain that the financial statements are *not* materially misstated. Zero risk would be certainty, and a 100 percent risk would be complete uncertainty.

When the auditor decides that a lower acceptable audit risk on an audit is appropriate, there are three potential effects:

- More evidence is required to increase audit assurance that there are no material misstatements. It is difficult to implement increased evidence accumulation after the field work has commenced because acceptable audit risk applies to the entire audit. It is expensive and often impractical to increase evidence in every part of an audit.
- The engagement may require more experienced staff. Public accounting firms should staff all engagements with qualified staff, but for low acceptable audit risk clients, special care is appropriate in staffing.
- The engagement will be reviewed more carefully than usual. Public accounting firms need to be sure that the working papers and other matters on all audits are adequately reviewed. When acceptable audit risk is low, there is often more extensive review, including a review by personnel who were not assigned to the engagement.

Inherent risk is a measure of the auditor's assessment of the likelihood that there are material misstatements in a segment before considering the effectiveness of the internal controls. If, for example, the auditor concludes that there is a high likelihood of material misstatement in an account such as accounts receivable, the auditor would conclude that inherent risk for accounts receivable is high.

When the auditor concludes that there is a high inherent risk for an account or a class of transactions, the same three potential effects are appropriate as for the lower acceptable audit risk. However, it is easier and more common to implement increased evidence accumulation for inherent risk than for acceptable audit risk because inherent risk can usually be isolated to one or two accounts or a class of transactions. For example, if inherent risk is high only for accounts receivable, the auditor can restrict the evidence expansion to the audit of accounts receivable.

PREPLAN THE AUDIT

OBJECTIVE 7-2

Apply the steps involved in preplanning the audit.

Most preplanning takes place early in the engagement, frequently in the client's office, to the extent that this is practical. Preplanning involves the following steps: decide whether to accept or continue doing the audit for the client, identify the client's reasons for the audit, obtain an engagement letter, and select staff for the engagement.

CLIENT ACCEPTANCE AND CONTINUANCE

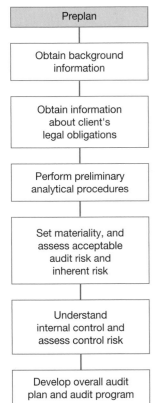

Even though obtaining and retaining clients is not easy in a competitive profession such as public accounting, a public accounting firm must use care in deciding which clients are acceptable. The firm's legal and professional responsibilities are such that clients who lack integrity or argue constantly about the proper conduct of the audit and fees can cause more problems than they are worth. Some public accounting firms may refuse clients in what they perceive to be a high-risk industry such as high technology, health, and casualty insurance, and may even discontinue auditing existing clients in such industries.

New client investigation   Before accepting a new client, most public accounting firms investigate the company to determine its acceptability. To the extent possible, the prospective client's standing in the business community, financial stability, and relations with its previous public accounting firm should be evaluated. For example, many public accounting firms use considerable caution in accepting new clients in newly formed, rapidly growing businesses. Many of these businesses fail financially and expose the public accounting firm to significant potential liability.

For prospective clients that have previously been audited by another public accounting firm, the new (successor) auditor is *required* by the rules of conduct of the institutes and *ordre* of chartered accountants and by the rules of conduct of CGAAC and by incorporating acts such as the *Canada Business Corporations Act* to communicate with the predecessor auditor. The purpose of the requirement is to help the successor auditor evaluate whether to accept the engagement. The communication may, for example, inform the successor auditor that the client lacks integrity or that there have been disputes over accounting principles, audit procedures, or fees.

The burden of initiating the communication rests with the successor auditor. Permission must be obtained from the client before the communication can be made because of the confidentiality requirement in the rules of conduct of the professional accounting bodies. Professional courtesy suggests that the predecessor auditor is required to respond to the request for information. In the event there are legal problems or disputes between the client and the predecessor, the latter's response can be limited to stating that no information will be provided. The successor should seriously consider the desirability of accepting a prospective engagement, without considerable investigation, if a client will not permit the communication or the predecessor will not provide a comprehensive response.

Even when a prospective client has been audited by another public accounting firm, other investigations are needed. Sources of information include local lawyers, other public accountants, banks, and other businesses. In some cases, the auditor may hire a professional investigator to obtain information about the reputation and background of the key members of management. More extensive investigation is appropriate when there has been no previous auditor, when a predecessor auditor will not provide the desired information, or if any indication of problems arises from the communication.

Many practitioners take advantage of the Internet as a search tool to learn more about the potential new client and its key operations by studying available client Web sites and by using search engines for other sites that discuss the potential client. In addition, they use data base search tools or customized search engines to examine financial data or recent publications about the client. This information is useful in the client acceptance decision and throughout the audit if the client is accepted.

Continuing clients   Considering whether or not to continue doing the audit of an existing client is as important a decision as deciding whether or not to accept a new client. For that reason, many public accounting firms evaluate existing clients annually to determine whether there are reasons for not continuing to do the audit. Previous conflicts over such things as the appropriate scope of the audit, the type of opinion to issue, or fees may cause the auditor to discontinue association. The auditor may also determine that the client lacks basic integrity and therefore should no longer be a client. If there is a lawsuit against a public accounting firm by a client or a suit against the client by the public accounting firm, the firm probably should not do the audit because its independence could be questioned.

Even if none of the previously discussed conditions exist, the public accounting firm may decide not to continue doing audits for a client because of excessive risk. For example, a public accounting firm might decide that there is considerable risk of a regulatory conflict between a governmental agency and a client which could result in financial failure of the client and ultimately, lawsuits against the public accounting firm. Even if the engagement is profitable, the risk may exceed the short-term benefits of doing the audit.

Investigation of new clients and re-evaluation of existing ones are an essential part of deciding acceptable audit risk. Assume that a potential client is in a reasonably risky industry and has management with a reputation of integrity but who is also known to take aggressive financial risks. If the public accounting firm decides that acceptable audit risk is extremely low, it may choose not to accept the engagement. If the public accounting firm concludes that acceptable audit risk is low but the client is still acceptable, it is likely to affect the fee proposed to the client. Audits with a low acceptable audit risk will normally result in higher audit costs, which should be reflected in higher audit fees.

Wall Street Journal
www.wsj.com

BIG ACCOUNTING FIRMS WEED OUT RISKY CLIENTS

In a *Wall Street Journal* article, Lee Berton discussed the impact of extensive lawsuits against CPAs by their clients on the firms' willingness to accept or continue auditing risky clients. Excerpts from the article follow:

. . . Big accounting firms say they have begun dropping risky audit clients to lower their risk of lawsuits for allegedly faulty audits. New companies, which have a particularly high chance of failure, are affected most, because almost nothing triggers lawsuits against accountants faster than company failures.

But established companies are getting the ax, too. KPMG Peat Marwick, the fourth-biggest U.S. accounting firm, is currently dropping 50 to 100 audit clients annually, up from only zero to 20 five years ago, says Robert W. Lambert, the firm's new director of risk management. "When a client we audit goes bust," he says, "it costs us a bundle in court if we're sued by investors, whether we win or lose the case."

Mr. Lambert says that legal costs were "staggering" for a lawsuit filed in a federal court in Texas alleging a faulty review of a bank's books by Peat. The bank was taken over by the federal government in 1992 after big losses. The jury ruled in Peat's favour in 1993, but the firm had to spend $7 million to defend itself "even though the fee for the job was only $15,000," Mr. Lambert says. "We just can't afford to take on risky audit clients anymore."

Lawrence Weinbach, managing partner of Arthur Anderson & Co., another leading accounting firm, says his organization has either dropped or declined to audit more than 100 companies over the past two years. "When the company has a risky profile and its stock price is volatile, we're just not going to jump in and do the audit and invite a lawsuit," says Mr. Weinbach.

. . . "No risky client can pay us enough money to defend ourselves after the client develops problems," asserts J. Michael Cook, chairman of Deloitte & Touche, the third biggest U.S. accounting firm. "We must reduce our legal risks to remain viable."

Source: Excerpted from an article by Lee Berton, "Big Accounting Firms Weed Out Risky Clients," *Wall Street Journal* (June 26, 1995), p. B1.

IDENTIFY CLIENT'S REASONS FOR AUDIT

Two major factors affecting the appropriate evidence to accumulate are the likely statement users and their intended uses of the statements. It will be shown in Chapter 8 that the auditor is likely to accumulate more evidence when the statements are to be used extensively. This is often the case for publicly held companies, those with extensive indebtedness, and companies that are to be sold in the near future.

The most likely uses of the statements can be determined from previous experience in the engagement and discussion with management. Throughout the engagement, the auditor may get additional information as to why the client is having an audit and the likely uses of the financial statements. This information may affect the auditor's assessment of acceptable audit risk.

OBTAIN AN ENGAGEMENT LETTER

A clear understanding of the terms of the engagement should exist between the client and the public accounting firm. The terms should be in writing to minimize misunderstandings. This is typically done using an engagement letter.

The engagement letter is an agreement between the public accounting firm and the client for the conduct of the audit and related services. It should specify whether the auditor will perform an audit, a review, or a compilation, plus any other services such as tax returns or management services. It should also state any restrictions to be imposed on the auditor's work, deadlines for completing the audit, assistance to be provided by the client's personnel in obtaining records and documents, and schedules to be prepared for the auditor. It often includes an agreement on fees. The engagement letter is also a means of informing the client that the auditor is not responsible for the discovery of all acts of fraud.

The engagement letter does not affect the public accounting firm's responsibility to external users of audited financial statements, but it can affect legal responsibilities to the client. For example, if the client sued the public accounting firm for failing to find a material misstatement, one defence a public accounting firm could use would be a signed engagement letter stating that a review, rather than an audit, was agreed upon.

Engagement letter information is important in planning the audit principally because it affects the timing of the tests and the total amount of time the audit and other services will take. If the deadline for submitting the audit report is soon after the balance sheet date, a significant portion of the audit must be done before the end of the year. When the auditor is preparing tax returns and a management letter, or if client assistance is not available, arrangements must be made to extend the amount of time for the engagement. Client-imposed restrictions on the audit could affect the procedures performed and possibly even the type of audit opinion issued. An example of an engagement letter for the audit of Hillsburg Hardware Ltd. is given in Figure 7-2. The financial statements for Hillsburg Hardware Ltd. are included on pages 127–129.

FIGURE 7-2
Engagement Letter

BORITZ, KAO, KADOUS & CO., Chartered Accountants
Halifax, Nova Scotia B3M 3J5

June 14, 19X8

June 14, 1998

Mr. Rick Chulick, President
Hillsburg Hardware Ltd.
2146 Willow Street
Halifax, Nova Scotia
B3H 3F9

Dear Mr. Chulick:

Thank you for reappointing us as your auditors for the year ending December 31, 1998. The purpose of this letter is to confirm our mutual understanding of the terms of our engagement

It will be the responsibility of J. E. Boritz to make sure that management receives quality service. J. E. Boritz will, as considered necessary, call upon other individuals with specialized knowledge, either in this office or elsewhere in our firm.

While auditing and reporting on your annual financial statements is to be the recurring basic service we provide, we would also like to assist you on issues as they arise throughout the year. Hence, we hope that you will call J. E. Boritz whenever you feel J. E. Boritz can be of assistance.

Audit of Financial Statements

The purpose of our annual engagement to audit financial statements is to evaluate the fairness of presentation of the statements in conformity with generally accepted accounting principles.

Our audit will be conducted in accordance with generally accepted auditing standards. Those standards require that we plan and perform an audit to obtain reasonable assurance that the financial statements are free of material misstatement. An audit includes examining, on a test basis, evidence supporting the amounts and disclosures in the financial statements. An audit also includes assessing the accounting principles used and significant estimates by management, as well as evaluating the overall financial statement presentation.

It should be noted that an audit conducted in accordance with generally accepted auditing standards is based on selective tests. Because detailed examination is not performed on all transactions, there is a risk that material fraud or error may exist but not be detected.

The objective of our audit is the expression of an opinion on financial statements. Our ability to express that opinion, and the wording of our opinion, will be dependent on the facts and circumstances at the date of our report. If our audit report requires qualification, the reasons therefore will be discussed with you prior to its issuance.

Year 2000

Neither our audit of the Company's financial statements for the year ending December 31, 1998, nor any reviews or other services provided pursuant to this engagement letter, will provide any assurances, nor will we express any opinion, that the Company's systems or any other systems, such as those of the Company's vendors, service providers, customers, unconsolidated subsidiaries or joint ventures in which the Company has an investment, or other third parties, are Year 2000 compliant. In addition, we are not engaged to perform, nor will we perform as part of this engagement, any procedures to test whether the Company's systems or any other systems are Year 2000 compliant or whether the plans and activities of the Company or any third parties are sufficient to address and correct systems or any other problems that might arise because of the Year 2000, nor will we express any opinion or provide any other assurances with respect to these matters.

Management's Responsibility

We direct your attention to the fact that the financial statements are the responsibility of management. In this regard, management has the responsibility for designing effective internal controls, for properly recording transactions in the accounting records, for making appropriate accounting estimates, for safeguarding assets, and for the overall accuracy of the financial statements.

Other Communications Arising from the Audit

In connection with the planning and the performance of our audit, we will communicate to you, to the extent that they come to our attention, fraud and significant deficiencies in the design or operation of the internal control structure that could adversely affect the Company's ability to record, process, summarize, and report financial data.

We may also have other comments for management on matters we have observed and possible ways to improve the efficiency of operations or other recommendations concerning the internal control structure.

With respect to these other communications, it is our practice to discuss all comments, if appropriate, with the level of management responsible for the matters prior to their communication to you.

Coordination of the Audit

Our audit is scheduled for performance and completion this year as follows:

Audit Performance Schedule	Begin	Complete
Planning	August 1, 1998	September 1, 1998
Interim	September 1, 1998	September 24, 1998
Year End	February 1, 1999	February 18, 1999
Report on Audit of Financial Statements		March 10, 1999

Assistance to be supplied by your personnel, including preparation of schedules and analyses of accounts, is described in a separate attachment. Timely completion of this work will facilitate the conclusion of our audit.

We are, of course, available to assist you in other areas that might arise.

Fees

Our fees are based on the amount of time required at various levels of responsibility, plus out-of-pocket expenses (travel, printing, telephone, etc.), payable upon presentation of our invoices. We will notify you immediately of any circumstances we encounter which could significantly affect our initial estimate of total fees.

We appreciate the opportunity to be of service to you and believe this letter accurately summarizes the significant items of our engagement. If you agree with the terms of our engagement as described, please sign the copy of this letter in the space provided and return it to us.

Yours very truly,

J. E. Boritz

J. E. Boritz
Boritz, Kao, Kadous & Co.

Accepted By: *Rick Chulick*
Title: President
Date: June 21, 1998

Note: This engagement letter is based upon an engagement letter provided by Deloitte and Touche during 1998.

SELECT STAFF FOR THE ENGAGEMENT

Assigning the appropriate staff to the engagement is important to meet the generally accepted auditing standards of Section 5100 and to promote audit efficiency. The general standard states in part:

> The examination should be performed and the report prepared by a person or persons having adequate technical training and proficiency in auditing . . .

Staff must, therefore, be assigned with that standard in mind. On larger engagements, there are likely to be one or more partners and staff at several experience levels doing the audit. Specialists in such technical areas as statistical sampling and computer auditing may also be assigned. On smaller audits, there may be only one or two staff members.

A major consideration affecting staffing is the need for continuity from year to year. An inexperienced staff assistant is likely to become the most experienced nonpartner on the engagement within a few years. Continuity helps the public accounting firm maintain familiarity with the technical requirements and closer interpersonal relations with the client's personnel.

Another consideration is that the persons assigned be familiar with the client's industry. This is discussed shortly.

To illustrate the importance of assigning appropriate staff to engagements, consider a computer manufacturing client with an extensive inventory of computers and computer parts. Inherent risk for inventory has been assessed as high. It is essential for the staff person doing the inventory portion of the audit to be experienced in auditing inventory. In addition, he or she should have a good understanding of the computer manufacturing industry.

OBTAIN BACKGROUND INFORMATION

OBTAIN KNOWLEDGE OF CLIENT'S INDUSTRY AND BUSINESS

OBJECTIVE 7-3

Know appropriate background information to obtain about an audit client.

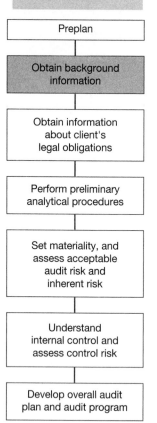

An extensive understanding of the client's business and industry and knowledge about the company's operations are essential for doing an adequate audit. Most of this information is obtained at the client's premises, especially for a new client.

There are three primary reasons for obtaining a good understanding of the client's industry. First, many industries have unique accounting requirements that the auditor must understand to evaluate whether the client's financial statements are in accordance with generally accepted accounting principles. For example, if an auditor is doing an audit of a city, the auditor must understand municipal accounting requirements. There are also unique accounting requirements for construction companies, railroads, not-for-profit organizations, financial institutions, and many other organizations.

Second, the auditor can often identify risks in the industry that may affect the auditor's assessment of acceptable audit risk, or even whether auditing companies in the industry is advisable. As stated earlier, certain industries are riskier than others, such as the high-tech and biomedical industries.

Finally, there are inherent risks that are typically common to all clients in certain industries. Understanding those risks aids the auditor in identifying the client's inherent risks. Examples include potential inventory obsolescence inherent risk in the fashion clothes industry, accounts receivable collection inherent risk in the consumer loan industry, and reserve for loss inherent risk in the casualty insurance industry.

Knowledge of the client's industry can be obtained in different ways. These include discussions with the auditor in the firm who was responsible for the engagement in previous years and other auditors in the firm currently on similar engagements, as well as conferences with the client's personnel. Many of the larger public accounting firms have industry specialists who can be consulted for their expertise. Smaller firms that do not have the expertise can consult the practice advisory service of their professional body. There are often industry audit guides, textbooks, and technical magazines available for the auditor to study in most major industries. Some auditors follow the practice of subscribing to specialized journals for those industries to which they devote a large amount of time. Considerable knowledge can also be obtained by participating actively in industry associations and training programs.

Knowledge about the client's business that differentiates it from other companies in its industry is also needed. That knowledge will help the auditor more effectively assess acceptable audit risk and inherent risk, and will also be useful in designing analytical procedures.

Section 5140 of the *CICA Handbook* requires the auditor to obtain knowledge of the entity's business in order to conduct the audit. Paragraph 5140.03 states, "In performing an audit, the auditor should obtain and apply knowledge of the entity's business in a continuous and cumulative manner." The section goes on to indicate that the auditor's knowledge of the business is a basis for helping the auditor plan and carry out the audit, including:

- Determining materiality levels and assessing inherent risk
- Obtaining an understanding of internal control
- Identifying the sources and nature of audit evidence available
- Designing audit procedures
- Understanding the substance of transactions
- Assessing whether sufficient appropriate evidence is available
- Assessing the appropriateness of management's selection and application of accounting principles
- Evaluating management's overall financial statement presentation

Companies filing their financial statements with a securities commission or whose securities are traded in a public market and all life insurance enterprises are required under paragraph 1701.16 of the *CICA Handbook* to disclose segment information by industry and by geographic area and the amount of export sales. Auditors must have sufficient knowledge of a company's business to enable them to evaluate whether segmented information should be disclosed and to determine whether the client's disclosure of segmented information is appropriate.

The auditor's *permanent files* frequently include the history of the company, a list of the major lines of business, and a record of the most important accounting policies in previous years. Study of this information and discussions with the client's personnel aid in understanding the business.

MANY PUBLIC ACCOUNTING FIRMS RE-ORGANIZE TO FOCUS ON INDUSTRIES

A high level of knowledge of a client's industry and business is so critical to quality audits and providing value-added tax and consulting services that many public accounting firms have re-organized to focus on industry lines. For example, KPMG LLP has re-organized its practice around lines of business such as the following: Financial Services; Health Care & Life Sciences; Manufacturing, Retailing & Distribution; Information, Communications & Entertainment; and Public Services. Re-organizing along industry lines may help public accounting firms such as KPMG LLP better understand their clients' businesses and provide additional value-added services.

KPMG International
www.kpmg.com

TOUR THE PLANT AND OFFICES

A tour of the client's facilities is helpful in obtaining a better understanding of the client's business and operations because it provides an opportunity to observe operations firsthand and to meet key personnel. The actual viewing of the physical facilities aids in understanding physical safeguards over assets and in interpreting accounting data by providing a frame of reference in which to visualize such assets as inventory in process, data processing equipment, and factory equipment. A knowledge of the physical layout also facilitates getting answers to questions later in the audit.

The tour may also help the auditor identify inherent risks. For example, if the auditor observes unused equipment and potentially unsalable inventory, it will affect the assessment of inherent risks for equipment and inventory. Discussions with nonaccounting employees during the tour and throughout the audit are useful in maintaining a broad perspective.

IDENTIFY RELATED PARTIES

Transactions with related parties are important to auditors because they must be *disclosed in the financial statements* if they are material. Generally accepted accounting principles require disclosure of the nature of the related-party relationship; a description of transactions, including dollar amounts; and amounts due from and to related parties. Transactions with related parties are not arms-length transactions. There is, therefore, a risk that they were not valued at the same amount as they would have been if the transactions had been with an independent party. Most auditors assess inherent risk as high for related parties and related party transactions, both because of the accounting disclosure requirements and the lack of independence between the parties involved in the transactions.

A party is considered to be a *related party* in Section 3840 of the *CICA Handbook* when it "has the ability to exercise, directly or indirectly, control or significant influence over [the operating and financial decisions of another party]." A *related-party transaction* is any transaction between the client and a related party. Common examples include sales or purchase transactions between a parent company and its subsidiary, exchanges of equipment between two companies owned by the same person, and loans to officers. A less common example, described in Section 3841 as *economic dependence*, is the potential for exercise of significant influence on an audit client by, for example, its most important supplier or customer, lender or borrower.

Because related-party transactions must be disclosed, it is important that all related parties be *identified and included in the permanent files* early in the engagement. Finding undisclosed related-party transactions is thereby facilitated. Common ways of identifying related parties include inquiry of management, review of filings with regulatory bodies such as securities commissions, and examination of shareholders' listings to identify principal shareholders.

EVALUATE NEED FOR OUTSIDE SPECIALISTS

When the auditor encounters situations requiring specialized knowledge, it may be necessary to consult a specialist. Section 5360 of the *CICA Handbook*, "Using the Work of a Specialist," establishes the requirements for selecting specialists and reviewing their work. Section 5365, "Communications with Actuaries," applies together with 5360 when the specialist is an actuary. Examples include using a diamond expert in evaluating the replacement cost of diamonds and an actuary for determining the appropriateness of the recorded value of insurance loss reserves. Another common use of specialists is consulting with lawyers on the legal interpretation of contracts and titles. In the previously discussed example of a large inventory of computers and computer parts, the public accounting firm may decide to engage a specialist if no one within the firm is qualified to evaluate whether the inventory is obsolete.

The auditor should have a sufficient understanding of the client's business to recognize the need for a specialist. The auditor should evaluate the specialist's professional qualifications and understand the objectives and scope of the specialist's work. The auditor should also consider the specialist's relationship to the client, including circumstances that might impair the specialist's objectivity.

OBTAIN INFORMATION ABOUT CLIENT'S LEGAL OBLIGATIONS

OBJECTIVE 7-4

Know appropriate information to obtain about an audit client's legal obligations.

Three closely related types of legal documents and records should be examined early in the engagement: articles of incorporation and bylaws, minutes of board of directors' and shareholders' meetings, and contracts. Some information, such as contracts, must be disclosed in the financial statements. Other information, such as authorizations in the board of directors' minutes, is useful in other parts of the audit. Early knowledge of these legal documents and records enables auditors to interpret related evidence throughout the engagement and to make sure there is proper disclosure in the financial statements.

ARTICLES OF INCORPORATION AND BYLAWS

The *articles of incorporation*, granted by the federal government or by the province in which the company is incorporated, is the legal document necessary for recognizing a corporation as a separate entity. It includes the exact name of the corporation, the date of incorporation, the kinds and amounts of capital stock the corporation is authorized to issue, and the types of business activities the corporation is authorized to conduct. In specifying the kinds of capital stock, it also includes such information as the voting rights of each class of stock, preferences and conditions necessary for dividends, and prior rights in liquidation.

The *bylaws* include the rules and procedures adopted by the shareholders of the corporation. They specify such things as the fiscal year of the corporation, the frequency of shareholder meetings, the method of voting for directors, and the duties and powers of the corporate officers.

The auditor must understand the requirements of the articles of incorporation and the bylaws in order to determine whether the financial statements are properly presented. The correct disclosure of the shareholders' equity, including the proper payment of dividends, depends heavily on these requirements.

MINUTES OF MEETINGS

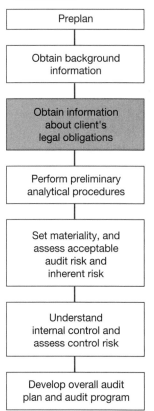

The *corporate minutes* are the official record of the meetings of the board of directors and shareholders. They include summaries of the most important topics discussed at these meetings and the decisions made by the directors and shareholders. The auditor should read the minutes to obtain information that is relevant to performing the audit. There are two categories of relevant information in minutes: authorizations and discussions by the board of directors affecting inherent risk.

Common authorizations in the minutes include compensation of officers, new contracts and agreements, acquisitions of property, loans, and dividend payments. While reading the minutes, the auditor should identify relevant authorizations and include the information in the working papers by making an abstract of the minutes or by obtaining a copy and underlining significant portions. Some time before the audit is completed, there must be a follow-up of this information to be sure that management has complied with actions taken by the shareholders and the board of directors. As an illustration, the authorized compensation of officers should be traced to each individual officer's payroll record as a test of whether the correct total compensation was paid. Similarly, the auditor should compare the authorizations of loans with notes payable to make certain that these liabilities are recorded.

Information included in the minutes affecting the auditor's assessment of inherent risk are likely to involve more general discussions. To illustrate, assume that the minutes state that the board of directors discussed two topics: changes in its industry that affect the usefulness of existing machinery and equipment, and a possible lawsuit by Environment Canada for chemical seepage at a plant in Ontario. The first discussion is likely to affect the inherent risk of obsolete equipment and the second one the inherent risk of an illegal act.

CONTRACTS

Clients become involved in different types of contracts that are of interest to the auditor. These can include such diverse items as long-term notes and bonds payable, stock options, pension plans, contracts with vendors for future delivery of supplies, software usage and maintenance contracts, government contracts for completion and delivery of manufactured products, royalty agreements, union contracts, and leases.

Most contracts are of primary interest in individual parts of the audit and, in practice, receive special attention during the different phases of the detailed tests. For example, the provisions of a pension plan would receive substantial emphasis as a part of the audit of the unfunded liability for pensions. The auditor should review and abstract the documents early in the engagement to gain a better perspective of the organization and to become familiar with potential problem areas. Later these documents can be examined more carefully as a part of the tests of individual audit areas.

The existence of contracts often affects the auditor's assessed inherent risk. To illustrate, assume that the auditor determines early in the audit that the client has signed several sales contracts with severe nonperformance clauses committing the company to deliver specified quantities of its product at agreed-upon prices during the current and next five years. The inherent risk for total sales, liabilities for penalties, and sales commitment disclosures are likely to be assessed as high in this situation.

PERFORM PRELIMINARY ANALYTICAL PROCEDURES

OBJECTIVE 7-5

Discuss the nature and purposes of preliminary analytical procedures.

Chapter 6 discussed the timing of analytical procedures and the four purposes of performing them. Doing analytical procedures during the planning phase is an essential part of conducting both efficient and effective audits. For a brief review, you should examine the four purposes of analytical procedures on pages 174 to 176 and especially Figure 6-2 on page 176.

Instead of restating the importance of analytical procedures during the planning phase, one example of analytical procedures typically done during planning is provided for each of the four purposes shown in Table 7-1.

TABLE 7-1

EXAMPLES OF ANALYTICAL PROCEDURES PERFORMED DURING PLANNING

PURPOSE	ANALYTICAL PROCEDURE PERFORMED DURING THE PLANNING PHASE
Understand the client's industry and business	Calculate key ratios for the client's business and compare them to industry averages.
Assess going concern	Calculate the debt to equity ratio and compare it to previous years and successful companies in the industry.
Indicate possible misstatements	Compare the gross margin to prior years, looking for large fluctuations.
Reduce detailed tests	Compare prepaid expenses and related expense accounts to prior years.

SUMMARY OF THE PURPOSES OF AUDIT PLANNING

There are several purposes of the planning procedures discussed in this section. A major purpose is to provide information to aid the auditor in assessing acceptable audit risk and inherent risk. These assessments will affect the auditor's client acceptance or continuation decision, the proposed audit fee, and the auditor's evidence decisions. A second purpose is to obtain information that requires follow-up during the audit. Doing so is one step in obtaining sufficient appropriate audit evidence. Examples include identifying approvals in the minutes of such items as dividends and officers' salaries, and searching for the names of related parties to help the auditor determine if related party transactions exist. Other purposes include staffing the engagement and obtaining an engagement letter. Figure 7-3 summarizes the four major parts of audit planning discussed in this section and the key components of each part, with a brief illustration of how a public accounting firm applied each component to a continuing client, Hillsburg Hardware Ltd.

FIGURE 7-3

Key Planning Parts: Preplan, Obtain Background Information, Obtain Information About Client's Legal Obligations, Preliminary Analytical Procedures Applied to Hillsburg Hardware Ltd.

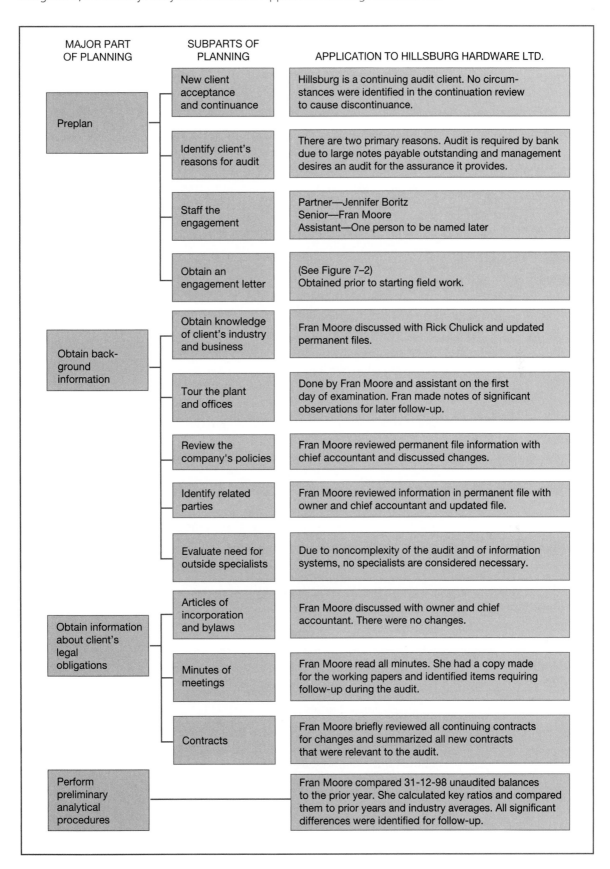

MAJOR PART OF PLANNING	SUBPARTS OF PLANNING	APPLICATION TO HILLSBURG HARDWARE LTD.
Preplan	New client acceptance and continuance	Hillsburg is a continuing audit client. No circumstances were identified in the continuation review to cause discontinuance.
	Identify client's reasons for audit	There are two primary reasons. Audit is required by bank due to large notes payable outstanding and management desires an audit for the assurance it provides.
	Staff the engagement	Partner—Jennifer Boritz Senior—Fran Moore Assistant—One person to be named later
	Obtain an engagement letter	(See Figure 7–2) Obtained prior to starting field work.
Obtain background information	Obtain knowledge of client's industry and business	Fran Moore discussed with Rick Chulick and updated permanent files.
	Tour the plant and offices	Done by Fran Moore and assistant on the first day of examination. Fran made notes of significant observations for later follow-up.
	Review the company's policies	Fran Moore reviewed permanent file information with chief accountant and discussed changes.
	Identify related parties	Fran Moore reviewed information in permanent file with owner and chief accountant and updated file.
	Evaluate need for outside specialists	Due to noncomplexity of the audit and of information systems, no specialists are considered necessary.
Obtain information about client's legal obligations	Articles of incorporation and bylaws	Fran Moore discussed with owner and chief accountant. There were no changes.
	Minutes of meetings	Fran Moore read all minutes. She had a copy made for the working papers and identified items requiring follow-up during the audit.
	Contracts	Fran Moore briefly reviewed all continuing contracts for changes and summarized all new contracts that were relevant to the audit.
Perform preliminary analytical procedures		Fran Moore compared 31-12-98 unaudited balances to the prior year. She calculated key ratios and compared them to prior years and industry averages. All significant differences were identified for follow-up.

WILL IT STAND UP IN COURT?

Rhonda McMillan had been the in-charge auditor on the audit of Blaine Construction Corp. in 1993. Now she is sitting here, in 1999, in a room full of lawyers who are asking her questions about the 1993 audit. Blaine was sold to another company in 1994 at a purchase price that was based primarily on the 1993 audited financial statements. Several of the large construction contracts showed a profit in 1993 using the percentage of completion method, but ultimately resulted in large losses for the buyer. Since Rhonda's firm audited the 1993 financial statements, the buyer is trying to make the case that Rhonda's firm failed in its audit of contract costs and revenues.

The buyer's lawyer is taking Rhonda's deposition and is asking her about the audit work she did on contracts. Referring to the working papers, his examination goes something like this:

Lawyer: Do you recognize this exhibit, and if you do, would you please identify it for us?

Rhonda: Yes, this is the summary of contracts in progress at the end of 1993.

Lawyer: Did you prepare this document?

Rhonda: I believe the client prepared it, but I audited it. My initials are right here in the upper right-hand corner.

Lawyer: When did you do this audit work?

Rhonda: I'm not sure; I forgot to date this one. But it must have been about the second week in March because that's when we did the field work.

Lawyer: Now I'd like to turn your attention to this tick mark next to the Baldwin contract. You see where it shows Baldwin, and then the red sort of cross-like mark?

Rhonda: Yes.

Lawyer: In the explanation for that mark, it says: "Discussed status of job with Elton Burgess. Job is going according to schedule and he believes that the expected profit will be earned." Now my question is, Ms. McMillan, what exactly was the nature and content of your discussion with Mr. Burgess?

Rhonda: Other than what is in the explanation to this tick mark, I have no idea. I mean, this all took place six years ago. I only worked on the engagement that one year, and I can hardly even remember that.

WORKING PAPERS

According to the *CICA Handbook*, paragraph 5145.02,

> Working papers are the [written or electronic] records kept by the auditor of procedures applied and the results thereof, information obtained and conclusions reached in performing his or her examination [in accordance with GAAS] and preparing his or her report.

Working papers should include all the information the auditor considers necessary to conduct the examination adequately and to provide support for the auditor's report.

OBJECTIVE 7-6

**Explain the purposes
of audit working
papers.**

The overall objective of working papers is to aid the auditor in providing reasonable assurance that an adequate audit was conducted in accordance with generally accepted auditing standards. More specifically, the working papers, as they pertain to the current year's audit, provide a basis for planning the audit, a record of the evidence accumulated and the results of the tests, data for determining the proper type of auditor's report, and a basis for review by supervisors and partners. Increasingly, working papers are maintained in computerized files, with the only paper component consisting of documentation provided by the client or external parties.

Basis for planning the audit   If the auditor is to plan the current year's audit adequately, the necessary reference information must be available in the working papers. The papers include such diverse planning information as descriptive information about internal control, a time budget for individual audit areas, the audit program, and the results of the preceding year's audit.

Record of the evidence accumulated and the results of the tests   The working papers are the primary means of documenting that an adequate audit was conducted in accordance with GAAS. If the need arises, the auditor must be able to demonstrate to regulatory agencies, such as the British Columbia Securities Commission, and to the courts that the audit was well planned and adequately supervised; the evidence accumulated was appropriate, sufficient, and timely; and the auditor's report was proper considering the results of the examination.

Data for determining the proper type of auditor's report   The working papers provide an important source of information to assist the auditor in deciding the appropriate auditor's report to issue in a given set of circumstances. The data in the papers are useful for evaluating the adequacy of audit scope and the fairness of the financial statements. In addition, the working papers contain information needed to assist the client in the preparation of the financial statements.

Basis for review by managers and partners   The working papers are the primary frame of reference used by supervisory personnel to evaluate whether sufficient appropriate evidence was accumulated to justify the auditor's report.

In addition to the purposes directly related to the auditor's report, the working papers can also serve as the basis for preparing tax returns, filings with the provincial securities commissions, and other reports. They are a source of information for issuing communications to the audit committee and management concerning various matters, such as internal control weaknesses or operations recommendations. Working papers also provide a frame of reference for training personnel and aid in planning and coordinating subsequent audits.

OBJECTIVE 7-7

**Discuss and apply the
concepts behind the
preparation and
organization of audit
working papers.**

Each public accounting firm establishes its own approach to preparing and organizing working papers, and the beginning auditor must adopt his or her firm's approach. The emphasis in this text is on the general concepts common to all working papers.

Figure 7-4 illustrates the contents and organization of a typical set of papers. They contain virtually everything involved in the examination. There is a definite logic to the type of working papers prepared for an audit and the way they are arranged in the files, even though different firms may follow somewhat different approaches. In the figure, the working papers start with more general information, such as corporate data in the permanent files, and end with the financial statements and auditor's report. In between are the working papers supporting the auditor's tests.

FIGURE 7-4
Working Paper
Contents and
Organization

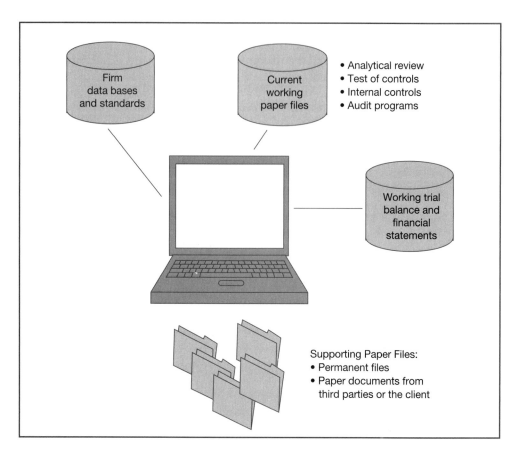

- Analytical review
- Test of controls
- Internal controls
- Audit programs

Supporting Paper Files:
- Permanent files
- Paper documents from third parties or the client

PERMANENT FILES

Permanent files are intended to contain data of a *historical or continuing nature* pertinent to the current examination. These files provide a convenient source of information about the audit that is of continuing interest from year to year. The permanent files typically include the following:

- Extracts or copies of such company documents of continuing importance as the articles of incorporation, bylaws, bond indentures, and contracts. The contracts are pension plans, leases, software usage and maintenance agreements, stock options, and so on. Each of these documents is of significance to the auditor for as many years as it is in effect.

- Analyses, from previous years, of accounts that have continuing importance to the auditor. These include accounts such as long-term debt, shareholders' equity accounts, goodwill, and capital assets. Having this information in the permanent files enables the auditor to concentrate on analyzing only the changes in the current year's balance while retaining the results of previous years' audits in a form accessible for review.

- Information related to the understanding of internal control and assessment of control risk. This includes organization charts, flowcharts, questionnaires, and other internal control information, including enumeration of controls and weaknesses in the system.

- The results of analytical procedures from previous years' audits. Among these data are ratios and percentages computed by the auditor, and the total balance or the balance by month for selected accounts. This information is useful in helping the auditor decide whether there are unusual changes in the current year's account balances that should be investigated more extensively.

Analytical procedures and the understanding of internal control and assessment of control risk are included in the current period working papers rather than in the permanent file by many public accounting firms.

The current files include all working papers applicable to the year under audit. There is one set of permanent files for each client and a set of current files for each year's audit. The types of information included in the current file are briefly discussed in the sections that follow. As firms strive towards a paperless environment, much of this information is prepared and stored electronically.

Risk assessment and materiality Prior to commencing controls testing or detail testing, conclusions need to be reached on materiality, acceptable audit risk, inherent risks, and control risks. Reasoning and conclusions are documented, and the resulting overall audit approach is documented. Analytical procedures for planning purposes may also be included in this section.

Audit program The *audit program* is kept in the relevant section with that section's working papers (e.g., accounts receivable), although some firms may also keep the audit program in a separate file. As the audit progresses, each auditor initials the program for the audit procedures performed and records the date of completion. The inclusion in the working papers of a well-designed audit program completed in a conscientious manner is evidence of a high-quality audit.

General information Some working papers include current period information that is of a general nature rather than designed to support specific financial statement amounts. This includes such items as staff scheduling and budgets, abstracts or copies of minutes of the board of directors' meetings, abstracts of contracts or agreements not included in the permanent files, notes on discussions with the client, working-paper review comments, subsequent events analysis, and summary documentation indicating audit conclusions by section.

Working trial balance Since the basis for preparing the financial statements is the general ledger, the amounts included in that record are the focal point of the examination. As early as possible after the balance sheet date, the auditor obtains or prepares a copy of the general ledger accounts and their year-end balances (frequently in electronic form). Once incorporated into working papers, this schedule is the working trial balance.

The technique used by many firms is to have the auditor's working trial balance in the same grouping format as the financial statements. Each line item on the trial balance is supported by a *lead schedule*, containing the detailed accounts from the general ledger making up the line item total. Each detailed account on the lead schedule is, in turn, supported by appropriate schedules evidencing the audit work performed and the conclusions reached. As an example, the relationship between cash as it is stated on the financial statements, the working trial balance, the lead schedule for cash, and the supporting working papers is presented in Figure 7-5. As the figure indicates, cash on the financial statements is the same as on the working trial balance and the total of the detail on the cash lead schedule. Initially, figures for the lead schedule were taken from the general ledger. The audit work performed resulted in an adjustment to cash that would be evidenced in the detail schedules and reflected on the lead schedule, the working trial balance, and the financial statements.

Adjusting and reclassification entries When the auditor discovers material misstatements in the accounting records, the financial statements must be corrected. For example, if the client failed to reduce inventory properly for obsolete raw materials, an adjusting entry can be suggested by the auditor to reflect the realizable value of the inventory. Even though adjusting entries discovered in the audit are typically prepared by the auditor, they must be approved and made by the client because the books and records are the client's and management has primary responsibility for the fair presentation of the statements. It is therefore important to remember that when the auditor believes that an adjusting or reclassification is required, the auditor must

FIGURE 7-5

Relationship of
Working Papers to
Financial Statements

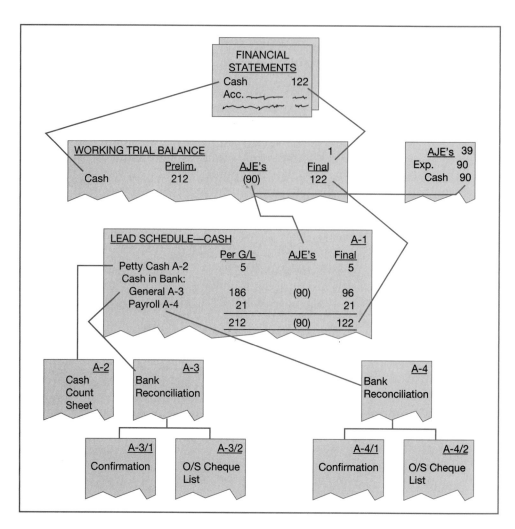

ask management to make the entry. Figure 7-5 illustrates an adjustment of the general cash account for $90. Use of automated working-paper software facilitates the necessary posting of such entries to multiple levels of working papers, from the working paper where the adjustment was described to the lead schedule to the working trial balance and through to the financial statements.

Reclassification entries are frequently made in the statements to present accounting information properly, even when the general ledger balances are correct. A common example is the reclassification for financial statement purposes of material credit balances in accounts receivable to accounts payable. Because the balance in accounts receivable on the general ledger reflects the accounts receivable properly from the point of view of operating the company on a day-to-day basis, the reclassification entry is not included in the client's general ledger.

Only those adjusting and reclassification entries that significantly affect the fair presentation of financial statements must be made. The determination of when a misstatement should be adjusted is based on *materiality*. The auditor should keep in mind that several immaterial misstatements that are not adjusted could result in an overall material misstatement when the misstatements are combined. It is common for auditors to summarize on a separate working paper all adjusting and reclassification entries that have not been recorded or posted to the accounts in the books or the working papers as a means of determining their cumulative effect.

Supporting schedules   The largest portion of working papers includes the detailed schedules prepared by the client or the auditors in support of specific amounts on the financial statements. Many different types of schedules are used. Use of the appropriate type for a given aspect of the audit is necessary to document the adequacy of the audit and to fulfill the other objectives of working papers. Following are the major types of supporting schedules:

- *Analysis.* An analysis is designed to show the *activity in a general ledger account* during the entire period under examination, tying together the beginning and ending balances. This type of schedule is normally used for accounts such as marketable securities, notes receivable, allowance for doubtful accounts, capital assets, long-term debt, and all equity accounts. The common characteristic of these accounts is the significance of the activity in the account during the year. In most cases, the working papers for analysis have cross-references to other working papers.
- *Trial balance or list.* This type of schedule consists of the *details that make up a year-end balance* of a general ledger account. It differs from an analysis in that it includes only those items constituting the end-of-the-period balance. Common examples include aged trial balances or lists in support of trade accounts receivable, trade accounts payable, repairs and maintenance expenses, legal expense, and miscellaneous income. An example is included in Figure 7-6 on page 218.
- *Reconciliation of amounts.* A reconciliation *supports a specific amount* and is normally expected to tie the amount recorded in the client's records to another source of information. Examples include the reconciliation of bank balances with bank statements, the reconciliation of subsidiary accounts receivable balances with confirmations from customers, and the reconciliation of accounts payable balances with vendors' statements. An example is included on page 679.
- *Tests of reasonableness.* A test of reasonableness schedule, as the name implies, contains information that enables the auditor to evaluate whether the client's balance appears to include a misstatement considering the circumstances in the engagement. Frequently, auditors test amortization expense, the provision for income taxes, and the allowance for doubtful accounts by tests of reasonableness. These tests are primarily analytical procedures.
- *Summary procedures.* Another type of schedule *summarizes the results* of a specific audit procedure performed. Examples are the summary of the results of accounts receivable confirmation and the summary of inventory observations.
- *Examination of supporting documents.* A number of special-purpose schedules are designed to *show detailed tests performed*, such as examination of documents during tests of transactions or cutoffs. These schedules show no totals, and they do not tie in to the general ledger because they document only the tests performed and the results found. The schedules must, however, state a definite positive or negative conclusion about the objective of the test.
- *Informational.* This type of schedule contains information as opposed to audit evidence. These schedules include information for tax returns and data such as time budgets and the client's working hours, which are helpful in administration of the engagement.
- *Outside documentation.* Much of the content of the working papers consists of the outside documentation gathered by auditors, such as confirmation replies and copies of client agreements. Although not "schedules" in the real sense, these are indexed and interfiled, and procedures are indicated on them in the same manner as on the other schedules.

PREPARATION OF WORKING PAPERS

The proper preparation of schedules to document the audit evidence accumulated, the results found, and the conclusions reached is an important part of the audit. The auditor must recognize the circumstances requiring the need for a schedule and the appropriate design of schedules to be included in the files. Although the design depends on the objectives involved, working papers should possess certain characteristics:

- Each working paper should be properly identified with such information as the client's name, the period covered, a description of the contents, the initials of the preparer, the date of preparation, and an index code. Where automated working-paper software is used, defaults can be set up in the software, simplifying this process.
- Working papers should be indexed and cross-referenced to aid in organizing and filing. One type of indexing is illustrated in Figure 7-5. The lead schedule for cash has been indexed as A-1, and the individual general ledger accounts making up the total cash on the financial statements are indexed as A-2 through A-4. The final indexing is for the schedules supporting A-3 and A-4.
- Completed working papers must clearly indicate the audit work performed. This is accomplished in three ways: by a written statement in the form of a memorandum, by initials on the audit procedures in the audit program, and by notations directly on the working paper schedules. Notations on working papers are accomplished by the use of *tick marks*, which are *symbols* written adjacent to the detail on the body of the schedule. These notations must be clearly explained at the bottom of the working paper.
- Each working paper should include sufficient information to fulfill the objectives for which it was designed. If the auditor is to prepare working papers properly, the auditor must be aware of his or her goals. For example, if a working paper is designed to list the detail and show the verification of support of a balance sheet account, such as prepaid insurance, it is essential that the detail on the working paper reconcile with the trial balance.
- The conclusions that were reached about the segment of the audit under consideration should be plainly stated.

The common characteristics of proper working-paper preparation are indicated in Figure 7-6.

FIGURE 7-6
Common Characteristics of Proper Working Papers

| Client Renaldo Machine Corp. | | | | Schedule reference | | C-1 |

Audit area Notes Receivable —Customers

Balance sheet date 30/11/98

Initials of Preparer J.B.
and date prepared 23/12/98

Customer's Name and Address	Interest Rate	Dates		Face Amount 30/11/98	Accrued Interest 30/11/98
		Issued	Maturity		
Craig Metal Works Ltd., Saskatoon, Sask.	12%	4/10/98	31/12/98	✓ 150 000 00 Ⓟ	2 850 00 a
Pedlar Hardware Co., York, Ont.	14%	15/11/98	7/1/99	✓ 89 000 00 Ⓟ	519 17 a
Gaber Forge Ltd., Waterloo, Ont.	11%	9/10/98	8/12/98	✓ 200 000 00 Ⓟ	3177 78 a
Dunlop Mfg. Ltd., Toronto, Ont.	15%	10/11/98	2/1/99	✓ 72 000 00 Ⓟ	600 00 a
Beritz Appliance Corp., Waterloo, Ont.	14%	20/11/98	12/1/99	✓ 125 000 00 Ⓟ	486 11 a
Haywood Hinge Inc., Hamilton, Ont.	13%	21/10/98	20/12/98	✓ 56 000 00 Ⓟ	808 89 a
Grimm Copper Inc., Vancouver, B.C.	12%	30/10/98	25/12/98	✓ 170 000 00 Ⓟ	1 756 67 a
	Cross-reference to general ledger			862 000 00 F T/B	10 198 62 a F T/B

Tick-mark symbols

F	Footed
T/B	Agrees with the trial balance
✓	Note examined
P	Positive confirmation sent, covering face, maturity, interest rate, and accrued interest
Ⓟ	Positive confirmation reply received - no material exceptions noted (C - 2)
a	Interest computations verified

} Explanation of audit steps performed

The collectibility of all notes was discussed with the controller. All seem collectible. In my opinion no loss provision is necessary. J.B. —— Auditor's conclusion

OWNERSHIP OF WORKING PAPERS

The working papers prepared during the engagement, including those prepared by the client for the auditor, are the *property of the auditor*. The only time anyone else, including the client, has a legal right to examine the papers is when the papers are subpoenaed by a court as legal evidence or when they are required by the public accountant's professional organization in connection with disciplinary proceedings or practice inspection. At the completion of the engagement, working papers are retained on the public accounting firm's premises for future reference. Many firms follow the practice of microfilming the working papers after several years to reduce storage costs.

CONFIDENTIALITY OF WORKING PAPERS

The need to maintain a confidential relationship with the client was discussed in Chapter 3. It was noted that the rules of conduct of the professional accounting bodies require their members not to disclose any confidential information obtained in the course of a professional engagement except with the consent of the client or, as was noted above, when required by the courts or by the professional accounting associations.

During the course of the examination, auditors obtain a considerable amount of information of a confidential nature, including officer salaries, product pricing and advertising plans, and product cost data. If auditors divulged this information to outsiders or to client employees who have been denied access, their relationship with management would be seriously strained. Furthermore, having access to the working papers would give employees an opportunity to alter information on them. For these reasons, care must be taken to protect the working papers at all times.

Ordinarily, the working papers can be provided to someone else only with the express permission of the client; the client owns the data on the working papers. This is the case even if a public accountant sells his or her practice to another public accounting firm. Permission is not required from the client, however, if the working papers are subpoenaed by a court or are used in connection with disciplinary hearings or practice inspection conducted by the auditor's professional body.

SUMMARY OF WORKING PAPERS

Working papers are an essential part of every audit for effectively planning the audit, providing a record of the evidence accumulated and the results of the tests, deciding the proper type of auditor's report, and reviewing the work of assistants. Public accounting firms establish their own policies and approaches for working-paper preparation to make sure that these objectives are met. High-quality public accounting firms make sure that working papers are properly prepared and are appropriate for the circumstances in the audit.

THE BURDEN OF PROOF

Jury studies conducted by a professional liability insurance company in the United States show that jurors consider CPAs to be experts in documentation. Therefore, when practitioners are faced with a liability suit and have fallen short of that expectation, they are likely to be judged negligent. On the other hand, even an informal note documenting a brief telephone conversation can sway a jury in the CPA's favour. Legally, the burden of proof rests with the plaintiff, but as a practical matter, the burden to document falls on the CPA. While there is not a Canadian study supporting these findings, it seems reasonable that public accountants in Canada would find similar support in the courts for appropriate documentation.

Source: Ric Rosario, "Making Documents Pay Off," *Journal of Accountancy* (February 1995), p. 70.

Acceptable audit risk — a measure of how willing the auditor is to accept that the financial statements may be materially misstated after the audit is completed and an unqualified opinion has been issued (p. 200).

Analysis working paper — a supporting schedule that shows the activity in a general ledger account during the entire period under audit (p. 217).

Articles of incorporation — a legal document granted by the federal or provincial jurisdiction in which a company is incorporated that recognizes a corporation as a separate entity. It includes the name of the corporation, the date of incorporation, capital stock the corporation is authorized to issue, and the types of business activities the corporation is authorized to conduct (p. 209).

Bylaws — the rules and procedures adopted by a corporation's shareholders, including the corporation's fiscal year and the duties and powers of its officers (p. 209).

Corporate minutes — the official record of the meetings of a corporation's board of directors and shareholders, in which corporate issues such as the declaration of dividends and the approval of contracts are documented (p. 209).

Current files — all working papers applicable to the year under audit (p. 215).

Engagement letter — an agreement between the public accounting firm and the client as to the terms of the engagement for the conduct of the audit and related services (p. 203).

Inherent risk — a measure of the auditor's assessment of the likelihood that there are material misstatements in a segment before considering the effectiveness of the internal controls (p. 201).

Lead schedule — a working paper that contains the detailed accounts from the general ledger making up a line item total in the working trial balance (p. 215).

Permanent files — auditors' working papers that contain data of a *historical or continuing nature* pertinent to the current audit, such as copies of articles of incorporation, bylaws, bond indentures, and contracts (p. 214).

Preplanning the audit — involves deciding whether to accept or continue doing the audit for the client, identifying the client's reasons for the audit, obtaining an engagement letter, and selecting staff for the engagement (p. 201).

Reconciliation of amounts working paper — a schedule that supports a specific amount; it normally ties the amount recorded in the client's records to another source of information, such as a bank statement or a confirmation (p. 217).

Related party — affiliated company, principal owner of the client company, or any other party with which the client deals such that one of the parties can influence the management or operating policies of the other (p. 208).

Related party transaction — any transaction between the client and a related party (p. 208).

Supporting schedule working paper — a detailed schedule prepared by the client or the auditor in support of a specific amount on the financial statements (p. 216).

Trial balance or list working paper — a supporting schedule of the details that make up the year-end balance of a general ledger account (p. 217).

Working papers — the records kept by the auditor of the procedures applied, the tests performed, the information obtained, and the pertinent conclusions reached in the engagement (p. 212).

Working trial balance — a listing of the general ledger accounts and their year-end balances (p. 215).

7-1   What benefits does the auditor derive from planning audits?

7-2   Identify the seven major steps in planning audits.

7-3   What are the responsibilities of the successor and predecessor auditors when a company is changing auditors?

7-4   What factors should an auditor consider prior to accepting an engagement?

7-5   What is the purpose of an engagement letter? What subjects should be covered in such a letter?

7-6   List the four types of information the auditor should obtain or review as a part of gaining background information for the audit, and provide one specific example of how the information will be useful in conducting an audit.

7-7   When a public accountant has accepted an engagement from a new client that is a manufacturer, it is customary for the public accountant to tour the client's plant facilities. Discuss the ways in which the public accountant's observations made during the course of the plant tour will be of help as he or she plans and conducts the audit.

7-8   An auditor often tries to acquire background knowledge of the client's industry as an aid to his or her audit work. How does the acquisition of this knowledge aid the auditor in distinguishing between obsolete and current inventory?

7-9   Define what is meant by a "related party." What are the auditor's responsibilities for related parties and related-party transactions?

7-10   Jennifer Bailey is an experienced senior auditor who is in charge of several important audits for a medium-sized firm. Her philosophy of conducting audits is to ignore all previous years' and permanent working papers until near the end of the audit as a means of keeping from prejudicing herself. She believes this enables her to perform the audit in a more independent manner because it eliminates the tendency of simply doing the same things in the current audit that were done on previous audits. Near the end of the audit, Bailey reviews the working papers from the preceding year, evaluates the significance of any items she has overlooked, and modifies her evidence if she considers it necessary. Evaluate Bailey's approach to conducting an audit.

7-11 Your firm has performed the audit of Danko Inc. for several years, and you have been assigned the responsibility for the current audit. How would your review of the articles of incorporation and bylaws for this audit differ from that of the audit of a client that was audited by a different public accounting firm in the preceding year?

7-12 For the audit of Flin Flon Manufacturing Company Ltd., the audit partner asks you to carefully read the new mortgage contract with the Bank of Manitoba and abstract all pertinent information. List the information in a mortgage that is likely to be relevant to the auditor.

7-13 Identify four types of information in the client's minutes of the board of directors' meetings that are likely to be relevant to the auditor. Explain why it is important to read the minutes early in the engagement.

7-14 List the purposes of working papers and explain why each purpose is important.

7-15 Explain why it is important for working papers to include each of the following: identification of the name of the client, period covered, description of the contents, initials of the preparer, date of the preparation, and an index code.

7-16 Define what is meant by a "permanent file of working papers," and list several types of information typically included. Why does the auditor not include the contents of the permanent file with the current year's working papers?

7-17 Distinguish between the following types of current-period supporting schedules and state the purpose of each: analysis, trial balance, and tests of reasonableness.

7-18 Why is it essential that the auditor not leave questions or exceptions in the working papers without an adequate explanation?

7-19 What type of working papers can be prepared by the client and used by the auditor as a part of the working-paper file? When client assistance is obtained in preparing working papers, describe the proper precautions the auditor should take.

7-20 Who owns the working papers? Under what circumstances can they be used by other people?

7-21 A public accountant sells his auditing practice to another public accounting firm and proposes to include all the working papers as a part of the purchase price. What rule(s) of professional conduct are violated by this proposed action? Is there anything the public accountant can do so as not to break the rule(s)?

MULTIPLE CHOICE QUESTIONS

7-22 The following questions concern the planning of the engagement. Select the best response.

a. Which of the following is an effective audit planning and control procedure that helps prevent misunderstandings and inefficient use of audit personnel? Arranging
   (1) to provide the client with copies of the audit programs to be used during the audit.
   (2) a preliminary conference with the client to discuss audit objectives, fees, timing, and other information.
   (3) to have the auditor prepare and post any necessary adjusting or reclassification entries prior to final closing.
   (4) to make copies, for inclusion in the working papers, of those client-supporting documents examined by the auditor.

b. An auditor is planning an audit engagement for a new client in a business with which he is unfamiliar. Which of the following would be the most useful source of information during the preliminary planning stage, when the auditor is trying to obtain a general understanding of audit problems that might be encountered?
   (1) Client manuals of accounts and charts of accounts.
   (2) Prior-year working papers of the predecessor auditor.
   (3) Latest annual and interim financial statements issued by the client.
   (4) Industry audit guides from professional accounting bodies.

c. The independent auditor should acquire an understanding of a client's internal audit function to determine whether the work of internal auditors will be a factor in determining the nature, timing, and extent of the independent auditor's procedures. The work performed by internal auditors might be such a factor when the internal auditor's work includes

   (1) verification of the mathematical accuracy of invoices.
   (2) review of administrative practices to improve efficiency and achieve management objectives.
   (3) study and evaluation of internal controls.
   (4) preparation of internal financial reports for management purposes.

   (AICPA adapted)

7-23 The following questions pertain to the predecessor/successor auditor relationship. Choose the best response.

a. When approached to perform an audit for the first time, the public accountant should make inquiries of the predecessor auditor. This is a necessary procedure because the predecessor may be able to provide the successor with information that will assist the successor in determining
   (1) whether the company follows the policy of rotating its auditors.
   (2) whether, in the predecessor's opinion, internal control of the company has been satisfactory.
   (3) whether the predecessor's work should be used.
   (4) whether the engagement should be accepted.

b. Hawkins requested permission to communicate with the predecessor auditor and review certain portions of the predecessor's working papers. The prospective client's refusal to permit this will bear directly on Hawkins's decision concerning the
   (1) adequacy of the preplanned audit program.
   (2) integrity of management.
   (3) ability to establish consistency in application of accounting principles between years.
   (4) apparent scope limitation.

c. What is the responsibility of a successor auditor with respect to communicating with the predecessor auditor in connection with a prospective new audit client?
  (1) The successor auditor should obtain permission from the prospective client to contact the predecessor auditor.
  (2) The successor auditor has *no* responsibility to contact the predecessor auditor.
  (3) The successor auditor should contact the predecessor regardless of whether the prospective client authorizes contact.
  (4) The successor auditor need not contact the predecessor if the successor is aware of all available relevant facts.

(AICPA adapted)

7-24 The following questions concern working papers. Choose the best response.

a. Which of the following is not a primary purpose of audit working papers?
  (1) To coordinate the examination.
  (2) To assist in preparation of the auditor's report.
  (3) To support the financial statements.
  (4) To provide evidence of the audit work performed.

b. Audit working papers are used to record the results of the auditor's evidence-gathering procedures. When preparing working papers, the auditor should remember that working papers should be
  (1) kept on the client's premises so that the client can have access to them for reference purposes.
  (2) the primary support for the financial statements being examined.
  (3) considered as a part of the client's accounting records that are retained by the auditor.
  (4) designed to meet the circumstances and the auditor's needs on each engagement.

c. Which of the following eliminates voluminous details from the auditor's working trial balance by classifying and summarizing similar or related items?
  (1) Account analyses
  (2) Supporting schedules
  (3) Control accounts
  (4) Lead schedules

d. During an audit engagement, pertinent data are compiled and included in the audit working papers. The working papers primarily are considered to be
  (1) support for the auditor's representations as to compliance with generally accepted auditing standards.
  (2) a client-owned record of conclusions reached by the auditors who performed the engagement.
  (3) evidence supporting financial statements.
  (4) a record to be used as a basis for the following year's engagement.

e. Although the quantity, type, and content of working papers vary with the circumstances, the working papers generally include
  (1) the auditing procedures followed and the testing performed in obtaining evidential matter.
  (2) copies of those client records examined by the auditor during the course of the engagement.
  (3) an evaluation of the efficiency and competence of the audit staff assistants by the partner responsible for the audit.
  (4) the auditor's comments concerning the efficiency and competence of client management personnel.

(AICPA adapted)

7-25 The following questions concern the use of analytical procedures during the planning phase of an audit. Select the best response.

a. Analytical procedures used in planning an audit should focus on identifying
  (1) material weaknesses in the internal controls.
  (2) areas that may represent specific risks relevant to the audit.
  (3) the predictability of financial data from individual transactions.
  (4) the various assertions that are embodied in the financial statements.

b. A basic premise underlying the application of analytical procedures is that
  (1) the study of financial ratios is an acceptable alternative to the investigation of unusual fluctuations.
  (2) plausible relationships among data may reasonably be expected to exist and continue in the absence of known conditions to the contrary.
  (3) these procedures *cannot* replace tests of controls and tests of details of balances.
  (4) statistical tests of financial information may lead to the discovery of material errors or fraud and other irregularities in the financial statements.

DISCUSSION QUESTIONS AND PROBLEMS

7-26 Two public accountants were talking about their profession while golfing one day. One commented that she thought that the decision to continue as auditor for a client was as important as the decision whether to accept a company as a new client. Her golfing partner asked her what she meant.

Required

Explain to the second golfer what the first golfer meant.

7-27 Janet Chow, a senior manager in a public accounting firm, is explaining to a new manager, Reinhard Mueller, that planning is a very important part of every audit and that her planning includes a preliminary conference with the client to discuss audit objectives, fees, timing, and other topics. Reinhard replies that he thought the engagement letter covered those issues and that he thought the preliminary conference was a waste of time.

Required

Explain the value of the preliminary conference to Reinhard, including why both it and the engagement letter are important.

7-28 In late spring, you are advised of a new assignment as the in-charge accountant of your public accounting firm's recurring annual audit of a major client, Lancer Inc. You are given the engagement letter for the audit covering the current fiscal year and a list of personnel assigned to this engagement. It is your responsibility to plan and supervise the field work for the engagement.

Required

Discuss the necessary preparation and planning for the Lancer Inc. annual audit *prior* to beginning field work at the client's office. In your discussion, include the sources you should consult, the type of information you should seek, the preliminary plans and preparation you should make for the field work, and any actions you should take relative to the staff assigned to the engagement.

(AICPA adapted)

7-29 Generally accepted accounting principles set certain requirements for disclosure of related parties and related-party transactions. There is also an Assurance and Related Services Guideline that discusses related party transactions and economic dependence. For this problem, you are expected to research appropriate *CICA Handbook* material.

Required

a. Define "related party" as used for generally accepted accounting principles, and explain the disclosure requirements for related parties and related-party transactions.

b. Explain why disclosure of related-party transactions is relevant information for decision makers.

c. List the most important related parties who are likely to be involved in related-party transactions.

d. List several different types of related-party transactions that could take place in a company.

e. Discuss ways the auditor can determine the existence of related parties and related-party transactions.

f. For each type of related-party transaction, discuss different ways the auditor can evaluate whether it is recorded on an arm's-length basis assuming that the auditor knows the transaction exists.

g. Suppose you knew that material related-party transactions had occurred and were transacted at significantly less favourable terms than ordinarily occur when business is done with independent parties. The client refuses to disclose these facts in the financial statements. What would your responsibilities be?

h. Why is disclosure of information about economic dependence so important for decision makers?

7-30 The minutes of the board of directors of the Marygold Catalogue Company Ltd. for the year ended December 31, 1998, were provided to you.

MEETING OF FEBRUARY 16, 1998

Ruth Ho, chair of the board, called the meeting to order at 4:00 P.M. The following directors were in attendance:

Margaret Aronson	Claude La Rose
Fred Brick	Lucille Renolds
Henri Chapdelaine	J.T. Schmidt
Ruth Ho	Marie Titard
Homer Jackson	Roald Asko

The minutes of the meeting of October 11, 1997, were read and approved.

Marie Titard, president, discussed the new marketing plan for wider distribution of catalogues in the western market. She made a motion for approval of increased expenditures of approximately $50,000 for distribution costs which was seconded by Asko and unanimously passed.

The unresolved dispute with Revenue Canada over the tax treatment of leased office buildings was discussed with Harold Moss, the tax partner from Marygold's public accounting firm, Moss & Lawson. In Mr. Moss's opinion, the matter would not be resolved for several months and could result in an unfavourable settlement.

J. T. Schmidt moved that the computer equipment that was no longer being used in the Kingston office, since new equipment had been acquired in 1997, be donated to the Kingston Vocational School for use in their repair and training program. Margaret Aronson seconded the motion and it unanimously passed.

Annual cash dividends were unanimously approved as being payable April 30, 1998 for shareholders of record April 15, 1998, as follows:

Class A common — $10 per share
Class B common — $5 per share

Officers' bonuses for the year ended December 31, 1997, were approved for payment March 1, 1998, as follows:

Marie Titard — President	$26,000
Lucille Renolds — Vice-President	$12,000
Roald Asko — Controller	$12,000
Fred Brick — Secretary-Treasurer	$9,000

Meeting adjourned 6:30 P.M.

Fred Brick, Secretary

MEETING OF SEPTEMBER 15, 1998

Ruth Ho, chair of the board, called the meeting to order at 4:00 P.M. The following directors were in attendance:

Margaret Aronson	Claude La Rose
Fred Brick	Lucille Renolds
Henri Chapdelaine	J. T. Schmidt
Ruth Ho	Marie Titard
Homer Jackson	Roald Asko

The minutes of the meeting of February 16, 1998, were read and approved. Marie Titard, president, discussed the improved sales and financial condition for 1998. She was pleased with the results of the catalogue distribution and cost control for the company. No action was taken.

The nominations for officers were made as follows:

President — Marie Titard
Vice-President — Lucille Renolds
Controller — Roald Asko
Secretary-Treasurer — Fred Brick

The nominees were elected by unanimous voice vote.

Salary increases of 6 percent, exclusive of bonuses, were recommended for all officers for 1999. Marie Titard moved that such salary increases be approved, seconded by J. T. Schmidt, and unanimously approved.

	SALARY	
	1998	**1999**
Marie Titard, President	$90,000	$95,400
Lucille Renolds, Vice-President	$60,000	$63,600
Roald Asko, Controller	$60,000	$63,600
Fred Brick, Secretary-Treasurer	$40,000	$42,400

Roald Asko moved that the company consider adopting a pension/profit-sharing plan for all employees as a way to provide greater incentive for employees to stay with the company. Considerable discussion ensued. It was agreed without adoption that Asko should discuss the legal and tax implications with lawyer Cecil Makay and a public accounting firm reputed to be knowledgeable about pension and profit-sharing plans, Able and Bark.

Roald Asko discussed expenditure of $58,000 for acquisition of a new computer for the Kingston office to replace equipment that was purchased in 1997 and has proven ineffective. A settlement has been tentatively reached to return the equipment for a refund of $21,000. Asko moved that both transactions be approved, seconded by Jackson, and unanimously adopted. Fred Brick moved that a loan of $36,000, from the Kingston Bank, be approved. The interest is floating at 2 percent above prime. The collateral is to be the new computer equipment being installed in the Kingston office. A chequing account, with a minimum balance of $2,000 at all times until the loan is repaid, must be opened and maintained if the loan is granted. Seconded by La Rose and unanimously approved.

Lucille Renolds, chair of the audit committee, moved that the public accounting firm of Moss & Lawson be selected again for the company's annual audit and related tax work for the year ended December 31, 1999. Seconded by Aronson and unanimously approved.

Meeting adjourned 6:40 P.M.

Fred Brick, Secretary

Required

a. How do you, as the auditor, know that all minutes have been made available to you?

b. Read the minutes of the meetings of February 16 and September 15. Use the following format to list and explain information that is relevant for the 1998 audit:

INFORMATION RELEVANT TO 1998 AUDIT	AUDIT ACTION REQUIRED
1.	
2.	

c. Read the minutes of the meeting of February 16, 1998. Did any of that information pertain to the December 31, 1997, audit? Explain what the auditor should have done during the December 31, 1997, audit with respect to 1998 minutes.

7-31 CA has been the auditor of Niles Ltd., a medium-sized manufacturing company, for just over two years. After CA billed the company for the first year audit, Mr. Hiles, the president, called CA to his office to discuss the audit fee, expressing surprise and concern as to its size. CA pointed out that an audit fee for a first-time audit is always higher than normal and gave Mr. Hiles several examples of the work he had to do that would not be required in subsequent years.

CA reminded Mr. Hiles that they had previously discussed this point in broad terms and Mr. Hiles accepted the explanation. CA suggested that the audit fee for subsequent years could be reduced if the staff of Niles Ltd. were to prepare some of the schedules for CA's working papers. Mr. Hiles agreed with this suggestion.

For the second year audit, Niles Ltd.'s staff prepared several of the schedules, and CA was able to reduce his fee. However, Mr. Hiles, on receiving the billing for the second year's audit fee, was still concerned as to its size.

When discussing the results of the audit with CA, Mr. Hiles expressed surprise as to the quantity of schedules that had to be prepared by his staff, particularly considering the fact that CA and his staff prepared additional working papers themselves. He asked CA what were the purposes of audit working papers. Mr. Hiles also expressed concern about all the information in the working papers on his company being in CA's files and asked who owned the working papers.

Required

a. What are the purposes or functions of audit working papers? (Include the benefits to the client and the auditor.)

b. What records may be included in audit working papers?

c. What factors affect the public accountant's judgment of the type and content of the working papers for a particular engagement?

d. Who owns or has access to audit working papers?

(CICA adapted)

7-32 Do the following with regard to the working paper for ABC Company Inc. shown on page 225.

a. List the deficiencies in the working paper.

b. For each deficiency, state how the working paper could be improved.

c. Prepare an improved working paper using an electronic spreadsheet software program. Include an indication of the audit work done as well as the analysis of the client data. (Instructor's option)

7-33 You are engaged in the annual audit of the financial statements of Maulack Corp., a medium-sized wholesale company that manufactures light fixtures. The company has 25 shareholders. During your review of the minutes, you observe that the president's salary has been increased substantially over the preceding year by action of the board of directors. His present salary is much greater than salaries paid to presidents of companies of comparable size and is clearly excessive. You determine that the method of computing the president's salary was changed for the year under audit. In previous years, the president's salary was consistently based on sales. In the latest year, however, his salary was based on net income before income taxes. Maulack Corp. is in a cyclical industry and would have had an extremely profitable year except that the increase in the president's salary siphoned off much of the income that would

ABC Company Inc.
Notes Receivable
31/12/98

Acct 110

Maker

Date	Apex Co.	Ajax, Inc.	J.J. Co.	P. Smith	Martin-Peterson	Tent Co.
Made	15/6/97	21/11/97	1/11/97	26/7/98	12/5/97	3/9/98
Due	15/6/99	Demand	$200/mo	$1000/mo	Demand	$400/mo
Face amount	5000<	3591<	13180<	25000<	2100<	12000<
Value of Security	none	none	24000	50000	none	10000
Notes:						
Beg. bal.	4000^{PWP}	3591^{PWP}	12780^{PWP}	—	2100^{PWP}	—
Additions				25000		12000
Payments	>(1000)	>(3591)	>(2400)	>(5000)	>(2100)	>(1600)
End bal.						
① Current	3000 ✓	—	2400 ✓	12000	—	4800
② Long term	—	—	7980	8000	—	5600
③ Total	3000 C	-0-	10380 C	20000 C	-0-	10400 C
	и	и	и	и	и	и
Interest						
Rate	5%	5%	5%	5%	5%	6%
Pd. to date	none	paid	31/12/98	30/9/98	paid	30/11/98
Beg. bal.	104^{PWP}	-0-^{PWP}	24^{PWP}	-0-	-0-^{PWP}	-0-
④ Earned	175 ✓	102 ✓	577 ✓	468 ✓	105 ✓	162 ✓
Received	-0-	>(102)	>(601)	>(200)	>(105)	>(108)
⑤ Accrued at						
31/12/98	279	-0-	-0-	268	-0-	54
	и	и	и	и	и	и

✓ - Tested
PWP - Agrees with prior year's working papers.
① Total of $22,200 agrees with working trial balance.
② Total of 21,580 agrees with working trial balance.
③ Total of $43,780 agrees with working trial balance.
④ Total of $1,589 agrees with miscellaneous income analysis in operations W/P.
⑤ Total of $601 agrees with A/R lead schedule.

have accrued to the shareholders. The president is a substantial shareholder.

Required

a. What is the implication of this condition on the fair presentation of the financial statements?

b. Discuss your responsibility for disclosing this situation.

c. Discuss the effect, if any, that the situation has on your auditor's opinion as to
   (1) the fairness of the presentation of the financial statements.
   (2) the consistency of the application of accounting principles.

(AICPA adapted)

7-34 Winston Black was an audit partner in the firm of Henson, Davis & Co. He was in the process of reviewing the working papers for the audit of a new client, Gallivan Resources Inc. Gallivan was in the business of heavy construction. Black was conducting his first review after the field work was substantially complete. Normally, he would have done an initial review during the planning phase as required by his firm's policies; however, he had been overwhelmed by an emergency with his largest and most important client. He rationalized not reviewing audit-planning information because (1) the audit was being overseen by Sarah Beale, a manager in whom he had confidence, and (2) he could "recover" from any problems during his end-of-audit review.

Later Black found that he was confronted with a couple of problems. First, he found that the firm may have accepted Gallivan without complying with its new client acceptance procedures. Gallivan came to Henson, Davis & Co. on a recommendation from a friend of Black's. Black got credit for the new business, which was important to him because it would affect his compensation from the firm. Because Black was busy, he told Beale to conduct a new client acceptance review and let him know if there were any problems. He never heard from Beale and assumed everything was okay. In reviewing Beale's pre-audit planning documentation, he saw a check mark in the box "contact prior auditors" but found no details indicating what was done. When he asked Beale about this, she responded with the following:

> I called Gardner Smith [the responsible partner with Gallivan's prior audit firm] and left a voice-mail message for him. He never returned my call. I talked to Don Gallivan, and he told me that he informed Gardner about the change and that Gardner said, "Fine, I'll help in any way I can." Don said Gardner sent over copies of analyses of fixed assets and equity accounts, which Don gave to me. I asked Don why his company replaced Gardner's firm, and he told me it was over the tax contingency issue and the size of its fee. Other than that, Don said the relationship was fine.

The tax contingency issue that Beale referred to was a situation where Gallivan had entered into litigation with a bank from which it had received a loan. The result of the litigation was that the bank forgave several hundred thousand dollars in debt. This was a windfall to Gallivan, who recorded it as a gain, taking the position that it was nontaxable. The prior auditors disputed this position and insisted that a contingent tax liability existed that required disclosure. This upset Gallivan, but it agreed in order to receive an unqualified opinion. Before hiring Henson, Davis & Co. as its new auditors, Gallivan requested that Henson, Davis review the situation. Henson, Davis believed the contingency as remote and agreed to the elimination of the disclosure.

The second problem involved a long-term contract with a customer in Montreal. Under GAAP, Gallivan was required to recognize income on this contract using the percentage-of-completion method. The contract was partially completed as of year end and had a material effect on the financial statements. When Black went to review the copy of the contract in the working papers, he found three things. First, there was a contract summary that set out its major features. Second, there was a copy of the contract written in French. Third, there was a signed confirmation confirming the terms and status of the contract. The space requesting information about any contract disputes was left blank, indicating no such problems.

Black's concern about the contract was that in order to recognize income in accordance with GAAP, the contract had to be enforceable. Often, contracts contain a cancellation clause that might mitigate enforceability. Because he was not able to read French, Black couldn't tell whether or not the contract contained such a clause. When he asked Beale about this, she responded that she had asked the company's vice-president for the Montreal division about the contract, and he told her that it was their standard contract. The company's standard contract did have a cancellation clause in it, but it required mutual agreement and could not be cancelled unilaterally by the buyer.

Required

a. Do you believe that Henson, Davis & Co. complied with generally accepted auditing standards in its acceptance of Gallivan Resources Inc. as a new client? If not, what can the firm do at this point in the engagement to resolve the deficiency?

b. Do you believe that sufficient audit work has been done with regard to Gallivan's Montreal contract? If not, what more should be done?

c. Have Black and Beale conducted themselves in accordance with generally accepted auditing standards? Explain.

7-35 Horatio Ltd., a public company listed on a Canadian stock exchange, produces a variety of agricultural products, primarily feed, seed, and fertilizer. It has a fertilizer manufacturing plant in a large Canadian city and a seed and feed processing plant in a nearby smaller centre. The company has been in an expansionary phase for the past few years.

In late January 1999, Ms. Kabola, the vice-president of Horatio Ltd., made an appointment to see CA. When they met in CA's office a few days later, Ms. Kabola informed CA that the company was holding its annual shareholders' meeting on February 20, 1999, and that the Board of Directors planned to introduce a motion to replace its current auditors. She felt that the motion would easily pass since the annual meetings were always sparsely attended. Ms. Kabola asked CA if he would accept the appointment as the new auditor. CA indicated he would be pleased to consider the matter, but that he would have to carry out a short investigation before giving a definite answer. He promised to give his answer by the end of January, which was about a week later.

During their brief conversation, Ms. Kabola indicated considerable dissatisfaction with the current auditors: "They were fine until a couple of years ago, but I guess we've outgrown them. They don't seem to understand the capital market. Their reports are very important in terms of the image we present to investors, but lately they've been nothing but a hindrance. This year they went too far, and we won't tolerate it. We have some major plans for the next couple of years and need all the capital we can get. We pay our auditors good money for their reports. I don't see how they can expect us to pay them for setting us back, but we'll cross that bridge when we get their bill."

When asked what "major plans" they had, Ms. Kabola replied, "Well, for a start, we are currently negotiating the purchase of a well-known fertilizer trademark for $150,000. We're almost certain of buying it, and when we do, it'll mean a 50 percent increase in sales. So we're looking into the possibility of building a new fertilizer plant. There is a tremendous shortage of fertilizer these days, so the price is right and we can make some great profits if we move as fast as possible. We'll account for that trademark consistently with previous years, so I'm sure there will be no problem there. When we get the new plant in full operation, we'll be able to expand our markets into other parts of Canada and perhaps the U.S., but that's further down the road."

After Ms. Kabola left, CA pondered the situation. He had some familiarity with Horatio Ltd. because last year his wife had inherited a sizeable block of the company's shares and he had taken note of any news about the company. CA recalled having seen a news item in the financial press a few days ago, and after a moment, found it in his office. It was an article about the financial and accounting effect of pollution problems on certain companies and contained the following paragraph about Horatio Ltd.:

One of the companies affected by the new pollution regulations is Horatio Ltd., a growing firm in the booming fertilizer business. It will be required to install some very costly equipment — so costly, in fact, that management says there may be some doubt about the continued economic viability of the city plant, putting about 400 jobs in jeopardy. Pressed on the impact of this equipment on earnings, Ms. Kapola, the vice-president, admitted that the impact would not be felt right away because the company plans to expense the new equipment according to what accountants call the sinking-fund method of amortization. Also, the government allows a 50 percent write-off on such equipment for tax purposes, in effect giving the company a loan to finance the equipment. The company plans to discount this "loan" in its financial statements. So far, Horatio Ltd. seems to be proceeding with its plans for plant expansion scheduled to begin later this year.

CA then obtained a copy of the latest annual report of Horatio Ltd. and summarized from it the following financial statements:

Horatio Limited
Balance Sheet — as at December 31, 1998

	1998	1997
	(In thousands of dollars)	
Assets		
Current assets		
Cash	$ 432	$ 468
Trade accounts receivable (less allowance for bad debts $42,000 in 1998; $116,000 in 1997)	763	625
Inventories, at lower of cost and net realizable value	956	351
Prepaid expenses	32	26
	$2,183	$1,470
Capital assets		
Land — cost	950	950
Plant and equipment — cost	$1,414	$1,030
Less — accumulated amortization	952	756
	462	274
Deferred charges (note 1)	54	3
	$4,139	$3,179
Liabilites and Shareholders' Equity		
Current liabilities		
Bank loans	$ 103	$ 10
Trade accounts payable	928	492
Accrued liabilities	73	76
	$1,104	$ 578
Mortgage payable (note 2)	182	200
Accrued income tax liability	171	121
Shareholders' equity		
Common shares — authorized 1,000,000 shares of no par value — issued and outstanding 433,000 in 1998 and 368,000 in 1997 (note 3)	2,300	1,950
Retained earnings	382	330
	$4,139	$3,179

Horatio Limited
Income Statement, for the year ended December 31, 1998

	1998	1997
	(In thousands of dollars)	
Sales	$6,328	$4,296
Cost of sales	4,206	2,817
Gross margin	$2,122	$1,479
Expenses		
Selling and administration	$1,136	$ 865
Amortization	188	146
Other (net)	609	316
	$1,933	$1,327
Income before taxes	$ 189	$ 152
Income taxes	94	76
Net income for the year	$ 95	$ 76
Basic Earnings per Share	$ 0.24	$ 0.22

Horatio Limited
Notes to the financial statements, December 31, 1998

(1) Deferred charges

Included in deferred charges are the following items:

Extraneous expenditures re plant renovations	$51,000
Trade marks (net of amortization)	3,000
	$54,000

The $51,000 expenditures were incurred to replace materials destroyed as a result of a fire while the plant was being renovated. Because the fire resulted directly from the disruptive conditions existing at the time of the renovations and would not have otherwise occurred, management considers the cost to be properly recoverable out of income from the renovated plant which is scheduled to reach full production in 1999.

The trademarks were purchased in 1993 and are being amortized to income on a straight-line basis over a fifteen-year period. The amortization less applicable income taxes, is included in expenses under "Other (net). "

(2) Mortgage payable

The mortgage is secured by the plant building and land. It is repayable at a rate of $18,000 per year plus interest at 7 percent.

(3) Common shares issued

During the year, 65,000 common shares were issued for cash of $350,000.

Auditor's Report

To the Shareholders of Horatio Ltd.:

We have audited the balance sheet of Horatio Ltd. as of December 31, 1998, and the statements of income, retained earnings and cash flow [the latter two were not summarized by CA] for the year then ended. These financial statements are the responsibility of the company's management. Our responsibility is to express an opinion on these financial statements based on our audit.

We conducted our audit in accordance with generally accepted auditing standards. Those standards require that we plan and perform an audit to obtain reasonable assurance whether financial statements are free of material misstatement. An audit includes examining, on a test basis, evidence supporting the amounts and disclosures in the financial statements. An audit also includes assessing the accounting principles used and significant estimates made by management, as well as evaluating the overall financial statement presentation.

During the year, the company experienced a loss of $51,000 as a result of a fire in its plant. Recognition of this loss has been deferred until the renovated area of the plant attains production capacity. In our opinion, this loss should have been shown as an extraordinary item in the income statement, in which case the income statement for the year ended December 31, 1998, would have shown income before extraordinary items for the year of $95,000 ($0.24 per share), extraordinary loss of $51,000 ($0.13 per share), and net income for the year of $44,000 ($0.11 per share).

In our opinion, except for the failure to recognize the fire loss as set out in the preceding paragraph, these financial statements present fairly, in all material respects, the financial position of Horatio Ltd. as of December 31, 1998, and the results of its operations and the changes in its cash flow position for the year then ended in accordance with generally accepted accounting principles.

Porter, Quantum & Co.

Chartered Accountants
Big Town
January 18, 1999

Required

a. Outline the steps CA should take and the matters he should consider before accepting the engagement.

b. Outline the reservations that might be required in the auditor's report for the year ended December 31, 1999, if CA accepts the engagement. Give your reasons and restrict your answer to the available information.

(CICA adapted)

8

MATERIALITY AND RISK

EXPLAIN TO ME ONE MORE TIME THAT YOU DID A GOOD JOB, BUT THE COMPANY WENT BROKE

Maxwell Spencer is a senior partner in his firm, and one of his regular duties is to attend the firm's annual training session for newly hired auditors. He loves doing this because it gives him a chance to share his many years of experience with inexperienced people who have bright and receptive minds. He covers several topics formally during the day and then sits around and "shoots the breeze" with participants during the evening hours. Here we listen to what he is saying.

Suppose you are a retired 72-year-old man. You and your wife, Minnie, live on your retirement fund which you elected to manage yourself, rather than receive income from an annuity. You concluded that your years in business gave you the ability to earn a better return than the annuity would provide.

So when you retired and got your bundle, you called your broker and discussed with him what you should do with it. He told you that the most important thing was to protect your principal, and recommended that you buy bonds. You settled on three issues that your broker and his firm believed were good ones, with solid balance sheets: (1) an entertainment company that was building a series of amusement parks across Canada, (2) a fast-growing alternative energy company, and (3) a major life insurance company. All you have to do is sit back and clip your coupons.

Ah, but the best made plans of mice and men ... First, the entertainment company goes broke and you can look forward to recovering only a few cents on the dollar over several years. Then, the alternative energy company fails, and you *might* get something back—eventually. Finally, the life insurance company is closed by the government and has to default on all of its outstanding bonds. A recovery plan is initiated, but don't hold your breath. Your best strategy is to apply for a job at McDonald's. They hire older people, don't they?

Now what could the auditors of these three entities ever say to you about how they planned and conducted their audits and decided to issue an unqualified opinion that would justify that opinion in your mind? You don't care about business failure versus audit failure, or risk assessment and reliability of audit evidence, or any of that technical mumbo jumbo. The auditors were supposed to be there for *you* when *you* needed them, and they weren't. And materiality? Anything that would have indicated a problem is material for you.

The message is, folks, that it's a lot easier to sweat over doing a tough audit right than it is to justify your judgments and decisions after it's too late. And God help you if you think that a harmed investor will ever see things from your point of view.

The scope paragraph in an auditor's report includes two important phrases that are directly related to materiality and risk. These phrases are emphasized in bold print in the following two sentences of a standard scope paragraph.

> I conducted my audit in accordance with generally accepted auditing standards. Those standards require that I plan and perform an audit to **obtain reasonable assurance** whether the financial statements are **free of material misstatement**.

The phrase **obtain reasonable assurance** is intended to inform users that auditors do not guarantee or ensure the fair presentation of the financial statements. The phrase communicates there is some *risk* that the financial statements are not fairly stated even when the opinion is unqualified.

The phrase **free of material misstatements** is intended to inform users that the auditor's responsibility is limited to *material* financial information. Materiality is important because it is impractical for auditors to provide assurances on immaterial amounts.

Thus, materiality and risk are fundamental concepts that are important to planning the audit and designing the audit approach. This chapter will show how these concepts fit into the planning phase of the audit.

MATERIALITY

OBJECTIVE 8-1

Apply the concept of materiality to the audit.

Materiality was first discussed on pages 43–46 as a major consideration in determining the appropriate auditor's report to issue. The concepts of materiality discussed in this chapter are directly related to those in Chapter 2. We suggest you reread pages 43–46 before you study the following material.

Paragraph 5130.05 of the *CICA Handbook* defines materiality in the following way:

> A misstatement or the aggregate of all misstatements in financial statements is considered to be material if, in the light of the surrounding circumstances, it is probable that the decision of a person who is relying on the financial statements, and who has a reasonable knowledge of business and economic activities (the user), would be changed or influenced by such misstatement or the aggregate of all misstatements.

The auditor's responsibility is to determine whether financial statements are materially misstated. If the auditor determines that there is a material misstatement, he or she will bring it to the client's attention so a correction can be made. If the client refuses to correct the statements, a qualified or an adverse opinion must be issued, depending on how material and pervasive the misstatement is. Auditors must, therefore, have a thorough knowledge of the application of materiality.

A careful reading of the *CICA Handbook* definition reveals the difficulty auditors have in applying materiality in practice. The definition emphasizes the decisions of users who have a reasonable knowledge of business and economic activities and who rely on the statements to make decisions. Auditors, therefore, must have knowledge of the likely users of their clients' statements and the decisions that are being made. For example, if an auditor knows financial statements will be relied on in a buy–sell agreement for the entire business, the amount that the auditor considers material

FIGURE 8-1
Steps in Applying
Materiality

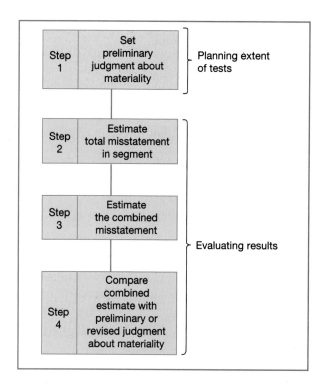

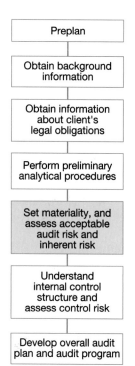

may be smaller than for an otherwise similar audit. In practice, auditors often do not know who the users are or what decisions will be made.

There are four closely related steps in applying materiality. They are shown in Figure 8-1 and discussed in this section. The steps start with setting a preliminary judgment about materiality. Estimation of the amount of misstatements in each segment takes place throughout the audit. The final two steps are done near the end of the audit during the engagement completion phase.

CICA Auditing Guideline AuG-7, "Applying Materiality and Audit Risk Concepts in Conducting an Audit," suggests that an auditor be concerned with three levels of misstatement in assessing whether or not there is a material misstatement:

1. Identified misstatements (IM) — the actual misstatements discovered in the sample tested; they have not been corrected by management.
2. Likely misstatements — the projection of the actual misstatement in the sample to the population; the misstatements have not been corrected by management. The sum of the likely misstatements in the financial statements is called the *likely aggregate misstatement.*
3. Further possible misstatements — the misstatements over and above the likely aggregate misstatement that result from the imprecision in the sampling process. The sum of likely aggregate misstatement plus further possible misstatements is called the *maximum possible misstatement* (MPM).

The auditor is sure of an identified misstatement because it was determined to be the misstatement in the sample. The projection of that error to the population — the likely misstatement — is based on the assumption that the sample is representative of the population. The auditor is fairly certain about the likely aggregate misstatement when he or she is talking to the client about making an adjustment; if the likely aggregate misstatement exceeds materiality, the auditor will require an adjustment.

Further possible misstatement is based on the imprecision in the sampling process. There are two risks: (1) the sample may not be representative, and (2) the auditor may misinterpret evidence.[1] The auditor recognizes that further possible misstatements

---

[1]These two risks are called sampling risk and nonsampling risk respectively. They are discussed in detail in Chapter 11.

are possible but not probable. It would not be appropriate to ask the client to make an adjustment for further possible misstatements by virtue of their very definition. The auditor may or may not require an adjustment when the maximum possible misstatement exceeds materiality.[2]

SET PRELIMINARY JUDGMENT ABOUT MATERIALITY

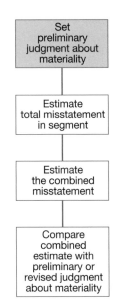

Set preliminary judgment about materiality

Estimate total misstatement in segment

Estimate the combined misstatement

Compare combined estimate with preliminary or revised judgment about materiality

Ideally, an auditor decides early in the audit the combined amount of misstatements in the financial statements that would be considered material. Paragraph 5130.30 states, "The auditor should make preliminary decisions as to materiality . . . at the planning stage of the engagement"; this is the preliminary judgment about materiality in step 1 of Figure 8-1. This judgment need not be quantified but often is. It is called a preliminary judgment about materiality because it is a professional judgment and may change during the engagement if circumstances change. Since materiality is defined in the context of users of financial statements, such a change would be unlikely unless additional information regarding users was obtained during the audit.

The preliminary judgment about materiality is thus the maximum amount by which the auditor believes the statements could be misstated and still *not* affect the decisions of reasonable users. (Conceptually, this would be an amount that is $1 less than materiality as defined in Section 5130. Preliminary materiality is defined in this manner as a convenience in application.) This judgment is one of the most important decisions the auditor makes. It requires considerable professional judgment.

The reason for setting a preliminary judgment about materiality is to help the auditor plan the appropriate evidence to accumulate. If the auditor sets a low dollar amount, more evidence is required than for a high amount. Examine again the financial statements of Hillsburg Hardware Ltd., on pages 127–129. What do you think is the combined amount of misstatements that would affect decisions of reasonable users? Do you believe a $100 misstatement would affect users' decisions? If so, the amount of evidence required for the audit is likely to be beyond that for which the management of Hillsburg Hardware can pay. Do you believe a $1 million misstatement would be material? Most experienced auditors would say that amount is far too large as a combined materiality amount.

The auditor may change the preliminary judgment about materiality during the audit if, for example, a new user of the financial statements is identified. Whenever that is done, the new judgment is called a revised judgment about materiality. Reasons for using a revised judgment can include a change in one of the factors used to determine the preliminary judgment or a decision by the auditor that the preliminary judgment was too small or, more likely, too large.

FACTORS AFFECTING JUDGMENT

Several factors affect setting a preliminary judgment about materiality for a given set of financial statements. The most important of these are discussed below.

Materiality is a relative rather than an absolute concept A misstatement of a given magnitude might be material for a small company, whereas the same dollar error could be immaterial for a large one. For example, a total error of $1 million would be extremely material for Hillsburg Hardware Ltd. because, as shown on page 127, total assets are about $3 million and net income before tax is about $285,000. It would be immaterial for a company such as IBM, which has total assets and net income of several billion dollars. Hence, it is not possible to establish any dollar-value guidelines for a preliminary judgment about materiality applicable to all audit clients.

Bases are needed for evaluating materiality Since materiality is relative, it is necessary to have bases for establishing whether misstatements are material. The CICA

---

[2]For a more extensive discussion of this topic see Leslie, Donald A., Albert D. Teitlebaum, and Rodney J. Anderson, *Dollar-Unit Sampling*, Toronto: Copp Clark Pitman, 1979, pp. 19–23.

Research Study *Materiality: The Concept and Its Application to Auditing*[3] includes an extensive discussion of the methods auditors presently use to compute their preliminary judgments about materiality. Assurance and Related Services Guideline AuG-7, "Applying Materiality and Audit Risk Concepts in Conducting an Audit," also suggests bases. The suggested bases include:

1. 5 percent to 10 percent of net income before taxes. This number can be fairly volatile so most auditors use normalized net income (i.e., net income adjusted for unusual and non-recurring items such as a large inventory writedown) or average net income.
2. $\frac{1}{2}$ percent to 5 percent of gross profit.
3. $\frac{1}{2}$ percent to 1 percent of total assets.
4. $\frac{1}{2}$ percent to 5 percent of shareholders' equity.
5. $\frac{1}{2}$ percent to 1 percent of revenue.
6. The weighted average of methods 1 to 5.
7. A reducing percentage of the greater of revenue and assets.
8. $\frac{1}{2}$ percent to 2 percent of expenses as suggested by the guideline for nonprofit entities.

Current practice also includes exponential models, in which materiality starts low for small bases, rises exponentially, and then levels off. Also, scaled amounts are used that are larger than the percentages shown above. Those methods that use a range of percentages generally suggest that the largest percentage be used for smaller entities and the smallest percentage be used for larger entities. For example, under method 1, 10 percent would be used if the entity was small and 5 percent if it was very large; some percentage between 5 percent and 10 percent would be used for entities between the two extremes.

Assume that for a given company, an auditor decided that a misstatement of income before taxes of $100,000 or more would be material, but a misstatement of $250,000 or more would be material for the balance sheet. Paragraph 5130.26 of the *CICA Handbook* suggests it would be inappropriate for the auditor to use a preliminary judgment about materiality of $250,000 for both income before taxes and the balance sheet. The auditor must therefore plan to find all misstatements affecting income before taxes that exceed the preliminary judgment about materiality of $100,000. Since most misstatements affect both the income statement and balance sheet, the auditor will not be greatly concerned about the possibility of misstatement on the balance sheet exceeding $250,000, and will use a materiality level of $100,000 for most tests. However, some misstatements, such as misclassifying a long-term asset as a current asset, affect only the balance sheet. The auditor will therefore also need to plan the audit with the $250,000 preliminary judgment about materiality for certain tests of the balance sheet assets and liabilities.

Qualitative factors also affect materiality   Certain types of misstatements are likely to be more important to users than others, even if the dollar amounts are the same. The auditors cannot plan to detect smaller amounts but must react if they are discovered. For example, amounts involving fraud and other irregularities are usually considered more important than unintentional errors of equal dollar amounts because fraud reflects on the honesty and reliability of the management or other personnel involved. To illustrate, most users would consider an intentional misstatement of inventory as being more important than clerical errors in inventory of the same dollar amount. In addition, while the amount of the fraud may be less than materiality, the impact of the fraud on the entity may be much in excess of materiality. For example, assume materiality for an entity with worldwide operations was $200,000. An

---

[3]Leslie, Donald A., *Materiality: The Concept and Its Application to Auditing*, Toronto: CICA, 1985, pp. 20–21.

illegal payment in another country of $25,000 would be less than materiality but could lead, if the illegal payment were to be discovered by the authorities in the other country, to fines or seizure in that country of the entity's assets which were many times the amount of the payment and much in excess of $200,000.

ILLUSTRATIVE GUIDELINES

The CICA currently does not provide specific materiality guidelines to practitioners. The concern is that such guidelines might be applied without considering all the complexities that should affect the auditor's final decision. In addition, Leslie shows in *Materiality* that no single base works well in all situations.[4]

To show the application of materiality, illustrative guidelines are provided. They are intended only to help you better understand the concept of applying materiality in practice. The guidelines are stated in Figure 8-2 in the form of a policy guideline for a public accounting firm.

FIGURE 8-2
Illustrative Materiality
Guidelines

MCCUTCHEON & WILKINSON, CHARTERED ACCOUNTANTS
Edmonton, Alberta T6G 1N4
(403) 432-6900

POLICY STATEMENT   Sally J. Wilkinson
No. 32 IC   Karen McCutcheon
Title: Materiality Guidelines

Professional judgment is to be used at all times in setting and applying materiality guidelines. As a general guideline the following policies are to be applied:

1. The combined total of misstatements in the financial statements exceeding 10 percent is normally considered material. A combined total of less than 5 percent is presumed to be immaterial in the absence of qualitative factors. Combined misstatements between 5 percent and 10 percent require the greatest amount of professional judgment to determine their materiality.
2. The 5 percent to 10 percent must be measured in relation to the appropriate base. Many times there is more than one base to which errors should be compared. The following guides are recommended in selecting the appropriate base:
   a. *Income statement.* Combined misstatements in the income statement should ordinarily be measured at 5 percent to 10 percent of operating income before taxes. A guideline of 5 percent to 10 percent may be inappropriate in a year in which income is unusually large or small. When operating income in a given year is not considered representative, it is desirable to substitute as a base a more representative income measure, such as normalized net income before taxes or average operating income for a three-year period.
      In the case of clients who operate in industries where operating income before taxes is not considered to be a useful base, $\frac{1}{2}$ percent to 1 percent of revenue will be used as a guideline.
   b. *Balance sheet.* Combined misstatements in the balance sheet should originally be evaluated for total assets. For total assets the guideline should be between $\frac{1}{2}$ and 1 percent, applied in the same way as for the income statement. An alternative is to use $\frac{1}{2}$ percent to 5 percent of shareholders' equity.
3. Qualitative factors should be carefully evaluated on all audits. In many instances they are more important than the guidelines applied to the income statement and balance sheet. The intended uses of the financial statements and the nature of the information on the statements, including footnotes, must be carefully evaluated.
4. If the guideline for the income statement is less than those selected for the balance sheet, the lesser amount should be used as a guideline for all misstatements that affect operating income before taxes. Misstatements such as misclassification errors would be evaluated using the greater amount.

APPLICATION TO HILLSBURG HARDWARE LTD.

Using the illustrative guidelines for McCutcheon & Wilkinson in Figure 8-2, it is now possible to decide on a preliminary judgment about materiality for Hillsburg Hardware Ltd. The guidelines are as follows:

---

[4]Leslie, Donald A., *Materiality: The Concept and Its Application to Auditing*, Toronto: CICA, 1985, pp. 20–37.

	PRELIMINARY JUDGMENT ABOUT MATERIALITY			
	MINIMUM		MAXIMUM	
	Percentage	Dollar Amount	Percentage	Dollar Amount
Revenue (net sales)	$\frac{1}{2}$	36,000	1	72,000
Net income before taxes	5	14,000	10	29,000
Total assets	$\frac{1}{2}$	15,000	1	31,000
Shareholders' equity	$\frac{1}{2}$	5,600	5	56,000
Gross profit	$\frac{1}{2}$	10,000	5	100,000

Assuming the auditor for Hillsburg Hardware decided that the general guidelines are reasonable, the first step would be to evaluate whether any qualitative factors significantly affect the materiality judgment. If not, considering the income statement base first, the auditor must decide that if combined misstatements on the income statement were less than $14,000, the statements would be considered fairly stated. If the combined misstatements exceeded $29,000, the statements would not be considered fairly stated. If the misstatements were between $14,000 and $29,000, a more careful consideration of all facts would be required. The auditor then applies the same process to the other three bases. Given the suggested guidelines calculated above and the fact that Hillsburg Hardware is a small company with few users of financial statements, the auditor would probably decide to use the larger of the bases, $100,000, as the preliminary judgment about materiality. Gross profit is also a base that fluctuates less from year to year than net income since small companies may have fluctuating income levels.

Dollar-Unit Sampling[5] suggests that the preliminary judgment about materiality be adjusted for the effect of *net anticipated* misstatements to determine materiality available for unanticipated misstatements.

The illustration that follows is an example of adjusting for the effect of net anticipated misstatements:

Preliminary judgment about materiality		$150,000
Less		
Anticipated misstatements from specific tests	$20,000	
Carry forward misstatements from the previous year	30,000	
Anticipated client corrections	(15,000)	35,000
Materiality available for unanticipated misstatements		$115,000

The auditor, in the above example, is simply reducing the preliminary judgment of $150,000 for net anticipated misstatements of $35,000 to determine that $115,000 will be available for unanticipated misstatements. A useful analogy would be that of an individual going on a date who has $60 for dinner and a show, but needs $10 for cab fare at the end of the evening. The amount available for spending for the evening is $50, not $60. Similarly, the amount available for unanticipated misstatements is really $115,000, not $150,000.

Some auditors allocate materiality to segments once they have determined materiality available for unanticipated misstatements. They use the amounts allocated to determine sample sizes and the amount of testing required. However, most auditors use total materiality available for unanticipated misstatements in audit planning on the grounds that the auditor is concerned about the aggregate misstatement in the financial statements as a whole and not in the misstatement in a particular account balance.

---

[5]Leslie, Donald A., Albert D. Teitlebaum, and Rodney J. Anderson, *Dollar-Unit Sampling*, Toronto: Copp Clark Pitman, 1979, pp. 178–179.

ESTIMATE MISSTATEMENT AND COMPARE

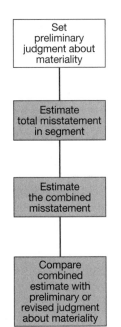

Set preliminary judgment about materiality

Estimate total misstatement in segment

Estimate the combined misstatement

Compare combined estimate with preliminary or revised judgment about materiality

The first step in applying materiality involves planning, whereas the last three (steps 2, 3, and 4 in Figure 8-1) result from performing audit tests. The last three steps are discussed in greater detail in later chapters; this section only shows their relationship to the first step.

When the auditor performs audit procedures for each segment of the audit, a worksheet is kept of all misstatements found. For example, assume the auditor finds six client errors in a sample of 200 in testing inventory costs (identified misstatement). These misstatements are used to estimate the *total* misstatements in inventory (step 2). The total is referred to as an "estimate" or often a "projection" because only a sample, rather than the entire population, was audited. Estimation of projected misstatement is required by Section 5130. The projected misstatement amounts (likely misstatements) for each account are combined on the worksheet (step 3), and then the combined misstatement (likely aggregate misstatement) is compared to materiality (step 4).

Table 8-1 is used to illustrate the last three steps in applying materiality. For simplicity, only three accounts are included and the calculation of likely misstatements for accounts receivable and for inventory are shown. The preliminary judgment about materiality is $50,000. The likely misstatements are calculated based on actual audit tests. Assume, for example, that in auditing inventory, the auditor found $3,500 of net overstatement errors in a sample of $50,000 of the total population of $450,000. One way to calculate the estimate of the misstatements is to make a direct projection from the sample to the population and add an estimate for sampling error (further possible misstatements). The calculation of the direct projection (likely misstatement) is:

$$\frac{\text{Net misstatements in the sample (\$3,500)}}{\text{Total sampled (\$50,000)}} \times \frac{\text{Total recorded population value}}{\text{(\$450,000)}} = \frac{\text{Direct projection estimate (\$31,500)}}{}$$

The estimate for sampling error results because the auditor has sampled only a portion of the population (this is discussed in detail in Chapters 11, 12, and 14). It is the amount by which a projected likely misstatement amount could be different from an actual (and unknown) total as a result of the sample not being representative. In this simplified example, the estimate for sampling error is assumed to be 50 percent of the direct projection of the misstatement amounts for the accounts where sampling was used (accounts receivable and inventory).

In combining the misstatements in Table 8-1, observe that the likely misstatements for the three accounts add to $43,500. The total sampling error (further possible misstatements) quite often is different from the sum of the sampling errors since varying levels of certainty must be incorporated and the total is usually calculated as a numeric range. It is shown here, adding up to the sum of the individual sampling errors for convenience. Sampling error represents the maximum error in account details not audited.

It is unlikely that this maximum error amount would exist in all accounts subjected to sampling. Thus, sampling methodology provides for determining a combined sampling error that takes this into consideration. Again, this is discussed in detail in Chapters 11, 12 and 14.

TABLE 8-1

ILLUSTRATION OF COMPARISON OF MAXIMUM POSSIBLE MISSTATEMENT TO PRELIMINARY JUDGMENT ABOUT MATERIALITY

ACCOUNT	MAXIMUM POSSIBLE MISSTATEMENT		
	Likely Misstatement	*Sampling Error*	*Total*
Cash	$ 0	N/A	$ 0
Accounts receivable	$12,000	$ 6,000[1]	$18,000
Inventory	$31,500	$15,750[2]	$47,250
Total estimated misstatement amount	$43,500	$21,750	$65,250
Preliminary judgment about materiality			$50,000

N/A = Not applicable; cash audited 100%.
(1) 12,000 × 50% (assumed)
(2) 31,500 × 50% (assumed)

Table 8-1 shows that maximum possible misstatement for the three accounts of $65,250 exceeds the preliminary judgment about materiality of $50,000. Furthermore, the major area of difficulty is inventory, where the maximum possible misstatement is $47,250. Because the estimated maximum possible misstatement exceeds the preliminary judgment, the financial statements are not acceptable. The auditor can either determine whether the estimated aggregate misstatement actually exceeds $50,000 by performing additional audit procedures or require the client to make an adjustment for likely misstatements. Assuming additional audit procedures are performed, they would be concentrated in the inventory area.

If the estimated maximum possible misstatement for inventory had been $24,000 ($16,000 plus $8,000 sampling error), the auditor probably would not need to expand audit tests, since the total maximum possible misstatement would be less ($18,000 + $24,000 = $42,000) than the $50,000 preliminary judgment. It is likely that the auditor would have accepted the balances in the three accounts.

RISK

Risk in auditing means that the auditor accepts some level of uncertainty in performing the audit function. The auditor recognizes, for example, that there is uncertainty about the appropriateness of evidence, uncertainty about the effectiveness of a client's internal control, and uncertainty as to whether the financial statements are fairly stated when the audit is completed.

An effective auditor recognizes that risks exist and deals with those risks in an appropriate manner. Most risks that auditors encounter are difficult to measure and require careful thought for an appropriate response. For example, assume the auditor determines that the client's industry is undergoing significant technological changes which affect both the client and the client's customers. This change may affect the obsolescence of the client's inventory, collectibility of accounts receivable, and perhaps even the ability of the client's business to continue. Responding to these risks properly is essential to achieving a quality audit.

The remainder of this chapter deals mostly with the risks that affect planning the engagement to determine the appropriate evidence to accumulate by applying the CICA's audit risk model. It concludes by showing the relationship between materiality and risk.

ILLUSTRATION CONCERNING RISKS AND EVIDENCE

Before discussing the audit risk model, an illustration for a hypothetical company is provided in Table 8-2 as a frame of reference for the discussion. The illustration shows that the auditor has decided on a "medium" willingness to accept the risk that material misstatements exist after the audit is complete for all five cycles (A). It is common for auditors to want an equal likelihood of misstatements for each cycle after the audit is finished to permit the issuance of an unqualified opinion. Next, the table shows that there are differences among cycles in the frequency and size of expected misstatements (B). For example, there are almost no misstatements expected in the payroll and personnel cycle, but many in inventory and warehousing. The reason may be that the payroll transactions are highly routine, whereas there may be considerable complexities in recording inventory. Similarly, internal control is believed to differ in effectiveness among the five cycles (C). For example, internal controls in payroll and personnel are considered highly effective, whereas those in inventory and warehousing are considered ineffective.

The previous considerations (A, B, C) affect the auditor's decision about the appropriate extent of evidence to accumulate (D). For example, because the auditor expects few misstatements in payroll and personnel (B) and internal control is effective (C), the auditor plans for less evidence collection in the payroll and personnel cycle (D) than for inventory and warehousing. Recall that the auditor has the same (medium) level of willingness to accept material misstatements after the audit is finished for all five cycles (A), but a different extent of evidence is needed for various

TABLE 8-2

ILLUSTRATION OF DIFFERING EVIDENCE AMONG CYCLES

		SALES AND COLLECTION CYCLE	ACQUISITION AND PAYMENT CYCLE	PAYROLL AND PERSONNEL CYCLE	INVENTORY AND WAREHOUSING CYCLE	CAPITAL AND ACQUISITION REPAYMENT CYCLE
A	Auditor's willingness to permit material misstatements to exist after completing the audit (acceptable audit risk)	Low willingness (medium)	Low willingness (medium)	Low willingness (medium)	Low willingness (medium)	Low willingness (medium)
B	Auditor's assessment of expectation of material misstatement before considering internal control (inherent risk)	Expect some misstatements (medium)	Expect many misstatements (high)	Expect few misstatements (low)	Expect many misstatements (high)	Expect few misstatements (low)
C	Auditor's assessment of effectiveness of internal control to prevent or detect material misstatements (control risk)	Medium effectiveness (medium)	High effectiveness (low)	High effectiveness (low)	Low effectiveness (high)	Medium effectiveness (medium)
D	Extent of evidence the auditor plans to accumulate (planned detection risk)	Medium level (medium)	Medium level (medium)	Low level (high)	High level (low)	Medium level (medium)

cycles. The difference is caused by differences in the auditor's expectations of misstatements and assessment of internal control.

AUDIT RISK MODEL FOR PLANNING

OBJECTIVE 8-5

Describe the audit risk model and its components.

The primary way that auditors deal with risk in planning audit evidence is through the application of the audit risk model. The source of the audit risk model is the professional literature in the *CICA Handbook* in Section 5130, "Materiality and Audit Risk in Conducting an Audit," and in Assurance and Related Services Guideline AuG-7, "Applying Materiality and Audit Risk Concepts in Conducting an Audit." A thorough understanding of the model is essential to effective auditing and to the study of the remaining chapters of this book.

The audit risk model is used primarily for planning purposes in deciding how much evidence to accumulate in each cycle. It is usually stated as follows:

$$AAR = IR \times CR \times PDR$$

where

AAR = acceptable audit risk (AuG-7 refers to this risk as audit risk)
IR = inherent risk
CR = control risk
PDR = planned detection risk (AuG-7 refers to this risk as detection risk)

ACCEPTABLE AUDIT RISK

As stated in Chapter 7, *acceptable audit risk* is a measure of how willing the auditor is to accept that the financial statements may be materially misstated after the audit is completed and an unqualified opinion has been reached.[6] When the auditor decides

---

[6]"The Parable of Bert and Ernie" by Stephen Aldersley in *CAmagazine* (March 1988), pp. 60–61, illustrates two different audit situations where the risk of misstatements occurring is similar but where the consequences of failing to detect

(continues on next page)

on a lower acceptable audit risk, it means the auditor wants a higher level of assurance. Auditors sometimes refer to the terms "audit assurance," "overall assurance," or "level of assurance" instead of "acceptable audit risk." Audit assurance or any of the equivalent terms is the complement of acceptable audit risk, that is, one minus acceptable audit risk. For example, acceptable audit risk of 2 percent is the same as audit assurance of 98 percent. In other words, acceptable audit risk of 2 percent means the auditor is willing to accept a 2 percent risk that there are material errors in the financial statements. At the same time, a 98 percent level of assurance has been obtained that the financial statements are free of material errors. Zero risk would be certainty, and a 100 percent risk would be complete uncertainty. Complete assurance (zero risk) of the accuracy of financial statements is not economically practical. It has already been established in Chapter 5 that the auditor cannot guarantee the complete absence of material misstatements.

Using the audit risk model, there is a direct relationship between acceptable audit risk and planned detection risk, and an inverse relationship between acceptable audit risk and planned evidence. For example, as the level of audit risk decreases (i.e., the auditor wants *more assurance*), more evidence needs to be gathered (planned detection risk is reduced, and *more assurance* is needed from audit evidence). As stated in Chapter 7, auditors also often assign more experienced staff or have an additional independent review of the working papers for a client with lower acceptable audit risk.

INHERENT RISK

As stated in Chapter 7, *inherent risk* is a measure of the auditor's assessment of the likelihood that a material misstatement might occur in the first place, that is, before considering the effectiveness of internal accounting controls. Inherent risk is the susceptibility of the financial statements to material misstatement, assuming no internal controls. If the auditor concludes that there is a high likelihood of misstatement, ignoring internal controls, the auditor would conclude that inherent risk is high. Internal controls are ignored in setting inherent risk because they are considered separately in the audit risk model as control risk. In Table 8-2 inherent risk (B) has been assessed high for inventory and lower for payroll and personnel and capital acquisitions and repayments. The assessment was likely based on discussions with management, knowledge of the company, and results in prior year audits. For example, there may be thousands of inventory transactions of many different types, with prior year files showing many errors. Payroll, personnel, and capital acquisition transactions could occur less frequently and be more frequently checked by outside parties (e.g., banks may process payroll and contracts may be reviewed externally for capital acquisitions). Factors to be examined when assessing inherent risk are discussed commencing on page 247.

CONTROL RISK

Control risk is a measure of the auditor's assessment of the likelihood that misstatements exceeding a tolerable amount in a segment will not be prevented or detected by the client's internal control. Control risk represents (1) an assessment of whether a client's internal control is effective for preventing or detecting misstatements and

---

[6] *(continued)* the misstatements are quite different. This is a classic tale. The author tells you that if you make a mistake with the small business, you must deal with Bert, who studied under Boris Karloff. "He's short, carries a long, mean-looking whip and wears boots with sharp studs . . . . but . . . you can usually buy him a beer and convince him to ignore it." However, if you make the same kind of mistake with the big business, you have to deal with Ernie, "who wields an axe." But first, Ernie will call a public meeting, tell everyone what a lousy job you did, and that he'll "have your head for it." Both Bert and Ernie will end up going away as long as you have met "the Standard," but if you haven't, "you might wish Ernie had been able to use his equipment after all." It is an excellent discussion of audit risk in the context of a large versus small business.

(2) the auditor's intention to rely on internal controls and thus assign a value to control risk below maximum (100 percent) as part of the audit plan. For example, assume the auditor concludes that internal control is completely ineffective to prevent or detect misstatements. That is the likely conclusion for inventory and warehousing in Table 8-2 (C). The auditor would therefore assign 100 percent risk factor to control risk. The more effective internal control, the lower the risk factor that *could* be assigned to control risk.

Before auditors can use a control risk of less than 100 percent, they must do three things: obtain an understanding of the client's internal control, evaluate how well it should function based on the understanding, and test internal control for effectiveness. The first of these is the *understanding* requirement that relates to all audits. The latter two are the *assessment of control risk* steps that are required when the auditor *chooses* to assess control risk at a level below maximum.

Understanding internal control, assessing control risk, and their impact on evidence requirements are so important that the entire next chapter is devoted to that topic. However, it should be noted that the auditor can choose to place no reliance on internal controls after an understanding has been obtained. Then control risk must be set at 100 percent regardless of the actual effectiveness of the underlying internal control. Use of the audit risk model in this circumstance then causes the auditor to control audit risk entirely through a low level of planned detection risk (assuming inherent risk is high).

PLANNED DETECTION RISK

Planned detection risk is a measure of the risk that audit evidence for a segment will fail to detect material misstatements, should such misstatements exist. There are two key points about planned detection risk. First, it is dependent on the other three factors in the model. Planned detection risk will change only if the auditor changes one of the other factors. Second, it determines the amount of evidence the auditor plans to accumulate inversely with the size of planned detection risk. Using the complement of detection risk, at 5 percent detection risk, the auditor needs to provide 95 percent assurance that the evidence collected will detect material errors. If planned detection risk is reduced to 2 percent, the auditor needs to accumulate more evidence (to obtain 98 percent assurance that evidence collected will detect material errors). For example, in Table 8-2 (D) planned detection risk is low for inventory and warehousing which causes planned evidence to be high. The opposite is true for payroll and personnel, which has high planned detection risk, thus requiring less evidence gathering.

A numerical example is provided to solve for detection risk, even though it is not practical in practice to measure as precisely as these numbers imply. The numbers used are for the inventory and warehousing cycle in Table 8-2.

$AAR = 5\%$ (medium risk to be accepted)
$IR = 100\%$ (high risk of errors expected, no reliance intended)
$CR = 100\%$ (low effectiveness of internal controls, no reliance intended)

$$AAR = IR \times DR \times PDR \quad \text{or}$$

$$PDR = \frac{AAR}{IR \times CR}$$

$$PDR = \frac{0.05}{1 \times 1} = 0.05 \text{ or } 5\%$$

(Auditor plans 5 percent risk of not detecting errors and seeks 95 percent assurance from substantive tests, as discussed in Chapter 14.)

Figure 8-3 shows how these audit risk model components interact. The inventory and warehousing cycle may have material errors present. This is represented by the material errors falling into the control risk tray, which has some holes in it and thus

FIGURE 8-3
Audit Risk Model
Components

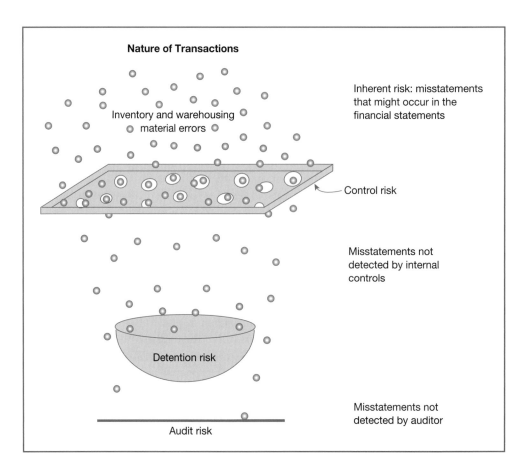

acts as a sieve. There may not be any material errors or there may be many. Since inherent risk for the inventory and warehousing cycle has been assessed as high, there are many material errors falling into the control risk tray, and inherent risk has been set at 100 percent. The purpose of internal controls is to prevent, detect, and correct material errors in the financial statements. The auditor has decided that in the inventory and warehousing cycle, there is low effectiveness in internal controls, so the control risk tray has holes in it, letting material errors escape, and thus control risk has been set at 100 percent (no reliance). For the auditor to obtain reasonable assurance that the financial statements are free of material error, these errors must be caught in the detection risk bowl, so that they can be brought to the attention of management for correction. The bowl is large enough so that 95 percent assurance of catching these errors through evidence gathering will occur (5 percent detection risk). When inherent risk is set at maximum and there is no reliance on internal controls (also set at maximum), then planned detection risk is equal to acceptable audit risk, here a 5 percent risk that misstatements will not be detected.

If control risk had been 0.50 instead of 1.0, planned detection risk would be 0.10 and planned evidence could therefore be reduced. Using Figure 8-3, this means that there would be fewer holes in the control risk tray (more errors would be detected by internal controls), and the size of the detection risk bowl could be smaller (less evidence would be required).

RELATIONSHIPS BETWEEN AUDIT RISK MODEL COMPONENTS

The acceptable audit risk desired affects the amount of evidence to be gathered. As audit risk decreases, assurance required increases and more evidence must be gathered, making the audit more costly. Think in terms of the number of audits conducted by all public accountants. What portion of these audits could include material misstatements without having an adverse effect on society? More undetected material misstatements could result in the audit being perceived as having less value.

Inherent risk and planned detection risk have an inverse relationship. Using Figure 8-3, we can see that when more material errors are likely to exist (inherent risk assessed as higher), if control risk stays the same, the detection risk bowl must be larger (more evidence to be gathered and lower detection risk).

Similarly, if inherent risk stays constant but control risk is higher (there are more holes in the control risk tray, letting more material errors through), then we again have to increase the size of our detection risk bowl (more evidence gathering needed and smaller detection risk). This is also an inverse relationship between the two types of risk.

CHANGING AUDIT RISK FOR BUSINESS RISK

OBJECTIVE 8-6

Consider the impact of business risk on acceptable audit risk.

Business risk is the risk that the auditor or audit firm will suffer harm, which paragraph 5130.15 describes as "risk of loss or injury to his or her professional practice from litigation, adverse publicity, or other events," because of a client relationship, even though the auditor's report rendered for the client was correct. For example, if a client declares bankruptcy after an audit is completed, there is a strong likelihood of a lawsuit against the public accounting firm even if the quality of the audit was good.

There is a difference of opinion among auditors about business risk: they are divided about whether it should be considered in planning the audit. Opponents of modifying the amount of evidence collected to account for business risk contend that auditors do not provide audit opinions with different levels of assurance and, therefore, should not provide more or less assurance because of business risk. Proponents contend that it is appropriate for auditors to accumulate additional evidence on audits where legal exposure is high. In all cases, it is agreed that the auditor cannot reduce the amount of audit evidence collected when business risk is minimal.

When auditors modify evidence for business risk, it is done by control of acceptable audit risk. The authors believe a reasonably low acceptable audit risk is always desirable, but in some circumstances an even lower risk is needed because of business risk factors. Research has indicated that several factors affect business risk and therefore acceptable audit risk. Only three of those are discussed here: the degree to which external users rely on the statements, the likelihood that a client will have financial difficulties after the auditor's report is issued, and the integrity of management.

The degree to which external users rely on the statements   When external users place heavy reliance on the financial statements, it is appropriate that acceptable audit risk be decreased. When the statements are heavily relied on, a great social harm could result if a material misstatement were to remain undetected in the financial statements. The cost of additional evidence can be more easily justified when the loss to users from material misstatements is substantial. Several factors are good indicators of the degree to which statements are relied on by external users:

- *Client's size.* Generally speaking, the larger a client's operations, the more widely used the statements will be. The client's size, measured by total assets or total revenues, will have an effect on acceptable audit risk.
- *Distribution of ownership.* The statements of publicly held corporations are normally relied on by many more users than those of private or closely held corporations. For these companies, the interested parties include the provincial securities administrators such as the Alberta Securities Commission, perhaps even the SEC, financial analysts, creditors, suppliers, the government, and the general public. The availability of financial statements on the Internet allows for easy downloading of financial statement information for publicly traded companies. Therefore, distribution of these financial statements is potentially increasing due to technology.
- *Nature and amount of liabilities.* When statements include a large number of liabilities, they are more likely to be used extensively by actual and potential creditors than when there are few liabilities.

U.S. Securities and Exchange Commission
www.sec.gov

The likelihood that a client will have financial difficulties after the auditor's report is issued If a client is forced to file for bankruptcy or suffers a significant loss after completion of the audit, there is a greater chance of the auditor's being required to defend the quality of the audit than if the client were under no financial strain. The loss could be due to fraud, the loss of a major customer, or a computer disaster that cripples the company for a period of time. There is a natural tendency for those who lose money in a bankruptcy or because of a stock price reversal to file suit against the auditor. This can result from the honest belief that the auditor failed to conduct an adequate audit or from the users' desire to recover part of their loss regardless of the adequacy of the audit work.

In situations in which the auditor believes the chance of financial failure or loss is high, and there is a corresponding increase in business risk for the auditor, the acceptable level of audit risk should be reduced. If a subsequent challenge does occur, the auditor will then be in a better position to defend the audit results successfully. The total audit evidence and costs will increase, but this is justifiable because of the additional risk of lawsuits the auditor faces.

It is difficult for an auditor to predict financial failure before it occurs, but certain factors are good indicators of its increased probability:

- *Liquidity position.* If a client is constantly short of cash and working capital, it indicates a future problem in paying bills. The auditor must assess the likelihood and significance of a weak liquidity position getting worse.
- *Profits (losses) in previous years.* When a company has rapidly declining profits or increasing losses for several years, the auditor should recognize the future solvency problems the client is likely to encounter. It is also important to consider the changing profits relative to the balance remaining in retained earnings.
- *Method of financing growth.* The more a client relies on debt as a means of financing, the greater the risk of financial difficulty if the client's operations become less successful. It is also important to evaluate whether permanent assets are being financed with short-term or long-term loans. Large amounts of required cash outflows during a short period of time can force a company into bankruptcy.
- *Nature of the client's operations.* Certain types of businesses are inherently riskier than others. For example, other things being equal, there is a much greater likelihood of bankruptcy of a start-up technology company dependent on one product than a diversified food manufacturer.
- *Competence of management.* Competent management is constantly alert for potential financing difficulties and modifies its operating methods to minimize the effects of short-run problems. The ability of management must be assessed as a part of the evaluation of the likelihood of bankruptcy.

Management's integrity As discussed in Chapter 7, as a part of new client investigation and continuing client evaluation, if a client has questionable integrity, the auditor is likely to assess acceptable audit risk lower or not accept or even resign from the audit. Companies with low integrity often conduct their business affairs in a manner that results in conflicts with their shareholders, regulators, and customers. These conflicts in turn often reflect on the users' perceived quality of the audit and can result in lawsuits and other disagreements. An obvious example of a situation in which management's integrity is questionable is prior criminal conviction of a key member of management. Other examples of questionable integrity might include frequent disagreements with previous auditors, Revenue Canada, the provincial securities commission, or the stock exchange where the company is listed. Frequent turnover of key financial and internal audit personnel and ongoing conflicts with labour unions and employees may also indicate integrity problems.

To assess acceptable audit risk, the auditor must first assess each of the factors affecting acceptable audit risk. Table 8-3 illustrates the methods used by auditors to assess each of the three factors already discussed. It is easy to see after examining Table 8-3 that the assessment of each of the factors is highly subjective, which means

TABLE 8-3

METHODS
PRACTITIONERS USE TO
ASSESS ACCEPTABLE
AUDIT RISK

FACTORS	METHODS USED BY PRACTITIONERS TO ASSESS ACCEPTABLE AUDIT RISK
External users' reliance on financial statements	• Examine the financial statements, including footnotes. • Read minutes of board of directors' meetings to determine future plans. • Examine filings with the provincial securities commission for a publicly held company. • Discuss financing plans with management.
Likelihood of financial difficulties	• Analyze the financial statements for financial difficulties using ratios and other analytical procedures. • Examine historical and projected cash flow statements for the nature of cash inflows and outflows.
Management integrity	• Follow the procedures discussed in Chapter 7 for client acceptance and continuance.

that the overall assessment is also highly subjective. A typical evaluation of acceptable audit risk is high, medium, or low, where a low acceptable audit risk assessment means a "risky" client requiring more extensive evidence, assignment of more experienced personnel, and/or a more extensive review of working papers. As the audit progresses, additional information about the client is obtained and acceptable audit risk may be modified.

ASSESSING ACCEPTABLE AUDIT RISK IN PRACTICE

Henry Rinsk, of Links, Rinsk & Rodman, Public Accountants, is the partner responsible for the audit of Hungry Food Restaurants Ltd., a chain of nine Manitoba family restaurants. The firm has audited Hungry Food for ten years and has always found management competent, cooperative, and easy to deal with. Hungry Food is family-owned with a business succession plan in place, profitable, and liquid and has little debt. Management has a reputation in the community for high integrity and good relationships with employees, customers, and suppliers.

After meeting with the other partners as part of the firm's annual client continuation meeting, Henry recommends that acceptable audit risk for Hungry Food be assessed as high. For Links, Rinsk & Rodman, this means no expansion of evidence, a "standard" review of working papers, and a "standard" assignment of personnel to the engagement.

INHERENT RISK

OBJECTIVE 8-7

Consider the impact of several factors on the assessment of inherent risk.

The inclusion of inherent risk in the audit risk model is one of the most important concepts in auditing. It implies that auditors should attempt to predict where misstatements are most and least likely in the financial statement segments. This information affects the total amount of evidence the auditor is required to accumulate and influences how the auditor's efforts to gather the evidence are allocated among the segments of the audit.

There is always some risk that the client has made misstatements that are individually or collectively large enough to make the financial statements misleading. The misstatements can be intentional or unintentional, and they can affect the dollar balance in accounts or disclosure. Inherent risk can be low in some instances and extremely high in others.

The audit risk model shows the common impact that inherent and control risks have on detection risk. For example, an inherent risk of 40 percent and a control risk of 60 percent affect detection risk and planned evidence the same as an inherent risk of 60 percent and a control risk of 40 percent. In both cases, multiplying *IR* by *CR* results in a denominator in the audit risk model of 24 percent. The combination of inherent risk and control risk can be thought of as the *expectation of misstatements after considering the effect of internal controls*. Inherent risk is the expectation of misstatements before considering the effect of internal controls.

At the start of an audit, there is not much that can be done about changing inherent risk. Instead, the auditor must *assess the factors* that make up the risk and *modify audit evidence* to take them into consideration. The auditor should consider several major factors when assessing inherent risk:

- Nature of the client's business, including the nature of the client's products and services
- Nature of data processing systems and extent of use of data communications
- Integrity of management
- Client motivation
- Results of previous audits
- Initial versus repeat engagement
- Related parties
- Nonroutine transactions
- Judgment required to record account balances and transactions correctly
- Assets that are susceptible to misappropriation
- Makeup of the population

NATURE OF THE CLIENT'S BUSINESS

Inherent risk for certain accounts is affected by the nature of the client's business. For example, there is a greater likelihood of obsolete inventory for an electronics manufacturer than for a steel fabricator. Similarly, loans receivable for a small loan company that makes unsecured loans are less likely to be collectible than those of a bank which makes only secured loans. Inherent risk is most likely to vary from business to business for accounts such as inventory, accounts and loans receivable, and property, plant, and equipment. The nature of the client's business should have little or no effect on inherent risk for accounts such as cash, notes, and mortgages payable. Information gained while obtaining knowledge about the client's industry and business, as discussed in Chapter 7, is useful for assessing this factor.

CICA RISK ALERT

The CICA's Assurance Standards department publishes irregular bulletins that provide an overview of current issues that may affect assessment of inherent risk and that may be of significance to public accountants who perform audits and review engagements.

NATURE OF DATA PROCESSING SYSTEMS

When programs are customized by an understaffed information systems group, there is a greater likelihood of programming errors than when an organization is using standard packaged software, thus increasing the likelihood of material error. (The system acquisition or development process is briefly summarized in the Appendix.)

The physical configuration of data processing systems affects the complexity of information systems. More complex systems are harder to understand and manage, thus increasing the likelihood of error. For example, a centralized data processing system with 15 data entry stations located on a single floor is easier to manage than a large financial institution's systems, where there are multiple central processing units, decentralized computing at minicomputers in regional centres, branches with microcomputers and automated teller machines processing transactions locally or transmitting to central locations, and electronic funds transfer transactions that are processed internationally. The scope of potential error is magnified a hundred fold in the more complex scenario. (The differences between centralized, decentralized, and distributed systems are summarized briefly in the Appendix.)

INTEGRITY OF MANAGEMENT

When management is dominated by one or a few individuals who lack integrity, the likelihood of significantly misrepresented financial statements is greatly increased. For example, a lack of integrity of management has been found to exist in the great majority of significant accountants' liability cases. As stated in Chapter 7 and earlier in this chapter, management integrity affects the auditor's assessment of acceptable audit risk and, in extreme cases, may cause the auditor to reject the client.

When management has an adequate level of integrity for the auditor to accept the engagement, but cannot be regarded as completely honest in all dealings, auditors normally reduce acceptable audit risk and also increase inherent risk. For example, management may deduct capital items as repairs and maintenance expense on tax returns. The public accounting firm should first evaluate the cycles or accounts for which management is most likely to make misstatements. A higher level of inherent risk is appropriate wherever the auditor believes material misstatements may occur.

CLIENT MOTIVATION

In many situations, management may believe that it would be advantageous to misstate the financial statements. For example, if management receives a percentage of total profits as a bonus, there may be a tendency to overstate net income. Similarly, if a bond indenture requirement includes a specification that the current ratio must remain above a certain level, the client may be tempted to overstate current assets or to understate current liabilities by an amount sufficient to meet the requirement. Also, there may be considerable motivation for intentional understatement of income when management wants the company to pay less income taxes. If management lacks integrity, some specific type of motivation may then lead management to misstate financial reports.

RESULTS OF PREVIOUS AUDITS

Errors found in the previous year's audit have a high likelihood of occurring again in the current year's audit. This is because many types of errors are systemic in nature, and organizations are often slow in making changes to eliminate them. Therefore, an auditor would be negligent if the results of the preceding year's examination were ignored during the development of the current year's audit program. For example, if the auditor found a significant number of errors in pricing inventory, inherent risk would likely be high, and extensive testing would have to be done in the current audit as a means of determining whether the deficiency in the client's system had been corrected. If, however, the auditor has found no errors for the past several years in conducting tests of an audit area, the auditor is justified in reducing inherent risk, provided that changes in relevant circumstances have not occurred.

INITIAL VERSUS REPEAT ENGAGEMENT

Auditors gain experience and knowledge about the likelihood of misstatements after auditing a client for several years. The lack of previous years' audit results would cause most auditors to use a larger inherent risk for initial audits than for repeat engagements in which no material misstatements had been found. Most auditors set a high inherent risk in the first year of an audit and reduce it in subsequent years as they gain experience.

RELATED PARTIES

Transactions between parent and subsidiary companies and those between management and the corporate entity are examples of related-party transactions as defined by the *CICA Handbook's* Section 3840, "Related Party Transactions." These transactions do not occur between two independent parties dealing at "arm's length." Therefore, a greater likelihood exists of their misstatement, which should cause an increase in inherent risk. Determining the existence of related parties was discussed in Chapter 7.

NONROUTINE TRANSACTIONS

Transactions that are unusual for the client are more likely to be incorrectly recorded by the client than routine transactions because the client lacks experience in recording them. Examples include fire losses, major property acquisitions, and lease agreements. Knowledge of the client's business and review of minutes of meetings, as discussed in Chapter 7, are useful to learn about nonroutine transactions.

JUDGMENT REQUIRED TO RECORD ACCOUNT BALANCES AND TRANSACTIONS CORRECTLY

Many account balances require estimates and a great deal of management judgment. Examples are allowance for uncollectible accounts receivable, obsolete inventory, liability for warranty payments, and bank loan loss reserves. Similarly, transactions for major repairs or partial replacement of assets are examples requiring considerable judgment to record the information correctly.

ASSETS THAT ARE SUSCEPTIBLE TO MISAPPROPRIATION

The auditor should be concerned about the risk of possible defalcation in situations in which it is relatively easy to convert company assets to personal use. Such is the case when currency, marketable securities, or highly marketable inventory are not closely controlled. When the likelihood of defalcation is high, inherent risk is increased.

MAKEUP OF THE POPULATION

The individual items making up the total population also frequently affect the auditor's expectation of material misstatement. For example, most auditors would use a higher inherent risk for accounts receivable when most accounts are significantly overdue than when most accounts are current. Similarly, the potential for misstatements in inventory purchased several years ago would normally be greater than for inventory purchased in the past few months. Transactions with affiliated companies, amounts due from officers, cash disbursements made payable to cash, and accounts receivable outstanding for several months are examples of situations requiring a larger inherent risk and therefore greater investigation because there is usually a higher likelihood of misstatement than in more typical transactions.

ASSESSING INHERENT RISK

The auditor must evaluate the preceding factors and decide on an appropriate inherent risk factor for each cycle, account, and audit objective. Some factors, such as the integrity of management, will affect many or perhaps all cycles, whereas others, such as nonroutine transactions, will affect only specific accounts or audit objectives. Although the profession has not established standards or guidelines for setting inherent risk, the authors believe auditors are generally conservative in making such assessments. Most auditors would probably set inherent risk at well above 50 percent, even in the best of circumstances, and at 100 percent when there is any reasonable possibility of significant misstatements. For example, assume that in the audit of inventory, the auditor notes that (1) a large number of errors were found in the previous year and (2) inventory turnover has slowed in the current year. Many auditors would probably set inherent risk at a relatively high level (some would use 100 percent) for each audit objective for inventory in this situation.

SUMMARY OF RISKS

OBJECTIVE 8-8

Discuss the relationship among the components of risk.

Figure 8-4 summarizes the factors that affect acceptable audit risk, inherent risk, and control risk. Based on the determined acceptable audit risk, the conclusion reached with respect to inherent risk, and both the conclusion and extent of reliance determined for control risk, the auditor determines the planned detection risk and the planned audit evidence to be accumulated.

FIGURE 8-4
Factors Influencing
Risks

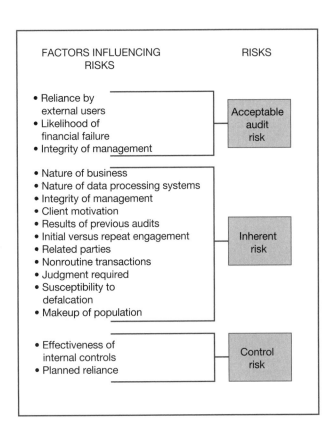

OTHER
MATERIALITY
AND RISK
CONSIDERATIONS

AUDIT RISK FOR
SEGMENTS

OBJECTIVE 8-9

Discuss risk for
segments and
measurement
difficulties.

Both control risk and inherent risk are typically estimated for each cycle, each account, and often even each audit objective and are likely to vary from cycle to cycle, account to account, and objective to objective on the same audit. Internal controls may be more effective for inventory-related accounts than for those related to capital assets. Control risk would therefore also be different for different accounts depending on the effectiveness of the controls. Factors affecting inherent risk, such as susceptibility to defalcation and routineness of the transactions, are also likely to differ from account to account. For that reason, it is normal to have inherent risk vary for different accounts in the same audit unless there is some strong overriding factor of concern, such as management integrity.

Acceptable audit risk is ordinarily set by the auditor for the entire audit and held constant for each major cycle and account. Auditors normally use the same acceptable audit risk for each segment because the factors affecting acceptable audit risk are related to the entire audit, not individual accounts. For example, the extent to which financial statements are relied on for users' decisions is usually related to the overall financial statements, not just one or two accounts.

In some cases, however, a *lower* audit risk may be more appropriate for one account than for others. In the previous example, if the auditor had decided to use an acceptable audit risk of medium for the audit as a whole, he or she might decide to reduce acceptable audit risk to low for inventory if inventory was used as collateral for a short-term loan.

Some auditors use the same acceptable audit risk for each segment, whereas others use a higher acceptable audit risk for each segment than that desired for the financial statements as a whole. The argument for using a higher acceptable audit risk for each segment is the effect of the interactions of the various accounts and transactions making up the financial statements and the synergy of multiple tests. Stated differently, if all individual segments of the audit are completed at an acceptable audit risk of a given level, the auditor can be assured that the audit risk for the financial statements as a whole will be lower.

In the illustrations that follow in this and subsequent chapters, a common acceptable audit risk is used for segments and for the financial statements as a whole.

Because control risk and inherent risk may vary from cycle to cycle, account to account, or objective to objective, planned detection risk and required audit evidence will also vary. This conclusion should not be surprising. The circumstances of each engagement are different, and the extent of evidence needed will depend on the unique circumstances. For example, inventory might require extensive testing on an engagement due to weak internal controls and concern about obsolescence due to technological changes in the industry. On the same engagement, accounts receivable may require little testing because of effective internal controls, fast collection of receivables, excellent relationships between the client and customers, and good audit results in previous years. Similarly, for a given audit of inventory, an auditor may assess that there is a higher inherent risk of a valuation misstatement because of the higher potential for obsolescence, but a low inherent risk of a classification misstatement because there is only purchased inventory.

RELATING RISKS TO BALANCE-RELATED AUDIT OBJECTIVES

It is common in practice to assess inherent and control risks for each audit objective. Auditors are able to effectively associate most risks with different objectives. It is reasonably easy to determine the relationship between a risk and one or two objectives. For example, obsolescence in inventory would be unlikely to affect any objective other than valuation.

MEASUREMENT LIMITATIONS

One major limitation in the application of the audit risk model is the difficulty of measuring the components of the model.[7] In spite of the auditor's best efforts in planning, the assessments of acceptable audit risk, inherent risk, control risk, and, therefore, planned detection risk are highly subjective and are approximations of reality at best. Imagine, for example, attempting to assess precisely inherent risk by determining the impact of factors such as the misstatements discovered in prior years' audits and technology changes in the client's industry.

To offset this measurement problem, many auditors use broad and subjective measurement terms, for example, "low," "medium," and "high." Audit firms have developed automated systems that help the auditor to ensure that the appropriate questions have been answered and assist in the documentation and tabulation of conclusions reached. Table 8-5 shows how auditors can use the information to decide on the appropriate amount of evidence to accumulate for a particular transaction cycle. For example, in situation 1, the auditor has decided to accept a high acceptable audit risk for an account or objective. The auditor has concluded that there is a low risk of misstatement in the cycle (inherent risk) and that internal controls are effective. Therefore, a high detection risk is appropriate. As a result, a low level of evidence is needed. Situation 3 is at the opposite extreme. If both inherent and control risks are high but the auditor wants a low acceptable audit risk, considerable evidence is required. The other three situations fall between the two extremes.

It is equally difficult to measure the amount of evidence implied by a given planned detection risk. A typical audit program that is intended to reduce detection risk to the planned level is a combination of several audit procedures, each using a different type of evidence which is applied to different audit objectives. Auditors' measurement methods are too imprecise to permit an accurate quantitative measure of the combined evidence. Instead, auditors subjectively evaluate whether sufficient evidence has been planned to satisfy a planned detection risk of low, medium, or

---

[7]The interested reader is referred to Cushing, Barry E. and James K. Loebbecke, "Analytical Approaches to Audit Risk: A Survey and Analysis," *Auditing: A Journal of Practice and Theory* (Fall 1983), pp. 23–41.

TABLE 8-5

RELATIONSHIPS OF
RISK TO EVIDENCE

SITUATION	ACCEPTABLE AUDIT RISK	INHERENT RISK	CONTROL RISK	PLANNED DETECTION RISK	AMOUNT OF EVIDENCE REQUIRED
1	High	Low	Low	High	Low
2	Low	Low	Low	Medium	Medium
3	Low	High	High	Low	High
4	Medium	Medium	Medium	Medium	Medium
5	High	Low	Medium	Medium	Medium

high. Presumably, measurement methods are sufficient to permit an auditor to know that more evidence is needed to satisfy a low planned detection risk than for medium or high. Considerable professional judgment is needed to decide how much more. Continuing research in audit firms is used to help auditors to determine the mix of evidence required and to devise more effective means of gathering evidence as the nature of business transactions change. Some firms have an emphasis on controls reliance (where possible), while others decide that analytical review and tests of details should be emphasized instead.

In applying the audit risk model, auditors are concerned about both over- and under-auditing, but most auditors are more concerned about the latter. Under-auditing exposes the public accounting firm to legal liability and loss of professional reputation.

Because of the concern to avoid under-auditing, auditors typically assess risks conservatively. For example, an auditor might not assess either control risk or inherent risk below 0.5 even when the likelihood of misstatement is low. In these audits, a low risk might be 0.5, medium 0.8, and high 1.0, if the risks are quantified.

TESTS OF DETAILS OF BALANCES EVIDENCE PLANNING WORKSHEET

Practising auditors develop various types of spreadsheets, templates, or computerized links to aid in relating the considerations affecting audit evidence to the appropriate evidence to accumulate. One such spreadsheet in printed form is included in Figure 8-5 (on page 252) for the audit of accounts receivable for Hillsburg Hardware Ltd. The nine balance-related audit objectives introduced in Chapter 5 are included in the columns at the top of the spreadsheet. Rows one and two are acceptable audit risk and inherent risk, which were studied in this chapter. Materiality is included at the bottom of the worksheet. The engagement in-charge, Fran Moore, made the following decisions in the audit of Hillsburg Hardware Ltd.:

- *Materiality.* The preliminary judgment about materiality was set at $100,000 (5 percent of gross profit of $1,992,000).
- *Acceptable audit risk.* Fran assessed acceptable audit risk as high because of the good financial condition of the company, high management integrity, and the relatively few users of the financial statements.
- *Inherent risk.* Fran assessed inherent risk as low for all balance-related audit objectives except valuation. In past years, there have been audit adjustments to the allowance for uncollectible accounts because it was found to be understated.

Planned detection risk would be approximately the same for each balance-related audit objective in the audit of accounts receivable for Hillsburg Hardware Ltd. if the only three factors the auditor needed to consider were acceptable audit risk, inherent risk, and materiality. The evidence planning spreadsheet shows that other factors must be considered before making the final evidence decisions. Control risk for the different transaction types is examined separately, as is the impact of analytical procedures. These are studied in subsequent chapters and will be integrated into the evidence planning spreadsheet at that time.

FIGURE 8-5
Evidence Planning Spreadsheet to Decide Tests of Details of Balances for Hillsburg
Hardware Ltd. — Accounts Receivable

	Detail tie-in	Existence	Completeness	Accuracy	Classification	Cutoff	Valuation	Rights and Obligations	Presentation and Disclosure
Acceptable audit risk	high	high	high	high	high	high	high	high	high
Inherent risk	low	low	low	low	low	low	medium	low	low
Control risk–Sales									
Control risk–Cash receipts									
Control risk–Additional controls									
Analytical procedures									
Planned detection risk for tests of details of balances									
Planned audit evidence for tests of details of balances									

Materiality $100,000

RELATIONSHIP OF MATERIALITY AND RISK AND AUDIT EVIDENCE

OBJECTIVE 8-10

Discuss how materiality and risk are related and integrated into the audit process.

The concepts of materiality and risk in auditing are closely related and inseparable. Materiality is a measure of magnitude or size while risk is a measure of uncertainty. Taken together they measure the uncertainty of amounts of a given magnitude. For example, the statement that the auditor plans to accumulate evidence such that there is only a 5 percent risk (acceptable audit risk) of failing to uncover misstatements exceeding materiality of $25,000 (materiality) is a precise and meaningful statement. If the statement eliminates either the risk or materiality portion, it would be meaningless. A 5 percent risk without a specific materiality measure could imply that a $100 or $1 million misstatement is acceptable. A $25,000 overstatement without a specific risk could imply that a 1 percent or 80 percent risk is acceptable.

As a general rule, there is a fixed relationship between materiality, risk, and audit evidence. If one of those components is changed, then one or both of the remaining components must also change to achieve the same acceptable audit risk. For example, if evidence is held constant and materiality is decreased, then the risk that a material but undiscovered misstatement could exist must increase. Similarly, if materiality were held constant and risk reduced, the required evidence would increase.

Refer again to Figure 8-3, where the different components of the audit risk model interact to achieve the specified acceptable audit risk. Planned evidence (the complement of planned detection risk) is used to offset any changes in inherent or control risks for a particular transaction cycle to achieve the targeted acceptable audit risk. Note that materiality is not present in the figure—materiality does not affect any of the four risks and the risks have no effect on materiality. Yet materiality is used in addition to the risks to determine the planned evidence required.

EVALUATING RESULTS

After the auditor plans the engagement and accumulates audit evidence, results of the audit can also be stated in terms of the audit risk model. However, research has shown that using the planning model to evaluate total audit results may result in an understatement of achieved audit risk.[8] Achieved audit risk is the numeric value of audit risk using the assessed inherent risk; the value of control risk after documenting, evaluating and testing internal controls (or the set value based on nonreliance); and the achieved detection risk.

During evaluation, the relationships can be used, but professional judgement is required to ensure that sufficient evidence has been collected rather than simple reliance on the formula.

The relationships show us that when insufficient evidence has been collected to achieve a specified audit risk, the following ways can be used to reduce achieved audit risk to the targeted level:

- *Reduce inherent risk.* Because inherent risk is assessed by the auditor based on the client's circumstances, this assessment is done during planning and is typically not changed unless new facts are uncovered as the audit progresses.
- *Reduce control risk.* Assessed control risk is affected by the client's internal controls and the auditor's tests of those controls. Auditors can reduce control risk by more extensive tests of controls if the client has effective controls.
- *Reduce achieved detection risk by increasing substantive audit tests.* Auditors reduce achieved detection risk by accumulating evidence using analytical procedures and tests of details of balances. Additional audit procedures, assuming that they are effective, and larger sample sizes both reduce achieved detection risk.

Subjectively combining these three factors to achieve an acceptably low audit risk requires considerable professional judgment. Some firms develop sophisticated approaches using computer modelling to help their auditors make those judgments, while other firms simply use automation to record the decisions made by each audit team.

Audit results are studied more extensively in later chapters.

REVISING RISKS AND EVIDENCE

The audit risk model is a *planning* model, and it is therefore of limited use in evaluating results. Great care must be used in revising the risk factors when the actual results are not as favourable as planned.

No difficulties occur when the auditor accumulates planned evidence and concludes that the assessment of each of the risks was reasonable or better than originally thought. The auditor will conclude that sufficient appropriate audit evidence has been collected for that account or cycle.

Special care must be exercised when the auditor decides, on the basis of accumulated evidence, that the original assessment of control risk or inherent risk was

---

[8]Research on U.S. Statement of Auditing Standards 47, which provides an evaluation form of the audit planning model, indicates that the formula can result in an understatement of achieved audit risk if the formula is used to evaluate total evidence collected.

understated or that acceptable audit risk was overstated. This is less problematic if the auditor has conducted inherent risk evaluation and completed tests of controls prior to commencing test of details work. However, if work is being done concurrently, adjustments to the field work process become more difficult.

In such a circumstance, the auditor should follow a two-step approach. First, the auditor must revise the original assessment of the appropriate risk. It would violate due care to leave the original assessment unchanged if the auditor knows it is inappropriate. Second, the auditor should consider the effect of the revision on evidence requirements, *without the use of the audit risk model*. Research in auditing has shown that if a revised risk is used in the audit risk model to determine a revised planned detection risk, there is a danger of not increasing the evidence sufficiently. Instead, the auditor should carefully evaluate the implications of the revision of the risk and modify evidence appropriately, outside of the audit risk model.

For example, assume that the auditor confirms accounts receivable and, based on the misstatements found, concludes that the original control risk assessment as low was inappropriate. The auditor should revise the estimate of control risk upward and carefully consider the effect of the revision on the additional evidence needed in the sales and collection cycle. This should be done without recalculating planned detection risk.

SUMMARY

This chapter discussed the effects of materiality and relevant risks on audit planning. The purpose of using materiality and risks is to help the auditor accumulate sufficient appropriate audit evidence in the most efficient way possible. Figure 8-6 shows the relationship of materiality and the most important risks discussed in this chapter to the evidence decisions discussed in Chapter 6.

FIGURE 8-6
Relationship of Materiality, Risks, and Available Evidence to Audit Planning

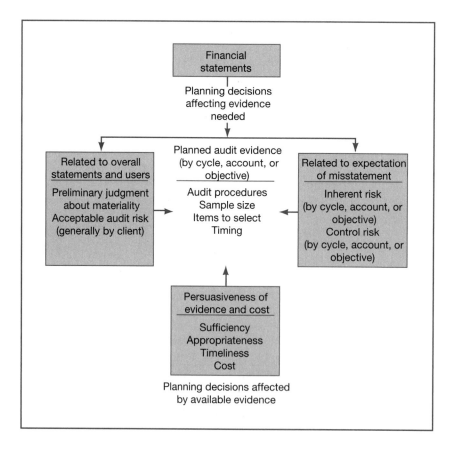

APPENDIX   EFFECTS OF INFORMATION SYSTEMS SOFTWARE ACQUISITION AND HARDWARE CONFIGURATION ON EVIDENCE COLLECTION PROCESSES

SOFTWARE ACQUISITION

Organizations employ a wide variety of software, serving a broad range of purposes, such as providing the user interface, providing security, managing hardware and software, communicating information, and recording and processing transactions. Here, we focus on the process used to obtain software that serves the organization's needs.

Information Technology Control Guidelines[9] breaks down the software acquisition process into three general categories:

- In-house development (employees within the entity determine user requirements and build the software using one of many alternative development approaches)
- Systems acquisition (software is acquired from an outside vendor and implemented as is, or modified and implemented)
- Turnkey software development (custom software development is contracted to an outside party)

The type of process used will affect the nature of controls that need to be examined by the auditor.

Again, using the terminology of *Information Technology Control Guidelines*, the acquisition process is broken down into five phases:

1. *Investigation.* In this first phase, it is determined whether the proposed system should actually be obtained.
2. *Requirements analysis and initial design.* Then it is necessary to identify and document the overall functionality and purpose of the proposed system.
3. *Development [or acquisition] and system testing.* Specific functionality of the new system is identified, it is developed/acquired and tested.
4. *Conversion, implementation, and post-implementation review.* Data is converted from the old to the new system, live running of the system commences, and the system is evaluated to determine whether it satisfies the entity's needs.
5. *Ongoing maintenance.* Necessary changes to the system are undertaken as needed.

For the evidence gathering process, as part of the knowledge of business documentation, the auditor will determine what types of systems are in place, paying particular attention to those of financial or operational significance. The auditor will then make inquiries regarding the information systems change process: are information systems developed, modified, or acquired, and have there been any changes in the current year? Where changes have taken place, the auditor may be required to conduct a conversion audit (discussed in Chapter 16), as well as assess changes to controls due to the new or modified systems.

The complexity of the software development or acquisition process needs to be determined to assess inherent risks. Thus, an overview of the process would be gathered during the knowledge of business documentation for the client. Controls over the acquisition or development process are part of the control environment and general information systems controls. These general controls need to be documented and should reliance be placed in software programs during the audit, would need to be tested, as discussed further in the next chapter.

---

[9] Canadian Institute of Chartered Accountants, *Information Technology Control Guidelines*, 3rd Edition, 1998, pp. 95–96.

HARDWARE CONFIGURATION[10]

As part of the knowledge of business, the auditor would determine the type of equipment in use by the entity, where it was located, how it was interconnected, and whether data communications or Internet/Intranet access was occurring. This helps to determine the complexity and scope of further controls that need to be documented and evaluated.

The simpler hardware structures are a *centralized* system (where all processing is done from a single central system, requiring that users be logged onto that system to conduct business activity) and *decentralized* systems (where each location of a multiple location system has stand-alone, independent processing). Such pure systems exist in smaller businesses, but are otherwise rare. For centralized systems, the auditor must document controls primarily at that one location, while for decentralized systems, multi-location issues, such as commonality of software, need to be considered.

Most larger systems now are *distributed* systems, where computing or files are shared among users and computing facilities. For example, a *local area network* is a distributed system, since computing can be accomplished at the individual computer level or the common file server can be used. An organization with a head office computer and branch location computing systems which transmit information to the head office is using a distributed system. Financial institution automated teller machines and point of sale terminals can also be components of distributed systems. In such systems, controls over each category of software and hardware need to be documented. Frequently, specialist assistance will be required to conduct the control documentation and evaluation process.

ESSENTIAL TERMS

Acceptable audit risk — a measure of how willing the auditor is to accept that the financial statements may be materially misstated after the audit is completed and an unqualified audit opinion has been issued; see also *audit assurance* (p. 239).

Achieved audit risk — the numeric value of audit risk using the assessed inherent risk; the value of control risk after documenting, evaluating and testing internal controls (or the set value based on nonreliance); and the achieved detection risk (page 253).

Audit assurance — a complement to *acceptable audit risk*; an acceptable audit risk of 2 percent is the same as audit assurance of 98 percent; also called *overall assurance* and *level of assurance* (p. 240).

Audit risk model — a formal model reflecting the relationships among acceptable audit risk (*AAR*), inherent risk (*IR*), control risk (*CR*), and planned detection risk (*PDR*); $AAR = IR \times CR \times PDR$ (p. 239).

Business risk — risk that the auditor or audit firm will suffer harm because of a client relationship, even though the auditor's report rendered for the client was correct (p. 243).

Control risk (CR) — a measure of the auditor's assessment of the likelihood that misstatements exceeding materiality in a segment will not be prevented or detected by the client's internal controls (p. 240).

Direct projection method of estimating misstatement — net misstatements in the sample, divided by the total sampled, multiplied by the total recorded population value; see also *likely misstatement* (p. 237).

Further possible misstatements — the misstatements over and above the likely aggregate misstatement that result from the imprecision in the sampling process (p. 232).

Identified misstatement — the actual misstatement discovered in the sample tested; the misstatement has not been corrected by management (p. 232).

Inherent risk (IR) — a measure of the auditor's assessment of the likelihood that there are material misstatements in a segment before considering the effectiveness of internal controls (p. 240).

Likely misstatement — the projection of the actual misstatement in the sample to the population; the misstatement has not been corrected by management; see also *direct projection method of estimating misstatement* (p. 232).

Materiality — the magnitude of an omission or misstatement of accounting information that, in the light of surrounding circumstances, makes it *probable* that the judgment of a reasonable person relying on the informa-

---

[10]For further explanations of hardware configuration, consult your accounting information systems or management information systems text, for example: Bodnar, George H., and William S. Hopwood, *Accounting Information Systems*, Seventh Edition, Prentice Hall, 1998; and McNurlin, Barbara C. and Ralph H. Sprague, Jr., *Information Systems Management in Practice*, Fourth Edition, Prentice Hall, 1998.

tion would have been changed or influenced by the omission or misstatement (p. 231).

Planned detection risk (PDR) — a measure of the risk that audit evidence for a segment will fail to detect misstatements exceeding materiality, should such misstatements exist; $PDR = AAR / (IR \times CR)$ (p. 241).

Preliminary judgment about materiality — the maximum amount by which the auditor believes that the statements could be misstated and still *not* affect the decisions of reasonable users; used in audit planning (p. 233).

Revised judgment about materiality — a change in the auditor's preliminary judgment made when the auditor determines that the preliminary judgment was too large or too small (p. 233).

Risk — the acceptance by auditors that there is some level of uncertainty in performing the audit function (p. 238).

Sampling error — error that results because the auditor has sampled only a portion of the population (p. 237).

REVIEW QUESTIONS

8-1   Chapter 7 introduced the seven parts of the planning phase of an audit. Which part is the evaluation of materiality and risk?

8-2   Define the meaning of the term "materiality" as it is used in accounting and auditing. What is the relationship between materiality and the phrase "obtain reasonable assurance" used in the auditor's report?

8-3   Explain why materiality is important but difficult to apply in practice.

8-4   What is meant by "setting a preliminary judgment about materiality"? Identify the most important factors affecting the preliminary judgment.

8-5   What is meant by "using bases for setting a preliminary judgment about materiality"? How would those bases differ for the audit of a manufacturing company and a government unit such as a school board?

8-6   Assume Rosanne Madden, a public accountant, is using 5 percent of net income before taxes as her major guideline for evaluating materiality. What qualitative factors should she also consider in deciding whether misstatements may be material?

8-7   Distinguish between the terms "materiality available for unanticipated misstatements" and "preliminary judgment about materiality." How are they related to each other?

8-8   Differentiate between identified misstatements, likely misstatements, and further possible misstatements. Explain why all three are important.

8-9   Explain why an auditor would adjust the preliminary judgment about materiality in calculating the materiality available for unanticipated misstatements.

8-10   How would the conduct of an audit of a medium-sized company be affected by the company's being a small part of a large conglomerate as compared with its being a separate entity?

8-11   Define the "audit risk model" and explain each term in the model.

8-12   What is meant by "planned detection risk"? What is the effect on the amount of evidence the auditor must accumulate when planned detection risk is increased from medium to high?

8-13   Explain the causes of an increased or decreased planned detection risk.

8-14   Define what is meant by inherent risk. Identify four factors that make for *high* inherent risk in audits.

8-15   Explain why inherent risk is estimated for segments rather than for the overall audit. What is the effect on the amount of evidence the auditor must accumulate when inherent risk is increased from medium to high for a segment? Compare your answer with the one for 8-12.

8-16   Explain the effect of extensive misstatements found in the prior year's audit on inherent risk, planned detection risk, and planned audit evidence.

8-17   Explain what is meant by the term "acceptable audit risk." What is its relevance to evidence accumulation?

8-18   Explain the relationship between acceptable audit risk and the legal liability of auditors.

8-19   State the two categories of circumstances that affect acceptable audit risk, and list the factors that the auditor can use to indicate the degree to which each category exists.

8-20   Auditors have not been successful in measuring the components of the audit risk model. How is it possible to use the model in a meaningful way without a precise way of measuring the risk?

8-21   Explain the circumstances when the auditor should revise the components of the audit risk model and the effect of the revisions on planned detection risk and planned audit evidence.

MULTIPLE CHOICE QUESTIONS

8-22   The following questions deal with materiality. Choose the best response.

a.   Which one of the following statements is correct concerning the concept of materiality?

(1)   Materiality is determined by reference to guidelines established by the CICA.

(2)   Materiality depends only on the dollar amount of an item relative to other items in the financial statements.

(3)   Materiality depends on the nature of an item rather than the dollar amount.

(4)   Materiality is a matter of professional judgment.

b.   The concept of materiality will be least important to the public accountant in determining the

(1)   scope of the audit of specific accounts.

(2)   specific transactions that should be reviewed.

(3)   effects of audit exceptions upon the auditor's report.

(4) effects of the public accountant's direct financial interest in a client upon the accountant's independence.

(AICPA adapted)

8-23 The following questions concern materiality, risk, or evidence. Choose the best response.

a. Edison Corporation has a few large accounts receivable that total $1,400,000. Victor Corporation has a great number of small accounts receivable that also total $1,400,000. The importance of a misstatement in any one account is, therefore, greater for Edison than for Victor. This is an example of the auditor's concept of
  (1) materiality.
  (2) comparative analysis.
  (3) reasonable assurance.
  (4) relative risk.

b. Which of the following elements ultimately determines the specific auditing procedures that are necessary in the circumstances to afford a reasonable basis for an opinion?
  (1) Auditor judgment
  (2) Materiality
  (3) Inherent risk
  (4) Reasonable assurance

c. Which of the following *best* describes the element of inherent risk that underlies the application of generally accepted auditing standards, particularly the examination and reporting standards?
  (1) Intercompany transactions are usually subject to less detailed scrutiny than arm's-length transactions with outside parties.
  (2) Inventories may require more attention by the auditor on an engagement for a merchandising enterprise than on an engagement for a public utility.
  (3) Cash audit work may have to be carried out in a more conclusive manner than inventory audit work.
  (4) The scope of the examination need *not* be expanded if errors that arouse suspicion of fraud are of relatively insignificant amounts.

(AICPA adapted)

d. Which of the following statements is *not* correct about materiality?
  (1) An auditor's consideration of materiality is influenced by the auditor's perception of the needs of a reasonable person who will rely on the financial statements.
  (2) The concept of materiality recognizes that some matters are important for fair presentation of financial statements in conformity with GAAP, while other matters are *not* important.
  (3) An auditor considers materiality for planning purposes in terms of the largest aggregate level of misstatements that could be material to any one of the financial statements.

(4) Materiality judgments are made in light of surrounding circumstances and necessarily involve both quantitative and qualitative judgments.

e. In considering materiality for planning purposes, an auditor believes that misstatements aggregating $10,000 would have a material effect on an entity's income statement, but that misstatements would have to aggregate $20,000 to materially affect the balance sheet. Ordinarily, it would be appropriate to design auditing procedures that would be expected to detect misstatements that aggregate
  (1) $15,000
  (2) $10,000
  (3) $20,000
  (4) $30,000

8-24 The following questions deal with the audit risk model. Choose the best response.

a. Which of the following statements is not correct about materiality?
  (1) The concept of materiality recognizes that some matters are important for fair presentation of financial statements in conformity with GAAP, while other matters are not important.
  (2) An auditor considers materiality for planning purposes in terms of the largest aggregate level of misstatements that could be material to any one of the financial statements.
  (3) Materiality judgments are made in light of surrounding circumstances and necessarily involve both quantitative and qualitative judgments.
  (4) An auditor's consideration of materiality is influenced by the auditor's perception of the needs of a reasonable person who will rely on the financial statements.

b. Inherent risk and control risk differ from planned detection risk in that they
  (1) arise from the misapplication of auditing procedures.
  (2) may be assessed in either quantitative or nonquantitative terms.
  (3) exist independently of the financial statement audit.
  (4) can be changed at the auditor's discretion.

c. In considering materiality for planning purposes, an auditor believes that misstatements aggregating $10,000 would have a material effect on an entity's income statement, but that misstatements would have to aggregate $20,000 to materially affect the balance sheet. Ordinarily, it would be appropriate to design auditing procedures that would be expected to detect misstatements that aggregate
  (1) $10,000
  (2) $15,000
  (3) $20,000
  (4) $30,000

8-25 The following are different types of misstatements that can be encountered on an audit:
1. The use of a method of valuing inventory that is not in accordance with generally accepted accounting principles
2. Accidental failure to disclose a lawsuit for patent infringement when the amount of the liability is unknown
3. The recording as capital assets expenditures that should have been recorded as repairs and maintenance
4. The inclusion of invalid accounts in accounts receivable by preparing fictitious sales invoices to nonexisting customers

Required

a. Assuming the amounts are equally material, rank the types of misstatements listed above in terms of the difficulty of uncovering each one. (*Most difficult* is first.) Give reasons to support your answers.

b. Discuss whether auditors should have the same responsibility for uncovering the most difficult-to-find misstatement as for discovering the least difficult one. Consider this from the point of view of the auditors and the users of financial statements.

8-26 Shown below and on page 260 are statements of earnings and financial position for Prairie Stores Corporation.

Required

a. Use professional judgment in reaching a preliminary judgment about materiality based on revenue, net income before taxes, total assets, and shareholders' equity. Your conclusions should be stated in terms of percentages and dollars.

b. Assume you complete the audit and conclude that your preliminary judgment about materiality has been exceeded. What should you do?

c. As discussed in part (b), likely net earnings from continuing operations *before* income taxes were used as a base for materiality when completing the audit. Discuss why most auditors use *before* tax net earnings instead of *after* tax net earnings when calculating materiality based on the income statement.

8-27 The following are terms discussed in Chapter 8:
1. Preliminary judgment about materiality
2. Estimate of the combined misstatements
3. Acceptable audit risk
4. Inherent risk
5. Estimated total misstatement in a segment
6. Control risk
7. Planned detection risk
8. Achieved detection risk

Required

a. Identify which items are *audit planning decisions* requiring professional judgment.

b. Identify which items are *audit conclusions* resulting from the application of audited procedures and requiring professional judgment.

c. Under what circumstances is it acceptable to change those items in part (a), after the audit is started? Which items can be changed after the audit is 95 percent completed?

8-28 Describe what is meant by "acceptable audit risk." Explain why each of the following statements is true.

	Statement of Earnings Prairie Stores Corporation		
	For the 53 Weeks Ended May 3, 1999	**For the 52 Weeks Ended**	
		April 28, 1998	**April 29, 1997**
Revenue			
Net sales	$8,351,149	$6,601,255	$5,959,587
Other income	59,675	43,186	52,418
	8,410,824	6,644,441	6,012,005
Costs and expenses			
Cost of sales	5,197,375	4,005,548	3,675,369
Marketing, general, and administrative expenses	2,590,080	2,119,590	1,828,169
Provision for loss on restructured operations	64,100	—	—
Interest expense	141,662	46,737	38,546
	7,993,217	6,171,875	5,542,084
Earnings from continuing operations before income taxes	417,607	472,566	469,921
Income taxes	196,700	217,200	214,100
Earnings from continuing operations	220,907	255,366	255,821
Provision for loss on discontinued operations, net of income taxes	$20,700	—	—
Net earnings	$200,207	$255,366	$255,821

Statement of Financial Position
Prairie Stores Corporation

Assets		May 3, 1999		April 28, 1998
Current assets				
Cash		$39,683		$37,566
Temporary investments (at cost, which approximates market)		123,421		271,639
Receivables, less allowances of $16,808 in 1999 and $17,616 in 1998		899,752		759,001
Inventories				
Finished product	680,974		550,407	
Raw materials and supplies	443,175		353,795	
		1,124,149		904,202
Deferred income tax benefits		9,633		10,468
Prepaid expenses		$57,468		$35,911
Current assets		2,254,106		2,018,787
Land, buildings, equipment, at cost, less accumulated amortiziation		1,393,902		1,004,455
Investments in affiliated companies and sundry assets		112,938		83,455
Goodwill and other intangible assets		99,791		23,145
Total assets		**$3,860,737**		**$3,129,842**

Liabilities and Shareholders' Equity				
Current liabilities				
Notes payable		$280,238		$113,411
Current portion of long-term debt		64,594		12,336
Accounts and drafts payable		359,511		380,395
Accrued salaries, wages, and vacations		112,200		63,557
Accrued income taxes		76,479		89,151
Other accrued liabilities including goods and services tax		321,871		269,672
Current liabilities		1,214,893		928,522
Long-term debt		730,987		390,687
Other noncurrent liabilities		146,687		80,586
Accrued income tax liability		142,344		119,715
Shareholders' equity		2,234,911		1,519,510
Total liabilities				
Common stock issued, 51,017 shares in 1999 ad 50,992 in 1998		200,195		199,576
Retained earnings		1,425,631		1,410,756
Shareholders' equity		1,625,826		1,610,332
Total liabilities and shareholders' equity		**$3,860,737**		**$3,129,842**

a. A public accounting firm should attempt to achieve the same acceptable audit risk for all audit clients when circumstances are similar.

b. A public accounting firm should decrease acceptable audit risk for audit clients when external users rely heavily on the statements.

c. A public accounting firm should decrease acceptable audit risk for audit clients when there is a reasonably high likelihood of a client's filing bankruptcy.

d. Different public accounting firms should attempt to achieve reasonably similar acceptable audit risks for clients with similar circumstances.

8-29 State whether each of the following statements is true or false, and give your reasons.

a. The audit evidence accumulated for every client should be approximately the same, regardless of the circumstances.

b. If acceptable audit risk is the same for two different clients, the audit evidence for the two clients should be approximately the same.

c. If acceptable audit risk, inherent risk, and control risk are approximately the same for two different clients, the audit evidence for the two clients should be approximately the same.

8-30 The following questions deal with the use of the audit risk model.

a. Assume that the auditor is doing a first-year municipal audit of Sackville, New Brunswick, and concludes that internal control is not likely to be effective.

(1) Explain why the auditor is likely to set both inherent and control risks at 100 percent for most segments.

(2) Assuming (1), explain the relationship of acceptable audit risk to planned detection risk.

(3) Assuming (1), explain the effect of planned detection risk on evidence accumulation compared with its effect if planned detection risk were larger.

b. Assume that the auditor is doing the third-year municipal audit of Sackville, New Brunswick, and concludes that internal controls are effective and inherent risk is low.
  (1) Explain why the auditor is likely to set inherent and control risks for material segments at a higher level than, say, 40 percent, even when the two risks are low.
  (2) For the audit of fixed asset accounts, assume inherent and control risks of 50 percent each and an acceptable audit risk of 5 percent. Calculate planned detection risk.
  (3) For (2), explain the effect of planned detection risk on evidence accumulation compared with its effect if planned detection risk were smaller.

c. Assume that the auditor is doing the fifth-year municipal audit of Sackville, New Brunswick, and concludes that acceptable audit risk can be set high, and inherent and control risks should be set low.
  (1) What circumstances would result in these conclusions?
  (2) For the audit of repairs and maintenance, inherent and control risk are set at 20 percent each. Acceptable audit risk is 5 percent. Calculate planned detection risk.
  (3) How much evidence should be accumulated in this situation?

8-31 Following are six situations that involve the audit risk model as it is used for planning audit evidence requirements. Numbers are used only to help you understand the relationships among factors in the risk model.

RISK	SITUATION					
	1	2	3	4	5	6
Acceptable audit risk	5%	5%	5%	5%	1%	1%
Inherent risk	100%	40%	60%	20%	100%	40%
Control risk	100%	60%	40%	30%	100%	60%
Planned detection risk	—	—	—	—	—	—

Required

a. Explain what each of the four risks mean.

b. Calculate planned detection risk for each situation.

c. Using your knowledge of the relationships among the foregoing factors, state the effect on planned detection risk (increase or decrease) of changing each of the following factors while the other two remain constant. Cite two situations from the table to support your comments.
  (1) A decrease in acceptable audit risk
  (2) A decrease in control risk
  (3) A decrease in inherent risk
  (4) An increase in control risk and a decrease in inherent risk of the same amount

d. Which situation requires the greatest amount of evidence and which requires the least?

8-32 Following are six situations that involve the audit risk model as it is used for planning audit evidence requirements in the audit of inventory.

RISK	SITUATION					
	1	2	3	4	5	6
Acceptable audit risk	High	High	Low	Low	High	Medium
Inherent risk	Low	High	High	Low	Medium	Medium
Control risk	Low	Low	High	High	Medium	Medium
Planned detection risk	—	—	—	—	—	—
Planned evidence	—	—	—	—	—	—

Required

a. Explain what low, medium, and high mean for each of the four risks and planned evidence.

b. Fill in the blanks for planned detection risk and planned evidence using the terms "low," "medium," or "high."

c. Using your knowledge of the relationships among the foregoing factors, state the effect on planned evidence (increase or decrease) of changing each of the following five factors while the other four remain constant.
  (1) An increase in acceptable audit risk
  (2) An increase in control risk
  (3) An increase in planned detection risk
  (4) An increase in inherent risk
  (5) An increase in inherent risk and a decrease in control risk of the same amount

8-33 Using the audit risk model, state the effect on control risk, inherent risk, acceptable audit risk, and planned evidence for each of the following independent events. In each of the events (a) to (k), circle one letter for each of the three independent variables and planned evidence: I = increase, D = decrease, N = no effect, and C = cannot determine from the information provided. Explain your reasoning.

a. The client's management materially increased long-term contractual debt:

  Control risk I D N C   Acceptable audit risk I D N C
  Inherent risk I D N C   Planned evidence   I D N C

b. The company changed from a privately held company to a publicly held company:

  Control risk I D N C   Acceptable audit risk I D N C
  Inherent risk I D N C   Planned evidence   I D N C

c. The auditor decided to assess control risk at a level below maximum; it was previously assessed at maximum.

  Control risk I D N C   Acceptable audit risk I D N C
  Inherent risk I D N C   Planned evidence   I D N C

d. The account balance increased materially from the preceding year without apparent reason:

  Control risk I D N C   Acceptable audit risk I D N C
  Inherent risk I D N C   Planned evidence   I D N C

e. You determined through the planning phase that working capital, debt to equity ratio, and other indicators of financial condition had improved during the past year:

Control risk   I D N C   Acceptable audit risk   I D N C
Inherent risk   I D N C   Planned evidence   I D N C

f. This is the second year of the engagement and there were few misstatements in the previous year. The auditor also decided to increase reliance on internal control:

Control risk   I D N C   Acceptable audit risk   I D N C
Inherent risk   I D N C   Planned evidence   I D N C

g. About halfway through the audit, you discover that the client is constructing its own building during idle periods, using factory personnel. This is the first time the client has done this and it is being done at your recommendation:

Control risk   I D N C   Acceptable audit risk   I D N C
Inherent risk   I D N C   Planned evidence   I D N C

h. In discussions with management, you conclude that management is planning to sell the business in the next few months. Because of the planned changes, several key accounting personnel quit several months ago for alternative employment. You also observe that the gross margin percent has significantly increased compared with that of the preceding year:

Control risk   I D N C   Acceptable audit risk   I D N C
Inherent risk   I D N C   Planned evidence   I D N C

i. There has been a change in several key management personnel. You believe that management is somewhat lacking in personal integrity, compared with the previous management. You believe it is still appropriate to do the audit:

Control risk   I D N C   Acceptable audit risk   I D N C
Inherent risk   I D N C   Planned evidence   I D N C

j. In auditing inventory, you obtain an understanding of internal control and perform tests of controls. You find it significantly improved compared with that of the preceding year. You also observe that due to technology changes in the industry, the client's inventory may be somewhat obsolete:

Control risk   I D N C   Acceptable audit risk   I D N C
Inherent risk   I D N C   Planned evidence   I D N C

8-34   The existence of risk is implicit in the phrase "in my opinion" that appears in the auditor's report. The auditor is indicating that he or she is accepting some risk that the opinion rendered may be incorrect. In planning and executing an audit, the auditor strives to reduce this risk to a level that is acceptable to the client, the users, and himself or herself.

Required

Discuss the steps that the auditor takes to reduce the risk to an acceptable level. What guidance do the professional standards provide to the auditor?

8-35   Some accountants have suggested that the auditor's report should include a statement of materiality level and acceptable audit risk that the auditor used in conducting the audit.

Required

a. The proponents of such disclosure believe that the information would be useful to users of the financial statements being reported on. Explain fully why you think they have this view.

b. Some accountants oppose such disclosure. Explain why you think they are not in favour of it.

c. What is your position on the issue?

![CASES]

8-36   In the audit of Whirland Chemical Corp., a large publicly traded company, you have been assigned the responsibility for obtaining background information for the audit. Your firm is auditing the client for the first time in the current year as a result of a dispute between Whirland and the previous auditor over the proper valuation of work-in-process inventory and the inclusion in sales of inventory that has not been delivered but has for practical purposes been completed and sold.

Whirland Chemical has been highly successful in its field in the past two decades, primarily because of many successful mergers negotiated by Lynn Randolph, the president and chairperson of the board. Even though the industry as a whole has suffered dramatic setbacks in recent years, Whirland continues to prosper, as evidenced by its constantly increasing earnings and growth. Only in the last two

years have the company's profits turned downward. Lynn Randolph has a reputation for having been able to hire an aggressive group of young executives by the use of relatively low salaries combined with an unusually generous profit-sharing plan.

A major difficulty you face in the new audit is the lack of highly sophisticated accounting records for a company the size of Whirland. Lynn Randolph believes that profits come primarily from intelligent and aggressive action based on forecasts, not by relying on historical data that come after the fact. Most of the forecast data are generated by the sales and production department rather than by the accounting department. The personnel in the accounting department do seem competent but somewhat overworked and underpaid relative to other employees. One of the recent changes, one month prior to the year end, that will potentially improve the record keeping is the installation of more sophisticated computer software. All the accounting records are being converted from batch systems to an on-line system. Major areas such as inventory and sales are included in the new system and expected to be fully functional by the middle of the next year. The new inquiry reporting capabilities are being reserved for production and marketing on the grounds that these areas are more essential to having current information than the accounting functions.

The first six months' financial statements for the current year include a profit of approximately only 10 percent less than the first six months of the preceding year, which is somewhat surprising considering the reduced volume and the disposal of a segment of the business, Mercury Supply Inc. The disposal of this segment was considered necessary because it had become increasingly unprofitable over the past four years. At the time of its acquisition from Brian Randolph, who is a brother of Lynn Randolph's, the company was highly profitable and it was considered a highly desirable purchase. The major customer of Mercury Supply Inc. was the Mercury Corporation, which is owned by Brian Randolph. Gradually the market for its products declined as the Mercury Corporation began diversifying and phasing out its primary products in favour of more profitable business. Even though Mercury Corporation is no longer buying from Mercury Supply Inc., it compensates for this by buying a large volume of other products from Whirland Chemical.

The only major difficulty Whirland faces right now, according to financial analysts, is underfinancing. There is an excessive amount of current debt and long-term debt because of the depressed capital markets. Management is reluctant to obtain equity capital at this point because the increased number of shares would decrease the earnings per share even more than 10 percent. At the present time, Lynn Randolph is negotiating with several cash-rich companies in the hope of being able to merge with them as a means of overcoming the capital problems.

Required

a. List the major concerns you should have in the audit of Whirland Corp. and explain why they are potential problems.

b. State the appropriate approach to investigating the significance of each item you listed in (a).

8-37 Pamela Albright is the manager of the audit of Stanton Enterprises Ltd., a public company that manufactures formed steel subassemblies for other manufacturers. Albright is planning the 1999 audit and is considering an appropriate amount for planning materiality, and the appropriate inherent risks. Summary financial statement information is shown in Exhibit I on page 264.

Additional relevant planning information is summarized below:

1. Stanton has been a client for four years and Albright's firm has always had a good relationship with the company. Management and the accounting people have always been cooperative, honest, and have had a positive attitude about the audit and financial reporting. No material misstatements were found in the prior year's

audit. Albright's firm has monitored the relationship carefully because when the audit was obtained, Leonard Stanton, the CEO, had the reputation of being a "high-flyer" and had been through bankruptcy at an earlier time in his career.

2. Leonard Stanton runs the company in an autocratic way, primarily because of a somewhat controlling personality. He believes that it is his job to make all the tough decisions. He delegates responsibility to others but is not always willing to delegate a commensurate amount of authority.

3. The industry in which Stanton participates has been in a favourable cycle for the past few years, and that trend is continuing in the current year. Industry profits are reasonably favourable and there are no competitive or other apparent threats on the horizon.

4. Internal controls for Stanton are evaluated as reasonably effective for all cycles but not unusually strong. Although Stanton supports the idea of control, Albright has been disappointed that management has continually rejected Albright's recommendation to establish an internal audit function.

5. Stanton has a contract with its employees that if earnings before taxes, interest expense, and pension cost exceed $7.8 million for the year, an additional contribution must be made to the pension fund equal to 5 percent of the excess.

Required

a. You are to play the role of Pamela Albright in the December 31, 1999, audit of Stanton Enterprises Ltd. Make a preliminary judgment of materiality. Prepare a working paper showing your calculations.

b. Make an acceptable audit risk decision for the current year as high, medium, or low, and support your answer.

c. Perform analytical procedures for Stanton Enterprises Ltd. that will help you identify accounts that may require additional evidence in the current year's audit. Document the analytical procedures you perform and your conclusions.

d. The evidence planning spreadsheet to decide tests of details of balances for Stanton's accounts receivable is shown in Exhibit II on page 265. Use the information in the case and your conclusions in parts (a) to (c) to complete the following rows of the evidence planning spreadsheet: Acceptable audit risk, Inherent risk, and Analytical procedures. Also fill in tolerable misstatement at the bottom of the spreadsheet. Make any assumptions you believe are reasonable and appropriate, and document them.

8-38 Excerpts from a court case appear on page 265. The lawyer is in the process of examining his client, a public accountant, accused of negligence in the conduct of an audit.

Lawyer: Were you aware that the statements were being used by the creditor who was owed $100,000 that was secured by inventory?

Auditor: Yes, he was one of several users.

Lawyer: How did your audit strategy take into account the needs of this creditor?

Auditor: We assessed the engagement as being slightly riskier than usual.

Lawyer: And how did you determine materiality to be $250,000?

Auditor: We used principles in accordance with generally accepted auditing standards, namely:

- 5 percent to 10 percent of income before income taxes of $6 million, being $300,000 to $600,000
- 0.5 percent to 1 percent of total assets of $50 million, being $250,000 to $500,000

Because of the riskiness of this engagement, we adopted a conservative approach and took a lower materiality level than we would otherwise have chosen.

Required

In accordance with generally accepted auditing standards:

a. List the factors that you would consider in this situation. How would materiality affect the extent of audit testing? List any other matters that would be relevant.

b. Discuss the relationship between materiality and audit risk. Were these concepts appropriately considered in the situation described above?

(CICA adapted)

EXHIBIT I

STANTON ENTERPRISES LTD.
Summary Financial Statements

Balance Sheet	Preliminary 31-12-99	Audited 31-12-98
Cash	$243,689	$133,981
Trade accounts receivable	3,544,009	2,224,921
Allowance for uncollectible accounts	(120,000)	(215,000)
Inventories	4,520,902	3,888,400
Prepaid expenses	29,500	24,700
Total current assets	8,218,100	6,057,002
Property, plant, and equipment:		
At cost	12,945,255	9,922,534
Less accumulated amortization	(4,382,990)	(3,775,911)
	8,562,265	6,146,623
Goodwill	1,200,000	345,000
Total Assets	$17,980,365	$12,548,625
Accounts payable	$2,141,552	$3,226,789
Bank loan payable	150,000	—
Accrued liabilities including goods and services tax	723,600	598,020
Income taxes payable	1,200,000	1,059,000
Current portion of long term debt	240,000	240,000
Total current liabilities	4,455,152	5,123,809
Long-term debt	960,000	1,200,000
Shareholders' equity:		
Common stock	3,719,921	2,333,801
Retained earnings	8,845,292	3,891,015
Total shareholders' equity	12,565,213	6,224,816
Total liabilities and shareholders' equity	$17,980,365	$12,548,625

Combined Statement of Income and Retained Earnings	Preliminary 31-12-99	Audited 31-12-98
Sales	$43,994,931	$32,258,015
Cost of goods sold	24,197,212	19,032,229
Gross profit	19,797,719	13,225,786
Selling, general, and administrative expenses	10,572,221	8,900,432
Pension cost	1,117,845	865,030
Interest expense	83,376	104,220
	11,773,442	9,869,682
Income before taxes	8,024,277	3,356,104
Income tax expense	1,820,000	1,141,000
Net income	6,204,277	2,215,104
Beginning retained earnings	3,891,015	2,675,911
	10,095,292	4,891,015
Dividends declared	(1,250,000)	(1,000,000)
Ending retained earnings	$ 8,845,292	$ 3,891,015

EXHIBIT II

STANTON ENTERPRISES LTD.
Evidence Planning Spreadsheet to Decide Tests of Details of Balances for Accounts Receivable

	Detail tie-in	Existence	Completeness	Accuracy	Classification	Cutoff	Valuation	Rights and obligations	Presentation and disclosure
Acceptable audit risk									
Inherent risk									
Control risk–Sales									
Control risk–Cash receipts									
Control risk–Additional controls									
Analytical procedures									
Planned detection risk for tests of details of balances									
Planned audit evidence for tests of details of balances									

Materiality

9

THE STUDY OF INTERNAL CONTROL AND ASSESSMENT OF CONTROL RISK

GOOD INTERNAL CONTROLS PREVENT MORE DEFALCATIONS THAN GOOD AUDITORS FIND

When Able & Co. issued its audit report on the Foundation for the Coalition of Canadian Athletes (FCCA), it included a qualification that is common for such charities (see *CICA Handbook,* paragraph 5510.I). The qualification explained that the auditors could verify only those revenues that were actually recorded on the organization's books. Because many contributions came in the form of cash and were received from many sources, there was no way to know what the total contributions should be.

Shortly after the firm's tenth consecutive audit of FCCA, Phil Able was informed that FCCA's general ledger accountant was found to have embezzled $2 million during the past four years. FCCA wanted to know how this could have occurred without Phil Able discovering it. Able responded that he would have to know how the fraud was carried out in order to answer the question.

After an extensive investigation and criminal trial against the perpetrators (the accountant and her husband), the following facts came to light: The FCCA's camp facility was in a different province than its home office. Funds were collected from campers and taken to a local bank by an independent person for transmittal to the home office. The funds were given to the bank in exchange for a cashier's cheque that was sent to the general ledger accountant who, in turn, sent it to the home office cash receipts clerk. She also recorded the revenue using the information on the cashier's cheque and related documentation. Since the funds were never deposited into the local FCCA bank account, there was no external record established. To perpetrate the fraud, the accountant periodically deposited one of the cheques in an account she and her husband controlled, with a name and endorsement "FCCA — West Branch." Obviously, she did not record the revenue for these defalcations.

When the auditors conducted their review of internal controls at FCCA, they regularly interviewed employees about how the system functioned. During the course of those discussions, they were never told about the procedure for transmitting funds from the camp. It is not clear that anyone in the home office, other than the embezzler, was aware of it. Given the denial in the auditor's report and the conduct of its audit, Able & Co. wasn't held responsible for the loss. It helped FCCA implement new controls to prevent a similar occurrence, but, nevertheless, the FCCA changed auditors.

OBJECTIVE 9-1

Discuss the nature of internal control and its importance to both management and the auditor.

Chapter 9 is the third chapter dealing with planning the audit and designing an audit approach. The subject of internal control is sufficiently important in the audit process to merit a separate generally accepted auditing standard:

> A sufficient understanding of internal control is to be obtained to plan the audit and to determine the nature, timing, and extent of tests to be performed. When control risk is assessed below maximum, sufficient appropriate audit evidence should be obtained through tests of controls to support the assessment.

The shaded part of the chart included in the margin on page 268 shows where obtaining an understanding of the client's internal control and assessing control risk fit into planning the audit. The study of internal control, assessment of control risk, and related evidence gathering is a major component in the audit risk model studied in Chapter 8. Control risk is "CR" in the audit risk model. It was shown in Chapter 8 that planned audit evidence can be reduced when there are effective internal controls. This chapter shows why and how this can done.

To understand how internal control is used in the audit risk model, knowledge of key internal control concepts is needed. Accordingly, this chapter focuses on the meaning and objectives of internal control from both the client's and the auditor's point of view, the components of internal control, and the auditor's methodology for fulfilling the requirements of the second examination standard. Professional guidance in considering internal control is found in Sections 5200–5220 of the *CICA Handbook*. Many practitioners consider it to be the most complex auditing standard in the literature.

CLIENT AND AUDITOR CONCERNS

In designing a system for control, management is likely to have some of the same concerns auditors have in evaluating the system, as well as additional or different concerns. This section examines the concerns of both clients and auditors.

CLIENT CONCERNS

The reason a company establishes a system of control is to help meet its own goals. Paragraph 5200.03 of the *CICA Handbook* states:

> Internal control consists of the policies and procedures established and maintained by management to assist in achieving its objective of ensuring, as far as practical, the orderly and efficient conduct of the entity's business.

The system consists of many specific *policies and procedures* designed to provide management with reasonable assurance that the goals and objectives that it believes

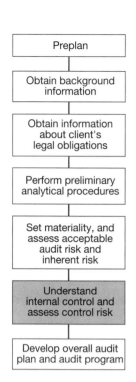

Preplan

Obtain background information

Obtain information about client's legal obligations

Perform preliminary analytical procedures

Set materiality, and assess acceptable audit risk and inherent risk

Understand internal control and assess control risk

Develop overall audit plan and audit program

to be important to the entity will be met. These policies and procedures are often called *controls*, and collectively they comprise the entity's *internal control*.

The focus box shows alternative definitions of control that have been used in the last few years, and how these definitions are broadening the concept of control.

BROADENING THE CONCEPTS OF INTERNAL CONTROL

1992 — Committee of Sponsoring Organizations (COSO) Internal Control — Integrated Framework

The Committee of Sponsoring Organizations (COSO) was formed in the United States by a group of several professional and academic accounting organizations to develop materials that would help organizations better control their operations. COSO published *Internal Control — Integrated Framework* in 1992.

1995 — CICA's Criteria on Control Board (CoCo)[1]

The CICA formed the Criteria on Control Board to adapt *Internal Control — Integrated Framework* for a Canadian environment and to build on the COSO framework. CoCo believes that the guidance it provides through its publications will allow organizations to enhance and improve their controls. *Guidance on Control*, the first in a series of publications produced by CoCo for directors, managers, owners, investors, lenders, and auditors was published in 1995. CoCo (page 4) uses a broader definition of control than the *CICA Handbook:*

> Control comprises those elements of an organization (including its resources, systems, processes, culture, structure and tasks) that, taken together, support people in the achievement of the organization's objectives.

This broader focus is primarily people-centred. It emphasizes that the organization does not exist without its people, although the intent is to work toward the organization's goals.

Control systems must be *cost beneficial*. The controls adopted are selected by comparing the costs to the organization relative to the benefits expected. One benefit to management, but certainly not the most important, is the reduced cost of an audit when the auditor evaluates internal control as good or excellent and assesses control risk as much below maximum (i.e., as low).

Management typically has the following four objectives in designing effective internal control.

Maintaining reliable control systems   Management must have reliable control systems so that it will have accurate information for carrying out its operations and producing financial statements. A wide variety of information is used for making critical business decisions. For example, the price to charge for products is based in part on information about the cost of making the products. Information must be reliable and timely if it is to be useful to management for decision making.

---

[1]Criteria on Control Board, *Guidance on Control*, Toronto: Canadian Institute of Chartered Accountants, 1995, pp. iii and 4. The interested reader is directed to the *Preface to Guidance Issued by the Criteria on Control Board* and other publications of CoCo.

Safeguarding assets   The physical assets of a company can be stolen, misused, or accidentally destroyed unless they are protected by adequate controls. The same is true of nonphysical assets such as important records (e.g., confidential business proposals or research and development data), and accounting records (e.g., accounts receivable balances, financial details). Safeguarding certain assets and records has become increasingly important since the advent of computer systems. Large amounts of information stored on computer media such as a disk or cartridge tape can be destroyed or stolen if care is not taken to protect them. Management safeguards assets by controlling access and by comparisons of assets with records of those assets.

Optimizing the use of resources   The controls within an organization are meant to optimize use of resources by preventing unnecessary duplication of effort and waste in all aspects of the business, and by discouraging other inefficient use of resources.

There may at times be a conflict between operational efficiency and safeguarding assets and records or providing reliable information. There is a cost attached to fulfilling these two objectives and, to the extent that the cost exceeds the benefits, the results may be operationally inefficient.

Management institutes procedures and rules to meet the goals of the company. Internal control is meant to provide reasonable assurance that these are followed by company personnel.

Preventing and detecting error and fraud   The internal controls of a company play an important role in the prevention and detection of error or fraud and other irregularities. Management must weigh cost versus benefit when considering this objective. The cost of preventing a particular misstatement should be balanced against the likelihood of the misstatement occurring and the amount of the misstatement that could occur.

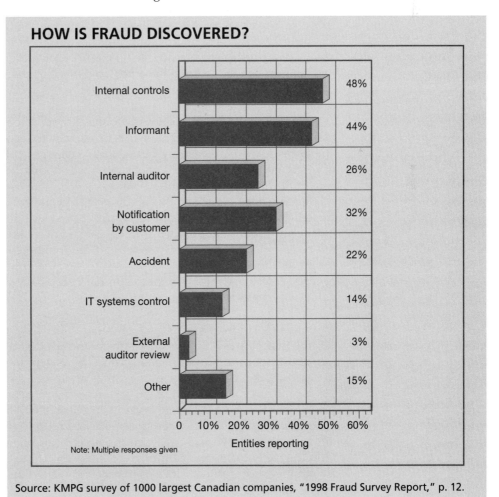

HOW IS FRAUD DISCOVERED?

Internal controls	48%
Informant	44%
Internal auditor	26%
Notification by customer	32%
Accident	22%
IT systems control	14%
External auditor review	3%
Other	15%

0   10%   20%   30%   40%   50%   60%
Entities reporting

Note: Multiple responses given

Source: KMPG survey of 1000 largest Canadian companies, "1998 Fraud Survey Report," p. 12.

As discussed on page 267, the study of internal control and the resultant assessment of control risk are important to auditors and are specifically included as a generally accepted auditing standard. The second examination standard is:

> A sufficient understanding of internal control should be obtained to plan the audit. When control risk is assessed below maximum, sufficient appropriate audit evidence should be obtained through tests of controls to support the assessment.

Paragraph 5200.05 points out that "Management's internal control objectives for the entity go beyond financial statement objectives." In other words, there are aspects of internal control that are of interest to management but not to the auditor; consequently, the auditor does not concern himself or herself with those aspects of internal control in planning the audit. An example would be internal controls that have been set up by management to ensure that accurate information about the company's market share is collected and provided to the company's marketing department.

The *CICA Handbook* in paragraph 5200.07 defines internal control that is relevant to the audit and the auditor as

> those policies and procedures established and maintained by management that affect the auditor's assessment of control risk relating to specific financial statement assertions at the account balance or class of transactions level.

Paragraph 5200.07 states that internal control "in the context of the audit" is comprised of the entity's *control environment* and *control systems* installed by management. The auditor should consider both components together and not separately. Both of these components of internal control will be discussed under Objective 9-3.

The auditor is interested primarily in controls that relate to the first of management's internal control objectives: maintaining reliable control systems. This is the area that directly impacts the financial statements and their related assertions, and therefore impacts the auditor's objective of determining that the financial statements are fairly stated. The financial statements are not likely to reflect generally accepted accounting principles correctly if the controls affecting the reliability of financial reporting are inadequate. On the other hand, the statements can be fairly stated even if the controls do not promote efficiency and effectiveness in the company's operations.

As stated in Chapter 5, auditors have significant responsibility for the discovery of management and employee fraud and, to a lesser degree, certain types of illegal acts. Auditors are therefore also concerned with a client's controls over the safeguarding of assets and compliance with applicable laws and regulations if they affect the fairness of the financial statements.

It has already been stated that auditors should emphasize controls concerned with the reliability of data for *external reporting purposes*, but controls affecting internal management information, such as budgets and internal performance reports, should not be completely ignored. These types of information are often important sources for the auditor because they can be used to develop expectations for analytical procedures. If the controls over these internal reports are considered inadequate, the value of the reports as evidence diminishes.

Emphasis on controls over classes of transactions The emphasis by auditors is on controls over classes of transactions rather than on account balances. The reason is that the accuracy of the output of the accounting system (account balances) is heavily dependent upon the accuracy of the inputs and processing (transactions). For example, if products sold, units shipped, or unit selling prices are incorrectly billed to customers for sales, both sales and accounts receivable will be misstated. If controls are adequate to ensure billings, cash receipts, sales returns and allowances, and charge-offs are correct, the ending balance in accounts receivable is likely to be correct.

In the study of internal control and assessment of control risk, therefore, auditors are primarily concerned with the transaction-related audit objectives discussed in

TABLE 9-1

SALES TRANSACTION-
RELATED AUDIT
OBJECTIVES

TRANSACTION-RELATED AUDIT OBJECTIVES — GENERAL FORM	SALES TRANSACTION-RELATED AUDIT OBJECTIVES
Occurrence	Recorded sales are for shipments made to nonfictitious customers.
Completeness	Existing sales transactions are recorded.
Accuracy	Recorded sales are for the amount of goods shipped and are correctly billed and recorded.
Classification	Sales transactions are properly classified.
Timing	Sales are recorded on the correct dates.
Posting and Summarization	Sales transactions are properly included in the data files and are correctly summarized.

Chapter 5. These objectives were discussed in detail on pages 142–144. Table 9-1 illustrates the development of transaction-related audit objectives for sales transactions.

During the study of internal control and assessment of control risk, the auditor does not, however, ignore internal controls over account balances. For example, transaction-related audit objectives typically have no effect on three balance-related audit objectives: valuation, rights and obligations, and presentation and disclosure. The auditor is likely to make a separate evaluation as to whether management has implemented internal controls for each of these three balance-related audit objectives.

KEY CONCEPTS

There are three basic concepts underlying the study of internal control and assessment of control risk: management's responsibility, reasonable assurance, and inherent limitations.

MANAGEMENT'S RESPONSIBILITY

Management, not the auditor, must establish and maintain the entity's controls. This concept is consistent with the requirement that management, not the auditor, is responsible for the preparation of financial statements in accordance with generally accepted accounting principles.

REASONABLE ASSURANCE

A company should develop internal controls that provide reasonable, but not absolute, assurance that the financial statements are fairly stated. Internal controls are developed by management after considering both the costs and benefits of the controls. Management is often unwilling to implement an ideal system because the costs may be too high. For example, it is unreasonable for auditors to expect the management of a small company to hire several additional accounting personnel to bring about a small improvement in the reliability of accounting data. It is often less expensive to have auditors do more extensive auditing than to incur higher internal control costs.

INHERENT LIMITATIONS

Internal controls cannot be regarded as completely effective, regardless of the care followed in their design and implementation. Even if systems personnel could design an ideal system, effectiveness of the system would depend on the competency and dependability of the people using it. For example, assume that a procedure for counting inventory is carefully developed and requires two employees to count independently. If neither of the employees understands the instructions or if both are careless in doing the counts, the count of inventory is likely to be wrong. Even if the count is right, management might override the procedure and instruct an employee to increase the count of quantities in order to improve reported earnings. Similarly, the employees might decide to overstate the counts intentionally to cover up a theft of inventory by one or both of them. This is called *collusion*.

Because of these inherent limitations of controls and because auditors cannot have more than reasonable assurance of the controls' effectiveness, there is almost always some level of control risk greater than zero. Therefore, even with the most effectively designed internal controls, the auditor must obtain audit evidence beyond testing the controls for every material financial statement account.

METHOD OF INFORMATION PROCESSING

The control concepts discussed in this chapter apply to all accounting systems regardless of complexity. There are major differences between a simple computerized accounting system using purchased software for a small service company and a complex distributed system for an international manufacturing business. Nevertheless, the control objectives are the same, and the methodology discussed in this chapter is applicable to both.

For simplicity, most illustrations in this chapter apply to simple computerized systems. These are considered to be batch-based systems or on-line data entry systems in centralized configurations, or using a local area network (LAN) with a single server. For a description of types of configurations, consult the Appendix to Chapter 8. Unique considerations in more advanced systems are studied in Chapter 22.

ELEMENTS OF INTERNAL CONTROL

OBJECTIVE 9-3

Understand that internal control consists of the control environment and control systems and discuss what these terms mean.

A company's internal control includes two basic categories of policies and procedures that management designs and implements to provide reasonable assurance that its control objectives will be met. These are called the *elements of internal control* and consist of (1) the control environment and (2) control systems. Figure 9-1 on page 276 shows how automated information systems have *general computer controls* as part of those control systems. General controls are those computer controls that can affect multiple transaction cycles and thus multiple classes of transactions. Controls for a particular transaction cycle are often called *application controls*. These can consist of manual control procedures, fully automated control procedures, or control procedures that are assisted by the computer systems, and are described in more detail later in the chapter. For convenience, the term "procedures" is often dropped during discussion, and the phrase "manual controls," for example, would be used to describe manual control procedures.

The elements of internal control contain many control-related policies and procedures. The auditor is concerned primarily with those relating to preventing or detecting material misstatements in the financial statements. Those aspects will be the focus of the remainder of the chapter.

THE CONTROL ENVIRONMENT

The essence of an effectively controlled organization lies in the attitude of its management. If top management believes control is important, others in the organization will sense that and respond by conscientiously observing the policies and procedures established. On the other hand, if it is clear to members of the organization that control is not an important concern to top management and is given "lip service" rather than meaningful support, it is almost certain that control objectives will not be effectively achieved.

The *control environment* consists of the actions, policies, and procedures that reflect the overall attitudes of top management, the directors, and the owners of an entity about control and its importance to the entity. For the purpose of understanding and assessing the control environment, the auditor should consider the nine factors taken from Section 5200 of the *CICA Handbook* listed below. The nine factors, which individually and collectively enhance or diminish internal control in an entity, are:

- Management philosophy and operating style
- The functioning of the board of directors and its committees, particularly the audit committee
- Organizational structure
- Methods of assigning authority and responsibility
- Management control methods
- Systems development methodology
- Personnel policies and practices
- Management reaction to external influences
- Internal audit

MANAGEMENT PHILOSOPHY AND OPERATING STYLE

Management should operate ethically and honestly and encourage like behaviour among employees. "Actions speak louder than words" is a saying that most of us have heard since childhood. Management, through its activities, provides clear signals to employees about the importance of control. For example, does management take significant risks or is it risk-averse? Do policies exist to protect information and ensure privacy and confidentiality? Are profit plans and budget data set as "best possible" plans or "most likely" targets? Can management be described as "fat and bureaucratic," "lean and mean," dominated by one or a few individuals, or "just right"? Does management use aggressive accounting to ensure budgets and goals are met? Understanding these and similar aspects of management's philosophy and operating style gives the auditor a sense of its attitude about control.

THE BOARD OF DIRECTORS AND AUDIT COMMITTEE

The board and its committees should take an active role in running the company and not simply rubber-stamp management's activities. Does the audit committee meet with the auditors, both external and internal, and support them in their activities? Can the external or internal auditors go to the audit committee with concerns about the company's operations knowing they will be heard? By understanding how the board and its committees, especially the audit committee, work, the auditor will be able to assess how active an oversight role they take with respect to the entity's accounting and financial reporting policies and practices.

ORGANIZATION STRUCTURE

The entity's organizational structure defines the lines of responsibilities and authority that exist. Does the entity have an appropriate organizational structure for planning, directing, and controlling operations? Are authority and responsibility assignments within the organization structure clear? Is there an information systems steering committee that oversees the development and management of information systems? By understanding the client's organizational structure, the auditor can learn the management and functional elements of the business and perceive how control-related policies and procedures can be carried out.

METHODS OF ASSIGNING AUTHORITY AND RESPONSIBILITY

The methods of communicating assignment of authority and responsibility must take into account the reporting relationships and responsibilities existing within the entity and the entity's culture. Care must be taken that issues such as the entity's policy on ethical and social issues and organizational goals and objectives are considered. The communications might include such methods as memoranda from top management about the importance of control and control-related matters, formal organizational and operating plans, employee job descriptions and related policies, and policy documents covering employee behaviour such as conflicts of interest and formal codes of conduct, including policies forbidding software copyright violation.

MANAGEMENT CONTROL METHODS

These are the methods that management uses to supervise the entity's activities. Do policies exist indicating the status of electronic communications? Have logical access and monitoring methods (e.g., passwords and logging) been implemented that reinforce rights of usage as defined? Management methods that monitor the activities of others enhance the effectiveness of internal control in two ways. First, the conduct of such methods sends a clear message about the importance of control. Second, the methods serve to detect misstatements that may have occurred.

An example that illustrates management control methods is an effective *budgeting system* including subsequent periodic reports of the results of operations compared to budgets. An organization that has effective planning identifies material differences between actual results and the plan, and takes appropriate corrective action at the proper management level.

SYSTEMS DEVELOPMENT METHODOLOGY

Management has the responsibility for the development and implementation of the entity's systems and procedures. The auditor should know whether management has a methodology for developing and modifying automated and manual systems and procedures or whether change occurs on an *ad hoc* basis. Where custom program development is routinely undertaken, formal methodologies with appropriate checkpoints should exist, as well as a method of evaluating systems once they have been implemented. Policies to monitor ongoing program changes should also exist. When software systems are purchased, management should ensure that the software is consistent with organizational objectives.

PERSONNEL POLICIES AND PRACTICES

An important aspect of any system of controls is personnel. If employees are competent and trustworthy, other controls can be absent and reliable financial statements will still result. Honest, efficient people are able to perform at a high level even when there are few other controls to support them. Even if there are numerous other controls, incompetent or dishonest people can reduce the system to a shambles. Even though personnel may be competent and trustworthy, people have certain innate shortcomings. They can, for example, become bored or dissatisfied, personal problems can disrupt their performance, or their goals may change.

Because of the importance of competent, trustworthy personnel in providing effective control, the method by which persons are hired, evaluated, and compensated is an important part of internal control.

MANAGEMENT REACTION TO EXTERNAL INFLUENCES

While external influences are beyond management's control, management should be aware of these influences and be prepared to react appropriately. For example, management (and its tax advisors) should be so knowledgeable of the tax laws in filing corporate tax returns that an audit by Revenue Canada would not uncover any surprises.

Management should be aware of changes in the economy and in technology in the entity's industry. For example, a retailing company should be aware of a downturn in the economy that could lead to reduced sales. The company should probably reduce its level of inventory in such a situation.

INTERNAL AUDIT

An effective, competent, independent, and well-trained internal audit department, which reports to the audit committee of the board of directors, can greatly enhance the operations of an entity by monitoring the effectiveness of other control-related policies and procedures and by performing operational audits (discussed further in Chapter 25).

In addition to its role in the entity's control environment, an adequate internal audit staff can contribute to reduced external audit costs by providing direct assistance to the external auditor. Section 5230 defines the way internal auditors affect the external auditor's evidence accumulation. If the external auditor obtains evidence that supports the competence, integrity, and objectivity of internal auditors, then the external auditor can rely on the internal auditors' work in a number of ways.

SUMMARY

The auditor is interested in the control environment as a reflection of management's commitment to internal control for the entity. If the auditor concludes that management is actively attempting to develop strong internal control through some or all the nine factors listed above, then the auditor can conclude that the entity's internal control can likely be relied on. On the other hand, if the auditor finds that management is not committed to a positive control environment, the information contained in the company's records is likely not to be very reliable.

MANAGEMENT'S RISK ASSESSMENT

Risk assessment for financial reporting is *management's* identification and analysis of risks relevant to the preparation of financial statements in conformity with generally accepted accounting principles. For example, if a company frequently sells products at a price below inventory cost because of rapid technology changes, it is essential for the company to incorporate adequate controls to overcome the risk of overstating inventory.

Management's risk assessment differs from, but is closely related to, the auditor's risk assessment discussed in Chapter 8. Management assesses risks as a part of designing and operating internal controls to minimize errors and irregularities. Auditors assess risks to determine the amount of evidence needed in the audit. If management effectively assesses and responds to risks, the auditor will typically accumulate less evidence than when management fails to identify or respond to significant risks.

CONTROL SYSTEMS

Paragraphs 5200.13 through 5200.15 of the *CICA Handbook* describe control systems as having two components: the *accounting system*, which includes policies and procedures that management implements and supports that involve the collection, transcribing, processing, and reporting of data; and the *control procedures*, which include the policies and procedures that management implements and supports that enhance the reliability of the data. The data that are collected, transcribed, processed, and reported include financial data, production data, marketing data, and personnel data, as well as other information needed to operate the entity. The control procedures include segregation of duties, suitable authorization procedures, appropriate documents and records, adequate safeguards over assets and records, and independent verification of performance and recorded data.

When an organization uses automated information systems, *general control systems and procedures* are used to describe control systems and procedures that could affect multiple classes of transactions. This text has divided control systems into components. This division means that, for purposes of discussion in this text, there will be four elements of internal control: (1) the control environment, (2) general control systems and procedures, (3) the accounting system, and (4) the accounting system control procedures. Figure 9-1 on page 276 places these elements in a hierarchy, showing how preceding elements of internal control affect following elements.

GENERAL COMPUTER CONTROL SYSTEMS

General (computer) control systems affect multiple classes of transactions (also called *applications*) and are intended to establish a framework of overall control over information systems processing activities.[2] As shown in Figure 9-1, they are grouped into the following types of control systems, containing policies and procedures:

---

[2]Further details are available from EDP-3, EDP auditing guideline, "Risk Assessment and Internal Control — EDP Characteristics and Considerations," *CICA Handbook* and from *Information Technology Guidelines*, 3rd Edition, Canadian Institute of Chartered Accountants, Chapters 2–7.

FIGURE 9-1
Elements of Internal
Control

MANUAL INFORMATION SYSTEM	AUTOMATED SYSTEMS
Control Environment	Control Environment
	General Control Systems and Procedures
	• Organization and management controls
	• Systems acquisitions, development, and maintenance controls
	• Operations and information systems support
Accounting System*	Application System*
Accounting System* Control Procedures	Application System* Control Procedures
• Manual controls	• Manual controls
	• Computer-assisted controls
	• Fully automated controls

*"Accounting systems" and "application systems" are used as synonymous terms.

- *Organization and management controls.* Policies and procedures related to controls should be established, and segregation of incompatible functions should exist.
- *Systems acquisition, development, and maintenance controls.* Application systems could be purchased, developed, or otherwise acquired. Once acquired, changes may need to be made. Established methodologies and control systems should be in place to provide reasonable assurance that the systems are authorized and efficient and function in a manner consistent with organizational objectives.
- *Operations and information systems support.* Systems should be available when needed and used for authorized purposes. This section covers employee operational training, adequate documentation of day-to-day procedures, business continuity planning and information systems recovery, and physical and logical security.

The actual activities used to implement the control systems are termed general (computer) control procedures. Table 9-2 provides examples of specific objectives, and the general control procedures used to implement the objectives for each general control system. For the purposes of brevity, the examples are illustrative only, and do not include all of the procedures that an organization would require to achieve the specific objective.

General controls at Hillsburg Hardware are included in the Appendix. Examples of policies and procedures associated with automated systems have been included in the previously discussed control environment. Specific controls that affect transaction cycles are also discussed in the remainder of this chapter.

THE ACCOUNTING SYSTEM

An accounting system has several subcomponents, typically made up of classes of transactions such as sales, sales returns, collections, acquisitions, and so on. For each class of transactions, the accounting system must satisfy all six transaction-related audit objectives identified in Table 9-1 on page 271. For example, the sales accounting system should be designed to assure that all shipments of goods by a company are correctly recorded as sales (completeness and accuracy objectives) and reflected in the financial statements in the proper period (timing objective). The system must also avoid duplicate recording of sales and recording a sale if a shipment did not occur (occurrence objective).

For a small company with active involvement by the owner, a simple computerized accounting system involving primarily one honest, competent accountant may provide an adequate accounting system. A larger company requires a more complex system which includes carefully defined responsibilities and written procedures.

TABLE 9-2

EXAMPLES OF GENERAL CONTROL PROCEDURES FOR A SPECIFIC GENERAL CONTROL WITHIN EACH CATEGORY OF GENERAL CONTROL SYSTEM

GENERAL CONTROL SYSTEM	SPECIFIC GENERAL CONTROL OBJECTIVE	GENERAL CONTROL POLICY OR PROCEDURE
Organization and management controls	Individuals using the organization's systems should have access to only those systems required to do their job effectively. (Segregation of duties)*	1. Managers are to describe necessary access rights by job description. 2. Unique user identification codes and passwords are to be assigned to each employee.
Systems acquisition, development, and maintenance controls	Current authorized versions of payroll programs are in use at all times. (Authorization of transactions and activities)*	1. Management is to monitor government budgets to understand the timing of payroll table changes. 2. The software supplier is to be contacted to ensure that updated payroll software is received on a timely basis.
Operations and information systems support	On-line systems should be fully operational between 8:00 A.M. and 6:00 P.M., Monday through Saturday. (Safeguards over use of assets)*	Duplicate hardware resources are to be kept functional for hardware systems.

*The phrase in parentheses shows the specific type of control procedure required, based on categories used with respect to accounting system control procedures. The difference is that general control procedures affect multiple classes of transactions. For example, functional allocation of access rights applies to sales, purchasing, and general ledger systems.

THE CONTROL PROCEDURES

Control procedures are the policies and procedures that help ensure that necessary actions are taken to address risks in the achievement of the entity's objectives. There are potentially many policies and procedures in any entity that could be classified as control procedures. Major categories of controls are discussed below.

APPROPRIATE SEGREGATION OF DUTIES

Six general categories of activities should be separated from one another. These are custody of assets, recording or data entry of transactions, systems development or acquisition and maintenance, computer operations, reconciliation, and authorization of transactions and activities. The first five are discussed in this section, but, because of its importance, authorization of transactions and activities is discussed separately.

Custody of assets The reason for not permitting the person who has temporary or permanent custody of an asset to account for that asset is to protect the firm against defalcation. Indirect access, such as access to cheque signature images, also must be separate. When one person performs both custody and accounting functions, there is an excessive risk of that person's disposing of or using the asset for personal gain and adjusting the records to relieve himself or herself of responsibility. If the cashier, for example, receives cash and is responsible for data entry for cash receipts and sales, it is possible for the cashier to take the cash received from a customer and adjust the customer's account by failing to record a sale or by recording a fictitious credit to the account.

Recording or data entry of transactions If each department or division in an organization were responsible for preparing its own records and reports, there would be a tendency to bias the results to improve its reported performance. In order to ensure unbiased information, record keeping is typically included in a separate accounting department under the controller.

Systems development or acquisition and maintenance   Systems development or acquisition comprises activities that create (or purchase) new methods of processing transactions, thus changing the way information is entered, displayed, reported, and posted against files or data bases. Maintenance activities involve changes to these processes. These functions should be monitored to ensure that only authorized programs and systems consistent with management objectives are put into place. A programmer who could enter data could enter transactions (e.g., a wage rate increase) and then suppress the printout showing the transaction. Two job functions in this grouping are:

- *Systems analyst.* The systems analyst is responsible for the general design of the system. The analyst sets the objectives of the overall system and the specific design of particular applications.
- *Programmer.* Based on the individual objectives specified by the systems analyst, the programmer develops special flowcharts for the application, prepares computer instructions, tests the program, and documents the results.

As described further in Objective 9-7, if there is inadequate control over software systems or over individual programs, then the auditor would be unable to rely on activities handled by those systems. For example, imagine being unable to rely on interest calculations made by a bank or on the aging in the accounts receivable aged trial balance. These types of situations occur when the auditor is unable to rely on system or program changes.

Computer operations   These job functions include basic procedures such as handling output reports and taking backup copies of information, and more complex functions such as set-up of functional access rights in password systems or development of information systems recovery procedures. Help-desk or computer support personnel may also be included in this area. Personnel who have physical access to media or the capability to set access rights could steal confidential information or give themselves the right to do anything on the system. Separation from authorization, data entry of transactions, or the ability to change programs makes it harder for personnel to suppress a trail of their activities.

Some organizations have a librarian to provide physical custody of the media holding the computer programs, transaction files, and other important computer records. The librarian provides a means of important physical control over these records and releases them only to authorized personnel.

Reconciliation   Reconciliation involves comparing information from two or more sources, or independently verifying the work that has been completed by others. For example, independent preparation of a bank reconciliation by the accounting manager from the accounts receivable or accounts payable personnel would detect unauthorized use or disbursements of cash.

For batch-based computer systems, a *data control group* handles the flow of transactions from users, passing the transactions to data entry after logging the number of them then matching output to logged details to help ensure that all transactions have been recorded, before passing the transactions and reports back to users. An *independent check* by someone other than the data entry person of key information entered, such as payroll rates or customer credit limits, also serves as a form of *data control function.*

When the entity has systems development or maintenance functions, a *quality assurance function* tests the functioning of the new systems or changes, helping ensure that inadvertent errors or unauthorized functions have not been introduced.

Naturally, the extent of separation of duties depends heavily on the size of the organization. In many small companies, it is not practical to segregate the duties to the extent suggested. In these cases, audit evidence may require modification.

PROPER AUTHORIZATION OF TRANSACTIONS AND ACTIVITIES

If possible, it is desirable to prevent persons who authorize transactions from having control over the related assets. For example, the same person should not authorize the payment of a vendor's invoice and also sign the cheque in payment of the bill. The authorization of a transaction and the handling of the related asset by the same person increase the possibility of defalcation within the organization. A person who authorizes transactions and handles computer operations could suppress printouts documenting the transactions. Similarly, a programmer who could authorize transactions could set up a fictitious supplier, authorize payments to that supplier, then alter the accounts payable programs so that the transactions did not print on reports.

Authorization also includes authorization of new programs or changes to programs since this affects the way that transactions are processed.

Every transaction must be properly authorized if controls are to be satisfactory. If any person in an organization could acquire or expend assets at will, complete chaos would result. Authorization can be either *general* or *specific*. General authorization means that management establishes policies for the organization to follow. Subordinates are instructed to implement these general authorizations by approving all transactions within the limits set by the policy. Examples of general authorization are the issuance of fixed price lists for the sale of products, credit limits for customers, and fixed re-order points for making purchases. General authorization can be implemented manually or embedded within computer programs, for example, where computer systems check for and reject orders if they cause a customer's accounts receivable balance to exceed the established credit limit.

Specific authorization has to do with individual transactions. Management is often unwilling to establish a general policy of authorization for some transactions. Instead, it prefers to make authorizations on a case-by-case basis. One example is the authorization of a sales transaction by the sales manager for a used-car company. Another example is that grocery clerks are authorized to reverse only small dollar transactions; for larger transactions, a supervisor must insert a key or type a password before the transaction can be completed.

There is also a distinction between authorization and approval. Authorization is a policy decision for either a general class of transactions or specific transactions. Approval is the implementation of management's general authorization decisions. For example, assume management sets a policy authorizing the order of inventory when there is less than a three-week supply on hand. That is a general authorization. When a department orders inventory, the purchasing agent approves the order to indicate that the authorization policy has been met.

ADEQUATE DOCUMENTS AND RECORDS

Documents and *records* are the physical objects (paper or electronic files) on which transactions are entered and summarized. They include such diverse items as sales invoices, purchase orders, subsidiary records, sales journals, and employee time cards. Both documents of original entry and records on which transactions are entered are important, but the inadequacy of documents normally causes greater control problems.

Documents and computer files perform the function of transmitting information throughout the client's organization and among different organizations. These records must be adequate to provide reasonable assurance that all assets are properly controlled and all transactions correctly recorded. For example, if the receiving department fills out a receiving report when material is obtained, the accounts payable department can verify the quantity and description on the vendor's invoice by comparing it with the information on the receiving report.

Certain relevant principles dictate the proper design and use of documents, electronic transactions, and input screens. These should be:

- Prenumbered or automatically numbered consecutively to facilitate control over missing records, and to aid in locating records when they are needed at a later date (significantly affects the transaction-related audit objective of completeness).

- Prepared at the time a transaction takes place, or as soon thereafter as possible. When there is a longer time interval, records are less credible and the chance for misstatement is increased (affects the transaction-related audit objective of timing).
- Sufficiently simple and described to ensure that they are clearly understood.
- Designed for multiple use whenever possible to minimize the number of different forms. For example, a properly designed and used shipping document can be the basis for releasing goods from storage to the shipping department, informing billing of the quantity of goods to bill the customer and the appropriate billing date, and updating the perpetual inventory records.
- Constructed in a manner that encourages correct preparation. This can be done by providing a degree of internal check within the form or record. For example, a document might include instructions for proper routing, blank spaces for authorizations and approvals, and designated column spaces for numerical data. Input screens would label fields that are to be entered, provide input entry edits (e.g., checking on valid date), and prevent users from proceeding until all relevant information has been completed.

Chart of accounts A control closely related to documents and records is the *chart of accounts*, which classifies transactions into individual balance sheet and income statement accounts. The chart of accounts is an important control because it provides the framework for determining the information presented to management and other financial statement users. The chart of accounts is helpful in preventing classification errors if it accurately and precisely describes which type of transactions should be in each account.

Systems manuals The procedures for proper record keeping should be spelled out in systems manuals to encourage consistent application. The manuals should provide sufficient information to facilitate adequate record keeping and the maintenance of proper control over assets. These could include procedural manuals, software user manuals, program documentation, and computer operations procedures.

ADEQUATE SAFEGUARDS OVER ACCESS TO AND USE OF ASSETS AND RECORDS

It is essential to have adequate internal control to protect assets and records. If assets are left unprotected, they can be stolen. If records are not adequately protected, they can be stolen, damaged, or lost. In the event of such an occurrence, the accounting process as well as normal operations could be seriously disrupted. When a company is highly computerized, it is especially important to protect its computer equipment, programs, and data files. The equipment and programs are expensive and essential to operations. The data files are the records of the company and, if damaged, could be costly, or even impossible, to reconstruct.

The most important type of protective measure for safeguarding assets and records is the use of physical precautions. An example is the use of storerooms for inventory to guard against pilferage. When the storeroom is under the control of a competent and knowledgeable employee, there is also further assurance that obsolescence is minimized. Fireproof safes and safety deposit vaults for the protection of assets such as currency and securities are other important physical safeguards.

There are three categories of controls related to safeguarding data processing equipment, programs, and data files. As with other types of assets, *physical controls* are used to protect the computer facilities. Examples are locks on doors to the computer room and terminals, adequate storage space for software and data files to protect them from loss, and proper fire-extinguishing systems. *Access controls* deal with ensuring that only authorized people can use the equipment and have access to software and data files. An example is an on-line access password system. *Backup* and *recovery procedures* are steps an organization can take in the event of a loss of equipment, programs, or data. For example, having a backup copy of programs and critical data files stored in a safe remote location together with information systems recovery procedures is important for maintaining business continuity.

INDEPENDENT VERIFICATION OF PERFORMANCE AND THE ACCURACY OF RECORDED AMOUNTS

The last category of control procedures is the careful and continuous review of the other four, often referred to as *independent check on performance* or *internal verification*. The need for independent checks arises because internal control tends to change over time unless there is a mechanism for frequent review. Personnel are likely to forget or intentionally fail to follow procedures, or become careless unless someone observes and evaluates their performance. In addition, both fraudulent and unintentional misstatements are possible, regardless of the quality of the controls.

An essential characteristic of the persons performing internal verification procedures is independence from the individuals originally responsible for preparing the data. The least expensive means of internal verification is the separation of duties in the manner previously discussed. For example, when the bank reconciliation is performed by a person independent of the accounting records and handling of cash, there is an opportunity for verification without incurring significant additional costs.

Computerized accounting systems can be designed so that many internal verification procedures can be automated as part of the system, such as separate addition of subsidiary files for agreement to general ledger totals.

MONITORING

Monitoring activities deal with ongoing or periodic assessment of the quality of internal control performance by management to determine that controls are operating as intended and that they are modified as appropriate for changes in conditions. Information for assessment and modification comes from a variety of sources including studies of existing internal controls, internal auditor reports, exception reporting on control activities, reports by regulators such as the Office of the Superintendent of Financial Institutions, feedback from operating personnel, and complaints from customers about billing charges.

INTERNAL AUDIT FUNCTION

For many companies, especially larger ones, an internal audit department is essential to effective monitoring. For an internal audit function to be effective, it is important that the internal audit staff be independent of both the operating and accounting departments, and that it report directly to a high level of authority within the organization, either top management or the audit committee of the board of directors.

In addition to its role in monitoring an entity's internal controls, an adequate internal audit staff can contribute to reduced external audit costs by providing direct assistance to the external auditor, as was mentioned previously.

SIZE OF BUSINESS AND INTERNAL CONTROL

The size of a company does have a significant effect on the nature of internal control and the specific controls. Obviously, it is more difficult to establish adequate separation of duties in a small company.[3] It would also be unreasonable to expect a small firm to have internal auditors. However, if the various components of internal control are examined, it becomes apparent that most are applicable to both large and small companies. Even though it may not be common to formalize policies in manuals, it is certainly possible for a small company to have competent, trustworthy personnel with clear lines of authority; proper procedures for authorization, execution, and

---

[3]A useful source of information about internal control and the small business is the CICA Audit Technique Study, *Audit of a Small Business*, Toronto: CICA, 1994.

recording of transactions; adequate documents, records, and reports; physical controls over assets and records; and, to a limited degree, checks on performance.

A major control available in a small company is the knowledge and concern of the top operating person, who is frequently an owner-manager. Knowledge about and personal interest in the organization and a close relationship with the personnel (often called "executive controls") make possible careful evaluation of the competence of the employees and the effectiveness of the overall system. For example, internal control can be significantly strengthened if the owner conscientiously performs such duties as signing all cheques after carefully reviewing supporting documents, reviewing bank reconciliations, examining accounts receivable statements sent to customers, approving credit, examining all correspondence from customers and vendors, and approving bad debts.

SUMMARY OF INTERNAL CONTROL

A summary of the three elements of internal control discussed in the preceding sections (control environment, accounting system, control procedures) is included in Table 9-3.

TABLE 9-3

ELEMENTS AND SUBELEMENTS OF INTERNAL CONTROL

INTERNAL CONTROL			
Control Environment	**General Control Systems and Procedures**	**Accounting Systems**	**Control Procedures**
Subelements of control environment: • management philosophy and operating style • organizational structure • audit committee • methods of assigning authority and responsibility • management control methods • internal audit function • personnel policies and procedures • external influences • systems development methodology	Types of general controls: • organization and management • systems acquisition, development, and maintenance • operations and information systems support	Transaction-related audit objectives that must be satisfied: • occurrence • completeness • accuracy • classification • timing • posting and summarization	Categories of control procedures: • adequate separation of duties • proper authorization of transactions and activities • adequate documents and records • physical control over assets and records • independent checks on performance

OVERVIEW OF UNDERSTANDING INTERNAL CONTROL FOR AUDIT PLANNING PURPOSES AND ASSESSING CONTROL RISK

The remainder of the chapter deals with how auditors obtain information about internal control and use that information as a basis for audit planning. To help understand how the auditor accomplishes this, an overview of the relevant parts of obtaining an understanding of internal control, assessing control risk, and relating the results to tests of financial statement balances is shown in summary form below and in more detail in Figure 9-2. The process described by Figure 9-2 is discussed first. The remainder of the chapter deals with ways that practitioners implement the first three parts.

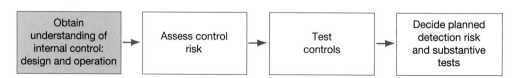

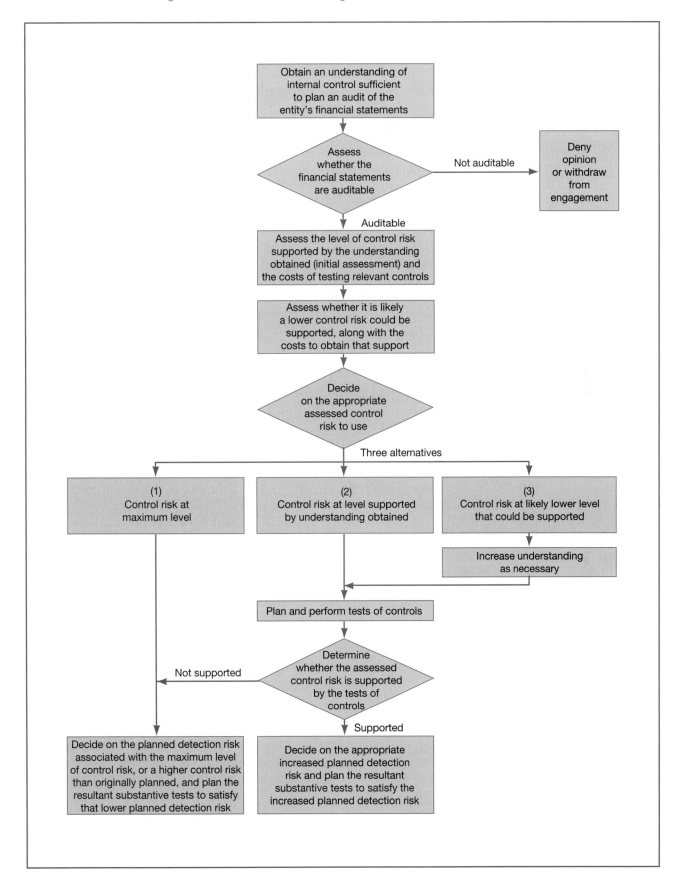

Paragraph 5205.05 of the *CICA Handbook* requires the auditor to obtain sufficient understanding of the client's internal control to plan the examination for every audit. The extent of that understanding must, at a minimum, be sufficient to adequately plan the examination in terms of four specific planning matters.

OBJECTIVE 9-4

Describe the
requirements of
understanding
internal control and
assessing control risk.

Auditability   The auditor must obtain information about the integrity of management and the nature and extent of the accounting records to be satisfied that sufficient appropriate audit evidence is available to support the financial statement balances and the auditor's report.

Potential material misstatements   The understanding should allow the auditor to identify the types of potential errors or fraud and other irregularities that might affect the financial statements, and to assess the risk that such misstatements might occur in amounts that are material to the financial statements.

Planned detection risk   Control risk in the planning form of the audit risk model directly affects detection risk for each audit objective $[PDR = AR \; / \; (IR \times CR)]$. Information about internal control is used to assess control risk for each control objective, which in turn affects planned detection risk and planned audit evidence.

Design of tests   The information obtained should allow the auditor to design effective tests of the financial statement balances. Such tests include tests for monetary correctness of both transactions and balances, as well as analytical procedures. These are discussed in more detail in Chapter 10.

UNDERSTANDING
INTERNAL CONTROL
FOR DESIGN AND
IMPLEMENTATION

Each of the four elements of internal control must be studied and understood. In obtaining that understanding, the auditor should consider two aspects: (1) the *design* of the various policies and procedures within each control element and (2) whether they have been implemented or placed in *operation*.

Understanding the control environment   Information is obtained about the control environment for each of the subcomponents discussed earlier in the chapter. The auditor then uses the understanding as a basis for assessing management's and the directors' attitudes and awareness about the importance of control. For example, the auditor might determine the nature of a client's budgeting system as a part of understanding the design of the control environment. The operation of the budgeting system might then be evaluated in part by inquiry of budgeting personnel to determine budgeting procedures and follow-up of differences between budget and actual amounts. The auditor might also examine client schedules comparing actual results to budgets.

Understanding general controls   The nature and level of complexity of automation in the information systems used at the organization will affect the amount of effort required by the auditor to understand general controls. The auditor obtains information about the organizational structure of the information systems processing department, the hardware and software configuration of computing systems, and a general description of the types of automated systems in use. This is used to plan the extent of work required to understand general controls. For example, if the organization has programmers on staff and many of its financial systems use customized software, then the auditor will need to spend time documenting the processes used to authorize, design, test, implement, and change such software. The Appendix provides a brief description of some general control systems and procedures at Hillsburg Hardware Ltd. This description is typical of small to medium-sized businesses. For further information on general controls, the reader should refer to the CICA's *Information Technology Control Guidelines*, 3rd edition.

Understanding the accounting system   To understand the design of the accounting system, the auditor determines (1) the major classes of transactions of the entity; (2) how those transactions are initiated; (3) what accounting records and data files exist and their nature; (4) how transactions are processed from initiation to completion, including a description of processing handled by computer programs; and (5) the nature and details of the financial reporting process followed. Typically, this is accomplished and documented by a *narrative description* of the system or by *flow-charting*. (These are described later in the chapter.) The operation of the accounting system is often determined by tracing one or a few transactions through the accounting system (called a *transaction walk-through*).

Understanding the control procedures   Auditors obtain an understanding of the control environment, general computer controls, and accounting system in a similar manner for most audits, but obtaining an understanding of control procedures varies considerably. For smaller clients, it is common to identify few or even no control procedures because controls are often ineffective due to limited personnel. In that case, a high assessed level of control risk is used; that is, control risk is assessed at maximum. For clients with extensive controls where the auditor believes controls are likely to be excellent, it is often appropriate to identify many controls during the controls understanding phase. In still other audits, the auditor may identify a limited number of controls during this phase and then identify additional controls later in the process. The extent to which controls are identified is a matter of audit judgment. A methodology for identifying controls is studied later in the chapter.

ASSESSMENT AND DECISIONS

Once an understanding of internal control that is sufficient for audit planning is obtained, two major assessments must be made. The assessment of auditability is undertaken as part of the client acceptance or client continuance process. As shown in Figure 9-2, these also require the auditor to make certain decisions.

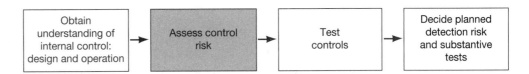

Assess whether the financial statements are auditable   The first assessment is whether the entity is auditable. Two primary factors determine auditability: the control environment, with an emphasis on the integrity of management, and the adequacy of accounting methods. Many audit procedures rely to some extent on the representations of management. For example, it is difficult for the auditor to evaluate whether inventory is obsolete without an honest assessment by management. If management lacks integrity, management may provide false representations causing the auditor to rely on unreliable evidence.

The accounting records serve as a direct source of audit evidence for most audit objectives. If the accounting records are deficient, necessary audit evidence may not be available. For example, if the client has not kept duplicate sales invoices and vendors' invoices, it would normally not be possible to do an audit. Unless the auditor can identify an alternative source of reliable evidence, or unless appropriate records can be constructed for the auditor's use, the only recourse may be to consider the entity unauditable.

When it is concluded that the entity is not auditable, the auditor discusses the circumstances with the client (usually at the highest level) and either withdraws from the engagement or issues a denial form of auditor's report.

Determine the level of control risk supported by the understanding obtained
After obtaining an understanding of internal control, the auditor makes an initial assessment of control risk. Control risk is a measure of the auditor's expectation that internal controls *will neither prevent material misstatements* from occurring *nor detect and correct them* if they have occurred.

The initial assessment is made for each transaction-related audit objective for each major type of transaction. For example, the auditor makes an assessment of the existence objective for sales and a separate assessment for the completeness objective. There are different ways to express this expectation. Some auditors use a subjective expression such as high, moderate, or low. Others use numerical probabilities such as 1.0, 0.6, or 0.2.

The initial assessment usually starts with consideration of the control environment and then of general computer controls. If the attitude of management is that control is unimportant, it is doubtful that general controls or detailed control procedures will be reliable. If general controls are inadequate, then the individual automated systems affecting the transaction cycles will not be reliable. The best course of action in that case is to assume that control risk for all transaction-related audit objectives is at maximum (such as high or 1.0). On the other hand, if management's attitude is positive, the auditor then considers the specific policies and procedures within the subelements of the control environment, the accounting system, and control procedures. Those policies and procedures are used as a basis for an assessment below maximum.

There are two important considerations about the assessment. First, the auditor does not have to make the assessment in a formal, detailed manner. In many audits, particularly of smaller companies, the auditor assumes that the control risk is at maximum whether or not it actually is. The auditor's reason for taking this approach is that he or she has concluded that it is more economical to audit the financial statement balances more extensively rather than to conduct tests of controls. Second, even though the auditor believes control risk is low, the level of control risk *assessed* is limited to that level supported by the evidence obtained. For example, suppose the auditor believes that control risk for unrecorded sales is low but has gathered little evidence in support of control procedures for the completeness objective. The auditor's assessment of control risk for unrecorded sales must either be moderate or high. It could be low only if additional evidence was obtained in support of the pertinent controls.

Assess whether it is likely that a lower assessed control risk could be supported
When the auditor believes that actual control risk may be significantly lower than the initial assessment (i.e., actual controls in place are likely significantly better), he or she may decide to support a lower assessed control risk. The most likely case where this occurs is when the auditor has identified a limited number of controls during the understanding phase. Based on the results of the initial assessment, the auditor now believes that additional controls can be identified and tested to further reduce assessed control risk.

Decide on the appropriate assessed control risk   After the auditor completes the initial assessment and considers whether a lower assessed control risk is likely, he or she is in a position to decide which assessed control risk should be used: either a level already supported in the initial assessment, or an even lower level that would need to be justified by further testing. The decision as to which level to use is essentially an economic one, recognizing the trade-off between the costs of testing relevant controls and the costs of substantive tests that would be avoided by reducing assessed control risk. Assume, for example, that for the existence and accuracy transaction-related audit objectives for sales, the auditor believes that the cost of confirming accounts receivable could be reduced by $5,000 by incurring $2,000 to support a lower assessed control risk. It would be cost effective to incur the $2,000 additional cost.

TESTS OF CONTROLS

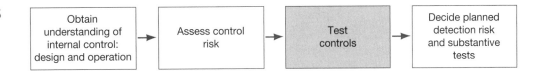

Assessing control risk requires the auditor to consider the design of controls to evaluate whether they would be effective in meeting specific transaction-related audit objectives. Some evidence will have been gathered in support of the design of the controls, as well as that they have been implemented, during the understanding phase. In order to use specific controls as a basis for assessing control risk below maximum, however, specific evidence must be obtained about their *effectiveness* throughout all (or most of) the period under audit. The procedures to gather evidence about design and placement in operation during the understanding phase are called *procedures to obtain an understanding*. The procedures to test effectiveness of controls in support of assessing control risk below maximum are called *tests of controls*. Both are discussed in more detail later in the chapter.

Where the results of tests of controls support the design of controls as expected, the auditor proceeds to use the same assessed control risk. If, however, the tests of controls indicate the controls did not operate effectively, the assessed level of control risk must be reconsidered. For example, the tests may indicate that frequent program changes occurred during the year or that the person applying the control made frequent errors. In such situations, a higher assessed level of control risk would be used unless additional controls relating to the same transaction-related audit objectives could be identified and found effective.

PLANNED DETECTION RISK AND SUBSTANTIVE TESTS

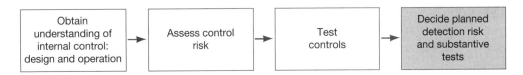

The result of the preceding steps is the determination of the assessed level of control risk, for each objective, for each of the entity's major transaction types. Where the assessed level of control risk is below maximum, it will be supported by specific tests of controls. These assessments are then related to the balance-related audit objectives for the accounts affected by the major transaction types. The appropriate level of detection risk for each balance-related audit objective is then determined using the audit risk model. The relationship of detection risk to audit objectives and the selection and design of audit procedures for substantive tests of financial statement balances are discussed and illustrated in Chapters 10 and 14.

PROCEDURES TO OBTAIN THE NECESSARY UNDERSTANDING

| Obtain understanding of internal control: design and operation | Assess control risk | Test controls | Decide planned detection risk and substantive tests |

OBJECTIVE 9-5

Know how to obtain the necessary understanding of the client's internal control.

In practice, the study of a client's internal control and assessment of control risk varies considerably from client to client. For smaller clients, many auditors obtain a level of understanding sufficient only to assess whether the statements are auditable, evaluate the control environment for management's attitude, and determine the adequacy of the client's accounting system. Often, for efficiency, control procedures are ignored, control risk is assumed to be maximum, and detection risk is therefore low. This approach is defined by paragraph 5205.02 of the *CICA Handbook* as a substantive audit approach. Approach 1 in Figure 9-2 on page 283 is a substantive approach.

For many larger clients, especially for repeat engagements, the auditor plans on a low assessed level of control risk for most parts of the audit before the audit starts. This approach is defined by paragraph 5205.02 of the *CICA Handbook* as a combined audit approach. Approaches 2 and 3 in Figure 9-2 are combined approaches. Having determined that internal controls can be relied on, the auditor first obtains an understanding of the control environment and the accounting system at a fairly detailed level, then identifies specific controls that will reduce control risk and makes an assessment of control risk, then tests the controls for effectiveness. The auditor can conclude that control risk is low only after all three steps are completed. The three steps discussed above are now explained in more detail to illustrate further how the study of a client's internal control and assessment of control risk are done.

PROCEDURES RELATING TO DESIGN AND IMPLEMENTATION

The auditor's task in obtaining an understanding of internal control is to find out about the elements of internal control, see that they have been implemented, and document the information obtained in a useful manner. The following are procedures relating to design and implementation.

Update and evaluate auditor's previous experience with the entity Most audits of a company are done annually by the same public accounting firm. Except for initial engagements, the auditor begins the audit with a great deal of information about the client's internal controls developed in prior years. Because systems and controls usually don't change frequently, this information can be updated and carried forward to the current year's audit.

Make inquiries of client personnel A logical starting place for updating information carried forward from the previous audit or for obtaining information initially is with appropriate client personnel. Inquiries of client personnel at the management, supervisory, and staff level will usually be conducted as part of obtaining an understanding of the design of internal control. Care must be taken to document the information collected.

Read client's policy and systems manuals To design, implement, and maintain its internal controls, an entity must have extensive documentation of its own. This includes policy manuals and documents (e.g., a corporate code of conduct) and systems manuals and documents (e.g., an accounting manual and an organization chart). This information is studied by the auditor and discussed with company personnel to assure that it is properly interpreted and understood.

Examine documents and records The subelements of the control environment, the details of the accounting system, and the application of control procedures will involve the creation of many documents and records. These will have been presented to some degree in the policy and systems manuals. By inspecting actual completed documents and records, the auditor can bring the contents of the manuals to life and better understand them. Inspection also provides evidence that the control policies and procedures have been placed in operation.

Observe the entity's activities and operations In addition to inspecting completed documents and records, the auditor can observe client personnel in the process of preparing them and carrying out their normal accounting and control activities. When the client uses paperless systems, this may require the running of test transactions through the system to verify the understanding, or specialist computer audit assistance, as discussed in Chapter 22. This further enhances understanding and verifies that control policies and procedures have been implemented.

Observation, documentation, and inquiry can be conveniently and effectively combined in the form of the transaction walk-through mentioned earlier. With that procedure, the auditor selects one or a few documents for the initiation of a transaction type and traces it (them) through the entire accounting process. At each stage of processing, the auditor makes inquiries and observes current activities, in addition to inspecting completed documentation for the transaction or transactions selected.

DOCUMENTATION OF THE UNDERSTANDING

Three commonly used methods of documenting the understanding of internal control are narratives, flowcharts, and internal control questionnaires. These may be used separately or in combination, as discussed below.

Narrative A narrative is a written description of a client's internal controls. A proper narrative of an accounting system and related controls includes four characteristics:

- The origin of every document and record in the system. For example, the description should state where customer orders come from and how sales invoices arise.
- All processing that takes place. For example, if sales amounts are determined by a computer program that multiplies quantities shipped by stored standard prices, that should be described.
- The disposition of every document and record in the system. The updating of computer files, method of storing of documents, and transferral to customers or discarding of documents should be described.
- An indication of controls relevant to the assessment of control risk. These typically include separation of duties (e.g., separating recording cash from handling cash), authorization and approvals (e.g., credit approvals), and internal verification (e.g., comparison of unit selling price to sales contracts).

Flowchart An internal control flowchart is a symbolic, diagrammatic representation of the client's documents and their sequential flow in the organization. An adequate flowchart includes the same four characteristics identified above for narratives.

Flowcharting is advantageous primarily because it can provide a concise overview of the client's system which is useful to the auditor as an analytical tool in evaluation. A well-prepared flowchart aids in identifying inadequacies by facilitating a clear understanding of how the system operates. For most uses, it is superior to narrative descriptions as a method of communicating the characteristics of a system, especially to show adequate separation of duties. It is easier to follow a diagram than to read a description. It is also usually easier to update a flowchart, particularly one that is stored electronically, than a narrative.

It would be unusual to use both a narrative and a flowchart to describe the same system, since both are intended to describe the flow of documents and records in an accounting system. Sometimes a combination of a narrative and flowchart is used. The decision to use one or the other or a combination of the two is dependent on two factors: relative ease of understanding by current- and subsequent-year auditors and relative cost of preparation.

Internal control questionnaire An internal control questionnaire asks a series of questions about the controls in each audit area, including the control environment, as a means of indicating to the auditor aspects of internal control that may be inadequate. In most instances, it is designed to require a "yes" or "no" response, with "no" responses indicating potential internal control deficiencies. Where automated working paper software is used, the responses can be automatically linked and cross-referenced to supporting documentation and weakness investigation working papers.

The primary advantage of the questionnaire is the ability to cover each audit area thoroughly and reasonably quickly at the beginning of the audit. The primary disadvantage is that individual parts of the client's systems are examined without providing an overall view. In addition, a standard questionnaire is often inapplicable to some audit clients, especially smaller ones.

Figure 9-3 illustrates part of an internal control questionnaire for the sales and collection cycle of Hillsburg Hardware Ltd. The questionnaire is also designed for use with the six transaction-related audit objectives. Notice that each objective (A through F) is a transaction-related objective as it applies to sales transactions (see shaded portions). The same is true for all other audit areas.

We believe the use of both questionnaires and flowcharts is highly desirable for understanding the client's system. Flowcharts provide an overview of the system,

FIGURE 9-3

Partial Internal Control Questionnaire for Sales

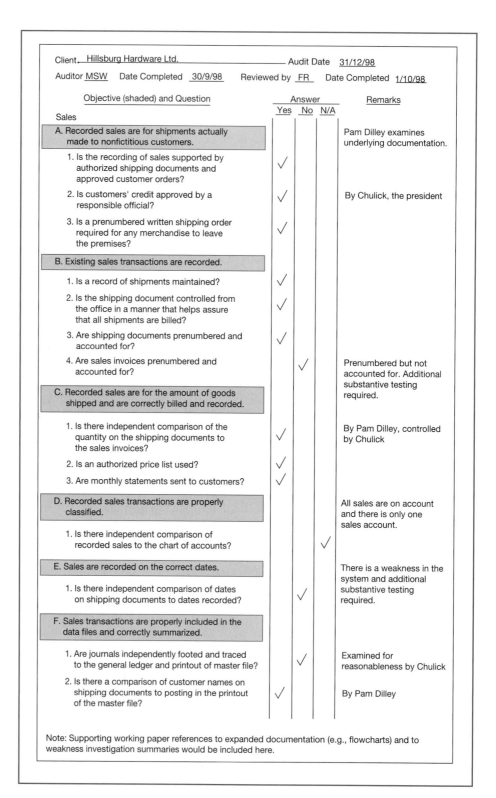

| Client Hillsburg Hardware Ltd. | Audit Date 31/12/98 |
| Auditor MSW Date Completed 30/9/98 | Reviewed by FR Date Completed 1/10/98 |

Objective (shaded) and Question	Yes	No	N/A	Remarks
Sales				
A. Recorded sales are for shipments actually made to nonfictitious customers.				Pam Dilley examines underlying documentation.
1. Is the recording of sales supported by authorized shipping documents and approved customer orders?	✓			
2. Is customers' credit approved by a responsible official?	✓			By Chulick, the president
3. Is a prenumbered written shipping order required for any merchandise to leave the premises?	✓			
B. Existing sales transactions are recorded.				
1. Is a record of shipments maintained?	✓			
2. Is the shipping document controlled from the office in a manner that helps assure that all shipments are billed?	✓			
3. Are shipping documents prenumbered and accounted for?	✓			
4. Are sales invoices prenumbered and accounted for?		✓		Prenumbered but not accounted for. Additional substantive testing required.
C. Recorded sales are for the amount of goods shipped and are correctly billed and recorded.				
1. Is there independent comparison of the quantity on the shipping documents to the sales invoices?	✓			By Pam Dilley, controlled by Chulick
2. Is an authorized price list used?	✓			
3. Are monthly statements sent to customers?	✓			
D. Recorded sales transactions are properly classified.				All sales are on account and there is only one sales account.
1. Is there independent comparison of recorded sales to the chart of accounts?			✓	
E. Sales are recorded on the correct dates.				There is a weakness in the system and additional substantive testing required.
1. Is there independent comparison of dates on shipping documents to dates recorded?		✓		
F. Sales transactions are properly included in the data files and correctly summarized.				
1. Are journals independently footed and traced to the general ledger and printout of master file?		✓		Examined for reasonableness by Chulick
2. Is there a comparison of customer names on shipping documents to posting in the printout of the master file?	✓			By Pam Dilley

Note: Supporting working paper references to expanded documentation (e.g., flowcharts) and to weakness investigation summaries would be included here.

and questionnaires are useful checklists to remind the auditor of many different types of controls that should exist. When properly used, a combination of these two approaches should provide the auditor with an excellent description of the system.

It is often desirable to use the client's narratives or flowcharts and have the client fill out the internal control questionnaire, as long as any subsequent reliance on controls is adequately substantiated with testing. When understandable and reliable narratives, flowcharts, and questionnaires are not available from a client, which is frequently the case, the auditor must prepare them.

ASSESSING CONTROL RISK

| Obtain understanding of internal control: design and operation | → | Assess control risk | → | Test controls | → | Decide planned detection risk and substantive tests |

OBJECTIVE 9-6

Know how to assess control risk for each major type of transaction.

Once the auditor has obtained descriptive information and evidence in support of the design and operation of internal control, an assessment of control risk by transaction-related audit objective can be made. This is normally done separately for each major type of transaction in each transaction cycle. For example, in the sales and collection cycle, the types of transactions usually involve sales, sales returns and allowances, cash receipts, and the provision for and write-off of uncollectible accounts.

IDENTIFY TRANSACTION-RELATED AUDIT OBJECTIVES

The first step in the assessment is to identify the transaction-related audit objectives to which the assessment applies. This is done by applying the transaction-related audit objectives introduced earlier, which are stated in general form, to each major type of transaction for the entity.

IDENTIFY SPECIFIC CONTROLS

The next step is to identify the specific controls that contribute to accomplishing each transaction-related audit objective. The auditor identifies pertinent controls by proceeding through the descriptive information about the client's system. Those policies and procedures that, in his or her judgment, provide control over the transaction involved are identified. In doing this, it is often helpful to refer back to the types of controls that *might* exist, and ask if they *do* exist. For example: Is there adequate segregation of duties and how is it achieved? Are the documents used well designed? Are there controls over inputting to the computer system?

In making this analysis, it is unnecessary to consider *every* control. The auditor should identify and include those controls that are expected to have the greatest impact on meeting the transaction-related audit objectives. These are often termed *key controls*. The reason for including only key controls is that they will be sufficient to achieve the transaction-related audit objectives and should provide audit efficiency.

IDENTIFY AND EVALUATE WEAKNESSES

Weaknesses are defined as the *absence of adequate controls*, which increases the risk of misstatements existing in the financial statements. If, in the judgment of the auditor, there are inadequate controls to satisfy one of the transaction-related audit objectives, expectation of such a misstatement occurring increases. For example, if no internal verification of the valuation of payroll transactions is taking place, the auditor may conclude there is a weakness in internal control.

A four-step approach can be used for identifying significant weaknesses.

Identify existing controls Because weaknesses are the absence of adequate controls, the auditor must first know which controls exist. The methods for identifying existing controls have already been discussed.

FIGURE 9-4
Weaknesses in Internal
Control

Client __Airtight Machine Inc.__

Weaknesses in Internal Control

Cycle __Sales and Collection__

Schedule __P-3__

Prepared by __JR__

Period __31/12/98__

Weakness	Compensating Control	Potential Misstatement	Materiality	Effect on Audit Evidence
1. The accounts receivable clerk approves credit memos and has access to cash.	The owner reviews all credit memos after they are recorded. He knows all customers.	N/A	N/A	N/A
2. There is no independent verification or review of order entry or credit note data entered into the system.[a]	None	Clerical errors in billings to customers, posting to data files, and account classification	Potentially material	Increase substantive tests of transactions for sales to 125 transactions.

[a] Included in the internal control letter.

Identify the absence of key controls Internal control questionnaires, narratives, and flowcharts are useful to identify areas in which key controls are lacking and the likelihood of misstatements is thereby increased. When control risk is assessed as moderate or high, there is usually an absence of controls.

Determine potential material misstatements that could result This step is intended to identify specific errors or fraud and other irregularities that are likely to result from the absence of controls. The importance of a weakness is proportionate to the magnitude of the errors or fraud and other irregularities that are likely to result from it.

Consider the possibility of compensating controls A compensating control is a control elsewhere in the system that offsets a weakness. A common example in a smaller company is active involvement of the owner. When a compensating control exists, the weakness is no longer a concern because the potential for misstatement has been sufficiently reduced.

Figure 9-4 shows the documentation of weaknesses for the sales and collection cycle of Airtight Machine Inc. The Effect on Audit Evidence column shows the effect of the weakness on the auditor's planned audit program.

THE CONTROL RISK MATRIX

Many auditors use a *control matrix* to assist in the control-risk assessment process. Most controls affect more than one transaction-related audit objective, and often several different controls affect a given transaction-related audit objective. These complexities make a control risk matrix a useful way to help assess control risk. The control risk matrix is used to assist in identifying both controls and weaknesses, and in assessing control risk.

Figure 9-5 illustrates the use of a control risk matrix for sales transactions of Airtight Machine Inc. In constructing the matrix, the transaction-related audit objectives for sales were listed as column headings, and pertinent controls that were identified were listed as headings for the rows. In addition, where significant weaknesses were identified, they were also entered as row headings below the listing of key controls. The body of the matrix was then used to show how the controls contribute to the accomplishment of the transaction-related audit objectives, and how weaknesses impact the objectives. In this illustration, a "C" was entered in each cell where a control partially or fully satisfied an objective, and a "W" was entered to show the impact of the weaknesses.

FIGURE 9-5

Control Risk Matrix for Sales Transactions — Airtight Machine Inc.

	INTERNAL CONTROL	SALES TRANSACTION-RELATED AUDIT OBJECTIVES: *Recorded sales are for shipments made to nonfictitious customers (occurrence)*	*Existing sales transactions are recorded (completeness)*	*Recorded sales are for the amount of goods shipped and are correctly billed and recorded (accuracy)*	*Recorded sales are properly classified (classification)*	*Sales are recorded on the correct dates (timing)*	*Sales transactions are properly included in the master files and correctly summarized (posting and summarization)*
ILLUSTRATIVE KEY CONTROLS	Credit is approved before shipment occurs	C					
	Sales are supported by authorized shipping documents which are attached to the duplicate sales invoice	C					
	Separation of duties among billing, recording sales, and handling cash receipts	C	C				C
	An approved price file is used to determine unit selling prices			C			
	Shipping documents are forwarded to billing daily and billed the subsequent day		C			C	
	Shipping documents and duplicate sales invoice numbers are accounted for weekly by computer		C			C	
	Shipping documents are batched daily by quantity shipped	C	C	C		C	C
	Statements are mailed to all customers each month	C		C			C
	There is an adequate chart of accounts				C		
	Sales journal is reviewed monthly for reasonableness of total and compared to the general ledger for sales and sales returns						C
WEAKNESS	Lack of internal verification of the data entry of customer number, quantities, and related information for sales invoices and credit memos			W	W		W
	Assessed control risk	low	low	mod	mod	low	mod

C = The control partially or fully satisfies the sales transaction-related audit objective.
W = Weakness identified in Figure 9-4.
Note: Automated systems would have each of the "C" or "W" cells linked or cross-referenced to supporting working papers.

ASSESS CONTROL RISK

Once controls and weaknesses have been identified and related to transaction-related audit objectives, there can be an assessment of control risk. Again, the control risk matrix is a useful tool for that purpose. Referring to Figure 9-5, the auditor assessed control risk for Airtight's sales by reviewing each column for pertinent controls and weaknesses, and asking, What is the likelihood that a material misstatement of the type to be controlled would not be prevented or detected and corrected by these controls, and what is the impact of the weaknesses? If the likelihood is high, then control risk is high, and so forth.

INTERNAL CONTROL LETTER AND RELATED MATTERS

During the course of obtaining an understanding of the client's internal control and assessing control risk, auditors obtain information that is of interest to the audit committee in fulfilling its responsibilities. Generally, such information concerns significant deficiencies in the design or operation of internal control (weaknesses).

Audit committee communications   Section 5220 suggests that the auditor communicate significant internal control weaknesses to an "appropriate representative of management." The most logical representative would be the audit committee, and the communication should be done as a part of every audit examination. If the client does not have an audit committee, then the communication should go to the person (or persons) in the organization who has (have) overall responsibility for internal control, such as the board of directors or the owner-manager. The communication may be oral or written. An illustrative internal-control-related-matters letter is shown in Figure 9-6.

Management letters   In addition to significant weaknesses in internal control, auditors often observe less significant internal control-related matters, as well as opportunities for the client to make operational improvements. These types of matters

FIGURE 9-6
Internal-Control-Related-Matters Letter

CHESLEY & BEDARD
Chartered Accountants
2016 Village Boulevard
Ottawa, Ontario K1S 5B6

February 12, 1999

Audit Committee
Airtight Machine Inc.
1729 Athens Street
Ottawa, Ontario K1N 6N5

Dear Members of the Audit Committee:

In planning and performing our audit of the financial statements of Airtight Machine Inc. for the year ended December 31, 1998, we considered its internal control in order to determine our auditing procedures for the purpose of expressing our opinion on the financial statements and not to provide assurance on internal control. However, we noted certain matters involving internal control and its operation that we consider to be of such significance that we believe they should be reported to you. The matters being reported involve circumstances coming to our attention relating to significant deficiencies in the design or operation of internal control that, in our judgment, could adversely affect the organization's ability to record, process, summarize, and report financial data consistent with the assertions of management in the financial statements.

The matter noted is that there is a lack of independent verification of the data entry of the customer's name, product number, and quantity shipped on sales invoices and credit memos. As a consequence, errors in these activities could occur and remain uncorrected, adversely affecting both recorded net sales and accounts receivable. This deficiency is particularly significant because of the large size of the average sale of Airtight Machine Inc.

This report is intended solely for the information and use of the audit committee, board of directors, management, and others in Airtight Machine Inc.

Very truly yours,

Chesley & Bedard

Chesley & Bedard

should also be communicated to the client. The form of communication is often a separate letter for that purpose, called a *management letter*. This letter needs to be clearly identified as a derivative report to indicate that the purpose of the engagement was not to determine weaknesses in internal control but that they were identified as a by-product of the audit. The letter would also indicate that the auditors may not have found all weaknesses.

IMPACT OF GENERAL CONTROLS

OBJECTIVE 9-7

Understand how the quality of general controls affects the auditor's ability to rely on computer-assisted or fully automated controls.

As described earlier and shown in Figure 9-1, general (computer) controls are controls over automated information systems with respect to organization and management; systems acquisition, development and maintenance; and operations and information systems support. Table 9-2 provided examples of general (computer) control procedures.

Since general controls affect multiple transaction cycles, the quality of general controls should be assessed prior to the decision on whether reliance will be placed on controls or procedures in automated accounting systems. This occurs because there are three types of controls that can occur in automated accounting systems (see Figure 9-1). These are:

Manual control procedures. These controls are performed by individuals that do not rely on reports or screens prepared by automated information systems. For example, goods received from a supplier are counted and recorded on a receiving report then compared to the bill of lading that came with the shipment on the truck.

Computer-assisted control procedures. These controls are performed by individuals with the assistance of a computer report or computer information. For example, inventory counts are recorded in the computer system. A report is printed identifying differences between the perpetual records and the inventory count so that a different count team can verify the discrepancy.

Fully automated control procedures. These controls are performed using only automated information systems, with no manual or human intervention. For example, every morning, prior to commencing sales order processing, the accounts receivable subsystem automatically adds the accounts receivable open item file and transfers the total to a reconciliation file, where another program compares the total to the accounts receivable balance in the general ledger. If there is a difference, a warning message is sent to the accounts receivable data entry clerk.

When identifying key controls in a system, the auditor may have identified a combination of manual, computer-assisted, or fully automated controls. For example, when considering credit approval prior to shipment, a manual control would require that each shipment be manually approved and initialled. A computer-assisted control would have the computer system print a report for the credit manager of questionable orders. The credit manager would review the report and release accepted orders for shipment. A fully automated control would have the computer system automatically reject all orders that caused customers to exceed their credit limit.

For an auditor to consider placing reliance upon either a computer-assisted or fully automated control, the auditor must have reasonable assurance that general controls over the computerized portion of the controls are effective. In particular, program change controls and access controls must be effective.

- *Program change controls.* There should be sufficient controls in place to ensure that programs throughout the year were adequately controlled. This provides reasonable assurance that there were no unauthorized program changes and that programs functioned consistently throughout the year.
- *Access controls.* Physical and logical access controls should exist to prevent unau-

thorized access to programs and data, and to document access so that accountability can be established. If unauthorized access to programs or data can be obtained, then the auditor would not be able to place reliance on the results of those programs or data throughout the year.

Should the auditor conclude that general controls are adequate, then the auditor has the choice of relying on any of the different types of controls in the accounting system that are identified as key controls (i.e., manual, computer-assisted, or fully automated). Should general controls be poor, then the auditor may be able to rely on only manual controls. Alternatively, the auditor may decide to assess control risk at maximum and not rely on any internal controls.

TESTS OF CONTROLS

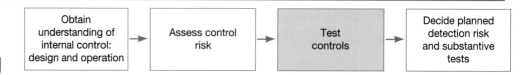

OBJECTIVE 9-8

Understand the process of designing and performing tests of controls as a basis for further study.

The controls that the auditor has identified in the assessment as reducing control risk (the key controls) must be supported by tests of controls to make sure they have been operating effectively throughout all, or most of, the audit period. For example, in Figure 9-5, each key control must be supported by sufficient tests of controls.

PROCEDURES FOR TESTS OF CONTROLS

Four types of audit procedures are used to support the operation of key internal controls. They are as follows:

Make inquiries of appropriate entity personnel   Although inquiry is not generally a strong source of evidence about the effective operation of controls, it is an appropriate form of evidence. For example, the auditor may determine that unauthorized personnel are not allowed access to computer files by making inquiries of the person who controls passwords.

Examine documents, records, and reports   Many controls leave a clear trail of documentary evidence. Suppose, for example, that when a customer order is received, it is used to update a customer accounts receivable record, which is approved for credit using the computer system. Orders that cause the customer to exceed the credit limit are printed and reviewed by the sales manager. The sales manager initials the listing for those orders that are to be accepted. (See the first and second key controls in Figure 9-5.) The auditor examines the credit exception report and ensures that required signatures or initials are present. Since this is a computer-assisted control (preparation of the exception report), the auditor reviews the general controls file to ensure that general controls are adequate prior to the conduct of this test. The auditor may examine a personal guarantee in a bank loan file if there is a need to increase credit, and this provides supporting evidence of the credit-granting process.

Observe control-related activities   Other types of control-related activities do *not* leave an evidential trail. For example, separation of duties relies on specific persons performing specific tasks, and there is typically no documentation of the separate performance. (See the third key control listed in Figure 9-5.) For controls that leave no documentary evidence, the auditor generally observes them being applied. For computer-based controls, the auditor may consider the use of test data to determine whether the control is functioning. Test data are fictitious transactions entered in controlled circumstances, processed through the client systems. The auditor compares anticipated results to results that actually occurred from processing the transactions.

Reperform client procedures   There are also control-related activities for which there are related documents and records, but their content is insufficient for the auditor's purpose of assessing whether controls are operating effectively. For example, assume prices on sales invoices are to be verified to a standard price list by client personnel as an internal verification procedure, but no indication of performance is entered on the sales invoices. (See the fourth key control in Figure 9-5.) In these cases, it is common for the auditor to actually reperform the control activity to see whether the proper results were obtained. For this example, the auditor can reperform the procedure by tracing the sales prices to the authorized price list in effect at the date of transaction. Reperformance can also be automated. For example, if the company uses a complex algorithm to calculate its allowance for bad debts based on sales throughout the year, the algorithm could be duplicated and recalculated using generalized audit software (general purpose testing software with audit modules). If no misstatements are found, the auditor can conclude that the procedure is operating as intended.

EXTENT OF PROCEDURES

The extent to which tests of controls are applied depends on the intended assessed level of control risk. The lower the assessed level of control risk, the more extensive the tests of controls must be both in terms of the number of controls tested and the extent of tests of each control. For example, if the auditor wants to use a low assessed level of control risk, a larger sample size for documentation, observation, and reperformance procedures should be applied.

Reliance on evidence from prior year's audit   If evidence was obtained in the prior year's audit that indicates a key control was operating effectively, and the auditor determines that it is still in place, the extent of the tests of that control may be reduced to some extent in the current year. For example, in such circumstances, the auditor might use a reduced sample size in testing a control that leaves documentary evidence.

Testing less than the entire audit period   Ideally, tests of controls should be applied to transactions and controls for the entire period under audit. However, it is not always possible to do so. Where less than the entire period is tested, the auditor should determine whether changes in controls occurred in the period not tested and obtain evidential matter about the nature and extent of any changes.

RELATIONSHIP OF TESTS OF CONTROLS TO PROCEDURES TO OBTAIN AN UNDERSTANDING

You will notice that there is a significant overlap between tests of controls and procedures to obtain an understanding. Both include inquiry, inspection, and observation. There are two primary differences in the application of these common procedures between phases. Section 5205 states, "The auditor needs to understand internal control only as it applies to the financial statements as a whole and to relevant assertions relating to significant account balances or classes of transactions." In other words, the procedures to gain an understanding are applied only to certain control policies and procedures that have been instituted by the client. The auditor will obtain knowledge about the design of the relevant policies and procedures and determine whether or not they have been implemented. Tests of controls, on the other hand, are only applied when control risk has been assessed below maximum, and then only to key controls.

The second difference is that procedures to obtain an understanding are performed only on one or a few transactions or, in the case of observations, at a single point in time. Tests of controls are performed on larger samples of transactions (perhaps 20 to 100), and often observations are made at more than one point in time.

For key controls, tests of controls other than reperformance are essentially an *extension* of related procedures to obtain an understanding. For that reason, when auditors plan at the outset to obtain a low assessed level of control risk, they will combine both types of procedures and perform them simultaneously.

Table 9-4 illustrates this concept in more detail. Where only the required minimum study of internal control is planned, the auditor will conduct a transaction walk-through. In so doing, the auditor determines that the audit documentation is complete and accurate, and observes that the control-related activities described are in operation.

When the control risk is assessed below maximum, a transaction walk-through is performed and a larger sample of documents is inspected for indications of the effectiveness of the operation of controls. (The determination of appropriate sample size is discussed in Chapters 11 and 12.) Similarly, when observations are made, they will be more extensive and often at several points in time. Also, reperformance is an important test of some controls.

TABLE 9-4

RELATIONSHIP OF PLANNED ASSESSED LEVEL OF CONTROL RISKS AND EXTENT OF PROCEDURES

	PLANNED ASSESSED LEVEL OF CONTROL RISK	
TYPE OF PROCEDURE	*High Level:* *Obtaining an Understanding Only*	*Lower Level:* *Tests of Controls*
Inquiry	Yes — extensive	Yes — some
Inspection	Yes — with transaction walk-through	Yes — using sampling
Observation	Yes — with transaction walk-through	Yes — at multiple times
Reperformance	No	Yes — using sampling

TWO AUDIT APPROACHES

OBJECTIVE 9-9

Understand the two audit approaches.

Section 5205 defines two approaches an auditor may take for a specific financial statement assertion: the *substantive* approach, where the auditor does not rely on internal controls; and the *combined* approach, where the auditor assesses control risk below maximum and does rely on internal controls.[4] Each will be discussed in turn below.

A substantive approach is used when the auditor cannot rely on the internal controls with respect to a particular assertion or when it is not cost-effective to rely on the controls for that assertion. Control risk is set at maximum for that assertion; planned detection risk will therefore be low and extent of evidence will be high. The auditor will obtain a sufficient understanding of the control environment and the accounting system to plan the audit and document the understanding and the control risk assessment; there would be no tests of controls.

A combined approach is used when the auditor can rely on the internal controls with respect to a particular assertion and control risk can be assessed at below maximum. Because control risk is set at below maximum for that assertion, planned detection risk will therefore be medium or high and extent of evidence will be medium or low respectively. The auditor will obtain a sufficient understanding of the control environment, the accounting system, and the control procedures to plan the audit and document the understanding and the control risk assessment; controls would be tested to support the assessment below maximum with the extent of testing varying inversely with the assessment as pointed out on page 297.

---

[4]Paragraphs 5205.02–.04, 5205.18–.24, and Appendix D to Sections 5200–5220 in the *CICA Handbook* explain the two approaches in more detail.

APPENDIX GENERAL CONTROL SYSTEMS AND PROCEDURES AT HILLSBURG HARDWARE LTD.

Hillsburg Hardware Ltd. uses an industry standard, local area network with a single central server. All software used is standard packaged software. There are no onsite data processing personnel, and operating functions are shared among accounting and general staff. The receptionist is responsible for initiating backup before she leaves in the evening. The general manager keeps a copy offsite at his home. The controller is responsible for maintaining password security profiles (that control access rights).

Organization and management controls. Management has a policy of establishing segregation of duties as much as possible with the existing personnel. Functions considered incompatible with respect to financial systems have been separated.

Systems acquisition, development, and maintenance controls. All software used is packaged software. The software has not been modified, and there is no intention to modify the software. Software was obtained only in object code (machine language), so it cannot be modified by Hillsburg Hardware personnel, even if they wanted to.

Operations and informations systems support. The company offices are open from 8:00 A.M. to 5:00 P.M. The network is left on and running 24 hours a day. A maintenance contract has been signed with a major support organization to provide onsite support in the event of equipment failure. Staff were initially trained in the software packages used, and have software manuals to refer to in the event of queries. The controller has prepared a set of instructions (about three pages) that would be used in the event that a major disaster destroyed the building and the local area network. These instructions would allow Hillsburg Hardware Ltd. personnel to resume operations at the local area network owned by their support organization for a fee of $500 per hour.

ESSENTIAL TERMS

Accounting system — the set of manual and/or computerized procedures that collect, record, and process data and report the resulting information (p. 276).

Application controls — (synonymous with *control procedures*) — the set of manual, computer-assisted, or fully automated controls that comprise the controls for a particular transaction stream (p. 272).

Assessed control risk — a measure of the auditor's expectation that internal controls will neither prevent material misstatements from occurring nor detect and correct them if they have occurred; control risk is assessed for each transaction-related audit objective in a cycle or class of transactions (p. 291).

Chart of accounts — a listing of all the entity's accounts, which classifies transactions into individual balance sheet and income statement accounts (p. 280).

Collusion — a cooperative effort among employees to defraud a business of cash, inventory, or other assets (p. 272).

Computer-assisted controls — controls that have a manual component and a computerized component, such as an individual using a computerized exception report to complete a task (p. 295).

Control environment — the actions, policies, and procedures that reflect the overall attitudes of top management, directors, and owners of an entity about control and its importance to the entity (p. 272).

Control procedures — (synonymous with *application controls*) the set of manual and/or computerized procedures that enhance the reliability of information generated by the accounting system. They include segregation of duties, suitable authorization procedures, appropriate documents and records and controls over input, adequate safeguards over assets and records, and independent verification of performance and recorded data (p. 277).

Control risk — see *assessed control risk*.

Control risk matrix — a methodology used to help the auditor assess control risk by matching key internal controls and internal control weaknesses with transaction-related audit objectives (p. 292).

Flowchart — a diagrammatic representation of the client's documents and records, and the sequence in which they are processed (p. 289).

Fully automated control — a control that is undertaken without human intervention, such as a credit check where transactions are automatically rejected (p. 295).

General authorization — company-wide policies for the approval of all transactions within stated limits (p. 279).

General computer control systems and procedures — internal controls for automated information systems pertaining to more than one transaction cycle that could be considered part of the control environment (pervasive) or are more detailed (p. 275).

Generalized audit software — general purpose software capable of reading and testing client data using special purpose modules such as extraction, sampling, and plotting (p. 297).

Independent checks — internal control activities designed for the continuous internal verification of other controls (p. 281).

Internal control — the policies and procedures instituted and maintained by the management of an entity in order to (1) maintain reliable control systems, (2) safeguard assets including records, (3) optimize the use of entity resources, and (4) prevent and detect error and fraud. Internal control can provide only reasonable, not absolute, assurance that management's objectives are met (p. 272).

Internal control letter — a letter from the auditor to the audit committee or senior management detailing significant weaknesses in internal control (p. 294).

Internal control questionnaire — a series of questions about the controls in each audit area used as a means of gaining an understanding of internal control (p. 289).

Internal control weakness — the absence of adequate controls; increases the risk of misstatements in the financial statements (p. 291).

Management letter — the auditor's written communication to management to point out less significant weaknesses in internal control and possibilities for operational improvements (p. 294).

Monitoring — management's ongoing and periodic assessment of the quality of internal control performance to determine that controls are operating as intended and modified when needed (p. 281).

Narrative — a written description of a client's internal controls, including the origin, processing, and disposition of documents and records, and the relevant control procedures (p. 289).

Procedures to obtain an understanding — procedures used by the auditor to gather evidence about the design and implementation of specific controls (p. 287).

Risk assessment — management's identification and analysis of risks relevant to the preparation of financial statements in accordance with generally accepted accounting principles (p. 275).

Separation of duties — segregation of the following activities in an organization: custody of assets, authorization, recording/data entry, systems development/acquisition and maintenance, and computer operations and reconciliation (p. 277).

Specific authorization — case-by-case approval of transactions not covered by company-wide policies (p. 279).

Tests of controls — audit procedures to test the effectiveness of controls in support of control risk assessed below maximum (p. 287).

Transaction-related audit objectives — six audit objectives that must be met before the auditor can conclude that the total for any given class of transactions is fairly stated. The general transaction-related audit objectives are occurrence, completeness, accuracy, classification, timing, and posting and summarization (p. 270).

Transaction walk-through — the tracing of selected transactions through the accounting system (p. 285).

REVIEW QUESTIONS

9-1 Chapter 7 introduced the seven parts of the planning phase of audits. Which part is understanding internal control and assessing control risk? Which parts precede and follow that understanding and assessing?

9-2 Compare management's concerns about internal control with those of the auditor.

9-3 Frequently, management is more concerned about internal controls that promote operational efficiency than about those that result in reliable financial data. How can the independent auditor persuade management to devote more attention to controls affecting the reliability of accounting information when management has this attitude?

9-4 State the six transaction-related audit objectives.

9-5 What is meant by the "control environment"? What are the factors the auditor must evaluate to understand it?

9-6 What is the relationship between the control environment and control systems?

9-7 What is the relationship between the control environment and general controls? Between general controls and application controls?

9-8 The separation of operational responsibility from record keeping is meant to prevent different types of misstatements than the separation of the custody of assets from accounting. Explain the difference in the purposes of these two types of separation of duties.

9-9 Distinguish between general and specific authorization of transactions, and give one example of each type.

9-10 For each of the following, give an example of a physical control the client can use to protect the asset or record:
1. Petty cash
2. Cash received by retail clerks
3. Accounts receivable records
4. Raw material inventory
5. Perishable inventory held for distribution
6. Manufacturing supplies and small tools
7. Manufacturing equipment
8. Marketable securities

9-11 Explain what is meant by "independent checks on performance," and give five specific examples.

9-12 Distinguish between obtaining an understanding of internal control and assessing control risk. Also explain the methodology the auditor uses for each of them.

9-13 Define what is meant by a "control" and a "weakness in internal control." Give two examples of each in the sales and collection cycle.

9-14 Frank James, a highly competent employee of Brinkwater Sales Corporation, had been responsible for accounting-related matters for two decades. His devotion to the firm and his duties had always been exceptional, and over the years he had been given increased responsibility.

Both the president of Brinkwater and the partner of an independent public accounting firm in charge of the audit were shocked and dismayed to discover that James had embezzled more than $500,000 over a 10-year period by not recording billings in the sales journal and subsequently diverting the cash receipts. What major factors permitted the defalcation to take place?

9-15 Jeanne Maier, a public accountant, believes it is appropriate to obtain an understanding of internal control about halfway through the audit, after she is familiar with the client's operations and the way the system actually works. She has found through experience that filling out internal control questionnaires and flowcharts early in the engagement is not beneficial because the system rarely functions the way it is supposed to. Later in the engagement, it is feasible to prepare flowcharts and questionnaires with relative ease because of the knowledge already obtained on the audit. Evaluate her approach.

9-16 Distinguish between the objectives of an internal control questionnaire and the objectives of a flowchart for documenting information about a client's internal control. State the advantages and disadvantages of each of these two methods.

9-17 Explain what is meant by "significant deficiencies" as they relate to internal control. What should the auditor do when he or she has discovered significant deficiencies in internal control?

9-18 Examine the control risk matrix in Figure 9-5, page 293. Explain the purpose of the matrix. Also explain the meaning and effect of an assessment of control risk as low compared to one of medium.

9-19 Explain what is meant by "tests of controls." Write one inspection of documents test of control and one reperformance test of control for the following internal control: hours of time cards are re-added by an independent payroll clerk and initialled to indicate performance.

9-20 Distinguish between a substantive approach and a combined approach in auditing a financial statement assertion.

MULTIPLE CHOICE QUESTIONS

9-21 The following are general questions about internal control. Choose the best response.

a. When considering internal control, an auditor must be aware of the concept of reasonable assurance which recognizes that the
   (1) employment of competent personnel provides assurance that management's control objectives will be achieved.
   (2) establishment and maintenance of internal control is an important responsibility of the management and *not* of the auditor.
   (3) cost of internal control should *not* exceed the benefits expected to be derived therefrom.
   (4) separation of incompatible functions is necessary to ascertain that the internal control is effective.

b. When an auditor issues an unqualified opinion, it is implied that the
   (1) entity's internal control is in conformity with criteria established by its audit committee.
   (2) entity has *not* violated provisions of the *Canada Business Corporations Act*.
   (3) likelihood of management fraud is minimal.
   (4) financial records are sufficiently reliable to permit the preparation of financial statements.

c. Taylor Sales Corp. maintains a large full-time internal audit staff that reports directly to the chief accountant. Audit reports prepared by the internal auditors indicate that the system is functioning as it should and that the accounting records are reliable. The public accountant will probably
   (1) eliminate tests of controls.
   (2) increase the depth and study and evaluation of controls related to achievement of Taylor Sales Corp.'s corporate policies.
   (3) avoid duplicating the work of the internal audit staff.
   (4) place limited reliance on the work of the internal audit staff.

d. What is the independent auditor's principal purpose in obtaining an understanding of internal control and assessing control risk?
   (1) To maintain a state of independence in mental attitude in all matters related to the audit.
   (2) To comply with generally accepted accounting principles.
   (3) To obtain a measure of assurance of management's efficiency.
   (4) To determine the nature, timing, and extent of subsequent audit work.

(AICPA adapted)

9-22 The following questions deal with specific internal control situations. Choose the best response.

a. In general, a material internal control weakness may be defined as a condition under which material errors or fraud and other irregularities would ordinarily *not* be detected within a timely period by
   (1) an auditor during the normal obtaining of an understanding of internal control and assessment of control risk.
   (2) a controller when reconciling accounts in the general ledger.
   (3) employees in the normal course of performing their assigned functions.
   (4) the chief financial officer when reviewing interim financial statements.

b. Which of the following statements with respect to suggested auditor communication of significant weaknesses in internal control is correct?

(1) Such communication is required to be in writing.

(2) Such communication must include a description of all weaknesses.

(3) Such communication is the principal reason for testing and evaluating internal controls.

(4) Such communication is incidental to the auditor's understanding of internal control and assessment of control risk.

c. Section 5220 suggests that the auditor who becomes aware of significant internal control weaknesses communicate this information to the

(1) shareholders.

(2) internal auditors.

(3) audit committee and senior management.

(4) person in charge of the area where the weakness was found.

(AICPA adapted)

9-23   The following questions deal with examining internal controls or assessing control risk. Choose the best response.

a. The ultimate purpose of assessing control risk is to contribute to the auditor's evaluation of the

(1) factors that raise doubts about the auditability of the financial statements.

(2) operating effectiveness of internal controls.

(3) risk that material misstatements exist in the financial statements.

(4) possibility that the nature and extent of substantive tests may be reduced.

b. An auditor uses assessed control risk to

(1) indicate whether materiality thresholds for planning and evaluation purposes are sufficiently high.

(2) evaluate the effectiveness of the entity's internal controls.

(3) identify transactions and account balances where inherent risk is at the maximum.

(4) determine the acceptable level of detection risk for financial statement assertions.

c. On the basis of audit evidence gathered and evaluated, an auditor decides to increase assessed control risk from that originally planned. To achieve an audit risk level that is substantially the same as the planned audit risk level the auditor would

(1) increase inherent risk.

(2) increase materiality levels.

(3) decrease substantive testing.

(4) decrease planned detection risk.

(AICPA adapted)

DISCUSSION QUESTIONS AND PROBLEMS

9-24   Each of the following internal controls has been taken from a standard internal control questionnaire used by a public accounting firm for assessing control risk in the payroll and personnel cycle.

1. Approval of the department head or supervisor on time cards is required prior to preparing payroll.

2. All prenumbered time cards are accounted for before beginning data entry for preparation of cheques.

3. Persons preparing the payroll do not perform other payroll duties (e.g., timekeeping, distribution of cheques) or have access to payroll data files or cash.

4. Program change control procedures over payroll calculation methods are adequate.

5. All voided and spoiled payroll cheques are properly mutilated and retained.

6. The personnel department requires an investigation of an employment application from new employees. The investigation includes checking the employee's background, former employers, and references.

7. Written termination notices, with properly documented reasons for termination and approval of an appropriate official, are required.

8. All cheques not distributed to employees are returned to the treasurer for safekeeping.

Required

a. For each internal control procedure, identify the type(s) of control activities to which it applies (e.g., adequate documents and records or physical control over assets and records).

b. For each internal control procedure, identify the transaction-related audit objective(s) to which it applies.

c. For each internal control procedure, identify a specific error or fraud and other irregularity that is likely to be prevented if the procedure exists and is effective.

d. For each control, list a specific misstatement that could result from the absence of the control.

e. For each control, identify one audit test the auditor could use to uncover misstatements resulting from the absence of the control.

9-25   The following are errors or fraud and other irregularities that have occurred in Fresh Foods Grocery Store Ltd., a wholesale and retail grocery company.

1. The incorrect price was used on sales invoices for billing shipments to customers because the wrong price was entered into a computer file.

2. A vendor's invoice was paid twice for the same shipment. The second payment arose because the vendor sent a duplicate copy of the original two weeks after the payment was due.

3. Employees in the receiving department took sides of beef for their personal use. When a shipment of meat was received, the receiving department filled out a receiving report and forwarded it to the accounting department for the amount of goods actually received. At that time, two sides of beef were put in an employee's pickup truck rather than in the storage freezer.

4. During the physical count of inventory of the retail grocery, one counter wrote down the wrong description of several products and miscounted the quantity.

5. A salesperson sold an entire carload of lamb at a price below cost because she did not know the cost of lamb had increased in the past week.

6. On the last day of the year, a truckload of beef was set aside for shipment but was not shipped. Because it was still on hand, it was counted as inventory. The shipping document was dated the last day of the year so it was also included as a current-year sale.

Required

a. For each error or fraud and other irregularity, identify one or more types of controls that were absent.

b. For each error or fraud or other irregularity, identify the objectives that have not been met.

c. For each error or fraud or other irregularity, suggest a control to correct the deficiency.

9-26 The division of the following duties is meant to provide the best possible controls for the Meridian Paint Company Ltd., a small wholesale store.

*1. Assemble supporting documents for general and payroll cash disbursements.

*2. Sign general disbursement cheques.

*3. Input information to prepare cheques for printing and signature, resulting in payments being recorded in the accounts payable, payments subsidiary system.

*4. Mail cheques to suppliers and deliver cheques to employees.

5. Cancel supporting documents to prevent their re-use.

*6. Update credit limit for customers in the order entry system.

*7. Input shipping and billing information to bill customers in the order entry system.

*8. Open the mail and prepare a prelisting of cash receipts.

*9. Enter cash receipts data in the accounts receivable subsystem used to prepare the cash receipts listing, and update the accounts receivable master file.

*10. Prepare daily cash deposits.

*11. Deliver daily cash deposits to the bank.

*12. Assemble the payroll time cards and input the data into the payroll system to prepare payroll cheques.

*13. Sign payroll cheques.

14. Retrieve journal entries from all subsystems (i.e., order entry, accounts receivable, accounts payable and payments, payroll) to update the general ledger at the end of each month and review all accounts for unexpected balances.

15. Print the aged accounts receivable trial balance and review accounts outstanding more than 90 days.

16. Print monthly statements for customers using the accounts receivable system, then mail the statements to customers.

17. Reconcile the monthly statements from vendors with the supplier balances according to the accounts payable system.

18. Reconcile the bank account.

Required

You are to divide the accounting-related duties 1 through 18 among Robert Smith, Karen Wong, and Barbara Chiu. All of the responsibilities marked with an asterisk are assumed to take about the same amount of time and must be divided equally between Smith and Wong. Both employees are equally competent. Chiu, who is president of the company, is not willing to perform any functions designated by an asterisk but is willing to perform a maximum of two of the other functions.

(AICPA adapted)

9-27 Recently, while eating lunch with some friends at a cafeteria at your university, you observe a practice that is somewhat unusual. As you reach the end of the cafeteria line, a server asks how many persons are in your party. He then totals the food purchases on the trays for all of your party and writes the number of persons included in the group on your bill. He hands you the bill and asks you to pay when you finish eating. Near the end of the meal, you decide you want a piece of pie and coffee so you return to the line, select your food, and again go through the line. The server goes through the same procedures, but this time he staples the second bill to the original and returns it to you.

When you leave the cafeteria, you hand the stapled bills to the cashier, who totals the two bills, takes your money, and puts the bills on a spindle.

Required

a. What internal controls has the cafeteria instituted for its operations?

b. How can the manager of the cafeteria evaluate the effectiveness of the controls?

c. How do these controls differ from those used by fast-food outlets?

d. What are the costs and benefits of the cafeteria's system?

9-28 Lew Pherson and Marie Violette are friends who are employed by different public accounting firms. One day during lunch they are discussing the importance of internal control in determining the amount of audit evidence required for an engagement. Pherson expresses the view that internal control must be carefully evaluated in all companies, regardless of their size, in basically the same manner. His public accounting firm requires a standard internal control questionnaire on every audit as well as a flowchart of every transaction area. In addition, he says the firm requires a careful evaluation of the system and a modification in the evidence accumulated based on the controls and weaknesses in the system.

Violette responds by saying she believes internal control cannot be adequate in many of the small companies she audits although she recognizes that the *CICA Handbook* requires her to "obtain a sufficient understanding." She disagrees with the *Handbook* Recommendations and goes on to say, "Why should I spend a lot of time obtaining an understanding of internal control and assessing control risk when I know it has all kinds of weaknesses before I start? I would rather spend the time it takes to fill out all those forms in testing whether the statements are correct."

Required

a. Express in general terms the most important difference between the nature of the potential controls available for large and small companies.

b. Criticize the positions taken by Pherson and Violette, and express your own opinion about the similarities and differences that should exist in understanding internal control and assessing control risk for different-sized companies.

9-29 The following are partial descriptions of internal control for companies engaged in the manufacturing business:

1. Every day hundreds of employees clock in using time cards at Generous Motors Corporation. The timekeepers collect these cards once a week and deliver them to the computer department. There the data on these time cards are entered into the computer. The information entered into the computer is used in the preparation of the labour cost distribution records, the payroll journal, and the payroll cheques. The treasurer, Mrs. Webber, compares the payroll journal with the payroll cheques, signs the cheques, and returns them to Mr. Strode, the supervisor of the computer department. The payroll cheques are distributed to the employees by Mr. Strode.

2. The smallest branch of Connor Cosmetics Inc. in Medicine Hat employs Mary Cooper, the branch manager, and her sales assistant, Jane Hendrix. The branch uses a bank account in Medicine Hat to pay expenses. The account is kept in the name of "Connor Cosmetics Inc. — Special Account." To pay expenses, cheques must be signed by Mary Cooper or by the treasurer of Connor Cosmetics, John Winters. Cooper receives the cancelled cheques and bank statements. She reconciles the branch account herself and files cancelled cheques and bank statements in her records. She also periodically prepares reports of disbursements and sends them to the home office.

Required

a. List the weaknesses in internal control for each of the above. To identify the weaknesses, use the methodology that was discussed in the chapter.

b. For each weakness, state the type of misstatement(s) that is (are) likely to result. Be as specific as possible.

c. How would you improve internal controls for each of the two companies?

(AICPA adapted)

9-30 You are a manager with a public accounting firm. In the course of reviewing a file prepared by a new senior staff accountant, you notice there is no letter to the client concerning weaknesses in internal control over purchases and payments. You also note that the senior commented in the file that she had obtained the necessary understanding of internal control over purchases and payments to plan the audit and found internal control to be so weak that she planned to assess control risk assessment at maximum. When you ask her about the apparent lack of communication, she says no letter was sent because she did not think the requirements of Section 5220 of the *CICA Handbook* applied.

Required

Prepare a response to the senior explaining why you (and your firm) believe that such a letter is required by Section 5220 of the *Handbook*.

9-31 Yvon Anthony, a public accountant, prepared the flowchart on page 305, which portrays the raw materials purchasing function of one of Anthony's clients, Mann Manufacturing Company, from the preparation of initial documents through the vouching of invoices for payment in accounts payable. Assume all documents are prenumbered.

Required

Identify the weaknesses of internal control that can be determined from the flowchart. Use the methodology discussed in the chapter. Include internal control weaknesses resulting from activities performed or not performed.

(AICPA adapted)

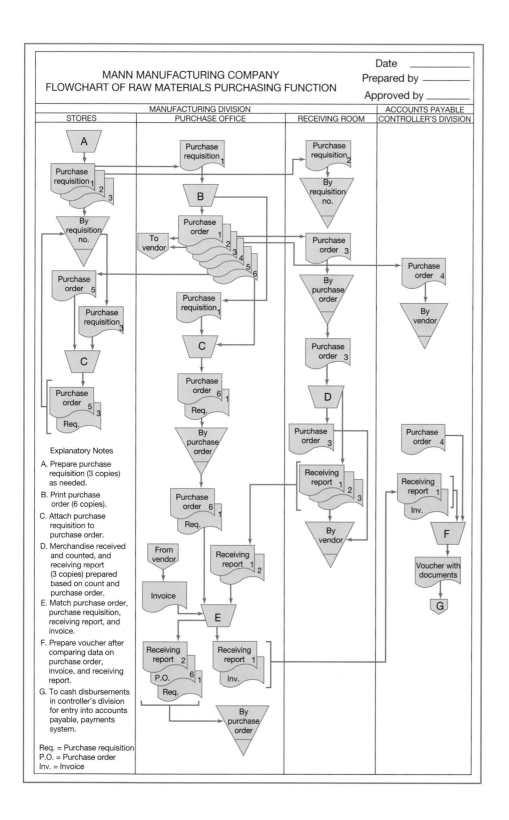

MANN MANUFACTURING COMPANY
FLOWCHART OF RAW MATERIALS PURCHASING FUNCTION

Date _____
Prepared by _____
Approved by _____

MANUFACTURING DIVISION | ACCOUNTS PAYABLE
STORES | PURCHASE OFFICE | RECEIVING ROOM | CONTROLLER'S DIVISION

Explanatory Notes

A. Prepare purchase requisition (3 copies) as needed.

B. Print purchase order (6 copies).

C. Attach purchase requisition to purchase order.

D. Merchandise received and counted, and receiving report (3 copies) prepared based on count and purchase order.

E. Match purchase order, purchase requisition, receiving report, and invoice.

F. Prepare voucher after comparing data on purchase order, invoice, and receiving report.

G. To cash disbursements in controller's division for entry into accounts payable, payments system.

Req. = Purchase requisition
P.O. = Purchase order
Inv. = Invoice

CASE

9-32 Filmore and Gus, Chartered Accountants, are the auditors of Campbells' Toy Store (CTS), a local retail operation, and you, CA, are in charge of the audit. In January 1999, you completed the inventory count and internal control testing. All procedures ran smoothly and no discrepancies were found. It is now March 2, 1999, and you are at the CTS offices to start the February 28 year-end audit. The controller, Gina Cooper, is explaining an incident that occurred before year end.

> We lost control of our microcomputer system temporarily. At noon on February 14, 1999, our computer system shut down. A red heart then appeared on all the computer screens, with "Happy Valentine's Day" written under it. This went on for an hour, after which the computer system started working again.
>
> It appears that someone introduced a computer virus into our system that affected every program in the network. The virus program was activated by a time and date: noon on Valentine's Day. Once the program had run its course, our system returned to normal.

> We have no way of knowing just what else this program did. Such unauthorized programs can change data in the computer, erase files, cause general damage, or do all three. Sometimes, even when the perpetrator intends no harm, an unauthorized program can cause unintended results. We still don't know how this virus got into the system. It could have been entered by one of our employees playing a joke or by someone breaking into our computer through our modem access, or the program could have come in through one of the purchased programs we use. We have spent a lot of time and money trying to remove this program and appear to have succeeded.

After you explained the virus incident to the audit partner, he asked you to provide him with a memo discussing the auditing implications of this event. In addition, the partner wants you to recommend controls that could be instituted to prevent viruses from entering CTS's computer system in the future.

Required

Prepare the memo to the partner.

(CICA adapted)

INTEGRATED CASE APPLICATION

ABC AUDIT — PART I

This case study of ABC Ltd. is presented in four parts. Each part deals with the material in the chapter in which that part appears. However, the parts are connected in such a way that in completing all four, you will gain a better understanding of how the parts of the audit are interrelated and integrated by the audit process. The parts appear in the following locations:

Part I — Understand internal control and assess control risk for acquisition and payment cycle, Chapter 9, pages 307–308.

Part II — Design tests of controls, Chapter 12, page 424.

Part III — Determine sample sizes using attribute sampling and evaluate results, Chapter 12, pages 424–425.

Part IV — Evaluate the results of analytical procedures and tests of details of balances, Chapter 13, page 500.

Background Information

ABC Ltd. is a medium-sized manufacturing company with a December 31 year end. You have been assigned the responsibility of auditing the acquisition and payments cycle and one related balance sheet account, accounts payable. The general approach to be taken will be to reduce assessed control risk to a low level, if possible, for the two main types of transactions affecting accounts payable: purchases and cash disbursements. The following are furnished as background information:

Exhibit I — A summary of key information from the audit of the acquisition and payment cycle and accounts payable in the prior year's audit.

Exhibit II — A flowchart description of the accounting system and internal controls for the acquisition and payment cycles on page 307.

Part I

The purpose of Part I is to obtain an understanding of internal control and assess control risk for ABC Ltd.'s acquisition and cash disbursement transactions.

Required

a. Study Exhibits I and II to gain an understanding of ABC's internal control for the acquisition and payment cycle.

b. Assess control risk as high, medium, or low on an objective-by-objective basis for the acquisition and payment cycle's internal controls considering both internal controls and weaknesses. You should use a matrix similar to the one in Figure 9-5, page 293, for the assessment (a template file containing this matrix is available from your instructor). There should be one matrix for acquisitions and a separate one for cash disbursements. The source of the internal controls and weaknesses is the information in Exhibit II on page 308.

EXHIBIT I

Information Relating to Audit of Accounts Payable — Previous Year

Accounts payable, 31-12-98	
Number of accounts	52
Total accounts payable	$163,892.27
Range of individual balances	$27.83 – $14,819.62
Materiality for the audit	$45,000
Transactions, 1998	
Acquisitions:	
Number of acquisitions	3,800
Total acquisitions	$2,933,812
Cash disbursements:	
Number of disbursements	2,600
Total cash disbursements	$3,017,112
Results of audit procedures — tests of controls for acquisitions (sample size of 100):	
Purchase order not approved	2
Purchase quantities, prices, and/or extensions not correct	1
Transactions charged to wrong general ledger account	1
Transactions recorded in wrong period	1
No other exceptions	
Results of audit procedures — cash disbursements (sample size of 100):	
Cash disbursement recorded in wrong period	1
No other exceptions	
Results of audit procedures — accounts payable	
20 percent of vendors' balances were verified: combined net understatement amounts were projected to the population as follows:	
Three cutoff misstatements	$4,873.28
One difference in amounts due to disputes and discounts	$1,103.12
No adjustment was necessary, since the total projected error was not material.	

EXHIBIT II

ABC Ltd. — Acquisition and Payment Cycle

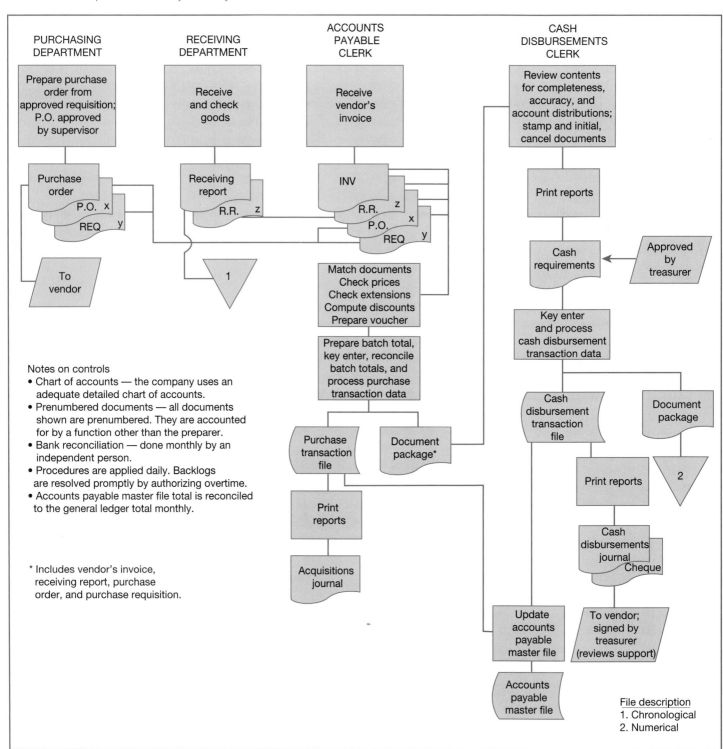

PURCHASING DEPARTMENT

Prepare purchase order from approved requisition; P.O. approved by supervisor

Purchase order
P.O. x
REQ y

To vendor

Notes on controls
- Chart of accounts — the company uses an adequate detailed chart of accounts.
- Prenumbered documents — all documents shown are prenumbered. They are accounted for by a function other than the preparer.
- Bank reconciliation — done monthly by an independent person.
- Procedures are applied daily. Backlogs are resolved promptly by authorizing overtime.
- Accounts payable master file total is reconciled to the general ledger total monthly.

* Includes vendor's invoice, receiving report, purchase order, and purchase requisition.

RECEIVING DEPARTMENT

Receive and check goods

Receiving report
R.R. z

1

ACCOUNTS PAYABLE CLERK

Receive vendor's invoice

INV
R.R. z
P.O. x
REQ y

Match documents
Check prices
Check extensions
Compute discounts
Prepare voucher

Prepare batch total, key enter, reconcile batch totals, and process purchase transaction data

Purchase transaction file

Document package*

Print reports

Acquisitions journal

CASH DISBURSEMENTS CLERK

Review contents for completeness, accuracy, and account distributions; stamp and initial, cancel documents

Print reports

Cash requirements

Approved by treasurer

Key enter and process cash disbursement transaction data

Cash disbursement transaction file

Document package

Print reports

2

Cash disbursements journal
Cheque

Update accounts payable master file

To vendor; signed by treasurer (reviews support)

Accounts payable master file

File description
1. Chronological
2. Numerical

10

OVERALL AUDIT PLAN AND AUDIT PROGRAM

HOW MUCH AND WHAT KIND OF TESTING WILL GET THE JOB DONE?

Professor Al Baker and Partner Ellen Holland have known each other for years, and it seems that their debate has been ongoing for years. Ellen is a partner in the Halifax office of a national accounting firm. Al is an auditing professor at a nearby university. They get together once a month for lunch, and the conversation always gets around to auditing theory versus practice. Take, for example, their most recent discussion.

Professor Al: A shortcoming of GAAS is that it offers too many choices of approach. An auditor can do an audit with virtually no testing of detailed transactions by relying on analytical procedures, observation, and inquiry, and testing details of balances for only significant items. In our highly competitive audit market, I am concerned that firms, including yours, will take the lowest cost approach instead of being sufficiently concerned about quality.

Partner Ellen: Auditors must understand internal control on all audits, and when control risk is assessed as below maximum, some tests of controls are always done to support that assessment. Detailed cutoff tests are always performed, and it is appropriate to concentrate on significant items in tests of details of balances.

Professor Al: That sounds great in theory, but there are certain things that only detailed testing will find, such as employee or management fraud.

Partner Ellen: Well, our clients want our opinion on their financial statements at as low a cost as possible. If we looked for fraud in every audit, our costs would go through the roof and our opinion would not be available on a timely basis. As you well know, searching for fraud is not the responsibility of the auditor. We provide recommendations to our clients for improving their internal control, which is the best way for clients to deal with fraud.

The first six steps in the planning process shown in the margin on page 311 are primarily for the purpose of helping the auditor develop an effective and efficient audit plan and audit program. As was indicated in Chapter 6, the audit program includes a listing of all of the audit procedures to be used to gather sufficient appropriate audit evidence. The related details for each procedure regarding sample size, the items to select, and the timing of the tests are also included.

The most important consideration in developing the audit plan and audit program is the planning form of the audit risk model:

$$AAR = IR \times CR \times PDR$$

where

$$
\begin{aligned}
AAR &= \text{acceptable audit risk} \\
IR &= \text{inherent risk} \\
CR &= \text{control risk} \\
PDR &= \text{planned detection risk}
\end{aligned}
$$

In previous chapters, we have discussed these variables. Reviewing the relationships, AAR (acceptable audit risk) is set by the auditor. IR (inherent risk) is based on the nature of the potential misstatements that could occur, while CR (control risk) is the risk that those potential misstatements are not detected by client controls. The auditor can choose whether or not to rely on controls but cannot decrease CR past the level supported by client controls. PDR (planned detection risk) can be solved by reworking the formula to

$$PDR = \frac{AAR}{IR \times CR}$$

PDR is thus a dependent variable. Solving for PDR, based on the other three variables, indicates the resulting risk and thus the amount of evidence that needs to be accumulated. In this chapter, the relationship between these variables and the dependent variable (PDR) is studied.

The audit plan and audit program are discussed in terms of four types of audit tests. First, the nature of each type of test is defined and discussed. Next, the relative emphasis on the different types of tests that result from differing audit plans is studied. The chapter ends with a summary of the audit process as developed in this and the previous five chapters.

TYPES OF TESTS

Auditors use four basic types of tests to determine whether financial statements are fairly stated: procedures to obtain an understanding of internal control, tests of controls, analytical procedures, and tests of details of balances. The first two types of test are performed to assess control risk, whereas the last two are substantive tests. Substantive tests are used to reduce planned detection risk. All audit procedures fall into one, and sometimes more than one, of these four categories.

PROCEDURES TO OBTAIN AN UNDERSTANDING OF INTERNAL CONTROL

The methodology and procedures used to obtain an understanding of internal control were studied in Chapter 9. During that phase of an audit, the auditor must focus attention on both the design and the operation of aspects of internal control to the extent necessary to plan the rest of the audit effectively. A critical point made in Chapter 9 was that the understanding obtained must be supported with evidence. The purpose of the procedures performed, then, is to provide both understanding and evidence to support that understanding. Five types of audit procedures that relate to the auditor's understanding of internal control were identified in Chapter 9:

- Update and evaluate the auditor's previous experience with the entity.
- Make inquiries of client personnel.
- Read clients' policy and systems manuals.
- Examine documents and records.
- Observe entity activities and operations.

TESTS OF CONTROLS

A major use of the auditor's understanding of internal control is to assess control risk for each transaction-related audit objective. Examples are assessing the accuracy objective for sales transactions as low and the existence objective as moderate. Where the auditor believes control policies and procedures are effectively designed, and where it is efficient to do so, he or she will elect to assess control risk at a level that reflects that evaluation. In making this risk assessment, however, the auditor must limit assessed control risk to the level supported by evidence. The procedures used to obtain such evidence are called *tests of controls*.

Tests of controls are performed to determine the effectiveness of both the design and operation of specific internal controls. These tests include the following types of procedures:

- Make inquiries of appropriate client personnel.
- Examine documents, records, and reports.
- Observe control-related activities.
- Reperform client procedures.

The first two procedures are the same as those used to obtain an understanding of internal control. Thus, performing tests of controls can be thought of as a continuation of the audit procedures used to obtain an understanding of internal control. The main difference is that with tests of controls, the objective is more specific and the tests are more extensive. For example, if the client's budgeting process is to be used as a basis for assessing a low level of risk that expenditures are misclassified, in addition to the procedures described in the example given for obtaining an understanding, the auditor might also select a recent budget report, trace its contents to source records, prove its mathematical accuracy, examine all variance reports and memos that flow from it, talk to responsible personnel about the follow-up actions they took, and examine documentation in support of those actions. In effect, when the auditor decides to assess control risk below maximum level for any transaction-related audit objective, the procedures used to obtain an understanding of internal control are combined with the tests of controls. The amount of additional evidence required for tests of controls will depend on the amount and extensiveness of evidence obtained in gaining the understanding.

The purpose of tests of controls is to determine whether all six transaction-related audit objectives have been satisfied for each class of transactions. For example, the auditor will perform tests of controls to test whether recorded transactions occurred and actual transactions are recorded. The auditor also performs these tests to determine if recorded sales transactions are accurately recorded, recorded in the appropriate time period, correctly classified, and accurately summarized and posted to the general ledger and master files. If the auditor is confident that transactions were correctly recorded in the journals and correctly posted, he or she can be confident that general ledger totals are correct.

To illustrate typical tests of controls, it is useful to return to the control risk matrix for Airtight Machine Inc. in Figure 9-5, page 293. For each of the 10 controls included in Figure 9-5, Table 10-1 identifies a test of controls that might be performed to test its effectiveness. Notice that no test of control is performed for the weakness in Figure 9-5. It would make no sense to determine if the absence of a control is being adequately performed.

TABLE 10-1

ILLUSTRATION OF TESTS OF CONTROLS

ILLUSTRATIVE KEY CONTROLS	TYPICAL TESTS OF CONTROLS
Credit is approved before shipment occurs.	Examine credit exception report to determine the existence of authorized initials indicating credit approval (documentation).
Sales are supported by authorized shipping documents, which are attached to the duplicate sales invoice.	Examine a sample of duplicate sales invoices to determine that each one is supported by an attached authorized shipping document (documentation).
Separation of duties between billing, recording sales, and handling cash receipts.	Observe whether personnel responsible for handling cash have no accounting responsibilities and inquire as to their duties (observation and inquiry).
An approved price file is used to determine unit selling prices.	Observe whether a price file is used when invoices are prepared, and determine whether approved procedures are used to make price changes (observation and documentation).
Shipping documents are forwarded to billing daily and billed the subsequent day.	Observe whether shipping documents are forwarded daily to billing and observe when they are billed (observation).
Shipping documents and duplicate sales invoice numbers are accounted for weekly by computer.	Account for a sequence of duplicate sales invoice and shipping documents and trace each to the sales journal (documentation and reperformance).
Shipping documents are batched daily by quantity shipped.	Examine a sample of daily batches, re-add the shipping quantities, and trace totals to reconciliation with input reports (reperformance).
Statements are mailed to all customers each month.	Observe whether statements are mailed for a month and inquire about whose responsibility it is (observation and inquiry).
There is an adequate customer master file.	Examine a sample of sales invoices to determine whether each one has an account number and that the account number is correct (documentation and reperformance).
The sales journal is reviewed monthly for reasonableness of total and compared to the general ledger for sales and sales returns.	Re-add the sales journal for one month, and trace the total to the general ledger (reperformance).

DUAL PURPOSE TESTS

A substantive test is a procedure designed to test for dollar amounts of errors or fraud and other irregularities directly affecting the correctness of financial statement balances. Such errors or fraud and other irregularities are a clear indication of misstatements of the accounts. The two main types of substantive procedure, analytical procedures and detailed tests of balances, are directed to significant account balances or classes of transactions because of the potential for a misstatement occurring (inherent risk) and because of the potential for a misstatement not being prevented or detected (control risk).

An auditor may perform auditing procedures that are both tests of controls and substantive procedures on the same sample of transactions or account balances for efficiency; such procedures are known as *dual purpose tests*. Dual purpose tests provide evidence of whether or not the controls being tested were operating effectively during the period and of whether there are misstatements in the data produced by the accounting system. Reperformance always simultaneously provides evidence about both controls and monetary correctness.

Figure 10-1 illustrates a dual purpose test. For simplicity, two assumptions are made. First, only sales and cash receipts transactions and three general ledger balances make up the sales and collection cycle. Second, the beginning balances in cash ($47) and accounts receivable ($96) were audited in the previous year and are considered correct. If the auditor verifies that sales ($660) and collection ($590) transactions were correctly recorded in the journals and posted in the general ledger, he or she can conclude that the ending balance in accounts receivable ($166) and sales ($660) are correct. (Cash disbursements [$563] will have to be audited before the auditor can reach a conclusion about the balance in cash in bank.) The auditor verifies the recording and summarizing of transactions by the dual purpose test. In this example, there will be one set of procedures for sales and another for cash receipts.

FIGURE 10-1

Relationship of Transactions to Journals and General Ledger

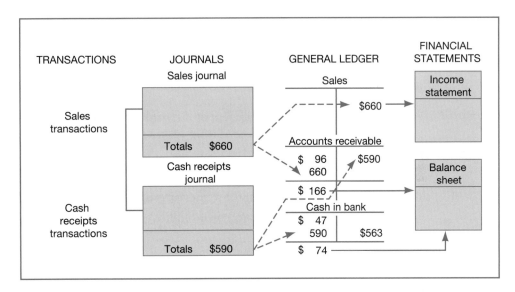

ANALYTICAL PROCEDURES

As discussed in Chapter 6, analytical procedures involve comparisons of recorded amounts to expectations developed by the auditor. They often involve the calculation of ratios by the auditor for comparison with previous years' ratios and other related data. For example, in Figure 10-1 the auditor could compare sales, collections, and accounts receivable in the current year to amounts in previous years and calculate the gross margin percentage for comparison to previous years.

There are four purposes of analytical procedures, all of which were discussed in Chapter 6: understand the client's business, assess the entity's ability to continue as a going concern, indicate the presence of possible misstatements in the financial statements, and reduce detailed audit tests. All of these help the auditor decide the extent of other audit tests. To illustrate, if analytical procedures indicate there may be misstatements, more extensive investigation may be needed. An example is an unexpected change in the current year's gross margin percentage compared to the previous year's. Other tests may be needed to determine if there is a misstatement in sales or cost of goods sold that caused the change. On the other hand, if no material fluctuations are found using analytical procedures and the auditor concludes that fluctuations should not have occurred, other tests may be reduced. Section 5301, Analysis, and the third examination standard of GAAS indicate that analytical procedures are used by the auditor to gain "sufficient appropriate audit evidence." Analytical procedures are both a substantive procedure and a planning procedure to be used in designing the nature, extent, and timing of other audit procedures. When used as a substantive procedure, they would be performed at a more detailed level (paragraph 5301.10).

TESTS OF DETAILS OF BALANCES

Paragraph 5300.04 states that "substantive procedures are used to gain evidence as to the validity of the data produced by the systems underlying the preparation of financial statements." In order to avoid confusion, this text will use the terms "analytical procedures" and "tests of details of balances" to describe the two components when they are considered as separate activities and the term "substantive procedures" to describe the aggregate testing for dollar misstatements directly affecting the correctness of financial statement balances.

Tests of details of balances focus on the ending general ledger balances for both balance sheet and income statement accounts, but the primary emphasis in most tests of details of balances is on the balance sheet. (Terms such as "detailed tests" and "direct tests of balances" may be used interchangeably with "tests of details of balances.") Examples include direct communication in writing with customers for accounts receivable, physical examination of inventory, and examination of vendors' statements for accounts payable. These tests of ending balances are essential to the conduct of the audit because, for the most part, the evidence is obtained from a source independent of the client and, thus, is considered to be highly reliable.

Examine Figure 10-1 to see the role of tests of details of balances in the audit. There are three general ledger accounts in the figure: sales, accounts receivable, and cash in bank. Detailed tests of the balances in these accounts would be performed. These would include audit procedures such as confirmation of receivables balances, sales cutoff tests, and review of the bank account reconciliation. The extent of these tests depends on the results of tests of controls and analytical procedures for these accounts.

Tests of details of balances have the objective of establishing the monetary correctness of the accounts they relate to and, therefore, are substantive tests. For example, confirmations test for monetary errors or fraud and other irregularities and are therefore substantive. Similarly, counts of inventory and cash on hand are also substantive tests.

SUMMARY OF TYPES OF TESTS

Figure 10-2 summarizes the types of tests. Procedures to obtain an understanding of internal control and tests of controls are concerned with evaluating whether controls are sufficiently effective to justify reducing control risk and thereby reducing substantive audit tests. Analytical procedures emphasize the overall reasonableness of transactions and the general ledger balances, and tests of details of balances emphasize the ending balances in the general ledger. Together the four types of audit tests enable the auditor to gather sufficient appropriate audit evidence to express an opinion on the financial statements.

Figure 10-2 also shows the relationships of the types of tests to the audit risk model. Observe that all four types of tests are used to satisfy sufficient appropriate audit evidence requirements. Also observe that procedures to obtain an understanding and tests of controls reduce control risk, whereas the two substantive tests are used to satisfy planned detection risk.

FIGURE 10-2

Types of Audit Tests

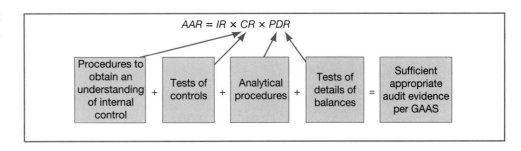

Figure 10-3 shows how the four types of tests are used to obtain assurance in the audit of one account, accounts receivable. The totals in the account are taken from Figure 10-1, page 313. It is apparent from examining Figure 10-3 that the auditor obtained a higher overall assurance for accounts receivable than the assurance obtained from any one test. The auditor can increase overall assurance by increasing the assurance obtained from any of the tests.

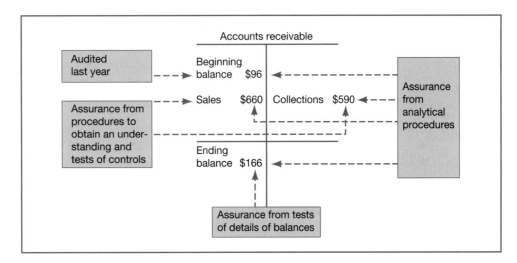

RELATIONSHIP BETWEEN TESTS AND EVIDENCE

Only certain types of evidence (confirmation, documentation, and so forth) are obtained through each of the four types of tests. Table 10-2 summarizes the relationship between types of tests and types of evidence. Several observations about Table 10-2 follow:

OBJECTIVE 10-2

Discuss the relative costs of each type of audit test, the relationships between types of tests and types of evidence, and the relationships among types of tests.

- Procedures to obtain an understanding of internal control and tests of controls involve only documentation, observation, inquiry, and reperformance.
- More types of evidence are obtained using tests of details of balances than by using any other type of test. Only tests of details of balances involve confirmation and physical examination.
- Inquiries of clients are made with every type of test.
- Documentation and reperformance are used for every type of test except analytical procedures.

RELATIVE COSTS

The types of tests are listed in order of increasing cost as follows:

- Analytical procedures
- Procedures to obtain an understanding of internal control and tests of controls
- Tests of details of balances

The reason analytical procedures are least costly is the relative ease of making calculations and comparisons. Often, considerable information about potential mis-

TABLE 10-2

RELATIONSHIP
BETWEEN TYPES OF
TESTS AND EVIDENCE

TYPE OF TEST	TYPE OF EVIDENCE						
	Physical Examination	Confirmation	Documentation	Observation	Inquiries of the Client	Reperformance	Analytical Procedures
Procedures to obtain an understanding of internal control			✓	✓	✓		
Tests of controls			✓	✓	✓	✓	
Analytical procedures					✓		✓
Tests of details of balances	✓	✓	✓		✓	✓	

statements can be obtained by simply comparing two or three numbers. Frequently, auditors calculate these ratios using computer software at almost no cost.

Tests of controls are also low in cost because the auditor is making inquiries and observations, examining such things as initials on documents and outward indications of other control procedures and performing reperformance which includes recalculations and tracings. Frequently, tests of controls can be done on a large number of items in a few minutes, especially if computer-based work, such as the use of test data, is included.

Tests of details of balances are almost always considerably more costly than any of the other types of procedures. It is costly to send confirmations and to count assets. Because of the high cost of tests of details of balances, auditors usually try to plan the audit to minimize their use.

Naturally, the cost of each type of evidence varies in different situations. For example, the cost of an auditor's test counting inventory (a substantive test of the details of the inventory balance) frequently depends on the nature and dollar value of the inventory, its location, and the number of different items.

RELATIONSHIP BETWEEN TESTS OF CONTROLS AND SUBSTANTIVE TESTS

To understand better the nature of tests of controls and substantive tests, an examination of how they differ is useful. An exception in a test of controls is only an indication of the likelihood of errors or fraud and other irregularities affecting the dollar value of the financial statements, whereas an exception in a substantive test is a financial statement misstatement. Exceptions in tests of controls are often referred to as "control test deviations." Thus, control test deviations are significant only if they occur with sufficient frequency to cause the auditor to believe there may be material dollar misstatements in the statements. Substantive tests should then be performed to determine whether dollar misstatements have actually occurred.

As an illustration, assume that the client's controls require an independent clerk to verify the quantity, price, and extension of each supplier's invoice, after which the clerk must initial the original invoice to indicate performance. A test of control audit procedure would be to examine a sample of suppliers' invoices for the initials of the person who verified the quantitative data. If there are a significant number of documents without a signature, the auditor should follow up with tests to determine if there are any monetary misstatements. This can be done by extending the tests of the suppliers' invoices to include verifying prices to purchase orders, extensions, and footings (reperformance) or by increasing the sample size for the confirmation of accounts payable (test of details of balances). Of course, even though the control is not operating effectively, the invoices may be correct. This will be the case if the persons originally preparing the supplier invoices did a conscientious and competent job. Similarly, even if there is an initial, there may be monetary misstatements due to initialling without performance or with careless performance of the internal control procedure. For these reasons, paragraph 5210.18 includes reperformance as one of the several auditing procedures performed as tests of controls. Some auditors prefer to reperform only when there is an indication of the need to do so.

TRADE-OFF BETWEEN TESTS OF CONTROLS AND SUBSTANTIVE TESTS

As explained in Chapter 9, there is a trade-off between tests of controls and substantive tests. The auditor makes a decision during planning about whether to assess control risk below maximum. If control risk is assessed at maximum, the auditor would follow a substantive approach; if control risk is assessed below maximum, the auditor would follow a combined approach. Tests of controls must be performed to determine whether the assessed control risk is supported. If it is, planned detection risk in the audit risk model is increased and substantive procedures can therefore be reduced. Figure 10-4 shows the relationship between substantive tests and control risk assessment (including tests of controls) at differing levels of internal control effectiveness.

The shaded area in Figure 10-4 is the maximum assurance obtainable from control risk assessment and tests of controls. For example, at any point to the left of point A, assessed control risk is 1.0 because the auditor evaluates internal control as ineffective. Any point to the right of point B results in no further reduction of control risk because the public accounting firm has established the minimum assessed control risk that it will permit.

After the auditor decides the effectiveness of the client's internal controls, it is appropriate to select any point within the shaded area of Figure 10-4 consistent with the level of control risk the auditor decides is appropriate. To illustrate, assume that the auditor contends that internal control effectiveness is at point C. Tests of controls at the C_1 level would provide the minimum control risk, given internal control. The auditor could choose to perform no tests of controls (point C_3) which would support a control risk of 1.0. Any point between the two, such as C_2, would also be appropriate. If C_2 is selected, the audit assurance from tests of controls is C_3–C_2 and from substantive tests is C–C_2. The auditor will likely select C_1, C_2, or C_3 based upon the relative cost of tests of controls and substantive tests.

FIGURE 10-4

Audit Assurance from Substantive Tests and Tests of Controls at Different Levels of Control Effectiveness

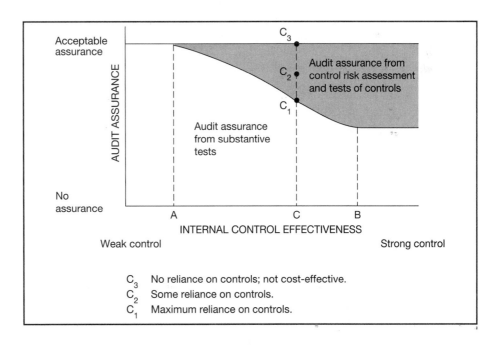

C_3 No reliance on controls; not cost-effective.
C_2 Some reliance on controls.
C_1 Maximum reliance on controls.

EVIDENCE MIX

OBJECTIVE 10-3

Understand the meanings of evidence mix and how it should be varied in different circumstances.

There are significant variations in the extent to which the four types of tests can be used in different audits for differing levels of inherent risk and internal control effectiveness. There can also be variations from cycle to cycle within a given audit, from account balance to account balance within a particular cycle, and even between assertions for a particular account balance.[1] Figure 10-5 shows the evidence mix for four different audits. In each case, considerable time was spent accumulating knowledge of business data, as well as completing analytical review for planning purposes. Assume sufficient appropriate audit evidence was accumulated for all audits. Audit 1 is a large company, while Audits 2 through 4 are medium-sized companies. An analysis of each audit follows.

Analysis of Audit 1 — sophisticated internal controls   This client is a large company with sophisticated internal controls. The auditor, therefore, performs extensive tests of controls and relies heavily on the client's internal control to reduce substantive tests. Extensive analytical procedures are also performed to reduce tests of details of balances which are, therefore, minimized. Because of the emphasis on tests of controls and analytical procedures, this audit can be done less expensively than other types of audits.

Analysis of Audit 2 — medium, some controls   This company is medium-sized, with some controls and some inherent risks. The auditor has, therefore, decided to do a medium amount of testing for all types of tests except analytical procedures, which will be done extensively.

FIGURE 10-5

Variations in Evidence Mix

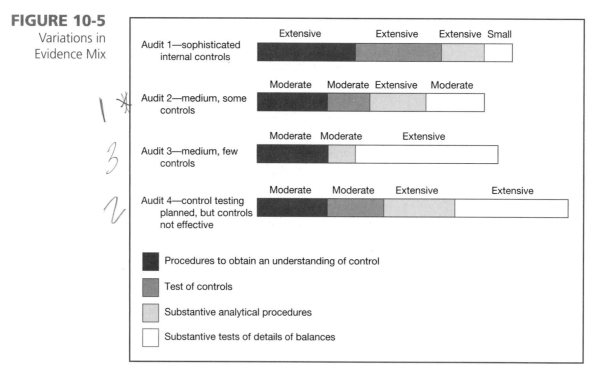

Note: Auditors in all the audits have knowledge of business and have completed planning analytical procedures.

---

[1]The interested reader is referred to the audit planning worksheet for an account balance presented as Exhibit 3 in an article by Professor J. Efrim Boritz in *CAmagazine* (August 1988), p. 58. The exhibit shows how the auditor achieves assurance for the different accounts receivable assertions from different audit procedures.

Analysis of Audit 3 — medium, few controls This company is medium-sized, but has few effective controls and significant inherent risks. Management has decided that it is not cost-effective to implement better internal controls. No tests of controls are done because reliance on internal control is inappropriate when controls are insufficient. The emphasis is on tests of details of balances, but some analytical procedures are also done. The reason for limiting analytical procedures is the auditor's expectations of misstatements in the account balances. The cost of the audit is likely to be relatively high because of the amount of detailed substantive testing.

Analysis of Audit 4 — medium, ineffective controls The original plan on this audit was to follow the approach used in Audit 2. However, the auditor found extensive control test deviations and significant misstatements using dual purpose tests and analytical procedures. The auditor, therefore, concluded that the internal controls were not effective. Extensive tests of details of balances are performed to offset the unacceptable results of the other tests. The costs of this audit are higher because tests of controls and dual purpose tests were performed but could not be used to reduce tests of details of balances.

Figure 10-5 shows the relative mix of audit evidence types. It does not reflect total audit cost since the costs associated with the tests will vary, depending on the specific test selected and the extent of computerized support used for conducting the tests.

DESIGN OF THE AUDIT PROGRAM

OBJECTIVE 10-4

Know the methodology for the design of an audit program.

A combined audit approach is appropriate for most audits; such an approach includes both tests of controls and substantive procedures. The audit program for most audits is designed in three parts: tests of controls, analytical procedures, and tests of details of balances. There will likely be a separate set of subaudit programs for each transaction cycle. An example in the sales and collection cycle might be tests of controls audit programs for sales and cash receipts; an analytical procedures audit program for the entire cycle; and tests of details of balances audit programs for cash, accounts receivable, bad-debt expense, allowance for uncollectible accounts, and miscellaneous accounts receivable.

TESTS OF CONTROLS

The tests of controls audit program normally includes a descriptive section documenting the understanding obtained about internal control. It is also likely to include a description of the procedures performed to obtain an understanding of internal control and the assessed control risk. Both of these affect the tests of controls audit program. The methodology to design tests of controls is shown in Figure 10-6. The first three steps in the figure were described in Chapter 9. When controls are effective and planned control risk is low (i.e., the auditor chooses to rely on internal controls), a combined approach will be used and there will be tests of controls. Some dual purpose tests may also be included. If control risk is assessed at maximum, the auditor will use a substantive audit approach (i..e., only substantive procedures will be used). The procedures already performed in obtaining an understanding of internal control may affect tests of controls.

Audit procedures The approach to designing tests of controls emphasizes satisfying the transaction-related audit objectives developed in Chapter 5. A three-step approach is followed when control risk is assessed below maximum:

1. Apply the transaction-related audit objectives to the class of transactions being tested, such as sales.
2. Identify specific controls to be relied upon that should reduce control risk for transaction-related audit objectives.
3. For all internal controls to which reduction in control risk is attributed (key controls), develop appropriate tests of controls. Where relevant, design appropriate

FIGURE 10-6
Methodology for
Designing Tests of
Controls

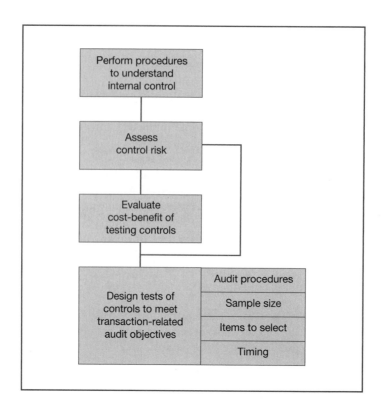

dual purpose tests, considering weakness in internal control and expected results of the tests of controls, for the potential types of errors or fraud and other irregularities related to those transaction-related audit objectives.

This three-step approach to designing tests of controls is summarized in Figure 10-7. The approach is illustrated in several chapters in the text. For example, see Table 12-3 on page 382 for an application of the three-step procedure for the audit of sales transactions. Each of the steps corresponds to a column in Table 12-4.

ANALYTICAL PROCEDURES

Many auditors perform extensive analytical procedures on all audits because they are relatively inexpensive. As stated in Chapter 6, analytical procedures are performed at three different stages of the audit: in the planning stage to help the auditor decide the other evidence needed to satisfy acceptable audit risk, during the audit in conjunction with tests of details of balances as part of substantive procedures, and near the end of the audit as a final test of reasonableness.

Section 5301, Analysis, requires the use of analytical procedures during both the planning phase and the completion phase of the audit; use of analytical procedures as a substantive procedure is optional.

Choosing the appropriate analytical procedures requires the auditor to use professional judgment. The appropriate use of analytical procedures and illustrative ratios are included in Chapter 6. There are also examples in several subsequent chapters. For example, page 464 illustrates several analytical procedures for the audit of accounts receivable.

TESTS OF DETAILS OF BALANCES

The methodology for designing tests of details of balances is oriented to the balance-related audit objectives developed in Chapter 5 (pages 145–147). For example, if the auditor is verifying accounts receivable, the planned tests must be sufficient to satisfy each of the objectives. In planning tests of details of balances to satisfy those objectives, many auditors follow a methodology such as the one shown in Figure 10-8 (page 322) for accounts receivable. The design of these tests is normally the most dif-

FIGURE 10-7

Three-Step Approach to Designing Tests of Controls

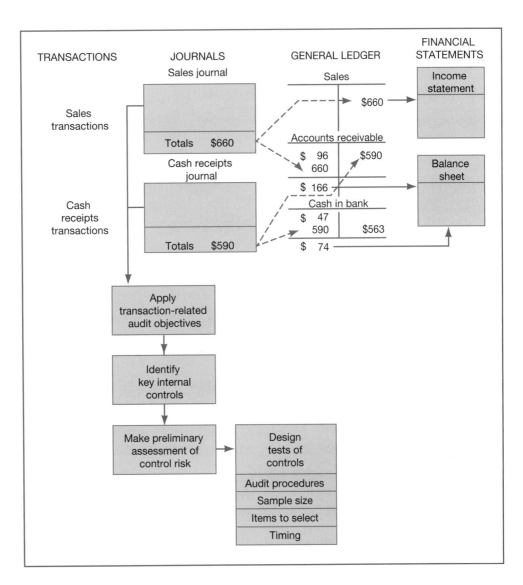

ficult part of the entire planning process. Designing such procedures is subjective and requires considerable professional judgment.

A discussion of the key decisions in designing tests of details of balances as shown in Figure 10-8 follows.

Set materiality and assess acceptable audit risk and inherent risk for accounts receivable Setting the preliminary judgment about materiality for the audit as a whole is an auditor decision that was discussed in Chapter 8. A lower materiality would result in more testing of details than a higher amount. Some auditors may allocate materiality to individual balances, but most do not. Analytical review for planning purposes, used together with a good knowledge of business and the industry, allows the auditor to identify obvious warning signals.

As discussed in Chapter 8, acceptable audit risk is normally decided for the audit as a whole, rather than by cycle. An exception might be when the auditor believes that a misstatement of a specific account, such as accounts receivable, would negatively affect users more than the same size misstatement of any other account. For example, if accounts receivable is pledged to a bank as security on a loan, audit risk may be set lower for sales and collections than for other cycles.

Inherent risk is assessed by identifying any aspect of the client's history, environment, or operations that indicates a high likelihood of misstatement in the current

FIGURE 10-8

Methodology for Designing Tests of Details of Financial Statement Balances — Accounts Receivable

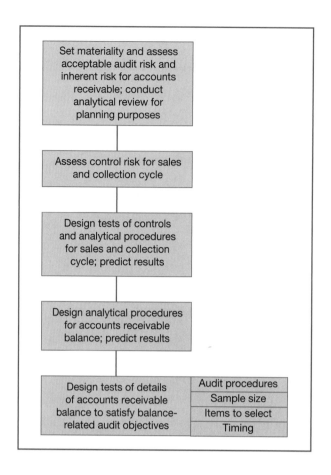

year's financial statements. This emphasizes the need for a broad-based knowledge of business that links risks to the external business environment. Considerations affecting inherent risk (discussed in Chapter 8) applied to accounts receivable include makeup of accounts receivable, nature of the client's business, initial engagement, and so on. An account balance for which inherent risk has been assessed as high would result in more evidence accumulation than for an account with low inherent risk.

Inherent risk also can be extended to individual audit objectives. For example, because of adverse economic conditions in the client's industry, the auditor may conclude that there is a high risk of uncollectible accounts receivable (realizable-value objective). Inherent risk could still be low for all other objectives.

Assess control risk Control risk is evaluated in the manner discussed in Chapter 9 and in earlier parts of this chapter. That methodology would be applied to both sales and collection in the audit of accounts receivable. Effective controls reduce control risk and therefore the evidence required for substantive procedures; inadequate controls increase the substantive evidence needed.

Design tests of controls and analytical procedures and predict results The methodology for designing tests of controls and analytical procedures was discussed earlier in this section and will be illustrated in subsequent chapters. The tests are designed with the expectation that certain results will be obtained. These predicted results affect the design of tests of details of balances as discussed below.

Design tests of details of balances to satisfy balance-related audit objectives The planned tests of details of balances include audit procedures, sample size, items to select, and timing. Procedures must be selected and designed for each account and each balance-related audit objective within each account. The balance-related audit objectives for accounts receivable are shown on page 462.

A difficulty the auditor faces in designing tests of details of balances is the need to predict the outcome of the tests of controls and analytical procedures before they are performed. This is necessary because the auditor should design tests of details of balances during the planning phase, but the appropriate design depends on the outcome of the other tests. In planning tests of details of balances, the auditor usually predicts that there will be few or no exceptions in tests of controls and analytical procedures, unless there are reasons to believe otherwise. If the results of the tests of controls and analytical procedures are not consistent with the predictions, the tests of details of balances will need to be changed as the audit progresses.

The discussion about the approach to designing tests of details of balances applied to accounts receivable is summarized in Figure 10-9. The unshaded portion of the upper part of the figure is the financial information being audited. The light shading in the lower left is the design of tests of controls as discussed in Figure 10-7. The figure shows that the tests of controls affect the design of the tests of details of balances.

FIGURE 10-9
Approach to Designing Tests of Details of Balances

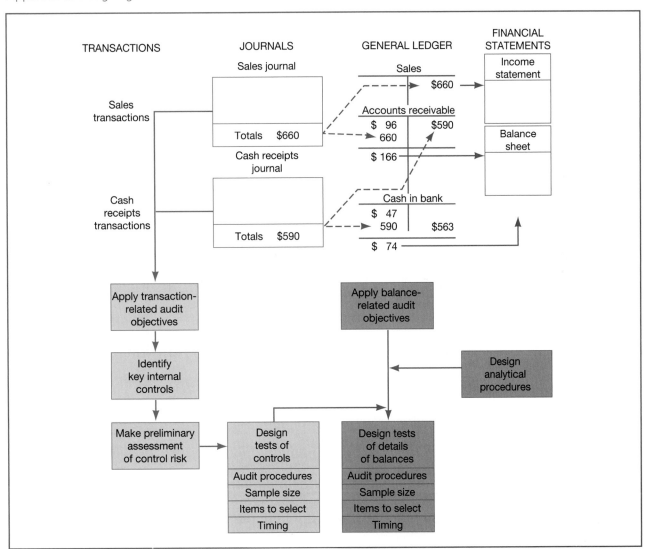

Note: These tests are in the context of planning processes for the overall audit.

The lower right portion shows the design of tests of details of balances and the factors affecting that decision.

One of the most difficult parts of auditing is properly applying the factors that affect tests of details of balances. Each of the factors is subjective, requiring considerable professional judgment. The impact of each factor on tests of details of balances is equally subjective. For example, if inherent risk is reduced from medium to low, there is agreement that tests of details of balances can be reduced. Deciding the specific effect on audit procedures, sample size, timing, and items to select is a difficult decision.

LEVEL OF DISAGGREGATION OF PLANNING ACTIVITIES

The various planning activities discussed in Chapters 5 through 10 are applied at different levels of disaggregation, depending on the nature of the activity. Table 10-3 shows the primary planning activities and the levels of disaggregation normally applied. These levels of disaggregation range from the overall audit to the audit objective for each account. For example, when the auditor obtains background information about the client's business and industry, it pertains to the overall audit. As the audit progresses, the information will first be used in assessing acceptable audit risk and inherent risk and later is likely to affect tests of details of balances. The level of disaggregation in Table 10-3 could be greater than indicated; for example, inherent risk could be assessed at the transaction level.

TABLE 10-3

DISAGGREGATION LEVEL TO WHICH PLANNING ACTIVITIES ARE APPLIED

			LEVEL OF DISAGGREGATION		
PLANNING ACTIVITY	Overall Audit	Cycle	Account	Transaction-Related Audit Objective	Balance-Related Audit Objective
Preplan audit	P				
Obtain background information	P				
Obtain information about client's legal obligations	P				
Set preliminary judgment about materiality	P				
Conduct analytical procedures for planning purposes	P				
Assess acceptable audit risk	P				
Assess inherent risk			P		

Understand internal control
  Control environment
  Accounting system
  Control procedures
	P	P
		P			

Identify key internal controls				P	
Identify internal control weaknesses				P	
Assess planned control risk				P	
Design tests of controls				P	
Assess control risk achieved				P	
Design substantive analytical procedures			P		
Design tests of details of balances					P

P = Primary level to which planning activity is applied.

ILLUSTRATIVE AUDIT PROGRAM

Table 10-4 shows the tests of details of balances segment of an audit program for accounts receivable. The format used relates the audit procedures to the balance-related audit objectives. Notice that most procedures satisfy more than one objective. Also, more than one audit procedure is used for each objective. Audit procedures can be added or deleted as the auditor considers necessary. Sample size, items to select, and timing can also be changed for most procedures.

TABLE 10-4

TESTS OF DETAILS OF BALANCES AUDIT PROGRAM FOR ACCOUNTS RECEIVABLE

SAMPLE SIZE	ITEMS TO SELECT	TIMING*	TESTS OF DETAILS OF BALANCES AUDIT PROCEDURES	Detail tie-in	Existence	Completeness	Accuracy	Classification	Cutoff	Realizable value	Rights	Presentation and disclosure
Trace 20 items; foot 2 pages and all subtotals	Random	I	1. Obtain an aged list of receivables: trace open items to supporting invoice detail, foot schedule and trace to general ledger.	x								
All	All	Y	2. Obtain an analysis of the allowance for doubtful accounts and bad debt expense: test accuracy, examine authorization for write-offs, and trace to general ledger.	x	x	x	x			x		
100	30 largest 70 random	I	3. Obtain direct confirmation of accounts receivable and perform alternative procedures for nonresponses.		x	x	x	x	x		x	
NA	NA	Y	4. Review accounts receivable control account for the period. Investigate the nature of, and review support for, any large or unusual entries or any entries not arising from normal journal sources. Also investigate any significant increases or decreases in sales toward year end.		x		x	x	x		x	x
All	All	Y	5. Review receivables for any that have been assigned or discounted.								x	x
NA	NA	Y	6. Investigate collectibility of account balances.							x		
All	All	Y	7. Review lists of balances for amounts due from related parties or employees, credit balances, and unusual items, as well as notes receivable due after one year.		x			x				x
30 transactions for sales and cash receipts; 10 for credit memos	50% before and 50% after year end	Y	8. Determine that proper cutoff procedures were applied at the balance sheet date to ensure that sales, cash receipts, and credit memos have been recorded in the correct period.						x			

*I = Interim; Y = Year end; NA = Not applicable.

The audit program in Table 10-4 was developed after consideration of all the factors affecting tests of details of balances and is based on several assumptions about inherent risk, control risk, and the results of tests of controls and analytical procedures. As indicated, if those assumptions are materially incorrect, the planned audit program will require revision. For example, analytical procedures could indicate potential errors for several balance-related audit objectives, tests of controls results could indicate weak internal controls, or new facts could cause the auditor to change inherent risk.

AUDIT PROGRAMS USED IN PRACTICE

Most large public accounting firms develop their own standard audit programs, organized by industry, linked by audit objective often to data bases including lists of expected controls and likely audit tests. Smaller firms often purchase similar audit programs from outside organizations. Standard audit programs are normally computerized and can easily be modified to meet the circumstances of individual audit engagements. One example of standard audit programs available for purchase is the CICA's *Professional Engagement Manual (PEM). PEM* is available in paper form, on diskette, or on CD-ROM and contains audit programs as well as general and industry-specific checklists that auditors can use and modify for individual engagements.

Standard audit programs, whether developed internally or purchased from an outside organization, can dramatically increase audit efficiency if they are used properly. They should *not* be used, however, as a substitute for an auditor's professional judgment. Because each audit is different, it is usually necessary to add, modify, or delete steps within a standard audit program in order to accumulate sufficient and competent evidence.

Professional Engagement Manual
www.cica.ca/cica/cicawebsite.nsf/public/99250

RELATIONSHIP OF TRANSACTION-RELATED AUDIT OBJECTIVES TO BALANCE-RELATED AUDIT OBJECTIVES

OBJECTIVE 10-5

Understand the relationship between transaction-related audit objectives and balance-related audit objectives.

It has already been shown that tests of details of balances must be designed to satisfy balance-related audit objectives for each account and the extent of these tests can be reduced when transaction-related audit objectives have been satisfied by tests of controls. It is, therefore, important to understand how each transaction-related audit objective relates to each balance-related audit objective. The following transaction-related audit objectives have a direct relationship with the balance-related audit objective:

TRANSACTION-RELATED AUDIT OBJECTIVE	BALANCE-RELATED AUDIT OBJECTIVE
Occurrence	Existence or completeness
Completeness	Existence or completeness
Accuracy	Accuracy
Classification	Classification
Timing	Cutoff
Posting and summarization	Detail tie-in

This direct relationship can be illustrated by looking at sales transactions. If there are controls to ensure that all sales transactions that occur are recorded in the accounts receivable, then these controls can provide assurance with respect to the completeness balance-related audit objective.

However, even when all transaction-related audit objectives are met, the auditor will still rely primarily on substantive tests of balances to meet the following balance-related audit objectives: realizable value, rights and obligations, and presentation and disclosure, since few internal controls are related to these audit objectives. Some substantive tests of balances are also likely for the other balance-related audit objectives, depending on the results of the tests of controls.

The relationship of transaction-related audit objectives to balance-related audit objectives is shown in greater detail in Figure 14-3, page 463. That figure shows how transaction-related audit objectives for sales and cash receipts affect accounts receivable balance-related audit objectives. Notice in Figure 14-3 that the existence transaction-related audit objective for sales affects the existence balance-related audit objective for accounts receivable, whereas the existence transaction-related audit objective for cash receipts affects the completeness balance-related audit objective for accounts receivable. The reason is that sales increase accounts receivable, whereas cash receipts decrease accounts receivable.

SUMMARY OF THE AUDIT PROCESS

OBJECTIVE 10-6

Integrate the four phases of the audit process.

The four phases of an audit were introduced at the end of Chapter 5. Considerable portions of Chapters 6 through 10 have discussed the different aspects of the process. Figure 10-10 on page 328 shows the four phases for the entire audit process. Table 10-5 on page 329 shows the timing of the tests in each phase for an audit with a December 31 balance sheet date.

PHASE I: PLAN AND DESIGN AN AUDIT APPROACH

Chapters 6 through 10 have emphasized various aspects of planning the audit. At the end of phase I, the auditor should have a well-defined audit plan and a specific audit program for the entire audit.

Obtaining information during preplanning, obtaining background information, obtaining information about the client's legal obligations, and performing preliminary analytical procedures (first four boxes in Figure 10-10) help to assess acceptable audit risk and inherent risk. Excellent knowledge of business with linkages to the external environment assists in the evaluation of these risks. An understanding of internal control is required to provided a planned control risk. Assessments of materiality, acceptable audit risk, inherent risk, and control risk are used to develop an overall audit plan and audit program.

PHASE II: PERFORM TESTS OF CONTROLS

Performance of the tests of controls occurs during this phase. The objectives of phase II are (1) to obtain evidence in support of the specific controls that contribute to the auditor's assessed control risk (i.e., where it is reduced below maximum) and (2) when dual purpose tests are used, to obtain evidence in support of the monetary correctness of transactions. The former objective is met by performing tests of controls, and the latter by performing substantive procedures. Many of both types of tests are conducted simultaneously on the same transactions. When controls are not considered effective, or when control deviations are discovered, substantive tests can be expanded in phase III.

Since the results of tests of controls are a major determinant of the extent of substantive procedures (i.e., analytical procedures and tests of details of balances), they are often performed two or three months before the balance sheet date or during regular quarterly visits to the client. This helps the auditor plan for contingencies, revise the audit program for unexpected results, and complete the audit as soon as possible after the balance sheet date.

FIGURE 10-10
Summary of the
Audit Process

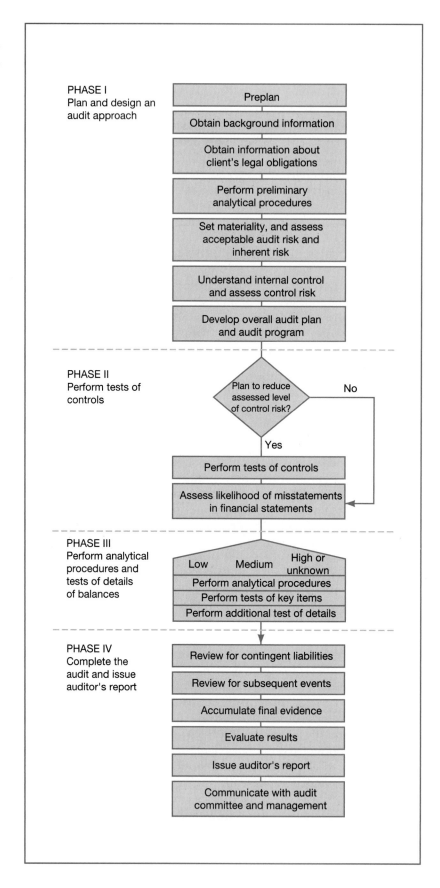

PHASE I
Plan and design an
audit approach

Preplan

Obtain background information

Obtain information about
client's legal obligations

Perform preliminary
analytical procedures

Set materiality, and assess
acceptable audit risk and
inherent risk

Understand internal control
and assess control risk

Develop overall audit plan
and audit program

PHASE II
Perform tests of
controls

Plan to reduce
assessed level
of control risk?   No

Yes

Perform tests of controls

Assess likelihood of misstatements
in financial statements

PHASE III
Perform analytical
procedures and
tests of details
of balances

Low   Medium   High or
unknown
Perform analytical procedures
Perform tests of key items
Perform additional test of details

PHASE IV
Complete the
audit and issue
auditor's report

Review for contingent liabilities

Review for subsequent events

Accumulate final evidence

Evaluate results

Issue auditor's report

Communicate with audit
committee and management

PHASE III: PERFORM ANALYTICAL PROCEDURES AND TESTS OF DETAILS OF BALANCES

The objective of phase III is to obtain sufficient additional evidence to determine whether the ending balances and footnotes in financial statements are fairly stated. The nature and extent of the work will depend heavily on the findings of the two previous phases.

There are two general categories of phase III procedures: analytical procedures and tests of details of balances. Analytical procedures are those that assess the overall reasonableness of transactions and balances. Tests of details of balances are specific procedures intended to test for monetary errors or fraud and other irregularities in the balances in the financial statements. Certain key transactions and amounts are so important that each one must be audited. Other items can be sampled.

Table 10-5 shows most analytical procedures being done both before and after the balance sheet date. Because of their low cost, it is common to use analytical procedures whenever they are relevant. They are frequently done early with preliminary data prior to year end as a means of planning and directing other audit tests to specific areas. But the greatest benefit from calculating ratios and making comparisons occurs after the client has finished preparing its financial statements. Ideally, these analytical procedures are done before tests of details of balances so that they can then be used to determine how extensively to test balances. They are also used as a part of performing tests of balances and during the completion phase of the audit.

Table 10-5 also shows that tests of details of balances are normally done last. On some audits, all are done after the balance sheet date. When clients want to issue statements soon after the balance sheet date, however, the more time-consuming tests of details of balances will be done at interim dates prior to year end with additional work being done to "roll forward" the audited interim-date balances to year end. (This involves substantive work on journal entries and other activities during this period.) Substantive tests of balances performed before year end provide less assurance and are not normally done unless internal controls are effective.

PHASE IV: COMPLETE THE AUDIT

After the first three phases are completed, it is necessary to accumulate some additional evidence for the financial statements, summarize the results, issue the auditor's report and perform other forms of communication. This phase has several parts.

Review for contingent liabilities Contingent liabilities are potential liabilities that must be disclosed in the client's footnotes. Auditors must make sure the disclosure is adequate. A considerable portion of the search for contingent liabilities is done during the first three phases, but additional testing is done during phase IV. Contingent liabilities are studied in Chapter 21.

TABLE 10-5

TIMING OF TESTS

Phase I	Plan and design audit approach. Update understanding of internal control. Update audit program. Perform preliminary analytical procedures.	31-8-98	
Phase II	Perform tests of controls for first 9 months of the year.	30-9-98	
Phase III	Confirm accounts receivable. Observe inventory.	31-10-98	
	Count cash. Perform cutoff tests. Request various other confirmations.	31-12-98	Balance sheet date
	Do analytical procedures, complete tests of controls, and do most tests of details of balances.	7-1-99	Books closed
Phase IV	Summarize results, review for contingent liabilities, review for subsequent events, accumulate final evidence including analytical procedures, and finalize audit.	8-3-99	Last date of field work
	Issue auditor's report.	15-3-99	

Review for subsequent events   Occasionally, events occurring subsequent to the balance sheet date but before the issuance of the financial statements and auditor's report will have an effect on the information presented in the financial statements. Specific review procedures are designed to bring to the auditor's attention any subsequent events that may require recognition in the financial statements. Review for subsequent events is also studied in Chapter 21 .

Accumulate final evidence   In addition to the evidence obtained for each cycle during phases I and II and for each account during phase III, it is also necessary to gather evidence for the financial statements as a whole during the completion phase. This evidence includes performing final analytical procedures; evaluating the going concern assumption; obtaining a client representation letter; and reading the annual report to make sure that the financial statements and the auditor's report have been accurately reproduced in the annual report, that the annual report is consistent with the financial statements, and that there are no material misstatements of fact in the annual report.

Issue auditor's report   The type of auditor's report issued depends on the evidence accumulated and the audit findings. The appropriate reports for differing circumstances were studied in Chapter 2.

Communicate with audit committee and management   The auditor should communicate internal control-related matters to and discuss any problems encountered on the audit with the audit committee or senior management. In addition, paragraphs 5135.20, 5136.28, and 5405.13 require the auditor to communicate certain other matters to the audit committee or management upon completion of the audit or sooner. Although not required, auditors often also make suggestions to management to improve business performance.

ESSENTIAL TERMS

Analytical procedures — use of comparisons and relationships to determine whether account balances or other data appear reasonable (p. 313).

Audit evidence mix — the combination of the four types of tests to obtain sufficient appropriate audit evidence for a cycle. There are likely to be variations in the mix from cycle to cycle depending on the circumstances of the audit (p. 318).

Dual purpose tests — the performing of auditing procedures that are both tests of controls and substantive procedures on the same sample of transactions or account balances for efficiency (p. 313).

Phases of the audit process — the four aspects of a complete audit: (1) plan and design an audit approach, (2) perform tests of controls, (3) perform analytical procedures and tests of details of balances, and (4) complete the audit and issue the auditor's report (p. 327).

Procedures to obtain an understanding — procedures used by the auditor to gather evidence about the design and implementation of specific controls (p. 311).

Tests of controls — audit procedures to test the effectiveness of controls in support of a reduced assessed control risk (p. 311).

Tests of details of balances — audit procedures testing for monetary errors or fraud and other irregularities to determine whether the nine balance-related audit objectives have been satisfied for each significant account balance (p. 314).

Types of tests — the four categories of audit tests auditors use to determine whether financial statements are fairly stated: procedures to obtain an understanding of internal control, tests of controls, analytical procedures, and tests of details of balances (p. 311).

REVIEW QUESTIONS

10-1   What are the four types of tests auditors use to determine whether financial statements are fairly stated? Identify which tests are performed to assess control risk and which tests are performed to achieve planned detection risk.

10-2   What is the purpose of tests of controls? Identify specific accounts on the financial statements that are affected by performing tests of controls for the acquisition and payment cycle.

10-3   Distinguish between a test of controls and a substantive procedure. Give two examples of each.

10-4   Explain what is meant by "reperformance." Give an example.

10-5 State a test of controls audit procedure to test the effectiveness of the following control: approved wage rates are used in calculating employees' earnings. State a test of controls audit procedure to determine whether approved wage rates are actually used in calculating employees' earnings.

10-6 An auditor may perform tests of controls and substantive procedures simultaneously as a matter of audit convenience. However, the substantive procedures and sample size are, in part, dependent upon the results of the tests of controls. How can the auditor resolve this apparent inconsistency?

10-7 Evaluate the following statement: Tests of sales and collection transactions are such an essential part of every audit that I like to perform them as near the end of the audit as possible. By that time, I have a fairly good understanding of the client's business and its internal controls because confirmations, cutoff tests, and other procedures have already been completed.

10-8 Explain how the calculation and comparison to previous years of the gross margin percentage and the ratio of accounts receivable to sales are related to the confirmation of accounts receivable and other tests of the accuracy of accounts receivable.

10-9 Distinguish between a combined audit approach and a substantive audit approach. Give one example of when each might be appropriate for the acquisition and payment cycle.

10-10 Assume that the client's internal controls over the recording and classifying of capital asset additions are considered weak because the individual responsible for recording new acquisitions has inadequate technical training and limited experience in accounting. How would this situation affect the evidence you should accumulate in auditing permanent assets as compared with another audit in which the controls are excellent? Be as specific as possible.

10-11 For each of the seven types of evidence discussed in Chapter 6, identify whether it is applicable for procedures to obtain an understanding of internal control, tests of controls, analytical procedures, and tests of details of balances.

10-12 Rank the following types of tests in terms of cost, from most to least costly: analytical procedures, tests of details of balances, procedures to gain an understanding of internal controls, and tests of controls.

10-13 In Figure 10-4 on page 317, explain the difference among C_3, C_2, and C_1. Explain the circumstances under which it would be a good decision to obtain audit assurance from substantive tests at part C_1. Do the same for parts C_2 and C_3.

10-14 The following are three decision factors related to the assessed level of control risk: effectiveness of internal controls, cost-effectiveness of a reduced assessed level of control risk, and results of tests of controls. Identify the combination of conditions for these three factors that is required before a reduction in substantive procedures is permitted.

10-15 Figure 10-5 on page 318 illustrates variations in the emphasis on different types of audit tests. What are the benefits to the auditor of identifying the best mix of tests?

10-16 State the three-step approach to designing tests of controls.

10-17 Explain the relationship between the methodology for designing tests of transactions in Figure 10-6 (page 320) to the methodology for designing tests of details of balances in Figure 10-8 (page 322).

10-18 Why is it desirable to design tests of details of balances before performing tests of controls? State the assumptions the auditor must make in doing that. What does the auditor do if the assumptions prove to be incorrect?

10-19 Explain the relationship of materiality available for unanticipated misstatements, inherent risk, and control risk to planned tests of details of balances.

10-20 List the nine balance-related audit objectives in the verification of the ending balance in inventory, and provide one useful audit procedure for each of the objectives.

10-21 Why do auditors frequently consider it desirable to perform audit tests throughout the year rather than wait until year end? List several examples of evidence that can be accumulated prior to year end.

MULTIPLE CHOICE QUESTIONS

10-22 The following questions concern types of audit tests. Choose the best response.

a. The auditor looks for an indication on duplicate sales invoices to see if the invoices have been verified. This is an example of
   (1) a test of details of balances.
   (2) an analytical procedure.
   (3) a dual purpose test.
   (4) a test of controls.

b. Analytical procedures may be classified as being primarily
   (1) substantive procedures.
   (2) tests of ratios.
   (3) tests of controls.
   (4) tests of details of balances.

c. Failure to detect material dollar misstatements in the financial statements is a risk that the auditor mitigates primarily by
   (1) performing tests of controls.
   (2) evaluating internal control.
   (3) obtaining a client representation letter.
   (4) performing substantive procedures.

d. Before reducing assessed control risk, the auditor obtains a reasonable degree of assurance that internal control is operating as planned. The auditor obtains this assurance by performing
   (1) analytical procedures.
   (2) substantive procedures.
   (3) tests of controls.
   (4) tests of trends and ratios.

e. The auditor faces a risk that the examination will not detect material misstatements that occur in the accounting process. In regard to minimizing this risk, the auditor relies primarily on

(2) substantive procedures.
(3) tests of controls.
(4) internal control.
(1) statistical analysis.

(AICPA adapted)

10-23 The following questions deal with tests of controls. Choose the best response.

a. Which of the following statements relating to tests of controls is most accurate?
(1) Auditing procedures cannot concurrently provide both evidence of the effectiveness of internal control and evidence required for substantive procedures.
(2) Tests of controls ordinarily should be performed as of the balance sheet date or during the period subsequent to that date.
(3) Tests of controls include observations of the proper segregation of duties that ordinarily may be limited to the normal audit period.
(4) Tests of controls should be based on proper application of an appropriate statistical sampling plan.

b. The two phases of the auditor's involvement with internal control are sometimes referred to as "understanding and assessment" and "tests of controls." In the tests of controls phase, the auditor attempts to
(1) obtain sufficient appropriate audit evidence to afford a reasonable basis for the auditor's opinion.
(2) obtain assurances that informative disclosures in the financial statements are reasonably adequate.
(3) obtain a reasonable degree of assurance that the client's controls are in use and are operating as planned.
(4) obtain knowledge and understanding of the client's prescribed procedures and methods.

c. Which of the following is ordinarily considered a test of controls audit procedure?
(1) Send confirmation letters to banks.
(2) Obtain or prepare reconciliation of bank accounts as of the balance sheet date.
(3) Count and list cash on hand.
(4) Examine signatures on cheques.

(AICPA adapted)

DISCUSSION QUESTIONS AND PROBLEMS

10-24 The following are 11 audit procedures taken from an audit program:

1. Add the supplier balances in the accounts payable master file, and compare the total with the general ledger.
2. Examine vendors' invoices to verify the ending balance in accounts payable.
3. Compare the balance in employee benefits expense with previous years. The comparison takes the increase in employee benefits rates into account.
4. Discuss the duties of the cash disbursements bookkeeper with him or her, and observe whether he or she has responsibility for handling cash or preparing the bank reconciliation.
5. Confirm accounts payable balances directly with vendors.
6. Use generalized audit software to run a gap test on the cheques issued during the year. (Print a list of cheque numbers omitted from the normal cheque number sequencing.)
7. Examine the treasurer's initials on monthly bank reconciliations as an indication of whether they have been reviewed.
8. Examine vendors' invoices and other documentation in support of recorded transactions in the acquisitions journal.
9. Multiply the commission rate by total sales, and compare the result with commission expense.
10. Examine vendors' invoices and other supporting documents to determine whether large amounts in the repair and maintenance account should be capitalized.
11. Examine the initials of vendors' invoices that indicate internal verification of pricing, extending, and footing by a clerk.

Required

a. Indicate whether each procedure is a test of controls, an analytical procedure, or a test of details of balances.

b. Identify the type of evidence for each procedure.

10-25 The following are audit procedures from different transaction cycles:

1. Create test data equivalent to one day's cheque issuance. Compare the total cash disbursement amount on the cheque listing to the general ledger posting.
2. Select a sample of entries from the accounts payable history file, and trace each one to the related vendor's invoice to determine if one exists.
3. Compute inventory turnover for each major product and compare with previous years.
4. Confirm a sample of notes payable balances, interest rates, and collateral with lenders.
5. Add the accounts payable balances in the supplier master file, and compare the total with the general ledger.
6. Examine documentation for acquisition transactions before and after the balance sheet date to determine whether the transactions are recorded in the proper period.
7. Observe whether cash is prelisted daily at the time it is received by the president's secretary.
8. Inquire of the credit manager whether each account receivable on the aged trial balance is collectible.

Required

a. For each audit procedure, identify the transaction cycle being audited.

b. For each audit procedure, identify the type of evidence.

c. For each audit procedure, identify whether it is a test of controls or a substantive procedure.

d. For each substantive audit procedure, identify whether it is a test of details of balances or an analytical procedure.

e. For each test of controls, identify the transaction-related audit objective or objectives being satisfied.

f. For each test of details of balances procedure, identify the balance-related audit objective or objectives being satisfied.

10-26 The following are independent internal controls commonly found in the acquisition and payment cycle. Each control is to be considered independently.

1. At the end of each month, an accounting clerk accounts for all prenumbered receiving reports (documents evidencing the receipt of goods) issued during the month, and he traces each one to the related vendor's invoice and purchase journal entry. The clerk's tests do not include testing quantity or description of the merchandise received.

2. The cash disbursement bookkeeper is prohibited from handling cash. The bank account is reconciled by another person even though the bookkeeper has sufficient expertise and time to do it.

3. Before a cheque is prepared to pay for purchases by the accounts payable department, the related purchase order and receiving report are attached to the vendor's invoice being paid. A clerk compares the quantity on the invoice with the receiving report and purchase order, compares the price with the purchase order, recomputes the extensions, re-adds the total, and examines the account number indicated on the invoice to determine whether it is properly classified. He indicates his performance of these procedures by initialling the invoice.

4. Before a cheque is signed by the controller, she examines the supporting documentation accompanying the cheque. At that time, she initials each vendor's invoice to indicate her approval.

5. After the controller signs the cheques, her secretary writes the cheque number and the date the cheque was issued on each of the supporting documents to prevent their re-use.

Required

a. For each of the internal controls, state the transaction-related audit objective(s) the control is meant to fulfill.

b. For each control, list one test of controls the auditor could perform to test the effectiveness of the control.

c. For each control, list one test of controls involving reperformance that the auditor could perform to determine whether financial errors or fraud and other irregularities are actually taking place.

10-27 The following internal controls for the acquisition and payment cycle were selected from a standard internal control questionnaire.

1. Vendors' invoices are recalculated prior to payment.

2. Approved price lists are used for acquisitions.
3. Prenumbered receiving reports are prepared as support for purchases and are numerically accounted for.
4. Dates on receiving reports are compared with vendors' invoices before entry into the accounts payable system.
5. The accounts payable system is updated, balanced, and reconciled to the general ledger monthly.
6. Account classifications are reviewed by someone other than the preparer.
7. All cheques are signed by the owner or the manager.
8. The cheque signer compares data on supporting documents with cheques.
9. All supporting documents are cancelled after entry.
10. Cheques are mailed by the owner or manager or a person under his or her supervision after signing.

Required

a. For each control, state which transaction-related audit objective(s) is (are) applicable.

b. For each control, write an audit procedure that could be used to test the control for effectiveness.

c. For each control, identify a likely misstatement, assuming the control does not exist or is not functioning.

d. For each likely misstatement, identify a substantive audit procedure to determine if the misstatement exists.

10-28 Jennifer Schaefer, a public accountant, follows the philosophy of performing interim tests of controls on every December 31 audit as a means of keeping overtime to a minimum. Typically, the interim tests are performed some time between August and November.

Required

a. Evaluate her decision to perform interim tests of controls.

b. Under what circumstances is it acceptable for her to perform no additional tests of controls work as part of the year-end audit tests?

c. If she decides to perform no additional testing, what is the effect on other tests she performs during the remainder of the engagement?

10-29 In the box at the top of the right-hand column are several decisions that the auditor must make in an audit. Letters indicate alternative conclusions that could be made.

Required

a. Identify the sequence in which the auditor should make decisions 1 through 4.

b. For the audit of sales, collections, and accounts receivable, an auditor reached the following conclusions: A, D, E, and H. Put the letters in the appropriate sequence, and evaluate whether the auditor's logic was reasonable. Explain your answer.

DECISIONS	ALTERNATIVE CONCLUSIONS
1. Determine whether it is cost-effective to perform tests of controls	A. It is cost-effective B. It is not cost-effective
2. Perform tests of details of balances	C. Perform reduced tests D. Perform expanded tests
3. Assess internal control risk	E. Controls are effective F. Controls are not effective
4. Perform tests of controls	G. Controls are effective H. Controls are not effective

c. For the audit of inventory and related inventory cost records, an auditor reached the following conclusions: B, C, E, and G. Put the letters in the appropriate sequence, and evaluate whether the auditor used good professional judgment. Explain your answer.

d. For the audit of property, plant, and equipment and related acquisition records, an auditor reached the following conclusions: A, C, F, and G. Put the letters in the appropriate sequence, and evaluate whether the auditor used good professional judgment. Explain your answer.

e. For the audit of payroll expenses and related liabilities, an auditor recorded the following conclusions: D and F. Put the letters in the appropriate sequence, and evaluate whether the auditor used good professional judgment. Explain your answer.

10-30 The following are three situations in which the auditor is required to develop an audit strategy:

1. The client has inventory at approximately 50 locations in the three Maritime provinces. The inventory is difficult to count and can be observed only by travelling by automobile. The internal controls over acquisitions, payments, and perpetual records are considered effective. This is the fifth year that you have done the audit, and audit results in past years have always been excellent.

2. This is the first year of an audit of a medium-sized company that is considering selling its business because of severe underfinancing. A review of the acquisition and payment cycle indicates that controls over disbursements are excellent, but controls over accounts payable cannot be considered effective. The client lacks receiving reports and a policy as to the proper timing to record acquisitions. When you review the general ledger, you observe that there are many adjusting entries to correct accounts payable.

3. You are doing the audit of a small loan company with extensive receivables from customers. Controls over granting loans, collections, and loans outstanding are considered effective, and there is extensive follow-up of all outstanding loans weekly. You have recommended a computer system for the past two years, but management believes the cost is too great, given the company's low profitability. Collections are an ongoing problem because many of the customers have severe financial problems. Because of adverse economic conditions, loans receivable have significantly increased and collections are less than normal. In previous years, you have had relatively few adjusting entries.

Required

a. For audit one, recommend an evidence mix for the four types of tests for the audit of inventory and cost of goods sold. Justify your answer.

b. For audit two, recommend an evidence mix for the audit of acquisitions and accounts payable. Justify your answer.

c. For audit three, recommend an evidence mix of the audit of outstanding loans. Justify your answer.

10-31 Brad Jackson was assigned to the audit of a client that had not been audited by any public accounting firm in the preceding year. In conducting the audit, he did no testing of the beginning balance of accounts receivable, inventory, or accounts payable on the grounds that the auditor's report was being limited to the ending balance sheet, the income statement, and the cash flow. No comparative financial statements are to be issued.

Required

a. Explain the error in Jackson's reasoning.

b. Suggest an approach Jackson can follow in verifying the beginning balance in accounts receivable.

c. Why does the same problem not exist in the verification of beginning balances on continuing audit engagements?

10-32 Kim Bryan, a new staff auditor, is confused by the inconsistency of the three audit partners to whom she has been assigned on her first three audit engagements. On the first engagement, she spent a considerable amount of time in the audit of cash disbursements by examining cancelled cheques and supporting documentation, but almost no time was spent in the verification of capital assets. On the second engagement, a different partner had her do less intensive tests in the cash disbursements area and take smaller sample sizes than in the first audit even though the company was much larger. On her most recent engagement under a third audit partner, there was a thorough test of cash disbursement transactions, far beyond that of the other two audits, and an extensive verification of capital assets. In fact, this partner insisted on a complete physical examination of all capital assets recorded on the books. The total audit time on the most recent audit was longer than that of either of the first two audits in spite of the smaller size of the company. Bryan's conclusion is that the amount of evidence to accumulate depends on the audit partner in charge of the engagement.

Required

a. State several factors that could explain the difference in the amount of evidence accumulated in each of the three audit engagements as well as the total time spent.

b. What could the audit partners have done to help Bryan understand the difference in the audit emphasis on the three audits?

c. Explain how these three audits are useful in developing Bryan's professional judgment. How could the quality of her judgment have been improved on the audits?

10-33 The following are parts of a typical audit for a company with a fiscal year end of July 31.

1. Confirm accounts payable.
2. Do tests of controls for acquisitions and payroll.
3. Do other tests of details of balances for accounts payable.
4. Do tests for review of subsequent events.
5. Preplan the audit.
6. Issue the auditor's report.
7. Understand internal control and assess control risk.
8. Do analytical procedures for accounts payable.
9. Set acceptable audit risk and decide preliminary judgment about materiality.

Required

a. Put parts 1 through 9 of the audit in the sequential order in which you would expect them to be performed in a typical audit.

b. Identify those parts that would frequently be done before July 31.

CASES

10-34 Yope Plastics Limited (YPL) is a federally incorporated company that manufactures moulded plastics for household and some industrial uses. It has a large number of customers throughout Canada. Some items are custom made but most are for stock. It is estimated that sales for the current year will be approximately $5,800,000 and net income $265,000. Major assets are accounts receivable ($1,400,00) and inventories ($1,700,000 of which $500,000 is raw materials, $200,000 work in process and $1,000,000 finished goods). Major liabilities are bank debt amounting to $900,000 and accounts payable and accruals of $650,000. The year end is December 31.

The company has been managed by Mr. Yope, the owner, assisted by Mr. Grey, a competent but rather unimaginative treasurer/controller. The accounting systems have been adequate but not elaborate. No serious weaknesses in internal control have existed. The owner has had a rule-of-thumb method of calculating inventory balances in interim periods which is based on his knowledge of the operations and a tour of the plant. The inventory computed in this way by the owner has always coincided fairly closely with the audited inventory figure at the year end. The general ledger inventory accounts have been updated annually at the December 31 year end.

The annual financial statements have been used for Mr. Yope's own purposes, for income tax purposes, and for the bank. The financial statements were basically prepared by the auditor, who also prepared a number of detailed back-up schedules.

Fairly, Small & Co. has been the auditor for many years, is very familiar with the company, and, among other services, carries out a statutory audit. Mrs. Keen, C.A., has just been appointed partner responsible for the client as a result of the retirement of one of the five partners in the firm. She has been involved with the audit ever since joining the firm as a student a few years previously. The senior who will be in charge of the field work this year has had two years' experience with the client and will have two assistants working for him from time to time.

The audit has always been routine and there has never been any trouble except for minor arguments over fees. Mr. Yope has always been very cooperative but is not at all knowledgeable on accounting and financial matters. His background is engineering and he is an inventor. In the past, the auditors have reviewed internal control and done some preliminary planning in the month of October. Minimum reliance has been placed on the internal control system because the work has been heavily concentrated on the year-end amounts. Tests of controls have not been necessary except in the sales system to obtain reasonable assurance that all sales were recorded. The inventory count, cash count, and cutoff information were taken at December 31 of each year, and the receivable, payable, and other confirmations were as at December 31 and mailed in mid- to late January. The year-end audit work was usually started in mid-February and finished in early March, which was the usual date of the auditor's report.

On March 31, 1998, Many Conglomerate Limited (MCL), also a federally incorporated company, purchased all the shares of YPL. Mr. Yope was retained as general manager, and Mr. Grey was also retained. In June 1998, MCL sent an accounting and systems person who

1. instructed Mr. Grey regarding a monthly and year-end reporting package and a new chart of accounts. No substantial changes were found to be necessary except as noted below with respect to inventories.
2. devised and installed a cost system which enabled general ledger accounts to be updated on a monthly basis to account separately for raw materials, work in process, and finished goods.
3. prepared a budget for the coming year and instituted a budgeting system covering revenues and expenses and key balance sheet items.

Since then, Mrs. Keen has learned that Mr. Grey has adapted reasonably well to the monthly reporting and that the new inventory system does not seem to be causing major problems. However, Mr. Yope insists that it is too expensive and still relies on his rule of thumb. Mr. Grey has not yet come to grips with the budgeting system. Under the new system, the monthly trial balances (general ledger, accounts receivable, etc.) are usually ready by the 12th of the following month, and it takes about one additional day to prepare the reporting package for MCL. Mrs. Keen has also learned that YPL is planning to take its physical inventory at October 31, 1998, and then to rely on the general ledger entries between that date and the year end.

Fairly, Small & Co. has been informed that it will continue as auditor of YPL and that the company year end will remain at December 31. Mrs. Keen has also been informed of the following matters by Giant and Co., the auditor of MCL:

1. A normal scope statutory audit will be satisfactory for consolidation purposes. However, Fairly, Small & Co. is expected to ensure that the year-end reporting package provided by the company to MCL for consolidation purposes is reconciled to the audited financial statements prepared for shareholders. It will also be expected to initial each page of the package for identification purposes and ship it directly to Giant and Co.
2. Giant and Co. will be relying on Fairly, Small & Co.'s report.
3. The audit has to be completed and the report signed by January 31, 1999.

Required

a. What further information should Mrs. Keen obtain from Giant and Co. and for what reasons?

b. Prepare a memorandum from Mrs. Keen to her senior staff member who will be running the field work, outlining for him, in point form, the nature of the changes that must be made to the previous year's auditing approach so that he can prepare a detailed audit program. The memorandum should cover
   (1) general matters of which the audit staff should be made aware;
   (2) changes which will be necessary in the review and evaluation of internal controls;
   (3) changes in the nature and timing of other auditing procedures, particularly those relating to major asset and liability accounts.

The memorandum should be comprehensive in describing the changes in the approach required but should not be a detailed list of auditing procedures, since the intention is that the senior prepare such a list. The memorandum should also point out areas where the change in approach would eliminate the necessity for work that was done in previous years.

(CICA adapted)

10-35 McClain Plastics has been an audit client of Belcor, Rich, Smith & Barnes (BRS&B), a public accounting firm, for several years. McClain Plastics was started by Evers McClain, who owns 51 percent of the company's stock. The balance is owned by about 200 shareholders, who are investors with no operational responsibilities. McClain Plastics makes products that have plastic as their primary material. Some are made to order, but most products are made for inventory. An example of a McClain manufactured product is a plastic chair pad that is used in a carpeted office. Another is a plastic bushing that is used with certain fastener systems.

McClain has grown from a small two-product company, when it first engaged BRS&B, to a successful diverse company. At the time Randall Sessions of BRS&B became manager of the audit, annual sales had grown to $20 million and profits to $1.9 million. Historically, the company presented no unusual audit problems, and BRS&B had issued an unqualified opinion every year.

The audit approach that BRS&B always used on the audit of McClain Plastics was a *substantive* audit approach. Under this approach, the in-charge auditor obtained an understanding of internal control, but control risk was assumed to be at maximum. Extensive analytical procedures were done on the income statement, and unusual fluctuations were investigated. Detailed audit procedures emphasized balance sheet accounts. The theory was that if the balance sheet accounts were correct at year end, and had been audited as of the beginning of the year, then retained earnings and the income statement must be correct.

Part I

In evaluating the audit approach for McClain for the current year's audit, Sessions believed that a substantive approach was certainly within the bounds of generally accepted auditing standards but was really only appropriate for the audits of small companies. In his judgment, McClain Plastics, with sales of $20 million and 46 employees, had reached the size where it was not economical, and probably not wise, to concentrate all the tests on the balance sheet. Therefore, he designed an audit program that emphasized identifying internal controls in all major transaction cycles and included tests of controls, a *combined* approach. The intended economic benefit of this combined approach was that the time spent testing controls would be more than offset by reduced tests of details of the balance sheet accounts.

In planning tests of inventories, Sessions used the Audit Risk Model included in the *CICA Handbook* to determine the number of inventory items BRS&B would test at year end. Because of the number of different products, features, sizes, and colours, McClain's inventory consisted of 2,450 different items. These were maintained on a perpetual inventory management system that used a relational data base.

In using the Audit Risk Model for inventories, Sessions believed that an audit risk of 5 percent was acceptable. He assessed inherent risk as high (100 percent) because inventory, by its nature, is subject to many types of misstatements. Based on his understanding of the relevant transaction cycles, Sessions believed that internal controls were good. He therefore assessed control risk as moderate (50 percent), prior to performing tests of controls. Sessions also planned to use analytical procedures for tests of inventory. These planned tests included comparing gross profit margins by month and reviewing for slow moving items. Sessions felt that these tests would provide assurance of 40 percent. Substantive tests of details would include tests of inventory quantities, costs, and net realizable values at an interim date two months prior to year end. Cutoff tests would be done at year end. Inquiries and analytical procedures would be relied on for assurance about events between the interim audit date and fiscal year end.

Required

a. Decide which of the following would likely be done under both a combined approach and a substantive approach:
   (1) Assess acceptable audit risk.
   (2) Assess inherent risk.
   (3) Obtain an understanding of internal control.
   (4) Assess control risk at less than maximum.
   (5) Perform analytical procedures

(6) Assess planned detection risk.

b. What advantages does the combined approach Sessions planned to use have over the substantive approach previously used in the audit of McClain Plastics?

c. What advantage does the substantive approach have over the combined approach?

Part II

The engagement partner agreed with Sessions' recommended approach. In planning the audit evidence for detailed inventory tests, the Audit Risk Model was applied with the following results:

$$TDR = \frac{AAR}{IR \times CR \times APR}$$

where,

TDR = test of details risk
AAR = acceptable audit risk
CR = control risk
APR = analytical procedures risk
PDR = APR × TDR

therefore, using Sessions' assessments and judgments as described above,

$$TDR = \frac{0.05}{1.0 \times 0.5 \times 0.6}$$

$$TDR = 0.17$$

Required

a. Explain what 0.17 means in this audit.

b. Calculate TDR assuming that Sessions had assessed control risk at 100 percent and all other risks as they are stated.

c. Explain the effect of your answer in requirement (b) on the planned audit procedures and sample size in the audit of inventory compared with the 0.17 calculated by Sessions.

Part III

Although the planning went well, the actual testing yielded some surprises. When conducting tests of controls over acquisitions and additions to the perpetual inventory, the staff person performing the tests found that the exception rates for several important controls were significantly higher than expected. As a result, the staff person considered internal control weak, supporting an 80 percent control risk rather than the 50 percent level used. Accordingly, the staff person reworked the audit risk model as follows:

$$TDR = \frac{0.05}{1.0 \times 0.8 \times 0.6}$$

$$TDR = 0.10$$

Ten percent test of details risk still seemed to the staff person to be in the moderate range, so he recommended no increase in planned sample size for substantive tests.

Required

Do you agree with the staff person's revised judgments about the effect of tests of controls on planned substantive tests? Explain the nature and basis of any disagreement.

10-36 It is September 1998. You, CA, have recently been assigned to the audit of the Canadian Chocolate Corp. (CCC). The partner who has just assumed responsibility for the engagement has asked you to prepare a planning memo. The memo is to discuss all significant matters that need to be considered in arriving at an audit opinion on the consolidated financial statements for the fiscal year ending December 31, 1998. You have obtained the information set out below.

CCC is a public company whose head office is located in Metrotown, Canada. The company's sole business is the manufacturing of chocolate candy products; it is one of the largest chocolate candy producers in North America. Prior to 1998, it had two Canadian subsidiaries (one located in Western Canada and the other in Eastern Canada), several subsidiaries located in the United States, and one in Brazil. All subsidiaries have a December 31 year-end.

Head office uses three experienced internal audit teams to perform various internal verification procedures at the subsidiary locations. For each of the past seven years, the company has engaged your firm, Sommer & Friedlan, Chartered Accountants, to render an opinion on the consolidated financial statements. In addition, your firm audits each Canadian subsidiary. The U.S. subsidiaries are audited by a national U.S. firm, Marti & Rosti. A local Sao Paulo firm, Carvalho & Frietas, audits the Brazilian operation, which follows the same accounting policies as the Canadian operations.

Products and technology are regularly transferred among the North American enterprises. The subsidiary in Brazil, however, operates as a virtually independent entity because of currency and other government-imposed restrictions. The Brazilian subsidiary's dividend payments are limited to 15 percent of each year's opening retained earnings. The subsidiary's major contribution has been its success to date in ensuring that the cocoa contracts, negotiated with government-controlled corporations in Brazil and neighbouring countries, are filled on time and that the company continues to obtain cocoa beans of high quality.

CCC manufactures 12 chocolate candy products that are retailed in Canada. All subsidiaries are manufacturers, but each foreign location manufactures only 10 products that are marketed in the country. All development and manufacturing of new products are done by the Canadian companies. New products, although marketed internationally, are not manufactured by the foreign subsidiaries until success in the foreign markets seems assured. All testing of new products is conducted in specific regions in Canada and the United States. Research and development costs are allocated among all companies on the basis of the relative size of their total assets. In addition, there are substantial common costs such as advertising that are allocated on the same basis. Products that have been successfully launched have usually enjoyed a comfortable level of profitability, recouping the significant start-up costs (for any special capital equipment, introductory advertising campaigns, and other expenditures) within a reasonable period of time.

The chocolate-bar market has a very rigid retail price structure. Cost control is therefore crucial.

The product concentrations of the two main raw-material components, chocolate and sugar, vary from country to country, according to local consumer preferences. The variations in mix can cause a variation of up to 5 percent in the total cost of the raw material used for each product brand.

Head office arranges the purchase of all cocoa beans from South American producers; the Brazilian company acts as purchasing agent. Because the prices are quite volatile, CCC obtains all cocoa bean purchases through contracts that fix, in advance, the price for each delivery date. Head office schedules the deliveries direct to each subsidiary on or about April 1 and November 1 each year. The beans are stored in silos at the manufacturing plants.

Sugar is purchased from regional suppliers by each subsidiary and is also obtained through contracts with anticipated quarterly deliveries. The last delivery date is December 1 each year. The sugar is stored in warehouses adjacent to the bean silos. CCC uses pile rotation procedures to ensure that the oldest sugar is used first. Perpetual inventory records are maintained at each location to account for changes in the quantity of these two important commodities. CCC does not perform a physical count on these items but adjusts the perpetual records when either a silo or a pile is totally depleted. To arrive at an inventory cost at each quarter end, CCC uses the contract price of the latest shipment. Head office's accounting policy is to value raw-material inventories at cost unless the replacement cost expressed in the local currency is lower.

Final processing consists of adding and mixing various flavour ingredients to the semi-processed chocolate and refrigerating the product. After 24 hours, the product is cut and wrapped, at which point it is placed in display boxes of 24 bars and sent to the warehouse for shipment. If a product remains unshipped for three months, the wrapping is removed and the bars are shipped to various surplus stores for bulk sale at reduced prices. If the anticipated net realizable value is below cost, CCC's policies require this inventory to be written down to the lower amount.

It is common for semi-processed chocolate to be shipped among operating subsidiaries, especially among the U.S. subsidiaries and between the Western Canada subsidiary and Western U.S. subsidiaries. Transfer prices are calculated by head office each time there is a transfer. The subsidiaries' executives are often dissatisfied with the prices.

In the past, CCC has concentrated most of its advertising on the most successful long-established brands. Ten of the twelve products are more than six years old. The "Treat" bar has been the worldwide top seller among all CCC's products for the past 10 years. Its "Chocnut" candies, introduced 14 years ago, have placed third in worldwide CCC's sales in five of the last seven years. In recent times, however, the company has found its overall market share decreasing because of aggressive marketing by its chief competitor, Sweet Corporation. In addition, there have been a number of problems in marketing new products. The last successful launch was six years ago. Products introduced annually since then have failed to sell well enough to cover their start-up costs. Only two of these products are still manufactured and will be discontinued if the new "Food for the Modern Adult" line proves successful.

CCC is determined to increase its overall North American market share. Accordingly, the company hired two new advertising agencies (one in Canada and the other in the United States) to conduct the "Food for the Modern Adult" campaign. This is the most ambitious campaign the company has ever mounted to promote new products. Four new products were launched simultaneously in North America on July 1, 1998.

Preliminary analysis of market potential were conducted earlier in the year in several test centres in the United States and Canada. Management has incorporated these analyses in its product projections, presented in Exhibit I on page 339. The United States is expected to account for 75 percent of total sales of the new product line and Canada for 25 percent.

Two new subsidiaries (one in Canada and one in the United States) have been established during 1998 to produce the four products, and all capital programs are complete. A new policy established by head office requires that the two new subsidiaries share all costs related to the four new products. All costs incurred to date in connection with the new products have, however, been allocated to all the subsidiaries, including the two new subsidiaries. It is expected that the new subsidiaries will experience a loss this year.

Under the current five-year contracts that commenced on April 1, 1998, with the advertising agencies, head office is committed to spending large sums to advertise the new products. The total contract cost of the U.S. campaign will be US$2.25 billion, and the total contract cost of the Canadian campaign will be CAN$1 million.

Head office has also arranged for a redeemable coupon campaign. Coupons were mailed to potential customers before June 30, 1998, to coincide with the new product launching. As set out in Exhibit II on page 339, these coupons will provide for a reduction in the selling price of the four products.

In CCC's experience, 5 percent of the coupons will be redeemed within the first year. In the second and subsequent years of such campaigns, it is normal for approximately 1 percent of the total number of coupons issued to be redeemed in each quarter until the expiry date, December 31, 2000. The company will give the retailer US$0.0175 or CAN$0.0175 per coupon to cover handling charges. The service fee to be paid to the agencies that have agreed to handle the retailers' claims is US$0.02 or CAN$0.02 per coupon.

Earlier this year, one of the U.S. subsidiaries was the victim of an extortion attempt. The extortionists demanded US$24 million from the company. When CCC refused to comply, the extortionists carried out their threat to poison "Treat" bars in three large U.S. cities, apparently chosen at random. As a result, six people died and twelve others became seriously ill. The company responded by removing every "Treat" bar from the shelves of all U.S. retailers and destroying the stock. The company also introduced a tamper-proof wrapper for new stock and hired a professional public relations firm to undertake a special campaign to rebuild consumer confidence in the bar.

All costs were transferred to the head office to allow for one consolidated insurance claim. The company has estimated that the total cost resulting from the poisoning is about CAN$25 million: $2 million for the new wrapping machinery, $8 million for the products destroyed, $2 million for the public relations firm, and $13 million for profits lost through reduced product sales. CCC's insurance covers 80 percent of profits lost through reduced product sales. CCC has informed you that it does not want to include the insurance settlement in income in the current year but wants to defer and amortize the amount over a five-year term (on the same basis as the costs of machinery and equipment are amortized).

Legal proceedings have been commenced against CCC and its subsidiaries by the estates of the deceased parties and by those who became ill. They are suing for US$450 million.

Required

Draft the memo for the partner.

EXHIBIT I
New Product Analysis

PRODUCT	PROJECTED AVERAGE ANNUAL SALES (UNITS)	ESTIMATED DEVELOPMENT COST	SELLING PRICE (Notes 1&2)	ESTIMATED ACCEPTANCE
Product 1	7,500,000	$4,000,000	$0.50	excellent
Product 2	5,000,000	4,000,000	0.85	excellent
Product 3	2,800,000	4,000,000	0.85	good
Product 4	1,200,000	4,000,000	1.00	fair–good

Note 1: Prices are in U.S. currency if the product is manufactured and sold in the United States and in Canadian currency if manufactured and sold in Canada.

Note 2: The production costs account for 45 percent of the selling prices.

EXHIBIT II
Coupon Redemption Program

PRODUCT	REDEMPTION COUPONS ISSUED	VALUE (Note 1)
Product 1	20,000,000	$0.05
Product 2	18,000,000	0.10
Product 3	15,000,000	0.15
Product 4	10,000,000	0.20

Note 1: Redemption values are in U.S. currency if the product is manufactured and sold in the United States and Canadian currency if manufactured and sold in Canada.

(CICA adapted)

11

AUDIT SAMPLING CONCEPTS

GOOD AUDITING OFTEN RESULTS IN IMPROVED CASH FLOWS

Sandy Previtz is a new internal audit staff person who has been with Erhardt Freight Corp. (EFC), a long-haul trucking company, only a year. Before being hired by EFC, she was an auditor for a public accounting firm for five years. She is now doing internal audit work on the sales and receivables function.

The sales transaction document for a long-haul trucking company is a freight bill evidencing a shipment for a customer. EFC has an extremely high growth rate, reaching a current volume of several thousand shipments a day. The accounting for all the freight bills, and the related receivables, is a massive accounting and systems problem. The problem is more complex because EFC is adding new customers and shipping agents daily. EFC's solution to this record-keeping problem has been to develop and implement a new state-of-the-art computerized information system. The parts of the system that have the biggest effect on the audit relate to the aging of accounts receivable and estimation of an appropriate allowance for uncollectible freight bills. By law, these bills must be paid within seven days.

Previtz decides to copy EFC's accounts receivable data file, take a statistical sample of outstanding freight bills, and estimate an aging from the bills. She gets approval from the head of internal auditing, Martha Harris, and makes arrangements with EFC's chief financial officer, Hal Stenson, to have the file copied and to proceed.

Previtz's initial sample consists of 300 items, selected at random from approximately 20,000 outstanding freight bills. She projects an aging from the sample and applies a formula to obtain a range estimate of the necessary allowance for uncollectible accounts. When she compares this to the company's recorded allowance, it appears that the recorded amount may be understated by as much as $1 million, clearly a material amount.

When Previtz informs Harris of the situation, Harris calls a meeting with Stenson and asks Previtz to attend. At the meeting, Previtz explains that her findings are based on a statistical estimate, that the confidence interval she obtained had an upper limit of $1 million and a lower limit of only $200,000, which is not a material amount, and that the interval was determined with a confidence level of 95 percent. After some discussion of the meaning of the relevant statistical terms and procedures, Stenson states: "I certainly don't want to make an adjustment to the books based on this wide range estimate, and I hope you both agree with me."

Harris tells Stenson in no uncertain terms that as long as the confidence limit indicates that there could be a material misstatement, EFC must continue to obtain evidence to resolve any doubts. She agrees with him that it is uncomfortable making an adjustment based on a wide confidence interval, but that the solution is to expand the sample until it is clear whether or not the allowance is materially misstated. After further discussion, Stenson finally agrees that the potential embarrassment of incorrect financial statements is not worth the risk and tells Harris to go ahead.

Previtz's second sample increases the overall sample size to 600 items, and shows approximately the same results. However, at Harris's request, the items are analyzed from both a management and an accounting standpoint. When Harris and Previtz meet with Stenson to discuss the updated information, Harris points out that the real problem is not the allowance but the fact that receivables are out of control and that EFC faces a risk of a significant loss in cash flows if management does not do something about it. Stenson quickly agrees and responds by hiring a team of temporary workers to analyze the aging of all 20,000 freight bills and to institute a large-scale collection effort. He also decides to make an adjustment to the allowance account based on the results of the second sample. Not only does the company's detailed analysis improve its cash flows, it also shows that Sandy Previtz's statistical estimate was right on target.

AICPA's Auditing Standards Board
www.aicpa.org/

The *CICA Handbook* in paragraph 5300.11 states that the auditor does not examine all the available evidence but rather examines samples from the available population, although sampling is not specifically defined. The AICPA's Auditing Standards Board in SAS 39 defines audit sampling as:

> The application of an audit procedure to less than 100 percent of the items within an audit balance or class of transactions for the purpose of evaluating some characteristics of the balance or class.

"Application of an audit procedure" in this definition means dealing with three aspects of audit sampling: (1) planning the sample, (2) selecting the sample and performing the tests, and (3) evaluating the results. As the chapter title implies, this chapter discusses sampling concepts, as applied to tests of controls or tests of details. The sales and collection cycle and its transactions are used as a frame of reference for discussing these concepts, but the concepts apply to any cycle. Chapter 12 applies these concepts to tests of controls, and Chapter 14 applies audit sampling to tests of details of balances. Figure 11-1, which uses the same information as Figure 10-2 on page 315, shows how audit sampling is related to the types of audit tests.

Chapter 12 and Chapter 14 are directly related to Chapter 11 in that the auditor must decide the audit procedures he or she plans to perform before applying audit sampling. Four topics are discussed at the beginning of this chapter as background knowledge about applying audit sampling to tests of controls and tests of details:

FIGURE 11-1

How Audit Sampling Is Related to the Types of Audit Tests

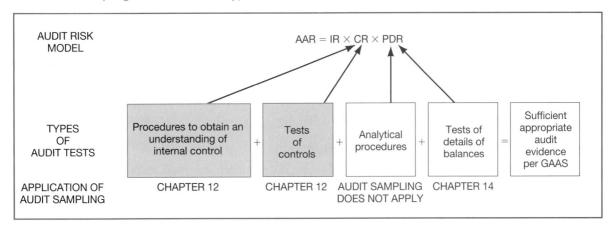

representative samples, statistical versus nonstatistical sampling, nonprobabilistic sample selection, and probabilistic sample selection. The types of audit sampling methodologies are then reviewed. Next, the steps involved in planning, selecting, and evaluating a sample are described. Lastly, the impact of such important aspects as documentation and professional judgment are discussed.

Chapter 12 applies audit sampling to tests of controls by integrating the sampling process into the audit of the sales and collection cycle. Chapter 13 discusses overall analytical procedures as well as providing specific examples for the sales and collection cycle. Chapter 14 then integrates sampling concepts into the completion of the tests in the sales and collection cycle by applying them to the audit of accounts receivable.

REPRESENTATIVE SAMPLES

OBJECTIVE 11-1

Explain the concept of representative sampling.

Whenever an auditor selects a sample from a population, the objective is to obtain a *representative* one. A representative sample is one in which the characteristics in the sample of audit interest are approximately the same as those of the population. This means that the sampled items are similar to the items not sampled. For example, assume that a client's internal controls require a clerk to attach a shipping document to every duplicate sales invoice, but the procedure is not followed exactly 3 percent of the time. If the auditor selects a sample of 100 duplicate sales invoices and finds 3 missing, the sample is highly representative. If two or four such items are found in the sample, the sample is reasonably representative. If many missing items or none are found, the sample is *nonrepresentative*.

In practice, auditors do not know whether a sample is representative, even after all testing is completed. Auditors can, however, increase the likelihood of a sample being representative by using care in its design, selection, and evaluation. Two things can cause a sample result to be nonrepresentative: nonsampling error and sampling error. The risk of these occurring is termed *nonsampling risk* and *sampling risk*; both can be controlled.

Nonsampling risk (nonsampling error) occurs when audit tests do not uncover existing exceptions in the sample. In the previous example in which three shipping documents were not attached to duplicate sales invoices, if the auditor concluded that no exceptions existed, there is a nonsampling error.

The two causes of nonsampling error are the auditor's failure to recognize exceptions and inappropriate or ineffective audit procedures. An auditor might fail to recognize an exception because of exhaustion, boredom, or lack of understanding of what constitutes an exception. Take for example the control of attaching a shipping document to the duplicate sales invoice. An exception would be defined as a missing document or a shipping document that does not agree to the sales invoice. An ineffective audit procedure for these exceptions would be the selection of a sample of shipping documents to determine if each is attached to a set of duplicate sales invoices, rather than examining a sample of duplicate sales invoices. The auditor in this case would be unable to determine whether there were numerous sales invoices unsupported by shipping documents, since such sales invoices could not be selected. Careful design of audit procedures and proper supervision and instruction are ways to reduce nonsampling risk.

Sampling risk (sampling error) is an inherent part of sampling that results from testing less than the entire population. Even with zero nonsampling error, there is always a chance that a sample is not representative. For example, if a population has a 3 percent exception rate, the auditor could easily select a sample of 100 items containing no exceptions or many.

There are two ways to control sampling risk: increase sample size and use an appropriate method of selecting sample items from the population. Increasing sample size will reduce sampling risk, and vice versa. At the extreme, testing all the items of a population will have a zero sampling risk (since this is no longer sampling). Using an appropriate sampling method will reasonably assure representativeness. This does not eliminate or even reduce sampling risk, but it does allow the auditor to measure the sample risk associated with a given sample size in a reliable manner.

STATISTICAL VERSUS NONSTATISTICAL SAMPLING

OBJECTIVE 11-2

Distinguish between statistical and nonstatistical sampling.

Audit sampling methods can be divided into two broad categories: statistical and nonstatistical. These categories have important similarities and differences. They are similar in that they both involve the three steps identified in the introduction: (1) plan the sample, (2) select the sample and perform the tests, and (3) evaluate the results. The purpose of planning the sample is to make sure that the audit tests are performed in a manner that provides the desired sampling risk and minimizes the likelihood of nonsampling error. Selecting the sample involves deciding how to select sample items from the population. Performing the tests involves examining documents and performing other audit tests. Evaluating the results involves drawing conclusions based on the audit tests. To illustrate, assume that an auditor selects a sample of 100 duplicate sales invoices from a population, tests each to determine if a shipping document is attached, and determines that there are three exceptions. Deciding that a sample size of 100 is needed is a part of planning the sample. Deciding which 100 items to select from the population is a sample selection problem. Doing the audit procedure for each of the 100 items and determining that there were 3 exceptions constitutes performing the tests. Reaching conclusions about the likely exception rate in the total population when there is a sample exception rate of 3 percent is evaluating the results.

Statistical sampling differs from nonstatistical sampling in that, through the application of mathematical rules, it allows the quantification (measurement) of sampling risk in planning the sample (step 1) and evaluating the results (step 3). (You may remember calculating a statistical result at a 95 percent confidence level in a statistics course. The 95 percent confidence level provides a 5 percent sampling risk.) The quantification of sampling risk is appropriate only when the auditor selects the sample (step 2) using a *probabilistic* sample, which is discussed shortly.

In nonstatistical sampling, the auditor does not quantify sampling risk. Instead, the auditor selects those sample items that he or she believes will provide the most useful information in the circumstances (i.e., *nonprobabilistic* samples are chosen), and conclusions are reached about populations on a judgmental basis. For that reason, the selection of nonprobabilistic samples is often termed *judgmental sampling*.

It is equally acceptable under professional standards for auditors to use either statistical or nonstatistical sampling methods. However, it is essential that either method be applied with due care. All steps of the process must be followed carefully. When statistical sampling is used, the sample must be a probabilistic one, and appropriate statistical evaluation methods must be used with the sample results to make the sampling risk computations.

TABLE 11-1

RELATIONSHIP OF
METHODS OF
SELECTING SAMPLES
TO EVALUATING
RESULTS

| METHOD OF | METHOD OF EVALUATING RESULTS | |
SELECTING SAMPLE	*Statistical*	*Nonstatistical*
Probabilistic	Preferable to use statistical	Acceptable to use nonstatistical
Nonprobabilistic	Not acceptable to use statistical	Mandatory to use nonstatistical

It is also acceptable to make nonstatistical evaluations by using probabilistic selection, but many practitioners prefer not to do so. They believe that statistical measurement of sampling risk is inherent in those samples, and should not be ignored. It is *never* acceptable, however, to evaluate a nonprobabilistic sample as if it were a statistical sample. A summary of the relationship of probabilistic and nonprobabilistic selection to statistical and nonstatistical evaluation is shown in Table 11-1.

There are three types of sample selection methods commonly associated with nonstatistical audit sampling and three types of sample selection methods commonly associated with statistical audit sampling. These are listed below and discussed in the following sections.

The nonprobabilistic (judgmental) sample selection methods are:

- Directed sample selection
- Block sample selection
- Haphazard sample selection

Probabilistic sample selection methods are:

- Simple random sample selection
- Systematic sample selection
- Probability proportionate-to-size sample selection

Stratified sample selection can be applied to both nonprobabilistic and probabilistic sample selection methods.

NONPROBABILISTIC SAMPLE SELECTION

Nonprobabilistic sample selection methods are those that do not meet the technical requirements for probabilistic sample selection. Since these methods are not based on strict mathematical probabilities, the representativeness of the sample may be difficult to determine. The information content of the sample, including its representativeness, will be based on the knowledge and skill of the auditor in applying his or her judgment in the circumstances.

DIRECTED SAMPLE SELECTION

Directed sample selection is the selection of each item in the sample based on some judgmental criteria established by the auditor. The auditor does not rely on equal chances of selection, but, rather, deliberately selects items according to the criteria. Some auditors consider certain directed samples to be a form of analytical review. The important issue is ensuring that the test is clearly defined and its audit role identified. The criteria may relate to representativeness, or they may not. Commonly used criteria are the following:

Items most likely to contain misstatements Frequently, auditors are able to identify which population items are most likely to be misstated. Examples are receivables outstanding for a long time, purchases from and sales to officers and affiliated companies, and unusually large or complex transactions. These kinds of items can be efficiently investigated by the auditor, and the results can be applied to the population on a judgmental basis. The reasoning underlying the evaluation of such samples is often that if none of the items selected contain misstatements, then it is highly unlikely that a material misstatement exists in the population.

Items containing selected population characteristics   The auditor may be able to describe the various types and sources of items that make up the population and design the sample to be representative by selecting one or more items of each type. For example, a sample of cash disbursements might include some from each month, each bank account or location, and each major type of acquisition.

Large dollar coverage   A sample can often be selected to cover such a large portion of total population dollars that the risk of drawing an improper conclusion by not examining small items is not a concern. For example, all transactions that have a value in excess of materiality could be examined. This is a practical approach on many audits, especially smaller ones. There are also statistical methods that are intended to accomplish the same effect.

BLOCK SAMPLE SELECTION

A block sample is the selection of several items in sequence. Once the first item in the block is selected, the remainder of the block is chosen automatically. One example of a block sample is the selection of a sequence of 100 sales transactions from the sales journal for the third week of March. A total sample of 100 could also be selected by taking 5 blocks of 20 items each, 10 blocks of 10, or 50 blocks of 2.

It is ordinarily acceptable to use block samples only if a reasonable number of blocks are used. If few blocks are used, the probability of obtaining a nonrepresentative sample is too great, considering the possibility of such things as employee turnover, changes in the accounting system, and the seasonal nature of many businesses.

A common use of block testing is testing cutoff. The auditor would select a block of invoices, receiving documents, and shipping documents spanning both sides of the year-end date to ensure that the transactions were recorded in the proper period.

HAPHAZARD SAMPLE SELECTION

When the auditor goes through a population and selects items for the sample without regard to their size, source, or other distinguishing characteristics, he or she is attempting to select without bias. This is called a *haphazard sample*.

The most serious shortcoming of haphazard sample selection is the difficulty of remaining completely unbiased in the selection. Because of the auditor's training and "cultural bias," certain population items are more likely than others to be included in the sample. For example, auditors may be inclined to select larger amounts or amounts from the middle of a period, or to avoid round dollar amounts.

Although haphazard and block sample selection appear to be less logical than directed sample selection, they are often useful as audit tools and should not be ignored. In some situations, the cost of more complex sample selection methods outweighs the benefits obtained from using them. For example, assume that the auditor wants to trace credits from the accounts receivable transaction history files to the duplicate bank deposit slips and other authorized sources as a test for fictitious credits in the data files. A haphazard or block approach is simpler and much less costly than other selection methods in this situation, and would be employed by many auditors.

PROBABILISTIC SAMPLE SELECTION

As previously indicated, to measure sampling risk, statistical sampling requires a probabilistic sample. There are three methods commonly used by auditors to obtain probabilistic samples: simple random sample selection, systematic sample selection, and stratified sample selection.

SIMPLE RANDOM SAMPLE SELECTION

A simple random sample is one in which every possible combination of elements in the population has an equal chance of constituting the sample. Simple random sampling is used to sample populations that are not segmented for audit purposes. For example, the auditor may wish to sample the client's cash disbursements for the year. A simple random sample of 60 items contained in the cash disbursements journal might be selected for that purpose. Appropriate auditing procedures would be applied to the 60 items selected, and conclusions would be drawn and applied to all cash disbursement transactions recorded for the year.

Random number tables When a simple random sample is obtained, a method must be used that assures that all items in the population have an equal chance of selection. Suppose that in the above example there were a total of 12,000 cash disbursement transactions for the year. A simple random sample of one transaction would be such that each of the 12,000 transactions would have an equal chance of being selected. This would be done by obtaining a *random number* between 1 and 12,000. If the number were 3,895, the auditor would select and test the 3,895th cash disbursement transaction recorded in the cash disbursements journal.

Random numbers are a series of digits that have equal probabilities of occurring over long runs and that have no discernible pattern. An example of a commonly used random number table is the *Table of 105,000 Random Decimal Digits*, published by the U.S. Interstate Commerce Commission. A page from that table appears in Table 11-2. This table has numbered rows and columns, with five digits in each column. This format is convenient for reading the table and documenting the portion of the table used. The presentation of the digits as five-digit numbers is purely arbitrary.

It is easy, but time-consuming, to select samples using a random number table. For example, assume that the auditor is selecting a sample of 100 sales invoices from a file of prenumbered sales invoices beginning with document number 3272 and ending

TABLE 11-2

RANDOM NUMBER TABLE

ROW	COLUMN							
	(1)	**(2)**	**(3)**	**(4)**	**(5)**	**(6)**	**(7)**	**(8)**
1000	37039	97547	64673	31546	99314	66854	97855	99965
1001	25145	84834	23009	51584	66754	77785	52357	25532
1002	98433	54725	18864	65866	76918	78825	58210	76835
1003	97965	68548	81545	82933	93545	85959	63282	61454
1004	78049	67830	14624	17563	25697	07734	48243	94318
1005	50203	25658	91478	08509	23308	48130	65047	77873
1006	40059	67825	18934	64998	49807	71126	77818	56893
1007	84350	67241	54031	34535	04093	35062	58163	14205
1008	30954	51637	91500	48722	60988	60029	60873	37423
1009	86723	36464	98305	08009	00666	29255	18514	49158
1010	50188	22554	86160	92250	14021	65859	16237	72296
1011	50014	00463	13906	35936	71761	95755	87002	71667
1012	66023	21428	14742	94874	23308	58533	26507	11208
1013	04458	61862	63119	09541	01715	87901	91260	03079
1014	57510	36314	30452	09712	37714	95482	30507	68475
1015	43373	58939	95848	28288	60341	52174	11879	18115
1016	61500	12763	64433	02268	57905	72347	49498	21871
1017	78938	71312	99705	71546	42274	23915	38405	18779
1018	64257	93218	35793	43671	64055	88729	11168	60260
1019	56864	21554	70445	24841	04779	56774	96129	73594
1020	35314	29631	06937	54545	04470	75463	77112	77126
1021	40704	48823	65963	39359	12717	56201	22811	24863
1022	07318	44623	02843	33299	59872	86774	06926	12672
1023	94550	23299	45557	07923	75126	00808	01312	46689
1024	34348	81191	21027	77087	10909	03676	97723	34469
1025	92277	57115	50789	68111	75305	53289	39751	45760
1026	56093	58302	52236	64756	50273	61566	61962	93280
1027	16623	17849	96701	94971	94758	08845	32260	59823
1028	50848	93982	66451	32143	05441	10399	17775	74169
1029	48006	58200	58367	66577	68583	21108	41361	20732
1030	56640	27890	28825	96509	21363	53657	60119	75385

with 8825. Since the invoices use four digits, it is necessary to use four digits in the random number table. Assuming the first four digits of each five-digit set were used, and the arbitrary starting point in the random number table in Table 11-2 is row 1009, column 2, then reading down, the first invoice for inclusion in the sample is 3646. The next usable number is 6186 since the next three numbers are all outside the population range.

Computer generation of random numbers It is useful to understand the use of random number tables as a means of understanding the concept of selecting simple random samples. However, most random samples obtained by auditors are obtained by using computer programs. There are three main types of these: electronic spreadsheet programs, random number generators, and generalized audit software programs.

The advantages of using computer programs in selecting random samples are time savings, reduced likelihood of auditor error in selecting the numbers, and automatic documentation. To illustrate computer generation of random numbers, Figure 11-2 shows a printout from a spreadsheet program. In the application illustrated, the auditor wishes to sample 30 items from a population of documents numbered from 140,672 to 253,590. The program requires only input parameters and the use of a predefined spreadsheet function by the auditor for a sample to be selected. The auditor can use the spreadsheet to generate random dates or ranges of sets of numbers (such as page and line numbers). It also provides output in both sorted and selection orders by means of the spreadsheet sort function.

Replacement versus nonreplacement sampling Random numbers may be obtained with replacement or without replacement. In *replacement sampling*, an element in the population can be included in the sample more than once, whereas in nonreplacement sampling, an element can be included only once. If the random number corresponding to an element is selected more than once in nonreplacement sampling, it is not included in the sample a second time. Although both selection approaches are consistent with sound statistical theory, auditors rarely use replacement sampling.

SYSTEMATIC SAMPLE SELECTION

In systematic selection (also known as *systematic sampling*), the auditor calculates an *interval* and then methodically selects the items for the sample based on the size of the interval. The interval is determined by dividing the population size by the number of sample items desired. For example, if a population of sales invoices ranges from 652 to 3151 and the desired sample size is 125, the interval is 20 [(3,151 − 651) ÷ 125]. The auditor must now select a random number between 0 and 19 to determine the starting point for the sample. If the randomly selected number is 9, the first item in the sample is invoice number 661 (652 + 9). The remaining 124 items are 681 (661 + 20), 701 (681 + 20), and so on through item 3141.

The advantage of systematic sampling is its *ease of use*. For most populations, the systematic sample can be drawn quickly, the approach automatically puts the numbers in sequence, and the appropriate documentation is easy to develop.

A major problem with systematic selection is the possibility of bias. Because of the way systematic selection works, once the first item in the sample is selected, all other items are chosen automatically. This causes no problem if the characteristic of interest, such as a possible control deviation, is distributed randomly throughout the population; however, in some cases, characteristics of interest may not be randomly distributed. For example, if a control deviation occurred at a certain time of the month or with certain types of documents, a systematic sample could have a higher likelihood of failing to be representative than a simple random sample. It is important, therefore, when systematic selection is used, to consider possible patterns in the population data that could cause sample bias.

A variation of systematic sample selection by unit of interest is used by the probability-proportionate-to-size (PPS) sampling methods, described in the next

FIGURE 11-2

Random Selection by
Use of a Computer

RANGE

Lower   140,672
Upper   253,590

RANDOM NUMBERS

SELECTION ORDER		NUMERICAL ORDER	
		Sequence	*Number*
1	140,812	16	145,532
2	235,629	20	147,191
3	235,546	9	157,188
4	204,629	11	157,271
5	174,042	1	160,134
6	158,448	13	161,264
7	230,376	12	164,471
8	249,493	17	168,253
9	180,681	19	170,651
10	178,869	22	173,379
11	175,649	23	189,273
12	161,610	4	191,667
13	177,096	30	195,509
14	245,601	28	197,544
15	181,370	3	200,259
16	205,785	29	212,731
17	209,811	18	214,303
18	144,631	27	216,013
19	150,707	25	220,151
20	158,354	8	221,762
21	205,598	6	223,313
22	243,695	2	231,675
23	191,338	14	234,929
24	229,621	24	238,267
25	247,089	5	239,244
26	165,653	21	240,240
27	145,121	7	245,985
28	154,306	10	248,634
29	170,990	15	248,964
30	236,540	26	252,584

Source: Random selection prepared courtesy of PricewaterhouseCoopers, 1998, using @RAND function of spreadsheet software.

section. Here, the individual dollar is considered the unit of interest. The interval is determined based upon a statistical formula, and the transactions associated with that dollar interval are selected.

STRATIFIED SAMPLE SELECTION

When a sample is *stratified* it is split into smaller sets where each set has a similar characteristic. For example, stratification can occur by dollar amount (sales over $50,000, sales under that amount), by location (foreign vs. domestic) or by another criteria, such as whether commissions will be paid (sales from head office vs. made by travelling sales personnel). This can improve the efficiency of the audit by focusing work on transactions that may be more readily subject to material error.

After data is stratified, the sample will be selected using one of the methods previously discussed (either probabilistic or nonprobabilistic).

STATISTICAL SAMPLING METHODOLOGIES

OBJECTIVE 11-4

Describe three statistical audit sampling methodologies.

Once the decision has been made to conduct statistical sampling, the auditor may choose from three broad categories of statistical sampling: attribute, probability-proportionate-to-size (PPS), and variable. (Discovery sampling is also described, but this is a subset of attribute sampling.) These methods are based upon underlying sampling distributions, such as binomial or normal distributions, which are beyond the scope of this text. Review your statistics text to examine these distributions. All three categories of sampling can be used for tests of controls or tests of details, although attribute sampling is normally used for controls testing while PPS and variables sampling are normally used for tests of details testing.

ATTRIBUTE SAMPLING

Attribute sampling is used to estimate the *proportion* of items in a population containing a characteristic or *attribute* of interest. This proportion is called the *occurrence rate* or *exception rate* and is the ratio of the items containing the specific attribute to the total number of population items. The occurrence rate is usually expressed as a percentage. For example, an auditor might conclude that the exception rate for the internal verification of sales invoices is approximately 3 percent, meaning that invoices are not properly verified 3 percent of the time. This methodology is designed to answer the question, How many items contain errors?

Auditors are interested in the occurrence of the following types of exceptions in populations of accounting data: (1) deviations from client's established controls, (2) monetary errors or fraud and other irregularities in populations of transaction data, and (3) monetary errors or fraud and other irregularities in populations of account balance details. Knowing the occurrence rate of such exceptions is particularly helpful for the first two types of exceptions, which relate to transactions. Therefore, auditors make extensive use of audit sampling that measures the occurrence or exception rate in performing tests of controls. With the third type of exception, the auditor usually needs to estimate the total dollar amount of the exceptions because a judgment must be made about whether the exceptions are material. When the auditor wants to know the total amount of a misstatement, he or she will use methods that measure dollars, not the exception or occurrence rate, such as PPS or variables methodologies.

The statistical sampling method most commonly used for tests of controls is *attribute sampling*. Whenever attribute sampling is used in this text, it refers to attribute statistical sampling for physical units. Both attribute sampling and nonstatistical sampling have attributes, which are the characteristics being tested for in the population, but attribute sampling is a statistical method. Attribute sampling is used primarily for tests of controls, but auditors also use attribute sampling for substantive procedures, particularly when performing dual purpose tests.

Attribute sampling may be based on physical units (e.g., invoices) or monetary units (e.g., dollars). In the case of the former, the occurrence or exception rate would be a percentage; in the case of the latter, the exception would be a monetary amount.

An example of attribute sampling applied to tests of controls is shown in Chapter 12.

Discovery sampling This special type of attribute sampling is used when the auditor is looking for very few or near zero deviations. For example, if the auditor suspects that fraud or other irregularities exist in the data, the sample size needs to be designed to provide the assurance of finding at least one example of the fraud or other irregularity. This method can also be used for tests of detail in situations where few or no misstatements are expected, for example where calculations are performed by a computer program.

PROPORTIONATE-TO-SIZE SAMPLING

PPS sampling is also known as *monetary unit sampling* (MUS) or *dollar unit sampling* (DUS). PPS is a modified form of attribute sampling that focuses on a single unit of currency (in Canada, the dollar), rather than on a physical unit. In the balance of the text, the term monetary unit sampling (MUS) is used to refer to this form of sampling.

In physical unit sampling, the sampling unit is usually a document, such as a cheque, or a transaction, such as a sale. In monetary unit sampling, the sampling unit is the individual dollar. If sales for the year were made up of 15,000 transactions with a dollar value of $30,000,000, the sampling unit for physical unit attribute sampling would be an invoice, while the sampling unit for monetary unit sampling would be each of the 30,000,000 dollars. In the case of the former, each of the 15,000 invoices would have an equal chance of selection; in the case of the latter, each of the 30,000,000 dollars would have an equal chance of selection.

Monetary unit sampling allows the result of the testing to be stated in dollar terms. This allows the auditor to specify a dollar range of potential errors for a specified confidence level. It also increases the probability that larger invoices, totalling larger dollar amounts than smaller invoices, will be selected, since an invoice including 150,000 dollars will have a greater probability of being selected than one containing only 15 dollars. Monetary unit sampling is appropriate for tests of controls or for tests of details.

VARIABLES SAMPLING

Variables sampling is used when the auditor desires a dollar or quantitative conclusion with respect to the test conducted. The general class of methods called variables sampling includes several techniques. Those described in this section are difference estimation, ratio estimation, and mean-per-unit estimation.

Difference estimation   Difference estimation is used to measure the estimated total misstatement amount when there is both a recorded value and an audited value for each item in the sample. An example is confirming a sample of accounts receivable and determining the difference (misstatement) between the client's recorded amount and the amount the auditor considers correct for each selected account. The auditor makes an estimate of the population misstatement based on the number of misstatements, average misstatement size, and individual misstatement size in the sample. The result is stated as a point estimate plus or minus a computed precision interval at a stated confidence level.

Difference estimation frequently results in smaller sample sizes than any other method, and it is relatively easy to use. For that reason, difference estimation is used frequently by auditors.

Ratio estimation   Ratio estimation is similar to difference estimation except that the point estimate of the population misstatement is determined by multiplying the portion of sample dollars misstated by the total recorded book value. The ratio estimate results in even smaller sample sizes than difference estimation if the size of the misstatements in the population is proportionate to the recorded value of the items. If the size of the individual misstatements is independent of the recorded value, the difference estimate results in smaller sample sizes.

Mean-per-unit estimation   In mean-per-unit estimation, the auditor is concerned with the audited value rather than the error amount of each item in the sample. Except for the definition of what is being measured, the mean-per-unit estimate is calculated in exactly the same manner as the difference estimate. The point estimate of the audited value is the average audited value of items in the sample times the population size. The computed precision interval is computed on the basis of the audited value of the sample items rather than the misstatements. When the auditor has computed the upper and lower confidence limits, a decision is made about the acceptability of the population by comparing these amounts with the recorded book value.

PLANNING, SELECTING, AND EVALUATING A SAMPLE

OBJECTIVE 11-5

Describe the steps in planning, selecting, and evaluating a sample. Define the terms used during this process.

Audit sampling is applied to tests of controls and tests of details through a set of 14 well-defined steps. The steps are divided into three sections: plan the sample, select the sample and perform the audit procedures, and evaluate the results. It is important to follow these steps carefully as a means of ensuring that both the auditing and the sampling aspects of the process are properly applied. The steps provide an outline of the discussion that follows. Table 11-7, shown at the end of the discussion, compares these steps for tests of controls (e.g., attribute sampling) and tests of details (e.g., MUS sampling).

PLAN THE SAMPLE

1. State the objectives of the audit test.
2. Decide if audit sampling applies.
3. Define attributes and exception or error conditions.
4. Define the population.
5. Define the sampling unit.
6. Specify tolerable exception rate or specify materiality.
7. Specify acceptable risk of assessing control risk too low or acceptable risk of incorrect acceptance.
8. Estimate the population exception rate or the misstatements in the population.
9. Determine the initial sample size.

SELECT THE SAMPLE AND PERFORM THE AUDIT PROCEDURES

10. Select the sample.
11. Perform the audit procedures.

EVALUATE THE RESULTS

12. Generalize from the sample to the population.
13. Analyze exceptions or misstatements.
14. Determine the acceptability of the population.

The general process of each step is described in this chapter, and related definitions are provided for new terms. Chapter 12 provides an example of tests of controls using nonstatistical and physical unit attribute sampling, while Chapter 14 does the same for tests of details using nonstatistical and MUS sampling.

1. STATE THE OBJECTIVES OF THE AUDIT TEST

The overall objectives of the test must be stated in terms of the transaction cycle being tested. Typically, the overall objective of tests of controls is to test the application of controls and to determine whether the transactions contain monetary errors or fraud and other irregularities. For tests of details, the auditor determines the maximum amount of overstatement and understatement that could exist while still providing a sample with no misstatements (or for the number of misstatements that was found). The objectives of the audit test are normally decided as a part of designing the audit program.

2. DECIDE IF AUDIT SAMPLING APPLIES

In this section the term "population" is used. The population represents the body of data about which the auditor wishes to generalize.

Audit sampling applies whenever the auditor plans to reach conclusions about a population based on a sample. The auditor should examine the audit program and decide those audit procedures for which audit sampling applies. For example, in the following partial audit program, sampling could be used for procedures 3 through 5.

1. Review sales transactions for large and unusual amounts (analytical procedure or directed sample).

2. Observe whether the duties of the accounts receivable clerk are separate from the handling of cash (test of control).
3. Examine a sample of duplicate sales invoices for
   (a) credit approval by the credit manager (test of control)
   (b) the existence of an attached shipping document (test of control)
   (c) inclusion of a chart of accounts number (test of control)
4. Select a sample of shipping documents, and trace each to related duplicate sales invoices for existence (test of control).
5. Compare the quantity on each duplicate sales invoice with the quantity on related shipping documents (test of control).

Audit sampling is inappropriate for the first two procedures in this audit program. The first is an analytical procedure for which sampling is inappropriate. The second is an observation procedure for which no documentation exists to perform audit sampling.

For tests of details, while it is common to sample in many accounts, there are situations when sampling does not apply. For the population shown in the table below (which is taken from Problem 14-27 on page 494), the auditor may decide to audit only items over $5,000 and ignore all others because the total of the smaller ones is immaterial. In this case, the auditor has not sampled. Similarly, if the auditor is verifying capital asset additions and there are many small additions and one extremely large purchase of a building, the auditor may decide to ignore the small items entirely. Again the auditor has not sampled.

POPULATION ITEM	RECORDED AMOUNT	POPULATION ITEM	RECORDED AMOUNT	POPULATION ITEM	RECORDED AMOUNT	POPULATION ITEM	RECORDED AMOUNT
1	$1,410	11	$2,270	21	4,865	31	935
2	9,130	12	50	22	770	32	5,595
3	660	13	5,785	23	2,305	33	930
4	3,355	14	940	24	2,665	34	4,045
5	5,725	15	1,820	25	1,000	35	9,480
6	8,210	16	3,380	26	6,225	36	360
7	580	17	530	27	3,675	37	1,145
8	44,110	18	955	28	6,250	38	6,400
9	825	19	4,490	29	1,890	39	100
10	1,155	20	17,140	30	27,705	40	8,435
							$207,295

3. DEFINE ATTRIBUTES AND EXCEPTION OR ERROR CONDITIONS

TERM RELATED TO PLANNING	TEST OF CONTROL (E.G., FOR ATTRIBUTE SAMPLE)	TEST OF DETAIL (E.G., FOR MUS SAMPLE)
Define the item of interest.	Identify the characteristic or *attribute* of interest.	Individual dollars
Define exceptions or errors.	Define the control deviation (an *exception*).	Normally any monetary difference (an *error*)

Whenever audit sampling is used, the auditor must carefully define the characteristics (*attributes*) being tested and the exception conditions. Unless a precise statement of what constitutes an attribute is made in advance, the staff person who performs the audit procedure will have no guidelines for identifying exceptions.

Attributes of interest and exception conditions come directly from the audit procedures for which the auditor has decided to use audit sampling. For example, based on the portion of the partial test of control audit program described in step 2, the first attribute that can be tested by means of sampling is whether the duplicate sales invoice is approved for credit (procedure 3a). A deviation condition in a manual system would be lack of initials indicating credit approval. The absence of the defined attribute for any sample item will be an exception for that attribute.

Audit sampling for tests of details of balances measures monetary misstatements in the population. Thus, the misstatement conditions are any conditions that represent a monetary misstatement in a sample item. In auditing accounts receivable, for example, any client misstatement in a sample item is a misstatement.

4. DEFINE THE POPULATION

The auditor can define the population to include whatever data are desired, but he or she must sample from the entire population as it has been defined. The auditor may generalize *only* about that population that has been sampled. For example, in performing tests of controls of sales, the auditor generally defines the population as all recorded sales for the year. If the auditor samples from only one month's transactions, it is invalid to draw conclusions about the invoices for the entire year.

It is important that the auditor carefully define the population in advance, being consistent with the objectives of the audit tests. For different tests in the audit program of the same cycle, it may be necessary to define more than one population for a given set of audit procedures. For example, if the auditor intends to trace from sales invoices to shipping documents and from shipping documents to duplicate sales invoices, there are two populations (i.e., one population of shipping documents and another of duplicate sales invoices).

The population for tests of details using MUS or other dollar-based tests is defined as the *recorded dollar population*. The auditor then evaluates whether the recorded population is overstated or understated. For example, the population of accounts receivable on page 353 consists of 40 accounts totalling $207,295. Most accounting populations subject to audit would contain far more items totalling a much larger dollar amount.

Stratified sampling   As mentioned earlier, the purpose of stratification is to permit the auditor to emphasize certain population items and de-emphasize others. In most audit sampling situations, auditors want to emphasize the larger recorded values; therefore, stratification is typically done on the basis of the size of recorded dollar values.

For example, examining the population in the table on page 353, there are many different ways to stratify the population. One such method follows:

STRATUM	STRATUM CRITERIA	NUMBER IN POPULATION	DOLLARS IN POPULATION
1	>$10,000	3	$88,955
2	$ 5,000 – $10,000	10	71,235
3	<$ 5,000	27	47,105
		40	$207,295

It is also important to test the population for completeness and detail tie-in before a sample is selected to ensure that all population items will be properly subjected to sample selection.

5. DEFINE THE SAMPLING UNIT

The major consideration in defining the physical sampling unit when conducting tests of controls is making it consistent with the objectives of the audit tests. Thus, the definition of the population and the planned audit procedures usually dictate the appropriate sampling unit. For example, if the auditor wants to determine how frequently the client fails to fill a customer's order, the sampling unit must be defined as the customer's order. If, however, the objective is to determine whether the proper quantity of the goods described on the customer's order is correctly shipped and billed, it is possible to define the sampling unit as the customer's order, the shipping document, or the duplicate sales invoice.

The sampling unit for nonstatistical audit sampling in tests of details of balances is almost always the item making up the account balance. For accounts receivable, it is the customer account name or number, or unpaid invoice, on the accounts receivable list. For statistical sampling, such as MUS, the definition of the sampling unit is an individual dollar.

Having the individual dollar as the sampling unit for MUS results in an automatic emphasis on physical units with larger recorded balances. Since the sample is selected on the basis of individual dollars, an account with a large balance has a greater chance of being included than an account with a small balance. For example, in accounts receivable confirmation, an account with a $5,000 balance has a 10 times greater probability of selection than one with a $500 balance, as it contains 10 times as many dollar units. As a result, there is no need to use stratified sampling with MUS. Stratification occurs automatically.

6. SPECIFY TOLERABLE EXCEPTION RATE OR SPECIFY MATERIALITY

TERM RELATED TO PLANNING	TEST OF CONTROL (E.G., FOR ATTRIBUTE SAMPLE)	TEST OF DETAIL (E.G., FOR MUS SAMPLE)
Specify tolerable exception rate (TER).	Specify the exception rate the auditor will permit in the population.	N/A
Specify materiality.	N/A	Use overall materiality available for the audit.

Establishing the tolerable exception rate (TER) requires *professional judgment* on the part of the auditor. TER represents the exception rate that the auditor will permit in the population and still be willing to use the assessed control risk and/or the amount of monetary errors or fraud and other irregularities in the transactions established during planning. For example, assume that the auditor decides that TER for the attribute of sales invoice credit approval is 6 percent. That means that the auditor has decided that even if 6 percent of the duplicate sales invoices are not approved for credit, the credit approval control is still effective in terms of the assessed control risk included in the audit plan.

TER is the result of an auditor's judgment. The suitable TER is a question of materiality and is therefore affected by both the definition and the importance of the attribute in the audit plan.

TER has a significant impact on sample size. A larger sample size is needed for a low TER than for a high TER. For example, a larger sample is required for a TER of 4 percent than for a TER of 6 percent.

For sampling for tests of details, materiality is used during the sampling process. It was stated in Chapter 8 that there were two methods for considering materiality: (1) materiality would *not* be allocated to individual accounts in planning the audit (the method adopted by the text); (2) materiality would be allocated to individual accounts at the planning stage. MUS uses method (1): the preliminary judgment about materiality is used to directly determine the tolerable misstatement amount for the audit of each account. Other sampling techniques (e.g., variables estimation) require method (2) and require the auditor to determine tolerable misstatement for each account by allocating the preliminary judgment about materiality over the accounts to be audited.

7. SPECIFY ACCEPTABLE RISK OF ASSESSING CONTROL RISK TOO LOW OR ACCEPTABLE RISK OF INCORRECT ACCEPTANCE

TERM RELATED TO PLANNING	TEST OF CONTROL (E.G., FOR ATTRIBUTE SAMPLE)	TEST OF DETAIL (E.G., FOR MUS SAMPLE)
Acceptable risk of assessing control risk too low (ARACR)	The risk that the auditor is willing to take of accepting a control as effective when the true population exception rate is greater	N/A
Acceptable risk of incorrect acceptance (ARIA)	N/A	The risk that the auditor is willing to take of accepting a balance as correct when the true misstatement is greater than materiality

Whenever a sample is taken, there is a risk that the quantitative conclusions about the population will be incorrect. This is always true unless 100 percent of the population is tested. As has already been stated, this is the case with both nonstatistical and statistical sampling.

For audit sampling in tests of controls, that risk is called the *acceptable risk of assessing control risk too low* (ARACR). ARACR is the risk that the auditor is willing to take of accepting a control as effective (or a rate of monetary errors or fraud and other irregularities as tolerable) when the true population exception rate is greater than the tolerable exception rate (TER). To illustrate, assume that TER is 6 percent, ARACR is 10 percent, and the true population exception rate is 8 percent. The control in this case is not acceptable because the true exception rate of 8 percent exceeds TER. The auditor, of course, does not know the true population exception rate. The ARACR of 10 percent means that the auditor is willing to take a 10 percent risk of concluding that the control is effective after all testing is completed, even when it is ineffective. If the auditor finds the control effective in this illustration, he or she will have over-relied on the system of internal control (used a lower assessed control risk than justified). ARACR is the auditor's measure of sampling risk.

In choosing the appropriate ARACR in a situation, the auditor must use his or her best judgment. Since ARACR is a measure of the risk that the auditor is willing to take, the main consideration is the extent to which the auditor plans to reduce assessed control risk as a basis for the extent of tests of details of balances. The lower the assessed control risk, the lower will be the ARACR chosen and the planned extent of tests of details of balances. Referring to Figure 9-2 (page 283), the most common situation where audit sampling would be used for tests of controls is when the auditor decides to assess control risk at a lower level than can be supported by understanding internal control (alternative 3). If the auditor decides to assess control risk at maximum (alternative 1), tests of controls are not performed. If control risk is assessed at the level supported by understanding internal control (alternative 2), tests of controls are often restricted to inquiry and transaction walk-through tests.

For nonstatistical sampling, it is common for auditors to use ARACR of high, medium, or low instead of a percentage. A low ARACR implies that the tests of controls are important and would correspond to a low assessed control risk and reduced substantive tests of details of balances.

The auditor can establish different TER and ARACR levels for different attributes of an audit test. For example, it is common for auditors to use higher TER and ARACR levels for tests of credit approval than for tests of the existence of duplicate sales invoices and bills of lading. This is because the exceptions for the latter are likely to have a more direct impact on the correctness of the financial statements than the former.

Table 11-3 presents illustrative guidelines for establishing TER and ARACR. The guidelines should not be interpreted as representing broad professional standards; however, they are typical of the types of guidelines public accounting firms issue to their staff.

TABLE 11-3

GUIDELINES FOR ARACR AND TER FOR NONSTATISTICAL SAMPLING: TESTS OF CONTROLS

FACTOR	JUDGMENT	GUIDELINE
Assessed control risk. Consider: Nature, extent, and timing of substantive tests (extensive planned substantive tests relate to higher assessed control risk and vice versa) Quality of evidence available for tests of controls (a lower quality of evidence available results in a higher assessed control risk and vice versa).	• Lowest assessed control risk • Moderate assessed control risk • Higher assessed control risk • Maximum control risk	• ARACR of low • ARACR of medium • ARACR of high • ARACR is not applicable
Significance of the transactions and related account balances that the internal controls are intended to affect.	• Highly significant balances • Significant balances • Less significant balances	• TER of 4% • TER of 5% • TER of 6%

Note: The guidelines should recognize that there may be variations in ARACRs based on audit considerations. The guidelines above are the most conservative that should be followed.

For tests of details, acceptable risk of incorrect acceptance (ARIA) is the risk that the auditor is willing to take of accepting a balance as correct when the true misstatement in the balance is greater than materiality. ARIA is the equivalent term to acceptable risk of assessing control risk too low (ARACR) for tests of controls.

There is an inverse relationship between ARIA and required sample size. If, for example, the auditor decides to reduce ARIA from 10 percent to 5 percent, the required sample size would increase. By reducing ARIA, we are increasing the required sampling assurance from 90 percent to 95 percent that the balance is correct, thus resulting in a larger sample size (i.e., the gathering of more evidence).

The primary factor affecting the auditor's decision about ARIA is assessed control risk in the audit risk model. When internal controls are effective, control risk can be reduced, permitting the auditor to increase ARIA. This, in turn, reduces the sample size required for the test of details of the related account balance.

A difficulty students often have is understanding how ARACR and ARIA affect evidence accumulation. In Chapter 10 it was shown that tests of details of balances for monetary errors or fraud and other irregularities can be reduced if internal controls are found to be effective through assessing control risk below maximum and performing tests of controls. The effects of ARACR and ARIA are consistent with that conclusion. If the auditor concludes that internal controls may be effective, control risk can be assessed at less than maximum. A lower control risk requires a lower ARACR in testing the controls, which in turn requires a larger sample size. If controls are found to be effective, control risk can remain low, which permits the auditor to increase ARIA (through use of the audit risk model), thereby requiring a smaller sample size in the related substantive tests of details of balances. The relationship between ARACR and ARIA is shown in Figure 11-3.

Besides control risk, ARIA is also directly affected by acceptable audit risk and inversely by other substantive tests already performed or planned for the account balance. For example, if acceptable audit risk is reduced, ARIA should also be reduced. If analytical procedures were performed and indicate that the account balance is fairly stated, ARIA should be increased. Stated differently, the analytical procedures are evidence in support of the account balance; therefore, less evidence from the detailed test of the balance using sampling is required to achieve acceptable audit risk. The same conclusion is appropriate for the relationship among dual purpose tests, ARIA, and sample size for tests of details of balances. The various relationships affecting ARIA are summarized in Table 11-4.

FIGURE 11-3
Effect of ARACR and
ARIA on Required
Evidence

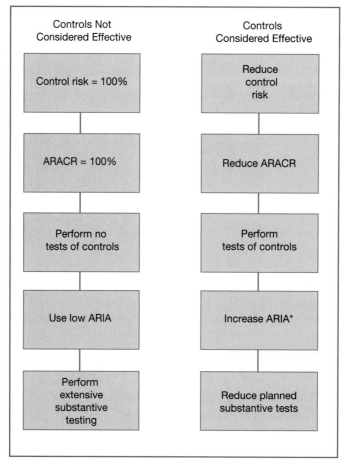

*Assumes tests of controls were satisfactory, which permits control risk to remain low.

TABLE 11-4

RELATIONSHIP
AMONG FACTORS
AFFECTING ARIA,
EFFECT ON ARIA, AND
REQUIRED SAMPLE
SIZE FOR AUDIT
SAMPLING

FACTOR AFFECTING ARIA	EXAMPLE	EFFECT ON ARIA	EFFECT ON SAMPLE SIZE
Effectiveness of internal controls (control risk)	Internal controls are effective (reduced control risk)	Increase	Decrease
Acceptable audit risk	Likelihood of bankruptcy is low (increased acceptable audit risk)	Increase	Decrease
Analytical procedures	Analytical procedures performed with no indications of likely misstatements	Increase	Decrease

8. ESTIMATE THE POPULATION EXCEPTION RATE OR THE MISSTATEMENTS IN THE POPULATION

TERM RELATED TO PLANNING	TEST OF CONTROL (E.G., FOR ATTRIBUTE SAMPLE)	TEST OF DETAIL (E.G., FOR MUS SAMPLE)
Estimated population exception rate (EPER)	The advance estimate of the percentage of exceptions in the population	N/A
Estimated misstatements in the population	N/A	The advance estimate of total dollar error in the population

When conducting tests of controls, an *advance estimate* of the population exception rate (EPER) should be made to plan the appropriate sample size. If the EPER is low, a relatively small sample size will satisfy the auditor's tolerable exception rate. When the expected exception rate is low, a less precise estimate of EPER can be used. To be more precise, an estimate of the population exception rate must be based on more data, that is, a larger sample.

It is common to use the results of the preceding year's audit to make this estimate. If the prior year's results are not available, or if they are considered unreliable, the auditor can take a small *preliminary sample* of the current year's population for this purpose. It is not critical that the estimate be precise because the current year's sample exception rate is ultimately used to estimate the population characteristics.

Note that if a preliminary sample is used, it can be included in the ultimate sample, as long as appropriate sample selection procedures are followed. For example, assume that an auditor takes a preliminary sample of 30 items to estimate the EPER that considers the entire population. Later, if the auditor decides that a total sample size of 100 is needed, only 70 additional items will need to be properly selected and tested.

Similarly, for tests of details sampling, the auditor makes this estimate based on prior experience with the client and by assessing inherent risk, considering the results of tests of controls and of analytical procedures already performed.

9. DETERMINE THE INITIAL SAMPLE SIZE

Four factors determine the initial sample size for audit sampling for tests of controls: population size, TER, ARACR, and EPER. Population size is not nearly as significant a factor as the others and typically can be ignored.

An important characteristic of nonstatistical sampling compared to statistical methods is the need to decide the sample size using professional judgment for nonstatistical methods rather than by calculation using a statistical formula. Once the three major factors affecting sample size have been determined, it is possible for the auditor to determine an initial sample size.

The initial sample size is called that because the exceptions in the actual sample must be evaluated before it is possible to know whether the sample is sufficiently large to achieve the objectives of the tests.

Sensitivity of sample size to a change in the factors   To properly understand the concepts underlying sampling in auditing, it is helpful to understand the effect of changing any of the four factors that determine sample size while the other factors are held constant. Table 11-5 illustrates the effect of increasing each of the four factors; a decrease will have the opposite effect.

A combination of two factors has the greatest effect on sample size: TER minus EPER. The difference is the *precision* of the planned sample estimate. For example, if TER (tolerable exception rate) is 5 percent and EPER (estimated population exception rate) is 2 percent, then precision is 3 percent. A smaller precision, which is called a more precise estimate, requires a larger sample.

Auditors using nonstatistical sampling for tests of details similarly determine the initial sample size judgmentally considering the factors discussed so far. Table 11-6

TABLE 11-5

EFFECT ON SAMPLE SIZE OF CHANGING FACTORS

TYPE OF CHANGE	EFFECT ON INITIAL SAMPLE SIZE
Increase acceptable risk of assessing control risk too low	Decrease
Increase tolerable deviation rate	Decrease
Increase estimated population deviation rate	Increase
Increase population size	Increase (minor effect)

FACTOR	CONDITIONS LEADING TO SMALLER SAMPLE SIZE	CONDITIONS LEADING TO LARGER SAMPLE SIZE
a. **Control risk (ARACR).** Affects acceptable risk of incorrect acceptance.	Low control risk	High control risk
b. **Risk for other substantive tests related to the same assertion** (including analytical procedures and other relevant substantive tests). Affects acceptable risk of incorrect acceptance.	Low risk associated with other relevant substantive tests	High risk associated with other relevant substantive tests
c. **Acceptable audit risk.** Affects acceptable risk and incorrect acceptance.	High acceptable audit risk	Low acceptable audit risk
d. **Materiality.**	Larger materiality	Smaller materiality
e. **Inherent risk.** Affects estimated misstatements in the population.	Low inherent risk	High inherent risk
f. **Expected size and frequency of misstatements.** Affects estimated misstatements in the population.	Smaller misstatements or lower frequency	Larger misstatements or higher frequency
g. **Number of items in the population.**	Almost no effect on sample size unless population is very small	Almost no effect on sample size unless population is very small

summarizes the primary factors that influence sample size for nonstatistical sampling of tests of details and how sample size is affected.

When the auditor uses stratified sampling, the sample size must be allocated among the strata. Typically, auditors allocate a higher portion of the sample items to larger population items. For example, in the example from Problem 14-27, allocating a sample size of 15, the auditor might decide to select all three accounts from stratum 1, and six each from strata 2 and 3. Observe that audit sampling does not apply to stratum 1 because all population items are being audited.

For MUS sampling, sample size is determined using a statistical formula.

10. SELECT THE SAMPLE

After the auditor has computed the initial sample size for the audit sampling application, he or she must choose the items in the population to be included in the sample. The sample can be chosen by using any of the probabilistic or nonprobabilistic methods discussed earlier in the chapter. It is important for the auditor to use a method that will permit meaningful conclusions about the sample results.

For stratified sampling, the auditor selects samples independently from each stratum.

Monetary unit samples are samples selected with probability proportionate to size (PPS). Such samples are of individual dollars in the population. Auditors cannot, however, audit individual dollars. Therefore, the auditor must determine the physical unit to perform the audit tests. For example, the auditor could select a random sample of population items and determine that dollar number 7,376 is to be selected. However, to perform the audit procedures, the auditor must identify the population item that corresponds to the 7,376th dollar, for example, the twelfth invoice transaction.

11. PERFORM THE AUDIT PROCEDURES

The auditor performs the test of control audit procedures by examining each item in the sample to determine whether it is consistent with the definition of the attribute and maintains a record of all the exceptions found. When audit procedures have been completed for a test of control sampling application, there will be a sample size and a number of exceptions for each attribute.

To perform the test of detail audit procedures, the auditor applies the appropriate audit procedures to each item in the sample to determine whether it is correct or contains a misstatement. For example, in the confirmation of accounts receivable, the auditor mails the sample of confirmations in the manner described in Chapter 14 and determines the amount of misstatement in each account confirmed. For nonresponses, alternative procedures are used to determine the misstatements. The auditor tracks the recorded value and the audited value so that the aggregate client misstatement can be determined.

The auditor cannot expect meaningful results from using audit sampling unless the audit procedures are applied carefully.

12. GENERALIZE FROM THE SAMPLE TO THE POPULATION

For tests of controls, the *sample exception rate* (SER) can be easily calculated from the actual sample results. SER equals the actual number of exceptions divided by the actual sample size.

It is improper for the auditor to conclude that the population exception rate is exactly the same as the sample exception rate; the chance that they are exactly the same is too small. For nonstatistical methods, there are two ways to generalize from the sample to the population.

1. Add an estimate of sampling error to SER to arrive at a computed upper exception rate (CUER) for a given acceptable risk of assessing control risk too low. It is extremely difficult for auditors to make sampling error estimates using nonstatistical sampling because of the judgment required to do so; therefore, this approach is generally not used.

2. Subtract the sampling exception rate from the tolerable exception rate, which is calculated sampling error (TER – SER = calculated sampling error), and evaluate whether calculated sampling error is sufficiently large to indicate that the true population exception rate is acceptable. Most auditors using nonstatistical sampling follow this approach. For example, if an auditor takes a sample of 100 items for an attribute and finds no exceptions (SER = 0), and TER is 5 percent, calculated sampling error is 5 percent (TER of 5 percent – SER of 0 = 5 percent). On the other hand, if there had been four exceptions, calculated sampling error would have been 1 percent (TER of 5 percent – SER of 4 percent). It is much more likely that the true population exception rate is less than or equal to the tolerable exception rate in the first case than in the second one. Therefore, most auditors would probably find the population acceptable based on the first sample result, and not acceptable based on the second.

In practice, auditors tend to test controls when they expect no exceptions. When exceptions are found, it is more likely that the controls cannot be relied on, unless the situation(s) causing the control exception can be isolated (as discussed in the next section).

In addition, the auditor's consideration of whether sampling error is sufficiently large will depend on sample size. For example, if the sample size in the above example had been only 20 items, the auditor would have been much less confident that finding no exceptions was an indication that the true population exception rate did not exceed TER than finding no exceptions in a sample of 100 items. Note that under the second approach, the auditor does not make an estimate of the computed upper exception rate.

When generalizing tests of details, the auditor deals with dollar amounts rather than with exceptions. The auditor must generalize from the sample to the population by (1) projecting misstatements from the sample results to the population and (2) considering sampling error and sampling risk (ARIA). For example, assume that the auditor discovered three misstatements that netted to $389 overstatement. Can the auditor conclude that accounts receivable is overstated by $389? No, the auditor is interested in the *population* results (further possible misstatement is described in

Chapter 8), not those for the sample (identified misstatement is defined in Chapter 8). It is therefore necessary to project from the sample to the population to estimate the population misstatement.

The first step is making a *point estimate,* which was defined as likely misstatement in Chapter 8. There are different ways to calculate the point estimate, but a common way is to assume that misstatements in the unaudited population are proportional to the misstatements in the sample. That calculation must be done for each stratum and then totalled, rather than for the total misstatements in the sample. Thus, the point estimate of the misstatement is determined by using a weighted-average method. For example, if the $389 total error were comprised as follows:

STRATUM	SAMPLE SIZE	DOLLARS AUDITED Recorded Value	Audited Value	CLIENT MISSTATEMENT
1	3	$ 88,955	$ 91,695	$(2,740)
2	6	43,995	43,024	971
3	6	13,105	10,947	2,158
	15	$146,055	$145,666	$ 389

then the point estimate would be calculated as shown:

STRATUM	CLIENT MISSTATEMENT ÷ RECORDED VALUE FROM SAMPLE	×	RECORDED BOOK VALUE FOR STRATUM	=	POINT ESTIMATE OF MISSTATEMENT
1	$(2,740) / $88,955		$88,955		$(2,740)
2	971 / 43,995		71,235		1,572
3	2,158 / 13,105		47,105		7,757
Total					$ 6,589

The point estimate of the error in the population is $6,589, indicating an overstatement. The point estimate, by itself, is not an adequate measure of the population misstatement, however, because of sampling error. In other words, because the estimate is based on a sample, it will be close to the true population misstatement, but it is unlikely that it is exactly the same. The auditor must consider the possibility that the true population misstatement is greater than the amount of misstatement that is tolerable in the circumstances whenever the point estimate is less than the tolerable misstatement amount. This must be done for both statistical and nonstatistical samples.

13. ANALYZE EXCEPTIONS OR MISSTATEMENTS

In addition to determining the SER for each attribute control tested and evaluating whether the true but unknown exception rate is likely to exceed the tolerable exception rate, it is necessary to analyze individual exceptions to determine the breakdown in the internal controls that caused them. Exceptions could be caused by carelessness of employees, misunderstood instructions, intentional failure to perform procedures, or many other factors. The nature of an exception and its cause have a significant effect on the qualitative evaluation of the system. For example, if all the exceptions in the tests of internal verification of credit authorization for sales invoices occurred while the person normally responsible for performing the tests was on vacation, this would affect the auditor's evaluation of the internal controls and the subsequent investigation. The auditor could choose to test the period substantively when the employee was on vacation, and rely on internal controls for the remainder of the year.

Misstatements discovered during tests of details could be caused by control exceptions. For example, in confirming accounts receivable, suppose that all misstatements resulted from the client's failure to record returned goods. The auditor would determine why that type of misstatement occurred so often, the implications of the misstatements on other audit areas, the potential impact on the financial statements, and the effect on company operations.

An important part of misstatement analysis is deciding whether any modification of the audit risk model is needed. If the auditor concluded that the failure to record the returns discussed in the previous paragraph resulted from a breakdown of internal controls, it might be necessary to reassess control risk. That, in turn, would probably cause the auditor to reduce ARIA, which would increase planned sample size. As discussed in Chapter 8, revisions of the audit risk model must be done with extreme care because the model is intended primarily for planning, not evaluating results.

14. DETERMINE THE ACCEPTABILITY OF THE POPULATION

For tests of controls, it was shown under "12. Generalize from the Sample to the Population" that most auditors subtract SER from TER when they use nonstatistical sampling and evaluate whether the difference, which is calculated sampling error, is sufficiently large. If the auditor concludes that the difference is sufficiently large, the control being tested can be used to reduce assessed control risk as planned, provided a careful analysis of the cause of exceptions does not indicate the possibility of other significant problems with internal controls.

When the auditor concludes that TER – SER is too small to conclude that the population is acceptable, the auditor must take specific action. Three courses of action can be followed.

Revise TER or ARACR This alternative should be followed only when the auditor has concluded that the original specifications were too conservative. Relaxing either TER or ARACR may be difficult to defend if the auditor is ever subject to review by a court or a quasi-legal body such as a commission.

Expand the sample size An increase in the sample size has the effect of decreasing the sampling error if the actual sample exception rate does not increase. Of course, SER may also increase or decrease if additional items are selected.

Revise assessed control risk If the results of the tests of controls do not support the planned assessed control risk, the auditor should revise assessed control risk upward. The effect of the revision is likely to increase tests of details of balances. For example, if tests of controls of credit approval indicate that those procedures are not being followed, the auditor may not be able to rely on the control and will therefore conduct additional substantive tests at year end. This is most likely to be done through tests of the bad debt allowance for accounts receivable and of bad debt expense for the year.

The decision whether to increase sample size until sampling error is sufficiently small or to revise assessed control risk must be made on the basis of cost versus benefit. If the sample is not expanded, it is necessary to revise assessed control risk upward and therefore perform additional substantive tests. The cost of additional tests of controls must be compared with the cost of additional substantive tests. If an expanded sample continues to produce unacceptable results, additional substantive tests will then be necessary.

If the original test performed is testing transactions for monetary errors or fraud and other irregularities, and an exception rate higher than that assumed is indicated, the response would generally be the same as for tests of controls.

For tests of details, an auditor using nonstatistical sampling cannot formally measure sampling error and therefore must subjectively consider the possibility that the true population misstatement aggregated with other misstatements exceeds materiality. This is done by considering (1) the difference between the point estimate and materiality, (2) the extent to which items in the population have been audited 100 percent, (3) whether misstatements tend to be offsetting or in only one direction, (4) the amounts of individual misstatements, and (5) sample size. To continue the example above, suppose that materiality is $40,000. In that case, the auditor may conclude that there is little chance, given the point estimate of $6,589, that the true population misstatement exceeds that amount.

Suppose that materiality is $12,000, only $5,411 greater than the point estimate. In that case, other factors would be considered. For example, if the larger items in the population were audited 100 percent (as was done here), any unidentified misstatements would be restricted to smaller items. If the misstatements tend to be offsetting and are relatively small in size, the auditor may conclude that the true population misstatement is likely to be less than materiality. Also, the larger the sample size, the more confident the auditor can be that the point estimate is close to the true population value. Therefore, the auditor would be more willing to accept that the true population misstatement is less than tolerable misstatement in this example, where the sample size is considered large, than where it is considered moderate or small. On the other hand, if one or more of these other conditions is different, the chance of a misstatement in excess of the tolerable amount may be judged to be high, and the recorded population unacceptable.

Even if the amount of likely misstatement is not considered material, the auditor must wait to make a final evaluation until the entire audit is completed. For example, the estimated total misstatement and estimated sampling error in accounts receivable must be combined with estimates of misstatements in all other parts of the audit to evaluate the effect of all misstatements on the financial statements as a whole.

For MUS and variables sampling, a formal decision rule is used for deciding the acceptability of the population. The decision rule used for MUS is similar to that used for nonstatistical sampling, but it is sufficiently different to merit discussion. The decision rule will be illustrated in Chapter 14, along with the illustration of a specific sample selection.

SUMMARY OF SAMPLING STEPS

Table 11-7 summarizes the steps used in sampling. It is apparent from the table that planning is an essential part of using any type of sampling. The purposes of planning are to make sure that the audit procedures are properly applied and that the sample

TABLE 11-7

SUMMARY OF AUDIT SAMPLING STEPS

STEPS — AUDIT SAMPLING FOR TESTS OF CONTROLS	STEPS — AUDIT SAMPLING FOR TESTS OF DETAILS
Plan the Sample 1. State the objectives of the audit test. 2. Decide if audit sampling applies. 3. Define attributes and exception conditions. 4. Define the population. 5. Define the sampling unit. 6. Specify tolerable exception rate. 7. Specify acceptable risk of assessing control risk too low. 8. Estimate the population exception rate. 9. Determine the initial sample size.	**Plan the Sample** 1. State the objectives of the audit test. 2. Decide if audit sampling applies. 3. Define misstatement conditions. 4. Define the population. 5. Define the sampling unit. 6. Specify materiality. 7. Specify acceptable risk of incorrect acceptance. 8. Estimate misstatements in the population. 9. Determine the initial sample size.
Select the Sample and Perform the Audit Procedures 10. Select the sample. 11. Perform the audit procedures.	**Select the Sample and Perform the Audit Procedures** 10. Select the sample. 11. Perform the audit procedures.
Evaluate the Results 12. Generalize from the sample to the population. 13. Analyze the exceptions. 14. Determine the acceptability of the population.	**Evaluate the Results** 12. Generalize from the sample to the population. 13. Analyze the misstatements. 14. Determine the acceptability of the population.

size is appropriate for the circumstances. Sample selection is also important and must be done with care to avoid nonsampling errors. Performing the audit procedures must be done carefully to correctly determine the number of exceptions or the value of errors in the sample. It is the most time-consuming part of audit sampling.

Evaluating the results for tests of controls includes making an estimate of sampling error and comparing it to the tolerable exception rate, while for tests of details, dollar values must be extrapolated, with decision rules and methodologies varying depending upon the sampling method chosen. Exceptions or errors must be analyzed and, finally, acceptability of the population determined.

OTHER CONSIDERATIONS

For the sake of greater continuity, in the preceding discussion, we bypassed four important aspects of using sampling that are now discussed: random selection versus statistical measurement, adequate documentation, management letters, and the need for professional judgment.

RANDOM SELECTION VERSUS STATISTICAL MEASUREMENT

Students often do not understand the distinction between random (probabilistic) selection and statistical measurement. It should now be clear that random selection is a part of statistical sampling but is not, by itself, statistical measurement. To have statistical measurement, it is necessary to generalize mathematically from the sample to the population.

It is acceptable to use random selection procedures without drawing statistical conclusions, but this practice is questionable if a reasonably large sample size has been selected. Whenever the auditor takes a random sample, regardless of his or her basis for determining its size, there is a *statistical measurement inherent in the sample*. Since there is little or no cost involved in computing the upper exception rate, we believe that it should be done whenever possible. It would, of course, be inappropriate to draw a statistical conclusion unless the sample were randomly selected or selected using a formal methodology, such as interval selection with a random start.

ADEQUATE DOCUMENTATION

It is important that the auditor retain adequate records of the procedures performed, the methods used to select the sample and perform the tests, the results found in the tests, and the conclusions drawn. This is necessary as a means of evaluating the combined results of all tests and as a basis for defending the audit if the need arises. Documentation is equally important for statistical and nonstatistical sampling. Examples of the type of documentation commonly found in practice are included in the case illustrations for Hillsburg Hardware Ltd. in Chapters 12 and 14 .

MANAGEMENT LETTERS

Documentation, evaluation, or testing of internal controls may lead to the discovery of a variety of internal control exceptions. These should be communicated to management regardless of the nature of the exceptions.

NEED FOR PROFESSIONAL JUDGMENT

A criticism occasionally levelled against statistical sampling is that it reduces the use of professional judgment. A review of the 14 steps discussed in this chapter for sampling shows how unwarranted this criticism is. For proper application of sampling, it is necessary to use professional judgment in most of the steps. For example, selection of the initial sample size depends primarily on the TER, ARACR, and EPER. Choosing the first two requires the exercise of high-level professional judgment; the latter requires a careful estimate. Similarly, the final evaluation of the acceptability of the population for any form of sampling must also be based on high-level professional judgment.

Acceptable risk of assessing control risk too low (ARACR) — the risk that the auditor is willing to take of accepting a control as effective or a rate of monetary errors or fraud and other irregularities as tolerable, when the true population exception rate is greater than the tolerable exception rate (p. 356).

Attribute — the characteristic being tested for in the population (p. 350).

Attribute sampling — a statistical, probabilistic method of sample evaluation that results in an estimate of the proportion of items in a population containing a characteristic or attribute of interest (p. 350).

Block sampling — a nonprobabilistic method of sample selection in which items are selected in measured sequences (p. 346).

Confidence level — statement of probability (p. 344).

Difference estimation — a form of sampling used to estimate the difference between the recorded value and the audited value (p. 351).

Directed sample selection — a nonprobabilistic method of sample selection in which each item in the sample is selected based on some judgmental criteria established by the auditor (p. 345).

Discovery sampling — a form of attribute sampling designed to look for one or very low occurrences (p. 350).

Estimated population exception rate (EPER) — exception rate the auditor expects to find in the population before testing begins (p. 359).

Exception rate — the percentage of items in a population that include exceptions in prescribed controls or monetary correctness (p. 350).

Haphazard selection — a nonprobabilistic method of sample selection in which items are chosen without regard to their size, source, or other distinguishing characteristics (p. 346).

Initial sample size — sample size determined by professional judgment (nonstatistical sampling) or by statistical tables (attribute sampling) (p. 359).

Judgmental sampling — use of professional judgment rather than statistical methods to select sample items for audit tests (p. 344).

Monetary unit sampling (MUS) — a modified form of attribute sampling that focuses on a single unit of currency (in Canada, the dollar), rather than on a physical unit (p. 351).

Nonprobabilistic sample selection — a method of sample selection in which the auditor uses professional judgment to select items from the population (p. 345).

Nonsampling risk — the chance of exception when audit tests do not uncover existing exceptions in the sample; caused by failure to recognize exceptions and by inappropriate or ineffective audit procedures; synonymous with nonsampling error (p. 343).

Nonstatistical sampling — the auditor's use of professional judgment to select sample items, estimate the population values, and estimate sampling risk (p. 344).

Occurrence rate — the ratio of items in a population that contain a specific attribute to the total number of population items (p. 350).

Population —the body of data about which the auditor wishes to generalize (p. 352).

Probabilistic sample selection — a method of sample selection in which it is possible to define the set of all possible samples, every possible sample has a known probability of being selected, and the sample is selected by a random process (p. 346).

Probability proportionate-to-size sampling — see *monetary unit sampling* (p. 351).

Random number table — a listing of independent random digits conveniently arranged in tabular form to facilitate the selection of random numbers with multiple digits (p. 347).

Random sample — a sample in which every possible combination of elements in the population has an equal chance of being selected (p. 347).

Representative sample — a sample with the same characteristics as those of the population (p. 343).

Sample exception rate (SER) — the number of exceptions in the sample divided by the sample size (p. 361).

Sampling distribution — a frequency distribution of the results of all possible samples of a specified size that could be obtained from a population containing some specific parameters (p. 350).

Sampling risk — the chance of exception inherent in tests of less than the entire population; may be reduced by using an increased sample size and using an appropriate method of selecting sample items from the population (p. 343).

Statistical sampling — the use of mathematical measurement techniques to calculate formal statistical results and quantify sampling risk (p. 344).

Systematic selection — a probabilistic method of sampling in which the auditor calculates an interval (the population size divided by the number of sample items desired) and selects the items for the sample based on the size of the interval and a randomly selected number between zero and the sample size (p. 348).

Tolerable exception rate (TER) — the exception rate that the auditor will permit in the population and still be willing to use the assessed control risk and/or the amount of monetary errors or fraud and other irregularities in the transactions established during planning (p. 355).

11-1 State what is meant by a "representative sample," and explain its importance in sampling audit populations.

11-2 Explain the major difference between statistical and nonstatistical sampling. What are the three main parts of statistical and nonstatistical methods?

11-3 Explain the difference between replacement sampling and nonreplacement sampling. Which method do auditors usually follow? Why?

11-4 Explain what is meant by a "random number table." Describe how an auditor would select 35 random numbers from a population of 1,750 items by using a random number table.

11-5 Describe systematic sample selection, and explain how an auditor would select 35 numbers from a population of 1,750 items using this approach. What are the advantages and disadvantages of systematic sample selection?

11-6 What is the purpose of using nonstatistical sampling for (a) tests of controls and (b) tests of details?

11-7 Explain what is meant by "block sampling," and describe how an auditor could obtain 5 blocks of 20 sales invoices from a sales journal.

11-8 Define each of the following terms:
a. Acceptable risk of assessing control risk too low (ARACR)
b. Acceptable risk of incorrect acceptance (ARIA)
c. Estimated population exception rate (EPER)
d. Sample exception rate (SER)
e. Tolerable exception rate (TER)

11-9 Describe what is meant by a "sampling unit." Explain why the sampling unit for verifying the existence of recorded sales differs from the sampling unit for testing for the possibility of omitted sales.

11-10 How is TER determined?

11-11 Distinguish between a sampling error and a nonsampling error. How can each be reduced?

11-12 What major difference between tests of controls and tests of details of balances makes attribute sampling inappropriate for tests of details of balances?

11-13 Explain the difference between an attribute and an exception condition. State the exception condition for the following audit procedure: the duplicate sales invoice has been initialled indicating the performance of internal verification.

11-14 Define "stratified sampling," and explain its importance in auditing. How could an auditor obtain a stratified sample of 30 items from each of 3 strata in the confirmation of accounts receivable?

11-15 Distinguish between the point estimate of the total misstatements (likely misstatement) and the true value of the misstatements in the population. How can each be determined?

11-16 State the relationship between the following:
a. ARACR and sample size
b. Population size and sample size
c. TER and sample size
d. EPER and sample size

11-17 Define what is meant by "sampling risk." Does sampling risk apply to nonstatistical sampling, MUS, attribute sampling, and variables sampling? Explain.

11-18 Explain what is meant by "analysis of exceptions," and discuss its importance.

11-19 Outline a situation for which discovery sampling would be used.

11-20 Distinguish between random selection and statistical measurement. State the circumstances under which one can be used without the other.

11-21 List the major decisions the auditor must make in using sampling. Indicate which decisions apply to specific forms of sampling. State the most important considerations involved in making each decision.

11-22 The following items apply to sampling from large populations. Select the most appropriate response for each question.

a. From a random sample of items listed from a client's inventory count, a public accountant estimates with a 10 percent ARACR that the CUER is between 4 percent and 6 percent. The accountant's major concern is that there is one chance in 20 that the true deviation rate in the population is
(1) more than 6 percent.
(2) less than 6 percent.
(3) more than 4 percent.
(4) less than 4 percent.

b. If all other factors specified in a sampling plan remain constant, changing the ARACR from 10 percent to 5 percent would cause the required sample size to

(1) increase.
(2) remain the same.
(3) decrease.
(4) become indeterminate.

c. In a random sample of 1,000 records, an auditor determines that the SER is 2 percent. The auditor can state that the exception rate in the population is
(1) not more than 3 percent.
(2) not less than 2 percent.
(3) probably about 2 percent.
(4) not less than 1 percent.

d. If all other factors specified in a sampling plan remain constant, changing the TER from 8 percent to 12 percent would cause the required sample size to
(1) increase.
(2) remain the same.

(3) decrease.

(4) become indeterminate.

(AICPA adapted)

e. If an auditor wishes to select a random sample that must have a 10 percent ARACR and a TER of 10 percent, the size of the sample to be selected will decrease as the estimate of the

(1) population exception rate increases.

(2) population exception rate decreases.

(3) population size increases.

(4) ARACR increases.

(AICPA adapted)

11-23 The following questions relate to physical unit attribute sampling and monetary unit attribute sampling. Select the most appropriate response.

a. In a dollar-unit sampling plan, the probability that any given account balance will be included in the sample is proportionate to

(1) the number of accounts in the population.

(2) the confidence level chosen for the sample.

(3) the size of the account balance.

(4) the TER chosen by the auditor.

b. Attribute sampling plans would be most appropriate in auditing situations where the auditor is performing

(1) tests of controls.

(2) analytical review procedures.

(3) tests of details of balances.

(4) none of the above.

(CICA adapted)

11-24 The following questions refer to the use of sampling in auditing. For each one, select the best response.

a. Felix Santos decides to use stratified sampling. The basic reason for using stratified sampling rather than unrestricted random sampling is to

(1) give every element in the population an equal chance of being included in the sample.

(2) reduce as much as possible the degree of variability in the overall population.

(3) allow the person selecting the sample to use his or her own judgment in deciding which elements should be included in the sample.

(4) reduce the required sample size from a nonhomogeneous population.

b. In an examination of financial statements, a public accountant will generally find stratified sampling techniques to be most applicable to

(1) recomputing net wage and salary payments to employees.

(2) confirming accounts receivable for residential customers at a large electric utility.

(3) reviewing supporting documentation for additions to capital assets.

(4) tracing hours worked from the payroll summary back to the individual time cards.

c. From prior experience, a public accountant is aware that cash disbursements contain a few unusually large disbursements. In using statistical sampling, the public accountant's best course of action is to

(1) increase the sample size to lessen the effect of the unusually large disbursements.

(2) eliminate any unusually large disbursements that appear in the sample.

(3) continue to draw new samples until no unusually large disbursements appear in the sample.

(4) stratify the cash disbursements population so that the unusually large disbursements are reviewed separately.

d. The auditor's failure to recognize an error in an amount or an error in an internal control data processing procedure is described as a

(1) standard error of the mean.

(2) statistical error.

(3) sampling error.

(4) nonsampling error.

e. An auditor makes separate tests of controls and tests of details of balances in the accounts payable area, which has good internal control. If the auditor uses statistical sampling for both of these tests, the acceptable risk established for the test of details of balances is normally

(1) greater than that for tests of controls.

(2) less than that for tests of controls.

(3) the same as that for tests of controls.

(4) totally independent of that for tests of controls.

f. How should an auditor determine the tolerable misstatement required in establishing a statistical sampling plan?

(1) By the materiality of an allowable margin of error the auditor is willing to accept.

(2) By the amount of risk the auditor is willing to take that material misstatements will occur in the accounting process.

(3) By the amount of reliance the auditor will place on the results of the sample.

(4) By reliance on a table of random numbers.

(AICPA adapted)

11-25

a. For each of the following independent problems, design an unbiased random sampling plan using the random number table in Table 11-2. The plan should include defining the sampling unit, establishing a numbering system for the population, and establishing a correspondence between the random number table and the population. After the plan has been designed, select the first five sample items from the random number table for each problem. Use a starting point of row 1009, column 1, for each problem. Read down the table using the leftmost digits in the column. When you reach the last item in a column, go to the top of the next column.

1. Prenumbered sales invoices in a sales journal where the lowest invoice number is 1 and the highest is 6211.
2. Prenumbered bills of lading where the lowest document number is 21926 and the highest is 28511.

b. Use an available random number generator in a spreadsheet or other source to obtain the above samples with the computer. (Instructor's option)

11-26 For the examination of the financial statements of Scotia Inc., Rosa Schellenberg, a public accountant, has decided to apply nonstatistical audit sampling in the tests of sales transactions. Based on her knowledge of Scotia's operations in the area of sales, she decides that the estimated population deviation rate is likely to be 3 percent and that she is willing to accept a 5 percent risk that the true population exception rate is not greater than 6 percent. Given this information, Schellenberg selects a random sample of 150 sales invoices from the 5,000 prepared during the year and examines them for exceptions. She notes the following exceptions in her working papers. There is no other documentation.

INVOICE NO.	COMMENT
5028	Sales invoice had incorrect price but a subsequent credit note was sent out as a correction.
6791	Voided sales invoice examined by auditor.
6810	Shipping document for a sale of merchandise could not be located.
7364	Sales invoice for $2,875 has not been collected and is six months past due.
7625	Client unable to locate the printed duplicate copy of the sales invoice.
8431	Invoice was dated three days later than the date of the shipping document.
8528	Customer purchase order is not attached to the duplicate sales invoice.
8566	Billing is for $100 less than it should be due to a pricing error.
8780	Client unable to locate the printed duplicate copy of the sales invoice.
9169	Credit not authorized, but the sale was for only $7.65.

Required

a. Which of the preceding should be defined as an exception?
b. Explain why it is inappropriate to set a single acceptable TER and EPER for the combined exceptions.
c. State the appropriate analysis of exceptions for each of the exceptions in the sample.

11-27 An audit partner is developing an office training program to familiarize her professional staff with statistical decision models applicable to the audit of dollar-value balances. She wishes to demonstrate the relationship of sample sizes to population size and variability and the auditor's specifications as to tolerable misstatement and ARIA. The partner prepared the table on page 370 to show comparative population characteristics and audit specifications of the two populations.

Required

In items (1) through (5) below, you are to indicate for the specific case from the table the required sample size to be selected from population 1 relative to the sample from population 2.

(1) In case 1 the required sample size from population 1 is _____.

(2) In case 2 the required sample size from population 1 is _____.

(3) In case 3 the required sample size from population 1 is _____.

(4) In case 4 the required sample size from population 1 is _____.

(5) In case 5 the required sample size from population 1 is _____.

Your answer should be selected from the following responses:

a. Larger than the required sample size from population 2.
b. Equal to the required sample size from population 2.
c. Smaller than the required sample size from population 2.
d. Indeterminate relative to the required sample size from population 2.

(AICPA adapted)

11-28 You have just completed the accounts receivable confirmation process in the audit of Danforth Paper Company Ltd., a paper supplier to retail shops and commercial users. Following are the data related to this process:

Accounts receivable recorded balance	$2,760,000
Number of accounts	7,320

	CHARACTERISTICS OF POPULATION 1 RELATIVE TO POPULATION 2		AUDIT SPECIFICATIONS AS TO A SAMPLE FROM POPULATION 1 RELATIVE TO A SAMPLE FROM POPULATION 2	
	Size	Estimated Population Exception Rate	Tolerable Misstatement	ARIA
Case 1	Equal	Equal	Equal	Lower
Case 2	Equal	Larger	Larger	Equal
Case 3	Larger	Equal	Smaller	Higher
Case 4	Smaller	Smaller	Equal	Higher
Case 5	Larger	Equal	Equal	Lower

A nonstatistical sample was taken as follows:

All accounts over $10,000 (23 accounts)	$465,000
77 accounts under $10,000	$81,500
Materiality	$100,000

Inherent and control risk are both high.
No relevant analytical procedures were performed.

The following are the results of the confirmation procedures:

	RECORDED VALUE	AUDITED VALUE
Items over $10,000	$465,000	$432,000
Items under $10,000	81,500	77,150
Individual misstatements for items under $10,000:		
Item 12	5,120	4,820
Item 19	485	385
Item 33	1,250	250
Item 35	3,975	3,875
Item 51	1,850	1,825
Item 59	4,200	3,780
Item 74	2,405	0
	19,285	14,935

Required

Evaluate the results of the nonstatistical sample. Consider both the direct implications of the misstatements found and the effect of using a sample.

11-29 Sampling, whether statistical or judgmental, is an integral part of the audit process. Its use raises fundamental auditing issues which have become the subject of professional literature and studies. A decision to use sampling involves a number of practical and conceptual considerations.

Required

Describe these considerations.

(CICA adapted)

CASE

11-30 CA's firm is joint auditor of the TC Bank and is responsible this year for the audit of securities. As in prior years, audit procedures have been carried out during the year on security transactions and balances recorded in the books. CA is planning the physical security count on October 31, the bank's fiscal year end. In prior years, this count had been carried out over a three-day period by a task force of auditors from both audit firms. The count continued 24 hours a day with teams of counters working 8-hour shifts until all the securities had been counted. During this period, the auditors took over control of the vaults so that the routine bank operations in the vault were effectively suspended (this suspension could range from one to three business days, depending on whether the count commenced Friday evening).

CA had discussed the forthcoming physical count with bank officials and some reservations had been expressed. First, the anticipated two-day disruption of the securities department in the current year was very inconvenient to the bank. Second, the audit fee was increasing each year and the officials questioned the justification of the cost of the count in sheer hours alone. And third, since the bank's computer department had complete records of all security transactions and certificates held on data files, it was suggested that a more modern approach to the count might be adopted. Further, CA knew that the count was inconvenient to his firm's staff planning as a large portion of the staff were needed to do this job during a busy time of the year.

After the meeting with bank officials, CA wondered whether the count might be done on a statistical sampling basis similar to sampling techniques used by his firm in verifying receivables. He sat down to draft a memorandum on this approach for consideration by his partners.

Required

Outline the points to be included in CA's memorandum under the following headings:

a. Audit objectives of the physical count.

b. Description and assessment of various statistical sampling techniques in terms of achieving the audit objectives.

c. Recommendations, taking into account any other considerations.

Note: For the purpose of your answer, ignore any statutory requirements of external bank auditors.

(CICA adapted)

12

AUDIT OF THE SALES AND COLLECTION CYCLE: TESTS OF CONTROLS

THE CHOICE IS SIMPLE — RELY ON INTERNAL CONTROL OR RESIGN

City Finance Inc. is one of the largest clients managed out of the Montreal office of a Big Five firm. It is a financial services conglomerate with almost 200 offices in Canada and the United States, as well as branch offices overseas. The company has over 200,000 accounts receivable and processes millions of sales and other transactions annually.

The company's computer centre is in a large environmentally controlled room containing several large mainframe computers and a great deal of ancillary equipment. There are two complete on-line systems, one serving as a backup for the other, as systems failure would preclude operations in all of the company's branches.

The company has an excellent system of checks and balances where branch office transaction totals are reconciled to head office data processing control totals daily, which in turn are reconciled to outside bank account records monthly. Whenever this regular reconciliation process indicates a significant out-of-balance condition, procedures are initiated to resolve the problem as quickly as possible. There is a large internal audit staff that oversees any special investigative efforts that are required.

Because City Finance Inc. is a public company, it must file its annual report with the Quebec and Ontario securities commissions within 90 days after its fiscal year end. In addition, the company likes to announce annual earnings and issue its annual report as soon after year end as reasonably feasible. Under these circumstances, there is always a great deal of pressure on the CA firm to complete the audit expeditiously.

A standard audit planning question is, How much shall we rely on internal control? In the case of the City Finance audit, there is only one

OBJECTIVE 12-1

Identify the classes of transactions and accounts in the sales and collection cycle.

The overall objective in the audit of the sales and collection cycle is to evaluate whether the account balances affected by the cycle are fairly presented in accordance with generally accepted accounting principles. The following are typical accounts included in the sales and collection cycle:

- Sales
- Sales returns and allowances
- Bad-debt expense
- Cash discounts taken
- Trade accounts receivable
- Allowance for uncollectible accounts
- Cash in the bank (debits from cash receipts)

The goods and services tax is collected by an entity and remitted to the federal government; the entity merely acts as a conduit for the government. Accordingly, in Figure 5-3 on page 128, the Hillsburg Hardware trial balance shows *goods and services tax payable* (the liability) and *goods and services tax receivable* (the contra account to the liability) as being in the acquisitions and payment cycle, which is discussed in Chapter 16.

For example, look at the adjusted trial balance for Hillsburg Hardware Ltd. on page 128. Accounts on the trial balance affected by the sales and collection cycle are identified by the letter *S* in the left margin. Each of the above accounts is included, except cash discounts taken. For other audits, the names and the nature of the accounts may vary, of course, depending on the industry and client involved. There are differences in account titles for a service company, a retail company, and an insurance company, but the basic concepts are the same. To provide a frame of reference for understanding the material in this chapter, a retail outlet with consumers and commercial customers is assumed.

A brief summary of the way accounting information flows through the various accounts in the sales and collection cycle is illustrated in Figure 12-1 by the use of T-accounts. This figure shows that there are five classes of transactions included in the sales and collection cycle:

- Sales (cash and sales on account)
- Cash receipts
- Sales returns and allowances
- Charge-off of uncollectible accounts
- Bad-debt expense

Figure 12-1 also shows that with the exception of cash sales, every transaction and amount ultimately is included in two balance sheet accounts, accounts receivable or allowance for uncollectible accounts.

For the most part, the audit of the sales and collection cycle can be performed independently of the audit of other cycles and subjectively combined with the other parts of the audit as the evidence accumulation process proceeds. Auditors must keep in mind that the concept of materiality requires them to consider the combination of

FIGURE 12-1
Accounts in the Sales
and Collection Cycle

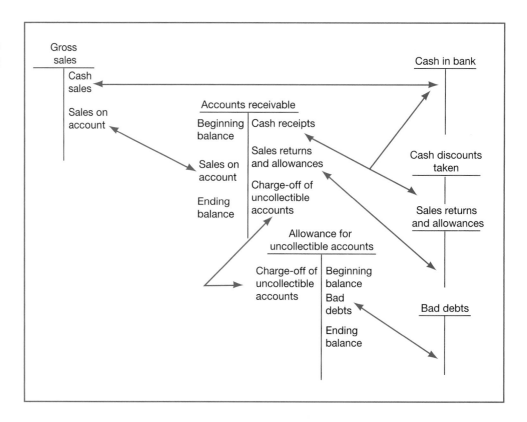

misstatements in all parts of the audit before making a final judgment on the fair presentation of the financial statements. This is done by continuously summarizing errors and integrating regular file review throughout the engagement with the many parts of the audit.

The types of audit tests discussed in Chapter 10, and shown in Figure 10-2 on page 315, are all used extensively in the audit of the sales and collection cycle. Tests of controls are used primarily to test the effectiveness of internal controls over the five classes of transactions in the cycle and to test the dollar amounts of these same five classes of transactions. Analytical procedures are used to test the relationships among the account balances in the cycle, both to one another and to prior years' balances. Tests of details of balances are used to verify ending account balances, primarily accounts receivable. Tests of controls are studied in this chapter.

NATURE OF THE SALES AND COLLECTION CYCLE

The sales and collection cycle involves the decisions and processes necessary for the transfer of the ownership of goods and services to customers after they are made available for sale. It begins with a request by a customer and ends with the conversion of material or service into an account receivable, and ultimately into cash.

The cycle includes several classes of transactions, accounts, and business functions, as well as a number of documents, reports and records. Information that could be included in computer data files is shown in Figure 12-2. The classes of transactions, accounts, business functions, and documents are shown in Table 12-1. Semi-permanent information and transaction information are updated during normal processing within the sales and collection cycle, as discussed in the remainder of this chapter.

The nature of computer processing used within a transaction cycle determines potential controls available in the system. For example, transactions can be processed using groups of transactions (also called *batch processing*), or they can be processed one at a time with immediate update against the data files (called *on-line processing*). Many companies use both methods. Payroll may be processed weekly in batch mode,

FIGURE 12-2

Typical Information
Included in Accounts
Receivable or Sales
Computer Data Files

SEMI-PERMANENT INFORMATION	TRANSACTION INFORMATION
Semi-permanent information is often called *master file data*. It is established when a customer starts purchasing, and is updated as customer information changes.	This information is based on customer activity, and there is normally one transaction for each activity, such as a sale or cash payment.
Customer number or code	Customer number or code
Customer name	Customer name
Customer billing address	Transaction type (sale, credit, payment, adjustment)
Customer shipping address	
Customer phone number	Transaction date
Credit limit	Transaction amount
Payment terms (includes applicable discounts)	Transaction detail (item detail)
Year-to-date sales	Transaction tracking (the individual who entered the transaction)
Current balance outstanding	

while sales orders received over the telephone may be recorded as received. The nature of the controls available to monitor the transactions are thus different. A summary of these differences is shown in Table 12-2.

TABLE 12-1

CLASSES OF
TRANSACTIONS,
ACCOUNTS, BUSINESS
FUNCTIONS, AND
RELATED DOCUMENTS
AND REPORTS FOR THE
SALES AND
COLLECTION CYCLE

CLASSES OF TRANSACTIONS	ACCOUNTS	BUSINESS FUNCTIONS	DOCUMENTS AND REPORTS
Sales	Sales Accounts receivable	Processing customer orders	Customer order
		Granting credit	Customer order
		Shipping goods	Shipping document
		Billing customers and recording sales	Sales invoice Sales journal/history report Summary sales report Accounts receivable trial balance Monthly statements
Cash receipts	Cash in bank (debits from cash receipts) Accounts receivable	Processing and recording cash receipts	Remittance advice Bank deposit detail Cash receipts journal
Sales returns and allowances	Sales returns and allowances Accounts receivable	Processing and recording sales returns and allowances	Credit memo Sales returns and allowances journal
Charge-off of uncollectible accounts	Accounts receivable Allowance for uncollectible accounts	Charging off uncollectible accounts receivable	Uncollectible account authorization form
Bad-debt expense	Bad-debt expense Allowance for uncollectible accounts	Providing for bad debts	Journal entry authorization
Master file change	Customer master file accounts	Maintaining semi-permanent data	Master file change form

Note: "Journal" and "history report" are synonymous terms.

TABLE 12-2

CONTROL DIFFER-
ENCES BETWEEN
BATCH AND ON-LINE
SYSTEMS

CONTROL CATEGORY	BATCH SYSTEMS	ON-LINE SYSTEMS
Audit trails	Transactions can readily be traced from source transaction through to general ledger posting. Groups of documents are totalled and entered into the system, and reports are printed showing the document details and the totals. These totals can be traced to transaction history reports or transaction journals, and from there to the general ledger.	Transactions may be initiated and entered without source documents (e.g., be initiated by a telephone call and entered directly into a system). Paper will normally be produced when the goods are picked or shipped, with daily or weekly summaries printed. Controls such as document sequencing are used to ensure that all transactions are completed. A full audit trail may be available in electronic form only.
Error detection and correction	Since transactions are processed in groups, if one transaction is in error, the entire batch of transactions may be rejected from subsequent processing. Each transaction must be correct before all transactions can be processed.	The focus is on preventing incorrect transactions from being entered. For example, systems should check for invalid customer numbers and reasonableness of dates or amounts prior to processing individual transactions.
Segregation of duties	Segregation can be achieved by separating the functions of totalling and counting of source documents from data entry. A person other than the data entry person should verify that the control totals entered match the control totals prepared from source documents. This verification function may be called *data control*.	Decentralization to departments can result in individual users performing traditionally incompatible functions, such as entering and verifying cash receipts and sales and accounts receivable, and updating credit limits. Passwords could be used to separate some of these functions. Alternatively, independent preparation and review of exception reports could compensate for such segregation problems.

Effects on other transactions or on other subsystems   For both batch and on-line systems, a transaction could cause other automatic transactions. For example, shipment of goods to customers could result in the automatic generation of a supplier purchase order if quantities fell below a certain level. Automatic postings to the general ledger could occur based on time or based on user initiation.

For both batch and on-line systems, it may be possible to identify who has entered transactions by associating user identification codes (user IDs) with the data entry person. This assists with segregation of duties.

BUSINESS FUNCTIONS IN THE CYCLE AND RELATED DOCUMENTS AND RECORDS

The business functions for a cycle are the key activities that an organization must complete to execute and record business transactions. Column three of Table 12-1 identifies the nine business functions in a typical sales and collection cycle. An understanding of these business functions for the sales and collection cycle promotes understanding of how an audit of the cycle is conducted. Students often also find it difficult to envision which documents and records exist in any given audit area and how they flow through the client's organization. The business functions for the sales and collection cycle and the most common documents and records used in each function are examined in this section.

PROCESSING CUSTOMER ORDERS

The request for goods by a customer is the starting point for the entire cycle. Legally, it is an offer to buy goods under specified terms.

Customer order   This is a request for merchandise by a customer. It may be received by telephone, by letter, electronically, by a printed form that has been sent to prospective and existing customers, through salespeople, or in other ways.

GRANTING CREDIT

OBJECTIVE 12-2

Describe the business functions and the related documents and records in the sales and collection cycle.

Before goods are shipped, a properly authorized person or computer program must *approve credit* to the customer for sales on account. Weak practices in credit approval or in changing the credit limit in the master file frequently result in excessive bad debts and accounts receivable that may be uncollectible. For most firms, credit approval is handled by having credit limits established when the customer is set up in the customer master file. Sales are automatically authorized as long as the account receivable stays within the authorized credit limit. Once the balance approaches the credit limit, exception reports are printed for the credit manager, or other methods are used to determine whether credit limits should be extended or individual sales should continue to be approved.

SHIPPING GOODS

This critical function is the first point in the cycle where company assets are given up. Most companies recognize sales when goods are shipped. A shipping document is prepared at the time of shipment; this can be done automatically by the computer based on sales order information. The shipping document, which is frequently a multicopy bill of lading, is essential to the proper billing of shipments to customers. Companies that maintain perpetual inventory records also update them based on shipping information.

Shipping document   This document is prepared to initiate the shipping of goods, indicating the description of the merchandise, the quantity shipped, and other relevant data. The original document is sent to the customer, and one or more copies are retained. It is also used as a signal to bill the customer. One type of shipping document is a bill of lading, which is a written contract between the carrier and the seller concerning the receipt and shipment of goods. Often bills of lading include only the number of boxes or kilograms shipped, rather than complete details of quantity and description. Throughout the text, we assume that complete details are included on bills of lading or on the internally generated shipping documents. Details of shipment are entered into the computer system so that perpetual inventory records can be updated and the billing process can commence.

BILLING CUSTOMERS AND RECORDING SALES

Since the billing of customers is the means by which the customer is informed of the amount due for the goods, it must be done correctly and on a timely basis. The most important aspects of billing are making sure that all shipments made have been billed, that no shipment has been billed more than once, and that each shipment is billed for the proper amount. Billing at the proper amount is dependent on charging the customer for the quantity shipped at the authorized price. The authorized price includes consideration of freight charges, insurance, and terms of payment.

In most systems, billing of the customer includes preparation of a multicopy sales invoice and updating of the sales transactions file, customer master file, and general ledger files for sales and accounts receivable. This information is used to generate the sales journal and, along with cash receipts and miscellaneous credits, allows preparation of the accounts receivable trial balance. Point-of-sale systems, such as those seen at many retail counters, often combine data entry and update for shipment, inventory, sales systems, and cash receipts with the entry of a single transaction.

Sales invoice   This is a document indicating the description and quantity of goods sold, the price including freight, insurance, terms, and other relevant data. Typically, it is printed by the computer after the customer number, quantity, and destination of goods shipped are entered. The sales invoice is the method of indicating to the customer the amount of a sale and due date of a payment. The original invoice is sent to the customer, and one or more copies are retained.

Sales journal   This is a listing of the sales history transaction file on a daily, weekly, monthly, or yearly basis. A detailed sales journal includes each sales transaction. It usually indicates gross sales for different classifications, such as product lines, the entry to accounts receivable, and miscellaneous debits and credits such as goods and services tax collected. The sales journal can also include sales returns and allowances transactions.

Summary sales report   This is a listing that summarizes sales for a period. The report typically includes information analyzed by key components such as customer, salesperson, product, and territory.

Accounts receivable trial balance   This is a listing of the amount owed by each customer at a point in time. It is prepared directly from the accounts receivable data files. It is most frequently an *aged* trial balance, showing how old the accounts receivable components of each customer's balance are as of the report date. This report can be printed showing only balances forward (i.e., the total owed by each customer) or on an open item basis (i.e., showing all sales invoices that have not been paid).

Monthly statement   This is a document sent to each customer indicating the monthly beginning balance of accounts receivable, the amount and date of each sale, cash payments received, credit memos issued, and the ending balance due. It is, in essence, a copy of the customer's portion of the accounts receivable activity.

PROCESSING AND RECORDING CASH RECEIPTS

The preceding four functions are necessary for getting the goods into the hands of customers, properly billing them, and reflecting the information in the accounting records. The result of these four functions is sales transactions. The remaining five functions involve the collection and recording of cash, sales returns and allowances, charge-off of uncollectible accounts, providing for bad-debt expense, and maintenance of semi-permanent information contained in customer master files.

Processing and recording cash receipts includes receiving, depositing, and recording cash. Cash includes both currency and cheques. The most important concern is the possibility of theft. Theft can occur before receipts are entered in the records or later. The most important consideration in the handling of cash receipts is that all cash must be deposited in the bank at the proper amount on a timely basis and recorded in the cash receipts transaction file, which is used to prepare the cash receipts journal and update the customer master and general ledger files. Remittance advices are important for this purpose.

Remittance advice   This is a document that accompanies the sales invoice mailed to the customer and can be returned to the seller with the cash payment. It is used to indicate the customer name, the sales invoice number, and the amount of the invoice when the payment is received. Often, a second copy of the sales invoice is used as a remittance advice. Alternatively, the customer may list the invoice numbers and amount paid on the cheque stub, which then serves as a remittance advice. If the customer fails to identify the invoices being paid with his or her payment, the data entry person must later allocate the payment to specific invoices. A remittance advice is used to permit the immediate deposit of cash and to improve control over the custody of assets.

Bank deposit detail This is a list prepared by an independent person (someone who has no responsibility for recording sales or accounts receivable) when cash is received. This could take the form of a listing of cheques received or a duplicate bank deposit slip. It is used to verify whether cash received was recorded and deposited at the correct amounts and on a timely basis.

Cash receipts journal This is a listing of cash receipts from collections, cash sales, and all other cash receipts. It indicates total cash received, the credit to accounts receivable at the gross amount of the original sale, trade discounts taken, and other debits and credits. The daily entries in the cash receipts journal are supported by remittance advices. The journal is generated for any time period from the cash receipts transactions included in the computer files.

PROCESSING AND RECORDING SALES RETURNS AND ALLOWANCES

When a customer is dissatisfied with the goods purchased, the seller frequently accepts the return of goods or grants a reduction in the charges. The company normally prepares a receiving report for the returned goods and returns them to inventory. Returns and allowances must be correctly and promptly recorded. *Credit memos* are normally issued for returns and allowances to aid in maintaining control and to facilitate record keeping.

Credit memo This is a document indicating a reduction in the amount due from a customer because of returned goods or an allowance granted. It often takes the same general form as a sales invoice, but it supports reductions in accounts receivable rather than increases.

Sales returns and allowances journal This is a listing of sales returns and allowances. It performs the same function as the sales journal. Many companies record these transactions using the same system as that used for the recording of sales. Transactions would thus be listed in the sales journal rather than a separate journal.

CHARGING OFF UNCOLLECTIBLE ACCOUNTS RECEIVABLE

Despite the diligence of credit departments, it is not unusual for some customers not to pay their bills. When the company concludes that an amount is no longer collectible, it must be charged off. Typically, this occurs after a customer files bankruptcy or the account is turned over to a collection agency. Proper accounting requires an adjustment for these uncollectible amounts.

Uncollectible account authorization form This is an internal document, indicating authority to write off an account receivable as uncollectible.

PROVIDING FOR BAD DEBTS

The provision for bad debts must be sufficient to allow for the current period sales that the company will be unable to collect in the future. For most companies, the provision represents a residual, resulting from management's end-of-period adjustment of the allowances for uncollectible accounts. Period-end reports or journal entries are used to document this adjustment.

CUSTOMER MASTER FILE CHANGE

The customer master file is a file for maintaining semi-permanent data used for processing sales, payments, and other transactions associated with customers. The master file information is provided by the customer, and reviewed and approved prior to set-up. Approval is necessary for the credit limit and payment terms in particular or for changes to these fields. It is also important that customers provide changes, such as shipping addresses, in writing, since an incorrect shipping address would result in goods being shipped to an incorrect (or unauthorized) location. This approval may be evidenced by a master file change form. The changes can then be authorized by an appropriate individual prior to entry.

The outstanding balance field in the customer master file is updated for sales, sales returns and allowances, and cash receipts. The total of the individual outstanding account balances in the customer master file equals the total balance of accounts receivable in the general ledger. A printout of the accounts receivable master file shows, by customer, the balance of accounts receivable at that time. It is also sometimes called "the accounts receivable subsidiary ledger" or "subledger." If the company has a data base, then the master file data is directly linked to the transaction data. Other computer installations have separate transaction files for unpaid transactions, sales, sales returns and allowances, and cash receipts that are used to update individual accounts receivable balances in the master file as entered, daily or weekly. Figures 5-5A, B, and C illustrate typical transaction flows for manual, batch, and data base systems.

EFFECT OF GENERAL CONTROLS

OBJECTIVE 12-3

Describe the impact of general controls on application controls in the sales and collection cycle.

As described in Chapter 9, general controls can be part of the control environment and part of individual applications or transaction cycles. Prior to assessing the individual transaction cycle, the auditor documents general controls that are pervasive and that affect multiple transaction cycles. For example, access and control policies and program change control procedures affect multiple cycles. If unauthorized individuals could establish or change credit limits, this would cause problems with collectibility of accounts. Access controls could then be tested as general controls, providing some control assurance for each application cycle that is affected. Similarly, the existence of excellent program change controls that have been tested would allow the auditor to place reliance on programs within each of the transaction cycles. Poor program change controls would suggest that the auditor could potentially rely on only manual controls in the transaction cycle. If unauthorized individuals could change how the accounts receivable aging is calculated or how invoices are calculated, the transactions would be unreliable. Thus, prior to documenting controls and assessing control risk in an individual cycle, the auditor reviews the general controls working-paper file to determine the controls in place, and whether reliance can be placed on these controls. Frequently, this assessment is completed by a specialist within the auditor's firm and in particular is based on the auditor's risk assessment process.

Following are the key areas that the auditor would review as part of general controls:

- Organization structure and job responsibilities within the data processing department
- Program change controls
- Physical access and security
- Logical access and security
- Documentation of programs and operations

These categories of general controls can include complex areas, such as data communications, data base management systems, Internet applications, electronic data interchange, and electronic funds transfer, as discussed further in Chapter 22.

METHODOLOGY FOR DESIGNING TESTS OF CONTROLS FOR SALES

The methodology for obtaining an understanding of internal controls and designing tests of controls for sales is shown in Figure 12-3. That methodology was studied in general terms in Chapters 9 and 10. It is applied specifically to sales in this section. The bottom box in Figure 12-3 shows the four evidence decisions the auditor must make. This section deals with deciding the appropriate audit procedures. For the timing decision, the tests are usually performed at an interim date if internal controls are

FIGURE 12-3
Methodology for
Designing Tests of
Controls for Sales

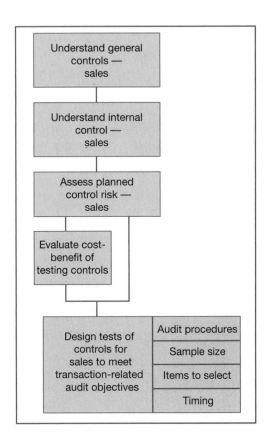

effective, but they can also be done after the balance sheet date. Decisions on the appropriate sample size and the items to select are studied under Objective 12-9.

Figure 12-3 is supported by Table 12-3, which summarizes the application of the methodology in the figure. Table 12-3 lists the specific transaction-related audit objectives for sales along with related key controls and common tests of controls for the objectives. Table 12-3 is referred to frequently throughout the section.

**UNDERSTAND
GENERAL CONTROLS
— SALES**

Certain general controls, such as access controls, will vary based upon the transaction cycle. The auditor needs to determine how password changes and other forms of security have been operationalized in the cycle. For example, some systems have passwords that allow entry into all functions of a cycle, while some systems have passwords that can be tailored to individual menu items. If a company has the latter type of system, it may be able to restrict master file changes and credit note generation. If these restrictions were not possible, then the auditor would look for other types of controls, such as the printing and review of reports that identify master file changes that have taken place.

The nature of programs in use affects the relevance of program change controls. When a company has purchased a software package and is unable to change the package, program change controls are considered excellent, since the programs cannot be changed. If the company has custom developed software with appropriate standards, documentation, and testing, controls over program changes are also likely to be assessed as good. When a company has informal program change procedures, poor testing, or no formal authorization of program changes, for example, program change controls are considered poor. This suggests that the auditor cannot rely on programs during the audit.

TABLE 12-3

SUMMARY OF TRANSACTION-RELATED AUDIT OBJECTIVES, KEY CONTROLS AND TESTS OF CONTROLS FOR SALES

TRANSACTION-RELATED AUDIT OBJECTIVE	KEY INTERNAL CONTROLS: MANUAL SYSTEMS	KEY INTERNAL CONTROLS: BATCH SYSTEMS	KEY INTERNAL CONTROLS: ON-LINE SYSTEMS	KEY INTERDEPENDENT INTERNAL CONTROLS	COMMON TESTS OF CONTROLS
Recorded sales are for shipments actually made to nonfictitious customers (occurrence).	• Recording of sales is supported by authorized shipping documents and approved customer purchase orders.	• Same as manual	• N/A. Likely no sales order documents.	• Review of exception reports that include unusual or large items extracted from transaction or master files.	• Examine copies of sales invoices for supporting bills of lading and customers' purchase orders. • Review the sales journal, general ledger, or trial balance for large or unusual items.*
	• Credit is approved before shipment takes place using manual review.	• Orders causing balances to exceed credit limits are printed on an exception report and are not processed for shipment.	• Orders causing balances to exceed credit limits require the entry of a supervisor password prior to shipment.††	• Orders causing balances to exceed credit limits are printed on an exception report and must be approved by a credit manager prior to shipment.	• Examine customer purchase order for credit approval. • Use test data to verify that orders causing balances to exceed credit limits are printed on exception reports. • Verify that password system has separate functionality for data entry and credit approval and that appropriate persons are assigned these functions. • Examine credit exception report for approval.
	• Sales invoices are prenumbered and properly accounted for (also satisfies completeness).	• Computer automatically generates sequential invoice numbers.	• Same as batch.	• Computer provides a report of missing invoice numbers, which are followed up by an independent person.	• Account for integrity of numerical sequence of sales invoices using block test. • Use generalized audit software to identify gaps in invoice numbers assigned.
	• N/A	• Only customer numbers existing in the customer master file are updated when they are entered.	• Sales invoices cannot be entered if the customer number is invalid.	• N/A	• Examine printouts of transactions rejected by the computer due to invalid customer numbers.† • Observe rejection of invalid customer numbers when entered by data entry staff into on-line system.
	• Approval is required to commence selling goods to a new customer or to change semi-permanent billing information.	• Approval is required to enter new customers or to change information for existing customers.	• A separate password is required to update customer master file information.	• Master file changes are printed on numerically controlled reports and reviewed by management.	• Examine master file change forms for authorization and compare to current master file information. • Review paper customer files for credit authorization forms and approval to accept customer.
	• Monthly statements are sent to customers; complaints receive independent follow-up (also satisfies posting and summarization).	• Same as manual.	• Same as manual.	• Same as manual.	• Observe whether statements are mailed, and examine customer correspondence files.

TABLE 12-3 (CONTINUED)

TRANSACTION-RELATED AUDIT OBJECTIVE	KEY INTERNAL CONTROLS: MANUAL SYSTEMS	KEY INTERNAL CONTROLS: BATCH SYSTEMS	KEY INTERNAL CONTROLS: ON-LINE SYSTEMS	KEY INTERDEPENDENT INTERNAL CONTROLS	COMMON TESTS OF CONTROLS
Existing sales transactions are recorded (completeness).	• Shipping documents (i.e., bills of lading or internal shipping documents) are prenumbered and accounted for.	• Same as manual.	• Same as manual.	• Computer checks for gaps in shipping document numbers and prints a report of missing numbers for independent follow-up.	• Account for integrity of numerical sequence of shipping documents using block test. • Trace shipping documents to resultant sales invoices and entry into sales history file and accounts receivable customer master file. • Verify independent follow-up of exception reports.
Recorded sales are for the amount of goods shipped and are correctly billed and recorded (accuracy).	• Determination that prices, terms, freight, and discounts are properly authorized. • Shipping documents are matched to invoices. • Invoices are prepared using prices from an approved price list.	• Invoices are prepared using prices, terms, freight, and discounts established in master files. • Same as manual. • Approved unit selling prices are entered into the master files and used for all sales. • Batch totals are compared with computer summary reports.	• Same as batch. • Shipping details are automatically used as the invoicing source. • Same as batch. • Invoice calculations (extensions, additions, taxes) are automatically calculated.	• Exception reports are reviewed by management.	• Recompute information on sales invoices. • Examine approved computer printout of unit selling prices and compare to invoice details.†† • Trace details on sales invoices to shipping documents, price lists, and customers' purchase orders. • Compare inventory selling prices in master files to approved master file change forms and invoice details. • Examine file of batch totals for initials of data control clerk; compare totals to summary reports.†† • Prepare test data and run through invoicing program to ensure program is functioning as required.
Sales transactions are classified to the correct account (classification).	• Adequate chart of accounts is used. • Internal review and verification is completed (also satisfies timing).	• Invoices can be posted only to valid customer accounts. • Posting is done automatically to sales account based upon batch totals.	• Invoices can only be prepared for valid customer accounts. • Posting is done automatically to sales account based upon periodic totals.	• Management reviews exception reports of unusual customer data.	• Review customer master file listing for adequacy. • Examine documents supporting sales transactions for proper classification. • Examine indication of internal verification on affected documents. • Use test date to verify that transactions are posted to correct general ledger accounts or conduct manual walk-through of transactions through programs.

383

TABLE 12-3
(CONTINUED)

TRANSACTION-RELATED AUDIT OBJECTIVE	KEY INTERNAL CONTROLS: MANUAL SYSTEMS	KEY INTERNAL CONTROLS: BATCH SYSTEMS	KEY INTERNAL CONTROLS: ON-LINE SYSTEMS	KEY INTERDEPENDENT INTERNAL CONTROLS	COMMON TESTS OF CONTROLS
Sales are recorded on the correct dates (timing).	• Procedures requiring billing and recording of sales on a daily basis are performed as close to time of occurrence as possible.	• Same as manual. • System checks reasonableness of date entered.	• Same as manual. • System checks reasonableness of date entered.	• Management reviews sales and cost of sales analytical reports for reasonableness.	• Compare dates of recorded sales transactions with dates on shipping records. • Examine documents for unbilled shipments and unrecorded sales. • Verify management walk-through of analytical reports.
Sales transactions are updated correctly to the customer master file, and the posting to the general ledger summed these transactions correctly (posting and summarization).	• Transactions are summarized on a timely basis for posting to the general ledger. • Subsidiary accounts receivable records are periodically balanced to the general ledger.	• Customer master file is periodically printed for independent review. • Customer master file totals are compared with general ledger balance monthly and differences are investigated.	• Same as batch. • Same as batch.	• Aged accounts receivable trial balance are reviewed for reasonableness. • Run-to-run totals are compared and reconciled (i.e., previous monthly accounts receivable total plus transactions reconciles to current month totals).	• Examine initials on general ledger account reconciliation indicating comparison. • Trace sales journal entries to copies of sales orders, sales invoices, and shipping documents. • Foot journals and trace postings to general ledger and accounts receivable master files. • Use generalized audit software to add up the outstanding accounts receivable transactions and the balances in the accounts receivable master file. Compare both independent totals to the accounts receivable general ledger balance.

* This analytical procedure can also apply to other objectives, including completeness, accuracy, and timing.

† This control would be tested on many audits by using the computer.

†† This control could also be considered an interdependent control, since both a computer based and personal action are required.

Problems with program change procedures or with access controls can have a strong impact on the auditor's assessment of control risk. The auditor may choose not to rely on any internal controls for clients with such control weaknesses.

UNDERSTAND INTERNAL CONTROL — SALES

Chapter 9 discussed how auditors obtain an understanding of internal control. A typical approach for sales is to conduct interviews, review internal audit working papers, study the clients' flowcharts, prepare an internal control questionnaire, and perform walk-through tests of sales. Figures 12-6 (page 397) and 12-7 (page 398) include an organization chart and a flowchart for Hillsburg Hardware Ltd. that are used to demonstrate the design of tests of controls audit procedures.

ASSESS PLANNED CONTROL RISK — SALES

The auditor uses the information obtained in understanding internal control to assess control risk. There are four essential steps to this assessment, all of which were discussed in Chapter 9.

- First, the auditor needs a framework for assessing control risk. The framework for all classes of transactions is the six transaction-related audit objectives. For sales, these are shown for Hillsburg Hardware in Figure 12-8 on page 399. These six objectives are the same for every audit of sales.
- Second, the auditor must identify the key internal controls and weaknesses for sales. These are also shown on page 399. The controls and weaknesses will be different for every audit.
- After identifying the controls and weaknesses, the auditor relates them to the objectives and cross-references them to supporting working papers. This is also shown on page 399 with Ws and Cs in appropriate columns.
- Finally, the auditor assesses control risk for each objective by evaluating the controls and weaknesses for each objective. This step is a critical one because it affects the auditor's decisions about both tests of controls and substantive tests. It is a highly subjective decision. The bottom of page 399 shows the auditor's conclusions for Hillsburg Hardware Ltd.

The section that follows discusses the key control activities for sales. A knowledge of these control activities is important for identifying the key controls and weaknesses for sales, which is the second step in assessing control risk.

Adequate separation of duties Proper separation of duties helps to prevent various types of misstatements, both intentional and unintentional. To prevent fraud, it is important that anyone responsible for inputting sales and cash receipts transaction information into the computer be denied access to cash. It is also desirable to separate the credit-granting functions from the sales function, since credit checks are intended to offset the natural tendency of sales personnel to optimize volume even at the expense of high bad-debt write-offs. It is equally desirable that personnel responsible for doing internal comparisons are independent of those entering the original data. For example, comparison of batch control totals to summary reports and comparison of customer master file totals to the general ledger balance should be done by someone independent of those who input sales and cash receipt transactions.

Proper authorization The auditor is concerned about authorization at *three key points*: credit must be properly authorized before a sale takes place; goods should be shipped only after proper authorization; and prices, including base terms, freight, and discounts, must be authorized. The first two controls are meant to prevent the loss of company assets by shipping to fictitious customers or those who will fail to pay for the goods. Price authorization is meant to make sure the sale is billed at the price set by company policy.

Adequate documents and records Since each company has a unique system of originating, processing, and recording transactions, it may be difficult to evaluate whether its procedures are designed for maximum control; nevertheless, adequate record-keeping procedures must exist before most of the transaction-related audit objectives can be met. Some companies, for example, automatically prepare a multi-copy prenumbered sales invoice at the time a customer order is received. Copies of this document are used to approve credit, authorize shipment, record the number of units shipped, and bill customers. Under this system, there is almost no chance of the failure to bill a customer if all invoices are accounted for periodically. Under a different system, in which the sales invoice is prepared only after a shipment has been made, the likelihood of failure to bill a customer is high unless some compensating control exists.

Prenumbered documents An important characteristic of documents for sales is the use of prenumbering, which is meant to prevent both the failure to bill or record sales and the occurrence of duplicate billings and recording thereof. Of course, it does not do much good to have prenumbered documents unless they are properly accounted for. An example of the use of this control is the filing, by a billing clerk, of a copy of all shipping documents in sequential order after each shipment is billed, with someone else periodically accounting for all numbers and investigating the reason for any missing documents. Another example is programming the computer to prepare a listing of unused numbers at month's end with follow-up by appropriate personnel.

Mailing of monthly statements The mailing of monthly statements by someone who has no responsibility for handling cash or preparing the sales and accounts receivable records is a useful control because it encourages a response from customers if the balance is improperly stated. For maximum effectiveness, all disagreements about the balance in the account should be directed to a designated official who has no responsibility for handling cash or recording sales or accounts receivable.

Internal verification procedures The use of independent persons for checking the processing and recording of sales transactions is essential for fulfilling each of the six transaction-related audit objectives. Examples of these procedures include accounting for the numerical sequence of prenumbered documents, checking the accuracy of document preparation, and reviewing reports for unusual or incorrect items. Examples include review of balances exceeding credit limits, approval of master file change reports, and examination of sales statistics.

EVALUATE COST BENEFIT OF TESTING CONTROLS

After the auditor has identified the key internal controls and weaknesses and assessed control risk, he or she decides whether substantive tests will be reduced sufficiently to justify the cost of performing tests of controls. Whenever it is practical, auditors make this decision before completing a matrix such as the one illustrated in Figure 12-8 on page 399. It makes little sense to incur the cost of identifying controls and assessing control risk below maximum if there will be no reduction of substantive tests.

Figure 12-3 and Table 12-3 are referred to during the subsequent discussion. Figure 12-3 (page 381) shows the methodology for designing tests of controls for sales. Table 12-3 (page 382) provides detailed examples used throughout the chapter.

Transaction-related audit objectives (column 1) The transaction-related audit objectives included in Table 12-3 are derived from the framework developed in Chapters 5 and 9. Although certain internal controls satisfy more than one objective, it is desirable to consider each objective separately to facilitate a better assessment of control risk.

Key internal controls (columns 2 through 5)   The internal controls for sales are designed to achieve the six transaction-related audit objectives discussed in Chapters 5 and 9. If the controls necessary to satisfy any one of the objectives are inadequate, the likelihood of misstatements related to that objective is increased, regardless of the controls for the other objectives. The methodology for determining existing controls was studied in Chapter 9.

The source of the controls in these columns is the controls from a control risk matrix such as the one illustrated on page 399. A control may satisfy more than one audit objective if there is more than one C for that control on the control risk matrix.

Common tests of controls (column 6)   For each internal control on which the auditor chooses to rely, he or she designs a test of control to verify its effectiveness. Observe that the tests of controls in column 6 in Table 12-3 relate directly to the internal controls.

DESIGN TESTS OF CONTROLS FOR SALES

For each control on which the auditor plans to rely to reduce assessed control risk, he or she must design one or more tests of controls to verify its effectiveness. In most audits, it is relatively easy to determine the nature of the test of the control from the nature of the control. For example, if the internal control is having the sales programs identify orders that cause customers to go over their credit limit and having the orders printed for subsequent approval, the test of control would include verifying that the program is functioning as designed and examining the credit exception report for approval.

The last column in Table 12-3 shows examples of tests of control for key internal controls in columns 2 through 5. For example, the first key internal control is "Recording of sales is supported by authorized shipping documents and approved customer purchase orders." The test of control is "Examine copies of sales invoices for supporting bills of lading and customers' purchase orders." For this test, it is important that the auditor start with sales invoices and examine documents in support of the sales invoices rather than go in the opposite direction. If the auditor traced from shipping documents to sales invoices, it would be a test of completeness. Direction of tests is discussed further on page 389.

A common test of control for sales is accounting for a sequence of various types of documents, such as duplicate sales invoices selected from the sales journal, watching for omitted and duplicate numbers or invoices outside the normal sequence, called a "block test." This test simultaneously provides evidence of both the existence and completeness objectives. Should the auditor choose to use generalized audit software, then a gap test can be conducted by scanning the entire transaction history file and identifying any gaps in the numeric sequence. Types of computer-assisted audit tests (CAATs) are described in the Appendix.

The appropriate tests of controls for separation of duties are ordinarily restricted to the auditor's observations of activities and discussions with personnel. For example, it is possible to observe whether the billing clerk has access to cash when opening incoming mail or depositing cash. It is usually also necessary to ask personnel what their responsibilities are and if there are any circumstances where their responsibilities are different from the normal policy. For example, the employee responsible for billing customers may state that he or she does not have access to cash. Future discussion may elicit that when the cashier is on vacation, that person takes over the cashier's duties. Allocation of password functionality should also be reviewed to ensure that individuals have not been assigned functions that are incompatible.

Several of the tests of controls in Table 12-3 can be performed using the computer. For example, one of the key internal controls to prevent fraudulent or fictitious transactions is the inclusion of procedures that ensure that only approved information was entered into the customer master files. If a nonexistent customer number is entered into the computer, it would be rejected. A test of control for on-line data entry systems is for the auditor to attempt to enter nonexistent customer numbers into the computer to make sure that the computer control is in operation.

DUAL PURPOSE OR WEAKNESS INVESTIGATION TESTS

Some of the procedures listed in Table 12-3 are performed on every audit regardless of the circumstances, whereas others are dependent on the adequacy of the controls and the results of the tests of controls. Tests that can be used to quantify the extent of potential error can be used as dual purpose tests (for assessing control risk and also as a substantive test) or for quantifying the potential dollar effect of monetary errors or fraud or other irregularities due to control weaknesses.

The audit procedures used are affected by the internal controls and the nonquantitative tests of controls for that objective. Some of the tests are dual purpose tests introduced in Chapter 10. In any event, the purpose of all tests in column 6 is to test the controls and assist the auditor in assessing control risk.

Materiality, results of the prior year, and the other factors discussed in Chapter 8 also affect the procedures used. Some of the audit procedures employed when internal controls are inadequate are discussed in a later section.

Determining the proper tests of controls procedures for sales is relatively difficult because the nature of client systems vary considerably.

In subsequent paragraphs, the procedures frequently *not* performed are emphasized, since they are the ones requiring an audit decision. The procedures are discussed in the same order in which they were included in Table 12-3. It should be noted that some procedures fulfill more than one objective.

Recorded sales occurred   For this objective, the auditor is concerned with the possibility of *three types of misstatements*: sales being included in the journals for which no shipment was made, sales recorded more than once, and shipments being made to nonexistent customers and recorded as sales. The first two types of misstatements can be intentional or unintentional; the last type is always intentional. As might be imagined, the inclusion of fraudulent sales is rare. The potential consequences are significant because they lead to an overstatement of assets and income.

There is an important difference between finding intentional and unintentional overstatements of sales. An unintentional overstatement normally also results in a clear overstatement of accounts receivable, which can often be easily found through confirmation procedures. For fraud, the perpetrator will attempt to conceal the overstatement, making it more difficult for auditors to find. Substantive tests of transactions may be necessary to discover overstated sales in these circumstances.

The appropriate tests of controls for testing the occurrence objective depends on where the auditor believes the misstatements are likely to take place. Many auditors do tests of controls for the occurrence objective only if they believe that a control weakness exists so that the potential error can be quantified; therefore, the nature of the tests depends on the nature of the potential misstatement as follows:

Recorded sale for which there was no shipment   The auditor can trace from selected entries in the sales journal to make sure that related copies of the shipping and other supporting documents exist. If the auditor is concerned about the possibility of a fictitious duplicate copy of a shipping document, it may be necessary to trace the amounts to the perpetual inventory records as a test of whether inventory was reduced. This would not be possible for paperless systems, which require advanced auditing techniques, as discussed in Chapter 22.

Sale recorded more than once   Duplicate sales can be determined by reviewing a numerically sorted list of recorded sales transactions for duplicate invoice or shipping document numbers or by running generalized audit software tests to identify all duplicated numbers.

Shipment made to nonexistent customers This type of fraud normally occurs only when the person recording sales is also in a position to authorize shipments or alter master file data. When internal controls are weak, it is difficult to detect fictitious shipments.

Another effective approach to detecting the three types of misstatements of sales transactions discussed above is to trace the *credit* in the accounts receivable master file to its source. If the receivable was actually collected in cash or the goods were returned, there must originally have been a sale. If the credit was for a bad-debt charge-off or a credit memo, or if the account was still unpaid at the time of the audit, intensive follow-up by examining shipping and customer order documents is required, since each of these could indicate an inappropriate sales transaction.

It should be kept in mind that *the ordinary audit is not primarily intended to detect fraud* unless the effect on the financial statements is material. Tests of controls to quantify potential errors should be necessary only if the auditor is concerned about the occurrence of fraud or material error due to inadequate controls.

Existing sales transactions are recorded In many audits, the auditor is not as concerned about the completeness objective on the ground that overstatements of assets and income are a greater concern in the audit of sales transactions than their understatement. If there are inadequate controls, which is likely if the client does no independent internal matching between shipping documents and sales transactions to the sales journal, substantive procedures will be necessary.

An effective procedure to test for unbilled shipments is tracing selected shipping documents from a file in the shipping department to related duplicate sales invoices and the sales journal. To conduct a meaningful test using this procedure, the auditor must be confident that all shipping documents are included in the sample population. This can be done by accounting for a numerical sequence of the documents.

Direction of tests It is important that auditors understand the difference between tracing from source documents to the journals and tracing from the journals back to supporting documents. The former is a test for *omitted transactions* (completeness objective), whereas the latter is a test for *nonexistent transactions* (occurrence objective).

In testing for the occurrence objective, the starting point is the journal. A sample of invoice numbers is selected *from* the journal and traced *to* duplicate sales invoices, shipping documents, and customer orders. In testing for the completeness objective, the likely starting point is the shipping document. A sample of shipping documents is selected and traced *to* duplicate sales invoices and the sales journal as a test of omissions.

When designing audit procedures for the occurrence and completeness objectives, the starting point for tracing the document is essential. This is referred to as the *direction of tests*. For example, if the auditor is concerned about the occurrence objective but traces in the wrong direction (from shipping documents to the journals), a serious audit deficiency exists. The direction of the tests is illustrated in Figure 12-4.

When testing for the other five transaction-related audit objectives, the direction of tests is usually not relevant. For example, the accuracy of sales transactions can be tested by tracing from a duplicate sales invoice to a shipping document or vice versa.

Recorded sales are accurately recorded The accurate recording of sales transactions concerns shipping the amount of goods ordered, accurately billing for the amount of goods shipped, and accurately recording the amount billed in the accounting records.

Reperformance to ensure the accuracy of each of these aspects is ordinarily conducted in every audit.

Typical reperformance tests include recomputing information in the accounting records to verify whether it is proper. A common approach is to start with entries in

FIGURE 12-4
Direction of Tests
for Sales

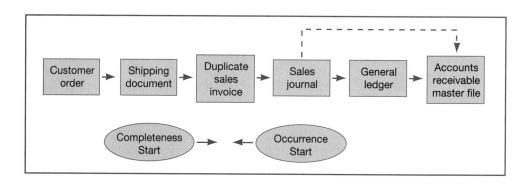

the sales journal and compare the total of selected transactions with customer master file totals and duplicate sales invoices. Prices on the duplicate sales invoices are normally compared with an approved price list, extensions and footings are recomputed, and the details listed on the invoices are compared with shipping records for description, quantity, and customer identification. Where reliance is placed on computer-based systems to perform mathematical calculations, the auditor may use test data to ensure that these programs are functioning as described. Test data as an audit tool is described further in the Appendix. Frequently, customer purchase orders are also examined for the same information.

The comparison of tests of controls and substantive procedures for the accuracy objective is a good example of how audit time can be saved when effective internal controls exist. In manual systems, the test of controls for this objective takes almost no time because it involves examining only an initial or other evidence of internal verification. The test data approach can also be effective since only a small number of transactions need be processed to verify that programs are functioning correctly. Since the sample size for substantive procedures can be reduced if this control is effective, a significant saving will result from performing the test of controls due to its lower cost.

Recorded sales are properly classified   Charging the correct general ledger account is less of a problem in sales than in some other transaction cycles, but it is still of some concern. When there are cash and credit sales, it is important not to debit accounts receivable for a cash sale or to credit sales for collection of a receivable. It is also important not to classify sales of operating assets, such as buildings, as sales. For those companies using more than one sales classification, such as companies issuing segmented earnings statements, proper classification is essential.

It is common to test sales for proper classification as part of testing for accuracy. The auditor examines supporting documents to determine the proper classification of a given transaction and compares this with the actual account to which it is charged. Most computer-based systems, whether batch or on-line, are set to post to the appropriate sales general ledger account automatically. The auditor then must determine the controls in place to ensure that unusual transactions are recorded to the correct account.

Sales are recorded on the correct dates   It is important that sales be billed and recorded as soon after shipment takes place as possible to prevent the unintentional omission of transactions from the records and to make sure sales are recorded in the proper period. At the same time that tests of controls with respect to the accuracy objective are being performed, it is common to compare the date on selected bills of lading or other shipping documents with the date on related duplicate sales invoices and the sales journal or sales history file. Significant differences indicate a potential cutoff problem. Many computer systems require that the shipping date match the invoice date, or that the invoice date is within a specified time period of the current date.

Sales transactions are properly updated in the customer master file and correctly summarized The proper inclusion of all sales transactions in the customer master file is essential because the accuracy of these records affects the client's ability to collect outstanding receivables. Similarly, the sales transactions must be correctly totalled and posted to the general ledger if the financial statements are to be correct. In every audit, it is necessary to perform some clerical accuracy tests by footing the journals and tracing the totals and details to the general ledger and the master files to check whether there are intentional or unintentional misstatements in the processing of sales transactions. For most large systems, this is accomplished using generalized audit software, whereby the auditor obtains the client data files and performs mechanical accuracy testing (such as footings or other calculations) using computer software.

The extent of such tests is affected by the quality of the internal controls. Tracing individual transactions to a posting source is typically done as a part of fulfilling other transaction-related audit objectives, but footing the sales journal and tracing the totals to the general ledger is done as a separate procedure.

The distinction between posting and summarization and other transaction-related audit objectives is that posting and summarization includes footing journals, transaction or open item files, master file records, and ledgers and tracing from one to the other. Whenever footing and comparisons are restricted to these sources, the process is posting and summarization. In contrast, accuracy involves comparing documents with each other or with journals and data file records. To illustrate, comparing a duplicate sales invoice with either the sales journal or master file entry is an accuracy objective procedure. Tracing a sales transaction from a sales history file to an open item file and balancing the open item file to the customer master file is a posting and summarization procedure.

SUMMARY OF METHODOLOGY FOR SALES

It is essential to understand the relationships among the columns in Table 12-3. The first column includes the six transaction-related audit objectives. The general objectives are the same for any class of transactions, but the specific objectives vary for sales, cash receipts, or any other classes of transactions. Columns 2 through 5 list one or more illustrative internal controls *for each transaction-related audit objective* for different types of systems, distinguishing between manual, batch, and on-line. The fifth column provides examples of interdependent controls. These controls require both a programmed and manual component to satisfy the audit objective. Many of these controls are supervisory controls, whereby a manager or supervisor would review an exception report or a monthly report for unusual information, and then conduct follow-up activities.

It is essential that any given control be related to one or more specific objective(s). A test of control is meaningless unless it tests a specific control. The table contains at least one test of control in column 6 for internal controls identified in columns 2 through 5.

DESIGN AND PERFORMANCE FORMAT AUDIT PROCEDURES

The information presented in Table 12-3 is intended to help auditors *design audit programs* that satisfy the transaction-related audit objectives in a given set of circumstances. If certain objectives are important in a given audit or when the controls are different for different clients, the methodology helps the auditor design an effective and efficient audit program.

After the appropriate audit procedures for a given set of circumstances have been designed, they must be performed. It is likely to be inefficient to do the audit procedures as they are stated in the design format of Table 12-3. In converting from a design to a performance format, procedures are combined. This will

- eliminate duplicate procedures.
- make sure that when a given document is examined, all procedures to be performed on that document are done at that time.

- enable the auditor to do the procedures in the most effective order. For example, by footing the journal and reviewing the journal for unusual items first, the auditor gains a better perspective in doing the detailed tests.

The process of converting from a design to a performance format is illustrated for the Hillsburg Hardware Ltd. case application. The design format is shown in Table 12-5 on pages 401–402. The performance format is on page 403 in Table 12-6.

SALES RETURNS AND ALLOWANCES

OBJECTIVE 12-5

Apply the methodology for controls over sales transactions to controls over sales returns and allowances.

The transaction-related audit objectives and the client's methods of controlling misstatements are essentially the same for processing credit memos as those described for sales, with two important differences. The first relates to *materiality*. In many instances, sales returns and allowances are so immaterial that they can be ignored in the audit altogether. The second major difference relates to *emphasis on objectives*. For sales returns and allowances, the primary emphasis is normally on testing the existence of recorded transactions as a means of uncovering any diversion of cash from the collection of accounts receivable that has been covered up by a fictitious sales return or allowance.

Although the emphasis for the audit of sales returns and allowances is often on testing the existence of recorded transactions, the *completeness* objective cannot be ignored. Unrecorded sales returns and allowances can be material and can be used by a company's management to overstate net income.

Naturally, the other objectives should not be ignored. But because the objectives and methodology for auditing sales returns and allowances are essentially the same as for sales, we will not include a detailed study of the area. The reader should be able to apply the same logic to arrive at suitable controls and tests of controls to verify the amounts.

SALES CAN BE RETURNED (AND COME BACK TO HAUNT YOU)

Don Sheelen sought to aggressively increase the market share of Regina Co. in the competitive vacuum cleaner market following its initial public offering in 1985. However, new products which were rushed to market without adequate testing suffered from a high defect rate. By 1987, the company was flooded with product returns. In the third quarter of 1987 alone, more than 40,000 vacuums were returned in one product line, representing 16 percent of sales.

To protect earnings and the company's stock price, Sheelen conspired with his chief financial officer to not record the sales returns, which by now were so substantial that they had to be stored in a separate warehouse. Under Sheelen's and the CFO's direction, Regina employees altered the company's computer system so that the returns were not recorded on Regina's books. When the fraud unravelled in 1988, the company was forced to declare bankruptcy. Sheelen pleaded guilty to one count of mail and securities fraud and was fined $25,000 and sentenced to one year in a minimum security correctional facility.

Sources: John A. Byrne, "How Don Sheelen Made a Mess that Regina Couldn't Clean Up," *Business Week* (February 12, 1990), pp. 46–50; Michael C. Knapp, *Contemporary Auditing: Issues and Cases*, West Publishing, 1993, pp. 79–85.

Business Week
www.businessweek.com

INTERNAL CONTROLS AND TESTS OF CONTROLS FOR CASH RECEIPTS

OBJECTIVE 12-6

Determine the client's internal controls over cash receipts transactions, design and perform tests of controls, and assess related control risk.

The same methodology used for designing tests of controls over sales transactions is used for designing tests of controls over cash receipts. Similarly, cash receipts tests of controls audit procedures are developed around the same framework used for sales; that is, given the transaction-related audit objectives, key internal controls for each objective are determined and tests of controls are developed for each control to ensure the control is working and to determine monetary errors for each objective. As in all other audit areas, the tests of controls depend on the controls the auditor has identified to reduce the assessed level of control risk.

Key internal controls and common tests of controls to satisfy each of the internal control objectives for cash receipts are listed in Table 12-4. This summary is similar to the previous one for sales. The differences are that key internal controls are shown in one column, rather then spread across four columns, and the tests of controls are split into two columns. The first column of tests of controls are controls that are used to detect whether controls have been followed (termed "general tests of controls"). The second column of tests of controls, used for quantification of potential errors, could serve as dual purpose tests.

The detailed discussion of the internal controls and tests of controls that was included for the audit of sales is not included for cash receipts. Instead, the audit procedures that are most likely to be misunderstood are explained in more detail.

An essential part of the auditor's responsibility in auditing cash receipts is identification of weaknesses in internal control that increase the likelihood of fraud. In expanding on Table 12-4, the emphasis will be on those audit procedures that are designed primarily for the discovery of fraud. However, the reader should keep in mind throughout this discussion that the nonfraud procedures included in the table are the auditor's primary responsibility. Those procedures that are not discussed are omitted only because their purpose and the methodology for applying them should be apparent from their description.

DETERMINE WHETHER CASH RECEIVED WAS RECORDED

The most difficult type of cash defalcation for the auditor to detect is that which occurs *before the cash is recorded* in the cash receipts journal or other cash listing, especially if the sale and cash receipt are recorded simultaneously. For example, if a grocery store clerk takes cash and intentionally fails to register the receipt of cash on the cash register, it is extremely difficult to discover the theft. To prevent this type of fraud, internal controls such as those included in the third objective in Table 12-4 are implemented by many companies. The type of control will, of course, depend on the type of business. For example, the controls for a retail store in which the cash is received by the same person who sells the merchandise and rings up the cash receipts (termed "point-of-sale" or "POS" systems) should be different from the controls for a company in which all receipts are received through the mail several weeks after the sales have taken place. In a point-of-sale system, the sale must be recorded for the customer to receive a receipt. This may also remove the item from inventory, but most important, it provides a control total that must be reconciled to the total cash (including credit card vouchers) that is received during the day.

It is normal practice to trace from *prenumbered remittance advices, prelists of cash receipts,* or the duplicate bank deposit slip to the cash receipts journal and subsidiary accounts receivable records as a test of the recording of actual cash received. This test will be effective only if the cash details were listed on a cash register tape or some other prelisting at the time the cash was received.

PREPARE PROOF OF CASH RECEIPTS

A useful audit procedure to test whether all recorded cash receipts have been deposited in the bank account is a *proof of cash receipts*. In this test, the total cash receipts recorded in the cash receipts data files for a given period, such as a month, are reconciled with the actual deposits made to the bank during the same period.

TRANSACTION-RELATED AUDIT OBJECTIVE	KEY INTERNAL CONTROL	GENERAL TESTS OF CONTROLS	QUANTITATIVE/DUAL PURPOSE TESTS OF CONTROLS
Recorded cash receipts are for funds actually received by the company (occurrence).	Separation of duties between handling cash and record keeping or data entry.	Observe separation of duties.	Review the cash receipts journal, general ledger, and accounts receivable master file or trial balance for large and unusual amounts.*
	Independent reconciliation or review of bank accounts.	Observe independent reconciliation of bank account.	Trace from cash receipts listing to duplicate deposit slip and bank statements.
Cash received is recorded in the cash receipts journal (completeness).	Separation of duties between handling cash and record keeping.	Discussion with personnel and observation.	Trace from remittances or prelisting to duplicate bank deposit slip and cash receipts journal.
	Use of remittance advices or a prelisting of cash.	As above.	
	Immediate endorsement of incoming cheques.	Observe immediate endorsement of incoming cheques.	
	Internal verification of the recording of cash receipts.	Examine indication of internal verification.	
	Regular monthly statements to customers.	Observe whether monthly statements are sent to customers.	
Cash receipts are deposited and recorded at the amount received (accuracy).	Approval of cash discounts.	Examine remittance advices for proper approval.	Examine remittance advices and sales invoices to determine whether discounts allowed are consistent with company policy.
	Regular reconciliation of bank accounts.	Review monthly bank reconciliations.	
	Comparison of batch totals to duplicate deposit slips and computer summary reports.	Examine file of batch totals for initials of data control clerk; compare totals to summary reports.	
Cash receipts are properly classified (classification).	Use of adequate chart of accounts or automatic posting to specified accounts.	Review chart of accounts and computer-assigned posting accounts.	Examine documents supporting cash receipts for proper classification.
Cash receipts are recorded on correct dates (timing).	Procedure requiring recording of cash receipts on a daily basis.	Observe unrecorded cash at any point in time.	Compare dates of deposits with dates in the cash receipts journal.
Cash receipts are properly included in the customer master file and are correctly summarized (posting and summarization).	Regular monthly statements to customers.	Observe whether statements are mailed.	Foot journals and trace postings to general ledger and accounts receivable master file.
	Use of properly approved master file change forms.	Examine master file change forms for proper authorization.	
	Comparison of accounts customer master file or aged accounts receivable trial balance totals with general ledger balance.	Examine documentation verifying that comparison was completed.	

* This analytical procedure can also apply to other objectives, including completeness, accuracy, and timing.

There may be a difference in the two due to deposits in transit and other items, but the amounts can be reconciled and compared. The procedure is not useful in discovering cash receipts that have not been recorded in the journals or time lags in making deposits, but it can help uncover recorded cash receipts that have not been deposited, unrecorded deposits, unrecorded loans, bank loans deposited directly into the bank account, and similar misstatements. A proof of cash receipts and cash disbursements is illustrated in Chapter 20 on page 664. This somewhat time-consuming procedure is ordinarily used only when the controls are weak. In rare instances in which controls are extremely weak, the period covered by the proof of cash receipts may be the entire year.

<table>
<tr>
<td>

TEST TO DISCOVER LAPPING OF ACCOUNTS RECEIVABLE

</td>
<td>

Lapping of accounts receivable, which is a common type of defalcation, is the postponement of entries for the collection of receivables to *conceal an existing cash shortage.* The defalcation is perpetrated by a person who handles cash receipts and then enters them into the computer system. He or she takes the cash, defers recording the cash receipts from one customer, and covers the shortages with the receipts of another customer. These in turn are covered from the receipts of a third customer a few days later. The employee must continue to cover the shortage through repeated lapping, replace the stolen money, or find another way to conceal the shortage.

This defalcation can be easily prevented by separation of duties. It can be detected by comparing the name, amount, and dates shown on remittance advices with cash receipts journal entries and related duplicate deposit slips. Since the procedure is relatively time-consuming, it is ordinarily performed only when there is a specific concern with defalcation because of a weakness in internal control.

</td>
</tr>
</table>

AUDIT TESTS FOR UNCOLLECTIBLE ACCOUNTS

OBJECTIVE 12-7

Apply the methodology for controls over the sales and collection cycle to write-offs of uncollectible accounts receivable.

Dun & Bradstreet Canada Limited
www.dnb.ca

Occurrence of recorded write-offs is the most important transaction-related audit objective that the auditor should keep in mind in the verification of the write-off of individual uncollectible accounts. A major concern in testing accounts charged off as uncollectible is the possibility of the client covering up a defalcation by charging off accounts receivable that have already been collected. The major control for preventing this type of misstatement is proper authorization of the write-off of uncollectible accounts by a designated level of management only after a thorough investigation of the reason the customer has not paid.

Normally, verification of the accounts charged off takes relatively little time. A typical procedure is the examination of approvals by the appropriate person. For a sample of accounts charged off, it is also usually necessary for the auditor to examine correspondence in the client's files establishing the uncollectibility of the accounts. In some cases, the auditor will also examine credit reports such as those provided by Dun & Bradstreet Canada Limited or Creditel. After the auditor has concluded that the accounts charged off by general journal entries are proper, selected items should be traced to listings of the accounts receivable master file or to a transactions file as a test of the records.

ADDITIONAL INTERNAL CONTROLS OVER ACCOUNT BALANCES

The preceding discussion emphasized internal controls and tests of controls for the five classes of transactions that affect account balances in the sales and collection cycle. If the internal controls for these classes of transactions are determined to be effective and the related tests of controls support the conclusions, the likelihood of misstatements in the financial statements is reduced.

In addition, there may be internal controls directly related to account balances that have not been identified or tested as a part of tests of controls. For the sales and collection cycle, these are most likely to affect three balance-related audit objectives: valuation, rights and obligations, and presentation and disclosure.

Valuation is an essential balance-related audit objective for accounts receivable because collectibility of receivables is often a major financial statement item and has been an issue in a number of accountants' liability cases. It is, therefore, common for inherent risk to be high for the valuation objective.

Several controls are common for the valuation objective. One that has already been discussed is credit approval by an appropriate person. A second is the preparation of a periodic aged accounts receivable trial balance for review and follow-up by appropriate management personnel. A third control is a policy of charging off uncollectible accounts when they are no longer likely to be collected.

Rights and obligations and presentation and disclosure are rarely a significant problem for accounts receivable. Therefore, employing competent accounting personnel is usually sufficient control for these two balance-related audit objectives.

EFFECT OF RESULTS OF TESTS OF CONTROLS

The results of the tests of controls have a significant effect on the remainder of the audit, especially on the tests of details of balances part of substantive procedures. The parts of the audit most affected by the tests of controls for the sales and collection cycle are the balances in *accounts receivable, cash, bad-debt expense,* and *allowance for doubtful accounts.* Furthermore, if the results of the tests are unsatisfactory, it is necessary to do additional substantive testing for the propriety of sales, sales returns and allowances, charge-off of uncollectible accounts, and processing of cash receipts.

At the completion of the tests of controls, it is essential to *analyze each control test exception* to determine its cause and the implication of the exception on assessed control risk, which may affect the supported detection risk and thereby the substantive procedures.

The most significant effect of the results of the tests of controls in the sales and collection cycle is on the confirmation of accounts receivable. The type of confirmation, the size of the sample, and the timing of the test are all affected. The effect of the tests on accounts receivable, bad-debt expense, and allowance for uncollectible accounts is considered in Chapter 14.

Figure 12-5 illustrates the major accounts in the sales and collection cycle and the types of audit tests typically used to audit these accounts. This figure also shows how the audit risk model discussed in Chapter 8 relates to the audit of the sales and collection cycle.

FIGURE 12-5

Types of Audit Tests for the Sales and Collection Cycle (see Figure 12-1 on page 374 for accounts)

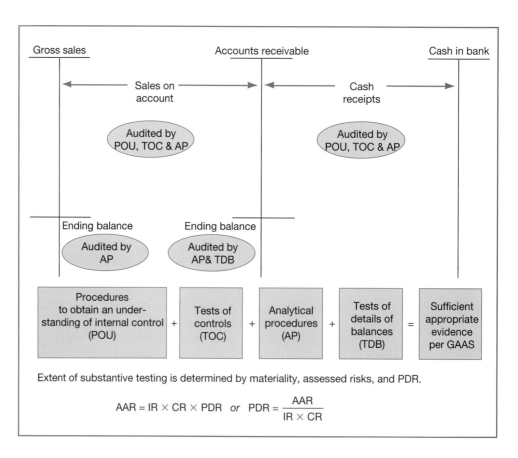

The concepts for testing the sales and collection cycle presented in this chapter are now illustrated for Hillsburg Hardware Ltd. The company's financial statements and the general ledger trial balance were shown in Chapter 5. Additional information was included in other chapters. A study of this case is intended to illustrate a methodology for designing audit procedures and integrating different parts of the audit.

Hillsburg Hardware Ltd. is a retail hardware outlet that focuses on selling high-quality power tools to individuals and the home improvement construction market. It is based in Eastern Canada. Preliminary analytical review was conducted and shows continued maintenance of profit margins (for details, see Chapter 13). This is the fourth year of the audit of this client, and there have never been any significant misstatements discovered in the tests. During the current year, a major change has occurred. The chief accountant left the firm and has been replaced by Erma Swanson. There has also been some turnover of other accounting personnel.

The overall assessment by management is that the accounting personnel are reasonably competent and highly trustworthy. The president, Rick Chulick, has been the chief operating officer for approximately 10 years. He is regarded as a highly competent, honest individual who does a conscientious job. The following information is provided from the auditor's files:

- *The organization chart and flowchart of internal control prepared for the audit.* This information is included in Figures 12-6 and 12-7. Sales returns and allowances for this client are too immaterial to include in the flowchart or to verify in the audit.
- *Internal controls and weaknesses, and assessment of control risk for sales and cash receipts.* An appropriate approach to identifying and documenting internal controls and weaknesses and assessing control risk is included for sales in Figure 12-8 on page 399 and for cash receipts in Figure 12-9 on page 400. There are several things the auditor, Francine Martel, did to complete each matrix. First, she identified internal controls from flowcharts, internal control questionnaires, and discussions with client personnel. Only flowcharts are available in the Hillsburg case. Second, she identified weaknesses using the same sources. Third, she decided which transaction-related audit objectives are affected by the internal controls and weaknesses. Finally, she assessed control risk using the information obtained in the preceding three steps. The objective-by-objective matrix in Figures 12-8 and 12-9 was used primarily to help Francine Martel effectively assess control risk.

FIGURE 12-6

Hillsburg Hardware
Organization Chart:
Personnel

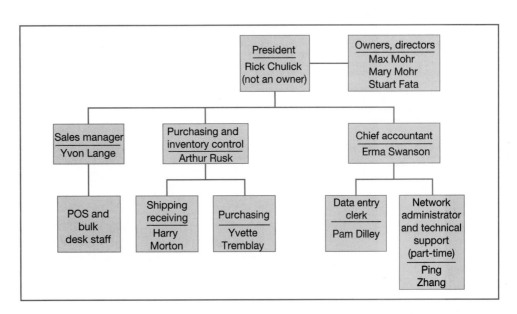

FIGURE 12-7

Hillsburg Hardware Ltd. — Flowchart of Sales and Cash Receipts

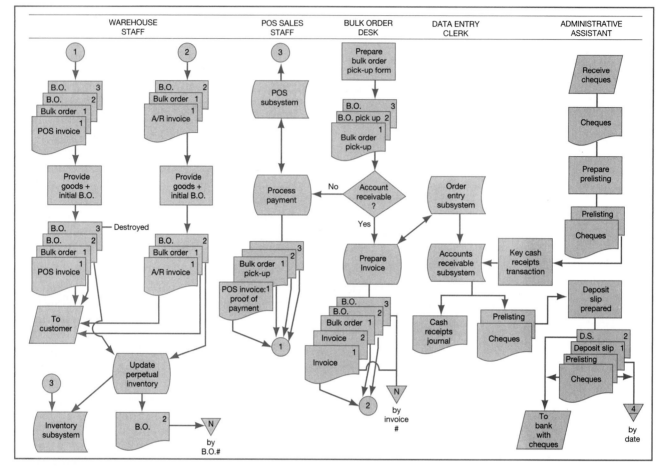

Notes

1. All correspondence is sent to the president.
2. An exception report of missing bulk order numbers is printed weekly by the data entry clerk. The chief accountant discusses this with the warehouse staff supervisor to ensure that follow-up is undertaken.
3. All subsystems are posted to the general ledger on a daily basis after the close of the store. The order-entry subsystem is also posted to the accounts receivable subsystem on a daily basis.
4. All prices in the point-of-sale (POS) system are based on prices in the master file. Should an override be necessary (e.g., due to damaged goods), the sales manager must enter his password to approve the price change. All such overrides will be printed on an exception report by the data entry clerk on a weekly basis. These are reviewed by the chief accountant.
5. All prices used for accounts receivable are based on the same prices as the point-of-sale system, with the customer discount applied. Customer discounts are negotiated at the time of customer approval, and range from 10 percent to 25 percent, based on the customer's projected and actual sales volume. An authorized customer signature is required on all accounts receivable invoices that matches the signature on the in-house credit card.
6. Changes to the price master file and the customer master file for credit limits must be co-approved by the sales manager and the chief accountant on a master file change form. These are entered by the data entry clerk, and a sequentially numbered master file change report printed. This report is reviewed by the chief accountant for accuracy of data entry.
7. Payment at the POS desks can be made by cash, credit card, or debit card. Stand-alone credit card authorization and debit card entry machines are used to process non-cash payments. Daily totals (i.e., cash drawer, debit card totals, credit card totals) must equal the total sales recorded at each POS terminal.

8. There are two POS terminals for immediate payment and two bulk order desk terminals, where staff can inquire regarding inventory status and can prepare accounts receivable invoices using the order entry system for pre-authorized customers.
9. Warehouse staff compare bulk order quantities to amounts paid for or invoiced prior to providing goods, and initial the customer invoice. Customers sign copy 2 of the bulk order to indicate that goods have been taken.
10. An aged accounts receivable trial balance is printed weekly by the data entry clerk for follow-up by the chief accountant. At this time, the trial balance total is compared to the general ledger accounts receivable balance.
11. Statements are sent to customers monthly.
12. The administrative assistant stamps incoming cheques with a restrictive endorsement immediately upon receipt.
13. Deposits are made daily by the administrative assistant. Cash from the POS terminals is counted, recorded on the duplicate deposit slip, and added to the total of cheques received for the day.
14. Daily cash receipts postings from the POS system and the accounts receivable system are reconciled to the duplicate deposit slip by the data entry clerk.
15. The bank account is reconciled by the chief accountant on a monthly basis.
16. All bad-debt expenses and write-offs of bad debts are approved by the president after being initiated by the chief accountant.
17. Financial statements are printed monthly by the data entry clerk and reviewed by the chief accountant and the president.
18. All management (i.e., sales, purchasing and inventory control, chief accountant, and the president) meet on a weekly basis to review exception reports and discuss weekly internal financial results. These meetings are not minuted.

- *Tests of controls for each internal control.* The tests of controls for sales are included in the third and fifth columns of Table 12-5 (page 401) and for cash receipts in the same columns in Table 12-6 (page 403). The source of the internal controls is Figure 12-8 for sales and Figure 12-9 for cash receipts. Francine decided the appropriate tests for each control.

FIGURE 12-8
Control Risk Matrix for Hillsburg Hardware — Sales

		SALES TRANSACTION-RELATED OBJECTIVES					
		Recorded sales are for shipments actually made to nonfictitious customers (occurrence).	Existing sales transactions are recorded (completeness).	Recorded sales are for the amount of goods shipped and are correctly billed and recorded (accuracy).	Sales transactions are properly classified (classification).	Sales are recorded on the correct dates (timing).	Sales transactions are updated correctly to the customer master file and the posting to the general ledger summed these transactions correctly (posting and summarization).
CONTROLS	Scanned POS sales must be paid by cash or credit card. (C1) **P**	C		C			
	All external and internal credit card purchases require customer signature on the invoice. (C2)	C					
	Bulk order pick up form is matched to invoice and initialled. (C3)	C		C			
	Credit is approved prior to customer account being established. (C4)	C					
	Monthly statements are sent to accounts receivable customers. (C5)	C		C			C
	Bulk order forms are pre-numbered, and the number is entered on the invoice. Computer system flags missing numbers on an exception report. (C6) **P**		C	C			
	POS invoices and accounts receivable invoices are automatically numbered by the computer. (C7) **P**		C	C			
	All invoices are prepared using prices in the inventory master file. (C8) **P**			C			
	Accounts receivable terms are based on the customer master file. (C9) **P**			C			
	Price overrides must be approved by sales manager password. (C10) **P**			C			
	Sales manager overrides are printed on an exception report and reviewed by the chief accountant. (C11) **P**			C			
	Sales control account is coded into computer system and all POS and bulk sales are posted to that account. (C12) **P**				C		
	The invoice date is automatically the computer system date. (C13) **P**					C	
	Posting to the data files is automatically handled by the computer system. (C14) **P**						C
	Aged accounts receivable trial balance is compared to general ledger balance monthly. (C15)						C
WEAKNESS	Evidence of follow up on exception report of missing bulk order numbers is not documented. (W1)	W					
	Assessed control risk	Medium	Low	Low	Low	Low	Low

Note: **P**—These controls are either programmed controls or interdependent controls (where part of the control is programmed and part of the control is handled by a person).

C = Control

W = Weakness

INTERNAL CONTROL	Recorded cash receipts are for funds actually received by the company (occurrence)	Cash received is recorded in the cash receipts journal (completeness)	Cash receipts are deposited at the amount received (accuracy)	Cash receipts transactions are properly classified (classification)	Cash receipts are recorded on the correct dates (timing)	Cash receipts are properly included in the customer master file and are correctly summarized (posting and summarization)
CONTROLS						
Accountant reconciles bank account. (C1)	C		C			
Cheques are stamped with a restrictive endorsement. (C2)		C				
Statements are sent to customers monthly. (C3)		C	C			
Bank deposit slip reconciled to POS and accounts receivable postings. (C4)	C	C	C			
Cash is automatically posted to cash and accounts receivable accounts. (C5)				C		
System date is used for data entry. (C6)					C	
Cash receipts are deposited daily. (C7)					C	
Entry of correct customer number results in automatic posting to that customer master file record. (C8)						C
Accountant compares accounts receivable master file total with general ledger account. (C9)						C
WEAKNESSES						
Prelisting of cash is not used to verify recorded cash receipts. (W1)		W				
Administrative assistant handles cheques after they are returned from cash receipts. (W2)		W				
Data entry clerk has access to cash receipts and maintains accounts receivable records. (W3)		W				
Assessed control risk	Low	High	Low	Low	Low	Low

CASH RECEIPTS TRANSACTION-RELATED AUDIT OBJECTIVES

C = Control
W = Weakness

TABLE 12-5

INTERNAL CONTROLS AND TESTS OF CONTROLS FOR HILLSBURG HARDWARE LTD. — SALES* (DESIGN FORMAT)

TRANSACTION-RELATED AUDIT OBJECTIVE	EXISTING CONTROL†	TESTS OF CONTROL, GENERAL	WEAKNESS	TESTS OF CONTROL, DUAL PURPOSE
Recorded sales are for shipments actually made to nonfictitious customers (occurrence).	Scanned POS sales must be paid by cash or credit card. (C1) All external and internal credit card purchases require customer signature on the invoice. (C2) Bulk order pick-up form is matched to invoice and initialled. (C3) Credit is approved prior to customer account being established. (C4) Monthly statements are sent to accounts receivable customers. (C5)	Review POS procedures manual and discuss with POS staff. (6) Examine a sample of invoices for customer signature. (13.1) Examine a selection of invoices for matching bulk order form and initial. (13.3, 13.4) Examine a sample of master file change forms for evidence of approval. (14.1, 14.2) Observe whether monthly statements are mailed. (7)	Evidence of follow-up on exception report of missing bulk order numbers is not documented. (W1)	Use generalized audit software to print a list of customers exceeding their credit limit. (4.1)
Existing sales transactions are recorded (completeness).	Bulk order forms are prenumbered, and the number is entered on the invoice. Computer system flags missing numbers on an exception report. (C6) POS invoices and accounts receivable invoices are automatically numbered by the computer. (C7)	Review sample of sales invoice for bulk order form number. (13.2) Observe system in use, and observe incremental assignment of invoice numbers. (1.2, 2.1)		Use generalized audit software to print a report of all gaps in the bulk order forms. (4.2) Use generalized audit software to print a report of all gaps in the invoice numbers. (4.3, 4.4)
Recorded sales are for the amount of goods shipped and are correctly billed and recorded (accuracy).	All invoices are prepared using prices in the inventory master file. (C8) Accounts receivable terms are based on the customer master file. (C9) Price overrides must be approved by sales manager password. (C10) Sales manager's overrides are printed on an exception report and reviewed by the chief accountant. (C11)	Observe invoice preparation process. (1.3, 2.2) Request bulk order staff to enter a different term, and see if computer rejects it. (2.3) Request staff to override a price, and observe whether sales manager password is required. (1.4, 2.4) Discuss disposition of exception report with chief accountant and review report for evidence of review. (8)		Use generalized audit software to print a report of unusual credit terms, and trace to customer master file approval form. (4.5, 4.7)
Sales transactions are properly classified (classification).	Sales control account is coded into computer system, and all POS and bulk sales are posted to that account. (C12)	Examine a daily sales summary to verify account allocation. (5.1)		
Sales are recorded on the correct dates (timing).	The invoice date is automatically the computer system date. (C13)	Observe invoice preparation process. (1.5, 2.5)		

TABLE 12-5 (CONTINUED)

TRANSACTION-RELATED AUDIT OBJECTIVE	EXISTING CONTROL†	TESTS OF CONTROL, GENERAL	WEAKNESS	TESTS OF CONTROL, DUAL PURPOSE
Sales transactions are updated correctly to the customer master file, and the posting to the general ledger summed these transactions correctly (posting and summarization).	Posting to the data files is automatically handled by the computer system. (C14) Aged accounts receivable trial balance is compared to general ledger balance monthly. (C15)	Conduct walk-through testing to verify that posting process is functioning correctly for daily posting. (5.1, 5.2, 5.3)		Compare aged accounts receivable trial balance total to general ledger. (4.6)

* The procedures are summarized into a performance format in Figure 12-10. The number in parentheses after the procedure refers to Figure 12-10.

† Only the primary (key) control(s) for each objective is (are) shown. Most objectives are also affected by one or more additional controls.

Notice that certain objectives in Tables 12-5 and 12-6 have only programmed controls (e.g., sales classification and timing and cash receipts classification), or existing controls are such that there are weaknesses (e.g., occurrence in Table 12-5; completeness in Table 12-6). The tests of controls listed in the fifth columns of Tables 12-5 and 12-6 are dual purpose tests designed to determine if the client's accounting transactions exist, are complete, are accurate, are properly classified, are recorded on the correct dates, and are summarized in the journals and correctly posted to the appropriate ledger. Tests such as these, described in Chapter 10, are both tests of controls and substantive procedures. As was suggested earlier in this chapter, the purpose of such tests is to assist the auditor in assessing control risk and also in quantifying the potential amount of error when conducted as substantive tests.

Francine decided on the tests of controls for each transaction-related audit objective listed in the third and fifth columns of Table 12-5 (sales) and Table 12-6 (cash receipts) for the different objectives after considering assessed control risk, the tests of controls listed in the third column, and weaknesses of internal control for that objective.

Notice that the objective-by-objective format in Tables 12-5 and 12-6 is used to help Francine more effectively determine the appropriate tests. She could have chosen tests of controls just as easily by selecting tests of controls for each internal control included in Figures 12-8 and 12-9. Most audit firms use automated working-paper software that allows them to simultaneously work on audit objective assessment and the preparation of audit testing plans without the preparation of multiple lists, as shown in this text. The multiple lists are shown here to assist students in assimilation of the audit process.

- *Tests of controls audit program in a performance format.* The tests of controls in Table 12-5 and Table 12-6 are combined into one audit program in Figure 12-10 (page 404). The cross-referencing of the numbers in parentheses shows that no procedures have been added to or deleted from Figure 12-10. The reasons Francine prepared the performance format audit program were to eliminate audit procedures that were included more than once in Tables 12-5 and 12-6 and to include them in an order that permits audit assistants to complete the procedures as efficiently as possible. Note the large number of programmed controls, walk-through tests, and general tests. These illustrate that in automated systems, where programmed controls can be relied on due to good general controls, the time spent on control testing can be reduced, since the effort required to conduct these tests is considerably less than the effort required to conduct sampling and tests of attributes through sampling. The generalized audit software tests are conducted at the same time as the substantive tests for accounts receivable (discussed further in Chapter 14).

TABLE 12-6

INTERNAL CONTROLS AND TESTS OF CONTROLS FOR HILLSBURG HARDWARE LTD. — CASH RECEIPTS*
(DESIGN FORMAT)

TRANSACTION-RELATED AUDIT OBJECTIVE	EXISTING CONTROL†	TEST OF CONTROL, GENERAL	WEAKNESS	TESTS OF CONTROL, DUAL PURPOSE
Recorded cash receipts are for funds actually received by the company (ocurrence).	Accountant reconciles bank account. (C1) Bank deposit slip reconciled to POS and accounts receivable postings. (C4)**	Observe whether Swanson reconciles the bank account. (9)		Review the journals and transaction files for unusual transactions and amounts using GAS. (4.7) Summarize and prepare analysis of credits using GAS. (4.7, 4.8) Prepare a proof of cash receipts. (18) Examine a sample of daily reconciliations, verifying agreement to postings and to bank statement. (16)
Cash received is recorded in the cash receipts journal (completeness).	Cheques are stamped with a restrictive endorsement. (C2) Statements are sent to customers monthly. (C3)	Observe whether a restrictive endorsement is used on cash receipts. (10) Observe whether monthly statements are mailed. (7)	Prelisting of cash is not used to verify recorded cash receipts. (W1) Administrative assistant handles cheques after they are returned from data entry. (W2) Data entry clerk has access to cash receipts and maintains accounts receivable records. (W3)	Obtain the prelisting of cash receipts, and trace amounts to the cash receipts journal, testing for names, amounts, and dates. (19) Compare the prelisting of cash receipts with the duplicate deposit slip, testing for names, amounts, and dates. (16)
Recorded cash receipts are deposited at the amount received (accuracy).	Accountant reconciles bank account. (C1) Statements are sent to customers monthly. (C3)	Observe whether Swanson reconciles the bank account. (9) Observe whether monthly statements are mailed. (7)		The procedures for the occurrence objective also fulfill this objective.
Cash receipts are properly classified (classification).	Cash is automatically posted to cash and accounts receivable accounts. (C5)	Conduct walk-through. (5.4)		Examine prelisting for proper account classification. (17)
Cash receipts are recorded on correct dates (timing).	System date is used for data entry. (C6) Cash receipts deposited daily. (C4)	Observe system use. (3.1) Observe whether bank deposits are made daily. (11)		Trace the total from the cash receipts journal to the bank statement, testing for a delay in deposit. (16)
Cash receipts are properly included in the customer master file and are correctly summarized (posting and summarization).	Accountant compares aged accounts receivable trial balance total with general ledger account. (C9) Entry of correct customer number results in automatic posting to that customer master file record. (C8)	Observe whether Swanson compares total with general ledger account. (12) Observe data entry and conduct walk-through test. (3)		Foot and cross-foot the cash receipts journal using GAS, and trace totals to the general ledger on a test basis. (4.8)

GAS = generalized audit software.
* The procedures are summarized into a performance format in Figure 12-10. The number in parentheses after the procedure refers to Figure 12-10.
† Only the primary (key) control(s) for each objective is (are) shown. Most objectives are also affected by one or more additional controls.
** This control also satisfies completeness and accuracy.

TESTS OF CONTROLS AUDIT PROCEDURES FOR SALES AND CASH RECEIPTS
(Sample Size and the Items in the Sample Are Not Included)

Tests of Programs

1. Observe use of POS system to verify that

    1.1 POS sales must be paid by cash or credit card.

    1.2 POS invoices are automatically numbered by the computer.

    1.3 Invoices are prepared using prices automatically pulled from the inventory master file.

    1.4 Price overrides must be approved using the sales manager password. (Request an attempt to enter an override.)

    1.5 Invoice date is equal to computer system date.

2. Observe use of bulk order desk and accounts receivable sales data entry to verify that

    2.1 Accounts receivable invoices are automatically numbered by the computer.

    2.2 Invoices are prepared using prices automatically pulled from the inventory master file and

    2.3 Credit terms are pulled automatically from the customer master file. (Request an attempt to enter an incorrect credit term.)

    2.4 Price overrides must be approved using the sales manager password. (Request an attempt to enter an override.)

    2.5 Invoice date is equal to computer system date.

3. Observe cash receipts data entry process to verify that

    3.1 System data is used for data entry.

Tests of Data Using Generalized Audit Software — Included with Substantive Field Work of Accounts Receivable

4. Obtain transaction history file, open item accounts receivable file and customer master file, and conduct the following tests:

    4.1 List customers with balances exceeding their credit limit.

    4.2 List gaps in bulk order form numbers.

    4.3 List gaps in POS invoice numbers.

    4.4 List gaps in accounts receivable invoice numbers.

    4.5 List customers with discount terms exceeding 25 percent.

    4.6 Foot open item file and customer master file and agree to general ledger.

    4.7 Summarize debits and credits by customer. Prepare graphs displaying analysis of debit and credit patterns.

    4.8 Summarize cash receipts and prepare totals by day and month.

Walk-through Tests

5. Conduct walk-through tests of three transactions for each of the following activities to verify that programs are functioning as described:

    5.1 POS daily sales summary is posted to correct general ledger accounts.

    5.2 Accounts receivable daily sales are posted to correct general ledger accounts.

    5.3 Sales transactions are posted to correct customer master file accounts.

    5.4 Cash receipts are posted to correct general ledger accounts.

6. Review system procedures and discuss with personnel to verify that procedures are being followed as described.

7. Observe whether monthly statements are mailed.

8. Discuss disposition of exception reports with appropriate member of management independently to verify consistency of treatment.

9. Observe whether the accountant reconciles the bank account.

10. Observe whether a restrictive endorsement is used on cash receipts.

11. Observe whether bank deposits are made daily.

12. Observe whether the accountant compares the accounts receivable trial balance total with the general ledger account.

Tests for Billing of Customers and Recording of Sales in the Accounts

13. Select a sample of customer invoices using a random selection process and

    13.1 Ensure that the invoice copy has a customer signature.

        If the sale was for bulk goods:

    13.2 Verify that the bulk order form number was entered onto the invoice.

    13.3 Verify that the bulk goods order form product description and quantity matches the invoice details.

    13.4 Locate the warehouse copy of the bulk goods order form and verify that the customer signature on the warehouse copy of the bulk goods order form matches the signature on the invoice copy.

14. Select a sample of customer master file change forms using a random selection process, and

    14.1 Verify that appropriate approvals are present.

    14.2 Trace to printout, confirming data entry of the change and verifying presence of chief accountant's initials.

Tests for Processing Cash Receipts and Recording the Amounts in the Records

15. Obtain the December prelistings of cash receipts, and trace amounts to the cash receipts journal, testing for names, amounts, and dates.

16. Compare the prelisting of cash receipts with the duplicate deposit slip, testing for names, amounts, and dates. Trace the total from the cash receipts journal to the duplicate bank deposit slip, and the total per the duplicate bank deposit slip to the bank statement, testing for a delay in deposit. For these dates, also trace the totals to the POS system and accounts receivable sales system totals.

17. Examine prelisting for proper account classification.

18. Prepare a proof of cash receipts.

19. Trace selected entries from the cash receipts journal to entries in the customer master file, and test for dates and amounts.

20. Trace selected credits from the accounts receivable master file to the cash receipts journal, and test for dates and amounts.

APPLICATION OF ATTRIBUTE SAMPLING

OBJECTIVE 12-9

Conduct attribute sampling for tests of controls.

To illustrate the sampling for the tests of controls concepts of Chapter 11, the sampling for the tests described in Figure 12-10 is now conducted. The only parts of the tests of the sales and collection cycle included here are the tests of payment approval by the customer, shipment verification of bulk orders, and approval of customer master file changes. It should be kept in mind that the procedures for Hillsburg Hardware Ltd. were developed specifically for that client and would probably not be applicable for a different audit. The audit procedures for these tests are taken from steps 13 and 14 of Figure 12-10.

The detailed sampling process is shown in Figure 12-11 for step 13. Involving the examination of invoices and supporting bulk order forms, it has the largest number of audit steps. Selection and testing of customer master file forms would be handled in a similar manner, and is shown in summary form only (Figure 12-14).

OBJECTIVES, DECIDING IF SAMPLING APPLIES, POPULATION, AND SAMPLING UNIT

Most auditors use some type of preprinted form or software template to document each attributes sampling application. An example of a commonly used form is given in Figure 12-12. The top part of the form includes a definition of the objective, the population, and the sampling unit.

DEFINE THE ATTRIBUTES OF INTEREST

The attributes used in this application are taken directly from the audit program. The procedures that can be used as attributes for a particular application of attributes sampling depend on the definition of the sampling unit. In this case, all the proce-

FIGURE 12-11
Random Sample for Testing Sales

	(1)	(2)	(3)	(4)	(5)
1086	77339	64605	4 82583	18 85011	00955
1087	61714	57933	5 37342	26000	32 93611
1088	15232	48027	15832	19 62924	11509
1089	41447	34275	10779	20 83515	33 63899
1090	23244	43524	16382	21 36840	34 73581
1091	53460	83542	25224	22 70378	35 49604
1092	53442	16897	6 61578	05032	36 81825
1093	55543	19096	04130	23104	37 60534
1094	18185	63329	02340	23 63111	38 41768
1095	02372	45690	7 38595	23121	39 73818
1096	51715	35492	8 61371	24 87132	40 81585
1097	24717	16785	9 42786	25 86585	21858
1098	78002	32604	10 87295	26 93702	99438
1099	35995	08275	11 62405	27 43313	03249
1100	29152	86922	31508	28 42703	41 59638
		Start			
1101	84192	↓ 90150	02904	26835	17174
1102	21791	—— 24764	12 53674	30093	42 45134
1103	63501	05040	13 71881	17759	43 91881
1104	07149	1 69285	14 55481	24889	44 67061
1105	59443	98962	15 74778	96920	45 65620
1106	39059	2 58021	28485	29 43052	↑ 99001
1107	73176	3 58913	22638	30 69769	21102
1108	11851	09065	96033	02752	End 58232
1109	37515	25668	16 55785	31 66463	52758
1110	45324	00016	17 46818	04373	75360

Population = 3600 to 9452
Correspondence — First 4 digits in table
Route — Read down to end of column; start at top of the next column.
Sample size — 45, represented by sequential numbers 1 to 45.

FIGURE 12-12
Attribute Sampling
Data Sheet

Client	Hillsburg Hardware Ltd.	Year end	31/12/98
Audit Area	Tests of Controls—Billing Function and Recording of Sales	Pop. size	5,853

Define the objective(s) Examine duplicate sales invoices and related documents to determine if the system has functioned as intended and as described in the audit program

Define the population precisely (including stratification, if any) POS invoices and credit sales invoices for the period 1/1/98 to 31/12/98. First POS number = 140 672. Last POS number = 253 590. First credit sales invoice number = 3600. Last credit sales invoice number = 9452.

Define the sampling unit, organization of population items, and random selection procedures Sales invoice number, POS invoice numbers, and credit recorded in the sales files sequentially; random sampling.

Description of Attributes	Planned Audit				Actual Results			
	EPER	TER	ARACR	Initial sample size	Sample size	Number of exceptions	Sample exception rate	CUER
1. Invoice copy has customer signature. (13.1)	0	3	10	76				
For Bulk Sales: 2. Bulk order form number entered on invoice details. (13.2)	2	8	10	48				
3. Bulk order form details match invoice details. (13.3)	0	4	10	57				
4. Warehouse copy of bulk order form has customer signature. (13.4)	1	4	10	96				
5. Customer signature on warehouse copy of bulk order form matches signature on invoice. (13.4)	0	3	10	76				

Intended use of sampling results:

1. Effect on Audit Plan:

2. Recommendations to Management:

dures in the billing function can be included. The attributes used for this case are listed in Figure 12-12.

The definition of the attribute is a critical part of attribute sampling. The decision as to which attributes to combine and which ones to keep separate is the most important aspect of the definition. If all possible types of attributes, such as customer name, date, price, and quantity, are separated for each procedure, the large number of attributes makes the problem unmanageable. However, if all the procedures are combined into one or two attributes, greatly dissimilar misstatements are evaluated together. Somewhere in between is a reasonable compromise.

| ESTABLISH TER, ARACR, AND EPER, AND DETERMINE INITIAL SAMPLE SIZE | The TER (tolerable exception rate) for each attribute is decided on the basis of the auditor's judgment of what exception rate is material. The failure to have a customer signature on an invoice would be highly significant since this could mean an inability to collect funds from a credit card organization or for a credit sale. Therefore, as indicated in Figure 12-12, the lowest TER (3 percent) is chosen for attribute 1. The incorrect billing of the customer for bulk sales represents potentially significant misstatements, but no misstatement is likely to apply to the full amount of the invoice. As a result, a 4 percent TER is chosen for matching of the bulk order form details and customer signature on that form. The second attribute has a higher TER since it is of less importance for the audit. The last item is also important, since it helps verify the authenticity of the customer. |

An ARACR (acceptable risk of assessing control risk too low) of 10 percent is chosen because there are numerous other controls, such as programmed controls and management review of exception reports.

The estimated population exception rate (EPER) is based on previous years' results, modified upward slightly due to the change in personnel. Initial sample size for each attribute is determined from Table 12-7 on the basis of the above considerations. This information is summarized for all attributes in Figure 12-15 on page 411. For convenience in selection and evaluation, the auditor decided to select a sample of 75 for attribute 1, 50 for attributes 2 and 3, 100 for attribute 5, and 75 for attribute 4. Based on past experience, the decision was made to select 30 samples from the POS invoices and the remainder from credit sales invoices, since these have a greater proportion of bulk sales orders.

SELECT THE SAMPLE

The random selection for the case is straightforward except for the need for different sample sizes for different attributes. This problem can be overcome by selecting a random sample of 50 for use on all five attributes followed by another sample of 25 for attributes 1 and 5, and an additional 25 for attribute 4. Figure 11-2 illustrates how the first 30 items were selected from the POS system using a spreadsheet template. The documentation for the selection of the 45 numbers is illustrated in Figure 12-11. This brings the total to 75 items selected. An additional 25 would be selected in a similar manner.

PERFORM THE PROCEDURES AND GENERALIZE TO THE POPULATION

The audit procedures that are included in the audit program and summarized in the attribute sampling data sheet must be carefully performed for every item in the sample. As a means of documenting the tests and providing information for review, it is common to include a worksheet of the results. Some auditors prefer to include a worksheet containing a listing of all items in the sample; others prefer to limit the documentation to identifying the exceptions. This latter approach is followed in the example (Figure 12-13 on page 410). Figure 12-14 on page 410 summarizes the sampling process for the testing of master file change forms.

At the completion of the testing, the exceptions are tabulated to determine the number of exceptions in the sample for each attribute. This enables the auditor to compute the sample exception rate and determine the computed upper exception rate (CUER) using Table 12-8 on page 412. The exceptions for attribute 1 were considered not to be true exceptions since signatures are not required on invoices for purchases made by cash on POS invoices, although they are required for all other types of purchases. Exception information is summarized in Figure 12-15 (page 411) and Table 12-9 (page 413).

EXCEPTION ANALYSIS

The final part of the application consists of analyzing the deviations to determine their cause and drawing conclusions about each attribute tested. For every attribute for which CUER exceeds TER, it is essential that some conclusion concerning follow-up action be drawn and documented. The exception analysis and conclusions

TABLE 12-7

DETERMINING SAMPLE SIZE FOR ATTRIBUTE SAMPLING

ESTIMATED POPULATION EXCEPTION RATE (IN PERCENTAGE)	5 PERCENT ARACR TOLERABLE EXCEPTION RATE (IN PERCENTAGE)										
	2	3	4	5	6	7	8	9	10	15	20
0.00	149	99	74	59	49	42	36	32	29	19	14
.25	236	157	117	93	78	66	58	51	46	30	22
.50	*	157	117	93	78	66	58	51	46	30	22
.75	*	208	117	93	78	66	58	51	46	30	22
1.00	*	*	156	93	78	66	58	51	46	30	22
1.25	*	*	156	124	78	66	58	51	46	30	22
1.50	*	*	192	124	103	66	58	51	46	30	22
1.75	*	*	227	153	103	88	77	51	46	30	22
2.00	*	*	*	181	127	88	77	68	46	30	22
2.25	*	*	*	208	127	88	77	68	61	30	22
2.50	*	*	*	*	150	109	77	68	61	30	22
2.75	*	*	*	*	173	109	95	68	61	30	22
3.00	*	*	*	*	195	129	95	84	61	30	22
3.25	*	*	*	*	*	148	112	84	61	30	22
3.50	*	*	*	*	*	167	112	84	76	40	22
3.75	*	*	*	*	*	185	129	100	76	40	22
4.00	*	*	*	*	*	*	146	100	89	40	22
5.00	*	*	*	*	*	*	*	158	116	40	30
6.00	*	*	*	*	*	*	*	*	179	50	30
7.00	*	*	*	*	*	*	*	*	*	68	37

ESTIMATED POPULATION EXCEPTION RATE	10 PERCENT ARACR										
	2	3	4	5	6	7	8	9	10	15	20
0.00	114	76	57	45	38	32	28	25	22	15	11
.25	194	129	96	77	64	55	48	42	38	25	18
.50	194	129	96	77	64	55	48	42	38	25	18
.75	265	129	96	77	64	55	48	42	38	25	18
1.00	*	176	96	77	64	55	48	42	38	25	18
1.25	*	221	132	77	64	55	48	42	38	25	18
1.50	*	*	132	105	64	55	48	42	38	25	18
1.75	*	*	166	105	88	55	48	42	38	25	18
2.00	*	*	198	132	88	75	48	42	38	25	18
2.25	*	*	*	132	88	75	65	42	38	25	18
2.50	*	*	*	158	110	75	65	58	38	25	18
2.75	*	*	*	209	132	94	65	58	52	25	18
3.00	*	*	*	*	132	94	65	58	52	25	18
3.25	*	*	*	*	153	113	82	58	52	25	18
3.50	*	*	*	*	194	113	82	73	52	25	18
3.75	*	*	*	*	*	131	98	73	52	25	18
4.00	*	*	*	*	*	149	98	73	65	25	18
4.50	*	*	*	*	*	218	130	87	65	34	18
5.00	*	*	*	*	*	*	160	115	78	34	18
5.50	*	*	*	*	*	*	*	142	103	34	18
6.00	*	*	*	*	*	*	*	182	116	45	25
7.00	*	*	*	*	*	*	*	*	199	52	25
7.50	*	*	*	*	*	*	*	*	*	52	25
8.00	*	*	*	*	*	*	*	*	*	60	25
8.50	*	*	*	*	*	*	*	*	*	68	32

*Sample is too large to be cost-effective for most audit applications.

Notes:

1. This table assumes a large population.
2. Sample sizes are the same in certain columns even when expected population exception rates differ, because of the method of constructing the tables. Sample sizes are calculated for attributes sampling using the expected number of exceptions in the population, but auditors can deal more conveniently with expected population exception rates. For example, in the 15 percent column for tolerable exception rate, at an ARACR of 5 percent, initial sample size for most EPERs is 30. One exception, divided by a sample size of 30, is 3.3 percent. Therefore, for all EPERs greater than zero but less than 3.3 percent, initial sample size is the same.

FIGURE 12-13
Exceptions Found During Inspection of Sample Items for Attributes

1. *Invoice copy has customer signature. (13.1)*

   Three exceptions found.

   POS invoices # 160134, 168253, and 240240 did not have customer signatures. These were all cash sales (i.e., not paid by credit card or debit card).

2. *Bulk order form number entered on invoice.*

   Four exceptions found.

   POS invoice # 248964 missing bulk order number, although copy was attached.

   Credit sales invoice # 5802, 6137, and 8713 missing bulk order number, although copy was attached.

   No exceptions found for attributes 3, 4, and 5.

FIGURE 12-14
Testing of Master File Change Forms

Objectives: As defined in Figure 12-10; authorization of master file change forms and proof of data entry verification.

Sampling: Applies to use of master file change forms throughout the year.

Population: Master file change forms used throughout the year. First form number used: 1201. Last form used: 1632.

TER: 5	**ARACR:** 10	**EPER:** 0	**Initial Sample Size:** 45

Results of Performing Procedures: Three exceptions found, on form # 1288, 1510, and 1599. In the first instance, signature of sales manager was missing. In the second and third, the signature of the chief accountant was missing. In all cases, the indicated person was on holidays. Also for the latter two forms, the data entry report was initialled by the sales manager, since the chief accountant was absent.

	No. of Exceptions	Sample Exception Rate	CUER
Attribute 1	3	6.7	14.2
Attribute 2	2	4.4	11.4

reached are illustrated in Table 12-9 and summarized at the bottom of the data sheet in Figure 12-15.

DETERMINE THE ACCEPTABILITY OF THE POPULATION

The controls tested for attributes 1 through 5 of the billing function and recording of sales can be relied on, even though the bulk order invoice number was not recorded on the sales invoice, since there were no deviations in any of the other controls. Thus, the sales population is acceptable. Master file change forms and data entry verification reports were approved using existing policies, except where the designated individual was absent. However, this enables a single individual to approve credit and customer master file changes, which could lead to manipulation. The auditor should conduct additional testing by examining master file changes during the period when one of these two individuals was absent or on holiday. Assume that once additional testing was done, no unusual transactions were discovered. The auditor can then accept the population, although additional testing of the bad-debt allowance is still advisable.

IMPACT OF TEST OF CONTROLS RESULTS ON AUDIT PLANNING

After the tests of controls have been performed, it is essential to *analyze each test of control exception* to determine its cause and the implication of the exception on assessed control risk, which may affect the supported detection risk and thereby the substantive procedures.

For Hillsburg Hardware, assume that there were no other deviations beyond those described and analyzed in Table 12-9. This means that the auditor can accept the

FIGURE 12-15
Attribute Sampling
Data Sheet, Completed

Client Hillsburg Hardware Ltd.

Audit Area Tests of Controls—Billing Function and Recording of Sales

Year end 31/12/98

Pop. size 5,853

Define the objective(s) Examine duplicate sales invoices and related documents to determine if the system has functioned as intended and as described in the audit program.

Define the population precisely (including stratification, if any) POS invoices and credit sales invoices for the period 1/1/98 to 31/12/98. First POS number = 140 672. Last POS number = 253 590. First credit sales invoice number = 3600. Last credit sales invoice number = 9452.

Define the sampling unit, organization of population items, and random selection procedures Sales invoice number, POS invoice numbers, and credit recorded in the sales files sequentially; random sampling.

Description of Attributes	Planned Audit				Actual Results			
	EPER	TER	ARACR	Initial sample size	Sample size	Number of exceptions	Sample exception rate	CUER
1. Invoice copy has customer signature. (13.1)	0	3	10	76	75	0	0	3
For Bulk Sales: 2. Bulk order form number entered on invoice details. (13.2)	2	8	10	48	50	4	8	15.4
3. Bulk order form details match invoice details. (13.3)	0	4	10	57	50	0	0	4.5
4. Warehouse copy of bulk order form has customer signature. (13.4)	1	4	10	96	100	0	0	2.3
5. Customer signature on warehouse copy of bulk order form matches signature on invoice. (13.4)	0	3	10	76	75	0	0	3

Intended use of sampling results:

1. **Effect on Audit Plan:** Controls tested using attributes #1, 3-5 can be relied upon. Policies and procedures to remedy #2 should be discussed with management. No additional audit procedures required since no financial impact.

2. **Recommendations to Management:** See attached weakness investigation.

OBJECTIVE 12-10

Determine the impact of the results of tests of controls on the overall audit plan.

planned control risk in all areas except valuation (due to the exceptions found with master file changes).

UPDATE THE EVIDENCE PLANNING SPREADSHEET

After completing tests of controls, the auditor should complete rows 3 through 5 of the evidence planning spreadsheet. Recall from Chapter 9 that the control risk rows could have been completed before the tests of controls were done, and then modified if the test results were not satisfactory. An updated evidence planning spreadsheet is

TABLE 12-8

EVALUATING SAMPLE RESULTS USING ATTRIBUTE SAMPLING

	ACTUAL NUMBER OF DEVIATIONS FOUND										
SAMPLE SIZE	0	1	2	3	4	5	6	7	8	9	10
5 PERCENT ARACR											
25	11.3	17.6	*	*	*	*	*	*	*	*	*
30	9.5	14.9	19.5	*	*	*	*	*	*	*	*
35	8.2	12.9	16.9	*	*	*	*	*	*	*	*
40	7.2	11.3	14.9	18.3	*	*	*	*	*	*	*
45	6.4	10.1	13.3	16.3	19.2	*	*	*	*	*	*
50	5.8	9.1	12.1	14.8	17.4	19.9	*	*	*	*	*
55	5.3	8.3	11.0	13.5	15.9	18.1	*	*	*	*	*
60	4.9	7.7	10.1	12.4	14.6	16.7	18.8	*	*	*	*
65	4.5	7.1	9.4	11.5	13.5	15.5	17.4	19.3	*	*	*
70	4.2	6.6	8.7	10.7	12.6	14.4	16.2	18.0	19.7	*	*
75	3.9	6.2	8.2	10.0	11.8	13.5	15.2	16.9	18.4	20.0	*
80	3.7	5.8	7.7	9.4	11.1	12.7	14.3	15.8	17.3	18.8	*
90	3.3	5.2	6.8	8.4	9.9	11.3	12.7	14.1	15.5	16.8	18.1
100	3.0	4.7	6.2	7.6	8.9	10.2	11.5	12.7	14.0	15.2	16.4
125	2.4	3.7	4.9	6.1	7.2	8.2	9.3	10.3	11.3	12.2	13.2
150	2.0	3.1	4.1	5.1	6.0	6.9	7.7	8.6	9.4	10.2	11.0
200	1.5	2.3	3.1	3.8	4.5	5.2	5.8	6.5	7.1	7.7	8.3
10 PERCENT ARACR											
20	10.9	18.1	*	*	*	*	*	*	*	*	*
25	8.8	14.7	19.9	*	*	*	*	*	*	*	*
30	7.4	12.4	16.8	*	*	*	*	*	*	*	*
35	6.4	10.7	14.5	18.1	*	*	*	*	*	*	*
40	5.6	9.4	12.8	15.9	19.0	*	*	*	*	*	*
45	5.0	8.4	11.4	14.2	17.0	19.6	*	*	*	*	*
50	4.5	7.6	10.3	12.9	15.4	17.8	*	*	*	*	*
55	4.1	6.9	9.4	11.7	14.0	16.2	18.4	*	*	*	*
60	3.8	6.3	8.6	10.8	12.9	14.9	16.9	18.8	*	*	*
70	3.2	5.4	7.4	9.3	11.1	12.8	14.6	16.2	17.9	19.5	*
80	2.8	4.8	6.5	8.3	9.7	11.3	12.8	14.3	15.7	17.2	18.6
90	2.5	4.3	5.8	7.3	8.7	10.1	11.4	12.7	14.0	15.3	16.6
100	2.3	3.8	5.2	6.6	7.8	9.1	10.3	11.5	12.7	13.8	15.0
120	1.9	3.2	4.4	5.5	6.6	7.6	8.6	9.6	10.6	11.6	12.5
160	1.4	2.4	3.3	4.1	4.9	5.7	6.5	7.2	8.0	8.7	9.5
200	1.1	1.9	2.6	3.3	4.0	4.6	5.2	5.8	6.4	7.0	7.6

* Over 20 percent.

Note: This table presents computed upper deviation rates as percentages. Table assumes a large population.

shown in Figure 12-16. The spreadsheet is used to determine the extent of substantive tests required for the cycle.

The most significant effect of the results of the tests of controls in the sales and collection cycle is on the confirmation of accounts receivable. The type of confirmation, the size of the sample, and the timing of the test are all affected by the results of tests of controls. The effect of the tests on accounts receivable, bad-debt expense, and allowance for uncollectible accounts is further considered in Chapter 14.

COMMUNICATION WITH MANAGEMENT

In addition to adjusting the audit procedures, the auditor should ensure that management is informed of all exceptions and that the impact of the exceptions is appropriately discussed. In some instances, the auditor will conduct such a discussion verbally, but in many instances, a *management letter* will be issued, in which the excep-

TABLE 12-9

ANALYSIS OF EXCEPTIONS

ATTRIBUTE	NUMBER OF EXCEPTIONS	NATURE OF EXCEPTIONS	EFFECT ON THE AUDIT AND OTHER COMMENTS
1, sales	3	Three POS invoices paid by cash did not have customer signatures. Each invoice was for less than $50.	No effect on the audit. Hillsburg policy has been clarified that cash purchase invoices do not require customer signature.
2, sales	4	One POS invoice and three credit sales invoices did not have the bulk order number on the face of the invoice, although the invoice copy was attached.	These omissions would show on the bulk order form exception report showing missing bulk order numbers. Management indicated that, unfortunately, new employees often forget to record this number, resulting in an excessive number of items on the exception report. This usually eases off. Since this does not have a financial effect on the audit (there were no errors in goods shipped), no further audit work is required.
1, master file changes	3	Three master file change forms for new credit accounts were approved by only the sales manager *or* the chief accountant.	Additional work on the bad-debt allowance should be completed in the event that bad credit risks have been approved. Master file changes submitted during the period of these managers' absence should be reviewed for unusual items.
2, master file changes	2	Two data entry verification reports of master file changes were verified by the sales manager rather than by the chief accountant.	See above.

tion is discussed, the implications of the exception explained, and recommendations for improvement in procedures identified. For the sales and collection cycle, the auditor might communicate in writing the exceptions with respect to master file change form approval, and recommend that another individual provide a second signature on these forms in the event of the sales manager's or chief accountant's absence. The likely individual recommended to do this would be the president of the organization.

APPENDIX   COMPUTER-ASSISTED AUDIT TESTS

The general term *computer-assisted audit tests* (CAAT) is used to describe tests that the auditor conducts using computer software or using the data or systems of the client. The audit objectives of these tests do not change, but the actual form of the tests must change as the client system changes, just as other aspects of the audit change with a change in audit client.

The two most common forms of CAATs are test data and generalized audit software.

Test data   This includes the use of fictitious transactions to determine whether client programs are functioning as described. For Hillsburg Hardware, test data is used to determine whether the system rejects transactions that it should reject, such as invalid customer numbers, unapproved prices, unapproved credit terms, or invalid dates. This is the most common use of test data since the client data files need not be disrupted, and the testing can be performed quickly and efficiently.

Should the auditor wish to determine whether programs are calculating invoice extensions correctly, then test data would need to be prepared that shows the expected result, and then the data entered into the client system. Such a test would

FIGURE 12-16

Evidence Planning Spreadsheet to Determine Tests of Details of Balances for Hillsburg Hardware Ltd. — Accounts Receivable

	Detail tie-in	Existence (or occurrence)	Completeness	Accuracy	Classification	Cutoff	Valuation	Rights and obligations	Presentation and disclosure
Acceptable audit risk	high	high	high	high	high	high	high	high	high
Inherent risk	low	low	low	low	low	low	medium	low	low
Control risk – Sales	low	medium	low	low	low	low	high	not applicable	not applicable
Control risk – Cash receipts	low	high	low	low	low	low	not applicable	not applicable	not applicable
Control risk – Additional controls	none	none	none	none	none	none	none	low	low
Analytical procedures									
Planned detection risk for tests of details of balances									
Planned audit evidence for tests of details of balances									

Materiality $100,000

result in an invoice being calculated and posted against a client account. A credit transaction would need to be created to reverse this invoice test from the client records (i.e., customer master file, transaction files, general ledger, and inventory files). Some of the inconvenience could be avoided by also establishing a fictitious client, but then we have inserted deliberate fictitious transactions in our client's systems. This is the major drawback of test data. It is also a point-in-time test and verifies that the programs being tested are functioning as tested as of the time of the test. The auditor needs to conduct additional tests to determine that these same programs were used during the duration of the period under audit.

An integrated test facility (discussed further in Chapter 22) overcomes the problems with test data by allowing the auditor to use test data in a test environment where it does not affect client accounting records. However, it can be used only with clients who have established such a capability during the initial set-up of their accounting systems.

Generalized audit software   This consists of a software package that is used by the auditor to run routines against client data. Two common such packages in Canada are Audit Command Language for Personal Computers (ACL-PC) and Interactive Data Extraction and Analysis (I.D.E.A.). The auditor obtains a copy of the client data files and runs one or more of the following types of activities against the data file. The examples shown are typical tests that would be run against the customer master file together with open item accounts:

Mathematical calculations: addition of debit and credit amounts, extensions

Aging functions: aging of the accounts to re-create figures in the aged accounts receivable trial balance

Comparisons: between the outstanding balance and the credit limit

Sampling: using random, dollar-unit, interval, or stratification

Certain functions of generalized audit software are often referred to as "parallel simulation," which is the reperformance of activities conducted by the client. For example, if the auditor re-creates the aged accounts receivable trial balance using client data, this is parallel simulation. This is a dual purpose test since it ensures the mechanical accuracy of the aging process (a substantive test), while also verifying that the client's aging program is functioning correctly (a controls test).

Examples of test data and generalized audit software are discussed in those chapters where transaction cycles are tested (primarily Chapters 15, 16, and 18), providing examples linked to specific audit objectives. Computer-assisted audit techniques are discussed further in Chapter 22.

ESSENTIAL TERMS

In addition to these terms, see pages 378–379 for descriptions of the key documents and records used in the sales and collection cycle.

Batch processing — transaction processing using groups of transactions (p. 374).

Business functions for the sales and collection cycle — the key activities that an organization must complete to execute and record business transactions for sales, cash receipts, sales returns and allowances, charge-off of uncollectible accounts, and bad debts (p. 376).

Classes of transactions in the sales and collection cycle — the categories of transactions for the sales and collection cycle in a typical company: sales, cash receipts, sales returns and allowances, charge-off of uncollectible accounts, and bad-debt expense (p. 373).

Computer-assisted audit tests — tests that the auditor conducts using computer software or using the data or systems of the client (p. 413).

Data control function — independent verification of control total and source document detail to that keyed into the system by data entry (p. 376).

Design format audit program — the audit procedures resulting from the auditor's decisions about the appropriate audit procedures for each audit objective; this audit program is used to prepare a performance format audit program (p. 391).

Interdependent controls — controls that require both a programmed and manual component to satisfy an audit objective (p. 381).

Lapping of accounts receivable — the postponement of entries for the collection of receivables to conceal an existing cash shortage; a common type of defalcation (p. 395).

On-line processing —the processing of transactions one at a time with an immediate update against the data files (p. 374).

Performance format audit program — the audit procedures for a class of transactions organized in the format that they will be performed; prepared from a design format audit program (p. 391).

Proof of cash receipts — an audit procedure to test whether all recorded cash receipts have been deposited in the bank account by reconciling the total cash receipts recorded in the cash receipts journal for a given period with the actual deposits made to the bank (p. 393).

Sales and collection cycle — involves the decisions and processes necessary for the transfer of the ownership of goods and services to customers after they are made available for sale; begins with a request by a customer and ends with the conversion of material or service into an account receivable, and ultimately into cash (p. 374).

Semi-permanent (or master file) data — in the sales and collection cycle, data that is established when a customer starts purchasing and updated as customer information changes; generally used for the processing of multiple transactions (p. 375).

Tests of controls in the sales and collection cycle — audit procedures performed to determine the effectiveness of both the design and operations of specific internal controls. They include audit procedures testing for monetary errors or fraud and other irregularities to determine whether the six transaction-related audit objectives have been satisfied for each class of transactions in the sales and collection cycle (p. 387).

Transaction information — information based on customer activity. There is normally one transaction for each activity. In the sales and collection cycle, examples include sale or cash payment transactions (p. 375).

Transaction-related audit objectives in the sales and collection cycle — the six objectives that the auditor must satisfy for each class of transactions in the sales and collection cycle (p. 386).

Weakness investigation tests — tests conducted to determine whether a material error or material misstatement could occur due to a control weakness (p. 388).

12-1 Describe the nature of the following documents and records, and explain their use in the sales and collection cycle: bill of lading, sales invoice, customer master file, credit memo, remittance advice, and monthly statement to customers.

12-2 Explain the importance of proper credit approval for sales. What effect do adequate controls in the credit function have on the auditor's evidence accumulation?

12-3 Distinguish between bad-debt expense and charge-off of uncollectible accounts. Explain why they are audited in completely different ways.

12-4 List the transaction-related audit objectives for the verification of sales transactions. For each objective, state one internal control that the client can use to reduce the likelihood of misstatements.

12-5 State two tests of controls the auditor can use to verify the following sales objective: Recorded sales are stated at the proper amount.

12-6 List the most important duties that should be segregated in the sales and collection cycle. Explain why it is desirable that each duty be segregated.

12-7 Explain how prenumbered shipping documents and sales invoices can be useful controls for preventing misstatements in sales.

12-8 What three types of authorizations are commonly used as internal controls for sales? For each authorization, state a test of controls that the auditor could use to verify whether the control was effective in preventing misstatements.

12-9 Explain the purpose of footing and cross-footing the sales journal and tracing the totals to the general ledger.

12-10 What is the difference between the auditor's approach in verifying sales returns and allowances and that for sales? Explain the reasons for the difference.

12-11 Explain why auditors usually emphasize the detection of fraud in the audit of cash. Is this consistent or inconsistent with the auditor's responsibility in the audit? Explain.

12-12 List the transaction-related audit objectives for the verification of cash receipts. For each objective, state one internal control that the client can use to reduce the likelihood of misstatements.

12-13 List several audit procedures the auditor can use to determine whether all cash received was recorded.

12-14 Explain what is meant by "proof of cash receipts," and state its purpose.

12-15 Explain what is meant by "lapping," and discuss how the auditor can uncover it. Under what circumstances should the auditor make a special effort to uncover lapping?

12-16 What audit procedures are most likely to be used to verify accounts receivable charged off as uncollectible? State the purpose of each of these procedures.

12-17 State the relationship between the confirmation of accounts receivable and the results of the tests of controls.

12-18 Under what circumstances is it acceptable to perform tests of controls for sales and cash receipts at an interim date?

12-19 Deirdre Brandt, a public accountant, tested sales transactions for the month of March in an audit of the financial statements for the year ended December 31, 1999. Based on the excellent results of the tests of controls, she decided to significantly reduce her substantive tests of details of balances at year end. Evaluate this decision.

12-20 Danny Ng, a public accountant, has decided to use attribute sampling during the audit of sales transactions. There are 100,000 sales transactions, and the preliminary assessment of control risk is low.

Required

a. Identify the factors Danny should use to decide an appropriate TER. Compare the sample size for a TER of 6 percent with that of 3 percent, all other factors being equal.

b. Identify the factors Danny should use to decide an appropriate ARACR. Compare the sample size for an ARACR of 10 percent with that of 5 percent, all other factors being equal.

c. Assume Danny selected 100 sales invoices to test for matching shipping documents with customer signatures. Determine the CUER at a 5 percent ARACR if three exceptions existed in the sample. Explain the meaning of the statistical results in auditing terms.

MULTIPLE CHOICE QUESTIONS

12-21 The following questions deal with internal controls in the sales and collection cycle. Choose the best response.

a. For effective internal control, the billing information should be entered by the
   (1) sales department.
   (2) accounting department.
   (3) shipping department.
   (4) credit and collection department.

b. A company policy should clearly indicate that defective merchandise returned by customers is to be delivered to the
   (1) inventory control clerk.
   (2) sales clerk.
   (3) receiving clerk.
   (4) accounts receivable clerk.

c. For good internal control, the credit manager should be responsible to the
   (1) treasurer.
   (2) sales manager.
   (3) customer service manager.
   (4) controller.

d. For good internal control, the billing department should be under the direction of the
   (1) controller.
   (2) sales manager.

(3) treasurer.

(4) credit manager.

(AICPA adapted)

12-22 For each of the following types of misstatements, parts (a) through (c), select the control that should have prevented the misstatement.

a. A manufacturing company received a substantial sales return in the last month of the year, but the credit memorandum for the return was not prepared until after the auditors had completed their field work. The returned merchandise was included in the physical inventory.

(1) Receiving reports are prepared for all materials received, and such reports are numerically controlled.

(2) Aging schedules of accounts receivable are prepared periodically.

(3) Credit memoranda are prenumbered and all numbers are accounted for.

(4) A reconciliation of the trial balance of customers' accounts with the general ledger control is prepared periodically.

b. The sales manager credited a salesman, Sean Boyle, with sales that were actually "house account" sales. Later, Boyle divided his excess sales commissions with the sales manager.

(1) The summary sales entries are checked periodically by persons independent of sales functions.

(2) The internal auditor compares the sales commission statements with the cash disbursements record.

(3) Customer purchase orders are reviewed and approved by persons independent of the sales department.

(4) Customer purchase orders are prenumbered, and all numbers are accounted for.

c. Copies of sales invoices show different unit prices for apparently identical items.

(1) Prices should be automatically placed on invoices from master file data.

(2) Differences reported by customers are satisfactorily investigated.

(3) All sales invoices are compared with the customers' purchase orders.

(4) Statistical sales data are compiled and reconciled with recorded sales.

(AICPA adapted)

12-23 The following questions deal with audit evidence for the sales and collection cycle. Choose the best response.

a. Auditors sometimes use comparison of ratios as audit evidence. For example, an unexplained decrease in the ratio of gross profit to sales may suggest which of the following possibilities?

(1) Unrecorded sales.

(2) Merchandise purchases being charged to selling and general expense.

(3) Unrecorded purchases.

(4) Fictitious sales.

b. To verify that all sales transactions have been recorded, a test of controls should be completed on a representative sample drawn from

(1) the shipping clerk's file of duplicate copies of bills of lading.

(2) the billing clerk's file of customer purchase orders.

(3) a file of duplicate copies of sales invoices for which all prenumbered forms in the series have been accounted.

(4) entries in the sales journal.

c. A public accountant is examining the financial statements of a small telephone company and wishes to test whether customers are being billed. One procedure that she might use is to

(1) trace a sample of postings from the billing control to the general ledger accounts receivable account.

(2) balance the outstanding amounts according to the customer master file to the general ledger control account.

(3) check a sample of listings in the telephone directory to the billing control.

(4) confirm a representative number of accounts receivable.

(AICPA adapted)

12-24 The following items are concerned with sampling in the sales and collection cycle. Choose the best response.

a. The auditor decides to set control risk at low for a particular control. The auditor should use

(1) A high ARACR

(2) A low ARACR

(3) A high TER

(4) A high TER

b. The auditor determines that the CUER for a particular control exceeds the TER. Which of the following is the least likely action the auditor would take?

(1) Analyze the exceptions

(2) Expand the sample size

(3) Revise TER

(4) Revise control risk

12-25 Items 1 through 8 are selected questions of the type generally found in internal control questionnaires used by auditors to obtain an understanding of internal control in the sales and collection cycle. In using the questionnaire for a particular client, a "yes" response to a question indicates a possible internal control, whereas a "no" indicates a potential weakness.

1. Are sales invoices independently compared with customers' orders for prices, quantities, extensions, and footings?

2. Are sales orders, invoices, and credit memoranda issued and filed in numerical sequence, and are the sequences accounted for periodically?

3. Are the selling function and cash register functions independent of the cash receipts, shipping, delivery, and billing functions?

4. Are all C.O.D., scrap, equipment, and cash sales accounted for in the same manner as charge sales, and is the record keeping independent of the collection procedure?

5. Is the collection function independent of, and does it constitute a check on, billing and recording sales?

6. Are customer master files balanced regularly to general ledger control accounts by an employee independent of billing functions?

7. Are cash receipts entered in the accounts receivable system by persons independent of the mail-opening and receipts-listing functions?

8. Are receipts deposited intact daily on a timely basis?

Required

a. For each of the questions above, state the transaction-related audit objectives being fulfilled if the control is in effect.

b. For each control, list a test of control to test its effectiveness.

c. For each of the questions above, identify the nature of the potential financial misstatements.

d. For each of the potential misstatements in part (c), list an audit procedure to determine whether a material error exists.

12-26 The following errors or fraud and other irregularities are included in the accounting records of Joyce Manufacturing Ltd.:

1. The credit limit for a new customer was entered as $20,000 rather than $2,000 into the customer master file.

2. A material sale was unintentionally recorded for the second time on the last day of the year. The sale had originally been recorded two days earlier.

3. Cash paid on accounts receivable was stolen by the mail clerk when the mail was opened.

4. Cash paid on accounts receivable that had been prelisted by a secretary was stolen by the bookkeeper who enters cash receipts and accounts receivable in the accounts receivable system. He failed to enter the transactions.

5. A shipment to a customer was not billed because of the loss of the bill of lading.

6. Merchandise was shipped to a customer, but no bill of lading was prepared. Since billings are prepared from bills of lading, the customer was not billed.

7. A sale to a residential customer was unintentionally classified as a commercial sale.

Required

a. Identify whether each misstatement is an error or a fraud or other irregularity.

b. For each misstatement, state a control that should have prevented it from occurring on a continuing basis.

c. For each misstatement, state an audit procedure that could uncover it.

12-27 The following are commonly performed tests of controls audit procedures in the sales and collection cycle:

1. Examine sales returns for approval by an authorized official.

2. Account for a sequence of shipping documents, and examine each one to make sure a duplicate sales invoice is attached.

3. Account for a sequence of sales invoices, and examine each one to make sure a duplicate copy of the shipping document is attached.

4. Compare the quantity and description of items on shipping documents with the related duplicate sales invoices.

5. Enter test transactions, and observe that both invalid customer numbers and orders that cause the customer balance to exceed the customer credit limit are rejected.

6. Add the sales transactions using generalized audit software, providing subtotals by date. Trace the daily total to the posting in the general ledger sales account.

7. Reconcile the recorded cash receipts on the prelisting of cash receipts with the cash receipts listing and the bank statement for a one-month period.

Required

a. State which of the six transaction-related audit objectives each of the audit procedures fulfills.

b. Identify the type of evidence used for each audit procedure, such as confirmation or observation.

12-28 The following are selected transaction-related audit objectives and audit procedures for sales transactions:

TRANSACTION-RELATED AUDIT OBJECTIVES

1. Recorded sales occurred.

2. Existing sales are recorded.

3. Sales transactions are updated correctly to the customer master file and are correctly summarized.

PROCEDURES

1. Trace a sample of shipping documents to related duplicate sales invoices and the sales journal to make sure the shipment was billed.

2. Examine a sample of duplicate sales invoices to determine if each one has a shipping document attached.

3. Examine a sample of shipping documents to determine if each one has a duplicate sales invoice number written on the bottom left corner.

4. Trace a sample of duplicate sales invoices to related shipping documents filed in the shipping department to make sure a shipment was made.

5. Determine whether the customer master file total agrees to the accounts receivable general ledger balance.

Required

a. For each objective, identify at least one specific misstatement that could occur.

b. Describe the differences between the purposes of the first and second objectives.

c. For each objective, identify one test of control.

d. For each test of control, state the internal control that is being tested. Also, identify or describe a misstatement that the client is trying to prevent by use of the control.

12-29 The following are common audit procedures for tests of sales and cash receipts:

1. Compare the quantity and description of items on duplicate sales invoices with related shipping documents.

2. Trace recorded cash receipts to the cash receipts journal and compare the customer name, date, and amount of each one.

3. Compare unit selling prices on duplicate sales invoices to the inventory master file.

4. Examine the sales journal for related-party transactions, notes receivable, and other unusual items.

5. Select a sample of customer purchase orders and trace the document to related shipping documents, vendors' invoices, and sales journal for comparison of name, date, and amount.

6. Perform a proof of cash receipts.

7. Examine a sample of remittance advices for approval of cash discounts.

Required

a. State which transaction-related audit objective each of the audit procedures fulfills.

b. For each test of control, state a dual purpose test (if possible) that could be used to determine whether there was a monetary misstatement.

12-30 Appliances Repair and Service Corp. bills all customers rather than collecting in cash when services are provided. All mail is opened by Tom Gyders, treasurer. Gyders, an accountant, is the most qualified person in the company who is in the office daily. He can, therefore, solve problems and respond to customers' needs quickly. Upon receipt of cash, he immediately prepares a listing of the cash and a duplicate deposit slip. Cash is deposited daily. Gyders uses the listing to enter the financial transactions in the computerized accounting records. He also contacts customers about uncollected accounts receivable. Because he is so knowledgeable about the business and each customer, he grants credit, authorizes all sales allowances, and charges off uncollectible accounts. The owner is extremely pleased with the efficiency of the company. He can run the business without spending much time there because of Gyders's effectiveness.

Imagine the owner's surprise when he discovers that Gyders has committed a major theft of the company's collections. Gyders did so by not recording sales, recording improper credits to recorded accounts receivable, and overstating receivables.

Required

a. Given that cash was prelisted, went only to the treasurer, and was deposited daily, what internal control deficiency permitted the fraud?

b. What are the benefits of a prelisting of cash? Who should prepare the prelisting and what duties should that person *not* perform?

c. Assume an appropriate person, as discussed in part (b), prepares a prelisting of cash. What is to prevent that person from taking the cash after it is prelisted but before it is deposited?

d. Who should deposit the cash, given your answer to part (b)?

12-31 You were asked in September 1999 by the board of management of your church to review its accounting procedures. As part of this review, you have prepared the following comments relating to the collections made at weekly services and record keeping for members' pledges and contributions:

1. The finance committee is responsible for preparing an annual budget based on the anticipated needs of the various church committees and for the annual fall "pledge campaign" during which most members make a commitment to contribute a certain amount to the church over the following year.

2. The financial records are maintained by the treasurer who has authority to sign cheques drawn on the church bank account.

3. The ushers each Sunday take up the collection during the services and place it uncounted in a deposit bag in the church safe. The term "safe" is a misnomer: the lock does not work and the door is merely closed. This fact is well known to church members since most have ushered at one time. The board of management and finance committee are not concerned since they believe that the members, as good church-goers, can be trusted.

4. The treasurer, who is retired, comes in Monday morning, counts the collection and deposits it into the church's bank account. Some members use predated numbered envelopes but most do not. The treasurer does not keep a record of members' contributions.

5. The treasurer issues receipts to each member every January based on the amounts pledged for the preceding year by that member. The contributions up to 1998 had always exceeded the amounts pledged so that the value of receipts given out was less than total contributions; the excess was recorded as "loose" or "open" collection. In 1999, the total of the receipts given out by the treasurer exceeded the total funds received by the church.

6. The church is registered as a charity under the *Income Tax Act* and is required to file a return each year to comply with its rules. The chairperson of the finance committee is upset because the church has received a letter from Revenue Canada in connection with the return for 1999 because the return showed receipts given exceeded the funds actually received. The letter indicated that such differences could result in removal of the church's ability to issue income tax receipts.

Required

Identify the weaknesses and recommend improvements in procedures for

a. collections made at weekly services.

b. record keeping for members' pledges and contributions. Use the methodology for identifying weaknesses that was discussed in Chapter 9. Organize your answer sheets as follows:

WEAKNESS	RECOMMENDED IMPROVEMENT

(AICPA adapted)

12-32 Lenter Supply Corp. is a medium-sized distributor of wholesale hardware supplies in southern Manitoba. It has been a client of yours for several years and has instituted excellent internal control for sales at your recommendation.

In providing control over shipments, the client has prenumbered "warehouse removal slips" that are used for every sale. It is company policy never to remove goods from the warehouse without an authorized warehouse removal slip. After shipment, two copies of the warehouse removal slip are sent to billing for the computerized preparation of a sales invoice. One copy is stapled to the duplicate copy of a prenumbered sales invoice, and the other copy is filed numerically. In some cases, more than one warehouse removal slip is used for billing one sales invoice. The smallest warehouse removal slip number for the year is 14682 and the largest is 37521. The smallest sales invoice number is 47821 and the largest is 68507.

In the audit of sales, one of the major concerns is the effectiveness of the controls in making sure that all shipments are billed. You have decided to use audit sampling in testing internal controls.

Required

a. State an effective audit procedure for testing whether shipments have been billed. What is the sampling unit for the audit procedure?

b. Assuming that you expect no deviations in the sample but are willing to accept a TER of 3 percent, at a 10 percent ARACR, what is the appropriate sample size for the audit test? You may complete this assignment using nonstatistical sampling or attribute sampling.

c. Design a random selection plan for selecting the sample from the population using the random number table. Select the first 10 sample items using Table 11-2 on page 348. Use a starting point of row 1013, column 3.

d. Your supervisor suggests the possibility of performing other sales tests with the same sample as a means of efficiently using your audit time. List two other audit procedures that could conveniently be performed using the same sample, and state the purpose of each of the procedures.

e. Is it desirable to test the existence of sales with the random sample you have designed in part (c)? Why or why not?

12-33 The following is a partial audit program for the audit of cash receipts.

1. Review the cash receipts journal for large and unusual transactions.

2. Trace entries from the prelisting of cash receipts to the cash receipts journal to determine if each is recorded.

3. Compare customer name, date, and amount on the prelisting with the cash receipts journal.

4. Examine the related remittance advice for entries selected from the prelisting to determine if cash discounts were approved.

5. Trace entries from the prelisting to the deposit slip to determine if each has been deposited.

Required

a. Identify which audit procedures could be tested using attribute sampling.

b. What is the appropriate sampling unit for the tests in part (a)?

c. List the attributes for testing in part (a).

d. Assume an ARACR of 5 percent and a TER of 8 percent for tests of controls. The estimated population deviation rate for tests of controls is 2 percent. What is the initial sample size for each attribute?

12-34 The following questions concern the determination of the proper sample size in attributes sampling using the following table:

	1	2	3	4	5	6	7
ARACR (in percentage)	10	5	5	5	10	10	5
TER (in percentage)	6	6	5	6	20	20	2
EPER (in percentage)	2	2	2	2	8	2	0
Population size	1,000	100,000	6,000	1,000	500	500	1,000,000

Required

a. For each of the columns numbered 1 through 7, decide the initial sample size using nonstatistical methods.

b. For each of the columns numbered 1 through 7, determine the initial sample size needed to satisfy the auditor's requirements using attribute sampling from the appropriate part of Table 12-8.

c. Using your understanding of the relationship between the following factors and sample size, state the effect on the initial sample size (increase or decrease) of changing each of the following factors while the other three are held constant:
(1) An increase in ARACR
(2) An increase in the TER
(3) An increase in the EPER
(4) An increase in the population size

d. Explain why there is such a large difference in the sample sizes for columns 3 and 6.

e. Compare your answers in part (b) with the results you determined in part (a). Which of the four factors appears to have the greatest effect on the initial sample size? Which one appears to have the least effect?

f. Why is the sample size referred to as the initial sample size?

12-35 The following are auditor judgments and audit sampling results for six populations. Assume large population sizes.

	1	2	3	4	5	6
EPER (in percentage)	2	0	3	1	1	8
TER (in percentage)	6	3	8	5	20	15
ARACR (in percentage)	5	5	10	5	10	10
Actual sample size	100	100	60	100	20	60
Actual number of exceptions in the sample	2	0	1	4	1	8

Required

a. For each population, did the auditor select a smaller sample size than is indicated by using attribute sampling tables for determining sample size? Evaluate selecting either a larger or smaller size than those determined in the tables.

b. Calculate the SER and CUER for each population.

c. For which of the six populations should the sample results be considered unacceptable? What options are available to the auditor?

d. Why is analysis of the deviations necessary even when the populations are considered acceptable?

e. For the following terms, identify which is an audit decision, a nonstatistical estimate made by the auditor, a sample result, and a statistical conclusion about the population:
(1) EPER
(2) TER
(3) ARACR
(4) Actual sample size
(5) Actual number of exceptions in the sample
(6) SER
(7) CUER

12-36 CA conducts a medium-sized audit practice in Anytown, Canada. On August 8, 1998, CA was approached by Smith, the majority shareholder of Smith Wholesalers Limited, to conduct an audit for the company for the year ended June 30, 1999. Having available time, CA, without hesitation, accepted Smith's offer to be appointed auditor at the company's annual shareholders' meeting held on August 31, 1998.

On September 7, 1998, CA received a letter from Smith Wholesalers Limited indicating CA's appointment as auditor for the fiscal period July 1, 1998, to June 30, 1999. CA immediately confirmed the acceptance of the audit engagement by telephoning Smith and at the same time made an appointment to visit the premises to meet the officers and acquire full details of the business, its accounting system, internal controls, and related data.

On the first visit to the premises in late September, 1998, CA obtained the following information:

1. Smith Wholesalers Limited was incorporated under the *Canada Business Corporations Act* and commenced operations on July 1, 1998. A review of the audited financial statements for the year ended June 30, 1998, revealed nothing unusual with respect to the company.

2. Smith Wholesalers Limited is a wholesaler of a broad line of products. All sales are made by the company's own sales force which operates in most geographical areas of the country. Sales are coordinated by Zee who acts as both vice-president of marketing and sales manager.

3. The company operates out of a large warehouse with the administrative offices, the shipping department, and the receiving department all located within this building.

4. The company employs:

   Smith — President and General Manager

   Zee — Vice-President, Marketing, and Sales Manager

   White — Accountant, Data Entry Clerk, and Cashier

   Thom — Shipper and Warehouse Supervisor

   Bee — Receiver and Inventory Control Clerk (entry of inventory receipts)

   3 warehouse employees

   10 salespersons

5. Excerpts from the company's formal sales policy revealed the following:
   i) Credit Sales
      Credit will be granted to low-risk customers only. All other sales are C.O.D. All credit sales and write-offs of uncollectible accounts must be approved by Zee.
   ii) Volume Discounts
      Volume discounts on orders shipped in excess of certain predetermined quantities are granted. All volume discounts must be approved by Zee.
   iii) Special Sales
      Special sales prices will be permitted from time to time for new products to help penetrate the market or for products approaching market obsolescence. All special sales prices must be approved by Zee.
   iv) Company Objectives
      As per Smith: "Our products sell easily. We are seeking long-term growth with a strong reputation for integrity. We, as a company, will not tolerate practices that reflect poorly on the company or its valued customers."

6. The company maintains all records necessary for the operation of a good system of internal control.

Early in March 1999, CA and the audit staff commenced the audit of Smith Wholesalers Limited. CA assigned a recently hired student to perform the tests of controls over sales. CA instructed the student to carry out the following audit program and report back when completed:

Sales Audit Program

1. Select, on a judgmental basis, a sample of sales invoices covering the entire fiscal period, ensuring that the sample includes all types of sales that the company makes.
2. Compare the sales invoice to the bill of lading and to the customer purchase order, noting description of goods, quantities, and approvals.
3. Agree pricing per the invoice to inventory master file, verifying approval where necessary for volume discounts or special sales prices, and recompute the mathematical calculations on the invoice.
4. Trace the sales invoice to the Sales Journal and to the Accounts Receivable Aged Trial Balance for credit sales, and to the Cash Receipts Journal for C.O.D. sales.
5. Add and cross-add the Sales Journal and Cash Receipts Journal for one month and match to General Ledger posting.
6. Account for the numerical sequence of 100 sales invoices and 100 bills of lading.
7. Scan the Customer Master File looking for unusual credit or payment terms.

The student took the audit program, selected a sample, and tested the system as required by the audit program. No exceptions to or deviations from the established system were noted except for the following:

Invoice 14350 — September 12, 1998 — N Ltd. — $8,000

The invoice indicated a volume discount of 10 percent allowed to the customer; however, the quantity ordered was below the stipulated quantity stated in the company policy for volume discounts. Upon inquiry, the sales manager indicated that the discount was allowed because this was a partial shipment to N Ltd., which was a potentially large customer.

Invoice 27771 — January 15, 1999 — Q Ltd. — $6,000

The invoice indicated a special discount for a new product. The student noted that this product had been sold regularly for approximately six months to other customers in the same locality covered by Q Ltd. Upon inquiry, the sales manager indicated that Q Ltd. was a new customer; thus the special sales price discount was allowed.

Invoice 30002 — February 12, 1999 — J Ltd. — $4,000

The student noted this credit sale invoice because J Ltd. was a customer of another of CA's clients who has had extreme difficulty in collecting from J Ltd. due to J Ltd.'s poor financial position.

The student presented the working papers and related comments to CA for review. CA agreed to all of the comments noted by the student but added that J Ltd.'s account should be confirmed on June 30.

Late in June, 1999, while CA and the audit staff were at the company completing the controls testing and preparing for the remainder of the audit, Smith asked CA to join him in his office. Once the door was closed, Smith stated:

> Something is wrong with our 1999 financial statements. Profits are not nearly what I expected. Sales are up but the gross margin is shrinking. I have just noticed that the cash flow has dwindled to the point where I may have to borrow some money to meet working capital requirements and to pay Zee the bonus based on gross sales that I negotiated with Zee in July of last year. Frankly, I am concerned.

Required

a. Comment upon CA's actions in accepting the audit.

b. With respect to the preparation, conduct, and evaluation of the results of the audit of sales transactions, has CA complied with generally accepted auditing standards? Explain.

c. What investigative procedures should CA perform to either confirm or refute Smith's concerns? In your answer, explain briefly the purpose of each of the procedures that you have listed.

d. Briefly explain the distinction made in the *CICA Handbook* between tests of controls and substantive procedures.

12-37 CA is the auditor of GR Ltd., the largest retailer of compact discs and cassette tapes in the city of Q. The company is a wholly-owned subsidiary of a nationwide wholesale music distributor. The ownership of the retail operation enables the parent company's management to keep abreast of changes in consumer buying patterns and tastes, thereby making the distributorship more quickly responsive to changes in demand than would otherwise be the case.

The merchandise inventory of GR Ltd. averages about 140,000 items of 15,000 different titles, 84 percent of which are CDs. In addition, there is a relatively small stock of peripheral items such as cleaners, catalogues, and ear plugs.

In order to provide current information on which CDs are selling, and to provide accurate inventory information for stock control, re-ordering, and financial statement preparation, GR uses point-of-sale computer terminals operating online with the parent company's computer.

All items are identifiable by the manufacturer's alphanumeric code which identifies the manufacturer as well as the title. For the perpetual inventory system, GR Ltd. converts the alphanumeric code for each CD to a strictly numeric code. This code, which is fixed in length, is printed on labels by the staff and affixed to each CD when the CD is received and put into stock.

When a customer makes a purchase or returns merchandise, the sales clerk keys the following into the POS terminal:

1. A four-digit sales clerk identifier code
2. ENTER
3. A one-digit transaction code (sale or return)
4. CD stock number of first CD sold or returned, if a CD; a one-digit code for other items
5. ENTER
6. Quantity of the specific items being purchased or returned
7. ENTER
8. Unit price
9. ENTER
10. Repeats steps 4 through 9 for each item
11. TOTAL (POS terminal displays the merchandise total, adds the automatically computed sales tax and GST, and displays the amount due or refundable)
12. Amount tendered
13. ENTER (causing the computer to calculate and display the change due)
14. END

The transaction is held by the computer without processing until the transaction is terminated by pressing the END key. This delay permits the staff to void the transaction if an error has been made during entry. When the END key is depressed, the inventory information (items 3, 4, and 6 above) is used to update the inventory master file. While the transaction is being entered, the terminal prints a sales slip. The sales slip is not released by the terminal until the transaction is completed with the END key. Voided sales slips must be approved by the store manager or the assistant manager.

As part of his internal control review, CA has undertaken to assess the controls embodied in GR Ltd.'s sales and inventory systems. As part of this internal control review, CA proposed to use test transactions to determine which controls were operating in the computerized sales entry portion of the system, as described above.

Required

a. List the controls that should be programmed into the sales entry system described above. List only those programmed controls that relate to the processing of individual sale and return transactions.

b. Describe the transactions that you would include in your set of test transactions, and state which controls each transaction would test.

c. Explain procedures that CA could follow in conducting the above tests in order to protect the integrity of GR Ltd.'s inventory master file.

ABC AUDIT — PART II

In Part I of this case study (pages 306–308), you obtained an understanding of internal control and made an initial assessment of control risk for each transaction-related audit objective for acquisition and cash disbursement transactions. The purpose of Part II is to continue the assessment of control risk by deciding the appropriate tests of controls.

Assume that in Part I, it was determined that the key internal controls are the following:

1. Segregation of the purchasing, receiving, and cash disbursement functions

2. Review of supporting documents and signing of cheques by an independent, authorized person

3. Use of prenumbered cheques, properly accounted for

4. Use of prenumbered purchase orders, properly accounted for

5. Use of prenumbered document package, properly accounted for

6. Internal verification of document package prior to preparation of cheques

7. Preparation and reconciliation of batch totals during data entry

8. Independent monthly reconciliation of bank statement

For requirements (a) and (b), you should follow a format similar to the one illustrated for cash receipts in the first three columns of Table 12-4, page 394. You should prepare one matrix for acquisitions and a separate one for cash disbursements. Observe that the first column in each matrix should include the same information as the top row in the spreadsheet you prepared for the Integrated Case on page 306. Also, the key internal controls include only those eight from above and the tests of controls include only those you develop in requirement (a).

Required

a. Design tests of controls audit procedures that will provide appropriate evidence for each of these controls. Do not include more than two tests of controls for each internal control.

b. Although controls appear to be well designed and test of control deviations are not expected, last year's results indicate that misstatements may still exist. Therefore, you decide to perform dual purpose tests for acquisitions and cash disbursements. Design dual purpose substantive procedures for each internal control objective. Do not include more than two substantive procedures for any internal control objective. Use Tables 12-4 on page 394 and 12-5 on page 401 as frames of reference.

c. Combine the test of controls and substantive procedures designed in requirements (a) and (b) into a performance format. Include both tests of acquisitions and cash disbursements in the same audit program. Use Figure 12-10 on page 404 as a frame of reference for preparing the performance format audit program.

ABC AUDIT — PART III

In Part II of the ABC Ltd. Integrated Application Case audit application, a tests of controls audit program was designed for acquisitions and cash disbursements. In Part III, sample sizes will be determined using nonstatistical or attribute sampling, and the results of the tests will be evaluated.

Required

a. Use the performance format audit program you prepared for acquisitions and cash disbursements from Part II to prepare a sampling data sheet. Use Figure 12-12 on page 407 as a frame of reference for preparing the data sheet. Complete all parts of the data sheet except those parts that are blank in Figure 12-12. Use the following additional information to complete this requirement:
   1. Prepare only one sampling data sheet.
   2. Decide the appropriate sampling unit, and select all audit procedures that are appropriate for that sampling unit from the performance format audit program that you prepared in Part II.
   3. Use judgment in deciding EPER, TER, and ARACR for each attribute. Assume that planned assessed control risk is low for each procedure.

b. Design a random sample plan using a table of random numbers or an electronic spreadsheet (instructor's option) for the attribute with the largest sample size in requirement (a). Select the first 10 random numbers using Table 11-2 on page 348 or the electronic spreadsheet. Document the design and 10 numbers selected using appropriate documentation.

c. Assume that you performed all audit procedures included in Part II using the sample sizes in requirement (a). The only exceptions found when you performed the tests were one missing indication of internal verification on a vendor's invoice, one acquisition of inventory transaction recorded for $200 more than the amount stated in the vendor's invoice (the vendor was also overpaid by $200), and one vendor's invoice recorded as an acquisition 18 days after the receipt of the goods. Complete the sampling data sheet prepared in part (a). Use Figure 12-15 as a frame of reference for completing the data sheet.

d. Develop the sampling data sheet using an electronic spreadsheet. (Instructor's option)

13

ANALYTICAL REVIEW AND THE AUDIT OF THE SALES AND COLLECTION CYCLE

COULD DIFFERENT ANALYTICAL REVIEW TOOLS HAVE HELPED THIS AUDIT?

The early 1980s saw many Canadian and American financial institutions fail. In the U.S., this prompted a study of the audit procedures undertaken at these failed institutions.

Could analytical review at Lincoln Savings and Loan (LSL) have helped identify transactions the substance of which was not equal to their form? Merle et al. seemed to think a more holistic analytical review process could have done so. At LSL, inflated real-estate transactions were used to keep a company in business that should have gone bankrupt or had interventions from legislators. The consequences were both public and private costs and private tragedies. The U.S. government spent several billion dollars on LSL, among other savings and loans institutions. In late 1992, Ernst & Young paid $400 million to settle four lawsuits with the U.S. government (including LSL). In 1993, Arthur Andersen agreed to pay $85 million on five similar savings and loan lawsuits (including LSL), and Deloitte & Touche paid nearly $5 million. Many individual investors lost their life savings, which caused at least one suicide.

Researchers examining the LSL audit determined that auditors used analytical review to consider economic reasonableness of transactions. A strategic auditing approach that related the audit to environmental factors would have also used analytical review to consider business activities in the context of the current economic climate, the nature of

regulatory changes on real-estate market values, and the impact of potential management biases.

Sources: (1) Bell, T., F. Marrs, I. Solomon and H. Thomas, *Auditing Organizations Through a Strategic-System Lens: The KPMG Business Measurement Process*, 1997, pp. 21–24; (2) Connelly, M., "Victim of S & L Loss Kills Self," *Los Angeles Times*, November 29, 1990, p. B1; (3) Knapp, M. C., "Lincoln Savings and Loan Association," Case 1.5 in *Contemporary Auditing: Issues and Cases*, Second Edition, West Publishing Company (1996), pp. 55–68; (4) Merle, M. E, B. W. Mayhew, and W. L. Felix, Jr., "Understanding the Client's Business: Lessons from Lincoln Savings and Loan," unpublished working paper (1996).

Lincoln Savings and Loan illustrates the importance of the "knowledge of business" of an entity in the planning process. Analytical review processes can be used to assess the reasonableness of overall business results and groups of transactions, and the likelihood of business failure.

This chapter expands on analytical review concepts discussed in Chapter 6. Chapter 6 described the overall role of analytical review and the types of analytical review, and provided some examples. This chapter starts by summarizing the role of analytical review during the audit process. The sales and collection cycle of Hillsburg Hardware is used as a frame of reference to examine the different assurance levels that can be obtained from analytical review. Judgmental, mathematical, and statistical tools are used to illustrate these assurance levels.

ANALYTICAL REVIEW AND THE AUDIT PROCESS

Figure 6-2 on page 176 showed that analytical review is required during both the planning and completion phases of the audit. It is optional during the testing phase.

RISK ASSESSMENT AND PLANNING

The audit planning process relies heavily on the audit risk model (AAR = IR × CR × PDR). Analytical review is important in helping the auditor establish preliminary assessments for each of these risk components. To determine an acceptable audit risk, the auditor needs to evaluate whether the business will likely continue as a going concern. Analytical review using ratios and comparisons to other businesses, such as competitors within the industry, is crucial to this process. The industry as a whole must also be examined for economic trends in relation to the Canadian and international economies.

Inherent risks in particular cycles could be affected by relationships with customers, suppliers, or strategic partners. For example, growth of a particular customer could indicate an economic dependency relationship, which has several effects on the audit. First, the business viability of the customer needs to be considered when assessing the viability of the audit client. Second, the nature of the transactions occurring with that customer could affect inherent or control risks. And third, this relationship might need to be disclosed in the financial statements. An analytical review comparing sales by customer on a year-to-year basis would highlight these changes for the auditor.

> **OBJECTIVE 13-1**
>
> Describe the impact of analytical review on the phases of the audit process.

KNOWLEDGE OF BUSINESS AND PLANNING

Where does risk assessment end and gathering of knowledge of business begin? These two terms are entwined and should be considered together. In the past, knowledge of business has frequently focused inward towards the business, including perhaps the local economy. However, examining this knowledge in relation to the business's external relationships reflects an awareness that the business needs those relationships to survive, prosper, and meet its goals. For example, without access to capital markets, a business could not raise money. With poor union relationships, a business would have unstable labour relations. Analytical review is one of the knowledge-of-business evidence gathering tools (others include discussion with management and research of external documentation, such as press releases and published financial statements).

TESTING

Analytical review can be used to identify unusual patterns in data, allowing the auditor to conduct targeted audit procedures. These patterns could also indicate the need for additional substantive tests. The matching of predicted data (using past patterns) to actual client data could also indicate that further substantive tests are *not* required. The analytical review can be used as a substantive test to provide assurance levels of low, medium, or high, thus affecting the overall testing mix. This will be illustrated by looking at one product line sold by Hillsburg Hardware.

COMPLETION PHASE

At the completion of the audit, the same analytical techniques used in risk assessment and planning will again be used to assess the ongoing condition of the business. They will also be used to examine subsequent events. This is described further in Chapter 21.

ANALYTICAL REVIEW AND PLANNING

OBJECTIVE 13-2

Explain the uses of analytical review during the knowledge of business and planning phases of the audit.

As described in Chapter 6 on page 177, there are five major types of analytical procedures. During the planning process, the auditor will likely have preliminary financial statements prepared by the client. Thus, it will be possible to readily perform the first three of these types, where client data is compared with industry data, with similar prior-period data (past financial statements), and with client-determined expected results (budgets). The first two are illustrated here, but not the third, since Hillsburg does not have budgets. The analytical review should be completed with an awareness of the organization's strategy, linkages to the external environment, and likelihood of business continuity. Figure 13-1 illustrates some information that has been collected on Hillsburg Hardware in the current and prior years. This awareness allows the auditor to step back and examine the overall reasonableness of the analysis.

FIGURE 13-1
Hillsburg Hardware
Knowledge of Business

Organizational Strategies
- Price competitively
- Focus on local repair and maintenance contractors to provide business loyalty
- Improve/maintain infrastructure to provide high-quality service
- Maintain profitability by managing costs

Environmental Linkages
- Excellent links with local and regional suppliers
- Good working relationship with national suppliers
- Working with local and regional business service organizations
- Competition from large chains reducing margins on some products
- Increase in local repair and maintenance contractor business as total percentage of sales due to membership and points programs
- Employees' participation in profit sharing and purchasing of some shares from the original owners

Business Continuity
- Business is continuing to maintain profits in the face of increasing competition
- Niche market approach is being used to combat this competition
- Business has invested in new technology for both accounting and marketing purposes (e.g., local area network with on-line order entry and perpetual inventory, Web site for promotional purposes, internal media, and printing technologies)
- Management is proactive rather than simply responsive

ORGANIZATIONAL STRATEGIES

As an organization, the entity under audit will have certain objectives. A not-for-profit organization could have a set service to be provided, while a profit-oriented organization may have specific profit targets as well as goals articulated in terms of its customers, suppliers, employees, and service areas. For example, a manufacturing business may have a certain quality target, as well as a growth target. A service organization may have a diversification strategy. These strategies help shape financial expectations and explain financial results in the context of an industry. A niche provider would be expected to have a higher than industry-average profit margin, while a low cost leader would be expected to have lower than industry-average profits.

ENVIRONMENTAL LINKAGES

An important part of modern auditing is recognizing that the business cannot function on its own. It needs, among others, suppliers, customers, employees, strategic business partners, and access to capital to achieve its organizational objectives. There will be impediments to success, such as competitors, raw material shortages, and labour unrest, that occur during the life of the business. As part of the knowledge of business, the auditor needs to be aware of the strength of positive linkages, and the potential problems that may arise in the business horizon. This comes from a broad assessment of the industry and economy within which the business operates.

BUSINESS CONTINUITY

GAAP assumes that the business will be continuing for at least another year. Risk of business failure affects the auditor's assessment of acceptable audit risk (AAR). Thus, while reviewing organizational goals and the business environment, and while conducting analytical review, the auditor specifically assesses the likelihood of the business continuing to operate.

Figure 13-2 shows that Hillsburg Hardware seems to be coping well in its chosen market. Hillsburg Hardware is located in Hillsburg, a thriving suburban town that has tripled in growth in the last five years. Thus, although revenues and profits appear to be stable, this stability must be viewed in the context of a market that is three times larger. The business strategy of maintaining size at approximately the same level while focusing on a niche market seems to be working well. In the face of increasing competition, it seems reasonable that the company can maintain its position since the local market size overall is growing. Business continuity in the short term (the next two to three years) seems likely based on this brief overview.

ANALYTICAL REVIEW: CLIENT AND INDUSTRY DATA

Figure 13-2 shows comparative financial statements for Hillsburg Hardware, providing current preliminary figures and audited figures for the prior two years. Selected ratios with comparison to industry data are shown in Figure 13-3.[1] An important part of examining these figures is establishing expectations. As a niche provider, Hillsburg Hardware would be expected to have higher profits than the industry averages. However, competitive pressures are driving profits in the other direction. We would expect inventory turnover to be increased due to higher levels of automation.

Review of Figure 13-3 shows some surprises that will need to be investigated using discussion with management. Short-term debt-paying ability is worse than the industry in all areas, and has been consistently so for all three years. The spread

---

[1]Industry data used in Figure 13-3 are fictitious. *Common size* statements could also be completed. Common size statements are financial statements in which the auditor converts the dollar amount of each account balance to a percentage of some relevant amount, such as total assets. The financial statements are thus shown as a percentage of total assets, allowing public financial statements to be compared. This was considered inappropriate for Hillsburg Hardware since it is a private company and comparison to public companies could be misleading.

FIGURE 13-2
Hillsburg Hardware
Comparative Financial
Statements

HILLSBURG HARDWARE LTD.
BALANCE SHEET
December 31, 1998
(in thousands)

	Preliminary 1998	Audited 1997	Audited 1996
Assets			
Current assets			
Cash	$ 41	$ 9	$ 52
Trade accounts receivable (net)	948	818	732
Other accounts receivable	47	53	58
Inventories	1,493	1,677	1,751
Prepaid expenses	21	21	21
Total current assets	2,550	2,578	2,614
Capital assets			
Land	$ 173	$ 173	$ 173
Buildings	1,625	1,625	1,625
Delivery equipment	188	123	153
Furniture and fixtures	127	82	82
	2,113	2,003	2,033
Less: Accumulated amortization	1,596	1,517	1,436
Net book value of capital assets	517	486	597
Total assets	$3,067	$3,064	$3,211
Liabilities and Shareholders' Equity			
Current liabilities			
Trade accounts payable	$ 236	$ 203	$ 240
Notes payable	167	167	167
Accrued payroll	67	66	67
Accrued payroll benefits	6	6	6
Accrued interest and dividends payable	102	59	61
Estimated income tax	39	39	32
Goods and services tax payable	42	52	55
Total current liabilities	659	592	628
Long-term liabilities			
Notes payable	$1,206	$1,373	$1,566
Accrued income tax liability	37	37	43
Other accrued payables	41	41	49
Total long-term liabilities	1,284	1,451	1,658
Shareholders' equity			
Capital stock	$ 250	$250	$ 250
Retained earnings	874	771	675
Total shareholders' equity	1,124	1,021	925
Total liabilities and shareholders' equity	$3,067	$3,064	$3,211
Sales	$7,721	$7,619	$7,750
Less: Goods and services tax	505	533	542
Returns and allowances	62	57	50
Net sales	7,154	7,029	7,158
Cost of goods sold	5,162	5,065	5,150
Gross profit	1,992	1,964	2,008
Selling expense			
Salaries and commissions	$ 387	$ 388	$ 389
Sales payroll benefits	71	70	70
Travel and entertainment	56	46	36
Advertising	131	85	120
Sales and promotional literature	16	59	48
Sales meetings and training	46	15	28
Miscellaneous sales expense	34	28	29
Total selling expense	741	691	720
Administrative expense			
Executive and office salaries	$ 276	$ 301	$ 333
Administrative payroll benefits	34	35	40
Travel and entertainment	28	35	42
Stationery and supplies	38	68	75
Postage	12	31	36

FIGURE 13-2
(Continued)

	1998	1997	1996
Telephone and telecommunications	36	26	27
Dues and memberships	3	3	3
Rent	16	16	16
Legal fees and retainers	14	12	14
Audit fees	12	12	12
Amortization—building and equipment	73	73	75
Bad-debt expense	166	166	158
Insurance	44	43	45
Office repairs and maintenance	57	35	28
Miscellaneous office expense	47	51	53
Miscellaneous general expense	26	22	29
Total administrative expense	882	929	986
Total selling and administrative expense	1,623	1,620	1,706
Earnings from operations	369	344	302
Other income and expense			
Interest expense	120	135	155
Gain on sale of assets	(36)		
	84	135	155
Earnings before income taxes	285	209	147
Income taxes	87	63	44
Net income	198	146	103
Retained earnings at January 1, 1998	771	675	622
	969	821	725
Dividends	95	50	50
Retained earnings at December 31, 1998	$ 874	$ 771	$ 675

FIGURE 13-3

Hillsburg Hardware and Industry Ratios

	Hillsburg 1998	Industry 1998	Hillsburg 1997	Industry 1997	Hillsburg 1996	Industry 1996
Short-term debt-paying ability						
Current ratio	3.87	5.20	4.35	5.10	4.16	4.90
Average accounts receivable turnover	8.67	12.15	9.82	12.25	10.59	12.15
Average inventory turnover	3.26	5.20	2.96	4.90	2.94	4.70
Average days to sell	112.07	61.00	123.52	59.00	124.10	57.00
Ability to meet long-term debt obligations						
Debt-to-equity ratio	1.14	2.51	1.42	2.53	1.79	2.55
Times interest earned	3.08	5.50	2.55	5.60	1.95	5.70
Operating and performance ratios						
Gross profit	0.26	0.31	0.26	0.32	0.26	0.31
Profit-margin ratio	0.05	0.07	0.05	0.08	0.04	0.09
Return on total assets ratio	0.12	0.09	0.11	0.09	0.09	0.10

Note: These are different from the illustrations in Chapter 6 since prior year data has been incorporated, affecting all ratios that use averages.

seems to be worsening. This could be due to the increased use of electronic data interchange and just-in-time inventory by many of the larger organizations, which is something that Hillsburg may not be able to implement. Accounts receivable turnover has worsened for Hillsburg but improved for the industry. This may be due to Hillsburg's increased reliance on local contractors for sales.

Debt-to-equity ratio is better at Hillsburg than in the industry overall. Gross profit and profit margin have remained stable both at Hillsburg and within the industry overall, with Hillsburg consistently below the industry average. Return on total assets at Hillsburg is improving marginally.

What do these figures tell us? Industry comparisons can be problematic because the industry may not be representative of the business being audited. For example, the retail hardware industry is becoming overtaken by large "depot" stores, leaving small independents such as Hillsburg to carve out a different type of market. On the other hand, a comparison to industry statistics indicates the overall profitability and trends within the industry, providing a context for the individual business. If the industry overall is doing poorly, the auditor would be surprised to see our client doing the opposite, and would need to seek an explanation.

ANALYTICAL REVIEW: CLIENT DATA WITH PRIOR PERIODS

This form of analysis can readily be prepared, since most firms are using lead sheet/trial balance software which allows for a variety of calculations as soon as preliminary general ledger balances are available. Accounts can be compared on a total dollar basis or on a percentage basis with prior years, highlighting differences over specific dollar or percentage amounts. Vertical analysis can also be completed for the income statement, whereby the sales figure is shown as 100 percent, and the remaining figures on the income statement are shown as a percentage of sales. Figure 13-4 provides comparative analysis for Hillsburg Hardware, highlighting dollar changes over $100,000 (the preliminary materiality figure) or percentage changes over 10 percent with an asterisk. Figure 13-5 (on page 435) provides ratio analyses for the same years. These analyses were prepared using spreadsheet software.

These figures should be evaluated in the context of expectations of the business. Discussions with Hillsburg management revealed that there has been investment in infrastructure, and that printing capabilities have been brought in-house. Figure 13-4 is examined for expected changes that should have occurred and for unexpected changes. Figure 13-5 is examined for trends.

Expected changes   Expected changes in a business would relate to balances that should have changed in the aggregate for balance sheet items or where differences would be expected from year to year. For example, accumulated amortization should change, amortization expense should change, and accruals are unlikely to be exactly the same from year to year. In addition, where management has specified business activities, such as expansion or changes in employees' roles (e.g., outsourcing or bringing in-house activities that were performed externally), then these accounts should change accordingly.

Figure 13-4 shows that capital assets of delivery equipment and furniture and fixtures have increased. Perhaps the new computer equipment and infrastructure costs are included here. Deferred taxes and other accrued payables are exactly the same as last year, which may indicate that these accounts have not been finalized. Sales salaries and commissions are similar to prior years, with executive and office salaries lower than the prior year. Since profit sharing has been put into place, we would expect these costs to be higher, unless there are fewer employees doing more work. Stationery and supplies have decreased, perhaps because of the movement in-house of the printshop capabilities (in-house costs should be less than external costs). Amortization of building and equipment is identical to the prior year when it should be higher due to acquisitions. There was mention of a customer points program, but there is no accrual for points earned but not yet collected by customers.

FIGURE 13-4

Hillsburg Hardware Comparative Analysis of Financial Statements

HILLSBURG HARDWARE LTD.
BALANCE SHEET
December 31, 1998
(in thousands)

	Preliminary 1998	Change (000s)	Change	Audited 1997	Change (000s)	Change	Audited 1996
Assets							
Current assets							
Cash	$ 41	$32	356%*	$ 9	$(43)	–83%*	$ 52
Trade accounts receivable (net)	948	130*	16%*	818	86	12%*	732
Other accounts receivable	47	(6)	–11%*	53	(5)	–9%*	58
Inventories	1,493	(184)*	–11%*	1,677	(74)	–4%	1,751
Prepaid expenses	21	0	0%	21	0	0%	21
Total current assets	2,550	(28)	–1%	2,578	(36)	–1%	2,614
Capital assets							
Land	$ 173	0	0%	$ 173	0	0%	$ 173
Buildings	1,625	0	0%	1,625	0	0%	1,625
Delivery equipment	188	65	53%*	123	(30)	–20%*	153
Furniture and fixtures	127	45	55%*	82	0	0%	82
	2,113	110*	5%	2,003	(30)	–1%	2,033
Less: Accumulated amortization	1,596	79	5%	1,517	81	6%	1,436
Net book value of capital assets	517	31	6%	486	(111)*	–19%*	597
Total assets	$3,067	3	0%	$3,064	(147)*	–5%	$3,211
Liabilities and Shareholders' Equity							
Current liabilities							
Trade accounts payable	$ 236	33	16%*	$ 203	(37)	–15%*	$ 240
Notes payable	167	0	0%	167	0	0%	167
Accrued payroll	67	1	2%	66	(1)	–1%	67
Accrued payroll benefits	6	0	0%	6	0	0%	6
Accrued interest and dividends payable	102	43	73%*	59	(2)	–3%	61
Estimated income tax	39	0	0%	39	7	22%*	32
Goods and services tax payable	42	(10)	–19%*	52	(3)	–5%	55
Total current liabilities	659	67	11%*	592	(36)	–6%	628
Long-term liabilities							
Notes payable	$1,206	(167)*	–12%*	$1,373	(193)*	–12%*	$1,566
Accrued income tax liability	37	0	0%	37	(6)	–14%*	43
Other accrued payables	41	0	0%	41	(8)	–16%*	49
Total long-term liabilities	1,284	(167)*	–12%*	1,451	(207)*	–12%	1,658
Shareholders' equity							
Capital stock	$ 250	0	0%	$ 250	0	0%	$ 250
Retained earnings	874	103*	13%*	771	96	14%*	675
Total shareholders' equity	1,124	103*	10%*	1,021	96	10%*	925
Total liabilities and shareholders' equity	$3,067	3	0%	$3,064	(147)*	–5%	$3,211

*Indicates dollar changes over $100,000 (the preliminary materiality figure) or percentage changes over 10 percent.

FIGURE 13-4
(Continued)

HILLSBURG HARDWARE LTD.

COMBINED STATEMENT OF INCOME AND RETAINED EARNINGS

for Year Ending December 31, 1998
(in thousands)

	Preliminary 1998	Change (000s)	Change	Audited 1997	Change (000s)	Change	Audited 1996
Sales	$7,721	$102*	1%	$7,619	$(131)*	–2%	$7,750
Less: Goods and services tax	505	(28)	–5%	533	(9)	–2%	542
Returns and allowances	62	5	9%	57	7	14%*	50
Net sales	7,154	125*	2%	7,029	(129)*	–2%	7,158
Cost of goods sold	5,162	97	2%	5,065	(85)	–2%	5,150
Gross profit	1,992	28	1%	1,964	(44)	–2%	2,008
Selling expense							
Salaries and commissions	$ 387	(1)	0%	$ 388	(1)	0%	$ 389
Sales payroll benefits	71	1	1%	70	0	0%	70
Travel and entertainment	56	10	22%*	46	10	28%*	36
Advertising	131	46	54%*	85	(35)	–29%*	120
Sales and promotional literature	16	(43)	–73%*	59	11	23%*	48
Sales meetings and training	46	31	207%*	15	(13)	–46%*	28
Miscellaneous sales expense	34	6	21%*	28	(1)	–3%	29
Total selling expense	741	50	7%	691	(29)	–4%	720
Administrative expense							
Executive and office salaries	$ 276	(25)	–8%	301	(32)	–10%*	333
Administrative payroll benefits	34	(1)	–3%	35	(5)	–13%*	40
Travel and entertainment	28	(7)	–20%*	35	(7)	–17%*	42
Stationery and supplies	38	(30)	–44%*	68	(7)	–9%	75
Postage	12	(19)	–61%*	31	(5)	–14%*	36
Telephone and telecommunications	36	10	38%*	26	(1)	–4%	27
Dues and memberships	3	0	0%	3	0	0%	3
Rent	16	0	0%	16	0	0%	16
Legal fees and retainers	14	2	17%*	12	(2)	–14%*	14
Audit fees	12	0	0%	12	0	0%	12
Amortization—building and equipment	73	0	0%	73	(2)	–3%	75
Bad-debt expense	166	0	0%	166	8	5%	158
Insurance	44	1	2%	43	(2)	–4%	45
Office repairs and maintenance	57	22	63%*	35	7	25%*	28
Miscellaneous office expense	47	(4)	–8%	51	(2)	–4%	53
Miscellaneous general expense	26	4	18%*	22	(7)	–24%*	29
Total administrative expense	882	(47)	–5%	929	(57)	–6%	986
Total selling and administrative expense	1,623	3	0%	1,620	(86)	–5%	1,706
Earnings from operations	369	25	7%	344	42	14%*	302
Other income and expense							
Interest expense	120	(15)	–11%*	135	(20)	–13%*	155
Gain on sale of assets	(36)	(36)	ERR		0	ERR	
	84	(51)	–38%*	135	(20)	–13%*	155
Earnings before income taxes	285	76	36%*	209	62	42%*	147
Income taxes	87	24	38%*	63	19	43%*	44
Net income	198	52	36%*	146	43	42%*	103
Retained earnings at January 1, 1998	771	96	14%*	675	53	9%	622
	969	148*	18%*	821	96	13%*	725
Dividends	95	45	90%*	50	0	0%	50
Retained earnings at December 31, 1998	$ 874	103*	13%*	$ 771	96	14%*	$ 675

*Indicates dollar changes over $100,000 (the preliminary materiality figure) or percentage changes over 10 percent.

FIGURE 13-5
Hillsburg Hardware,
Internal Ratios

	1998	1997	1996
Short-term debt-paying ability			
Current ratio	3.87	4.35	4.16
Quick ratio	1.50	1.40	1.25
Cash ratio	0.06	0.02	0.08
Average accounts receivable turnover	8.74	9.83	10.59
Average days to collect	41.74	37.13	34.47
Average inventory turnover	3.26	2.96	2.94
Average days to sell	112.07	123.52	124.10
Average days to convert inventory to cash	153.82	160.64	158.57
Ability to meet long-term debt obligations			
Debt-to-equity ratio	1.14	1.42	1.79
Tangible net assets-to-equity ratio	0.98	0.98	0.98
Times interest earned	3.08	2.55	1.95
Operating and performance ratios			
Gross profit	0.26	0.26	0.26
Earnings per share (on 1,000 shares)	0.20	0.15	0.10
Efficiency ratio	13.84	14.46	11.99
Profit margin ratio	0.05	0.05	0.04
Profitability ratio	0.12	0.11	0.09
Return on total assets ratio	0.12	0.11	0.09
Return on common equity ratio	0.18	0.26	0.34
Book value per common share	1.12	1.02	0.93

Note: These are different from the illustrations in Chapter 6, since prior year data has been incorporated, affecting all ratios that use averages.

Thus, some changes are shown in the financial statements as expected, but overall there is a clear signal that many year-end accruals and calculations have not been completed.

Unexpected changes   These changes represent increases or decreases in accounts that the auditor would expect to be stable. Changes could be unusually large in absolute magnitude or as a percentage. These changes are then examined to determine whether they are consistent with organizational strategies or represent potential areas of further audit investigation. Some changes may send a "mixed signal."

Looking at Hillsburg's balance sheet, we can see that trade accounts receivable have increased overall by a significant amount, $130,000, while sales have increased only by $102,000. This is a "mixed signal" change, since we would expect increased accounts receivable with the sales-mix change to repairs and maintenance companies rather than sales to the end consumer. However, such a large accounts receivable increase could also indicate potential collectibility or cutoff errors. Fixed assets have increased by $110,000, and trade accounts payable have increased by $33,000, when they had decreased in the prior year. The capital asset increase is consistent with infrastructure increase, while the accounts payable increase needs to be viewed in the context of increased sales. Accrued interest and dividends payable have increased by $43,000, but dividends have increased by $45,000. This therefore seems to be a reasonable increase.

Selling expenses have increased overall by $50,000. Costs for promotional literature have declined significantly, while advertising and travel and entertainment have increased. Executive and office salaries, stationery and supplies, and postage have all increased, as have office repairs and maintenance. These changes are consistent with bringing marketing and printing in-house, and with an increased use of telecommunications to distribute information. The increase in telephone and telecommunications costs supports this.

In general, the changes in financial statements support management information about the business objectives and the linkages with the external environment.

Other anomalies Often called a "reasonableness check," this is a review of figures for consistency across accounts and for the existence of patterns that we would expect when analyzing financial statements or groups of accounts. For example, an increase in sales would often also result in an increase in returns and allowances and in bad-debt expenses. Figure 13-4 shows that this pattern is unreasonable. We have increased sales, but bad-debt expense remains unchanged from the prior year.

Trends Figure 13-4 is not useful for an examination of trends since income and expenses were generally down in 1997 from 1996, and then increased again in 1998. Based on a discussion with management, we would expect margins generally to be similar, although we would find differences in particular product lines. Figure 13-5 supports the success of Hillsburg's niche strategy in terms of profits. The profit margin ratio has improved marginally, while the profitability ratio has improved and stabilized. However, there are warning signs in liquidity. Cash position seems alarmingly low, with only $41,000 in cash on hand. This does not even cover one month's wages. The higher accounts payable balance could be explained by management's attempt to stretch payables. We should discuss with management whether it has an operating line of credit or other cash sources (such as shareholder loans). Accounts receivable turnover has declined, while inventory turnover has improved marginally, providing opposing forces on liquidity.

These trends indicate that although profitability seems to be stable, using preliminary figures, this may be an example of high profits but poor liquidity due to the investments in infrastructure and marketing that have been made by the company. As part of the audit, the auditor would want to discuss with management how it plans to carry the business through this potential liquidity problem.

IMPACT ON INDIVIDUAL TRANSACTION CYCLES

General knowledge of a business, risk assessments, discussion with management, information systems controls, results of analytical review, and examination of prior year audit results are used during planning. Individual audit objectives are assessed, and the extent and type of audit evidence to be gathered for the individual transaction cycles are determined. For example, comments above indicate that for Hillsburg, valuation of accounts receivable may be a problem. This would result in increased testing of year-end accounts receivable balances and the bad-debt expense. Large sums have been spent in fixed assets, stationery and supplies, and office repairs and maintenance. Controls in purchasing and payables would need to be reviewed to help ensure that these expenditures have been properly allocated and approved. Depending on the quality and reliability of these controls, the auditor would then decide to what extent detailed testing would be required. Physical inspection of significant new assets would be included.

PROFESSIONAL JUDGMENT AND IMPACT ON AUDIT APPROACH

As shown with the above illustration, analytical review in the planning stage is very subjective, requiring considerable professional judgment. Judgment is used to determine the type and extent of analytical review. It is also used to link the quantitative results to knowledge of the client, its environment, and organizational strategies. The auditor needs to have the experience to derive expectations for the analytical review, so that once calculations have been completed, they can be interpreted meaningfully. When calculations deviate significantly from expectations and cannot be adequately explained by the client, then the audit risk model should be adjusted accordingly.

For example, although an overall assessment seems to indicate that Hillsburg Hardware is a viable business, it seems to have continued liquidity problems. If there is no plan to improve access to cash, the auditor may choose to lower audit risk. If there are fewer employees doing the same level of work, there may be an increased likelihood of errors, increasing inherent risk, control risk (if there are also segregation problems), or both.

The use of computerized modelling, risk tables, and review and guidance by experienced personnel all assist the auditor in the development and use of the appropriate analytical review techniques. Low assurance levels are obtained using judgmental comparisons of annual results. Medium assurance levels can be obtained if predetermined expectations are used when conducting the comparisons. High assurance can be obtained if regression analysis is used to develop expectations when conducting comparisons. In all cases, significant fluctuations are examined further or subjected to tests of details. As the desired assurance increases, the extent of quantified processes and rules increase for the steps of expectation building and fluctuation identification.

ANALYTICAL PROCEDURES ASSURANCE LEVELS

OBJECTIVE 13-3

Describe how substantive analytical procedures can be used to achieve low, medium, or high levels of assurance using the 12 steps required to conduct analytical review as a framework.

During the testing stage of the audit, analytical procedures serve as substantive procedures. Using the sales transactions as an example, Table 13-1 summarizes the audit assurance that can be obtained from analytical review procedures[2] and describes the effects on detailed testing, assuming no controls reliance.

Table 13-1 identifies analytical review procedure effects on substantive testing when there is no controls reliance. As controls reliance increases, tests of details can be decreased still further. For example, where controls reliance is set to a high level, and high audit assurance is obtained through analytical techniques including regression analysis, tests of details could be set at minimal, including perhaps bank confirmations and selected verification of high-risk transactions or balances.

TABLE 13-1

ANALYTICAL REVIEW PROCEDURES AND EFFECT ON DETAILED TESTING BY ASSURANCE LEVEL

SAMPLE ANALYTICAL REVIEW PROCEDURES	EFFECT ON DETAILED TESTING (ASSUMING NO CONTROLS RELIANCE)
Low Audit Assurance — Experience • Compare annual results to prior years; investigate significant fluctuations (greater than materiality) • Compare monthly results to prior years; investigate significant fluctuations (greater than materiality allocated to monthly amounts).	• High assurance required from detailed testing
Medium Audit Assurance — Trend Extrapolation • Develop expectations of annual results using ratio and trend analysis. • Conduct analytical review as described under "low audit assurance."	• Medium assurance required from detailed testing
High Audit Assurance — Statistical • Develop expectations of annual results using regression analysis. • Conduct analytical review as described under "low audit assurance."	• Low assurance required from detailed testing

[2]Based on *Analytical Review*, a CICA research study by D. G. Smith, 1983, Chapter 5.

To obtain assurance from analytical review procedures, auditors need to follow a specific, formalized process, similar in many respects to the specific process followed for sampling. The 12 steps in this process[3], illustrated with sales and cost of goods sold transactions in the next few sections, are as follows:

1. Define results to be examined and relationship When examining sales, the auditor would look at sales dollars, cost of goods sold, and possibly the units sold and units produced. The relationship is used to define how the results are related, for example, with dollar amounts, "sales: cost of sales" describes a ratio relationship. Relationships should be carefully selected to ensure that they are plausible. Sales should vary with cost of sales for a distributorship or a manufacturing company where good markets for the company products exist. Such a relationship would be less plausible for a service organization charging different prices for services based on the size of the client. The comparison of results should also be operationally independent. For example, in a retail organization, cost of sales may be calculated as a fixed percentage of sales. There, comparing sales to cost of sales amounts serves no purpose except as a check of mechanical accuracy. Independence would exist if sales were recorded by an accounting department and cost of sales recorded by the manufacturing department (two independent internal sources), or if one of these amounts was independently verified by other audit procedures.

2. State objectives of the review The audit assertions being tested are described, as well as the affected accounts. For example, in sales, the auditor could intend to obtain assurance regarding the completeness and accuracy of recorded sales and cost of sales. The absence of fluctuations could provide assurance, while the presence of fluctuations could be explained, perhaps due to the addition of a new, high-margin customer group.

3. Decide on examination methods The examination method used will affect the possible assurance level that can be obtained from the analytical procedures technique. As listed in Table 13-1, the left column describes review procedures associated with specific assurance levels. Low assurance relies significantly on the quality of experience of the individual auditor. Trend extrapolation is useful when the entity has stable growth patterns. Statistical techniques such as regression analysis permit more complexity in the analysis, such as broadening the number of results being considered, while providing a disciplined approach. This requires having a sufficient number of data observations and may require a specialist's supervision.

4. Define significant fluctuations A key assumption when conducting analytical review is that reported balances that are predicted will conform to past experiences of the entity under audit. When analytical review is conducted using annual figures, significance would normally be overall audit materiality. When more detailed numbers are used, such as monthly figures, the auditor needs to assess the size of monthly errors that could aggregate to an annual material error. For example, the auditor may choose to investigate fluctuations in a particular month that exceed 25 percent of materiality.

5. Specify intended reliance The components of the audit risk model are used to determine how analytical procedures can contribute to the intended reliance for one or more audit objectives. Assessed inherent risk, assessed control risk, the desired audit assurance, and the evidence obtained from any other audit procedures are used to specify the reliance intended.

---

[3]Ibid.

6. Select the method of computation The software to complete the calculation is chosen. This could be an audit firm's internally developed software or package software such as spreadsheets.

7. Control nonsampling risk In the context of analytical review, as with statistical sampling, nonsampling risk occurs when the auditor misinterprets evidence obtained and thus fails to detect an error. Auditors should be adequately trained and supervised to minimize this risk.

8. Ensure audit control This includes steps undertaken by the auditor to obtain accurate, complete, and authorized data for the test, as well as maintaining control over the conduct of the analytical procedure. For example, should comparative calculations be prepared by the entity's financial accounting software, the auditor would need to ensure that these calculations are appropriately formulated.

9. Make the comparison This is a mechanical step whereby the results are compared as determined by the previous steps, using the chosen method and software.

10. Identify significant fluctuations The auditor will have defined the dollar value or magnitude of fluctuations to be investigated. The absence of an expected fluctuation may also require investigation, where, for example, a seasonal increase in sales in a retail organization did not occur. Normal fluctuations, such as seasonal trends or business cycles, could be readily explained, while an unexpected fluctuation, such as an unusually low gross profit for a particular month, may require a test of details follow-up.

11. Investigate significant fluctuations Those fluctuations identified in the previous step as requiring further follow-up are documented in the working papers. The auditor records explanations provided by the entity's management and staff, and also documents the results of work done to corroborate any explanations received.

12. State conclusions Based on the work done in the previous steps, the auditor has either no fluctuations to investigate or has completed additional work on significant fluctuations. This allows the auditor to specify whether the intended reliance was achieved.

Table 13-2 on page 441 summarizes these steps for an example using the sales cycle data for Brink Power Tools at Hillsburg Hardware from Figure 13-6.

LOW ANALYTICAL REVIEW ASSURANCE USING EXPERIENCE

OBJECTIVE 13-4

Describe the processes used to obtain a low level of assurance from analytical review using the auditor's professional experience.

The analytical review conducted in the earlier part of this chapter provided minimal audit assurance for the financial results of Hillsburg Hardware. Instead, that analytical review assists in updating the auditor's knowledge of business for Hillsburg Hardware and in the risk analysis process that forms part of the audit planning process. Having completed the preliminary planning and conducted control risk assessment, the auditor now intends to obtain some substantive assurance on the sales and cost of goods sold transactions using analytical review.

Figure 13-6 shows additional data that was obtained from Hillsburg Hardware so that this analytical review could be conducted. Table 13-2 summarizes the analytical procedures conducted for low, medium, and high substantive assurance levels. The first two steps are common to all three assurance levels. The auditor decides to examine the sales of Brink's power tools, which provided over 35 percent of annual sales and close to 80 percent of gross profit for the 1998 fiscal year, as follows. (These figures are obtained from Figure 13-2 and from adding the monthly totals in Figure 13-6.)

FIGURE 13-6
Hillsburg Hardware
Brink Power Tools Data

YEAR AND PERIOD	CUMULATIVE PERIODS	SALES OF BRINK POWER TOOLS (000s)	COST OF SALES (000s)	UNITS SOLD (EACH)	UNITS RECEIVED (EACH)	UNITS IN PERIOD-END INVENTORY (EACH)
1996 1	1	$ 124	$ 69	2105	2316	211
2	2	134	74	2231	2442	421
3	3	161	89	2694	2905	632
4	4	141	77	2358	2568	842
5	5	151	83	2526	2737	1053
6	6	160	88	2694	2905	1263
7	7	175	96	2947	3158	1474
8	8	191	105	3200	3410	1684
9	9	201	110	3368	2947	1263
10	10	223	122	3747	3326	842
11	11	230	126	3873	3452	421
12	12	185	102	3115	2947	253
		2,076	1,141			
1997 1	13	155	85	2610	2821	463
2	14	167	92	2821	3031	674
3	15	201	111	3368	3579	884
4	16	176	97	2947	3158	1095
5	17	189	104	3200	3410	1305
6	18	200	110	3368	3579	1516
7	19	219	121	3663	3873	1726
8	20	239	131	4000	4210	1937
9	21	251	138	4252	3831	1516
10	22	279	154	4673	4252	1095
11	23	288	158	4842	4421	674
12	24	231	127	3873	3705	505
		2,595	1,428			
1998 1	25	170	100	2863	3073	716
2	26	184	110	3073	3284	926
3	27	221	122	3705	3915	1137
4	28	176	107	3242	3452	1347
5	29	190	115	3494	3705	1558
6	30	210	122	3705	3915	1768
7	31	241	132	4042	4252	1979
8	32	263	144	5094	4589	1474
9	33	277	152	4673	4547	1347
10	34	307	168	5473	4715	589
11	35	316	174	5305	4884	168
12	36	272	140	4294	4673	547
		2,827	1,586			

YEAR	TOTAL SALES (FIGURE 13-2) (in thousands)	BRINK'S TOOLS SALES (FIGURE 13-6)		TOTAL GROSS PROFIT (FIGURE 13-2)	BRINK'S TOOLS GROSS PROFIT (FIGURE 13-6)	
1996	$7,750	$2,076	26.8%	$2,008	$1,141	56.8%
1997	$7,619	$2,595	34.1%	$1,964	$1,428	72.7%
1998	$7,721	$2,827	36.6%	$1,992	$1,586	79.6%

The above figures show that in 1998, Hillsburg's total sales were $7,721,000, with a total gross profit of $1,992,000. Of those sales, $2,827,700 were of Brink's tools, a line of tools that Hillsburg has been selling for over 15 years. These power tools are an extremely broad range, from lightweight drills to table saws and other fixed tools. They are provided at various quality and strength levels, appealing to people undertaking home repairs, small businesses, and large construction organizations alike. These versatile products contributed 79.6 percent of Hillsburg's gross profit in the current year, allowing the company to continue to maintain the broad product range that is required by a hardware company, even though other products may not carry significant profits. Since these products are so important to the company's continued

TABLE 13-2

SUMMARY OF SALES ANALYTICAL PROCEDURES FOR THREE LEVELS OF ASSURANCE AT HILLSBURG HARDWARE

PROCEDURE STEP	LOW ASSURANCE	MEDIUM ASSURANCE	HIGH ASSURANCE
1. Define results to be examined and relationship.	Sales: cost of sales and cost of sales: units	Sales: cost of sales and cost of sales: units	Sales: cost of sales and cost of sales: units
2. State objectives of the review.	Substantive assurance on completeness and accuracy of sales and cost of sales	Substantive assurance on completeness and accuracy of sales and cost of sales	Substantive assurance on completeness and accuracy of sales and cost of sales
3. Decide on examination methods.	Compare current to prior. Use numeric and graphic methods.	Use techniques from low assurance, plus trend analysis and additional comparisons.	Use regression analysis.
4. Define significant fluctuations.	Monthly variance of greater than 25% of materiality ($25,000)	Monthly variance of greater than 25% of materiality ($25,000)	Monthly variance of greater than 25% of materiality ($25,000)
5. Specify intended reliance.	Low	Medium	High
6. Select the method of computation.	Spreadsheet	Spreadsheet	Auditor's internal regression software
7. Control nonsampling risk.	Written instructions to staff; supervision	Written instructions to staff; supervision	Written instructions to staff; supervision
8. Ensure audit control.	Reconcile monthly sales and cost of goods sold to general ledger. Audit staff to perform analytical review.	Reconcile monthly sales and cost of goods sold to general ledger. Audit staff to perform analytical review.	Reconcile monthly sales and cost of goods sold to general ledger. Audit staff to perform analytical review.
9. Make the comparison.	See Figures 13-4, 13-5, 13-6.	See also Figures 13-8, 13-9, 13-10.	See Figures 13-11 and 13-12.
10. Identify significant fluctuations.	Annual sales variation is significant enough to pursue monthly analysis. Sales: CGS* in periods 4, 5, and 6 in 1998 is unusual, and CGS* units in periods 8, 10, and 12 do not appear to be normal.	In addition to the periods with unusual data already identified, periods 1 and 2 are identified as unusual.	No additional fluctuations found. All fluctuations discovered with previous techniques were identified.
11. Investigate significant fluctuations.	Some sales not recorded; inventory stolen. See Figure 13-13.	One account allocation error, duplicate payment, and cutoff error. See Figure 13-13.	No additional investigation required. See Figure 13-13.
12. State conclusions.	Reliance on analytical review procedures is warranted.	Reliance on analytical review procedures is warranted.	Reliance on analytical review procedures is warranted.

*Cost of goods sold/cost of sales.

survival, the auditor determines that additional audit focus is required on this product line.

Since sales, cost of sales, and physical inventory are handled by different individuals and different computer subsystems at Hillsburg, the auditor determines that the relationships between sales and cost of sales and between cost of sales and physical units can be used to provide assurance from analytical procedures for the sales and cost of sales accounts. This comprises the first and second steps of the analytical procedures process (Table 13-2).

Examination methods (step 3) will consist of comparing current to prior sales, cost of goods sold, and units sold information. Thus, the expectation for the current year is based on the prior year's figures. Significant annual fluctuations for all three methods (step 4) are considered to be materiality of $100,000, and 25 percent of materiality, or $25,000, for monthly amounts. Step 5, intended assurance, is low. Spreadsheet software will be used to perform the calculations (step 6), and nonsampling risk (step 7) will be controlled for by providing written instructions to assistants, and by carefully reviewing their work. The information in Figure 13-6 was provided by management. To ensure audit control (step 8), the auditor compared monthly sales and cost of goods sold figures to the general ledger postings, and relied upon internal control testing in the inventory transaction cycle for the units sold, which are obtained from the perpetual inventory system.

Some of the calculations (step 9) were already completed during preliminary planning. Figure 13-3 shows that gross profit stayed consistent at 26 percent. Figure 13-4 shows that net sales has increased by 2 percent, a dollar magnitude of $125,000, well over materiality. This is a significant increase in sales (step 10), so the auditor decides to graph sales, cost of sales, and units sold, shown in Figure 13-7 (parts A through C).

FIGURE 13-7A
Hillsburg Hardware
1997 and 1998
Brink Power Tools Data

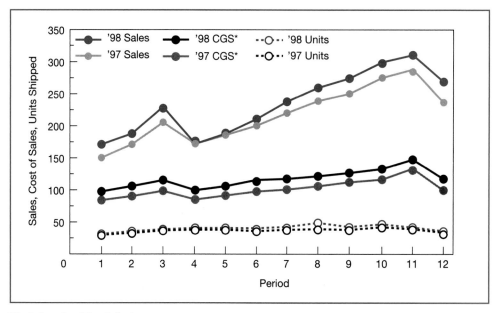

*Cost of goods sold/cost of sales.

FIGURE 13-7B
Hillsburg Hardware
1997 and 1998
Brink Power Tools Sales
and Cost of Sales Data

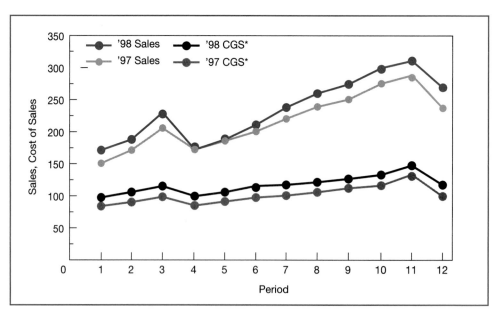

*Cost of goods sold/cost of sales.

FIGURE 13-7C

Hillsburg Hardware
1997 and 1998
Brink Power Tools Cost
of Sales and Units Sold
(in 50s) Data

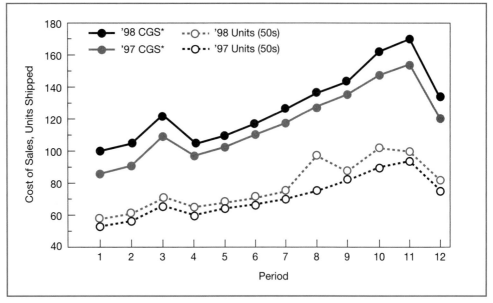

*Cost of goods sold/cost of sales.

FIGURE 13-7D

Hillsburg Hardware
1997 and 1998
Brink Power Tools Sales
and Cost of Sales Data
After Correction of
Errors in Periods 4, 5,
and 6

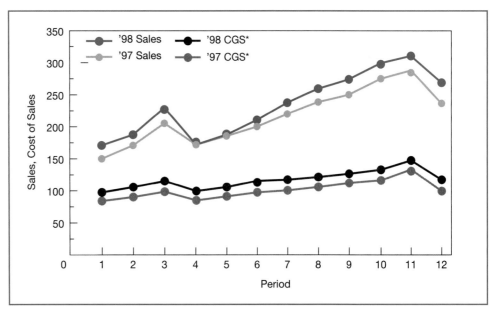

*Cost of goods sold/cost of sales.

From Figure 13-7B, the auditor sees something irregular about the sales figures in periods 4, 5, and 6, while Figure 13-7C shows drastic bumps in the units shipped graph for periods 8 and 10.

Investigation of these periods leads to the discovery of the errors summarized in Figure 13-13. The sales not recorded were due to a problem with procedures in the shipping area. Goods were shipped using trucking company bill of lading forms, omitting the company's standard packing slips. The shipments were entered in the perpetual inventory system but not invoiced. This was done by a part-time employee who is no longer with the company. Subsequent investigation by the company indicates that there were no further incidences of this type of activity.

The theft of the large number of units is more complex and requires considerable digging to track down. The auditor commences the investigation by a discussion

FIGURE 13-7E
Hillsburg Hardware
1997 and 1998
Brink Power Tools Cost
of Sales and Units Sold
(in 50s) Data After
Correction of Errors in
Periods 8 and 10

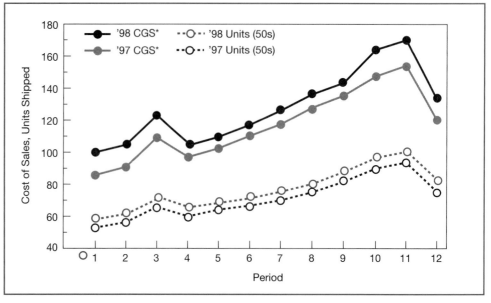

*Cost of goods sold/cost of sales.

with the shipping supervisor, who is also surprised with the graphic results. The auditor asks about inventory adjustments, and the supervisor responds that since he was the only one who made inventory adjustments, he did not print that report regularly from the computer system. On request, the supervisor prints the history report of inventory adjustments for the entire year and notes that there were two days where unusually large adjustments to the inventory quantities had been made. The supervisor does not recall making those adjustments. It takes two days of discussion with employees and review of time records to determine that on both of those days, a Sunday, there was only one person present in the warehouse. The supervisor was not on the company premises on either of these days. (Normal company policy dictates having two persons present, but one had called in sick on both occasions.) When confronted, that person admits to having observed the supervisor's password, made the inventory adjustments, and having a friend come with a truck to steal the goods. The person is immediately let go and charges are laid.

Figure 13-7 parts D and E show how the graphs look when corrections are made for the missed sales and the stolen units removed from the units sold. The conclusion to these procedures (step 12) is that the auditor can place reliance on these analytical review procedures.

This section illustrated how numerical and graphic analyses can be used together effectively. Numeric analysis provides an indication of magnitude, while graphic analysis allows the auditor to observe unusual patterns for further investigation.

MODERATE ANALYTICAL REVIEW ASSURANCE USING TREND EXTRAPOLATION

Since many of the analytical review steps are the same for medium level assurance as for low assurance (Table 13-2), only those steps that are different are discussed here. For step 3, the auditor decides to use an additional prior year to determine trends in sales and cost of goods sold, and to review patterns on a monthly basis, since the intended reliance (step 4) is medium rather than low. The expectation of the current year's results is thus based on trends extrapolated from the prior two years.

The auditor commences the comparisons (step 9) with the analyses shown in Figures 13-8 and 13-9, calculating average unit sales prices and monthly gross profit. These calculations show that average sales prices varied between $58.91 and $59.64 during 1996 and 1997. Many months in 1998 also were within this range. However, periods 4, 5, 6, 8, and 10 were lower. These periods had errors, as described in the pre-

FIGURE 13-8

Hillsburg Hardware
Brink Power Tools
Comparative Analysis

YEAR AND PERIOD		CUMU-LATIVE PERIODS	SALES OF BRINK POWER TOOLS (000s)	COST OF SALES (000s)	UNITS SOLD (EACH)	AVERAGE UNIT SALES PRICE ($)	MONTHLY GROSS PROFIT (%)
1996:	1	1	124	69	2105	58.91	44.35
	2	2	134	74	2231	60.06	44.78
	3	3	161	89	2694	59.76	44.72
	4	4	141	77	2358	59.80	45.39
	5	5	151	83	2526	59.78	45.03
	6	6	160	88	2694	59.39	45.00
	7	7	175	96	2947	59.38	45.14
	8	8	191	105	3200	59.69	45.03
	9	9	201	110	3368	59.68	45.27
	10	10	223	122	3747	59.51	45.29
	11	11	230	126	3873	59.39	45.22
	12	12	185	102	3115	59.39	44.86
			2,076	1,141			
1997	1	13	155	85	2610	59.39	45.16
	2	14	167	92	2821	59.20	44.91
	3	15	201	111	3368	59.68	44.78
	4	16	176	97	2947	59.72	44.89
	5	17	189	104	3200	59.06	44.97
	6	18	200	110	3368	59.38	45.00
	7	19	219	121	3663	59.79	44.75
	8	20	239	131	4000	59.75	45.19
	9	21	251	138	4252	59.03	45.02
	10	22	279	154	4673	59.70	44.80
	11	23	288	158	4842	59.48	45.14
	12	24	231	127	3873	59.64	45.02
			2,595	1,428			
1998	1	25	170	100	2863	59.38*	41.18*
	2	26	184	110	3073	59.88*	40.22*
	3	27	221	122	3705	59.65	44.80
	4	28	176	107	3242	54.29*	39.20*
	5	29	190	115	3494	54.38*	39.47*
	6	30	210	122	3705	56.68*	41.90*
	7	31	241	132	4042	59.62	45.23
	8	32	263	144	5094	51.63*	45.25
	9	33	277	152	4673	59.28	45.13
	10	34	307	168	5473	56.09*	45.28
	11	35	316	174	5305	59.57	44.94
	12	36	272	140	4294	63.34*	48.53*
			2,827	1,586			
Totals:							
1996			$2,076,000	$1,141,000	34,858	59.56	45.04
1997			$2,595,000	$1,428,000	43,617	59.50	44.97
1998			$2,827,000	$1,586,000	48,963	57.74	43.90

*Unusual

OBJECTIVE 13-5

Explain how combinations of analytical procedures can be used to obtain a moderate level of assurance using trend analysis.

vious section. Period 12 has a higher than usual average sales price. Monthly gross profit calculations similarly pinpoint periods 1 and 2 as having an abnormally low gross profit.

Figure 13-13 summarizes the results of investigation (step 11) of these errors. In period 1, a warehouse equipment purchase was incorrectly coded and posted to cost of goods sold, while in period 2, a duplicate payment was made to Brink's for one invoice. In period 12, there was a cutoff error, whereby a group of shipments made early on January 2 was recorded in December in error. Figure 13-10 shows how an overall comparison of unit sale increases and changes in the overall percentage of cost of goods sold uses trend analysis to explain changes in total sales and in cost of sales.

The results of these calculations and investigations allow the auditor to conclude that reliance on the analytical procedures is warranted.

AVERAGE SELLING PRICE PER UNIT CALCULATIONS

	1998	1997	1996
Units Shipped	48,963	43,617	34,858
Sales dollars	$2,827,000	$2,595,000	$2,076,000
Average selling price per unit	$57.74	$59.50	$59.56

Unusual 1998 months: (gross profit or average selling price)	Period	Average Selling Price / Unit	
	1	59.38	Too high
	2	59.88	Too high
	4	54.29	Too high
	5	54.38	Too low
	6	56.68	Too low
	8	51.63	Too low
	10	56.09	Too low
	12	63.34	Too high

Potential Understatement of Sales

	1996	1997	1998
Unit sales	34,858	43,617	
Percent increase		25.13%	
Expected unit sales			54,578
Actual unit sales			48,963
Potential understatement of sales, in units			(5,615)
Average sales price			$57.74
Potential understatement of sales, in dollars			($324,210)
Actual sales increase in dollars			
1997 sales		$2,595,000	
1998 sales		$2,827,000	$232,000
			($92,210)
Periods 4, 5, 6 sales not recorded			$44,700
Units stolen, periods 8 and 10 @ $57.74			$64,958
Cutoff error, period 12			($17,100)
Unexplained difference, immaterial			$348

Potential Overstatement of Cost of Sales

	1996	1997	1998
Cost of sales percentage	54.96%	55.03%	56.10%
Change from prior year		0.07%	1.07%
Potential overstatement of cost of sales at 1% of sales			$28,270
Less: Equipment purchase allocation error			(6,300)
Duplicate payment to supplier			(9,100)
Remaining potential overstatement of cost of sales			$12,870

HIGH ASSURANCE FROM ANALYTICAL PROCEDURES USING STATISTICAL TECHNIQUES

Regression analysis provides for statistical prediction of the current year's results based on prior results. An equation can be developed to provide a description of the relationships in past years which is then used to predict the current year's results. Because the equation is an average, the predicted results most likely will not agree with the actual results. However, software can be used to indicate which differences are statistically significant and thus warrant further investigation. This process allows the auditor to quantify in statistical terms which fluctuations require further investigation. More complex relationships than those used here can be explored. For example, rather than simply using units to predict cost of goods sold or cost of goods sold to predict sales, the auditor could also include items such as advertising costs or

OBJECTIVE 13-6

Describe the characteristics of regression analysis (a statistical analytical procedures technique), and explain how regression analysis can be used to obtain a high level of assurance from analytical review.

adjustments for seasonality. This requires having sufficient data observations available from the client, and may require additional auditor training or the use of specialized assistance during the conduct of the analysis.

Regression analysis has advantages and disadvantages over other analytical procedures similar to those of statistical sampling over non-statistical sampling.

Advantages of regression analysis are as follows:

- The probability that a particular account differs from expectations by a material amount can be quantified. Thus the degree of confidence that can be placed on the procedure and the precision are used to quantify results.
- Several independent variables can be used simultaneously to predict a dependent variable. Techniques such as multiple linear regression and logarithmic techniques can be used for such equations. This permits the auditor to include variables that relate in a nonlinear way or to take into account complexities such as seasonality.
- A disciplined approach is used, which provides consistency in application. This provides objective audit assurance that the auditor can use to reduce the extent of other substantive tests.

Disadvantages of regression analysis are as follows:

- Minimum numbers of observations are required to have an adequate base for the regression projection. Such information may not be readily available in the format needed by the auditor.
- Specialized assistance may be required to formulate the regression analysis, examine results, and investigate unusual data patterns.

Due to the quantification and specific methods used by regression analysis, this technique can be used to provide high assurance levels. The same data presented in Figure 13-6 is used for this analysis. Since several steps in Table 13-2 are common (such as calculation of materiality levels), only differences with previous analytical procedures are discussed.

In step 3, examination methods, the auditor decides to use regression analysis to test the relationships of sales to cost of sales and cost of sales to units shipped. The auditor used past experience with the client to develop the expectation that there will be a degree of association between these variables (called *correlation*).

Audit expectations are formalized by developing the regression model using the first 24 months of data. Figures 13-10 and 13-12 show the output of *STAR: Statistical Techniques for Analytical Review*, a software product developed specifically for audit use of regression analysis. The first section of these figures identifies the input data, while the second section, development of auditor expectations, shows the regression models developed (Figures 13-11 and 13-12 express these models in terms of general statistical variables x and y over time, t):

(FIGURE 13-11) SALES: COST OF SALES	(FIGURE 13-12) COST OF SALES: UNITS
Sales = -0.69 + (1.8247 × Cost of Sales)	Sales = 0.46 + (0.0326 × units shipped)

Figures 13-11 (pages 448 and 449) and 13-12 (page 450) also indicate that the correlation of the variables exceeds 99 percent, showing that there is a high level of association between the variables being examined.

Intended reliance on the regression analysis technique is high, so the auditor has used the reliability factor of 3.0 (determined with reference to statistical tables).

Next, *STAR* is used to project results for periods 25 through 36, and actual results are compared to projected results. First, note that both Figures 13-11 and 13-12 have a warning that "there is an indication of discontinuity between base and projection

FIGURE 13-11
Hillsburg Hardware,
Regression of Sales:
Cost of Sales

STAR: STATISTICAL TECHNIQUES FOR ANALYTICAL REVIEW

[Identification of input information]
SPECIFICATIONS FOR MODEL — SALES AND COS

Variables Specified

Y	Column C	Test
X1	Column D	Predicting

Observations

Base, 1–24	24
Projection, 25–36	12
Total	36

Data Profile

Periods per year	Time Series
Seasonal adjustment requested	12
	No

Type of Test

Monetary precision (MP)	Audit
Reliability factor (R)	100
Direction of test	3.0
	Understatement

Report Mathematical Details	No

[Development of auditor expectations]
STEPWISE MULTIPLE REGRESSION MODEL

	Input Data		Regression Function	
Description	**Mean**	**Standard Error**	**Constant or Coefficient**	**Standard Error**
Constant			−0.69	
Predicting variables				
X1 Column D	107.04	23.98	1.8247	0.0063
Test variable				
Y Column C	194.63	43.76		
Y' Expectation			194.63	0.7224

Coefficient of correlation (100% = perfect) exceeds 99%

Expectation [Y' (t)] for observation t:
Y'(t) = −0.69 + 1.8247*X1(t)

[Graphic data to assist with analyzing unusual data patterns]
THERE IS AN INDICATION OF DISCONTINUITY BETWEEN BASE AND PROJECTION PROFILES.
This type of discontinuity does not invalidate the model, but it may affect the differences to be audited. If it is not eliminated, it may result in invalid models in future years. Examine the plot of residuals to identify the cause.

FIGURE 13-11
(Continued)

PLOT OF RESIDUALS

Obs. No.	Recorded Amount	Regression Estimate	Residual (Difference)	Residuals Graphed in Units of One Standard Error
				-4 -3 -2 -1 0 1 2 3 4
1	124	125	-1	
2	134	134	0	
3	161	162	-1	
4	141	140	1	
5	151	151	0	
6	160	160	0	
7	175	174	1	
8	191	191	0	
9	201	200	1	
10	223	222	1	
11	230	229	1	
12	185	185	0	
13	155	154	1	
14	167	167	0	
15	201	202	-1	
16	176	176	0	
17	189	189	0	
18	200	200	0	
19	219	220	-1	
20	239	238	1	
21	251	251	0	
22	279	280	-1	
23	288	288	0	
24	231	231	0	
25	170	182	-12	
26	184	200	-16	
27	221	222	-1	
28	176	195	-19	
29	190	209	-19	
30	210	222	-12	
31	241	240	1	
32	263	262	1	
33	277	277	0	
34	307	306	1	
35	316	317	-1	
36	272	255	17	

[Numeric calculation of expected results, and comparison to actual results]
AUDIT TEST FOR UNDERSTATEMENT USING MP = 100, R = 3.0

Obs. No.	Recorded Amount	Regression Estimate	Residual (Difference)	Threshold	Excess <1>	Optional Test Selection Interval	Sample
25	170	182	-12	2	10	36	5
26	184	200	-16	2	14	33	6
27	221	222	-1				
28	176	195	-19	2	16	32	6
29	190	209	-19	2	17	34	6
30	210	222	-12	2	10	31	7
31	241	240	1				
32	263	262	1				
33	277	277	0				
34	307	306	1				
35	316	317	-1				
36	272	255	17	<2>			
	2,827	2,887	-60				30

<1> Significant difference in direction of test. Perform further analysis and inquiry to obtain and corroborate explanation. Perform optional test of details only if difference cannot be explained. Computed sample sizes less than 5 are set to the lesser of 5 and REGRESSION ESTIMATE / (MP/R).
<2> Significant difference in opposite direction to that of test. Seek an explanation.

[List of variables used has been removed since it duplicates Figure 13–6.]

Source: Analysis courtesy of Deloitte & Touche, 1998.

FIGURE 13-12

Hillsburg Hardware, Regression of Cost of Sales: Units

STAR: STATISTICAL TECHNIQUES FOR ANALYTICAL REVIEW

[Identification of input information]
SPECIFICATIONS FOR MODEL — COS AND UNITS

Variables Specified

Y	Column D	Test
X1	Column E	Predicting

Observations

Base, 1–24	24
Projection, 25–36	12
Total	36

Data Profile

	Time Series
Periods per year	12
Seasonal adjustment requested	No

Type of Test

	Audit
Monetary precision (MP)	100
Reliability factor (R)	3.0
Direction of test	Overstatement

Report Mathematical Details	No

[Development of auditor expectations]
STEPWISE MULTIPLE REGRESSION MODEL

	Input Data		Regression Function	
Description	**Mean**	**Standard Error**	**Constant or Coefficient**	**Standard Error**
Constant			0.46	
Predicting variables				
X1 Column E	3,269.79	735.44	0.0326	0.0002
Test variable				
Y Column D	107.04	23.98		
Y' Expectation			107.04	0.6278

Coefficient of correlation (100% = perfect) exceeds 99%

Expectation [Y' (t)] for observation t:
$Y'(t) = 0.46 + 0.0326 * X1(t)$

[Graphic data to assist with analyzing unusual data patterns]
THERE IS AN INDICATION OF DISCONTINUITY BETWEEN BASE AND PROJECTION PROFILES.
This type of discontinuity does not invalidate the model but it may affect the differences to be audited. If it is not eliminated, it may result in invalid models in future years. Examine the plot of residuals to identify the cause.

FIGURE 13-12
(Continued)

PLOT OF RESIDUALS

Obs. No.	Recorded Amount	Regression Estimate	Residual (Difference)	Residuals Graphed in Units of One Standard Error
				−4 −3 −2 −1 0 1 2 3 4
1	69	69	0	* (≈0)
2	74	73	1	* (≈+1)
3	89	88	1	* (≈+1)
4	77	77	0	* (≈−1)
5	83	83	0	* (≈0)
6	88	88	0	* (≈0)
7	96	97	−1	* (≈−1)
8	105	105	0	* (≈0)
9	110	110	0	* (≈0)
10	122	123	−1	* (≈−1)
11	126	127	−1	* (≈−1)
12	102	102	0	* (≈0)
13	85	86	−1	* (≈−1)
14	92	92	0	* (≈−1)
15	111	110	1	* (≈+1)
16	97	97	0	* (≈+1)
17	104	105	−1	* (≈−1)
18	110	110	0	* (≈0)
19	121	120	1	* (≈+1)
20	131	131	0	* (≈0)
21	138	139	−1	* (≈−1)
22	154	153	1	* (≈+1)
23	158	158	0	* (≈0)
24	127	127	0	* (≈0)
25	100	94	6	* (≈+4)
26	110	101	9	* (≈+4)
27	122	121	1	* (≈+1)
28	107	106	1	* (≈+1)
29	115	114	1	* (≈+1)
30	122	121	1	* (≈+1)
31	132	132	0	* (≈0)
32	144	167	−23	* (≈−4)
33	152	153	−1	* (≈−2)
34	168	179	−11	* (≈−4)
35	174	173	1	* (≈+1)
36	140	140	0	* (≈−1)

[Numeric calculation of expected results, and comparison to actual results]
AUDIT TEST FOR OVERSTATEMENT USING MP = 100, R = 3.0

Obs. No.	Recorded Amount	Regression Estimate	Residual (Difference)	Threshold	Excess <1>	Optional Test Selection Interval	Sample
25	100	94	6	2	4	33	3
26	110	101	9	2	7	36	3
27	122	121	1				
28	107	106	1				
29	115	114	1				
30	122	121	1				
31	132	132	0				
32	144	167	−23	<2>			
33	152	153	−1				
34	168	179	−11	<2>			
35	174	173	1				
36	140	140	0				
	1,586	1,601	−15				6

<1> Significant difference in direction of test. Performs further analysis and inquiry to obtain and corroborate explanation. Perform optional test of details only if difference cannot be explained. Computed sample sizes less than 5 are set to the lesser of 5 and RECORDED AMOUNT / (MP/R).

<2> Significant difference in opposite direction to that of test. Seek an explanation.

[List of variables used has been removed, since it duplicates Figure 13–6.]

Source: Analysis courtesy of Deloitte & Touche, 1998.

profiles." This means that the data in the third year does not have the same levels of association as in the first two years. A plot of residuals is provided for analysis (a residual measures the difference between the predication and the actual results). Examining the scatter diagram of residuals in Figures 13-11 and 13-12, the first two years are seen as scattered somewhat evenly about zero, while in the third year, there are several residuals with high negative values, with uneven scattering about zero. These diagrams inform the auditor that there may be large differences between the predicted values and the actual values. These could be due to changes in relationships between the components of the model or due to errors in the client's records.

The program used materiality (described as monetary precision) and the reliability factor to establish a cutoff point for each projection so that unusual differences could be identified. The last sections of Figure 13-11 and 13-12 list the client figures (recorded amount), the projected amount (regression estimate), the difference between these two figures (residual difference), and the statistically calculated threshold that requires investigation ($2,000). Periods exceeding the threshold are identified, with directions indicating that the auditor should perform further analysis, inquiry, or sampling, or seek explanations. Thus, depending on the auditor's judgment, a variety of techniques could be used to investigate the differences found.

Figure 13-11 indicates the following potential errors:

- Observation #25, 26, 28 to 30 (the months 1, 2, 4 to 6) potential overstatement of cost of sales: Figure 13-13 and our previous analytical procedures found errors consistent with these directions (monthly periods 1 and 2 had overstatements of cost of sales, while periods 4 through 6 had understatements of sales).
- Observation # 26 (month 12) potential understatement of cost of sales: Figure 13-13 and our previous analytical procedures indicated overstatement of sales.

Figure 13-12 also points out potential problems to the first two periods indicating the following additional potential error:

- Observation # 32 and 34 (the months 8 and 10): Figure 13-12 and our previous procedures found significant numbers of stolen units in these periods.

At Hillsburg Hardware, all unusual fluctuations were due to errors or irregularities in the accounts that needed to be corrected or remedied. Fluctuations could also be due to:

- unusual business factors, such as damage to inventory or unusual weather conditions affecting purchasing patterns
- an extreme result generated in the ordinary course of business, such as increased competition in a particular period
- any other factors which render the regression equation invalid due to a shift in the relationship between the variables being scrutinized

The Hillsburg Hardware examples for analytical procedures have shown that techniques targeted to achieve medium and high levels of assurance can identify significant potential errors in the accounts, as summarized in Figure 13-13. However, when relationships are more complex or a large number of relationships need to be investigated, statistical techniques are easier to perform and are more likely to identify all significant variances than trend analysis techniques.

MONTHLY PERIOD DESCRIPTION	ACCOUNT IMPACTS: OVER (UNDER)				
	Sales	Cost of Goods Sold	Accounts Receivable	Fixed Assets	Accounts Payable
Low assurance — experience					
4 $16,900 sales under	($16,900)		($16,900)		
5 $17,300 sales under	(17,300)		(17,300)		
6 $10,500 sales under	(10,500)		(10,500)		
8 765 units stolen, recorded in CGS					
10 360 units stolen, recorded in CGS					
Medium assurance — trend extrapolation					
1 $6,300 equipment purchase charged to cost of sales in error		$ 6,300		($6,300)	
2 $9,100 duplicate payment made to a supplier, charged to cost of sales		9,100			$9,100
12 $17,100 cutoff error, sale from January 2 recorded as December 31, cost of sales recorded in January	17,100		17,100		
High assurance — statistical, regression analysis					
No additional errors					
	($27,600)	$15,400	($27,600)	($6,300)	$9,100

ESSENTIAL TERMS

Common size financial statements — financial statements in which the auditor converts the dollar amount of each account balance to a percentage of some relevant amount, such as total assets (p. 429).

Correlation — the degree of association that one variable has to another. If the variables change in the same direction, the correlation is positive. If they change in opposite directions, it is negative (p. 447).

Nonsampling risk [for analytical procedures] — the risk that the auditor will misinterpret evidence obtained and thus fail to detect an error (p.439).

Trend extrapolation — analytical procedures that use ratio analysis or similar techniques to develop expectations of annual results (p. 444).

REVIEW QUESTIONS

13-1 Describe how analytical procedures can be used during the knowledge of business and planning phases of the audit.

13-2 Peter Li, a student-in-accounts at an accounting firm, has completed analytical procedures comparing internal client data for Abracadabra Company. Since there are no other companies providing supplies for the magic industry, Peter believes that no additional analytical procedures are required. Assess his position.

13-3 When an auditor conducts comparative analytical procedures, he or she looks for both expected changes and unexpected changes. Why?

13-4 Explain how the results of analytical procedures affect individual transaction cycles.

13-5 Jane Berger has conducted analytical procedures using the current and prior comparative financial statements. John Polakowsky has completed regression analysis using purchasing and production data. What assurance levels can be obtained from these techniques? Provide advantages and disadvantages for both techniques.

13-6 List the 12 steps required to conduct structured analytical procedures.

13-7 How does the auditor decide the dollar value of a significant fluctuation when conducting analytical procedures?

13-8 Provide an example of an analytical procedure for each of the three intended assurance levels: low, medium, and high.

13-9 What techniques would an auditor use to investigate significant fluctuations discovered during analytical procedures?

13-10 How can spreadsheet software be used to assist with the analytical procedures process?

13-11 Compare the advantages of graphic presentation methods to numeric methods in analytical procedures.

13-12 List the advantages and disadvantages of analytical procedures using statistical methods.

13-13 Assume that Federoco Limited has no significant errors or irregularities in its accounts. Analytical procedures have identified several significant fluctuations. What could have caused these fluctuations?

13-14 The following questions deal with analytical procedures. Choose the best response.

a. The auditor will likely obtain each of the following benefits from using analytical procedures except
   (1) better understanding of the client.
   (2) a sense of potential problem areas.
   (3) better communication with the client's employees.
   (4) possible reduction of other audit tests.

b. Analytical procedures used in planning an audit should focus on identifying
   (1) material weaknesses in internal control.
   (2) the predictability of financial data from certain transactions.
   (3) the management assertions in the financial statement.
   (4) areas that may represent specific risks relevant to the audit.

c. Analytical procedures
   (1) are required during the planning phase of the audit.
   (2) are required in gaining a knowledge of control procedures.
   (3) are a required substantive procedure.
   (4) are only used when control risk is assessed as high.

d. Regression analysis has the advantage of
   (1) requiring no special skills or experience.
   (2) requiring a disciplined approach that provides consistency in application.
   (3) requiring no judgment by the auditor.
   (4) requiring only two observations.

13-15 The following questions deal with analytical procedures. Choose the best response.

(a) As a result of using analytical procedures, the audior determines that the gross profit has declined from 30 percent in 1998 to 20 percent in 1999. The auditor should
   (1) document management's plans for reversing this trend.

(2) write a memo to management suggesting that all prices should be carried.
(3) require footnote disclosure.
(4) consider the possibility of an error in the financial statements.

b. Which of the following is not an analytical procedure?
   (1) calculating inventory turnover and comparing it to prior years
   (2) calculating year over year change in accounts receivable for several years
   (3) calculating the year over year change in accounts payable for several years
   (4) calculating the earnings per share for the current year

c. Analytical procedures used in planning an audit should focus on
   (1) identifying possible scope limitations and gathering evidence in assessing control risk factors.
   (2) enhancing the understanding of the entity's business and the transactions and events that have occurred since the last audit.
   (3) aggregating data at a low level and substantiating management's assertions that are embodied in the financial statement.
   (4) discovering material weaknesses in internal control.

d. Which of the following statements is not true?
   (1) The reliability of analytical procedures does depend on the accuracy of the underlying data.
   (2) Comparing the current year's results with the prior year provides a high audit assurance.
   (3) The auditor must use judgment and experience in interpreting the results of analytical procedures.
   (4) There is an inverse relationship between the assurance provided by analytical procedures and the assurance required from detailed testing.

13-16 You learned in Chapter 1, Chapter 5 and subsequent chapters that many of the accounts of a company are related, and changes should occur in the same direction. For example, a decrease in capital assets is not usually compatible with an increase in amortization expense as a percent of capital assets.

You have applied low assurance analytical procedures to the accounts in the sales and collection cycle with the following results:

- Days' sales in receivables have increased.

- Sales have decreased.

- The allowance for doubtful accounts has decreased as a percentage of accounts receivable.

Required

Assuming that you have decided that there are possible misstatements in accounts mentioned in the bullets, indicate what may have caused the contradictory results.

For example, the increase in amortization expense as a percent of capital assets referred to above could have been caused by amortization expense being taken or assets that had been disposed of.

13-17 You learned in Chapter 1, Chapter 5 and subsequent chapters that many of the accounts of a company are related, and changes should occur in the same direction. For example, a decrease in capital assets is not usually compatible with an increase in amortization expense as a percent of capital assets.

You have applied low assurance analytical procedures to accounts in the inventory and warehousing cycle with the following results:

- Inventory has increased.
- Gross margin has increased.

Required

Assuming that you have decided that there are possible misstatements in the accounts mentioned in the bullets, indicate what may have caused the contradictory results.

For example, the increase in amortization expense as a percent of capital assets referred to above could have been caused by amortization expense being taken or assets that had been disposed of.

13-18 Analytical procedures are substantive tests that are extremely useful in the initial audit planning stage.

Required

a. Explain why analytical procedures are considered to be substantive tests.

b. Describe the analytical procedures an auditor might use to reduce the evidence gathered by confirmation of accounts receivable.

13-19 A senior partner stated, "Analytical procedures are a useful technique except that the wrong people in the firm are performing the procedures."

Required

State what you think the partner meant.

13-20 An auditor has conducted a comparative analytical review for Bogsworth Company and has found significant differences in the following accounts:

Fixed assets
Accumulated depreciation
Accounts receivable
Accrued liabilities
Shareholders' capital
Cost of goods sold
Gross profit
Advertising expenses
Salespeople's commissions

Required

For each of the accounts:

a. Specify a ratio that could be used to analyze the account.

b. Specify whether the auditor's expectation should be either "no difference anticipated" or "difference anticipated" when a company is experiencing gradual sales growth.

c. Explain how the auditor's expectations in (b) would be developed.

CASE

13-21 "We have had a fairly good year," said the president of Frankruary Limited. "Sales exceeded $2 million for the first time in our history, though net income didn't keep pace with the sales increase because of higher labour costs."

Frankruary Limited is a Canadian manufacturing company. Its factory and most if its sales branches are located in Western Canada, but it also has sales branches and warehouse facilities in Toronto, Montreal, and Halifax. The company sells a number of industrial products, divided into "Product Line A" and "Product Line B." The industry is highly competitive in both price and quality, and technological developments have been quite rapid, subjecting most products to a substantial obsolescence risk.

The company's accounting functions are located at the factory; the sales branches and warehouses maintain only payroll, petty cash, and inventory records, which are subject to review by head office. The company's four principal officers (the president, the sales manager, the product development manager, and the factory manager) own substantially all of its shares and manage the company in a highly individualistic manner.

Assume that you are the manager in charge of the Frankruary Limited audit. Most of the field work for the 1998 examination has been completed, and the audit senior has presented the working-paper file to you for review. In the file are the following financial statements for the fiscal years ended June 30, 1998, 1997, and 1996. See Exhibit I on pages 457 and 458. (The 1997 and 1996 figures are those reported in the audited financial statements, but the 1998 figures are those prepared by the chief accountant prior to the audit.)

Required

a. In your review of the audit file of Frankruary Limited for the year ended June 30, 1998, which specific matters shown in the financial statements (other than financial statement presentation) would you be particularly interested in investigating before completing the audit?

b. Comment on the company's financial position.

(CICA adapted)

EXHIBIT I
Financial Statement
for Frankruary Limited

Frankruary Limited

BALANCE SHEETS AS AT JUNE 30

	1998	1997	1996
Cash	$ 148,000	$ 234,000	$ 210,000
Accounts receivable:			
Trade	387,000	263,000	219,000
Employees	8,000	6,000	5,000
Income taxes recoverable	10,000	—	—
Land sale	130,000	—	—
Allowance for doubtful accounts	(15,000)	(15,000)	(15,000)
Inventories:			
Raw material (cost)	69,000	72,000	78,000
Finished goods (standard cost):			
Product line A	204,000	124,000	84,000
Product line B	166,000	156,000	149,000
Shop supplies (cost)	23,000	—	—
	$1,130,000	$ 840,000	$ 730,000
Land (cost)	$ 150,000	$ 200,000	$ 200,000
Plant and equipment (cost)	1,600,000	1,600,000	1,600,000
Accumulated amortization	(870,000)	(800,000)	(685,000)
	$ 880,000	$1,000,000	$1,115,000
	$2,010,000	$1,840,000	$1,845,000
Bank loan	$ 170,000	$ 110,000	$ 80,000
Accounts payable	374,000	304,000	241,000
Trade notes payable	97,000	34,000	21,000
Incomes taxes payable	—	9,000	8,000
Due to shareholder	—	12,000	100,000
Current portion of mortgage	75,000	60,000	60,000
	$ 716,000	$ 529,000	$ 510,000
Mortgage (6%) – less current portion	440,000	500,000	560,000
Deferred incomes taxes	71,000	68,000	63,000
	$1,227,000	$1,097,000	$1,133,000
Common share capital	$ 210,000	$ 200,000	$ 200,000
Contributed surplus	50,000	50,000	50,000
Retained earnings	523,000	493,000	462,000
	$ 783,000	$ 743,000	$ 712,000
	$2,010,000	$1,840,000	$1,845,000

INCOME STATEMENTS FOR YEARS ENDED JUNE 30

	1998	1997	1996
Sales	$2,100,000	$1,800,000	$1,700,000
Cost of sales	1,690,000	1,380,000	1,320,000
Gross profit	$ 410,000	$ 420,000	$ 380,000
Selling and administrative expenses:			
Advertising and promotion	$ 117,000	$ 77,000	$ 51,000
Bad debts	10,000	7,000	6,000
Amortization	10,000	15,000	15,000
Insurance	7,000	7,000	7,000
Salaries	182,000	160,000	150,000
Sundry	28,000	12,000	11,000
Utilities and telephone	26,000	22,000	20,000
	$ 380,000	$ 300,000	$ 260,000
Operating income	$ 30,000	$ 120,000	$ 120,000
Other expense (income):			
Interest and bank charges	$ 63,000	$ 41,000	$ 38,000
Profit on sale of land	(80,000)	—	—
Cash discounts and sundry	(1,000)	(3,000)	(4,000)
	$ (18,000)	$ 38,000	$ 34,000
Income before tax	$ 48,000	$ 82,000	$ 86,000

EXHIBIT I
(Continued)

Income taxes:			
Current	$ (10,000)	$ 21,000	$ 20,000
Deferred	3,000	5,000	8,000
	$ (7,000)	$ 26,000	$ 28,000
Net income for the year	$ 55,000	$ 56,000	$ 58,000
Dividends paid	$ 25,000	$ 25,000	$ 25,000

SCHEDULES OF GROSS PROFIT FOR YEARS ENDED JUNE 30

Product Line A	**1998**	**1997**	**1996**
Sales	$ 850,000	$ 825,000	$ 800,000
Cost of sales:			
Material (standard)	$ 417,000	$ 386,000	$ 378,000
Labour (standard)	231,000	160,000	156,000
Overhead (standard)	84,000	56,000	50,000
Standard cost variances	(22,000)	(2,000)	1,000
Amortization	20,000	35,000	35,000
	$ 730,000	$ 635,000	$ 620,000
Gross profit	$ 120,000	$ 190,000	$ 180,000

Product Line B			
Sales	$1,250,000	$ 975,000	$ 900,000
Cost of sales:			
Material (standard)	$ 482,000	$ 347,000	$ 323,000
Labour (standard)	297,000	223,000	207,000
Overhead (standard)	173,000	113,000	103,000
Standard cost variances	(32,000)	(3,000)	2,000
Amortization	40,000	65,000	65,000
	$ 960,000	$ 745,000	$ 700,000
Gross profit	$ 290,000	$ 230,000	$ 200,000
Total gross profit	$ 410,000	$ 420,000	$ 380,000

Note: The overhead standards shown above do not include amortization; however, when the finished goods are transferred to inventory, a factor for amortization is added to the material-labour-overhead standard to get the inventory carrying cost.

14

COMPLETING THE TESTS IN THE SALES AND COLLECTION CYCLE: ACCOUNTS RECEIVABLE

WHEN MORE ISN'T BETTER

On Cindy Veinot's first audit assignment, she is asked to handle the confirmation of accounts receivable. She is excited because it was one of the areas in her auditing class that she felt confident she understood. The audit client is a retailer with a large number of customer accounts. In previous years, Cindy's firm confirmed these accounts using negative confirmations. Last year, 200 negative confirmations were sent. Confirmations were sent one month prior to year end. Those that were returned showed only timing differences; none represented a misstatement in the client's books.

The tentative audit plan for the current year is to do about the same as the prior year. Before the current year's planned confirmation date, Cindy performs a review of internal controls over sales and cash receipts transactions. She discovers that a new system for sales transactions has been implemented, but the client is having considerable problems getting it to work properly. There are a significant number of misstatements in recording sales during the past few months. Cindy's tests of controls and substantive tests of sales transactions also identify similar misstatements.

When Cindy takes her findings to her supervisor and asks her what to do, she responds, "No problem, Cindy. Just send 300 confirmation requests instead of the usual 200. And be sure you get a good random sample so we can get a good projection of the results." Cindy is seriously bothered by this instruction. She recalls from her auditing class that negative confirmation requests aren't considered to be good evidence when there are weak controls. Because customers are asked to respond only when there are differences, the auditor cannot be confident of the correct value for each misstatement in the sample. If this is so, then the results of using negative confirmations will be misleading even if a request is sent to *every* account. Cindy concludes that expanding the sample size is the wrong solution. When Cindy talks with her supervisor about her point of view, this time she responds, "You are absolutely right. I spoke too quickly. We need to sit down and think about a better strategy to find out if accounts receivable is materially misstated."

Chapter 14 is concerned with using analytical procedures and tests of details of balances for the accounts in the sales and collection cycle to reduce planned detection risk to a sufficiently low level. The accounts included in the sales and collection cycle for a typical company are shown in Figure 12-1 on page 374. Figure 12-4 on page 390 illustrates relationships among the major accounts, the types of audit tests, and the audit risk model.

Analytical procedures are used to reduce planned detection risk for all accounts in the cycle. Tests of details of balances focus on balance sheet accounts, which include accounts receivable, allowance for uncollectible accounts, and cash in bank for the sales and collection cycle. Because it is interacting with all other cycles, cash in bank is treated separately in Chapter 20. This chapter, therefore, emphasizes the audit of accounts receivable and allowance for uncollectible accounts, using analytical procedures and tests of details of balances. Figure 14-1 shows the relationship between these two types of tests and planned detection risk, using the audit risk model.

To help the reader maintain perspective, refer to Figure 10-10 on page 328. Tests of controls for the sales and collection cycle, which were studied in Chapter 12, are done in phase II of the audit process. Tests of details of balances for the sales and collection cycle, which are studied here, are done in phase III.

FIGURE 14-1

Relationship Between Analytical Procedures and Tests of Details of Balances to Planned Detection Risk

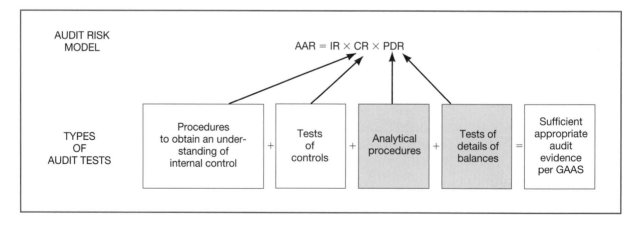

METHODOLOGY FOR DESIGNING TESTS OF DETAILS OF BALANCES

Figure 14-2 shows the methodology that auditors follow in determining the appropriate tests of details of balances for accounts receivable. The methodology was introduced in Chapter 10 and is now applied to the audit of accounts receivable. This methodology integrates both the audit risk model and the types of audit tests that are shown in Figure 14-1.

Determining the appropriate tests of details of balances evidence is complicated because it must be decided on an objective-by-objective basis and there are several interactions that affect the evidence decision. For example, the auditor must consider inherent risk, which may differ by objective, and control risk, which also may vary by objective.

To help manage the decision-making process for the appropriate tests of details of balances, auditors often use an evidence planning spreadsheet. This spreadsheet was first introduced in Chapter 8 (Figure 8-5, page 252) and further amplified in Chapter 12 (Figure 12-10 pages 404–405). The completed evidence planning spreadsheet is included as Figure 14-8 on page 482. This spreadsheet is directly related to the methodology in Figure 14-2. Both figures are discussed as we proceed.

FIGURE 14-2
Methodology for Designing Tests of Details of Balances for Accounts Receivable

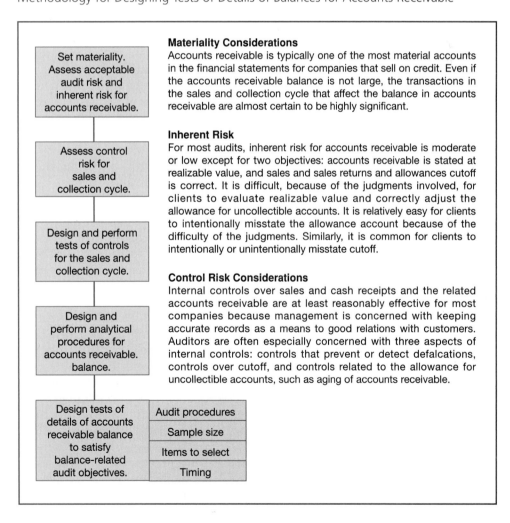

ACCOUNTS RECEIVABLE BALANCE-RELATED AUDIT OBJECTIVES

OBJECTIVE 14-2

Know the nine accounts receivable balance-related audit objectives.

The nine general balance-related audit objectives are the same for every account balance and are applied to accounts receivable as accounts receivable balance-related audit objectives. The general objectives were first introduced in Chapter 5. These nine objectives applied to accounts receivable are:[1]

- Accounts receivable in the aged trial balance agree with related customer master file amounts, and the total is correctly added and agrees with the general ledger (detail tie-in).
- Recorded accounts receivable exist (existence).
- Existing accounts receivable are included (completeness).
- Accounts receivable are accurate (accuracy).
- Accounts receivable are properly classified (classification).
- Cutoff for accounts receivable is correct (cutoff).
- Accounts receivable is stated at realizable value (valuation).
- The client has rights to accounts receivable (rights and obligations).
- Accounts receivable presentation and disclosures are proper (presentation and disclosure).

The columns in the evidence planning spreadsheet in Figure 14-8 include the balance-related audit objectives. The auditor uses the factors in the rows to aid in assessing planned detection risk for accounts receivable, by objective. All of these factors are decided during audit planning. They were studied in Chapters 8 through 13.

SET MATERIALITY AND ASSESS ACCEPTABLE AUDIT RISK AND INHERENT RISK

Setting materiality starts with the auditor making the preliminary judgment about materiality for the entire financial statements. Figure 14-8 shows that materiality was set at $100,000 for the Hillsburg Hardware audit by including the amount on the bottom of the evidence planning spreadsheet.

Acceptable audit risk is assessed for the financial statements as a whole and is not usually allocated to various accounts or objectives. Figure 14-8 shows an acceptable audit risk of high for every objective, which will permit a higher planned detection risk for accounts receivable than if acceptable audit risk were low.

Inherent risk is assessed for each objective for an account such as accounts receivable. It was assessed at low for all objectives except valuation for Hillsburg Hardware.

ASSESS CONTROL RISK FOR THE SALES AND COLLECTION CYCLE

The methodology for assessing control risk was studied in general in Chapter 9 and applied to sales and cash receipts transactions in Chapter 12. The framework used to identify control activities and internal control weaknesses was a control risk matrix. An example is included in Figures 12-8 (page 399) and 12-9 (page 400).

The internal controls studied in Chapter 12 relate specifically to transaction-related audit objectives for classes of transactions. The two primary classes of transactions in the sales and collection cycle are sales and cash receipts.

The auditor must relate control risk for transaction-related audit objectives to balance-related audit objectives in deciding planned detection risk and planned evidence for tests of details of balances. For the most part, the relationship is straightforward. Figure 14-3 shows the relationship for the two primary classes of transactions in the sales and collection cycle. For example, assume that the auditor concluded that control risk for both sales and cash receipts transactions is low for the accuracy transaction-related audit objective. The auditor can, therefore, conclude that controls for the accuracy balance-related audit objective for accounts receivable are effective because the only transactions that affect accounts receivable are sales and cash receipts. Of course, if sales returns and allowances and charge-off of uncollectible accounts receivable are significant, assessed control risk must also be considered for these two classes of transactions.

---

[1]Detail tie-in is included as the first objective here, as compared with being Objective 6 in Chapter 5, because tests for detail tie-in are normally done first.

FIGURE 14-3

Relationship Between
Transaction-Related
and Balance-Related
Audit Objectives for
the Sales and
Collection Cycle

ACCOUNTS RECEIVABLE BALANCE-RELATED AUDIT OBJECTIVES

CLASS OF TRANSACTIONS	TRANSACTION-RELATED AUDIT OBJECTIVES	Detail tie-in	Existence	Completeness	Accuracy	Classification	Cutoff	Valuation	Rights	Presentation and disclosure
Sales	Occurrence		X							
	Completeness			X						
	Accuracy				X					
	Classification					X				
	Timing						X			
	Posting and summarization	X								
Cash receipts	Occurrence			X						
	Completeness		X							
	Accuracy				X					
	Classification					X				
	Timing						X			
	Posting and summarization	X								

Two aspects of the relationships in Figure 14-3 deserve special mention:

- For sales, the occurrence transaction-related audit objective affects the existence balance-related audit objective, but for cash receipts the occurrence transaction-related audit objective affects the completeness balance-related audit objective.
- A similar relationship exists for the completeness transaction-related audit objective. The reason for this somewhat surprising conclusion is that an increase of sales increases accounts receivable, but an increase of cash receipts decreases accounts receivable. For example, recording a sale that did not occur violates the occurrence transaction-related audit objective and existence balance-related audit objective (both overstatements). Recording a cash receipt that did not occur violates the occurrence transaction-related audit objective, but it violates the completeness balance-related audit objective for accounts receivable, because a receivable that is still outstanding is no longer included in the records.
- Three accounts receivable balance-related audit objectives are not affected by assessed control risk for classes of transactions. These are valuation, rights and obligations, and presentation and disclosure. When the auditor wants to reduce assessed control risk below maximum for these three objectives, separate controls are identified and tested. This was discussed in Chapter 9.

Figure 14-8 on page 482 includes three rows for assessed control risk: one for sales, one for cash receipts, and one for additional controls related to the accounts receivable balance. The source of each control risk for sales and cash receipts is the control risk matrix, assuming that the tests of controls results supported the original assessment. The auditor makes a separate assessment of control risk for objectives related only to the accounts receivable balance.

Chapter 12 dealt with deciding audit procedures and sample size for tests of controls and evaluating the results of those tests. The results of the tests of controls determine whether assessed control risk for sales and cash receipts needs to be revised. The evidence planning spreadsheet in Figure 14-8 shows three rows for control risk based on the completion and evaluation of those tests.

DESIGN AND PERFORM ANALYTICAL PROCEDURES

OBJECTIVE 14-3

Design and perform analytical procedures for accounts in the sales and collection cycle.

As discussed in Chapter 6, analytical procedures are done during three phases of the audit: during planning, when performing detailed tests in phase III, and as a part of completing the audit. Those affecting accounts receivable or the sales cycle that are done during planning and when performing detailed tests are discussed in this chapter.

Most year-end analytical procedures are done after the balance sheet date but before tests of details of balances. It makes little sense to perform extensive analytical procedures before the client has recorded all transactions for the year and finalized the financial statements. Where auditors also provide assurance on quarterly financial results, analytical review procedures are updated periodically throughout the year.

Table 14-1 presents examples of the major types of ratios and comparisons for the sales and collection cycle and potential misstatements that may be indicated by the analytical procedures. It is important to observe in the "Possible Misstatement" column that both balance sheet and income statement accounts are affected. For example, when the auditor performs analytical procedures for sales, evidence is being obtained about both sales and accounts receivable.

In addition to the analytical procedures in Table 14-1, there should also be a review of accounts receivable for large and unusual amounts. Individual receivables that deserve special attention are large balances; accounts that have been outstanding for a long time; receivables from affiliated companies, officers, directors, and other related parties; and credit balances. The auditor should review the listing of accounts (aged trial balance) or run exception tests against the customer master file at the balance sheet date to determine which accounts should be investigated further.

TABLE 14-1

ANALYTICAL PROCEDURES FOR SALES AND COLLECTIONS

ANALYTICAL PROCEDURE	POSSIBLE MISSTATEMENT
Compare gross margin percentage with previous years (by product line).	Overstatement or understatement of sales and accounts receivable.
Compare sales by month (by product line) over time.	Overstatement or understatement of sales and accounts receivable.
Examine relationship between sales and cost of sales, for example, using regression analysis.	Understatement or overstatement of sales and accounts receivable.
Compare sales returns and allowances as a percentage of gross sales with previous years (by product line).	Overstatement or understatement of sales returns and allowances and accounts receivable.
Compare individual customer balances over a stated amount with previous years.	Misstatements in accounts receivable and related income statement accounts.
Compare bad-debt expense as a percentage of gross sales with previous years.	Uncollectible accounts receivable that have not been provided for.
Compare number of days that accounts receivable are outstanding with previous years.	Overstatement or understatement of allowance for uncollectible accounts and bad-debt expense.
Compare aging categories as a percentage of accounts receivable with previous years.	Overstatement or understatement of allowance for uncollectible accounts and bad-debt expense.
Compare allowance for uncollectible accounts as a percentage of accounts receivable with previous years.	Overstatement or understatement of allowance for uncollectible accounts.

The auditor's conclusion about analytical procedures for the sales and collection cycle is incorporated into the third row from the bottom on the evidence planning spreadsheet in Figure 14-8. Analytical procedures are substantive tests and therefore reduce the extent to which the auditor needs to test details of balances, if the analytical procedures' results are favourable.

PRACTICE APPLICATION OF ANALYTICAL PROCEDURES FOR GROSS MARGIN

Lesley Stopps, a public accountant, is the auditor for Great Western Lumber Company Ltd., a wholesale wood milling company. Lesley calculates the gross margin by three product lines and obtains industry information from published data as follows:

	1998 GROSS MARGIN %		1997 GROSS MARGIN %		1996 GROSS MARGIN %	
	Great Western	Industry	Great Western	Industry	Great Western	Industry
Hardwood	36.3	32.4	36.4	32.5	36.0	32.3
Softwood	23.9	22.0	20.3	22.1	20.5	22.3
Plywood	40.3	50.1	44.2	54.3	45.4	55.6

In discussing the results, the controller states that Great Western has always had a higher gross margin on hardwood products than the industry because it focuses on the markets where it is able to sell at higher prices instead of emphasizing volume. The opposite is true of plywood where it has a reasonably small number of customers, each of which demands lower prices because of high volume. The controller states that competitive forces have caused reductions in plywood gross margin for both the industry and Great Western in 1997 and 1998. Great Western has traditionally had a somewhat lower gross margin for softwood than the industry until 1998, when the gross margin went up significantly due to aggressive selling.

Stopps observed that most of what the controller said was reasonable given the facts. Hardwood gross margin for the industry was stable and approximately 3.5 to 4 percent lower than Great Western's every year. Industry gross margin for plywood has declined annually but is about 10 percentage points higher than Great Western's. Industry gross margin for softwood has been stable for the three years, but Great Western's has increased by a fairly large amount.

The change in Great Western's softwood gross margin from 20.3 percent to 23.9 percent is a concern to Stopps, so she goes through a three-step procedure.

1. Calculate the potential misstatement and evaluate the materiality of that amount. She calculates 23.9% − 20.3% × softwood sales and concludes the amount is potentially material.
2. Identify potential causes of the change:
   • overstatement of sales
   • overstatement of ending inventory (understatement of cost of goods sold)

DESIGN TESTS OF DETAILS OF ACCOUNTS RECEIVABLE

The appropriate tests of details of balances depend upon the factors incorporated into the evidence planning spreadsheet in Figure 14-8. The second row from the bottom shows planned detection risk for each accounts receivable balance-related audit objective. Planned detection risk for each objective is an auditor decision, decided by subjectively combining the conclusions reached about each of the factors listed above that row.

Combining the factors that determine planned detection risk is complex because the measurement for each factor is imprecise and the appropriate weight to be given each factor is highly judgmental. On the other hand, the relationship between each factor and planned detection risk is well established. Figure 8-3 on page 242 illustrated these relationships. Figure 14-4 contrasts how changes in inherent and control risks affect detection risk and thus the planned audit evidence for tests of details of

FIGURE 14-4
Contrasted Planned Evidence for Tests of Details of Balances

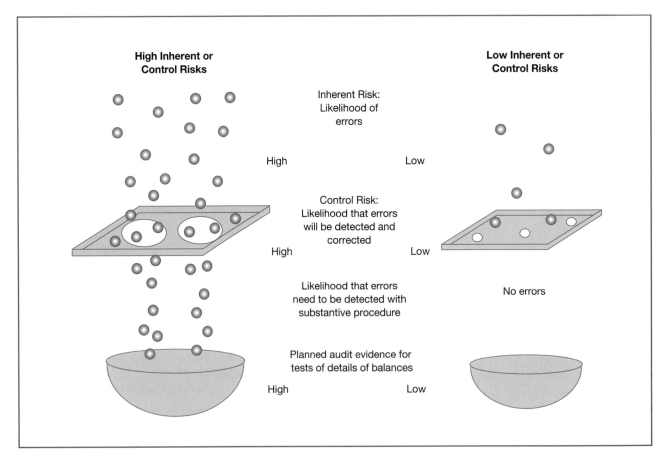

balances. For example, the left side of the diagram shows high inherent risk (many errors likely) and high control risk (the control risk "tray" has large holes in it). The right side shows low inherent risk (few errors likely) and low control risk (the control risk "tray" has only a few very small holes). The auditor knows that a high inherent risk or high control risk decreases planned detection risk and increases planned substantive tests, whereas good results from dual purpose tests can lead to increased planned detection risk and decreased planned substantive tests.

The bottom row in Figure 14-8 shows the planned audit evidence for tests of details of balances for accounts receivable, by objective. As discussed in Chapters 8 and 10, planned audit evidence is the complement of planned detection risk.

The conclusion that planned audit evidence for a given objective is high, medium, or low is implemented by the auditor deciding the appropriate audit procedures, sample size, items to select, and timing. The remainder of this chapter discusses these issues.

TESTS OF DETAILS OF BALANCES

OBJECTIVE 14-4

Design and perform tests of details of accounts receivable for each balance-related audit objective.

Tests of details of balances for all cycles emphasize balance sheet accounts, but income statement accounts are not ignored because they are verified more as a byproduct of the balance sheet tests. For example, if the auditor confirms account receivable balances and finds overstatements due to mistakes in billing customers, there are overstatements of both accounts receivable and sales.

Confirmation of accounts receivable is the most important test of details of accounts receivable. Confirmation is discussed briefly in studying the appropriate tests for each of the balance-related audit objectives, then separately in more detail.

The discussion of tests of details of balances for accounts receivable that follows assumes that the auditor has completed an evidence planning spreadsheet similar to the one in Figure 14-8 and has decided planned detection risk for tests of details for each balance-related audit objective. The audit procedures selected and their sample size will depend heavily on whether planned evidence for a given objective is low, medium, or high. The discussion focuses on accounts receivable balance-related audit objectives.

ACCOUNTS RECEIVABLE ARE CORRECTLY ADDED AND AGREE WITH THE CUSTOMER MASTER FILE AND THE GENERAL LEDGER

Most tests of accounts receivable and the allowance for uncollectible accounts are based on the *aged trial balance*. An aged trial balance is a listing of the balances in the accounts receivable customer master file at the balance sheet date. It includes the individual total balances outstanding and a breakdown of each balance by the time passed between the date of sale and the balance sheet date. An illustration of a typical aged trial balance summary, in this case for Hillsburg Hardware Ltd., is given in Figure 14-5. Notice that the total is the same as accounts receivable on the general ledger trial balance on page 128. This is an aged trial balance summary because it includes only totals for each customer. If the open item transactions were used to produce the aged trial balance, then the individual unpaid invoices would be listed to produce a detailed aged trial balance.

Testing the information on the aged trial balance for mechanical accuracy is a necessary audit procedure. It is ordinarily done before any other tests to assure the auditor that the population being tested agrees with the general ledger and accounts receivable master file. The total column and the columns depicting the aging must be test footed, and the total on the trial balance compared to the general ledger. In addition, a sample of individual balances should be traced to supporting documents, such as duplicate sales invoices, to verify the customer name, balance, and proper aging. The extent of the testing for detail tie-in depends on the number of accounts involved, the degree to which the customer master file data have been tested as a part of tests of controls, and the extent to which the schedule has been verified by an internal auditor or other independent person before it is given to the auditor.

For most large clients, this testing is most effectively completed using generalized

FIGURE 14-5

Aged Trial Balance Summary for Hillsburg Hardware Ltd.

Account Number	Customer	Balance 31/12/98	Aging, Based on Invoice Date				
			0-30 days	31-60 days	61-90 days	91-120 days	over 120
01011	Adams Supply Ltd.	7,329	4,511	2,818			
01044	Argonaut, Inc.	1,542	1,542				
01100	Atwater Brothers	10,519	10,519				
01191	Beekman Bearings Corp.	4,176	3,676		500		
01270	Brown and Phillips	3,000				3,000	
01301	Christopher Plumbing Ltd.	789					789
09733	Travellers Equipment Ltd.	2,976	2,976				
09742	Underhill Parts and Maintenance	8,963	8,963				
09810	UJW Co. Ltd.	5,111	1,811	1,700	1,600		
09907	Zephyr Plastics Corp.	14,300	9,300	5,000			
		1,009,800	785,856	128,466	55,432	34,446	5,600

Hillsburg Hardware Ltd. Accounts Receivable Aged Trial Balance 31/12/99. Schedule Prepared by Client. Approved by. Date 5/1/99.

audit software. The auditor obtains a copy of both the customer master file and the outstanding accounts receivable transactions. By performing the additions, aging, and subtotalling for each customer, the auditor conducts the dual purpose tests of verifying that the programs performing these functions are working correctly as well as quantifying any error. At the same time, samples for confirmation can be selected and unusual transactions identified using the auditor's criteria. For example, balances that exceed their credit limits, or outstanding transactions over a certain size, or extremely old outstanding transactions could be listed. These would be used during tests of the relevant audit objectives.

RECORDED ACCOUNTS RECEIVABLE EXIST

The most important test of details of balances for determining the existence of recorded accounts receivable is the confirmation of customers' balances. When customers do not respond to confirmations, auditors also examine supporting documents to verify the shipment of goods and evidence of subsequent cash receipts to determine whether the accounts were collected. Normally, auditors do not examine shipping documents or evidence of subsequent cash receipts for any account in the sample that is confirmed, but these documents are used extensively as alternative evidence for nonresponses.

EXISTING ACCOUNTS RECEIVABLE ARE INCLUDED

It is difficult to test for account balances omitted from the aged trial balance except by comparing the customer master file to the file of outstanding transactions and to the general ledger. For example, if the client accidentally excluded an account receivable from a manually prepared trial balance, the only way it would likely be discovered is by footing the accounts receivable trial balance and reconciling the balance with the control account in the general ledger.

If all sales to a customer were omitted from the sales journal or were not entered into the order entry system, the understatement of accounts receivable would be almost impossible to uncover by tests of details of balances. For example, auditors rarely send accounts receivable confirmations with zero balances, in part because research shows that customers are unlikely to respond to requests that indicate balances are understated. The understatement of sales and accounts receivable is best uncovered by tests of controls for shipments made but not recorded (completeness objective for tests of sales transactions) and by analytical procedures.

ACCOUNTS RECEIVABLE ARE ACCURATE

Confirmation of accounts selected from the accounts receivable trial balance is the most common test of details of balances for the accuracy of accounts receivable. When customers do not respond to confirmation requests, auditors examine supporting documents, in the same way as described for the existence objective. Tests of the debits and credits to particular customers' balances are done by examining supporting documentation for shipments and cash receipts.

ACCOUNTS RECEIVABLE ARE PROPERLY CLASSIFIED

It is normally relatively easy to evaluate the classification of accounts receivable by reviewing the aged trial balance for material receivables from affiliates, officers, directors, or other related parties. If notes receivable or accounts that should not be classified as a current asset are included with the regular accounts, these should also be segregated. Finally, if the credit balances in accounts receivable are significant, it is appropriate to reclassify them as accounts payable.

There is a close relationship between the classification objective as discussed here and the presentation and disclosure objective. Classification concerns determining whether the client has correctly separated different classifications of accounts receivable. Presentation and disclosure concern making sure the classifications are properly presented. For example, under the classification objective, the auditor determines if receivables from related parties have been separated on the aged trial balance. Under the presentation and disclosure objective, the auditor determines if related-party transactions are correctly shown in the financial statements.

CUTOFF FOR ACCOUNTS RECEIVABLE IS CORRECT

Cutoff misstatements can occur for *sales*, *sales returns and allowances*, and *cash receipts*. They take place when current period transactions are recorded in the subsequent period or subsequent period transactions are recorded in the current period.

The objective of cutoff tests is the same regardless of the type of transaction, but the procedures vary. The objective is to verify whether transactions near the end of the accounting period are recorded in the proper period. The cutoff objective is one of the most important in the cycle because misstatements in cutoff can significantly affect current period income. For example, the intentional or unintentional inclusion of several large, subsequent period sales in the current period or the exclusion of several current-period sales returns and allowances can materially overstate net earnings.

In determining the reasonableness of cutoff, a threefold approach is needed: first, decide on the appropriate *criteria for cutoff*; second, evaluate whether the client has established *adequate procedures* to ensure a reasonable cutoff; and third, *test* whether a reasonable cutoff was obtained.

Sales cutoff   The criterion used by most merchandising and manufacturing clients for determining when a sale takes place is the *shipment of goods*, but some companies record invoices at the time title passes. The passage of title can take place before shipment (as in the case of custom-manufactured goods), at the time of shipment, or subsequent to shipment. For the correct measurement of current-period income, the method must be in accordance with generally accepted accounting principles and consistently applied.

The most important part of evaluating the client's method of obtaining a reliable cutoff is to determine the procedures in use. When a client issues prenumbered shipping documents sequentially, it is usually a simple matter to evaluate and test cutoff. Moreover, the segregation of duties between the shipping and the billing function also enhances the likelihood of recording transactions in the proper period. However, if shipments are made by company truck, the shipping records are not numbered, and shipping and billing department personnel are not independent of each other, it may be difficult, if not impossible, to be assured of an accurate cutoff.

When the client's internal controls are adequate, the cutoff can usually be verified by obtaining the shipping document number for the last shipment made at the end of the period and comparing this number with current and subsequent period recorded sales. As an illustration, assume the shipping document number for the last shipment in the current period is 1489. All recorded sales before the end of the period should bear a shipping document number preceding number 1490. There should also be no sales recorded in the subsequent period for a shipment with a shipping document numbered 1489 or lower. This can easily be tested by comparing recorded sales with the related shipping document for the last few days of the current period and the first few days of the subsequent period.

Sales returns and allowances cutoff Generally accepted accounting principles require that sales returns and allowances be *matched with related sales* if the amounts are material. For example, if current period shipments are returned in the subsequent period, the proper treatment of the transactions is the inclusion of the sales return in the current period. (The returned goods would be treated as current period inventory.) For most companies, however, sales returns and allowances are recorded in the *accounting period in which they occur*, under the assumption of approximately equal, offsetting errors at the beginning and end of each accounting period. This is acceptable as long as the amounts are not significant.

When the auditor is confident that the client records all sales returns and allowances promptly, the cutoff tests are simple and straightforward. The auditor can examine supporting documentation for a sample of sales returns and allowances recorded during several weeks subsequent to the closing date to determine the date of the original sale. If the amounts recorded in the subsequent period are significantly different from unrecorded returns and allowances at the beginning of the period under audit, an adjustment must be considered. If internal controls for recording sales returns and allowances are evaluated as ineffective, a larger sample is needed to verify cutoff.

Cash receipts cutoff For most audits, a proper cash receipt cutoff is *less important* than either the sales or the sales returns and allowances cutoff because the improper cutoff of cash affects only the cash and the accounts receivable balances, not earnings. Nevertheless, if the misstatement is material, it could affect the fair presentation of these accounts, particularly when cash is a small or negative balance.

It is easy to test for a cash receipts cutoff misstatement (frequently referred to as "holding the cash receipts open") by tracing recorded cash receipts to subsequent period bank deposits on the bank statement. If there is a delay of several days, this could indicate a cutoff misstatement.

The confirmation of accounts receivable may also be relied on to some degree to uncover cutoff misstatements for sales, sales returns and allowances, and cash receipts, especially when there is a long interval between the date the transaction took place and the recording date. However, when the interval is only a few days, mail delivery delays may cause confusion of cutoff misstatements with normal reconciliation differences. For example, if a customer mails and records a cheque to a client for payment of an unpaid account on December 30 and the client receives and records the amount on January 5, the records of the two organizations will be different on December 31. This is not a cutoff misstatement, but a *reconcilable difference* due to the delivery time; it will be difficult for the auditor to evaluate whether a cutoff misstatement or a timing difference occurred when a confirmation reply is the source of information. This type of situation requires additional investigation such as inspection of underlying documents.

ACCOUNTS RECEIVABLE IS VALUED CORRECTLY

Tests of the *valuation* objective are performed to evaluate the account *allowance for uncollectible accounts*. Generally accepted accounting principles require that accounts receivable be stated at the amount that will ultimately be collected, which is gross accounts receivable less the allowance. The client's estimate of the total amount that is uncollectible is represented by the allowance for uncollectible accounts. Although it is not possible to predict the future precisely, it is necessary for the auditor to evaluate whether the allowance is reasonable considering all available facts.

The starting point for the evaluation of the allowance for uncollectible accounts is to review the results of the tests of controls that are concerned with the client's credit policy. If the client's credit policy has remained unchanged and the results of the tests of credit policy and credit approval are consistent with those of the preceding year, the change in the balance in the allowance for uncollectible accounts should reflect only changes in economic conditions and sales volume. However, if the client's credit policy or the degree to which it correctly functions have significantly changed, great care must be taken to consider the effects of these changes as well.

A common way to evaluate the adequacy of the allowance is to examine carefully the noncurrent accounts on the aged trial balance to determine which ones have not been paid subsequent to the balance sheet date. The size and age of unpaid balances can then be compared with similar information from previous years to evaluate whether the amount of noncurrent receivables is increasing or decreasing over time. The examination of credit files, discussions with the credit manager, and review of the client's correspondence file may also provide insights into the collectibility of the accounts. These procedures are especially important if a few large balances are noncurrent and are not being paid on a regular basis.

There are two pitfalls in evaluating the allowance by reviewing individual noncurrent balances on the aged trial balance. First, the current accounts are ignored in establishing the adequacy of the allowance even though some of these amounts will undoubtedly become uncollectible. Second, it is difficult to compare the results of the current year with those of previous years on such an unstructured basis. If the accounts are becoming progressively uncollectible over a period of several years, this fact could be overlooked. A way to avoid these difficulties is to establish the history of bad-debt charge-offs over a period of time as a frame of reference for evaluating the current year's allowance. As an example, if historically a certain percentage of the total of each age category becomes uncollectible, it is relatively easy to compute whether the allowance is properly stated. If 2 percent of current accounts, 10 percent of 30- to 90-day accounts, and 35 percent of all balances over 90 days ultimately become uncollectible, these percentages can easily be applied to the current year's aged trial balance totals and the result compared with the balance in the allowance account. Of course, the auditor has to be careful to modify the calculations for changed conditions.

Bad-debt expense   After the auditor is satisfied with the allowance for uncollectible accounts, it is easy to verify bad-debt expense. Assume that (1) the beginning balance was verified as a part of the previous audit, (2) the uncollectible accounts charged off were verified as a part of the tests of controls, and (3) the ending balance in the allowance account has been verified by various means. Then bad-debt expense is simply a residual balance that can be verified by a reperformance test.

THE CLIENT HAS RIGHTS TO ACCOUNTS RECEIVABLE

The client's rights to accounts receivable ordinarily cause no audit problems because the receivables usually belong to the client, but in some cases a portion of the receivables may have been pledged as collateral, assigned to someone else, factored, or sold at discount. Normally, the client's customers are not aware of the existence of such matters; therefore, the confirmation of receivables will not bring it to light. A review of the minutes, discussions with the client, confirmation with banks, and the examination of correspondence files are usually sufficient to uncover instances in which the client has limited rights to receivables.

In addition to testing for the proper statement of the dollar amount in the general ledger, the auditor must also determine that information about the account balance resulting from the sales and collection cycle is properly presented and disclosed in the financial statements. The auditor must decide whether the client has properly combined amounts and disclosed related-party information in the statements. To evaluate the adequacy of the presentation and disclosure, the auditor must have a thorough understanding of generally accepted accounting principles and presentation and disclosure requirements.

An important part of the evaluation involves deciding whether material amounts requiring separate disclosure have actually been separated in the statements. For example, paragraph 3020.01 and Section 3840 of the *CICA Handbook* require that receivables from officers and affiliated companies be segregated from accounts receivable from customers if the amounts are material. Similarly, under Section 1701, it is necessary for companies over a certain size to disclose information about revenues, operations, and assets for different segments of the business as well as information about export sales. The proper aggregation of general ledger balances in the financial statements also requires combining account balances that individually are not relevant for external users of the statements. If all accounts included in the general ledger were disclosed separately on the statements, most statement users would be more confused than enlightened.

As a part of proper disclosure, the auditor is also required to evaluate the adequacy of the *footnotes*. Required footnote disclosure includes information about the pledging, discounting, factoring, assignment of accounts receivable, and amounts due from related parties. Of course, in order to evaluate the adequacy of these disclosures, it is first necessary to know of their existence and to have complete information about their nature. This is generally obtained in other parts of the audit, as discussed in the previous section. One of the major lawsuits in the history of the profession, the *Continental Vending* case, discussed in Chapter 4, revolved primarily around the adequacy of the footnote disclosure of receivables.

CONFIRMATION OF ACCOUNTS RECEIVABLE

One of the most important audit procedures is the *confirmation of accounts receivable*. This multi-purpose technique is used to satisfy the *existence, accuracy*, and *cutoff* objectives.

CICA HANDBOOK REQUIREMENTS

OBJECTIVE 14-5

Obtain and evaluate accounts receivable confirmations.

Two major audit procedures were required by the *CICA Handbook*: the *confirmation of accounts receivable* and the *physical examination of inventory*. These requirements are probably a result of the 1938 landmark U.S. legal case, *McKesson and Robbins*, in which a massive fraud involving fictitious accounts receivable and inventory was not uncovered in the audit. There was ample support to demonstrate that the confirmation of receivables and the physical observation of inventory would have brought the fraud to light, but at that time neither of these procedures was normally performed. Both Canada and the U.S. required confirmation and physical examination.

In 1996, the Auditing Standards Board issued a new *CICA Handbook* Section 5303, "Confirmation." Section 5303 defines a confirmation as "the process of obtaining and evaluating a direct communication from a third party in response to a request for information concerning one or more assertions underlying one or more financial statement items." One of the most important changes in the new section is that confirmations of receivables would continue to be required except in cases where the auditor has assessed the combined inherent risk and control risk as low and where the auditor concludes, in planning the audit, that confirmation would be ineffective. If the auditor did not confirm receivables, he or she would gain the required assurance by other means such as review of subsequent payments or examination of documentation supporting the receivable balance.

Although the remaining sections in this chapter refer specifically to the confirmation of accounts receivable from customers, the concepts apply equally to other receivables such as notes receivable, amounts due from officers, and employee advances.

ASSUMPTIONS UNDERLYING CONFIRMATIONS

An auditor makes two assumptions when accepting a confirmation as evidence. The first is that the person returning the confirmation is independent of the company and thus will provide an unbiased response. If this assumption is invalid, as would be the case if the confirmation of a fraudulent accounts receivable was sent to a company owned by an associate of the person committing the fraud, the value of the returned confirmation becomes zero. The second assumption is that the person returning the confirmation has knowledge of the account and the intent of the confirmation, and has carefully checked the balance to his or her books and records to ensure that the confirmation is in agreement. However, this second assumption may also not always be valid. Research has shown that some people return confirmations without really checking the balance; such a confirmation would have no value.

In many cases, the auditor is able to assess the independence of the person returning the confirmation, but sometimes a relationship may exist of which the auditor is not aware. Furthermore, it is almost always impossible for an auditor to know how much care was taken in checking the balance before the confirmation was signed and returned. Thus, weaknesses may exist in the confirmation of receivables. However, despite the possibility of weakness, confirmation is a procedure on which auditors rely.

In performing confirmation procedures, the auditor must decide the type of confirmation to use, timing of the procedures, sample size, and individual items to select. Each of these is discussed, along with the factors affecting the decision.

CONFIRMATION DECISIONS

Type of confirmation Two common types of confirmations are used for confirming accounts receivable: *positive* and *negative*. A *positive confirmation* is a communication addressed to the debtor requesting him or her to confirm directly whether the balance as stated on the confirmation request is correct or incorrect. Figure 14-6 illustrates a positive confirmation in the audit of Island Hardware Ltd. A variation of the first type of confirmation includes a listing of outstanding invoices making up the balance or a copy of the client customer statement attached by the auditor to the confirmation request. The listing of invoices is useful when the debtor uses a voucher system for accounts payable, while attaching the statement makes it easier for the debtor to respond.

A second type of positive confirmation, often called a *blank confirmation form*, does not state the amount on the confirmation but requests the recipient to fill in the balance or furnish other information. Because blank forms require the recipient to determine the information requested before signing and returning the confirmation, they are considered more reliable than confirmations that include the information. Research shows, however, that response rates are usually lower for blank confirmation forms. These forms are preferred for accounts payable confirmations when the auditor is searching for understatement of accounts payable.

A *negative confirmation* is also addressed to the debtor but requests a response only when the debtor disagrees with the stated amount. Figure 14-7 illustrates a negative confirmation in the audit of Island Hardware Ltd. that is a gummed label and would be attached to a customer's monthly statement. Often, the client can print the auditor's negative confirmation request directly onto the customer statements.

A positive confirmation is *more reliable* evidence because the auditor can perform follow-up procedures if a response is not received from the debtor. With a negative confirmation, failure to reply can only be regarded as a correct response even though the debtor may have ignored the confirmation request.

Offsetting the reliability disadvantage, negative confirmations are *less expensive* to send than positive confirmations, and thus more can be distributed for the same total

FIGURE 14-6
Positive Confirmation

Cockburn, Pedlar & Co.

Chartered Accountants
Cabot Bldg.
P.O. Box 123
3 King Street North
St. John's, Newfoundland A1C 3R5

Garner Hardware
80 Main Street
Cornerbrook, Newfoundland
A2H 1C8

August 15, 1998

To Whom It May Concern:

Re: Island Hardware Ltd.
    In connection with our audit of the financial statements of the above company, we would appreciate receiving from you confirmation of your account. The company's records show an amount receivable from you of $175.00 on June 30, 1998.
    Do you agree with this amount? If you do, please sign this letter in the space below. However, if you do not, please note at the foot of this letter or on the reverse side the details of any differences.
    Please return this letter directly to us in the envelope enclosed for your convenience.

Sincerely,

Cockburn, Pedlar & Co.

Cockburn, Pedlar & Co.

Per:

Please provide Cockburn, Pedlar & Co. with this information.

_____

The above amount was owing by me (us) at the date mentioned.

_____

cost. Negative confirmations cost less because there are no second requests and no follow-up of nonresponses. The determination of which type of confirmation to use is an auditor's decision, and it should be based on the facts in the audit. Positive confirmations are more effective in the following circumstances:

- When there are individual balances of relatively large amounts
- When there are few debtors
- When there is evidence or suspicion of fraud or serious error

FIGURE 14-7
Negative Confirmation

AUDITOR'S ACCOUNT CONFIRMATION

Please examine this statement carefully. If it does NOT agree with your records, please report any exceptions directly to our auditors

Cockburn, Pedlar & Co.
Cabot Bldg.
P.O. Box 123
3 King Street North
St. John's, Newfoundland
A1C 3R5

who are making an examination of our financial statements. A stamped, addressed envelope is enclosed for your convenience in replying.

Do not send your remittance to our auditors.

When these conditions do not exist, it is appropriate to use negative confirmations.

Typically, when negative confirmations are used, the auditor puts considerable emphasis on the effectiveness of internal control as evidence of the fairness of accounts receivable, and assumes the large majority of the recipients will provide a conscientious reading and response to the confirmation request. Negative confirmations are often used for audits of municipalities, retail stores, banks, and other industries in which the receivables are due from the general public. In these cases, more weight is placed on tests of controls than on confirmations.

It is also common to use a combination of positive and negative confirmations by sending positive requests to accounts with large balances and negative requests to those with small balances.

The discussion of confirmations to this point shows that there is a continuum for the type of confirmation decision, starting with using no confirmation in some circumstances, to using only negatives, to using both negatives and positives, to using only positives. The primary factors affecting the decision are the materiality of total accounts receivable, the number and size of individual accounts, control risk, inherent risk, the effectiveness of confirmations as audit evidence, and the availability of other audit evidence.

Timing   The most reliable evidence from confirmations is obtained when they are sent as close to the balance sheet date as possible, as opposed to confirming the accounts several months before year end. This permits the auditor to test directly the accounts receivable balance on the financial statements without making any inferences about the transactions taking place between the confirmation date and the balance sheet date. However, as a means of completing the audit on a timely basis, it is frequently convenient to confirm the accounts at an interim date. This is permissible if internal controls are adequate and can provide reasonable assurance that sales, cash receipts, and other credits are properly recorded between the date of the confirmation and the end of the accounting period. Other factors the auditor is likely to consider in making the decision are the materiality of accounts receivable and the auditor's exposure to lawsuits because of the possibility of client bankruptcy and similar risks.

If the decision is made to confirm accounts receivable prior to year end, it may be necessary to test the transactions occurring between the confirmation date and the balance sheet date by examining such internal documents as duplicate sales invoices, shipping documents, and evidence of cash receipts, in addition to performing analytical procedures of the intervening period.

Sample size   The main considerations affecting the number of confirmations to send are as follows:

- Materiality
- Inherent risk (relative size of total accounts receivable, number of accounts, prior year results, and expected misstatements)
- Control risk
- Achieved detection risk from other substantive tests (extent and results of analytical procedures and other tests of details)
- Type of confirmation (negatives normally require a larger sample size)

These factors are discussed further in the context of audit sampling for Hillsburg Hardware at the end of this chapter.

Selection of the items for testing   Some type of *stratification is desirable* with most confirmations. A typical approach to stratification is to consider both the size of the outstanding balance and the length of time an account has been outstanding as a basis for selecting the balances for confirmation. In most audits, the emphasis should be on confirming larger and older balances, since these are most likely to include a significant misstatement. But it is also important to sample some items from every material stratum of the population. In many cases, the auditor selects all accounts above a certain dollar amount and selects a statistical sample from the remainder.

MAINTAINING CONTROL	After the items for confirmation have been selected, the auditor must maintain control of the confirmations until they are returned from the debtor. If the client's assistance is obtained in preparing the confirmations, enclosing them in envelopes, or putting stamps on the envelopes, close supervision by the auditor is required. A return address must be included on all envelopes to make sure that undelivered mail is received by the public accounting firm. Similarly, self-addressed return envelopes accompanying the confirmations must be addressed for delivery to the public accounting firm's office. It is even important to mail the confirmations *outside* the client's office. All these steps are necessary to ensure independent communication between the auditor and the customer.

FOLLOW-UP ON NONRESPONSES	It is inappropriate to regard confirmations mailed but not returned by customers as significant audit evidence. For example, nonresponses to positive confirmations do not provide audit evidence. Similarly, for negative confirmations, the auditor should not conclude that the recipient received the confirmation request and verified the information requested. Negative confirmations do, however, provide some evidence of the existence assertion.

It is common when the auditor does not receive a response to a positive confirmation request to send a second and even a third request for confirmation. Even with these efforts, some debtors will not return the confirmation. Section 5303, "Confirmations," suggests two alternatives: (1) perform *alternative procedures*, or (2) treat the nonresponse as an error to be projected from the sample to the population in order to assess its materiality. The objective of alternative procedures is to determine by a means other than confirmation whether the nonconfirmed account existed and was properly stated at the confirmation date. The alternative procedures would include examining the following documentation to verify the validity and valuation of individual sales transactions making up the ending balance in accounts receivable.

Subsequent cash receipts Evidence of the receipt of cash subsequent to the confirmation date includes examining remittance advices, entries in the cash receipts records, or perhaps even subsequent credits in the supporting records. On the one hand, the examination of evidence of subsequent cash receipts is a highly useful alternative procedure because it is reasonable to assume that a customer would not make a payment unless it was an existing receivable. On the other hand, the fact of payment does not establish whether there was an obligation on the date of the confirmation. In addition, care should be taken to match specifically each unpaid sales transaction with evidence of its payment as a test for disputes or disagreements over individual outstanding invoices.

Duplicate sales invoices These are useful in verifying the actual issuance of a sales invoice and the actual date of the billing.

Shipping documents These are important in establishing whether the shipment was actually made and as a test of cutoff.

Correspondence with the client Usually, the auditor does not need to review correspondence as a part of alternative procedures, but correspondence can be used to disclose disputed and questionable receivables not uncovered by other means.

The extent and nature of the alternative procedures depend primarily upon the materiality of the nonresponses, the types of misstatements discovered in the confirmed responses, the subsequent cash receipts from the nonresponses, and the auditor's conclusions about internal control. It is normally desirable to account for all unconfirmed balances with alternative procedures even if the amounts are small, as a means of properly generalizing from the sample to the population.

THE BOOKS ARE BURNING

The Regina Co., a manufacturer of vacuum cleaners, overstated income by failing to record sales returns. This irregularity in sales returns was not sufficient to allow the company to meet its earnings targets, so the company generated 200 fictitious sales invoices totalling $5.4 million at the end of the June 30, 1988, fiscal year.

Although auditors usually test sales cutoff and confirm accounts receivable, these fictitious sales were cleverly disguised. The bogus invoices were prepared in the same amounts as other existing sales transactions and they were prepared only for large customers who were unlikely to respond to accounts receivable confirmation requests. The CFO also made sure that the fraudulent invoices were not sent to Regina's regular customers and were concealed from members of the accounting staff who were not involved in the scheme.

The auditors' alternative procedures failed to detect the scheme, most likely because the amounts on the fraudulent invoices matched existing sales invoices. The audit firm defended itself by saying, "If you're a good book-cooker, it's almost impossible to detect."

Sources: John A. Byrne, "How Don Sheelen Made a Mess That Regina Couldn't Clean Up," *Business Week*, February 12, 1990, pp. 46–50; Michael C. Knapp, *Contemporary Auditing: Issues and Cases*, West Publishing, 1993, pp. 79–85.

ANALYSIS OF DIFFERENCES

When the confirmation requests are returned by the customer, it is necessary to determine the reason for any reported differences. In many cases, they are caused by timing differences between the client's and the customer's records. It is important to distinguish between these and *exceptions*, which represent misstatements of the accounts receivable balance. The most commonly reported types of differences in confirmations follow.

Payment has already been made   Reported differences typically arise when the customer has made a payment prior to the confirmation date, but the client has not received the payment in time for recording before the confirmation date. Such instances should be carefully investigated to determine the possibility of a cash receipts cutoff misstatement, lapping, or a theft of cash.

Goods have not been received   These differences typically result because the client records the sale at the date of shipment and the customer records the purchase when the goods are received. The time the goods are in transit is frequently the cause of differences reported on confirmations. These should be investigated to determine the possibility of the customer not receiving the goods at all or the existence of a cutoff misstatement on the client's records.

The goods have been returned   The client's failure to record a credit memo could result from timing differences or the improper recording of sales returns and allowances. Like other differences, these must be investigated.

Clerical errors and disputed amounts The most likely case of reported differences in a client's records occurs when the customer states that there is an error in the price charged for the goods, the goods are damaged, the proper quantity of goods was not received, and so forth. These differences must be investigated to determine whether the client is in error and what the amount of the error is.

In most instances, the auditor asks the client to reconcile the difference and, if necessary, communicates with the customer to resolve any audit disagreements. Naturally, the auditor must carefully verify the client's conclusions on each significant difference.

DRAWING CONCLUSIONS

When all differences have been resolved, including those discovered in performing alternative procedures, it is important to *re-evaluate internal control*. Each client misstatement must be analyzed to determine whether it was consistent or inconsistent with the original assessed level of control risk. If there is a significant number of misstatements that is inconsistent with the assessment of control risk, then it is necessary to revise the assessment and consider the effect of the revision on the audit.

It is also necessary to generalize from the sample to the entire population of accounts receivable. Even though the sum of the misstatements in the sample may not significantly affect the financial statements, the auditor must consider whether the population is likely to be materially misstated. This conclusion can be reached by using statistical sampling techniques or a nonstatistical basis. Projection of misstatements was discussed in Chapter 8 and is further explained in the example at the end of this chapter.

The auditor should always evaluate the *qualitative* nature of the misstatements found in the sample, regardless of the dollar amount of the projected misstatement. Even if the projected misstatement is less than materiality, the misstatements found in a sample can be symptomatic of a more serious problem.

The final decision about accounts receivable and sales is whether sufficient evidence has been obtained through analytical procedures, tests of controls, cutoff procedures, confirmation, and other substantive procedures to justify drawing conclusions about the correctness of the stated balance.

CASE ILLUSTRATION — HILLSBURG HARDWARE, PART III

OBJECTIVE 14-6

Design audit procedures for the audit of accounts receivable, using an evidence planning spreadsheet as a guide.

The Hillsburg Hardware Ltd. case illustration used in Chapter 12 continues here to include the determination of the tests of details of balances audit procedures in the sales and collection cycle. Table 14-2 includes selected comparative trial balance information for the sales and collection cycle for Hillsburg Hardware Ltd. Some of that information is used to illustrate several analytical procedures in Table 14-3. None of the analytical procedures indicated potential misstatements except the ratio of the allowance of uncollectible accounts to accounts receivable. The explanation at the bottom of Table 14-3 comments on the potential error.

Fran Moore prepared the evidence planning spreadsheet in Figure 14-8 as an aid to help her decide the extent of planned tests of details of balances. The source of each of the rows is as follows:

- *Materiality*. The preliminary judgment about materiality was set at $100,000.
- *Assessed audit risk*. Fran assessed audit risk as high (0.05) because of the good financial condition of the company, its financial stability, and the relatively few users of the financial statements. Although the financial statements show some liquidity problems (as discussed in Chapter 13), the company has a large working capital line of credit, and the majority shareholders have indicated a willingness to make available up to $500,000 in personal funds as shareholder loans.
- *Inherent risk*. Fran assessed inherent risk as low for all objectives except valuation. In past years, there have been audit adjustments to the allowance for uncollectible accounts because it was found to be understated.

TABLE 14-2

SELECTED
COMPARATIVE
INFORMATION FOR
HILLSBURG
HARDWARE LTD.—
SALES AND
COLLECTION CYCLE

	AMOUNT (IN THOUSANDS)		
	31-12-98	31-12-97	31-12-96
Sales	$ 7,721	$ 7,619	$ 7,750
Sales returns and allowances	62	57	50
Gross profit	1,992	1,964	2,008
Accounts receivable	1,010	895	801
Allowance for uncollectible accounts	62	77	69
Accounts receivable (net)	948	818	732
Bad-debt expense	166	166	158
Total current assets	2,500	2,578	2,614
Total assets	3,067	3,064	3,211
Net earnings before taxes	285	209	147
Number of accounts receivable	258	221	209
Number of accounts receivable with balances over $35,000	9	7	6

TABLE 14-3

ANALYTICAL
PROCEDURES FOR
HILLSBURG
HARDWARE LTD.—
SALES AND
COLLECTION CYCLE

	31-12-98	31-12-97	31-12-96
Gross profit percent	25.8%	25.8%	25.9%
Sales returns and allowances/gross sales	0.8%	0.7%	0.6%
Bad-debt expense/net sales	2.2%	2.2%	2.0%
Allowance for uncollectible accounts/accounts receivable	6.1%	8.6%	8.6%
Number of days receivables outstanding	45.4	40.9	38.0
Net accounts receivable/total current assets	37.9%	31.7%	28.0%

Note: Allowance as a percentage of accounts receivable has declined from 8.6 percent to 6.1 percent. Number of days receivable outstanding and economic conditions do not justify this change. Potential misstatement is approximately $25,250 ($1,010,000 × [0.086 − 0.061]).

- *Control risk.* Assessed control risk for sales and collections is taken from the assessment of control risk matrix for sales and cash receipts, modified by the results of the tests of controls. The control risk matrix is shown in Figures 12-8 and 12-9 on pages 399 and 400. The results of the tests of controls in Chapter 12 were consistent with the preliminary assessments of control, except for the valuation objective. The initial assessment was low, but tests of controls results changed the assessment to high.
- *Analytical procedures.* Fran chose to use analytical procedures to obtain medium levels of assurance from additional analytical procedures, as described in Table 14-3. These analytical procedures resulted in the detection of certain errors, as summarized in Figure 13-13 on page 453. All of these errors have been corrected in Hillsburg's accounts.
- *Planned detection risk and planned audit evidence.* These two rows are decided for each objective based on the conclusions in the other rows.

Table 14-4 shows the tests of details audit program for accounts receivable, by objective, and for the allowance for uncollectible accounts. The audit program reflects the conclusions for planned audit evidence on the planning spreadsheet in Figure 14-8. Table 14-5 (page 481) shows the audit program in a performance format. The audit procedures are identical to those in Table 14-4 except for procedure 2, which is an analytical procedure. The numbers in parentheses are a cross-reference between the two tables.

**USING
MONETARY UNIT
SAMPLING TO
SELECT AND
EVALUATE
CONFIRMATIONS**

To illustrate the sampling for tests of details described in Chapter 11, monetary unit sampling is now conducted using accounts receivable data. Since Hillsburg Hardware has numerous accounts receivable, only portions of the population will be shown during this illustration.

The steps followed are based on the 14 steps in planning, selecting, and evaluating a sample, as shown in Chapter 11, starting on page 352.

TABLE 14-4

BALANCE-RELATED AUDIT OBJECTIVES AND AUDIT PROGRAM FOR HILLSBURG HARDWARE LTD. — SALES AND COLLECTION CYCLE (DESIGN FORMAT)

OBJECTIVE 14-7

Apply monetary unit sampling to tests of details of accounts receivable.

BALANCE-RELATED AUDIT OBJECTIVE	AUDIT PROCEDURE
Accounts receivable in the aged trial balance agree with related master file amounts, and the total is correctly added and agrees with the general ledger. (detail tie-in)	Foot open item file and customer master file and agree to general ledger. (1.1, 1.2)
The accounts receivable on the aged trial balances exist. (existence)	Confirm accounts receivable using positive confirmations. Confirm all amounts over $35,000 and a statistical sample of the remainder. (7) Perform alternative procedures for all confirmations not returned on the first or second request. (8) Use generalized audit software (GAS) to provide reports of: • All customers with balances exceeding their credit limit (1.3) • All customers with discount terms exceeding 25% (1.4) • Debit and credit totals by customer (1.5) • Customers with balances over $35,000 (1.6) • A dollar-unit sample of the remainder (1.6)
Existing accounts receivable are included in the aged trial balance. (completeness)	Agree details of customers selected using GAS to the aged accounts receivable trial balance listing. (6)
Accounts receivable on the aged trial balances are properly classified. (classification)	Review the receivables listed on the aged trial balance for notes and related party receivables. (3) Inquire of management whether there are any related party notes or long-term receivables included in the trial balances. (4)
Transactions in the sales and collection cycle are recorded in the proper period. (cutoff)	Select the last 40 sales transactions from the current year's sales journal and the first 40 from the subsequent year's, and trace each to the related shipping documents, checking for the date of actual shipment and the correct recording. (11) Review large sales returns and allowances after the balance sheet date to determine whether any should be included in the current period. (12)
Accounts receivable is stated at realizable value. (valuation)	Use GAS to reperform aging for the aged accounts receivable trial balance. Agree totals by aging category to the trial balance listing. (1.7, 1.8) Discuss with the credit manager the likelihood of collecting older accounts. Examine subsequent cash receipts and the credit file on all accounts over 90 days, and evaluate whether the receivables are collectible. (9) Evaluate whether the allowance is adequate after performing other audit procedures relating to collectibility of receivables. (10)
The client has rights to the accounts receivable on the trial balance. (rights and obligations)	Review the minutes of the board of directors' meetings for any indication of pledged or factored accounts receivable. (5) Inquire of management whether any receivables are pledged or factored. (5)
Accounts in the sales and collection cycle and related information are properly presented and disclosed. (presentation and disclosure)	Review the minutes of the board of directors' meetings for any indication of pledged or factored accounts receivable. (5) Inquire of management whether any receivables are pledged or factored. (5)

Note: The procedures are summarized into a performance format in Table 14-5. The number in parentheses after the procedure refers to Table 14-5.

TABLE 14-5

TESTS OF DETAILS OF BALANCES AUDIT PROGRAM FOR HILLSBURG HARDWARE LTD. — SALES AND COLLECTION CYCLE (PERFORMANCE FORMAT)

1. Obtain a copy of the customer master file and the accounts receivable open item transaction file as of December 31 and:
   1.1 Foot both the customer master file and the accounts receivable open item file.
   1.2 Agree the totals of the two files to each other and to the general ledger account balance.
   1.3 List all customers with balances exceeding their credit limit.
   1.4 List all customers with discount terms exceeding 25 percent.
   1.5 Provide a report that shows total debits and credit totals of open items by customer.
   1.6 List customer and transaction details for all customers exceeding $35,000, and a dollar unit sample of customers with balances below $35,000.
   1.7 Reperform the aging of the open items to derive the aged accounts receivable trial balance by customer.
   1.8 Agree the totals by aging category to the client-prepared aged accounts receivable trial balance.
2. Calculate analytical procedures indicated in carry-forward working papers (not included) and follow up any significant changes from prior years.
3. Review the receivables listed on the aged trial balance for notes and related party receivables.
4. Inquire of management whether there are any related-party, notes, or long-term receivables included in the trial balance.
5. Review the minutes of the board of directors' meetings and inquire of management to determine whether any receivables are pledged or factored.
6. Agree details of customers selected using GAS to the aged accounts receivable trial balance listing.
7. Confirm accounts receivable using positive confirmations. Confirm all amounts over $35,000 and a nonstatistical sample of the remainder.
8. Perform alternative procedures for all confirmations not returned on the first or second request.
9. Discuss with the credit manager the likelihood of collecting older accounts. Examine subsequent cash receipts and the credit file on all larger accounts over 90 days, and evaluate whether the receivables are collectible.
10. Evaluate whether the allowance is adequate after performing other audit procedures relating to collectibility of receivables.
11. Select the last 40 sales transactions from the current year's sales journal and the first 40 from the subsequent year's, and trace each to the related shipping documents, checking for the date of actual shipment and the correct recording.
12. Review large sales returns and allowances after the balance sheet date to determine whether any should be included in the current period.

OBJECTIVES, DECIDING IF SAMPLING APPLIES, POPULATION, AND SAMPLING UNIT

When auditors sample for tests of details of balances, the objective is to determine whether the account balance being audited is fairly stated. The audit objective here is to determine the amount of monetary error associated with the existence, accuracy, and cutoff of accounts receivable. This will be accomplished by sending and evaluating confirmations of the accounts receivable balance as of December 31. Sampling can be used to select the smaller items to be confirmed, since the auditor has decided that all amounts greater than $35,000 will be confirmed. Any monetary error between the recorded amount in the customer master file or the open item invoice amount and the confirmed amount is considered to be an error condition.

Hillsburg Hardware has total accounts receivable outstanding of $1,010,000. Since the sampling unit is defined as an individual dollar, the population size is equal to the total outstanding accounts receivable. However, the population is being divided into two strata. High dollar amounts over $35,000 are all being confirmed. A sample will thus be selected from the remainder.

The population for each stratum consists of the total of uncollected sales invoice amounts in that dollar range.

SPECIFY MATERIALITY AND THE ACCEPTABLE RISK OF INCORRECT ACCEPTANCE (ARIA), PROVIDE AN ESTIMATE OF TOTAL DOLLAR ERROR IN THE POPULATION, AND DETERMINE SAMPLE SIZE

Materiality The preliminary judgment about materiality is normally the basis for the tolerable misstatement amount used. If misstatements in non-dollar-unit-sampling tests (i.e., any other tests of details) were expected, tolerable misstatement would be materiality less those amounts. Tolerable misstatement may be different for overstatements or understatements. For this example, tolerable misstatement for both overstatements and understatements is $100,000, the materiality figure for Hillsburg Hardware for total accounts receivable. Fran expects that errors would more likely occur in the smaller accounts so has allocated 60 percent of that amount, or $60,000, to the stratum of smaller amounts.

FIGURE 14-8

Evidence Planning Spreadsheet to Determine Tests of Details of Balances for Hillsburg Hardware Ltd. — Accounts Receivable

	Detail tie-in	Existence (or occurrence)	Completeness	Accuracy	Classification	Cutoff	Valuation	Rights and obligations	Presentation and disclosure
Acceptable audit risk	high	high	high	high	high	high	high	high	high
Inherent risk	low	low	low	low	low	low	medium	low	low
Control risk – Sales	low	medium	low	low	low	low	high	not applicable	not applicable
Control risk – Cash receipts	low	high	low	low	low	low	not applicable	not applicable	not applicable
Control risk – Additional controls	none	none	none	none	none	none	none	low	low
Analytical procedures	good results	good results	good results	good results	good results	good results	unaccept-able results	not applicable	not applicable
Planned detection risk for tests of details of balances	high	medium	high	high	high	high	low	high	high
Planned audit evidence for tests of details of balances	low	medium	low	low	low	low	high	low	low

Materiality $100,000

Acceptable risk of incorrect acceptance   Setting ARIA is a matter of professional judgment and is often reached with the aid of the audit risk model. It is 5 percent for this example.

Estimate of the population exception rate   Normally the estimate of the population exception rate for MUS is zero, as it is most appropriate to use MUS when no misstatements or only a few are expected. Where misstatements are expected, the total dollar amount of expected population misstatements is estimated and then expressed as a percentage of the population recorded value. In this example, some overstatement is expected. Based on past experience, a 0.5 percent expected exception rate is used.

Assumption of the average percent of misstatement for population items that contain a misstatement   To determine the sample size, the auditor also needs to make assumptions about how much error there will be in items that contain a misstatement. This is termed *tainting* in *Dollar Unit Sampling: A Practical Guide for Auditors.*[2]

---

[2]See Leslie, Donald A., Albert D. Teitlebaum, and Rodney J. Anderson, *Dollar Unit Sampling: A Practical Guide for Auditors,* Toronto: Copp Clark Pitman, 1979, pp. 122–123 and 390.

Again there may be a separate assumption for the upper and lower bounds. This is also a matter of professional judgment. Assumptions should be based on the auditor's knowledge of the client and past experience, and if less than 100 percent is used, the assumptions must be clearly defensible. For this example, 50 percent is used for overstatements and 100 percent for understatements.

These assumptions are summarized as follows:

Tolerable misstatement (same for upper and lower)	$100,000
Tolerable misstatement allocated to lower dollar strata	$60,000
Average percent of misstatement assumption, overstatements	50%
Average percent of misstatement assumption, understatements	100%
ARIA	5%
Accounts receivable — recorded value	$1.01 million
Accounts receivable — amounts less than $35,000	$600,000
Estimated misstatement in accounts receivable	0.5%

The *sample size* for the strata of amounts less than $35,000 is calculated as follows:

	UPPER BOUND	LOWER BOUND
Tolerable misstatement	60,000	60,000
Average percent of error assumption (divide by):	0.50	1.00
equals	120,000	60,000
Recorded population value (divide by):	600,000	600,000
Allowable percent error bound (TER)	20%	10%
Estimated population exception rate (EPER)	0.5%	0
Required sample size from the attributes table (Table 12-7, page 409)		
5% ARACR, 20% and 10% TER, and 0.5% and 0 EPER	22	29

Since only one sample is taken for both overstatements and understatements, the *larger* of the two computed sample sizes would be used, in this case 29 items. Normally, generalized audit software is used to determine sample size and to actually select the sample items, once the auditor has determined the ARIA, ARACR, TER, and the EPER. The sample is selected using a statistical formula. High tolerable error rates for a specific procedure such as confirmations are acceptable where the auditor also relies on other audit procedures, such as tests of controls and analytical procedures.

In auditing the sample, finding any understatement amounts will cause the lower bound to exceed the tolerable limit because the sample size is based on no expected misstatements. On the other hand, several overstatement amounts might be found before the tolerable limit for the upper bound is exceeded. Where the auditor is concerned about unexpectedly finding a misstatement that would cause the population to be rejected, he or she can guard against it by arbitrarily increasing sample size above the amount determined by the tables. For example, in this illustration, the auditor might use a sample size of 35 instead of 29.

SELECT THE SAMPLE AND PERFORM THE AUDIT PROCEDURES

For the purposes of illustrating sample selection, Table 14-6 contains part of the population of unpaid invoices less than $35,000, consisting of 12 items totalling $7,376. Assume that the auditor wants to select a monetary unit sample of four accounts from this portion of the population.

Four digits are needed from a random number table or computer program. Using the first four digits in the random number table, Table 11-2 on page 348, with a starting point of row 1002, column 4, the usable random numbers are 6586, 1756, 850, and 6499. The population physical unit items that contain these random dollars are determined by reference to the cumulative total column. They are items 11 (containing dollars 6,577 through 6,980), 4 (dollars 1,699 through 2,271), 2 (dollars 358 through 1,638), and 10 (dollars 5,751 through 6,576). These will be audited, and the result for each physical unit will be applied to the random dollar it contains.

The statistical methods used to evaluate monetary unit samples permit the inclu-

TABLE 14-6

ACCOUNTS
RECEIVABLE
POPULATION

POPULATION ITEM (PHYSICAL UNIT)	RECORDED AMOUNT	CUMULATIVE TOTAL (DOLLAR UNIT)
1	$ 357	$ 357
2	1,281	1,638
3	60	1,698
4	573	2,271
5	691	2,962
6	143	3,105
7	1,425	4,530
8	278	4,808
9	942	5,750
10	826	6,576
11	404	6,980
12	396	7,376

sion of a physical unit in the sample more than once. That is, in the previous example, if the random numbers had been 6,586, 1,756, 856, and 6,599, the sample items would be 11, 4, 2, and 11. Item 11 would be audited once but would be treated as two sample items statistically, and the sample total would be four items because four monetary units were involved.

One problem using MUS (monetary unit sampling) selection is that population items with a zero recorded balance have no chance of being selected even though they could contain misstatements. Similarly, small balances that are significantly understated have little chance of being included in the sample. This problem can be overcome by doing specific audit tests for zero- and small-balance items, assuming that they are of concern.

Another problem is the inability to include negative balances, such as credit balances in accounts receivable, in the MUS sample. It is possible to ignore negative balances for MUS selection and test those amounts by some other means. An alternative is to treat them as positive balances (which is readily done with audit software by simply using absolute values) and add them to the total number of monetary units being tested; however, this complicates the evaluation process.

Fran determined from earlier generalized audit software tests that credit amounts were insignificant, and decided that no separate audit work would be done on those amounts.

Fran ensured that audit staff on the engagement properly handled the accounts receivable confirmation process. Confirmations were prepared and mailed, second requests were sent, discrepancies were reviewed, and alternative procedures were conducted for those items selected for which no replies were received.

GENERALIZE FROM THE SAMPLE TO THE POPULATION

GENERALIZING FROM THE SAMPLE TO THE POPULATION WHEN NO MISSTATEMENTS ARE FOUND USING MUS

Assume that during the audit, no misstatements were uncovered in the sample. The auditor next wants to determine the maximum amount of overstatement and understatement amounts that could exist in the population and still provide a sample with no misstatements. These are the upper misstatement bound and the lower misstatement bound, respectively. Assuming an ARIA of 5 percent, and using Table 12-8 on page 412, both the upper and lower bounds are determined by locating the intersection of the sample size (35) and the actual number of misstatements (0) in the same manner as for attribute sampling. The CUER of 8.2 percent on the table represents both the upper and lower bound, *expressed as a percentage.*

Thus, based on the sample results and the misstatement bounds from the table, the auditor can conclude with a 5 percent sampling risk that no more than 8.2 percent of the dollar units in the population are misstated. To convert this percent into *dollars,* the auditor must make an assumption about the average percent of misstatement for population dollars that contain a misstatement. This assumption significantly affects the misstatement bounds. To illustrate this, first Fran's assumptions are shown, that is, a 50 percent misstatement assumption for overstatements and a 100 percent assumption for understatements, and a second assumption is shown with a 100 percent misstatement assumption for overstatements and a 200 percent assumption for understatements.

Assumption 1 (Fran's) Overstatement amounts equal 50 percent; understatement amounts equal 100 percent; misstatement bounds at a 5 percent ARIA are

> Upper misstatement bound = $600,000 × 8.2% × 50% = $24,600
> Lower misstatement bound = $600,000 × 8.2% × 100% = $49,200

The assumption is that, on the average, those population items that are misstated are misstated by the full dollar amount of the recorded value. Since the misstatement bound is 8.2 percent, the dollar value of the misstatement is not likely to exceed $24,600 (8.2 percent times 50 percent of the total recorded dollar units in the population). If all the amounts are overstated, there is an overstatement of $24,600. If they are all understated, there is an understatement of $49,200.

The assumption of 100 percent or 50 percent misstatements is very conservative, especially for overstatements. Assume that the actual population exception rate is 8.2 percent. The following two conditions both have to exist before the $24,600 properly reflects the true overstatement amount:

1. All amounts have to be overstatements. Offsetting amounts would have reduced the amount of the overstatement.
2. All population items misstated have to be 50 percent misstated. There could not, for example, be a misstatement such as a cheque written for $226 that was recorded as $262. This would be only a 13.7 percent misstatement (262 − 226 = 36 overstatement; 36/262 = 13.7%).

In the calculation of the misstatement bounds of $24,600 overstatement and $49,200 understatement, the auditor did not calculate a point estimate and precision amount as described in the next section on judgmental sampling. This is because the tables used include both a point estimate and a precision amount to derive the upper exception rate. Even though the point estimate and precision amount are not calculated for MUS, they are implicit in the determination of misstatement bounds and can be determined from the tables. For example, in this illustration, the point estimate is zero and the statistical precision is $24,600 for overstatement and $49,200 for understatement.

Assumption 2 Overstatement amounts equal 100 percent; understatement amounts equal 200 percent; misstatement bounds at a 5 percent ARIA are

> Upper misstatement bound = $600,000 × 8.2% × 100% = $49,200
> Lower misstatement bound = $600,000 × 8.2% × 200% = $98,400

The justification for a larger percent for understatements is the potential for a larger misstatement in percentage terms. For example, an accounts receivable recorded at $20 that should have been recorded at $200 is understated by 900 percent [(200 − 20)/20], whereas one that is recorded at $200 that should have been recorded at $20 is overstated by 90 percent [(200 − 20)/200].

Items containing large understatement amounts may have a small recorded value, due to those misstatements. As a consequence, because of the mechanics of MUS, few of them will have a chance of being selected in the sample. Because of this, some auditors select an additional sample of small items to supplement the monetary unit sample whenever understatement amounts are an important audit concern.

Appropriate percent of misstatement assumption The appropriate assumption to make regarding the overall percent of misstatement in those population items containing a misstatement is an auditor's decision. The auditor must set these percentages based on personal judgment in the circumstances. In the absence of convincing information to the contrary, most auditors believe it is desirable to assume a 100 percent amount for both overstatements and understatements. This approach is considered highly conservative, but it is easier to justify than any other assumption. In fact, the reason upper and lower limits are referred to as misstatement bounds when MUS is used, rather than maximum likely misstatement or the commonly used statistical term "confidence limit," is due to widespread use of that conservative assumption. Unless stated otherwise, the 100 percent misstatement assumption is used in the chapter and problem materials when no misstatements are found.

GENERALIZING WHEN MISSTATEMENTS ARE FOUND

This section presents the evaluation method used when there are misstatements in the sample. The same illustration is continued; the only change is the assumption about the misstatements. The sample size remains at 35 and the recorded value is still $600,000, but now five misstatements in the sample are assumed. The misstatements are shown in Table 14-7.

The following changes to the process of generalizing need to be incorporated:

- *Overstatement and understatement amounts are dealt with separately and then combined.* First, initial upper and lower misstatement bounds are calculated separately for overstatement and understatement amounts. Next, a point estimate of overstatements and understatements is calculated. The point estimate of understatements is used to reduce the initial upper misstatement bound, and the point estimate of overstatements is used to reduce the initial lower misstatement bound. The method and rationale for these calculations will be illustrated by using the four overstatement and one understatement amounts in Table 14-7.
- *A different misstatement assumption is made for each misstatement, including the zero misstatements.* When there were no misstatements in the sample, an assumption was required as to the average percent of misstatement for the population items misstated. The misstatement bounds were calculated showing several different assumptions. Now that misstatements have been found, sample information is available to use in determining the misstatement bounds. The misstatement assumption is still required, but it can be modified based on this actual misstatement data.

Where misstatements are found, a 100 percent assumption for all misstatements is not only exceptionally conservative, it is inconsistent with the sample results. A common assumption in practice, and the one followed in this book, is that the actual sample misstatements are representative of the population misstatements. This assumption requires the auditor to calculate the percent that each sample item is misstated (misstatement ÷ recorded balance) and apply that percent to the population. The calculation of the percent for each misstatement is shown in the last column in Table 14-7. As will be explained shortly, a misstatement assumption is still needed for the zero misstatement portion of the computed results. For this example, a 50 percent misstatement assumption is

TABLE 14-7

MISSTATEMENTS FOUND

CUSTOMER NO.	RECORDED ACCOUNTS RECEIVABLE AMOUNT	AUDITED ACCOUNTS RECEIVABLE AMOUNT	MISSTATEMENT	MISSTATEMENT ÷ RECORDED AMOUNT
2073	$ 6,200	$ 6,100	$ 100	0.016
5111	12,910	12,000	910	0.070
5206	4,322	4,450	(128)	(0.030)
7642	23,000	22,995	5	0.0002
9816	8,947	2,947	6,000	0.671

TABLE 14-8

PERCENT MISSTATEMENT BOUNDS

NUMBER OF MISSTATEMENTS	UPPER PRECISION LIMIT FROM TABLE	INCREASE IN PRECISION LIMIT RESULTING FROM EACH MISSTATEMENT (LAYERS)
0	0.082	0.082
1	0.129	0.047
2	0.169	0.04
3	0.20*	0
4	0.20*	0

*Table 12-9 (page 413) indicates these as being over 20 percent; differences would be small.

used for the zero misstatement portion for overstatements and 100 percent for understatement misstatement bounds.

- *The auditor must deal with layers of the computed upper exception rate (CUER) from the attribute sampling table.* The reason for doing so is that there is a different misstatement assumption for each misstatement. Layers are calculated by first determining the CUER from the table for each misstatement and then calculating each layer. Table 14-8 shows the layers in the attribute sampling table for the example at hand. The layers were determined by reading across the table for a sample size of 100, from the 0 through 4 exception columns.

- *Misstatement assumptions must be associated with each layer.* The most common method of associating misstatement assumptions with layers is to be conservative by associating the largest dollar misstatement percents with the largest layers. Table 14-9 shows the association. For example, the largest average misstatement was 0.671 for customer 9816. That misstatement is associated with the layer factor of 0.047, the largest layer where misstatements were found. The portion of the upper precision limit related to the zero misstatement layer has a misstatement assumption of 50 percent, which is still conservative. Table 14-9 shows the calculation of misstatement bounds before consideration of offsetting amounts.

The upper misstatement bound was calculated as if there were no understatement amounts, and the lower misstatement bound was calculated as if there were no overstatement amounts.

TABLE 14-9

ILLUSTRATION OF CALCULATING INITIAL UPPER AND LOWER MISSTATEMENT BOUNDS

NUMBER OF MISSTATEMENTS (1)	UPPER PRECISION LIMIT PORTION* (2)	RECORDED VALUE (3)	UNIT ERROR ASSUMPTION (4)	MISSTATEMENT BOUND PORTION (COLUMNS 2 × 3 × 4) (5)
Overstatements				
0	0.082	$600,000	0.50	$24,600
1	0.047	$600,000	0.671	18,922
2	0.04	$600,000	0.070	1,680
3	0	$600,000	0.016	0
4	0	$600,000	0.0002	0
Upper precision limit	0.169			
Initial misstatement bound				$45,202
Understatements				
0	0.082	$600,000	1.00	$49,200
1	0.047	$600,000	0.03	1,692
Lower precision limit	0.129			
Initial misstatement bound				$50,982

*ARIA of 5 percent. Sample size of 100.

Adjustment for offsetting amounts Most MUS users believe that the approach just discussed is overly conservative when there are offsetting amounts. If an understatement misstatement is found, it is logical and reasonable that the bound for overstatement amounts should be lower than it would be had no understatement amounts been found, and vice versa. The adjustment of bounds for offsetting amounts is made as follows: (1) a point estimate of misstatements is made for both understatement and overstatement amounts, and (2) each bound is reduced by the opposite point estimate.

The point estimate for overstatements is calculated by multiplying the average overstatement amount in the dollar units audited by the recorded value. The same approach is used for calculating the point estimate for understatements. In the example, there is one understatement amount of 3 cents per dollar unit in a sample of 35. The understatement point estimate is therefore $360 (0.03/35 × $600,000). Similarly, the overstatement point estimate is $12,981 [(0.67+0.07+ 0.016 + 0.0002)/ 35 × $600,000].

Table 14-10 shows the adjustment of the bounds that follow from this procedure. The initial upper bound of $45,202 is reduced by the estimated most likely understatement error of $514 to an adjusted bound of $44,688. The initial lower bound of $49,200 is reduced by the estimated most likely overstatement amount of $12,981 to an adjusted bound of $36,219. Thus, given the methodology and assumptions followed, the auditor concludes that there is a 5 percent risk that accounts receivable is overstated by $44,688 or more, or understated by more than $36,219. It should be noted that if the misstatement assumptions were changed, the misstatement bounds would also change. The reader should be advised that the method used to adjust the bounds for offsetting amounts is but one of several in current use. The method illustrated here is taken from Leslie, Teitlebaum, and Anderson.[3] All the methods in current use are reliable and somewhat conservative.

Summary The following seven steps summarize the calculation of the adjusted misstatement bounds for monetary unit sampling when there are offsetting amounts. The calculation of the adjusted upper misstatement bound for the four overstatement amounts in Table 14-7 is used to illustrate. The evaluation process for MUS is complex and is best handled using computer software.

TABLE 14-10

ILLUSTRATION OF CALCULATING ADJUSTED MISSTATEMENT BOUNDS

NUMBER OF MISSTATEMENTS	UNIT MISSTATEMENT ASSUMPTION	SAMPLE SIZE	RECORDED POPULATION	POINT ESTIMATE	BOUNDS
Initial overstatement bound					$45,202
Understatement misstatement					
1	0.030	35	$600,000	$514	(514)
Adjusted overstatement bound					$44,688
Initial understatement bound					$49,200
Overstatement misstatements					
1	0.671				
2	0.070				
3	0.016				
4	0.0002				
Sum	0.7572	35	$600,000	$12,981	(12,981)
Adjusted understatement bound					$36,219

[3]See Leslie, Teitlebaum, and Anderson, *op. cit.*

STEPS TO CALCULATE ADJUSTED MISSTATEMENT BOUNDS	CALCULATION FOR OVERSTATEMENTS IN TABLE 14-7
1. Determine misstatement for each sample item, keeping overstatements and understatements separate.	Table 14-7 Four overstatements
2. Calculate misstatement per dollar unit in each sample item (misstatement/recorded value).	Table 14-7 0.016, 0.07, 0.0002, 0.671
3. Layer misstatements per dollar unit from highest to lowest, including the percent misstatement assumption for sample items not misstated.	Table 14-9 0.5, 0.671, 0.07, 0.016, 0.0002
4. Determine upper precision limit for attribute sampling table, and determine the percent misstatement bound for each misstatement (layer).	Table 14-9 Total of 16.9 percent for four misstatements; calculate five layers
5. Calculate initial upper and lower misstatement bounds for each layer and total.	Table 14-9 Total of $45,202 and $50,892
6. Calculate point estimate for overstatements and understatements.	Table 14-10 $514 for understatements
7. Calculate adjusted upper and lower misstatement bounds.	$44,688 adjusted overstatement limit and $36,219 adjusted understatement limit

ANALYZE THE MISSTATEMENTS AND DECIDE THE ACCEPTABILITY OF THE POPULATION

Fran and her staff analyzed the errors described in Table 14-7. The first two overstatement errors were due to accumulated discounts taken by customers that had not been properly removed from the accounts receivable. The understatement was due to a credit note that had accidentally been issued twice, and the large $6,000 difference was due to a change in discount rate. This customer had reached such a high volume of purchases that it was moved to a higher discount level, but Hillsburg staff did not implement the discount on a timely basis. In addition to calculating misstatement bounds, Fran will discuss with Hillsburg staff their management of discounts to ensure that these errors are corrected and to determine how future errors can be prevented. Fran could also have initiated additional substantive procedures to further quantify the extent of the dollar errors associated with discount differences.

Whenever a statistical method is used, a *decision rule* is needed to decide whether the population is acceptable. The decision rule for MUS is as follows:

> If *both* the lower misstatement bound (LMB) and upper misstatement bound (UMB) fall between the understatement and overstatement tolerable misstatement amounts, accept the conclusion that the book value is not misstated by a material amount; otherwise, conclude that the book value is misstated by a material amount.

This decision rule is illustrated on page 490. The auditor should conclude that both the LMB and UMB for situations 1 and 2 fall completely within both the understatement and overstatement tolerable misstatements. Therefore, the conclusion that the population is not misstated by a tolerable misstatement amount is accepted. For situations 3, 4, and 5, either LMB or UMB, or both, are outside tolerable misstatements. Therefore, the population book value is rejected.

For the audit of accounts receivable amounts below $35,000, Fran set the lower misstatement bound and upper misstatement bound at $60,000. Table 14-10 indicates that with the errors discovered, the overstatement bound is $44,688 and the understatement bound is $36,219. Thus, the population book value is accepted since these amounts fall within the stated bounds.

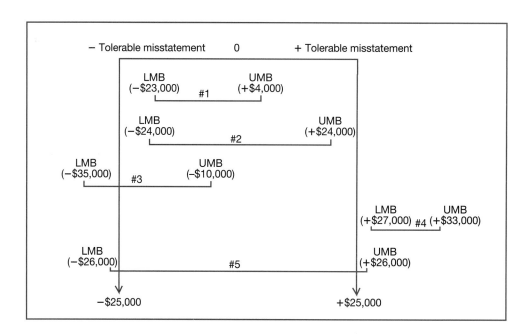

ACTION WHEN A POPULATION IS REJECTED

When one or both of the error bounds lie outside the tolerable misstatement limits and the population is not considered acceptable, the auditor has several options. Fran could wait until tests of other audit areas were completed to see if materiality of $100,000 was exceeded for the aggregated misstatements. Alternatively, she could perform expanded tests in other areas, increase the sample size (as explained on page 363), ask that the account balance be adjusted, or request the client correct the population (which would then have to be re-audited). If the aggregated errors exceed materiality and the client will not adjust the accounts, the auditor will have to consider refusing to give an unqualified opinion.

Use of judgmental sampling Fran could have alternatively determined that judgmental sampling could be used to select the items to be confirmed below $35,000. She would then have followed 14 steps similar to those outlined in Chapter 11, as applied to nonstatistical rather than statistical sampling.

ESSENTIAL TERMS

Accounts receivable balance-related audit objectives — the nine specific audit objectives used to help the auditor decide the appropriate audit evidence for accounts receivable (p. 462).

Aged trial balance — a listing of the balances in the accounts receivable master file at the balance sheet date broken down according to the amount of time passed between the date of sale and the balance sheet date (p. 467).

Alternative procedure — the follow-up of a positive confirmation not returned by the debtor with the use of documentation evidence to determine whether the recorded receivable exists and is collectible (p. 476).

Blank confirmation form — a letter, addressed to the debtor, requesting the recipient to fill in the amount of the accounts receivable balance; considered a positive confirmation (p. 473).

Cutoff misstatements — misstatements that take place as a result of current period transactions being recorded in a subsequent period, or subsequent period transactions being recorded in the current period (p. 469).

Evidence planning spreadsheet — a working paper used to

help the auditor decide whether planned audit evidence for tests of details of balances should be low, medium, or high for each balance-related audit objective (p. 461).

Negative confirmation — a letter, addressed to the debtor, requesting a response only if the recipient disagrees with the amount of the stated account balance (p. 473).

Positive confirmation — a letter, addressed to the debtor, requesting that the recipient indicate directly on the letter whether the stated account balance is correct or incorrect and, if incorrect, by what amount (p. 473).

Tainting — the average percent of misstatement for population dollars that contain a misstatement (used with MUS sampling) (p. 482).

Timing difference in an accounts receivable confirmation — a reported difference in a confirmation from a debtor that is determined to be a timing difference between the client's and debtor's records and therefore not a misstatement (p. 470).

Valuation of accounts receivable — the amount of the outstanding balances in accounts receivable that will ultimately be collected (p. 470).

14-1 Distinguish between tests of details of balances and tests of controls for the sales and collection cycle. Explain how the tests of controls affect the tests of details.

14-2 Cynthia Roberts, a public accountant, expresses the following viewpoint: "I do not believe in performing tests of controls for the sales and collection cycle. As an alternative, I send a lot of negative confirmations on every audit at an interim date. If I find a lot of misstatements, I analyze them to determine their cause. If internal controls are inadequate, I send positive confirmations at year end to evaluate the amount of the misstatements. If the negative confirmations result in minimal misstatements, which is often the case, I have found that internal controls are effective without bothering to perform tests of controls, and the CICA's confirmation requirement has been satisfied at the same time. In my opinion, the best test of internal controls is to go directly to third parties." Evaluate her point of view.

14-3 List five analytical procedures for the sales and collection cycle. For each test, describe a misstatement that could be identified.

14-4 Identify the nine accounts receivable balance-related audit objectives. For each objective, list one audit procedure.

14-5 Which of the nine accounts receivable balance-related audit objectives can be partially satisfied by confirmations with customers?

14-6 State the purpose of footing the total column in the client's aged accounts receivable trial balance, tracing individual customer names and amounts to the customer master file, and tracing the total to the general ledger. Is it necessary to trace each amount to the master file? Why or why not?

14-7 Distinguish between accuracy tests of gross accounts receivable and tests of the realizable value of receivables.

14-8 Explain why you agree or disagree with the following statement: "In most audits, it is more important to test carefully the cutoff for sales than for cash receipts." Describe how you perform each type of test assuming the existence of prenumbered documents.

14-9 Evaluate the following statements: "In many audits in which accounts receivable are material, the requirement of confirming customer balances is a waste of time and would not be performed by competent auditors if it were not required by the CICA. When inherent risk is low, internal control is excellent, and there are many small receivables from customers who do not recognize the function of confir-

mation, confirming customer balances is a meaningless procedure. Examples include well-run utilities and department stores. In these situations, tests of controls are far more effective than confirmations." Assume these statements were made in the context of the previous *CICA Handbook* requirement that auditors confirm accounts receivable; evaluate the statements in the context of the discussion of the *CICA Handbook* Section 5303, "Confirmations," in the chapter.

14-10 Distinguish between a positive and a negative confirmation, and state the circumstances in which each should be used. Why do public accounting firms frequently use a combination of positive and negative confirmations on the same audit?

14-11 In what circumstances is it acceptable to confirm accounts receivable prior to the balance sheet date?

14-12 State the most important factors affecting the sample size in confirmations of accounts receivable.

14-13 In Chapter 11, one of the points brought out was the need to obtain a representative sample of the population. How can this concept be reconciled with the statement in this chapter that the emphasis should be on confirming larger and older balances since these are most likely to contain misstatements?

14-14 An auditor is determining the appropriate sample size for testing inventory valuation using MUS. The population has 2,620 valued at $12,625,000. The tolerable misstatement for both understatements and overstatements is $500,000 at a 10 percent ARIA. No misstatements are expected in the population. Calculate the preliminary sample size using a 100 percent average misstatement assumption.

14-15 Define what is meant by "alternative procedures" and explain their purpose. Which alternative procedures are the most reliable? Why?

14-16 Explain why the analysis of differences is important in the confirmation of accounts receivable even if the misstatements in the sample are not material.

14-17 State three types of differences that might be observed in the confirmation of accounts receivable that do not constitute misstatements. For each, state an audit procedure that would verify the difference.

14-18 What is the relationship of each of the following to the sales and collection cycle: flowcharts, assessing control risk, tests of controls, and tests of details of balances?

14-19 The following questions concern analytical procedures in the sales and collection cycle. Choose the best response.

a. As a result of analytical procedures, the independent auditor determines that the gross profit percentage has declined from 30 percent in the preceding year to 20 percent in the current year. The auditor should
   (1) evaluate management's performance in causing this decline.
   (2) investigate the credit manager's performance.

   (3) require footnote disclosure.
   (4) consider the possibility of a misstatement in the financial statements.

b. Once a public accountant has determined that accounts receivable have increased due to slow collections in a "tight money" environment, the public accountant would be likely to
   (1) review the going concern ramifications.
   (2) review the credit and collection policy.

(3) increase the balance in the allowance for bad-debt account.

(4) expand tests of collectibility.

c. In connection with his review of key ratios, the public accountant notes that Pyzi Inc. had accounts receivable equal to 30 days' sales at December 31, 1997, and to 45 days' sales at December 31, 1998. Assuming that there had been no changes in economic conditions, clientele, or sales mix, this change most likely would indicate

(1) a steady increase in sales in 1998.

(2) a steady decrease in sales in 1998.

(3) an easing of credit policies in 1998.

(4) a decrease in accounts receivable relative to sales in 1998.

(AICPA adapted)

14-20 The following questions deal with confirmation of accounts receivable. Choose the best response.

a. In connection with her examination of the Beke Supply Corp. for the year ended August 31, 19X1, Sylvia Lowe, a public accountant, has mailed accounts receivable confirmations to three groups as follows:

GROUP NUMBER	TYPE OF CUSTOMER	TYPE OF CONFIRMATION
1	Wholesale	Positive
2	Current retail	Negative
3	Past-due retail	Positive

The confirmation responses from each group vary from 10 percent to 90 percent. The most likely response percentages are

(1) Group 1 — 90 percent; Group 2 — 50 percent; Group 3 — 10 percent

(2) Group 1 — 90 percent; Group 2 — 10 percent; Group 3 — 50 percent

(3) Group 1 — 50 percent; Group 2 — 90 percent; Group 3 — 10 percent

(4) Group 1 — 10 percent; Group 2 — 50 percent; Group 3 — 90 percent

b. The negative form of accounts receivable confirmation request is particularly useful except when

(1) internal control surrounding accounts receivable is considered to be effective.

(2) a large number of small balances are involved.

(3) the auditor has reason to believe the persons receiving the requests are likely to give them consideration.

(4) individual account balances are relatively large.

c. Which of the following is the best argument against the use of negative confirmations of accounts receivable?

(1) The cost per response is excessively high.

(2) There is *no* way of knowing if the intended recipients received them.

(3) Recipients are likely to feel that the confirmation is a subtle request for payment.

(4) The inference drawn from receiving no reply may not be correct.

d. The return of a positive confirmation of accounts receivable without an exception attests to the

(1) collectibility of the receivable balance.

(2) accuracy of the receivable balance.

(3) accuracy of the aging of accounts receivable.

(4) accuracy of the allowance for bad debts.

(AICPA adapted)

DISCUSSION QUESTIONS AND PROBLEMS

14-21 The following are common tests of details of balances for the audit of accounts receivable.

1. Obtain a list of aged accounts receivable, foot the list, and trace the total to the general ledger.

2. Trace 35 accounts to the customer master file or open item transaction file for name, amount, and age categories.

3. Examine and document collections on accounts receivable for 20 days after the engagement date.

4. Request 25 positive and 65 negative confirmations of accounts receivable.

5. Perform alternative procedures on accounts not responding to second requests by examining subsequent collection documentation and shipping reports or sales invoices.

6. Test the sales cutoff by tracing entries in the sales journal for 15 days before and after the engagement date to shipping reports, if available, and/or sales invoices.

7. Determine and disclose accounts pledged, discounted, sold, assigned, or guaranteed by others.

8. Evaluate the materiality of credit balances in the aged trial balance.

Required

For each audit procedure, identify the balance-related audit objective or objectives it partially or fully satisfies.

14-22 The following misstatements are sometimes found in the sales and collection account balances:

1. Cash received from collections of accounts receivable in the subsequent period are recorded as current period receipts.

2. The allowance for uncollectible accounts is inadequate due to the client's failure to reflect depressed economic conditions in the allowance.

3. Several accounts receivable are in dispute due to claims of defective merchandise.

4. The pledging of accounts receivable to the bank for a loan is not disclosed in the financial statements.

5. Goods shipped and included in the current period sales were returned in the subsequent period.

6. Long-term interest-bearing notes receivable from affiliated companies are included in accounts receivable.

7. The aged accounts receivable trial balance total does not equal the amount in the general ledger.

Required

a. For each misstatement, identify the balance-related audit objective to which it pertains.

b. For each misstatement, list an internal control that should prevent it.

c. For each misstatement, list one test of details of balances audit procedure that the auditor can use to detect it.

14-23 The following are audit procedures in the sales and collection cycle.

1. Examine a sample of shipping documents to determine if each has a sales invoice number included on it. A 1 (ii)

2. Discuss with the sales manager whether any sales allowances have been granted after the balance sheet date that may apply to the current period. E 3 (f)

3. Add the open item accounts receivable data file, calculate aging totals, agree the aging totals to the columns on the aged trial balance, and compare the total with the general ledger. F 3 (a)

4. Observe whether the controller makes an independent comparison of the total on the general ledger with the trial balance of accounts receivable. D 1 (iv)

5. For the month of May, count the approximate number of shipping documents filed in the shipping department, and compare the total with the number of sales invoices in the sales journal. F 3 (f)

6. Compare the date on a sample of shipping documents throughout the year with related duplicate sales invoices. G 2

7. Examine a sample of customer purchase orders and see if each has a credit authorization. A 1 (i)

8. Send letters directly to former customers whose accounts have been charged off as uncollectible to determine if any accounts have actually been paid. B 3 (b)

9. Examine the customer master file to see if each customer has an indication of C for a regular customer, N for interest-bearing receivables, and R for related parties. C 3 (e)

10. Compare the date on a sample of shipping documents a few days before and after the balance sheet date with related sales journal transactions. F 3 (f)

11. Compute the ratio of allowance for uncollectible accounts to accounts receivable, and compare with previous years. G 2

12. Examine a sample of noncash credits in the open item accounts receivable file to determine if supporting approval exists. C 1 (i)

Required

a. For each procedure, identify the applicable type of audit evidence.

b. For each procedure, identify which of the following it is:
   (1) Test of controls
   (2) Analytical procedure
   (3) Test of details of balances

c. For those procedures you identified as a test of controls, which transaction-related audit objective(s) is(are) being satisfied? p. 382

d. For those procedures you identified as a test of details of balances, which balance-related audit objective(s) is(are) being satisfied? p. 467

14-24 André Auto Parts Inc. sells new parts for foreign automobiles to auto dealers. Company policy requires that a prenumbered shipping document be issued for each sale. At the time of pickup or shipment, the shipping clerk writes the date on the shipping document. The last shipment made in the fiscal year ended August 31, 1998, was recorded on document 2167. Shipments are billed in the order that the billing clerk receives the shipping documents.

For late August and early September, shipping documents are billed on sales invoices as follows:

SHIPPING DOCUMENT NO.	SALES INVOICE NO.
2163	4332
2164	4326
2165	4327
2166	4330
2167	4331
2168	4328
2169	4329
2170	4333
2171	4335
2172	4334

The August and September sales journals have the following information included:

SALES JOURNAL — AUGUST 1998

DAY OF MONTH	SALES INVOICE NO.	AMOUNT OF SALE
30	4326	$ 726.11
30	4329	1,914.30
31	4327	419.83
31	4328	620.22
31	4330	47.74

SALES JOURNAL — SEPTEMBER 1998

DAY OF MONTH	SALES INVOICE NO.	AMOUNT OF SALE
1	4332	$2,641.31
1	4331	106.39
1	4333	852.06
2	4335	1,250.50
2	4334	646.58

Required

a. What are the generally accepted accounting principles requirements for a correct sales cutoff?

b. Which sales invoices, if any, are recorded in the wrong accounting period, assuming a periodic inventory? Prepare an adjusting entry to correct the financial statement for the year ended August 31, 1998.

c. Assume that the shipping clerk accidentally wrote August 31 on shipping documents 2168 through 2172. Explain how that would affect the correctness of the financial statements. How would you, as an auditor, discover that error?

d. Describe, in general terms, the audit procedures you would follow in making sure cutoff for sales is accurate at the balance sheet date.

e. Identify internal controls that would reduce the likelihood of cutoff errors. How would you test each control?

14-25 John Gossling, a public accountant, is examining the financial statements of a manufacturing company with a significant amount of trade accounts receivable. Gossling is satisfied that the accounts are properly summarized and classified and that allocations, reclassifications, and valuations are made in accordance with generally accepted accounting principles. He is planning to use accounts receivable confirmation requests to satisfy the third examination standard as to trade accounts receivable.

Required

a. Identify and describe the two forms of accounts receivable confirmation requests, and indicate the factors Gossling will consider in determining when to use each.

b. Assume that Gossling has received a satisfactory response to the confirmation requests. Describe how he could evaluate collectibility of the trade accounts receivable.

c. What are the implications to a public accountant if, during his or her examination of accounts receivable, some of a client's trade customers do not respond to the request for positive confirmation of their accounts?

d. What auditing steps should a public accountant perform if there is no response to a second request for a positive confirmation?

(AICPA adapted)

14-26 You have been assigned to the confirmation of aged accounts receivable for the Blank Paper Company Ltd. audit. You have tested the trial balance and selected the accounts for confirming. Before the confirmation requests are mailed, the controller asks to look at the accounts you intend to confirm to determine whether she will permit you to send them.

She reviews the list and informs you that she does not want you to confirm six of the accounts on your list. Two of them have credit balances, one has a zero balance, two of the other three have a fairly small balance, and the remaining balance is highly material. The reason she gives is that she feels the confirmations will upset these customers because

"they are kind of hard to get along with." She does not want the credit balances confirmed because it may encourage the customers to ask for a refund.

In addition, the controller asks you to send an additional 20 confirmations to customers she has listed for you. She does this as a means of credit collection for "those stupid idiots who won't know the difference between a public accountant and a credit collection agency."

Required

a. Is it acceptable for the controller to review the list of accounts you intend to confirm? Discuss.

b. Discuss the appropriateness of sending the 20 additional confirmations to the customers.

c. Assuming the auditor complies with all the controller's requests, what is the effect on the auditor's opinion?

14-27 The following are the entire outstanding accounts receivable for Jake's Bookbinding Company Ltd. The population is smaller than would ordinarily be the case for statistical sampling, but an entire population is useful to show how to select samples by monetary unit sampling.

POPULATION ITEM	RECORDED AMOUNT	POPULATION ITEM	RECORDED AMOUNT
1	$1,410	21	$4,865
2	9,130	22	770
3	660	23	2,305
4	3,355	24	2,665
5	5,725	25	1,000
6	8,210	26	6,225
7	580	27	3,675
8	44,110	28	6,250
9	825	29	1,890
10	1,155	30	27,705
11	2,270	31	935
12	50	32	5,595
13	5,785	33	930
14	940	34	4,045
15	1,820	35	9,480
16	3,380	36	360
17	530	37	1,145
18	955	38	6,400
19	4,490	39	100
20	17,140	40	8,435
			$207,295

Required

a. Select a random sample of 10 items using systematic MUS sampling. Use a starting point of 1857. Identify the physical units selected. Explain how you determined the interval to be used.

b. Which sample items will always be included in the systematic MUS sample regardless of the starting point? Will that also be true of random MUS sampling?

c. Which method is preferable in terms of ease of selection in this case?

d. Why would an auditor use MUS?

ACCOUNTS RECEIVABLE PER RECORDS		ACCOUNTS RECEIVABLE PER CONFIRMATION	FOLLOW-UP COMMENTS BY AUDITOR
1.	$2,728.00	$2,498.00	Pricing errors on two invoices.
2.	$5,125.00	-0-	Customer mailed cheque 269; company received cheque 3/10.
3.	$3,890.00	$1,190.00	Merchandise returned 30/9 and counted in inventory; credit was issued 6/10.
4.	$ 791.00	$ 815.00	Footing error on an invoice.
5.	$ 548.00	$1,037.00	Goods were shipped 28/9, sale was recorded on 6/10.
6.	$3,115.00	$3,190.00	Pricing error on a credit memorandum.
7.	$1,540.00	-0-	Goods were shipped on 29/9; customer received goods 3/10; sale was recorded on 30/9.

14-28 In the audit of Price Seed Company Ltd. for the year ended September 30, the auditor set a tolerable misstatement of $50,000 at an ARIA of 10 percent. An MUS sample of 100 was selected from an accounts receivable population that had a recorded balance of $1,975,000. The table above shows the differences uncovered in the confirmation.

Required

a. Calculate the upper and lower misstatement bounds on the basis of the client misstatements in the sample.

b. Is the population acceptable as stated? If not, what options are available to the auditor at this point? Which option should the auditor select? Explain.

14-29 You intend to use MUS as a part of the audit of several accounts for Roynpower Manufacturing Inc. You have done the audit for the past several years, and there has rarely been an adjusting entry of any kind. Your audit tests of all tests of controls for the transactions cycles were completed at an interim date, and control risk has been assessed as low. You therefore decide to use an ARIA of 10 percent for all tests of details of balances.

You intend to use MUS in the audit of the three most material asset balance sheet account balances: accounts receivable, inventory, and marketable securities. You feel justified in using the same ARIA for each audit area because of the low assessed control risk.

The recorded balances and related information for the three accounts are as follows:

	RECORDED VALUE
Accounts receivable	$ 3,600,000
Inventory	4,800,000
Marketable securities	1,600,000
	$10,000,000

Net earnings before taxes for Roynpower are $2,000,000. You decide that materiality will be $100,000 for the client.

The audit approach will be to determine the total sample size needed for all three accounts. A sample will be selected from all $10 million, and the appropriate testing for a sample item will depend on whether the item is a receivable, inventory, or marketable security. The audit conclusions will pertain to the entire $10 million, and no conclusion will be made about the three individual accounts unless significant misstatements are found in the sample.

Required

a. Evaluate the audit approach of testing all three account balances in one sample.

b. Calculate the required sample size for all three accounts.

c. Calculate the required sample size for each of the three accounts assuming you decide that the tolerable misstatement in each account is $100,000. (Recall that tolerable misstatement equals preliminary judgment about materiality for MUS.)

d. Assume that you select the random sample using a seven-digit random number table. How would you identify which sample item in the population to audit for the number 4,627,871? What audit procedures would be performed?

e. Assume you select a sample of 100 sample items for testing and you find one misstatement in inventory. The recorded value is $987.12, and the audit value is $887.12. Calculate the misstatement bounds for the three combined accounts, and reach appropriate audit conclusions.

14-30 You are doing the audit of Peckinpah Tire and Parts Inc., a wholesale auto parts company. You have decided to use MUS for the audit of accounts receivable and inventory. The following are the recorded balances:

Accounts receivable	$12,000,000
Inventory	$23,000,000

You have already made the following judgments:

Preliminary judgment about materiality	$800,000
Acceptable audit risk	5%
Inherent risk:	
Accounts receivable	80%
Inventory	100%
Assessed control risk:	
Accounts receivable	50%
Inventory	80%

Substantive analytical procedures have been planned for inventory but not for accounts receivable. The analytical procedures for inventory are expected to have a 60 percent chance of detecting a material misstatement should one exist.

You have concluded that it would be difficult to alter sample size for accounts receivable confirmation once confirmations are sent and replies are received. However, inventory tests could be re-opened without great difficulty.

After discussions with the client, you believe that the accounts are in about the same condition this year as they were last year. Last year no misstatements were found in the confirmation of accounts receivable. Inventory tests revealed an overstatement amount of about 1 percent.

Required

a. Plan the sample size for the confirmation of accounts receivable using MUS.

b. Plan the sample size for the test of pricing of inventories using MUS.

c. Plan the combined sample size for both the confirmation of accounts receivable and the price tests of inventory using MUS.

d. Using an electronic spreadsheet, generate a list of random dollars in generation order and in ascending order for the sample of accounts receivable items determined in part (a). (Instructor's option)

14-31 You have been assigned to the first examination of the accounts of the North Battleford Corp. for the year ending March 31, 1999. Accounts receivable were confirmed on December 31, 1998, and at that date the receivables consisted of approximately two hundred accounts with balances totalling $956,750. Seventy-five of these accounts with balances totalling $650,725 were selected for confirmation. All but 20 of the confirmation requests have been returned; 30 were signed without comments, 14 had minor differences which have been cleared satisfactorily, while 11 confirmations had the following comments:

1. We are sorry but we cannot answer your request for confirmation of our account as Duck Lake Inc. uses an accounts payable voucher system.

2. The balance of $1,050 was paid on December 13, 1998.

3. The balance of $7,750 was paid on January 5, 1999.

4. The balance noted above has been paid.

5. We do not owe you anything at December 31, 1998, as the goods, represented by your invoice dated December 30, 1998, number 25,050, in the amount of $11,550, were received on January 5, 1999, on FOB destination terms.

6. An advance payment of $2,500 made by us in November 1998 should cover the two invoices totalling $1,350 shown on the statement attached.

7. We never received these goods.

8. We are contesting the propriety of this $12,525 charge. We think the charge is excessive.

9. Amount okay. As the goods have been shipped to us on consignment, we will remit payment upon selling the goods.

10. The $10,000, representing a deposit under a lease, will be applied against the rent due to us during 2000, the last year of the lease.

11. Your credit memo dated December 5, 1998, in the amount of $440 cancels the balance above.

Required

What steps would you take to clear satisfactorily each of the above 11 comments?

(AICPA adapted)

14-32 You have examined the financial statements of Boiestown Limited for several years. Internal control for accounts receivable is very satisfactory. Boiestown Limited operates on a calendar-year basis. An interim audit, which included confirmation of the accounts receivable, was performed on August 31 and indicated that the accounting for cash, sales, sales returns and allowances, and receivables was reliable.

The company's sales are principally to manufacturing concerns. There are about 1,500 active trade accounts receivable of which about 35 percent represent 65 percent of the total dollar amount. The accounts receivable are maintained alphabetically in a master file of accounts receivable.

Shipping document data are entered into a computerized system that produces a sales invoice and sales journal, and updates the open item transaction files and the customer master file.

All cash receipts are in the form of customers' cheques. Information for cash receipts is obtained from the remittance advice portions of the customers' cheques. The person who enters the receipts into the computer system compares the remittance advices with the list of cheques, which was prepared by another person when the mail was received. As for sales, a cash receipts journal, an updated open item transaction file, and a customer master file are prepared when the cash receipts information is entered.

Summary totals are produced monthly by the system for updating the general ledger file accounts such as cash, sales, and accounts receivable. An aged accounts receivable trial balance is prepared monthly.

Required

Prepare the additional audit procedures necessary for testing the balances in the sales and collection cycle. (Ignore bad debts and allowance for uncollectible accounts.)

(AICPA adapted)

14-33 In the confirmation of accounts receivable for the Millbank Service Company Inc., 85 positive and no negative confirmations were mailed to customers. This represents 35 percent of the dollar balance of the total accounts receivable. For all nonresponses, second requests were sent, but 10 customers still did not respond. The decision was made to perform alternative procedures on the 10 unanswered confirmation requests. An assistant is asked to conduct the alternative procedures and report to the senior auditor after completing his tests on two accounts. He prepared the following information for the working papers:

1. Confirmation request no. 9
   Customer name: Jolene Milling Co.
   Balance: $3,621 at December 31, 1998
   Subsequent cash receipts per the accounts receivable
   open item file:
   January 15, 1999 — $1,837
   January 29, 1999 — $1,263
   February 6, 1999 — $1,429

2. Confirmation request no. 26
   Customer name: Rosenthal Repair Service Ltd.
   Balance: $2,500 at December 31, 1998
   Subsequent cash receipts per the accounts
   receivable open item file:

February 9, 1999 — $500
Sales invoices per the accounts receivable open item
file (I examined the duplicate invoice):
September 1, 1998 — $4,200

Required

a. If you were called upon to evaluate the adequacy of the sample size, the type of confirmation used, and the percentage of accounts confirmed, what additional information would you need?

b. Discuss the need to send second requests and perform alternative procedures for nonresponses.

c. Evaluate the adequacy of the alternative procedures used for verifying the two nonresponses.

14-34   During his interim audit visit, Charles Ai determined that one of the subsidiary companies of Mega Big Limited had experienced some very serious problems with respect to the credit management and collection of trade accounts receivable. During the first six months of the year, the accounts receivable of this subsidiary had almost doubled, the number of days' sales in accounts receivable had increased from 39 days to 64 days, and bad-debt expense had risen sharply. Charles recommended that these problems be investigated immediately.

The board shared Charles' concern and agreed that corrective measures be taken at the earliest opportunity. It believes that this problem has arisen, in part, because this subsidiary (like others in the group) operates autonomously, maintains its own accounting records, and establishes its own policies in such areas as credit and collections. The parent company's controller is in the process of organizing an investigation of these collection problems, but in view of the seriousness of the situation and the apparent need for standardized policies and procedures for all subsidiary companies, the board of directors has requested that Charles assist the controller in this investigation. The board specifically requested that Charles prepare an outline of the steps that should be taken to investigate the nature and causes of the credit and collection problems, assist the controller in conducting the investigation, and prepare a full report to the board at the conclusion of the investigation.

Required

Prepare an outline of the steps that should be taken to investigate the nature and causes of the credit and collection problems. (Do *not* consider the possibility of fraud.)

CASES

14-35   You are auditing the sales and collection cycle for Maritime Cabinets Limited, a small manufacturer of high-quality furniture in Nova Scotia. Maritime makes cabinets to order for local contractors and home renovators, and some stock items for local furniture stores and hardware stores. The company has a reputation for excellent cabinet work and weak record keeping. The cabinet-makers have a reputation of doing all aspects of their job well, but due to a shortage of accounting personnel, there is no time for internal verification or careful performance. In previous years, your public accounting firm has found quite a few errors in billings, collections, and accounts receivable. As was mentioned, most of the manufacturing is to order so the two largest assets are accounts receivable and property, plant, and equipment.

The company has several large loans payable to a local bank, and the bank has told management that it is reluctant to extend more credit, especially considering the declining market for high-quality furniture. In the past, loans from the owners have made up the cash deficits, but in the past year, the owners simply have not been able to raise any more money personally.

In previous years, the response you have had to confirmation requests has been frustrating at best. The response rate has been extremely low, and those who did respond did not know the purpose of the confirmation or their correct outstanding balance. You have had the same experience in confirming receivables at other businesses in the area.

You conclude that control over cash is excellent and that the likelihood of fraud is extremely small. You are less confident about unintentional errors in billing and recording of sales, cash receipts, accounts receivable, and bad debts.

Required

a. Identify major factors affecting acceptable audit risk in this audit.

b. What inherent risks are you concerned about?

c. In this audit of the sales and collection cycle, which types of tests are you likely to emphasize?

d. For each of the following, explain whether you plan to emphasize the test and give reasons.
   (1) Tests of controls
   (2) Analytical procedures
   (3) Test of details of balances

14-36   Loofa Limited is a dry goods chain selling mainly staples: practical clothing for the family, work clothes, shoes, notions, piece goods, and a relatively small amount of housewares. Its 170 stores are distributed across the country. Ten years ago, the president authorized the introduction of a credit card system, and within 2 years the company had issued 300,000 credit cards. In 1999, some 450,000 credit cards were in circulation with about 430,000 showing monthly activity. Seventy percent of the company's sales are made on credit, with some 75 percent of the credit sales made to company credit card holders and the other credit sales being made to holders of other credit cards.

The credit card system is one of several computerized systems processed on the company's computer. Relevant procedures for the computerized credit card system are as follows:

1. There are 140 stores located in areas other than the head office location. All credit card purchases are stored

locally in the point of sales systems and then transmitted at night in a batch to head office, along with a header record that includes the number of transactions and a control total. The control totals and record counts are automatically verified by the head office computer system before the transactions are used to update individual customer records.

2. Cyclical billing is done at head office. Credit card holders have been divided into groups, the size of the group having been determined by dividing the number of customers (credit cards) by the number of working days in the month. Each group is billed once a month.

3. Remittances received by mail or in person at head office, write-offs, and other adjustments including service charges on overdue accounts are processed at head office.

4. The credit department at head office is responsible for the issue of credit cards and for a weekly advice to all stores of cards that have been inactive for 90 days and of delinquent credit cards. Credit cards are delinquent as soon as:
   (i) the customer exceeds his or her credit limit;
   (ii) the customer has made no payments for 60 days since the last billing;

(iii) the credit card is reported stolen; or
(iv) the customer has given notice of cancellation.

In addition to the above information, the auditor finds the following in the accounts:

Accounts receivable — credit cards	$8,218,374 Debit
Allowance for doubtful accounts (manually controlled)	1,221,000 Credit

During the discussion of the computerized system, the data processing manager indicated that he could have one of his programmers extract information from the credit card data files (i.e., customer master, transaction history, or open item transactions) according to the auditor's specifications.

Required

a. As auditor, assuming you accept the data processing manager's offer, describe with reasons the information you would ask to have extracted from the client data files.

b. How would you ensure that no credit card data would be excluded from the query programs prepared by the client programmer?

(CICA adapted)

INTEGRATED CASE APPLICATION

ABC AUDIT — PART IV

Parts I (pp. 306–308), II (p. 424), and III (pp. 424–425) of this case study dealt with obtaining an understanding of internal control and assessing control risk for transactions affecting accounts payable of ABC Ltd. In Part IV, we begin the audit of the accounts payable balance itself by addressing analytical procedures.

Assume that your understanding of internal control over purchases and cash disbursements and the related tests of controls supports an assessment of the control risk as low. Assume also that analytical procedures support the overall reasonableness of the balance. Accounts payable at December 31, 1998, are included in Exhibit I (page 499).

Required

a. List those relationships, ratios, and trends that you believe will provide useful information about the overall reasonableness of accounts payable.

b. Prepare an audit program in a design format for tests of details of balances for accounts payable. Before preparing the audit program, you should review the Hillsburg Hardware Ltd. Case Illustration starting on page 478. You should prepare a matrix similar to the one in Figure 14-8 (page 482) for accounts payable. Assume that assessed control risk is low for all transaction-related audit objectives and that analytical procedures results were satisfactory for those balance-related audit objectives

where analytical procedures are relevant. The design format audit program should include audit procedures for each audit objective.

c. Prepare an audit program for accounts payable in a performance format, using the audit procedures for part (b).

d. Suppose for requirement (b) that (1) assessed control risk had been high rather than low for each transaction-related audit objective, (2) inherent risk had been high for each balance-related audit objective, and (3) analytical procedures had indicated a high potential for misstatements. What would the effect have been on the audit procedures and sample sizes for part (b)?

e. Exhibit II (pages 500 and 501) presents six replies to the request for information from 20 vendors specified in Exhibit III (page 502). These are the replies for which follow-up indicates a difference between the vendor's balance and the company's records. The auditor's follow-up findings are indicated on each reply. Calculate the estimated misstatement in accounts payable based on the misstatements in accounts payable confirmations and other relevant information provided in this case. Be sure to consider likely misstatements in accounts payable not confirmed and sampling error. Prepare a spreadsheet similar to the one illustrated in Exhibit IV on page 503 to aid in your analysis. The exception for Fiberchem is analyzed as an illustration. Assume that ABC took a complete physical inventory at December 31, 1998, and the auditor concluded that recorded inventory reflected all inventory on hand at the balance sheet date.

Use a computer with appropriate software to prepare this spreadsheet and analysis. (Instructor's option)

f. Based on the confirmation responses and your analysis in part (e), what are your conclusions about the fairness of the recorded balance in accounts payable for ABC Ltd. and your assessments of control risk as low for all transaction-related objectives?

EXHIBIT I

ABC Ltd. Trial Balance of Trade Accounts Payable December 31, 1998

Vendor	Amount	Vendor	Amount
Advent Sign Mfg. Co. Ltd.	$2,500.00	M & A Milling Ltd.	4,662.00
Alder Insurance Co.	660.00	Maritime Power	3,698.15
Bauer and Adamson	86.00	Midatlantic Gas Corp.	2,442.10
Bleyl & Sons Ltd.	1,500.00	Monsanto Chemical Canada Ltd.	14,622.15
Can-Amer Computing Service	1,211.00	Nielsen Enterprises	437.56
Central Steel, Inc.	8,753.00	Norris Industries, Inc.	9,120.00
Chelsea Development Corp.	1,800.00	Pare Tile Corp.	320.00
Commercial Supply Ltd.	3,250.00	Permaloy Manufacturing	3,290.00
Country Electric Ltd.	980.00	Petro-Canada	11,480.00
Diamond Janitorial Service	750.00	Polein Drill and Bit Ltd.	2,870.16
Dictaphone Corp.	675.00	Propec Inc.	510.00
Douglas Equipment Ltd.	6,425.00	Rayno Sales and Service	1,917.80
Ellison, Robt. & Assoc.	346.10	Reames Construction, Inc.	4,500.00
FMC Corp.	15,819.00	Remington Supply Co. Ltd.	9,842.10
Fiberchem Inc.	6,315.80	Ritter Engineering Corp.	1,200.00
Fuller Travel	943.00	Roberts Bros. Service	189.73
GAFCO, Inc.	5,750.00	S & S Truck Painting	819.00
Glade Specialties	1,000.00	Sanders, Geo. A. & Co.	346.00
Granger Supply Corp.	4,250.00	Semco, Inc.	50.20
Hesco Services	719.62	Shell Oil	12,816.27
Innes, Brush & Co. CAs	1,500.00	Stationery Supply Ltd.	619.12
J & L Plastics Corp.	1,412.00	Thermal Tape Co. Ltd.	123.00
Judkins Co. Ltd.	2,500.00	Todd Machinery, Inc.	6,888.12
Kazco. Mfg. Corp.	1,627.30	Valco Sales Ltd.	1,429.00
Kedman Company	19.27	Vermax Corp.	284.00
Koch Plumbing Contractors	2,750.00	Waco Electronics, Inc.	126.33
Kohler Products Inc.	10,483.23	Western Maritimes Supply Ltd.	2,369.62
Lakeshore Inc.	1,850.00	Williams Controls, Inc.	1,915.00
Landscape Services Ltd.	420.00	Xerox Canada Inc.	3,250.00
Lundberg Coatings, Inc.	2,733.10	Yates Supply Co.	919.70
		Total	$192,085.53

Other related information:

• The vendors with the greatest volume of transactions during the year are:

Central Steel, Inc.	Monsanto Chemical Canada Ltd.
Commercial Supply Ltd.	Norris Industries, Inc.
FMC Corp.	Petro-Canada
Fiberchem Inc.	Remington Supply Co. Ltd.
GAFCO, Inc.	Shell Oil

EXHIBIT II
Replies to Requests for
Information

STATEMENT FROM ADVENT SIGN MFG. CO. LTD.

ABC Ltd.
Halifax, NS

Amounts Due as of December 31, 1998:

First progress billing per contract	$2,500,00(1)
Second progress billing per contract	1,500.00(2)
Total due	$4,000.00

Auditor's Notes:

(1) Agrees with accounts payable listing.

(2) Progress payment due as of December 31, 1998, per contract for construction of new custom electric sign. Sign installed on January 15, 1999.

STATEMENT FROM FIBERCHEM INC.

ABC Ltd.
Halifax, NS

Amounts Due as of December 31, 1998:

INVOICE NO.	DATE	AMOUNT	BALANCE DUE
8312	22-11-98	$2,217.92	$2,217.92
8469	02-12-98	2,540.11	4,758.03
8819	18-12-98	1,557.77	6,315.80(1)
9002	30-12-98	2,403.42(2)	8,719.22

Auditor's Notes:

(1) Agrees with accounts payable listing.

(2) Goods received December 31, 1998. Due to New Year's Eve shutdown, recorded on January 2, 1999.

STATEMENT FROM FULLER TRAVEL

ABC Ltd.
Halifax, NS

Amounts Due as of December 31, 1998:

TICKET NO.	DATE	AMOUNT	BALANCE DUE
843 601 102	04-12-98	$280.00(2)	$280.00
843 601 819	12-12-98	280.00(2)	560.00
843 602 222	21-12-98	383.00(1)	943.00
843 602 919	26-12-98	383.00(2)	1,326.00

Auditor's Notes:

(1) Ticket not used and returned for credit. Credit given on January 1999 statement.

(2) The total of these items of $943.00 agrees with accounts payable listing.

EXHIBIT II
(Continued)

STATEMENT FROM NORRIS INDUSTRIES, INC.

ABC Ltd.
Halifax, NS

Amounts Due as of December 31, 1998:

INVOICE NO.	DATE	AMOUNT	BALANCE DUE
14896	27-12-98	$9,120.00	$9,120.00(1)
15111	27-12-98	4,300.00(2)	13,420.00

Auditor's Notes:

(1) Agrees with accounts payable listing.

(2) Goods shipped FOB Norris Industries' plant on December 21, 1998, arrived at ABC Ltd. on January 4, 1999.

STATEMENT FROM PETRO-CANADA

ABC Ltd.
Halifax, NS

Amounts Due as of December 31, 1998:

INVOICE NO.	DATE	AMOUNT	BALANCE DUE
DX10037	02-12-98	$2,870.00	$2,870.00
DX11926	09-12-98	2,870.00	5,740.00
DX12619	16-12-98	2,870.00	8,610.00
DX14777	23-12-98	2,870.00	11,480.00(1)
DX16908	30-12-98	2,870.00(2)	14,350.00

Auditor's Notes:

(1) Agrees with accounts payable listing.

(2) Goods shipped FOB ABC Ltd. Arrived on January 3, 1999.

STATEMENT FROM REMINGTON SUPPLY CO. LTD.

ABC Ltd.
Halifax, NS

Amounts Due as of December 31, 1998:

INVOICE NO.	DATE	AMOUNT	BALANCE DUE
141702	11-11-98	$3,712.09(2)	$3,712.09
142619	19-11-98	1,984.80(1)	5,696.89
142811	04-12-98	2,320.00(2)	8,016.89
143600	21-12-98	3,810.01(2)	11,826.90
143918	26-12-98	3,707.00(3)	15,533.90

Auditor's Notes:

(1) Paid by ABC Ltd. on December 28, 1998. Payment in transit at year end.

(2) The total of these items of $9,842.10 agrees with accounts payable listing.

(3) Goods shipped FOB Remington Supply on December 26, 1998, arrived at ABC Ltd. on January 3, 1999.

EXHIBIT III

ABC Ltd. Sample of
Accounts Payable
Selection for
Confirmation
December 31, 1998

HIGH-VOLUME ITEMS

1.	Central Steel, Inc.	$ 8,753.00
2.	Commercial Supply Ltd.	3,250.00
3.	FMC Corp.	15,819.00
4.	Fiberchem Inc.	6,315.80
5.	GAFCO, Inc.	5,750.00
6.	Monsanto Chemical Canada Ltd.	14,622.15
7.	Norris Industries, Inc.	9,120.00
8.	Petro-Canada	11,480.00
9.	Remington Supply Co. Ltd.	9,842.10
10.	Shell Oil	12,816.27

OTHER MATERIAL ITEMS

11.	Kohler Products Inc.	10,483.23

RANDOM SAMPLE OF ADDITIONAL ITEMS

12.	Advent Sign Mfg. Co. Ltd.	2,500.00
13.	Country Electric Ltd.	980.00
14.	Fuller Travel	943.00
15.	J & L Plastics Corp.	1,412.00
16.	M & A Milling Ltd.	4,662.00
17.	Permaloy Manufacturing	3,290.00
18.	S & S Truck Painting	819.00
19.	Todd Machinery, Inc.	6,888.12
20.	Western Maritime Supply Ltd.	2,369.62
	TOTAL TESTED	$132,115.29

EXHIBIT IV

ABC Ltd. Analysis of Trade Accounts Payable December 31, 1998

VENDOR	BALANCE PER BOOKS	AMOUNT CONFIRMED BY VENDOR	DIFFERENCE: BOOKS OVER (UNDER) AMOUNT CONFIRMED	TIMING DIFFERENCE: NO MISSTATEMENT	MISSTATEMENT IN ACCOUNTS PAYABLE DR (CR)	MISSTATEMENT IN RELATED ACCOUNTS		BRIEF EXPLANATION
						Balance Sheet Misstatement DR (CR)	Income Statement Misstatement DR (CR)	
Fiberchem	6,315.80	8,719.22	(2,403.42)		(2,403.42)		2,403.42	Unrecorded A/P: Dr Purchases Cr A/P

15

AUDIT OF THE PAYROLL AND PERSONNEL CYCLE

THE STAFF AUDITOR MUST NEVER "SIMPLY FOLLOW ORDERS"

Leslie Scott graduated with a Masters of Accountancy degree from a major university and was enthusiastically recruited by several large CA firms. She joined the audit staff of the firm she liked best and was assigned to some of her office's better audit engagements. During her first "busy season," she was working on the audit of Sysco, Inc., a software development company. Because it was the busy season, the engagement team was working 60 to 70 hours per week.

Her immediate supervisor on the Sysco audit was Bob Stith. Bob had been with the firm three years longer than Leslie, and worked on the Sysco audit the previous year. He was supervising Leslie's work on capitalized software development costs. In preparing herself, Leslie had read *CICA Handbook* Section 3450 ("Research and Development Costs") and had a good understanding of the accounting rules concerning the capitalization of such costs. She understood, for example, that costs could not be capitalized until after technological feasibility was established either through detail program design or product design and the completion of a working model, confirmed by testing.

Bob Stith drafted an audit program for capitalized software development costs. The steps were fairly general, but Bob added several oral instructions. He told Leslie to verify the payroll costs which were a significant part of the development cost and to talk to Jack Smart, Sysco's controller, about whether the projects with capitalized costs had reached the technological feasibility stage. Leslie tested the payroll costs and found no misstatements. She also made inquiries of Smart and was told that the appropriate stage was reached. Leslie documented Smart's representation in the working papers and went on to the next area assigned to her.

Later, Leslie began to have second thoughts. She understood that management's representations were a weak form of audit evidence, and she was concerned about whether Jack Smart was the most knowledgeable person about the technical status of software projects. To resolve her concerns, she decided to talk to the responsible software engineers about one of the projects to confirm Smart's representations. She intended to clear this with Stith, but he was at another client's office that morning, so she proceeded on her own initiative. The engineer she talked to on the first project told her that he was almost finished with a working model but hadn't tested it yet. She decided to inquire about another project and discovered the same thing. Leslie documented these findings on a working paper and planned to discuss the situation with Stith as soon as he returned to the job.

When Leslie (somewhat proud of herself) told Stith of her findings and showed him the working paper, he told her the following:

> Listen Leslie, I told you just to talk to Jack. You shouldn't do procedures that you're not instructed to do. I want you to destroy this working paper and don't record the wasted time. We're under a lot of time pressure, and we can't bill Sysco for procedures that aren't necessary. Jack knows what he's talking about. There's nothing wrong with the capitalized software development costs. The fact that Sysco has working products that it's selling indicates that technological feasibility was reached.

Leslie was extremely distressed with this reaction from Stith but followed his instructions. She later talked to the audit partner about the situation during her annual counselling session. He mollified her concerns by pointing out that Stith was an experienced senior and probably had a broader perspective of the situation than she had as the staff assistant. Rather than worry, she should try and learn as much from working with the senior as she could.

The following fall, the OSC conducted an investigation of Sysco and found, among other things, that it had overstated capitalized software development costs. The OSC brought an action against both the management of Sysco and its auditors.

The payroll and personnel cycle involves the employment and payment of all employees, regardless of classification or method of determining compensation. The employees include executives on straight salary plus bonus, office workers on monthly salary with or without overtime, salespeople on a commission basis, and factory and unionized personnel paid on an hourly basis.

The cycle is important for several reasons. First, the salaries, wages, employee benefits (e.g., Canada Pension, employment insurance, health and dental care, etc.), and other employer costs (e.g., workers' compensation) are a major expense in all companies. Second, labour is such an important consideration in the valuation of inventory in manufacturing and construction companies that the improper classification and allocation of labour can result in a material misstatement of net income. Finally, payroll is an area in which large amounts of company resources can be wasted through inefficiency or stolen through fraud.

The Hillsburg Hardware Ltd. trial balance on pages 128–129 in Chapter 5 includes typical general ledger accounts affected by the payroll and personnel cycle. They are identified as payroll and personnel accounts by the letter P in the left column. In larger companies, many general ledger accounts are often affected by payroll. It is common, for example, for large companies to have 50 or more payroll expense accounts. Payroll also affects work-in-process and finished goods inventory accounts for manufacturing companies.

As with the sales and collection cycle, the audit of the payroll and personnel cycle includes obtaining an understanding of internal control, assessment of control risk, tests of controls, analytical procedures, and tests of details of balances. Accordingly, the first part of this chapter deals with the nature of the cycle, including documents and records, its primary functions, and internal controls. The second part includes tests of controls for the cycle. The third part discusses analytical procedures. Finally, the fourth part of the chapter focuses on verification by tests of details of balances of the related liability and expense accounts. These accounts include all salaries and wage expense accounts, employee benefits, and the liability for accrued wages, employee withholdings, employee benefits, and similar items connected with payroll.

There are several important differences between the payroll and personnel cycle and other cycles in a typical audit.

- *There is only one class of transactions for payroll.* Most cycles include at least two classes of transactions. For example, the sales and collection cycle includes both sales and cash receipts transactions and often sales returns and charge-off of uncollectibles. Payroll has only one class because the receipt of services from employees and the payment for those services through payroll occur within a short time period.
- *Transactions are far more significant than related balance sheet accounts.* Payroll-related accounts such as accrued payroll and withheld taxes are usually small compared to the total amount of transactions for the year.
- *Internal controls over payroll are effective for almost all companies, even small ones.* The reasons for effective controls are harsh federal and provincial penalties for errors in withholding and paying payroll taxes, and employee morale problems if employees are not paid or are underpaid.

Because of these three characteristics, auditors typically emphasize tests of controls and analytical procedures in the audit of payroll. Tests of details of balances often take only a few minutes.

The way in which accounting information flows through the various accounts in the payroll and personnel cycle is illustrated by T-accounts in Figure 15-1. In most

FIGURE 15-1

Accounts in the Payroll and Personnel Cycle

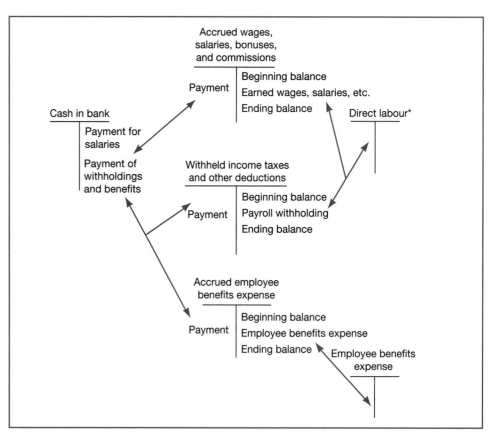

*Separate operating accounts for payroll also normally include officers' salaries and bonuses, office salaries, sales salaries and commissions, and indirect manufacturing labour. These accounts have the same relationship to accrued wages and withheld taxes and other deductions that is shown for direct labour.

Some companies use a payroll service that performs all of the above functions.

systems, the accrued wages and salaries account is used only at the end of an accounting period. Throughout the period, expenses are charged when the employees are actually paid rather than when the labour costs are incurred. The accruals for labour are recorded by adjusting entries at the end of the period for any earned but unpaid labour costs.

FUNCTIONS IN THE CYCLE, RELATED DOCUMENTS AND RECORDS, AND INTERNAL CONTROLS

OBJECTIVE 15-1

Describe the payroll and personnel cycle and the pertinent documents, records, functions, and internal controls.

The payroll and personnel cycle begins with the hiring of personnel and ends with payment to the employees for the services performed and to the government and other institutions for employee withholdings (i.e., income tax, Canada [or Quebec] Pension Plan, employment insurance), and employee benefits (i.e., required contributions by the employer for the Canada [or Quebec] Pension Plan, employment insurance, workers' compensation, hospital insurance plans, provincial health and education taxes; and voluntary or negotiated employer contributions to company pension, medical, or dental plans). In between, the cycle involves obtaining services from the employees consistent with the objectives of the company and accounting for the services in a proper manner.

Column 3 of Table 15-1 identifies the five business functions in a typical payroll and personnel cycle. The table also shows the relationships among the business functions, classes of transactions, accounts, and documents and records. The business functions and related documents are discussed in this section. In addition, there is a discussion of key internal controls to prevent errors or fraud and other irregularities in providing data and to ensure the safety of assets.

PERSONNEL AND EMPLOYMENT

The personnel (or human resources) department provides an independent source for interviewing and hiring qualified personnel. The department is also an independent source of records for the internal verification of wage information.

Personnel records   These are records that include such data as the date of employment, personnel investigations, rates of pay, authorized deductions, performance evaluations, and termination of employment.

Deduction authorization forms   These are forms authorizing payroll deductions, including the number of exemptions for withholding of income taxes (TD-1), Canada

TABLE 15-1

CLASSES OF TRANSACTIONS, ACCOUNTS, BUSINESS FUNCTIONS, AND RELATED DOCUMENTS AND RECORDS FOR THE PAYROLL AND PERSONNEL CYCLE

CLASS OF TRANSACTIONS	ACCOUNTS	BUSINESS FUNCTIONS	DOCUMENTS AND RECORDS
Payroll	Payroll cash All payroll expense accounts All payroll withholding accounts All payroll accrual accounts	Personnel and employment Master file change	Personnel records Deduction authorization form Rate authorization form
		Timekeeping and payroll preparation	Time card Job time ticket Summary payroll report Payroll journal Payroll master file Payroll transaction and history files
		Payment of payroll	Payroll cheque
		Preparation of employee withholdings and benefit remittance forms and payment of taxes	Form T-4 Employee withholdings and benefit remittance forms

Savings Bonds, charitable contributions, union dues, government or private insurance, and pension, medical, or dental plans.

Rate authorization form   This is a form authorizing the rate of pay. The source of the information is a labour contract, authorization by management, or, in the case of officers, authorization from the board of directors.

Internal controls   From an audit point of view, the most important internal controls in personnel involve formal methods of informing the timekeeping and payroll preparation personnel of new employees, the authorization of initial and periodic changes in pay rates, and the termination date of employees no longer working for the company. As a part of these controls, segregation of duties is extremely important. No individual with access to time cards, payroll records, or cheques should also be permitted access to personnel records. A second important control is the adequate investigation of the competence and trustworthiness of new employees.

<table>
<tr><td>

TIMEKEEPING AND PAYROLL PREPARATION

</td><td>

This function is of major importance in the audit of payroll because it directly affects payroll expense for the period. It includes the preparation of time cards or time records by employees; the summarization and calculation of gross pay, deductions, and net pay; the preparation of payroll cheques; and the preparation of payroll records. There must be adequate controls to prevent misstatement in each of these activities.

</td></tr>
</table>

Time card or time record   A time card is a document indicating the time an employee started and stopped working each day and the number of hours the employee worked. For many employees, the time card is prepared automatically by time clocks. Time cards are usually submitted weekly. Alternatively, many companies assign each employee a magnetic stripe card. Each employee "swipes" the card through a time clock, and a computer system tracks the employee's time, producing electronic records and printed reports of the time worked.

Job time ticket   This document indicates particular jobs on which a factory employee worked during a given time period. This form is used only when an employee works on different jobs or in different departments. Use of electronic systems and magnetic stripe cards allows companies to track time spent on specific jobs using computer systems rather than by handling job tickets for each job.

Summary payroll report   This computer-generated document summarizes payroll for a period in various forms. One summary lists the totals debited to each general ledger account for payroll charges. These will equal gross payroll for the period. Another common summary for a manufacturing company lists the totals charged to various jobs in a job cost accounting system. Similarly, commissions earned by each salesperson may be summarized.

Payroll journal   This is a journal for recording payroll cheques. It typically indicates gross pay, withholdings, and net pay. The payroll journal is generated for any time period from the payroll transactions included in the computer files. The totals from the journal are also included in the payroll master file by employee. Journal totals are posted to the general ledger by the computer.

Payroll master file   This file summarizes each payroll transaction by employee and maintains total employee wages paid for the year to date. The master file is updated from payroll computer transaction files. The total of the individual employee earnings in the master file equals the total balance of gross payroll in various general ledger accounts.

Payroll transaction and history files   The transaction record for each employee includes gross pay for each payroll period, deductions from gross pay, net pay, cheque number, and date. This information is used to update the payroll master file.

Internal controls   Adequate control over the time in the time records includes the use of a time clock or other method of making certain that employees are paid for the number of hours they worked. There should also be controls to prevent anyone from checking in for several employees or submitting a fraudulent time record.

The summarization and calculation of the payroll can be controlled by well-defined policies for the payroll department, separation of duties to provide automatic cross-checks, reconciliation of payroll hours with independent production records, and independent internal verification of all important data. For example, payroll policies should require a competent, independent person to recalculate actual hours worked, review for the proper approval of all overtime, and examine time records for erasures and alterations or for unusually long hours. Similarly, batch control totals over hours worked can be calculated when payroll time cards are used and compared to the actual hours entered by the computer. Finally, a printout of wage and withholding rates included in the computer files can be obtained and compared to authorized rates in the personnel files.

Controls over the preparation of payroll cheques include preventing those responsible for preparing the cheques from having access to time records, signing or distributing cheques, or independently verifying payroll output. In addition, the cheques should be prenumbered and verified through independent bank reconciliation procedures.

When manufacturing labour affects inventory valuation, special emphasis should be put on controls to make sure labour is distributed to proper account classifications. There must also be adequate internal controls for recording job time records and other relevant payroll information in the cost accounting records. Independent internal verification of this information is an essential control.

A MOBILE WORK FORCE

In 1996, the AICPA's information technology division published a listing of the top fifteen technologies that may affect public accountants. One of these top technologies is telecommuting — an arrangement under which an employee works at a site other than the employer's central location. It is becoming increasingly common for employees to work at home in order to meet family and other personal obligations.

A company must have unique internal controls in place when employees work off-site. For example, controls should be in place to ensure that (1) recorded payments to off-site employees are for work *actually performed* (existence objective); (2) all payroll transactions involving off-site employees are recorded (completeness); and (3) payroll transactions for off-site employees are recorded on the correct dates (timing).

Source: *Journal of Accountancy*, January 1996, pp. 25–28.

PAYMENT OF PAYROLL

The actual signing and distribution of the cheques must be properly handled to prevent their theft.

Payroll cheque   This is a cheque written to the employee for services performed. The cheque is prepared as a part of the payroll preparation function, but the authorized signature makes the cheque an asset. The amount of the cheque is the gross pay less taxes and other deductions withheld. After the cheque is cashed and returned to the company from the bank, it is referred to as a cancelled cheque. It is now common for paycheques to be directly deposited into employees' bank accounts.

Internal controls   Controls over cheques should include limiting the authorization for signing the cheques to a responsible employee who does not have access to time-keeping or the preparation of the payroll, the distribution of payroll by someone who is not involved in the other payroll functions, and the immediate return of unclaimed cheques for redeposit. If a cheque-signing machine is used to replace a manual signature, the same controls are required; in addition, the cheque-signing machine must be carefully controlled.

Most companies use an *imprest payroll account* to prevent the payment of unauthorized payroll transactions. An imprest payroll account is a separate payroll account in which a small balance is maintained. A cheque for the exact amount of each net payroll is transferred from the general account to the imprest account immediately before the distribution of the payroll. The advantages of an imprest account are that it limits the client's exposure to payroll fraud, allows the delegation of payroll cheque-signing duties, separates routine payroll expenditures from irregular expenditures, and facilitates cash management. It also simplifies the reconciliation of the payroll bank account if it is done at the low point in the payment cycle.

Where employee payments are made directly into their bank account, independent verification of the reports produced by the bank or payroll service provider should occur in lieu of the independent cheque-signature process.

| PREPARATION OF T-4S AND EMPLOYEE WITHHOLDINGS AND BENEFITS REMITTANCE FORMS | The timely preparation and mailing of T-4s and employee withholdings and benefits remittance forms is required by federal and provincial laws. |

T-4 form This form is issued for each employee summarizing the earnings record for the calendar year. The information includes gross pay, income taxes withheld, other withholdings, and taxable benefits such as employer contributions to government or privately sponsored medical plans. The same information is also submitted to Revenue Canada and, if appropriate, provincial tax authorities. This information is prepared from the payroll master file and is normally prepared by computer.

Employee withholdings and benefits remittance forms These forms are submitted to the federal government and to other organizations for the payment of withholdings and employee benefits. The nature and due date of the forms vary depending on the type of withholding or benefit. For example, federal income tax withholding, Canada (or Quebec) Pension Plan withholding, and employment insurance withholding are due monthly, and workers' compensation is due quarterly. These forms are prepared from information in the payroll master file or payroll history file.

Internal controls The most important control in the preparation of these returns is a well-defined set of policies that carefully indicate when each form must be filed. Most computerized payroll systems include the preparation of payroll tax returns using the information on the payroll transaction and master files. The independent verification of the output by a competent individual is an important control to prevent misstatements and potential liability for taxes and penalties.

| TESTS OF CONTROLS | Figure 15-2 shows the methodology for designing tests of controls for the payroll and personnel cycle. It is the same methodology used in Chapter 12 for the sales and collection cycle. |

OBJECTIVE 15-2

Design and perform tests of controls for the payroll and personnel cycle.

Internal control for payroll is normally highly structured and well controlled in order to control cash disbursed and to minimize employee complaints and dissatisfaction. It is common to use electronic data-processing techniques to prepare all journals and payroll cheques. In-house systems are often used, as are outside service centre systems such as banks or financial institutions. Thus, general controls such as control over program changes or program updates and over access to data files must be evaluated. It is usually not difficult to establish good control in the payroll and personnel cycle. For factory and office employees, there are usually a large number of relatively homogeneous, small amount transactions. There are fewer executive payroll transactions, but they are ordinarily consistent in timing, content, and amount. Because of relatively consistent payroll concerns from company to company, high-

FIGURE 15-2

Methodology for Designing Tests of Controls for the Payroll and Personnel Cycle

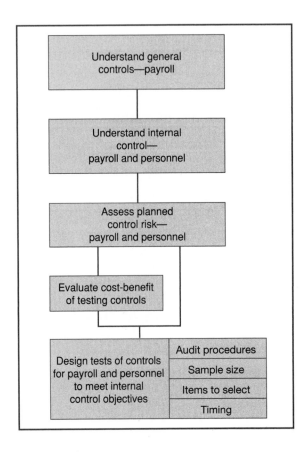

quality computer software packages are available, resulting in good controls over program changes. Consequently, auditors seldom expect to find exceptions in testing payroll transactions. Occasionally control test deviations occur, but most monetary errors or fraud and other irregularities are corrected by internal verification controls or in response to employee complaints.

INTERNAL CONTROLS AND TESTS OF CONTROLS

Tests of controls procedures are the *most important* means of verifying account balances in the payroll and personnel cycle. The emphasis on tests of controls is due to the lack of independent third-party evidence, such as confirmation for verifying accrued wages, withholdings, accrued benefits payable, and other balance sheet accounts. Furthermore, in most audits, the amounts in the balance sheet accounts are small and can be verified with relative ease if the auditor is confident that payroll transactions are correctly entered into the computer and that withholding and benefit remittance forms are properly prepared.

Even though the tests of controls are the most important part of testing payroll, many auditors spend little time in this area. In many audits, there is a minimal risk of material misstatements even though payroll is frequently a significant part of total expenses. There are three reasons for this: employees are likely to complain to management if they are underpaid, all payroll transactions are typically uniform and uncomplicated, and payroll transactions are extensively audited by federal and provincial governments for income tax withholding and for Canada Pension, employment insurance, and health care payments.

Following the same approach used in Chapter 12 for tests of sales and cash receipts transactions, the internal controls and tests of controls for each objective and related monetary misstatements are summarized in Table 15-2. Again, the reader should recognize that

- The internal controls will vary from company to company; therefore, the auditor must identify the controls and weaknesses for each organization.
- Controls the auditor intends to use for reducing assessed control risk must be tested with tests of controls.

TABLE 15-2

SUMMARY OF TRANSACTION-RELATED AUDIT OBJECTIVES, KEY CONTROLS, AND TESTS OF CONTROLS FOR PAYROLL

TRANSACTION-RELATED AUDIT OBJECTIVE	KEY INTERNAL CONTROL	COMMON TESTS OF CONTROLS	
Recorded payroll payments are for work actually performed by existing employees (occurrence).	Time records are approved by supervisors. Time clock is used to record time. Adequate personnel files. Separation of duties between personnel, timekeeping, and payroll disbursements. Only employees existing in the computer data files are accepted when they are entered. Authorization to issue cheques.	Examine the cards or listings for indication of approvals. Examine time records. Review personnel policies. Review organization chart, discuss with employees, and observe duties being performed. Examine printouts of transactions rejected by the computer as having nonexistent employee numbers, or determine whether invalid entries are accepted at point of entry.[†] Examine payroll records for evidence of approval.	Review the payroll journal, general ledger, and payroll earnings records for large or unusual amounts.*[†] Compare cancelled cheques with payroll journal for name, amount, and date. Examine cancelled cheques for proper endorsement. Compare cancelled cheques with personnel records.
Existing payroll transactions are recorded (completeness).	Payroll cheques are prenumbered and accounted for. Independent preparation of bank reconciliation.	Account for a sequence of payroll cheques, or conduct gap testing.[†] Discuss with employees and observe reconciliation.	Reconcile the disbursements in the payroll journal with the disbursements on the payroll bank statement. Prove the bank reconciliation.
Recorded payroll transactions are for the amount of time actually worked and at the proper pay rate; withholdings are properly calculated (accuracy).	Internal verification of calculations and amounts. Batch totals are compared with computer summary reports. Authorization of wage rate, salary, or commission rate. Authorization of withholdings, including amounts for insurance and Canada Savings Bonds.	Examine indication of internal verification. Examine file of batch totals for initials of data control clerk; compare totals to summary reports.[†] Examine payroll records for indication of internal verification. Examine authorizations in personnel file.	Recompute hours worked from time records. Compare pay rates with union contract, approval by board of directors, or other source. Recompute gross pay.[†] Check withholdings by reference to appropriate tables[†] and authorization forms in personnel file. Recompute net pay.[†] Compare cancelled cheque with payroll journal for amount.
Payroll transactions are properly classified (classification).	Adequate chart of accounts. Internal verification of classification.	Review chart of accounts. Examine indication of internal verification; determine that software posts to correct accounts.[†]	Compare classification with chart of accounts or procedures manual. Review time records for employee department and job records for job assignment, and trace through to labour distribution.
Payroll transactions are recorded on the correct dates (timing).	Procedures require recording transactions as soon as possible after the payroll is paid. Internal verification.	Examine the procedures manual and observe when recording takes place. Examine indication of internal verification.	Compare date of recorded cheque in the payroll journal with date on cancelled cheques and time records. Compare date on cheque with date the cheque cleared the bank.
Payroll transactions are properly included in the payroll master file and transaction files; they are properly summarized (posting and summarization).	Internal verification of payroll file contents. Comparison of payroll master file with payroll general ledger totals.	Examine indication of internal verification. Examine initialled summary total reports indicating comparisons have been made.	Test clerical accuracy by footing the payroll journal and tracing postings to general ledger and the payroll master file.[†]

* This analytical procedure can also apply to other objectives, including completeness, valuation, and timeliness.

[†] This control would be tested on many audits by using the computer, possibly with generalized audit software.

- The tests of controls will vary depending on the assessed control risk and the other considerations of the audit, such as the effect of payroll on inventory. Where an outside service organization is used to process payroll, the auditor must consider whether controls at the client are sufficient to ensure that the transaction-related audit objectives are satisfied. If not, the auditor may need to request evidence regarding controls at the service organization, including the existence of a service auditor's report on controls, discussed in Chapter 23.
- The tests of controls are not actually performed in the order given in Table 15-2. The tests of controls are performed in as convenient a manner as possible, using a performance format audit program.

The purposes of the internal controls and the meaning and methodology of audit tests that can be used for payroll should be apparent from the description in Table 15-2. An extended discussion of these procedures is therefore not necessary.

PAYROLL WITHHOLDINGS AND BENEFITS REMITTANCE FORMS AND PAYMENTS

Payroll taxes are an important consideration in many companies, both because the amounts are often material and because the potential liability for failure to file timely forms can be severe.

Preparation of payroll withholdings and benefits remittance forms   As a part of understanding the internal control structure, the auditor should review the preparation of at least one of each type of employee withholding and benefits remittance form that the client is responsible for filing. There is a potential liability for unpaid balances and penalty and interest if the client fails to prepare the forms properly.

A detailed reconciliation of the information on the remittance forms and the payroll records may be necessary when the auditor believes that there is a reasonable chance that the remittance forms may be improperly prepared. Indications of potential errors in the forms include the payment of penalties and interest in the past for improper payments, new personnel in the payroll department who are responsible for the preparation of the remittance forms, the lack of internal verification of the information, and the existence of serious liquidity problems for the client.

Payment of the taxes withheld and other withholdings and benefits on a timely basis   It is desirable to test whether the client has fulfilled its legal obligation in submitting payments for all payroll withholdings and benefits as a part of the payroll tests even though the payments are usually made from general cash disbursements. The withholdings of concern in these tests are such items as taxes, Canada (or Quebec) Pension Plan, employment insurance, union dues, insurance, and Canada Savings Bonds. The auditor must first determine the client's requirements for submitting the payments. The requirements are determined by reference to such sources as tax laws, Canada Pension Plan rules, employment insurance rules, union contracts, and agreements with employees. After the auditor knows the requirements, it is easy to determine whether the client has paid the proper amount on a timely basis by comparing the subsequent payment with the payroll records.

INVENTORY AND FRAUDULENT PAYROLL CONSIDERATIONS

Auditors often extend their procedures considerably in the audit of payroll under the following circumstances: (1) when payroll significantly affects the valuation of inventory and (2) when the auditor is concerned about the possibility of material fraudulent payroll transactions.

Relationship between payroll and inventory valuation   In audits in which payroll is a significant portion of inventory, a frequent occurrence for manufacturing and construction companies, the improper account classification of payroll can significantly affect asset valuation for accounts such as work in process, finished goods, or construction in process.

For example, the overhead charged to inventory at the balance sheet date can be overstated if the salaries of administrative personnel are inadvertently or intentionally charged to indirect manufacturing overhead. Similarly, the valuation of inventory is affected if the direct labour cost of individual employees is improperly charged to the wrong job or process. When some jobs are billed on a cost-plus basis, revenue and the valuation of inventory are both affected by charging labour to incorrect jobs.

When labour is a material factor in inventory valuation, there should be special emphasis on testing the internal controls over proper classification of payroll transactions. Consistency from period to period, which is essential for classification, can be tested by reviewing the chart of accounts and procedures manuals. It is also desirable to trace job records or other evidence of an employee's having worked on a particular job or process to the accounting records that affect inventory valuation. For example, if each employee must account for all of his or her time on a weekly basis by allocating individual job numbers, a useful test is to trace the recorded hours of several employees for a week to the related job-cost records to make sure each has been properly recorded. It may also be desirable to trace from the job-cost records to employee summaries as a test for nonexistent payroll charges being included in inventory.

<table>
<tr><td>

**TESTS FOR
NONEXISTENT
PAYROLL**

</td><td>

Although auditors are not primarily responsible for the detection of fraud, they must extend audit procedures when internal controls over payroll are inadequate. There are several ways employees can significantly defraud a company in the payroll area. This discussion is limited to tests for the two most common types — nonexistent employees and fraudulent hours.

The issuance of payroll cheques to individuals who do not work for the company (nonexistent employees) frequently results from the continuance of an employee's remuneration after his or her employment has been terminated. Usually, the person committing this type of defalcation is a payroll clerk, supervisor, fellow employee, or perhaps the former employee. For example, under some systems, a supervisor could clock in daily for an employee and approve the time record at the end of the time period. If the supervisor also distributes paycheques, considerable opportunity for defalcation exists.

Certain procedures can be performed on cancelled cheques as a means of detecting defalcation. A procedure used on payroll audits is comparing the names on cancelled cheques with time cards and other records for authorized signatures and reasonableness of the endorsements. It is also common to scan endorsements on cancelled cheques for unusual or recurring second endorsements as an indication of a possible fraudulent cheque. The examination of cheques that are recorded as voided is also desirable to make sure they have not been fraudulently used. Where employees are paid automatically by bank deposits to the employees' accounts, the auditor can look for duplicated bank account numbers or for common employee addresses.

A test for nonexistent employees is tracing selected transactions recorded in the payroll journal to the personnel department to determine whether the employees were actually employed during the payroll period. The endorsement on the cancelled cheque written out to an employee can be compared with the authorized signature on the employee's withholding authorization forms.

A procedure that tests for proper handling of terminated employees is selecting several files from the personnel records for employees who were terminated in the current year to determine whether each received his or her termination pay in accordance with company policy. Continuing payments to terminated employees is tested by examining the payroll records in the subsequent period to ascertain that the employee is no longer being paid. Naturally, this procedure is not effective if the personnel department is not informed of terminations.

In some cases, where employees are paid by cheque, the auditor may request a surprise payroll payoff. This is a procedure in which each employee must pick up and sign for his or her cheque in the presence of a supervisor and the auditor. Any cheques that have not been claimed must be subject to an extensive investigation to determine whether an unclaimed cheque is fraudulent. Surprise payoff is frequently expensive and in some cases may even cause problems with a labour union, but it may be the only likely means of detecting a defalcation.

</td></tr>
</table>

Fraudulent hours exist when an employee reports more time than was actually worked. Because of the lack of available evidence, it is usually difficult for an auditor to determine whether an employee records more time on his or her time card or time record than was actually worked. One procedure is reconciling the total hours paid according to the payroll records with an independent record of the hours worked, such as those often maintained by production control. Alternatively, it may be possible to observe an employee clocking in more than one time card under a buddy approach. However, it is ordinarily easier for the client to prevent this type of defalcation by adequate controls than for the auditor to detect it.

ANALYSIS OF EXCEPTIONS AND CONCLUSIONS

As mentioned previously, most internal controls for payroll are highly structured and well controlled. It is common to use electronic data-processing techniques. In-house systems are often used, as are outside service centre systems and electronic funds transfers. It is usually not difficult to establish good control in payroll. For factory and office employees, there are usually a large number of relatively homogeneous, small amount transactions. There are fewer executive payroll transactions, but they are ordinarily consistent in timing, content, and amount. Because of relatively consistent payroll concerns from company to company, high-quality computer software packages are available. Consequently, auditors seldom expect to find exceptions in testing payroll transactions. Occasionally control test deviations occur, but most monetary errors are corrected by internal verification controls or in response to employee complaints. There are, however, specific types of errors that give the auditor particular concern in auditing payroll transactions:

- Classification errors in charging labour to inventory and job cost accounts. As previously indicated, these can result in misstated earnings.
- Computational errors when a computerized system is used. Recall that one of the primary characteristics of the computer is processing consistency. If a calculation error is made for one item, it is probably made on every other similar item. As indicated, these errors are rare due to the high quality of most software packages.
- Any errors that indicate possible fraud, particularly relating to the executive payroll.

Generally, the tests of controls performed in the payroll cycle will use *attribute sampling* under a plan that assumes a zero deviation rate. Sampling size should be large enough to give the auditor a reasonable chance of finding at least one deviation if an intolerable number of deviations exists.

If classification errors are found through this procedure, the sample selected for attributes will often then be used to make an estimate of the total monetary error involved. Sample expansion is usually necessary, however, to achieve a precise enough estimate to conclude whether the total error is material in amount.

If a computational error or one indicating possible fraud is found, specific investigation will be required to determine what allowed such an error to occur. Generally, further sampling and estimation are not done; rather, a nonstatistical approach based on the circumstances is taken.

If no exceptions are found, or if those found are not alarming or unexpected, the auditor will conclude that assessed control risk can be reduced as planned, and he or she will proceed with the tests of details of balances of the affected accounts without modification.

ANALYTICAL PROCEDURES

OBJECTIVE 15-3

Design and perform analytical procedures for the payroll and personnel cycle.

The use of analytical procedures is as important in the payroll and personnel cycle as it is in every other cycle. Table 15-3 illustrates analytical procedures for the balance sheet and income statement accounts in the payroll and personnel cycle. Most of the relationships included in Table 15-3 are highly predictable and are therefore useful for uncovering areas in which additional investigation is desirable. The auditor should consider any changes in business policies or business practices when conducting the analytical procedures.

TABLE 15-3

ANALYTICAL
PROCEDURES FOR THE
PAYROLL AND
PERSONNEL CYCLE

ANALYTICAL PROCEDURE	POSSIBLE MISSTATEMENT
Compare payroll expense account balance with previous years (adjusted for pay rate increases and increases in volume).	Misstatement of payroll expense accounts
Compare direct labour as a percentage of sales with previous years.	Misstatement of direct labour
Compare commission expense as a percentage of sales with previous years.	Misstatement of commission expense
Compare payroll benefits expense as a percentage of salaries and wages with previous years (adjusted for changes in the benefits rates)	Misstatement of payroll benefits expense and payroll benefits liability
Compare accrued payroll benefits accounts with previous years.	Misstatement of accrued payroll benefits and payroll benefits expense

TESTS OF DETAILS OF BALANCES FOR LIABILITY AND EXPENSE ACCOUNTS

OBJECTIVE 15-4

Design and perform tests of details for the account balances related to the payroll and personnel cycle.

Figure 15-3 summarizes the methodology for deciding the appropriate tests of details of balances for payroll liability accounts. The methodology is the same as that followed in Chapter 14 for accounts receivable. Normally, however, payroll-related liabilities are less material than accounts receivable; therefore, there is less inherent risk.

The verification of the liability accounts associated with payroll, often termed *accrued payroll expenses*, ordinarily is straightforward if internal controls are operating effectively. When the auditor is satisfied that payroll transactions are being properly recorded in the payroll journal and the related employee withholding and benefits remittance forms are being accurately prepared and promptly paid, the tests of details of balances should not be time-consuming.

The two major objectives in testing payroll-related liabilities are to determine whether (1) accruals in the trial balance are stated at correct amounts (accuracy), and (2) transactions in the payroll and personnel cycle are recorded in the proper period (cutoff). The primary concern in both objectives is to make sure there are no understated or omitted accruals. The major liability accounts in the payroll and personnel cycle are now discussed.

AMOUNTS WITHHELD FROM EMPLOYEES' PAY

Income taxes withheld, but not yet disbursed, can be tested by comparing the balance with the payroll journal, the withholding remittance form prepared in the subsequent period, and the subsequent period cash disbursements. Other withheld items such as the Canada (or Quebec) Pension Plan, employment insurance, union dues, Canada Savings Bonds, and insurance can be verified in the same manner. If internal controls are operating effectively, cutoff and accuracy can easily be tested at the same time by these procedures.

ACCRUED SALARIES AND WAGES

The accrual for salaries and wages arises whenever employees are not paid for the last few days or hours of earned wages until the subsequent period. Salaried personnel usually receive all of their pay except overtime on the last day of the month, but frequently several days of wages for hourly employees are unpaid at the end of the year.

The correct cutoff and valuation of accrued salaries and wages depend on company policy, which should be followed consistently from year to year. Some companies calculate the exact hours of pay that were earned in the current period and paid in the subsequent period, whereas others compute an approximate proportion. For example, if the subsequent payroll results from three days' employment during the

FIGURE 15-3

Methodology for Designing Tests of Details of Balances for Payroll Liabilities

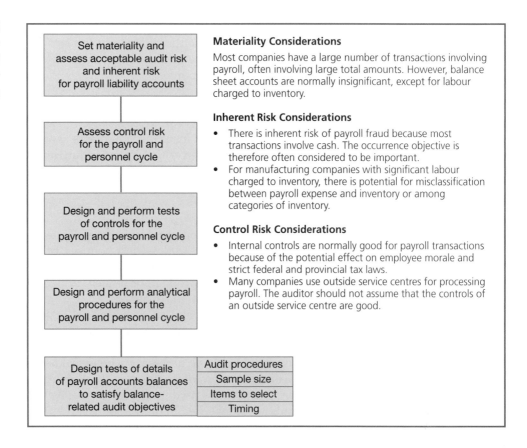

Set materiality and assess acceptable audit risk and inherent risk for payroll liability accounts

Assess control risk for the payroll and personnel cycle

Design and perform tests of controls for the payroll and personnel cycle

Design and perform analytical procedures for the payroll and personnel cycle

Design tests of details of payroll accounts balances to satisfy balance-related audit objectives

| Audit procedures |
| Sample size |
| Items to select |
| Timing |

Materiality Considerations

Most companies have a large number of transactions involving payroll, often involving large total amounts. However, balance sheet accounts are normally insignificant, except for labour charged to inventory.

Inherent Risk Considerations

- There is inherent risk of payroll fraud because most transactions involve cash. The occurrence objective is therefore often considered to be important.
- For manufacturing companies with significant labour charged to inventory, there is potential for misclassification between payroll expense and inventory or among categories of inventory.

Control Risk Considerations

- Internal controls are normally good for payroll transactions because of the potential effect on employee morale and strict federal and provincial tax laws.
- Many companies use outside service centres for processing payroll. The auditor should not assume that the controls of an outside service centre are good.

current year and two days' employment during the subsequent year, the use of 60 percent of the subsequent period's gross pay as the accrual is an example of an approximation.

Once the auditor has determined the company's policy for accruing wages and ensures it is consistent with that of previous years, the appropriate audit procedure to test for cutoff and valuation is evaluating the reasonableness of the method then recalculating the client's accrual. The most likely error of any significance in the balance is the failure to include the proper number of days of earned but unpaid wages.

ACCRUED COMMISSIONS

The same concepts used in verifying accrued salaries and wages are applicable to accrued commissions, but the accrual is often more difficult to verify because companies frequently have several different types of agreements with salespeople and other commissioned employees. For example, some salespeople might be paid a commission every month and earn no salary, while others will get a monthly salary plus a commission paid quarterly. In some cases, the commission varies for different products and may not be paid until several months after the end of the year. In verifying accrued commissions, it is necessary first to determine the nature of the commission agreement and then to test the calculations based on the agreement. It is important to compare the method of accruing commissions with previous years for purposes of consistency. If the amounts are material, it is also common to confirm the amount that is due directly with the employees.

ACCRUED BONUSES

In many companies, the year-end unpaid bonuses to officers and employees are such a major item that the failure to record them would result in a material misstatement. The verification of the recorded accrual can usually be accomplished by comparing it with the amount authorized in the minutes of the board of directors.

ACCRUED VACATION PAY, SICK PAY, OR OTHER BENEFITS

The consistent accrual of these liabilities relative to those of the preceding year is the most important consideration in evaluating the fairness of the amounts. The company policy for recording the liability must first be determined, followed by the recalculation of the recorded amounts.

ACCRUED EMPLOYEE BENEFITS

This account will include the employer's share of Canada (or Quebec) Pension Plan payments and employment insurance payments as well as workers' compensation. The employer's share can be verified by examining remittance forms prepared in the subsequent period to determine the amount that should have been recorded as a liability at the balance sheet date.

TESTS OF DETAILS OF BALANCES FOR EXPENSE ACCOUNTS

Several accounts in the income statement are affected by payroll transactions. The most important are officers' salaries and bonuses, office salaries, sales salaries and commissions, and direct manufacturing labour. There is frequently a further breakdown of costs by division, product, or branch. Fringe benefits such as dental insurance may also be included in the expenses.

There should be relatively little additional testing of the income statement accounts in most audits beyond the analytical procedures, tests of controls, and related tests of liability accounts, which have already been discussed. Extensive additional testing should only be necessary when weaknesses are found in internal control, significant errors are discovered in the liability tests, or major unexplained variances are found in the analytical procedures. Nevertheless, some income statement accounts are often tested in the personnel and payroll cycle. These include officers' compensation, commissions, and total payroll.

Officers' compensation   It is common to verify whether the total compensation of officers is the amount authorized by the board of directors because disclosure of the salaries and other compensation of the top five officers is required by certain provincial securities commissions. Verification of the officers' compensation is also warranted because some individuals may be in a position to pay themselves more than the authorized amount. The usual audit test is to obtain the authorized salary of each officer from the minutes of the board of directors' meetings and compare it with the related earnings record.

Commissions   Commission expense can be verified with relative ease if the commission rate is the same for each type of sale and the necessary sales information is available in the accounting records. The total commission expense can be verified by multiplying the commission rate for each type of sale by the amount of sales in that category. If the calculations are complex, the auditor may decide that these calculations should be tested using generalized audit software or automated audit techniques. If the desired information is not available, it may be necessary to test the annual or monthly commission payments for selected salespeople and trace those to the total commission payments. When the auditor believes it is necessary to perform these tests, they are normally done in conjunction with tests of accrued liabilities.

Employee benefits expense   Employee benefits expense for the year can be tested by first reconciling the total payroll on each employee benefits remittance form with the total payroll for the entire year. Total employee benefits expense can then be recomputed by multiplying the appropriate rate by the payroll. The calculation is frequently time-consuming because the benefits are usually applicable on only a portion of the payroll and the rate may change part way through the year if the taxpayer's financial statements are not on a calendar-year basis. On most audits, the calculation is costly and is unnecessary unless analytical procedures indicate a problem that cannot be resolved through other procedures. When the auditor believes that the test is necessary, it is ordinarily done in conjunction with tests of employee benefits accruals.

Total payroll A closely related test to the one for employee benefits is the reconciliation of total payroll expense in the general ledger with the T-4 Summary that the company must send in to Revenue Canada by the end of February each year. The objectives of the test are to determine whether payroll transactions were charged to a non-payroll account or not recorded in the payroll journal at all. The audit objectives are certainly relevant, but it is questionable whether the procedure is useful in uncovering the type of error for which it was intended. Since the T-4 Summary and the payroll are usually both prepared directly from the payroll master file, the errors, if any, are likely to be in both records. The procedure may be worthwhile in rare situations, but it is usually unnecessary. Tests of controls are a better means of uncovering these two types of errors in most audits.

SUMMARY

Figure 15-4 illustrates the major accounts in the payroll and personnel cycle and the types of audit tests used to audit these accounts. This figure also shows how the audit risk model discussed in Chapter 8 relates to the audit of the payroll and personnel cycle.

FIGURE 15-4

Types of Audit Tests for the Payroll and Personnel Cycle

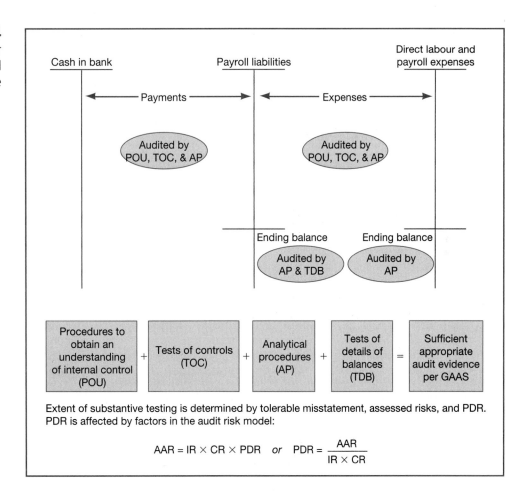

Accrued payroll expenses — the liability accounts associated with payroll including accounts for accrued salaries and wages, accrued commissions, accrued bonuses, accrued benefits, and accrued employee benefits (p. 516).

Employee withholdings and benefits remittance forms — forms that the employer submits to federal and provincial authorities for the payment of withholdings and employee benefits (p. 510).

Imprest payroll account — a bank account to which the exact amount of payroll for the pay period is transferred by cheque from the employer's general cash account (p. 510).

Payroll and personnel cycle — the transaction cycle that begins with the hiring of personnel, includes obtaining and accounting for services from the employees, and ends with payment to the employees for the services per-formed and to the government and other institutions for withheld and accrued employee benefits (p. 505).

Payroll master file — a computer file for recording each pay-roll transaction for each employee and maintaining total employee wages paid and related data for the year to date (p. 508).

Personnel records — records that include such data as the date of employment, personnel investigations, rates of pay, authorized deductions, performance evaluations, and termination of employment (p. 507).

T-4 form — a form issued to each employee summarizing the earnings record for the calendar year (p. 510).

Time card — a document indicating the time that the employee started and stopped working each day and the number of hours worked (p. 508).

15-1 Identify five general ledger accounts that are likely to be affected by the payroll and personnel cycle in most audits.

15-2 Explain the relationship between the payroll and per-sonnel cycle and inventory valuation.

15-3 List five tests of controls that can be performed for the payroll cycle, and state the purpose of each control being tested.

15-4 Explain why the percentage of total audit time in the cycle devoted to performing tests of controls is usually far greater for the payroll and personnel cycle than for the sales and collection cycle.

15-5 Evaluate the following comment by an auditor: "My job is to determine whether the payroll records are fairly stated in accordance with generally accepted accounting principles, not to find out whether the client is following proper hiring and termination procedures. When I conduct an audit of payroll, I keep out of the personnel department and stick to the time cards, journals, and payroll cheques. I don't care whom the client hires and whom it fires, as long as it properly pays the employees it has."

15-6 Distinguish between the following payroll audit pro-cedures and state the purpose of each: (1) Trace a random sample of prenumbered time cards to the related payroll cheques in the payroll register, and compare the hours worked with the hours paid, and (2) trace a random sample of payroll cheques from the payroll register to the related time cards, and compare the hours worked with the hours paid. Which of these two procedures is typically more impor-tant in the audit of payroll? Why?

15-7 In auditing payroll withholding and payroll benefits expense, explain why emphasis should normally be on eval-uating the adequacy of the employee withholding and bene-fits remittance forms preparation procedures rather than on the employee withholding and benefits liability. If the prepa-ration procedures are inadequate, explain the effect that this will have on the remainder of the audit.

15-8 List several analytical procedures for the payroll and personnel cycle, and explain the type of error that might be indicated when there is a significant difference in the com-parison of the current year with previous years' results for each of the tests.

15-9 Explain the circumstances under which an auditor should perform audit tests primarily designed to uncover fraud in the payroll and personnel cycle. List three audit pro-cedures that are primarily for the detection of fraud, and state the type of fraud that the procedure is meant to uncover.

15-10 Distinguish between a payroll master file, a T-4 form, and an employee benefits remittance form. Explain the pur-pose of each.

15-11 List the supporting documents and records that the auditor will examine in a typical payroll audit in which the primary objective is to detect fraud.

15-12 List the five types of authorizations in the payroll and personnel cycle, and state the type of misstatement that is enhanced when each authorization is lacking.

15-13 Explain why it is common to verify total officers' compensation even when the tests of controls results in pay-roll are excellent. What audit procedures can be used to ver-ify officers' compensation?

15-14 Explain what is meant by an "imprest payroll account." What is its purpose as a control over payroll?

15-15 List several audit procedures that the auditor can use to determine whether recorded payroll transactions are recorded at the proper amount.

15-16 Explain how attribute sampling can be used to test the payroll and personnel cycle.

15-17 The following questions concern internal controls in the payroll and personnel cycle. Choose the best response.

a. A factory supervisor at Steblecki Corporation discharged an hourly worker but did *not* notify the payroll department. The supervisor then forged the worker's signature on time cards and work tickets and, when giving out the cheques, diverted the payroll cheques drawn from the discharged worker to his own use. The most effective procedure for preventing this activity is to
   (1) have a paymaster who has *no* other payroll responsibility distribute the payroll cheques.
   (2) have someone other than persons who prepare or distribute the payroll obtain custody of unclaimed payroll cheques.
   (3) require written authorization for all employees added to or removed from the payroll.
   (4) from time to time, rotate persons distributing the payroll.

b. A public accountant reviews Shah Ltd.'s payroll procedures. An example of an internal control weakness is to assign to a department supervisor the responsibility for
   (1) initiating requests for salary adjustments for subordinate employees.
   (2) distributing payroll cheques to subordinate employees.
   (3) reviewing and approving time reports for subordinates.
   (4) interviewing applicants for subordinate positions prior to hiring by the personnel department.

c. From the standpoint of good internal control, distributing payroll cheques to employees is best handled by the
   (1) accounting department.
   (2) personnel department.
   (3) treasurer's department.
   (4) employee's departmental supervisor.

(AICPA adapted)

15-18 The following questions concern audit testing of the payroll and personnel cycle. Choose the best response.

a. A computer operator perpetrated a theft by preparing erroneous T-4 forms. The operator's income tax withheld was overstated by $2,000 and the income tax withheld from all other employees was understated. Which of the following audit procedures would detect such a fraud?
   (1) Multiplication of the applicable rate by the individual's gross taxable earnings.
   (2) Using employees' TD-1 forms and withholding tables to determine whether deductions authorized per pay period agree with amounts deducted per pay period.
   (3) Footing and crossfooting of the payroll register followed by tracing postings to the general ledger.
   (4) Vouching cancelled cheques to income tax withholding remittance forms.

b. In the audit of which of the following types of profit-oriented enterprises would the auditor be most likely to place special emphasis on tests of controls for proper classifications of payroll transactions?
   (1) A service organization
   (2) A wholesaling organization
   (3) A retailing organization
   (4) A manufacturing organization

c. A common audit procedure in the audit of payroll transactions involves tracing selected items from the payroll journal to employee time cards that have been approved by supervisory personnel. This procedure is designed to provide evidence in support of the audit proposition that
   (1) only proper employees worked and their pay was properly computed.
   (2) all employees worked the number of hours for which their pay was computed.
   (3) jobs on which employees worked were charged with the appropriate labour cost.
   (4) internal controls relating to payroll disbursements are operating effectively.

(AICPA adapted)

15-19 Items 1 through 9 are selected questions typically found in internal control questionnaires used by auditors to obtain an understanding of internal controls in the payroll and personnel cycle. In using the questionnaire for a client, a "yes" response to a question indicates a possible internal control, whereas a "no" indicates a potential weakness.

1. Does an appropriate official authorize initial rates of pay and any subsequent changes in rates?

2. Are written notices required documenting reasons for termination?

3. Are formal records such as time cards used for keeping time?

4. Is approval by a department head or supervisor required for all time cards before they are submitted for processing?

5. Does anyone verify pay rates and overtime hours before payroll cheques are prepared?

6. Does an adequate means exist for identifying jobs or products, such as work orders, job numbers, or some similar identification provided to employees to ensure proper coding of time records?

7. Are employees paid by cheques prepared by persons independent of timekeeping?

8. Are authorized procedures used to set up direct deposit payments, independent of payroll data entry processes?

9. Is a continuing record maintained of all unclaimed wages?

Required

a. For each of the questions, state the transaction-related audit objective(s) being fulfilled if the control is in effect.

b. For each control, list a test of the control to test its effectiveness.

c. For each of the questions, identify the nature of the potential financial misstatement(s) if the control is not in effect.

d. For each of the potential misstatements in part (c), list a control audit procedure for determining whether a material error exists.

15-20 Following are some of the tests of controls procedures frequently performed in the payroll and personnel cycle. (Each procedure is to be done on a sample basis.)

1. Reconcile the monthly payroll total for directing manufacturing labour with the labour cost distribution.

2. Examine the time card for the approval of a supervisor.

3. Recompute hours on the time card and compare the total with the total hours for which the employee has been paid.

4. Compare the employee name, date, wage rate, and bank account number from the payroll distribution report received from the bank to the authorized input forms sent to the bank.

5. Trace the hours from the employee time cards to job tickets to make sure that the totals reconcile, and trace each job ticket to the job-cost record.

6. Account for a sequence of payroll cheques in the payroll journal.

7. Select employees from the personnel files who have been terminated, and determine whether their termination pay was in accordance with the union contract. As part of this procedure, examine two subsequent periods to determine whether the terminated employee is still being paid.

Required

Identify the transaction-related audit objective(s) of each of the procedures.

15-21 The following misstatements are included in the accounting records of Lathen Manufacturing Ltd.:

1. Direct labour was unintentionally charged to job 620 instead of job 602 by the payroll clerk when he entered the job tickets. Job 602 was completed and the costs were expensed in the current year, whereas job 620 was included in work in process.

2. Jane Block and Frank Demery take turns "punching in" for each other every few days. The absent employee comes in at noon and tells the supervisor that he or she had car trouble or some other problem. The supervisor does not know the employee is getting paid for the time.

3. The supervisor submits a fraudulent time card for a former employee each week and delivers the related payroll cheque to the employee's house on the way home from work. They split the amount of the paycheque.

4. Employees frequently overlook recording their hours worked on job-cost tickets as required by the system. Many of the client's contracts are on a cost-plus basis.

5. The payroll clerk prepares a cheque to the same nonexistent person every week when entering payroll transactions in the microcomputer system, which also records the amount in the payroll journal. The clerk submits it along with all other payroll cheques for signature. When the cheques are returned to the clerk for distribution, the clerk takes the cheque and deposits it in a special bank account bearing that person's name.

6. In withholding income taxes from employees, the computer operator overrides the standard tax calculation, taking $2.00 extra from dozens of employees each week and crediting the amount to the operator's own employee earnings record.

Required

a. For each misstatement, state a control that should have prevented it from occurring on a continuing basis.

b. For each misstatement, state a test of control audit procedure that could uncover it.

15-22 The following audit procedures are typical of those found in auditing the payroll and personnel cycle.

1. Examine evidence of double-checking payroll wage rates and overtime calculations by an independent person.

2. Obtain a schedule of all payroll liabilities and trace to the general ledger.

3. Select a sample of 20 cancelled payroll cheques and account for the numerical sequence.

4. Foot and cross-foot the payroll journal using audit software, and trace the totals to the general ledger.

5. For accrued expenses, examine subsequent payments and supporting documents such as employee benefits remittance forms and receipts received.

6. Select a sample of 20 cancelled payroll cheques, and trace to the payroll journal for name, date, and amounts.

7. Compute direct labour, indirect labour, and commissions as a percentage of net sales, and compare with prior years.

8. Examine owner approval of rates of pay and withholdings.

9. Compute employment insurance expense as a percentage of total wages and salaries.

10. Discuss with management any payroll liabilities at the last engagement date that are not provided for currently.

11. Scan journals for all periods for unusual transactions to determine if they are recorded properly.

12. Select a sample of 40 entries in the payroll journal, and trace each to an approved time card.

Required

a. Select the type of test for each audit procedure from the following:
   (1) Test of controls
   (2) Analytical procedure
   (3) Test of details of balances

b. For each test of control, identify the applicable transaction-related audit objective(s).

c. For each test of details of balances, identify the applicable balance-related audit objective(s).

15-23 The following are steps in the methodology for designing tests of controls and tests of details of balances for the payroll and personnel cycle:

1. Design tests of details of balances for payroll and personnel.

2. Evaluate risk for payroll expense and liability accounts.

3. Evaluate cost-benefit of assessing control risk as low for payroll.

4. Design and perform payroll- and personnel-related analytical procedures.

5. Identify controls and weaknesses in internal control for the payroll and personnel cycle.

6. Obtain an understanding of payroll and personnel cycle internal controls.

7. Evaluate tests of controls results.

8. Design payroll and personnel cycle tests of controls.

9. Assess inherent risk for payroll-related accounts.

Required

a. Identify those steps that are tests of controls and those that are tests of details of balances.

b. Put steps that are tests of controls in the order of their performance in most audits.

c. Put the tests of details of balances in their proper order.

15-24 In comparing total employee benefits expense with the preceding year, Marilyn Brendin, public accountant, observed a significant increase, even though the total number of employees had only increased from 175 to 195. To investigate the difference, she selected a large sample of payroll disbursement transactions and carefully tested the withholdings for each employee in the sample by referring to Canada Pension Plan, employment insurance, and other benefits withholding tables. In her test, she found no exceptions; therefore, she concluded that employee benefits expense was fairly stated.

Required

a. Evaluate Brendin's approach to testing employee benefits expense.

b. Discuss a more suitable approach for determining whether employee benefits expense was properly stated in the current year.

15-25 As part of the audit of McGree Plumbing and Heating Ltd., you have responsibility for testing the payroll and personnel cycle. Payroll is the largest single expense in the client's trial balance, and hourly wages make up most of the payroll total. Employees are paid every two weeks. A unique aspect of the business is the extensive overtime incurred by employees on some days. It is common for employees to work only three or four days during the week but to work long hours while they are on the job. McGree's management has found that this actually saves money, in spite of the large amount of overtime, because the union contract requires payment for all travel time. Since many of the employees' jobs require long travel times and extensive startup costs, this policy is supported by both McGree and the employees.

You have already carefully evaluated and tested the payroll and personnel cycle's internal control and concluded that it contains no significant weaknesses. Your tests included tests of the time cards, withholdings, pay rates, the filing of all required employee withholding and benefits remittance forms, payroll cheques, and all other aspects of payroll.

As part of the year-end tests of payroll, you are responsible for verifying all accrued payroll as well as the company's liability for withholdings and accrued benefits. The accrued factory payroll includes the last six working days of the current year. The client has calculated accrued wages by taking 60 percent of the subsequent period's gross payroll and has recorded it as an adjusting entry to be reversed in the subsequent period.

Required

List all audit procedures you would follow in verifying accrued payroll and the liability for withholdings and accrued employee benefits.

15-26 In the audit of Larnet Manufacturing Corp., the auditor concluded that internal controls were inadequate because of the lack of segregation of duties. As a result, the decision was made to have a surprise payroll payoff one month before the client's balance sheet date. Since the auditor had never been involved in a payroll payoff, she did not know how to proceed.

Required

a. What is the purpose of a surprise payroll payoff?

b. What other audit procedures can the auditor perform that may fulfill the same objectives?

c. Discuss the procedures that the auditor should require the client to observe when the surprise payroll payoff is taking place.

d. At the completion of the payroll payoff, there are frequently several unclaimed cheques. What procedures should be followed for these?

15-27 Kowal Manufacturing Corp. employs about 50 production workers and has the following payroll procedures:

The factory supervisor interviews applicants and on the basis of the interview either hires or rejects them. When the applicant is hired, he or she prepares a TD-1 form (Personal Tax Credit Return) and gives it to the supervisor. The supervisor writes the hourly rate of pay for the new employee in the corner of the TD-1 form and then gives the form to a payroll clerk as notice that the worker has been employed. The supervisor verbally advises the payroll department of rate adjustments.

A supply of blank time cards is kept in a box near the entrance to the factory. Each worker takes a time card on Monday morning, fills in his or her name, and notes in pencil his or her daily arrival and departure times. At the end of the week the workers drop the time cards in a box near the door to the factory.

On Monday morning, the completed time cards are taken from the box by a payroll clerk. One of the payroll clerks then records the payroll transactions using a microcomputer system, which records all information for the payroll journal that was calculated by the clerk and automatically updates the employees' earnings records and general ledger. Employees are automatically removed from the payroll when they fail to turn in a time card.

The payroll cheques are manually signed by the chief accountant and given to the supervisor. The supervisor distributes the cheques to the workers in the factory and arranges for the delivery of the cheques to the workers who are absent. The payroll bank account is reconciled by the chief accountant, who also prepares the various employee withholdings and benefits remittance forms.

Required

a. List the most serious weaknesses in internal control and state the misstatements that are likely to result from the weaknesses. In your audit of Kowal's payroll, what will you emphasize in your audit tests? Explain.

b. List your suggestions for improving the Kowal Manufacturing Corp.'s internal controls for the factory hiring practices and payroll procedures.

(AICPA adapted)

15-28 During the first-year audit of Omato Wholesale Stationery Ltd., you observe that commissions amount to almost 25 percent of total sales, which is somewhat higher than in previous years. Further investigation reveals that the industry typically has larger sales commissions than Omato and that there is significant variation in rates depending on the product sold.

At the time a sale is made, the salesperson records his or her commission rate and the total amount of the commissions on the office copy of the sales invoice. When sales are entered into the microcomputer system for the recording of sales, the debit to sales commission expense and credit to accrued sales commission are also recorded. As part of recording the sales and sales commission expense, the accounts receivable clerk verifies the prices, quantities, commission rates, and all calculations on the sales invoices. Both the customer master and the salespersons' commission master files are updated when the sale and sales commission are recorded. On the fifteenth day after the end of the month, the salesperson is paid for the preceding month's sales commissions.

Required

a. Develop an audit program to verify sales commission expense assuming that no audit tests have been conducted in any audit area to this point.

b. Develop an audit program to verify accrued sales commissions at the end of the year assuming that the tests you designed in part (a) resulted in no significant misstatements.

15-29 Dunlop Ltd., a property management company, has a subsidiary, Riber Ltd., that is constructing an office building to be operated as a rental property by Dunlop. The building is being constructed by an independent contractor on the basis of direct costs plus 20 percent. Direct costs are defined as material used and labour costs incurred in the construction. The 20 percent is intended to cover overhead and profit.

At August 31, 1999, the degree of completion is estimated at 75 percent. Brett Dunlop, president of Dunlop, has just asked you as Dunlop's and Riber's auditor to conduct an investigation of the labour costs which are about $1 million over estimates. Dunlop has some concerns about the contractor's honesty. He says that he is satisfied with the material costs, however.

A review of the contract between Riber and the contractor and a talk with Dunlop reveal the following:

1. Wage rates, specified in the contract, are based on union contracts. The rates vary with the trade and worker's experience.

2. Employees are paid by the contractor. The payroll records are kept by an independent computer service bureau. The contractor sends a monthly payroll summary by employee to Riber to support her invoice.

3. Brett Dunlop explained that construction workers' mobility made it very difficult to verify that employees listed on the monthly summary actually worked on the site. He added that he had no confidence in the time-keeping system used on the site.

4. The contract provides Riber with the right to examine the books of the contractor.

Required

List the procedures you would perform to carry out the investigation requested by Dunlop. State why you would perform each procedure.

(CICA adapted)

15-30 Carrie Ahwahli is the auditor of Abbolah Ltd., a large manufacturing company with several plants across Canada. All accounting records are automated using a combination of software packages and customized programming.

In prior years Abbolah had never recorded accrued vacation pay in its accounts but instead had recognized the expense when vacations were taken by the employees. This was considered reasonable since employees took their vacation throughout the year. For the year ended December 31, 1998, however, the company decided to set up the liability at that date for accrued vacation pay. This coincided with changes in personnel policies requiring employees to take their holidays in specified time periods during the year.

The company employs approximately 2,400 employees, each of whom belongs to one of four unions. Employees' entitlement to vacation pay is based on length of service (calculated from the month of employment) and varies according to the terms of each union contract. Some specific variations in calculations are required based on sick-leave entitlements as well.

Complete personnel information for all employees is maintained on a payroll master file which is updated weekly. An "Employee Status Report" containing all master file details for specified employees is produced on request.

A specially written computer program was prepared to determine the amount of accrued vacation pay, since the standard software packages used by the company could not handle the calculations. This program extracted the relevant data from the payroll master file as at December 31, 1998, calculated the amount of accrued vacation pay for each employee, recorded the details in a separate data file, and printed a summarized report showing only the grand total of the accrued vacation pay.

Required

a. How could an audit trail be provided to enable Carrie to perform tests of details of the accrued vacation pay? What practical difficulties may arise?

b. Explain briefly how Carrie could use either test data or generalized audit software to check the accuracy of the computer program.

(CICA adapted)

15-31 In many companies, labour costs represent a substantial percentage of total dollars expended in any one account-

ing period. One of the auditor's primary means of verifying payroll transactions is by a detailed payroll test.

You are making an annual examination of Lethbridge Inc., a medium-sized manufacturing company. You have selected a number of hourly employees for a detailed payroll test. The following worksheet outline has been prepared.

COLUMN NUMBER	HEADING
1	Employee number
2	Employee name
3	Job classification
	Hours worked:
4	Straight time
5	Premium time
6	Hourly rate
7	Gross earnings
	Deductions:
8	Income tax withheld
9	Canada Pension Plan withheld
10	Employment insurance withheld
11	Union dues
12	Amount of cheque
13	Cheque number
14	Account number charged
15	Description of account

Required

a. What factors should the auditor consider in selecting his or her sample of employees to be included in any payroll test?

b. Using the column numbers above as a reference, state the principal way(s) that the information for each heading would be verified.

c. In addition to the payroll test, the auditor employs a number of other audit procedures in the verification of payroll transactions. List five additional procedures that may be employed and the corresponding audit objective.

(AICPA adapted)

CASE

15-32 A long-time client of your firm, Watran Limited is a company incorporated under the *Canada Corporations Act*. It is engaged in the manufacture and construction of prefabricated homes for various mining communities across the northern frontier of Canada.

The executive, sales, and administrative offices are located in a major Canadian city. The company has two manufacturing plants — one in Eastern Canada and one in Western Canada. There are seven field work crews, each under the supervision of a supervisor. The work crews move from community to community erecting the prefabricated homes.

Last year you worked on the audit examination of the company. The partner of your firm responsible for the audit has asked you to carry out a one-day preliminary audit survey of the company payroll in preparation for the audit of the

financial statements for the year ending December 31, 1999.

In your initial discussion with the controller, you learn that the company has purchased a payroll software package and, after running parallel for the month of June, adopted the new payroll system effective July 1, 1999.

The controller tells you that the new payroll system should solve the weaknesses in internal control over field crew wages that your firm mentioned in its 1998 Management Letter. To refresh your memory, you refer to the prior year's audit file and find the following notes relating to the old manual payroll system of the company:

- Field crews are paid each Friday using cheques manually prepared by the crew supervisor. Each supervisor maintains an imprest bank account for this purpose. The supervisors prepare weekly payroll journals from their time record books, and each one sends one copy of the weekly journal sheet to Head Office. A cheque is mailed to each crew supervisor to replenish his or her imprest account (7 crews, 7 supervisors, 54 crew workers).

- Labour payrolls based on time clock records are submitted to the bank for preparation of weekly paycheques at both of the manufacturing plants. Plant employees are paid every two weeks by direct deposit from payroll accounts at banks located close to the plants (total plant labour force: 112).

- Salaried employees are paid twice a month by direct deposit. Calculations are made by the bank based on wage rates and authorized deduction rates supplied by the company. The salaried personnel include:

  Executive officers
  Sales staff
  Plant supervisory staff
  Head office administrative staff
  Office staff at plants
  Field crew supervisors
  (Total salaried employees: 56)

- Certain executives, sales personnel, plant supervisory staff, and field crew supervisors receive bonuses twice a year based on performance criteria.

- No employee of the company works under a union agreement.

At this point, you obtain additional information from the controller about the new payroll software package and the related procedures:

- The package handles both hourly payroll (wages) and salaried payroll.

- The following information is maintained in the payroll master file:
  — "hourly" — employee name, number, and personal information; regular and overtime wage rates; wages and deductions accumulated to date
  — "salary" — employee name, number, and personal information; monthly salary rate; salary and deductions to date

- Hours worked by wage earners are sent in every two weeks by the field crew supervisors and the payroll clerk at each manufacturing plant. Preprinted coding forms are used for this purpose. One form is prepared for each employee.

- Preprinted "personnel change notices" are prepared by the payroll department on the advice of various department heads for all payroll changes (e.g., new employees, terminations, rate changes).

- All employees are now paid every two weeks.

- Cheques are prepared and signed by computer (using a stored image file).

- Separate payroll journals are printed for salaried employees, Eastern Plant Labour, Western Plant Labour, and each of the seven field crews.

- Job-cost distribution reports are printed for each pay period.

- Paycheques are mailed to plant superintendents and field crew supervisors with a copy of the related payroll journal.

- Salary cheques are distributed or mailed by the payroll department.

- Bonus information is supplied by the controller twice each year.

Your day at the client's office is over. Tomorrow afternoon you must report back to the partner in charge of the audit.

Required

a. List the points to be included in the memorandum to the partner outlining your suggested approach to the audit of the payroll systems and the payroll costs of Watran Limited for the year ending December 31, 1999. It is *not necessary* to describe the new systems in your answer. *Do not* list detailed procedures.

b. Prepare a list of audit procedures that would be used to test the controls in place in the new payroll system. Organize your procedures by audit objective.

c. From the information available, identify the weaknesses that existed under the old manual payroll system and discuss the extent to which they have been corrected under the new system.

d. Identify any new weaknesses that are now present under the new system. Indicate the potential consequences of these weaknesses and provide recommendations to management for improvement.

(CICA adapted)

16

AUDIT OF THE ACQUISITION AND PAYMENT CYCLE

FALSE PURCHASES CAMOUFLAGE OVERSTATED PROFITS

On November 25, 1992, Comptronix Corporation announced that members of its senior management team had overstated profits and that there would be material adjustments to the prior year's audited financial statements. In its subsequent investigation, the Securities and Exchange Commission (SEC) determined that Comptronix's chief executive officer (CEO), chief operating officer (COO), and the controller/treasurer colluded to overstate assets and profits by recording fictitious sales, accounts receivable, and purchases of equipment on account.

To camouflage the fraud, the executives made it appear that collections from customers were received on the nonexistent receivables and that payments were made to fictitious accounts payable to vendors. They even prepared cash disbursement cheques to the phony vendors, but retained the unendorsed cheques and deposited them into the company's disbursement account on which they had been drawn. These fraudulent disbursements were recorded in the accounting records as payments against the nonexistent accounts payable, which eliminated the phony liabilities.

The senior executives circumvented Comptronix's existing internal controls by bypassing the purchasing and receiving departments so that no one at Comptronix could discover the scheme. Comptronix employees usually created a fairly extensive paper trail for equipment purchases. Company internal controls over acquisition and cash disbursement transactions typically required a purchase order, receiving report, and vendor invoice before payment could be authorized by the COO or controller/treasurer, who were both participants in the fraud. As a result, the executives were able to

Comptronix Corporation
www.comptronix.com

The third major transaction cycle discussed in this text is the acquisition of and payment for goods and services from outsiders. The acquisition of goods and services includes such items as the purchase of raw materials, equipment, supplies, utilities, repairs and maintenance, and research and development. The cycle does not include the acquisition and payment of employees' services or the internal transfers and allocations of costs within the organization. The former are a part of the payroll and personnel function, and the latter are audited as part of the verification of individual assets or liabilities. The acquisition and payment cycle also excludes the acquisition and repayment of capital (interest-bearing debt and owners' equity), which are considered separately in Chapter 19.

The audit of the acquisition and payment cycle is studied in Chapters 16 and 17. In this chapter, the format for discussing internal control introduced in earlier chapters is repeated. The first part of the chapter deals with the nature of the acquisition and payment cycle, including documents and records, and its primary functions and internal controls. The second part discusses tests of controls for the cycle related to key internal controls. The final part covers tests of details of accounts payable, the major balance sheet account in the cycle, and applies both tests of controls and tests of details to the audit of a system change, called a *conversion audit*. It emphasizes the relationship between tests of controls and tests of details of balances. In Chapter 17, several other important balance sheet accounts that are a part of the acquisition and payment cycle are examined. These are manufacturing equipment, prepaid insurance, and accrued liabilities. The chapter also discusses tests of details of income statement accounts included in the acquisition and payment cycle.

The acquisition and payment cycle includes two distinct classes of transactions—acquisitions of goods and services and cash disbursements for those acquisitions. Purchases returns and allowances is also a class of transactions, but, for most companies, the amounts are immaterial.

There are a larger number and variety of accounts in the acquisition and payment cycle in a typical company than for any other cycle. Examine the trial balance for Hillsburg Hardware Ltd. on pages 128–129. Accounts affected by the acquisition and payment cycle are identified by the letter "A" in the left column. Notice first that accounts affected by the cycle include asset, liability, expense, and miscellaneous income accounts, and second, the large number of accounts affected. It is not surprising, therefore, that it often takes more time to audit the acquisition and payment cycle than any other cycle.

The way the accounting information flows through the various accounts in the acquisition and payment cycle is illustrated by T-accounts in Figure 16-1. To keep the

FIGURE 16-1
Accounts in the
Acquisition and
Payment Cycle

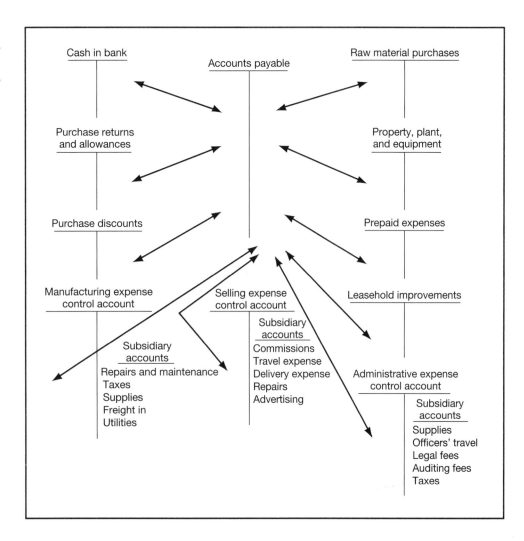

illustration manageable, only the control accounts are shown for the three major categories of expenses used by most companies. For each control account, examples of the subsidiary expense accounts are also given.

Figure 16-1 shows that every transaction is either debited or credited to accounts payable. Because many companies make some purchases directly by cheque or through petty cash, the figure is an oversimplification. We assume that cash transactions are processed in the same manner as transactions flowing through accounts payable.

NATURE OF THE CYCLE

OBJECTIVE 16-1

Describe the acquisition and payment cycle, the pertinent documents and records, functions, and internal controls.

The acquisition and payment cycle involves the decisions and processes necessary for obtaining the goods and services for operating a business. The cycle typically begins with the initiation of a purchase requisition by an authorized employee who needs the goods or services and ends with payment for the benefits received. Although the discussion that follows deals with a small manufacturing company that makes tangible products for sale to third parties, the same principles apply to a service company, a government unit, or any other type of organization.

Column 3 of Table 16-1 identifies the five business functions in a typical acquisition and payment cycle. The table shows the relationships among the classes of transactions, accounts, business functions, and documents and records. The business

TABLE 16-1

CLASSES OF TRANSACTIONS, ACCOUNTS, BUSINESS FUNCTIONS, AND RELATED DOCUMENTS AND RECORDS FOR THE ACQUISITION AND PAYMENT CYCLE

CLASSES OF TRANSACTIONS	ACCOUNTS	BUSINESS FUNCTIONS	DOCUMENTS AND RECORDS
Acquisitions	Inventory Property, plant, and equipment Prepaid expenses Leasehold improvements Accounts payable Manufacturing expenses Selling expenses Administrative expenses	Processing purchase orders	Purchase requisition Purchase order Vendor master file Purchase transaction file
		Receiving goods and services Recognizing the liability Vendor master file changes	Receiving report Acquisitions journal Summary acquisitions report Vendor's invoice Debit memo Vendor transaction file Voucher Vendor master file Accounts payable trial balance Vendor's statement
Cash disbursements	Cash in bank (from cash disbursements) Accounts payable Purchase discounts	Processing and recording cash disbursements	Cheque Cheque transaction file Cash disbursements journal

functions and related documents are discussed in this section. In addition, there is a discussion of key internal controls to prevent misstatements and to ensure the safety of assets.

PROCESSING PURCHASE ORDERS

The request for goods or services by the client's personnel is the starting point for the cycle. The exact form of the request and the required approval depend on the nature of the goods and services and company policy.

Purchase requisition   This is a request for goods and services by an authorized employee. It may take the form of a request for such acquisitions as materials by a shop supervisor or the storeroom supervisor, outside repairs by office or factory personnel, or insurance by the vice-president in charge of property and equipment.

Purchase order   This document records the description, quantity, and related information for goods and services that the company intends to purchase. This document is frequently used to indicate authorization to procure goods and services. Purchase order details are retained in a *purchase order transaction file.*

Vendor master file   This file sums individual acquisitions, cash disbursements, and acquisition returns and allowances for each vendor. Those companies that have automated purchasing systems ensure that authorized vendor information, such as credit terms, contact name, and shipping terms, is established and recorded in the vendor master file. The file also keeps track of total purchase commitments and total liabilities (unpaid invoices) by vendor.

Purchase order transaction file   As purchase commitments are made, transaction details are recorded in the purchase order file. Automated systems automatically number the purchase orders sequentially and assist in tracking purchase commitments, expected delivery dates, and items that have been back-ordered (i.e., when the vendor currently does not have stock, but shipments are expected later).

Internal controls   Proper *authorization* for acquisitions and changes to the vendor master file is an essential part of this function because it ensures that the goods and services acquired are for authorized company purposes, and it avoids the acquisition of excessive or unnecessary items. Most companies permit general authorization for the acquisition of regular operating needs, such as inventory at one level and acquisitions of capital assets or similar items at another. For example, acquisitions of capital assets in excess of a specified dollar limit may require board of directors' action; items acquired relatively infrequently, such as insurance policies and long-term service contracts, are approved by certain officers; supplies and services costing less than a designated amount are approved by supervisors and department heads; and some types of raw materials and supplies are re-ordered automatically whenever they fall to a predetermined level, often by direct communication with vendors' computers. Where automatic purchase orders are generated, care must be taken to ensure that re-order points are monitored so that only those goods still required by the company are purchased.

After an acquisition has been approved, an order to acquire the goods and services must be initiated. An order is issued to a vendor for a specified item at a certain price to be delivered at or by a designated time. The order is usually in writing and is a legal document that is an offer to buy. For most routine items, a purchase order is used to indicate the offer.

It is common for companies to establish purchasing departments to ensure an adequate quality of goods and services at a minimum price. For good internal control, the purchasing department should not be responsible for authorizing the acquisition or receiving the goods. All purchase orders should be prenumbered and should include sufficient columns and spaces to minimize the likelihood of unintentional omissions on the form when goods are ordered.

RECEIVING GOODS AND SERVICES

The receipt by the company of goods and services from the vendor is a critical point in the cycle because it is the point at which most companies first recognize the acquisition and related liability on their records. When goods are received, adequate control requires examination for description, quantity, timely arrival, and condition.

Receiving report   This document is prepared at the time tangible goods are received and indicates the description of goods, the quantity received, the date received, and other relevant data. The receipt of goods and services in the normal course of business represents the date that clients normally recognize the liability for an acquisition. Where an organization has automated purchase order systems, the receipt needs to be entered into the computer system to signal that the goods have been received. This information would also be used to update perpetual inventory systems.

Internal controls   Most companies have the receiving department initiate a receiving report as evidence of the receipt and examination of goods. One copy is normally sent to the storeroom, where it is used to update the quantity fields of the computer records, and another to the accounts payable department for its information needs. To prevent theft and misuse, it is important that the goods be *physically controlled* from the time of their receipt until their disposal. The personnel in the receiving department should be independent of the storeroom personnel and the accounting department. Finally, the accounting records should transfer responsibility for the goods as they are transferred from receiving to storage and from storage to manufacturing.

The proper recognition of the liability for the receipt of goods and services requires *prompt and accurate* recording. The initial recording has a significant effect on the recorded financial statements and the actual cash disbursement; therefore, great care must be taken to include only existing company acquisitions at the correct amounts.

Acquisitions journal This journal lists acquisition transactions. A detailed acquisitions journal includes each acquisition transaction. It usually includes several classifications for the most significant types of acquisitions, such as the purchase of inventory, repairs and maintenance, supplies, the entry to accounts payable, and miscellaneous debits and credits. The acquisitions journal can also include acquisition returns and allowances transactions if a separate journal is not used. The acquisitions journal is generated for any time period from the acquisition transactions included in the computer files. Individual transaction amounts are posted to the vendor master file and journal totals are posted to the general ledger.

Summary acquisitions report This report summarizes acquisitions for a period. The report typically includes information analyzed by key components such as account classification, type of inventory, and division.

Vendor's invoice This document indicates such things as the description and quantity of goods and services received, price including freight, cash discount terms, and date of the billing. It is an essential document because it specifies the amount of money owed to the vendor for an acquisition.

Debit memo This document indicates a reduction in the amount owed to a vendor because of returned goods or an allowance granted. It often takes the same general form as a vendor's invoice, but it supports reductions in accounts payable rather than increases.

Vendor transaction file This file, detailing transactions of individual vendors, indicates both the details of the vendor's invoice and debit memo details from accounts payable. Payments to vendors are deducted from outstanding transactions and recorded in a cheque transaction file. Unpaid transactions are used to prepare the *accounts payable trial balance*. The sum of the unpaid transactions should always agree to the sum of liabilities in the vendor master file and to the general ledger accounts payable total.

Voucher This document is frequently used by organizations to establish a formal means of recording and controlling acquisitions. Vouchers include a cover sheet or folder for containing documents and a package of relevant documents such as the purchase order, copy of the packing slip, receiving report, and vendor's invoice. After payment, a copy of the cheque is added to the voucher package.

Vendor master file As described earlier, this summary file sums individual acquisitions, cash disbursements, and acquisition returns and allowances for each vendor. The master file is updated from the purchase order, receiving report, invoice, returns and allowances, and cash disbursements transaction files. The total of the individual account balances in the master file equals the total balance of accounts payable in the general ledger.

Accounts payable trial balance This is a listing of the amount owed by each vendor at a point in time. It is prepared directly from the accounts payable master file and open item transaction files. It can be prepared in summary form (showing totals only by vendor) or in detail (showing the current month's transactions plus any unpaid transactions making up the opening balance).

Vendor's statement This statement, prepared monthly by the vendor, indicates a customer's beginning balance, acquisitions, returns and allowances, payments, and ending balance. These balances and activities are the vendor's representations of the transactions for the period and not the client's. Except for disputed amounts and timing differences, the client's accounts payable transaction file details and vendor master file totals should be the same as the vendor's statement.

Internal controls In some companies, the recording of the liability for acquisitions is made on the basis of the receipt of goods and services, and in other companies, it is deferred until the vendor's invoice is received. In either case, the accounts payable department typically has responsibility for verifying the propriety of acquisitions. This is done by comparing the details on the purchase order, the receiving report, and the vendor's invoice to determine that the descriptions, prices, quantities, terms, and freight on the vendor's invoice are correct. Typically, extensions, footings, and account distribution are also verified.

The level of automation of the accounts payable system varies. Some organizations simply record the total amount of the vendor invoice into the accounts payable system. In that case, it is important that all of the above steps, including recalculation of the vendor invoice, are completed before the invoice is entered into the system. For highly integrated computer systems, the vendor invoice details entered manually or received electronically include each line of the invoice (i.e., the item number, description, quantity, price, and terms). The computer systems can then make the comparison to the purchase order details and recalculate the vendor invoice. Accurate and authorized entry by the organization personnel of receiving order details is important so that the system can confirm that the quantity received is equal to the quantity ordered and the quantity billed by the vendor.

An important control in the accounts payable and information processing departments is requiring that those personnel who record acquisitions *do not have access* to cash, marketable securities, and other assets. Adequate documents and records, proper procedures for record keeping, and independent checks on performance are also necessary controls in the accounts payable function.

PROCESSING AND RECORDING CASH DISBURSEMENTS

For most companies, payment is made by computer-prepared cheques from information included in the acquisition transactions file at the time goods and services are received. Cheques are typically prepared in a multi-copy format, with the original going to the payee, one copy being filed with the vendor's invoice and other supporting documents, and another copy being filed numerically. In most cases, individual cheques are recorded in a cash disbursements (cheque) transactions file.

Cheque This is the means of paying for the acquisition when payment is due. After the cheque is signed by an authorized person, it is an asset. Therefore, signed cheques should be mailed by the signer or a person under his or her control. When cashed by the vendor and cleared by the client's bank, it is referred to as a "cancelled cheque."

Cash disbursements journal This journal is for recording cash disbursement transactions. The cash disbursements journal is generated for any time period from the cash disbursement (cheque) transactions included in the computer files. Details from the transaction file are posted to the vendor transaction file and vendor master file. Transaction totals are posted to the general ledger.

Internal controls The most important controls in the cash disbursements function include the signing of cheques by an individual with proper authority, separation of responsibilities for signing the cheques and performing the accounts payable function, and careful examination of the supporting documents by the cheque signer at the time the cheque is signed.

The cheques should be prenumbered and printed on special paper that makes it difficult to alter the payee or amount. Care should be taken to provide physical control over blank, voided, and signed cheques. It is also important to have a method of cancelling the supporting documents to prevent their re-use as support for another cheque at a later time. A common method is to mark the documents as "entered" when recorded in the computer system and to write the cheque number on the supporting documents when cheques are issued or documents are paid (e.g, electronic bank transfer).

Wall Street Journal
www.wsj.com

ARE COMPANIES THROWING MONEY AWAY?

Howard Schultz is the president of an accounts payable auditing firm. Mr. Schultz's firm specializes in analyzing acquisitions and cash disbursements for its clients. In an article written for the *Wall Street Journal*, Mr. Schultz states that auditors in his firm find that clients often overpay vendors. Excerpts from the article follow:

> In working with more than 1,000 companies, we have seen the same errors crop up with enough regularity to convince us that overpayments are intrinsic to the process of buying and selling. These problems usually begin with the fact that in most large companies the person or department that places the order is not the same party that pays the bill . . .
>
> . . . Adding to the problem is the dizzying array of price promotions and special allowances that vendors offer, causing prices to fluctuate from month to month, or sometimes day to day. These marketing promotions, which may be anything from limited-time-only discounts to refund offers, turn simple invoices into complicated documents. Corporate payment clerks usually don't have time to sift through the details to be sure that a company gets credit for all the special discounts it may be entitled to. And many vendors offer refunds and other incentives after the sale — but it's up to the buyer to request credit for them . . .

Mr. Schultz points out that companies can reduce losses from overpayments by implementing the following strategies:
- Re-evaluate the purchasing and payment processes by improving communication between the marketing and finance departments.
- Be alert to the dangers of automation. Sometimes automated systems can be too complicated for clerical staff.
- Pay attention to peaks and transitional periods because companies are usually more vulnerable to errors during these times.
- Watch for patterns of overpayment, including repeated failure to take advantage of trade allowances or discounts for early payment.

Source: Howard Schultz, "Washing Away the Sin of Overpayment," *Wall Street Journal*, August 9, 1993, p. A.12.

TESTS OF CONTROLS

In a typical audit, the most time-consuming accounts to verify by tests of details of balances are accounts receivable, inventory, capital assets, accounts payable, and expense accounts. Of these five, four are directly related to the acquisition and payment cycle. The net time saved can be dramatic if the auditor can reduce the tests of details of the accounts by using tests of controls to verify the effectiveness of internal controls for acquisitions and cash disbursements. It should not be surprising, therefore, that tests of controls for the acquisition and payment cycle receive a considerable amount of attention in well-conducted audits, especially when the client has effective internal controls.

Tests of controls for the acquisition and payment cycle are divided into two broad areas: *tests of acquisitions* and *tests of payments*. Acquisition tests concern four of the five functions discussed earlier in the chapter: processing purchase orders, vendor master file changes, receiving goods and services, and recognizing the liability. Tests of payments concern the fifth function, processing and recording cash disbursements.

The six transaction-related audit objectives developed in Chapters 5 and 9 are again used as the frame of reference for designing tests of controls for acquisition and cash disbursement transactions. For each objective, the auditor must go through the same logical process that has been discussed in previous chapters. First, the auditor must understand the general controls applicable to the cycle and the cycle's internal controls to determine which controls exist. After the auditor has identified existing controls and weaknesses for each objective, an initial assessment of control risk can be made for each objective. At this point, the auditor must decide which controls he or she plans to test to satisfy the initial assessment of control risk. After the auditor has developed the audit procedures for each objective, the procedures can be combined into an audit program that can be efficiently performed. Figure 16-2 summarizes that methodology. It is the same one used in Chapter 12 for sales and cash receipts. Again, the emphasis in the methodology is on determining the appropriate audit procedures, sample size, items to select, and timing.

VERIFYING ACQUISITIONS

Key internal controls and common tests of controls for each transaction-related audit objective are summarized in Table 16-2. An assumption underlying the internal controls and audit procedures is the existence of a separate acquisitions process for recording all acquisitions.

FIGURE 16-2

Methodology for Designing Tests of Controls for the Acquisition and Payment Cycle

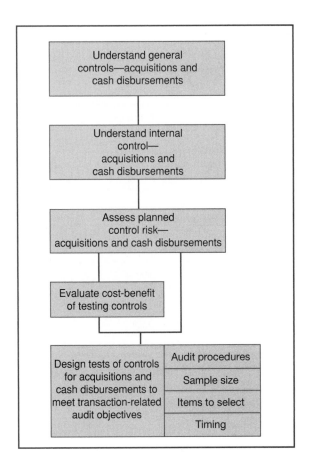

TABLE 16-2

SUMMARY OF TRANSACTION-RELATED AUDIT OBJECTIVES, KEY CONTROLS, AND TESTS OF CONTROLS FOR ACQUISITIONS

TRANSACTION-RELATED AUDIT OBJECTIVE	KEY INTERNAL CONTROL	COMMON TESTS OF CONTROLS	
Recorded acquisitions are for goods and services received, consistent with the best interests of the client (occurrence).	Existence of purchase requisition, purchase order, receiving report, and vendor's invoice attached to the voucher.[†]	Examine documents in voucher for existence.	Review the acquisitions journal, general ledger, and transaction files for large or unusual amounts.[*]
	Approval of acquisitions at the proper level.	Examine indication of approval.	Examine underlying documents for reasonableness and authenticity (vendors' invoices, receiving reports, purchase orders, and requisitions).
	Cancellation of documents to prevent their re-use.	Examine indication of cancellation.	
	Internal verification of vendors' invoices, receiving reports, purchase orders, and purchase requisitions.[†]	Examine indication of internal verification.[‡]	Trace inventory purchases to inventory files. Examine capital assets acquired.
	New vendors and changes to vendor file approved. Vendor master file independently examined periodically.	Examine master file change forms, and trace details to vendor master file. Discuss review process with management.	Review vendor master file for unusual credit terms, prices, or P.O. box addresses.[‡]
Existing acquisition transactions are recorded (completeness).	Purchase orders are prenumbered and accounted for.	Account for a sequence of purchase orders.[‡]	Trace from a file of receiving reports to the acquisitions journal.[†]
	Receiving reports are prenumbered and accounted for.[†]	Account for a sequence of receiving reports.[‡]	Trace from a file of vendors' invoices to the acquisitions journal.
	Vouchers are prenumbered and accounted for.	Account for a sequence of vouchers.[‡]	
Recorded acquisition transactions are accurate (accuracy).	Internal verification of calculations and amounts.	Examine indication of internal verification.[‡]	Compare recorded transactions in the acquisitions journal with the vendor's invoice, receiving report, and other supporting documentation.[†‡]
	Batch totals are compared with computer summary reports.	Examine file of batch totals for initials of data control clerk; compare totals to summary reports.[‡]	
	Approval of acquisitions for prices and discounts.	Examine indication of approval.	Recompute the clerical accuracy on the vendors' invoices, including discounts and freight.[‡]
Acquisition transactions are properly classified (classification).	Adequate chart of accounts.	Examine procedures manual and chart of accounts.	Compare classification with chart of accounts by reference to vendors' invoices.
	Automatic updates and posting.	Enter test transactions or observe entry, and trace to correct file.	
Acquisition transactions are recorded on the correct dates (timing).	Procedures require recording transactions as soon as possible after the goods and services have been received.	Examine procedures manual and observe whether unrecorded vendors' invoices exist.	Compare dates of receiving reports and vendors' invoices with dates in the acquisitions journal.[†]
	Transaction date must be system date (today's date) or a reasonable date.	Observe data entry process.	
Acquisition transactions are properly included in the vendor and inventory master files, and are properly summarized (posting and summarization).	Comparison of accounts payable master file or trial balance totals with general ledger balance.	Examine initials on general ledger accounts indicating comparison.	Test clerical accuracy by footing the journals and tracing postings to general ledger and accounts payable and inventory master files.

[*] This analytical procedure can also apply to other objectives including completeness, valuation, and timing.

[†] Receiving reports are used only for tangible goods and are therefore not available for services, such as utilities and repairs and maintenance. Frequently, vendors' invoices are the only documentation available.

[‡] This control would be tested on many audits by using the computer.

In studying Table 16-2, it is important to relate internal controls to objectives and to relate tests of controls to both internal controls and monetary misstatements that would be absent or present due to controls and weaknesses in the system. It should be kept in mind that a set of audit procedures for a particular audit engagement will vary with the internal controls and other circumstances.

Four of the objectives for acquisitions deserve special attention. A discussion of each of these objectives follows.

Recorded acquisitions are for goods and services received, consistent with the best interests of the client (occurrence)   If the auditor is satisfied that the controls are adequate for this objective, tests for improper and nonexistent transactions can be greatly reduced. Adequate controls are likely to prevent the client from including as a business expense or asset those transactions that primarily benefit management or other employees rather than the entity being audited. In some instances, improper transactions are obvious, such as the acquisition of unauthorized personal items by employees or the actual embezzlement of cash by recording a fraudulent purchase in the purchases journal. In other instances, the propriety of a transaction is more diffi-cult to evaluate, such as the payment of officers' memberships to country clubs, expense-paid vacations to foreign countries for members of management and their families, and management-approved illegal payments to officials of foreign coun-tries. If the controls over improper or nonexistent transactions are inadequate, exten-sive examination of supporting documentation is necessary.

Existing acquisitions are recorded (completeness)   Failure to record the acquisition of goods and services received directly affects the balance in accounts payable and may result in an overstatement of net income and owners' equity. Because of this, auditors are usually very concerned with the completeness objective. In some instances, it may be difficult to perform tests of details to determine whether there are unrecorded transactions, and the auditor must rely on controls for this purpose. In addition, since the audit of accounts payable generally takes a considerable amount of audit time, effective internal control, properly tested, can significantly reduce audit costs.

Acquisitions are accurately recorded (accuracy)   Since the accuracy of many asset, liability, and expense accounts depends on the correct recording of transactions in the acquisitions journal, the extent of tests of details of many balance sheet and expense accounts depends on the auditor's evaluation of the effectiveness of the internal con-trols over the accuracy of recorded acquisitions transactions. For example, if the audi-tor believes the capital assets are correctly recorded in the books of original entry, it is acceptable to vouch fewer current period acquisitions than if the controls are inade-quate.

When a client uses perpetual inventory records, the tests of details of inventory can also be significantly reduced if the auditor believes the perpetuals are accurate. The controls over the acquisitions included in the perpetuals are normally tested as a part of the tests of controls for acquisitions, and the controls over this objective play a key role in the audit. The inclusion of both quantity and unit costs in the inventory perpetual records permits a reduction in the tests of the physical count and the unit costs of inventory if the controls are operating effectively.

Acquisitions are correctly classified (classification)   The auditor can reduce the tests of details of certain individual accounts if he or she believes internal control is adequate to provide reasonable assurance of correct classification in the acquisitions journal. Although all accounts are affected to some degree by effective controls over classification, the two areas most affected are current period acquisitions of capital assets and all expense accounts, such as repairs and maintenance, utilities, and advertising. Since performing documentation tests of current period capital asset acquisitions and expense accounts for accuracy are relatively time-consuming audit procedures, the saving in audit time can be significant.

VERIFYING CASH DISBURSEMENTS

The same format used in Table 16-2 for acquisitions is also used in Table 16-3 for cash disbursements. The assumption underlying these controls and audit procedures is the existence of separate cash disbursements and acquisitions processes. The com-

TABLE 16-3

SUMMARY OF TRANSACTION-RELATED AUDIT OBJECTIVES, KEY CONTROLS, AND TESTS OF CONTROLS FOR CASH DISBURSEMENTS

TRANSACTION-RELATED AUDIT OBJECTIVE	KEY INTERNAL CONTROL	COMMON TESTS OF CONTROLS	
Recorded cash disbursements are for goods and services actually received (occurrence).	Adequate segregation of duties between accounts payable and custody of signed cheques. Examination of supporting documentation before signing of cheques by an authorized person. Approval of payment on supporting documents at the time cheques are signed.	Discuss with personnel and observe activities. Discuss with personnel and observe activities. Examine indication of approval.	Review the cash disbursements journal, general ledger, and vendor master file for large or unusual amounts.* Trace the cancelled cheque to the related acquisitions journal entry and examine for payee name and amount. Examine cancelled cheque for authorized signature, proper endorsement, and cancellation by the bank. Examine supporting documents as a part of the tests of acquisitions.
Existing cash disbursement transactions are recorded (completeness).	Cheques are prenumbered and accounted for. A bank reconciliation is prepared monthly by an employee independent of recording cash disbursements or custody of assets.	Account for a sequence of cheques.† Examine bank reconciliations and observe their preparation.	Reconcile recorded cash disbursements with the cash disbursements on the bank statement (proof of cash disbursements).
Recorded cash disbursement transactions are accurate (accuracy).	Internal verification of calculations and amounts. Monthly preparation of a bank reconciliation by an independent person.	Examine indication of internal verification.† Examine bank reconciliations and observe their preparation.	Compare cancelled cheques with the related acquisitions journal and cash disbursements journal entries.† Recompute cash discounts.† Prepare a proof of cash disbursements.
Cash disbursement transactions are properly classified (classification).	Adequate chart of accounts. Internal verification of classification.	Examine procedures manual and chart of accounts. Examine indication of internal verification.	Compare classification with chart of accounts by reference to vendors' invoices and acquisitions journal.
Cash disbursement transactions are recorded on the correct dates (timing).	Procedures require recording of transactions as soon as possible after the cheque has been signed. Transaction date must be system date.	Examine procedures manual and observe whether unrecorded cheques exist. Observe data entry process.	Compare dates on cancelled cheques with the cash disbursements journal. Compare dates on cancelled cheques with the bank cancellation date.
Cash disbursement transactions are properly included in the vendor master file and properly summarized (posting and summarization).	Internal verification of vendor master file contents. Comparison of vendor master file or trial balance totals with general ledger balance.	Examine indication of internal verification.† Examine initials on general ledger accounts indicating comparison.	Test clerical accuracy by footing journals and tracing postings to general ledger and vendor master file.†

*This analytical procedure can also apply to other objectives including completeness, accuracy, and timing.
†This control would be tested on many audits using the computer.

ments made about the methodology and process for developing audit procedures for acquisitions apply equally to cash disbursements.

Once the auditor has decided on procedures, the acquisitions and cash disbursements tests are typically performed concurrently. For example, for a transaction selected for examination from the acquisitions journal, the vendor's invoice and the receiving report are examined at the same time as the related cancelled cheque. Thus, the verification is speeded up without reducing the effectiveness of the tests.

ATTRIBUTE SAMPLING FOR TESTS OF CONTROLS

Because of the importance of tests of controls for acquisitions and cash disbursements, the use of attribute sampling is common in this audit area. The approach is basically the same as for the tests of controls of sales discussed in Chapter 12. It should be noted, however, with particular reference to the most essential transaction-related audit objectives presented earlier, that most of the important attributes in the acquisition and payment cycle have a direct monetary effect on the accounts. Furthermore, many of the types of errors or fraud and other irregularities that may be found represent a misstatement of earnings and are of significant concern to the auditor. For example, there may be inventory cutoff misstatements or an incorrect recording of an expense amount. Because of this, the tolerable exception rate selected by the auditor in tests of many of the attributes in this cycle is relatively low. Since the dollar amounts of individual transactions in the cycle cover a wide range, it is also common to segregate very large and unusual items and to test them on a 100 percent basis.

ACCOUNTS PAYABLE

Accounts payable are *unpaid obligations* for goods and services received in the ordinary course of business. It is sometimes difficult to distinguish between accounts payable and accrued liabilities, but it is useful to define a liability as an account payable if the total amount of the obligation is *known and owed at the balance sheet date*. The accounts payable account therefore includes obligations for the acquisition of raw materials, equipment, utilities, repairs, and many other types of goods and services that were received before the end of the year. The great majority of accounts payable can also be recognized by the existence of vendors' invoices for the obligation. Accounts payable should also be distinguished from interest-bearing obligations. If an obligation includes the payment of interest, it should be recorded properly as a note payable, contract payable, mortgage payable, or bond payable.

The methodology for designing tests of details for accounts payable is summarized in Figure 16-3. This methodology is the same as that used for accounts receivable in Chapter 14. It is common for accounts payable to be material and thus there may be several inherent risks. Internal controls are often ineffective for accounts payable because many companies depend on the vendors to bill them and remind them of unpaid bills. Tests of details for accounts payable, therefore, often need to be extensive.

INTERNAL CONTROLS

The effects of the client's internal controls on accounts payable tests can be illustrated by two examples. In the first, assume that the client has highly effective internal controls over recording and paying for acquisitions. The receipt of goods is promptly documented by prenumbered receiving reports; prenumbered vouchers are promptly and efficiently prepared and recorded in the acquisition transactions file and thus in the vendor master file. Cash disbursements are also made promptly when due, and the disbursements are immediately recorded in the cash disbursements transactions file and the vendor master file. On a monthly basis, individual accounts payable balances in the vendor master file are reconciled with vendors' statements, and the total is compared with the general ledger by an independent person. Under these circumstances, the verification of accounts payable should require

FIGURE 16-3
Methodology for
Designing Tests of
Details of Balances of
Accounts Payable

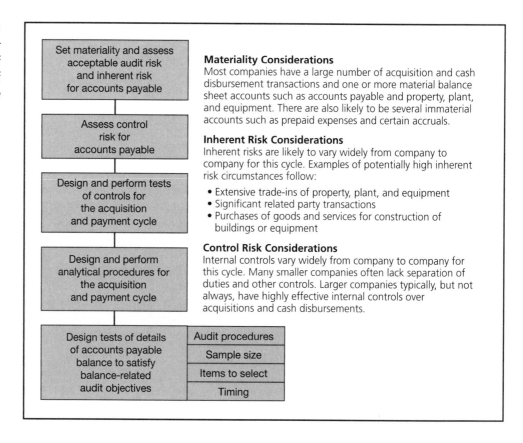

Materiality Considerations
Most companies have a large number of acquisition and cash disbursement transactions and one or more material balance sheet accounts such as accounts payable and property, plant, and equipment. There are also likely to be several immaterial accounts such as prepaid expenses and certain accruals.

Inherent Risk Considerations
Inherent risks are likely to vary widely from company to company for this cycle. Examples of potentially high inherent risk circumstances follow:

• Extensive trade-ins of property, plant, and equipment
• Significant related party transactions
• Purchases of goods and services for construction of buildings or equipment

Control Risk Considerations
Internal controls vary widely from company to company for this cycle. Many smaller companies often lack separation of duties and other controls. Larger companies typically, but not always, have highly effective internal controls over acquisitions and cash disbursements.

little audit effort once the auditor concludes that internal controls are operating effectively.

In the second example, assume that receiving reports are not used, the client defers recording acquisitions until cash disbursements are made, and, because of a weak cash position, bills are frequently paid several months after their due date. When an auditor faces such a situation, there is a high likelihood of an understatement of accounts payable; therefore, under these circumstances, extensive tests of details of accounts payable are necessary to determine whether accounts payable are properly stated at the balance sheet date.

The most important controls over accounts payable have already been discussed as part of the control and recording of acquisitions and cash disbursements. In addition to these controls, it is important to have a monthly reconciliation of vendors' statements with recorded liabilities and of the outstanding transaction file with the vendor master file and the general ledger. This should be done by an independent person.

ANALYTICAL PROCEDURES

The use of analytical procedures is as important in the acquisition and payment cycle as it is in every other cycle. Table 16-4 illustrates analytical procedures for the balance sheet and income statement accounts in the acquisition and payment cycle that are useful for uncovering areas in which additional investigation is desirable. Frequently, these ratios are calculated using the auditor's generalized audit software.

One of the most important analytical procedures for uncovering misstatements of accounts payable is comparing current-year expense totals to prior years. For example, by comparing current utilities expense to the prior year, the auditor may determine that the last utilities bill for the year was not recorded. Comparing expenses to prior years is an effective analytical procedure for accounts payable because expenses from year to year are relatively stable. Examples include rent, utilities, and other expenses billed on a regular basis.

TABLE 16-4	ANALYTICAL PROCEDURE	POSSIBLE MISSTATEMENT
ANALYTICAL PROCEDURES FOR ACQUISITION AND PAYMENT CYCLE	Compare acquisition-related expense account balances with prior years.	Misstatement of accounts payable and expenses.
	Review list of accounts payable for unusual, nonvendor, and interest-bearing payables.	Classification misstatement for nontrade liabilities.
	Compare individual accounts payable with previous years.	Unrecorded or nonexistent accounts, or misstatements.
	Calculate ratio such as purchases divided by accounts payable, and accounts payable divided by current liabilities.	Unrecorded or nonexistent accounts, or misstatements.

BALANCE-RELATED AUDIT OBJECTIVES FOR TESTS OF DETAILS

OBJECTIVE 16-5

Design and perform tests of details for accounts payable.

The overall objective in the audit of accounts payable is to determine whether accounts payable are fairly stated and properly disclosed. Eight of the nine balance-related audit objectives discussed in Chapter 5 are applicable to accounts payable. Realizable value is not applicable to liabilities.

The auditor should recognize the difference in emphasis between the audit of liabilities and the audit of assets. When assets are being verified, attention is focused on ensuring that the balance in the account is not overstated. The validity of recorded assets is constantly questioned and verified by confirmation, physical examination, and examination of supporting documents. The auditor should certainly not ignore the possibility of assets being understated, but the fact remains that the auditor is more concerned about the possibility of overstatement than understatement. The opposite approach is taken in verifying liability balances, that is, the main focus is on the discovery of understated or omitted liabilities.

The difference in emphasis in auditing assets and liabilities results directly from the *legal liability of public accountants*. If equity investors, creditors, and other users determine subsequent to the issuance of the audited financial statements that owners' equity was materially overstated, a lawsuit against the public accounting firm is fairly likely. Since an overstatement of owners' equity can arise either from an overstatement of assets or from an understatement of liabilities, it is natural for public accountants to emphasize those two types of misstatements. The probability of a successful lawsuit against a public accountant for failing to discover an understatement of owners' equity is far less likely.

Nevertheless, the auditing profession must avoid too much emphasis on protecting users from overstatements of owners' equity at the expense of ignoring understatements. If assets are consistently understated and liabilities are consistently overstated for large numbers of audited companies, the decision-making value of financial statement information is likely to decline. Therefore, even though it is natural for auditors to emphasize the possibility of overstating assets and understating liabilities, uncovering the opposite types of misstatement is also a significant responsibility.

TESTS OF DETAILS OF ACCOUNTS PAYABLE

The same balance-related audit objectives that were used as a frame of reference for verifying accounts receivable in Chapter 14 are also applicable to liabilities with three minor modifications. The most obvious difference in verifying liabilities is the non-applicability of the ownership objective. The second difference is in the rights and obligations objective. For assets, the auditor is concerned with the client's rights to the use and disposal of assets. For liabilities, the auditor is concerned with the client's obligations for the payment of the liability. If the client has no obligation to pay a liability, it should not be included as a liability. The third difference was discussed above: in auditing liabilities, the emphasis is on the search for understatements rather than for overstatements.

TABLE 16-5

BALANCE-RELATED
AUDIT OBJECTIVES
AND TESTS OF DETAILS
OF BALANCES FOR
ACCOUNTS PAYABLE

BALANCE-RELATED AUDIT OBJECTIVE	COMMON TESTS OF DETAILS OF BALANCES PROCEDURES	COMMENTS
Accounts payable in the accounts payable list agree with related master file, and the total is correctly added and agrees with the general ledger (detail tie-in).	Foot the accounts payable list.[†] Trace the total to the general ledger. Trace individual vendor's invoices to transaction file for names and amounts.	All pages need not ordinarily be footed if done manually. Unless controls are weak, tracing to transaction file should be limited.
Accounts payable in the accounts payable list exist (existence).	Trace from accounts payable list to vendors' invoices and statements. Confirm accounts payable, emphasizing large and unusual amounts.	Ordinarily receives little attention because the primary concern is with understatements.
Existing accounts payable are in the accounts payable list (completeness).	Perform out-of-period liability tests (see discussion).	These are essential audit tests for accounts payable.
Accounts payable in the accounts payable list are accurate (accuracy).	Perform same procedures as those used for existence objective and out-of-period liability tests.	Ordinarily, the emphasis in these procedures for accuracy is understatement rather than omission.
Accounts payable in the accounts payable list are properly classified (classification).	Review the list and master file for related parties, notes or other interest-bearing liabilities, long-term payables, and debit balances.	Knowledge of the client's business is essential for these tests.
Transactions in the acquisition and payment cycle are recorded in the proper period (cutoff).	Perform out-of-period liability tests (see discussion). Perform detailed tests as a part of physical observation of inventory (see discussion). Test for inventory in transit (see discussion).	These are essential audit tests for accounts payable. These are referred to as *cutoff tests*.
The company has an obligation to pay the liabilities included in accounts payable (obligations).	Examine vendors' statements and confirm accounts payable.	Normally, not a concern in the audit of accounts payable because all accounts payable are obligations.
Accounts in the acquisition and payment cycle are properly presented and disclosed (disclosure).	Review financial statements to make sure material related party, long-term, and interest-bearing liabilities are segregated.	Ordinarily not a problem.

[†]This test of details would be conducted on many audits using the computer.

Table 16-5 includes the balance-related audit objectives and common tests of details of balances procedures for accounts payable. The actual audit procedures will vary considerably depending on the nature of the entity, the materiality of accounts payable, the nature and effectiveness of internal controls, and inherent risk.

OUT-OF-PERIOD LIABILITY TESTS

OBJECTIVE 16-6

Know the importance of out-of-period tests for accounts payable and common tests.

Because of the emphasis on understatements in liability accounts, out-of-period liability tests are important for accounts payable. The extent of tests to uncover unrecorded accounts payable, frequently referred to as "the search for unrecorded accounts payable," depends heavily on assessed control risk and the materiality of the potential balance in the account. The same audit procedures used to uncover unrecorded payables are applicable to the accuracy objective. The audit procedures that follow are typical tests.

Examine underlying documentation for subsequent cash disbursements   The purpose of this audit procedure is to uncover payments made in the subsequent accounting period that represent liabilities at the balance sheet date. The supporting documentation is examined to determine whether a payment was for a current period obligation. For example, if inventory was received prior to the balance sheet date, it will be so indicated on the receiving report. Frequently, documentation for payments made in the subsequent period are examined for several weeks, especially when the client does not pay its bills on a timely basis. Any payment that is for a current period obligation should be traced to the accounts payable trial balance to make sure it has been included as a liability.

Examine underlying documentation for bills not paid several weeks after the year end   This procedure is carried out in the same manner as the preceding one and serves the same purpose. The only difference is that it is done for unpaid obligations near the end of the examination rather than for obligations that have already been paid. For example, in an audit with a March 31 year end, if the auditor examines the supporting documentation for cheques paid until June 28, bills that are still unpaid at that date should be examined to determine whether they are obligations of the year ended March 31. For large audit engagements, or for organizations with good internal controls, the auditor would limit these tests to a sample of transactions or reduce the period of investigation to a shorter period of time (perhaps two or three weeks).

Trace receiving reports issued before year end to related vendors' invoices   All merchandise received before the year end of the accounting period, indicated by the issuance of a receiving report, should be included as accounts payable. By tracing receiving reports issued at and before year end to vendors' invoices and making sure they are included in accounts payable, the auditor is testing for unrecorded obligations.

Trace vendors' statements that show a balance due to the accounts payable trial balance   If the client maintains a file of vendors' statements, any statement indicating a balance due can be traced to the listing to make sure it is included as an account payable.

Send confirmations to vendors with whom the client does business   Although the use of confirmations for accounts payable is less common than for accounts receivable, it is common testing for vendors omitted from the accounts payable list, omitted transactions, and misstated account balances. Sending confirmations to active vendors for whom a balance has not been included in the accounts payable list is a useful means of searching for omitted amounts. This type of confirmation is commonly referred to as "zero balance confirmation." Additional discussion of confirmation of accounts payable is deferred until later in the chapter.

CUTOFF TESTS

Cutoff tests for accounts payable are intended to determine whether transactions recorded a few days before and after the balance sheet date are included in the correct period. The five audit procedures discussed in the preceding section are directly related to cutoff for acquisitions, but they emphasize understatements. For the first three procedures, it is also appropriate to examine supporting documentation as a test of overstatement of accounts payable. For example, the third procedure is to trace receiving reports issued before year end to related vendors' invoices in order to test for unrecorded accounts payable. To test for overstatement cutoff amounts, the auditor should trace receiving reports issued *after* year end to related invoices to make sure they are not recorded as accounts payable (unless they are inventory in transit, which will be discussed shortly).

Since most cutoff tests have already been discussed, only two aspects are enlarged upon here: the examination of receiving reports and the determination of the amount of inventory in transit.

Relationship of cutoff to physical observation of inventory In determining that the accounts payable cutoff is correct, *it is essential that the cutoff tests be coordinated with the physical observation of inventory*. For example, assume that an inventory acquisition for $40,000 is received late in the afternoon of December 31, after the physical inventory is completed. If the acquisition is included in accounts payable and purchases, but excluded from inventory, the result is an understatement of net earnings of $40,000. Conversely, if the acquisition is excluded from both inventory and accounts payable, there is a misstatement in the balance sheet, but the income statement is correct. The only way the auditor will know which type of misstatement has occurred is to coordinate cutoff tests with the observation of inventory.

The cutoff information for purchases should be obtained *during the physical observation* of the inventory. At this time the auditor should review the procedures in the receiving department to determine that all inventory received was counted, and the auditor should record in his or her working papers the last receiving report number of inventory included in the physical count. During the year-end field work, the auditor should then test the accounting records for cutoff. The auditor should trace receiving report numbers to the accounts payable records to verify that they are correctly included or excluded.

For example, assume that the last receiving report number representing inventory included in the physical count was 3167. The auditor should record this document number and subsequently trace it and several preceding numbers to their related vendor's invoice and to the accounts payable list or the accounts payable transaction file to determine that they are all included. Similarly, accounts payable for purchases recorded on receiving reports with numbers larger than 3167 should be excluded from accounts payable.

When the client's physical inventory takes place before the last day of the year, it is still necessary to perform an accounts payable cutoff at the time of the physical count in the manner described in the preceding paragraph. In addition, the auditor must verify whether all acquisitions taking place between the physical count and the end of the year were added to the physical inventory and accounts payable. For example, if the client takes the physical count on December 27 for a December 31 year end, the cutoff information is taken as of December 27. During the year-end examination, the auditor must first test to determine whether the cutoff was accurate as of December 27. After determining that the December 27 cutoff is accurate, the auditor must test whether all inventory received subsequent to the physical count, but before the balance sheet date, was added to inventory and accounts payable by the client.

Inventory in transit A distinction in accounts payable must be made between acquisitions of inventory that are on an *FOB destination* basis and those that are on an *FOB origin* (or *FOB shipping point*) basis. With the former, title passes to the buyer when it is received for inventory. Therefore, only inventory received prior to the balance sheet date should be included in inventory and accounts payable at year end. When an acquisition is on an FOB origin basis, the inventory and related accounts payable must be recorded in the current period if shipment occurred before the balance sheet date.

Determining whether inventory has been purchased on an FOB destination or origin basis is done by examining vendors' invoices. The auditor should examine invoices for merchandise received shortly after year end to determine if they were on an FOB origin basis. For those that were, and when the shipment dates were prior to the balance sheet date, the inventory and related accounts payable must be recorded in the current period if the amounts are material.

RELIABILITY OF EVIDENCE

In determining the appropriate evidence to accumulate for verifying accounts payable, it is essential that the auditor understand the relative reliability of the three primary types of evidence ordinarily used: vendors' invoices, vendors' statements, and confirmations.

OBJECTIVE 16-7

Know the relative reliability of vendor's invoices, vendor's statements, and confirmations of accounts payable.

Distinction between vendors' invoices and vendors' statements In verifying the amount due to a vendor, the auditor should make a major distinction between vendors' invoices and vendors' statements. In examining vendors' invoices and related supporting documents, such as receiving reports and purchase orders, the auditor gets highly reliable *evidence about individual transactions*. A vendor's statement is not as desirable as invoices for verifying individual transactions because a statement only includes the total amount of the transaction. The units acquired, price, freight, and other data are not included. However, a statement has the advantage of including the ending balance according to the vendor's records. Which of these two documents is better for verifying the correct balance in accounts payable? *The vendor's statement is superior for verifying accounts payable* because it includes the ending balance. The auditor could compare existing vendors' invoices with the client's list and still not uncover missing ones, which is the primary concern in accounts payable. Which of these two documents is better for testing acquisitions in tests of control? *The vendor's invoice is superior for verifying transactions* because the auditor is verifying individual transactions and the invoice shows the details of the acquisitions.

Difference between vendors' statements and confirmations The most important distinction between a vendor's statement and a confirmation of accounts payable is the source of the information. A vendor's statement has been prepared by an independent third party, but it is in the hands of the client at the time the auditor examines it. This provides the client with an opportunity to alter a vendor's statement or to make particular statements unavailable to the auditor. A confirmation of accounts payable, which normally is a request for an itemized statement sent directly to the public accountant's office, provides the same information but can be regarded as more reliable. In addition, confirmations of accounts payable frequently include a request for information about notes and acceptances payable, as well as consigned inventory that is owned by the vendor but stored on the client's premises. An illustration of a typical accounts payable confirmation request is given in Figure 16-4.

Due to the availability of vendors' statements and vendors' invoices, which are both relatively reliable evidence because they originate from a third party, the confirmation of accounts payable is less common than confirmation of accounts receivable. If the client has adequate internal controls and vendors' statements are available for examination, then confirmations are normally not sent. However, when the client's internal controls are weak, when statements are not available, or when the auditor questions the client's integrity, then it is desirable to send confirmation requests to vendors. Because of the emphasis on understatements of liability accounts, the accounts confirmed should include large accounts, active accounts, accounts with a zero balance, and a representative sample of all others.

In most instances in which accounts payable are confirmed, it is done shortly after the balance sheet date. However, if assessed control risk is low, it may be possible to confirm accounts payable at an interim date as a test of the effectiveness of internal controls. Then if the confirmation indicates that the internal controls are ineffective, it is possible to design other audit procedures to test accounts payable at year end.

When vendors' statements are examined or confirmations are received, there must be a *reconciliation* of the statement or confirmation with the accounts payable list. Frequently, differences are caused by inventory in transit, cheques mailed by the client but not received by the vendor at the statement date, and delays in processing the accounting records. The reconciliation is of the same general nature as that discussed in Chapter 14 for accounts receivable. The documents typically used to reconcile the balances on the accounts payable list with the confirmation or vendor's statement include receiving reports, vendors' invoices, and cancelled cheques.

FIGURE 16-4
Accounts Payable
Confirmation Request

Roger Mead Ltd.
1600 Westmount Ave. N.
Kenora, Ontario
P9N 1X7

January 15, 1999

Szabo Sales Co. Ltd.
2116 King Street
Kenora, Ontario
P9N 1G3

To Whom It May Concern:

Our auditors, Adams and Lelik, CAs, are conducting an audit of our financial statements. For this purpose, please furnish directly to them, at their address noted below, the following information as of December 31, 1998.

(1) Itemized statements of our accounts payable to you showing all unpaid items;
(2) A complete list of any notes and acceptances payable to you (including any which have been discounted) showing the original date, dates due, original amount, unpaid balance, collateral and endorsers; and
(3) An itemized list of your merchandise consigned to us.

Your prompt attention to this request will be appreciated. A stamped, addressed envelope is enclosed for your reply.

Yours truly,

Sally Palm

Adams and Lelik
Chartered Accountants
215 Tecumseh Crescent
Kenora, Ontario
P9N 2K5

Roger Mead Ltd.
per Sally Palm

SAMPLE SIZE

Sample sizes for accounts payable tests vary considerably depending on such factors as the materiality of accounts payable, number of accounts outstanding, assessed control risk, and results of the prior year. When a client's internal controls are weak, which is not uncommon for accounts payable, almost all population items must be verified. In other situations, minimal testing is needed.

Statistical sampling is less commonly used for the audit of accounts payable than for accounts receivable. It is more difficult to define the population and determine the population size in accounts payable. Since the emphasis is on omitted accounts payable, it is essential that the population include all potential payables.

SUMMARY

Figure 16-5 illustrates the major accounts in the acquisition and payment cycle and the types of audit tests used to audit these accounts. This figure also shows how the audit risk model discussed in Chapter 8 relates to the audit of the acquisition and payment cycle.

AUDIT OF SYSTEM CONVERSIONS

OBJECTIVE 16-8

Apply audit objectives and design audit procedures for an accounts payable system conversion.

Organizations are not static. With time, as an organization grows or shrinks, or changes its business objectives, the procedures within an organization also change. Often, when the auditor returns to conduct the audit, he or she identifies minor changes in procedures, causing minor changes in risk assessments, internal control testing, and tests of details.

At other times, the organization has undertaken a major change in its systems by implementing a new computer system or has made major changes to a particular system. For example, a client that previously processed its accounts payable and cash disbursements manually could use a standard accounting software package. A large client could change a batch-processing accounts payable and cash disbursements system to an on-line processing system, as described in the focus box on the next page.

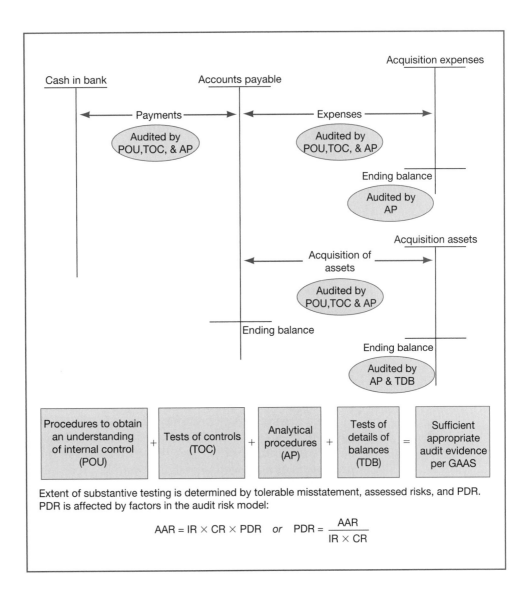

Extent of substantive testing is determined by tolerable misstatement, assessed risks, and PDR. PDR is affected by factors in the audit risk model:

$$AAR = IR \times CR \times PDR \quad or \quad PDR = \frac{AAR}{IR \times CR}$$

CONVERSION TO NEW SYSTEM HIDES $5 MILLION ERROR

A large pharmaceutical company had been using complex data processing methods for many years. They had custom programmed accounting systems and used data communications to send and receive orders and other business documents. The accounts payable system was falling behind — it was batch processing-based and not integrated with the purchasing system. Accordingly, the information systems personnel designed and tested many new programs for updating the accounts payable and purchasing systems. These systems were put in place at the company's year-end date, January 31. Systems were run parallel (i.e., both the old and new systems were used) for the month of January, with the new system used exclusively effective February 1. The auditors relied on the equivalency of the two systems and on the fact that the company normally had excellent controls in accounts payable and cash disbursements. However, due to excessive workload, goods received on January 31 were not recorded until February 1, and, *therefore, were recorded only in the new system.* Thus, accounts

When an organization changes an entire system or set of systems, there are three issues that the auditor needs to address:

- A new system of internal controls will need to be documented and evaluated.
- The auditor will need to audit the actual data conversion process.
- The auditor will need to determine whether accounting policies have been changed.

NEW SYSTEM OF INTERNAL CONTROLS

When new computer programs are put in place, the controls that are part of those programs will change. For example, if the system changes from batch to on-line, then controls to help ensure data entry accuracy will likely occur as information is entered, rather than be checked for a group of transactions. If a system changes from manual to automated, then new controls will be present in the programs, such as automatic calculation of invoice extensions, which previously needed to be completed manually. Also, activities done by persons handling these systems may change.

The auditor needs to document the new procedures, evaluate these procedures, and determine the effect on control risk. Should reliance on the programmed controls be tested, the auditor may have the option of using the same audit procedures as in prior years or may need to design new audit procedures, such as the creation of test transactions to determine that programs are functioning as intended. If the client has run its systems in parallel (i.e., run both the old and the new systems for a period of time), then the auditor can evaluate the new system by examining the records kept during this parallel process.

AUDITING THE DATA CONVERSION PROCESS

When computer systems are established for the first time, a major task is the creation of master files. For example, purchase orders cannot be processed nor accounts payable vendor invoices entered if the vendor and information such as name, address, and terms are not established in the vendor master file. Quantities ordered or received cannot be entered if the inventory item, description, and price do not exist in the inventory master file. The number of vendors could be in the hundreds, while the number of inventory items could number in the thousands.

Determining the audit procedures required involves a risk assessment process. Inherent risk may increase because these are new systems in place and employees may not be aware of the actions required. By determining the extent of employee training and the rigour of the implementation process, the auditor can assess whether inherent risk is affected. The rigour of the implementation process also affects control risk. If the implementation process is properly planned, conducted, and supervised, the auditor can rely on these controls. Conversely, if controls over the conversion process are poor or are not documented, the auditor must conduct tests of details. Table 16-6 combines the features of Tables 16-2 and 16-5 to describe audit objectives for the conversion of a batch system to an on-line system. Table 16-6 shows possible key controls, tests of controls, and tests of details that would be required should controls be absent.

Notice that two audit objectives are not included. Classification is not included since accuracy and agreement between the two systems ensures that classification is satisfied. The same is true for posting and summarization: if individual and total vendor amounts are correct and details from the old system agree to the new system, then posting and summarization are also satisfied.

Careful review of Table 16-6 shows that the tests can be simplified to the following three types:

- Tests comparing details from the new system to the old system (to verify that only accurate, authorized information has been established)
- Tests comparing details from the old system to the new system (to ensure accuracy and that no transactions have been omitted)
- Cutoff testing to ensure that transactions are included in only the proper system and have not been omitted

Thus, a *conversion audit* uses audit tests that we have used in other portions of our audit. The emphasis is on the accurate and authorized establishment of new master files and on the cutoff of transactions in the appropriate system.

DETERMINING WHETHER ACCOUNTING POLICIES HAVE CHANGED

This could be done concurrently with inventory costing. For example, if inventory is counted only at year end (a periodic system), it would be costed on a FIFO (first-in, first-out) basis, whereas most computer systems use average costing or weighted average costing. Should the method of inventory costing change, the auditor would need to gather and include sufficient evidence that there is adequate disclosure on the financial statements for this change in accounting policy.

TABLE 16-6

AUDIT OBJECTIVES, KEY CONTROLS, TESTS OF CONTROLS, AND TESTS OF DETAILS FOR SYSTEM CONVERSION OF ACCOUNTS PAYABLE

AUDIT OBJECTIVE	KEY INTERNAL CONTROL	COMMON TESTS OF CONTROLS	COMMON TESTS OF DETAILS
Only authorized vendors are established with balances for goods and services actually received (existence).	Agree vendor file details for each vendor from the new (on-line) system to the old (batch) system.	Review vendor file listings for evidence of agreement.	On a test basis, agree vendor file details for each vendor from the new (on-line) system to the old (batch) system
All vendor balances as of the date of conversion are included (completeness).	Agree aged accounts payable trial balance details from the old (batch) system to the new (on-line) system for each vendor and in total. Agree the total to the general ledger.	Review aged accounts payable trial balance listings for evidence of comparison.	On a test basis, agree aged accounts payable trial balance details from the old (batch) system to the new (on-line) system for each vendor and in total. Agree total to general ledger.
Details in the new system agree to details from the old system. New information is accurate (accuracy).	Same as for completeness.	Same as for completeness.	Same as for completeness.
Information is recorded in the appropriate system and is not omitted (cutoff).	Procedures exist to ensure appropriate cutoff of transactions (i.e., transactions are recorded only once in the proper system and are not omitted).	Conduct cutoff tests, as described on page 543, for receiving reports and vendor invoices.	Same as for tests of controls.

Accounts payable trial balance — a listing of the amount owed by each vendor at a point in time; prepared directly from the accounts payable master file (p. 532).

Acquisition and payment cycle — the transaction cycle that includes the acquisition of and payment for goods and services from suppliers outside the organization (p. 528).

Conversion audit — the audit procedures required when an organization changes its system to a different automated system (p. 528).

Debit memo — a document indicating a reduction in the amount owed to a vendor because of returned goods or an allowance granted (p. 532).

FOB origin — shipping contract in which title to the goods passes to the buyer at the time that the goods are shipped (p. 544).

FOB destination — shipping contract in which title to the goods passes to the buyer when the goods are received (p. 544).

Purchase order — a document prepared by the purchasing department indicating the description, quantity, and related information for goods and services that the company intends to purchase (p. 530).

Purchase requisition — request by an authorized employee to the purchasing department to place an order for inventory and other items used by an entity (p. 530).

Receiving report — a document prepared by the receiving department at the time tangible goods are received, indicating the description of the goods, the quantity received, the date received, and other relevant data; part of the documentation necessary for payment to be made (p. 531).

Vendor master file — a computer file for maintaining a record for each vendor of individual acquisitions, cash disbursements, and acquisition returns and allowances, and vendor balances (p. 532).

Vendor's invoice — a document that specifies the details of an acquisition transaction and amount of money owed to the vendor for an acquisition (p. 532).

Vendor's statement — a statement prepared monthly by the vendor, which indicates the customer's beginning balance, acquisitions, payments, and ending balance (p. 533).

REVIEW QUESTIONS

16-1 List five asset accounts, three liability accounts, and five expense accounts included in the acquisition and payment cycle for a typical manufacturing company.

16-2 List one possible internal control for each of the six transaction-related audit objectives for cash disbursements. For each control, list a test of control to test its effectiveness.

16-3 List one possible control for each of the six transaction-related audit objectives for acquisitions. For each control, list a test of control to test its effectiveness.

16-4 Evaluate the following statements by an auditor concerning tests of acquisitions and payments: "In selecting the acquisitions and cash disbursements sample for testing, the best approach is to select a random month and test every transaction for the period. Using this approach enables me to thoroughly understand internal control because I have examined everything that happened during the period. As a part of the monthly test, I also test the beginning and ending bank reconciliations and prepare a proof of cash for the month. At the completion of these tests, I feel I can evaluate the effectiveness of internal control."

16-5 What is the importance of cash discounts to the client, and how can the auditor verify whether they are being used in accordance with company policy?

16-6 What are the similarities and differences in the objectives of the following two procedures?

1. Select a random sample of receiving reports and trace them to related vendors' invoices and acquisitions journal entries, comparing the vendor's name, type of material and quantity acquired, and total amount of the acquisition.

2. Select a random sample of acquisitions journal entries and trace them to related vendors' invoices and receiving reports, comparing the vendor's name, type of material and quantity acquired, and total amount of the acquisition.

16-7 If an audit client does not have prenumbered cheques, what type of misstatement has the greatest chance of occurring? Under the circumstances, which audit procedure can the auditor use to compensate for the weakness?

16-8 What is meant by a "voucher"? Explain how its use can improve an organization's internal controls.

16-9 Explain why most auditors consider the receipt of goods and services the most important point in the acquisition and payment cycle.

16-10 Explain the relationship between tests of the acquisition and payment cycle and tests of inventory. Give specific examples of how these two types of tests affect each other.

16-11 Explain the relationship between tests of the acquisition and payment cycle and tests of accounts payable. Give specific examples of how these two types of tests affect each other.

16-12 A public accountant examines all unrecorded invoices on hand as of February 28, 1999, the last day of field work. Which of the following misstatements is most likely to be uncovered by this procedure? Explain.

1. Accounts payable are overstated at December 31, 1998.

2. Accounts payable are understated at December 31, 1998.

3. Operating expenses are overstated for the twelve months ended December 31, 1998.

4. Operating expenses are overstated for the two months ended February 28, 1999.

16-13 Explain why it is common for auditors to send confirmation requests to vendors with "zero balances" on the client's accounts payable listing but uncommon to follow the same approach in verifying accounts receivable.

16-14 Distinguish between a vendor's invoice and a vendor's statement. Which document should ideally be used as evidence in auditing acquisition transactions and which for directly verifying accounts payable balances? Why?

16-15 It is less common to confirm accounts payable at an interim date than accounts receivable. Explain why.

16-16 In testing the cutoff of accounts payable at the balance sheet date, explain why it is important that auditors coordinate their tests with the physical observation of inventory. What can the auditor do during the physical inventory to enhance the likelihood of an accurate cutoff?

16-17 Distinguish between FOB destination and FOB origin. What procedures should the auditor follow concerning acquisitions of inventory on an FOB origin basis near year end?

16-18 John has discovered that his client converted to an integrated set of software packages one month prior to the year end. During the last month of the fiscal year, the client ran systems parallel. John decides that he can do the audit as usual because the old system is still in operation. Next year, he will have to audit only the new system because the old system will no longer be in use. Evaluate John's decision regarding the audit.

MULTIPLE CHOICE QUESTIONS

16-19 The following questions concern internal controls in the acquisition and payment cycle. Choose the best response.

a. Effective internal control over the purchasing of raw materials should usually include all of the following procedures except
   (1) systematic reporting of product changes that will affect raw materials.
   (2) determining the need for raw materials prior to preparing the purchase order.
   (3) obtaining third-party, written quality and quantity reports prior to payment for the raw materials.
   (4) obtaining financial approval prior to making a commitment.

b. Budd, the purchasing agent of Lake Hardware Wholesalers Ltd., has a relative who owns a retail hardware store. Budd arranged for hardware to be delivered by manufacturers to the retail store on a COD basis, thereby enabling his relative to buy at Lake's wholesale prices. Budd was probably able to accomplish this because of Lake's poor internal control over
   (1) purchase orders.
   (2) purchase requisitions.
   (3) cash receipts.
   (4) perpetual inventory records.

c. Which of the following is an internal control that would prevent paid disbursement documents from being presented for payment a second time?
   (1) The date on cash disbursement documents should be within a few days of the date that the document is presented for payment.
   (2) Unsigned cheques should be prepared by individuals who are responsible for signing cheques.
   (3) Cash disbursement documents should be approved by at least two responsible management officials.
   (4) The official signing the cheque should compare the cheque with the documents and should deface the documents.

(AICPA adapted)

16-20 The following questions concern accumulating evidence in the acquisition and payment cycle. Choose the best response.

a. In comparing the confirmation of accounts payable with suppliers and confirmation of accounts receivable with debtors, the true statement is that
   (1) confirmation of accounts payable with suppliers is a more widely accepted auditing procedure than is confirmation of accounts receivable with debtors.
   (2) statistical sampling techniques are more widely accepted in the confirmation of accounts payable than in the confirmation of accounts receivable.
   (3) as compared with the confirmation of accounts payable, the confirmation of accounts receivable will tend to emphasize accounts with zero balances at the balance sheet date.
   (4) it is less likely that the confirmation request sent to the supplier will show the amount owed her than that the request sent to the debtor will show the amount due from him.

b. Which of the following audit procedures is best for identifying unrecorded trade accounts payable?
   (1) Examining unusual relationships between monthly accounts payable balances and recorded cash payments
   (2) Reconciling vendors' statements to the file of receiving reports to identify items received just prior to the balance sheet date
   (3) Reviewing cash disbursements recorded subsequent to the balance sheet date to determine whether the related payables apply to the prior period
   (4) Investigating payables recorded just prior to and just subsequent to the balance sheet date to determine whether they are supported by receiving reports

c. In auditing accounts payable, an auditor's procedures most likely would focus primarily on management's assertion of
   (1) existence or occurrence.
   (2) completeness.
   (3) presentation and disclosure.
   (4) valuation or allocation.

16-21 Questions 1 through 8 are typically found in questionnaires used by auditors to obtain an understanding of internal control in the acquisition and payment cycle. In using the questionnaire for a particular client, a "yes" response to a question indicates a possible internal control, whereas a "no" indicates a potential weakness.

1. Is the purchasing function performed by personnel who are independent of the receiving and shipping functions and the payables and disbursing functions?

2. Are all vendors' invoices routed directly to accounting from the mailroom?

3. Are all receiving reports prenumbered and the numerical sequence checked by a person independent of cheque preparation or by the computer system?

4. Are all extensions, footings, discounts, and freight terms on vendors' invoices checked for accuracy?

5. Does a responsible employee review and approve the invoice account distribution before it is recorded in the acquisitions system?

6. Are cheques recorded in the cash disbursement system as they are prepared?

7. Are all supporting documents properly cancelled at the time the cheques are signed?

8. Is the custody of cheques after signature and before mailing handled by an employee independent of all payable, disbursing, cash, and general ledger functions?

Required

a. For each of the preceding questions, state the transaction-related audit objective(s) being fulfilled if the control is in effect.

b. For each internal control, list a test of control to test its effectiveness.

c. For each of the preceding questions, identify the nature of the potential financial misstatement(s) if the control is not in effect.

d. For each of the potential misstatements in part (c), list a substantive audit procedure that can be used to determine whether a material misstatement exists.

16-22 Following are some of the tests of controls frequently performed in the acquisition and payment cycle. Each is to be done on a sample basis.

1. Trace transactions recorded in the purchase journal to supporting documentation, comparing the vendor's name, total dollar amounts, and authorization for acquisition.

2. Account for a sequence of receiving reports and trace selected ones to related vendors' invoices and acquisitions journal entries.

3. Review supporting documents for clerical accuracy, propriety of account distribution, and reasonableness of expenditure in relation to the nature of the client's operations.

4. Examine documents in support of acquisition transactions to make sure each transaction has an approved vendor's invoice, receiving report, and purchase order included.

5. Foot the cash disbursements transaction file, trace postings for selected days to the general ledger, and trace postings of individual payments to the accounts payable transaction file.

6. Account for a numerical sequence of cheques in the cash disbursements data file, and examine all voided or spoiled cheques for proper cancellation.

7. Prepare a proof of cash disbursements for an interim month.

8. Compare dates on cancelled cheques with dates on the cash disbursements listing and the bank cancellation date.

Required

State the purpose(s) of each procedure.

16-23 The following misstatements are included in the accounting records of Westgate Manufacturing Corp.

1. Telephone expense (account 2112) was unintentionally charged to repairs and maintenance (account 2121).

2. Acquisitions of raw materials are frequently not recorded until several weeks after the goods are received due to the failure of the receiving personnel to forward receiving reports to accounting. When pressure from a vendor's credit department is put on Westgate's accounting department, it searches for the receiving report, records the transactions in the acquisitions journal, and pays the bill.

3. The accounts payable clerk prepares a monthly cheque to Story Supply Ltd. for the amount of an invoice owed and submits the unsigned cheque to the treasurer for payment along with related supporting documents that have already been approved. When she receives the signed cheque from the treasurer, she records it as a debit to accounts payable and deposits the cheque in a personal bank account for a company named Story Ltd. A few days later she records the invoice in the acquisitions journal again, resubmits the documents and a new cheque to the treasurer, and sends the cheque to the vendor after it has been signed.

4. The amount of a supplier invoice is entered as $6,412.87 instead of $4,612.87. The cheque is also issued and mailed for this amount.

5. The accounts payable clerk intentionally held onto and did not mail seven large cheques written on December 26 to prevent cash in the bank from having a negative balance. They were mailed on January 2 of the subsequent year.

6. Each month a fraudulent receiving report is submitted to accounting by an employee in the receiving department. A few days later he sends Westgate an invoice for the quantity of goods ordered from a small company he

owns and operates in the evening. A cheque is prepared, and the amount is paid when the receiving report and the vendor's invoice are matched by the accounts payable clerk.

Required

a. For each misstatement, identify the transaction-related audit objective that was not met.

b. For each misstatement, state a control that should have prevented it from occurring on a continuing basis.

c. For each misstatement, state a substantive audit procedure that could uncover it.

16-24 The following auditing procedures were performed in the audit of accounts payable:

1. Examine supporting documents for cash disbursements several days before and after year end.

2. Examine the acquisition and payment journals for the last few days of the current period and first few days of the succeeding period, looking for large or unusual transactions.

3. Trace from the general ledger trial balance and supporting working papers to determine if accounts payable, related parties, and other related assets and liabilities are properly included on the financial statements.

4. For liabilities that are payable in a foreign currency, determine the exchange rate and check calculations.

5. Discuss with the controller whether any amounts included on the accounts payable list are due to related parties, debit balances, or notes payable.

6. Obtain vendors' statements from the controller, and reconcile to a listing of accounts payable.

7. Obtain vendors' statements directly from vendors, and reconcile to the listing of accounts payable.

8. Obtain the accounts payable aged trial balance listing and the accounts payable open transaction file. Re-add the data file, and agree totals to the listing and to the general ledger.

Required

a. For each procedure, identify the type of audit evidence used.

b. For each procedure, use the following matrix to identify which balance-related audit objective(s) was (were) satisfied. (Procedure 1 is completed as an illustration.)

AUDIT PROCEDURE	BALANCE-RELATED AUDIT OBJECTIVE							
	Detail tie-in	Existence	Completeness	Accuracy	Classification	Cutoff	Obligations	Presentation and disclosure
1			X			X		
2								
3								
4								
5								
6								
7								
8								

c. Evaluate the need to have certain objectives satisfied by more than one audit procedure.

16-25 In testing cash disbursements for Immanuel Klein Ltd., you have obtained an understanding of internal control. The controls are reasonably good, and no unusual audit problems have arisen in previous years.

Although there are not many personnel in the accounting department, there is a reasonable separation of duties in the organization. There is a separate purchasing agent who has responsibility for ordering goods and a separate receiving department for counting the goods when they are received and for preparing receiving reports. There is a separation of duties between recording acquisitions and cash disbursements, and all information is recorded in the two subsystems independently. The controller reviews all supporting documents before signing the cheques and ensures independent mailing to the respective vendors.

All aspects of internal control seem satisfactory to you, and you perform minimum tests of 15 transactions as a means of assessing control risk. In your tests, you discover the following exceptions:

1. Two items in the acquisitions journal have been misclassified.

2. Three invoices had not been initialled by the controller, but there were no dollar misstatements evident in the transactions.

3. Five receiving reports were recorded in the acquisitions journal at least two weeks later than their date on the receiving report.

4. One invoice had been paid twice. The second payment was supported by a duplicate copy of the invoice. Both copies of the invoice had been marked "paid."

5. One cheque amount in the cash disbursements journal was for $100 less than the amount stated on the vendor's invoice.

6. One voided cheque was missing.

7. Two receiving reports for vendors' invoices were missing from the transaction packet. One vendor's invoice had an extension error, and the invoice had been initialled to verify that the amount had been checked.

Required

a. Identify whether each of exceptions 1 through 7 was a control test deviation, a monetary error or fraud and other irregularities, or both.

b. For each exception, identify which transaction-related audit objective was not met.

c. What is the audit importance of each of these exceptions?

d. What follow-up procedures would you use to determine more about the nature of each exception?

e. How would each of these exceptions affect the balance of your audit? Be specific.

f. Identify internal controls that should have prevented each misstatement.

16-26 You are the staff auditor testing the combined purchase and cash disbursements journal for a small audit client. Internal control is regarded as reasonably effective, considering the number of personnel.

The in-charge auditor has decided that a sample of 80 items should be sufficient for this audit because of the excellent controls and gives you the following instructions:

1. All transactions selected must exceed $100.

2. At least 50 of the transactions must be for purchases of raw material because these transactions are typically material.

3. It is not acceptable to include the same vendor in the sample more than once.

4. All vendors' invoices that cannot be located must be replaced with a new sample item.

5. Both cheques and supporting documents are to be examined for the same transactions.

6. The sample must be random, after modifications for instructions 1 through 5.

Required

a. Evaluate each of these instructions for testing acquisition and cash disbursements transactions.

b. Explain the difficulties of applying each of these instructions to attributes sampling.

16-27 You were in the final stages of your examination of the financial statements of Ozine Corporation for the year ended December 31, 1998, when you were consulted by the corporation's president. He believes that there is no point to your examining the 1999 acquisitions data files and testing data in support of 1999 entries. He stated that (1) bills pertain-

ing to 1998 that were received too late to be included in the December acquisitions data files were recorded as of the year end by the corporation by journal entry, (2) the internal auditor made tests after the year end, and (3) he would furnish you with a letter certifying that there were no unrecorded liabilities.

Required

a. Should a public accountant's test for unrecorded liabilities be affected by the fact that the client made a journal entry to record 1998 bills that were received late? Explain.

b. Should a public accountant's test for unrecorded liabilities be affected by the fact that a letter is obtained in which a responsible management official certifies that, to the best of his or her knowledge, all liabilities have been recorded? Explain.

c. Should a public accountant's test for unrecorded liabilities be eliminated or reduced because of the internal audit tests? Explain.

d. Assume that the corporation, which handled some government contracts, had no internal auditor but that an auditor from the Auditor General's office spent three weeks auditing the records and was just completing her work at this time. How would the public accountant's unrecorded liability test be affected by the work of the auditor from the Auditor General's office?

e. What sources in addition to the 1999 acquisitions data files should the public accountant consider to locate possible unrecorded liabilities?

(AICPA adapted)

16-28 Because of the small size of the company and the limited number of accounting personnel, the Dry Goods Wholesale Company Ltd. initially records all acquisitions of goods and services at the time that cash disbursements are made. At the end of each quarter when financial statements for internal purposes are prepared, accounts payable are recorded by adjusting journal entries. The entries are reversed at the beginning of the subsequent period. Except for the lack of a purchasing system, the controls over acquisitions are excellent for a small company. (There are adequate prenumbered documents for all receipt of goods, proper approvals, and adequate internal verification wherever possible.)

Before the auditor arrives for the year-end audit, the bookkeeper prepares adjusting entries to record the accounts payable as of the balance sheet date. The aged trial balance is listed as of the year end, and a manual schedule is prepared adding the amounts that were entered in the following month. Thus, the accounts payable balance equals the aged trial balance plus the following month's journal entry for invoices received after the year end. All vendors' invoices supporting the journal entry are retained in a separate file for the auditor's use.

In the current year, the accounts payable balance has increased dramatically because of a severe cash shortage. (The cash shortage apparently arose from expansion of inventory and facilities rather than lack of sales.) Many accounts have remained unpaid for several months and the client is getting pressure from several vendors to pay the bills. Since the company had a relatively profitable year, management is anxious to complete the audit as early as possible so that the audited statements can be used to obtain a large bank loan.

Required

a. Explain how the lack of a complete aged accounts payable trial balance will affect the auditor's tests of controls for acquisitions and cash disbursements.

b. What should the auditor use as a sampling unit in performing tests of acquisitions?

c. Assuming that no misstatements are discovered in the auditor's tests of controls for acquisitions and cash disbursements, how will that result affect the verification of accounts payable?

d. Discuss the reasonableness of the client's request for an early completion of the audit and the implications of the request from the auditor's point of view.

e. List the audit procedures that should be performed in the year-end audit of accounts payable to meet the cutoff objective.

f. State your opinion as to whether it is possible to conduct an adequate audit in these circumstances.

16-29 Mincin, a public accountant, is the auditor of the Raleigh Corporation. Mincin is considering the audit work to be performed in the accounts payable area for the current year's engagement.

The prior year's working papers show that confirmation requests were mailed to 100 of Raleigh's 1,000 suppliers. The selected suppliers were based on Mincin's sample that was designed to select accounts with large dollar balances. A substantial number of hours were spent by Raleigh and Mincin resolving relatively minor differences between the confirmation replies and Raleigh's accounting records. Alternative audit procedures were used for those suppliers who did not respond to the confirmation requests.

Required

a. Identify the accounts payable balance-related audit objectives that Mincin must consider in determining the audit procedures to be followed.

b. Identify situations in which Mincin should use accounts payable confirmations, and discuss whether Mincin is required to use them.

c. Discuss why the use of large dollar balances as the basis for selecting accounts payable for confirmation might not be the most effective approach, and indicate more effective procedures that could be followed when selecting accounts payable for confirmation.

(AICPA adapted)

16-30 As part of the June 30, 1999, audit of accounts payable of Milner Products Ltd., the auditor sent 22 confirmations of accounts payable to vendors in the form of

requests for statements. Four of the statements were not returned by the vendors, and five vendors reported balances different from the amounts recorded on Milner's vendor transaction file. The auditor made duplicate copies of the five vendors' statements to maintain control of the independent information and turned the originals over to the client's accounts payable clerk to reconcile the differences. Two days later, the clerk returned the five statements to the auditor with the information on the working papers as follows:

Statement 1	Balance per vendor's statement	$ 6,618.01
	Payment by Milner June 30, 1999	(4,601.01)
	Balance per transaction file	$ 2,017.00
Statement 2	Balance per vendor's statement	$ 9,618.93
	Invoices not received by Milner	(2,733.18)
	Payment by Milner June 15, 1999	(1,000.00)
	Balance per transaction file	$ 5,885.75
Statement 3	Balance per vendor's statement	$26,251.80
	Balance per master file	$20,516.11
	Difference cannot be located due to the vendor's failure to provide details of its account balance	$ 5,735.69
Statement 4	Balance per vendor's statement	$ 6,170.15
	Credit memo issued by vendor on July 15, 1999	(2,360.15)
	Balance per transaction file	$ 3,810.00
Statement 5	Balance per vendor's statement	$ 8,619.21
	Payment by Milner July 3, 1999	(3,000.00)
	Unlocated difference not followed up due to minor amount	215.06
	Balance per transaction file	$ 5,834.27

Required

a. Evaluate the acceptability of having the client perform the reconciliations, assuming the auditor intends to perform adequate additional tests.

b. Describe the additional tests that should be performed for each of the five statements that included differences.

c. What audit procedures should be performed for the non-responses to the confirmation requests?

16-31 The physical inventory for Ajak Manufacturing Ltd. was taken on December 30, 1998, rather than December 31 because the client had to operate the plant for a special order on the last day of the year. At the time of the client's physical count, you observed that purchases represented by receiving report number 2631 and all preceding ones were included in the physical count, whereas inventory represented by succeeding numbers was excluded. On the evening of December 31, you stopped by the plant and noted that inventory represented by receiving report numbers 2632 and 2634 was received subsequent to the physical count, but prior to the end of the year. You later noted that the final inventory on the financial statements contained only those items included in the physical count. In testing accounts payable at December 31, 1998, you obtain a schedule from the client to aid you in testing the adequacy of the cutoff. The schedule includes the information in the table at the top of page 556 that you have not yet resolved.

RECEIVING REPORT NUMBER	AMOUNT OF VENDOR'S INVOICE	AMOUNT PRESENTLY INCLUDED IN OR EXCLUDED FROM ACCOUNTS PAYABLE*	INFORMATION ON THE VENDOR'S INVOICE		
			Invoice Date	Shipping Date	FOB Origin or Destination
2631	$2,619.26	Included	30-12-98	30-12-98	Origin
2632	3,709.16	Excluded	26-12-98	15-12-98	Destination
2633	5,182.31	Included	31-12-98	26-12-98	Origin
2634	6,403.00	Excluded	16-12-98	27-12-98	Destination
2635	8,484.91	Included	28-12-98	31-12-98	Origin
2636	5,916.20	Excluded	3-1-99	31-12-98	Destination
2637	7,515.50	Excluded	5-1-99	26-12-98	Origin
2638	2,407.87	Excluded	31-12-98	3-1-99	Origin

*All entries to record inventory purchases are recorded by the client as a debit to purchases and a credit to accounts payable.

Required

a. Explain the relationship between inventory and accounts payable cutoff.

b. For each of the receiving reports, state the misstatement in inventory or accounts payable, if any exists, and pre-pare an adjusting entry to correct the financial statements, if a misstatement exists.

c. Which of the misstatements in part (b) are most impor-tant? Explain.

CASES

16-32 You are provided with the following information about internal control relating to materials purchases for the Lau Machinery Corp., a medium-sized firm that builds spe-cial machinery to order.

Materials purchase requisitions are first approved by the plant supervisor, who then sends them to the purchasing department. A prenumbered purchase order is prepared in triplicate by one of several department employees. Employ-ees account for all purchase order numbers. The original copy is sent to the vendor. The receiving department is sent the second copy to use for a receiving report. The third copy is kept on file in the purchasing department along with the requisition.

Delivered materials are immediately sent to the store-room. The receiving report, which is a copy of the purchase order, is sent to the purchasing department. A copy of the receiving report is sent to the storeroom. Materials are issued to factory employees subsequent to a verbal request by one of the supervisors.

When the mailroom clerk receives vendors' invoices, the clerk forwards them to the purchasing department employee who placed the order. The invoice is compared with the pur-chase order on file for price and terms by the employee. The invoice quantity is compared with the receiving depart-ment's report. After checking footings, extensions, and dis-counts, the employee indicates approval for payment by initialling the invoice. The invoice is then forwarded to the accounting department. Vendor name, date, gross and net invoice amounts, and account distribution are entered into the computer system for updating the acquisitions data and vendor transaction file, and filed by payment due date. The vendor's invoice is filed in the accounting department. The purchase order and receiving report are filed in the purchas-ing department.

The accounting department requisitions prenumbered cheques from the cashier. They are prepared using the com-puter system (to record cash disbursements and update accounts payable) and then returned to the cashier, who puts them through the cheque-signing machine. After accounting for the sequence of numbers, the cashier sends the cheques to the accounting department. There the cheques are placed in envelopes and sent to the mailroom. At the end of each month, an aged accounts payable trial balance is printed and the total is compared with the general ledger balance. Any differences disclosed are investigated.

Required

PART 1

a. Prepare a flowchart for the acquisition and payment cycle for Lau Machinery Corp.

b. List the controls in existence for each of the six transac-tion-related audit objectives for acquisitions.

c. For each control in part (b), list one test of controls to ver-ify its effectiveness.

d. List the most important internal control weaknesses for acquisitions and payments.

e. Design an audit program to test internal control. The pro-gram should include, but not be limited to, the tests of controls from part (c) and procedures to compensate for the weaknesses in part (d).

PART 2

In confirming accounts payable at December 31, 1998, the following procedures are suggested to you for the Lau Machinery Corp.

1. Obtain a list of accounts payable at December 31, 1998, from the client and
   (i) foot the list.
   (ii) compare the total with the balance shown in the general ledger.
   (iii) compare the amounts shown on the list with the balances in the accounts payable master file.

2. Select accounts to confirm.
   (i) Select each account with a balance payable in excess of $2,000.
   (ii) Select a random sample of 50 other accounts over $100.
   (iii) Indicate the accounts to be confirmed on the accounts payable list, make a copy of the list, and give it to the accounts payable clerk along with instructions to type the vendor's name, address, and balance due on confirmations.

3. Compare the confirmations with the accounts payable master file.

4. Have the client's controller sign each confirmation.

5. Have the accounts payable clerk insert the confirmations and return envelopes addressed to the public accounting firm in the client's envelopes. The envelopes are also to be stamped and sealed by the clerk. This should all be done under the auditor's control.

6. Mail the confirmations.

Required

Assume that the results of tests of controls in Part 1 support your preliminary assessment of control risk in the acquisition and payment cycle. Evaluate the procedures for confirming accounts payable.

16-33 You have been assigned to the audit of Compu Co. (CC), a new client of your firm, Neer & Farr, Chartered Accountants. You are responsible for the accounts payable section of this year's audit. You have prepared the following description of the accounts payable system from discussions with CC staff.

Head office of CC processes the accounts payable for its branch offices. When a new branch is set up on the automated accounts payable system, it is requested to send to head office a detailed accounts payable trial balance and an accounts payable vendor list, approved by the manager of the branch. The accounts payable vendor list includes vendor name, address, discount terms, and other descriptive information, such as telephone number and personal contact.

The head office accounts payable department consists of an accounts payable supervisor and three clerks.

The accounts payable supervisor assigns and records vendor codes on the original vendor list provided by the branch manager. Vendor codes are assigned alphanumerically, based on the vendor's name. This list is used as a source of input to the computer system, and a photocopy of the list is returned to the branch for its reference.

The branch manager approves the invoices and codes them as to general ledger allocation prior to sending them to head office for payment. The supervisor reviews the allocation of the invoices and passes them on to one of the clerks. Each clerk is responsible for specific branches. The clerks scan the vendor list, call up the vendor file on the screen, and enter the invoice details into the system. If the vendor is not on the vendor list, the clerks check for similar names on the screen to verify that the vendor has not been set up since the vendor list was printed and then add a new vendor using the standard method. The clerks then record the invoice against this new vendor.

By means of an error message, the system identifies invoices that have already been entered for payment so that invoices that have inadvertently been entered twice are detected. However, the accounts payable clerks are able to override this error message since it is sometimes necessary for an invoice to be entered twice (e.g., if partial payment was made earlier and the balance is now being paid in full). Once an invoice has been entered for payment, the accounts payable clerk files the invoice alphabetically by vendor name.

Cheques are run Mondays and Thursdays, based on due dates. Because of the high volume of cheques processed, the accounts payable supervisor signs all cheques. However, cheques for amounts greater than $50,000 must also be signed by the head office controller. The cheques are mailed directly to suppliers from head office. A copy of the cheque register, showing which invoices have been paid, is sent to the branch.

The partner on the CC engagement has requested that you prepare a memo that identifies the control strengths and weaknesses in CC's accounts payable system and analyzes their impact on this year's audit (i.e., identifying tests of controls and compensating audit procedures needed). The memo should also provide practical recommendations for the resolution of the accounts payable system weaknesses.

Required

Prepare the memo requested by the partner.

(CICA adapted)

17

COMPLETING THE TESTS IN THE ACQUISITION AND PAYMENT CYCLE: VERIFICATION OF SELECTED ACCOUNTS

IMPROPER CLASSIFICATIONS HIDE A GREATER NET LOSS

TV Communications Network (TVCN), a Denver-based wireless cable television company, materially understated losses in its 1992 financial statements by improperly recording $2.5 million of expenses as a direct decrease in shareholders' equity. The misstatement took the company from an actual 1992 net loss of $4.7 million to a reported loss of only $2.2 million.

According to the investigation by the Securities and Exchange Commission (SEC), the expenses charged to equity were from disbursements for the development and distribution of brochures promoting the company's business prospects. The payments should have been expensed and reflected in the income statement as advertising expense.

The internal controls associated with the advertising expenses were clearly inadequate. TVCN typically did not have invoices or other documentation available when the payments were made by the company's president, who controlled the bank account. Because of the lack of adequate documentation, when the financial statements were prepared, TVCN employees responsible for recording the expenses did not have sufficient information to classify the disbursements properly. The SEC found that even when documentation was available, the accounts in which the transactions were recorded conflicted with the supporting documentation.

Unfortunately, TVCN's auditor relied on inquiry of the company president as the primary source of evidence about the nature of the advertising payments. In his substantive testing of transactions exceeding $10,000, the auditor relied on the company controller to identify all transactions meeting the criteria for review. Needless to say, the controller didn't present all transactions exceeding $10,000. As you might expect, the SEC brought charges against the auditor for failing to comply with generally accepted auditing standards.

Source: *Accounting and Auditing Enforcement Release No. 534*
Commerce Clearing House, Inc., Chicago.

OBJECTIVE 17-1

Recognize the many accounts besides accounts payable that are part of the acquisition and payment cycle.

An important characteristic of the acquisition and payment cycle is the large number of accounts involved. These include the following:

- Accounts payable
- Accrued professional fees
- Accrued property taxes
- Buildings
- Cash in the bank
- Commercial franchises
- Cost of goods sold
- Goods and Services Tax payable
- Income tax expense
- Income taxes payable
- Insurance expense
- Inventory
- Land
- Leases and leasehold improvements
- Manufacturing equipment
- Organization costs
- Patents, trademarks, and copyrights
- Prepaid insurance
- Prepaid rent
- Prepaid taxes
- Professional fees
- Property taxes
- Rent expense
- Supplies
- Travel expense
- Utilities

Since the audit procedures for many of these accounts are similar, an understanding of the appropriate methodology for each can be obtained by studying the following selected account balances:

- Cash in bank — affected by all transaction cycles (Chapter 20)
- Inventory — represents tangible assets and is typically used up in one year (Chapter 18)
- Prepaid insurance — represents prepaid expenses (Chapter 17)
- Manufacturing equipment — represents long-lived tangible assets (Chapter 17)
- Accounts payable — represents specific liabilities for which the amounts and the dates of the future payments are known (Chapter 16)

- Accrued property taxes — represents estimated liabilities (Chapter 17)
- Operations accounts — include several methods of verifying all accounts in this category (Chapter 17).

The methodology for designing tests of details of balances for the above accounts is the same as that shown in Figure 16-3 on page 540 for accounts payable. Each account is a part of the acquisition and payment cycle. Therefore, the only change required in the figure is the replacement of accounts payable with the account being audited. For example, if the account being discussed is accrued property taxes, simply substitute accrued property taxes for accounts payable in the first, second, and last boxes in the figure.

The types of audit tests used to audit the above accounts are the same as those shown in Figure 16-5 on page 547. Figure 16-5 also illustrates how the audit risk model discussed in Chapter 8 relates to the audit of these accounts.

Capital assets are assets that have expected lives of more than one year, are used in the business, and are not acquired for resale. The intention to use the assets as a part of the operation of the client's business and their expected life of more than one year are the significant characteristics that distinguish these assets from inventory, prepaid expenses, and investments.

Capital assets can be classified as follows:

- Land and land improvements
- Buildings and building improvements
- Manufacturing equipment
- Furniture and fixtures
- Autos and trucks
- Leasehold improvements
- Construction of property, plant, and equipment in process

AUDIT OF MANUFACTURING EQUIPMENT

In this section, the audit of manufacturing equipment is discussed as an illustration of an appropriate approach to the audit of all capital asset accounts. When there are significant differences in the verification of other types of capital assets, they are briefly examined.

OVERVIEW OF THE ACCOUNTS

OBJECTIVE 17-2

Design and perform the audit tests of manufacturing equipment and related accounts.

The accounts commonly used for manufacturing equipment are illustrated in Figure 17-1. The relationship of manufacturing equipment to the acquisition and payment cycle is apparent by examining the debits to the asset account. Since the source of debits in the asset account is the acquisitions journal, the accounting system has already been tested for recording the current period's additions to manufacturing equipment as part of the test of the acquisition and payment cycle. Because equipment additions are infrequent and may be subject to special controls, such as board of directors' approval, the auditor may decide not to rely heavily on these tests.

The primary accounting record for manufacturing equipment and other capital asset accounts is generally a property or capital asset master file with supporting purchase, disposal, and amortization transactions. The contents of the data files must be understood for a meaningful study of the audit of manufacturing equipment. The files will be composed of a set of records, one for each piece of equipment and other types of property owned. In turn, each record will include descriptive information, date of acquisition, original cost, current-year amortization,[1] and accumulated amor-

---

[1]The term "amortization" is used in *CICA Handbook* Section 3060, "Capital Assets," to describe the process of charging the cost of a capital asset to expense over its useful life. However, many organizations and accountants refer to the process as "depreciation," especially when using the term in connection with property, plant, and equipment. The text will use the term "amortization."

FIGURE 17-1
Manufacturing
Equipment and
Related Accounts

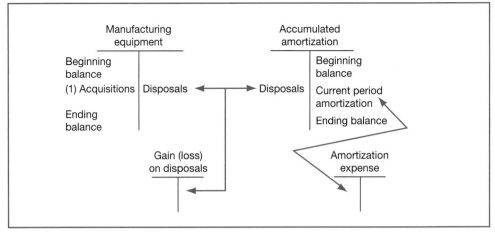

(1) Acquisitions of manufacturing equipment arise from the acquisition and payment cycle. See Figure 16-1 on page 529.

tization for the property. The totals of detailed transactions for each property item will equal the total in the master file for that piece of property, and the total of the master file for all items of property will equal the general ledger balances for the related accounts.

The files will also contain information about property acquired and disposed of during the year. Proceeds, gains, and losses will be included for disposals.

AUDITING MANUFACTURING EQUIPMENT

Manufacturing equipment is normally audited differently from current asset accounts for three reasons: (1) there are usually fewer current-period acquisitions of manufacturing equipment, (2) the amount of any given acquisition is often material, and (3) the equipment is likely to be kept and maintained in the accounting records for several years. Because of these differences, the emphasis in auditing manufacturing equipment is on the verification of current-period acquisitions rather than on the balance in the account carried forward from the preceding year. In addition, the expected life of assets over one year requires amortization and accumulated amortization accounts, which are verified as part of the audit of the assets. Additions should be traced to the capital cost allowance section of the tax working papers.

Although the approach to verifying manufacturing equipment is dissimilar from that used for current assets, several other accounts are verified in much the same manner. These include patents, copyrights, catalogue costs, and all capital asset accounts.

In the audit of manufacturing equipment, it is helpful to separate the tests into the following categories:

- Analytical procedures
- Verification of current-year acquisitions
- Verification of current-year disposals
- Verification of the ending balance in the asset account
- Verification of amortization expense
- Verification of the ending balance in accumulated amortization

ANALYTICAL PROCEDURES

As in all audit areas, the nature of the analytical procedures depends on the nature of the client's operations. Table 17-1 illustrates the type of ratio and trend analysis frequently performed for manufacturing equipment.

TABLE 17-1

ANALYTICAL
PROCEDURES FOR
MANUFACTURING
EQUIPMENT

ANALYTICAL PROCEDURE	POSSIBLE MISSTATEMENT
Compare amortization expense divided by gross manufacturing equipment cost with previous years.	Misstatement in amortization expense and accumulated amortization.
Compare accumulated amortization divided by gross manufacturing equipment cost with previous years.	Misstatement in accumulated amortization.
Compare monthly or annual repairs and maintenance, supplies expense, small tools expense, and similar accounts with previous years.	Expensing amounts that should be capital items.
Compare gross manufacturing cost divided by some measure of production with previous years.	Idle equipment or equipment that has been disposed of but not written off.

VERIFICATION OF CURRENT-YEAR ACQUISITIONS

The proper recording of current-year additions is important because of the long-term effect the assets have on the financial statements. The failure to capitalize a capital asset, or the recording of an acquisition at the improper amount, affects the balance sheet until the firm disposes of the asset. The income statement is affected until the asset is fully amortized.

Because of the importance of current-period acquisitions in the audit of manufacturing equipment, seven of the nine balance-related audit objectives for tests of details of balances are used as a frame of reference. (Realizable value and presentation and disclosure are discussed on page 568 in connection with the verification of ending balances.)

The balance-related audit objectives and common audit tests are shown in Table 17-2. As in all other audit areas, the actual audit tests and sample size depend heavily on materiality, inherent risk, assessed control risk, and the results of prior-year tests. Materiality is of special importance for verifying current-year additions. They vary from immaterial amounts in some years to a large number of significant acquisitions in others. Accuracy and classification are usually the major objectives for this part of the audit.

The starting point for the verification of current-year acquisitions is normally a schedule obtained from the client of all acquisitions recorded in the general ledger during the year. A typical schedule lists each addition separately and includes the date of the acquisition, vendor, description, notation of new or used, life of the asset for amortization purposes, amortization method, cost, and any relevant income tax information such as capital cost allowance rates and the investment tax credit if applicable. The client obtains this information from the property master file.

In studying Table 17-2, one should recognize the importance of examining vendors' invoices and related documents in verifying acquisitions of manufacturing equipment. That subject is discussed in the next section.

EXAMINATION OF SUPPORTING DOCUMENTATION

The most common audit test to verify additions is examination of vendors' invoices and receiving reports. Additional testing besides that which is done as a part of the tests of controls is frequently considered necessary to verify the current-period additions because of the complexity of many equipment transactions and the materiality of the amounts. It is ordinarily unnecessary to examine supporting documentation for each addition, but it is normal to verify large and unusual transactions for the entire year as well as a representative sample of typical additions. The extent of the verification depends on the auditor's assessed control risk for acquisitions and the materiality of the additions.

TABLE 17-2

BALANCE-RELATED
AUDIT OBJECTIVES
AND TESTS OF DETAILS
OF BALANCES FOR
MANUFACTURING
EQUIPMENT
ADDITIONS

BALANCE-RELATED AUDIT OBJECTIVE	COMMON TESTS OF DETAILS OF BALANCES PROCEDURES	COMMENTS
Current-year acquisitions in the acquisitions schedule agree with related data file amounts, and the total agrees with the general ledger (detail tie-in).	Foot the acquisitions schedule. Trace the total to the general ledger. Trace the individual acquisitions to the data files for amounts and descriptions.	These tests should be limited unless controls are weak. All increases in the general ledger balance for the year should reconcile to the schedule.
Current-year acquisitions as listed exist (existence).	Examine vendors' invoices and receiving reports. Physically examine assets.	It is uncommon to physically examine additions unless controls are weak or amounts are material.
Existing acquisitions are recorded (completeness).	Examine vendors' invoices of closely related accounts such as repairs and maintenance to uncover items that should be manufacturing equipment. Review lease and rental agreements.	This objective is one of the most important ones for manufacturing equipment.
Current-year acquisitions as listed are owned (ownership).	Examine vendors' invoices.	Ordinarily no problem for equipment. Property deeds, abstracts, and tax bills are frequently examined for land or major buildings.
Current-year acquisitions as listed are accurate (accuracy).	Examine vendors' invoices.	Extent depends on inherent risk and effectiveness of internal controls.
Current-year acquisitions as listed are properly classified (classification).	Examine vendors' invoices in manufacturing equipment account to uncover items that should be classified as office equipment, part of the buildings, or repairs. Examine vendors' invoices of closely related accounts such as repairs to uncover items that should be manufacturing equipment. Examine rent and lease expense for capitalizable leases.	The objective is closely related to tests for completeness. It is done in conjunction with that objective and tests for accuracy.
Current-year acquisitions are recorded in the proper period (cutoff).	Review transactions near the balance sheet date for proper period.	Usually done as a part of accounts payable cutoff tests.
The client has rights to current-year acquisitions (rights).	Examine vendors' invoices.	Ordinarily no problem for equipment. Property deeds and tax bills are frequently examined for land or major buildings.

AUDIT THAT WHICH IS UNCOMFORTABLE

"Although this landscaping plan is expensive, the project is long overdue. I heartily approve!" wrote the president of a West Coast company in an internal memo.

One year later, the internal audit department conducted a routine review of significant expenditures involving the construction, renovation, and maintenance of corporate properties. One of the disbursements selected for review was issued in connection with the relandscaping of the company's corporate headquarters.

The contractor was an established local commercial landscaping firm. Based on the disbursement vouchers and vendor invoices, project payments totalled almost $1,000,000, including $800,000 under a written contract plus $200,000 in planning, design work, and enhancements not covered under the contract. Each of 12 invoices had been approved by the vice-president responsible for corporate facilities or the recently retired former president.

When the auditors went to the facilities department to get the contract, design blueprint, bidding records, and other supporting documents, the manager informed them that the relandscaping had not been administered by his department but by the department's vice-president, who had approved most of the invoices.

The vice-president confirmed that:

- He had administered the project personally, with the knowledge and approval of the president.
- There was no need for bidding because of the quality and integrity of the landscaping firm, a vendor to the organization for over 20 years.

The auditors decided to probe further because the landscaping cost seemed excessive, there was no competitive bidding, and the contract was administered by high-level executives rather than those usually administering such contracts.

The contractor initially defended his pricing as reasonable, due to adverse soil and site conditions. However, after several intense meetings and discussion of possible legal action, the contractor reluctantly disclosed the true circumstances of the transaction. He was instructed by the vice-president and former president to price the project so that it would also cover extensive landscaping and building renovation at each of their homes. The internal auditor's review of the contractor's records confirmed that excess charges of almost $600,000 covered the cost of a pool, hot tub, deck, marble patio, sprinkler system, fountain, dock, landscaping, and extensive building renovation at the homes of both executives. The contractor also said that the former president had contacted him during the audit to discourage cooperation.

The company went public with the audit findings, and the investigative file was turned over to the prosecutor. As a result of their no contest pleas, the two executives were convicted of obtaining money under false pretenses. Virtually all losses were recovered through successful bonding claims.

Source: Courtenay Thompson, "Fraud in the Executive Suite,"
Internal Auditor (October 1993), pp. 68–69.

Tests for acquisitions are accomplished by comparing the charges on vendors' invoices with recorded amounts. The auditor must be aware of the client's capitalization policies to determine whether acquisitions are valued in accordance with generally accepted accounting principles and are treated consistently with those of the preceding year. For example, many clients automatically expense items that are less than a certain amount, such as $100. The auditor should be alert for the possibility of material transportation and installation costs, as well as the trade-in of existing equipment.

The auditor should also ensure that government grants for fixed assets are properly accounted for as required by Section 3800 of the *CICA Handbook*, "Accounting for Government Assistance."

In conjunction with testing current-period additions for existence and valuation, the auditor should also review recorded transactions for proper classification. In some cases, amounts recorded as manufacturing equipment should be classified as office equipment or as a part of the building. There is also the possibility that the client has improperly capitalized repairs, rents, or similar expenses.

The inclusion of transactions that should properly be recorded as assets in repairs and maintenance expense, lease expense, supplies, small tools, and similar accounts is a common client error. The error results from lack of understanding of generally accepted accounting principles and some clients' desire to avoid income taxes. The likelihood of these types of misclassifications should be evaluated in conjunction with obtaining an understanding of internal controls in the acquisition and payment cycle. If the auditor concludes that material misstatements are likely, it may be necessary to vouch the larger amounts debited to the expense accounts. It is a common practice to do this as a regular part of the audit of the capital asset accounts.

VERIFICATION OF CURRENT-YEAR DISPOSALS

Internal controls The most important internal control over the disposal of manufacturing equipment is the existence of a formal method to inform management of the sale, trade-in, abandonment, or theft of recorded machinery and equipment. If the client fails to record disposals, the original cost of the manufacturing equipment account will be overstated indefinitely, and the net book value will be overstated until the asset is fully amortized. Another important control to protect assets from unauthorized disposal is a provision for authorization for the sale or other disposal of manufacturing equipment. Finally, there should be adequate internal verification of recorded disposals to make sure assets are correctly removed from the accounting records.

Audit tests The two major objectives in the verification of the sale, trade-in, or abandonment of manufacturing equipment are that *existing disposals are recorded* and *recorded disposals are accurately valued.*

The starting point for verifying disposals is the client's schedule of recorded disposals. The schedule typically includes the date at which the asset was disposed of, the name of the person or firm acquiring the asset, the selling price, the original cost of the asset, the acquisition date, the accumulated amortization of the asset, and the capital cost allowance recapture, if any. Mechanical accuracy tests of the schedule are necessary, including footing the schedule, tracing the totals on the schedule to the recorded disposals in the general ledger, and tracing the cost and accumulated amortization of the disposals to the property master file. The proceeds from disposal should be traced to the capital cost section of the tax working papers. Where there is significant activity in these accounts, the auditor may use audit software to reperform the calculations. It is more effective to use spreadsheet software to reperform calculations than to do them by hand.

Because the failure to record disposals of manufacturing equipment no longer used in the business can significantly affect the financial statements, *the search for unrecorded disposals is essential.* The nature and adequacy of the controls over disposals affect the extent of the search. The following procedures are frequently used for verifying disposals:

- Review whether newly acquired assets replace existing assets.
- Analyze gains on the disposal of assets and miscellaneous income for receipts from the disposal of assets.
- Review plant modifications and changes in product line, taxes, or insurance coverage for indications of deletions of equipment.
- Make inquiries of management and production personnel about the possibility of the disposal of assets.

When an asset is sold or disposed of without having been traded in for a replacement asset, the *valuation* of the transaction can be verified by examining the related sales invoice and property master file. The auditor should compare the cost and accumulated amortization in the master file with the recorded entry in the general journal and recompute the gain or loss on the disposal of the asset for comparison with the accounting records.

Two areas deserve special attention in the valuation objective. The first is the *trade-in of an asset for a replacement.* When trade-ins occur, the auditor should ensure that the new asset is properly capitalized and that the replaced asset is properly eliminated from the records, considering the book value of the asset traded in and the additional cost of the new asset. The second area of special concern is the disposal of assets affected by *capital cost allowance recapture.* Since the recapture affects the current year's income tax expense and liability, the auditor must evaluate its significance. While discussion of the tax implications is beyond the scope of this text, the auditor should ensure that the proceeds on disposal are properly recorded in the tax working papers.

VERIFICATION OF ASSET BALANCE

Internal controls   The nature of the internal controls over existing assets determines whether it is necessary to verify manufacturing equipment acquired in prior years. Important controls include the use of a master file for individual capital assets, adequate physical controls over assets that are easily movable (e.g., tools, vehicles), assignment of identification numbers to each plant asset, and periodic physical count of capital assets and their reconciliation by accounting personnel. A formal method of informing the accounting department of all disposals of permanent assets is also an important control over the balance of assets carried forward into the current year.

Audit tests   Usually, the auditor does not obtain a list from the client of all assets included in the ending balance of manufacturing equipment. Instead, audit tests are determined on the basis of the master file.

Typically, the first audit step concerns the detail tie-in objective: manufacturing equipment as listed in the master file agrees with the general ledger. Examining a printout of the master file that totals to the general ledger balance is ordinarily sufficient. The auditor may choose to test foot a few pages or use generalized audit software to reconcile balances in the data files.

After assessing control risk for the existence objective, the auditor must decide whether it is necessary to verify the existence of individual items of manufacturing equipment included in the master file. If the auditor believes there is a high likelihood of significant missing capital assets that are still recorded in the accounting records, an appropriate procedure is selecting a sample from the master file and examining the actual assets. In rare cases, the auditor may believe that it is necessary that the client take a complete physical inventory of capital assets to make sure they actually exist. If a physical inventory is taken, the auditor normally observes the count.

Ordinarily, it is unnecessary to test the valuation of capital assets recorded in prior periods because presumably they were verified in previous audits at the time they were acquired. But the auditor should be aware that companies may occasionally have on hand manufacturing equipment that is no longer used in operations. If the amounts are material, the auditor should evaluate whether they should be written down to net realizable value or at least be disclosed separately as "nonoperating equipment."

A major consideration in verifying the ending balance in capital assets is the possibility of existing *legal encumbrances* (presentation and disclosure objective). A number of methods are available to determine if manufacturing equipment is encumbered. These include reading the terms of loan and credit agreements and mailing loan confirmation requests to banks and other lending institutions. Information with respect to encumbered assets may also be obtained through discussions with the client or confirmations with company lawyers. In addition, it is desirable to obtain information on possible liens by checking with the sheriff in the locale where the company operates. In Ontario, the auditor may obtain information from the Department of Corporate and Consumer Affairs, for a small fee, about the existence of encumbrances under the *Personal Property Security Act*. Other provinces have similar procedures for checking on liens and encumbrances.

The *proper presentation and disclosure* of manufacturing equipment in the financial statements must be carefully evaluated to ensure that generally accepted accounting principles are followed. Manufacturing equipment should include the gross cost and should ordinarily be separated from other permanent assets. Leased property should also be disclosed separately, and all liens on property must be included in the footnotes.

VERIFICATION OF AMORTIZATION EXPENSE

Amortization expense is one of the few expense accounts that is not verified as a part of tests of controls. The recorded amounts are determined by *internal allocations* rather than by exchange transactions with outside parties. When amortization expense is material, more tests of details of amortization expense are required than for an account that has already been verified through tests of controls.

The most important objectives for amortization expense are proper valuation and accuracy. These involve determining whether the client is following a *consistent amortization policy* from period to period and whether the client's *calculations are accurate*. In determining the former, there are four considerations: the useful life of current period acquisitions, the method of amortization, the estimated salvage value, and the policy of amortizing assets in the year of acquisition and disposition. The client's policies can be determined by having discussions with the client and comparing the responses with the information in the auditor's permanent files.

In deciding on the reasonableness of the useful lives assigned to newly acquired assets, the auditor must consider a number of factors: the actual physical life of the asset, the expected useful life (taking into account obsolescence and the company's normal policy of upgrading equipment), and established company policies on trading in equipment. Occasionally, changing circumstances may necessitate a re-evaluation of the useful life of an asset. When this occurs, a change in accounting estimate rather than a change in accounting principle is involved. The effect of this on amortization must be carefully evaluated.

A useful method of testing amortization is to make a calculation of its overall reasonableness. The calculation is made by multiplying the unamortized capital assets by the amortization rate for the year. In making these calculations, the auditor must of course make adjustments for current-year additions and disposals, assets with different lengths of life, and assets with different methods of amortization. The calculations can be made fairly easily if the public accounting firm includes in the permanent file a breakdown of the capital assets by method of amortization and length of life. If the overall calculations are reasonably close to the client's totals and if assessed control risk for amortization expense is low, tests of details for amortization can be minimized.

In many audits, it is also desirable to check the mechanical accuracy of amortization calculations. This is done by recomputing amortization expense for selected assets to determine whether the client is following a proper and consistent amortization policy. To be relevant, the detailed calculations should be tied in to the total amortization calculations by footing the amortization expense on the property master file and reconciling the total with the general ledger. Assuming the client maintains computerized amortization and amortization records, it may be advantageous to use the computer in testing the calculations.

VERIFICATION OF ACCUMULATED AMORTIZATION

The debits to accumulated amortization are normally tested as a part of the audit of disposals of assets, whereas the credits are verified as a part of amortization expense. If the auditor traces selected transactions to the accumulated amortization records in the property master file as a part of these tests, little additional testing should be required.

Two objectives are usually emphasized in the audit of accumulated amortization:

- Accumulated amortization as stated in the property master file agrees with the general ledger. This objective can be satisfied by test footing the accumulated amortization on the property master file and tracing the total to the general ledger.
- Accumulated amortization in the master file is properly valued.

In some cases, the life of manufacturing equipment may be significantly reduced because of such changes as reductions in customer demands for products, unexpected physical deterioration, or a modification in operations. Because of these possibilities and if the decline in asset value is permanent, it may be appropriate to write the asset down to net realizable value.

AUDIT OF PREPAID EXPENSES, DEFERRED CHARGES, AND INTANGIBLES

OBJECTIVE 17-3

Design and perform the audit tests of prepaid expenses.

Prepaid expenses, deferred charges, and intangibles are assets that vary in life from several months to several years. Their inclusion as assets results more from the concept of matching expenses with revenues than from their resale or liquidation value. The following are examples:

- Prepaid rent
- Organization costs
- Prepaid taxes
- Patents
- Prepaid insurance
- Trademarks
- Deferred charges
- Copyrights

One typical difference between these assets and others, such as accounts receivable and inventory, is the immateriality of the former in many audits. Frequently, analytical procedures are sufficient for prepaid expenses, deferred charges, and intangibles.

In this section, the audit of prepaid insurance is discussed as an account representative of this group because (1) it is found in most audits — virtually every company has some type of insurance, (2) it is typical of the problems frequently encountered in the audit of this class of accounts, and (3) the auditor's responsibility for the review of insurance coverage is an additional consideration not encountered in the other accounts in this category.

OVERVIEW OF PREPAID INSURANCE	The accounts typically used for prepaid insurance are illustrated in Figure 17-2. The relationship between prepaid insurance and the acquisition and payment cycle is apparent in examining the debits to the asset account. Since the source of the debits in the asset account is the purchase journal, the payments of insurance premiums have already been partially tested by means of the acquisition and cash disbursement transactions.	

INTERNAL CONTROLS

The internal controls for prepaid insurance and insurance expense can be divided into three categories: controls over the acquisition and recording of insurance, controls over the insurance register, and controls over the charge-off of insurance expense.

Controls over the acquisition and recording of insurance are a part of the acquisition and payment cycle. These should include proper authorization for new insurance policies and payment of insurance premiums consistent with the procedures discussed in that cycle.

A record of insurance policies in force and the due date of each policy (insurance register) is an essential control to make sure the company has adequate insurance at all times. The control should include a provision for periodic review of the adequacy of the insurance coverage by an independent qualified person.

After they have been completed, the detailed records of the information in the prepaid insurance register should be verified by someone independent of the person preparing them. A closely related control is the use of monthly "standard journal entries" for insurance expense. If a significant entry is required to adjust the balance in prepaid insurance at the end of the year, it indicates a potential misstatement in the recording of the acquisition of insurance throughout the year or in the calculation of the year-end balance in prepaid insurance.

AUDIT TESTS

Throughout the audit of prepaid insurance and insurance expense, the auditor should keep in mind that the amount in insurance expense is a residual based on the beginning balance in prepaid insurance, the payment of premiums during the year, and the ending balance. The only verifications of the balance in the expense account that are ordinarily necessary are analytical procedures and a brief test to be sure that the charges to insurance expense arose from credits to prepaid insurance. Since the payments of premiums are tested as part of the tests of controls and analytical procedures, the emphasis in the tests of details of balances is on prepaid insurance.

In the audit of prepaid insurance, a schedule is obtained from the client or prepared by the auditor that includes each insurance policy in force, policy number, insurance coverage for each policy, premium amount, premium period, insurance expense for the year, and prepaid insurance at the end of the year. An example of a schedule obtained from the client for the auditor's working papers is given in Figure 17-3 on pages 572 and 573. The auditor's tests of prepaid insurance are normally indicated on the schedule.

FIGURE 17-2

Prepaid Insurance and Related Accounts

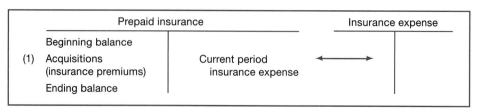

(1) Acquisitions of insurance premiums arise from the acquisition and payment cycle. This can be observed by examining Figure 16–1 on page 529.

Analytical procedures   A major consideration in the audit of prepaid insurance is the frequent *immateriality* of the beginning and ending balances. Furthermore, few transactions are debited and credited to the balance during the year, most of which are small and simple to understand. Therefore, the auditor can generally spend very little time verifying the balance. When the auditor plans not to verify the balance in detail, analytical procedures become increasingly important as a means of identifying potentially significant misstatements. The following are commonly performed analytical procedures of prepaid insurance and insurance expense:

- Compare total prepaid insurance and insurance expense with previous years as a test of reasonableness.
- Compute the ratio of prepaid insurance to insurance expense, and compare it with previous years.
- Compare the individual insurance policy coverage on the schedule obtained from the client with the preceding year's schedule as a test of the elimination of certain policies or a change in insurance coverage.
- Compare the computed prepaid insurance balance for the current year on a policy-by-policy basis with that of the preceding year as a test of an error in calculation.
- Review the *insurance coverage* listed on the prepaid insurance schedule with an appropriate client official or insurance broker for adequacy of coverage. The auditor cannot be an expert on insurance matters, but his or her understanding of accounting and the valuation of assets is important in making certain a company is not underinsured.

For many audits, no additional tests need be performed beyond the review for overall reasonableness unless the tests indicate a high likelihood of a significant misstatement or assessed control risk is high. The remaining audit procedures should be performed only when there is a special reason for doing so. The discussion of these tests is organized around the balance-related audit objectives for performing tests of details of asset balances. For convenience, certain objectives are combined and the order in which they are discussed is different from that previously used. Valuation is not applicable.

Insurance policies in the prepaid schedule are valid, and all existing policies are listed (existence and completeness)   The verification of existence and tests for omissions of the insurance policies in force can be tested in one of two ways: by referring to supporting documentation or by obtaining a confirmation of insurance information from the company's insurance agent. The first approach entails examining insurance invoices and policies in force. If these tests are performed, they should be done on a limited test basis. Sending a confirmation to the client's insurance agent is preferable because it is usually less time-consuming than vouching tests, and it provides 100 percent verification. The use of confirmations for this purpose has grown rapidly in the past few years.

The client has rights to all insurance policies in the prepaid schedule (rights)   The party who will receive the benefit if an insurance claim is filed has the rights. Ordinarily, the recipient named in the policy is the client, but when there are mortgages or other liens, the insurance claim may be payable to a creditor. The review of insurance policies for claimants other than the client is an excellent test of unrecorded liabilities and pledged assets.

Prepaid amounts on the schedule are accurate, and the total is correctly added and agrees with the general ledger (accuracy and detail tie-in)   The accuracy of prepaid insurance involves verifying the total amount of the insurance premium, the length of the policy period, and the allocation of the premium to unexpired insurance. The amount of the premium for a given policy and its time period can be verified simul-

FIGURE 17-3

Schedule of Prepaid
Insurance

<table>
<tr><td colspan="4" align="center">**Lesmann Company, Inc.**
Prepaid Insurance
31/12/98</td><td>**Schedule** F-2
Prepared by Client/JL
Approved by GG</td><td>**Date**
20/1/99
25/1/99</td></tr>
</table>

Insurer	Policy Number	Coverage	Term
Ever-ready Casualty Co.	IBB-79016 ②	Auto liability, collision, comprehensive, uninsured motorist—covers all autos owned and leased by the company	1/6/97–98 1/6/98–99
Interprovincial Insurance Co.	74-88-914 ②	Multi peril-Headquarters and plant, including contents	15/3/97–98 ① 15/3/98–99 ①
Standard Surety Co.	1973016 ②	Blanket Position Bond-$25,000	1/7/97–98
Commercial Bonding Co.	717-639 ②	Commercial Blanket Bond-$100,000	1/7/98–99

Reconciliation to Insurance Expense (General) Account:

Dependable Insurance	DIC-9161 ②	Personal property-Sales offices	1/1/98–31/12/98

Insurance Expense

① Policy term is 3 years, expiring 14/3/2000, premium shown is annual portion. Annual premium is estimated, subject to annual review and adjustment. Premium is payable in monthly installments under terms of contract. (See work paper section CC, Contracts Payable.)

② Reviewed policies; details of coverage in permanent file. Blanket Position Bond replaced by Commercial Blanket Bond on expiration.

③ Annual premium adjustment; traced to invoice and voucher

taneously by examining the premium invoice or the confirmation from an insurance agent. Once these two have been verified, the client's calculations of unexpired insurance can be tested by recalculation. The schedule of prepaid insurance can then be footed and the totals traced to the general ledger to complete the detail tie-in tests.

The insurance expense related to prepaid insurance is properly classified (classification) The proper classification of debits to different insurance expense accounts should be reviewed as a test of the income statement. In some cases, the appropriate expense account is obvious because of the type of insurance (e.g., insurance on a piece of equipment), but in other cases, allocations are necessary. For example, fire insurance on the building may require allocation to several accounts, including manufacturing overhead. Consistency with previous years is the major consideration in evaluating classification.

Insurance transactions are recorded in the proper period (cutoff) Cutoff for insurance expense is normally not a significant problem because of the small number of

Annual Premium	Unexpired Premium 1/1/98		Additions	Expense	Unexpired Premium 31/12/98	
6300	2625	PY		2625	—	✓
7000	—		7000	4083	C 2917	✓
12600	2625	PY	1800 ③	4425	—	✓
15100	—		15100	11954	C 3146	✓
1200	600	PY	—	600	—	✓
800	—		800	400	C 400	✓
	5850		24,700	24087	6463	
	Ʌ PY		Ʌ	Ʌ	Ʌ x GL	
500				500		
				24587		
				Ʌ GL		

PY — Agreed to prior year's schedule of prepaid insurance in working papers

Ʌ — Footed
x — Cross-footed
GL — Agreed to general ledger
C — Unearned premium confirmed by broker; confirmation filed at F-2/1
✓ — Verified calculation

policies and the immateriality of the amount. If the cutoff is checked at all, it is reviewed as a part of accounts payable cutoff tests.

Prepaid insurance is properly disclosed (presentation and disclosure) In most audits, prepaid insurance is combined with other prepaid expenses and included as a current asset. The amount is usually small and not a significant consideration to statement users.

AUDIT OF ACCRUED LIABILITIES

OBJECTIVE 17-4

Design and perform the audit tests of accrued liabilities.

Accrued liabilities are estimated unpaid obligations for services or benefits that have been received prior to the balance sheet date. Many accrued liabilities represent future obligations for unpaid services resulting from the passage of time but are not payable at the balance sheet date. For example, the benefits of property rental accrue throughout the year; therefore, at the balance sheet date, a certain portion of the total rent cost that has not been paid should be accrued. If the balance sheet date and the date of the termination of the rent agreement are the same, any unpaid rent is more appropriately called "rent payable" than an "accrued liability."

A second type of accrual is one in which the amount of the obligation must be estimated due to the uncertainty of the amount due. An illustration is accrued warranty costs with respect to a new or modified product: the company would have difficulty estimating the warranty expense since experience with established products would be of only very limited assistance. The following are common accrued liabilities, including payroll-related accruals discussed as a part of Chapter 15.

- Accrued officers' bonuses
- Accrued commissions
- Accrued income taxes
- Accrued interest
- Accrued payroll

- Accrued payroll taxes
- Accrued pension costs
- Accrued professional fees
- Accrued rent
- Accrued warranty costs

The verification of accrued expenses varies depending on the nature of the accrual and the circumstances of the client. For most audits, accruals take little audit time, but, in some instances, accounts such as accrued income taxes, warranty costs, and pension costs are material and require considerable audit effort. To illustrate, the audit of accrued property taxes is discussed in the next section.

AUDITING ACCRUED PROPERTY TAXES

The accounts typically used by companies for accrued property taxes are illustrated in Figure 17-4. The relationship between accrued property taxes and the acquisition and payment cycle is the same as for prepaid insurance and is apparent from examining the debits to the liability account. Since the source of the debits is the cash disbursement journal, the payments of property taxes have already been partially tested by means of the tests of the acquisition and payment cycle.

As for insurance expense, the balance in property tax expense is a residual amount that results from the beginning and ending balances in accrued property taxes and the payments of property taxes. Therefore, the emphasis in the tests should be on the ending property tax liability and payments. In verifying accrued property taxes, all nine balance-related audit objectives except realizable value are relevant, but two are of special significance:

1. Existing properties for which accrual of taxes is appropriate are on the accrual schedule. The failure to include properties for which taxes should be accrued would understate the liability (completeness). A material misstatement could occur, for example, if taxes on property were not paid before the balance sheet date and were not included as accrued property taxes.
2. Accrued property taxes are accurately recorded. The greatest concern in accuracy is the consistent treatment of the accrual from year to year (accuracy).

The primary methods of testing for the inclusion of all accruals are (1) to perform the accrual tests in conjunction with the audit of current-year property tax payments and (2) to compare the accruals with those of previous years. In most audits, there are few property tax payments, but each payment is often material and therefore it is common to verify each one.

FIGURE 17-4
Accrued Property Taxes and Related Accounts

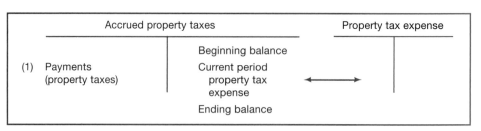

(1) Payments of property taxes arise from the acquisition and payment cycle. This can be observed by examining Figure 16–1 on page 529.

First, the auditor should obtain a schedule of property tax payments from the client and compare each payment with the preceding year's schedule to determine whether all payments have been included in the client-prepared schedule. It is also necessary to examine the permanent asset working papers for major additions and disposals of assets that may affect the property taxes accrual. If the client is expanding its operations, all property affected by local property tax regulations should be included in the schedule even if the first tax payment has not yet been made.

After the auditor is satisfied that all taxable property has been included in the client-prepared schedule, it is necessary to evaluate the reasonableness of the total amount of property taxes on each property being used as a basis to estimate the accrual. In some instances, the total amount has already been set by the taxing authority, and it is possible to verify the total by comparing the amount on the schedule with the tax bill in the client's possession. In other instances, the preceding year's total payments must be adjusted for the expected increase in property tax rates.

The auditor can verify the accrued property tax by recomputing the portion of the total tax applicable to the current year for each piece of property. In making this calculation, it is essential to use the same portion of each tax payment as the accrual that was used in the preceding year unless justifiable conditions exist for a change. After the accrual and property tax expense for each piece of property have been recomputed, the totals should be added and compared with the general ledger. In many cases, property taxes are charged to more than one expense account. When this happens, the auditor should test for proper classification by evaluating whether the proper amount was charged to each account.

A typical working paper showing the property tax expense, the accrued property taxes, and the audit procedures used to verify the balances is illustrated in Figure 17-5 on pages 576 and 577.

AUDIT OF OPERATIONS

OBJECTIVE 17-5

Design and perform the audit tests of income and expense accounts.

The audit of operations is meant to determine whether the income and expense accounts in the financial statements are fairly presented in accordance with generally accepted accounting principles. The auditor must be satisfied that each of the income and expense totals included in the income statement, as well as net earnings, is not materially misstated.

In conducting audit tests of the financial statements, the auditor must always be aware of the importance of the income statement to users of the statements. Many users rely more heavily on the income statement than on the balance sheet for making decisions. Equity investors, long-term creditors, union representatives, and frequently even short-term creditors are more interested in the ability of a firm to generate profit than in the liquidity value or book value of the individual assets.

Considering the purposes of the statement of earnings, the following two concepts are essential in the audit of operations:

1. The matching of periodic expense to periodic income is necessary for a proper determination of operating results.
2. The consistent application of accounting principles for different periods is necessary for comparability.

These concepts must be applied to the recording of individual transactions and to the combining of accounts in the general ledger for statement presentation.

APPROACH TO AUDITING OPERATIONS

The audit of operations cannot be regarded as a separate part of the total audit process. A misstatement of an income statement account will most often equally affect a balance sheet account, and vice versa. The audit of operations is so intertwined with the other parts of the audit that it is necessary to interrelate different aspects of testing operations with the different types of tests previously discussed. A

FIGURE 17-5
Schedule for Property
Taxes

			Burnaby Company, Inc.			Schedule	I-6	Date
			Property Tax Worksheet			Prepared by	Client/JL	15/1/99
			31/12/98			Approved by	GS	20/1/99

Tax Bill No.	Area Code	Assessing Authority	Property	Assessed Value ①	Total Tax ②	Period Covered ③
		West Coast Facilities				
526391	51	Fraser County				
			Westside Warehouse	400 000	16 000	1998
526392	51	Fraser County				
			Headquarters Bldg	250 000	10 000	1997
		Manitoba Facilities				
17923		Flin Flon County				
			Manufacturing Plant	2 000 000	23 000	1998

① Assessed valuation is defined by the laws of both provinces as 50 percent of "true and fair value." Assessments and taxes payable are on a calendar basis.

② Mill rates:

Fraser County   0.0400 ($40 per $1,000)

Flin Flon County   0.0115 ($11.50 per $1,000) for 1998

③ Taxes are payable as follows

West Coast site — one-half no later than April 30 and the balance no later than October 31, for the current calendar year.

Manitoba site — payable in full not later than December 31 following assessment date, which is June 30.

brief description of these tests serves as a review of material covered in other chapters; but more important, it shows the interrelationship of different parts of the audit with operations testing. The parts of the audit directly affecting operations are

- Analytical procedures
- Tests of controls
- Analysis of account balances
- Tests of details of balance sheet accounts
- Tests of allocations

This section emphasizes the operations accounts directly related to the acquisition and payment cycle, but the same basic concepts apply to the operations accounts in all other cycles.

Prepaid				Accrued			
Beginning Balance	Additions	Expense	Ending Balance	Beginning Balance	Additions	Payments	Ending Balance
1 250	16 000 #✓	15 867	1 383 x				
1 563	10 000 #✓	9 896	1 667 x				
				3 667	✓23 000	#22 834	38 33x
2 813	26 000	25 763	3 050	3 667	23 000	22 834	3 983 x
⋀ PY	⋀	⋀	⋀	⋀ PY	⋀	⋀	⋀

PY   Agreed to prior year's working paper
✓   Agreed to county tax due notice (identified in left column)
Traced to cancelled cheque and validated receipt
⋀ x Footed, cross-footed

ANALYTICAL PROCEDURES

Analytical procedures were first discussed in Chapter 6 as a general concept and have been referred to in subsequent chapters as a part of particular audit areas. Analytical procedures should be considered a part of the test of the fairness of the presentation of both balance sheet and income statement accounts. A few analytical procedures and their effect on operations in the acquisition and payment cycle are shown in Table 17-3.

TESTS OF CONTROLS

Tests of controls have the effect of simultaneously verifying balance sheet and operations accounts. For example, when an auditor concludes that internal controls provide reasonable assurance that transactions in the acquisitions journal exist and are accurately recorded, correctly classified, and recorded in a timely manner, then evidence exists as to the correctness of individual balance sheet accounts (e.g., accounts

TABLE 17-3

ANALYTICAL
PROCEDURES FOR
OPERATIONS

ANALYTICAL PROCEDURE	POSSIBLE MISSTATEMENT
Compare individual expenses with previous years.	Overstatement or understatement of a balance in an expense account.
Compare individual asset and liability balances with previous years.	Overstatement or understatement of a balance sheet account that would also affect an income statement account (i.e., a misstatement of inventory affects cost of goods sold).
Compare individual expenses with budgets.	Misstatement of expenses and related balance sheet accounts.
Compare gross margin percentage with previous years.	Misstatement of cost of goods sold and inventory.
Compare inventory turnover ratio with previous years.	Misstatement of cost of goods sold and inventory.
Compare prepaid insurance expense with previous years.	Misstatement of insurance expense and prepaid insurance.
Compare commission expense divided by sales with previous years.	Misstatement of commission expense and accrued commissions.
Compare individual manufacturing expenses divided by total manufacturing expenses with previous years.	Misstatement of individual manufacturing expenses and related balance sheet accounts.

payable, capital assets) and income statement accounts (e.g., advertising, repairs). Conversely, inadequate controls and misstatements discovered through tests of controls are an indication of the likelihood of misstatements in both the income statement and the balance sheet.

Understanding internal control and the related tests of controls to determine the appropriate assessed control risk is the most important means of verifying many of the operations accounts in each of the transaction cycles. For example, if the auditor concludes after adequate tests that assessed control risk can be reduced to low, the only additional verification of operating accounts such as utilities, advertising, and purchases should be analytical procedures and cutoff tests. However, certain income and expense accounts are not verified at all by tests of controls, and others must be tested more extensively by other means. These are discussed as we proceed.

ANALYSIS OF ACCOUNT BALANCES

For some accounts, the amounts included in the operations accounts must be analyzed even though the two previously mentioned tests have been performed. The meaning and methodology of analysis of accounts will be described first, followed by a discussion of when expense account analysis is appropriate.

Expense account analysis is the examination of underlying documentation of the individual transactions and amounts making up the total particular expense account. The underlying documents are similar in nature to those used for examining transactions as a part of tests of acquisitions transactions and include invoices, receiving reports, purchase orders, and contracts. Figure 17-6 illustrates a typical working paper showing expense analysis for legal expenses.

Thus, expense account analysis is closely related to tests of controls. The major difference is the degree of concentration on an individual account. Since the tests of controls are meant to assess the appropriate level of control risk, they constitute a general review that usually includes the verification of many different accounts. The analysis of expense and other operations accounts consists of the examination of the transactions in specific accounts to determine the propriety, classification, valuation, and other specific information about each account analyzed.

Assuming satisfactory classification results are found in tests of controls and sub-

FIGURE 17-6

Expense Analysis for Legal Expense

Fundy Corp.		Schedule	V-10	**Date**
General and Administrative Expenses		Prepared by	Client/JI	21/1/99
31/12/98		Approved by	SW	28/1/99

Acct. 913-Legal Expense

Paid to	For	Date	Amount
② Alexander J. Schweppe	Retainer—12 months @$500	Monthly	① 6 000 ✓
	Fundy vs. Carson—patent infringement suit	Apr. 14 Aug. 9	2 800 ✓ 3 109 ✓
② Smith, Tom & Ball	Consultation re: inquiry from Health and Welfare Canada	June 6 July 10	200 ✓ 200 ✓
③ L. Marvin Hall	Assistance in collecting overdue receivable from Star Mfg. Ltd.	Nov. 10	105 ✓
			12 414 GL Λ

① Per minutes of meeting of Board of Directors 10/1/99. Schweppe reappointed general counsel with retainer.

② Lawyer's letters requested { Received 23/1/99, all matters listed are covered therein; letters filed in General Section of working papers.

③ Lawyer's letters not requested. Per phone conversation with Mr. Hall, 15/1/99, he rarely represents the company, and his services have been limited to collection problems. The Star Mfg. matter was closed in October 1998, and he has not been involved in any other matters related to the company since that time.

✓ Examined statement and vouchers
Λ Footed
GL Agreed to general ledger

stantive tests of transactions, auditors normally restrict expense analysis to those accounts with a relatively high likelihood of material misstatement. For example, auditors often analyze repairs and maintenance expense accounts to determine if they erroneously include property, plant, and equipment transactions; rent and lease expense are analyzed to determine the need to capitalize leases; and legal expense is analyzed to determine whether there are potential contingent liabilities, disputes, illegal acts, or other legal issues that may affect the financial statements. Accounts such as utilities, travel expense, and advertising are rarely analyzed unless analytical procedures indicate high potential for material misstatement.

Frequently, the expense account analysis is done as a part of the verification of the related asset. For example, it is common to analyze repairs and maintenance as a part of verifying capital assets, rent expense as a part of verifying prepaid or accrued rent, and insurance expense as a part of testing prepaid insurance.

TESTS OF ALLOCATIONS

Several expense accounts that have not yet been discussed arise from the internal allocation of accounting data. These include expenses such as the amortization of capital assets and the amortization of copyrights and catalogue costs. The allocation of manufacturing overhead between inventory and cost of goods sold is an example of a different type of allocation that affects the expenses.

Allocations are important because they determine whether a particular expenditure is an asset or a current-period expense. If the client fails to follow generally accepted accounting principles or fails to calculate the allocation properly, the financial statements can be materially misstated. The allocation of many expenses such as the amortization of capital assets and the amortization of copyrights is required because the life of the asset is greater than one year. The original cost of the asset is verified at the time of acquisition, but the charge-off takes place over several years. Other types of allocations directly affecting the financial statements arise because the life of a short-lived asset does not expire on the balance sheet date. Examples include prepaid rent and insurance. Finally, the allocation of costs between current-period manufacturing expenses and inventory is required by generally accepted accounting principles as a means of reflecting all the costs of making a product.

Income statement accounts resulting from allocations are typically not verified as a part of tests of controls or tests of details of balance sheet accounts. Analytical procedures are used extensively for verifying allocations, but additional detailed testing is frequently needed.

In testing the allocation of expenditures such as prepaid insurance and manufacturing overhead, the two most important considerations are adherence to generally accepted accounting principles and consistency with the preceding period. The two most important audit procedures for allocations are tests for overall reasonableness and recalculation of the client's results. It is common to perform these tests as a part of the audit of the related asset or liability accounts. For example, amortization expense is usually verified as part of the audit of capital assets; the amortization of patents is tested as part of verifying new patents or the disposal of existing ones; and the allocations between inventory and cost of goods sold are verified as part of the audit of inventory.

REVIEW OF RELATED PARTY TRANSACTIONS

While the examination of underlying documents in the tests of controls is designed primarily to verify transactions with third parties, related transactions with affiliates and subdivisions within the client's organization are also included in the examination. The possibility of improper recording and disclosure of transactions between independent entities was discussed in Chapter 7 in the section dealing with related party transactions.

In 1999, the CICA's Assurance Standards Board issued Section 6010, "Audit of Related Party Transactions." The new section adopts a risk-based approach and provides guidance to the auditor for assessing inherent and control risks and ultimately determining the extent of substantive testing. Minimum procedures are set out in the new section.

When a client deals with related parties, Section 3840 of the *Handbook* requires that the nature of the relationship, the nature and extent of transactions, and amounts due to and from the related parties, including contractual obligations and contingencies, be properly disclosed for the financial statements to be in conformity with GAAP. Services and inventory acquired from related parties must be properly valued, and other exchange transactions must be carefully evaluated for propriety and reasonableness. Obviously, related party transactions must be audited more extensively than those with third parties.

Accrued liabilities — estimated unpaid obligations for services or benefits that have been received prior to the balance sheet date; include accrued commissions, accrued income taxes, accrued payroll, and accrued rent (p. 573).

Allocation — the division of certain expenses, such as amortization and manufacturing overhead, among several expense accounts (p. 568).

Capital asset master file — a computer file containing records for each piece of equipment and other types of property owned; the primary accounting record for manufacturing equipment and other capital asset accounts (p. 561).

Expense account analysis — the examination of underlying documentation of individual transactions and amounts making up the total of an expense account (p. 578).

Insurance register — a record of insurance policies in force and the due date of each policy (p. 570).

REVIEW QUESTIONS

17-1 Explain the relationship between tests of controls for the acquisition and payment cycle and tests of details of balances for the verification of capital assets. Which aspects of capital assets are directly affected by the tests of controls, and which are not?

17-2 Explain why the emphasis in auditing capital assets is on the current-period acquisitions and disposals rather than on the balances in the account carried forward from the preceding year. Under what circumstances would the emphasis be on the balances carried forward?

17-3 What is the relationship between the audit of property accounts and the audit of repair and maintenance accounts? Explain how the auditor organizes the audit to take this relationship into consideration.

17-4 List and briefly state the purpose of all audit procedures that might reasonably be applied by an auditor to determine that all capital assets retirements have been recorded on the books.

17-5 In auditing amortization expense, what major considerations should the auditor keep in mind? Explain how each can be verified.

17-6 Explain the relationship between the tests of controls for the acquisition and payment cycle and the tests of details of balances for verification of prepaid insurance.

17-7 Explain why the audit of prepaid insurance should ordinarily take a relatively small amount of audit time if the client's assessed control risk for acquisitions is low.

17-8 Distinguish between the evaluation of the adequacy of insurance coverage and the verification of prepaid insurance. Explain which is more important in a typical audit.

17-9 What are the major differences between the audit of prepaid expenses and other asset accounts such as accounts receivable or property, plant, and equipment?

17-10 Explain the relationship between accrued rent and the tests of controls for the acquisition and payment cycle. Which aspects of accrued rent are not verified as a part of the tests of controls?

17-11 In verifying accounts payable, it is common to restrict the audit sample to a small portion of the population items, whereas in auditing accrued property taxes it is common to verify all transactions for the year. Explain the reason for the difference.

17-12 Which documents are used to verify prepaid property taxes and the related expense accounts?

17-13 List three expense accounts that are tested as part of the acquisition and payment cycle or the payroll and personnel cycle. List three expense accounts that are not directly verified as a part of either of these cycles.

17-14 What is meant by "the analysis of expense accounts"? Explain how expense account analysis relates to the tests of controls that the auditor has already completed for the acquisition and payment cycle.

17-15 How would the approach for verifying repair expense differ from that used to audit amortization expense? Why would the approach be different?

17-16 List the factors that should affect the auditor's decision whether or not to analyze a particular account balance. Considering these factors, list four expense accounts that are commonly analyzed in audit engagements.

17-17 Explain how costs of goods sold for a wholesale company could in part be verified by each of the following types of tests:
a. Analytical procedures
b. Tests of controls
c. Analysis of account balances
d. Tests of details of balance sheet accounts
e. Tests of allocations

17-18 The following questions concern internal controls in the acquisition and payment cycle. Choose the best response.

a. If preparation of a periodic scrap report is essential in order to maintain adequate control over the manufacturing process, the data for this report should be accumulated in the
(1) production department.
(2) warehousing department.
(3) budget department.
(4) accounting department.

b. Which of the following is an internal control weakness related to factory equipment?
(1) Cheques issued in payment of purchases of equipment are not signed by the controller.
(2) Proceeds from sales of fully amortized equipment are credited to other income.
(3) All acquisitions of factory equipment must be made by the department in need of the equipment.
(4) Factory equipment replacements are generally made when estimated useful lives, as indicated in amortization schedules, have expired.

c. With respect to an internal control measure that will assure accountability for capital asset retirements, management should implement controls that include
(1) continuous analysis of miscellaneous revenue to locate any cash proceeds from sale of capital assets.
(2) periodic inquiry of plant executives by internal auditors as to whether any capital assets have been retired.
(3) continuous use of serially numbered retirement work orders.
(4) periodic observation of capital assets by the internal auditors.

(AICPA adapted)

17-19 The following questions concern analytical procedures in the acquisition and payment cycle. Choose the best response.

a. Which of the following comparisons would be most useful to an auditor in evaluating the results of an entity's operations?
(1) Current year revenue to budgeted current year revenue
(2) Current year warranty expense to current year contingent liabilities
(3) Prior year accounts payable to current year accounts payable
(4) Prior year payroll expense to budgeted current year payroll expense

b. The controller of Eigram Manufacturing, Inc., wants to use ratio analysis to identify the possible existence of idle equipment or the possibility that equipment has been disposed of without having been written off. Which of the following ratios would best accomplish this objective?
(1) Amortization expense/book value of manufacturing equipment

(2) Repairs and maintenance cost/direct labour costs
(3) Gross manufacturing equipment cost/units produced
(4) Accumulated amortization/book value of manufacturing equipment

17-20 The following questions concern the audit of asset accounts in the acquisition and payment cycle. Choose the best response.

a. In testing for unrecorded retirements of equipment, an auditor most likely would
(1) select items of equipment from the accounting records and then locate them during the plant tour.
(2) inspect items of equipment observed during the plant tour and then trace them to the equipment master file.
(3) compare amortization journal entries with similar prior-year entries in search of fully amortized equipment.
(4) scan the general journal for unusual equipment additions and excessive debits to repairs and maintenance expense.

b. Which of the following is the best evidence of real-estate ownership at the balance sheet date?
(1) Paid real-estate tax bills
(2) Insurance policy
(3) Original deed held in the client's safe
(4) Lawyer's statement on closing

(AICPA adapted)

17-21 The following questions concern the audit of liabilities or operations. Choose the best response.

a. Which of the following audit procedures is least likely to detect an unrecorded liability?
(1) Analysis and recomputation of amortization expense
(2) Analysis and recomputation of interest expense
(3) Reading of the minutes of meetings of the board of directors
(4) Mailing of standard bank confirmation forms

b. Which of the following best describes the independent auditor's approach to obtaining satisfaction concerning amortization expense in the income statement?
(1) Determine the method for computing amortization expense, and ascertain that it is in accordance with generally accepted accounting principles.
(2) Verify the mathematical accuracy of the amounts charged to income as a result of amortization expense.
(3) Reconcile the amount of amortization expense to those amounts credited to accumulated amortization accounts.
(4) Establish the basis for amortizable assets, and verify the amortization expense.

c. Before expressing an opinion concerning the results of operations, the auditor should proceed with the examination of the income statement by

(1) making net income comparisons to published industry trends and ratios.

(2) applying a rigid measurement standard designed to test for understatement of net income.

(3) analyzing the beginning and ending balance sheet inventory amounts.

(4) examining income statement accounts concurrently with the related balance sheet accounts.

(AICPA adapted)

DISCUSSION QUESTIONS AND PROBLEMS

17-22 The following three questions explore different problems related to the audit of capital assets.

a. During your year-end audit of Beechwood, Inc., you learn that the company developed a new type of heat pump and has capitalized all costs associated with the research on and development of it. Explain fully what action you would take and what you would say to management in your discussion about this issue.

b. Explain how an auditor determines real-estate ownership by a client.

c. Briefly discuss why an auditor would be interested in the payee(s) of a client's property insurance policies.

17-23 For each of the following misstatements in property, plant, and equipment accounts, state an internal control that the client could implement to prevent the misstatement from occurring and a substantive audit procedure that the auditor could use to discover the misstatement.

1. The asset lives used to amortize equipment are less than reasonable, expected useful lives.

2. Capitalizable assets are routinely expensed as repairs and maintenance, perishable tools, or supplies expense.

3. Construction equipment that is abandoned or traded for replacement equipment is not removed from the accounting records.

4. Amortization expense for manufacturing operations is charged to administrative expenses.

5. Tools necessary for the maintenance of equipment are stolen by company employees for their personal use.

6. Acquisitions of property are recorded at an improper amount.

7. A loan against existing equipment is not recorded in the accounting records. The cash receipts from the loan never reached the company because they were used for the down payment on a piece of equipment now being used as an operating asset. The equipment is also not recorded in the records.

17-24 The following types of internal controls are commonly employed by organizations for property, plant, and equipment:

1. A capital asset master file is maintained with a separate record for each capital asset.

2. Written policies exist and are known by accounting personnel to differentiate between capitalizable additions, freight, installation costs, replacements, and maintenance expenditures.

3. Purchases of capital assets in excess of $20,000 are approved by the board of directors.

4. Whenever it is practical, equipment is labelled with metal tags and is inventoried on a systematic basis.

5. Amortization charges for individual assets are calculated for each asset; recorded in a capital asset master file that includes cost, amortization, and accumulated amortization for each asset; and verified periodically by an independent clerk.

Required

a. State the purpose of each of the internal controls listed above. Your answer should refer to the type of misstatement that is likely to be reduced because of the control.

b. For each internal control, list one test of controls that the auditor can use to test for its existence.

c. List one test of controls for determining whether the control is actually preventing misstatements in property, plant, and equipment.

17-25 The following audit procedures were planned by Marissa Tomasetti, a public accountant, in the audit of the acquisition and payment cycle for Cooley Products, Inc.

1. Review the acquisitions journal for large and unusual transactions.

2. Send letters to several vendors, including a few for which the recorded accounts payable balance is zero, requesting them to inform us of their balance due from Cooley. Ask the controller to sign the letter.

3. Examine a sample of receiving reports, and determine whether each one has been matched to a vendor invoice.

4. Select a sample of equipment listed on capital asset master files, and inspect the asset to confirm its existence and to determine its condition.

5. Refoot the acquisitions data files, and trace totals to the general journal.

6. Calculate the ratio of equipment repairs and maintenance to total equipment, and compare with previous years.

7. Obtain a written statement from the client confirming that all capital assets accounts payable have been included in the current-period financial statements and have been accurately recorded, and that the collateral for each is included in the footnotes.

8. Use the prior year's properties master file together with the current year's transactions data file to derive ending

balances in asset cost and accumulated amortization. Compare to the general ledger ending balances.

9. For 20 nontangible acquisitions, select a sample of line items from the acquisitions transaction files and trace each to related vendors' invoices. Examine whether each transaction appears to be an appropriate expenditure for the client, and whether each was approved and recorded at the correct amount and date in the transaction file and charged to the correct account per the chart of accounts.

10. Examine invoices included in the client's unpaid invoice file at the auditor's report date to determine if they were recorded in the appropriate accounting period and at the correct amounts.

11. Recalculate the portion of insurance premiums on the client's unexpired insurance schedule that is applicable to future periods.

12. Observe data entry to ensure that documents are entered in the system. Observe that cheque numbers are entered on vendor invoices prior to cheque signature. When the cheque signer's assistant writes "paid" on supporting documents, watch whether she does it after the documents are reviewed and the cheques are signed.

Required

a. For each procedure, identify the type of evidence being used.

b. For each procedure, identify whether it is an analytical procedure, a test of controls, or a test of details of balances.

c. For each test of controls, identify the transaction-related audit objective(s) being met.

d. For each test of details of balances, identify the balance-related audit objective(s) being met.

17-26 Hardware Manufacturing Company Limited, a closely held corporation, has operated since 1994 but has not had its financial statements audited. The company now plans to issue additional capital stock to be sold to outsiders and wishes to engage you to examine its 1998 transactions and render an opinion on the financial statements for the year ended December 31, 1998.

The company has expanded from one plant to three and has frequently acquired, modified, and disposed of all types of equipment. Capital assets have a net book value of 70 percent of total assets and consist of land and buildings, diversified machinery and equipment, and furniture and fixtures. Some property was acquired by donation from shareholders. Amortization was recorded by several methods using various estimated lives.

Required

a. May you confine your examination solely to 1998 transactions as requested by this prospective client whose financial statements have not previously been examined? Why or why not?

b. Prepare an audit program for the January 1, 1998, opening balances of the land, building, and equipment and

accumulated amortization accounts of Hardware Manufacturing Company Limited. You need not include tests of 1998 transactions in your program.

(AICPA adapted)

17-27 The following program has been prepared for the audit of prepaid real-estate taxes of a client that pays taxes on 25 different pieces of property, some of which have been acquired in the current year.

1. Obtain a schedule of prepaid taxes from the client, and tie the total to the general ledger.

2. Compare the charges for annual tax payments with property tax assessment bills.

3. Recompute accrued/prepaid amounts for all payments on the basis of the portion of the year expired.

Required

a. State the purpose of each procedure.

b. Evaluate the adequacy of the audit program.

17-28 As part of the audit of different audit areas, it is important to be alert for the possibility of unrecorded liabilities. For each of the following audit areas or accounts, describe a liability that could be uncovered and the audit procedures that could uncover it.

a. Minutes of the board of directors' meetings

b. Land and buildings

c. Rent expense

d. Interest expense

e. Cash surrender value of life insurance

f. Cash in the bank

g. Officers' travel and entertainment expense

17-29 While you are having lunch with a banker friend, you explain to him how your firm conducts an audit in a typical engagement. You outline your philosophy of emphasizing the study of internal control, analytical procedures, tests of controls, and tests of details. At the completion of your explanation, he says, "That all sounds great except for a couple of things. At our bank, we currently stress the importance of a continuous earnings stream. You seem to be emphasizing fraud detection and a fairly stated balance sheet. We would rather see you put more emphasis on the income statement."

Required

How would you respond to your friend's comments?

17-30 Eugene Fikursky, a staff assistant, was asked to analyze interest and legal expense as a part of the first-year audit of Chinook Manufacturing Corp. In searching for a model to follow, Fikursky looked at other completed working papers in the current audit file and concluded that the closest thing to what he was looking for was a working paper for repair and maintenance expense account analysis. Following the approach used in analyzing repairs and maintenance, he made a schedule of all interest and legal expenses in excess of $500 and verified them by examining supporting documentation.

Required

a. Evaluate Fikursky's approach to verifying interest and legal expense.

b. Suggest a better approach to verifying these two account balances.

17-31 In performing tests of the acquisition and payment cycle for Oakville Manufacturing, Inc., the staff assistant did a careful and complete job. Since internal controls were evaluated as excellent before tests of controls were performed and were determined to be operating effectively on the basis of the lack of exceptions in the tests of controls, the decision was made to reduce significantly the tests of expense account analysis. The in-charge auditor decided to reduce, but not eliminate, the acquisition-related expense account analysis for repair expense, legal and other professional expense, miscellaneous expense, and utilities expense on the grounds that they should always be verified more extensively than normal accounts. The decision was also made to eliminate any account analysis for the purchase of raw materials, amortization expense, supplies expense, insurance expense, and the current-period additions to capital assets.

Required

a. List considerations in the audit other than the quality of internal controls that should affect the auditor's selection of accounts to be analyzed.

b. Assuming no significant problems were identified on the basis of the other considerations in part (a), evaluate the auditor's decision to reduce but not eliminate expense account analysis for each account involved. Justify your conclusions.

c. Assuming no significant problems were identified on the basis of the other considerations in part (a), evaluate the auditor's decision to eliminate expense account analysis for each account involved. Justify your conclusions.

17-32 Xavier Ltd. is a general contractor in the business of constructing high-rise buildings. The company subcontracts most of the construction work, on fixed-price contracts with penalty clauses, to various smaller specialized contractors.

The subcontractors submit monthly progress billings for each project. All such billings are subject to a 15 percent holdback by Xavier Ltd., which is payable 90 days after the project architect has certified that the subcontractor's portion of the work has been completed.

Xavier Ltd. treats the portions of the progress billings that are immediately payable as trade accounts payable but sets up the holdback portions in a separate general ledger account.

Required

List the audit procedures that you would perform to verify the balance reported by the company as "holdbacks payable" at its fiscal year end. Identify the audit objective of each audit procedure.

<hr>

CASES

17-33 You are doing the audit of the Ute Corporation for the year ended December 31, 1998. The schedule for the property, plant, and equipment and related allowance for amortization accounts has been prepared by the client (see Exhibit I on page 586). You have compared the opening balances with your prior year's audit working papers.

The following information is obtained during your audit:

1. All equipment is amortized on the straight-line basis (no salvage value taken into consideration) based on the following estimated lives: buildings—25 years, all other items — 10 years. The corporation's policy is to take one-half year's amortization on all asset acquisitions and disposals during the year.

2. On April 1, the corporation entered into a 10-year lease contract for a die-casting machine with annual rentals of $5,000, payable in advance every April 1. The lease is cancellable by either party (60 days' written notice is required), and there is no option to renew the lease or buy the equipment at the end of the lease. The estimated useful life of the machine is 10 years with no salvage value. The corporation recorded the die-casting machine in the machinery and equipment account at $40,400, the present value at the date of the lease, and $2,020, applic-

able to the machine, has been included in amortization expense for the year.

3. The corporation completed the construction of a wing on the plant building on June 30. The useful life of the building was not extended by this addition. The lowest construction bid received was $17,500, the amount recorded in the buildings account. Company personnel were used to construct the addition at a cost of $16,000 (materials—$7,500, labour—$5,500, and overhead—$3,000).

4. On August 18, $5,000 was paid for paving and fencing a portion of land owned by the corporation and used as a parking lot for employees. The expenditure was charged to the land account.

5. The amount shown in the machinery and equipment asset retirement column represents cash received on September 5, upon disposal of a machine purchased in July 1994 for $48,000. The bookkeeper recorded amortization expense of $3,500 on this machine in 1998.

6. Fredericton donated land and building appraised at $10,000 and $40,000, respectively, to the Ute Corporation for a plant. On September 1, the corporation began operating the plant. Since no costs were involved, the bookkeeper made no entry for the foregoing transaction.

EXHIBIT I

Ute Corporation Analysis of Property, Plant, and Equipment and Related Allowance for Amortization Accounts for Year Ended December 31, 1998

DESCRIPTION	FINAL 31/12/97	ADDITIONS	RETIREMENTS	PER BOOKS 31/12/98
Assets				
Land	$ 22,500	$ 5,000		$ 27,500
Buildings	120,000	17,500		137,500
Machinery and equipment	385,000	40,400	$26,000	399,400
	$527,500	$62,900	$26,000	$564,400
Allowance for Amortizaton				
Building	$ 60,000	$ 5,150		$ 65,150
Machinery and equipment	173,250	39,220		212,470
	$233,250	$44,370		$277,620

Required

a. In addition to inquiry of the client, explain how you would have found each of the given six items during the audit.

b. Identify likely errors in these accounts, with supporting computations at December 31, 1998. Disregard income tax implications.

(AICPA adapted)

17-34 A Canadian life insurance company maintains a large first mortgage investment portfolio. The mortgagors are all located in the province of the head office of the company. The president has advised Peter Forbes, the company's auditor for many years, that the mortgage manager had suddenly disappeared.

The president states that he feels the fees paid for the acquisition of mortgages are too high (i.e., finders' fees) and that there are possibilities that some mortgages have been granted for properties with appraised values that have been inflated. He then asks Peter to investigate the possibility of fraud in the mortgage department.

From his working papers on the current internal control review, Peter extracts the following pertinent facts:

- All cheques issued for finders' fees are prepared from cheque requisitions. These requisitions are prepared and signed by the mortgage manager. All requisitions are cross-referenced to the applicable cheques.
- All finders' fees cheques are prepared by the accounting department. They are prenumbered and signed by the vice-president of finance and the controller of the company after they review the finders' invoices.
- After the cheques are signed, they are sent to the mortgage manager for distribution to the payees.
- All such cheques are paid from the company's general bank account. The finders' invoices are filed in the mortgage department.
- The amount authorized by the company for finders' fees is 1 percent of the principal amount of the mortgage loans.
- No other cheque requests are prepared by the mortgage department.
- All properties for which mortgage loans are granted are

appraised by the mortgage manager. The mortgage manager decides on the mortgage loans to be granted.
- The company policy is not to grant mortgage loans on first mortgages in excess of 75 percent of the appraised value of the related property.
- The mortgage manager prepares all mortgage note documentation.
- Before the mortgage loan is granted, the finance committee board authorizes the mortgage loan amounts and interest rates and approves the mortgagors.
- The computer-prepared mortgage ledger indicates the mortgage principal, unpaid interest, mortgage terms, interest rate, and aggregate balance due for each mortgage. Finders' fees are not indicated in this ledger.
- Finders' fees paid are recorded in a separate general ledger account. The account indicates date paid, cheque number, and amount for each fee paid.
- All cheques received from mortgagors are sent directly from the mailroom to the mortgage department for identification of the mortgagors. The cheques are then submitted to the cash collections department for depositing. Mortgagors paying by means of payment withdrawal directly from their bank accounts are also handled by the mortgage department.

Peter's review of his files indicates that he has brought the internal control weaknesses, evident from the above facts, to the attention of the company's management in a recent memorandum of recommendations to strengthen internal controls and procedures. Management's written response (as in previous years) has been that it would review the procedures and take corrective action where warranted. Although Peter has repeatedly reminded the company to improve its procedures, it has not done so in the last five years.

Required

a. Outline the weaknesses in internal control, their potential consequences to the insurance company, and suggested recommendations for improvement that Peter would likely have included in his most recent management letter.

b. Outline audit procedures that Peter could conduct to quantify the dollar amount of any potential fraud. Specify the purpose of each audit procedure identified.

17-35 As the manager of the audit of Vernal Manufacturing Inc., you are investigating the operations accounts. The in-charge auditor assessed control risk for all cycles as low, supported by tests of controls. There are no major inherent risks affecting operations. Accordingly, in auditing the operations accounts, you decide to emphasize analytical procedures. The in-charge auditor prepared a schedule of the key income statement accounts that compares the prior year totals to the current year's and includes explanations of variances obtained from discussions with client personnel. That schedule is included in Exhibit II on page 588.

Required

a. Examine the schedule prepared by the in-charge auditor, and write a memorandum to the in-charge that includes criticisms and concerns about the audit work procedures performed and questions for the in-charge to resolve.

b. Evaluate the explanations for variances provided by client personnel. List any alternative explanations to those given.

c. Indicate which variances are of special significance to the audit and how they should affect additional audit procedures.

EXHIBIT II
Vernal Manufacturing Inc. Operations Accounts 31/12/98

ACCOUNT	PER G/L 31/12/97	PER G/L 31/12/98	CHANGE AMOUNT	CHANGE PERCENT	EXPLANATIONS BY CLIENT
Sales*	$8,467,312	$9,845,231	$1,377,919	16.3	Sales increase due to two new customers who account for 20% of volume. Larger returns due to need to cement relations with these customers.
Sales returns and allowances	(64,895)	(243,561)	(178,666)	275.3	
Gain on sale of assets	43,222	(143,200)	(186,422)	−431.3	
Interest income	243	223	(20)	−8.2	Trade-in of several sales cars that needed replacement.
Miscellaneous income	6,365	25,478	19,113	300.3	
	8,452,247	9,484,171	1,031,924	12.2	
Cost of goods sold:					
Beginning inventory	1,487,666	1,389,034	(98,632)	−6.6	Increase in these accounts due to increased volume with new customers as indicated above.
Purchases	2,564,451	3,430,865	866,414	33.8	
Freight in	45,332	65,782	20,450	45.1	
Purchase returns	(76,310)	(57,643)	18,667	−24.5	
Factory wages	986,755	1,145,467	158,712	16.1	
Factory benefits	197,652	201,343	3,691	1.9	
Factory overhead	478,659	490,765	12,106	2.5	
Factory amortization	344,112	314,553	(29,559)	−8.6	Inventory being held for new customers.
Ending inventory	(1,389,034)	(2,156,003)	(766,969)	55.2	
	4,639,283	4,824,163	184,880	4.0	
Selling, general and administrative:					
Executive salaries	167,459	174,562	7,103	4.2	Normal salary increases.
Executive benefits	32,321	34,488	2,167	6.7	
Office salaries	95,675	98,540	2,865	3.0	
Office benefits	19,888	21,778	1,890	9.5	
Travel and entertainment	56,845	75,583	18,738	33.0	Sales and promotional expenses increased in an attempt to obtain new major customers. Two obtained and program will continue.
Advertising	130,878	156,680	25,802	19.7	
Other sales expense	34,880	42,334	7,454	21.4	
Stationery and supplies	38,221	21,554	(16,667)	−43.6	Probably a misclassification; will investigate.
Postage	14,657	18,756	4,099	28.0	Normal increase.
Telephone	36,551	67,822	31,271	85.6	Normal increase.
Dues and memberships	3,644	4,522	878	24.1	Normal increase.
Rent	15,607	15,607	0	0.0	
Legal fees	14,154	35,460	21,306	150.5	Timing of billing for fees.
Accounting fees	16,700	18,650	1,950	11.7	Normal increase.
Amortization	73,450	69,500	(3,950)	−5.4	Normal change.
Bad debt expense	166,454	143,871	(22,583)	−13.6	Haven't reviewed yet for the current year.
Insurance	44,321	45,702	1,381	3.1	Normal change.
Interest expense	120,432	137,922	17,490	14.5	Normal change.
Other expense	5,455	28,762	23,307	427.3	Amount not material.
	1,087,592	1,212,093	124,501	11.4	
	5,726,875	6,036,256	309,381	5.4	
Income before taxes	2,725,372	3,447,915	722,543	26.5	Increase due to increased income before tax.
Income taxes	926,626	1,020,600	93,974	10.1	
Net income	$1,798,746	$2,427,315	$628,569	34.9	

*Sales are shown net of Goods and Services Taxes.

18

AUDIT OF THE INVENTORY AND WAREHOUSING CYCLE

DON'T IGNORE RED FLAGS

Kim, Zafar & Smale (KZ&S) had audited Finco Ltd., a commercial finance company owned by a large heavy equipment dealer, for the past seven years. When equipment was sold on credit by the dealer, the transaction was financed through Finco. If customers defaulted on their loan payments, Finco would repossess the equipment inventory.

In assessing inherent risk for repossessed inventory, the engagement senior, Kelly Haney, noted that the commercial finance industry was experiencing problems, and that Finco's management was aggressive in its choice of accounting policies and seemed quite concerned about earnings. Kelly believed that inherent risk should be increased at least to a medium level, leading to increased testing of the repossessed inventory. However, the engagement manager, Joan Nault, felt differently. Joan told Kelly, "Nothing has changed on this audit. Just state the risk is low and do the same amount of testing."

In determining the existence of repossessed equipment, KZ&S had always relied on internal reports from the branch managers who held the equipment. Based on the prior year's work, Kelly concluded that physical inspection was not necessary. In determining the value of equipment inventory, Kelly relied on discussions with management, the same as in the prior year. As in the past, management did not get appraisals of the equipment, stating that their familiarity with the industry allowed them to make reasonable estimates. The auditors accepted this without further challenge. Based on finding no significant exceptions, KZ&S issued an unqualified report.

When KZ&S conducted its audit of Finco the next year, Joan Nault had left the firm and a new manager was assigned. Conditions in the commercial finance industry had deteriorated even more during the

Inventory takes many different forms, depending on the nature of the business. For retail or wholesale businesses, the most important inventory is merchandise on hand which is available for sale. For hospitals, it includes food, drugs, and medical supplies. A manufacturing company has raw materials, purchased parts, and supplies for use in production; goods in the process of being manufactured; and finished goods available for sale. We have selected manufacturing company inventories for presentation in this text. However, most of the principles discussed apply to other types of businesses as well.

For the reasons that follow, the audit of inventories is often the most complex and time-consuming part of the audit:

- Inventory is generally a major item on the balance sheet, and it is often the largest item making up the accounts included in working capital.
- The inventory items are often in different locations, which makes physical control and counting difficult. Companies must have their inventory accessible for the efficient manufacture and sale of the product, but this dispersal creates significant audit problems.
- The diversity of the items in inventories creates difficulties for the auditor. Such items as jewels, chemicals, and electronic parts present problems of observation and valuation.
- The valuation of inventory is difficult due to such factors as obsolescence and the need to allocate manufacturing costs to inventory.
- There are several acceptable inventory valuation methods, but any given client must apply a method consistently from year to year. Moreover, an organization may prefer to use different valuation methods for different parts of the inventory, which is acceptable under GAAP.

The trial balance for Hillsburg Hardware Ltd. on pages 128–129 shows that only two accounts are affected by inventories and warehousing: inventory and cost of goods sold. However, both accounts are highly material. For a manufacturing company, a great many accounts are affected because labour, acquisitions of raw materials, and all indirect manufacturing costs affect inventory.

The physical flow of goods and the flow of costs in the inventory and warehousing cycle for a manufacturing company are shown in Figure 18-1. The direct tie-in of the inventory and warehousing cycle to the acquisition and payment cycle and to the payroll and personnel cycle can be seen by examining the debits to the raw materials, direct labour, and manufacturing overhead T-accounts. The direct tie-in to the sales and collection cycle occurs at the point where finished goods are relieved (credited) and a charge is made to cost of goods sold. This close relationship to other transaction cycles in the organization is a basic characteristic of the audit of the inventory and warehousing cycle.

FIGURE 18-1

Flow of Inventory and Costs

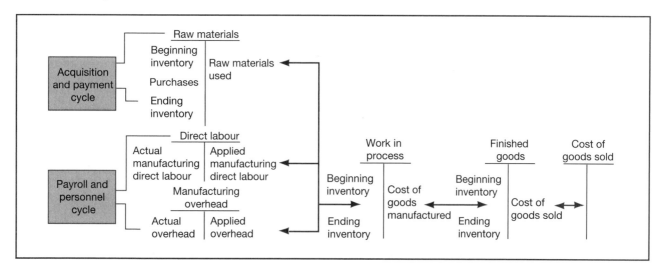

FUNCTIONS IN THE CYCLE AND INTERNAL CONTROLS

OBJECTIVE 18-1

Describe the inventory and warehousing cycle and the pertinent functions, documents, records, and internal controls.

The inventory and warehousing cycle can be thought of as comprising two separate but closely related systems: one involving the actual *physical flow of goods* and the other the *related costs*. As inventories move through the company, there must be adequate controls over both their physical movement and their related costs. A brief examination of the six functions making up the inventory and warehousing cycle will help you to understand these controls and the audit evidence needed to test their effectiveness.

PROCESS PURCHASE ORDERS

Purchase requisitions are used to inform the purchasing department for which inventory items to place orders. Requisitions may be initiated by stockroom personnel when inventory reaches a predetermined level, orders may be placed for the materials required to produce a particular customer order, or orders may be initiated on the basis of a periodic inventory count by a responsible person. Regardless of the method followed, the controls over purchase requisitions and the related purchase orders are evaluated and tested as part of the acquisition and payment cycle. Many organizations use only purchase orders, relying on automated systems to identify the need to obtain materials or products.

RECEIVE NEW MATERIALS

Receipt of the ordered materials is also part of the acquisition and payment cycle. Materials received should be inspected for quantity and quality. The receiving department produces a *receiving report* that becomes a part of the necessary documentation before payment is made. After inspection, the materials are sent to the storeroom and the receiving documents are typically sent to purchasing, the storeroom, and accounts payable. Control and accountability are necessary for all transfers.

STORE RAW MATERIALS	When materials are received, they are stored in the stockroom until needed for production. Materials are issued out of stock to production upon presentation of a properly approved materials requisition, work order, or similar document that indicates the type and quantity of materials needed. This requisition document is used to update the perpetual inventory master files and to make book transfers from the raw materials to work-in-process accounts.

PROCESS GOODS	The processing portion of the inventory and warehousing cycle varies greatly from company to company. The determination of the items and quantities to be produced is generally based on specific orders from customers, sales forecasts, predetermined finished goods inventory levels, or economic production runs. Frequently, a separate production control department is responsible for the determination of the type and quantity of items to be produced. Within the various production departments, provision must be made to account for the quantities produced, control of scrap, quality controls, and physical protection of the material in process. The production department must generate production and scrap reports so that the accounting department can reflect the movement of materials in the books and determine accurate costs of production.

In any company involved in manufacturing, an adequate *cost accounting system* is an important part of the processing of goods function. The system is necessary to indicate the relative profitability of the various products for management planning and control and to value inventories for financial statement purposes. There are two types of cost systems (although many variations and combinations of these systems are employed): *job cost* and *process cost*. The main difference is whether costs are accumulated by individual jobs when material is issued and labour costs incurred (job cost), or whether they are accumulated by particular processes, with unit costs for each process assigned to the products passing through the process (process cost).

Cost accounting records consist of master files, worksheets, and reports that accumulate material, labour, and overhead costs by job or process as the costs are incurred. When jobs or products are completed, the related costs are transferred from work in process to finished goods on the basis of production department reports.

STORE FINISHED GOODS	As finished goods are completed by the production department, they are placed in the stockroom awaiting shipment. In companies with good internal controls, finished goods are kept under physical control in a separate limited access area. The control of finished goods is often considered part of the sales and collection cycle.

SHIP FINISHED GOODS	Shipping of completed goods is an integral part of the sales and collection cycle. Any shipment or transfer of finished goods must be authorized by a properly approved shipping document. The controls for shipment have already been studied in previous chapters.

PERPETUAL INVENTORY FILES	One of the records for inventory that has not been previously discussed is perpetual inventory data files. Separate perpetual records are normally kept for raw materials and finished goods. Most companies do not use perpetuals for work in process.

The perpetual inventory master file normally includes only information such as item number, description, unit cost, quantity on hand, and quantity on order. The supporting transaction files contain supporting records of the units of inventory purchased and sold. Sales price information and vendor information could also be included in data files.

For acquisitions of raw materials, the perpetual inventory master file is updated automatically when acquisitions of inventory are processed as part of recording acquisitions. For example, when the computer system enters the number of units and unit cost for each raw material purchase, this information is used to update perpetual inventory master files along with the acquisitions journal and accounts payable master file. Chapter 16 described the recording of acquisition transactions.

Transfers of raw materials from the storeroom must be separately entered into the computer to update the perpetual records. Typically, only the units transferred need to be entered because the computer can determine the unit costs from the master file. Raw materials perpetual inventory data files that have unit costs include, for each raw material, beginning and ending units on hand, units and unit cost of each purchase, and units and unit cost of each transfer into production.

Finished goods perpetual inventory data files include the same type of information as raw materials perpetuals, but are considerably more complex if costs are included along with units. Finished goods costs include raw materials, direct labour, and manufacturing overhead, which often requires allocations and detailed record keeping. When finished goods perpetuals include unit costs, the cost accounting records must be integrated into the computer system.

SUMMARY OF INVENTORY DOCUMENTATION

The physical movement and related documentation in a basic inventory and warehousing cycle is shown in Figure 18-2. The figure re-emphasizes the important point that the recording of costs and movement of inventory as shown in the books must correspond to the physical movements and processes.

PARTS OF THE AUDIT OF INVENTORY

The overall objective in the audit of the inventory and warehousing cycle is to determine that raw materials, work in process, finished goods inventory, and cost of goods sold are fairly stated on the financial statements. The basic inventory and warehousing cycle can be divided into five distinct parts.

ACQUIRE AND RECORD RAW MATERIALS, LABOUR, AND OVERHEAD

This part of the inventory and warehousing cycle includes the first three functions in Figure 18-2: processing of purchase orders, receipt of raw materials, and storage of raw materials. The internal controls over these three functions are first studied then tested as part of performing tests of controls in the acquisition and payment cycle and the payroll and personnel cycle. At the completion of the acquisition and payment cycle, the auditor is likely to be satisfied that acquisitions of raw materials and manufacturing costs are correctly stated, and samples should be designed to ensure that these systems are adequately tested. Similarly, when labour is a significant part of inventory, the payroll and personnel cycle tests should verify the proper accounting for these costs.

OBJECTIVE 18-2

Explain the significance of the five parts of the inventory and warehousing cycle to the auditor.

TRANSFER ASSETS AND COSTS

Internal transfers include the fourth and fifth functions in Figure 18-2: processing the goods and storing finished goods. These two activities are not related to any other transaction cycles and therefore must be studied and tested as part of the inventory and warehousing cycle. The accounting records concerned with these functions are referred to as the *cost accounting records*.

SHIP GOODS AND RECORD REVENUE AND COSTS

The recording of shipments and related costs, the last function in Figure 18-2, is part of the sales and collection cycle. Thus, the internal controls over this function are studied and tested as part of auditing the sales and collection cycle. The tests of controls should include procedures to verify the accuracy of the perpetual inventory master files.

FIGURE 18-2

Functions in the Inventory and Warehousing Cycle

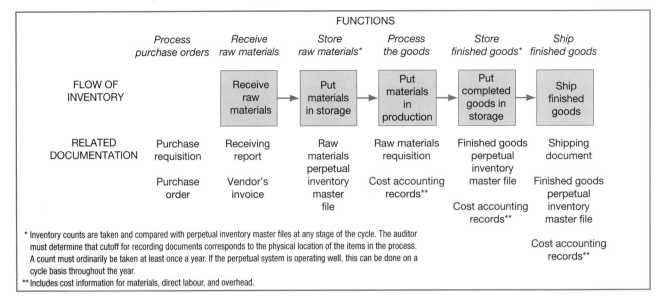

PHYSICALLY OBSERVE INVENTORY

Observing the client taking a physical inventory count is necessary to determine whether recorded inventory actually exists at the balance sheet date and is properly counted by the client. Inventory is the first audit area for which physical examination is an essential type of evidence used to verify the balance in an account. Physical observation is discussed further in this chapter.

PRICE AND COMPILE INVENTORY

Costs used to value the physical inventory must be tested to determine whether the client has correctly followed an inventory method that is in accordance with generally accepted accounting principles and is consistent with previous years. Audit procedures used to verify these costs are referred to as "price tests." In addition, the auditor must verify whether the physical counts were correctly summarized, the inventory quantities and prices were correctly extended, and the extended inventory was correctly footed. These tests are called "compilation tests."

Figure 18-3 summarizes the five parts of the audit of the inventory and warehousing cycle and shows the cycle in which each is audited. The first and third parts of the audit of the inventory and warehousing cycle have already been discussed in connection with the other cycles. The importance of the tests of these other cycles should be kept in mind throughout the remaining sections of this chapter.

AUDIT OF COST ACCOUNTING

OBJECTIVE 18-3

Design and perform audit tests of cost accounting.

The cost accounting systems and controls of different companies vary more than most other areas because of the wide variety of items of inventory and the level of sophistication desired by management. For example, a company that manufactures an entire line of farm machines would have completely different kinds of cost records and internal controls than a steel fabricating shop that makes and installs custom-made metal cabinets. Not surprisingly, small companies with owners who are actively involved in the manufacturing process need less sophisticated records than do large multi-product companies.

FIGURE 18-3
Audit of Inventory

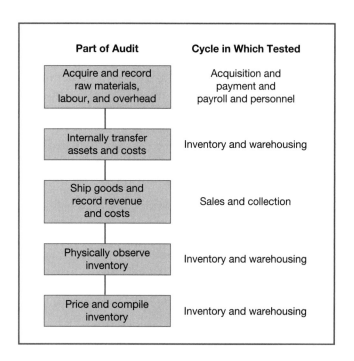

Part of Audit	Cycle in Which Tested
Acquire and record raw materials, labour, and overhead	Acquisition and payment and payroll and personnel
Internally transfer assets and costs	Inventory and warehousing
Ship goods and record revenue and costs	Sales and collection
Physically observe inventory	Inventory and warehousing
Price and compile inventory	Inventory and warehousing

COST ACCOUNTING CONTROLS

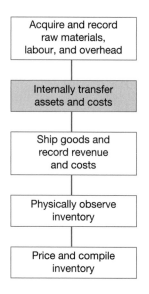

Cost accounting controls are those related to the physical inventory and the consequent costs from the point at which raw materials are requisitioned to the point at which the manufactured product is completed and transferred to storage. It is convenient to divide these controls into two broad categories: (1) physical controls over raw materials, work in process, and finished goods inventory; and (2) controls over the related costs.

Almost all companies need physical controls over their assets to prevent loss from misuse and theft. The use of physically segregated, limited access storage areas for raw material, work in process, and finished goods is one major control to protect assets. In some instances, the assignment of custody of inventory to specific responsible individuals may be necessary to protect the assets. Approved prenumbered documents for authorizing movement of inventory also protect the assets from improper use. Copies of these documents should be sent directly to accounting by the persons issuing them, bypassing people with custodial responsibilities. An example of an effective document of this type is an approved materials requisition for obtaining raw materials from the storeroom.

Perpetual inventory data files maintained by persons who do not have custody of or access to assets are another useful cost accounting control. Perpetual inventory data files are important for a number of reasons: they provide a record of items on hand, which is used to initiate production or purchase of additional materials or goods; they provide a record of the use of raw materials and the sale of finished goods, which can be reviewed for obsolete or slow-moving items; and they provide a record that can be used to pinpoint responsibility for custody as part of the investigation of differences between physical counts and the amounts shown on the records.

Another important consideration in cost accounting is the existence of adequate internal controls that integrate production and accounting records for the purpose of obtaining accurate costs for all products. The existence of adequate cost records aids management in pricing, controlling costs, and costing inventory.

The concepts in auditing cost accounting are no different from those discussed for any other transaction cycle. Figure 18-4 shows the methodology that the auditor should follow in determining which tests to perform. In auditing cost accounting, the auditor is concerned with four aspects: physical controls over inventory, documents and records for transferring inventory, perpetual inventory master files and transaction files, and unit cost records.

Physical controls   The auditor's tests of the adequacy of the physical controls over raw materials, work in process, and finished goods must be restricted to observation and inquiry. For example, the auditor can examine the raw materials storage area to determine whether the inventory is protected from theft and misuse by the existence of a locked storeroom. The existence of an adequate storeroom with a competent custodian in charge also ordinarily results in the orderly storage of inventory. If the auditor concludes that the physical controls are so inadequate that the inventory will be difficult to count, the auditor should expand his or her observation of physical inventory tests to ensure that an adequate count is carried out.

Documents and records for transferring inventory   The auditor's primary concerns in verifying the transfer of inventory from one location to another are that the recorded transfers are valid, the transfers that have actually taken place are recorded, and the quantity, description, and date of all recorded transfers are accurate. First, it is necessary to understand the client's internal controls for recording transfers before relevant tests can be performed. Once the internal controls are understood, the tests can easily be performed by examining documents and records. For example, a procedure to test the existence and accuracy of the transfer of goods from the raw materi-

FIGURE 18-4
Methodology for Designing Tests of Controls for Cost Accounting

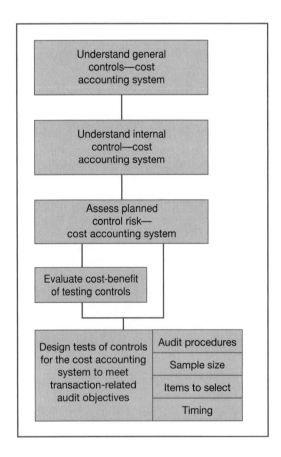

als storeroom to the manufacturing assembly line is accounting for a sequence of raw material requisitions, examining the requisitions for proper approval, and comparing the quantity, description, and date with the information on the raw material perpetual inventory transaction files. Similarly, completed production records can be compared with perpetual inventory files to be sure all manufactured goods were physically delivered to the finished goods storeroom.

Perpetual inventory master and transaction files   The existence of adequate perpetual inventory master files has a major effect on the *timing and extent* of the auditor's physical examination of inventory. For one thing, when there are accurate perpetual inventory master files, it is frequently possible to test the physical inventory prior to the balance sheet date. An interim physical inventory can result in significant cost savings for both the client and the auditor, and enables the client to receive the audited statements earlier. Perpetual inventory master files also enable the auditor to reduce the extent of the tests of physical inventory when the assessed level of control risk related to physical observation of inventory is low.

Tests of the perpetual inventory master files and supporting detail transaction files for the purpose of reducing the tests of physical inventory or changing their timing are done through the use of documentation. Documents to verify the purchase of raw materials can be examined when the auditor is verifying acquisitions as part of the tests of the acquisition and payment cycle. Documents supporting the reduction of raw materials inventory for use in production and the increase in the quantity of finished goods inventory when goods have been manufactured are examined as part of the tests of the cost accounting documents and records in the manner discussed in the preceding section. Support for the reduction in the finished goods inventory through the sale of goods to customers is ordinarily tested as part of the sales and collection cycle. Usually, it is relatively easy to test the accuracy of the perpetuals after the auditor determines how internal controls are designed and decides to what degree assessed control risk should be reduced.

Unit cost records   Obtaining accurate cost data for raw materials, direct labour, and manufacturing overhead is an essential part of cost accounting. Adequate cost accounting records must be integrated with production and other accounting records in order to produce accurate costs of all products. Cost accounting records are pertinent to the auditor in that the valuation of ending inventory depends on the proper design and use of these records.

In testing the inventory cost records, the auditor must first develop an understanding of general controls applicable to this cycle and of internal control. This is frequently somewhat time-consuming because the flow of costs is usually integrated with other accounting records, and it may not be obvious how internal control provides for the internal transfers of raw materials and for direct labour and manufacturing overhead as production is carried out.

Once the auditor understands internal control, the approach to internal verification involves the same concepts that were discussed in the verification of sales and acquisition transactions. Whenever possible, it is desirable to test the cost accounting records as part of the acquisition, payroll, and sales tests to avoid testing the records more than once. For example, when the auditor is testing acquisition transactions as part of the acquisition and payment cycle, it is desirable to trace the units and unit costs of raw materials to the perpetual inventory data files and the total cost to the cost accounting records. Similarly, when payroll costs data are maintained for different jobs, it is desirable to trace data from the payroll summary directly to the job cost record as a part of testing the payroll and personnel cycle.

A major difficulty in the verification of inventory cost records is determining the reasonableness of cost allocations. For example, the assignment of manufacturing overhead costs to individual products entails certain assumptions that can significantly affect the unit costs of inventory and therefore the fairness of the inventory valuation. In evaluating these allocations, the auditor must consider the reasonableness of both the numerator and the denominator that result in the unit costs. For example, in testing overhead applied to inventory on the basis of direct labour dollars, the overhead rate should approximate total actual direct labour dollars. Since total manufacturing overhead is tested as part of the tests of the acquisition and payment cycle and direct labour is tested as part of the payroll and personnel cycle, determining the reasonableness of the rate is not difficult. However, if manufacturing overhead is applied on the basis of machine hours, the auditor must verify the reasonableness of the machine hours by separate tests of the client's machine records. The major consideration in evaluating the reasonableness of all cost allocations, including manufacturing overhead, is consistency with previous years.

ANALYTICAL PROCEDURES

OBJECTIVE 18-4

Design and perform analytical procedures for the accounts in the inventory and warehousing cycle.

Analytical procedures are as important in auditing inventory and warehousing as in any other cycle. Table 18-1 includes several common analytical procedures and possible misstatements that may be indicated when fluctuations exist. Several of those analytical procedures have also been included in other cycles. An example is the gross margin percent.

TABLE 18-1

ANALYTICAL PROCEDURES FOR THE INVENTORY AND WAREHOUSING CYCLE

ANALYTICAL PROCEDURE	POSSIBLE MISSTATEMENT
Compare gross margin percentage with previous years.	Overstatement or understatement of inventory and cost of goods sold
Compare inventory turnover (costs of goods sold divided by average inventory) with previous years.	Obsolete inventory, which affects inventory and cost of goods sold
Compare unit costs of inventory with previous years.	Overstatement or understatement of inventory Overstatement or understatement of unit costs
Compare extended inventory value with previous years.	Misstatements in compilation, unit costs, or extensions which affect inventory and cost of goods sold
Compare current-year manufacturing costs with previous years (variable costs should be adjusted for changes in volume).	Misstatement of unit costs of inventory, especially direct labour and manufacturing overhead which affect inventory and cost of goods sold

TESTS OF DETAILS FOR INVENTORY

The methodology for deciding which tests of details of balances to do for inventory and warehousing is essentially the same as that discussed for accounts receivable, accounts payable, and all other balance sheet accounts. It is shown in Figure 18-5. Notice that test results of several other cycles besides inventory and warehousing affect tests of details of balances for inventory.

Because of the complexity of auditing inventory, two aspects of tests of details of balances are discussed separately: (1) physical observation and (2) pricing and compilation. These topics are studied in the next two sections.

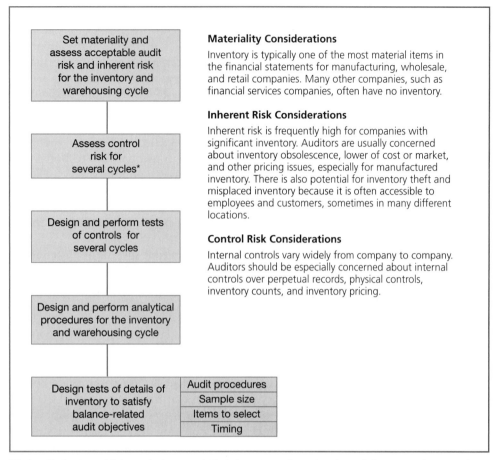

*Cycles affecting tests of balances for inventory include inventory and warehousing cycle (cost accounting system), sales and collection cycle (sales only), acquisition and payment cycle (acquisitions only), and payroll and personnel cycle.

PHYSICAL OBSERVATION OF INVENTORY

OBJECTIVE 18-5

Design and perform physical observation audit tests for inventory.

Prior to the late 1930s, auditors generally avoided responsibility for determining either the physical existence of or the accuracy of the count of inventory. Audit evidence for inventory quantities was usually restricted to obtaining a certificate from management as to the correctness of the stated amount. In 1938, the discovery of major fraud in the McKesson & Robbins Company in the United States caused a reappraisal by the accounting profession of its responsibilities relating to inventory. In brief, the financial statements for McKesson & Robbins at December 31, 1937, which were "certified" by a major accounting firm, reported total consolidated assets of $87 million. Of this amount, approximately $19 million was subsequently determined to be fictitious ($10 million in inventory and $9 million in receivables). Due primarily to its adherence to generally accepted auditing practices of that period, the auditing firm was not held directly at fault in the inventory area. However, it was noted that if certain procedures, such as observation of the physical inventory, had been carried out, the fraud would probably have been detected.

Paragraph 6030.05 of the *CICA Handbook* states:

> Observation of the client's physical stocktaking, whether this is done at the end of the financial period or at some other date, is considered a most useful auditing procedure in assessing the degree of care which management exercises in establishing the existence and condition of inventories.

This notion of physical attendance is reinforced by paragraph 6030.09:

> Generally accepted auditing procedures in respect of inventories should include: ... attendance by the auditors at the stocktaking, whether this is at the end of the financial period or at other times ...

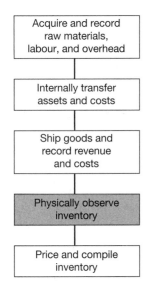

Acquire and record
raw materials,
labour, and overhead

Internally transfer
assets and costs

Ship goods and
record revenue
and costs

Physically observe
inventory

Price and compile
inventory

"If attendance at stocktaking is not practicable in the circumstances," paragraph 6030.10 permits the auditor to apply "other satisfactory procedures." The phrase "not practicable" is taken to mean not feasible in the circumstances and not merely inconvenient or difficult. For example, an auditor who was appointed after a company's year end would find it not practicable to count inventory; driving 100 km to attend an inventory count at a remote location may be neither practical nor convenient. If precluded, for any reason, from attending the physical stocktaking, the auditor must exercise judgment in deciding whether or not attendance was "practicable."

An essential point in the Section 6030 requirements is the distinction between the observation of the physical count and the responsibility for taking the count. The client has responsibility for setting up the procedures for taking an accurate physical inventory and actually making and recording the counts. The auditor's responsibility is to evaluate and observe the client's physical procedures and draw conclusions about the adequacy of those procedures and about the quantity and condition of the physical inventory.

Paragraph 6030.07 does permit the auditor to count the inventory at a time other than the client's stocktaking "if the accounting system provides a good internal control over the inventories."

CONTROLS

Regardless of the client's inventory record-keeping method, there must be a periodic physical count of the inventory items on hand. The client can take the physical count at or near the balance sheet date, at a preliminary date, or on a cycle basis throughout the year. The last two approaches are appropriate only if there are adequate perpetual inventory master files and transaction files.

In connection with the client's physical count of inventory, adequate controls include proper instructions for the physical count, supervision by responsible personnel, independent internal verification of the counts, independent reconciliations of the physical counts with perpetual inventory master files, and adequate control over count tags, sheets, or computerized records.

An important aspect of the auditor's understanding of the client's physical inventory controls is complete familiarity with them before the inventory-taking begins. This is obviously necessary to evaluate the effectiveness of the client's procedures, but it also enables the auditor to make constructive suggestions beforehand. If the inventory instructions do not provide adequate controls, the auditor must spend more time ensuring that the physical count is accurate.

AUDIT DECISIONS

The auditor's decisions in the physical observation of inventory are of the same general nature as in any other audit area: selection of audit procedures, timing, determination of sample size, and selection of the items for testing. The selection of the audit procedures is discussed throughout the section; the other three decisions are discussed briefly at this time.

Timing The auditor decides whether the physical count can be taken prior to year end primarily on the basis of the accuracy of the perpetual inventory files. When an interim physical count is permitted, the auditor observes it at that time and also tests the perpetuals for transactions from the date of the count to year end. When the perpetuals are accurate, it may be unnecessary for the client to count the inventory every year. Instead, the auditor can compare the perpetuals with the actual inventory on a sample basis at a convenient time. When there are no perpetuals and the inventory is material, a complete physical inventory must be taken by the client near the end of the accounting period and tested by the auditor at the same time.

Sample size Sample size in physical observation is usually difficult to specify in terms of the number of items because the emphasis during the tests is on observing the client's procedures rather than on selecting particular items for testing. A convenient way to think of sample size in physical observation is in terms of the total number of hours spent rather than the number of inventory items counted. The most important determinants of the amount of time needed to test the inventory are the adequacy of the internal controls over the physical counts, the accuracy of the perpetual inventory files, the total dollar amount and the type of inventory, the number of different significant inventory locations, and the nature and extent of misstatements discovered in previous years and other inherent risks. In some situations, inventory is such a significant item that dozens of auditors are necessary to observe the physical count, whereas in other situations, one person can complete the observation in a short time. Special care is warranted in the observation of inventory because of the difficulty of expanding sample size or reperforming tests after the physical inventory has been taken.

Selection of items The selection of the particular items for testing is an important part of the audit decision in inventory observation. Care should be taken to observe the counting of the most significant items and a representative sample of typical inventory items, to inquire about items that are likely to be obsolete or damaged, and to discuss with management the reasons for excluding any material items.

PHYSICAL OBSERVATION TESTS

The same balance-related audit objectives that have been used in previous sections for tests of details of balances provide the frame of reference for discussing the physical observation tests. However, before the specific objectives are discussed, some comments that apply to all the objectives are appropriate.

The most important part of the observation of inventory is determining whether the physical count is being taken in accordance with the client's instructions. To do this effectively, *it is essential that the auditor be present* while the physical count is taking place. When the client's employees are not following the inventory instructions, the auditor must either contact the supervisor to correct the problem or modify the physical observation procedures. For example, if the procedures require one team to count the inventory and a second team to recount it as a test of accuracy, the auditor should inform management if he or she observes both teams counting together.

Obtaining an adequate understanding of the client's business is even more important in physical observation of inventory than for most aspects of the audit because inventory varies so significantly for different companies. A proper understanding of the client's business and its industry enables the auditor to ask about and discuss such problems as inventory valuation, potential obsolescence, and existence of consignment inventory intermingled with owned inventory. A useful starting point for the auditor to become familiar with the client's inventory is a tour of the client's facilities, including receiving, storage, production, planning, and record-keeping areas. The tour should be led by a supervisor who can answer questions about production, especially about any changes in the past year.

Common tests of details audit procedures for physical inventory observation are shown in Table 18-2 on page 602. Detail tie-in and presentation and disclosure are the only balance-related audit objectives not included in the table. These objectives are discussed under compilation of inventory. The assumption throughout is that the client records inventory on prenumbered tags on the balance sheet date. In reality, smaller businesses may use inventory sheets rather than inventory tags. Larger businesses with heavily automated systems will not use tags at all. Rather, individuals will use hand-held scanners to scan each inventory location and item code, then manually enter the amount counted.

In addition to the detailed procedures included in Table 18-2, the auditor should walk through all areas where inventory is warehoused to make sure that all inventory has been counted and properly tagged. When inventory is in boxes or other containers, these should be opened during test counts. It is desirable to compare high dollar value inventory to counts in the previous year and inventory master files as a test of reasonableness. These two procedures should not be done until the client has completed its physical counts.

TABLE 18-2

BALANCE-RELATED AUDIT OBJECTIVES AND TESTS OF DETAILS OF BALANCES FOR PHYSICAL INVENTORY OBSERVATION

BALANCE-RELATED AUDIT OBJECTIVE	COMMON INVENTORY OBSERVATION PROCEDURES	COMMENTS
Inventory as recorded on tags exists (existence).	Select a random sample of tag numbers and identify the tag with that number attached to the actual inventory. Observe whether movement of inventory takes place during the count.	The purpose is to uncover the inclusion of nonexistent items as inventory.
Existing inventory is counted and tagged and tags are accounted for to make sure none are missing (completeness).	Examine inventory to make sure it is tagged. Observe whether movement of inventory takes place during the count. Inquire as to inventory in other locations. Account for all used and unused tags to make sure none are lost or intentionally omitted. Record the tag numbers for those used and unused for subsequent follow-up.	Special concern should be directed to omission of large sections of inventory. This test should be done at the completion of the physical count. This test should be done at the completion of the physical count.
Inventory is counted accurately (accuracy).	Recount client's counts to make sure the recorded counts are accurate on the tags (also check descriptions and unit of count, such as dozen or gross). Compare physical counts with perpetual inventory master file. Record client's counts for subsequent testing.	Recording client counts in the working papers on *inventory count sheets* is done for two reasons: to obtain documentation that an adequate physical examination was made, and to test for the possibility that the client might change the recorded counts after the auditor leaves the premises.
Inventory is classified correctly on the tags (classification).	Examine inventory descriptions on the tags and compare with the actual inventory for raw material, work in process, and finished goods. Evaluate whether the percent of completion recorded on the tags for work in process is reasonable.	These tests would be done as a part of the first procedure in the valuation objective.
Information is obtained to make sure sales and inventory purchases are recorded in the proper period (cutoff).	Record in the working papers for subsequent follow-up the last shipping document number used at year end. Make sure the inventory for that item was excluded from the physical count. Review shipping area for inventory set aside for shipment, but not counted. Record in the working papers for subsequent follow-up the last receiving report number used at year end. Make sure the inventory for that item was included in the physical count. Review receiving area for inventory that should be included in the physical count.	Obtaining proper cutoff information for sales and purchases is an essential part of inventory observation. The appropriate tests during the field work were discussed for sales in Chapter 12 and for purchases in Chapter 16.
Obsolete and unusable inventory are excluded or noted (valuation).	Test for obsolete inventory by inquiry of factory employees and management, and alertness for items that are damaged, rust- or dust-covered, or located in inappropriate places.	
The client has right to inventory recorded on tags (rights and obligations).	Inquire as to consignment or customer inventory included on client's premises. Be alert for inventory that is set aside or specially marked as indications of non-ownership.	

An important part of the audit of inventory is performing all the procedures necessary to make certain the physical counts were properly priced and compiled. *Pricing* includes all the tests of the client's unit prices to determine whether they are correct. *Compilation* includes all the tests of the summarization of the physical counts, the extension of price times quantity, footing the inventory summary, and tracing the totals to the general ledger.

PRICING AND COMPILATION CONTROLS

The existence of adequate internal control for unit costs that is integrated with production and other accounting records is important to ensure that reasonable costs are used for valuing ending inventory. One important internal control is the use of *standard cost records* that indicate variances in material, labour, and overhead costs and can be used to evaluate production. When standard costs are used, procedures must be designed to keep the standards updated for changes in production processes and costs. The review of unit costs for reasonableness by someone independent of the department responsible for developing the costs is also a useful control over valuation.

An internal control designed to prevent the overstatement of inventory through the inclusion of obsolete inventory is a formal review and reporting of obsolete, slow-moving, damaged, and overstated inventory items. The review, which should be done by a competent employee, includes reviewing perpetual inventory master files for inventory turnover, possibly using generalized audit software, and holding discussions with engineering or production personnel.

Compilation internal controls are needed to provide a means of ensuring that the physical counts are properly summarized, priced at the same amount as the unit perpetual records, correctly extended and totalled, and included in the general ledger at the proper amount. Important compilation internal controls are adequate documents and records for taking the physical count, adequate controls over program changes, and proper internal verification. If the physical inventory is taken on prenumbered tags and carefully reviewed before the personnel are released from the physical examination of inventory, there should be little risk of misstatement in summarizing the tags. The most important internal control over accurate determination of prices, extensions, and footings is adequate controls over the programs that perform these calculations, with internal verification or review of output reports by a competent, independent person.

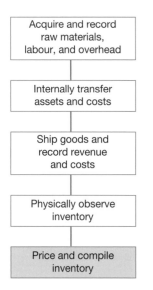

OBJECTIVE 18-6

Design and perform audit tests of pricing and compilation for inventory.

Acquire and record raw materials, labour, and overhead

Internally transfer assets and costs

Ship goods and record revenue and costs

Physically observe inventory

Price and compile inventory

PRICING AND COMPILATION PROCEDURES

Balance-related audit objectives for tests of details of balances are also useful in discussing pricing and compilation procedures. The objectives and related tests are shown in Table 18-3 (page 604), except for the cutoff objective. Physical observation, which was previously discussed, is a major source of cutoff information for sales and purchases. The tests of the accounting records for cutoff are done as part of sales (sales and collection cycle) and purchases (acquisition and payment cycle).

The frame of reference for applying the objectives is a listing of inventory obtained from the client that includes each inventory item's description, quantity, unit price, and extended value. The inventory listing is an inventory item description order with raw material, work in process, and finished goods separated. The total equals the general ledger balance.

The proper valuation (pricing) of inventory is often one of the most important and time-consuming parts of the audit. In performing pricing tests, three things about the client's method of pricing are extremely important: the method must be in accordance with generally accepted accounting principles, the application of the method must be consistent from year to year, and cost versus market value (replacement cost or net realizable value) must be considered. Because the method of verifying the pricing of inventory depends on whether items are purchased or manufactured, these two categories are discussed separately.

TABLE 18-3

BALANCE-RELATED AUDIT OBJECTIVES AND TESTS OF DETAILS OF BALANCES FOR INVENTORY PRICING AND COMPILATION

BALANCE-RELATED AUDIT OBJECTIVE	COMMON TESTS OF DETAILS OF BALANCES PROCEDURES	COMMENTS
Inventory in the inventory listing schedule agrees with the physical inventory counts, the extensions are correct, and the total is correctly added and agrees with the general ledger (detail tie-in).	Perform compilation tests (see existence, completeness, and accuracy objectives). Extend the quantity times the price on selected items. Foot the inventory listing schedules for raw materials, work in process, and finished goods. Trace the totals to the general ledger.	Unless controls are weak, extending and footing tests should be limited. For large inventories, these tests should be conducted using generalized audit software.
Inventory items in the inventory listing schedule exist (existence).	Trace inventory listed in the schedule to inventory tags and auditor's recorded counts for existence and description.	The next six objectives are affected by the results of the physical inventory observation. The tag numbers and counts verified as a part of physical inventory observation are traced to the inventory listing schedule as a part of these tests.
Existing inventory items are included in the inventory listing schedule (completeness).	Account for unused tag numbers shown in the auditor's working papers to make sure no tags have been added. Trace from inventory tags to the inventory listing schedules, and make sure inventory on tags is included. Account for tag numbers to make sure none have been deleted.	
Inventory items in the inventory listing schedule are accurate (accuracy).	Trace inventory listed in the schedule to inventory tags and auditor's recorded counts for quantity and description. Perform price tests of inventory. For a discussion of price tests, see text material on pages 603–606.	
Inventory items in the inventory listing schedule are properly classified (classification).	Compare the classification into raw materials, work in process, and finished goods by comparing the descriptions on inventory tags and auditor's recorded test counts with the inventory listing schedule.	
Inventory items in the inventory listing are stated at realizable value (valuation).	Perform test of lower of cost or market, selling price, and obsolescence.	
The client has rights to inventory items in the inventory listing schedule (rights and obligations).	Trace inventory tags identified as non-owned during the physical observation to the inventory listing schedule to make sure these have not been included. Review contracts with suppliers and customers and inquire of management for the possibility of the inclusion of consigned or other non-owned inventory, or the exclusion of owned inventory.	
Inventory and related accounts in the inventory and warehousing cycle are properly disclosed (presentation and disclosure).	Examine financial statements for proper presentation and disclosure, including: • Separate disclosure of raw materials, work in process, and finished goods. • Proper description of the inventory costing method. • Description of pledged inventory. • Inclusion of significant sales and purchase commitments.	Pledging of inventory and sales and purchase commitments are usually uncovered as a part of other audit tests.

Pricing purchased inventory The primary types of inventory included in this category are raw materials, purchased parts, and supplies. As a first step in verifying the valuation of purchased inventory, it is necessary to establish clearly whether FIFO, LIFO, weighted average, or some other valuation method is being used. It is also necessary to determine which costs should be included in the valuation of a particular item of inventory. For example, the auditor must find out whether freight, storage, discounts, and other costs are included and compare the findings with the preceding year's audit working papers to ensure that the methods are consistent.

In selecting specific inventory items for pricing, emphasis should be put on the larger dollar amounts and on products that are known to have wide fluctuations in price, but a representative sample of all types of inventory and departments should be included as well. Stratified variable or monetary unit sampling is commonly used in these tests.

The auditor should list the inventory items he or she intends to verify for pricing and request that the client locate the appropriate vendors' invoices. It is important that a sufficient number of invoices be examined to account for the entire quantity of inventory for the particular item being tested, especially for the FIFO valuation method. Examining a sufficient number of invoices is useful in uncovering situations in which clients value their inventory on the basis of the most recent invoice only and, in some cases, in discovering obsolete inventory. As an illustration, assume that the client's valuation of a particular inventory item is $12.00 per unit for 1,000 units, using FIFO. The auditor should examine the most recent invoices for acquisitions of that inventory item made in the year under audit until the valuation of all of the 1,000 units is accounted for. If the most recent acquisition of the inventory item were for 700 units at $12.00 per unit and the immediately preceding acquisition were for 600 units at $11.30 per unit, then the inventory item in question was overstated by $210.00 (300 × $0.70).

When the client has perpetual inventory master files that include unit costs of acquisitions, it is usually desirable to test the pricing by tracing the unit costs to the perpetuals rather than to vendors' invoices. In most cases, the effect is to reduce the cost of verifying inventory valuation significantly. Naturally, when the perpetuals are used to verify unit costs, it is essential to test the unit costs on the perpetuals to vendors' invoices as a part of the tests of the acquisition and payment cycle.

Pricing manufactured inventory The auditor must consider the cost of raw materials, direct labour, and manufacturing overhead in pricing work in process and finished goods. The need to verify each of these has the effect of making the audit of work-in-process and finished goods inventory more complex than the audit of purchased inventory. Nevertheless, such considerations as selecting the items to be tested, testing for whether cost or market value is lower, and evaluating the possibility of obsolescence also apply.

In pricing raw materials in manufactured products, it is necessary to consider both the unit cost of the raw materials and the number of units required to manufacture a unit of output. The unit cost can be verified in the same manner as that used for other purchased inventory — by examining vendors' invoices or perpetual inventory master files. Then it is necessary to examine engineering specifications, inspect the finished product, or find a similar method to determine the number of units it takes to manufacture a particular product.

Similarly, the hourly costs of direct labour and the number of hours it takes to manufacture a unit of output must be verified while testing direct labour. Hourly labour costs can be verified by comparison with labour payroll or union contracts. The number of hours needed to manufacture the product can be determined from engineering specifications or similar sources.

The proper manufacturing overhead in work in process and finished goods is dependent on the approach being used by the client. It is necessary to evaluate the method being used for consistency and reasonableness and to recompute the costs to determine whether the overhead is correct. For example, if the rate is based on direct labour dollars, the auditor can divide the total manufacturing overhead by the total direct labour dollars to determine the actual overhead rate. This rate can then be compared with the overhead rate used by the client to determine unit costs.

When the client has *standard cost records*, an efficient and useful method of determining valuation is the review and analysis of variances. If the variances in material, labour, and manufacturing overhead are small, this is evidence of reliable cost records.

Cost or market In pricing inventory, it is necessary to consider whether replacement cost or net realizable value is lower than historical cost. For purchased finished goods and raw materials, the most recent cost of an inventory item as indicated on a vendor's invoice of the subsequent period is a useful way to test for replacement cost. All manufacturing costs must be considered for work in process and finished goods for manufactured inventory. It is also necessary to consider the sales value of inventory items and the possible effect of rapid fluctuation of prices to determine net realizable value. Finally, it is necessary to consider the possibility of obsolescence in the evaluation process.

INTEGRATION OF THE TESTS

The most difficult part of understanding the audit of the inventory and warehousing cycle is grasping the interrelationship of the many different tests the auditor makes to evaluate whether inventory and cost of goods sold are fairly stated. Figure 18-6 and the discussion that follows are designed to aid the reader in perceiving the audit of the inventory and warehousing cycle as a series of integrated tests.

TESTS OF THE ACQUISITION AND PAYMENT CYCLE

> **OBJECTIVE 18-7**
>
> **Explain how the various parts of the audit of the inventory and warehousing cycle are integrated.**

Whenever the auditor verifies acquisitions as part of the tests of the acquisition and payment cycle, evidence is being obtained about the accuracy of raw materials purchased and all manufacturing overhead costs except labour. These acquisition costs either flow directly into cost of goods sold or become the most significant part of the ending inventory of raw material, work in process, and finished goods. In audits involving perpetual inventory master files, it is common to test these as a part of tests of controls procedures in the acquisition and payment cycle. Similarly, if manufacturing costs are assigned to individual jobs or processes, they are usually tested as part of the same cycle.

TESTS OF THE PAYROLL AND PERSONNEL CYCLE

When the auditor verifies labour costs, the same comments apply as for acquisitions. In most cases, the cost accounting records for direct and indirect labour costs can be tested as part of the audit of the payroll and personnel cycle if there is adequate advance planning.

TESTS OF THE SALES AND COLLECTION CYCLE

Although the relationship is less close between the sales and collection cycle and the inventory and warehousing cycle than between the two cycles previously discussed, it is still important. Most of the audit testing in the storage of finished goods as well as the shipment and recording of sales takes place when the sales and collection cycle is tested. In addition, if standard cost records are used, it may be possible to test the standard cost of goods sold at the same time that sales tests are performed.

TESTS OF COST ACCOUNTING

Tests of cost accounting are meant to verify the controls affecting inventory that were not verified as part of the three previously discussed cycles. Tests are made of the physical controls, transfers of raw material costs to work in process, transfers of costs

FIGURE 18-6

Interrelationship of
Various Audit Tests

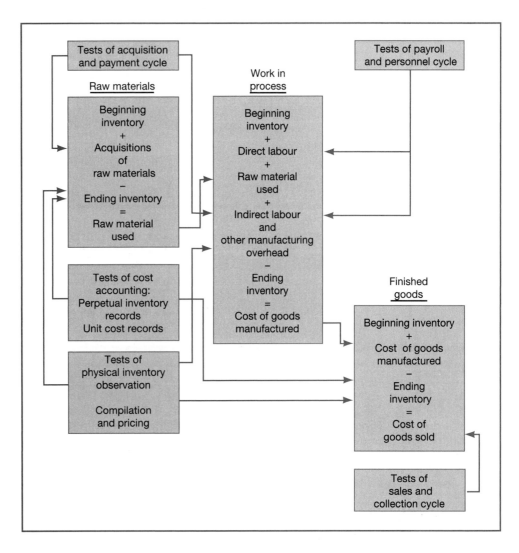

of completed goods to finished goods, perpetual inventory master files, and unit cost records.

PHYSICAL INVENTORY, COMPILATION, AND PRICING

In most audits, the underlying assumption in testing the inventory and warehousing cycle is that cost of goods sold is a residual of beginning inventory plus acquisitions of raw materials, direct labour, and other manufacturing costs minus ending inventory. When the audit of inventory and cost of goods sold is approached with this idea in mind, the importance of ending inventory becomes obvious. Physical inventory, compilation, and pricing are each equally important in the audit because a misstatement in any one results in misstated inventory and cost of goods sold.

In testing the physical inventory, it is possible to rely heavily on the perpetual inventory master files if they have been tested as part of one or more of the previously discussed tests. In fact, if the perpetual inventory master files are considered reliable, the auditor can observe and test the physical count at some time during the year and rely on the perpetuals to keep adequate records of the quantities.

When testing the unit costs, it is also possible to rely, to some degree, on the tests of the cost records made during the tests of transaction cycles. The existence of standard cost records is also useful for the purpose of comparison with the actual unit costs. If the standard costs are used to represent historical cost, they must be tested for reliability.

ESSENTIAL TERMS

Cost accounting controls — controls over physical inventory and the related costs from the point at which raw materials are requisitioned to the point at which the manufactured product is completed and transferred to storage (p. 595).

Cost accounting records — the accounting records concerned with the manufacture and processing of the goods and storing finished goods (p. 593).

Inventory and warehousing cycle — the transaction cycle that involves the physical flow of goods through the organization, as well as related costs (p. 590).

Inventory compilation tests — audit procedures used to verify whether physical counts of inventory were correctly summarized, inventory quantities and prices were correctly extended, and extended inventory was correctly footed (p. 594).

Inventory price tests — audit procedures used to verify the costs used to value physical inventory (p. 594).

Job cost system — the system of cost accounting in which costs are accumulated by individual jobs when material is used and labour costs are incurred (p. 592).

Perpetual inventory data files — continuously updated computerized records of inventory items purchased, used, sold, and on hand for merchandise, raw materials, and finished goods. The master file normally contains the balance of quantity on hand, as well as prices and description of items. The transaction files contain activity details, such as shipments (items sold) and receipts (goods purchased) (p. 592).

Process cost system — the system of cost accounting in which costs are accumulated for a process, with unit costs for each process assigned to the products passing through the process (p. 592).

Standard cost records — records that indicate variances between projected material, labour, and overhead costs, and the actual costs (p. 603).

REVIEW QUESTIONS

18-1 Give the reasons why inventory is often the most difficult and time-consuming part of many audit engagements.

18-2 Explain the relationship between the acquisition and payment cycle and the inventory and warehousing cycle in the audit of a manufacturing company. List several audit procedures in the acquisition and payment cycle that support your explanation.

18-3 What is meant by "cost accounting records," and what is their importance in the conduct of an audit?

18-4 Many auditors assert that certain audit tests can be significantly reduced for clients with adequate perpetual records that include both unit and cost data. What are the most important tests of the perpetual records that the auditor must make before he or she can reduce the assessed level of control risk? Assuming the perpetuals are determined to be accurate, which tests can be reduced?

18-5 Before the physical examination, the auditor obtains a copy of the client's inventory instructions and reviews them with the controller. In obtaining an understanding of inventory procedures for a small manufacturing company, these deficiencies are identified: shipping operations will not be completely halted during the physical examination, and there will be no independent verification of the original inventory count by a second counting team. Evaluate the importance of each of these deficiencies, and state its effect on the auditor's observation of inventory.

18-6 At the completion of an inventory observation, the controller requested a copy of all recorded test counts from the auditor to facilitate the correction of all discrepancies between the client's and the auditor's counts. Should the auditor comply with the request? Why or why not?

18-7 What major audit procedures are involved in testing for the ownership of inventory during the observation of the physical counts and as part of subsequent valuation tests?

18-8 In the verification of the amount of the inventory, the auditor should identify slow-moving and obsolete items. List the auditing procedures that could be employed to determine whether slow-moving or obsolete items have been included in inventory.

18-9 During the taking of physical inventory, the controller intentionally withheld several inventory tags from the employees responsible for the physical count. After the auditor left the client's premises at the completion of the inventory observation, the controller recorded nonexistent inventory on the tags and thereby significantly overstated earnings. How could the auditor have uncovered the misstatement assuming there are no perpetual records?

18-10 Explain why a proper cutoff of purchases and sales is heavily dependent on the physical inventory observation. What information should be obtained during the physical count to make sure cutoff is accurate?

18-11 Define what is meant by "compilation tests." List several examples of audit procedures to verify compilation.

18-12 List the major analytical procedures for testing the overall reasonableness of inventory. For each test, explain the type of misstatement that could be identified.

18-13 Included in the December 31, 1998, inventory of Kupitz Supply Ltd. are 2,600 deluxe ring binders in the amount of $5,902. An examination of the most recent purchases of binders showed the following costs: January 26, 1999, 2,300 at $2.42 each; December 6, 1998, 1,900 at $2.28 each; and November 26, 1999, 2,400 at $2.07 each. What is the misstatement in valuation of the December 31, 1998, inventory for deluxe ring binders assuming FIFO inventory valuation? What would your answer be if the January 26, 1999, purchase were for 2,300 binders at $2.12 each?

18-14 Ruswell Manufacturing Ltd. applied manufacturing overhead to inventory at December 31, 1998, on the basis of $3.47 per direct labour hour. Explain how you would evaluate the reasonableness of total direct labour hours and manufacturing overhead in the ending inventory of finished goods.

18-15 Each employee for Gedding Manufacturing Corp., a firm using a job-cost inventory costing method, must reconcile his or her total hours worked to the hours worked on individual jobs using a job time sheet at the time weekly payroll time cards are prepared. The job time sheet is then stapled to the time card. Explain how you could test the direct labour dollars included in inventory as part of the payroll and personnel tests.

18-16 Assuming that the auditor properly documents receiving report numbers as part of the physical inventory observation procedures, explain how he or she should verify the proper cutoff of purchases, including tests for the possibility of raw materials in transit, later in the audit.

MULTIPLE CHOICE QUESTIONS

18-17 The following questions concern internal controls in the inventory and warehousing cycle. Choose the best response.

a. In a company whose materials and supplies include a great number of items, a fundamental deficiency in control requirements would be indicated if
   (1) the cycle basis for physical inventory-taking had been used.
   (2) a perpetual inventory master file had not been maintained for items of small value.
   (3) the storekeeping function had been combined with production and record keeping.
   (4) minor supply items had been expensed when acquired.

b. For control purposes, the quantities of materials ordered may be omitted from the copy of the purchase order that is
   (1) forwarded to the receiving department.
   (2) forwarded to the accounting department.
   (3) retained in the purchasing department's files.
   (4) returned to the requisitioner.

c. Which of the following procedures would *best* detect the theft of valuable items from an inventory that consists of hundreds of different items selling for between $1 and $10 and a few items selling for hundreds of dollars?
   (1) Maintain a perpetual inventory master file of only the more valuable items with frequent periodic verification of the validity of the perpetuals.
   (2) Require an authorized officer's signature on all requisitions for the more valuable items.
   (3) Have an independent public accounting firm prepare an internal control report on the effectiveness of the administrative and accounting controls over inventory.
   (4) Have separate warehouse space for the more valuable items with sequentially numbered tags.

(AICPA adapted)

18-18 The following questions concern testing the client's internal controls for inventory and warehousing. Choose the best response.

a. When an auditor tests a client's cost accounting records, the auditor's tests are *primarily* designed to determine that
   (1) the internal controls are in accordance with generally accepted accounting principles and are functioning as planned.

   (2) quantities on hand have been determined based on acceptable cost accounting techniques that reasonably approximate actual quantities on hand.
   (3) physical inventories are in substantial agreement with book inventories.
   (4) costs have been properly assigned to finished goods, work in process, and cost of goods sold.

b. The accuracy of perpetual inventory transaction files may be established, in part, by comparing perpetual inventory records with
   (1) purchase orders.
   (2) purchase requisitions.
   (3) receiving reports.
   (4) vendor payments.

c. When evaluating inventory controls with respect to segregation of duties, a public accountant would be *least* likely to
   (1) observe procedures.
   (2) consider policy and procedure manuals.
   (3) inspect documents.
   (4) make inquiries.

(AICPA adapted)

18-19 The following questions deal with tests of details of balances and analytical procedures for inventory. Choose the best response.

a. An auditor would *most* likely learn of slow-moving inventory through
   (1) inquiry of store personnel.
   (2) inquiry of sales personnel.
   (3) physical observation of inventory.
   (4) review of perpetual inventory data files.

b. An inventory turnover analysis is useful to the auditor because it may detect
   (1) inadequacies in inventory pricing.
   (2) the optimum automatic re-order points.
   (3) the existence of obsolete merchandise.
   (4) methods of avoiding cyclical holding costs.

c. A public accountant examining inventory may appropriately apply attribute sampling in order to estimate the
   (1) dollar value of inventory.
   (2) average price of inventory items.
   (3) physical quantity of inventory items.
   (4) percentage of slow-moving inventory items.

(AICPA adapted)

DISCUSSION QUESTIONS AND PROBLEMS

18-20 Items 1 through 8 are selected questions typically found in questionnaires used by auditors to obtain an understanding of internal controls in the inventory and warehousing cycle. In using the questionnaire for a particular client, a "yes" response to a question indicates a possible internal control, whereas a "no" indicates a potential weakness.

1. Does the receiving department prepare prenumbered receiving reports and account for the numbers periodically for all inventory received, showing the description and quantity of materials?

2. Is all inventory stored under the control of a custodian in areas where access is limited?

3. Are all shipments to customers authorized by prenumbered shipping documents?

4. Is a detailed perpetual inventory master file maintained for raw materials inventory?

5. Are physical inventory counts made by someone other than storekeepers and those responsible for maintaining the perpetual inventory master file?

6. Are standard cost records used for raw materials, direct labour, and manufacturing overhead?

7. Is there a stated policy with specific criteria for writing off obsolete or slow-moving goods?

8. Is the clerical accuracy of the final inventory compilation checked by a person independent of those responsible for preparing it?

Required

a. For each of the preceding questions, state the purpose of the internal control.

b. For each internal control, list a test of control to test its effectiveness.

c. For each of the preceding questions, identify the nature of the potential financial misstatement(s) if the control is not in effect.

d. For each of the potential misstatements in part (c), list a substantive audit procedure to determine whether a material misstatement exists.

18-21 The cost accounting records are often an essential area to audit in a manufacturing or construction company.

Required

a. Why is it important to review the cost accounting records and test their accuracy?

b. For the audit of standard cost accounting records in which 35 parts are manufactured, explain how you would determine whether each of the following was reasonable for part no. 21.
   (1) Standard direct labour hours
   (2) Standard direct overhead rate
   (3) Standard overhead rate
   (4) Standard units of raw materials
   (5) Standard cost of a unit of raw materials
   (6) Total standard cost

18-22 Following are audit procedures frequently performed in the inventory and warehousing cycle for a manufacturing company.

1. Compare the client's count of physical inventory at an interim date with the perpetual inventory master file.

2. Trace the auditor's test counts recorded in the working papers to the final inventory compilation, and compare the tag number, description, and quantity.

3. Compare the unit price on the final inventory summary with vendors' invoices.

4. Read the client's physical inventory instructions, and observe whether they are being followed by those responsible for counting the inventory.

5. Account for a sequence of raw materials requisitions, and examine each requisition for an authorized approval.

6. Trace the recorded additions on the finished goods perpetual inventory master file to the records for completed production.

7. Account for a sequence of inventory tags, and trace each tag to the physical inventory to ensure it actually exists.

Required

State the purpose(s) of each of the procedures.

18-23 The following errors or omissions are included in the inventory and related records of Westbox Manufacturing Company Ltd.

1. An inventory item was priced at $12 each instead of at the correct cost of $12 per dozen.

2. During the physical inventory-taking, the last shipments for the day were excluded from inventory and were not included as a sale until the subsequent year.

3. The clerk in charge of the perpetual inventory master file altered the quantity on an inventory tag to cover up the shortage of inventory caused by its theft during the year.

4. After the auditor left the premises, several inventory tags were lost and were not included in the final inventory summary.

5. In recording raw materials purchases, the improper unit price was included in the perpetual inventory transaction file and master file. Therefore, the inventory valuation was misstated because the physical inventory was priced by referring to the perpetual records.

6. During the physical count, several obsolete inventory items were included.

7. Because of a significant increase in volume during the current year and excellent control over manufacturing overhead costs, the manufacturing overhead rate applied to inventory was far greater than actual cost.

Required

a. For each misstatement, state an internal control that should have prevented it from occurring.

b. For each misstatement, state a substantive audit procedure that could be used to uncover it.

18-24 Often an important aspect of a public accountant's examination of financial statements is his or her observation of the taking of physical inventory.

Required

a. What are the general objectives or purposes of the public accountant's observation of the taking of the physical inventory? (Do not discuss the procedures or techniques involved in making the observation.)

b. For what purposes does the public accountant make and record test counts of inventory quantities during his or her observation of the taking of the physical inventory? Discuss.

c. A number of companies employ outside service companies that specialize in counting, pricing, extending, and footing inventories. These service companies usually furnish a certificate attesting to the value of the inventory.

Assuming that the service company took the inventory on the balance sheet date:

   (1) How much reliance, if any, can the public accountant place on the inventory certificate of outside specialists? Discuss.

   (2) What effect, if any, would the inventory certificate of outside specialists have upon the type of auditor's report the public accountant would render? Discuss.

   (3) What reference, if any, would the public accountant make to the certificate of outside specialists in the auditor's report.

(AICPA adapted)

18-25 You encountered the following situations during the December 31, 19X7, physical inventory of Latner Shoe Distributing Corp.

a. Latner maintains a large portion of the shoe merchandise in 10 warehouses throughout eastern and central Canada. This ensures swift delivery service for its chain of stores. You are assigned alone to the Halifax warehouse to observe the physical inventory process. During the inventory count, several express trucks pulled in for loading. Although infrequent, express shipments must be attended to immediately. As a result, the employees who were counting the inventory stopped to assist in loading the express trucks. What should you do?

b (1) In one storeroom of 10,000 items, you have test counted about 200 items of high value and a few items of low value. You found no misstatements. You also note that the employees are diligently following the inventory instructions. Do you think you have tested enough items? Explain.

   (2) What would you do if you counted 150 items and found a substantial number of counting errors?

c. In observing an inventory of liquid shoe polish, you note that a particular lot is five years old. From inspection of

some bottles in an open box, you find that the liquid has solidified in most of the bottles. What action should you take?

d. During your observation of the inventory count in the main warehouse, you found that most of the prenumbered tags that had been incorrectly filled out are being destroyed and thrown away. What is the significance of this procedure and what action should you take?

18-26 In connection with her examination of the financial statements of Knutson Products Co. Ltd., an assembler of home appliances, for the year ended May 31, 1999, Raymonde Mathieu, public accountant, is reviewing with Knutson's controller the plans for a physical inventory at the company warehouse on May 31, 1999.

Finished appliances, unassembled parts, and supplies are stored in the warehouse, which is attached to Knutson's assembly plant. The plant will operate during the count. On May 30, the warehouse will deliver to the plant the estimated quantities of unassembled parts and supplies required for May 31 production, but there may be emergency requisitions on May 31. During the count, the warehouse will continue to receive parts and supplies and to ship finished appliances. However, appliances completed on May 31 will be held in the plant until after the physical inventory.

Required

What procedures should the company establish to ensure that the inventory count includes all items that should be included and that nothing is counted twice?

(AICPA adapted)

18-27 The table below shows sales, cost of sales, and inventory data for Aladdin Products Supply Inc., a wholesale distributor of cleaning supplies. Dollar amounts are in millions.

	1998	1997	1996	1995
Sales	$23.2	$21.7	$19.6	$17.4
Cost of sales	17.1	16.8	15.2	13.5
Beginning inventory	2.3	2.1	1.9	1.5
Ending inventory	2.9	2.3	2.1	1.9

Required

a. Calculate the following ratios using an electronic spreadsheet program (Instructor's option):
   (1) Gross margin as a percentage of sales
   (2) Inventory turnover

b. List several logical causes of the changes in the two ratios.

c. Assume that $500,000 is considered material for audit planning purposes for 1998. Could any of the fluctuations in the computed ratios indicate a possible material misstatement? Demonstrate this by using the spreadsheet program to perform a sensitivity analysis.

d. What should the auditor do to determine the actual cause of the changes?

18-28 The following calculations were made as of December 31, 1997, from the records of Scace Fishing Equipment Ltd., a wholesale distributor of fishing equipment.

	1998	1997	1996	1995
Gross margin as percentage of sales	26.4%	22.8%	22.7%	22.4%
Inventory turnover	56.1 days	47.9 days	48.3 days	47.1 days

Required

List several logical causes of the changes in the two ratios. What should the auditor do to determine the actual cause of the changes?

18-29 In an annual audit as at December 31, 1998, you find the following transactions near the closing date:

1. Merchandise costing $1,822 was received on January 3, 1999, and the related purchase invoice recorded January 5. The invoice showed the shipment was made on December 29, 1998, FOB destination.

2. Merchandise costing $625 was received on December 28, 1998, and the invoice was not recorded. You located it in the hands of the purchasing agent; it was marked "on consignment."

3. A packing case containing products costing $816 was standing in the shipping room when the physical inventory was taken. It was not included in the inventory because it was marked "Hold for shipping instructions." Your investigation revealed that the customer's order was dated December 18, 1998, but that the case was shipped and the customer billed on January 10, 1999. The product was a stock item of your client's.

4. Merchandise received on January 6, 1999, costing $720 was entered in the purchase register on January 7, 1999. The invoice showed shipment was made FOB supplier's warehouse on December 31, 1998. Since it was not on hand at December 31, it was not included in inventory.

5. A special machine, fabricated to order for a customer, was finished and in the shipping room on December 31, 1998. The customer was billed on that date and the machine excluded from inventory, although it was shipped on January 4, 1999.

Assume that each of the amounts is material.

Required

a. State whether or not the merchandise should be included in the client's inventory.

b. Give your reason for your decision on each item.

(AICPA adapted)

18-30 You have been engaged for the audit of Saskatoon Chemicals Ltd. for the year ended December 31, 1998. Saskatoon Chemicals is engaged in the wholesale chemical business and makes all sales at 25 percent over cost.

Following are portions of the client's sales and purchases accounts for the calendar year 1998.

SALES					
			BALANCE FORWARD		
Date	**Reference**	**Amount**	**Date**	**Reference**	**Amount**
31-12	Closing entry	$699,860			$658,320
			27-12	*SI#965	5,195
			28-12	SI#966	19,270
			28-12	SI#967	1,302
			31-12	SI#969	5,841
			31-12	SI#970	7,922
			31-12	SI#971	2,010
		$699,860			$699,860

* SI, sales invoice.

PURCHASES					
BALANCE FORWARD					
Date	**Reference**	**Amount**	**Date**	**Reference**	**Amount**
		$360,300	31-12	Closing entry	$385,346
28-12	† RR#1059	3,100			
30-12	RR#1061	8,965			
31-12	RR#1062	4,861			
31-12	RR#1063	8,120			
		$385,346			$385,346

† RR, receiving report.

You observed the physical inventory of goods in the warehouse on December 31, 1998, and were satisfied that it was properly taken.

When performing a sales and purchases cutoff test, you found that at December 31, 1998, the last receiving report that had been used was no. 1063 and that no shipments have been made on any sales invoices with numbers larger than no. 968. You also obtained the following additional information.

1. Included in the warehouse physical inventory at December 31, 1998, were chemicals that had been purchased and received on receiving report no. 1060 but for which an invoice was not received until 1999. The cost was $2,183.

2. In the warehouse at December 31, 1998, were goods that had been sold and paid for by the customer but which were not shipped out until 1999. They were all sold on sales invoice no. 965 and were not inventoried.

3. On the evening of December 31, 1998, there were two cars on the Saskatoon Chemicals company siding:
   (i) Car AR38162 was unloaded on January 2, 1999, and received on receiving report no. 1063. The freight was paid by the vendor.
   (ii) Car BAE74123 was loaded and sealed on December 31, 1998, and was switched off the company's siding on January 2, 1999. The sales price was $12,700, and the freight was paid by the customer. This order was sold on sales invoice no. 968.

4. Temporarily stranded at December 31, 1998, on a railroad siding were two cars of chemicals en route to the Sask-Man Pulp and Paper Co. Ltd. They were sold on sales invoice no. 966 and the terms were FOB destination.

5. En route to Saskatoon Chemicals on December 31, 1998, was a truckload of material that was received on receiving report no. 1064. The material was shipped FOB destination, and a freight charge of $75 was paid by Saskatoon Chemicals. However, the freight was deducted from the purchase price of $975.

6. Included in the physical inventory were chemicals exposed to rain in transit and deemed unsalable. Their invoice cost was $1,250, and freight charges of $350 had been paid on the chemicals.

Required

a. Compute the adjustments that should be made to the client's physical inventory at December 31, 1998.

b. Prepare the auditor's worksheet adjusting entries that are required as of December 31, 1998.

(AICPA adapted)

18-31 You are testing the summarization and cost of raw materials and purchased part inventories as part of the audit of Rubber Products and Supply Corp. There are 2,000 inventory items with a total recorded value of $648,500.

Your audit tests will compare recorded descriptions and counts with the final inventory listing, compare unit costs with vendors' invoices, and extend unit costs times quantity. A misstatement in any of those is defined as a difference. You plan to use monetary unit sampling.

You make the following decisions about the audit of inventory:

Tolerable misstatement (same for upper as for lower)	$16,000
Average percent of error assumption — overstatements	50%
Average percent of error assumption — understatements	100%
Acceptable risk of incorrect acceptance	5%
Estimated error rate in the population	. 5%

Required

a. What are the advantages of using monetary unit sampling in this situation?

b. What is the sample size necessary to achieve your audit objectives using monetary unit sampling?

c. Disregarding your answer to part (b), assume that a sample of 60 items is selected and that the following differences between book and audited values are identified (understatements are in parentheses). The book or recorded amounts are also shown.

ITEM NO.	DIFFERENCE	BOOK AMOUNT
1	$19	$700
2	11	136
3	(19)	820
4	40	250
5	90	300
6	38	210
7	(90)	2,150
8	70	300
9	(85)	950
Total	$74	

For each of the other 116 items in the sample, there was no difference between the book and the audited values.

Based on this sample, calculate the adjusted overstatement and understatement error bounds.

d. Is the book value misstated?

18-32 You are assigned to the December 31, 1997, audit of Sea Gull Airframes, Inc. The company designs and manufactures aircraft superstructures and airframe components.

You observed the physical inventory at December 31 and are satisfied it was properly taken. The inventory at December 31, 1997, has been priced, extended, and totalled by the client and is made up of about 5,000 inventory items with a total valuation of $8,275,000. In performing inventory price tests, you have decided to stratify your tests, and you conclude that you should have two strata: items with a total value over $5,000 and those with a value of less than $5,000. The book values are as follows:

	NO. OF ITEMS	TOTAL VALUE
More than $5,000	500	$4,150,000
Less than $5,000	4,500	4,125,000
	5,000	$8,275,000

In performing your pricing and extension tests, you have decided to test about 50 inventory items in detail. You have selected 40 of the over $5,000 items and 10 of those under $5,000 at random from the population. You find all items to be correct except for the following items A through G, which you believe may be misstated. You have tested the following items, to this point, exclusive of A through G.

	NO. OF ITEMS	TOTAL VALUE
More than $5,000	36	$360,000
Less than $5,000	7	2,600

Sea Gull Airframes uses a periodic inventory system and values its inventory at the lower of FIFO cost or market. You were able to locate all invoices needed for your examination. The seven inventory items in the sample which you believe may be misstated are shown at the top of page 614. The relevant data for determining the proper valuation are shown in the middle of page 614.

INVENTORY ITEMS POSSIBLY MISSTATED			
DESCRIPTION	QUANTITY	PRICE	TOTAL
A. L37 spars	3,000 m	$8.00/m	$24,000
B. B68 metal formers	3,000 cm	4.00/m	12,000
C. R01 metal ribs	1,500 m	10.00/m	15,000
D. St26 struts	1,000 m	8.00/m	8,000
E. Industrial hand drills	45 units	20.00 each	900
F. L803 steel leaf springs	40 pairs	69.00 each spring	276
G. V16 fasteners	$5\frac{1}{2}$ dozen	10.00/dozen	55

Note: Amounts are as stated on client's inventory.

In addition, you noted a freight bill for voucher 12-23 in the amount of $200. This bill was entered in the freight-in account. Virtually all freight was for the metal formers.

This is the first time Sea Gull Airframes has been audited by your firm.

Required

a. Review all information and determine the inventory misstatements of the seven items in question. State any assumptions you consider necessary to determine the amount of the misstatements.

b. Prepare a working-paper schedule on the computer to summarize your findings. (Instructor's option)

SEA GULL AIRFRAMES INFORMATION FOR PRICING FROM INVOICES					
VOUCHER NUMBER	VOUCHER DATE	DATE PAID	TERMS	RECEIVING REPORT DATE	INVOICE DESCRIPTION
7-68	01-08-93	21-08-93	Net FOB destination	01-08-93	77 V16 fasteners at $10 per dozen
11-81	16-10-97	15-11-97	Net FOB destination	18-10-97	1,100 m R01 metal ribs at $9.50 per metre; 2,000 m St26 struts at $8.20 per metre
12-06	08-12-97	30-12-97	2/10, n/30 FOB S.P.	10-12-97	1880 L803 steel leaf springs at $69 each
12-09	10-12-97	18-12-97	Net FOB destination	11-12-97	45 industrial hand drills at $20 each; guaranteed for four years
12-18	27-12-97	27-12-97	2/10, n/30 FOB S.P.	21-12-97	4,200 m L37 spars at $8 per metre
12-23	24-12-97	03-01-98	2/10, n/30 FOB destination	26-12-97	1,280 cm B68 metal formers at $4 per metre
12-61	29-12-97	08-01-98	Net FOB destination	29-12-97	1,000 m R01 metal ribs at $10 per metre; 800 m St26 struts at $8 per metre
12-81	31-12-97	20-01-98	Net FOB destination	06-01-98	2,000 m L37 spars at $7.50 per metre; 2,000 m R01 metal ribs at $10 per metre

CASES

18-33 Rakhi Grande has been assigned to the audit of Produce Distributors Inc. (PDI), a new client with his firm, Beaver & Jones, Chartered Accountants. The company is a wholesale distributor of produce, groceries, dry goods, and other related products to grocery store chains and independent grocers.

Rakhi's assistant, Charlie, who has limited experience with automated systems, has asked him for assistance in preparing a plan for the audit of PDI's year-end inventory. He specifically wants advice on which computer controls and what computer-generated information may be relied on and the audit procedures necessary to justify that reliance.

He has prepared the following notes on the client's system and planned count procedures:

System Notes

1. The financial inventory system is automated and fully integrated with other financial accounting systems (e.g., order entry, general ledger). Automatic updates to the inventory records occur at the same time as the shipping documents are printed. The computer system recalculates average cost of inventory items when receipt of goods is recorded.

2. Stock-out reports are printed daily. Because the incidence of negative quantities has significantly decreased over the last year, the client believes a small book-to-physical adjustment will be required.

3. The warehouse supervisor has a special password, allowing him to access and change inventory information to take into account expired, broken, and damaged goods. An expired, broken, and damaged goods report is printed monthly.

4. Fresh produce is shipped directly from suppliers to grocers based on direct shipping instructions that PDI has transmitted to suppliers over telephone lines. All accounting records are updated by the computer system. A numeric control sequence is automatically assigned by the computer system and is used by accounting to control paper flow.

5. PDI ships to several large grocery chains in response to purchase orders received over telephone lines. These orders are listed on a transfer report, and the shipping documents are then printed.

Count Procedures

1. Prenumbered count tags will be used. Product stock number, description, and location will be preprinted on the tags by the computer in both human-readable and machine-readable form. To record quantities counted, warehouse personnel will use optical scanning devices to read the preprinted information, and then manually enter the quantity counted into the computer system. Any changes to preprinted information such as change in location will also be entered manually.

2. Two discrepancy reports will be generated by the system: one identifying differences between quantities counted and perpetual records, and one listing missing count tags. The information will be followed up, and any changes to inventory records will be authorized by the warehouse supervisor.

Required

What advice should Rakhi give to Charlie?

(CICA adapted)

18-34 Pill Distribution Limited (PDL) is a new client with Sober & Klein, Chartered Accountants. PDL is one of the largest distributors to pharmacists in the province. Employing close to 300 people, the company has six branches across the province, each acting as a distribution centre. During the year, PDL implemented a new, automated inventory system to facilitate efficient distribution of the more than 10,000 different inventory items that PDL handles.

Goldie Brown is responsible for the audit engagement of PDL. PDL has a January 31 year end, and it is now September 1999.

Goldie has recently visited the client's premises and has documented details regarding the computer environment (see Exhibit I on page 616) as well as the new inventory system (see Exhibit II on page 617).

The partner on this engagement has asked Goldie to prepare a draft internal control letter to PDL management based on her review of the information in Exhibits I and II. He has also asked you to prepare a memo discussing the significant audit implications of this information.

Required

Prepare the draft internal control letter and the memo.

EXHIBIT I
Computer Environment

Hardware

PDL has a central mainframe computer with tape drives, disk drives, printers, and communications equipment. Each member of the data processing department has a terminal. There are no terminals in users' departments. There are several microcomputers in various other departments which are not linked to the mainframe computer.

Organization

The data processing manager, the software specialist, and several of the programmers have been employed by PDL for more than five years, and they are familiar with the applications programs.

Access Controls

The software specialist is responsible for setting up new users and changing passwords as required. Since she knows all the department heads, they usually tell her about new employees, changes in responsibilities, or employees' terminations. If she is absent, the hardware supplier's technical support group is contacted directly to make the changes.

Data Control

Data control staff are responsible for reviewing batch control sheets and retrieving the required tapes from the tape room. Data control staff are also responsible for entering new file numbers and destruction dates into the tape management system. Some tapes have not yet been recorded in the system as they have no internal labels.

Data Entry

All batch processing data (i.e., accounts payable, payroll, general ledger, accounts receivable) are entered by data entry clerks. The data entry supervisor is responsible for ensuring agreement between the batch totals submitted with the data and the totals compiled from the data entered. When these totals do not agree, the data entry supervisor telephones and checks the information with the preparer, and if necessary, makes the required correction, noting the name of the person spoken to, the time, and the date.

Program Management

The software specialist prepared "software standards" guidelines, which identify standards for documentation and testing. Unfortunately, she has not had time to revise the guidelines to cover the updated version of the operating system which was installed six months ago.

Programmers do all their work on new computer programs that cannot access production programs or live data. When the data processing manager is satisfied that a program is functioning as specified, he permits the programmer to copy the program into the production area of the computer.

Program changes are initiated by means of program-change request forms, which are completed by a programmer based upon information provided by the user departments.

Programming, testing, and documentation of most changes are handled similarly to that for new programs. Discussions with programmers have revealed that they have not been updating documentation for program changes due to pressures to complete the new inventory system.

Back-up and Recovery

The data processing manager prepared a back-up and recovery plan several years ago.

All data and program files are backed up daily and are kept on site. The previous day's back-up tapes are sent to the closest branch for storage. Inventory count tapes are kept for two years.

As part of its recovery plan, PDL shares the cost of a vacant data processing site with 20 other companies. This site contains the necessary wiring and telephone connections. In the event of a major disaster, the plan calls for the site to be operational within 24 hours. PDL's hardware supplier would route equipment to this site if it became available.

Microcomputer Support

One month ago, the company created a new position for microcomputer support services. The first task of the individual hired is to compile an inventory of the existing microcomputer applications. Subsequently, the individual will assist microcomputer users.

Users are constantly bringing in new software and copying software from one machine to another when they see something useful.

Employees need guidance on back-up procedures. Many are not backing up their programs or data.

EXHIBIT II

Inventory System

Order Entry via Hand-held Units

Approximately 400 pharmacists in the province have access to PDL's new inventory system. This system permits instantaneous transmission of information to PDL by means of a hand-held microcomputer that contains a built-in modem.

When ordering, the pharmacist enters the item number and quantity of the product into the hand-held unit. The modem, linked to a telephone, transmits the order and the pharmacist's number and password. Microcomputers located at head office receive and record orders on hard disks. A printout of the order also specifies the pharmacist's number, the time, and the date of the order.

Data control staff copy the orders from the microcomputers onto tapes. The tapes are then loaded into the mainframe. Data control staff then delete the details from the microcomputer hard disks. The orders are validated through an edit routine that checks the pharmacist number and item numbers. The orders are then processed during that night's shipping/invoicing run. All orders that cannot be processed are listed on a printed exception report that is given to the sales department for follow-up and correction.

Preparation of Shipping Document/Invoice

The filling and shipping of orders is completed at night. A six-part form, which includes the shipping document and the invoice, is printed at the branch closest to the pharmacist.

At the branch, invoices are placed in boxes which are put onto a conveyor system, and warehouse personnel read the invoice, place the goods into the box, and check off the items on the invoice.

Items are checked and wrapped in the packaging area. If the packer finds all the items listed on the invoice in the correct quantities, he or she then wraps the order and attaches all copies of the invoice to the package(s). The package(s) is (are) then shipped.

If all the items listed on the invoice are not in the box, or are present but not in the quantities ordered, the packer notes their unavailability on all copies of the invoice. The packer then removes one copy of the invoice, records details of the items and quantities actually shipped, and forwards this copy of the invoice to head office. The packer attaches the remaining copies of the invoice to the package(s) and ships it. The next day, head office prints and mails a credit note for the unshipped items directly to the pharmacist.

Perpetual Inventory Update

At the same time as shipping documents are printed, inventory records are updated. All items are costed on an average-cost basis.

Semi-annual Inventory Count and Costing

Semi-annually, the computer prints inventory count cards. The item number, description, and inventory location are printed at the top of each card. The count personnel record the quantity counted on the card and initial the card. All items are counted by teams of two, following appropriate count procedures; one member counts and the second member records the count.

Completed cards are forwarded to head office for data entry. After entry, reports are run to verify that all goods have been counted, and a report is printed listing all discrepancies between the physical and the perpetual records. These discrepancies are followed up at the branch, and changes due to the recount are separately entered into the perpetual records and costed.

The inventory count is costed using a modified costing approach to approximate the lesser of cost and net realizable value. The most recent purchase price in the files is used as the cost.

Separate inventory extension listings are printed for each branch, resulting in six reports of up to 10,000 items.

19

AUDIT OF THE CAPITAL ACQUISITION AND REPAYMENT CYCLE

LEARNING OBJECTIVES

Thorough study of this chapter will enable you to:

19-1 Identify the accounts and the unique characteristics of the capital acquisition and repayment cycle (pages 619–620).

19-2 Design and perform the audit tests of notes payable and related accounts and transactions (pages 620–625).

19-3 Describe the primary concerns in the design and performance of the audit of owners' equity transactions (pages 625–628).

19-4 Design and perform tests of controls and tests of details of balances for capital stock and retained earnings (pages 628–631).

A DISHONEST CLIENT WILL GET THE BEST OF THE AUDITOR ALMOST EVERY TIME

Burnaby Contractors Inc. entered into long-term construction contracts, recognizing income using the percentage of completion method of accounting. This method requires, among other things, an agreement with well-defined, enforceable terms, a reliable method of estimating costs to complete the contracts, and recognition of losses at the time they become known. As part of the audit of Burnaby, its auditors read the contracts for all projects in progress, test costs incurred to date, and assess the ultimate profitability of the contracts, including discussing them with management. A significant part of verifying income under percentage of completion is auditing costs incurred.

In the current year, management's records and schedules of projects indicate that all projects will result in a profit. For each project, there is a separate schedule showing estimated total revenue from the project, costs incurred in the current period, costs incurred to date, estimated total costs, percentage of completion, and profit recognized in the current period. The auditor discussed each project with management, performed audit tests to support the schedule, and concluded that the revenue, expenses, and project were reasonably stated. Reported income allowed Burnaby to meet several of the restrictive covenants in its loan agreement with the bank.

In fact, Burnaby had incurred a significant loss on one of its major projects. Burnaby engaged a subcontractor to do reconstructive work not anticipated in the original contract bid. In awarding the subcontract, Burnaby entered into an agreement with the subcontractor that the work would not be paid for until after its audit was completed. Management hid the subcontractor's invoices from the auditors as they were received. During the next year, management recognized this loss, but doctored the invoices so that it appeared that the "unexpected" additional cost was incurred during that year and that the previous year's statements were correct.

The fraudulent misstatement was discovered several years later when Burnaby went bankrupt and the public accounting firm was sued for performing inadequate audits by the bank that had loaned Burnaby funds to finance construction projects. The firm was ultimately found not responsible, but only after spending extensive time and large amounts of money defending its audit.

OBJECTIVE 19-1

Identify the accounts and the unique characteristics of the capital acquisition and repayment cycle.

The final transaction cycle discussed in this text relates to the acquisition of capital resources in the form of interest-bearing debt and owner's equity and the repayment of the capital. The capital acquisition and repayment cycle also includes the payment of interest and dividends. The following are the major accounts in the cycle:

- Notes payable
- Contracts payable
- Mortgages payable
- Capital stock — preferred
- Capital stock — common
- Retained earnings
- Bonds payable

- Interest expense
- Accrued interest
- Cash in the bank
- Dividends declared
- Dividends payable
- Proprietorship — capital account
- Partnership — capital account

Four characteristics of the capital acquisition and repayment cycle significantly influence the audit of these accounts:

1. *Relatively few transactions affect the account balances, but each transaction is often highly material in amount.* For example, bonds are infrequently issued by most companies, but the amount of a bond issue is normally large. Due to the large size of most bond issues, it is common to verify each transaction taking place in the cycle for the entire year as a part of verifying the balance sheet accounts. It is not unusual to see audit working papers that include the beginning balance of every account in the capital acquisition and repayment cycle and documentation of every transaction that occurred during the year.
2. *The exclusion of a single transaction could be material in itself.* Considering the effect of understatements of liabilities and owners' equity, which was discussed in Chapter 16, omission is a major audit concern.
3. *There is a legal relationship between the client entity and the holder of the stock, bond, or similar ownership document.* In the audit of the transactions and amounts in the cycle, the auditor must ensure that the significant legal requirements affecting the financial statements have been properly fulfilled and adequately disclosed in the statements.
4. *There is a direct relationship between the interest and dividends accounts and debt and equity.* In the audit of interest-bearing debt, it is desirable to verify simultaneously the related interest expense and interest payable. This holds true for owners' equity, dividends declared, and dividends payable.

The audit procedures for many of the accounts in the capital acquisition and repayment cycle can best be understood by selecting representative accounts for study. Therefore, this chapter discusses (1) the audit of notes payable and the related interest expense and interest payable to illustrate interest-bearing capital and (2) common stock, retained earnings, and dividends.

The methodology for determining tests of details of balances for capital acquisition accounts is the same as that followed for all other accounts. For example, the methodology for notes payable is shown in Figure 19-1.

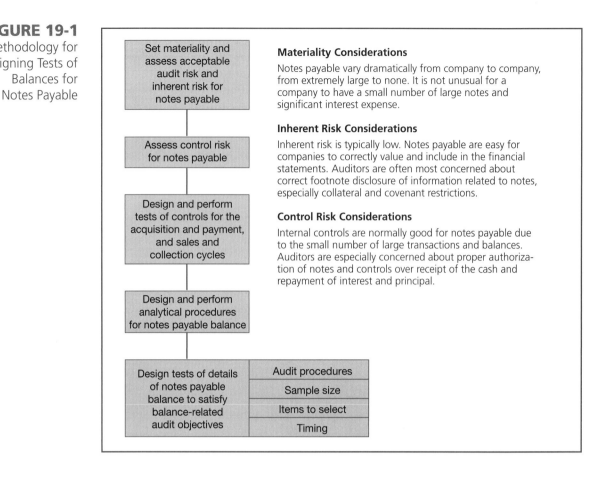

NOTES PAYABLE

A *note payable* is a legal obligation to a creditor, which may be unsecured or secured by assets. Typically, a note is issued for a period somewhere between one month and one year, but there are also long-term notes of over a year. Notes are issued for many different purposes, and the pledged property includes a wide variety of assets, such as securities, inventory, and capital assets. The principal and interest payments on the notes must be made in accordance with the terms of the loan agreement. For short-term loans, a principal and interest payment is usually required only when the loan becomes due; but for loans over 90 days, the note usually calls for monthly or quarterly interest payments.

OVERVIEW OF ACCOUNTS

The accounts used for notes payable and related interest are shown in Figure 19-2. It is common to include tests of principal and interest payments as a part of the audit of the acquisition and payment cycle because the payments are recorded in the cash disbursement journal. But due to their relative infrequency, in many cases no capital transactions are included in the tests of controls sample. Therefore, it is also normal to test these transactions as a part of the capital acquisition and repayment cycle.

OBJECTIVES

The objectives of the auditor's examination of notes payable are to determine whether

- The internal controls over notes payable are adequate.
- Transactions for principal and interest involving notes are properly authorized and recorded as defined by the six transaction-related audit objectives.
- The liability for notes payable and the related interest expense and accrued lia-

FIGURE 19-2
Notes Payable and the
Related Interest
Accounts

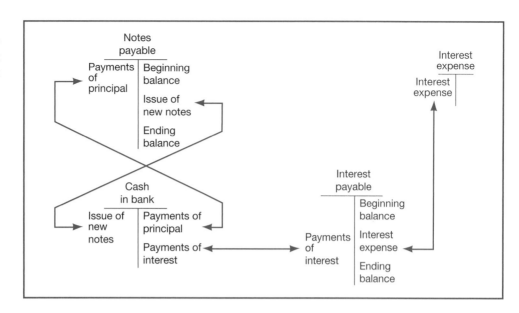

bility are properly stated as defined by eight of the nine balance-related audit objectives. (Realizable value is not applicable to liability accounts.)

INTERNAL CONTROLS

There are four important controls over notes payable:

Proper authorization for the issue of new notes Responsibility for the issuance of new notes should be vested in the board of directors or high-level management personnel. Generally, two signatures of properly authorized officials are required for all loan agreements. The amount of the loan, the interest rate, the repayment terms, and the particular assets pledged are all part of the approved agreement. Whenever notes are renewed, it is important that they be subject to the same authorization procedures as those for the issuance of new notes.

Adequate controls over the repayment of principal and interest The periodic payments of interest and principal should be controlled as part of the acquisition and payment cycle. At the time the note was issued, the accounting department should have received a copy in the same manner in which it receives vendors' invoices and receiving reports. The accounts payable department should automatically issue cheques for the notes when they fall due, again in the same manner in which it prepares cheques for acquisitions of goods and services. The copy of the note is the supporting documentation for payment.

Proper documents and records These include the maintenance of subsidiary records and control over blank and paid notes by a responsible person. Paid notes should be cancelled and retained under the custody of an authorized official.

Periodic, independent verification Periodically, the detailed note records should be reconciled with the general ledger and compared with the note holders' records by an employee who is not responsible for maintaining the detailed records. At the same time, an independent person should recompute the interest expense on notes to test the accuracy and propriety of the record keeping.

TESTS OF CONTROLS

Tests of notes payable transactions involve the issue of notes and the repayment of principal and interest. The audit tests are part of tests of controls for cash receipts

(Chapter 12) and cash disbursements (Chapter 16). Additional tests of controls are often performed as part of tests of details of balances due to the materiality of individual transactions.

Tests of controls for notes payable and related interest should emphasize testing the four important internal controls discussed in the previous section. In addition, the accurate recording of receipts from note proceeds and payments of principal and interest is emphasized.

ANALYTICAL PROCEDURES

Analytical procedures are essential for notes payable because tests of details for interest expense and accrued interest can frequently be eliminated when results are favourable. Table 19-1 illustrates typical analytical procedures for notes payable and related interest accounts.

TABLE 19-1

ANALYTICAL PROCEDURES FOR NOTES PAYABLE

ANALYTICAL PROCEDURE	POSSIBLE MISSTATEMENT
Recalculate approximate interest expense on the basis of average interest rates and overall monthly notes payable.	Misstatement of interest expense or accrued interest, or omission of an outstanding note payable.
Compare individual notes outstanding with the prior year.	Omission or misstatement of a note payable.
Compare total balance in notes payable, interest expense, and accrued interest with prior year.	Misstatement of interest expense, accrued interest, or notes payable.

FIGURE 19-3

Schedule of Notes Payable and Accrued Interest

Favron Corp.
Notes Payable

31/12/98

Schedule __AA-4__ Date
Prepared by __DB__ 12/1/99
Approved by __JL__ 16/1/99

Payee	Date Made	Due	Face Amount of Note	Security Description	Valuation	Balance at Beginning of Period
Bank of Westminister	30/9/97	30/9/98	10000	Investments	15000	10000
Fraser Trust Co.	30/9/98	30/9/99	10000	Investments	16000	
Fraser Trust Co.	31/10/98	31/10/99	10000	Capital Assets	22000	
			30000		53000	10000 ①

① –Traced to prior year audit working papers
② –Obtained copy of note included in permanent file
③ –Examined cancelled note and/or cheque
④ –Agreed to confirmation received from bank
⑤ –Traced to general ledger
⑥ –Recomputed expense; no differences noted
Ⅴ –Footed
x –Cross-footed

The auditor's independent estimate of interest expense, using average notes payable outstanding and average interest rates, tests the reasonableness of interest expense but also tests for omitted notes payable. An illustration of an auditor's working paper where such an analytical procedure has been performed is illustrated in Figure 6-3 on page 180. If actual interest expense had been materially larger than the auditor's estimate, one possible cause could be interest payments on unrecorded notes payable.

TESTS OF DETAILS OF BALANCES

The normal starting point for the audit of notes payable is a *schedule of notes payable and accrued interest* obtained from the client. A typical schedule is shown in Figure 19-3 on pages 622 and 623. The usual schedule includes detailed information of all transactions that took place during the entire year for principal and interest, the beginning and ending balances for notes and interest payable, and descriptive information about the notes, such as the due date, the interest rate, and the assets pledged as collateral.

When there are numerous transactions involving notes during the year, it may not be practical to obtain a schedule of the type shown in Figure 19-3. In that situation, the auditor is likely to request that the client prepare a schedule or computer spreadsheet of only those notes with unpaid balances at the end of the year. This would show a description of each note, its ending balance, and the interest payable at the end of the year, including the collateral and interest rate.

The objectives and common audit procedures are summarized in Table 19-2. Realizable value is not included in the table because it is not applicable to notes payable. The schedule of notes payable is the frame of reference for the procedures. The amount of testing depends heavily on materiality of notes payable and the effectiveness of internal controls.

	Notes				Interest			
Additions	Payments	Balance at End of Period	Rate Paid to		Accrued at Beginning of Period	Expense	Paid	Accrued at End of Period
	10000 ③	-0- ④	9.5% ④	Maturity	238	712 ⑥	950 ③	-0- x
10000 ②		10000 ④	10% ④	Maturity		250 ⑥		250 x
10000 ②		10000 ④	10% ④	Maturity		167 ⑥		167 x
20000	10000	20000 ⑤			238 ①	1129	950	417
⋎	⋎	⋎ x			⋎	⋎	⋎	⋎

TABLE 19-2

OBJECTIVES AND TESTS OF DETAILS OF BALANCES FOR NOTES PAYABLE AND INTEREST

BALANCE-RELATED AUDIT OBJECTIVES	COMMON TESTS OF DETAILS OF BALANCES PROCEDURES	COMMENTS
Notes payable in the notes payable schedule agree with the client's notes payable register or master file (detail tie-in).	Foot the notes payable list for notes payable and accrued interest.† Trace the totals to the general ledger. Trace the individual notes payable to the master file.	Frequently, these are done on a 100 percent basis because of the small population size.
Notes payable in the schedule exist (existence).	Confirm notes payable. Examine duplicate copy of notes for authorization. Examine corporate minutes for loan approval.	The existence objective is not as important as completeness or accuracy.
Existing notes payable are included in the notes payable schedule (completeness).	Examine notes paid after year end to determine whether they were liabilities at the balance sheet date. Obtain a *standard bank confirmation* that includes specific reference to the existence of notes payable from all financial institutions with which the client does business. (Bank confirmations are discussed more fully in Chapter 20.) Review the *bank reconciliation* for new notes credited directly to the bank account by the bank. Bank reconciliations are also discussed more fully in Chapter 20. Obtain confirmations from creditors who have held notes from the client in the past and are not currently included in the notes payable schedule. This is the same concept as a "zero balance" confirmation in accounts payable. Analyze interest expense to uncover a payment to a creditor who is not included in the notes payable schedule. This procedure is automatically done if the schedule is similar to the one in Figure 19-3 because all interest payments are reconciled with the general ledger. Examine paid notes for cancellation to make sure they are not still outstanding. They should be maintained in the client's files. Review the minutes of the board of directors for authorized but unrecorded notes.	This objective is important for uncovering both errors or fraud and other irregularities. The first three of these procedures are done on most audits. The others are frequently done only when internal controls are weak.
Notes payable and accrued interest on the schedule are accurate (accuracy).	Examine duplicate copies of notes for principal and interest rates. Confirm notes payable, interest rates, and last date for which interest has been paid with holders of notes. Recalculate accrued interest.†	In some cases, it may be necessary to calculate, using present-value techniques, the imputed interest rates, or the principal amount of the note. An example is when equipment is acquired for a note.†
Notes payable in the schedule are properly classified (classification).	Examine due dates on duplicate copies of notes to determine whether all or part of the notes are a noncurrent liability. Review notes to determine whether any are related party notes or accounts payable.	
Notes payable are included in the proper period (cutoff).	Examine duplicate copies of notes to determine whether notes were dated on or before the balance sheet date.	Notes should be included as current-period liabilities when dated on or before the balance sheet date.
The company has an obligation to pay the notes payable (rights and obligations).	Examine notes to determine whether the company has obligations for payment.	

TABLE 19-2

(CONTINUED)

BALANCE-RELATED AUDIT OBJECTIVES	COMMON TESTS OF DETAILS OF BALANCES PROCEDURES	COMMENTS
Notes payable, interest expense, and accrued interest are properly presented and disclosed (presentation and disclosure).	Examine duplicate copies of notes. Confirm notes payable. Examine notes, minutes, and bank confirmations for restrictions. Examine balance sheet for proper disclosure of noncurrent portions, related parties, assets pledged as security for notes, and restrictions resulting from notes payable.	Proper financial statement presentation, including footnote disclosure, is an important consideration for notes payable.

†This test could be completed using spreadsheet software or other computerized methods in audits where volume is high.

The three most important balance-related audit objectives in notes payable are as follows:

- Existing notes payable are included (completeness).
- Notes payable in the schedule are accurately recorded (accuracy).
- Notes payable are properly presented and disclosed (presentation and disclosure).

The first two objectives are important because a misstatement could be material if even one note is omitted or incorrect. Presentation and disclosure are important because generally accepted accounting principles require that the footnotes adequately describe the terms of notes payable outstanding and the assets pledged as collateral for the loans. If there are significant restrictions on the activities of the company required by the loans, such as compensating balance provisions or restrictions on the payment of dividends, these must also be disclosed in the footnotes.

SUMMARY

Figure 19-4 on page 626 illustrates the major accounts related to notes payable in the capital acquisition and repayment cycle and the types of audit tests used to audit these accounts. This figure also shows how the audit risk model discussed in Chapter 8 relates to the audit of these accounts in the cycle.

OWNERS' EQUITY

OBJECTIVE 19-3

Describe the primary concerns in the design and performance of the audit of owners' equity transactions.

A major distinction must be made in the audit of owners' equity between *publicly* and *closely held corporations* (also known as *private corporations*). Public companies are permitted by their articles of incorporation to issue shares to the public; closely held companies tend to be private companies with restricted share ownership. In most closely held corporations, there are few if any transactions during the year for capital stock accounts, and there are typically only a few shareholders. The only transactions entered in the owners' equity section are likely to be the change in owners' equity for the annual earnings or loss and the declaration of dividends, if any. The amount of time spent verifying owners' equity is frequently minimal for closely held corporations even though the auditor must test the existing corporate records.

For publicly held corporations, the verification of owners' equity is more complex due to the larger numbers of shareholders and frequent changes in the individuals holding the stock. In this section, the appropriate tests for verifying the major accounts — capital stock, retained earnings, and the related dividends — in a publicly held corporation are discussed. The other accounts in owners' equity are verified in much the same way as these.

FIGURE 19-4

Types of Audit Tests for the Capital Acquisition and Repayment Cycle — Notes Payable (see Figure 19-2 on page 621 for accounts)

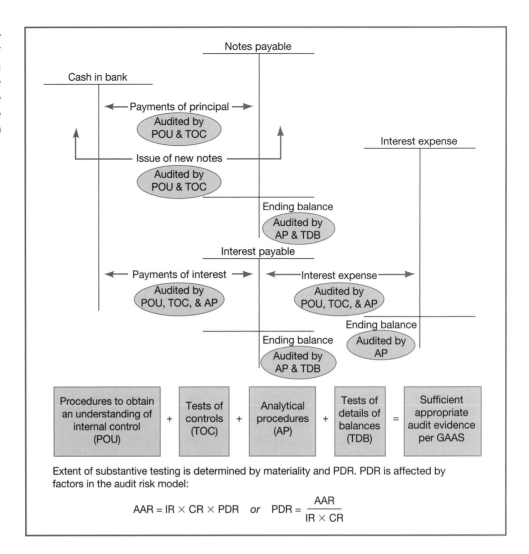

An overview of the specific owners' equity accounts discussed in this section is given in Figure 19-5.

OBJECTIVES

The objectives of the auditor's examination of owners' equity are to determine whether

- The internal controls over capital stock and related dividends are adequate.
- Owners' equity transactions are recorded properly as defined by the six transaction-related audit objectives.
- Owners' equity balances are properly presented and disclosed as defined by the balance-related audit objectives for owners' equity accounts. (Rights/obligations and realizable value are not applicable.)

INTERNAL CONTROLS

Several important internal controls are of concern to the independent auditor in owners' equity: proper authorization of transactions, proper record keeping, adequate segregation of duties between maintaining owners' equity records and handling cash and stock certificates, and the use of an independent registrar and stock transfer agent.

Proper authorization of transactions Since each owners' equity transaction is typically material, many of these transactions must be approved by the board of direc-

FIGURE 19-5
Owners' Equity and
Dividends Accounts

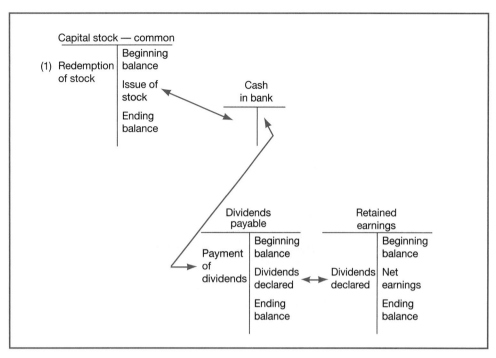

(1) Decrease cash

tors. The following types of owners' equity transactions usually require specific authorization.

- *Issuance of capital stock* The authorization includes the type of the equity to issue (e.g., preferred or common stock), number of shares to issue, issue price (also known as the stated value), privileges or conditions that attach to the stock, and date of the issue.
- *Repurchase or redemption of capital stock* The repurchase or redemption of common or preferred shares, the timing of repurchase (redemption), and the amount to pay for the shares should all be approved by the board of directors.
- *Declaration of dividends* The board of directors should authorize the form of dividends (e.g., cash or stock), the amount of the dividend per share, and the record and payment dates of the dividends.

Proper record keeping and segregation of duties When a company maintains its own records of stock transactions and outstanding stock, internal controls must be adequate to ensure that the actual owners of the stock are recognized in the corporate records, the correct amount of dividends is paid to the shareholders owning the stock as of the dividend record date, and the potential for employee fraud is minimized. The proper assignment of personnel and adequate record-keeping procedures are useful controls for these purposes.

The most important procedures for preventing misstatements in owners' equity are (1) well-defined policies for preparing stock certificates and recording capital stock transactions and (2) independent internal verification of information in the records. The client must be certain when issuing and recording capital stock that there is compliance with the relevant federal (for federally incorporated companies) or provincial (for provincially incorporated companies) laws governing corporations and the requirements in the articles of incorporation. For example, the classes of shares and the number of shares that the company is authorized to issue affect issuance and recording.

A control over capital stock used by most companies is the maintenance of stock certificate books and shareholders' capital stock master and transaction files. A *capi-*

tal stock certificate book is a record of the issuance and repurchase of capital stock for the life of the corporation. For large public corporations, these records would be automated rather than kept manually. There would normally be a book or file for each type (preferred or common) and each class (common, class A; common, class B; etc.). The record for a particular capital stock transaction includes such information as the certificate number, the number of shares issued, the name of the person to whom it was issued, and the issue date. When shares are repurchased, the capital stock certificate book should include the cancelled certificates and the date of their cancellation. A shareholders' capital stock master file is the record of the outstanding shares at any given time. The master file acts as a check on the accuracy of the capital stock certificate book or transaction details and the preferred and common stock balances in the general ledger. It is also used as the basis for the payment of dividends.

The disbursement of cash for the payment of dividends should be controlled in much the same manner as was described in Chapter 15 for the preparation and payment of payroll. Dividend cheques should be prepared from the capital stock certificate book by someone who is not responsible for maintaining the capital stock records. After the cheques are prepared, it is desirable to have an independent verification of the shareholders' names and the amount of the cheques and a reconciliation of the total amount of the dividend cheques with the total dividends authorized in the minutes. The use of a separate imprest dividend account is desirable to prevent the payment of a larger amount of dividends than was authorized.

Independent registrar and stock transfer agent   Some companies engage an independent registrar and stock transfer agent (usually one organization such as a trust company performs both tasks, but the job may be split between two such organizations) as a control to prevent the improper issue of share certificates and to maintain shareholder records. The function of an independent registrar is to ensure that stock is issued by a corporation in accordance with the capital stock provisions in the articles of incorporation and the authorization of the board of directors. The registrar is responsible for signing all newly issued share certificates and making sure old certificates are received and cancelled before a replacement certificate is issued when there is a change in the ownership of the stock.

Most large corporations also employ the services of a stock transfer agent for the purpose of maintaining the shareholder records, including those documenting transfers of share ownership. The employment of a transfer agent not only serves as a control over the share records by putting them in the hands of an independent organization but reduces the cost of record keeping. Many companies also have the transfer agent disburse cash dividends to shareholders, thereby further transferring internal control. Corporations should have adequate procedures to verify on a periodic basis that transfer agents perform only authorized transactions.

AUDIT OF CAPITAL STOCK

OBJECTIVE 19-4

Design and perform tests of controls and tests of details of balances for capital stock and retained earnings.

There are four main concerns in auditing capital stock:

- Existing capital stock transactions are recorded (completeness).
- Recorded capital stock transactions exist and are accurately recorded (existence and accuracy).
- Capital stock is accurately recorded (accuracy).
- Capital stock is properly presented and disclosed (presentation and disclosure).

The first two concerns involve tests of controls, and the last two involve tests of details of balances.

Existing capital stock transactions are recorded   This objective is easily satisfied when a registrar or transfer agent is used. The auditor can confirm with him or her whether any capital stock transactions occurred and the valuation of existing transactions. Review of the minutes of the board of directors' meetings, especially near the balance sheet date, and examination of client-held stock records are also useful to uncover issuances and repurchases of capital stock.

Recorded capital stock transactions exist and are accurately recorded The issuance of new capital stock for cash, the merger with another company through an exchange of stock, the donation of shares, and the repurchase of shares each require extensive auditing. Regardless of the controls in existence, it is normal practice to verify all capital stock transactions because of their materiality and permanence in the records. Existence can ordinarily be tested by examining the minutes of the board of directors' meetings for proper authorization.

Accurate recording of capital stock transactions for cash can be readily verified by confirming the amount with the transfer agent and tracing the amount of the recorded capital stock transactions to cash receipts. (In the case of repurchased shares, the amounts are traced to the cash disbursements journal.) In addition, the auditor must verify whether the correct amounts were credited to capital stock by referring to the articles of incorporation to determine the stated value of the capital stock.

When capital stock transactions involve stock dividends, acquisition of property for stock, mergers, or similar non-cash transfers, the verification of valuation may be considerably more difficult. For these types of transactions, the auditor must be certain that the client has correctly computed the amount of the capital stock issue in accordance with generally accepted accounting principles. For example, in the audit of a major merger transaction, the auditor has to evaluate whether the transaction is a purchase or, in very rare instances, a pooling of interests. Frequently, considerable research is necessary to determine which accounting treatment is correct for the existing circumstances. After the auditor reaches a conclusion as to the appropriate method, it is necessary to verify that the amounts were correctly computed.

Capital stock is accurately recorded The ending balance in the capital stock account is verified by first determining the number of shares outstanding at the balance sheet date. A confirmation from the transfer agent is the simplest way to obtain this information. When no transfer agent exists, the auditor must rely on examining the stock records and accounting for all shares outstanding in the stock certificate records, examining all cancelled certificates, and accounting for blank certificates. After the auditor is satisfied that the number of shares outstanding is correct, the recorded value in the capital account can be verified by multiplying the number of shares by the stated value of the stock. It is audited by verifying the share amounts of recorded transactions during the year and adding them to or subtracting them from the beginning balance in the account.

A major consideration in the accuracy of capital stock is verifying whether the number of shares used in the calculation of earnings per share is accurate. It is easy to determine the correct number of shares to use in the calculation when there is only one class of stock and a small number of capital stock transactions. The problem becomes much more complex when there are convertible securities, stock options, or stock warrants outstanding. It is important for the auditor to have a thorough understanding of Section 3500, "Earnings per Share," in the *CICA Handbook* before verifying the number of basic and fully diluted shares.

Capital stock is properly presented and disclosed The most important sources of information for determining proper presentation and disclosure are the articles of incorporation, the minutes of board of directors' meetings, and the auditor's analysis of capital stock transactions. The auditor should determine that there is a proper description of each class of stock, including such information as the number of shares issued and outstanding and any special rights of an individual class. The proper disclosure of stock options, stock warrants, and convertible securities should also be verified by examining legal documents or other evidence of the provision of these agreements.

AUDIT OF DIVIDENDS The emphasis in the audit of dividends is on the transactions rather than the ending balance. The exception is when there are dividends payable.

The six transaction-related audit objectives for transactions are relevant for dividends. However, dividends are usually audited on a 100 percent basis and cause few problems. The following are the most important objectives, including those concerning dividends payable:

- Recorded dividends occurred (occurrence).
- Existing dividends are recorded (completeness).
- Dividends are accurately recorded (accuracy).
- Dividends that exist are paid to shareholders (existence).
- Dividends payable are recorded (completeness).
- Dividends payable are accurately recorded (accuracy).

Existence of recorded dividends can be checked by examining the minutes of board of directors' meetings for the amount of the dividend per share and the dividend date. When the auditor examines the board of directors' minutes for dividends declared, the auditor should be alert to the possibility of unrecorded dividends declared, particularly shortly before the balance sheet date. A closely related audit procedure is reviewing the permanent audit working-paper file to determine if there are restrictions on the payment of dividends in bond indenture agreements or preferred stock provisions.

The accuracy of a dividend declaration can be audited by recomputing the amount on the basis of the dividend per share and the number of shares outstanding. If the client uses a transfer agent to disburse dividends, the total can be traced to a cash disbursement entry to the agent and also confirmed.

When a client keeps its own dividend records and pays the dividend itself, the auditor can verify the total amount of the dividend by recalculation and reference to cash disbursed. In addition, it is necessary to verify whether the payment was made to the shareholders who owned the stock at the dividend record date. The auditor can test this by selecting a sample of recorded dividend payments and tracing the payee's name on the cancelled cheque to the dividend records to ensure the payee was entitled to the dividend. At the same time, the amount and the authenticity of the dividend cheque can be verified.

Tests of dividends payable should be done in conjunction with declared dividends. Any unpaid dividend should be included as a liability.

AUDIT OF RETAINED EARNINGS For most companies, the only transactions involving retained earnings are net earnings for the year and dividends declared. But there may also be corrections of prior-period earnings, prior-period adjustments charged or credited directly to retained earnings, and the setting up or elimination of appropriations of retained earnings.

The starting point for the audit of retained earnings is an analysis of retained earnings for the entire year. The audit schedule showing the analysis, which is usually part of the permanent file, includes a description of every transaction affecting the account.

The audit of the credit to retained earnings for net income for the year (or the debit for a loss) is accomplished by simply tracing the entry in retained earnings to the net earnings figure on the income statement. The performance of this procedure must, of course, take place fairly late in the audit after all adjusting entries affecting net earnings have been completed.

An important consideration in auditing debits and credits to retained earnings other than net earnings and dividends is determining whether the transactions should have been included. For example, prior-period adjustments can be included in retained earnings only if they result from a change in accounting policy or are intended to correct an error in prior period financial statements. The auditor should ensure that the accounting is in accordance with "Accounting Changes," Section 1506 of the *CICA Handbook*.

Once the auditor is satisfied that the recorded transactions are appropriately classified as retained earnings transactions, the next step is to decide whether they are accurately recorded. The audit evidence necessary to determine accuracy depends on the nature of the transactions. If there is a requirement for an appropriation of retained earnings for a bond sinking fund, the correct amount of the appropriation can be determined by examining the bond indenture agreement.

Another important consideration in the audit of retained earnings is evaluating whether there are any transactions that should have been included but were not. If a stock dividend was declared, for instance, the market value of the securities issued should be capitalized by a debit to retained earnings and a credit to capital stock. Similarly, if the financial statements include appropriations of retained earnings, the auditor should evaluate whether it is still necessary to have the appropriation as of the balance sheet date. As an example, an appropriation of retained earnings for a bond sinking fund should be eliminated by crediting retained earnings after the bond has been paid off.

Of primary concern in determining whether retained earnings are correctly disclosed on the balance sheet is the existence of any restrictions on the payment of dividends. Frequently, agreements with bankers, shareholders, and other creditors prohibit or limit the amount of dividends the client can pay. These restrictions must be disclosed in the footnotes to the financial statements.

SUMMARY

Figure 19-6 on the following page illustrates the major accounts related to owners' equity in the capital acquisition and repayment cycle and the types of audit tests used to audit these accounts. This figure also shows how the audit risk model discussed in Chapter 8 relates to the audit of these accounts in the cycle.

ESSENTIAL TERMS

Capital acquisition and repayment cycle — the transaction cycle involving the acquisition of capital resources in the form of interest-bearing debt and owners' equity, and the repayment of the capital (p. 619).

Capital stock certificate book or records — a record of the issuance and repurchase of capital stock for the life of the corporation (p. 627).

Closely held corporation — a corporation whose stock is not publicly traded; typically, there are only a few shareholders and few, if any, capital stock account transactions during the year; also known as a *private corporation* (p. 625).

Independent registrar — an outside person or organization engaged by a corporation to ensure that its stock is issued

in accordance with capital stock provisions in the corporate charter and authorizations by the board of directors (p. 628).

Note payable — a legal obligation to a creditor, which may be unsecured or secured by assets (p. 620).

Private corporation — see *Closely held corporation*.

Publicly held corporation — a corporation whose stock is publicly traded; typically, there are many shareholders and frequent changes in the ownership of the stock (p. 625).

Stock transfer agent — an outside person or organization engaged by a corporation to maintain the shareholder records and often to disburse cash dividends (p. 628).

FIGURE 19-6

Types of Audit Tests for the Capital Acquisition and Repayment Cycle — Owners' Equity (see Figure 19-5 on page 627 for accounts)

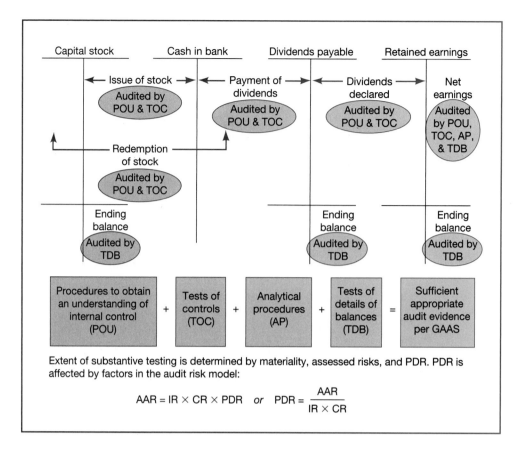

REVIEW QUESTIONS

19-1 List four examples of interest-bearing liability accounts commonly found in balance sheets. What characteristics do these liabilities have in common? How do they differ?

19-2 Why are liability accounts that are included in the capital acquisition and repayment cycle audited differently from accounts payable?

19-3 It is common practice to audit the balance in notes payable in conjunction with the audit of interest expense and interest payable. Explain the advantages of this approach.

19-4 With which internal controls should the auditor be most concerned in the audit of notes payable? Explain the importance of each.

19-5 Which analytical procedures are most important in verifying notes payable? Which types of misstatements can the auditor uncover by the use of these tests?

19-6 Why is it more important to search for unrecorded notes payable than for unrecorded notes receivable? List several audit procedures the auditor can use to uncover unrecorded notes payable.

19-7 What is the primary purpose of analyzing interest expense? Given this purpose, what primary considerations should the auditor keep in mind when doing the analysis?

19-8 Distinguish between the tests of controls and tests of details of balances for liability accounts in the capital acquisition and repayment cycle.

19-9 List four types of restrictions that long-term creditors often put on companies when granting them a loan. How can the auditor find out about each of these restrictions?

19-10 What are the primary objectives in the audit of owners' equity accounts?

19-11 Evaluate the following statement: "The articles of incorporation and the bylaws of a company are legal documents; therefore, they should not be examined by the auditors. If the auditor wants information about these documents, a lawyer should be consulted."

19-12 What are the major internal controls over owners' equity?

19-13 How does the audit of owners' equity for a closely held corporation differ from that for a publicly held corporation? In what respects are there no significant differences?

19-14 Describe the duties of a stock registrar and a transfer agent. How does the use of their services affect the client's internal controls?

19-15 What kinds of information can be confirmed with a transfer agent?

19-16 Evaluate the following statement: "The most important audit procedure to verify dividends for the year is a comparison of a random sample of cancelled dividend cheques with a dividend list that has been prepared by management as of the dividend record date."

19-17 When a transfer agent disburses dividends for a

client, how is the audit of dividends declared and paid affected? What audit procedures are necessary to verify dividends paid when a transfer agent is used?

19-18 What should be the major emphasis in auditing the retained earnings account? Explain your answer.

19-19 Explain the relationship between the audit of owners' equity and the calculations of earnings per share. What are the main auditing considerations in verifying the earnings per share figure?

MULTIPLE CHOICE QUESTIONS

19-20 The following multiple-choice questions concern interest-bearing liabilities. Choose the best response.

a. The auditor's program for the examination of long-term debt should include steps that require the
   (1) examination of any bond trust indenture.
   (2) inspection of the accounts payable master file.
   (3) verification of the existence of the bondholders.
   (4) investigation of credits to the bond interest income account.

b. During the year under audit, a company has completed a private placement of a substantial number of bonds. Which of the following is the most important step in the auditor's examination of bonds payable?
   (1) Examining the bond records maintained by the transfer agent.
   (2) Confirming the amount issued with the bond trustee.
   (3) Tracing the cash received from the issue to the accounting records.
   (4) Recomputing the annual interest cost and the effective yield.

c. Several years ago, Conway, Inc., secured a conventional real-estate mortgage loan. Which of the following audit procedures would most likely be performed by an auditor examining the mortgage balance?
   (1) Recomputing mortgage interest expense.
   (2) Examining the current year's cancelled cheques.
   (3) Reviewing the mortgage amortization schedule.
   (4) Inspecting public records of registered mortgages.

19-21 The following questions concern the audit of accounts in the capital acquisition and repayment cycle. Choose the best response.

a. During an examination of a public company, the auditor should obtain written confirmation regarding debenture transactions from the
   (1) client's lawyers.
   (2) internal auditors.
   (3) trustee.
   (4) debenture holders.

b. An audit program for the examination of the retained earnings account should include verification of
   (1) authorization for both cash and stock dividends.
   (2) market value used to charge retained earnings to account for a 2-for-1 stock split.
   (3) approval of the adjustment to the beginning balance as a result of a write-down of an account receivable.
   (4) approval of the adjustment to the beginning balance as a result of a change in the estimated life of certain fixed assets.

c. Where no independent stock transfer agents are employed and the corporation issues its own shares and maintains share records, cancelled stock certificates should
   (1) be defaced to prevent re-issuance and attached to their corresponding stubs.
   (2) be destroyed to prevent fraudulent re-issuance.
   (3) be defaced and sent to the Ministry of Corporate and Consumer Affairs.
   (4) not be defaced but segregated from other stock certificates and retained in a cancelled certificates file.

(AICPA adapted)

DISCUSSION QUESTIONS AND PROBLEMS

19-22 Items 1 through 6 are questions typically found in a standard internal control questionnaire used by auditors to obtain an understanding of internal control for notes payable. In using the questionnaire for a particular client, a "yes" response indicates a possible internal control, whereas a "no" indicates a potential weakness.

1. Are liabilities for notes payable incurred only after written authorization by a proper company official?

2. Is a notes payable master file maintained?

3. Is the individual who maintains the notes payable master file someone other than the person who approves the issue of new notes or handles cash?

4. Are paid notes cancelled and retained in the company files?

5. Is a periodic reconciliation made of the notes payable master file with the actual notes outstanding by an individual who does not maintain the master file?

6. Are interest expense and accrued interest recomputed periodically by an individual who does not record interest transactions?

Required

a. For each of the preceding questions, state the purpose of the control.

b. For each of the preceding questions, identify the type of financial statement misstatement that could occur if the control were not in effect.

c. For each of the potential misstatements in part (b), list an audit procedure that could be used to determine whether a material misstatement existed.

19-23 The following are frequently performed audit procedures for the verification of bonds payable issued in previous years.

1. Obtain a copy of the bond indenture agreement and review its important provisions.

2. Determine that each of the bond indenture provisions has been met.

3. Analyze the general ledger account for bonds payable, interest expense, and unamortized bond discount or premium.

4. Test the client's calculations of interest expense, unamortized bond discount or premium, accrued interest, and bonds payable.

5. Obtain a confirmation from the bondholder.

Required

a. State the purpose of each of the five audit procedures listed.

b. List the provisions for which the auditor should be alert in examining the bond indenture agreement.

c. For each provision listed in part (b), explain how the auditor can determine whether its terms have been met.

d. Explain how the auditor should verify the unamortized bond discount or premium.

e. List the information that should be requested in the confirmation of bonds payable with the bondholder.

19-24 In conducting an audit of a corporation that has a bond issue outstanding, the trust indenture is reviewed and a confirmation as to the issue is obtained from the trustee.

Required

List eight matters of importance to the auditor that might be found either in the indenture or in the confirmation obtained from the trustee. Explain briefly the reason for the auditor's interest in each of the items.

(AICPA adapted)

19-25 Fox Corp. is a medium-sized industrial client that has been audited by your public accounting firm for several years. The only interest-bearing debt owed by Fox Corp. is $200,000 in long-term notes payable held by the bank. The notes were issued three years previously and will mature in six more years. Fox Corp. is highly profitable, has no pressing needs for additional financing, and has excellent internal controls over the recording of loan transactions and related interest costs.

Required

a. Describe the auditing that you think would be necessary for notes payable and related interest accounts in these circumstances.

b. How would your answer differ if Fox Corp. were unprofitable, had a need for additional financing, and had weak internal controls?

19-26 The ending general ledger balance of $186,000 in notes payable for Sisam Manufacturing Inc. is made up of 20 notes to 8 different payees. The notes vary in duration anywhere from 30 days to 2 years and in amount from $1,000 to $10,000. In some cases, the notes were issued for cash loans; in other cases, the notes were issued directly to vendors for the purchase of inventory or equipment. The use of relatively short-term financing is necessary because all existing properties are pledged for mortgages. Nevertheless, there is still a serious cash shortage.

Record-keeping procedures for notes payable are not good, considering the large number of loan transactions. There is neither a notes payable master file nor an independent verification of ending balances; however, the notes payable records are maintained by a secretary who does not have access to cash.

The audit has been done by the same public accounting firm for several years. In the current year, the following procedures were performed to verify notes payable:

1. Obtain a list of notes payable from the client, foot the notes payable balances on the list, and trace the total to the general ledger.

2. Examine duplicate copies of notes for all outstanding notes included on the listing. Compare the name of the lender, amount, and due date on the duplicate copy with the list.

3. Obtain a confirmation from lenders for all listed notes payable. The confirmation should include the due date of the loan, the amount, and interest payable at the balance sheet date.

4. Recompute accrued interest on the list for all notes. The information for determining the correct accrued interest is to be obtained from the duplicate copy of the note. Foot the accrued interest amounts and trace the balance to the general ledger.

Required

a. What should be the emphasis in the verification of notes payable in this situation? Explain.

b. State the purpose of each of the four audit procedures listed.

c. Evaluate whether each of the four audit procedures was necessary. Evaluate the sample size for each procedure.

d. List other audit procedures that should be performed in the audit of notes payable in these circumstances.

19-27 The following covenants are extracted from the indenture of a bond issue outstanding from McMullen Corp. The indenture provides that failure to comply with its terms in any respect automatically advances the due date of the loan to the date of noncompliance (the regular date is 20 years hence).

Required

List any audit steps or reporting requirements that you feel should be taken or recognized in connection with each one of the following with respect to your audit of McMullen Corp.

a. The debtor company shall endeavour to maintain a working capital ratio of 2:1 at all times, and, in any fiscal year following a failure to maintain said ratio, the company shall restrict compensation of officers to a total of $250,000. Officers for this purpose shall include a chair of the board of directors, a president, all vice presidents, a secretary, and a treasurer.

b. The debtor company shall keep all property that is security for this debt insured against loss by fire to the extent of 100 percent of its actual value. Policies of insurance comprising this protection shall be filed with the trustee.

c. The debtor company shall pay all taxes legally assessed against the property that is security for this debt within the time provided by law for payment without penalty, and shall deposit receipted tax bills or equally acceptable evidence of payment of same with the trustee.

d. A sinking fund shall be deposited with the trustee by semi-annual payments of $300,000, from which the trustee shall, in his or her discretion, purchase bonds of this issue.

(AICPA adapted)

19-28 Evangeline Ltd. took out a 20-year mortgage on June 15, 1999, for $2,600,000 and pledged its only manufacturing building and the land on which the building stands as collateral. Each month subsequent to the issue of the mortgage, a monthly payment of $20,000 was paid to the mortgagor. You are in charge of the current-year audit for Evangeline, which has a balance sheet date of December 31, 1999. The client has been audited previously by your public accounting firm, but this is the first time Evangeline Ltd. has had a mortgage.

Required

a. Explain why it is desirable to prepare a working paper for the permanent file for the mortgage. What type of information should be included in the working paper?

b. Explain why the audits of mortgage payable, interest expense, and interest payable should all be done together.

c. List the audit procedures that should ordinarily be performed to verify the issue of the mortgage, the balance in the mortgage and interest payable accounts at December 31, 1999, and the balance in interest expense for the year 1999.

19-29 Items 1 through 6 are common questions found in internal control questionnaires used by auditors to obtain an understanding of internal control for owners' equity. In using the questionnaire for a particular client, a "yes" response

indicates a possible internal control, whereas a "no" indicates a potential weakness.

1. Does the company use the services of an independent registrar or transfer agent?

2. Are issues and retirements of stock authorized by the board of directors?

3. If an independent registrar and transfer agent are not used:
   (i) Are unissued certificates properly controlled?
   (ii) Are cancelled certificates mutilated to prevent their re-use?

4. Are common stock master files and stock certificate records periodically reconciled with the general ledger by an independent person?

5. Is an independent transfer agent used for disbursing dividends? If not, is an imprest dividend account maintained?

6. Are all entries in the owners' equity accounts authorized at the proper level in the organization?

Required

a. For each of the preceding questions, state the purpose of the control.

b. For each of the preceding questions, identify the type of potential financial statement misstatements if the control were not in effect.

c. For each of the possible misstatements in part (b), list an audit procedure the auditor could use to determine whether a material misstatement existed.

19-30 The following audit procedures are frequently performed by auditors in the verification of owners' equity:

1. Review the articles of incorporation and bylaws for provisions relating to owners' equity.

2. Review the minutes of the board of directors' meetings for the year for approvals related to owners' equity.

3. Analyze all owners' equity accounts for the year, and document the nature of any recorded change in each account.

4. Account for all certificate numbers in the capital stock book for all shares outstanding.

5. Examine the stock certificate book or records for any stock that was cancelled.

6. Recompute earnings per share.

7. Review debt provisions and senior securities with respect to liquidation preferences, dividends in arrears, and restrictions on the payment of dividends or the issue of stock.

Required

a. State the purpose of each of these seven audit procedures.

b. List the type of misstatements the auditors could uncover by the use of each audit procedure.

19-31 You are engaged in the audit of Muranaka Corp. Its records have not previously been audited by you. Muranaka has both an independent transfer agent and a registrar for its capital stock. The transfer agent maintains the record of shareholders, and the registrar checks that there is no overissue of stock. Signatures of both are required to validate certificates.

It has been proposed that confirmations be obtained from both the transfer agent and the registrar as to the stock outstanding at the balance sheet date. If such confirmations agree with the books, no additional work is to be performed for capital stock.

Required

If you agree that obtaining the confirmations as suggested would be sufficient in this case, give the justification for your position. If you disagree, state specifically all additional steps you would take and explain your reasons for taking them.

(AICPA adapted)

19-32 The Bergonzi Corporation is a medium-sized wholesaler of grocery products with 4,000 shares of stock outstanding to approximately 25 shareholders. Because of the age of several retired shareholders and the success of the company, management has decided to pay dividends six times a year. The amount of the bimonthly dividend per share varies depending on the profits, but it is ordinarily between $5 and $7 per share. The chief accountant, who is also a shareholder, prepares the dividend cheques, records the cheques in the dividend journal, and reconciles the bank account. Important controls include manual cheque signing by the president and the use of an imprest dividend bank account.

The auditor verifies the dividends by maintaining a schedule of the total shares of stock issued and outstanding in the permanent working papers. The total amount of stock outstanding is multiplied by the dividends per share authorized in the minutes to arrive at the current total dividend. This total is compared with the deposit that has been made to the imprest dividend account. Since the transfer of stock is infrequent, it is possible to verify dividends paid for the entire year in a comparatively short time.

Required

a. Evaluate the usefulness of the approach followed by the auditor in verifying dividends in this situation. Include both the strengths and the weaknesses of the approach.

b. List other audit procedures that should be performed in verifying dividends in this situation. Explain the purpose of each procedure.

19-33 In 1956, Claudette André and her brothers took over a small manufacturing company started by their father as a sideline to their regular occupations. What began as a small informal partnership eventually became a successful business, and when the sons of two of the original partners entered the firm, the need to formalize the relationship became obvious to everyone concerned. After lengthy dis-

cussions among themselves and with their lawyers and public accountants, they decided to enter into a clearly defined partnership agreement rather than to incorporate. The partnership agreement was completed in 1971.

The firm has continued to operate successfully without internal difficulties since that time. Great care has been taken by the firm to keep the affairs of the partnership entity and those of the individual partners completely separate. For example, if a personal transaction is paid by the partnership, the partner's capital account is charged.

Your firm has audited and provided accounting and tax advice to the partnership since the 1960s. The individuals involved in the audit over the years have concluded that internal controls are excellent. No unusual difficulties have been encountered in any year.

Required

a. How much does the fact that the business is a partnership rather than a corporation affect the audit of the capital and repayment cycle? Be specific.

b. How do the tests of controls for each of the cycles other than the capital acquisition and repayment cycle differ when the client is a partnership rather than a corporation?

c. How do the tests of details of balances for each of the cycles other than the capital acquisition and repayment cycle differ when the client is a partnership rather than a corporation?

(AICPA adapted)

19-34 Xiel Limited is a Canadian manufacturing company with a June 30 fiscal year end. Until recently, the company had financed its operations with equity capital, supplemented by bank loans and other current indebtedness.

On August 31, 1999, the company issued $10 million of 20-year 8 1/2 percent first mortgage sinking fund bonds, secured by a specific charge against certain company properties. The bonds were distributed to the public through a group of investment dealers for a fee equalling 2 percent of the par value of the issue. The bonds were sold to the public at 99.

A trust company agreed to act as a trustee under the bond indenture and was also appointed transfer agent and interest-paying agent. The company paid fees totalling $25,000 for legal, audit, printing, and other costs in connection with the issue.

The company's auditor of long standing retired in March of 2000. You were then appointed auditor. You have reviewed the company's accounting system and internal controls but have not yet performed any further audit procedures.

Required

List the audit procedures you should perform in order to form an opinion on the bond indebtedness and interest expense shown in the June 30, 2000, financial statements.

(CICA adapted)

19-35 The controller of Abracadabra Limited has presented Joan Smylowsky, the company's auditor, with the financial statements for the year ended June 30, 1999. The statements include the following statement of contributed surplus and retained earnings for the year.

Abracadabra Limited
Statement of Contributed Surplus and Retained Earnings
For the Year Ended June 30

	1999	1998
Contributed surplus		
Incentive grants (note 4)	$94,200	
Deduct:		
Cost of redemption of preferred shares in excess of their par values	40,000	
Balance at end of year	$54,200	
Retained earnings		
Balance, beginning of year	$1,025,000	$ 950,000
Net income for the year	128,000	105,000
	$1,153,000	$1,085,000
Deduct:		
Dividend on preferred shares	$30,000	$60,000
Extraordinary adjustments to company pension plan (note 5)	73,000	
	$ 103,000	
Balance at end of year	$1,050,000	$1,025,000

Abracadabra Limited
Notes to Financial statements
For the Year Ended June 30, 1999

Note 4

During the year, the company received the following grants from the Government of Canada:

Grant received relating to wage expenses of the year and future year for new jobs created by plant expansion	$44,200
Grant received relating to the acquisition of fixed assets for plant expansion	$50,000

Note 5

During the year, the benefits payable under the company's pension plan were modified. Accordingly, the company made past service payments to the trustees of the plan totalling $53,000.

The consulting actuaries carried out the normal biennial actuarial revaluation which is required by the company's pension plan. Accordingly, the company made payments to the trustees of the plan totalling $20,000.

Required

a. Outline audit procedures that Joan would apply to verify the items presented in the statement of contributed surplus and retained earnings. (Note: Ignore procedures related to "Net income for the year.")

b. Evaluate the financial statement presentation, and comment on alternatives recommended in the CICA Handbook.

(CICA adapted)

19-36 Exxtra Manufacturing Limited (EML) was incorporated by six shareholders seven years ago to manufacture a variety of electronic and mechanical toys. Since incorporation, EML has had a June 30 year end and has been profitable each year except for its first year.

A little over two years ago, several of the senior executives expressed dissatisfaction with the company's profit-sharing plan which provided a bonus based on income before income taxes. In order to retain the senior executives, a "phantom stock plan" (PSP) was devised by the six shareholders to improve management motivation. After considerable discussion among the six shareholders of EML and senior executives, an agreement for the PSP was reached, and the plan went into effect on July 1, 1998.

The accounting firm with which you are employed has been the auditor of EML since its incorporation. As senior on the EML audit, you performed the initial calculation of the book value computation at July 1, 1998, for the PSP. In preparing this calculation, you noted in EML's documentation on the PSP the following:

1. For the initial granting of notional units under the PSP, senior executives were granted units depending on their seniority and position in the company. For both the initial granting and the subsequent yearly June 30 grantings, no cash was or will be paid by the executives receiving the units.

2. Notional units can be sold to the company by the participants in the PSP once per year as of June 30 for cash. Sales by the participants are limited to 10 percent per year of their total holdings, except upon retirement or death when the participants or their heirs must sell 100 percent of the participants' notional units.

3. The prices at which the notional units are sold to the company are based on the June 30 book value per issued common shares according to EML's "financial statements, as presented fairly in accordance with generally accepted accounting principles" except that extraordinary gains and losses occurring after June 30, 1998, are to be excluded from subsequent computations of the book value per issued common shares.

4. The auditor of EML is required to "prepare a special report on the computation of book value per issued common share as of June 30 that gives reasonable assurance that the computation is in accordance with the agreement. Unless otherwise stated, the accounting principles used for the PSP are to be the same principles that have been adopted by EML."

5. One clause states that "accounting policies are to be chosen by the senior executives and approved by the six shareholders of the company. In the event of disagreement between the six shareholders and the senior executives, the auditor will choose the most appropriate policies, giving reasons for his or her choice."

The six shareholders of EML and the senior executives have asked you to prepare a report providing a thorough analysis of all important aspects (excluding tax issues) of the "phantom stock plan" and to recommend changes in the plan. In the same report, they have also asked you to comment on the appropriateness of each of the following accounting treatments for EML's financial statements and for the computation of the book value per issued common share for purposes of the PSP.

1. A new assembly plant was completed in January 1999 and will reach normal production levels in three years. Meanwhile, management of EML suggested the following accounting treatments:
   - Fixed manufacturing overhead is to be estimated in advance, and an absorption rate will be set assuming normal production levels. Any unabsorbed fixed manufacturing overhead at June 30 will be expensed each year.
   - Interest on funds borrowed to finance construction of the plant are to be capitalized in the plant account until normal production levels are reached.
   - Many new employees had to be hired for the new assembly plant and trained in the spring of 1999. Training costs of $100,000 have been deferred and will be amortized on a straight-line basis commencing in July 1999.
   - All manufactured products are to be recorded at standard cost using standards for fully trained employees. Any variances from the standards are to be expensed as they are known. In fiscal year 1999, variances of $28,500 were expensed.

2. A dividend of $200,000 was declared June 25, 1999, to shareholders of record on July 5, 1999, and is to be paid on July 15, 1999. The dividend was debited to retained earnings on June 25, 1999.

3. The company applied for and was awarded a government grant to subsidize construction and to create employment at the new assembly plant. On April 1, 1999, 75 percent of the grant was received as follows:
   - $500,000 towards the construction of the new plant; this amount was credited to contributed surplus;
   - $250,000 towards providing jobs over a three-year period ending April 1, 2003. This amount was credited to a deferred income account and is to be amortized to cost of goods sold on a straight-line basis over five years.

4. In January 1999, management revised its estimate of the remaining useful life of certain assets from eight to twelve years. This change had the effect of reducing amortization expense for the year ended June 30, 1999, by $80,000.

5. In the year ended June 30, 1999, some convertible preferred shares were converted into common shares. The credit to common share capital exceeded the book value of the common shares issued by $235,000.

6. As of July 1, 1998, $780,000 of unfunded past service pension obligation existed. EML paid $750,000 on January 15, 1999, to the administrator of the pension fund to reduce the past service obligation. Management of EML retroactively charged this sum to retained earnings at June 30, 1998, the date of the revision of the plan which gave rise to the past service obligation.

7. In February 1999, a capital loss was realized on the disposition of marketable securities. As a result of inflation, management anticipates that future capital gains will offset this capital loss. Therefore, the income tax benefit of the loss, $150,000, was recorded by debiting deferred income taxes and crediting administrative expense.

8. During 1999, EML commenced self-insurance for accident and theft losses under $100,000. In the year ended June 30, 1999, $92,500 was charged to extraordinary losses for accident and theft.

9. Management spent $1,000 for an appraisal of some unused land that the company had bought several years ago. The appraisal showed that the land had a value $180,000 higher than its cost. Management paid $9,000 to have the land cleared and levelled for future sale. The $180,000 less the $10,000 appraisal and clearing cost was debited to land and credited to appraisal increment.

Required

Prepare the report requested by the six shareholders and the senior executives of Exxtra Manufacturing Limited.

(CICA adapted)

20

AUDIT OF CASH BALANCES

SOCIETY EXPECTS A LOT FROM AUDITORS

Olar Brox was the controller of Ontcan Products Ltd. From 1993 through 1998, Olar paid himself an extra $2 million in "bonuses." He did this by transferring funds from the general account, writing cheques to himself from the payroll account, destroying the cheques when received from the bank, and making entries directly into the company's computer files to disguise the theft. Olar was able to do this because he had almost complete control of the company's accounting process.

Jocelyn Domm of Domm and Graham, a public accounting firm, was the partner on the Ontcan audit. Although Domm found a strong control environment at Ontcan and a good budgeting and reporting system, the company was relatively small and had limited segregation of duties. Accordingly, Domm assessed control risk at maximum and used a "substantive" approach to the audit. Domm applied tests of details of balances and analytical procedures to the year-end financial statements. She did no tests of controls.

Because Olar had lost all of the $2 million and Ontcan had no fidelity bond insurance, the company sued Domm and Graham for the loss, claiming breach of contract. Domm's defence was that she had done the audit in accordance with generally accepted auditing standards.

The trial revolved around the testimony of two expert witnesses. The witness for the company argued that even though the auditors took a substantive approach to the audit, they should have seen that Brox had the opportunity to commit the theft, extended their audit, and found the theft.

The expert for the defence argued that a substantive audit approach is allowed by generally accepted auditing standards. Olar manipulated the records so carefully that the substantive procedures of the various payroll accounts did not indicate that the theft had occurred. Because

The audit of cash balances is the last audit area studied because the evidence accumulated for cash balances depends heavily on the results of the tests in all the various transactions cycles. For example, if the understanding of internal control and audit tests of controls of the acquisition and payment cycle lead the auditor to believe that it is appropriate to assess control risk as low, the auditor can reduce the detailed tests of the ending balance in cash. If, however, the auditor concludes that assessed control risk should be higher, extensive year-end testing will likely be necessary.

TYPES OF CASH ACCOUNTS

It is important to understand the different types of cash accounts because the auditing approach to each varies. The following are the major types of cash accounts.

GENERAL CASH ACCOUNT

OBJECTIVE 20-1

Describe the major types of cash accounts maintained by business entities.

The general account is the focal point of cash for most organizations because virtually all cash receipts and disbursements flow through this account at some time. The disbursements for the acquisition and payment cycle are normally paid from this account, and the receipts of cash in the sales and collection cycle are deposited in the account. In addition, the deposits and disbursements for all other cash accounts are normally made through the general account. Most small companies have only one bank account — the general cash account.

IMPREST PAYROLL ACCOUNT

Some companies, as a means of improving internal control, establish a separate imprest bank account for making payroll payments to employees. In an imprest payroll account, a fixed balance, such as $1,000, is maintained in a separate bank account. Immediately before each pay period, one cheque is drawn on the general cash account to deposit the total amount of the net payroll in the payroll account. After all payroll cheques have cleared the imprest payroll account, the bank account should have a $1,000 balance. The only deposits into the account are of the periodic weekly (or semi-monthly) payroll, and the only disbursements are payments to employees. For companies with many employees, the use of an imprest payroll account can improve internal control and reduce the time needed to reconcile bank accounts.

BRANCH BANK ACCOUNT

For a company operating in multiple locations, it is frequently desirable to have a separate bank balance at each location. Branch bank accounts are useful for building public relations in local communities and permitting the decentralization of operations to the branch level.

In some companies, the deposits and disbursements for each branch are made to a particular bank account, and the excess cash is periodically sent to the main office general bank account. The branch account in this instance is much like a general account, but at the branch level.

A somewhat different type of branch account consists of one bank account for receipts and a separate one for disbursements. All receipts are deposited in the branch bank, and the total is transferred to the general account periodically. The disbursement account is set up on an *imprest basis* but in a different manner from an imprest payroll account. A fixed balance is maintained in the imprest account, and the authorized branch personnel use these funds for disbursements at their own discretion as long as the payments are consistent with company policy. When the cash balance has been depleted, an accounting is made to the home office and a reimbursement is made to the branch account from the general account *after* the expenditures have been approved. The use of an imprest branch bank account improves controls over receipts and disbursements.

IMPREST PETTY CASH FUND

A petty cash fund is actually not a bank account, but it is sufficiently similar to cash on deposit to merit inclusion in this section. It is used for small cash purchases that can be paid more conveniently and quickly by cash than by cheque. An imprest cash account is set up on the same basis as an imprest branch bank account, but the expenditures are normally for a much smaller amount. Typical expenses include minor office supplies, stamps, and small contributions to local charities. Usually a petty cash account does not exceed a few hundred dollars and may not be reimbursed more than once or twice each month.

CASH EQUIVALENTS

Excess cash accumulated during certain parts of the operating cycle that will be needed in the reasonably near future is often invested in short-term, highly liquid cash equivalents. Examples include term deposits, certificates of deposit, and money market funds. Cash equivalents, which can be highly material, are included in the financial statements as part of the cash account only if they are short-term investments that are readily convertible to known amounts of cash within a short time and there is little risk of a change in value from interest rate changes. Marketable securities and longer-term interest-bearing investments are not cash equivalents.

SUMMARY

Figure 20-1 on page 642 shows the relationship of general cash to the other cash accounts. All cash either originates from or is deposited in general cash. This chapter focuses on three types of accounts: the general cash account, the imprest payroll bank account, and the imprest petty cash fund. The others are similar to these and need not be discussed.

CASH IN THE BANK AND TRANSACTION CYCLES

OBJECTIVE 20-2

Describe the relationship of cash in the bank to the various transaction cycles.

A brief discussion of the relationship between cash in the bank and the other transaction cycles serves a dual function: it highlights the importance of the tests of various transaction cycles to the audit of cash, and it aids in further understanding the integration of the different transaction cycles. Figure 20-2 on page 643 illustrates the relationships of the various transaction cycles, the focal point being the general cash account.

An examination of Figure 20-2 on page 643 indicates why the general cash account is considered significant in almost all audits, even when the ending balance is immaterial. The amount of cash *flowing* into and out of the cash account is frequently larger than for any other account in the financial statements. Furthermore, the susceptibility of cash to defalcation is greater than for other types of assets because most other assets must be converted to cash to make them usable.

FIGURE 20-1

Relationship of General
Cash to Other Cash
Accounts

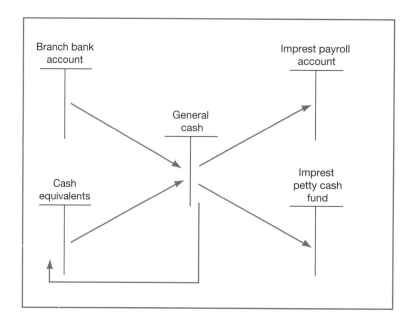

In the audit of cash, an important distinction should be made between verifying the client's reconciliation of the balance on the bank statement to the balance in the general ledger and verifying whether recorded cash in the general ledger correctly reflects all cash transactions that took place during the year. It is relatively easy to verify the client's reconciliation of the balance in the bank account to the general ledger, which is the primary subject of this chapter, but a significant part of the total audit of a company involves verifying whether cash transactions are properly recorded. For example, each of the following misstatements ultimately results in the improper payment of or the failure to receive cash, but none will normally be discovered as a part of the audit of the bank reconciliation:

- Failure to bill a customer.
- Billing a customer at a lower price than called for by company policy.
- A defalcation of cash by interception of collections from customers before they are recorded. The account receivable is charged off as a bad debt.
- Duplicate payment of a vendor's invoice.
- Improper payments of officers' personal expenditures.
- Payment for raw materials that were not received.
- Payment to an employee for more hours than he or she worked.
- Payment of interest to a related party for an amount in excess of the going rate.

If these misstatements are to be uncovered in the audit, their discovery must come about through the tests of controls that were discussed in the preceding chapters. The first three misstatements could be discovered as part of the audit of the sales and collection cycle, the next three in the audit of the acquisitions and payment cycle, and the last two in the tests of the payroll and personnel cycle and the capital acquisition and repayment cycle, respectively.

Entirely different types of misstatements are normally discovered as part of the tests of a bank reconciliation. For example,

- Failure to include a cheque that has not cleared the bank on the outstanding cheque list, even though it has been recorded in the cash disbursements journal
- Cash received by the client subsequent to the balance sheet date but recorded as cash receipts in the current year
- Deposits recorded as cash receipts near the end of the year, deposited in the bank, and included in the bank reconciliation as a deposit in transit

FIGURE 20-2
Relationships of Cash in the Bank and Transaction Cycles

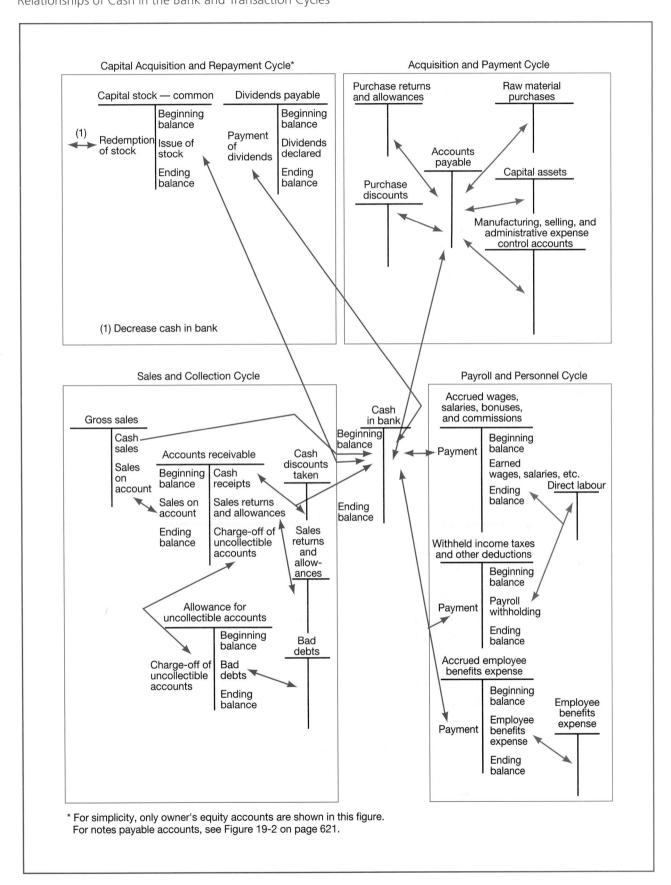

* For simplicity, only owner's equity accounts are shown in this figure.
  For notes payable accounts, see Figure 19-2 on page 621.

- Payments on notes payable that were debited directly to the bank balance by the bank but were not entered in the client's records

The appropriate methods for discovering the preceding misstatements by testing the client's bank reconciliation will become apparent as we proceed. At this point, it is important only that the reader distinguish between tests of controls that are related to the cash account and tests that determine whether the book balance reconciles to the bank balance.

AUDIT OF THE GENERAL CASH ACCOUNT

OBJECTIVE 20-3

Design and perform the audit tests of the general cash account.

On the trial balance of Hillsburg Hardware Ltd., on page 128, there is only one cash account. Notice, however, that all cycles, except inventory and warehousing, affect cash in the bank.

In testing the year-end balance in the general cash account, the auditor must accumulate sufficient evidence to evaluate whether cash, as stated on the balance sheet, is fairly stated and properly disclosed in accordance with six of the nine balance-related audit objectives used for all tests of details of balances. Rights to general cash, its classification on the balance sheet, and the realizable value of cash are not a problem.

The methodology for auditing year-end cash is essentially the same as for all other balance sheet accounts. This methodology is shown in Figure 20-3.

INTERNAL CONTROLS

Internal controls over the year-end cash balances in the general account can be divided into two categories: *controls over the transaction cycles* affecting the recording of cash receipts and disbursements and *independent bank reconciliations*.

FIGURE 20-3
Methodology for Designing Tests of Details of Balances for Cash in the Bank

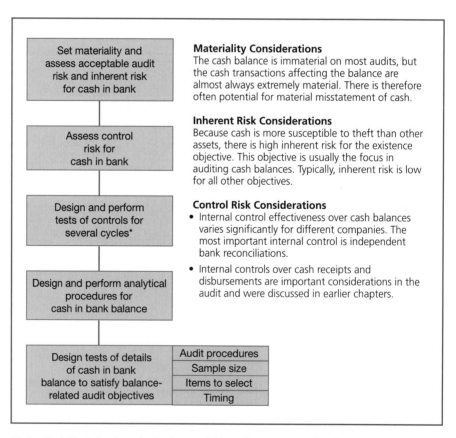

*Cycles affected include sales and collection, acquisition and payment, payroll and personnel, and capital acquisition and repayment.

Controls affecting the recording of cash transactions have been discussed in preceding chapters. For example, in the acquisition and payment cycle, major controls include the adequate segregation of duties between the cheque signing and the accounts payable functions, the signing of cheques by only a properly authorized person, the use of prenumbered cheques that are printed on special paper, adequate control of blank and voided cheques, careful review of supporting documentation by the cheque signer before cheques are signed, and adequate internal verification. If the controls affecting cash-related transactions are adequate, it is possible to reduce the audit tests of the year-end bank reconciliation.

A monthly *bank reconciliation* of the general bank account on a timely basis by someone independent of the handling or recording of cash receipts and disbursements is an essential control over the cash balance. The reconciliation is important to ensure that the books reflect the same cash balance as the actual amount of cash in the bank after consideration of reconciling items, but even more important, the *independent* reconciliation provides a unique opportunity for an internal verification of cash receipts and disbursements transactions. If the bank statements are received unopened by the reconciler and physical control is maintained over the statements until the reconciliations are complete, the cancelled cheques, duplicate deposit slips, and other documents included in the statement can be examined without concern for the possibility of alteration, deletions, or additions. A careful bank reconciliation by competent client personnel includes the following:

- Compare cancelled cheques with the cash disbursements journal for date, payee, and amount.
- Examine cancelled cheques for signature, endorsements, and cancellation.
- Compare deposits in the bank with recorded cash receipts for date, customer, and amount.
- Account for the numerical sequence of cheques, and investigate missing ones.
- Reconcile all items causing a difference between the book and bank balance, and verify their propriety.
- Reconcile total debits on the bank statement with the totals in the cash disbursements journal.
- Reconcile total credits on the bank statement with the totals in the cash receipts journal.
- Review month-end interbank transfers for propriety and proper recording.
- Follow up on outstanding cheques and stop-payment notices.

The first four of these internal procedures are directly related to the tests of controls that were discussed in previous chapters. The last five are directly related to the reconciliation of the book and bank balance and are discussed in greater detail later.

Because of the importance of monthly reconciliation of bank accounts, another common control for many companies is having a responsible employee review the monthly reconciliation as soon as possible after its completion.

ANALYTICAL PROCEDURES

In many audits, the year-end bank reconciliation is verified on a 100 percent basis. Testing the reasonableness of the cash balance is therefore less important than for most other audit areas.

It is common for auditors to compare the ending balance on the bank reconciliation, deposits in transit, outstanding cheques, and other reconciling items with the prior-year reconciliation. Similarly, auditors normally compare the ending balance in cash with previous months' balances. These analytical procedures may uncover misstatements in cash.

AUDIT PROCEDURES FOR YEAR-END CASH

A major consideration in the audit of the general cash balance is the possibility of fraud. The auditor must extend his or her procedures in the audit of year-end cash to determine the possibility of a material fraud when there are inadequate internal controls, especially the improper segregation of duties between the handling of cash and the recording of cash transactions in the journals. The study of cash in the following section assumes the existence of adequate controls over cash; therefore, fraud detection is not emphasized. At the completion of study of typical audit procedures for the verification of year-end cash, procedures designed primarily for the detection of fraud are discussed.

The starting point for the verification of the balance in the general bank account is obtaining a bank reconciliation from the client for inclusion in the auditor's working papers. Figure 20-4 shows a bank reconciliation after adjustments. Notice that the bottom figure in the working paper is the adjusted balance in the general ledger.

FIGURE 20-4

Working Paper for a Bank Reconciliation

Kao Foods Inc.			Schedule A-2 Date	
Bank Reconciliation			Prepared by DED 10/1/99	
31/12/98			Approved by SW 18/1/99	

Acct. 101 - General account—Bank of Columbia

Balance per Bank			109,713	A-2/1
Add:				
Deposits in transit ①				
30/12		10,017		
31/12		11,100	21,117	
Deduct				
Outstanding cheques ①				
#7993	16/12	3,068		
8007	16/12	9,763		
8012	23/12	11,916		
8013	23/12	14,717		
8029	24/12	37,998		
8038	30/12	10,000	(87,462)	
Other reconciling items: Bank error				
Deposit to payroll account credited				
to General account by bank, in error			(15,200)	A-3
Balance per bank, adjusted			28,168	T/B
			⋁	
Balance per books before adjustments			32,584	A-1
Adjustments:				
Unrecorded bank service charge		216		A-3
Non-sufficient funds cheque				
returned by bank, not collectible				
from customer		4,200	(4,416)	C-3/1
Balance per books, adjusted			28,168	A-1
			⋁	

① Cutoff bank statement procedures completed by DED   10/1/99

② Cutoff bank statement enclosures returned to client,
    acknowledged by M Smith   12/1/99

⋁ Footed

Although the bank reconciliation is normally prepared manually, or using a spreadsheet, many accounting systems allow the client to use computerized systems to prepare the list of outstanding cheques.

The frame of reference for the audit tests is the bank reconciliation. The balance-related audit objectives and common tests of details of balances are shown in Table 20-1. As in all other audit areas, the actual audit procedures depend on the considerations discussed in previous chapters. Also, because of their close relationship in the audit of year-end cash, the existence of recorded cash in the bank, accuracy, and inclusion of existing cash (completeness) are combined. These three objectives are the most important ones for cash and therefore receive the greatest attention.

The following three procedures are discussed thoroughly because of their importance and complexity.

Receipt of a bank confirmation   The direct receipt of a confirmation from every bank or other financial institution with which the client does business is necessary for every audit except when there are an unusually large number of inactive accounts. If

TABLE 20-1

BALANCE-RELATED AUDIT OBJECTIVES AND TESTS OF DETAILS OF BALANCES FOR GENERAL CASH IN THE BANK

BALANCE-RELATED AUDIT OBJECTIVE	COMMON TESTS OF DETAILS OF BALANCES PROCEDURES	COMMENTS
Cash in the bank as stated on the bank reconciliation foots correctly and agrees with the general ledger (detail tie-in).	Foot the outstanding cheque list and deposits in transit. Prove the bank reconciliation as to additions and subtractions, including all reconciling items. Trace the book balance on the reconciliation to the general ledger.	These tests are done entirely on the bank reconciliation, with no reference to documents or other records except the general ledger.
Cash in the bank as stated on the reconciliation exists (existence). Existing cash in the bank is included (completeness). Cash in the bank as stated on the reconciliation is accurate (accuracy).	(See extended discussion for each of these.) Obtain and test a bank confirmation. Obtain and test a cutoff bank statement. Test the bank reconciliation. Perform extended tests of the bank reconciliation. Prepare proof of cash. Test for kiting.	The first three procedures are the most important objectives for cash in the bank. The procedures are combined because of their close interdependence. The last three procedures should be done only when there are internal control weaknesses.
Cash receipts and cash disbursements transactions are recorded in the proper period (cutoff).	*Cash receipts* Count the cash on hand on the first day of the year and subsequently trace to deposits in transit and the cash receipts journal. Trace deposits in transit to subsequent period bank statement (cutoff bank statement). *Cash disbursements* Record the last cheque number used on the last day of the year and subsequently trace to the outstanding cheques and the cash disbursements journal. Trace outstanding cheques to subsequent period bank statement.	When cash receipts received after year end are included in the journal, a better cash position than actually exists is shown. It is called "holding open" the cash receipts journal. Holding open the cash disbursements journal reduces accounts payable and usually overstates the current ratio. The first procedure listed for receipts and disbursement cutoff tests requires the auditor's presence on the client's premises at the end of the last day of the year.
Cash in the bank is properly presented and disclosed (presentation and disclosure).	Examine minutes, loan agreements, and obtain confirmation for restrictions on the use of cash and compensating balances. Review financial statements to make sure (a) material savings accounts and guaranteed investment certificates, if access is restricted, are disclosed separately from cash in the bank, (b) cash restricted to certain uses and compensating balances are adequately disclosed, and (c) bank overdrafts are included as current liabilities.	An example of a restriction on the use of cash is cash deposited with a trustee for the payment of mortgage interest and taxes on the proceeds of a construction mortgage. A compensating balance is the client's agreement with a bank to maintain a specified minimum in its chequing account.

the bank does not respond to a confirmation request, the auditor must send a second request or ask the client to telephone the bank. As a convenience to CAs as well as to bankers who are requested to fill out bank confirmations, the CICA has approved the use of a *standard bank confirmation* form. Figure 20-5 is an illustration of such a completed standard bank confirmation. As shown in Figure 20-5, it is referred to as a *bank confirmation*. This standard form has been agreed upon by the CICA and the Canadian Banker's Association. Similarly, CGAAC and the Canadian Banker's Association have approved a similar bank confirmation form for use by CGAs.

The importance of bank confirmations in the audit extends beyond the verification of the actual cash balance. It is typical for the bank to confirm loan information and bank balances on the same form. The confirmation in Figure 20-5 includes three outstanding loans and a contingent liability. Information on liabilities to the bank for notes, mortgages, or other debt typically includes the amount of the loan, the date of the loan, its due date, interest rate, and the existence of collateral.

The auditor completes the sections labelled "client," "chartered accountant," "financial institution," and "confirmation date"; a signing officer from the client signs in the "client" box authorizing the bank to provide the information; and the auditor sends the confirmation to the bank. While the bank should exercise due care in completing the confirmation, errors can occur. The auditor may wish to communicate with the bank if there is any information on the returned confirmation about which he or she is dubious or if any information that was expected is not reported.

After the bank confirmation has been received, the balance in the bank account confirmed by the bank should be traced to the amount stated on the bank reconciliation. Similarly, all other information on the reconciliation should be traced to the relevant audit working papers. In any case, if the information is not in agreement, an investigation must be made of the difference.

Receipt of a cutoff bank statement   A *cutoff bank statement* includes a partial-period bank statement and the related cancelled cheques, duplicate deposit slips, and other documents included with bank statements, mailed by the bank directly to the public accounting firm's office. The purpose of the cutoff bank statement is to verify the reconciling items on the client's year-end bank reconciliation with evidence that is inaccessible to the client. To fulfill this purpose, the auditor requests that the client have the bank send directly to the auditor the statement for seven to ten days subsequent to the balance sheet date.

Many auditors prove the subsequent period bank statement if a cutoff statement is not received directly from the bank. The purpose of this proof is to test whether the client's employees have omitted, added, or altered any of the documents accompanying the statement. It is obviously a test for intentional misstatements. The auditor performs the proof in the month subsequent to the balance sheet date by (1) footing all the cancelled cheques, debit memos, deposits, and credit memos; (2) checking to see that the bank statement balances when the footed totals are used; and (3) reviewing the items included in the footings to make sure they were cancelled by the bank in the proper period and do not include any erasures or alterations.

Tests of the bank reconciliation   The reason for testing the bank reconciliation is to verify whether the client's recorded bank balance is the same amount as the actual cash in the bank except for deposits in transit, outstanding cheques, and other reconciling items. In testing the reconciliation, the cutoff bank statement provides the information for conducting the tests. Several major procedures are involved:

- Verify that the client's bank reconciliation is mathematically accurate.
- Trace the balance on the cutoff statement to the balance per bank on the bank reconciliation. A reconciliation cannot take place until these two are the same.
- Trace cheques included with the cutoff bank statement to the list of outstanding cheques on the bank reconciliation and to the cash disbursements journal. All

BANK CONFIRMATION

(Areas to be completed by client are marked §, while those to be completed by the financial institutions are marked †)

FINANCIAL INSTITUTION	CLIENT (Legal Name) §
(Name, branch, and full mailing address) §	Koa Foods Inc.
Bank of Columbia	St. Jacobs, Ontario
Westmount & Old Post Road	NOL 1KO
Waterloo, Ontario	The financial institution is authorized to provide the provide the details requested herein to the below-noted firm of accountants
L2L 5M1	§ *J Koa*
	Client's authorized signature
CONFIRMATION DATE § December 31, 1998	Please supply copy of the most recent credit facility agreement
(All information to be provided as of this date)	(initial if required) § _____
(See Bank Confirmation Completition Instructions)	

1. LOANS AND OTHER DIRECT AND CONTIGENT LIABILITIES (If balances are nil, please state.)

NATURE OF LIABILITY/ CONTINGENT LIABILITY †	INTEREST (Note rate per contract) RATE † DATE PAID TO †		DUE DATE †	DATE OF CREDIT FACILITY AGREEMENT †	AMOUNT AND CURRENCY OUTSTANDING †
Loan	8%	31/12/98	Demand	5/5/96	$90,000
Loan	9%	30/11/98	30/5/03	30/5/95	$120,000
Loan	10%	31/12/98	Demand	1/6/97	$20,000
Guarantee	N/A		N/A	1/1/90	$8,000

ADDITIONAL CREDIT FACILITY AGREEMENT(S)

Note the date(s) of any credit facility agreement(s) not drawn upon and not referenced above †

2. DEPOSITS/OVERDRAFTS

TYPE OF ACCONUT §	ACCOUNT NUMBER §	INTEREST RATE §	ISSUE DATE (if applicable) §	MATURITY DATE (if applicable) §	AMOUNT AND CURRENCY (Bracket if Overdraft) †
General	65422	—	—	—	$109,713
Payroll	65432	—	—	—	$4,000

EXCEPTIONS AND COMMENTS
(See Bank Confirmation Completion Instructions) †

STATEMENT OF PROCEDURES PERFORMED BY FINANCIAL INSTITUTION †
The above information was completed in accordance with the Bank Confirmation Completion Instructions.

Bill Brown
Authorized signature of financial institution

Branch Contact ___W. Brown   884-1921___
Name and telephone number

Please mail this form directly to our chartered accountant in the enclosed addressed envelope.

Name:	Kadous & Co.
Address:	P.O. Box 1939
	Waterloo, Ontario N2L 1G1
Telephone:	(905) 999-1234
Fax:	(905) 999-1235

Developed by the Canadian Bankers Association and the Canadian Institute of Chartered Accountants cheques that cleared the bank after the balance sheet date and were included in the cash disbursements journal should also be included on the outstanding cheque list. If a cheque was included in the cash disbursements journal, it should be included as an outstanding cheque if it did not clear before the balance sheet date. Similarly, if a cheque cleared the bank prior to the balance sheet date, it should not be on the bank reconciliation.

- Investigate all significant cheques included on the outstanding cheque list that have not cleared the bank on the cutoff statement. The first step in the investigation should be tracing the amount of any items not clearing to the cash disbursements journal. The reason for the cheque not being cashed should be discussed with the client, and if the auditor is concerned about the possibility of fraud, the vendor's accounts payable balance should be confirmed to determine whether the vendor has recognized the receipt of the cash in its records. In addition, the cancelled cheque should be examined prior to the last day of the audit if it becomes available.

- Trace deposits in transit to the subsequent bank statement. All cash receipts not deposited in the bank at the end of the year should be traced to the cutoff bank statement to ensure they were deposited shortly after the beginning of the new year.

- Account for other reconciling items on the bank statement and bank reconciliation. These include such items as bank service charges, bank errors and corrections, and unrecorded note transactions debited or credited directly to the bank account by the bank. These reconciling items should be carefully investigated to ensure they have been treated properly by the client.

SUMMARY OF AUDIT TESTS FOR THE GENERAL CASH ACCOUNT

Figure 20-6 illustrates the types of audit tests used to audit the general cash account. This figure also shows how the audit risk model discussed in Chapter 8 relates to the audit of the general cash account.

FIGURE 20-6

Types of Audit Tests Used for General Cash

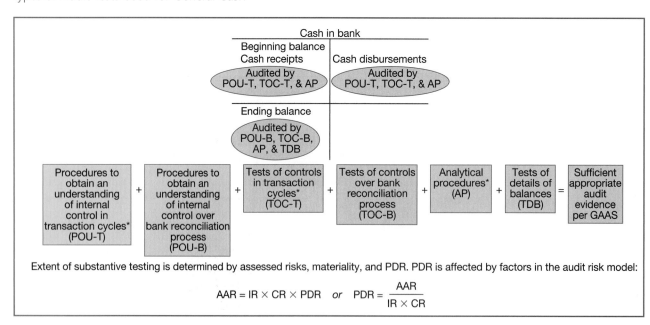

* Procedures to obtain an understanding of internal control, tests of controls in transaction cycles, and analytical procedures are done for the four transaction cycles included in Figure 20-2. The primary tests of the ending cash balance are tests of details of balances.

It is frequently necessary for auditors to extend their year-end audit procedures to test more extensively for the possibility of material fraud when there are material internal control weaknesses. Many fraudulent activities are difficult, if not impossible, to uncover; nevertheless, auditors are responsible for making a reasonable effort to detect fraud when they have reason to believe it may exist. The following procedures for uncovering fraud are discussed in this section: extended tests of the bank reconciliation, proofs of cash, and tests for kiting.

Extended tests of the bank reconciliation   When the auditor believes that the year-end bank reconciliation may be intentionally misstated, it is appropriate to perform extended tests of the year-end bank reconciliation. The purpose of the extended procedures is to verify whether all transactions included in the journals for the last month of the year were correctly included in or excluded from the bank reconciliation and to verify whether all items in the bank reconciliation were correctly included. Let us assume that there are material internal control weaknesses and that the client's year end is December 31. A common approach is to start with the bank reconciliation for November and compare all reconciling items with cancelled cheques and other documents in the December bank statement. In addition, all remaining cancelled cheques and deposit slips in the December bank statement should be compared with the December cash disbursements and receipts journals. All uncleared items in the November bank reconciliation and the December cash disbursements and receipts journals should be included in the client's December 31 bank reconciliation. Similarly, all reconciling items in the December 31 bank reconciliation should be items from the November bank reconciliation and December's journals that have not yet cleared the bank.

In addition to the tests just described, the auditor must also carry out procedures subsequent to the end of the year using the bank cutoff statement. These tests would be performed in the same manner as previously discussed.

Proof of cash   Auditors sometimes prepare a proof of cash when the client has material internal control weaknesses in cash. A proof of cash includes the following:

- A reconciliation of the balance on the bank statement with the general ledger balance at the beginning of the proof-of-cash period
- A reconciliation of cash receipts deposited with the cash receipts journal for a given period
- A reconciliation of cancelled cheques clearing the bank with the cash disbursements journal for a given period
- A reconciliation of the balance on the bank statement with the general ledger balance at the end of the proof-of-cash period

A proof of cash of this nature is commonly referred to as a four-column proof of cash — one column is used for each type of information listed above. A proof of cash can be performed for one or more interim months, the entire year, or the last month of the year. Figure 20-7 shows a four-column proof of cash for an interim month.

The auditor uses a proof of cash to determine whether

- All recorded cash receipts were deposited.
- All deposits in the bank were recorded in the accounting records.
- All recorded cash disbursements were paid by the bank.
- All amounts that were paid by the bank were recorded.

The concern in an interim-month proof of cash is not with adjusting account balances, but rather with reconciling the amounts per books and bank.

When the auditor does a proof of cash, he or she is combining tests of controls and tests of details of balances. For example, the proof of the cash receipts is a test of recorded transactions, whereas the bank reconciliation is a test of the balance in cash at a particular time. The proof of cash is an excellent method of comparing recorded

FIGURE 20-7

Interim Proof of Cash

R. Mathieu, Inc.

Interim Proof of Cash

31/12/98

Schedule_____ Date_____
Prepared by _DJ_ 15/7/98
Approved by _MT_ 17/7/98

Acct. 101-General account, Bank of Waterloo

		31/5/98	Receipts	Disbursements	30/6/98
Balance per Bank	①	121782.12	627895.20	631111.96	118565.36
Deposits in transit					
31/5	②	21720.00	<21720.00>		
30/6	②		16592.36		16592.36
Outstanding cheques					
31/5	③	36396.50		<36396.50>	
30/6	③			14800.10	<14800.10>
NSF cheques	④		<4560.00>	<4560.00>	
To allow for effect of a cash disbursement recorded as a credit item in Cash Receipts Journal			8500.00	8500.00	
Balance per books, adjusted		107105.62	626707.56	613455.56	120357.62
Balance per books, unadjusted		107105.62	626707.56	614957.04	118856.14
Bank debit memos	⑤			120.00	<120.00>
Payroll cheques erroneously entered in General Disbursements Journal	⑥			<1621.48>	1621.48
Balance per books, adjusted		107105.62	626707.56	613455.56	120357.62

① Per 30/6/98 bank statement
② Detailed listing filed below; traced to subsequent bank statements.
③ Outstanding-cheques list filed below: examined cancelled cheques.
④ Detailed listing filed below; all NSF items were deposited and had cleared as of 15/7/98.
⑤ Safety deposit rentals; traced to recording via journal entry. Requested list of contents of safety deposit boxes.
⑥ Traced to journal entry correcting error.

cash receipts and disbursements with the bank account and with the bank reconciliation. However, the auditor must recognize that the proof of cash disbursements is not for discovering cheques written for an improper amount, fraudulent cheques, or other misstatements in which the dollar amount appearing on the cash disbursements records is incorrect. Similarly, the proof of cash receipts is not useful for uncovering the theft of cash receipts or the recording and deposit of an improper amount of cash.

Tests for kiting Embezzlers occasionally cover a defalcation of cash by a practice known as *kiting*: transferring money from one bank to another and improperly recording the transaction. Near the balance sheet date, a cheque is drawn on one bank account and immediately deposited in a second account for credit before the end of the accounting period. In making this transfer, the embezzler is careful to make sure that the cheque is deposited at a late enough date so that it does not clear the first bank until after the end of the period. Assuming that the bank transfer is not recorded until after the balance sheet date, the amount of the transfer is recorded as an asset in both banks. Although there are other ways of perpetrating this fraud, each involves the basic device of increasing the bank balance to cover a shortage by the use of bank transfers.

A useful approach to test for kiting, as well as for unintentional errors in recording bank transfers, is listing all bank transfers made a few days before and after the balance sheet date and tracing each to the accounting records for proper recording. An example of a bank transfer schedule is included in Figure 20-8. The working paper shows that there were four bank transfers shortly before and after the balance sheet date.

There are several things that should be audited on the bank transfer schedule.

- *The accuracy of the information on the bank transfer schedule should be verified.* The auditor should compare the disbursement and receipt information on the schedule to the cash disbursements and cash receipts journals to make sure that it is accurate. Similarly, the dates on the schedule for transfers that were received and disbursed should be compared to the bank statement. Finally, cash disbursements and receipts journals should be examined to ensure that all transfers a few days before and after the balance sheet date have been included on the schedule. The tick mark explanations on the working paper in Figure 20-8 indicate that these steps have been taken.
- *The bank transfers must be recorded in both the receiving and disbursing banks.* If, for example, there was a $10,000 transfer from Bank A to Bank B, but only the disbursement was recorded, this would be evidence of an attempt to conceal a cash theft.

FIGURE 20-8
Bank Transfer Working Paper

			R. Mathieu, Inc.		Schedule	A-7 Date	
			Schedule of Bank Transfers		Prepared by	DED 10/1/99	
			December 31, 1998		Reviewed by	SW 18/1/99	

| | | | Disbursements | | | Receipts | |
Cheque No. (1)	Bank (2)	Amount (3)	Date Recorded in Books (4)	Date Paid by Bank (5)	Bank (6)	Date Recorded in Books (7)	Date Received by Bank (8)
2609	Waterloo	20,642 ✓	26-12-98	28-12-98 ❑	Huron Bank	28-12-98 ∅	28-12-98 ❑∅
2910	Waterloo	12,000 ✓	28-12-98 ✗	02-01-99 ❑	Federal Trust	30-12-98 ∅	31-12-98 ❑∅
2741	Waterloo	10,000 ✓	31-12-98 ✗	04-01-99 ❑	Federal Trust	31-12-98 ∅	02-01-99 ❑Ⓝ
2762	Waterloo	23,721 ✓	03-01-99 ⊗	05-01-99 ❑	Huron Bank	04-01-99 ∅	05-01-99 ❑∅

✓   Traced to cash disbursements journal
∅   Traced to cash receipts journal
✗   Cheque included as outstanding on bank reconciliation
⊗   Cheque not included as outstanding on bank reconciliation
Ⓝ   Receipt included as a deposit in transit
❑   Traced to bank statement
∅   Receipt not included as a deposit in transit

Note: Examined cash disbursements and cash receipts journals for cheques to and deposits from bank accounts. None included except those listed above

- *The date of the recording of the disbursements and receipts for each transfer must be in the same fiscal year.* In Figure 20-8, the dates in the two "date recorded in books" columns [columns (4) and (7)] are in the same period for each transfer; therefore, they are correct. If a cash disbursement was recorded in the current fiscal year and the receipt in the subsequent fiscal year, it might be an attempt to cover a cash shortage.
- *Disbursements on the bank transfer schedule should be correctly included in or excluded from year-end bank reconciliations as outstanding cheques.* In Figure 20-8, the 31-12-98 bank reconciliation should include outstanding cheques for the second and third transfers but not the other two. [Compare the dates in columns (4) and (5).] Understating outstanding cheques on the bank reconciliation indicates the possibility of kiting.
- *Receipts on the bank transfer schedule should be correctly included in or excluded from year-end bank reconciliations as deposits in transit.* In Figure 20-8, the 31-12-98 bank reconciliation should indicate a deposit in transit for the third transfer but not for the other three. (Compare the dates for each transfer in the last two columns.) Overstating deposits in transit on the bank reconciliation indicates the possibility of kiting.

Even though audit tests of bank transfers are usually fraud-oriented, they are often performed on audits in which there are numerous bank transfers, regardless of the internal controls. When there are numerous intercompany transfers, it is difficult to be sure that each is correctly handled unless a schedule of transfers near the end of the year is prepared and each transfer is traced to the accounting records and bank statements. In addition to the possibility of kiting, inaccurate handling of transfers could result in a misclassification between cash and accounts payable. Due to the materiality of transfers and the relative ease of performing the tests, many auditors believe that the tests should always be performed.

Summary of fraud-oriented procedures   In designing audit procedures for uncovering fraud, careful consideration should be given to the nature of the weaknesses in internal control, the type of fraud that is likely to result from the weaknesses, the potential materiality of the fraud, and the audit procedures that are most effective in uncovering the misstatement. When auditors are specifically testing for fraud, they should keep in mind that audit procedures other than tests of details of cash balances may also be useful. Examples of procedures that may uncover fraud in the cash receipts area include the confirmation of accounts receivable, tests for lapping, reviewing the general ledger entries in the cash account for unusual items, tracing from customer orders to sales and subsequent cash receipts, and examining approvals and supporting documentation for bad debts and sales returns and allowances. Similar tests can be used for testing for the possibility of fraudulent cash disbursements.

AUDIT OF THE PAYROLL BANK ACCOUNT

OBJECTIVE 20-5

Design and perform the audit tests of the payroll bank account.

Tests of the payroll bank reconciliation should take only a few minutes if there is an imprest payroll account and an independent reconciliation of the bank account such as that described for the general account. Typically, the only reconciling items are outstanding cheques, and, for most audits, the great majority clear shortly after the cheques are issued. In testing the payroll bank account balances, it is necessary to obtain a bank reconciliation, a bank confirmation, and a cutoff bank statement. The reconciliation procedures are performed in the same manner as those described for general cash. Naturally, extended procedures are necessary if the controls are inadequate or if the bank account does not reconcile with the general ledger imprest cash balance.

The discussion in the preceding paragraph should not be interpreted as implying that the audit of payroll is unimportant. A review of Chapter 15 should remind the reader that the most important audit procedures for verifying payroll are tests of controls. The most likely payroll misstatements will be discovered by those procedures rather than by checking the imprest bank account balance.

ELECTRONIC FUNDS TRANSFER

Many organizations use electronic funds transfers when they are transferring cash among banks, collecting from customers, paying employees, and paying vendors. Under these systems, cash is transferred instantly. For example, when Company A collects from Customer X, the cash is instantly transferred from Customer X's bank account to Company A's. No cheque is issued.

Electronic funds transfers have the potential to improve internal controls in that no cash is handled by employees. There is also potential risk of cash thefts through inappropriate cash transfers. It is essential that excellent internal controls be in place for electronic funds transfers.

AUDIT OF ELECTRONIC CASH TRANSACTIONS

As described in the focus box, many organizations are receiving cash or making cash payments electronically. For a typical small to medium-sized business, electronic cash receipts are used if the business sells to customers over the counter and accepts debit card payments from those customers. Electronic cash payments include automatic payments for loans, insurance, or payroll to employees. More sophisticated or larger businesses could use electronic data interchange (EDI) with their electronic funds transfers (EFTs), as discussed further in Chapter 22.

CONTROL OVER DEBIT CARD CASH RECEIPTS

When a business accepts debit card payments from its customers, the customer swipes his or her debit card and enters a personal identification number (PIN) to authorize the transfer of funds from the customer's bank account to the organization's bank account. At the same time, a two-part receipt is provided, with one copy going to the customer and the other to the organization.

OBJECTIVE 20-6

Describe the impact of electronic funds transfers on the audit of cash.

Although most debit card transactions are processed accurately, a very small percentage are not. The organization should therefore continue its cash reconciliation functions as part of the bank reconciliation for these electronic transactions. Most organizations keep track of payment methods automatically using their point-of-sale (POS) systems. Thus, the daily sales are broken down by cash, debit card, credit card, cheque, and accounts receivable. When performing the bank reconciliation, the debit card total should agree to the amounts automatically deposited in the bank statement. This reconciliation should be handled by a person independent of the POS function. These receipts should be tested as part of the sales, receivables transaction cycle.

CONTROL OVER ELECTRONIC PAYMENTS

Automatic pre-authorized monthly payments   Loan payments, interest payments, and insurance payments made on a monthly or other regular interval are based on a loan agreement or regular invoice. When the bank statement is sent to an organization, likely the only evidence of this payment will be a line on the bank statement showing the amount, a reference number, and possibly the name of the company that was paid.

The organization under audit should have controls to ensure that only authorized amounts are set up for payment, and that all automatic withdrawals are recorded in the accounts in the period made. These payments should be tested as part of the purchases, payments cycle.

Payroll payments As with a payroll paid by cheque, payroll payments made electronically should be paid using an imprest bank account.

Payment is usually initiated by the organization sending to the bank or other financial institution a set of forms or electronic data files specifying how much employees should be paid, what deductions should be made, the appropriate withholdings, and the bank accounts to which the funds should be transferred. The bank may (or may not) do the actual calculations, process payments, and send either a listing or a data file to the organization of payments made.

Again, there is a two-step authorization phase here. The first step covers master file information (i.e., wage rate, withholdings rates, bank account number, etc.), and the second covers the actual wages paid in a specific pay period. These controls should be documented, evaluated, and tested as part of the personnel and payroll cycle. As part of control over cash, a person independent of payroll should verify bank account numbers used for payments and should verify that payments from the imprest bank account match the payroll journal.

AUDIT OF ELECTRONIC RECEIPTS AND PAYMENTS

The extent of audit work conducted on the bank reconciliation depends on the assessed quality of internal controls. There are usually fewer outstanding bank transactions for electronic transactions than for paper transactions sent via mail since the timing difference between invoice and receipt is minimal.

When client personnel prepare the bank reconciliation, electronic payments should be agreed to an authorized schedule of such payments by date, payee account number, and amount. The auditor would review the authorized schedule of payments and controls over its preparation. Similarly, deposits would be traced to the client's POS system records.

For the imprest payroll account reconciliation, the auditor would review the documentation received from the bank and agree details to the reconciliation.

SUMMARY

For electronic receipts and payments, the discussion shows that there are changes in the types of controls required and the type of evidence available to the auditor. However, standard audit procedures are still used to verify existence, completeness, and accuracy.

AUDIT OF PETTY CASH

Petty cash is a unique account because it is frequently immaterial in amount, yet it is verified on most audits. The account is verified primarily because of the potential for defalcation and the client's expectation of an audit review even when the amount is immaterial.

INTERNAL CONTROLS OVER PETTY CASH

OBJECTIVE 20-7

Design and perform audit tests of petty cash.

The most important internal control for petty cash is the use of an imprest fund that is the responsibility of *one individual*. In addition, petty cash funds should not be mingled with other receipts, and the fund should be kept separate from all other activities. There should also be limits on the amount of any expenditure from petty cash, as well as on the total amount of the fund. The type of expenditure that can be made from petty cash transactions should be well defined by company policy.

Whenever a disbursement is made from petty cash, adequate internal controls require a responsible official's approval on a prenumbered petty cash form. The total of the actual cash and cheques in the fund plus the total unreimbursed petty cash forms that represent actual expenditures should equal the total amount of the petty cash fund stated in the general ledger. Periodically, surprise counts and a reconciliation of the petty cash fund should be made by the internal auditor or another responsible official.

When the petty cash balance runs low, a cheque payable to the petty cash custodian should be written on the general cash account for the reimbursement of petty cash. The cheque should be for the exact amount of the prenumbered vouchers that are submitted as evidence of actual expenditures. These vouchers should be verified by the accounts payable clerk and cancelled to prevent their re-use.

AUDIT TESTS FOR PETTY CASH

The emphasis in verifying petty cash should be on testing petty cash transactions rather than the ending balance in the account. Even if the amount of the petty cash fund is small, there is potential for numerous improper transactions if the fund is frequently reimbursed.

An important part of testing petty cash is first determining the client's procedures for handling the fund by discussing internal control with the custodian and examining the documentation of a few transactions. As a part of obtaining an understanding of internal control, it is necessary to identify internal controls and weaknesses. Even though most petty cash systems are not complex, it is often desirable to use a flowchart and an internal control questionnaire, primarily for documentation in subsequent audits. The tests of controls depend on the number and size of the petty cash reimbursements and the auditor's assessed level of control risk. When control risk is assessed at a low level and there are few reimbursement payments during the year, it is common for auditors not to test any further for reasons of immateriality. When the auditor decides to test petty cash, the two most common procedures are counting the petty cash balance and carrying out detailed tests of one or two reimbursement transactions. In such a case, the primary procedures should include footing the petty cash vouchers supporting the amount of the reimbursement, accounting for a sequence of petty cash vouchers, examining the petty cash vouchers for authorization and cancellation, and examining the attached documentation for reasonableness. Typical supporting documentation includes cash register tapes, invoices, and receipts.

Petty cash tests can ordinarily be performed at any time during the year, but, as a matter of convenience, they are typically done on an interim date. If the balance in the petty cash fund is considered material, which is rarely the case, it should be counted at the end of the year. Unreimbursed expenditures should be examined as part of the count to determine whether the amount of unrecorded expenses is material.

ESSENTIAL TERMS

Bank reconciliation — the monthly reconciliation, usually prepared by client personnel, of the differences between the cash balance recorded in the general ledger and the amount in the bank account (p. 645).

Branch bank account — a separate bank account maintained at a local bank by a branch of a company (p. 640).

Cash equivalents — excess cash invested in short-term, highly liquid investments, such as term deposits, certificates of deposit, and money market funds (p. 641).

Cutoff bank statement — a partial-period bank statement and the related cancelled cheques, duplicate deposit slips, and other documents included in bank statements, mailed by the bank directly to the auditor. The auditor uses it to verify reconciling items on the client's year-end bank reconciliation (p. 648).

Electronic data interchange (EDI) — the electronic transfer of business documents, such as invoices and purchase orders (p. 655).

Electronic funds transfer (EFT) — the electronic transfer of funds, either as payment or receipt (e.g., using a debit card) (p. 655).

General cash account — the primary bank account for most organizations; virtually all cash receipts and disbursements flow through this account at some time (p. 640).

Imprest payroll account — a bank account to which the exact amount of payroll for the pay period is transferred by cheque from the employer's general cash account (p. 640).

Imprest petty cash fund — a fund of cash maintained within the company for small cash acquisitions; its fixed balance is comparatively small, and it is periodically reimbursed (p. 641).

Kiting — the transfer of money from one bank account to another and improperly recording the transfer so that the amount is recorded as an asset in both accounts; used by embezzlers to cover a defalcation of cash (p. 652).

Proof of cash — a four-column working paper prepared by the auditor to reconcile the bank's record of the client's beginning balance, cash deposits, cleared cheques, and ending balance for the period with the client's records (p. 651).

Standard bank confirmation form — a form approved by the CICA and Canadian Banker's Association through which the bank responds to the auditor's request for information about the client's bank balances, loan information, and contingent liabilities (p. 648).

20-1   Explain the relationship between the initial assessed level of control risk, tests of controls for cash receipts, and tests of details of cash balances.

20-2   Explain the relationships between the initial assessed level of control risk, tests of controls for cash disbursements, and tests of details of cash balances. Give one example in which the conclusions reached about internal controls in cash disbursements would affect the tests of cash balances.

20-3   Why is the monthly reconciliation of bank accounts by an independent person an important internal control over cash balances? Which individuals would generally not be considered independent for this responsibility?

20-4   Evaluate the effectiveness and state the shortcomings of the preparation of a bank reconciliation by the controller in the manner described in the following statements: "When I reconcile the bank account, the first thing I do is sort the cheques in numerical order and find which numbers are missing. Next, I determine the amount of the uncleared cheques by referring to the cash disbursements journal. If the bank account reconciles at that point, I am all finished with the reconciliation. If it does not, I search for deposits in transit, cheques from the beginning outstanding cheque list that still have not cleared, other reconciling items, and bank errors until the bank account reconciles. In most instances, I can do the reconciliation in 20 minutes."

20-5   How do bank confirmations differ from positive confirmations of accounts receivable? Distinguish between them in terms of the nature of the information confirmed, the sample size, and the appropriate action when the confirmation is not returned after the second request. Explain the rationale for the differences between these two types of confirmations.

20-6   Evaluate the necessity of adhering to the following practice described by an auditor: "In confirming bank accounts I insist on a response from every bank with which the client has done business in the past two years, even though the account may be closed at the balance sheet date."

20-7   Describe what is meant by a "cutoff bank statement," and state its purpose.

20-8   Why are auditors usually less concerned about the client's cash receipts cutoff than the cutoff for sales? Explain the procedure involved in testing for the cutoff for cash receipts.

20-9   What is meant by an "imprest bank account" for a branch operation? Explain the purpose of using this type of bank account.

20-10   Explain the purpose of a four-column proof of cash. List two types of misstatements it is meant to uncover.

20-11   When the auditor fails to obtain a cutoff bank statement, it is common to "prove" the entire statement for the month subsequent to the balance sheet date. How is this done and what is its purpose?

20-12   Distinguish between lapping and kiting. Describe audit procedures that can be used to uncover each.

20-13   Assume that a client with excellent internal controls uses an imprest payroll bank account. Explain why the verification of the payroll bank reconciliation ordinarily takes less time than the tests of the general bank account even if the number of cheques exceeds those written on the general account.

20-14   Distinguish between the verification of petty cash reimbursements and the verification of the balance in the fund. Explain how each is done. Which is more important?

20-15   Why is there a greater emphasis on the detection of fraud in tests of details of cash balances than for other balance sheet accounts? Give two specific examples that demonstrate how this emphasis affects the auditor's evidence accumulation in auditing year-end cash.

20-16   Explain why, in verifying bank reconciliations, most auditors emphasize the possibility of a nonexistent deposit in transit being included in the reconciliation and an outstanding cheque being omitted rather than the omission of a deposit in transit and the inclusion of a nonexistent outstanding cheque.

20-17   Describe how audit procedures change when EFTs are used to receive cash or make payments.

20-18   The following questions deal with auditing year-end cash. Choose the best response.

a.   A public accountant obtains a January 10 cutoff bank statement for a client directly from the bank. Very few of the outstanding cheques listed on the client's December 31 bank reconciliation cleared during the cutoff period. A probable cause for this is that the client
   (1)   sent the cheques to the payees after year end.
   (2)   has overstated its year-end bank balance.
   (3)   is engaged in kiting.
   (4)   is engaged in lapping.

b.   The auditor should ordinarily mail confirmation requests to all banks with which the client has conducted any business during the year, regardless of the year-end balance, since

   (1)   the mailing of confirmation forms to all such banks is required by generally accepted auditing standards.
   (2)   the confirmation form also seeks information about indebtedness to the bank.
   (3)   this procedure will detect kiting activities that would otherwise not be detected.
   (4)   this procedure relieves the auditor of any responsibility with respect to nondetection of forged cheques.

c.   On December 31, 1998, a company erroneously prepared an accounts payable transaction (debit cash, credit accounts payable) for a transfer of funds between banks. A cheque for the transfer was drawn January 3, 1999. This resulted in overstatements of cash and accounts payable at December 31, 1998. Of the following proce-

dures, the *most* effective in disclosing this misstatement would be review of the
(1) schedule of interbank transfers.
(2) December 31, 1998, bank reconciliation for the two banks.
(3) December 1998 cheque register.
(4) support for accounts payable at December 31, 1998.

(AICPA adapted)

20-19 The following questions deal with discovering fraud in auditing year-end cash. Choose the best response.

a. Which of the following is one of the better auditing techniques to detect kiting?
(1) Prepare year-end bank reconciliations.
(2) Prepare a schedule of bank transfers from the client's books.
(3) Review composition of authenticated deposit slips.
(4) Review subsequent bank statements and cancelled cheques received directly from the banks.

b. The cashier of Baker Company Ltd. in Yorkton, Saskatchewan, covered a shortage in the branch petty cash fund with cash obtained on December 31 from a bank in Yorkton by cashing an unrecorded cheque drawn on the Regina branch of another bank used by the company. The auditor would discover this manipulation by
(1) preparing independent bank reconciliations as of December 31.
(2) confirming the December 31 bank balances.
(3) counting the petty cash fund at the close of business on December 31.
(4) investigating items returned with the bank cutoff statements.

c. A cash shortage may be concealed by transferring funds from one location to another or by converting negotiable assets to cash. Because of this, which of the following is vital? Simultaneous
(1) bank reconciliations
(2) verification
(3) confirmations
(4) surprise cash counts

(AICPA adapted)

DISCUSSION QUESTIONS AND PROBLEMS

20-20 The following are fraud and other irregularities that might be found in the client's year-end cash balance. (Assume the balance sheet date is June 30.)

1. A cheque was omitted from the outstanding cheque list on the June 30 bank reconciliation. It cleared the bank July 7.

2. A cheque was omitted from the outstanding cheque list on the bank reconciliation. It cleared the bank September 6.

3. Cash receipts collected on accounts receivable from July 2 to July 5 were included as June 29 and 30 cash receipts.

4. A loan from the bank on June 26 was credited directly to the client's bank account. The loan was not entered in the books as of June 30.

5. A cheque that was dated June 26 and disbursed in June was not recorded in the cash disbursements journal, but it was included as an outstanding cheque on June 30.

6. A bank transfer recorded in the accounting records on July 2 was included as a deposit in transit on June 30.

7. The outstanding cheques on the June 30 bank reconciliation were underfooted by $2,000.

Required

a. Assuming that each of these misstatements was intentional, state the most likely motivation of the person responsible.

b. What control could be instituted for each intentional misstatement to reduce the likelihood of occurrence?

c. List an audit procedure that could be used to discover each misstatement.

20-21 Following are misstatements an auditor might find through tests of controls or tests of details of cash balances:

1. The bookkeeper failed to record cheques in the cash disbursements journal that were written and mailed during the first month of the year.

2. The bookkeeper failed to record or deposit a material amount of cash receipts during the last month of the year. Cash is prelisted by the president's secretary.

3. The cash disbursements journal was held open for two days after the end of the year.

4. A cheque was paid to a vendor for a carload of raw materials that was never received by the client.

5. A discount on a purchase was not taken even though the cheque was mailed before the discount period had expired.

6. Cash receipts for the last two days of the year were recorded in the cash receipts journal for the subsequent period and listed as deposits in transit on the bank reconciliation.

7. A cheque written to a vendor during the last month of the year was recorded in the cash disbursements journal twice to cover an existing fraud. The cheque cleared the bank and did not appear on the bank reconciliation.

Required

a. List a substantive audit procedure to uncover each of the preceding misstatements.

b. For each procedure in part (a), state whether it is a test of details of cash balances or a test of controls.

20-22 The following audit procedures are concerned with tests of details of general cash balances.

1. Compare the bank clearing date with the date on the cancelled cheque for cheques dated on or shortly before the balance sheet date.

2. Trace deposits in transit on the bank reconciliation to the cutoff bank statement and the current year cash receipts journal.

3. Obtain a standard bank confirmation from each bank with which the client does business.

4. Compare the balance on the bank reconciliation obtained from the client with the bank confirmation.

5. Compare the cheques returned along with the cutoff bank statement with the list of outstanding cheques on the bank reconciliation.

6. List the cheque number, payee, and amount of all material cheques not returned with the cutoff bank statement.

7. Review the minutes of the board of directors' meetings, loan agreements, and bank confirmation for interest-bearing deposits, restrictions on the withdrawal of cash, and compensating balance agreements.

8. Prepare a four-column proof of cash.

Required

Explain the objective of each.

20-23 Patrick Yip-Chuk Inc. had weak internal control over its cash transactions. Facts about its cash position at November 30 were as follows:

The cash books showed a balance of $18,901.62, which included undeposited receipts. A credit of $100 on the bank's records did not appear on the books of the company. The balance per bank statement was $15,550. Outstanding cheques were no. 62 for $116.25, no. 183 for $150.00, no. 284 for $253.25, no. 8621 for $190.71, no. 8623 for $206.80, and no. 8632 for $145.28.

The cashier, Khalid Nasser, embezzled all undeposited receipts in excess of $3,794.41 and prepared the following reconciliations:

Balance, per books, November 30		$18,901.62
Add: Outstanding cheques		
8621	$190.71	
8623	206.80	
8632	145.28	442.79
		19,344.41
Less: Undeposited receipts		3,794.41
Balance per bank, November 30		15,550.00
Deduct: Unrecorded credit		100.00
True cash, November 30		$15,450.00

Required

a. Prepare a supporting schedule showing how much Khalid embezzled.

b. How did he attempt to conceal his theft?

c. Using only the information given, name two specific features of internal control that were apparently missing.

(AICPA adapted)

20-24 You are auditing general cash for Trail Supply Corp. for the fiscal year ended July 31. The client has not prepared the July 31 bank reconciliation. After a brief discussion with the owner, you agree to prepare the reconciliation with assistance from one of Trail Supply's clerks. You obtain the following information:

	GENERAL LEDGER	BANK STATEMENT
Beginning balance	$ 4,611	$ 5,753
Deposits		25,056
Cash receipts journal	25,456	
Cheques cleared		(23,615)
Cash disbursements journal	(21,811)	
July bank service charge		(87)
Note paid directly		(6,100)
NSF cheque		(311)
Ending balance	$ 8,256	$ 696

June 30 Bank Reconciliation

INFORMATION IN GENERAL LEDGER AND BANK STATEMENT	
Balance per bank	$5,753
Deposits in transit	600
Outstanding cheques	1,742
Balance per books	4,611

In addition, the following information is obtained:

1. Cheques clearing that were outstanding on June 30 totalled $1,692.

2. Cheques clearing that were recorded in the July disbursements journal totalled $20,467.

3. A cheque for $1,060 cleared the bank but had not been recorded in the cash disbursements journal. It was for an acquisition of inventory. Trail Supply uses the periodic inventory method.

4. A cheque for $396 was charged to Trail Supply but had been written on a different associated company's bank account.

5. Deposits included $600 from June and $24,456 for July.

6. The bank charged Trail Supply's account for a nonsufficient funds (NSF) cheque totalling $311. The credit manager concluded that the customer intentionally closed its account and the owner left the city. The cheque was turned over to a collection agency.

7. The bank deducted $5,800 plus interest from Trail Supply's account for a loan made by the bank under an agreement signed four months ago. The note payable was recorded at $5,800 on Trail Supply's books.

Required

a. Prepare a bank reconciliation that shows both the unadjusted and adjusted balances as per the books.

b. Identify the nature of adjustments required.

c. What audit procedures would you use to verify each item in the bank reconciliation?

20-25 Van Weelden Transport Ltd.'s head office is located in Winnipeg. It has a large branch in Brandon that maintains its own bank account. Cash is periodically transferred to the central account in Winnipeg. On the branch account's records, bank transfers are recorded as a debit to the home office clearing account and as a credit to the branch bank account. Similarly, the home office account is recorded as a debit to the central bank account and as a credit to the branch office clearing account. Gordon Whitefish is the head bookkeeper for both the home office and the branch bank accounts. Since he also reconciles the bank account, the senior auditor, Cindy Marintette, is concerned about the internal control weakness.

As a part of the year-end audit of bank transfers, Marintette asks you, a member of her staff, to schedule the transfers for the last few days in 1998 and the first few days of 1999. You prepare the following list:

AMOUNT OF TRANSFER	DATE RECORDED IN THE HOME OFFICE CASH RECEIPTS JOURNAL	DATE RECORDED IN THE BRANCH OFFICE CASH DISBURSEMENTS JOURNAL	DATE DEPOSITED IN THE HOME OFFICE BANK ACCOUNT	DATE CLEARED THE BRANCH BANK ACCOUNT
$12,000	27-12-98	29-12-98	26-12-98	27-12-98
26,000	28-12-98	2-1-99	28-12-98	29-12-98
14,000	2-1-99	30-12-98	28-12-98	29-12-98
11,000	26-12-98	26-12-98	28-12-98	3-1-99
15,000	2-1-99	2-1-99	28-12-98	31-12-98
28,000	7-1-99	5-1-99	28-12-98	3-1-99
37,000	4-1-99	6-1-99	3-1-99	5-1-99

Required

a. In verifying each bank transfer, state the appropriate audit procedures you should perform.

b. Identify the nature of adjusting journal entries required in the home office and the branch bank records.

c. State how each bank transfer should be included in the December 31, 1998, bank reconciliation of the home office account after your adjustments in part (b).

d. State how each bank transfer should be included in the December 31, 1998, bank reconciliation of the branch bank account after your adjustments in part (c).

20-26 Toyco Inc., a retail toy chain, honours two bank credit cards and makes daily deposits of credit card sales in two credit card bank accounts (Bank A and Bank B). Each day, Toyco batches its credit card sales slips, bank deposit slips, and authorized sales return documents. The total of the batch is reconciled to the total according to the point-of-sale terminals used by Toyco. Each week, detailed computer printouts of the general ledger credit card cash accounts are prepared. The credit card banks have been instructed to make an automatic weekly transfer of cash to Toyco's general bank account. The credit card banks charge back deposits that include sales to holders of stolen or expired cards.

The auditor conducting the examination of the Toyco financial statements has obtained the following copies of the detailed general ledger cash account printouts, the manually prepared bank reconciliations, and a summary of the bank statements, all for the week ended December 31.

Toyco Inc. — Detailed General Ledger Credit Card Cash Account Printouts

	BANK A DR. OR (CR.)	BANK B DR. OR (CR.)
Beginning balance, December 24, 1998	$12,100	$4,200
Deposits		
December 27, 1998	2,500	5,000
December 28, 1998	3,000	7,000
December 29, 1998	0	5,400
December 30, 1998	1,900	4,000
December 31, 1998	2,200	6,000
Cash transfer, December 27, 1998	(10,700)	0
Chargebacks, expired cards	(300)	(1,600)
Deposit errors (physically deposited in wrong account)	(1,400)	(1,000)
Redeposit of deposits made to the wrong account	1,000	1,400
Sales returns for week ending December 31, 1998	(600)	(1,200)
Ending balance, December 31, 1998	$9,700	$29,200

Toyco Inc. — Summary of the Bank Statements

	(CHARGES) OR CREDITS	
	BANK A	**BANK B**
Beginning balance, December 24, 1998	$10,000	$ 0
Deposits dated		
December 24, 1998	2,100	4,200
December 27, 1998	2,500	5,000
December 28, 1998	3,000	7,000
December 29, 1998	2,000	5,500
December 30, 1998	1,900	4,000
Cash transfers to general bank account		
December 27, 1999	(10,700)	0
December 31, 1999	0	(22,600)
Chargebacks		
Stolen cards	(100)	0
Expired cards	(300)	(1,600)
Deposit errors	(1,400)	(1,000)
Bank service charges	0	(500)
Bank charge (unexplained)	(400)	0
Ending balance, December 31, 1999	$8,600	$ 0

Toyco Inc. — Bank Reconciliations

	ADD OR (DEDUCT)	
CODE NO.	**BANK A**	**BANK B**
1. Balance per bank statement, December 31, 1999	$8,600	$ 0
2. Deposits in transit, December 31, 1999	2,200	6,000
3. Redeposit of deposits made to wrong account	1,000	1,400
4. Difference in deposits of December 29, 1999	(2,000)	(100)
5. Unexplained bank charge	400	0
6. Bank cash transfer not yet recorded	0	22,600
7. Bank service charges	0	500
8. Chargebacks not recorded, stolen cards	100	0
9. Sales returns recorded but not reported to the bank	(600)	(1,200)
10. Balance per general ledger, December 31, 1999	$9,700	$29,200

Required

Based on a review of the December 31 bank reconciliations and the related information available in the printouts and the summary of bank statements, describe what action(s) the auditor should take to obtain audit satisfaction *for each item* on the bank reconciliations. Assume that all amounts are material and that all computations are accurate. Organize your answer sheet as follows, using the appropriate code number *for each item* on the bank reconciliations:

CODE NO.	ACTION(S) TO BE TAKEN BY THE AUDITOR TO OBTAIN AUDIT SATISFACTION
1.	

20-27 Julian Gomes is the auditor of Jahafra Hotel, a small independent hotel, which has a November 30 year end. In order to give written instructions to his staff regarding the verification of year-end cash on hand, Julian reviewed his working papers of last year and contacted the client to make sure there were no changes. From his review, he obtained the following information:

1. Cash on hand consisted of undeposited receipts, imprest change funds, and imprest petty cash funds.

2. The hotel had three point-of-sale cash terminals and eight cashiers. Each of the cashiers was responsible for an imprest change fund of $500.

3. The following funds were also used:
   (i) Auxiliary change funds of $1,000, controlled by the office manager

   (ii) Three office petty cash funds of $50, each controlled by a different office staff member

   (iii) Undeposited receipts, controlled by the assistant hotel manager

4. The hotel's policy was to deposit receipts daily and intact.

5. In order to avoid the hotel's busy times of day, the year-end cash count was made at about 6:00 A.M., December 1.

6. Internal control over cash was satisfactory.

Required

Prepare an audit program regarding verification of year-end cash on hand for the assistant.

(CICA adapted)

21

COMPLETING THE AUDIT

GOOD REVIEW REQUIRES MORE THAN LOOKING AT WORKING PAPERS

Larry Bedard, an audit senior of Messier, Nixon & Royce, assigned staff assistant Clawson Lum the audit accounts payable for Westside Industries Ltd., a large equipment manufacturer. Accounts payable is a major liability account for a manufacturing company, and testing accounts payable cutoff is an important audit area. Testing primarily involves reviewing the liability recorded by the client by examining subsequent payments to supliers and other creditors to assure that they were properly recorded.

Bedard observed that Lum was spending a lot of time on the phone, apparently on personal matters. Shortly before the audit was completed, Lum announced that he was leaving the firm. In spite of Lum's distractions due to his personal affairs, he completed the audit work he was assigned within the budgeted time.

Because of Bedard's concern about Lum's work habits, he decided to review the working papers with extreme care. Every schedule he reviewed was properly prepared, with tick marks entered and explained by Lum, indicating that he had made an extensive examination of underlying data and documents and had found the client's balance to be adequate as stated. Specifically, there were no payments subsequent to year end for inventory purchases received during the audit period that had not been accrued by the Westside.

When Bedard finished the audit, he turned the working papers over to Kelsey Mayburn, an audit manager on the engagement, for her review. She had considerable knowledge about equipment manufacturers and about Westside Industries. Mayburn reviewed all the working papers, including analytical procedures performed during the audit. After performing additional analytical procedures during her review, she contacted Bedard to inform him that accounts payable didn't seem reasonable to her. She asked him to do some additional

After the auditor has completed the tests in specific audit areas, it is necessary to summarize the results and perform additional testing of a more general nature. This is the fourth and last phase of the audit, as shown in Figure 10-10 on page 328. The first four procedures for completing this audit phase are the major topics of this chapter. They are reviewing for contingent liabilities, reviewing for subsequent events, accumulating final evidence, and evaluating results. In addition, communications with the audit committee and management and subsequent discovery of facts existing at the date of the auditor's report are discussed.

REVIEW FOR CONTINGENT LIABILITIES

OBJECTIVE 21-1

Conduct a review for contingent liabilities.

Paragraph 3290.02 of the *CICA Handbook* defines a contingency as

> . . . an existing condition or situation involving uncertainty as to possible gain or loss to an enterprise that will ultimately be resolved when one or more future events occur or fail to occur.

The auditor is concerned both with the nature of the future event and with the amount involved. Just as he or she is concerned with recognizing a contingent liability, the auditor must also be able to recognize a recorded asset that is really a contingent asset and that has the effect of overstating the net worth of the business.

Three conditions indicate the existence of a *contingent liability*: (1) there is a potential future payment to an outside party that resulted from an existing condition, (2) there is uncertainty about the amount of the future payment, and (3) the outcome will be resolved by some future event or events. For example, contingencies include lawsuits that have been filed but not yet resolved.

This uncertainty of the future payment can vary from extremely likely to highly unlikely. Section 3290 of the *CICA Handbook* describes three levels of likelihood of occurrence and the appropriate financial statement treatment for each likelihood; the three levels are likely, unlikely, and not determinable. The ability to estimate the amount of the loss is also a factor that must be considered. Table 21-1 describes the various alternatives.

TABLE 21-1

LIKELIHOOD OF OCCURRENCE OF CONTINGENCIES AND FINANCIAL STATEMENT TREATMENT

LIKELIHOOD OF OCCURRENCE OF EVENT	FINANCIAL STATEMENT TREATMENT
Unlikely to occur	No disclosure is necessary unless the event will have a significant adverse financial effect, in which case footnote disclosure is suggested.
Not determinable	Footnote disclosure is necessary.
Likely to occur and the amount can be estimated	Financial statement accounts are adjusted.
Likely to occur and the amount cannot be estimated	Footnote disclosure is necessary.

Review for contingent liabilities and gains

Review for subsequent events

Accumulate final evidence

Evaluate results

Issue auditor's report

Communicate with audit committee and management

The decision as to the appropriate treatment requires considerable professional judgment. (A contingent gain should never be accrued, but rather, if its future confirmation is very likely, it should be disclosed in the notes.)

When the proper disclosure in the financial statements of material contingencies is through footnotes, the footnote should describe the nature of the contingency to the extent it is known, an estimate of the amount, or a statement that the amount cannot be estimated. The following is an illustration of a footnote related to pending litigation:

> The Company is a defendant in a legal action instituted in the Alberta Court of the Queen's Bench by Mountain Supply Ltd. for alleged product defect. The amount claimed is $792,000 and the Company is vigorously contesting the claim.
>
> The Company's legal counsel is unable, at the present time, to give any opinion with respect to the merits of this action. Settlement, if any, that may be made with respect to these actions is expected to be accounted for as a charge against income for the period in which settlement is made.

Certain contingent liabilities are of considerable concern to the auditor:

- Pending litigation for patent infringement, product liability, or other actions
- Income tax disputes
- Product warranties
- Notes receivable discounted
- Guarantees of obligations of others
- Unused balances in outstanding letters of credit

Auditing standards make it clear that management, not the auditor, is responsible for identifying and deciding the appropriate accounting treatment for contingent liabilities. In many audits, it is impractical for auditors to uncover contingencies without management's cooperation.

The auditor's objectives in verifying contingent liabilities are to evaluate the accounting treatment of known contingent liabilities and to identify, to the extent practical, any contingencies not already identified by management.

AUDIT PROCEDURES

Many of these potential obligations are ordinarily verified as an integral part of various segments of the engagement rather than as a separate activity near the end of the audit. For example, guarantees of obligations of others may be tested as part of confirming bank balances and loans from banks. Similarly, income tax disputes can be checked as part of analyzing income tax expense, reviewing the general correspondence file, and examining Revenue Canada reports and statements. Even if the contingencies are verified separately, it is common to perform the tests well before the last few days of completing the engagement to ensure their proper verification. The tests of contingent liabilities near the end of the engagement are more a review than an initial search.

The appropriate audit procedures for testing contingencies are less well defined than those already discussed in other audit areas because the primary objective at the initial stage of the tests is to determine the *existence* of contingencies. As the reader knows from the study of other audit areas, it is more difficult to discover unrecorded transactions or events than to verify recorded information. Once the auditor is aware that contingencies exist, the evaluation of their materiality and the disclosure required can ordinarily be satisfactorily resolved.

The following are some audit procedures commonly used to search for contingent liabilities. The list is not all-inclusive, and each procedure is not necessarily performed on every audit.

- Inquire of management (orally and in writing) regarding the possibility of unrecorded contingencies. In these inquiries, the auditor must be specific in describing the different kinds of contingencies that may require disclosure. Naturally, inquiries of management are not useful in uncovering the intentional failure to disclose existing contingencies, but if management has overlooked a particular type of contingency or does not fully comprehend accounting disclosure requirements, the inquiry can be fruitful. At the completion of the audit, management is typically asked to make a written statement as part of the letter of representation that it is aware of no undisclosed contingent liabilities.

- Review current and previous years' Revenue Canada notices of assessment. The reports may indicate areas in which disagreement over unsettled years is likely to arise. If an audit by Revenue Canada has been in progress for a long time, there is an increased likelihood of an existing tax dispute.
- Review the minutes of directors' and shareholders' meetings for indications of lawsuits or other contingencies.
- Analyze legal expense for the period under audit, and review invoices and statements from the client's law firms for indications of contingent liabilities, especially lawsuits and pending tax assessments.
- Obtain a confirmation from all major law firms performing legal services for the client as to the status of pending litigation or other contingent liabilities. This procedure is discussed in more depth shortly.
- Review existing working papers for any information that may indicate a potential contingency. For example, bank confirmations may indicate notes receivable discounted or guarantees of loans.
- Obtain letters of credit in force as of the balance sheet date, and obtain a confirmation of the used and unused balances.
- Read contracts, agreements, and related correspondence and documents.

EVALUATION OF KNOWN CONTINGENT LIABILITIES

If the auditor concludes that there are contingent liabilities, he or she must evaluate the significance of the potential liability and the nature of the disclosure that is necessary in the financial statements. The potential liability is sufficiently well known in some instances to be included in the statements as an actual liability. In other instances, disclosure may be unnecessary if the contingency is highly remote or immaterial. The public accounting firm may obtain a separate evaluation of the potential liability from its own law firm rather than relying on management or management's lawyers. The client's law firm is an advocate for the client and may lose perspective in evaluating the likelihood of losing the case and the amount of the potential judgment.

COMMITMENTS

Closely related to contingent liabilities are commitments to purchase raw materials or to lease facilities at a certain price, agreements to sell merchandise at a fixed price, bonus plans, profit-sharing and pension plans, royalty agreements, and similar items. For a commitment, the most important characteristic is the *agreement to commit the firm to a set of fixed conditions* in the future, regardless of what happens to profits or the economy as a whole. In a free economy, presumably the entity agrees to commitments as a means of bettering its own interests, but these commitments may turn out to be less or more advantageous than originally anticipated.

Paragraph 3280.01 of the *CICA Handbook* requires disclosure of the details of any contractual obligation that is significant to a client's current financial position or future operations. All commitments are ordinarily either described together in a separate footnote or combined in a footnote related to contingencies.

The search for unknown commitments is usually performed as part of the audit of each audit area. For example, in verifying sales transactions, the auditor should be alert for sales commitments. Similarly, commitments for the purchase of raw materials or equipment can be identified as part of the audit of each of these accounts. The auditor should also be aware of the possibility of commitments as he or she is reading contracts and correspondence files, and should therefore query management.

OBTAIN CONFIRMATION FROM CLIENT'S LAW FIRMS

A major procedure on which auditors rely for evaluating known litigation or other claims against the client and identifying additional ones is *sending a letter of inquiry to the client's law firms*. There are two categories of lawsuits: an *outstanding* or *asserted claim* exists when a suit has been brought or when the client has been notified that a suit will be brought; a *possible* or *unasserted claim* exists when no suit has been filed but is possible. An example of the latter is a situation in which the lawyer is aware of a violation of a patent agreement that could be damaging to the client.

The auditor relies on the lawyer's expertise and knowledge of the client's legal affairs to provide a professional opinion about the expected outcome of existing lawsuits and the likely amount of the liability, including court costs. The lawyer is also likely to know of pending litigation and claims that management may have overlooked.

As a matter of tradition, many public accounting firms analyze legal expense for the entire year and have the client send a standard lawyer's letter to every law firm with which it has been involved in the current or preceding year, plus any law firm that it occasionally engages. In some cases, this involves a large number of law firms, including some dealing in aspects of law that are far removed from potential lawsuits.

The standard letter of confirmation to the client's law firm, which should be prepared on the client's letterhead and signed by one of the company's officials, should include the following:

- A list, prepared by management, of outstanding and possible claims with which the lawyer has had significant involvement
- A description of the nature and the current status of each claim and possible claim
- An indication of management's evaluation of the amount and likelihood of loss or gain for each listed claim and possible claim
- A request that the lawyer reply to the client, with a signed copy going to the public accounting firm, advising whether management's descriptions and evaluations of the outstanding and possible claims are reasonable

    Lawyers are not required to mention any omission of possible claims in their response to the inquiry letter, and thus do not directly notify the auditor of them. Instead, lawyers discuss these possible claims with the client separately and inform management of its responsibility to inform the auditor.

    Whether management does so or not is its decision; Paragraph 6560.19 requires the auditor to obtain a letter of representation from management that it has disclosed *all* outstanding and possible claims. In short, unless management discloses the existence of possible claims to the auditor, the auditor has no means of discovering whether or not any such claims exist.

    Any differences between management's identification and assessment of outstanding and possible claims and the law firm's would be resolved, if possible, in a meeting of the law firm, the auditor, and management. Failure to resolve the differences would force the auditor to consider a reservation of opinion on the auditor's report.

- A request for information regarding any unlisted outstanding or potential legal actions or a statement that the client's list was complete

An example of a typical standard inquiry letter sent to a lawyer's office is shown in Figure 21-1. The letter should be sent towards the end of the audit so that the lawyer is communicating about contingencies up to approximately the date of the auditor's report.

FIGURE 21-1
Typical Inquiry of
Lawyer

PEPPERTREE PRODUCE INC.
293 Rue Crécy
Montréal, Québec

January 26, 1999

Rowan and Gunz
Barristers and Solicitors,
412 Côte des Neiges,
Montréal, Québec
H3C 1J7

To Whom It May Concern:

In connection with the preparation and audit of our financial statements for the fiscal period ended December 31, 1998, we have made the following evaluations of claims and possible claims with respect to which your firm's advice or representation has been sought:

Description	Evaluation
Calvert Growers vs. Peppertree Produce Inc., nonpayment of debt in the amount of $16,000, trial date not set.	Peppertree Produce Inc. disputes this billing on the grounds that the produce was spoiled and expects to successfully defend this action.
Desjardins, Inc. vs. Peppertree Produce Inc., damages for breach of contract in the amount of $40,000, trial date not set.	It is probable that this action will be successfully defended.
Foodex Ltd. has a possible claim in connection with apples sold to them by Peppertree Produce Inc. The apples apparently had not been properly washed by the growers to remove insect spray, and a number of Foodex Ltd.'s customers became ill after eating said apples.	No claim has yet been made, and we are unable to estimate possible ultimate loss.

Would you please advise us, as of February 28, 1999, on the following points:
a. Are the claims and possible claims properly described?
b. Do you consider that our evaluations are reasonable?
c. Are you aware of any claims not listed above that are outstanding? If so, please include in your response letter the names of the parties and the amount claimed.

This inquiry is made in accordance with the Joint Policy Statement of January, 1978, approved by the Canadian Bar Association and the Auditing Standards Committee of the Canadian Institute of Chartered Accountants.

Please address your reply, marked "Privileged and Confidential," to this company and send a signed copy of the reply directly to our auditors, Jeannerette & Cie, Contables Agrées, 1133 Rue Sherbrooke, Montréal, Québec, H3C 1M8.

Yours truly,

Charles D. Peppertree

Charles D. Peppertree, President

c.c. Jeannerette & Cie

LIMITED OR NONRESPONSES FROM LAW FIRMS

Law firms in recent years have become reluctant to provide certain information to auditors because of their own exposure to legal liability for providing incorrect or confidential information. The nature of the refusal of law firms to provide auditors with complete information about contingent liabilities falls into two categories: the refusal to respond due to a lack of knowledge about matters involving contingent liabilities, and the refusal to disclose information that the lawyer regards as confidential. As an example of the latter, the lawyer might be aware of a violation of a patent agreement that could result in a significant loss to the client if it were known (unasserted claim). The inclusion of the information in a footnote could actually cause the lawsuit and, therefore, be damaging to the client.

When the nature of the lawyer's legal practice does not involve contingent liabilities, the lawyer's refusal to respond causes no audit problems. It is certainly reasonable for lawyers to refuse to make statements about contingent liabilities when they are not involved with lawsuits or similar aspects of the practice of law that directly affect financial statements.

A serious audit problem does arise, however, when a lawyer refuses to provide information that is within the lawyer's jurisdiction and may directly affect the fair presentation of financial statements. If a lawyer refuses to provide the auditor with information about material existing lawsuits (outstanding claims) or possible claims, *the auditor's report would have to be modified to reflect the lack of available evidence*. The "Joint Policy Statement concerning communications with law firms regarding claims and possible claims in connection with the preparation and audit of financial statements," an appendix to Section 6560 of the *CICA Handbook*, has the effect of encouraging lawyers to cooperate with auditors in obtaining information about contingencies, as the law firm's confidential relationship with its clients will not be violated. The Joint Policy Statement was approved by the Canadian Bar Association, the Council of the Bermuda Bar Association, and the Auditing Standards Committee (now the Assurance Standards Board) of the CICA.

REVIEW FOR SUBSEQUENT EVENTS

OBJECTIVE 21-3

Conduct a post-balance sheet review for subsequent events.

The auditor must review transactions and events occurring after the balance sheet date to determine whether anything occurred that might affect the fair presentation or disclosure of the statements being audited. The auditing procedures required by Section 6550 "Subsequent Events" to verify these transactions and events are often referred to as the *review for subsequent events* or *post-balance sheet review*.

The auditor's responsibility for reviewing for subsequent events is normally limited to the period beginning with the balance sheet date and ending with the date of the auditor's report. Since the date of the auditor's report usually corresponds with the completion of the important auditing procedures in the client's office, the subsequent events review should be completed near the end of the engagement. Figure 21-2 shows the period covered by a subsequent events review and the timing of that review.

FIGURE 21-2
Period Covered by Subsequent Events Review

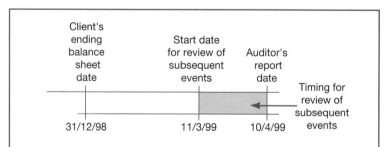

- The auditor is responsible for subsequent events occurring between 31/12/98 and 10/4/99.
- Most subsequent events audit procedures would be performed between approximately 11/3/99 and 10/4/99.

TYPES OF SUBSEQUENT EVENTS

Two types of subsequent events require consideration by management and evaluation by the auditor: those that have a direct effect on the financial statements and require adjustment and those that have no direct effect on the financial statements but for which disclosure is advisable.

Review for
contingent liabilities

Review for
subsequent events

Accumulate
final evidence

Evaluate results

Issue auditor's
report

Communicate with
audit committee
and management

Those that have a direct effect on the financial statements and require adjustment
These events or transactions provide additional information to management in determining the valuation of account balances as of the balance sheet date and to auditors in verifying the balances. For example, if the auditor is having difficulty determining the correct valuation of inventory because of obsolescence, the sale of raw material inventory as scrap in the subsequent period should be used as a means of determining the correct valuation of the inventory as of the balance sheet date.

Such subsequent period events as the following require an adjustment of account balances in the current year's financial statements if the amounts are material:

- The declaration of bankruptcy due to the deteriorating financial condition of a customer with an outstanding accounts receivable balance
- The settlement of litigation at an amount different from the amount recorded on the books
- The disposal of equipment not being used in operations at a price below the current book value
- The sale of investments at a price below recorded cost

Whenever subsequent events are used to evaluate the amounts included in the statements, care must be taken to distinguish between conditions that existed at the balance sheet date and those that came into being after the end of the year. The subsequent information should not be incorporated directly into the statements if the conditions causing the change in valuation did not take place until after year end. For example, the sale of scrap in the subsequent period would not be relevant in the valuation of inventory for obsolescence if the obsolescence took place after the end of the year. Also, an amount outstanding from a customer who declared bankruptcy after year end, due to uninsured fire damage to its premises, should not be removed from the accounts receivable balance until the year the damage took place.

Those that have no direct effect on the financial statements but for which disclosure is advisable Subsequent events of this type provide evidence of conditions that did not exist at the date of the balance sheet being reported on but are so significant that they require disclosure even though they do not require adjustment. Ordinarily, these events can be adequately disclosed by the use of footnotes, but occasionally one event may be so significant as to require supplementing the historical statements with statements that include the effect of the event as if it had occurred on the balance sheet date (i.e., *pro forma* statements).

Following are examples of events or transactions occurring in the subsequent period that may require disclosure rather than an adjustment in the financial statements:

- Decline in market value of investments
- Issuance of bonds or shares
- Decline in market value of inventory as a consequence of government action barring further sale of a product
- Uninsured loss of inventories as a result of fire or other disaster
- Purchase of a business or trademark

AUDIT TESTS

Audit procedures for the subsequent events review can be conveniently divided into two categories: procedures normally integrated as part of the verification of year-end account balances and those performed specifically for the purpose of discovering events or transactions that must be recognized as subsequent events.

The first category includes cutoff and valuation tests that are done as part of the tests of details of balances. For example, subsequent period sales and acquisition transactions are examined to determine whether the cutoff is accurate. Similarly, many valuation tests involving subsequent events are also performed as part of the verification of account balances. As an example, it is common to test the collectibility of accounts receivable by reviewing subsequent period cash receipts. It is also a normal audit procedure to compare the subsequent period purchase price of inventory with the recorded cost as a test of lower of cost or market valuation. The procedures for cutoff and valuation have been discussed sufficiently in preceding chapters and are not repeated here.

The second category of tests is performed specifically for the purpose of obtaining information that must be incorporated into the current year's account balances or footnotes. These tests include the following:

Inquire of management Inquiries vary from client to client but normally are about the existence of potential contingent liabilities or commitments, significant changes in the assets or capital structure of the company, the current status of items that were not completely resolved at the balance sheet date, and the existence of unusual adjustments made subsequent to the balance sheet date.

Inquiries of management about subsequent events must be held with the proper client personnel to obtain meaningful answers. For example, discussing tax or union matters with the accounts receivable supervisor would not be appropriate. Most inquiries should be made of the controller, the vice-presidents, or the president, depending on the information desired.

Correspond with law firms Correspondence with law firms, which was previously discussed, takes place as part of the search for contingent liabilities. In obtaining confirmation letters from law firms, the auditor must remember his or her responsibility for testing for subsequent events up to the date of the auditor's report. A common approach is to request that the law firm date and mail the letter as of the expected completion date for field work.

Review internal statements prepared subsequent to the balance sheet date The emphasis in the review should be on (1) changes in the business relative to results for the same period in the year under audit and (2) changes after year end. The auditor should pay particular attention to major changes in the business or environment in which the client is operating. The statements should be discussed with management to determine whether they are prepared on the same basis as the current period statements, and there should be inquiries about significant changes in operating results.

Review records prepared subsequent to the balance sheet date Journals, data files, and ledgers should be reviewed to determine the existence and nature of any transaction related to the current year. If the journals are not kept up to date, the documents relating to the journals should be reviewed.

Examine minutes prepared subsequent to the balance sheet date The minutes of shareholders' and directors' meetings subsequent to the balance sheet date must be examined for important subsequent events affecting the current period financial statements.

Obtain a letter of representation The letter of representation written by the client to the auditor formalizes statements the client has made about different matters throughout the audit, including discussions about subsequent events.

DUAL DATING

Chapter 2 discussed dating the auditor's report and introduced the notion of *dual dating*, or *double dating*, from Section 5405 of the *CICA Handbook*. Occasionally, the auditor determines that an important subsequent event occurred after the field work was completed but before the auditor's report was issued. The source of such information is typically management or the press. An example is the acquisition of another company by the audit client on April 23, when the last day of field work was April 11. In such a situation, paragraph 6550.06 of the *CICA Handbook* requires the auditor to extend audit tests for the newly discovered subsequent event to ensure that the client has correctly accounted for it (i.e., either adjusted the statements or disclosed the event). The auditor has two equally acceptable options for expanding subsequent event tests: expand the period of all subsequent events tests to the date at which the auditor is satisfied that the newly determined subsequent event is correctly stated, or restrict the review to matters related to the new subsequent event. For the first option, the auditor's report date would be changed, whereas for the second, the auditor's report would be *dual dated*. In the previous example of the acquisition, assume that the auditor returned to the client's premises and completed audit tests on April 30 pertaining only to the acquisition. The auditor's report would be dual dated as follows: April 11, 1999, except for note 17, for which the date is April 30, 1999.

ACCUMULATE FINAL EVIDENCE

The auditor has a few final accumulation responsibilities that apply to all cycles besides the search for contingent liabilities and the review for subsequent events. The four most important ones, as well as management discussion and analysis, are discussed in this section. All four are done late in the engagement.

FINAL ANALYTICAL PROCEDURES

OBJECTIVE 21-4

Design and perform the final steps in the evidence-accumulation segment of the audit.

Analytical procedures were introduced in Chapter 6, discussed as substantive tests in Chapter 13, and applied to specific cycles in several other chapters. As discussed in Chapter 6, analytical procedures are normally used as part of planning the audit, during the performance of detailed tests in each cycle as part of substantive procedures, and at the completion of the audit.

Analytical procedures done during the completion of the audit are useful as a final review for material misstatements or financial problems not noted during other testing, and to help the auditor take a final objective look at the financial statements. It is common for a partner to closely review the analytical procedures during the final review of working papers and financial statements. Typically, a partner has a good understanding of the client and its business because of ongoing relationships. Knowledge of the client's business and its business environment combined with effective analytical procedures help identify possible oversights in an audit. Section 5301 requires the auditor to use analytical procedures as part of the completion phase of the audit.

EVALUATION OF GOING CONCERN ASSUMPTION

The Commission to Study the Public's Expectation of Audits (Macdonald Commission) suggested in Recommendation 10 that management should disclose in the financial statements if "there is significant danger that [the company] may not be able to continue as [a going concern] throughout the foreseeable future."[1] The implication of this and other recommendations is that the auditor should pay particular attention to the going concern assumption during the audit but especially when performing the final review of the disclosures in the financial statements.

J.E. Boritz, in the CICA research study *The "Going Concern" Assumption: Accounting and Auditing Assumptions*, suggests that "auditors, as part of every audit, should independently examine the support for management's implicit or explicit assertion about the validity of the 'going concern' assumption."[2] He also suggests that the

[1]"50 Ways to Change Our Ways," *CAmagazine*, July 1988, page 42. The July issue of *CAmagazine* includes several articles dealing with the report of the Commission to Study the Public's Expectations of Audits (Macdonald Commission).

[2]Boritz, J.E., *The "Going Concern" Assumption: Accounting and Auditing Implications*, Toronto: Canadian Institute of Chartered Accountants, 1991, pages xiv and 102–104.

auditor should modify the auditor's report to reflect his or her concern about the client's ability to operate when the "degree of doubt" about the validity of the going concern assumption exceeds 50 percent.[3]

U.S. standards (SAS 59) require the auditor to evaluate whether there is a substantial doubt about a client's ability to continue as a going concern for at least one year beyond the balance sheet date. If the auditor concludes that there is substantial doubt, the auditor's report should include an explanatory paragraph following the opinion paragraph to describe that conclusion. International Standard on Auditing 570, "Going Concern," also requires the auditor to consider the appropriateness of the going concern assumption.

The Assurance Standards Board (ASB) issued the exposure draft "Auditor's Responsibility to Evaluate the Going Concern Assumption" in 1995, while the Accounting Standards Board issued the exposure draft "Going Concern" in 1996. The proposed new auditing *Handbook* Section would require the auditor to assess whether or not the organization being audited had a going concern problem and, if so, to consider the going concern problem in planning the audit. The exposure draft would require the auditor to ensure that his or her concerns about the going concern assumption were communicated to the audit committee and to obtain from management representations with respect to the validity of the going concern assumption and the appropriateness of the financial statement disclosures. Presently, *Handbook* Section 5510 suggests what the auditor should do on becoming aware of conditions that may lead to going concern problems. As of spring 1999, these two exposure drafts have been deferred (placed on hold). The ASB is monitoring international projects with a view to harmonization and considering comments on these exposure drafts requesting greater consistency between the two.

It is the conclusion of the authors that the auditor should follow the suggestions with respect to the going concern assumption proposed by Macdonald and Boritz.

CLIENT REPRESENTATION LETTER

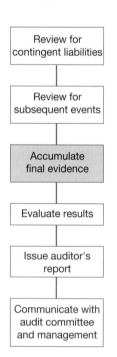

Review for contingent liabilities

Review for subsequent events

Accumulate final evidence

Evaluate results

Issue auditor's report

Communicate with audit committee and management

The *CICA Handbook* does not specifically require a letter of representation from a client, except in connection with communications with law firms (paragraph 6560.19). Such letters are, however, suggested in connection with prospectuses (paragraph 7100.14) and with review engagements (AuG-20). However, many public accounting firms in Canada do require a letter of representation covering many of the aspects of the audit. For that reason, the requirements of the AICPA in SAS 19 are instructive.

SAS 19 (AU 333) *requires the auditor to obtain a letter of representation* that documents management's most important oral representations during the audit. The client representation letter is prepared on the client's letterhead, addressed to the public accounting firm, and signed by high-level corporate officials, usually the president and chief financial officer.

There are two purposes of the client letter of representation:

- *To impress upon management its responsibility for the assertions in the financial statements.* For example, if the letter of representation includes a reference to pledged assets and contingent liabilities, honest management may be reminded of its unintentional failure to disclose the information adequately. To fulfill this objective, the letter of representation should be sufficiently detailed to act as a reminder to management.
- *To document the responses from management to inquiries about various aspects of the audit.* This provides written documentation of client representations in the event of disagreement or a lawsuit between the auditor and the client.

---

[3]Ibid., pages xiv–xv and 104–106.

The letter should be dated as of the auditor's report date to make sure there are representations related to the subsequent events review. The letter implies that it has originated with the client, but it is common practice for the auditor to prepare the letter and request the client to type it on the company's letterhead and sign it. Refusal by a client to prepare and sign the letter should probably cause the auditor to consider a qualified opinion or denial of opinion.

SAS 19 suggests many specific matters that should be included, when applicable, in a client representation letter. A few of these are:

- Management's acknowledgment of its responsibility for the fair presentation in the statements . . . in conformity with generally accepted accounting principles or [an appropriate disclosed] basis of accounting
- Availability of all financial records and related data
- Completeness and availability of all minutes of meetings of shareholders, directors, and committees of directors
- Information concerning related-party transactions and related amounts receivable or payable
- Plans or intentions that may affect the carrying value or classification of assets or liabilities
- Disclosure of compensating balances or other arrangements involving restrictions on cash balances and disclosure of lines of credit or similar arrangements

A client representation letter is a written statement from a non-independent source and therefore *cannot be regarded as reliable evidence*. The letter does provide minimal evidence that management has been asked certain questions, but its primary purpose is psychological and to protect the auditor from potential claims by management that it was unaware of its responsibilities.

OTHER INFORMATION IN ANNUAL REPORTS

Section 7500 of the *CICA Handbook* details the auditor's responsibility for information in the annual report of a company. The primary responsibility is to ensure that the financial statements and auditor's report are accurately reproduced in the annual report. If the company's annual report has not been issued, correcting any misstatement is relatively easy; the auditor can simply ask management to correct the misstatement in the report. On the other hand, if the financial statements and annual report have already been issued when the misstatement is discovered, the auditor must be satisfied that management will take "reasonable steps" to notify users about the misstatement. If the auditor is not so satisfied, notice should be given to the board of directors and consideration should be given to what further action should be taken.

The auditor should also read the entire annual report to ascertain if any of the other information in the annual report is inconsistent with the financial statements. For example, assume that the president's letter in the annual report refers to an increase in earnings per share from $2.60 to $2.93. The auditor is required to compare that information to the financial statements to make sure that it corresponds. If an error exists in the financial statements and they have not been issued, the auditor should have them corrected or issue a reservation of opinion; if they have been issued, the auditor should treat the error as a subsequent discovery of a misstatement (Section 5405) and notify management. If it is the annual report that requires revision, the auditor should notify management. If the auditor cannot gain satisfaction from management, including the audit committee and the board of directors, the auditor should consider what further action is warranted.

The auditor has responsibilities beyond searching for misstatements in the financial statements in the annual report or for inconsistencies between the financial statements and other material in the annual report; paragraph 7500.20 requires the auditor to advise management of any material misstatements of fact that are contained in the annual report. The annual report may include, for instance, information about a fictitious lucrative contract with the company, which would affect the following years' business and profits significantly. If management refuses to correct the misstatements, the auditor should advise the audit committee and the board of directors. If satisfaction is still not obtained by the auditor, further action should be considered.

MANAGEMENT DISCUSSION AND ANALYSIS

The academic and professional literature include descriptions of research and articles that indicate that users of financial statements and annual reports are interested in an entity's future as well as its past and present. While an entity's financial statements, including the notes to those statements, present information about the entity's financial position and financial history, until recently, there was little information to inform users of expectations of the entity's management for the foreseeable future. In addition, there was a belief that it would be helpful to users if management were to provide a narrative expressing its interpretation of the entity's financial position and operations.

Section 4250, "Future-Oriented Financial Information (FOFI)," was added to the *CICA Handbook* in 1989 to provide guidance on preparing such information with the financial statements but did not require that FOFI be provided. To date, few companies are providing information under Section 4250. There is an Assurance and Related Services Guideline AuG-6, "Examination of a Financial Forecast or Projection Included in a Prospectus or Other Public Offering Document" that provides guidance on handling FOFI included in a prospectus but does not deal with the auditor's involvement when such information is included in an annual report.

In Canada and the United States, securities regulators, recognizing that there is a limit to the amount of information that can be communicated by the financial statements, including the notes, are requiring that companies that borrow money from or sell stock to the public provide a comment from management in the annual report; the comment would be supplementary to the financial statements and provide information about management's expectations. Such a report has come to be known as *management discussion and analysis* (MD&A).

MD&A is generally required by securities administrators in Canada. For example, the Ontario Securities Commission (OSC) requires most of its larger registrants to provide MD&A in their annual reports and suggests that MD&A also be provided with interim financial statements.[4] The description of MD&A in the Ontario Securities Commission's (OSC) Policy Statement 5.10[5] is helpful in understanding the concept.

> MD&A is supplemental analysis and explanation which accompanies but does not form part of the financial statements. MD&A provides management with the opportunity to explain in narrative form its current financial situation and future prospects. MD&A is intended to give the investor the ability to look at the [company issuing the financial statements] through the eyes of management by providing a historical and prospective analysis of the business of the [issuer]. MD&A requirements ask management to discuss the dynamics of the business and to analyze the financial statements. Coupled with the financial statements this information should allow investors to assess [the issuing company's] performance and future prospects.

The auditor's role with respect to MD&A is the same as the auditor's role with respect to the annual report as required by Section 7500.

---

[4]The interested reader is referred to the Ontario Securities Commission Policy Statement 5.10, "Annual Information Form and Management's Discussion and Analysis of Financial Condition and Results of Operations," or to the comparable release from the securities administrators in the reader's province. Appreciation is expressed to Ms. Brenda Eprile, (then) Chief Accountant to the OSC, for providing the authors with a copy of Policy Statement 5.10.

[5]Ibid., page 20.

EVALUATE RESULTS

OBJECTIVE 21-5

Integrate the audit evidence gathered, and evaluate the overall audit results.

After performing all audit procedures in each audit area, the auditor must integrate the results into *one overall conclusion*. Ultimately, the auditor must decide whether sufficient appropriate audit evidence has been accumulated to warrant the conclusion that the financial statements are stated in accordance with generally accepted accounting principles.

Figure 21-3 (page 678) summarizes the parts of the audit that must be reviewed in the evaluation of results. The emphasis is on the conclusions reached through tests of controls, analytical procedures, and tests of details of balances for each of the five cycles shown in the figure. Five aspects of evaluating the results are discussed.

SUFFICIENCY OF EVIDENCE

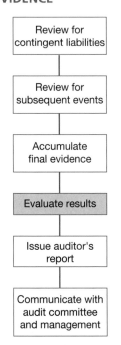

The final summarization of the adequacy of the evidence is a review by the auditor of the entire audit to determine whether all important aspects have been adequately tested considering the circumstances of the engagement. A major step in this process is reviewing the audit programs to make sure that all parts have been accurately completed and documented and that all audit objectives have been met. An important part of the review is deciding whether the audit program is adequate considering the problem areas that were discovered as the audit progressed. For example, if misstatements were discovered as part of the tests of sales, the initial plans for the tests of details of accounts receivable balances may have been insufficient. The final review should evaluate whether the revised audit program is adequate.

As an aid in drawing final conclusions about the adequacy of the audit evidence, auditors frequently use *completing the engagement checklists*. These are reminders of aspects of the audit that must not be overlooked. An illustration of part of a completing the engagement checklist is given in Figure 21-4 on page 679.

If the auditor concludes that he or she has *not* obtained sufficient evidence to draw a conclusion about the fairness of the client's representations, there are two choices: additional evidence must be obtained, or either a qualified opinion or a denial of opinion must be issued. The former is the more common choice as a client is not likely to agree to have a qualified auditor's report because of the auditor's failure to do sufficient work.

EVIDENCE SUPPORTING AUDITOR'S OPINION

An important part of evaluating whether the financial statements are fairly stated is summarizing the misstatements uncovered in the audit. Whenever the auditor uncovers misstatements that are in themselves material, entries should be proposed to the client to correct the statements. It may be difficult to determine the appropriate amount of adjustment because the true value of the misstatement is unknown; nevertheless, it is the auditor's responsibility to determine the required adjustment. In addition to the material misstatements, there are often a large number of immaterial misstatements discovered that are not adjusted at the time they are found. It is necessary to combine individually immaterial misstatements to evaluate whether the combined amount is material. The auditor can keep track of the misstatements and combine them in several different ways, but many auditors use a convenient method known as an *unadjusted misstatement worksheet* or *summary of possible adjustments*. It is relatively easy to evaluate the overall significance of several immaterial misstatements with this type of working paper. An example of an unadjusted misstatement worksheet is given in Figure 21-5 on page 679.

The auditor should consider carry-forward misstatements from the previous year in analyzing misstatements and the need for adjustment. For example, if closing inventory was understated by $15,000 in 1998 and overstated by $10,000 in 1999, the effect on income in 1999 would be $25,000. Although the individual misstatements may be immaterial, the combined effect might well be material and require adjustment.

FIGURE 21-3
Evaluating Engagement Results

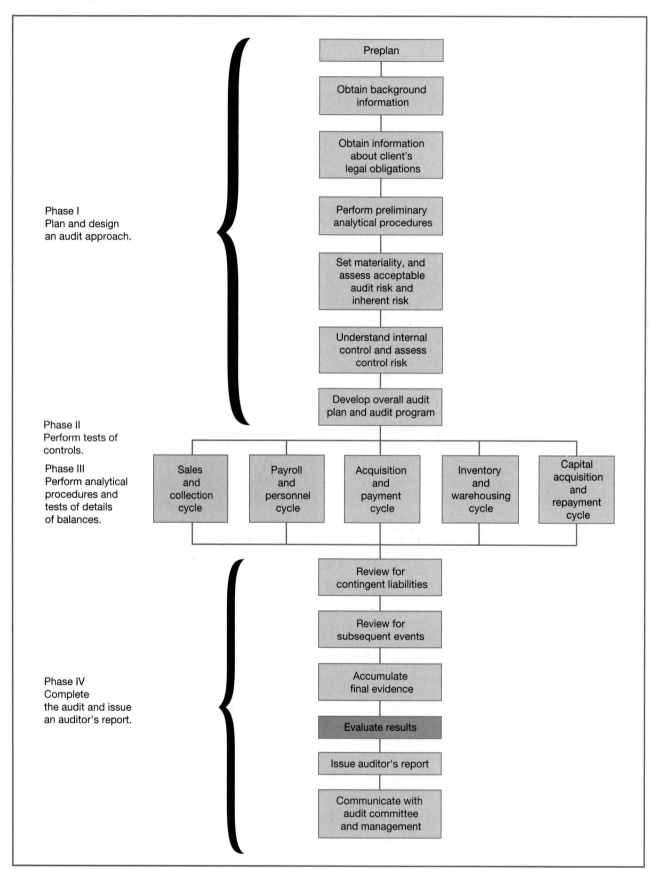

FIGURE 21-4
Completing the Engagement Checklist

	YES	NO	W/P Ref.
1. *Examination of prior year's working papers*			
a. Were last year's working papers and review notes examined for areas of emphasis in the current-year audit?	___	___	___
b. Was the permanent file reviewed for items that affect the current year?	___	___	___
2. *Internal control*			
a. Has internal control been adequately understood and reviewed?	___	___	___
b. Is the scope of the audit adequate in light of the assessed level of control risk?	___	___	___
c. Have all major weaknesses been included in a management letter and material weakness in a letter to the audit committee or senior management?	___	___	___
3. *General documents*			
a. Were all current-year minutes and resolutions reviewed, abstracted, and followed up?	___	___	___
b. Has the permanent file been updated?	___	___	___
c. Have all major contracts and agreements been reviewed and abstracted or copied to ascertain that the client complies with all existing legal requirements?	___	___	___

FIGURE 21-5
Unadjusted Misstatement Worksheet

Schedule A-3   Date
Prepared by PR 28/1/99
Approved by GS 31/1/99

Bradshaw Company, Inc.
Summary of Possible Adjustments

31/12/98

Possible Adjustments—Dr <Cr>

Workpaper Source		Total Amount	Current Assets	Noncurrent Assets	Current Liabilities	Noncurrent Liabilities	Sales and Revenues	Costs and Expenses	Income Tax
B-32	Unreimbursed petty cash vouchers	480	<480>		240			480	<240>
C-4	Possible underprovision in allowance for uncollectable accounts	4000	<4000>		2000			4000	<2000>
C-8	Accounts receivable/Sales cutoff misstatements	600	600		<300>		<600>		300
D-2	Difference between physical inventory and book figures	5200	5200		<2600>			<5200>	2600
H-7/2	Unrecorded liabilities	4850	2000	1850	<4350>			1000	<500>
V-10	Repairs expense items that should be capitalized	900		900	<450>			<900>	450
	Totals		3320	2750	<5460>		<600>	<620>	610

Conclusions:

The net effects of the above items are as follows:

Working capital	$<2140>
Total assets	6070
Net income	<610>
Materiality	$21000

None of these aggregate effects or of the individual items has a material effect on the financial statements in total or with respect to the components to which they pertain. On this basis, adjustment of any or all of the items is passed.

Paul Roberts
28/1/99

The schedule in Figure 21-5 includes both known misstatements that the client has decided not to adjust and projected misstatements, including sampling error. Observe that in the bottom left-hand portion of the working paper there is a comparison of possible adjustments to the preliminary judgment about materiality decided during planning.

If the auditor believes that he or she *has* sufficient evidence but that it does not warrant a conclusion of fairly presented financial statements, the auditor again has two choices: the statements must be revised to the auditor's satisfaction, or either a qualified or an adverse opinion must be issued. Notice that the options here are different from those in the case of obtaining insufficient evidence.

FINANCIAL STATEMENT DISCLOSURES

A major consideration in completing the audit is determining whether the disclosures in the financial statements are adequate. Throughout the audit, the emphasis in most examinations is on verifying the accuracy of the balances in the general ledger by testing the most important accounts on the auditor's trial balance. Another important task is to ensure that the account balances on the trial balance are correctly aggregated and disclosed on the financial statements. Naturally, adequate disclosure includes consideration of all of the statements including related footnotes.

The auditor actually prepares the financial statements from the trial balance in many small client audits and submits them to the client for approval. Having the auditor perform this function may seem to imply that the client is absolved of responsibility for the fair representation in the statements, but that is not the case. The auditor acts in the role of advisor when preparing the financial statements, but *management retains the final responsibility for approving the issuance of the statements.*

Review for adequate disclosure in the financial statements at the completion of the audit is not the only time the auditor is interested in proper disclosure. Unless the auditor is constantly alert for disclosure problems, it is impossible to perform the final disclosure review adequately. For example, as part of the examination of accounts receivable, the auditor must be aware of the need to separate accounts receivable, notes receivable, and other amounts due from affiliates and those due from customers. Similarly, there must be a segregation of current from noncurrent receivables and a disclosure of the factoring or discounting of notes receivable if such is the case. An important part of verifying all account balances is determining whether generally accepted accounting principles were properly applied on a basis consistent with that of the preceding year. The auditor must carefully document this information in the working papers to facilitate the final review.

As part of the final review for financial statement disclosure, many public accounting firms require the completion of a *financial statement disclosure checklist* for every engagement. This questionnaire is designed to remind the auditor of common disclosure problems encountered on audits and to facilitate the final review of the entire audit by an independent partner. An illustration of a partial financial statement disclosure checklist is given in Figure 21-6. Naturally, reliance on a checklist should not replace the auditor's own knowledge of generally accepted accounting principles. In any given audit, some aspects of the engagement require much greater expertise in accounting than can be obtained from such a checklist.

WORKING PAPER REVIEW

There are three main reasons why it is essential that the working papers be thoroughly reviewed by another member of the audit firm at the completion of the audit:

- *To evaluate the performance of inexperienced personnel.* A considerable portion of most audits is performed by audit personnel with less than four or five years of experience. These people may have sufficient technical training to conduct an adequate audit, but their lack of experience affects their ability to make sound professional judgments in complex situations.

FIGURE 21-6

Financial Statement
Disclosure Checklist:
Capital Assets

	YES	NO	W/P Ref.
1. Are the following disclosures in the financial statements or notes (Section 3060):			
a. Cost for each major category of capital assets?	___	___	___
b. The amount of amortization for the period?	___	___	___
c. Accumulated amortization, including the amount of any write-downs, for each major category of capital assets at the balance sheet date?	___	___	___
d. The amount of any write-downs during the period?	___	___	___
e. The amortization method used, including the amortization period or rate, for each major category of capital assets including leased assets? (also Section 3065)	___	___	___
f. The net carrying amount of a capital asset not being amortized because it is under construction or development, or has been removed from service for an extended period?	___	___	___
2. Are the nature, basis of measurement, amount, and related gains and losses of nonmonetary transactions disclosed? (Section 3830)	___	___	___
3. Has consideration been given to disclosure of fully amortized capital assets still in use?	___	___	___
4. Are carrying amounts of property mortgaged and encumbered by indebtedness disclosed? (Section 1500)	___	___	___
5. Is the carrying amount of property that is not a part of operations and is idle or held for investment or sale segregated?	___	___	___

Note: Information in parentheses refers to the *CICA Handbook*.

- *To make sure that the audit meets the public accounting firm's standard of performance.* Within any organization, the performance quality of individuals varies considerably, but careful review by top-level personnel in the firm assists in maintaining a uniform quality of auditing.
- *To counteract the bias that frequently enters into the auditor's judgment.* Auditors may attempt to remain objective throughout the audit, but it is easy to lose proper perspective on a long audit when there are complex problems to solve.

Except for a final independent review, which is discussed shortly, the review of the working papers should be conducted by someone who is knowledgeable about the client and the unique circumstances in the audit. Therefore, the initial review of the working papers prepared by any given auditor is normally done by the auditor's immediate supervisor. For example, the least experienced auditor's work is ordinarily reviewed by the audit senior; the senior's immediate supervisor, who is normally a supervisor or manager, reviews the senior's work and also reviews less thoroughly the papers of the inexperienced auditor. When several staff are working together at an engagement, team review by means of interview is used. The senior meets with staff on a daily basis, discusses the nature of findings, and ensures that these are appropriately recorded in the electronic working papers before the actual client documents are returned to the client. Finally, the partner assigned to the audit must ultimately review all working papers, but the partner reviews those prepared by the supervisor or manager more thoroughly than the others. Except for the final independent review, most of the working-paper review is done as each segment of the audit is completed.

INDEPENDENT REVIEW

At the completion of larger audits, the financial statements and the entire set of working papers are often reviewed by a completely independent reviewer who has not participated in the engagement. This reviewer, usually a partner, frequently takes an adversarial position to ensure the adequacy of the conduct of the audit. The audit team must be able to justify the evidence they have accumulated and the conclusions they have reached on the basis of the unique circumstances of the engagement.

Figure 21-7 summarizes the evaluation of the sufficiency of the evidence and the decision as to whether the evidence supports the opinion. The top portion of the figure shows the planning decisions that determine the planned audit evidence. It was taken from Figure 8-6 on page 254. The bottom portion shows how the auditor evaluates the sufficiency of the actual evidence by first evaluating whether the evidence gathered using substantive procedures was adequate to achieve the acceptable audit risk set for the audit given the auditor's assessment of inherent risk and control risk for the account and cycle and then making the same evaluation for the overall financial statements. The auditor also evaluates whether the evidence supports the audit opinion by first estimating misstatements in each account and then for the overall

FIGURE 21-7

Evaluating Results and Reaching Conclusions on the Basis of Evidence

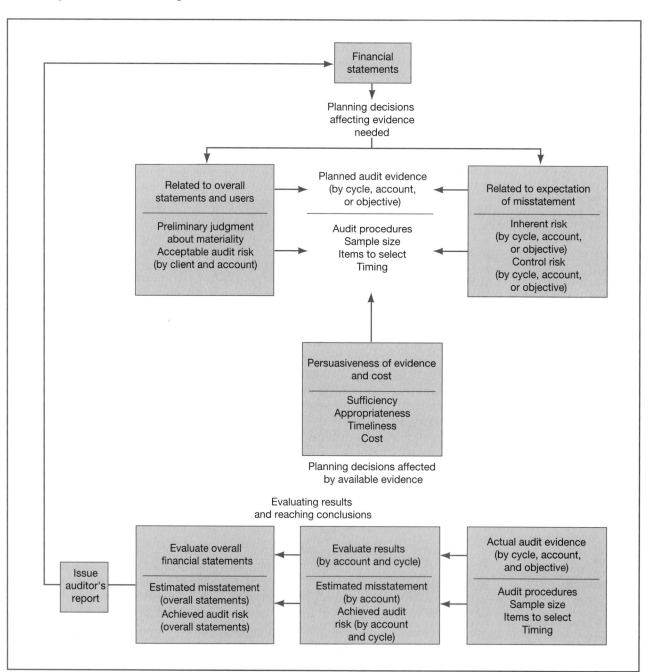

financial statements. In practice, both sets of evaluations are made at the same time. On the basis of these evaluations, the auditor's report is issued for the financial statements.

COMMUNICATE WITH THE AUDIT COMMITTEE AND MANAGEMENT

After the audit is completed, there are several potential communications from the auditor to client personnel. Most of these are directed to the audit committee or senior management, but communications with operating management are also common.

COMMUNICATE MISSTATEMENTS AND ILLEGAL ACTS

OBJECTIVE 21-6

Communicate effectively with the audit committee and management.

Section 5135 of the *CICA Handbook* requires the auditor to ensure that the appropriate level of management is informed of existing misstatements that are other than trivial. In addition, the auditor must ensure that the audit committee or similarly designated group (e.g., board of directors, board of trustees) is informed of all significant misstatements, whether or not they are adjusted. Misstatements include intentional (fraud and other irregularities) or unintentional (errors) misstatements. The audit committee can be informed by either the auditor or management, and this should be done on a timely basis. This requirement indicates the increased concern over the auditor's responsibility for the detection and prevention of misstatements.

Illegal acts are violations of laws or government regulations. Section 5136 requires the auditor to communicate illegal or possibly illegal acts, such as noncompliance with waste disposal regulations, to the audit committee or equivalent group on a timely basis. The audit committee may also expect the auditor to communicate such matters as unusual actions that increase the risk of loss to the company; actions that could cause serious embarrassment to the entity, such as breaches of the company's code of conduct; significant transactions that appear to be inconsistent with the ordinary course of business; or other matters. The audit committee's wishes should be discussed and clarified with the audit committee prior to the auditor's undertaking of the audit field work.

COMMUNICATE REPORTABLE INTERNAL CONTROL CONDITIONS

As discussed in Chapter 9, Section 5135 includes misstatements that indicate significant deficiencies in the design or operation of internal control in its definition of significant misstatements that must be reported to the audit committee. Although the auditor has no duty to report less significant internal control weaknesses identified during the audit to the client, he or she commonly does so as a client service. In addition, some auditors provide suggestions for improvements in internal control. In larger companies, this communication is made to the audit committee, and in smaller companies, to the owners or senior management. The nature and form of this communication were discussed in Chapter 9. Section 5220.07 requires the auditor to communicate to the audit committee, or equivalent, information about significant weaknesses in internal control discovered during the financial statement audit.

OTHER COMMUNICATION WITH AUDIT COMMITTEE

The auditor should communicate certain additional information obtained during the audit for audits where there is an audit committee or similarly designated body. Like all communications with the audit committee, the purpose is to keep the committee informed of auditing issues and findings that will assist it in performing its supervisory role for financial statements.

Audit committees were introduced in Chapter 3. It was pointed out there that their role as specified by the *Canada Business Corporations Act* was quite limited but that there were many useful functions the audit committee could perform. The following are issues that could be discussed with the audit committee, or a similarly designated body, by the auditor with the intent of keeping the audit committee informed:

Review for
contingent liabilities

Review for
subsequent events

Accumulate
final evidence

Evaluate results

Issue auditor's
report

Communicate with
audit committee
and management

- The auditor's responsibilities under generally accepted auditing standards, including responsibility for understanding and evaluating internal control and the concept of reasonable rather than absolute assurance
- Planning of the current audit, including such matters as the general approach, areas of perceived high risk, materiality and risk levels selected, planned reliance on other auditors (including the internal audit department), and timing of the audit
- The significant accounting principles and policies selected and applied to the financial statements, the existence of acceptable alternatives, and the acceptability of those selected by management
- Management's judgments and estimates of sensitive accounting-related issues and the auditor's conclusions about the reasonableness of them
- Disagreements with management about the scope of the audit, applicability of accounting principles, and wording of the auditor's report, whether or not satisfactorily resolved
- Difficulties encountered in performing the audit, such as lack of availability of client personnel, failure to obtain necessary information, and an unreasonable timetable in which to complete the audit
- Any unresolved matters arising from review of the entire annual report and identification of misstatements in reproducing the financial statements or the auditor's report, or of inconsistencies between the statements and other information in the report
- If the auditor becomes aware of any consultation with other accountants about accounting or auditing matters, the auditor's opinions about the subjects of these consultations
- Any major issues discussed with management in connection with the appointment of the auditor, including those related to the application of accounting principles, auditing standards, and fees

Communication with the audit committee normally takes place more than once during each audit and can be oral, written, or both. The *CICA Handbook* does not specify the form of communication but uses the terminology "communicate" or "inform." For example, issues dealing with the auditor's responsibilities and significant accounting policies are usually discussed early in the audit, preferably during the planning phase. Disagreements with management and difficulties encountered in performing the audit would be communicated after the audit is completed or earlier if the problems hinder the auditor's ability to complete the audit. The most important matters are communicated in writing to minimize misunderstanding and to provide documentation in the event of subsequent disagreement.

MANAGEMENT LETTERS

The purpose of a management letter (letter of recommendation) is to inform the client of the public accountant's recommendations for improving the client's business. The recommendations focus on suggestions for more efficient operations. The combination of the auditor's experience in various businesses and a thorough understanding gained in conducting the audit place the auditor in a unique position to provide management with assistance.

A management letter is different from a required communication on matters related to internal control discussed in Chapter 9. The latter is required whenever there are significant internal control weaknesses. A management letter is optional and is intended to help the client operate its business more effectively. Auditors write management letters for two reasons: to encourage a better relationship between the public accounting firm and management and to suggest additional tax and management advisory services that the public accounting firm can provide.

There is no standard format or approach for writing management letters. Each letter should be developed to meet the style of the auditor and the needs of the client, consistent with the public accounting firm's concept of management letters. It should be noted that many auditors combine the management letter with the required communication on internal control-related matters. On smaller audits, it is common for the auditor to communicate operational suggestions orally rather than by letter.

SUBSEQUENT DISCOVERY OF FACTS[6]

Identify the auditor's responsibilities when facts affecting the auditor's report are discovered after its issuance.

If the auditor becomes aware *after the audited financial statements have been released* that some information included in the statements is materially misleading, the auditor has an obligation under Section 5405 of the *CICA Handbook* to make certain that users who are relying on the financial statements are informed about the misstatements.

The *CICA Handbook* requires the auditor first to discuss the matter with management and, if required or appropriate, with the board of directors or the audit committee. The auditor also has an obligation, under the *Canada Business Corporations Act* (Section 171(7)) to notify each of the directors. The directors are required to prepare and issue revised financial statements or otherwise inform the shareholders. The directors must also inform the director of the Corporations Branch of the Department of Consumer and Corporate Affairs and may have to inform other regulatory agencies.

If a director or officer discovers a misstatement of any size, he or she is required to notify the audit committee *and* the auditor. The responsibilities of the former are not specified, but presumably it would notify its fellow directors. The auditor would first decide if the misstatement is material and, if so, notify each director.

The most likely case in which the auditor is faced with this problem occurs when the financial statements are determined to include a material misstatement subsequent to the issuance of an unqualified report. Possible causes of misstatements are the inclusion of material fictitious sales, the failure to write off obsolete inventory, or the omission of an essential footnote. Regardless of whether the failure to discover the misstatement was the fault of the auditor or the client, the auditor's responsibility remains the same.

The most desirable approach to follow if the auditor discovers that the statements are misleading is to request that the client issue an immediate revision of the financial statements containing an explanation of the reasons for the revision. The auditor may decide, after consideration of the misstatement, to revise the financial statements and issue a double dated auditor's report with respect to the misstatement. On the other hand, the auditor may decide that further work is required and a new auditor's report, with the current date, is necessary. The auditor's report, in any event, should clearly indicate that the previous statements were withdrawn and that they have been revised. This information would normally be in a paragraph following the opinion paragraph. If a subsequent period's financial statements were completed before the revised statements could be issued, it is acceptable to disclose the misstatements in the subsequent period's statements.

If the client refuses to cooperate in disclosing the misstated information, the auditor should inform the board of directors of this fact. In addition, the auditor should seek legal advice as to what he or she should do to discharge his or her responsibilities and consider resigning from the engagement.

It is important to understand that the subsequent discovery of facts requiring the recall or re-issuance of financial statements *does not arise from developments occurring after the date of the auditor's report*. For example, if an auditor believes that an accounts receivable is collectible after an adequate review of the facts at the date of the audi-

---

[6]The discussion in this section is more closely related to the auditor's report, which is the subject of Chapter 2, than it is to completing the audit. However, many students of auditing confuse the examination of subsequent period events as a part of post-balance sheet review with the subsequent discovery of facts existing at the balance sheet date. The latter is studied at this point to eliminate the confusion.

tor's report but the customer subsequently files bankruptcy, a revision of the financial statements is not required. The statements must be recalled or re-issued only when information that would indicate that the statements were not fairly presented *already existed at the auditor's report date*. If, in the previous example, the customer had filed for bankruptcy before the audit report date, there would be a subsequent discovery of facts.

In an earlier section, it was shown that the auditor's responsibility for subsequent events review begins on the balance sheet date and ends on the date of the completion of the field work. Any pertinent information discovered as part of the review can be incorporated in the financial statements before they are issued. Note that the auditor has no responsibility to search for subsequent facts of the nature discussed in this section, but if the auditor discovers that issued financial statements are improperly stated, he or she must take action to correct them. The auditor's responsibility for reporting on improperly issued financial statements does not start until the date of the auditor's report. Typically, an existing material misstatement is found as part of the subsequent year's audit, or it may be reported to the auditor by the client.

Figure 21-8 shows the difference in the period covered by the review for subsequent events and that for the discovery of facts after the auditor's report date. If the auditor discovers subsequent facts after the audit report date, but before the financial statements are issued, he or she would require that the financial statements be revised before they are issued.

FIGURE 21-8

Review for Subsequent Events and Subsequent Discovery of Facts

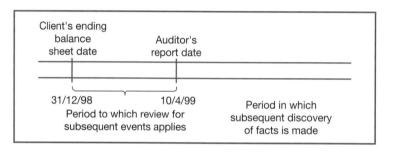

ESSENTIAL TERMS

Commitments — agreements that the entity will hold to a fixed set of conditions, such as the purchase or sale of merchandise at a stated price, at a future date, regardless of what happens to profits or to the economy as a whole (p. 667).

Completing the engagement checklist — a reminder to the auditor of aspects of the audit that may have been overlooked (p. 677).

Contingent liability — a potential future obligation to an outside party for an unknown amount resulting from activities that have already taken place (p. 665).

Dual-dated auditor's report — the use of one auditor's report date for normal subsequent events and a later date for one or more subsequent events that come to the auditor's attention after the field work has been completed (p. 672).

Financial statement disclosure checklist — a questionnaire that reminds the auditor of disclosure problems commonly encountered in audits and that facilitates the final review of the entire audit by an independent partner (p. 680).

Independent review — a review of the financial statements and the entire set of working papers by a completely independent reviewer to whom the audit team must justify the evidence accumulated and the conclusions reached (p. 681).

Inquiry of client's law firms — a letter from the client's legal counsel informing the auditor of pending litigation or any other information involving legal counsel that is relevant to financial statement disclosure (p. 668).

Letter of representation — a written communication from the client to the auditor formalizing statements that the client has made about matters pertinent to the audit (p. 674).

Management discussion and analysis (MD&A) — supplemental analysis and explanation by management that accompanies but does not form part of the financial statements (p. 676).

Other information in annual reports — information that is not a part of published financial statements but is published with them; must be read by auditors for inconsistencies with the financial statements and misleading information (p. 675).

Outstanding claim — a lawsuit that has been brought against a client; also known as an *asserted claim* (p. 668).

Possible claim — *see* unasserted claim.

Review for subsequent events — the auditing procedures performed by auditors to identify and evaluate subsequent events (p. 670).

Subsequent events — transactions and other pertinent events that occurred after the balance sheet date that affect the fair presentation or disclosure of the statements being audited (p. 670).

Unadjusted misstatement worksheet — a summary of immaterial misstatements not adjusted at the time they were found, used to help the auditor assess whether the combined amount is material; also known as a *summary of possible adjustments* (p. 677).

Unasserted claim — a potential legal claim against a client where the condition for a claim exists but no claim has been filed (p. 668).

Working paper review — a review of the completed audit working papers by another member of the audit firm to ensure quality and counteract bias (p. 680).

REVIEW QUESTIONS

21-1 Distinguish between a contingent liability and an actual liability, and give three examples of each.

21-2 In the audit of James Mobley Ltd., you are concerned about the possibility of contingent liabilities resulting in income tax disputes. Discuss the procedures you could use for an extensive investigation in this area.

21-3 Explain why the analysis of legal expense is an essential part of every audit engagement.

21-4 During the audit of the Merrill Manufacturing Corp., Ralph Pyson, a public accountant, has become aware of four lawsuits against the client through discussions with the client, reading corporate minutes, and reviewing correspondence files. How should Pyson determine the materiality of the lawsuits and the proper disclosure in the financial statements?

21-5 Distinguish between an outstanding (asserted) and a possible (unasserted) claim. Explain why a client's law firm may not reveal a possible claim.

21-6 Describe the action that an auditor should take if a law firm refuses to provide information that is within its jurisdiction and may directly affect the fair presentation of the financial statements.

21-7 Distinguish between subsequent events requiring adjustment and those requiring disclosure. Give two examples of each type.

21-8 In obtaining confirmations from law firms, Betty Chui's aim is to receive the confirmation letters as early as possible after the balance sheet date. This provides her with a signed letter from every law firm in time to investigate properly any exceptions. It also eliminates the problem of a lot of unresolved loose ends near the end of the audit. Evaluate Chui's approach.

21-9 Explain why an auditor would be interested in a client's future commitments to purchase raw materials at a fixed price.

21-10 What major considerations should the auditor take into account in determining how extensive the review of subsequent events should be?

21-11 Identify five audit procedures normally done as part of the review for subsequent events.

21-12 Distinguish between subsequent events occurring between the balance sheet date and the date of the auditor's report, and subsequent discovery of facts existing at the date of the auditor's report. Give two examples of each, and explain the appropriate action by the auditor in each instance.

21-13 Dorinda Robertson, a public accountant, believes that the final summarization is the easiest part of the audit if careful planning is followed throughout the engagement. She makes sure each segment of the audit is completed before she goes on to the next. When the last segment of the engagement is completed, she is finished with the audit. She believes that although this may cause each part of the audit to take a little longer, she makes up for it by not having to do the final summarization. Evaluate Robertson's approach.

21-14 Compare and contrast the accumulation of audit evidence and the evaluation of the adequacy of the disclosures in the financial statements. Give two examples in which adequate disclosure could depend heavily on the accumulation of evidence and two others in which audit evidence does not normally affect the adequacy of the disclosure significantly.

21-15 Explain the meaning of the following: The auditor should actively evaluate whether there is substantial doubt about the client's ability to continue as a going concern.

21-16 Distinguish between a client's letter of representation and a management letter, and state the primary purpose of each. List some items that might be included in each letter.

21-17 What is meant by "reading other financial information" in annual reports? Give an example of the type of information that the auditor would be examining.

21-18 Explain why you think securities regulators in certain jurisdictions require public companies to provide MD&A in their annual reports.

21-19 Distinguish between regular working-paper review and independent review, and state the purpose of each. Give two examples of important potential findings in each of these two types of review.

MULTIPLE CHOICE QUESTIONS

21-20 The following questions deal with contingent liabilities. Choose the best response.

a. The audit step most likely to reveal the existence of contingent liabilities is

(1) accounts payable confirmations.
(2) an inquiry directed to law firms.
(3) mortgage-note confirmation.
(4) a review of vouchers paid during the month following the year end.

b. When a contingency is resolved immediately subsequent to the issuance of a report that included an appropriate note on the contingency, the auditor should
   (1) inform the appropriate authorities that the report cannot be relied upon.
   (2) insist that the client issue revised financial statements.
   (3) inform the audit committee that the report cannot be relied upon.
   (4) take no action regarding the event.

(AICPA adapted)

21-21 The following questions concern letters of representation. Choose the best response.

a. A principal purpose of a letter of representation from management is to
   (1) serve as an introduction to company personnel and an authorization to examine the records.
   (2) remind management of its primary responsibility for financial statements.
   (3) discharge the auditor from legal liability for his or her examination.
   (4) confirm in writing management's approval of limitations on the scope of the audit.

(AICPA adapted)

b. A representation letter issued by a client
   (1) is essential for the preparation of the audit program.
   (2) is a substitute for testing.
   (3) does *not* reduce the auditor's responsibility.
   (4) reduces the auditor's responsibility only to the extent that it is relied upon.

c. The date of the management representation letter should coincide with the
   (1) balance sheet date.
   (2) date of the auditor's report.
   (3) date of the engagement agreement.
   (4) date of the latest subsequent event referred to in the notes to the financial statements.

(AICPA adapted)

d. Management's refusal to furnish a written representation on a matter the auditor considers essential constitutes
   (1) a scope limitation sufficient to preclude an unqualified opinion.
   (2) *prima facie* evidence that the financial statements are *not* presented fairly.
   (3) a violation of the *Canada Business Corporations Act*.
   (4) a GAAP violation sufficient to preclude an unqualified opinion.

(AICPA adapted)

21-22 The following questions deal with review of subsequent events. Choose the best response.

a. Subsequent events for reporting purposes are defined as events that occur subsequent to the
   (1) balance sheet date but prior to the date of the auditor's report.
   (2) balance sheet date.
   (3) date of the auditor's report.
   (4) date of the auditor's report and concern contingencies that are not reflected in the financial statements.

b. A major customer of an audit client suffers a fire just prior to completion of year-end field work. The audit client believes that this event could have a significant direct effect on the financial statements. The auditor should
   (1) advise management to adjust the financial statements.
   (2) advise management to disclose the event in notes to the financial statements.
   (3) disclose the event in the auditor's report.
   (4) withhold submission of the auditor's report until the extent of the direct effect on the financial statements is known.

c. An example of an event occurring in the period of the auditor's field work subsequent to the end of the year being audited that normally would not require disclosure in the financial statements or the auditor's report would be
   (1) issuance of a widely advertised capital stock issue with restrictive covenants.
   (2) decreased sales volume resulting from a general business recession.
   (3) serious damage to the company's plant from a widespread flood.
   (4) settlement of a large liability for considerably less than the amount recorded.

d. With respect to issuance of an auditor's report that is dual dated for a subsequent event occurring after the completion of field work but before issuance of the auditor's report, the auditor's responsibility for events occurring subsequent to the completion of field work is
   (1) limited to the specific event referred to in the auditor's report.
   (2) limited to all events occurring up to the date of issuance of the report.
   (3) extended to include all events occurring until the date of the last subsequent event referred to in the auditor's report.
   (4) extended to include all events occurring up to the date of submission of the report to the client.

e. Shona Karr has examined the financial statements of Lurch Corporation for the year ended December 31, 1998. Although Karr's field work was completed on February 27, 1999, Karr's auditor's report was dated February 28, 1999, and was received by the management of Lurch on March 5, 1999. On April 4, 1999, the management of Lurch asked that Karr approve inclusion of this report in its annual report to shareholders, which will include unaudited financial statements for the first quarter ended March 31, 1999. Karr approved the inclusion of this auditor's report in the annual report to shareholders. Under the circumstances, Karr is responsible for inquiring as to subsequent events occurring through
   (1) February 27, 1999.
   (2) February 28, 1999.
   (3) March 31, 1999.
   (4) April 4, 1999.

(AICPA adapted)

DISCUSSION QUESTIONS AND PROBLEMS

21-23 Kathy Choi, a public accountant, has completed the audit of notes payable and other liabilities for Valley River Electrical Services Ltd. and now plans to audit contingent liabilities and commitments.

Required

a. Distinguish between contingent liabilities and commitments, and explain why both are important in an audit.

b. Identify three useful audit procedures for uncovering contingent liabilities that Choi would likely perform in the normal conduct of the audit even if she had no responsibility for uncovering contingencies.

c. Identify three other procedures Choi would likely perform for the purpose of identifying undisclosed contingencies.

21-24 In an examination of Marco Corporation as of December 31, 1998, the following situations exist. No related entries have been made in the accounting records.

1. Marco Corporation has guaranteed the payment of interest on the 10-year, first mortgage bonds of Chen Corp., an affiliate. Outstanding bonds of Chen Corp. amount to $150,000 with interest payable at 8 percent per annum, due June 1 and December 1 each year. The bonds were issued by Chen on December 31, 1996, and all interest payments have been met by that company with the exception of the payment due December 1, 1998. The Marco Corporation states that it will pay the defaulted interest to the bondholders on January 15, 1999.

2. During the year 1998, Marco Corporation was named as a defendant in a suit for damages by Dalton Inc. for breach of contract. A decision adverse to Marco Corporation was rendered, and Dalton Inc. was awarded $40,000 in damages. At the time of the audit, the case was under appeal to a higher court.

3. On December 23, 1998, Marco Corporation declared a common share dividend of 1,000 shares with a stated value of $100,000 of its common stock, payable February 2, 1999, to the common shareholders of record December 30, 1998.

Required

a. Define "contingent liability."

b. Describe the audit procedures that you would use to learn about each of the above situations.

c. Describe the nature of the adjusting entries or disclosure, if any, that you would require for each of these situations.

(AICPA adapted)

21-25 The field work for the June 30, 1999, audit of Tracy Brewing Ltd. was finished August 19, 1999, and the completed financial statements, accompanied by the signed auditor's reports, were mailed September 6, 1999. In each of the highly material events (a through i), state the appropriate action (1 through 4) for the situation, and justify your

response. Possible actions are as follows:

1. Adjust the June 30, 1999, financial statements.

2. Disclose the information in a footnote in the June 30, 1999, financial statements.

3. Request the client to recall the June 30, 1999, statements for revision.

4. No action is required.

The events are as follows:

a. On December 14, 1999, the auditor discovered that a debtor of Tracy Brewing went bankrupt on October 2, 1999. The sale of goods took place April 15, 1999, but the amount appeared to be collectible on June 30, 1999, and August 19, 1999.

b. On August 15, 1999, the auditor discovered that a debtor of Tracy Brewing went bankrupt on August 1, 1999. The most recent sale had taken place April 2, 1998, and no cash receipts had been received since that date.

c. On December 14, 1999, the auditor discovered that a debtor of Tracy Brewing went bankrupt on July 15, 1999, due to declining financial health. The sale of goods had taken place January 15, 1999.

d. On August 6, 1999, the auditor discovered that a debtor of Tracy Brewing went bankrupt on July 30, 1999. The cause of the bankruptcy was an unexpected loss of a major lawsuit on July 15, 1999, resulting from a product deficiency suit by a different customer.

e. On August 6, 1999, the auditor discovered that a debtor of Tracy Brewing went bankrupt on July 30, 1999, for a sale that took place on July 3, 1999. The cause of the bankruptcy was a major uninsured fire on July 20, 1999.

f. On May 31, 1999, the auditor discovered an uninsured lawsuit against Tracy Brewing that had originated on February 28, 1999.

g. On July 20, 1999, Tracy Brewing settled a lawsuit out of court that had originated in 1996 and is currently listed as a contingent liability.

h. On September 14, 1999, Tracy Brewing lost a court case that had originated in 1998 for an amount equal to the lawsuit. The June 30, 1999, footnotes state that, in the opinion of legal counsel, there will be a favourable settlement.

i. On July 20, 1999, a lawsuit was filed against Tracy Brewing for a patent infringement action that allegedly took place in early 1999. In the opinion of legal counsel, there is a danger of a significant loss to the client.

21-26 Melanie Adams is a partner in a medium-sized public accounting firm and takes an active part in the conduct of every audit she supervises. She follows the practice of reviewing all working papers of subordinates as soon as it is convenient, rather than waiting until the end of the audit. When the audit is nearly finished, Adams reviews the working papers again to make sure she has not missed anything significant. Since she makes most of the major decisions on the audit, there is rarely anything that requires further investigation. When she completes the review, she prepares a pencil draft of the financial statements, gets them approved by management, and has them keyed, printed out, and assembled in her firm's office. No other partner reviews the working papers because Adams is responsible for signing the auditor's reports.

Required

a. Evaluate the practice of reviewing the working papers of subordinates on a continuing basis rather than when the audit is completed.

b. Is it acceptable for Adams to prepare the financial statements rather than make the client assume the responsibility?

c. Evaluate the practice of not having a review of the working papers by another partner in the firm.

21-27 Ruben Chavez, public accountant, has prepared a letter of representation for the president and controller to sign. It contains references to the following items:

1. Inventory is fairly stated at the lower of cost or market and includes no obsolete items.

2. All actual and contingent liabilities are properly included in the statements.

3. All subsequent events of relevance to the financial statements have been disclosed.

Required

a. Why is it desirable to have a letter of representation from the client concerning the above matters when the audit evidence accumulated during the course of the engagement is meant to verify the same information?

b. To what extent is the letter of representation useful as audit evidence? Explain.

c. List several other types of information commonly included in a letter of representation.

21-28 Generally accepted accounting practice recognizes that the balance sheet date is arbitrary but that the operations of an enterprise are continuous. The financial statements should therefore reflect the effects of some events that did not actually occur until after the balance sheet date. Several methods exist for reporting the effects of such events in the financial statements.

Required

a. Describe the criteria you would apply in determining whether and how to report in the financial statements events occurring subsequent to the balance sheet date.

b. Apply the criteria you described in part (a) to each of the following unrelated situations, explaining how you would determine which situation(s) should be reported in the December 31, 1999, financial statements of the affected company.

(1) On February 14, 2000, Xavier Limited acquired for cash the inventory and plant of a smaller competitor. The acquisition required most of Xavier's cash, which had amounted to 15 percent of its assets as at December 31, 1999.

(2) About 10 percent of the consolidated sales of Yarmora Limited and its subsidiaries have been made by a particular subsidiary (which is not wholly-owned). The financial situation of that subsidiary has deteriorated recently, and on February 15, 2000, the directors of the subsidiary decided on a voluntary liquidation. Although the liquidation will take some time, the directors expect that the shareholders will ultimately recover the book value of their shares. The financial statements of Yarmora are prepared on a consolidated basis.

(3) On February 15, 2000, Zabry Limited's largest customer, which had been responsible for 30 percent of Zabry's sales, signed a long-term purchase contract with a competitor of the company. The customer informed Zabry Limited that it no longer intended to purchase any of the company's products.

(CICA adapted)

21-29 In connection with your examination of the financial statements of Olars Mfg. Corporation for the year ended December 31, 1999, your review of subsequent events disclosed the following items:

1. January 3, 2000: The provincial government approved a plan for the construction of an express highway. The plan will result in the expropriation of a portion of land owned by Olars Mfg. Corporation. Construction will begin in late 2000. No estimate of the condemnation (expropriation) award is available.

2. January 4, 2000: The funds for a $25,000 loan to the corporation made by Mr. Olars, the president, on July 15, 1999, were obtained by him by a loan on his personal life insurance policy. The loan was recorded in the account "loan from officers." Mr. Olars's source of the funds was not disclosed in the company records. The corporation pays the premiums on the life insurance policy, and Mrs. Olars, wife of the president, is the beneficiary.

3. January 7, 2000: The mineral content of a shipment of ore which was en route on December 31, 1999, was determined to be 72 percent. The shipment was recorded at year end at an estimated content of 50 percent by a debit to raw material inventory and a credit to accounts payable in the amount of $20,600. The final liability to the vendor is based on the actual mineral content of the shipment.

4. January 15, 2000: As a result of a series of personal disagreements between Mr. Olars and his brother-in-law, the treasurer, the latter resigned, effective immediately, under an agreement whereby the corporation would purchase his 10 percent stock ownership at book value as of December 31, 1999. Payment is to be made in two equal amounts in cash on April 1, 2000, and October 1, 2000. In December 1999, the treasurer obtained a divorce from his wife, who was Mr. Olars's sister.

5. January 31, 2000: As a result of reduced sales, production was curtailed in mid-January and some workers were laid off. On February 5, 2000, all the remaining workers went on strike. To date, the strike is unsettled.

6. February 10, 2000: A contract was signed whereby Mammoth Enterprises purchases from Olars Mfg. Corporation all of the latter's capital assets (including rights to receive the proceeds of any property condemnation), inventories, and the right to conduct business under the name "Olars Mfg. Division." The effective date of the transfer will be March 1, 2000. The sale price was $500,000, subject to adjustment following the taking of a physical inventory. Important factors contributing to the decision to enter into the contract were the policy of the board of directors of Mammoth Enterprises to diversify the firm's activities and the report of a survey conducted by an independent market appraisal firm that revealed a declining market for Olars products.

Required

Assume that the items described above came to your attention prior to completion of your audit work on February 15, 2000. For *each* item:

a. Give the audit procedures, if any, that would have brought the item to your attention. Indicate other sources of information that may have revealed the item.

b. Discuss the disclosure that you would recommend for the item, listing all details that you would suggest should be disclosed. Indicate those items or details, if any, that should not be disclosed. Give your reasons for recommending or not recommending disclosure of the items or details.

(AICPA adapted)

21-30 The following unrelated events occurred after the balance sheet date but before the auditor's report was prepared:

1. The granting of a retroactive pay increase.

2. Determination by Revenue Canada of additional income tax due for a prior year.

3. Charging the entity with restriction of trade by the federal government.

4. Declaration of a stock dividend.

5. Sale of a capital asset at a substantial profit.

Required

a. Explain how each of the above items might have come to the auditor's attention.

b. Discuss the auditor's responsibility to recognize each of these items in connection with his or her report.

(AICPA adapted)

21-31 The philosophy of Barbara Hatton, public accountant, is that transactions taking place during the current audit period should be audited intensively but that subsequent transactions should be ignored. She believes each year should stand on its own and be audited in the year in which the transactions take place. According to Hatton, "If a transaction recorded in the subsequent period is audited in the current period, it is verified twice — once this year and again in next year's audit. That is a duplication of effort and a waste of time."

Required

a. Explain the fallacy in Hatton's argument.

b. Give six specific examples of information obtained by examining subsequent events that are essential to the current-period audit.

21-32 In analyzing legal expense for the Boastman Bottle Company, Bart Little, public accountant, observes that the company has paid legal fees to three different law firms during the current year. In accordance with his accounting firm's normal operating practice, Little requests standard confirmation letters as of the balance sheet date from each of the three law firms.

On the last day of field work, Little notes that one of the confirmations has not yet been received. The confirmation from the second law firm contains a statement to the effect that the law firm deals exclusively in registering patents and refuses to comment on any lawsuits or other legal affairs of the client. The confirmation letter from the third law firm states that there is an outstanding unpaid bill due from the client and recognizes the existence of a potentially material lawsuit against the client but refuses to comment further to protect the legal rights of the client.

Required

a. Evaluate Little's approach to requesting the confirmations and his follow-up on the responses.

b. What should Little do about each of the confirmations?

21-33 Betty Ann Jarrett, CA, was reading the annual report of Watgold Ltd. and noticed that the president's report contradicted several items in the audited financial statements included in the report.

Required

What are Betty Ann's responsibilities in this instance?

21-34 You are a partner in the public accounting firm of Lind and Hemming. One of your larger clients is Yukon Corp., a company incorporated under the *Canada Business Corporations Act*, which has a December 31 year end. Yukon's 1998 audit was completed in January 1999; the auditor's report was dated January 28, 1999.

It is now August 1999 and professional staff from your office are working at Yukon doing interim work on the December 31, 1999, audit. Yesterday, the senior in charge of the audit gave you a memo dated August 4, 1999, revealing that the staff have discovered that several large blocks of inventory were materially overpriced at December 31, 1998, and have since been written down to reflect their true value.

You have just finished reviewing again the 1998 working papers and have determined that the error was a sampling error; your firm does not appear to have been negligent.

Required

What action would you take and why? Support your answer.

CASES

21-35 You are in charge of the audit field work of a multinational public company with subsidiaries in Europe, Asia, and South America, which has expanded very rapidly over the last few years. Your firm has recognized that public accounting firms perform audit examinations in those countries in which subsidiaries are located. The following paragraphs are extracted from a letter received from one of these public accounting firms just prior to the issuance of your audit opinion on the consolidated financial statements. As in past years, your planned audit opinion contained no qualifications. The subsidiary audited by the public accounting firm that sent you the letter accounts for approximately 20 percent of consolidated sales, net income, and assets.

> Our review of cash expenditures revealed a number of payments to senior government officials amounting to approximately 50 percent of net income before taxes. These payments have been recorded as promotional expenses. We were unable to obtain documentary evidence to support the nature of these payments, but client management personnel claim that these payments were necessary in order to obtain government approval for some client sales contracts. We were informed that these payments represent donations to political campaign funds.
>
> Although we have no direct evidence, we believe that these payments have been instrumental in obtaining a number of very profitable contracts that contributed over 50 percent of sales.
>
> Finally, our discussions with client personnel, all of whom are citizens of this country, lead us to believe that they took it upon themselves to authorize these payments. We found no evidence to suggest that the payments were made known in advance to head office management. However, we cannot state whether head office management was subsequently informed of these payments.

Required

Discuss your professional responsibilities in this situation assuming the two following situations:

a. Donations to political campaign funds are legal in the subsidiary's country.

b. Donations to political campaign funds are illegal in the subsidiary's country.

(CICA adapted)

21-36 You are the senior on the audit of Dahlstrom Manufacturing Corp. Dahlstrom manufactures various sizes of cardboard boxes. These are customized both in terms of size and printing, and are used by producers of various types of retail food products. Your present task is to draft an internal control letter and a management letter to the company. Your firm prepares these letters using the following process:

1. As work is done, auditors who observe a possible internal control or management letter item fill out an electronic form (a word processing template) that shows a description of the item and a recommended solution.

2. The senior drafts both the internal control letter and the management letter using word processing software and the firm's standard formats.

   The standard formats:
   (i) Contain standard introduction and ending sections
   (ii) Require three segments for each item: description of finding or observation, possible consequences if item is not resolved, and suggestion(s) for resolution

3. The drafts are reviewed by the manager and discussed with appropriate client personnel. They are then finalized and delivered.

Following is a summary of the internal control and management letter items being suggested by the audit team, in the order in which they were documented. Each item is stated and then followed by a suggested solution.

1. In sampling sales invoices, it was noted that in a sample of 60 items, 4 items were recorded on a different date than the day that the goods were shipped.

   The company should batch invoices by the date of shipment, accounting for their numerical sequence, and ensure that the date of shipment is used when the invoices are input into the computer system.

2. While verifying prices on sales invoices, it was noticed that prices charged differed from catalogue prices in a number of instances. These price differences were authorized by regional sales managers as per company policy. However, we also received comments on our accounts receivable confirmation replies that some sales were in dispute, and the credit manager told us that there were some collection problems that arose from pricing differences.

   The company should consider reviewing its pricing policies and related practices.

3. In conducting our inventory observation, we noted that there was a large buildup of work-in-process inventory between the cutting and printing operations. Workers in the folding/gluing operation were observed idle, waiting for output from printing to continue their work.

   The company should consider reviewing the design of its production line, specifically the printing operation, for a possible bottleneck problem.

4. When we conducted our inventory observation, we noted a significant amount of cardboard stock [raw material to the production process] that had apparently not

been used for some time. It was still bound by strapping and covered with dust.

The client should determine whether this stock can be used in production, and if not, consider whether it can be sold.

5. In conducting our inventory observation, we observed several wall-hung fire extinguishers that were stamped with an expiration date prior to the date of our observation.

All fire extinguishers should be kept in working condition.

6. When we counted petty cash at the Oakridge location, we found that the fund contained a personal cheque for $240 prepared by the fund custodian. The custodian told us it represented a "temporary loan." This is not in accordance with company policy. We informed the Oakridge manager about this finding.

The Oakridge manager should review the policy on petty cash funds with the custodian and ensure adherence to the policy in the future.

7. In reviewing the cash accounts, we noted that some payroll bank accounts had not been reconciled for more than 60 days.

All bank accounts should be reconciled monthly.

8. During discussions, the manager of the Oakridge location told us that he was having difficulty making production decisions because of constant changes in sales forecasts being issued by marketing. He said that if he could receive more stable sales forecast data, he could save significantly on set-up costs and also reduce both raw material and work-in-process inventories.

The company should consider reviewing its sales forecasting system with the objective of providing more stable information that is effectively integrated with production planning.

Required

a. For each of the eight items, decide whether the item belongs in an internal control letter, a management letter, both, or neither. Justify your decisions.

b. Prepare a draft of the internal control letter for Dahlstrom Manufacturing Corp. using word-processing software. The letter should be properly organized and effectively written. Feel free to make any assumptions that you believe are reasonable and appropriate.

c. Prepare a draft of the management letter for Dahlstrom Manufacturing Corp. using word-processing solftware. Note that the management letter can refer to items included in the internal control letter without including details of these items. The letter should be properly organized and effectively written. Feel free to make any assumptions that you believe are reasonable and appropriate.

21-37 Brigitte Beckman is the senior in charge of the audit of Proctor Industries (PI), a public company in the business of wholesaling plumbing products. It is now November 3, 1999, five weeks after her client's year end, September 30,

1999, and one week before her firm, Evans & Martin, is required to discuss the auditor's report and financial statements with PI's audit committee. Her firm is also required to report to the audit committee on all significant accounting and auditing issues encountered during the audit and on any recommendations for improving the internal control systems.

PI's unconsolidated annual sales approximate $36 million. It operates through six regional branches with about equal sales volumes at each branch.

PI has a 60 percent interest in Minor Inc., a company located in the United Kingdom. Minor Inc. also has a September 30 year end and is audited by Schweitzer & Catts, Public Accountants.

Brigitte is at the client's premises reviewing the year-end working papers for Proctor Industries and notes the following items:

1. PI's unconsolidated net income before taxes is normally about $2 million. Her firm employs a rotational audit approach on PI. Two branches are subject to a complete examination each year; the others are reviewed for unusual or significant fluctuations.

2. The confirmation of accounts receivable of the PI branches examined had disclosed $18,000 in double billings. The audit staff member determined that this occurred because several sales invoices at one branch were recorded twice near year end. The audit staff member has concluded that it is not significant because the error was isolated to one branch. Brigitte knows that sales from each branch are summarized in a weekly computerized report that is sent to head office to enable the general ledger to be updated.

3. The allowance for doubtful accounts in PI is $200,000. Based on the work performed in this section of the audit, the audit staff member concluded that the allowance should be at least $250,000 and could be as high as $300,000.

4. Weekly cycle counts for inventory are performed at each branch, and the results are compared to the perpetual records. The perpetual records are used for year-end reporting purposes. The audit staff member assigned to the inventory section attended cycle counts in September at the two branches being examined. He checked a sample of quantities as counted by the PI cycle-counters and ensured that these quantities agreed to the perpetual records. They did in all but one case — one carton of 10 copper pipe fittings was incorrectly recorded in the perpetual records as containing 100 fittings. PI's warehouse manager explained to the auditor that this error was probably an isolated incident due to human error. The perpetuals were adjusted to reflect the proper quantity and cost.

5. Brigitte has contacted Schweitzer & Catts to obtain the financial statements for Minor Inc. However, the firm is unable to provide her with audited financial statements since the president of Minor Inc. refuses to sign the management representation letter. He disagrees with the revenue recognition policy insisted on by Schweitzer & Catts and intends to obtain opinions from other audit

firms on the issue. The financial statements, under the policy advocated by Schweitzer & Catts, show a net loss of $320,000 for the year.

6. There is a new item on PI's balance sheet called "Investments." The working papers show that this represents a cash payment in June 1999 of $100,000 for all of the common shares of Chemicals Inc. This company has always had an August 31 year end. Although Chemicals Inc. had previously never been audited, PI has requested, and Brigitte has completed, an audit of Chemicals Inc. for its August 31, 1999, year end. The audited balance sheet of Chemicals Inc. appears in Exhibit I. Chemicals Inc. manufactures household cleaning products. The equipment used in the manufacturing process is not complex and is inexpensive to replace. Chemicals Inc. has earned large profits in the past, mainly from government contracts. This year, the financial statements show an after-tax profit of $100,000.

7. An extract of the agreement to purchase Chemicals Inc. states that if the company earns more than $1 million per year in any of the next five years, the vendor may buy the common shares back for a price to be determined.

8. One of the legal letters for PI was returned with the following comment:

> Chemicals Inc. may be liable for damages arising from the alleged dumping of hazardous chemicals from its Bedford plant into the nearby Black River. As of the current data, a statement of claim has been filed. Chemicals Inc. denies these allegations.

The partner has asked Brigitte to prepare a memo on the above-noted items for his use in discussions with the audit committee. Brigitte should also prepare notes for the audit staff regarding any follow-up work that she considers necessary as a result of her review.

Required

Prepare the memo requested by the partner and the notes for the audit staff that Brigitte should write.

EXHIBIT I

CHEMICALS INC. EXTRACTS FROM AUDITED BALANCE SHEET AS AT AUGUST 31, 1999

Assets	
Accounts receivable	$ 900,000
Prepaid expenses	100,000
Inventory	400,000
Fixed assets, net	400,000
	$1,800,000
Liabilities and Shareholders' Equity	
Accounts payable	$500,000
Share capital	
100 common shares	50,000
Retained earnings	1,250,000
	$1,800,000

(CICA adapted)

22

AUDITING AUTOMATED INFORMATION SYSTEMS: SPECIAL TOPICS

JUST BECAUSE THE COMPUTER DID THE WORK DOESN'T MEAN IT'S RIGHT

Foster Wellman's audit client, Manion's Department Stores Inc., installed a software program that processed and aged customer accounts receivable. The aging, which indicated how long the customers' accounts were outstanding, was useful to Foster when evaluating the collectibiliy of those accounts.

Because Foster did not know whether the aging totals were computed correctly, he decided to test Manion's aging by using his own firm's audit software to recalculate the aging, using an electronic copy of Manion's accounts receivable data file. He reasoned that if the aging produced by his audit software was in reasonable agreement with Manion's aging, he would have evidence that Manion's aging was correct.

Foster was shocked when he found a material difference between his and Manion's calculated aging. Manion's manager of the IT function, Rudy Rose, investigated the discrepancy and discovered that programmer errors had resulted in design flaws in Manion's software used to calculate the aging. This outcome caused Foster to substantially increase the amount of his testing of the year-end balance of the allowance for uncollectible accounts.

Most organizations use automated information systems when processing financial and accounting information. To this point, the text has described internal controls in terms of basic computer-based systems. This chapter deals with complex automated systems and their effect on internal controls and auditing. Small businesses and special topics, such as disaster recovery planning, are also discussed.

Each of the topics covered deserves a separate chapter, due to the diversity of information systems and the scope of the topic. Thus, the purpose of this chapter is to provide a brief overview of the topics and key impacts on the audit process. The interested reader is provided with references on each topic for further study.

There are several reasons for initially using basic automated information systems. First, it is important that students understand such systems as they are used extensively in business and government. Second, we have found that students understand internal control concepts when they are studied in the less abstract context of noncomplex systems. Finally, and most important, most complex automated accounting systems rely extensively on types of procedures for control that are similar to those used in noncomplex systems.

There is no distinction between the audit concepts applicable to complex electronic data processing and those applicable to basic systems. When complex automated information systems are introduced, generally accepted auditing standards, professional rules of conduct, legal liability, and the basic concepts of evidence accumulation remain the same. However, some of the specific methods appropriate for implementing the basic auditing concepts and for collecting evidence do change as systems become more complex.

The Assurance Standards Board has issued a series of EDP Auditing Guidelines that are based on International Auditing Guidelines issued by the International Auditing Practices Committee (IAPC) of the International Federation of Accountants (IFAC). These guidelines are included in a separate section of Volume III of the *CICA Handbook*. They are a concise reference source and should be consulted as part of any study of information systems auditing.

This chapter is organized around the following topics:

- Effects on the audit process when clients have automated information systems
- Characteristics of advanced data processing systems: data base management systems, use of data communications or Internet, electronic data interchange, and paperless systems
- Effects of advanced systems on internal controls and control risk
- Disaster recovery planning
- Computer-assisted audit techniques for advanced systems
- Computer fraud
- Audit of a computer service bureau

REVIEW THE AUDIT PROCESS FOR AUTOMATED SYSTEMS

In Chapter 7, Figure 7-1 (page 200) provided a phased approach for planning an audit and designing an audit approach. Figure 22-1 shows how automated information systems affect every phase of this process and lists the chapters of the text where the audit process has been discussed for noncomplex automated information systems.

PREPLAN

OBJECTIVE 22-1

Summarize the impact of automated systems on the audit process.

During preplanning, the auditor determines whether to accept or continue to audit a client, obtains an engagement letter, and selects staff for the engagement. Where clients have complex automated information systems, the auditor must ensure that staff possessing sufficient information systems expertise are included in the audit team so that computer general controls and application controls can be appropriately documented, evaluated, and tested during subsequent phases of the audit. All of the system complexities discussed in this chapter require technical expertise on the part of the audit team. Preplanning was discussed in Chapter 7.

FIGURE 22-1

Planning an Audit Program and Designing an Audit Approach for Clients with Automated Information Systems

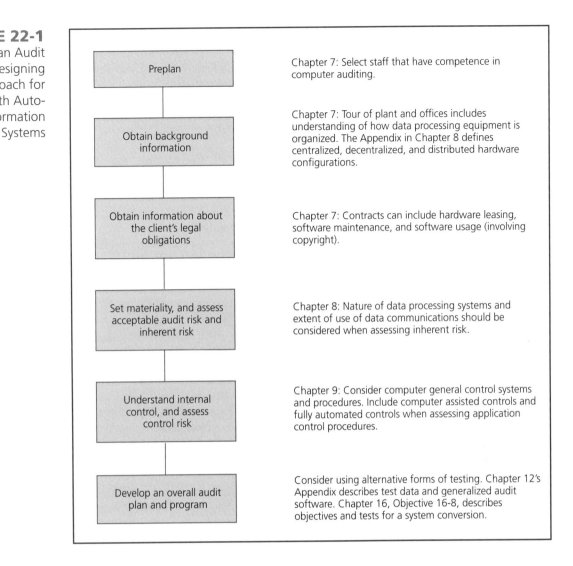

Preplan	Chapter 7: Select staff that have competence in computer auditing.
Obtain background information	Chapter 7: Tour of plant and offices includes understanding of how data processing equipment is organized. The Appendix in Chapter 8 defines centralized, decentralized, and distributed hardware configurations.
Obtain information about the client's legal obligations	Chapter 7: Contracts can include hardware leasing, software maintenance, and software usage (involving copyright).
Set materiality, and assess acceptable audit risk and inherent risk	Chapter 8: Nature of data processing systems and extent of use of data communications should be considered when assessing inherent risk.
Understand internal control, and assess control risk	Chapter 9: Consider computer general control systems and procedures. Include computer assisted controls and fully automated controls when assessing application control procedures.
Develop an overall audit plan and program	Consider using alternative forms of testing. Chapter 12's Appendix describes test data and generalized audit software. Chapter 16, Objective 16-8, describes objectives and tests for a system conversion.

OBTAIN BACKGROUND INFORMATION

Information about the entity's business environment, linkages to that environment, the industry, and the business itself are collected and analyzed to identify strengths of the business and potential risks, as described in Chapter 7. Is data processing centralized, decentralized, or distributed? To what extent are financial applications or other aspects of the business automated? Are potential complex applications such as data base management systems or paperless systems used? The nature of systems and their organization will affect risks, the nature of controls, and the types of testing that can be conducted by the auditor.

OBTAIN INFORMATION ABOUT THE CLIENT'S LEGAL OBLIGATIONS

Chapter 7 indicated that important business records and legal documents such as articles of incorporation and bylaws, minutes, and contracts should be reviewed. When automated information systems are in place, there could be contracts for hardware, software, or both. Hardware could be purchased or leased, with maintenance contracts. The existence of maintenance contracts helps the company ensure ongoing operations of the equipment. Software could also be purchased or leased, with the added concern of the nature of copyright. Does the entity have the right to make copies of the software for internal distribution, or are there specific use limitations on the software? This is important since violation of copyright agreements could bring fines, equipment seizure, or negative publicity to the organization (contingent liabilities).

SET MATERIALITY, AND ASSESS ACCEPTABLE AUDIT RISK AND INHERENT RISK

Figure 8-4 on page 249 summarizes the factors influencing risks discussed in Chapter 8. The nature of automated information systems is one of the components affecting inherent risk: simple systems using batch programming would be less prone to error than more complex systems. The focus box illustrates how custom programming, data communications, or paperless processing can cause errors.

The Toronto Star
www.torstar.com

> ### *TORONTO STAR* HIGHLIGHTS THE DOUBLE-BILLING COMPUTER
>
> Have you ever been double-billed on your credit card or debit card for a purchase? *The Toronto Star*, on November 2, 1996, explained how a consumer had been double-billed when the debit card reader "crashed" so that the consumer could not obtain her receipt. She was asked to process the transaction again by the processing centre but found that the transaction had been billed twice. The article goes on to point out that only 0.009 percent of transactions are double-billed. However, when there are over 100 million debit transactions, this means there are close to 10,000 duplicates. The moral of the story? Keep your paper receipts and check your statements! The article does not talk about other types of errors that can and do occur, such as money being removed from or deposited to incorrect accounts, increasing the overall error rate.
>
> Excess deposit errors also occur. *ComputerWorld Canada* indicated that the First National Bank of Chicago had deposited U.S.$924.8 million into each of 826 different chequing accounts, which was later identified as a programming error. One customer recorded his bank balance on his home telephone answering machine as $924,844,208.32 for posterity.
>
> Sources: *The Toronto Star*, Saturday, November 2, 1996, and *ComputerWorld Canada*, Vol. 12, No. 11, June 7, 1996.

UNDERSTAND INTERNAL CONTROL, AND ASSESS CONTROL RISK

Chapter 9 talked about the multiple types of internal controls that are needed to help entities achieve their goals efficiently and effectively. The control environment, general computer controls, and different types of application controls were described. As organizations and their systems become more complex, so do the types of controls. Specialists within the client organization and the audit firm are needed to assess these controls, provide recommendations for improvement, and assess control risk. Most readers are familiar with the concept of "hackers" — individuals who can bypass data communications controls. Many public accounting firms have internal experts who help assess the quality of data communications (including Internet) controls, as described in the focus box on ethical hacking.

DEVELOP AN OVERALL AUDIT PLAN AND PROGRAM

Figure 12-9 (page 400) in Chapter 12 describes the performance audit program for tests of controls audit procedures for sales and cash receipts. The audit program is based on Hillsburg Hardware, a hardware store with a point-of-sale system and a small local area network. Software is packaged software, with adequate audit trail and basic controls for batch processing and on-line data entry. Review of Figure 12-9 will show that it is possible to rely on programmed controls for many audit objectives and that the computer-assisted audit techniques of test data and generalized audit software can be used for many of the tests. When developing the audit plan and specific audit programs for cycles or audit objectives, the auditor must choose between available manual and automated techniques based on the auditor's expertise, the nature of the client systems, and the cost of the tests. As the nature of systems change, moving perhaps to complex data base systems or to paperless systems, the choices available to the auditor during testing also change. Additional types of computer-assisted audit tests for tests of controls and tests of details are described further in Objective 22-7. System changes, or "conversions," which were discussed adequately in Chapter 16, are not addressed here.

SUMMARY

Since the nature of automated information systems form part of the structure of the organization under audit, it would clearly affect every phase of the audit process. The rest of this chapter discusses specific topics in the context of the audit process.

WHAT ARE ADVANCED INFORMATION SYSTEMS?

OBJECTIVE 22-2

Identify five characteristics of advanced automated information systems.

An organization is likely to have advanced automated systems when its systems have one or more of the following characteristics:

- Custom-designed operational or strategic information systems
- Use of data base management systems
- Use of data communications (including Internet)
- Use of paperless systems such as electronic data interchange or electronic funds transfer
- A complex hardware or software processing configuration

The existence of each of these characteristics affects the nature of information systems processing at the organization and thus also affects the audit process. This section describes the characteristics, while subsequent sections describe the effects on internal controls.

**EXTENT OF CUSTOM-
DESIGNED
OPERATIONAL AND
STRATEGIC
INFORMATION
SYSTEMS[1]**

The Appendix to Chapter 8 described the forms of software acquisition as being in-house development, acquisition from an outside vendor, or turnkey software development (where an outsider prepares custom software). Here, we discuss the type of custom software as opposed to standard packaged software. Figure 22-2 summarizes the advantages and disadvantages of these two types of software.

Increased use of customization can improve a business entity's competitive advantage or efficiency of operations. However, should such systems fail or have errors, they increase costs and risks to the business. During the audit planning process, the auditor identifies the nature of such systems and the type of development process. In highly automated or integrated systems, auditors prefer to rely on the computer systems since it is more efficient to test programmed controls than to conduct tests of details. Where the system development process is complex or error prone, the auditor may assess the risk of program errors occurring as high, leading to an increased assessment of inherent risk and control risk.

When systems are so strategic that they could affect the ability of the entity to continue as a going concern if they fail, then the auditor takes a closer look at the disaster recovery planning process, as discussed in Objective 22-6. For example, if a bank's teller functions and automated teller machines could not function for a lengthy period of time, banks would be unable to provide basic services. Similarly, grocery stores with point-of-sale terminals would be unable to sell goods when their systems were down.

FIGURE 22-2
Advantages and
Disadvantages of
Custom Software and
Packaged Software

	CUSTOM SOFTWARE	PACKAGED SOFTWARE
ADVANTAGES	Tailored to meet company's exact needs.	Less costly than custom programming.
	The company conducts operations in its own often unique way.	Implementation can commence immediately after the package has been selected.
	Can more likely be used to gain strategic advantage than a software package.	Risk of system error and incorrect choice can be reduced by testing the software before purchase is made.
		Depending on the area, there are likely to be many packages available.
		Annual maintenance costs are low.
		Usually comes with user and other operating documentation.
		In-house technical analysis and programming personnel are likely not needed.
DISADVANTAGES	Very costly to develop.	The package may not "fit" the way the company does business or may be less efficient than customized systems.
	Lengthy program development times are common, from several months to several years.	Package evaluation process is costly and time-consuming.
	Rigorous testing program required to ensure that systems are error free.	In-house resources may be insufficient to resolve problems with system use or operations.
	Significant employee time is required for development, testing, and standard setting.	
	An iterative process that requires a high level of user and management involvement is needed to ensure greater likelihood of successful implementation.	

---

[1]See also Laudon, K. C. and J.P. Laudon, *Essentials of Management Information Systems,* Third Edition, 1999, p. 51.

USE OF DATA BASE MANAGEMENT SYSTEMS[2]

EDP Auditing Guideline #6, "EDP environments — data base systems," defines a data base system as consisting of two parts:

- The data base: the collection of data that is shared and used by different users for different purposes
- The data base management system: the software that is used to create, maintain, and operate the data base

Many software packages now sold use a data base as an underlying file structure, and automatically maintain the profile of the data base as part of the system. The use of such a software package does not normally indicate complexity or advanced automated information systems.

Complexity is introduced where a separate data base management system is acquired, and the client is required to set up a separate *data base administration* function to maintain the *data dictionary*[3]. With such systems, separate custom programs must be written to access and work with the data in the data base. Thus, the data base management system is separate from the application programs. Figure 22-3 illustrates how the data dictionary would be used to maintain the profile of the data base contents, while access to the data base through applications or a report writer is also handled by the data base management system.

USE OF DATA COMMUNICATIONS[4] (INCLUDING INTERNET)

Data communications are essentially the process of sending data electronically from one physical location to another. This can occur via microwave, satellite, or telephone lines. Sending or receiving data can expose the organization to risks if the method of sending or receiving exposes the organization's assets. Some of these risks are described in Objective 22-4 and in the focus box on page 702.

FIGURE 22-3
Data Base Components

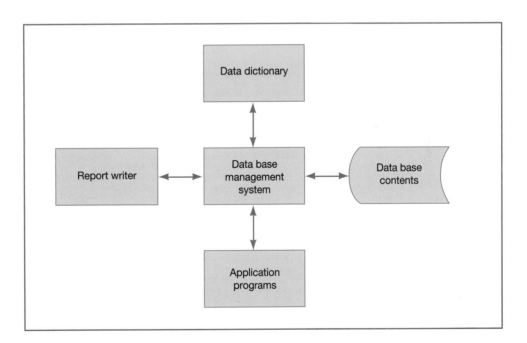

---

[2]Ibid., p. 206.

[3]Ibid., p. 235.

[4]Ibid.

There are many ways of sending information electronically. These include facsimile, electronic mail, the Internet, and dedicated communications systems for sending high volumes of data (e.g., some automated teller machines, transferral of data from a branch office to a head office). All forms of communication, whether electronic or paper-based, are subject to abuse. Mail fraud methods (e.g., employment scams, sale of inferior or nonexistent products) have been adopted by unethical individuals and companies using the new communications technologies. Organizations using any form of media need to exercise appropriate precautions to ensure that they do not purchase nonexistent or inferior products or fall prey to other abuses.

Central Intelligence Agency
www.lodci.gov/cia/
ciahome.html

Canadian Imperial Bank of
Commerce
www.cibc.com

The Globe & Mail
www.globeandmail.ca

Air Miles
www.airmiles.ca/english/
Default.asp

IS YOUR CLIENT'S ORGANIZATION SUSCEPTIBLE TO THESE THREATS?

Hackers altered the Central Intelligence Agency's home page, renaming it the Central Stupidity Agency and linking it to pornographic sites on the Internet.

****

Thousands of shoppers were left cashless when a burned-out cable darkened the Canadian Imperial Bank of Commerce's Computer Centre at about 11:30 a.m. on Monday, November 4, 1996. Three thousand five hundred automated banking machines and the debit-card network stayed down until 1:42 p.m.

****

Securities regulators in three countries were investigating an international stock sales scam in 1998 involving a group that used a Canadian brokerage firm's Web site to lend itself credibility. The Web site was developed to look like that of a legitimate brokerage house.

****

The confidential client data base on the Air Miles Web site was left unprotected, possibly for a year. The unencrypted information was downloaded by Terry Hamilton, a Toronto-based software developer in 1999. It contained names, addresses, e-mail addresses, home and business telephone numbers, and other personal details of up to 50,000 Air Miles card holders.

Sources: *ComputerWorld Canada*, Vol. 12, No. 22, November 8, 1996; *The Toronto Star*, November 5, 1996; *The Globe & Mail*, April 4, 1998; *Computing Canada*, Vol. 25, No. 5, February 5, 1999.

USE OF PAPERLESS SYSTEMS SUCH AS ELECTRONIC DATA INTERCHANGE[5] OR ELECTRONIC FUNDS TRANSFER[6]

Electronic data interchange (EDI) is an electronic method of sending documents between companies using a specified standard format. For example, a pharmaceutical manufacturer could mandate that its suppliers must accept standard purchase orders and submit invoices electronically. EDI is either implemented as a stand-alone system or integrated into the accounting systems. Stand-alone systems are used as

---

[5]See *Audit Implications of EDI*, The Canadian Institute of Chartered Accountants, 1996; and Splettstoesser, I. B., "Managing and Auditing Electronic Data Interchange," *The CPA Journal*, (November 1997) pp. 26–32.

[6]See Powell, R., "Auditing Electronic Funds Transfer," *IS Audit and Control Journal*, vol. II, 1994, pp. 48–51.

receiving and sending stations: transactions are often printed out, reviewed, and rekeyed into the appropriate application system. In integrated systems, the EDI transaction is automatically translated into a format that can be read by the application system. EDI transactions can be sent and received directly between two organizations having direct data communications links or by means of a value added network (VAN) acting as an electronic mailbox and forwarding service. Thus, there are no longer paper documents that move between organizations but rather electronic documents in a standard format.

Electronic funds transfer (EFT), also referred to as *electronic commerce* or *E-commerce*, is the transmission of cash equivalents using data communications. Examples include:

- Use of a debit card by a consumer to authorize the transfer of funds from the consumer's account to a merchant's account
- (As an extension of EDI) submission of appropriate transactions for the electronic payment of the invoice by the entity once the electronic invoice has been received and approved for payment
- Automatic payment of employee payroll from the company's bank account to the employee's bank account

COMPLEXITY OF HARDWARE OR SOFTWARE PROCESSING CONFIGURATION

Just as multiple physical operating locations for a client increase inherent risk, so do multiple locations of information systems processing. Such systems normally require the use of data communications. Control risks and control procedures associated with multiple data processing locations are further discussed under Objective 22-4.

We have already described two components of software complexity: the existence of a data base management system and the extent of software customization. There are many advanced forms of software, such as decision support systems, expert systems, data warehouses, and executive support systems[7]. The use of such systems requires staff with a high level of technical expertise. When an organization uses minicomputers, mainframes, and multiple local area networks, additional software layers[8] are necessary to manage these systems and keep them secure. The development of custom software systems, whether on a home page for the Internet, for a strategic business application, or for a separate data base system, requires knowledge of new and evolving programming languages[9].

The technical issues identified in the preceding paragraph are beyond the scope of this text and are best addressed in a management information systems course or a computer audit course.

---

[7]For definitions and descriptions of such systems, see any management information systems text, for example Laudon, K. C. and J. P. Laudon, *Essentials of Management Information Systems*, Third Edition, 1999, pp. 41, 383, 218.

[8]*Middleware* is a software product that connects two otherwise separate applications in order to pass data between them. *Network operating systems* are used to route and manage communications on the network and for the sharing of network resources. See Laudon, K. C. and J. P. Laudon, *Essentials of Management Information Systems*, Third Edition, 1999, pp. 243, 347.

[9]*Virtual Reality Modelling Language (VRML)* is a set of specifications for interactive, three-dimensional modelling on the World Wide Web that can organize multiple media, including animation, images, and sound. *Object-Oriented Programming (OOP)* combines data and the specific procedures that operate on those data into one *object*. *Structured Query Language (SQL)* is the most prominent data manipulation language used to manage data stored in data bases. See Laudon, K. C. and J. P. Laudon, *Essentials of Management Information Systems*, Third Edition, 1999, pp. 377, 187, 206.

EFFECTS OF
DATA BASE
MANAGEMENT
SYSTEMS ON
INTERNAL
CONTROLS

It is important for the auditor to be aware of the existence of a data base management system, since it affects all areas of general controls. These general controls include the following:

Organization and management controls The data base administrator requires specialized skills to establish and maintain the data base. He or she should be segregated from other functions, such as data authorization. Typical responsibilities of the data base administrator include creation and maintenance of the data dictionary, assistance with development of logical views of the data, allocation of physical storage for the data base, provision for backup, and security and privacy of the data elements.

Systems acquisition, development, and maintenance controls The systems development life cycle necessitates added controls to ensure that (1) the data base is developed in accordance with business needs and (2) programs accessing the data base are accurate and authorized and control concurrent options (to ensure that several individuals do not attempt to change the same data element at the same time).

Operations and information systems support This includes the need for security over the data dictionary and over access to the data base. The person in charge of this area works together with the data base administrator.

Each application cycle needs to be examined to ensure that the appropriate controls are in place:

- Since many departments may need to access key information, such as customer name and address, a single data "owner" should be assigned responsibility for defining access and security rules, such as who can use the data (access) and what functions they can perform (security).
- Passwords should be used to restrict access to the data base based on the security rules defined above.
- Segregation of duties should occur with respect to system design, data base design, data base administration, system operation, and authorization of data placed into the data base.

Figure 22-4 shows a business with a head office, a branch office, and an Internet home page that is used by customers for ordering goods. At point (1), head office initiates data communications to connect with the branch at point (2) using a communications channel (3) such as a public telephone line. Customers use Internet service providers to connect to the head office Internet home page at (4). The Internet home page is linked to the head office order entry software. The following unauthorized activities could occur at the numeric points of Figure 22-4:

1. A hacker could dial into the head office system, penetrating the systems and copying, altering, or removing data or programs.
2. A hacker could similarly dial into the branch office system, penetrating the systems and copying, altering, or removing data or programs.
3. The line could be tapped and data copied.
4. Orders could be placed using fraudulent credit cards. A hacker could penetrate the Web site and alter it by placing inappropriate material on the site. A hacker could penetrate the Web site and gain access to the accounting systems, with the same result as (2). Viruses could be transmitted and placed on the head office or branch office systems.

Table 22-1 summarizes the data communications risks and provides examples of control procedures that would be used to deal with each risk. When conducting the audit of entities that use data communications, the auditor needs to extend the

---

OBJECTIVE 22-3

Describe the impact of advanced data base systems on the understanding of internal controls.

OBJECTIVE 22-4

Describe the impact of the use of data communications, including the Internet, on the understanding of internal controls.

FIGURE 22-4
Potential Data
Communications
Risk Points

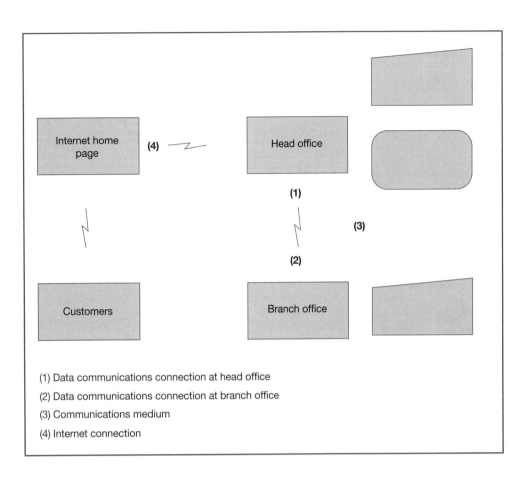

(1) Data communications connection at head office

(2) Data communications connection at branch office

(3) Communications medium

(4) Internet connection

assessment of general and application controls to the data communications process. Table 22-1 shows that controls previously discussed, such as the use of passwords and physical segregation, can be used to effectively deal with data communications risks.

TABLE 22-1

EXAMPLES OF DATA
COMMUNICATIONS
RISKS AND
CONTROLS[10]

DATA COMMUNICATIONS RISK	EXAMPLES OF CONTROL PROCEDURES TO DEAL WITH THE RISK
Inappropriate access to the accounting or other systems via data communications, with resulting loss of confidentiality or damage (see (1) and (2) on Figure 22-4).	Create multiple levels of passwords; change passwords regularly.
Data intercepted or copied during data communications (see (3) on Figure 22-4).	Ensure that confidential data is *encrypted* (scrambled) during transmission.
Inappropriate access to the accounting or other systems via the Internet, with resulting loss of confidentiality or damage (see (4) on Figure 22-4).	Physically segregate Internet home page equipment and software from other systems. Use *firewalls* (software and/or hardware that restricts access to and from Internet sites).
Viruses could be placed onto the head office or branch office systems, causing destruction of data or programs or disruption of service (see (4) on Figure 22-4).	Same as above. Also, acquire current anti-virus software, and keep the software current.

[10]See also Schwartau, W., "Creating Boundaries: Protecting Companies and Employees on the Information Superhighway," *IS Audit and Control Journal*, vol. I, 1996, pp. 28–32; and Sheehy, D. and G. Trites, "Access Denied," *CAmagazine* (September 1995), pp. 50–52.

TABLE 22-2

MULTIPLE INFORMATION PROCESSING LOCATIONS RISK	EXAMPLES OF CONTROL PROCEDURES TO REDUCE THE RISK
Data processed in multiple locations could become inconsistent (e.g., inventory prices).	One location has primary responsibility for updating the information. Exception reports are printed and differences between locations followed up.
Programs could be inaccurate or unauthorized at one or more locations.	Head office controls all program changes. Branch offices are sent only the source code.
Branches could have unauthorized access to head office programs and data or vice versa.	Clear responsibilities are assigned for data and program ownership and change rights. Adequate access control systems are used to enforce these rights (e.g., confidential passwords).
Some data sent from one location to another might not be received (i.e., incomplete or inaccurate transmissions).	Use control totals, record counts, and sequential numbering of transactions and follow up any missing or out-of-sequence data.

Related to data communications is the risk associated with multiple information processing locations. Table 22-2 describes examples of these risks and provides examples of control procedures that would reduce the risks.

As part of the knowledge of business, the auditor should have obtained system hardware and software configuration diagrams. These would inform the auditor about the extent of the complexity associated with data communications or multiple locations. General controls over data communications software and passwords are critical when assessing control risks associated with data communications. The auditor must be assured that controls are in place for:

- Accurate functioning of data communications software
- Custody of and periodic changes to *encryption keys* (codes used to scramble and unscramble data)
- Effective functioning of firewalls
- Effective controls over issuance, maintenance, and removal of passwords

Once these technical areas have been assessed, the auditor would then consider each application cycle, as discussed in Chapters 12 through 20.

EFFECTS OF PAPERLESS SYSTEMS ON CONTROL RISK

Many organizations are moving towards paperless systems in order to benefit from the cost savings and potential data integrity improvements associated with such systems (described in *Audit Implications of EDI*, a CICA Audit Technique Study). Three common effects of paperless systems on the auditor are as follows:

- The audit trail exists in automated form rather than on paper.
- It becomes necessary to rely on programmed controls rather than manual controls.
- Greater use of computer-assisted audit techniques (both tests of data and tests of programs) may be needed.

ELECTRONIC DATA INTERCHANGE

Figure 22-5 provides a simplified overview schematic diagram showing how Big Pharmaceutical Company (BPC) has implemented EDI with 200 of its suppliers. A typical EDI transaction would be a supplier purchase order. BPC uses its purchasing system to generate an electronic purchase order, which is sent to the EDI system with

FIGURE 22-5

Sample Summary
Schematic of an
EDI System

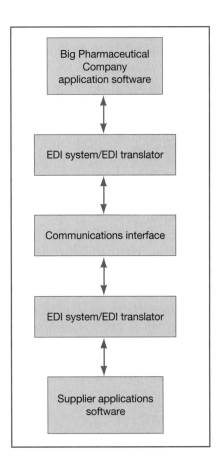

OBJECTIVE 22-5

**List the characteristics
of electronic data
interchange (EDI) and
electronic commerce
as examples of
paperless systems,
describing their
impact on the
understanding of
internal controls.**

its translator capabilities, where the purchase order is reformatted into the agreed-upon EDI standard format. The communication interfaces are used to send the transaction to the supplier and receive the transaction from the supplier. The supplier's EDI system translates the purchase order into a form that can be read by its systems. The supplier then sends an electronic acknowledgement back through the same set of software to confirm to BPC that the purchase order has been received.

This example indicates the following important characteristics of EDI systems:

- Transactions flow seamlessly from one party to another (e.g., client, supplier, VAN) with little or no physical evidence; electronic evidence is used instead.
- Authorization, completeness, and accuracy of transactions may not be as evident since controls are embedded within programs rather than performed by individuals.
- The extent of programmed controls depends on the type of EDI (i.e., stand-alone or integrated) and thus on the extent of paperless systems.
- Year-end balances of accounts receivable, accounts payable, and inventory are likely smaller when EDI is used in these application cycles since the lag between one party sending a transaction and the other receiving it is shorter.
- Preventive rather than detective controls are needed so that incorrect or unauthorized transactions are not processed by the systems.

**ELECTRONIC
COMMERCE**

Several examples of electronic commerce or electronic funds transfers (EFTs) were described on pages 702 and 703. Chapter 20 described the following types of EFTs and how they should be controlled and audited:

- Debit card cash receipts
- Automatic pre-authorized monthly payments
- Payroll payments

Here, we explain the effects of electronic funds transfer as an extension of the use of electronic data interchange. Figure 22-5 was used to explain how BPC ordered goods using EDI. Continuing the example, the supplier prepares the goods and ships them to BPC, providing both a paper shipping document with the goods and an electronic invoice that is submitted to BPC. BPC then uses its own application systems to compare the invoice to its purchase order. Once matched, an automatic transaction is initiated that approves payment of funds for the invoice. Funds are removed from BPC's bank account and automatically transferred to the supplier's bank account. At the same time, BPC sends an electronic remittance advice to the supplier. This example shows that, although there are no paper documents except for the document accompanying the goods, there is an *electronic audit trail* of activity supporting the purchase, invoicing, and payment of goods.

CONTROL AND AUDIT

When assessing internal controls, the auditor needs to evaluate and document controls in the communications layer, the EDI software, the electronic funds transfer software, and the applications software. Since year-end balances may be reduced, such year-end balances in accounts receivable, accounts payable, and inventory may be immaterial, reducing the need for tests of details of balances but increasing the need for tests of controls. Since data communications are involved, the auditor needs to address the risks covered in Objective 22-4 and consider en-route protection of information during EDI processing. Where funds are transferred electronically, there is an increased need for the enhanced security features of encryption, access control, and authentication (verifying the identity of parties to a transaction).

Advanced computer-assisted audit techniques[11] are usually required, as discussed in Objective 22-7.

DISASTER RECOVERY PLANNING

OBJECTIVE 22-6

Identify the five phases of disaster recovery planning (DRP). State the impact of DRP on the audit process.

Disaster recovery planning is also known as "business continuity planning." The purpose of such a plan is to enable a business to continue operations in the event of failure of part or all of its information systems. Something as simple as a hard drive crash (in which the reading head of the hard drive fails, destroying the head, the disk, and the data on it) can cause enormous problems if a company has not given careful thought to contingency procedures. Think of your own personal computer. What would you do if this terrible event occurred? The focus box below describes how an insurance company fared when it had a fire that destroyed some microcomputers and disk drives.

WOULD YOUR CLIENT RECOVER THIS QUICKLY FROM A MAJOR FIRE?

A major insurance company located in downtown Toronto on Bay Street occupied several floors of a high-rise building. On the tenth floor, there was a data centre housing mainframe computers, 20 disk drives, printers, and telecommunications equipment for communicating with

---

[11]See Zoladz, C., "Auditing in an Integrated EDI Environment," *IS Audit and Control Journal*, vol. II, 1994, pp. 36–40.

hundreds of insurance brokers and insurance offices. The data centre was physically segregated, with an automatic fire extinguishing system. On the ninth floor, immediately below the data centre, was an open area with microcomputers used by the actuaries (individuals who analyze mortality rates and thus determine how much the company should charge for life insurance). On the sixth floor was a tape vault, housing backup data and programs from the data centre.

On a Friday prior to a long weekend, the ninth floor open area caught fire. It was a massive fire, blackening the entire area and blowing out windows. Smoke filtered up to the tenth floor, where it seeped through holes in the data centre's walls (caused by previous movement of office partitions that had been attached to the data centre's walls). The operators (who had not been adequately trained) panicked and did not push the 15-cm wide red button beside the exit door that would have automatically shut off the power to all systems. Instead, they rapidly left the room. Although the fire extinguishing system was activated, smoke continued to seep in, and half of the disk drives crashed.

Large volumes of water poured onto the ninth floor, hitting the top of the tape vault and cracking it. (The tape vault was located in the building's "water well," the area to which water was supposed to flow so that it did not filter through the floors and ceilings of multiple floors.) Luckily, only about 5 cm of water settled in the bottom of the tape vault.

Saturday morning, a human chain of 300 people transferred backup media to Bay Street, where transport trucks loaded with mainframe computing equipment and peripherals waited, hooked up to the telephone cables at the front of the building. On Tuesday morning, the mainframe systems were up and running, as if nothing had happened to the tenth floor. The ninth floor actuaries were not so lucky. All of their backup media was kept in their desks on the ninth floor and had been destroyed.

However, one of the actuaries had gone on holiday one week prior to the fire. Thinking that he would do some work at home, he had taken a copy of the system with him when he left. Needless to say, he was a hero when he returned a week after the fire.

Gary Baker provided a concise article in *CAmagazine*[12] several years ago that breaks down the disaster recovery process into five phases. The phases are as follows:

1. **Management commitment to the concept of disaster recovery planning** Preparation of a DRP is time-consuming and requires the provision of funds and human resources. If management is not fully committed to this process, the resources will not be provided and the activity will falter.

2. **Ranking of business processes** The entity needs to ask, "What will happen if process X is not available?" Can the payroll be paid? Can goods be shipped out of the door? For organizations using paperless systems and electronic data interchange or electronic commerce, operations will likely cease if those systems are unavailable. Users need to identify what would happen if particular application processes were

---

[12]Baker, G., "Quick Recoveries," *CAmagazine* (August 1995), pp. 49–50, 53.

unavailable and the likely impact that this would have on the business. Baker suggests using one-day, three-day, and seven-day time frames when conducting this ranking.

3. Identifying minimum resources required   From step 2, the entity will have identified applications that were critical to ongoing operations. Resources required to restore these operations (and perhaps some noncritical systems as well) now need to be identified and costed. Where multiple alternatives exist, they should be similarly identified and costed.

4. Prepare a *data centre plan* and a *user plan*   The data centre plan addresses technical issues and procedures, such as obtaining hardware and software backup, and ensuring appropriate telecommunications access. The user plan identifies activities required to resume operations and can include manual alternative activities that would be completed if computing resources were unavailable.

5. Test the plan   This trial run will help both data processing personnel and users identify any shortcomings in the DRP and provide a subsequent schedule for remedying those shortcomings.

There are a variety of technical publications and articles that can be used by organizations to prepare a disaster recovery plan or to obtain more detailed guidance on the components of planning[13]. In addition to those issues mentioned by Baker, it is important that an entity have current offsite backup of its systems, carry adequate appropriate insurance coverage, and continue to maintain its disaster recovery plans once the DRP has initially been developed.

AUDIT IMPACT

The existence of an effective disaster recovery plan is linked to the auditor's assessment of the viability of the entity as a going concern. If an entity using integrated EDI, EFTs, and automated shipping systems were to lose its systems and not have an effective DRP, the entity would likely fail if it could not recover its systems within a short period of time. Thus, the auditor might consider either lowering the numeric value of acceptable audit risk or disclosing the lack of appropriate disaster recovery plans in a note to the financial statements.

ADVANCED COMPUTER-ASSISTED AUDIT TESTS

OBJECTIVE 22-7

Be familiar with the types of computer-assisted audit techniques, and provide examples of how such techniques can be used during the audit of advanced data processing systems.

The Appendix to Chapter 12 defined computer-assisted audit tests as "tests that the auditor conducts using computer software or the data or systems of the client." The Appendix went on to describe test data (the use of fictitious transactions to determine whether client programs are functioning as described) and generalized audit software[14] (a package that allows the auditor to run routines against client data).

In this section we describe four additional techniques:

- Integrated test facility
- Parallel simulation
- Program comparison software
- Fourth generation languages or generic report writers

---

[13]See, for example: Dwyer, P. D., A. H. Friedberg and K. S. McKenzie, "It Can Happen Here: The Importance of Continuity Planning," *IS Audit and Control Journal*, vol. 1, 1994, pp. 30–35.

[14]See also *Application of Computer Assisted Audit Techniques Using Microcomputers*, a CICA Audit Technique Study, 1994.

Table 22-3 defines each of these techniques, describes the audit purpose of the technique, and provides an example of actual use of the technique. These are not the only computer-assisted techniques available to auditors but rather a selection of those that are appropriate for the types of advanced systems that have been discussed in this chapter[15]. The auditor would likely enlist an information systems audit specialist to design, develop, test, and run these advanced techniques.

TABLE 22-3

SELECTED ADVANCED
COMPUTER-ASSISTED
AUDIT TECHNIQUES
AND THEIR
APPLICATIONS

COMPUTER-ASSISTED AUDIT TEST DEFINITION	AUDIT PURPOSE	EXAMPLE
Integrated test facility (ITF): The creation of a nonexistent branch or company as part of a system, running together with a live data file.	To allow the auditor to run fictitious transactions through client systems without affecting the general ledger or financial records of the business to examine the functioning of programs (test of control).	Companies within an industry group using EDI each have a nonexistent company on their system. Auditors use these companies to send transactions, and verify that acknowledgements are sent and that exception reports are printed for unusual transactions.
Parallel simulation (reperformance): Use of any form of software to fully repeat a program's processing.	To repeat the functioning of a program, verifying the results (test of control and test of detail).	An auditor calculates inventory quantity on hand times price, resulting in an extended value for each item. These values are added and compared to the general ledger. This verifies both the mathematical amount of any difference with the general ledger and that the program is performing calculations correctly.
Program comparison software: Software that allows the auditor to compare operating programs to auditor-tested versions of source code, looking for differences.	To identify potential unauthorized program changes (test of control).	An approved version of an accounts receivable aging program is compared to the accounts receivable aging program used to conduct the aging.
Fourth generation language or generic report writer: Software that uses an English-like or a menu-based interface to allow the reading of data files and the preparation of customized reports.	To access client data files and print reports or create data files for data of interest (test of detail).	A human resources data base is queried, and a list of all employees working more than 50 hours of overtime in a particular period is printed for auditor examination.

The integrated test facility was chosen for discussion since the capability of a fictitious entity (branch or corporation) is frequently built into EDI and EFTs systems so that these systems can be fully tested prior to implementation. The capability remains for audit use once the integrated test facility has been developed for the systems development purpose. The auditor must exercise caution to ensure that test transactions affect only the fictitious entity. If actual accounting records are affected, then reversal of test entries will require the client to initiate appropriate reversing transactions or have special programming completed. Parallel simulation, which can be completed using generalized audit software, can be applied to relatively simple calculations and processes or to complex calculations, as described in the opening vignette to this chapter. Source code comparison software can help the auditor rely on the program change

---

[15]For a more complete discussion of the different types of computer-assisted audit techniques, see Boritz, J.E., *Computer Control and Audit Guide*, Tenth Edition, 1999, Chapter 10.

controls at an entity. Due to the complexity of many data base structures, the report writer, which forms part of a data base management system query language, may be the only viable way for an auditor to conduct tests of a data base.

MAINTAINING
ADEQUATE AUDIT
CONTROL

No matter what audit technique is used by the auditor with a client, adequate control must be maintained to ensure the integrity of the test. Boritz discusses these controls at length[16]. When using data to test the client's programs, the auditor should ensure that the programs tested are those that are actually in use during normal processing. Since this is a point-in-time test, the auditor would also examine the quality of general computer controls prior to deciding whether reliance could be placed on these programs.

When testing client data files using software (e.g., generalized audit software, a report writer), the auditor must determine that the data file being used is complete and is the same as the actual data file used by the client. This is accomplished by reconciling control totals to the general ledger, having the audit software count the number of records, and comparing individual details to supporting evidence.

COMPUTER FRAUD

Computer fraud consists of fraud conducted with the assistance of computer software or hardware. The focus box below provides examples of different types of actual computer frauds.

OBJECTIVE 22-8

Review the sources of computer fraud. Identify controls that help to prevent computer fraud and audit tests that may detect computer fraud.

WOULD YOU OR YOUR CLIENT FALL VICTIM TO THESE TYPES OF FRAUD?

Adolescent steals over 500 AOL passwords A U.S. teenager, identified only as John Doe, sent Trojan Horse programs to AOL (America Online) users in electronic-mail messages that contained attachments. When the users received those messages and clicked on the attachments, the Trojan Horse programs were activated. Those programs would then record the AOL users' keystrokes, which included their passwords. The passwords could then be sold to others or used by John Doe to have "free" time on the World Wide Web.

****

Quebec software house builds in "delete audit trail" functions Tracking cash in a restaurant or store is easier with point-of-sale systems. A Quebec software house provided functions to purchasers to delete and remove the audit trail for transactions on certain days, in certain hours, or for specific itemized transactions. The owner of the software could then pocket the cash, avoiding income taxes and goods and service taxes.

****

Did Reuters steal information from a major competitor? The *New York Times* reported that London executives of Reuters parent organization obtained software codes and data base content from a former Bloomberg employee. This employee reportedly broke into Bloomberg computers and downloaded confidential data.

****

---

[16]Ibid.

> ***IRS employee steals tax payments*** An IRS employee admitted he stole refunds by changing the name of the payee on the refund cheques and depositing them. He then recorded the payment in the IRS computer systems. He was caught when he forgot to record one of the payments that he stole.
>
> **★★★★★★★★★★★★★★★**
>
> ***Use of stolen credit card numbers*** Five juveniles stole credit card numbers by compromising the security of an on-line encryption process. They then used the credit card numbers to purchase and ship computer equipment directly to their homes.

Examining these frauds, we can see that the following control failures occurred:

- *Compromise of access security features.* The theft of AOL computer time occurred due to someone obtaining confidential passwords. Theft of Bloomberg data may have occurred due to the bypass of firewall functionality or again due to password compromise. Stolen credit card numbers were obtained by compromising an encryption process (possibly by obtaining the encryption key).
- *Inappropriate programming.* Developers of the point-of-sale software house should have policies in place to prevent programs that enable illegal activities to take place.
- *Segregation of duties.* The IRS employee had access to both cash and recording of cash.

These types of controls have been discussed throughout this text. Thus, to prevent computer fraud, an organization should implement appropriate controls and remain vigilant in the exercise of those controls.

TESTING FOR COMPUTER FRAUD

When an auditor suspects fraud, current standards require that he or she communicate with the management level that is one level above the suspected fraud or with the audit committee, and that the auditor confirm or dispel doubts with respect to the fraud, particularly if there is suspicion that a material amount is involved. Each of the cycle chapters in this text have described how an auditor would conduct such tests.

For example, Chapter 16, audit of the acquisition and payment cycle, described potential fraud by employees' recording of fraudulent purchases in the purchases journal. These could be payments to fictitious suppliers for fictitious invoices or duplicated payments. Table 22-4 provides examples of potential frauds and computer-assisted audit techniques using generalized audit software that an auditor could use to search for such frauds. Remember, such audit techniques might not detect the fraud if the perpetrator does not use the types of data that are being searched for in the generalized audit test.

Whenever fraud is suspected, specialists in both the type of system being audited and forensic auditing (i.e., auditing for fraud) should be consulted before designing any tests and in examining results.

TABLE 22-4

EXAMPLES OF FRAUDS
AND GENERALIZED
AUDIT SOFTWARE
STEPS USED TO
SEARCH FOR THOSE
FRAUDS

FRAUD	GENERALIZED AUDIT SOFTWARE TEST
Fictitious employees included in payroll system and salary paid every month to these employees.	Search for duplicate social insurance numbers, invalid social insurance numbers, duplicate addresses, and addresses with post office boxes.
Invoices paid twice. Employee steals the second payment.	Search for duplicate invoice numbers.
Lapping. Employee steals cash and records receipts using cash received from another customer.	Test for unallocated cash (cash that is recorded but does not have an associated invoice number), preparing totals by customer for such cash.
Inventory is stolen and written off in the computer as an "adjustment."	Summarize inventory adjustments by inventory item. Use graphics to examine trends.

SMALL BUSINESS CONTROLS

Our discussions of internal control have indicated that small businesses frequently rely on owner/manager supervision. This is true whether a business uses manual or automated information systems. In this section, we examine the likely characteristics of a small business using the control framework of Figure 9-1 (page 276), Elements of Internal Control. For more detail, the reader should refer to *Audit of a Small Business*[17].

CONTROL ENVIRONMENT

The quality of the control environment depends on the attitudes of the owner/manager. If the owner/manager adequately supervises employees, hires only competent employees, and encourages practices such as the use of confidential passwords, then the organization will have a more positive control environment than a situation in which the owner is an absentee one and encourages the use of illegal copies of software.

GENERAL CONTROL SYSTEMS AND PROCEDURES

Organization and management controls There are often fewer people in the accounting department, perhaps even only one person; thus, segregation of duties may not be possible. Controls are often informal, lacking written authorization procedures. The owner/manager can readily override controls by personally performing clerical or operating functions.

OBJECTIVE 22-9

Describe how small businesses can adequately control their automated information systems.

Systems acquisition, development, and maintenance controls Use of packaged software is common in the accounting systems. There are a variety of software packages available which range in quality. Where programming is undertaken, controls over changes may be poor since an informal process will likely be used rather than a structured approach.

Operations and information systems support Primarily because of the small size of the organization, the information systems are likely to be simpler systems, using a centralized form of processing. The entity is unlikely to have in-house expertise on systems and would normally place reliance on software and hardware suppliers for system support and maintenance. Passwords may be in use but are in a simple form (i.e., the accounting personnel may have a single password that allows access to all systems and all functions).

---

[17]See *Audit of a Small Business*, a CICA Audit Technique Study, 1994, Chapters 1, 6, and 7.

When a software package is used and the entity is not capable of making changes to the software (since most software packages are provided only in machine code), certain controls in the software become important. For example, calculations in invoicing and inventory costing (mechanical accuracy), posting of transactions to subsidiary systems and to the general ledger (detail tie-in), and aging of accounts receivable (valuation) are all functions normally present in software packages which assist the business and on which the auditor can rely.

PRACTICAL CONTROLS TO BE EXERCISED BY THE OWNER/MANAGER

For controls to be practical in a small business, they need to be activities that can be performed in a short period of time; otherwise it is unlikely that an owner/manager will implement them.

Systems acquisition, development, and maintenance controls It is important that the owner/manager understand the nature of software used by the business and how business needs might change. This includes software maintenance needs. For example, if the company uses a payroll package, then the company should expect to receive an upgrade whenever tax rates change. The owner should ensure that authorized programs are implemented (i.e., only valid, copyrighted materials should be implemented). If program changes are implemented, an employee should be assigned to test and keep a record of changes.

Operations and information systems support Backups should be made daily, with at least two copies of recent data kept offsite. Although a formal disaster recovery plan may not be contemplated, the entity should have a current contact for hardware and software support in the event of system problems. As a minimum, documentation to provide for ongoing operations should be present, such as a list of the procedures that are normally completed on a daily, weekly, and monthly basis.

Application control procedures These procedures include *controls to prevent fraud*. The most important control concept here is the separation of authorization from the recording of transactions. As in other sizes of business, the owner/manager needs to remain vigilant to prevent computer fraud or other types of fraud. Chapters 12 through 20 indicate that the owner should perform certain key activities, such as signing payroll cheques with a supporting payroll journal, signing accounts payable cheques with supporting documentation, and reviewing master file information.

SUMMARY

When a small business has automated information systems, the required key controls are the same as those required in a small business using manual procedures. These are owner/manager controls. In addition, reliance on the computer programs may be useful. Activities to maintain ongoing operations, such as backup and operational documentation, should also be present.

Most small businesses have a lack of expertise in the selection, design, or operation of their automated information systems and frequently call on their accountant as a business advisor to help in these areas.

AUDIT OF A COMPUTER SERVICE ORGANIZATION

Some clients still have certain types of data processed at an independent computer service organization. For example, many companies have banks process their payrolls or have trust companies maintain their share and dividend records.

In a computer service organization operation, the client submits input data, either on paper forms or by means of data communications. The service organization processes it for a fee and provides the output transactions to the client along with the agreed-upon output. Generally, the service organization is responsible for designing the computer system and providing adequate controls to ensure that the processing is reliable.

OBJECTIVE 22-10

Discuss the special concerns of the auditor when the client's information is processed by a computer service organization.

The difficulty that the independent auditor faces when a computer organization is used is in determining the adequacy of the service organization's internal controls. The auditor cannot automatically assume that the controls are adequate simply because the service organization is an independent enterprise. If the client's service organization application involves the processing of significant financial data, the auditor must consider the need to understand and test the service organization's controls.

The extent of obtaining an understanding and testing of the service organization should be based on the same criteria that the auditor uses in evaluating a client's own internal controls. The depth of the understanding depends on the complexity of the system and the extent to which the auditor intends to assess control risk below maximum to reduce other audit tests. If the auditor concludes that active involvement with the service organization is the only feasible way to conduct the audit, it may be necessary to obtain an extensive understanding of the service organization's internal controls, test them by the use of test data and other tests of controls, and use the computer to perform tests of the type discussed in the preceding sections. Extensive testing of this nature is unlikely in most audits because most service organization applications are reasonably simple. When the client has controls that involve comparing the input details provided by the client to the output details provided by the service provider, reference to controls at the service provider may not be necessary. (This is known as the "black box" approach.) However, some review of the service centre is usually done.

In recent years, it has become increasingly common to have *one* independent auditor obtain an understanding of and test the service organization's internal control for the use of *all* customers and their independent auditors. The purpose of these independent reviews is to provide customers with a reasonable level of assurance of the adequacy of the service organization's internal controls and to eliminate the need for redundant audits by the service organization's customers' auditors. If the service organization has many customers and each one requires an understanding of the service organization's internal controls by its own independent auditor, the inconvenience to the service organization can be substantial. When the service organization's independent public accounting firm completes the audit of the controls and records, a special report under Section 5900, "Opinions on Control Procedures at a Service Organization," is issued indicating the scope of the audit and the conclusions. It is then the responsibility of the customer's auditor to decide the extent to which he or she wants to rely on the service organization's auditor's report. Section 5310, "Audit Evidence Considerations When an Enterprise Uses a Service Organization," is instructive in that regard.

ESSENTIAL TERMS

Communications channel — the medium used to transmit data from one location to another (e.g., microwave, satellite, telephone line) (p. 704).

Computer fraud — fraud conducted with the assistance of computer software or hardware (p. 712).

Computer service organization — an external organization that processes transactions or performs other information systems processing services (p. 715).

Data base — a collection of data that is shared and used by different users for different purposes (p. 701).

Data base management system — a system consisting of software used to create, maintain, and operate a data base (p. 701).

Data communications — the process of sending data electronically from one physical location to another (p. 715).

Disaster recovery planning (DRP) — activities and procedures required to maintain business operations in the event of failure of all or part of the business's information systems (p. 708).

E-commerce — see *Electronic funds transfers*.

Electronic audit trail — electronic storage of transactions and their audit trail rather than availability in paper form (p. 708).

Electronic commerce — see *Electronic funds transfers*.

Electronic data interchange — an electronic method of sending documents between companies using a specified standard format (p. 702).

Electronic funds transfers (EFTs) — the transmission of cash equivalents using data communications (also known as *electronic commerce* or *E-commerce*) (p. 703).

Encryption — the process of scrambling data so that it cannot be read directly (p. 706).

Encryption key — codes used to scramble and unscramble data (p. 706).

Fourth generation language — English-like programming language that allows the auditor to read data files and prepare customized reports (p. 711).

Firewall — software and/or hardware that is used to restrict access to and from Internet sites (p. 706).

Integrated test facility (ITF) — the creation of data for a nonexistent branch or company as part of a system, which is run together with a live data file (p. 711).

Parallel simulation — use of any form of software to fully repeat a program's processing (also known as *reperformance*) (p. 711).

Program comparison software — software that allows the auditor to compare operating programs to auditor-tested versions of source code, looking for differences (p. 711).

Report writer — software that uses an English-like or a menu-based interface to allow the reading of data files and the preparation of customized reports (often associated with data base management systems) (p. 711).

Strategic information system — a system that provides a competitive advantage or improves efficiency within an entity (p. 700).

Value added network (VAN) — an intermediary for an organization using EDI; translates, stores, and forwards EDI transactions (p. 703).

REVIEW QUESTIONS

22-1   List the phases of the audit. For each phase, provide at least one example of matters an auditor needs to consider when auditing automated information systems.

22-2   Contrast the terms "hacker" and "ethical hacker." What types of skills might an ethical hacker require?

22-3   List five characteristics of advanced automated information systems. Define each characteristic and provide an example.

22-4   Explain why the use of customized software is more likely to increase the complexity of information systems than the use of packaged software.

22-5   What is the difference between a software package that uses data base file structures and one that uses a data base management system? Why is the latter more likely to increase system complexity?

22-6   Identify the types of controls that are affected by the implementation of data base management systems. For each type of control, provide an example of the effects.

22-7   List four risks that face entities using data communications. Provide at least one example of how the risk could be mitigated.

22-8   Describe the risks associated with entities that process information using multiple locations. For each risk, provide a potential control.

22-9   List the three common effects of paperless systems on the auditor.

22-10   Describe five important characteristics of EDI systems that are significant to the auditor.

22-11   Identify audit and control issues associated with EDI and EFTs.

22-12   List the five phases of disaster recovery planning, and explain the importance of each phase. How does the quality of the disaster recovery plan affect the audit risk model?

22-13   List and define four advanced computer-assisted audit techniques. For each technique, provide an example of how it could be used in a payroll application cycle.

22-14   Define computer fraud. List three possible frauds in the purchases, payments cycle, and explain how such frauds might be detected using generalized audit software.

MULTIPLE CHOICE QUESTIONS

22-15   The following questions concern the audit risk model or audit approach. Choose the best answer.

a.   Medium Financial Corporation has a complex hardware configuration. There is a central computer, as well as branch computers and automated teller machines. An Internet banking interface is being considered. Several thousand transactions are processed each day. Given good internal controls, the likely audit approach would be
   (1)   a test of details approach only, due to the uniqueness of the system.
   (2)   controls testing only, due to the high volume of transactions processed.
   (3)   a combined audit approach, with reliance on specialist assistance.
   (4)   primary reliance on a service auditor's report, due to the outsourced software.

b.   Halloween Sales Limited uses custom software written by an outside software house. Contract personnel have been hired in the accounting department to help with the seasonal workload. These people use a common password. The most likely audit approach for the audit of accounts receivable
   (1)   would be combined since a high volume would make substantive testing costs prohibitive.
   (2)   would be substantive due to potential data integrity problems.
   (3)   would be oriented heavily towards control testing due to the high level of automation.
   (4)   cannot be determined due to insufficient information.

c.   At ABC Company, programmers work directly with user managers to identify the maintenance requirements of particular application systems. The programmer documents the needed change, tests it, and returns the pro-

gram to the user for placement into the production system. The program change process has the following effect on the audit risk model components:
(1) The inherent risk is decreased.
(2) The control risk is increased.
(3) The detection risk is increased.
(4) The detection risk is increased.

22-16 The following questions concern controls for automated information systems. Choose the best answer.

a. Small Manufacturing Company has only two staff members that get involved in accounting: the owner and a full-time bookkeeper/receptionist. Which of the following functions is it most important that the owner do, rather than the receptionist?
(1) Review of master file changes
(2) Transferral of backup tapes offsite
(3) Approval of programming standards
(4) Printing of accounts receivable aging report

b. Which of the following items should be assessed as part of a company's control environment?
(1) Program change procedures
(2) Cheque signature procedures
(3) Disaster recovery plans
(4) Document sequencing methods

c. JKM Company is an on-line Internet-based bookstore. Customers place orders, inputting their credit card numbers. All Internet electronic traffic is encrypted, but passwords are not required for customers. To prevent hackers from accessing JKM's accounting systems, JKM should
(1) use firewalls to restrict access of known problem Web sites.
(2) use dial-back methods to connect with all customers who want to place an order.
(3) use a dedicated, stand-alone computer for Web site systems.

(4) have detection software to prevent junk E-mail and other abuses.

d. To help ensure that only authorized payments for supplier invoices are sent using EDI, a company should
(1) match electronic fund transfer amounts to purchase orders.
(2) compare control totals of supplier invoices to control totals of payments sent.
(3) compare record counts sent to record counts received
(4) encrypt all Internet electronic traffic.

22-17 The following questions concern computer-assisted audit tests. Choose the best answer.

a. Which of the following is not a data communications risk?
(1) Viruses that are transmitted by e-mail
(2) Data stolen during transmission between locations
(3) Use of unauthorized programs
(4) Absence of firewalls to protect systems

b. Which of the following is not a computer-assisted audit task?
(1) Test data
(2) Program comparison software
(3) Generalized audit software
(4) Encryption testing

c. The key advantage of an integrated test facility over test data is that
(1) programs being developed can be tested for accuracy.
(2) test data can be run through actual production programs.
(3) programs can be tested for adequacy of documentation.
(4) the auditor can detect whether there is unauthorized coding in the programs.

DISCUSSION QUESTIONS AND PROBLEMS

22-18 Turner Valley Hospital plans to install a data base management system, Hosp Info, that will maintain patient histories including tests performed and their results, vital statistics and medical diagnoses. The system also will manage personnel and payroll, medical and non-medical supplies, and patient and provincial health care billings.

The decision was taken by the board of the hospital on the advice of a consultant who was a former employee of Medical Data Services Inc., the developer of Hosp Info.

Turner Valley Hospital's chief information officer has come to your accounting firm to ask for advice on what general controls she should ask Medical Data Services Inc. to install to preserve the integrity of the information in the system and to deal with privacy issues.

The system would permit data about patients to be entered by doctors, nurses and medical technologists.

Required

a. Describe in general terms the controls you would suggest for the system as a whole.

b. Considering the nature of Turner Valley Hospital, describe potential risks the hospital should be concerned about with respect to Hosp Info.

c. What are the advantages of such a data base management system?

22-19 Lifed & Verboten, Public Accountants, are the auditors of numerous credit unions in your city. The CFO of Ethnic Credit Union (ECU) recently called Sarah Lifed about his concerns with respect to one of his loan officers. ECU is a small credit union, with only 10 full-time employees. There are two loan officers who are responsible for approving and administering loans, recording interest rate changes in the master files, and recording pre-authorized payments. The CFO indicated that there have been a number of complaints about duplicated and incorrect loan payments. Upon investigation, incorrect interest rates were found and the duplicated payments were reversed. The CFO has requested that as part of your annual audit, you perform additional computer-assisted audit tests on member account and transaction data files to pinpoint potential errors in the data files and potential irregularities. Since ECU's records are stored in a data base, the firm uses ECU's report writer to run computer-assisted audit tests.

The following semi-permanent information is contained in the data base for each credit union member:

- Member's account number
- Member's name and address
- Sub-account code (1 = savings, 2 = personal loan, 3 = mortgage loan)
- Date account opened
- Last transaction date
- Current balance
- Interest rate (savings and loan accounts)
- Loan payment amount (personal and mortgage loan accounts)
- Interest amount — current month (savings and loan accounts)
- Interest amount — year-to-date (savings and loan accounts)
- Maturity date (personal and mortgage loan accounts)
- Overdue payments amount (personal and mortgage loan accounts)
- Number of loan payments — year-to-date (personal and mortgage loan accounts)
- Number of cash deposit transactions — year-to-date (savings accounts)
- Number of cash withdrawal transactions — year-to-date (savings accounts)
- Total cash deposits year-to-date (savings accounts)
- Total cash withdrawal — year-to-date (savings accounts)
- Original amount (personal and mortgage loan accounts)

The following information is retained for each transaction in the data base:

- Member's account number
- Member's sub-account number
- Transaction code
- Transaction date
- Transaction amount

Required

a. Identify potential errors that could occur and potential fraudulent activities that could be conducted by the loan officers. State whether each item is a potential error or a potential fraudulent activity.

b. For each potential error or potential fraudulent activity, identify a test that could be conducted using the report writer to investigate the likely occurrence of that error or activity.

22-20 Western Transport Limited (WTL) is a national trucking company. When goods are shipped, the shipment process is initiated using a waybill, recording weight, size, and number of goods moved. When the trucker records arrival at the destination, the waybill signed by the customer is scanned into the computer system and is used to trigger an automatic billing process. At month end, the waybill history file is interrogated and a revenue accrual is made to account for outstanding waybills. This accrual is based on the following formula:

DAYS OUTSTANDING	PERCENT ACCRUED
5 days and greater	100
4 days	75
3 days	50
2 days	25
1 day	—

Required

Identify the different methods that could be used by the auditor to determine the reasonableness of the monthly revenue accrual or to place reliance on the revenue accrual method.

22-21 Grocery Stores Inc. (GSI) is a regional chain of grocery stores. GSI stores are strategically spread throughout the province, outside major metropolitan areas. The great distances between the stores and the head office make the stores difficult to manage and control. For some time, GSI has been considering a variety of efficiency and image problems, hoping to find a way to improve its stable but lacklustre performance and attract additional capital.

One improvement that is to be implemented is the upgrading of the point-of-sale (POS) computer systems. Currently, each store uses old stand-alone equipment which is used to record sales and cash receipts. There is no tie-in to the inventory systems. Ted Bear, GSI's vice-president of store operations, believes that several benefits will occur with the new system. He wants to improve the stores' image not only with customers but also with potential investors. He wants to hold the line on expanding existing store facilities or hiring more checkout personnel by increasing the flow-through capacity at existing locations. In addition, he believes that the information provided by the on-line, real-time capture of sales and inventory data will improve GSI's management of stock, reduce carrying costs and out-of-stock conditions, and help reduce the alarming amount of "waste" and pilferage.

Mike Jones, the audit senior responsible for the GSI audit, has been called into the office of Pierre Brule, the partner in charge, to discuss GSI's proposed computer system.

Brule: Mike, I have just come from lunch with Ted Bear. He informed me that GSI will be taking steps to upgrade their POS systems.

Jones: When does it plan to convert to the new systems?

Brule: It plans to start phasing in the POS system in three months. The Cottage Country Store is to be converted first.

Then, if all goes well, the entire central region will be converted by year end.

Jones: That makes me a little uneasy. A lot of pre-implementation and development work is required, and I can't see the company making such a major change in such a short period of time given its limited resources.

Brule: The company has decided to outsource implementation, training, and operations to an independent software house, Royal Systems Ltd. (RSL). Since RSL has other retail clients, only some modifications are required to fit the system to GSI's needs. Once the system is operational, RSL will continue to operate and maintain the system (hardware and software) as an independent service bureau on GSI's behalf. RSL will own all of the equipment, related facilities, and software and will lease them to GSI. I have an overview schematic of the proposed system (see Exhibit I on page 721). I'd like you to look it over. I've agreed to meet with Ken Berryman (internal audit manager) and Andrea Martin (vice-president of finance) to discuss planning issues.

Jones: We can also consider computer-assisted audit testing, which we talked about briefly last year.

Brule: I'd like to discuss the POS system, its overall impact on our audit approach, and the impact that the implementation will have on GSI's control systems. Before our meeting, please draft a memorandum to me discussing the relevant issues and their impact on the audit.

Required

a. Identify the new risks for GSI due to the implementation of the POS system.

b. Provide recommendations to GSI for minimizing the risks identified.

c. How will the implementation affect the audit of GSI?

d. What should the role of internal audit be during the implementation?

e. How would your answers to the above parts change if RSL were to also act as a clearing house for debit card transactions?

22-22 Eastern Distributor Limited (EDL) is a rapidly growing distributor of health-care products operating in three regions — Ontario, Quebec, and the Maritimes. In the last three years, the company has experienced a 20 percent growth rate. Data processing operations are distributed. There is a minicomputer at head office in Montreal, with local area networks in Toronto and Halifax. Every night, head office connects to the branches, uploading the day's transactions and downloading master file changes. During 1998, a major ice storm devastated large parts of eastern Ontario and Quebec, with the head office systems square in the path of the storm. EDL was hit on several fronts:

- Electrical trunk lines were destroyed in the vicinity of the head office building; offices were without electricity for three weeks.

- The roof caved in on a section of the Montreal warehouse, destroying 25 percent of the inventory; another 10 percent was destroyed due to temperature changes.
- Trucks were stopped on many routes for 10 days as roads became impassable due to the ice storm.

During the three weeks of the head office power failure, the Toronto and Halifax branches operated as local systems. Since there was an intervening month end, they had to purchase and stockpile additional backup tapes so that backups could be taken every day. When power resumed, a specialist from the supplier software house was called to untangle the "data mess." Special programs were written so that each day's transactions could be separately processed. It took EDL more than three months to stabilize and recover its information systems.

Required

Identify the safeguards that EDL should have had in place prior to the storm that would have prevented the "data mess."

22-23 During the past six months, your company has consistently been losing competitive bids to a nearby company whose bids always seem to be slightly lower. Subsequent investigation reveals that an employee of your company in the payroll department has been stealing your bid data and selling it to the competitor for $5,000 per bid. Your company has offices in five buildings. Computing services are provided using five local area networks connected by a common carrier.

Required

a. Identify methods that the employee could be using to obtain the data.

b. For each method, identify at least one control that could have been used to detect or prevent the data theft.

22-24 It was a typical madhouse time on the night before a payroll run. Some employees were entering time cards; other employees were checking data entry lists to time cards and calling supervisors about employee numbers that they couldn't read. The system started slowing down, and then staff started getting ABORT—RETRY messages when they tried to execute programs. Initially, technical support staff suspected a cable break or an operating system failure. Diagnostics were run, revealing nothing. Finally, a staff member began running the SCAN virus detection program and uncovered a new virus that seemed to have originated from the central server. The virus cost the company about 25 person-hours in technical support and about 70 hours in overtime for payroll clerks, who stayed until 4 A.M.

The company has one local area network with 250 stations using linked central servers. Some stations have hard disks up to 20 gigabytes in size; some stations have no disk drives at all. Salespeople have laptop computers which they can use to dial in from remote locations to conduct customer inquiries and place customer orders.

EXHIBIT I

Overview of GSI's POS
System

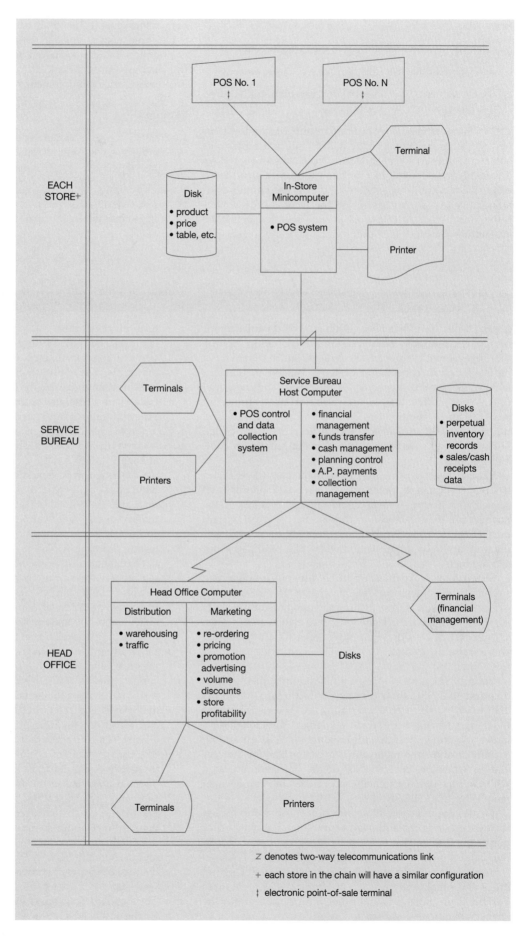

EACH STORE+

POS No. 1 ↕

POS No. N ↕

Terminal

Disk
• product
• price
• table, etc.

In-Store Minicomputer
• POS system

Printer

SERVICE BUREAU

Terminals

Printers

Service Bureau Host Computer
• POS control and data collection system

• financial management
• funds transfer
• cash management
• planning control
• A.P. payments
• collection management

Disks
• perpetual inventory records
• sales/cash receipts data

Terminals (financial management)

HEAD OFFICE

Head Office Computer

Distribution	Marketing
• warehousing • traffic	• re-ordering • pricing • promotion advertising • volume discounts • store profitability

Disks

Terminals

Printers

z denotes two-way telecommunications link

+ each store in the chain will have a similar configuration

↕ electronic point-of-sale terminal

Required

a. Identify the potential sources of the virus infection.

b. How could this virus infection have been prevented?

c. What elements of a disaster recovery plan are required for recovery from a virus infection?

22-25 Frank is the owner of Frankincents Machining Limited, a custom machining centre with 10 full-time employees and a part-time bookkeeper, Norma, who comes in two days a week. Norma convinced Frank to purchase a small business suite of accounting packages and a microcomputer with a laser printer. Norma has set up the records on the computer, and all accounting work is now handled using the accounting packages (i.e., order entry, accounts receivable, cash disbursements, general ledger, payroll). It took Norma about three months, and she initially had some difficulty balancing the subsystems, but everything seems to be functioning properly now. Frank did not consult with you, his accountant, prior to implementing the systems.

Required

a. Identify the risks associated with the current method of handling accounting records at Frankincents Machining Limited.

b. Identify those activities that Frank should handle in sales, accounts receivable, cash disbursements, and payroll. Explain why.

CASE

22-26 Miles Jones has been assigned as the audit senior responsible for a new client, Starfire Electric Limited (SEL). The engagement partner, Ms. Rogers, explained that SEL is a reputable private corporation located in Vancouver. It manufactures electrical components for residential and industrial uses. Major product lines include electrical fuses and circuit breakers for residential uses and heavy-duty breakers and transformers for industrial uses. During the current year, SEL also began producing electrical heating units for commercial applications.

SEL has been growing steadily over the past 10 years and has plants located in Vancouver, Calgary, and Winnipeg. It started with 10 employees and now employs over 200. Transformers are manufactured at the Vancouver plant, circuit breakers at the Calgary plant, and electrical fuses and heating units at the Winnipeg plant. In total, SEL produces about 600 products.

SEL has been experiencing some difficulty in obtaining supplies of plastics used as raw material in the production of circuit breakers. It is investigating the purchase of a plastics company located in the United States to ensure an adequate supply. SEL is considering a public offering after the year end to raise the estimated $10 million required to purchase this company.

Because SEL is considering a public offering, the directors decided that SEL should have its financial statements audited. A local chartered accounting firm had issued Notice to Readers for SEL since its incorporation. SEL looked for a larger accounting firm that could better serve its expanding operations and appointed your firm as auditors for the year ending September 30, 1999. Ms. Rogers has communicated with the previous accountants and has obtained an engagement letter from SEL.

Ms. Rogers asks you to prepare a planning memo for her review regarding the audit and accounting and other issues pertaining to this new assignment, along with your recommendations on how to deal with each of them.

After your meeting with Ms. Rogers, you visit SEL's head office and obtain the most recent financial statements (see Exhibit II on page 724) and other information about the client's operations as shown.

- Each plant operates as a separate profit centre, maintaining its own accounting system on a local area network. Each plant uses a copy of the head office programs. These programs are stored in object code (machine language) on the plant's server.

- Each plant is responsible for the control of its own computer operations, and each produces special-purpose reports for its own use using a general-purpose report writer as the need arises. The five accounting personnel at each location handle computer operations and the use of the report writer. File layouts are used to decide which data fields to access. Copies of new report formats are sent to head office as attachments to electronic mail messages when completed. Since these reports and new programs are produced as required, no formal testing procedures exist.

- Each plant also submits to head office a set of accounting reports and supplementary information. These are submitted in a standard format, electronically, for use in the preparation of combined corporate financial statements. The statements are prepared by the controller using a spreadsheet package.

- SEL's inventory consists of raw materials, work in progress, and finished goods. Raw materials include copper, used as a conductor in almost all of the components; silver, used for contacts in the electrical breakers; and plastic and steel, used in the casings for breakers and transformers. Most of the raw materials are purchased from suppliers in the United States.

- SEL uses a standard costing system to account for its inventory. A standard cost is prepared for each product by each plant based on its own production capacity, time and motion studies, and engineering estimates. Each standard cost consists of a raw material component, a direct labour component, and an overhead component that is based on direct labour hours. The costing and perpetual inventory systems were custom written by head office programmers.

- New standards are established once a year on April 1. The standard costs are entered in a standard cost master file and used to value inventories. Only two people at each plant have the password that allows them to change the standard cost master file. Password changes are controlled by the computer operators, who are informed orally of the need for change. The revaluation allowance resulting from the annual conversion of March 31 inventories to the new standard is amortized over the inventory turnover period. Normally, sales prices are updated at the same time by the sales supervisor using a separate password.

- The Vancouver plant's standard cost master file had been inadvertently changed during the performance of some computer program maintenance. The programs had been transmitted to the plant server from the head office systems by the head office's programming department. The head office programmers are attempting to determine the cause of the data changes to ensure that the problem does not recur. As a result of the inadvertent change, the books in Vancouver had been showing favourable variances in the direct labour and overhead components of $50,000 and $100,000 respectively. As of August 31, $60,000 of these variances has been allocated to cost of sales.

- The company Web page is maintained by head office personnel, with information on all of the different types of products and services. Since the Web page provides information only (customers cannot place orders), it is located directly on the head office server. Customers can view product information and send E-mail queries to anyone at the company using the Web page.

Required

Prepare the memo requested by the partner.

(CICA adapted)

EXHIBIT II
Starfire Electric
Limited Extracts

STARFIRE ELECTRIC LIMITED EXTRACTS FROM UNAUDITED BALANCE SHEET

(In thousands of dollars)

As at

	August 31, 1999	September 30, 1998
Assets		
Current		
Cash	$ 244	$ 54
Accounts receivable, net	4,771	4,601
Inventories	9,256	7,922
	14,271	12,577
Fixed assets, net	6,707	5,547
	$20,978	$18,124
Liabilities		
Current		
Accounts payable and accrued liabilities	$ 6,779	$ 5,892
Income taxes payable	45	54
Current portion of long-term debt	312	255
	7,136	6,201
Long-term debt	4,258	3,595
Deferred income taxes	1,401	1,274
Shareholders' Equity		
Share capital	$ 2	$ 2
Retained earnings	8,181	7,052
	8,183	7,054
	$20,978	$18,124

**STARFIRE ELECTRIC LIMITED EXTRACTS FROM UNAUDITED
STATEMENTS OF INCOME AND RETAINED EARNINGS**

(In thousands of dollars)

As at

	August 31, 1999 (11 months)	September 30, 1998 (12 months)
Net sales	$35,846	$31,454
Income before the following:	$ 3,017	$ 2,511
Amortization	954	750
Interest on long-term debt	350	386
Other interest	12	20
	1,316	1,156
Income before income taxes	1,701	1,355
Income taxes		
— current	445	574
— deferred	127	(115)
	572	459
Net income	1,129	896
Retained earnings at beginning of the period	7,052	6,156
Retained earnings at the end of the period	$ 8,181	$ 7,052

23

ASSURANCE SERVICES: ATTEST ENGAGEMENTS

SCEPTICISM APPLIES TO ALL TYPES OF ENGAGEMENTS

Menard Construction Ltd. was a contractor specializing in apartment complexes in Alberta. The owner of the construction company, Tony Menard, reached an agreement with a promoter named Alice Mayberry to serve as contractor on three projects Mayberry was currently marketing. One problem with the agreement was that Menard would not receive final payment for the construction work until all partnership units were sold.

The first partnership offering was completely sold and Menard was paid. Unfortunately, the next two partnerships were not completely sold. To solve this problem, Menard loaned money to relatives and key employees who bought the necessary interests for the partnerships to close so that Menard would receive the final payment.

When Menard Construction Ltd. had a review service performed by Renée Fortin, a public accountant and sole practitioner, the accounting records showed loans receivable from a number of employees and individuals named Menard. Fortin observed that the loans were made just before the second and third partnerships closed, and they were for amounts that were multiples of $15,000, the amount of a partnership unit. Fortin asked Menard to explain what happened. Menard told her, "When I received the money from the first partnership escrow, I wanted to do something nice for relatives and employees who had been loyal to me over the years. This is just my way of sharing my good fortune with the ones I love. The equality of the amounts is just a coincidence."

When Fortin considered the reasonableness of this scenario, she found it hard to believe. First, the timing was odd. Second, the amounts seemed to be an unusual coincidence. Third, if he really had wanted to do something special for these folks, why didn't he give them something, rather than loan them money? Fortin asked that the promoter, Mayberry, send her detailed information on the

> subscriptions for each partnership. Mayberry refused, stating that she was under legal obligation to keep all information confidential. When Fortin pressed Menard, he also refused further cooperation, although he did say he would "represent" to her that the loans had nothing to do with closing the partnerships so he could get his money. At this point, Fortin withdrew from the engagement.

In addition to being involved with audits of historical financial statements prepared in accordance with generally accepted accounting principles, public accountants commonly deal with situations involving other types of information, varying levels of assurance, and other types of reports. Because the partners of many public accounting firms believe that there is relatively little growth potential for financial statement auditing in their practices, they are increasingly looking to other types of services to provide additional revenues. Although opportunities still exist for review and compilation services, many practitioners believe that nontraditional services have even more potential. For example, forecasts and prospective financial statements are widely used by investors and other financial statement users; however, these users prefer some type of assurance about the reliability of the information provided. Many public accounting firms have the expertise to provide such assurance. Similarly, these firms are increasingly performing agreed-upon procedures engagements on a variety of information to provide some assurance about its reliability. One example discussed in the next chapter deals with the issuing of an opinion by a public accounting firm on whether a chemical company has put the appropriate procedures into place to satisfy the requirements of federal and provincial environmental acts. Even though such an engagement may not seem like auditing, many public accounting firms now perform such attestation services, or services called *direct reporting engagements* or *business advisory assistance*. These services are the subject of this and the next chapter of this text.

This chapter reviews the definition of assurance engagements and defines attest engagements and direct reporting engagements. It discusses eight specific types of engagements outside audits:

- Special attest engagement reports in which the auditor expresses an opinion on financial information other than financial statements or on compliance with a contractual agreement, or in which the public accountant applies certain auditing procedures to financial information
- Special attest engagements to report on internal control procedures at a service organization
- Review engagements and compilations
- Prospectuses
- Future-oriented financial information
- Reports on the application of accounting principles, auditing standards, or review standards
- Pension costs
- Pension fund financial statements

Chapter 24 describes direct reporting engagements and special services offered by accountants, including services related to environmental auditing and information systems. Chapter 25 covers internal auditing and comprehensive auditing.

Section 5020, "Association," of the *CICA Handbook* was introduced in Chapter 2. Recall that the section defines when a public accountant is associated with information and describes the accountant's responsibilities when he or she is associated.

This chapter describes the wide range of services that a public accountant can provide. It is very important that the public accountant properly communicate to users of information with which he or she is associated both the nature and extent of the association. There are a number of figures in this chapter that illustrate the various forms of communication that the public accountant may issue. In studying them, you should note similarities and differences between the auditor's report discussed in Chapter 2 and the communications in this chapter.

Engagement letters were discussed in Chapter 7; an illustration of an engagement letter appears in Figure 7-2 on page 204. The various topics discussed below suggest the need for an engagement letter describing exactly what work the public accountant, acting as auditor or accountant, will do for the client and the proposed communication that will describe the work done (e.g., Figure 23-2 on page 729). The need for an engagement letter that is tailored to reflect the circumstances of the engagement cannot be overemphasized.

ASSURANCE ENGAGEMENTS

During the past 20 years, public accountants have increasingly been asked to perform a variety of audit-like or assurance services for different purposes. For example, a public accountant might be asked to provide assurance on the reliability of computer software or with respect to the meeting of environmental standards by an entity. Existing standards dealt primarily with historical financial statements prepared according to generally accepted accounting principles, whereas the new services often dealt with other types of information. Accordingly, the guidance provided to accountants became difficult to formulate and communicate effectively without disrupting the cohesiveness of the existing standards in the *Handbook*.

The problem is addressed by the profession through the issuance of *CICA Handbook* Section 5025, "Standards for Assurance Engagements." The development of the section was a cooperative venture between the CICA's Assurance Standards Board and the Public Sector Accounting and Auditing Board (now the Public Sector Accounting Board). The section establishes the standards for all assurance engagements and applies to:

- Public and private sector engagements
- Attest engagements and direct reporting engagements
- Engagements such as audits that provide a high level of assurance and engagements such as reviews that provide a lower level of assurance

The section defines an *assurance engagement* as "an engagement where, pursuant to an accountability relationship between two or more parties, a practitioner is engaged to issue a written communication expressing a conclusion concerning a subject matter for which the accountable party is responsible." There are three parties to the relationship: (1) the practitioner, (2) the user(s), and (3) the person who is accountable (usually management). Figure 23-1 illustrates this relationship. The user could be any stakeholder who will use the information on which the assurance is provided.

The section was designed to provide guidance for a broader range of services than the existing standards in the *Handbook*. For example, the new section considers both attest engagements and direct reporting engagements. *Attest engagements* are engagements where the auditor expresses a conclusion on a written assertion about a subject prepared by a party accountable for the assertion, such as management. The assertion measures the subject matter using appropriate criteria. The special reports discussed in the remainder of this chapter are all attest engagements.

A *direct reporting engagement* is an engagement where the auditor *directly* expresses a conclusion on his or her evaluation of subject matter using certain criteria; management does not report in a direct reporting engagement. Perhaps the best example of a direct reporting engagement is the communication by the Auditor General to Parliament. In his report, the Auditor General, Denis Desautels, describes what was found as a result of audits performed by his office. Public sector auditing is discussed fur-

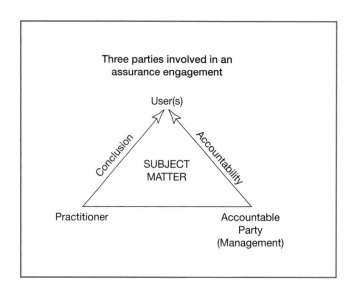

Three parties involved in an assurance engagement

ther in Chapter 25. Other types of direct reporting engagements are also discussed in Chapter 24.

The *criteria* referred to in the previous paragraph are the benchmark or standard against which the subject matter is measured. For example, the criteria in a financial statement audit are GAAP.

The general standard states that "Before undertaking an assurance engagement, the practitioner should have a reasonable basis for believing the engagement can be completed in accordance with the assurance standards." The practitioner and all others involved with the assurance engagement should have adequate proficiency to perform the engagement and should collectively possess adequate knowledge of the subject matter. In addition, the engagement should be performed with due care and an objective state of mind.

The practitioner should obtain some form of evidence that an accountability relationship exists (i.e., that management is responsible for the subject matter). The evidence will normally be an acknowledgment from management but may be in some other form.

The section requires the practitioner to identify or develop criteria that can be used to evaluate the subject matter. The importance of this requirement cannot be overemphasized. If the criteria are not suitable, the value of the assurance engagement is doubtful. The section suggests that the necessary characteristics are relevance, reliability, neutrality, understandability, and completeness. The section lists sources of criteria that may be considered generally accepted and suggests that they are preferred. Other sources are acceptable subject to certain conditions. Criteria that could result in the report being misleading should not be used.

There are three performance standards outlined in Section 5025:

- The work should be adequately planned, and there should be proper supervision.
- The practitioner should consider both significance (similar to materiality) and engagement risk (similar to audit risk) when planning and performing the engagement.
- Sufficient evidence should be gathered to support the conclusion the practitioner expresses in his or her report.

The reporting standards for Section 5025 indicate that, as a minimum, the report should:

1. Identify to whom the report is directed.

2. Describe the objective of the engagement.
3. Identify management's assertion in an attest engagement.
4. Distinguish between the responsibilities of management and the practitioner.
5. Identify the applicable standards in accordance with which the engagement was conducted.
6. Identify the criteria against which the subject matter was evaluated.
7. Provide a conclusion that states the level of assurance being conveyed and/or any reservation that the practitioner may have.
8. State the date of the report.
9. Identify the practitioner.
10. Identify the place of issue.

Note that the reporting standards are much like those of GAAS found in Section 5400 and discussed in Chapter 2.

There can be scope limitations leading to a qualification or a denial of opinion with an assurance engagement. There can also be a qualification or an adverse opinion with an assurance engagement when:

* In a direct reporting engagement, the subject matter does not conform to the criteria.
* In an attest engagement, the assertion made by management does not present fairly the criteria used or conformity of the subject matter with the criteria, or if essential information has not been presented or is presented in an inappropriate manner.

Figure 23-2 illustrates the form of communication that would be issued under Section 5025. The report is an attest report providing a high level of assurance. The criteria for the engagement are described in an appendix to the report not provided with this example. Note the extra paragraph following the opinion paragraph; it is an

FIGURE 23-2
Example of a Report on an Assurance Engagement

> **AUDITOR'S REPORT CONCERNING EFFECTIVENESS OF THE SYSTEM OF INTERNAL CONTROL OVER FINANCIAL REPORTING**
>
> To the Shareholders of Gaa Corp.
>
> We have audited management's assertion that Gaa Corp. maintained an effective system of internal control over financial reporting as of December 31, 1998, in relation to the criteria described in the appendix to this report. Management's assertion is included in the accompanying report "Report on Effectiveness of Internal Control at Gaa Corp." as of December 31, 1998. The maintenance of an effective system of internal control over financial reporting is the responsibility of management. Our responsibility is to express an opinion on management's assertion about the effectiveness of the internal control system based on our audit.
>
> We conducted our audit in accordance with generally accepted auditing standards. Those standards require that we plan and perform an audit to obtain reasonable assurance that management's assertion is free from significant misstatements. An audit includes examining, on a test basis, evidence supporting the content and disclosures in management's assertion. An audit also includes assessing the criteria used and the significant judgments made by management, as well as evaluating the overall presentation of management's assertion.
>
> In our opinion, management's assertion presents fairly, in all significant respects, the effectiveness of the system of internal control over financial reporting of Gaa Corp. as of December 31, 1998, based on the criteria referred to above.
>
> Because of the inherent limitations in any internal control system, errors or fraud and other irregularities may occur and not be detected. Also, projections of any evaluation of the internal control system over financial reporting to future periods are subject to the risk that the internal control system may become inadequate because of changes in conditions, or that the degree of compliance with the policies or procedures may deteriorate.
>
> Edmonton, Alberta
> February 7, 1999
>
> *Charles Co.*
> Chartered Accountants

example of additional information that the practitioner may wish to include to make the auditor's report more informative.

You should compare Figure 23-2 to Figure 2-1 on page 36 in order to understand the differences and similarities between a standard auditor's report and a report issued in connection with an assurance engagement.

SELECTED ATTEST REPORTS

Public accountants are frequently asked to prepare special reports. In preparing these reports, they may be acting as *auditors*, as stipulated in Sections 5805 and 5815 of the *CICA Handbook*, or as *accountants*, as stipulated in Section 9100. Each of these sections will be covered in turn. Although many of these reports are still referred to as "audit reports" in the *CICA Handbook*, this text uses the term "attest engagements" to keep terminology in line with the relatively new (1997) Section 5025 on assurance engagements. The text uses the term "auditor" for those engagements where a high level of assurance is required.

OBJECTIVE 23-2

Describe attest engagements to examine financial information, apply specified auditing procedures, and report on compliance.

Because the nature of an engagement is different from that of a regular audit, an engagement letter is essential in order to prevent misunderstandings as to what is wanted and what will be done.

It is important that the public accountant acting as auditor or accountant, when required to report in some specified form, ensure that his or her comments follow the form suggested in the *CICA Handbook*. At the same time, the public accountant must ensure that the communication he or she issues indicates the accountant's involvement and the nature of the responsibility assumed. The wording of the communication need not follow exactly that in the *CICA Handbook*.

REPORTS EXPRESSING AN AUDIT OPINION ON FINANCIAL INFORMATION OTHER THAN FINANCIAL STATEMENTS (SECTION 5805)

This section is concerned with an auditor's reporting on information such as employee bonuses, sales in a specified location where rent is based on sales, amounts calculated under a reporting insurance agreement, or the costs of a capital project.

The report, as discussed in Section 5805, differs from the auditor's report for a regular financial statement audit in two ways:

- Materiality is defined in terms of the element, account, or items involved rather than in relation to the overall statements. The effect ordinarily is to require more evidence than would be needed if the item being verified were just one of many parts of the statements (e.g., if the sales account were being reported on as part of a regular audit).
- The auditor should comply with the general and examination standards but does not have to comply with the reporting standards.

The report required under Section 5805, like that required under Section 5400 for audited financial statements, will be entitled "Auditor's Report," will identify the financial information, and will include three paragraphs: an introductory paragraph, a scope paragraph, and an opinion paragraph. Each are discussed in turn below:

The introductory paragraph

- Indicates that an audit was performed.
- Identifies the relevant portions of any agreement, statute, or regulation under which the financial information was prepared and explains any significant interpretations of the agreement, statute, or regulation made by management in preparing the information.
- Specifies the basis of accounting if other than GAAP.
- Indicates any lack of consistent application of either accounting principles or interpretation of the agreement, statute, or regulation by management from previous reports.
- States the respective responsibilities of management and the auditor.

The scope paragraph   This paragraph is similar to the scope paragraph for a financial statement audit with the exception that it refers to the financial information reported on.

The opinion paragraph   This paragraph includes the auditor's opinion on whether the financial information is presented fairly in all material respects, in accordance with GAAP or with the basis of accounting described in the introductory paragraph, and in accordance with any interpretations of the agreement, statute, or regulation by management.

Figure 23-3 illustrates a report for royalties, which is a specified account.

FIGURE 23-3
Example of a Report Under Section 5805

AUDITOR'S REPORT ON SCHEDULE OF ROYALTIES

To the Directors of Ace Corp.

We have audited the schedule of royalties applicable to engine production of the Q Division of Ten Limited for the year ended December 31, 1998, under the terms of a licence agreement dated May 14, 1993, between Ace Corp. and Ten Limited. We have been informed that, under Ten Limited's interpretation of the agreement referred to above, royalties were based on the number of engines produced after giving effect to a reduction for production retirements that were scrapped, but without a reduction for field returns that were scrapped, even though the field returns were replaced with new engines without charge to customers. The financial information is the responsibility of the management of Ten Limited. Our responsibility is to express an opinion on this financial information based on our audit.

We conducted our audit in accordance with generally accepted auditing standards. Those standards require that we plan and perform an audit to obtain reasonable assurance whether the financial information is free of material misstatement. An audit includes, on a test basis, evidence supporting the amounts and disclosures in the financial information. An audit also includes assessing the accounting principles used and significant estimates made by management, as well as evaluating the overall presentation of the financial information.

In our opinion, this schedule, when read together with the information set out in the introductory paragraph, presents fairly, in all material respects, the amount of royalties applicable to the number of engines produced by the Q Division of Ten Limited for the year ended December 31, 1998, in accordance with the provision of the agreement referred to above and the interpretations thereof.

Val D'Or, Québec
January 21, 1999

Adams + Ferrie
Chartered Accountants

REPORTS ON THE RESULTS OF APPLYING SPECIFIED AUDITING PROCEDURES TO FINANCIAL INFORMATION OTHER THAN FINANCIAL STATEMENTS (SECTION 9100)

This section is concerned with an accountant's application of prespecified auditing procedures to financial information. The engagement is not an assurance engagement and an expression of an opinion is not expected. Since the client specifies what auditing procedures are to be applied and the form of report that is to be issued, distribution of the report is normally restricted. The accountant reaches an agreement with the client with respect to all three issues before beginning the engagement. In this situation, the accountant should comply both with the general standard and the first examination standard.

The report should specify

- The financial information to which the procedures were applied.
- The procedures applied.
- The factual results of the procedures; negative assurance should not be expressed.
- That an audit was not performed; there should be a disclaimer of opinion.
- Any restrictions on circulation of the report.

Figure 23-4 is an illustration of such a report. It was prepared in the situation where the financial statements were audited but gross sales were not audited on a store-by-store basis.

FIGURE 23-4
Example of a Report
Under Section 9100

ACCOUNTANTS' REPORT IN CONNECTION WITH GROSS SALES

To Garner Limited

As requested by Okanagan Stores Limited, we report that the gross sales of the company's store at King Street, Kelowna, B.C. for the year ended June 30, 1999, are recorded in the amount of $790,000 in the general ledger sales account of the company and form part of the company's gross sales in its financial statements for the year then ended, on which we reported on August 3, 1999.

Our examination of the company's financial statements for the year ended June 30, 1999, was not directed to the determination of gross sales or other financial information of individual stores. We have not performed an audit of and accordingly do not express an opinion on the amount of gross sales referred to in the preceding paragraph.

It is understood that this report is to be used solely for computing percentage rental and is not to be referred to or distributed to any person who is not a member of management of Garner Limited or Okanagan Stores Limited.

Kelowna, B.C.
August 8, 1999

Carter & Wilhelm
Certified General Accountants

REPORTS ON COMPLIANCE WITH CONTRACTUAL AGREEMENTS, STATUTES, AND REGULATIONS (SECTION 5815)

This section is concerned with an auditor's report on a client's compliance with particular accounting and financial reporting requirements that have been included as terms of a contract or agreement, such as a loan agreement or a trust deed. For example, this report is often used to report to creditors on the client's compliance with restrictive covenants in a loan agreement or bond indenture, such as maintenance of a minimum current ratio or sinking fund payments. The auditor may express an opinion in this situation.

The auditor must comply with the general standard and the examination standards. The auditor should reach agreement with the client with respect to the terms of the engagement and the form of report.

The report required under Section 5815, like that required under Section 5400 for audited financial statements, will be entitled "Auditor's Report" and will include three paragraphs: an introductory paragraph, a scope paragraph, and an opinion paragraph. Each are discussed in turn below.

The introductory paragraph

- Indicates that compliance with criteria established by provisions of the agreement, statute, or regulation was audited.
- Identifies the relevant provisions of the agreement, statute, or regulation under which the financial information was prepared and explains any significant interpretations of the provisions of the agreement, statute, or regulation made by management in preparing the information.
- Indicates any lack of consistent application of interpretation of the agreement, statute, or regulation by management from previous reports.
- States the respective responsibilities of management and the auditor.

The scope paragraph This paragraph is similar to the scope paragraph for a financial statement audit except that reference is to compliance with the agreement described in the introductory paragraph.

The opinion paragraph This paragraph includes the auditor's opinion as to whether the entity has complied with, in all material respects, the criteria established by provisions of the agreement, statute, or regulation.

An illustration is provided in Figure 23-5.

FIGURE 23-5

Example of a Report Under Section 5815

AUDITOR'S REPORT

To Georgian Trust Company

We have audited Victoria Limited's compliance with the accounting and financial reporting matters of Sections 1 to 3 of the Trust Deed dated February 28, 1995, with Georgian Trust Company. Compliance with the criteria established by the provisions of the Trust Deed is the responsibility of the management of Victoria Limited. Our responsibility is to express an opinion on this compliance based on our audit.

We conducted our audit in accordance with generally accepted auditing standards. Those standards require that we plan and perform an audit to obtain reasonable assurance as to whether Victoria Limited complied with the criteria established by the provisions of the Trust Deed referred to above. Such an audit includes examining, on a test basis, evidence supporting compliance, evaluating the overall compliance with the Trust Deed, and, where applicable, assessing the accounting principles used and significant estimates made by management.

In our opinion, Victoria Limited is in compliance, in all material respects, with the accounting and financial reporting matters of Sections 1 to 3 of the Trust Deed dated February 28, 1995, with Georgian Trust Company as at December 31, 1998.

Lethbridge, Alberta
February 7, 1999

Tilly & Nanda

Chartered Accountants

OPINION ON CONTROL PROCEDURES AT A SERVICE ORGANIZATION

OBJECTIVE 23-3

Describe attest engagements to examine control procedures.

Some companies rely on a service organization to provide custodial services (e.g., provide security for a public warehouse), provide data-processing services (e.g., process payroll and issue payroll cheques), or manage assets (e.g., administer a company's pension plan). The auditor of such a company will require evidence that the service organization had internal controls in place to safeguard the company's assets and records and provide reliable and timely data to the company. The auditor could (1) gather the necessary evidence at the service organization (which is not necessarily a client) or have the service organization provide a confirmation in the case of custodial services, or (2) rely on an audit of the service organization's internal controls by another auditor. Section 5310 of the *CICA Handbook* describes how an auditor should assess the report of a service auditor.

An auditor may be engaged to report on a service organization's internal controls. Section 5900 describes "matters that an auditor would consider when engaged to express an opinion on the design, effective operation, and continuity of control procedures at a service organization."

There are two possible types of engagements:

- The auditor may be required to provide an opinion on the design and existence of control procedures at some date.
- The auditor may be required to provide an opinion on the design, effective operation, and continuity of control procedures during a period of time.

It is desirable that the auditor obtain a written engagement letter to clarify the scope and purpose of the engagement as well as the opinion to be rendered.

COMPARISON TO REQUIREMENTS FOR AUDITS

When auditors perform an audit of financial statements, they obtain an understanding of internal controls in accordance with the second examination standard. The scope of the study depends on the assessed level of control risk that will be used to determine the nature, timing, and extent of related substantive tests. When control risk is assessed below maximum, the auditor considers internal controls in effect for the entire audit period. Certain areas are *not* examined if control risk is assessed as maximum in those areas.

When the auditor is engaged to report on internal controls, however, all areas of control will be included unless specifically excluded by agreement. To clarify the controls reported on, the auditor will describe the controls using narrative, tables, flowcharts, or other appropriate forms of documentation in an attachment. The time period covered will be a matter of agreement. The service auditor must comply with the general standard and the first and third examination standards.

STEPS FOR OBTAINING AN UNDERSTANDING AND TESTING CONTROLS

Six steps, which are similar to those followed for a regular audit engagement, are followed when a public accountant is engaged to provide an opinion on internal control:

1. *Plan the scope of the engagement.* The auditor, client, and others involved first agree on the areas to be covered and timing of the study.
2. *Review the design of internal control.* Next, the auditor obtains information about the internal control objectives of the system and the control procedures used to achieve control. A preliminary assessment is made to determine the apparent controls and weaknesses. The procedures for accomplishing this step are the same as those discussed in Chapter 9.
3. *Perform tests of controls to determine conformity with prescribed procedures.* Appropriate audit procedures using such means as observation, inquiry, and tracing of transactions through the system must be performed to determine whether the control procedures needed to meet the control objectives were being followed.
4. *Evaluate the results of the understanding and tests of controls.* A final evaluation is made of whether the design of the control procedures results in the meeting of internal control objectives.
5. *Obtain written representations from management.*
6. *Prepare the appropriate report.* The type of report prepared depends on the purpose and scope of the engagement and the auditor's findings. Figure 23-6 shows a sample auditor's report prepared when the auditor makes a study and evaluation of the design and existence of control procedures at a point in time. Figure 23-7 shows a sample auditor's report when the auditor examines the design, effective operation, and continuity of control procedures.

FIGURE 23-6

Example of a Report on the Design and Existence of Control Procedures

---

AUDITOR'S REPORT ON CONTROL PROCEDURES

To Normandy Trust Ltd.:

We have examined the accompanying description of the stated internal control objectives of the Secur-Pension system of Normandy Trust Ltd. and the control procedures designed to achieve those objectives and have performed tests of the existence of those control procedures as at June 30, 1999. Our examination was made in accordance with generally accepted auditing standards and accordingly included such tests and other procedures as we considered necessary in the circumstances.

In our opinion, the control procedures included in the accompanying description were suitably designed to provide reasonable, but not absolute, assurance that the stated internal control objectives of the system described therein were achieved, and the control procedures existed as at June 30, 1999.

As we tested the existence of the control procedures only as at June 30, 1999, we do not express an opinion on whether the control procedures existed at any other time.

Red Deer, Alberta
July 15, 1999

Certified General Accountants

FIGURE 23-7

Example of a Report
When the Design,
Effectiveness, and
Continuity of Control
Procedures Are
Evaluated

AUDITOR'S REPORT ON CONTROL PROCEDURES

To Payroll Plus Ltd.:

I have examined the accompanying description of the stated internal control objectives of P Pay system of Payroll Plus Ltd. and the control procedures designed to achieve those objectives and have performed tests of the effectiveness of those control procedures for the period from September 1, 1998, to January 31, 1999. My examination was made in accordance with generally accepted auditing standards and accordingly included such tests and other procedures as I considered necessary in the circumstances.

In my opinion, the control procedures included in the accompanying description were suitably designed to provide reasonable, but not absolute, assurance that the stated internal control objectives of the system described therein were achieved, and the control procedures operated effectively from September 1, 1998, to January 31, 1999.

Halifax, Nova Scotia
February 28, 1999

Don Martens

Chartered Accountant

REVIEW AND COMPILATION SERVICES

OBJECTIVE 23-4

Understand review and compilation services that may be offered to clients.

Many public accountants are involved with nonpublic clients that do not have audits. A company may believe an audit is unnecessary due to the active involvement of the owners in the business, lack of significant debt, or absence of regulations requiring the company to have one. Common examples are smaller companies and professional organizations such as partnerships of physicians and lawyers.

These organizations often engage a public accountant to provide tax services and to assist in the preparation of accurate financial information without an audit. Providing these services is a significant part of the practice of many smaller public accounting firms. When a public accountant provides any services involving financial statements, certain requirements exist. The requirements for review engagements are covered in *CICA Handbook* Sections 8100, 8200, 8500, and 8600. Requirements for compilation engagements appear in Section 9200.

The assurance provided by reviews and compilations is considerably below audits, and the practitioners' reports are intended to convey that difference. Similarly, the extent of evidence accumulation differs among the three types of engagements (i.e., audit, review, and compilation). Figure 23-8 illustrates the difference in both the evidence accumulation and the level of assurance provided. The amount of assurance and extent of evidence accumulation, shown in Figure 23-8, are not well defined by the profession. This is because both evidence accumulation and assurance are subjective. Only a practitioner in the circumstances of an engagement can judge how much evidence is sufficient and what level of assurance has actually been attained.

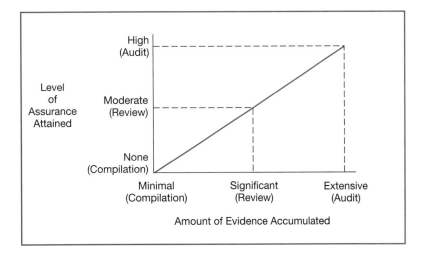

Table 23-1 compares audits, reviews, and compilations on a number of dimensions and, as such, is helpful in understanding the differences among the three types of engagement.

<table>
<tr><td>TERMS OF
ENGAGEMENT</td><td>While the *Handbook* sections covering review and compilation engagements do not require an engagement letter, they do require that the public accountant and the client reach an understanding and agreement regarding the services to be provided. A *written* agreement as to the nature and extent of services is most appropriate. The *1136 Tenants* case examined in Chapter 4 on page 99 is a good example of the problems that can arise if there is not a clear, written understanding between accountant and client. The engagement letter would include such items as follows:</td></tr>
</table>

- A description of the services to be provided.
- A discussion of the client's responsibility for providing complete and accurate information.
- A statement that an audit is not to be performed and that, consequently, no opinion will be expressed. In the case of a compilation engagement, the fact that no assurance results should be stated.
- A note on any restrictions on the distribution of the statements.
- A statement that each page of the statements should be clearly marked "unaudited."
- The probable content of the communication to be appended by the accountant.
- The fact that the engagement cannot be relied on to detect error or fraud and other irregularities.
- Other relevant exclusions, such as the fact that the engagement cannot be relied on to detect year 2000 problems or related programming difficulties.
- Possibly a comment to the effect that the statements do not satisfy any statutory requirements.

Figure 23-9 on page 738 provides an example of an engagement letter for a review of annual financial statements.

REVIEW

Review is defined by *CICA Handbook* paragraph 8100.05 as consisting primarily of "inquiry, analytical procedures and discussion . . . . with the limited objective of assessing whether the information being reported on is plausible within the framework of appropriate criteria." *Plausible* can be defined as being worthy of belief.

GENERAL REVIEW STANDARDS

Section 8100, "General Review Standards," discusses the acceptance of an engagement and the standards applicable to review engagements. These include knowledge of the client's business, review procedures, documentation, and reporting. Review engagements should be accepted by a public accountant only if the accountant believes that he or she has the necessary competence in the subject matter to be reported on.

Procedures suggested for reviews   Reviews imply a level of assurance somewhere between that of an audit and the absence of assurance provided by a compilation. A review does not include obtaining an understanding of internal controls or tests of controls, independent confirmation, or physical examination. The emphasis in reviews is on four broad areas:

- *Obtain knowledge of the client's business.* The information should be about the nature of the client's organization and business transactions; its accounting records and employees; the basis, form, and content of the financial statements; and accounting matters peculiar to the client's business and industry.

TABLE 23-1

COMPARISON OF AUDIT, REVIEW, AND COMPILATION ENGAGEMENTS

	AMOUNT OF EVIDENCE TO BE COLLECTED	PROCEDURES USED TO COLLECT EVIDENCE	LEVELS OF ASSURANCE PROVIDED	RELATIVE COST OF ENGAGEMENT	COMMUNICATION TITLE	ENGAGEMENT LETTER DESIRED	AREA PROFICIENCY REQUIRED IN	PUBLIC ACCOUNTANT REQUIRED TO BE OBJECTIVE?	KNOWLEDGE OF BUSINESS REQUIRED?	UNDERSTANDING OF INTERNAL CONTROL REQUIRED?	DOCUMENTATION REQUIRED?
Audit	Extensive	Inspection, Observation, Inquiry, Confirmation, Computation, Analysis	High	High	Auditor's Report	Yes	Auditing	Yes	Yes	Yes	Yes
Review	Significant	Inquiry, Analysis, Discussion, Others if necessary	Moderate	Moderate	Review Engagement Report	Yes	Review	Yes	Yes	No	Yes
Compilation	Minor	Computation	None	Low	Notice to Reader	Yes	Accounting	No	No	No	Not specifically stated but desirable

FIGURE 23-9

Example of an
Engagement Letter for
a Review Engagement

JOSEPHINE LIMITED
677 PETER STREET
WINNIPEG, MANITOBA
R3Y 1Z6

Attention: Josephine Collins, President

Dear Ms. Collins:

The purpose of this letter is to outline the nature of our involvement with the financial statements of Josephine Limited for the year ending December 31, 1999. As agreed, we will conduct a review, consisting primarily of inquiry, analytical procedures, and discussion in accordance with the standards applicable to review engagements.

Unless unanticipated difficulties are encountered, our report will be substantially in the following form:

> We have reviewed the balance sheet of Josephine Limited as at December 31, 1999, and the statements of income, retained earnings, and cash flows for the year then ended. Our review was made in accordance with generally accepted standards for review engagements and accordingly consisted primarily of inquiry, analytical procedures, and discussion related to information supplied to us by the company.
>
> A review does not constitute an audit, and consequently, we do not express an opinion on these financial statements.
>
> Based on our review, nothing has come to our attention that causes us to believe that these financial statements are not, in all material respects, in accordance with generally accepted accounting principles.
>
> This review does not constitute an audit. For example, it does not contemplate a study and evaluation of internal control, tests of accounting records, and responses to inquiries by obtaining audit evidence through inspection, observation, or confirmation and other procedures ordinarily performed during an audit. Accordingly, this review is not intended to, and will not, result in the expression of an audit opinion or the fulfilling of any statutory or other audit requirement. Since we are not accepting this engagement as auditor, we request that you do not record this as an auditing engagement in the minutes of your shareholders' meetings. You may wish to obtain legal advice concerning statutory auditing requirements.

It is understood that:

(a) you will provide the information required for us to complete this review;
(b) the responsibility for the accuracy and completeness of the representations in the financial statements remains with you;
(c) if our name is to be used in connection with the financial statements, you will attach our review engagement report when distributing the financial statements to third parties; and
(d) each page of the financial statements will be conspicuously marked "Unaudited."

This engagement cannot be relied on to prevent or detect error or fraud and other irregularities. We wish to emphasize that control over and responsibility for the prevention and detection of error or fraud and other irregularities remains with management.

The arrangements outlined in this letter will continue in effect from year to year unless evidenced by a new engagement letter.

If you have any questions about the contents of this letter, please raise them with us. If the services outlined are in accordance with your requirements and if the above terms are acceptable to you, please sign the copy of this letter in the space provided and return it to us. We appreciate the opportunity of continuing to be of service to your company.

Yours very truly,

Simunic & Stein
Chartered Accountants

The services and terms set out are as agreed.
Josephine Limited
Per   *Valerie Mann*

TABLE 23-2

PARTIAL LIST OF EXAMPLE INQUIRIES FOR REVIEW ENGAGEMENTS

PRELIMINARY CONSIDERATIONS

1. Are the services to be provided mutually agreed upon? Has desirability of obtaining an engagement letter been considered?

2. Is it clear that an auditor has not been appointed with respect to financial statements which are the subject of this engagement?

3. Are generally accepted accounting principles being used? If not, is the basis of accounting being used appropriate in the circumstances?

KNOWLEDGE OF BUSINESS

1. Nature of business

2. What are the major assets and liabilities, costs and expenses, and sources of revenue? Who are the major customers and suppliers?

3. Has a knowledge of the accounting system been obtained sufficient to understand the manner in which transactions are recorded, classified and summarized?

4. What books and records are kept?

5. Has appropriate consideration been given to:

   (a) prior period financial statements?
   (b) prior period working paper and related files?
   (c) prior period accounting problems?
   (d) reservations in the previous report?

FINANCIAL STATEMENT ITEMS

A series of questions are suggested about the various financial statement items.

OVERALL REVIEW

1. Has appropriate consideration been given to:

   (a) the inter-relationship of financial statement items?
   (b) a comparison of significant components of the statement of income (in light of current operating and economic conditions) with budgets and figures for preceding periods?

   (c) significant operating ratios?
   (d) identification of related parties and related party transactions?
   (e) whether or not the enterprise is economically dependent on anyone?
   (f) the need to obtain bank confirmation of specific matters?

2. Have inquiries been made concerning matters discussed at meetings, if any, of shareholders and directors and committees thereof that may affect the financial statements?

3. Has there been communication with other public accountants who have reviewed or audited the financial statements of significant components of the reporting enterprise?

4. Have there been any changes in accounting principles and, if so, have these changes been adequately disclosed?

5. Are there any events which occurred after the end of the financial period which would have significant effect on the financial statements or would be significant to readers of the financial statements?

6. Have all matters that in your professional judgment are important to support the content of your report been documented?

7. Do the financial statements agree with the records of the enterprise?

FINAL CONSIDERATIONS

1. Have the financial statements and the review engagement report been discussed with the client?

2. Is the client satisfied that the financial statements are complete and accurate?

3. Has a letter of representation been obtained? Does it contain all representations by the client which should be documented?

4. Based on the review performed, do the financial statements appear to be plausible in the circumstances within the framework of generally accepted accounting principles?

5. Is the form and content of the review engagement report appropriate to this engagement and is it dated to correspond with the date of substantial completion of the review?

- *Make inquiries of client personnel.* The objective of these inquiries is to determine whether the financial statements are fairly presented, assuming that management does not intend to deceive the accountant. The CICA Assurance and Related Services Guideline AuG-20, entitled "Performance of a Review of Financial Statements," lists illustrative inquiries. The list has been substantially reproduced in Table 23-2.

- *Perform analytical procedures.* These are meant to identify relationships and individual items that appear to be unusual. Analytical procedures performed during a review engagement would normally be less extensive than during an audit. The appropriate analytical procedures are the same as the ones already studied in Chapter 6 and in those chapters dealing with substantive procedures. Explanations for relationships and items that appear to be unusual would be obtained by inquiry of appropriate client personnel.

- *Have discussions with management concerning information received and the information being reported on.*

Generally accepted review standards The standards for review engagements are similar to generally accepted auditing standards, except that they deal with reviews and not audits. They are as follows:

General standard

The review should be performed and the review engagement report prepared by a person or persons having adequate technical training and proficiency in conducting reviews, and with due care and an objective state of mind.

Review standards

(i) The work should be adequately planned and properly executed. If assistants are employed, they should be properly supervised.

(ii) The public accountant should possess or acquire sufficient knowledge of the business carried on by the enterprise so that intelligent inquiry and assessment of information obtained can be made.

(iii) The public accountant should perform a review with the limited objective of assessing whether the information being reported on is plausible in the circumstances within the framework of an appropriate criteria. Such a review should consist of:

(a) inquiry, analytical procedures and discussion; and

(b) additional or more extensive procedures when the public accountant's knowledge of the business carried on by the enterprise and the results of the inquiry, and analytical procedures and discussion cause him or her to doubt the plausibility of such information.

Reporting standards

(i) The review engagement report should indicate the scope of the review. The nature of the review engagement should be made evident and be clearly distinguished from an audit.

(ii) The report should indicate, based on the review:

(a) whether anything has come to the public accountant's attention that causes him or her to believe that the information is not, in all material respects, in accordance with appropriate criteria; or

(b) that no assurance can be provided.

The report should provide an explanation of the nature of any reservations contained therein and, if readily determinable, their effect.

The requirement that the accountant have sufficient knowledge of the client's enterprise and type of business is made so that the accountant can assess whether the information to be reported on is plausible in the circumstances. The accountant would not be able to make the required inquiry and assessment of the information obtained without such knowledge. For instance, the accountant would not be able to assess the plausibility of manufactured inventory unless he or she had knowledge of the company's product and manufacturing processes.

The review standards should be appropriate to the particular engagement; for example, it is likely that procedures would differ between a review of financial statements and financial information. The review procedures do not preclude audit procedures if the accountant believes that more extensive procedures are required to assess plausibility. However, once the accountant decides to use more extensive procedures, such as audit procedures, the particular procedure must be carried out to completion. The accountant should not carry out an audit procedure to partial completion simply because the engagement is a review.

Materiality would be measured in the same manner as with an audit.

Negative assurance should be expressed only when the standards applicable to a review engagement described above have been met.

In addition to the reporting standards listed above, the communication should identify the information presented, state that a review does not constitute an audit, and state that the review, which consisted primarily of inquiry, analytical procedures, and discussion, was made in accordance with generally accepted standards for review engagements. The purpose of stating that a review does not constitute an audit is to ensure that financial statement users are aware that a review provides a lower level of assurance than an audit. The accountant should also state, except when a reservation is required, that nothing has come to his or her attention as a result of his or her review that causes him or her to believe that the information is not, in all material respects, in accordance with an appropriate disclosed basis of accounting, which, except in special circumstances, should be generally accepted accounting principles, or in the case of nonfinancial information, other appropriate criteria. In addition, each page of information reported on should be marked "unaudited."

Reservations may be required in the accountant's report when the review cannot be completed, when there is a departure from the appropriate criteria, or when the accountant concludes that the client's interpretation of an agreement or regulation is not reasonable. The reservation would be disclosed in a reservation paragraph in the review engagement report, which would appear immediately preceding the negative assurance paragraph. The reason for the reservation and the effect of the reservation on the information reported on should also be disclosed.

The discovery of a misstatement after the release of the report by the accountant should be treated in the same way as the discovery of a misstatement by an auditor after the release of audited financial statements.

Reviews of financial statements   Section 8200 provides guidelines that apply in addition to those in Section 8100 when the accountant is reporting on interim or annual financial statements. An example of a report that the accountant would issue is shown in Figure 23-10.

FIGURE 23-10

Example of a Report Under Section 8200

REVIEW ENGAGEMENT REPORT

To R. Fortin

I have reviewed the balance sheet of Leger Inc. as at December 31, 1998, and the statements of income, retained earnings, and cash flows for the year then ended. My review was made in accordance with generally accepted standards established for review engagements and accordingly consisted primarily of inquiry, analytical procedures, and discussion related to information supplied to me by the company.

A review does not constitute an audit, and consequently, I do not express an audit opinion on these financial statements.

Nothing has come to my attention as a result of my review that causes me to believe that these financial statements are not, in all material respects, in accordance with generally accepted accounting principles.

Montréal, Québec
February 18, 1999

a. Vachon

Chartered Accountant

Financial information other than financial statements   Section 8500 describes the sorts of financial information that might be included under this grouping. This section is parallel to Section 5805 and refers the accountant to Section 5805 for further guidance in this matter. When the information is prepared in accordance with an agreement or a regulation and that agreement requires interpretations, the report should refer to such interpretations. Figure 23-11 shows the form a communication might take when the auditor is reporting on financial information other than financial statements.

Reviews of compliance with agreements and regulations   Section 8600, besides describing the situations that fall under this heading, lists the steps that would be followed in these situations in addition to those listed in Section 8100. This section is parallel to Section 5815. The accountant should read the relevant provisions of the agreement or regulation, inquire about how the client monitors its compliance with

FIGURE 23-11
Example of a Report Under Section 8500

REVIEW ENGAGEMENT REPORT

To Kamloops Limited

At the request of Pacific Limited, I have reviewed the plant and equipment of Pacific Limited as at March 31, 1999 (calculated in accordance with the provisions of section X of the mortgage agreement with Kamloops Limited dated May 5, 1996, and the interpretations set out in note 1). My review was made in accordance with generally accepted standards for review engagements and accordingly consisted primarily of inquiry, analytical procedures, and discussion related to information supplied to me by the company.

A review does not constitute an audit, and consequently, I do not express an audit opinion on this plant and equipment.

Based on my review, nothing has come to my attention that causes me to believe that this plant and equipment are not presented fairly in accordance with (the provisions of section X of the mortgage agreement with Kamloops Limited dated May 5, 1996, and the interpretations set out in note 1).

Vancouver, B.C.
June 7, 1999

L. Daryl

Chartered Accountant

FIGURE 23-12
Example of a Report Under Section 8600

REVIEW ENGAGEMENT REPORT

To J. O'Sullivan

I have reviewed Separate Limited's compliance as at December 31, 1998, with covenants to be complied with described in sections 8 to 10 inclusive of the agreement dated November 3, 1997, with Waterloo Inc. My review was made in accordance with generally accepted standards for review engagements and accordingly consisted primarily of inquiry, analytical procedures, and discussion related to information supplied to me by the company.

A review does not constitute an audit, and consequently, I do not express an audit opinion on this matter.

Nothing has come to my attention as a result of my review that causes me to believe that the company is not in compliance with covenants to be complied with described in sections 8 to 10 inclusive of this agreement.

Calgary, Alberta
January 18, 1999

G. On

Certified General Accountant

---

the provisions, and consider whether the provisions have been consistently applied. In the review engagement report, the public accountant should identify the provisions of the agreement or regulation that establish the criteria on which his or her assessment of compliance is based. As well, any significant interpretations of the criteria made by the accountant when the criteria were nonspecific and any significant changes in interpretations from the previous year should be identified. Figure 23-12 presents an example of a report that the accountant might issue.

COMPILATION

Compilation services are intended to enable a public accounting firm to compete with bookkeeping firms. It is common for smaller public accounting firms to own one or more microcomputers and provide bookkeeping services, monthly or quarterly financial statements, and tax services for smaller clients.

In such engagements, discussed in Section 9200, the public accountant provides assistance in compiling financial statements but is not required to provide any assurance about the statements; the engagement is not an assurance engagement. The statements may be complete (i.e., include balance sheet, income statement, and statement of changes in financial position); they may be part of a complete set of financial statements; or they may be for the whole enterprise or for a part of the enterprise. The accountant assembles the information supplied by the client and ensures that it is arithmetically correct; the accountant is concerned with neither whether the information is either accurate or complete nor whether the financial statements comply with GAAP. Although the accountant should not be associated with false or misleading financial statements, determining whether the statements are false or misleading can be difficult because of his or her limited involvement.

Section 9200 sets out criteria for accepting a compilation engagement:

(a) the public accountant has no reason to believe that the information supplied to him or her for the purpose of compiling the financial statements is false or misleading; and

(b) he or she believes that the client understands that:

    (i) such statements may not be appropriate for general purpose use; and

    (ii) uninformed readers could be misled unless they are aware of the possible limitations of the statements, and of the public accountant's very limited involvement.

Professional standards There are standards that the public accountant must follow in performing a compilation engagement:

- The services should be performed and the communication should be prepared by a person or persons having adequate technical training and proficiency in accounting, and with due care.
- The work should be adequately planned and properly executed. If assistants are employed, they should be properly supervised.

If the public accountant ascertains that the financial statements may be false or misleading, he or she must obtain additional information and amend the statements or resign from the engagement.

Form of report The communication from the public accountant in a compilation engagement is entitled "Notice to Reader." Each page of the statements should either include the "Notice to Reader" heading itself or the statement "Unaudited — See Notice to Reader." The communication should

(a) state that the public accountant compiled the statement from information provided by management;

(b) state that the public accountant did not audit, review or otherwise attempt to verify the accuracy or completeness of such information;

(c) caution readers that the statement may not be appropriate for their purposes; and

(d) not express any form of opinion or negative assurance.

An example of a Notice to Reader appears in Figure 23-13.

Departures from generally accepted accounting principles should not be referred to in the report as this may suggest that the public accountant has a responsibility to detect and report all such departures.

Compilation standards also apply to the information actually included in a client's tax return. The Institute of Chartered Accountants of Ontario issued in its December 1998/January 1999 issue of *Checkmark* (a regular newsletter to members) a technical news services release concerning tax returns. The release stated that "members must attach a Notice to Reader to the financial information that they have compiled regardless of whether the information is prepared separately or included as part of a tax schedule." Thus, accountants should include a Notice to Readers with personal tax returns prepared on behalf of clients.

FIGURE 23-13

Example of Report
Under Section 9200

NOTICE TO READER

I have compiled the balance sheet of New B Ltd. as at March 31, 1999, and the statements of income, retained earnings, and cash flows for the year ended from information provided by management. I have not audited, reviewed, or otherwise attempted to verify the accuracy or completeness of such information. Readers are cautioned that this statement may not be appropriate for their purposes.

Halifax, N.S.
June 12, 1999

R. Fundy

Chartered Accountant

INTERIM FINANCIAL INFORMATION

Interim financial information may be audited, reviewed, or compiled by a public accountant. The decision depends on how much assurance is desired from the accountant's involvement and how timely the information must be. Estimates normally have to be made in order to prepare the information on a timely basis. Therefore, the information may not be as reliable as annual financial information. Since the objective of producing interim financial information is to provide up-to-date information to users of the statements, such information is usually not audited. Sections 8100, 8200, 8500, and 8600 should be consulted when interim financial information is reviewed. If it is compiled, Section 9200 is relevant.

PROSPECTUSES

> **OBJECTIVE 23-5**
>
> **Understand the auditor's involvement with prospectuses and other offering documents.**

Section 7100, "The Auditor's Involvement with Prospectuses and Other Offering Documents," does not just apply to prospectuses but to all offering documents (e.g., takeover bid circulars, issuer bid circulars, information circulars, statements of material facts) to the extent that they are similar. In other words, the requirements apply when the financial information being audited is similar to that found in a prospectus.

The auditor comments on three aspects of a prospectus to securities regulatory authorities:

- The auditor consents to inclusion of his or her auditor's report in the prospectus.
- The auditor comments on any unaudited or pro-forma financial information that is included.
- The auditor advises the authorities that the entire prospectus has been read and that it contains no misrepresentations insofar as information taken from the financial statements is concerned.

The auditor must seek assurance that the financial information in the prospectus conforms to the requirements of the appropriate securities act. Securities legislation is a provincial jurisdiction and may vary from province to province. There is no federal securities legislation in Canada in contrast to the United States, where securities are a federal, rather than a state, matter.

The auditor may also be requested to examine forecasts or projections included in the offering document. This involvement is discussed in a later section of this chapter.

AUDITED FINANCIAL STATEMENTS

The auditor normally has to report on comparative balance sheets and five-year comparative statements of income, retained earnings, and changes in financial position. Those statements should be reviewed to ensure that GAAP have been applied consistently over the five years and that any accounting changes and prior period adjustments have been accounted for correctly.

When audited financial statements in the five-year period have been audited by a predecessor auditor, he or she would have to consent to the inclusion of his or her auditor's report in the prospectus. The auditor's report would be similar to the standard report except that it would refer to the financial position at both year ends and the results of operations and changes in financial position for the five years.

UNAUDITED FINANCIAL STATEMENTS

When the audited financial statements to be included in a prospectus are not current, unaudited interim financial information is included. The auditor normally provides a comfort letter to the securities regulatory authorities about the unaudited information. A *comfort letter* is a letter addressed to the authorities that provides negative assurance on the interim financial statements and indicates that they are unaudited. Figure 23-14 is an example of a comfort letter.

Review procedures consisting primarily of inquiry, analysis, and discussion (which were discussed earlier in the chapter) would be applied to determine whether the interim financial statements are plausible and in accordance with generally accepted accounting principles. The work done on the statements is subject to the general and first examination standard. The auditor must possess a reasonable knowledge of the client's business, of accounting and internal control systems, and of the industry.

FIGURE 23-14
A Comfort Letter

APRIL 18, 1999
ONTARIO SECURITIES COMMISSION

To Whom It May Concern:

Re: Mariposa Limited

We are the above company's auditors, and on February 28, 1999, we reported on the following financial statements included in the prospectus to the sale and issue of 1,000,000 common shares:

Balance sheets as at December 31, 1998 and 1997;

Statements of income, retained earnings, and changes in financial position for each of the years in the five-year period ended December 31, 1998.

The prospectus includes the following unaudited interim financial statements:

Balance sheet as at March 31, 1999;

Statements of income, retained earnings, and cash flows for the three months ended March 31, 1999 and 1998.

We have not examined any financial statements of the company as at any date or for any period subsequent to December 31, 1998.

Although we have performed an examination for the year ended December 31, 1998, the purpose and therefore the scope of the examination was to enable us to express our opinion on the financial statements as at December 31, 1998, and for the year then ended, but not on the financial statements for any interim period within that year. Therefore, we are unable to and do not express any opinion on the unaudited balance sheet as at March 31, 1999, and the unaudited interim statements of income, retained earnings, and cash flows for the three months ended March 31, 1999 and 1998, included in the prospectus or on the financial position, results of operations, or cash flows as at any date or for any period subsequent to December 31, 1998.

We have, however, performed procedures that meet the standards established by the Canadian Institute of Chartered Accountants relating to unaudited interim financial statements in prospectuses. On the basis of these procedures, nothing has come to our attention that would cause us to believe that the unaudited interim financial statements are not presented, in all material respects, in accordance with generally accepted accounting principles.

The procedures referred to in the preceding paragraph do not constitute an audit and would not necessarily reveal material adjustments that might be required to present fairly, in all material respects, the financial position of the company as at March 31, 1999, and the results of its operations and the cash flows for the three months ended March 31, 1999 and 1998, in accordance with generally accepted accounting principles.

This letter is provided solely for the purpose of assisting you in discharging your statutory responsibilities and should not be relied on for any other purpose.

Markdale, Ontario
April 20, 1999

Bojarić & Company

Chartered Accountants

OTHER FINANCIAL INFORMATION

As was mentioned previously, the auditor must be satisfied that other financial information derived from the financial statements is not misleading. If, for example, the prospectus contained a summary of the dollars spent on capital additions, the auditor would want to ensure that the summary was not misleading.

The auditor must also read the complete prospectus and be satisfied that the contents, insofar as they relate to matters on which the auditor might reasonably be expected to have knowledge as a result of his or her examination, are not misleading. If not satisfied, the auditor would consider withholding his or her consent letter and consulting legal counsel.

PRO-FORMA FINANCIAL STATEMENTS

Pro-forma financial statements are historical financial statements adjusted to give effect to a specific transaction. For instance, a company might be issuing a prospectus to raise $1 million from the sale of bonds and planning to use the money to pay off short-term loans. The prospectus might include pro-forma financial statements that would show the new long-term debt and would not show the short-term loans that would be paid off.

The auditor should review pro-forma financial statements included in a prospectus to ensure that they have been properly compiled. Procedures could include:

- Obtaining evidence of completed transactions or firm commitments to proceed with transactions by inspection of agreements and correspondence
- Ensuring adjustments to historical statements are made and disclosed

A compilation report should be prepared by the auditor and included in the prospectus. An example of such a report, where the issuers propose to acquire another company, is shown in Figure 23-15.

FIGURE 23-15
Example of a Compilation Report on Pro-Forma Financial Statements

COMPILATION REPORT

To the Directors of Adam Limited

We have reviewed, as to compilation only, the accompanying pro-forma combined balance sheet of Adam Limited and Alicia Limited as at December 31, 1998, and the pro-forma combined statement of income for the year ended December 31, 1998. These pro-forma combined financial statements have been prepared solely for inclusion in the prospectus relating to the sale and issue of 100,000 shares of common stock and are based on the audited financial statements of Adam Limited and Alicia Limited as at December 31, 1998. The separate financial statements of Alicia Limited were examined and reported on by another auditor. In our opinion, these pro-forma combined financial statements have been properly compiled to give effect to the transactions and assumptions described in the notes thereto.

Calgary, Alberta
February 14, 1999

Kowalski & Butchart

Chartered Accountants

OTHER ISSUES

Section 7100 defines a preliminary prospectus as ". . . a formal filing signed by officers of the [company] and the underwriters and is used to provide preliminary information to investors." The section also discusses the comfort letter to be sent to the securities regulatory authorities about the audited and unaudited financial statements included in the preliminary prospectus. The auditor should issue the comfort letter containing negative assurance only when satisfied that it can properly be issued. Figure 23-16 is an example of a comfort letter for a preliminary prospectus.

The auditor issues a "consent letter" to the securities regulatory authorities consenting to the use of his or her auditor's report in the prospectus. The auditor must perform the appropriate review of the client's records for the period between the date of the audited statements and the date of the consent letter to ensure that all material subsequent events are properly disclosed. The auditor's consent letter should be

FIGURE 23-16

Example of a Comfort
Letter for a Preliminary
Prospectus

MAY 10, 1999
ALBERTA SECURITIES COMMISSION

To Whom It May Concern:

Re: Stuart Toys Limited

I refer to the preliminary prospectus of the above company dated May 10, 1999, relating to the sale and issue of 1,000,000 Class "B" common shares.

I have reported to the shareholders on the following financial statements in the preliminary prospectus:

Balance sheets as at December 31, 1998 and 1997;

Statements of income, retained earnings, and cash flows for each of the years in the five-year period ended December 31, 1998.

My report on the financial statements for 1998 was dated February 28, 1999.

I am withholding my signature from the draft report in the preliminary prospectus pending:
(a) reviewing events between the dates of the preliminary and final prospectuses;
(b) reviewing comments that may be issued by the Commission; and
(c) reading the final prospectus.

Based on the results of my audits of the financial statements referred to above and my limited inquiry and review procedures for the period from February 28, 1999, to the date of this letter, I have no reason to believe that the financial statements do not present fairly, in all material respects, the financial position of the company as at December 31, 1998 and 1997, and the results of its operations and cash flows for each of the years in the five-year period ended December 31, 1998, in accordance with generally accepted accounting principles.

This letter is provided solely for the purpose of assisting the Alberta Securities Commission in discharging its responsibilities and should not be relied on for any other purpose.

Yours truly,

Penden & Assoc.

Chartered Accountants

issued and the auditor's report signed when the requirements of the *Handbook* have been met, the underwriting agreement has been signed, and the final prospectus and financial statements in the prospectus have been signed. The consent letter is normally dated concurrently with the final prospectus. Figure 23-17 is an example of a consent letter.

ASSISTANCE TO UNDERWRITERS

The underwriters of an offering document may request the auditors to perform specific tasks, other than those required in connection with the financial statements, relating to the offering document. The underwriters, for example, may want additional assurance about accounts receivable as at the date of the consent letter, which will probably be later than the date of either the auditor's report or the date of the comfort letter.

Before addressing other matters, auditors must ensure that they are within their expertise. If the additional work is performed, the auditor's letter to the underwriter should:

- Describe the financial information examined.
- State that an audit was not performed and no opinion is expressed.
- Describe the procedures performed and the results.
- State that no assurance as to the sufficiency of the procedures for the underwriter's purposes is provided.
- Identify that the letter's distribution is restricted to the underwriter.

FIGURE 23-17

Example of a
Consent Letter

JUNE 22, 1999
ALBERTA SECURITIES COMMISSION

To Whom It May Concern:

Re: Stuart Toys Limited

We refer to the prospectus of the above company dated June 22, 1999, relating to the sale and issue of 1,000,000 Class "B" common shares.

We consent to the use in the above mentioned prospectus of our report dated February 28, 1999, to the directors of Stuart Toys Limited on the following financial statements:

Balance sheets as at December 31, 1998 and 1997;

Statements of income, retained earnings, and cash flows for each of the years in the five-year period ended December 31, 1998.

We report that we have read the prospectus and have no reason to believe that there are any misrepresentations in the information contained therein that is derived from the financial statements upon which we have reported or that is within our knowledge as a result of our audit of such financial statements.

This letter is provided to the Alberta Securities Commission to which it is addressed pursuant to the requirements of its securities legislation and not for any other purpose.

Yours truly,

Perden & Assoc.

Chartered Accountants

REPORTS ON THE APPLICATION OF ACCOUNTING PRINCIPLES, AUDITING STANDARDS, OR REVIEW STANDARDS

OBJECTIVE 23-6

Describe reports on the application of accounting principles, auditing standards, or review standards.

Public accountants are being asked by clients of other public accountants to give opinions with respect to accounting issues and the application of auditing or review standards, and to provide generic opinions. This practice by clients has been described by the public accounting profession as *opinion shopping*; it occurs when the client of one public accounting firm disagrees with that accounting firm's opinion about a particular accounting treatment and goes to another public accounting firm (i.e., shops) for an opinion supporting the client's position. The client seeking the second opinion might intentionally or unintentionally not provide the second firm with *all* the facts that the incumbent used, so that a potentially different opinion will be reached by the second firm. The Macdonald Commission and leaders of the profession have been critical of the practice because of its potential harmful impact on independence.

The Assurance Standards Board has issued a *Handbook* section, Section 7600, to deal with the problem of opinion shopping. The section does not attempt to stop the practice but rather sets some rules to be followed, so that the second public accounting firm provides its opinion using the same information as the incumbent.

The reporting accountant, the accountant asked for the second opinion, must come to agreement with the organization seeking the opinion on the nature of the engagement, the information to be provided by the organization, and the type of report wanted, plus any restrictions on its distribution. This agreement should be in the form of an engagement letter.

The reporting accountant should follow the general standard and examination standards (i) and (iii) of GAAS. If an entity requests the opinion, the reporting accountant should request permission from the entity to contact (and then contact) the entity's incumbent auditor. Paragraphs 7600.12 and 7600.14 stress that the reporting accountant should obtain "a written statement of all relevant facts and assumptions" from the party requesting the opinion. In the case of a request by the entity, paragraph 7600.12 states that the reporting accountant should "obtain a written statement from the entity [describing] the circumstances and nature of any relevant disagreements of the entity with its incumbent accountant or a third party."

The report should be in writing. Paragraph 7600.24 specifies the content of the report so that users of it will fully understand the context and content of the report issued by the reporting accountant.

FUTURE-ORIENTED FINANCIAL INFORMATION

OBJECTIVE 23-7

Describe examinations of future-oriented financial information.

In September 1989, the CICA issued Section 4250, "Future-Oriented Financial Information," which establishes accounting standards for such information. The CICA also issued Assurance and Related Services Guideline AuG-6, entitled "Examination of a Financial Forecast or Projection Included in a Prospectus or Other Public Offering Document." This Guideline is directed at prospective information included in offering documents.

Assurance and Related Services Guideline AuG-16, "Compilation of a Financial Forecast or Projection," was issued in 1993. It indicates the standards that the public accountant should follow when compiling a forecast or projection for a client who does not require the public accountant to provide any assurance.

Chapter 1 points out that Assurance and Related Services Guidelines do not have the force of Recommendations. Their intent is to provide guidance in the absence of Recommendations.

FORECASTS AND PROJECTIONS

Future-oriented financial information deals with the future, not with the past. Section 4250 describes two general types of future-oriented financial information: forecasts and projections. A *forecast* is prospective financial information prepared using assumptions reflecting management's judgment as to the most probable courses of action for the entity. The information is presented to the best of management's knowledge and belief. A *projection* is prepared using one or more assumptions (hypotheses) that do not necessarily reflect the most likely course of action in management's judgment.

USE OF PROSPECTIVE FINANCIAL STATEMENTS

Prospective financial statements are for either *general* use or *special* use. General use refers to use by any third party. An example of general use would be inclusion of a financial forecast in a prospectus for the sale of shares of a large public company. Special use refers to use by third parties with whom the responsible party is negotiating directly. An example of special purpose future-oriented financial information would be the inclusion of a financial projection in a takeover bid circular aimed at current shareholders of the company.

ACCEPTANCE OF THE ENGAGEMENT

The following discussion pertains to Assurance and Related Service Guideline AuG-6. As with other types of engagements performed by the public accountant, it is important to ensure that the nature and terms of involvement with future-oriented financial information are understood and agreed to by management, preferably in writing. Management should also acknowledge its responsibilities related to the financial information. AuG-6 identifies a number of matters that should be agreed to by management and the public accountant:

- The anticipated form of the financial forecast
- The period of time to be covered
- The fact that management will prepare and present the forecast in accordance with accounting standards established by the CICA and in accordance with any applicable securities requirements.
- The fact that management is responsible for the forecast: its presentation, the process of preparation, and the assumptions used.
- The fact that management is responsible for obtaining or developing appropriate support for the assumptions sufficient to enable the public accountant to report without reservation
- The need for the public accountant to have access to outside specialists and third party reports obtained by management (e.g., a feasibility study)
- The anticipated form and content of the public accountant's report
- The fact that the public accountant has no responsibility to update his or her report for events and circumstances occurring after the date of that report.

Professional standards There are standards that the public accountant should follow in examining prospective information. The services should be performed by someone with adequate technical training and proficiency in auditing, and the examination should be performed and the report prepared with due care. The work should be adequately planned, and any assistants should be properly supervised. Sufficient evidence should be obtained to provide a reasonable basis for the report. Important matters should be documented to indicate that sufficient appropriate evidence has been obtained.

Before accepting such an engagement, the public accountant should ensure the following:

- There is adequate support for the assumptions used to prepare the financial information. For example, management of a new company may not be able to provide such support.
- Any hypotheses used do not significantly impair the quality of the financial information.
- Management is willing to disclose all significant assumptions.
- The period to be covered by the forecast or projection does not extend beyond the point where future results can be reasonably estimated.
- Any hypotheses are not false or misleading. If they are, the public accountant cannot be involved with the financial information.

EXAMINATION OF PROSPECTIVE FINANCIAL STATEMENTS

An examination of future-oriented financial information involves evaluating the preparation of the future-oriented financial information and the underlying assumptions and assessing the plausibility of hypotheses. In addition, the public accountant would evaluate the presentation of the financial information for conformity with CICA presentation and disclosure guidelines (Section 4250) and ensure that accounting policies are consistent with those used in the historical financial statements. The public accountant would obtain a written letter of representation from management acknowledging its responsibility for preparing the forecast or projection and indicating that forecast figures are management's best estimate of the forecast results. Finally, the accountant would issue an examination report.

These evaluations are based primarily on accumulating evidence about the completeness and reasonableness of the underlying assumptions as disclosed in the prospective financial information. This requires the accountant to become familiar with the client's business and industry, to identify the significant matters on which the client's entity's future results are expected to depend ("key factors"), and to determine that appropriate assumptions have been included with respect to these.

In developing a knowledge of the industry and business, the public accountant should focus on areas such as:

- The availability and cost of resources that the client needs for continuing operations
- The nature and condition of markets in which the client operates
- Specific industry factors such as competition, sensitivity to economic conditions, accounting principles and practices, regulatory requirements, and technology
- Past performance by the client and its competitors

REPORTING

The accountant's report on an examination of financial statements should include:

- An identification of the financial information presented
- A description of the nature of the examination
- A statement that the examination of the financial information was made in accordance with AuG-6

- A statement that the public accountant assumes no responsibility to update the report for events and circumstances occurring after the report date
- The accountant's opinion as to whether the assumptions are suitably supported, consistent with the client's plans, and provide a reasonable basis for the information; the forecast or projection reflects these assumptions; and the information is prepared in conformity with the CICA's presentation and disclosure standards
- A caveat that the prospective results may not be achieved
- A disclaimer of opinion as to the achievability of the forecast or projection

For projections, the report would also:

- State that the assumptions used include a hypothesis.
- State that since a hypothesis need not be supported, procedures were limited to ensuring it was consistent with the purpose of the projection.
- Provide an opinion regarding the consistency of the hypothesis with the purpose of the projection.

Figure 23-18 is an example of a report on a financial forecast. The date of the report would be the date of the completion of the field work by the public accountant.

FIGURE 23-18
Example of a Report on a Financial Forecast

AUDITOR'S REPORT ON FINANCIAL FORECAST

To the Directors of Nomad Corp.

The accompanying financial forecast of Nomad Corp. consisting of a balance sheet as at June 30, 2000, and the statements of income, retained earnings, and changes in financial position for the period then ending has been prepared by management using assumptions with an effective date of June 30, 1999. We have examined the support provided by management for the assumptions, and the preparation and presentation of this forecast. Our examination was made in accordance with Auditing Guideline AuG-6 issued by the Canadian Institute of Chartered Accountants. We have no responsibility to update this report for events and circumstances occurring after the date of our report.

In our opinion, as of the date of this report, the assumptions developed by management are suitably supported and consistent with the plans of the Company, and provide a reasonable basis for the forecast; this forecast reflects such assumptions; and the financial forecast complies with the presentation and disclosure standards for forecasts established by the Canadian Institute of Chartered Accountants.

Since this forecast is based on assumptions regarding future events, actual results will vary from the information presented and the variations may be material. Accordingly, we express no opinion as to whether this forecast will be achieved.

Toronto, Ontario
August 15, 1999

McWhirt & Kedwell

Chartered Accountants

AUDIT OF PENSION COSTS AND OBLIGATIONS

OBJECTIVE 23-8

Describe the auditor's involvement with pension costs and obligations.

Assurance and Related Services Guideline AuG-2, "Audit of Pension Costs and Obligations," is intended to provide guidance to those auditing defined benefit pension plans as described in Section 3460, "Pension Costs and Obligations," of the *CICA Handbook*. The Assurance Standards Board of the CICA and the Council of the Canadian Institute of Actuaries (CIA) issued a Joint Policy Statement in March 1991 to facilitate communications between the actuary and the auditor. It describes when each can use the work of the other, how they should interact in carrying out their responsibilities, and how these responsibilities should be disclosed. This statement is included in Section 5365, "Communication with Actuaries."

The auditor should consider the following factors in planning the audit of pension costs and obligations:

- Materiality of the pension costs, assets, and obligations in relation to the sponsor's financial statements taken as a whole
- Number and type of pension plans and the provisions of each plan
- Extent to which the plan sponsor uses a service organization in the operation of the plan
- Timing of the pension plan valuation, the need for extrapolations, and the involvement of management and the actuary in determining the pension costs, assets, and obligations
- Use of the work and report of the actuary

In considering the use of the work and report of the actuary, Section 5365 would apply. Of particular concern is the assessment of the actuary's competence. The auditor would have to communicate with the actuary in order to ascertain whether the actuary's work is "appropriate for the purpose intended." Section 5365A lists a number of considerations for the auditor when he or she is using the actuary's work in connection with an audit of financial statements. Assurance and Related Services Guideline AuG-2 lists a number of considerations of which the auditor would seek confirmation from the actuary in the year of an actuarial valuation. It also lists what the concerns of the auditor would be in the years between actuarial valuations.

There are several matters regarding pension costs and obligations of which the auditor should be aware. The auditor should review the actuary's assumptions to assess whether they are reasonable and reflect the conditions that are likely to affect future events and whether they are internally and externally consistent. As a methodology for examining the appropriateness of the source data used by the actuary, the guideline suggests procedures from Section 5360, "Using the Work of a Specialist," which the auditor could apply.

The auditor must assess the actuary's work in a context of knowledge about the business and the actuary's methods, assumptions, and source data. The auditor should be reasonably assured that the source data is appropriate and that the financial statement assertions are in agreement with the actuary's findings. If the auditor reaches the conclusion that the actuary's work and report cannot be used, he or she should consider having the Review Committee of the CIA review the work of the actuary. If the committee is also not satisfied with the work of the actuary, the auditor should consider appointing another actuary. As a final measure, the auditor should contemplate qualifying the auditor's report.

The auditor must review management's extrapolation of pension costs and obligations. If the extrapolation was done by or with the assistance of an actuary, the auditor should communicate with the actuary to make certain that the extrapolation was accurate and properly done. If no actuary was involved, the auditor should consider consulting an actuary to review the extrapolation.

The auditor should also obtain a letter of representation from management that the pension costs, assets, and obligations were calculated and disclosed in accordance with Section 3460. The auditor should further think of getting management's representation on, among other details, source data, the completeness of the plans, the specific assumptions used, and the accuracy of the extrapolations.

The auditor should at the same time accumulate evidence to satisfy himself or herself about the existence, ownership, and valuation of the pension plan assets, considering their materiality relative to the total assets of the company. Section 3460 requires the basis of valuation of pension plan assets to be market value.

Finally, the auditor should ensure that contributions to and benefits paid by the pension plan are proper and that funding provisions and surplus withdrawals have been made with the approval of regulatory authority as well as having been accounted for properly in the sponsor's financial statements.

OTHER ASSURANCE GUIDELINES

Described other assurance and related services guidelines pertaining to attest engagements.

This section will briefly describe other assurance and related services guidelines that are of interest.

Comparative financial statements Assurance and Related Services Guideline AuG-8 discusses the auditor's responsibilities when the auditor reports on comparative financial statements on which he or she had previously reported. The guideline also considers financial statements reported on by another auditor.

Audit of pension fund financial statements Assurance and Related Services Guideline AuG-12, "Auditor's Report on Pension Fund Financial Statements Filed with a Regulator," provides guidance for auditing pension fund statements of a defined benefit pension plan under a regulatory requirement. The suggested report format is similar to the format of an audit report on compliance with regulations under Section 5815 except that a fourth paragraph is added stating that the pension fund financial statements and the auditor's report have been prepared for filing with the regulator and are not appropriate for any other purpose.

Financial statements of federally regulated financial institutions Assurance and Related Services Guideline AuG-14 provides guidance to auditors of financial institutions regulated by a federal act including banks, cooperative credit associations, insurance companies, and trust and loan companies.

Audit of actuarial liabilities of life insurance companies Assurance and Related Services Guideline AuG-15 provides guidance to auditors of life insurance companies in their audit of actuarial liabilities. The guideline discusses the role of the actuary in the valuation processes, as well as discussing the role of the auditor in auditing the actuarial liability.

Audit of financial statements affected by environmental matters Assurance and Related Services Guideline AuG-19 is designed to assist auditors who audit financial statements that are affected by environmental matters such as efforts by the entity to prevent or correct environmental damage or to deal with the consequences of violations of environmental laws. The guideline considers planning of the audit, use of specialists, and the possibility of material misstatements resulting from the environmental matters.

There are other Assurance and Related Services Guidelines in the *CICA Handbook* that are not discussed here but that are nonetheless important. In addition, new guidelines are continually being added to the *Handbook*. Chapter 24 describes guidelines in progress at the time of writing of this text.

ESSENTIAL TERMS

Assurance — the practitioner's degree of certainty that the conclusions stated in his or her report are correct (p. 726).

Assurance engagement — one where, pursuant to an accountability relationship between two or more parties, a practitioner is engaged to issue a written communication expressing a conclusion concerning a subject matter for which the accountable party is responsible (p. 727).

Attest engagement — one where the auditor expresses a conclusion on a written assertion about subject matter prepared by a party accountable for the assertion, such as management; the assertion measures the subject matter using appropriate criteria (p. 727).

Compilation engagement — non-audit engagement in which the public accountant provides assistance in compiling financial statements but is not expected to provide assurance about the statements (p. 742).

Direct reporting engagement — one where the auditor directly expresses a conclusion on his or her evaluation of the subject matter using certain criteria and where the accountable party is responsible for the subject matter (p. 727).

Forecast — prospective financial information prepared using assumptions as to the most probable courses of action for the entity (p. 749).

Future-oriented financial information (FOFI) — information about prospective results of operations, financial position, and/or changes in financial position based on assumptions about future economic conditions and courses of action; may be presented either as a forecast or projection (p. 749).

Opinion shopping — when a public accountant is asked by a client of another public accountant to give an opinion with respect to accounting issues or the application of auditing or review standards, or to provide a generic opinion (p. 748).

Projection — prospective financial information prepared using assumptions reflecting management's judgment as to the most probable course of action for the entity; prepared using one or more assumptions (hypotheses) that do not necessarily reflect the most likely course of action in management's judgment (p. 749).

Prospective financial statements — financial statements that deal with expected future data rather than with historical data (p. 749).

Prospectus — an offering document issued by an organization in connection with the issue, acquisition, or exchange of its securities; usually contains both financial and non-financial information (p. 744).

Review engagement — one that consists primarily of inquiry, analytical procedures, and discussion with the limited objectives of assessing whether the information being reported on is plausible within the framework of appropriate criteria (p. 736).

Service organization — an organization that, on behalf of other organizations, has custody of assets, processes or stores data, or initiates or executes transactions (p. 733).

REVIEW QUESTIONS

23-1 Distinguish between an "attest engagement" and a "direct reporting engagement."

23-2 Explain why criteria are so important with respect to assurance engagements.

23-3 Identify the three parties to an accountability relationship, and explain each of their roles. Why is the practitioner part of the relationship even though his or her role is indirect?

23-4 Give three examples of the special reports that a public accountant may be asked to issue. Explain why these reports would be requested.

23-5 How does materiality differ in special reports from that in reports prepared as part of any ordinary audit? Why?

23-6 Why is an engagement letter often considered more important in the case of special reports than in the case of a regular audit?

23-7 Why are reports expressing an opinion on financial information other than financial statements prepared by public accountants?

23-8 Why are reports on the results of applying specified auditing procedures to financial information other than financial statements prepared by public accountants?

23-9 Why are reports on compliance with contractual agreements prepared by public accountants?

23-10 What is an engagement to report on control procedures at a service organization? Describe the two types of engagement that the auditor might undertake when issuing such a report.

23-11 List and discuss the standards applicable to review engagements.

23-12 How do the general standards applicable to review engagements differ from generally accepted auditing standards?

23-13 Contrast the level of assurance provided by negative assurance discussed in Sections 8100, 8200, 8500, and 8600 of the *CICA Handbook* with the level of assurance provided by the opinion given in the auditor's report.

23-14 What is the intent of Section 9200, "Compilation Engagements," in the *CICA Handbook*?

23-15 Discuss the standards for compilation engagements, and explain why they differ from those for review engagements and audits.

23-16 The financial statements prepared for a compilation engagement may not be complete according to GAAP. Why is this exception permitted? Provide examples of information that might be excluded.

23-17 What are the three aspects of an auditor's involvement with a prospectus?

23-18 What financial statements are included in a prospectus?

23-19 What is "negative assurance" in the context of a prospectus? What is a "comfort letter"?

23-20 What are the auditor's responsibilities with respect to financial information (other than financial statements) included in a prospectus?

23-21 What is "opinion shopping"? Describe what actions a public accountant should take if requested to give an opinion on specific circumstances or transactions of an entity.

23-22 On what does the auditor comment in his or her comments on financial forecasts? On what does the auditor disclaim an opinion and why?

23-23 What should the auditor's comments on financial forecasts include?

23-24 What significant factors should an auditor consider in determining the nature, timing, and extent of audit procedures in the audit of pension costs and obligations?

23-25 What factors must an auditor consider when relying on an actuary in the audit of pension costs and obligations?

23-26 The following questions concern audits and reviews, assurance engagements, and compilations (related services). Choose the best response.

a. A public accountant normally performs enquiry analytical procedures and discussion in order to assess whether or not the information being reported on is plausible. If those procedures cause him or her to doubt the plausibility, the public accountant should
   (1) provide a reservation in the review engagement report.
   (2) resign.
   (3) perform a compilation engagement.
   (4) perform procedures similar to audit procedures.

b. A compilation is described as a "related service" because
   (1) the public accountant has no liability for errors.
   (2) the compilation is a form of consulting service.
   (3) no assurance is provided by the public accountant.
   (4) only the general standard of GAAS applies to compilations.

c. Section 7500 describes the auditor's responsibilities with respect to annual reports. Which of the following statements is not a part of Section 7500?
   (1) The auditor must be satisfied that MD&A is not inconsistent with the financial statements.
   (2) The auditor must be satisfied that the financial statements are accurately reproduced.
   (3) The auditor must be satisfied that the aims and objectives of the company as discussed in the President's Report have been approved by the Board of Directors.
   (4) The auditor must be satisfied that the annual report does not include any information that is inconsistent with the financial statements.

d. Which of the following statements about a compilation engagement is not true?
   (1) The compiled statements must comply with GAAP.
   (2) The accountant must be satisfied that the statements are not false or misleading.
   (3) The public accountant does not have to have an objective state of mind.
   (4) The public accountant should exercise due care.

23-27 The following questions relate to assurance services.

a. Which of the following is not true of a direct reporting assurance engagement?
   (1) There are no management representations.
   (2) There are only two parties in a direct reporting engagement: the practitioner and the user(s).
   (3) The criteria should be identified.
   (4) The engagement team is likely to include nonaccountants.

b. The greatest concern to the public accountant in a future-oriented financial information (FOFI) engagement is
   (1) that management's projections may not be met.
   (2) that users may believe that the public accountant's involvement ensures that the prospectus results will be achieved.
   (3) that management assumptions are not reasonable.
   (4) that the appropriate standards were followed in preparing the FOFI.

c. Which of the following engagements is not appropriate under Section 5805?
   (1) Audit of sales in a specific location of a chain of stores.
   (2) Audit of sales of a product produced under licence.
   (3) Audit of attendance at a rock concert.
   (4) Compliance with a debt covenant.

d. Which of the following statements best describes negative assurance?
   (1) The public accountant states that in his/her opinion the plausibility of the financial statements is not in doubt.
   (2) The public accountant states the there is no reason to not accept the plausibility of the financial statements.
   (3) The public accountant states that in his/her opinion the financial statements are plausible.
   (4) The public accountant states that there is a low probability the financial statements are not plausible.

23-28 Prentice Manufacturing Limited is a Canadian-controlled public company that issued shares to the public for the first time in 1975. The shares are listed on both Canadian and U.S. stock exchanges. Al Prentice, the president of the company, approaches Don Migwam, a public accountant, who is currently performing the interim audit of the company. The company has decided to issue interim financial statements for the first time.

Mr. Prentice would like to publish the interim results following Migwam's review and has asked him to do whatever is necessary to give his "certification" and suggest whatever changes are necessary to present these interim statements in accordance with generally accepted accounting principles. He informs Migwam that the three-month statement of earnings will also be circulated to minority shareholders in the United States and will therefore likely have to conform to the American accounting pronouncements (AICPA, FASB) as well as Canadian ones.

Required

Assume the role of Don Migwam, a public accountant. Outline the following:

a. The points you would include in a letter to Mr. Prentice on your responsibility with respect to the interim financial statements

b. The nature of any work you would have to perform in this regard

(CICA adapted)

23-29 Three public accountants, Annette, Maureen, and Carlos, were discussing various problems they encountered in their practices. The subject of the requirements in the *CICA Handbook* for consolidated financial statements arose, and the following conversation took place.

Annette: One of the things that causes me a lot of problems is the requirement that any company having subsidiaries must consolidate. That means even small private companies. I don't think that's reasonable. Some of my clients don't want, need, or understand consolidated statements, and surely don't want to pay for them.

Maureen: I agree. Several of our small clients refuse to present consolidated statements at all, claiming that they just don't need them. For our larger clients, we often report on a dual set of statements — one consolidated and the other prepared on a nonconsolidated basis for corporation purposes. We approach both problems by qualifying our report whenever statements are not consolidated. Many of the clients don't really care if we qualify on a technical point like that, and it saves a lot of trouble.

Carlos: Well, I'm inclined to agree with the *Handbook*. We'll generally give an adverse opinion where the statements are not consolidated in accordance with Section 1590. For clients issuing a dual set of statements, we address our report on the consolidated statements to the shareholders and our report on the nonconsolidated statements to the directors. Then our report to the directors contains a clean opinion. After the opinion paragraph, we have a final paragraph saying that because the statements are not prepared for issuance to the shareholders, they are prepared on a nonconsolidated basis and that the statements differ materially from the consolidated statements on which we reported to shareholders.

Annette: Whenever we are reporting on nonconsolidated financial statements, we change our opinion paragraph to say "in accordance with the basis of accounting outlined in Note X," instead of "in accordance with generally accepted accounting principles." Note X then outlines the basis of accounting (nonconsolidated) and the client's reasons for not consolidating the statements. This overcomes problems where a dual set of statements is issued or where the client simply refuses to consolidate.

Required

Discuss the viewpoints of each accountant — Annette, Maureen, and Carlos.

(CICA adapted)

23-30 Your firm has just accepted the audit appointment of Floss Ltd., a major confectionery retailer with more than 60 leased stores in shopping malls across Canada. Every lease calls for a base rent plus a percentage of the store's sales. The "sales escalation" clause in each lease requires Floss Ltd. to have its auditor issue a report to the lessor on the sales of the store covered by the lease. However, the leases do not specify the nature and extent of the audit effort or the form of the report.

The audited financial statements show only the aggregate figure for sales at all stores, and the previous audits had involved visiting only some of the locations each year on a rotating basis. The former auditors had not extended their procedures for the purposes of reporting to lessors, but had simply reported to individual lessors the following:

As requested by Floss Ltd., we report that the sales of the corporation's store in Penticton Plaza for the year ended September 30, 1999, are recorded in the amount of $ _____ in the general ledger sales account of the corporation.

Our examination of the corporation's financial statements for the year ended June 30, 1999, was not directed to the determination of sales of individual stores, nor have we examined the corporation's financial statements for the three-month period subsequent to June 30, 1999. We have not performed an audit of, and accordingly do not express an opinion on, the amount of sales referred to in the preceding paragraph.

This year several lessors, including one that owns nine malls containing Floss Ltd. stores, have objected to this report, stating that it provides them with no assurance that sales at individual store locations are fairly stated. You, as a representative of your firm, have explained to the management of Floss Ltd. that it would cost considerably more in time and audit effort to provide an audit opinion on sales at each particular store location.

The management of Floss Ltd. is very unhappy with the prospect of paying the extra costs for an individual audit of sales at each location. The chief financial officer has observed that "it seems to us that your firm should be able to give some reasonable intermediate level of assurance between nothing, which is what the former auditors' reports seem to indicate, and a full scope audit opinion." In particular, the officer has asked why your firm cannot simply report, solely on the basis of your financial statement audit, as follows:

As requested by Floss Ltd., we report that, in our opinion, the sales of the corporation's store at Hilltop Plaza (Hamilton, Ontario) for the year ended September 30, 1999, in the amount of $ _____ are fairly stated in all respects material to the financial statements taken as a whole.

Required

Discuss the three reporting approaches identified by the chief financial officer of Floss Ltd. and any other reporting approaches that could satisfy both Floss Ltd. management and the lessors.

(CICA adapted)

23-31 In late May, 1999, Sheila Chan, a public accountant, received a telephone call from Raimo, the treasurer of Karloan Limited, who disclosed that preliminary arrangements had been made with an investment dealer to underwrite an issue of 6 percent first mortgage bonds, to be dated June 30, 1999. He asked Sheila to prepare an auditor's report for the prospectus which would be used for selling the bonds to the public. Sheila's report would cover both the historical financial statements and the earnings forecasts to be included in the prospectus. Raimo also indicated that it had been decided to date the prospectus June 15 but to start preliminary advertising of the issue immediately.

Sheila's firm has been the auditor for one and a half years of Karloan Limited and its four subsidiaries, all of which have December 31 year ends. The financial statements of Karloan Limited have never been prepared on a consolidated basis, but Sheila's firm has issued unqualified opinions on the statements of all five companies since being appointed auditor. The company and all its subsidiaries are federal companies incorporated prior to 1990.

Required

a. Comment on any problems you see in connection with what Karloan Limited intends to do.

b. Assuming that the problems on which you commented in part (a) have been overcome, list the steps that Sheila would undertake in order to have her firm express an opinion on the financial statements included in the prospectus.

(CICA adapted)

23-32 You are doing a review engagement and the related tax work for Regency Tools, Inc., a tool and die company with $2,000,000 in sales. Inventory is recorded at $125,000. Prior year unaudited statements, prepared by the company without assistance from a public accounting firm, disclose that the inventory is based on "historical cost estimated by management." You obtain the following facts:

1. The company has been growing steadily for the past five years.

2. The unit cost of typical material used by Regency Tools has increased dramatically for several years.

3. The inventory cost has been approximately $125,000 for five years.

4. Management intends to use a value of $125,000 again for the current year-end financial statements.

When you discuss with management the need to get a physical count and an accurate inventory, the response is negative. Management is concerned about the effects on income taxes of a more realistic inventory. The company has never been audited and has always estimated the historical cost of inventory. You are convinced, based upon inquiry and ratio analysis, that a conservative evaluation would be $500,000 at historical cost.

Required

a. What are the generally accepted accounting principle requirements for valuation and disclosure of inventory for unaudited financial statements?

b. Identify the potential legal and professional problems that you face in this situation.

c. What procedures would you normally follow for a review engagement when the inventory is a material amount? Be as specific as possible.

d. How should you resolve the problem in this situation? Identify alternatives, and evaluate the costs and benefits of each.

23-33 Herbert Lewis, a public accountant, is in the process of completing two client engagements involving partnerships. One, U.K. Co., requires an audit for credit purposes whereas the other, Punch Co., involves the preparation of unaudited statements and schedules. Louis Geroux is a partner of both U.K. Co. and Punch Co., and, although the major owner, he holds less than 50 percent of the capital of each. Both businesses are new clients for Lewis.

Lewis informed Geroux that partners' salaries and interest on loans in each business must be reported separately in the financial statements and not hidden in the income statement expense figures. On hearing Lewis's comment, Geroux became very upset and said that he intended to check the matter out with another chartered accountant.

Approximately one week after Lewis's remark, Geroux met with Lewis and said that the other chartered accountant had told him that separate disclosure was not necessary. According to Geroux, the other chartered accountant gave the following arguments:

1. Separate disclosure is only necessary when salary and interest are not at fair values of services provided or at current interest rates.

2. The *CICA Handbook* does not require Lewis to approve of everything on financial statements that he prepares under a review engagement.

3. Materiality should be considered. Lewis should merely expand his materiality limits and ignore the issue.

4. Separate disclosure would be required if both companies were incorporated.

Geroux informed Lewis that he would consider inviting the other chartered accountant to take over the engagements if some reasonable compromise could not be worked out with Lewis.

Required

Assume that you are Herbert Lewis, and give a reply to Louis Geroux concerning each of the arguments raised. If Geroux refused to accept your point of view, what action would you take and why?

(CICA adapted)

23-34 Sunshine Mines Ltd. (SML) is a small public company in the process of developing a gold mine in the Canadian North. It has already staked a claim on a highly promising find and has conducted all the preliminary exploratory drilling. SML is now looking for funds to finance the approximately three years of preproduction mine development costs. SML had originally planned to raise these additional funds through the usual combination of long-term debt and short-term bank loans. However, a private investment house has approached the company with an offer of a "gold loan" to finance a portion of SML's requirements.

The investment house has a large inventory of gold that it is holding on its own account. The investment house expects gold to rise significantly in value over the next decade, so it does not want to sell its gold inventory and invest the proceeds. However, as long as the gold is held in commodity form, it earns no interest. Accordingly, the investment house is proposing to lend 100,000 ounces of gold to SML. The "interest rate" on the loan would be lower than the rate on a cash loan: about two-thirds of the cash interest rate. However, the interest would be payable in additional ounces of gold — not in currency — once SML reaches the production stage. SML's gold mining claims would be held as security for the loan. In this manner, the investment house would earn "interest" while still maintaining a gold investment, and SML would obtain some of the funds it needs for development simply by selling the original 100,000 ounces of gold.

Because of the unique nature of the proposed loan and the risks involved, the investment house is especially concerned about the possibility of SML defaulting on its payments. If SML's gold reserves are much smaller than projected, then production may never be sufficient to repay the loan. Accordingly, the investment house has asked your firm, Rousseau & Locke, Public Accountants, SML's auditors, to provide it with a special report or some kind of "gold flow" forecast to evaluate SML's ability to repay its loan. The partner assigned to the SML engagement has asked you to write a memo to him, recommending a reporting alternative that will satisfy the investment house and discussing issues that may arise in preparing the report.

Furthermore, the vice-president of finance is also concerned about the audit implications for the coming year's audit.

Required

Prepare the memo requested by the partner, and address the concerns of the vice-president of finance.

(CICA adapted)

23-35 Your public accounting firm is the auditor of Taylor Fruit Farms, Inc., a company located in Penticton, B.C., and incorporated under the laws of British Columbia. You have been requested by the management of Taylor to issue an opinion under Section 5815 of the *CICA Handbook* with respect to Taylor's compliance under the terms of a chattel mortgage issued by J.L. Lockwood Corp. as part of your audit of Taylor Fruit Farms, Inc. J.L. Lockwood Corp. is a supplier of irrigation equipment. Much of the equipment, including that supplied to Taylor, is sold on a secured contract basis. Taylor Fruit Farms is an audit client of yours, but Lockwood is not.

In addition to the present equipment, Taylor informs you that Lockwood is evaluating whether it should sell another $500,000 of equipment to Taylor Fruit Farms.

You have been requested to send them the report under Section 5815 concerning the following matters:

1. The current ratio has exceeded 2.0 in each quarter of the unaudited statements prepared by management and in the annual audited statements.

2. Total owners' equity is more than $800,000.

3. The company has not violated any of the legal requirements of British Columbia's fruit-growing regulations.

4. Management is competent and has made reasonable business decisions in the past three years.

5. Management owns an option to buy additional fruit land adjacent to its present property.

Required

a. Define the purpose of a report under Section 5815.

b. Is it necessary to conduct an audit of a company before issuing a report on compliance under Section 5815?

c. Would you include all five matters listed above in your report? If not, explain why you would exclude any from the report.

23-36 It is now March 1999. Margaret Monson, the owner of Major Products Manufacturing Inc., a small successful long-time audit client of your firm, has requested you to work with them in preparing three-year forecasted information for the year ending December 31, 2000, and two subsequent years. Monson informs you that she intends to use the forecasts, together with the audited financial statements, to seek additional financing to expand the business. Monson has had little experience in formal forecast preparation and counts on you to assist her in any way possible. She wants the most supportive opinion possible from your firm to add to the credibility of the forecast. She informs you that she is willing to do anything necessary to help you prepare the forecast.

First, she wants projections of sales and revenues and earnings from the existing business, which she believes could continue to be financed from existing capital.

Second, she intends to buy a company in a closely related business that is currently operating unsuccessfully. Monson states that she wants to sell some of the operating assets of the business and replace them with others. She believes that this will make the company highly successful. She has made an offer on the new business, subject to obtaining proper financing. She also informs you that she has received an offer on the assets that she intends to sell.

Required

a. Explain circumstances under which it would and would not be acceptable to undertake the engagement.

b. Why is it important that Monson understand the nature of your reporting requirements before the engagement proceeds?

c. With what information will Monson have to provide you before you can complete the forecasted statements? Be as specific as possible.

d. Discuss, in as specific terms as possible, the nature of the report you will issue with the forecasts, assuming that you are able to properly complete them.

23-37 O'Sullivan, a public accountant, has completed the audit of Sarawak Lumber Supply Co. Ltd. and has issued a standard unqualified report. In addition to a report on the overall financial statements, the company needs a special audit report on three specific accounts: sales, net fixed assets, and inventory valued at FIFO. The report is to be issued to Sarawak's lessor, who bases annual rentals on these three accounts. O'Sullivan was not aware of the need for the special report until after the overall audit was completed.

Required

a. Explain why O'Sullivan is unlikely to be able to issue the special audit report without additional audit tests.

b. What additional tests are likely to be needed before the special report can be issued?

c. Assume that O'Sullivan is able to satisfy all the requirements needed to issue the special report, and write the report. Make any necessary assumptions.

CASE

23-38 Medical Partnership (MP), a limited partnership, was formed in July 1999 to permit the sale of 10 partnership units at $400,000 per unit. The proceeds of $4 million together with a new first mortgage of $8 million are to be used to purchase four medical buildings that were constructed about three years ago. At present (September 1999), these four buildings are fully leased to doctors, dentists, laboratory companies, a drugstore chain, and related medical services companies.

MP will be purchasing the four medical buildings effective October 1, 1999, from Hogg Investments Limited (HIL), a company owned by the promoters of MP. HIL was incorporated several years ago, when the idea of constructing the four medical buildings on land near a new hospital was first conceived, in order to handle all business matters. HIL was incorporated solely to hold the group of medical-building assets. HIL has arranged the new first mortgage of $8 million required to purchase the four buildings.

MP will operate with one general partner, Medicmanagement Limited (ML), owned by HIL, and the 10 limited partners. ML will hold 0.01 percent of the ownership of MP but will have unlimited liability for MP's debts and obligations. The limited partners will be liable only to the extent of their equity contribution. The $400,000 minimum required investment exempts MP and its promoters from the requirements of provincial securities acts.

Since HIL's inception, its financial statements have always been audited by a firm of public accountants, which has issued unqualified auditor's reports each year. Income statements have been prepared for HIL for only the past two years because the company was previously in a startup stage.

In order to maintain the appearance of objectivity and independence, MP's promoters have decided to engage an independent accountant. They have recently approached your employer to assemble and report on the financial statements that they propose to include in a confidential sales document that is to be provided to prospective purchasers of an MP partnership unit. They would like the following in the document:

1. Pro-forma income statements for MP for each of the two years ended June 30, 1998 and 1999. These pro-forma statements would essentially be those of HIL, adjusted for pro-forma changes in interest expense, management fees and similar accounts, and changes in accounting policies. The promoters would like the income statements audited, preferably without a qualification. The auditors of HIL are willing to make their working papers available to you and to answer any questions.

2. Income statements and projected income statements of MP for each of the five years ended December 31, commencing with the year ended December 31, 1999.

You have been designated to prepare a report for the partner in charge of the tentative MP engagement. The partner wants your report to address the requests made by the promoters of MP. In addition, the partner wants to know what the major accounting and auditing issues are for this engagement.

You meet with the promoters of MP and the auditors of HIL, who provide you with the information listed below. The promoters also give you a draft copy of the income statement that they would like to see included in the confidential sales document (see Exhibit I). The auditors of HIL provide you with the audited income statement of that company for the 1999 and 1998 fiscal years (see Exhibit II).

1. The return-on-investment calculation in Exhibit I is based on net income plus (1) amortization, (2) interest on the mortgage, and (3) other noncash charges to arrive at a total that has been divided by the $4 million equity investment.

2. According to the promoters, adjustments have been made to Exhibit I on the assumption that a going concern will be sold to MP, whereas a startup operation is shown in Exhibit II. For example, expenses were incurred in paying for leasehold improvements and inducements to tenants. HIL has been writing them off over five years.

3. In Exhibit II, amortization has been recorded on a straight-line basis at an average rate of 5 percent a year on buildings and equipment.

4. The income statements in Exhibit I are based on recognizing revenue on an accrual basis, with no allowance for vacancies.

5. You have been provided with photographs of the four buildings.

6. An audit of the partnership's accounting records will occur if the units are sold by December 31, 1999.

7. The promoters expect your firm's income tax practitioners to assist with the marketing of the partnership units.

Required

Prepare the requested report.

(CICA adapted)

EXHIBIT I

Medical Partnership
Extracts from the
Draft Income
Statements
(in Thousands of
Dollars)

	Pro-forma years ended June 30		Projected years ending December 31		
	1998	**1999**	**1999**	**2000**	**For each of 2001, 2002, 2003**
Revenue	$ 3,620	$ 4,076	$ 4,150	$ 4,300	$ 4,730
Expenses					
Salaries and security	146	185	180	190	200
Utilities	110	127	130	140	150
Advertising (1)	50	50	40	30	30
Depreciation and amortization	360	360	360	360	360
Office	111	127	130	140	150
Mortgage interest	960	960	960	940	920
Property taxes	240	260	260	280	300
Waste disposal	97	110	115	125	135
Maintenance	135	178	185	195	205
Insurance	15	12	12	15	18
Professional fees	19	12	12	15	18
Management fee (2)	290	326	332	344	378
Other	101	115	118	125	130
	2,634	2,832	2,834	2,899	2,994
Operating profit	$ 986	$ 1,244	$ 1,316	$ 1,401	$ 1,736
Return-on-investment	58.9%	65.6%	66.5%	68.1%	75.9%

Pro-forma adjustments

1. Non-recurring start-up expenses have been deleted from the income figures because the limited partners do not incur these expenses.
2. A management fee of 8% of revenue is included in the pro-forma income figures for 1998 and 1999 because a newly negotiated management contract will apply to the partnership.
3. Other adjustments have been made to reflect pro-forma changes in interest and similar amounts and to reflect revised accounting policies.

EXHIBIT II

Hogg Investments
Limited Extracts from
the Audited Income
Statements:
Years Ended June 30
(in Thousands of
Dollars)

	1998	1999
Revenue	$3,666	$4,136
Expenses		
Salaries and security	146	185
Utilities	110	127
Advertising and inducements	837	629
Depreciation	355	379
Financing fees	150	150
Sign-up fees	510	405
Office	111	127
Start-up	393	358
Interest	976	966
Property taxes	240	260
Amortization	290	290
Waste disposal	97	110
Maintenance	135	178
Insurance	15	12
Professional fees	19	12
Other	101	115
	4,485	4,304
Operating loss	$ 819	$ 168

24

ASSURANCE SERVICES: DIRECT REPORTING ENGAGEMENTS AND BUSINESS ADVISORY SERVICES

AN ACCOUNTANT'S EDUCATION SHOULDN'T STOP WITH AN ACCOUNTING DESIGNATION

Bob, Joanne, Brigitte, and Tom all went to university together, and each received his or her accounting designation about 10 years ago. They get together for lunch regularly. Recently, Joanne announced that she had successfully obtained her CBV (Chartered Business Valuator) designation. As a tax practitioner, Joanne believed this would help her clients immensely with respect to tax planning. Groans (from Tom) and cheers (from the others) greeted her.

"Pretty late for you to do something like this. It's so hard to get back into studying, especially for the CBV program," commented Brigitte, who had obtained her CISA (Certified Information Systems Auditor) designation five years previously. Bob agreed. Bob is a CFA (Certified Financial Analyst) who practises in the Mergers and Acquisitions Department of a large public accounting firm.

Tom smiled and said, "You couldn't get me to write another exam! It's difficult enough keeping up to date in tax and accounting and auditing standards, as well as learning how to use all the different accounting software packages on the market. Getting some designation wouldn't help my clients with their software and accounting needs."

Bob, Joanne, Brigitte, and Tom reflect the changing face of accounting professionals. Having met the challenge of obtaining an

> accounting designation and working with a diversity of clients, Bob, Joanne, and Brigitte updated their educational qualifications and business experience to help them satisfy the needs of their clients. However, some practitioners, like Tom, feel that while ongoing education and experience are important, additional designations may not be appropriate for them.

Professional accounting organizations understand the need for specialization, and have decided it is time to officially recognize these realities. In June 1997, the CICA Board of Governors released *The First Report of the Specialization Implementation Task Force*, which provided a process for identifying and recognizing specialist designations. The October 1, 1998, issue of *The Bottom Line* (page 10) reported that the CICA was moving ahead with its first specialist certification and accreditation program, in the area of investigative and forensic accounting. Two other areas involved in ongoing accreditation discussions were identified: Canadian insolvency practitioners and the Information Systems Audit and Control Association.

There is a world of opportunity awaiting interested, qualified professionals. The April 1998 issue of *The Bottom Line* quotes a number of accounting firms that are expanding in the business advisory and consulting areas. Chapter 23 provided numerous attest reports that auditors can provide based on standards in the *CICA Handbook*. This chapter starts by providing examples of direct reporting and business advisory services (also known as "consulting"), then goes on to describe some of these engagements further. Such work is governed by the general assurance standards and by standards of other professional organizations or specialist publications. This chapter, which is intended as only an introduction, provides an indication of the breadth of professional practice.

Specific engagements discussed in this chapter include:

- WebTrust
- ISO-14000, Environmental Management Systems audits
- Forensic audits
- Business valuations
- Risk management services (e.g., business risk, treasury risk)
- Controls assessment services
- Information systems quality assurance services
- Information systems selection and implementation assistance

SPECIAL ENGAGEMENTS

OBJECTIVE 24-1

Describe direct reporting engagements and business advisory services.

Chapter 23 explained that assurance engagements could be either attest engagements or direct reporting engagements. The following discussion uses direct reporting as a basis, although attest engagements could also be appropriate in certain situations. The previous chapter, on page 727, defined a direct reporting engagement as an engagement in which the auditor directly expresses a conclusion on his or her evaluation of a subject matter using certain criteria and for which management does not report. For example, an auditor could be asked to evaluate the controls surrounding the use of electronic commerce in connection with purchases made using a company's Web page. Management provides a list of its business activities and business objectives, not a list of controls. Should the controls be of adequate quality, the auditor will be able to issue a WebTrust seal (see next section for more details) for placement on the Web page. The seal confirms to users of the Web page that acceptable control quality was achieved. The auditor uses published criteria when making the assessment of control quality.

Criteria used for a direct reporting engagement could be externally available, provided by a specific user, or established by agreement between the auditor and management. In a direct reporting engagement, the auditor is adding value by providing (or denying) assurance that the criteria have (or have not) been met.

Many organizations have voluntarily registered the entity as adhering to specific ISO (International Organization for Standardization) standards, such as ISO-9000 (quality assurance standards) and ISO-14000 (environmental management standards). The auditor uses the criteria associated with the international standards to confirm that the entity has met the ISO standards.

WHAT IS ISO?

This information is extracted from the Web page for the International Organization for Standardization or ISO (at **www.iso.ch**) , described as a worldwide federation of national standards bodies from some 130 countries, having one body from each country.

The ISO is a nongovernmental organization established in 1947. Its stated mission is to promote the development of standardization to facilitate the international exchange of goods and services and to develop cooperation in intellectual, scientific, technological, and economic activity.

The Web page notes that ISO is not an acronym but rather derived from the Greek word *isos*, meaning "equal." This international name was chosen so that acronyms would not change with the language used. Whatever the country, the short form is always ISO.

The organization indicates that international standards exist for the following reasons:

- To improve worldwide progress in trade liberalization
- To assist interpenetration of industry sectors
- To facilitate worldwide communications systems
- To provide global standards for emerging technologies
- To assist developing countries in creating infrastructures

The Web page also provides examples of widely adopted standards:

- An ISO film speed code for photographic equipment
- Telephone and banking cards for worldwide use
- Paper sizes
- ISO 9000 series for quality management and quality assurance
- ISO 14000 series for environmental management
- International codes for country names, currencies, and languages

The Web page explains who makes up ISO, who does the work, how standards are developed, how to order copies of materials, and many other related topics.

The distinction between assurance services and business advisory services can be blurred. Some firms would call the above "ISO standards examination business advisory services." Other firms reserve the term "business advisory services" for the completion of work that may not have any predetermined criteria. Some examples follow:

- The management of a manufacturing company observes that its gross profits are declining but is not sure why. The accountant is called in to identify what can be done: should quality control be improved or does overtime need to be reduced?

- The accountant is asked to assist in the selection and implementation of software and hardware for a new accounting system.
- During the annual financial statement audit, the auditor notices that there are significant weaknesses in general computer controls (perhaps program development controls or access controls are poor). Rather than simply stating that controls are poor in a management letter, the auditor will discuss with management how further assistance can be contracted in a special engagement to provide detailed guidance for general controls and a specific application cycle indicating how controls should be improved.

In theory, direct reporting engagements and attest engagements are those engagements that require specified standards (or criteria) to be used, while *business advisory services* relate to the completion of a specified task (or set of tasks) agreed upon by the accountant and the client. In practice, the term "business advisory services" may be used loosely to encompass almost any type of work that assists a client.

NEW SERVICES: WEBTRUST AND ISO-14000

WEBTRUST

> **OBJECTIVE 24-2**
>
> Describe two new services offered by public accountants, WebTrust and ISO-14000 Audits, and explain why these services are important to the public.

Chapter 22 described EDI, EFTs (electronic funds transfers), and the related hazards (i.e., stolen credit card numbers, amounts taken from or deposited to the wrong account, and duplicate payments charged to a customer). One of the reasons consumers might not purchase items via an Internet Web site is fear of credit card numbers being misused, either during the transaction or by the entity that is storing the information. Another reason could be that since the consumer cannot walk into a store and touch the goods, he or she may have doubts as to the goods' existence or whether they will really be shipped. These fears led to the idea for WebTrust.

The final report of the *CICA Task Force on Assurance Services*, dated January 1998, described how the CA/CPA WebTrust was successfully launched in the fall of 1997 with a joint press release issued by the CICA and the AICPA. The task force report and information about WebTrust itself are both available from the CICA Web page at **http://www.cica.ca**. The WebTrust principles (extracted from this Web site) specifically address the potential concerns of consumers:

- *Business practice disclosure*: The entity is to disclose its business practices for e-commerce transactions and execute those transactions using those disclosed business practices.
- *Transaction integrity*: Effective controls are maintained to ensure that customers' orders placed using e-commerce are completed and billed as agreed.
- *Information protection*: Effective controls are maintained to ensure that private customer information is protected.

In his book, Boritz[1] includes in a chapter on information systems assurance services a printout of the detail from **RocketRoger.Com**, the Web site used by "Rocket Roger" Clemens to market merchandise. The home page is typical with graphics of the baseball player, some background information, and the actual WebTrust seal. The remaining pages reproduced in the chapter do not describe the merchandise sold, but rather show the actual disclosures required under the standards of WebTrust. Following are some examples:

- The *Business practice disclosures* page indicates that goods are shipped within five business days of receipt of a credit card and money order purchase, and that credit cards are not charged before the goods are shipped. It also indicates shipping methods and provides contact points using e-mail, telephone, or mail for queries.

---

[1]Boritz, J.E., *Computer Control & Audit Guide*, Tenth Edition, 1999, Chapter 9.

- *Management assertions* indicate that business practices are disclosed and followed, that controls are in place to ensure that goods shipped match goods ordered, and that controls are in place to keep customer information private.

(The business practices page and management assertions, although specific, do not list the controls in place at the business. The auditor uses the standard WebTrust criteria and professional judgment to enable provision of an auditor's report.)

- The *Auditor's report* is one signed by Bennett Gold, Chartered Accountants, dated October 16, 1998. The auditor's report is linked to the CICA Web site where criteria for WebTrust are displayed. The report is addressed to management and has the following paragraphs:
  - An introductory paragraph indicating that an audit was conducted, defining criteria, and specifying a time period. It is explained that it is management's responsibility to provide the controls; the auditor is expressing an opinion on those controls.
  - A scope paragraph further defining the standards and explaining the type of work required.
  - An opinion paragraph indicating that the standards were met.
  - Additional explanatory and disclaimer paragraphs. The first indicates that fraud or errors may not be detected and that controls may change in the future. The second indicates that the WebTrust seal is symbolic of the contents of the report but does not provide assurance in itself. The third states that there is no representation regarding the quality of goods and services provided.

Reference to Chapter 23 will show that this is a standard format followed by special audit reports.

The controls used by businesses may be highly technical and may involve encryption, the use of firewalls (as discussed in Chapter 22), or other controls that the entity considers necessary. The WebTrust seal is initially obtained by an organization when those principles have been met using specified criteria. An electronic seal is placed upon the client's Web page, which is linked to the CICA (or AICPA) Web site so that consumers can obtain information about WebTrust and establish that the seal's authenticity is verified by Verisign, as well as find out about the standards associated with the seal. The seal must be periodically renewed by having an audit confirm that the standards are still in place and operating effectively.

ISO-14000 AUDITS AND ENVIRONMENTAL AUDITING

An auditor would be concerned with environmental issues in the audited financial statements because of possible contingent liabilities. What if the client is not complying with specific environmental legislation? There could be fines for violating the legislation. There could also be clean-up costs associated with inappropriately handling waste or dangerous substances. The public may prefer purchasing products from or investing in those companies that run their businesses responsibly, taking the environment into account.

With respect to the financial statement audit, Assurance and Related Services Guideline AuG-19, "Audit of Financial Statements Affected by Environmental Matters," released in January 1994, provides guidance. Audit of the actions undertaken by management with respect to specific legislation is a compliance audit (discussed in the next chapter), that is also a direct reporting engagement and requires significant expertise on the part of the auditor.

Legislative activity is a factor in improving the environment. In May 1997, *The Bottom Line* reported (on page 1) that British Columbia had amended its *Waste Management Act*. The act was quoted as purporting "zero tolerance" with respect to contaminated sites. Several provinces and the federal government also have some type of legislation with respect to cleanliness of water, discharge of pollutants, and use and disposal of dangerous substances. This type of regulation and a public that is environmentally conscious could lead more organizations to register for ISO-14000.

The ISO standards, set by the Geneva-based International Organization for Standardization, require that registered entities adhere to the published standards. Standards are lengthy and require that organizations establish policies and procedures associated with the standards, have internal processes that ensure that the standards are met, and submit to an independent review by an outside organization that is qualified to inspect that standard. *The Bottom Line* article states that KPMG was the first public accounting firm to be registered by the Standards Council of Canada to inspect (or audit) companies under the ISO-14000 series. Approximately 60 other organizations or individuals were already certified as auditors of ISO-14000 at that time. The audit team that conducts an ISO-14000 audit must have expertise in auditing, in the ISO standards, and in the practice of environmental management and/or auditing; have adequate knowledge of the business processes to plan the audit; and adhere to the standards of assurance engagements, as discussed in the previous chapter.

In addition to conducting ISO-14000 audits, professional accounting firms could conduct audits with respect to specific environmental legislation, assist organizations in improving their management of environmental pollutants, or perform other specified consulting assignments. Such work helps both the organization and the legislators to verify that appropriate actions are being taken in this area that affects us all.

FORENSIC AUDITING AND BUSINESS VALUATIONS

FORENSIC AUDITING

OBJECTIVE 24-3

Explain how accountants can provide services such as forensic auditing and business valuations.

Many insurance companies are concerned about the huge losses to fraud in their industry — estimated at about $1.3 billion per year in property and casualty alone.[2] Insurance adjusters (individuals within insurance companies who establish the amounts of specific insurance claims) and the lawyers of insurance companies may use accountants to help document fraudulent insurance claims, especially fire and lost business claims. Groups of insurance companies have established Special Investigation Units (SIUs), using ex-commercial crime unit police officers.[3] When arson or theft is suspected, these units may turn to auditors trained as forensic auditors, whose task is to quantify the loss and assist in identifying how the loss occurred.

These auditors use an expanded skill set to investigate suspected individuals or entities. Think of the types of questions that a financial statement auditor asks when deciding whether to accept or continue working with a client and when conducting a knowledge of business evaluation:

- What are the financial needs of the business or the owners?
- Are there any indications of financial problems leading to going-concern problems?
- Are there any indicators of potential problems with management's integrity?

The forensic auditor asks these questions in a slightly different way:

- Do the owners have financial needs that are not being met by the business?
- How do owners benefit from the business?
- Is an owner trying to run down one business to the benefit of another?

Information systems skills can help tremendously when the forensic auditor is given access to computerized records and needs to deal with logs or backup data due to the destruction of potentially incriminating E-mail or phone-mail evidence. There is a professional organization, called the Association of Certified Fraud Examiners, based in the United States, that has members worldwide including Canada. The association helps provide training to people in fraud prevention and detection.

---

[2]Lundy, D., "Forensics on Front Lines on Insurance Fraud," *The Bottom Line* (December 1996), p. 5.

[3]Ibid.

COULD YOU CATCH THESE CROOKS?

A group of Australian hackers had hacked into several defence contractors' systems, stealing confidential data. When the Canadian defence contractors were contacted, not one of them had detected the theft of its data.

****

Several laptop computers were stolen from the office of a public mining company. The laptops, used by field technicians, contained exploration results, showing where precious metals and mineral deposit ores were likely to be found. The company had not yet laid claim to any mining rights in the explored areas. The data on the laptop computers was not encrypted.

****

An individual obtained the passwords of several departments of a telecommunications company. He set up both a fictitious customer and a fictitious supplier. He purchased telecommunications equipment from this company (which he never paid for), then sold it back to the company (and was paid for the equipment).

****

Management conspired to inflate the financial results of the business prior to the sale of the business. Details of the activity were stored in electronic mail messages that had been deleted. These electronic mail messages were recovered from log files *after* the business had been sold.

In addition to insurance fraud, there are many types of crime investigations that can be assisted by the forensic auditor. These include white-collar crime and commercial crime (e.g., cheque and credit-card fraud, money laundering, extortion, mail fraud) estimated to exceed $12 billion a year.[4]

CA SAVES CN

Andre Lepage suspected foul play in Montreal's freight yard. The bills from a diesel-fuel distributor seemed to be too high. LePage spent many hours poring over supplier invoices and several nights skulking in the freight yard measuring tanker fuel levels. CN was paying for fuel it had never received.

The distributor was questioned and admitted guilt, returning the ill-gotten gains.

Lepage is both a CA and a licensed private investigator, with nine years of policing experience for CN's special investigation unit.[5]

These massive losses due to a variety of crimes help explain why specific CAs campaigned for "Investigative and Forensic Accounting" to be the first formal specialization designated by the CICA. For many years, the CICA has also had an

---

[4]Colapinto, R., "The New Fraud Squad," *CAmagazine* (May 1998), pp. 19–24.

[5]Ibid, p. 19. For a detailed description of the forensic auditing process, see McLaughlin, P., "The Bingo Haul," *CAmagazine* (December 1997), pp. 18–25.

investigative and forensic accounting interest group. Such groups are formal mechanisms whereby CAs with special interests can exchange information.

An auditor's professional scepticism, together with the supporting training, can be extremely useful in this specialized area.

BUSINESS VALUATIONS

"Obtaining the highest price in an open and unrestricted market is the goal of any business that's up for sale."[6] Qualified accountants are trained in business valuation, using methods such as net present value of projected cash flows to provide a value for the shares or assets of a business. The following focus box provides one example of why business valuations are needed.

IT WAS FINALLY TIME TO SELL

Helen's husband died suddenly of a heart attack, leaving her the majority shareholder of a specialized manufacturing business with revenues of $2 million. The managers did not listen to her, and she didn't understand the business very well, so the business suffered. After several years of losses, Helen started using a variety of consultants.

Finally, an acquaintance recommended a qualified accountant. The accountant, Diane, started with a business review, identifying efficiency problems and the need to trim excess management. Then quality control procedures were improved. A building was sold to bring in necessary capital. Helen was gradually building up her expertise, working with both the accountant and selected individuals in the business. An unprofitable segment was disposed of. The company became profitable, and profit sharing was implemented with key employees.

Helen had proven herself capable. After talking about selling the business for three years, she started getting serious in her talks with the general manager of the business, who was interested in taking it over. Diane called Bob, a qualified accountant who specialized in business valuations, and Helen engaged Bob to conduct a business valuation. The valuation would be used during negotiations between herself and her general manager.

In addition to providing an estimated value for the business, qualified accountants can, in their capacity as advisors to the vendors, arrange an auction process to sell a business. Cole describes the process of arranging an auction from potential purchaser identification through to negotiations and closing of a sale.[7]

Business valuations are required for numerous reasons. These could include marital breakdown, estate planning, or business mergers. The public accountant's analytical skills and professional judgment assist clients in this process.

BUSINESS ADVISORY SERVICES

For many years, public accountants have been saying that the financial statement audit market is saturated — there are only so many companies that are prepared to have financial statement audits! But look at the wonderful skill base that public

---

[6]Cole, S., "Going Once, Going Twice ... ," *CAmagazine* (January/February 1999), pp. 41–42, 50.

[7]Ibid, p. 42.

Describe four types of
business advisory
services provided by
accountants.

Arthur Andersen
www.arthurandersen.com

accountants bring with them and the variety of work that they do that can contribute to an accounting firm's growth. The services may be assurance services (if assurance based on criteria is provided) or business advisory services (if the work is a specific task or problem resolution and no assurance is provided).

In 1998, the firm of Arthur Andersen indicated that it expected growth to come from business risk consulting, while KPMG referred to the ISO practice, treasury risk management, and control and risk self-assessment.[8]

In this section, we will describe:

- Risk management services
- Controls assessment services
- Information systems quality assurance services
- Information systems selection and implemenation assistance

RISK MANAGEMENT SERVICES

In their article "Risky Business," Willis and Bradshaw state that risk analysis is a process that needs to be dealt with on a continuous basis, not as a "one-time, quick-fix exercise."[9] They use a fictitious business (see focus box below) to describe how risks could be identified.

MANAGING RISKS IS AN ONGOING BUSINESS PROCESS

Senior management and the board of directors held special meetings, with senior executives giving presentations to identify risks. Twenty-one risks were identified, all of them substantive and serious issues. Several were familiar: foreign exchange, year 2000 issues, and labour contract renewals. Others were familiar to specific executives but not to the entire group: competitors raiding top sales staff, quality of after-sales service, and difficulties in obtaining environmental permits. One was not a surprise but was usually not mentioned: gaps in succession planning.

The chair of the meeting then directed the discussion to "processes, patterns, and perspectives."

- ***Processes*: Coordinated processes for identifying and assessing risks, and for sharing information about risk.**
- ***Patterns*: Identifying frameworks, models, or classifications to help talk about risk and risk management.**
- ***Perspectives*: "Everyone has something different to say about risks."**

The company made a decision to broaden its risk identification and assessment process, involving others in the business, and then to develop a structured process to deal with those risks.

Think about the risk assessment process used during the conduct of a financial statement audit. We have used the audit risk model (AAR = IR × CR × PDR) to categorize risks and identify actions (audit procedures) used to mitigate risks. Running a business or specific operations within a business also exposes the organization and its goals to risks, both internal and external to the organization. When assessing audit

---

[8]Campbell, M., "Firms Launching New Services to Increase Access to Assurance Market," *The Bottom Line* (May 1, 1998), p. 17.

[9]Willis, A., and W. A. Bradshaw, "Risky Business," *CAmagazine* (August 1998), pp. 37–38.

risk and gathering knowledge of business, the auditor specifically evaluates the likelihood of business failure. Several firms use that knowledge to obtain engagements in business risk assessment or business risk management.

BUSINESS RISK MANAGEMENT

Students who have taken a business strategy course will recognize the process that businesses should follow when establishing goals or objectives:

- Define and prioritize objectives.
- Identify and analyze resources and risks associated with these objectives.
- Determine a strategy to achieve goals and overcome risks.
- Implement the strategy.
- Measure performance.
- Monitor, learn, adapt, and start again at the first step.

A similar process is followed for identifying and managing risks. Sophisticated software modelling tools are used to assist professional advisors in the risk assessment and evaluation process. One such product, *CARDmap*,[10] is a software tool used to pinpoint risks, identify controls that address the risk, and help identify gaps in the control process. It is used both by professionals to document their risk assessment work and as a self-help tool by clients of the firm.

Several of the large firms have developed "best practices data bases" using work completed for their clients. Client data is sanitized (i.e., generalized so that the client cannot be identified), and methods for dealing with risks and providing controls for those risks are included in the data base. Such data bases are used to help identify business risks and then to provide recommended business practices to mitigate the risk exposures. Also, when specific risks are identified, such as inadequate succession planning, the accounting firm can then provide specific solutions based on its experience to deal with that risk.

TREASURY RISK MANAGEMENT

The treasury function is the function within the organization that manages the liquid assets of the entity. This could be a relatively straightforward process of balancing accounts payable, accounts receivable, and long-term and short-term debt, or a complex process involving foreign exchange hedging, futures purchases, and the issuance or use of a variety of financial instruments. Activities include managing the organization's cash, conducting loan and investment activities, and possibly administering employee pension and other benefit plans. For large organizations, this can mean managing billions of dollars. For financial institutions, this function is at the heart of the business.

Like business risk management engagements, this type of business assurance service involves a structured approach. Qualified accountants with experience in the industry document and evaluate business processes, working closely with management to assess known risks as well as to identify potential additional risks. Liquid assets need to be available to pay debts or expand the business. If the liquid assets are not monitored, a business can risk losing everything. The following focus box indicates Web sites where best practices and resource information can be obtained about the treasury management function.

---

[10]Source: Promotional brochure entitled "CARDmap," provided by KPMG. The brochure states that CARDmap is a product developed by MCS Control Training and Design Inc.

The treasury risk management process could look at the existence and nature of cash flow monitoring (including the effects of electronic commerce), the use of technology for cash management, banking relationships, and borrowing and investing activities.

CONTROLS ASSESSMENT SERVICES

For the financial statement audit, the auditor needs to examine controls that affect financial statement results, perhaps focusing only on key controls, programmed controls, or management controls. An understanding of controls is necessary to design audit tests. During this examination of controls, the auditor could discover weaknesses or identify risks due to the nature of client application systems.

For example, in a financial institution, the auditor might discover that loans in the range of $5,000 to $25,000 are not being properly approved, with a greater risk of bad debts. The auditor might choose to do additional audit tests of the loan loss provision to compensate for this weakness during the financial statement audit. However, to improve the situation, the client financial institution may need to reorganize its personnel, change information systems, and change the nature of documentation used to handle these loans. The public accountant may be able to assist the client with a more detailed analysis of the internal controls, providing assistance with the redesign of procedures to improve the quality of controls while retaining or improving efficiency. Depending on the mandate of the engagement, the controls assessment service could be similar to an operational audit or value-for-money audit, as described in the next chapter.

INFORMATION SYSTEMS QUALITY ASSURANCE SERVICES

Many organizations are constantly changing some portion of their information systems. Recently, many financial institutions had to change their systems to enable the proper treatment of a new currency, the Euro. Changes with respect to the year 2000 (Y2K) problem are ongoing during 1999, with expected program changes required to systems as far into the future as 2010. Businesses are increasingly using electronic commerce to process transactions and need to update payroll programs as legislation brings changes. Some organizations have strategic information systems, systems that give the entity a strategic advantage over other entities. Such systems may need continued enhancement for the entity to maintain that leading edge.

Accountants can help with all these changes. Accountants with information systems experience may be called on to assist with the design, testing, or monitoring of these many information systems changes. For example, software auditors from the Dutch branch of Ernst & Young undertook independent testing of European software using the Euro so that the software could be accredited by BASDA (Business and Accounting Software Developers Association), a United Kingdom-based international trade association.[11] BASDA represents 260 developers and suppliers of business and accounting software (visit its Web site at **www.basda.org**).

Andrews and Trites[12] walk through the development and design process of a Web site for accountants. This process is similar to that used for design and development of other types of information systems. Accountants and auditors can help with the design and development of information systems since they have detailed knowledge of the businesses they have worked in and can apply this business knowledge when designing systems to achieve the organization's objectives.

INFORMATION SYSTEMS SELECTION AND IMPLEMENTATION ASSISTANCE

Many businesses look to their accountants for guidance in selecting business systems, implementing those systems, and even training personnel. Public accounting firms may have groups of personnel trained in the evaluation and selection process and others in the use of specific software packages (e.g., ACCPAC for small businesses, SAP for larger businesses). This latter group could undertake software customization, training, and implementation.

The Bottom Line has regular feature writers who address these processes. For example, R. Morochrove talks about the implementation and change process associated with respect to the year 2000 problems.[13] Although not stated in Morochrove's article, the Y2K problem has been responsible for many businesses implementing new software application systems rather than changing their existing ones. Other authors provide software reviews, such as Salmon,[14] who described features of ACCPAC for Windows and MYOB, two common accounting systems for small business.

[11]"The Euro: Panacea or Problem?" *IS Audit & Control Journal*, vol. VI, 1998, pp. 8–9.

[12]Andrews, J., and G. Trites, "Net Sales," *CAmagazine* (August 1997), pp. 13–15.

[13]Morochrove, R., "Millennium Bug: Small Businesses Seek Guidance from Accountants," *The Bottom Line* (September 1, 1998), p. 17.

[14]Salmon, A., "Latest ACCPAC Offers Key Accounting Features," *The Bottom Line* (December 1996), p. 22.

As the business world constantly changes, new types of businesses emerge and business practices change. Thus, accountants must also change in the way audits are conducted for such businesses.

All professional associations have some form of research activity. For example, the Certified General Accountants' Association has a federal Research Foundation, chartered in 1913, which sponsors research. The results of the research are published in articles or books and are available for purchase (at **www.cga-canada.org**). The CISA (Certified Information Systems Auditor) designation is provided by the Information Systems Audit and Control Association, which also has a Research Foundation. Research grants are provided to academics, and the association itself conducts research into topics that are technology-related, such as controls in electronic commerce (visit the Web site at **www.isaca.org**).

The CICA provides regular status reports on its Web page (at **www.cica.ca**) of the activities being undertaken by a variety of task forces and committees. The following, based on a review of material in progress by the Assurance Standards Board (ASB) as of spring 1999, describes some projects that are relevant to future financial statement auditing and other assurance services.

Audit risk model   The ASB is working cooperatively with the United Kingdom Auditing Practices Board and the U.S. Auditing Standards Board to gather information on the design and application of new audit methodologies being implemented by major firms. It will then assess the implications for auditing standards, particularly whether or not there is a need to modify the audit risk model.

Engagement contracts   Accountants are expected to use engagement letters to help clarify the nature of their relationship with a client. In September 1998, the ASB approved a project to develop a new *Assurance and Related Services Guideline*. The guideline is to describe best practices for engagement letters or contracts, including samples of model engagement letters or terms covering the range of services commonly offered by CAs in public practice.

Year 2000 specified procedures engagement for certain "brokers/dealers"   AuG-27, "The Year 2000 Issue — Specified Procedures Engagement Pursuant to the Requirements of Certain Regulatory Organizations," was published in March 1999. This guideline sets out the form for the public accountant's report and provides guidance about engagement performance with respect to the application of specified procedures required by some regulatory organizations for certain securities commission firm registrants. The specified procedures are described in a management-prepared "Narrative Report on Year 2000 Preparations" that is required by regulatory organizations.

New types of engagements are being considered both by the AICPA's (American Institute of Certified Public Accountants') Special Committee on Assurance Services and the CICA's Assurance Services Development Board. Two of these engagements are an expansion of the WebTrust type of engagements.[15] These are:

- *Reports on TPSPs (Third-party service providers).* A TPSP could be an ISP (Internet service provider) that provides data communications services or another third-party Web-hosting service that provides key processing and administers security relating to the Web site. Thus, in order for an auditor to provide a WebTrust report on a Web site, he or she must also consider the controls and activities of the TPSP. As with a third-party service centre, a TPSP would not wish multiple audit firms to come in and audit its controls so that a third-party report could be

---

[15]See also Sheehy, D., "Secure Transactions: Beyond Phase 1," *CAmagazine* (March 1999), pp. 43–44, 48.

prepared. The report would contain some of the attributes of Section 5025, "Standards for Assurance Engagements," as well as of Section 5900, "Opinions on Control Procedures at a Service Organization."

- *CATrust ("Certificate Authority — Trust").* A certificate authority is an entity that issues *certificates of authority*, also known as *digital signatures*. Digital signatures are a means of authenticating the origins of documents sent electronically. A task force has started the development of criteria that could be used for Certificate Authority or CATrust.

One final potential service we will discuss is *continuous auditing*, which has also been identified by the CICA Task Force on Assurance Services as an assurance service that should be offered. A study is underway to provide a conceptual framework for external continuous audits.[16] In a continuous audit, reports would be issued at short intervals or be made immediately, such as whenever a user accessed a Web site. It is expected that the continuous audit could focus on any type of information relevant to decision making. Some examples are:

- The authenticity, integrity, and nonrepudiation of electronic commerce transactions
- The effective operation of controls over a publicly accessible data base

SUMMARY

There are many different types of engagements that qualified accountants can complete for their clients. In all cases, a pivotal condition for the engagement is the proficiency of the public accountant to undertake the engagement. This requires a sound grasp of the subject matter being audited (which may be nonfinancial) and possibly a mastery of various types of information technology. The engagement team needs to have the required expertise.

ESSENTIAL TERMS

Business advisory services — services agreed on by an accountant and a client for the completion of a specific task (or set of tasks) (p. 766).

Business valuation — provision of a value for the shares or assets of a business (p. 768).

CATrust — a service being considered by the CICA to provide assurance with respect to certificate authorities (p. 776).

Certificate authority — an entity that issues certificates of authority, also known as *digital signatures* (p. 776).

Continuous auditing — the process of providing audit reports that cover an ongoing time period and are current up to the present date (p. 776).

Digital signatures — electronic signals that can be used to authenticate the point of origin of an electronic message (p. 776).

Forensic auditing — the process of quantifying losses due to crime and identifying how those losses occurred (p. 768).

ISO — International Organization for Standardization, a worldwide federation of national standards bodies from some 130 countries (p. 765).

ISO-14000 — standards provided by the International Organization for Standardization (ISO) with respect to environmental management (p. 767).

ISO-9000 — standards provided by the International Organization for Standardization (ISO) with respect to quality assurance management (p. 765).

ISP — Internet service provider that provides data communications services or third-party Web-hosting services, such as key processing and security administration (p. 775).

Sanitize [data] — generalize data so that the client cannot be identified (p. 772).

TPSP — third-party service provider; in the context of the Internet, organizations that provide data communications services or third-party Web-hosting services, such as key processing and security administration (p. 775).

---

[16]See also Shields, G., "Non-stop Auditing," *CAmagazine* (September 1998), pp. 39–40.

Treasury function — the function within an organization that manages the liquid assets of the entity (e.g., managing cash, conducting loan and investment activities, administering employee pension and benefit plans) (p. 772).

WebTrust seal — a seal placed on a Web site upon completion of an auditor's report, verifying compliance with standards with respect to business practices and controls over electronic commerce transactions (p. 767).

REVIEW QUESTIONS

24-1 What are the distinguishing characteristics of a direct reporting engagement?

24-2 Provide three examples of business advisory services.

24-3 What is the theoretical difference between an assurance engagement and a business advisory service?

24-4 List three reasons why consumers might not want to pay for goods electronically using the Internet. Explain how the WebTrust principles address these concerns.

24-5 Explain why international standards such as ISO-14000 are important. Why would an entity voluntarily register for ISO-14000?

24-6 Identify the different categories of expertise required to conduct an ISO-14000 audit.

24-7 Provide four examples indicating where a forensic auditor could assist in quantifying losses.

24-8 List the services that a business valuator can provide to a client.

24-9 Describe four types of business advisory services provided by accountants.

24-10 List five risks that could affect the ability of a business to continue operating.

24-11 List and explain the activities performed by a treasury function.

24-12 Describe categories of controls that could be evaluated by an auditor as part of a controls assessment service.

24-13 List the phases of the systems development life cycle (refer to an MIS textbook), and identify at least one activity that the accountant could undertake in each phase.

24-14 Describe the typical skills that an accountant would require to provide information systems selection and implementation assistance.

24-15 Provide an example of a continuous audit.

MULTIPLE CHOICE QUESTIONS

24-16 The following questions cover unusual reporting situations. Choose the best response.

a. A WebTrust engagement requires an auditor to provide assurance with respect to
  (1) the accuracy and authorization of electronic commerce transactions.
  (2) the controls over electronic data interchange transactions.
  (3) security over the data communications and data retrieval process.
  (4) controls over business practices and related controls over electronic commerce.

b. A forensic audit would provide information with respect to
  (1) losses occurring due to crime and how those losses might have occurred.
  (2) the reasons for a crime occurring.
  (3) losses occurring due to inefficient business practices.
  (4) weaknesses in internal control and the associated business costs.

24-17 The following questions concern assurance engagements or business advisory services. Choose the best answer.

a. The theoretical distinction between an assurance engagement and a business advisory engagement is that a business advisory engagement
  (1) requires that the business disclose relevant criteria.
  (2) may not have specified criteria but requires completion of a task.
  (3) requires that audit level assurance be provided.
  (4) is an engagement designed totally by the accountant.

b. One of the reasons that consumers may not purchase items using an electronic web site is due to concern over having their credit card numbers compromised. The WebTrust principle that addresses this concern is
  (1) business practice disclosure: the entity is to disclose its business practices for e-commerce transactions and execute the transactions using those disclosed business practices.
  (2) transaction integrity: effective controls are maintained to ensure that customers' orders placed using e-commerce are completed and billed as agreed.
  (3) information protection: effective controls are maintained to ensure that private customer information is protected.
  (4) firewall usage: hardware and software firewalls are used to coordinate and manage Internet traffic.

c. The purpose of treasury risk management is to identify risks associated with
  (1) the management of the liquid assets of an entity.
  (2) the likelihood of the business continuing as a going concern.
  (3) the inherent risk component of the audit risk model.
  (4) automated information systems controls.

24-18 Regional Airlines Limited (RAL) is a regional airline serving as a feeder for one of the national airlines. RAL's aggressive advertising campaign claims that RAL has "the most dependable service in Atlantic Canada."

Ingrid Knorr, the senior partner of Spletts & Toesser (ST), a medium-sized CA firm, has been responsible for the audit of RAL since its incorporation in 1975. Last Friday afternoon, just after the completion of the audit, RAL's general manager had a meeting with Ingrid. The general manager was agitated because the Ministry of Consumer Affairs had demanded that RAL provide support for its advertised claim to have the most dependable service.

The general manager wondered whether ST could issue "some kind of statement" on RAL's service performance. The statement would be used by RAL to support its advertising claims to the Ministry of Consumer Affairs and in its television advertising. He was not very specific about the nature of the engagement and left it to ST to design the approach to assess RAL's claims.

Since this is an unusual engagement, Ingrid asks you, a member of her audit staff, to prepare a memo on what the study would involve and how to report the results. She also wants you to assess the implications for ST of accepting the engagement.

Required

Draft the memo requested by the partner.

(CICA adapted)

24-19 Farmco Limited (Farmco), a privately owned apple farm, is highly debt leveraged. Two loans from XYZ Bank are currently outstanding: a long-term loan that is secured by the farm's land, building structure and equipment; and, a short-term demand loan that is secured by unharvested apples valued at net realizable value. Farmco also leases some of the farming equipment from a local supplier. It is now one month before the harvesting of the apples. The bank has given you a special assignment to assess the adequacy of the security for Farmco's loans.

Required

Discuss which audit procedures you would carry out in completing this assignment and why.

(CICA adapted)

24-20 Access Records Limited (ARL), which commenced operations on April 1 of the current year, is owned by the provincial government (50 percent) and three private companies (16 2/3 percent each). The provincial government currently maintains, on a manual basis, all descriptive information on land in the province, such as information on ownership, legal descriptions, etc. ARL's mandate is to computerize this information and to provide additional data not available from the manual system. The conversion of the manual system for several geographical regions of the province commenced on May 1, with a targeted completion of all regions two and one half years hence. The manual sys-

tems for each region will be maintained by ARL until each regional computerized system is operational.

The computer files are to be available to on-line users; those not on-line must obtain the information they need by going to designated government offices for hard copies. The prime users are market research firms, publishers of data bases, real-estate companies, and a variety of individuals and corporations. ARL charges the users a fee based on the information obtained. Computerization will permit additional descriptive information to be added to the data base. As a result, user fees will increase as a region is computerized. No other organization provides this information.

In calculating pretax income of ARL, the following items must be taken into account:

- In return for providing the original information, the provincial government receives a royalty for revenue generated from information that was previously available from the manual system. Two of the private companies receive a royalty for revenue generated from any new information that they gather and enter into the data base. The computer system automatically identifies charges for previously available information and charges for the new information.

- The three private companies are to receive, for 10 years, a 20 percent rate of return on the original cost of the computer equipment and technology they were required to provide to ARL. At the end of 10 years, the computer equipment and technology will become the property of ARL.

- One of the three private companies entered into a 10-year agreement to provide the land and building from which ARL operates. It receives a 12 percent rate of return per year on its investment in the land and building. All operating cost, including repairs and maintenance, property taxes, and necessary improvements, are to be paid by ARL.

- The shareholders of ARL are to receive interest at the rate of prime plus 1 percent on any funds lent to ARL.

If the private owners, in operating ARL, do not meet certain specified performance standards, the provincial government can acquire their shares at cost.

It is now September of the initial year of operations of ARL. Your employer, Martin and Partners, Chartered Accountants, has been engaged by ARL as auditor for the coming fiscal year, ending in March. ARL also wants your firm to consider some form of assurance that could be provided to the shareholders and other prime users who rely on the information from the computerized system for their operations.

You obtain the following information:

1. The cash contribution of the four owners totals $49 million. Another $30 to $50 million will be needed to complete the computerization. ARL will borrow the additional cash from a chartered bank, using ARL's assets as collateral.

2. Most of the total conversion cost of $70 to $90 million is for mapping, aerial photography, and computer graphics.

3. At the end of 10 years, the government is entitled to acquire, at fair market value, the 50 percent of the shares that it does not own. The private companies are entitled to a reduced royalty if the provincial government acquires their shares.

4. The user fee schedule is set by the provincial government.

5. Discounts are offered to volume users.

6. ARL intends to sell its technology to other provinces.

7. The province's auditor is permitted access to ARL's financial records.

Required

a. What type of report(s) could be provided to the provincial government and to the two private companies that receive royalties to provide assurance as to the accuracy of the royalty figures?

b. Identify the issues involved in preparing a report on computer controls at ARL. What general process would be followed in conducting the audit and in preparing the report?

c. ARL is considering expanding the system to provide for the provision of some information electronically, via the Internet, and has heard about WebTrust. Identify the advantages and disadvantages to ARL of initiating a WebTrust engagement for their Web site once it is developed.

d. Identify significant accounting and auditing matters that would need to be addressed with respect to the financial statement audit.

(CICA adapted)

24-21 Acme Manufacturing Limited (AML) consists of two operating divisions: Acme Plastics, which produces various plastic consumer products, and Acme Chemicals, which uses a by-product of Acme Plastics to produce various resins for sale to other companies for further processing. A summary process chart of the operations and additional comments are included in Exhibit I on page 780.

As a result of increasing public concern about environmental issues, Donna Rideout, the president of AML, has asked the audit engagement partner for AML to provide her with a proposal to conduct an environmental audit of the Acme Plastics division. The results will be used to provide an environmental "report card" for the division and will be included in the company's next annual report to its shareholders.

The partner has asked you to provide him with a memo that discusses the unique issues in accepting this type of engagement. Your memo should include a discussion of the audit approach for this engagement and the nature and content of the report that would be issued as a result of the environmental audit.

Required

Prepare the memo requested by the partner.

(CICA adapted)

CASES

24-22 The Pumpkin Patch is a franchise business operating retail stores for children's fashions. Tom and Wendy Koger had no previous business experience when they answered an advertisement for a Pumpkin Patch franchise outlet in a large new shopping mall. The terms of the franchise contract signed by the Kogers are summarized in Exhibit I on page 780I. The Kogers incorporated as Koger Limited (KL) on August 31, 1998, and opened their store on September 1, 1998. During fiscal 1998/99, KL's sales were consistently below the franchisor's forecasts. In early September 1999, when the bank manager refused to extend their line of credit, the Kogers arranged a luncheon meeting with Dan, a CA, to discuss their situation.

Dan: We met a year ago when you were seeking advice on acquiring the franchise. Was I of help to you?

Tom: We followed your advice on incorporating as one of our friends emphasized how important it was to have limited liability. But I decided that I could handle the bookkeeping on my microcomputer and that we would not need tax advice until we started making money. At the time, there seemed little point in seeing a lawyer as the franchisor had a standard "take it or leave it" franchise contract. (See Exhibit II.)

Wendy: We will soon have to place spring orders, and we are not sure whether to risk the money in additional inventory or

throw in the towel now. I don't understand why we are having such severe cash problems when we are almost making a profit. I have nightmares about the bank manager calling in the demand loan. We both enjoy the business and would like to make a go of it.

Dan: Can I see your August 31, 1999, financial statements?

Tom: Here are the 1999 operating statement and balance sheet (see Exhibit III on page 781). Our sales fluctuate seasonally, with a large peak in December and smaller peaks in April and August. Our clearance sale in January produces sales second only to December. March, September, and October are slow months.

Dan: What then is the problem?

Wendy: Simply that every month we spend more than we collect, and we have not drawn any salaries ourselves. Part of the problem is that the purchase orders that the franchisor places for us have not sold well, so we are now placing our own orders. But the main problem is that the first-year sales that the franchisor forecasted for us were about 15 percent too high: the mall has not yet attracted many customers. Also, our store is just too large. We need at least three salespeople on average to attend to customers and inhibit pilfering.

EXHIBIT I
Acme Plastics,
Summary Process Chart
and Additional
Comments

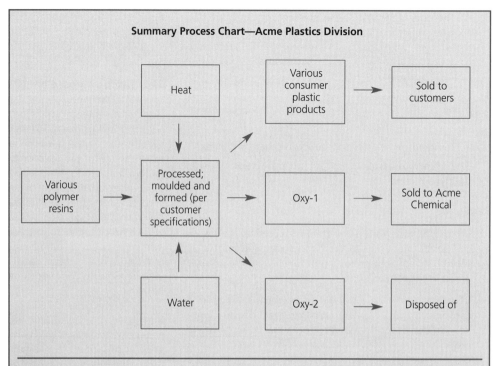

Summary Process Chart—Acme Plastics Division

Additional Comments

Polymer resins used for the process are purchased from U.S. suppliers and shipped to the plant in specially built tanker trucks used by AML. To avoid contamination of the various resins in transit, it is necessary to rinse the inside of each tank with water after each shipment.

Water, obtained from the nearby river, is also used in the process as both an ingredient and a coolant. The coolant water returning to the river is tested regularly to ensure compliance with local regulations.

The process requires considerable heat, which is produced by thermal generators that burn natural gas. The gas arrives by pipe-line from the local gas company. Some of the excess heat is recycled throughout the plant to reduce heating costs in winter.

The process produces two highly flammable liquid by-products, known as Oxy-1 and Oxy-2. Oxy-1 is packaged into 200 L drums and stored until sold to the Acme Chemical Division. Acme Chemical further processes it into a varnish resin and sells this product to various paint manufacturers.

At present, there is no commercially viable use for Oxy-2, which is also stored in 200 L drums and kept in a storage area at the back of the property. When necessary (about twice a year), Acme Plastics contracts We-Take-All Ltd., an independent waste disposal company, to have the drums removed.

EXHIBIT II
Summary of Pumpkin Patch Franchise Contract with the Kogers

Dan: What is your markup policy?

Tom: We have followed the franchisor's guideline of a 100 percent markup on purchase price. Our practice is to mark everything down 20 percent during clearance sales.

Dan: What markdown would it take to clear out your inventory?

Wendy: We would have to have a 50 percent-off sale to clear out about 80 percent, by value, of our inventory. But 50 percent would be madness since we would then be losing money.

Tom: Here are the franchisor's sales forecasts for the next five years, as well as our estimates based on the assumption that our new purchasing policy is a success and results in an increase in sales (see Exhibit IV on page 782).

1. At the beginning of August 1998, the Kogers signed a 10-year Pumpkin Patch franchise agreement, commencing September 1, 1998. The agreement specifies an initial franchise payment of $30,000, with monthly royalties of 7 percent of each month's sales. The franchisor agreed to give the Kogers merchandising advice during the first year. The franchisor supplies the Pumpkin Patch brand of quality clothing for children.

2. The franchisor selected the store site, signed a five-year lease with the mall, and sublet the store to the Kogers. The sublease is for five years commencing September 1, 1998, and requires monthly rental payments of $3,000 plus 2 percent of the month's sales. The Kogers were required to install and pay for fixtures in accordance with designs supplied by the franchisor. The franchise contract requires that the franchisee reimburse the franchisor for the $50,000 lease cancellation fee in the event that the lease is cancelled before the end of the five-year term.

3. The Kogers are required to maintain inventories above $150,000.

EXHIBIT III
Extracts from Financial
Statements of Koger
Limited

KOGER LIMITED EXTRACTS FROM BALANCE SHEET
As at August 31

	1999	1998
Assets		
Cash	$ 3,845	$ 9,000
Inventories	247,465	150,000
Fixtures	25,000	25,000
Less: amortization	(5,000)	—
Franchise fee	30,000	30,000
	$301,310	$214,000
Liabilities		
Accounts payable (Note 1)	$ 35,634	$ 14,000
Royalties payable	8,366	—
Bank loan (Note 2)	90,000	30,000
	134,000	44,000
Shareholders' Equity		
Share Capital (Note 3)	170,000	170,000
Less: loss for year	(2,690)	—
	167,310	170,000
	$301,310	$214,000

Note 1:

Includes $23,500 to suppliers other than the franchisor and $1,750 to the federal government for payroll deductions.

Note 2:

Bank demand loan granted under line of credit negotiated for $90,000 and secured by the Kogers' personal guarantees; interest on the loan is 13 percent.

Note 3:

Cash invested on incorporation in August 1998: represents $100,000 proceeds of first mortgage on the Koger family house and the balance from personal savings.

KOGER LIMITED EXTRACTS FROM STATEMENT OF OPERATIONS
For the year ended August 31, 1999

Sales		$272,144
Cost of sales	$141,000	
Credit card charge (1% of credit)		
card sales)	2,177	
Rent	41,443	
Royalties	19,050	
Utilities	3,000	
Amortization	5,000	
Bank loan interest	4,214	
Insurance	2,500	
Advertising	4,830	
Promotions	5,250	
Business taxes	2,000	
Miscellaneous	9,870	
Wages – regular	29,700	
– part-time	4,800	
		274,834
Profit (Loss)		$ (2,690)

EXHIBIT IV
Koger Limited
Five-Year Sales Forecast

	Franchisor's Forecast	Kogers' Forecast
1999	$330,000	$272,144 (actual)
2000	$412,500	$338,000
2001	$515,625	$464,063
2002	$644,531	$612,305
2003	$805,664	$805,664

The assumption underlying the Kogers' forecast is that the gap between the actual sales and the franchisor's forecast will decline each year until the actual equals the forecast in 2003. The Kogers recognize that this is an optimistic assumption, given the actual numbers of shoppers at the mall. However, the Kogers believe that if the new product lines prove to be successful, this forecast is attainable.

Dan: Let me look at the information, and I will prepare a report outlining my advice. First, I'll explain the process of cash flow management. Then, I'll outline alternative courses of action for you. Your business problems are pressing, so I won't worry about your tax situation now.

The franchisor has been unavailable to help the Kogers but has telephoned them several times about delays in making merchandise and franchise payments. During the last call, the possibility of the store's failing was discussed. In the event of failure, the franchisor stated that he would be prepared to take over ownership of the store and continue to manage the store but would pay only 65 percent of the cost for the year-end inventory. He considered much of the inventory ordered independently by the Kogers to be slow-moving. Any such payment would be net of anything owed to him by the Kogers. This sale would not be subject to the royalties and rental payments that are based on sales revenue. The Kogers would be reimbursed for the book value of the fixtures but would have to settle all outstanding liabilities.

Required

Draft a report to the Kogers in which you

a. Explain the process of cash management.

b. Identify and analyze options available to them regarding their store.

(CICA adapted)

24-23 Fruit Juice Company (FJC) Ltd. was federally incorporated in 1989 and is in the business of bottling, distributing, and promoting the sale of fruit juices. FJC holds a 7 percent share of the Canadian fruit-juice-bottling market. The company has a December 31 year end and has been audited by Rioux Paquin, Public Accountants, (RP) since 1989.

The fruit juice industry started doing well in the health-conscious 1980s and has been relatively unaffected by the recession of the early 1990s, as consumers have continued to buy juice products. Peak sales are in May and June when stores and restaurants stock up for the warm summer months.

FJC sells approximately 90 percent of its products in returnable containers. Customers pay a deposit when they purchase a bottle of juice. The deposit approximates the cost of the bottle to FJC.

FJC was founded by Leo McCulloch and Yen Chan. Leo McCulloch had many years of experience as an importer of concentrated juices. Yen Chan, an Asian investor who provided the financial backing for the venture, became a permanent resident of Canada in 1994. Yen Chan is the President and Chief Operating Officer, while Leo McCulloch has held the position of Vice-President, Operations. Both work out of FJC's Calgary head office. Yen Chan holds 62 percent of FJC common shares and Leo McCulloch 38 percent. There are no other shareholders. Extracts from the audited financial statements as at December 31, 1998, are shown in Exhibit V (on page 783).

Leo McCulloch realized that the amount of time he was spending on the business could cost him his marriage, so in February 1999, he decided to sell his shares in FJC and take early retirement. Yen Chan was not interested in purchasing Leo's shares and, therefore, Leo offered his shares to a group of investors, led by John Sing, a wealthy Toronto businessman. The investors incorporated a numbered company (123 Co.) to buy the common shares. An agreement in principle has been signed, and a draft purchase-and-sale agreement has been prepared by the lawyers who are acting for each of the parties.

The preliminary purchase price for Leo's shares in FJC, based on the December 31, 1998, audited financial statements, has been agreed at $5,369,000, with the effective date for the transaction to be June 30, 1999. The price was determined largely through capitalized-earnings calculations. This price is to be adjusted according to the formula contained in Clause 5.11 of the draft purchase-and-sale agreement, to take into account the financial position of FJC at June 30, 1999. (Extracts from the draft agreement appear in Exhibit VI (on page 784).)

The firm of Marviano and Duncan, Public Accountants, (M & D) has advised John Sing professionally for many years. The investors, through 123 Co., have recently engaged M & D to provide an audit opinion on the net-asset calculation that will be used to determine the final purchase price. Yen Chan has agreed to make the accounting records of FJC available to M & D if necessary. The investors are open to M & D's comments about any improvements to the draft purchase-and-sale agreement.

A draft June 30, 1999, balance sheet has been provided by the controller (see Exhibit VII on page 784). The engagement partner has met with the controller of FJC and has reviewed RP's December 31, 1998, audit working papers. She has dictated notes on the information she gathered (see Exhibit VIII on pages 784 and 785). She has also provided you with notes on her discussion with John Sing's lawyer (see Exhibit IX on page 785).

EXHIBIT V
Extracts from Financial
Statements of FJC

FRUIT JUICE COMPANY EXTRACTS FROM AUDITED BALANCE SHEET
As at December 31

	(in thousands of dollars)	
	1998	1997
Assets		
Cash	$ 5,666	$ 5,416
Accounts receivable	9,568	8,358
Inventory	10,205	9,205
Prepaid expenses	567	675
	26,006	23,654
Property, plant and equipment, net	5,697	5,587
Franchise rights	1,234	1,234
	6,931	6,821
Total assets	$32,937	$30,475
Liabilities and Shareholders' Equity		
Accounts payable and accrued liabilities	$ 5,557	$ 4,678
Income taxes payable	235	124
	5,792	4,802
Long-term debt	12,000	12,000
	17,792	16,802
Share capital — 1,000,000 common shares	4,000	4,000
Retained earnings	11,145	9,673
	15,145	13,673
Total liabilities and shareholders' equity	$32,937	$30,475

FRUIT JUICE COMPANY
EXTRACTS FROM AUDITED STATEMENT OF INCOME
AND RETAINED EARNINGS
For the years ended December 31

	(in thousands of dollars)	
	1998	1997
Revenue	$33,458	$29,859
Cost of sales	24,421	21,200
	9,037	8,659
Administration expenses	5,645	5,456
Selling expenses	935	1,152
	6,580	6,608
Income before income tax	2,457	2,051
Income taxes	985	923
Net income	1,472	1,128
Retained earnings, beginning of year	9,673	8,545
Retained earnings, end of year	$11,145	$ 9,673

Extracts from Accounting Policy Notes

Returnable Containers

Deposits on returnable containers are recorded as revenue when the bottles are shipped. When bottles are returned to FJC, the refunds of deposits are recorded as expenses.

Property, Plant, and Equipment

Amortization is calculated using the declining-balance method, based on the following annual rates:

Building	2%
Equipment	8%
Vehicles	15%

EXHIBIT VI

Extracts from the Draft
Purchase-and-Sale
Agreement

5.10 The preliminary purchase price of the shares is $5,369,000. This price is based on the December 31, 1998, audited financial statements.

5.11 The preliminary purchase price is to be increased (decreased) by 38 percent of the amount by which the net assets in the June 30, 1999, financial statements (as defined in clause 5.13 of this agreement) exceed (fall short of) $25,911,000.

5.12 The June 30, 1999, financial statements will be prepared in accordance with generally accepted accounting principles.

5.13 Net assets are defined as the sum of current assets and property, plant, and equipment less current liabilities but excluding deferred income taxes and lease obligations.

EXHIBIT VII

Fruit Juice Company
Extracts from Draft
Balance Sheet

As at June 30

(in thousands of dollars)

	1999
Assets	
Cash	$6,264
Accounts receivable	12,169
Inventory	8,135
Prepaid expenses	567
	27,135
Property, plant and equipment, net	5,781
Franchise rights	1,234
	7,015
Total assets	$34,150
Liabilities and Shareholders' Equity	
Acounts payable and accrued liabilities	$4,912
Income taxes payable	493
	5,405
Long-term debt	12,000
	17,405
Share capital — 1,000,000 common shares	4,000
Retained earnings	12,745
	16,745
Total liabilities and shareholders' equity	$34,150

EXHIBIT VIII

Partner's Notes from
Discussions with the
Controller and Review
of the December 31,
1998, Audit Working
Papers

1. In general, RP relied heavily on the internal controls of the company in changing the nature and reducing the extent of the year-end substantive testing. Tests of controls revealed no errors.

2. I have assessed risk on this special engagement as follows:
   - Risk is increased due to the use of the financial statements to determine the purchase price.
   - Risk is increased because it is a first-time engagement for M & D.
   - Risk is decreased because the company has good accounting systems and controls.

3. FJC rents a building from Angeline Developments Inc. In 1993, Angeline Developments increased the rent for the property by $5,300 a month, according to a rental agreement signed by both parties. Angeline Developments has never invoiced FJC for the additional rent, so FJC has never paid it. The auditors have been accruing this rent as a liability each year, despite the objections of FJC's controller, who says that it is not a true liability because history shows that the amounts will never be paid. At December 31, 1998, the accrual for the additional rent stood at $328,600.

   My main concern is that Angeline Developments, who is an audit client of mine, could really use the money as the company is in financial difficulty. Its managers would be really pleased if I reminded them about this money that they have forgotten to collect.

4. We were not informed in time to attend the June 30, 1999, inventory count, but personnel from RP were on hand to observe the count.

Continued

EXHIBIT VIII

Partner's Notes from
Discussions with the
Controller and Review
of the December 31,
1998, Audit Working
Papers
(Continued)

5. Our office's resource centre has obtained the following recent nationwide averages for the juice-bottling industry:

Current ratio	4.5:1
Days' sales in accounts receivable (250-day year)	70 days
Inventory turnover	2.5 times per year
Total debt to equity	5:1

6. FJC imports almost all its raw-material juice inputs in bulk in frozen concentrated form. These juices usually come from the U.S. or South America. About 60 percent of the frozen concentrate is orange juice.

7. In early 1999, FJC entered into an agreement with a Florida supplier of frozen concentrated orange juice. As part of this agreement, the supplier has provided FJC with a large holding tank for the type of juice that FJC uses at its Calgary bottling facility. If FJC were to buy this type of tank, it would have to pay between CAN$400,000 and $510,000 according to the controller. FJC has debited capital assets $400,000 and credited selling expenses $400,000 to record the transaction.

   Title to the tank will pass to FJC if it buys at least 3 million pounds of frozen concentrated orange juice a year for the 1999–2003 period at a price that is fixed at the start of the contract. However, this price cannot exceed, at any time, the prevailing market price. At December 31, 1998, the market price was CAN$2.52 a pound.

8. The concentrated juices that FJC buys normally produce juices in a 5-to-1 ratio. On average, half of the sale price of a bottle of juice consists of the cost of the concentrated juice ingredients.

9. A bottling machine appears to be the only leased asset, apart from the building. The lease was classified as an operating lease in the December 31, 1998, financial statements. The terms of the lease are as follows: monthly payments of $3,690 for 5 years, plus $0.02 for each bottle processed on the machine. The machine could have been bought for $113,240 at the inception of the lease.

10. All the accounting records are excellent except the property, plant, and equipment records. These books are in terrible condition with unreconciled differences of up to $250,000 in different places.

11. FJC supports stores and distributors who promote the sale of its products. This is called indirect advertising. Essentially, FJC pays its customers 50 percent of the cost of advertising regardless of the medium used. Customers are reimbursed the amount upon submission of proof that the amounts were expended to support the sale of FJC products. Customers usually take two to three months to submit this documentation because they must wait to pay the supplier of the advertising or promotion services before they can submit their claim. The annual cost of indirect advertising to FJC is nearly $3 million.

EXHIBIT IX

Notes from Discussion
with John Sing's Lawyer

1. Mr. Sing's lawyer would like a liability set up at June 30, 1999, for the 15 million pounds of frozen concentrated orange juice that FJC will have to purchase over the next five years.

2. Mr. Sing's lawyer is very concerned about one of FJC's bottling facilities. The property was purchased in 1993 from a trustee in bankruptcy who was selling off the assets of a bankrupt soft-drink bottler. Leaks of chemicals used in the soft-drink bottling have recently been found to have severely contaminated the ground water in the surrounding area. The lawyer would like M & D to conduct an environmental audit before the deal is finally closed. The lawyer has prepared the following draft of the auditor's report that he wants M & D to sign.

TO THE SHAREHOLDERS OF 123 CO. LTD.:

We have examined the environmental risks and exposure of the Fruit Juice Company as at June 30, 1999, in accordance with generally accepted auditing standards.

In our opinion, satisfactory cleanup in accordance with the applicable environmental legislation would cost $ _____ at June 30, 1999.

Public Accountants
City, Date

It is now July 1999. You are a qualified accountant with M & D and have been put in charge of this engagement. The engagement partner has asked you to provide her with a memo discussing the various issues raised. Your reasoning should be fully supported.

Required

Prepare the memo requested by the partner.

(CICA adapted)

25

ASSURANCE SERVICES: INTERNAL AUDITING AND COMPREHENSIVE AUDITING

AUDITING IN THE PUBLIC SECTOR

The mission of the Department of Advanced Education and Career Development is to set new directions for adult learning and to provide Albertans with an accessible, responsive, and affordable system of quality adult learning. It spent $1.1 billion in 1996–97.

The Auditor General of Alberta's work was comprised of the following:

An audit of the financial statements of the Department for the year ended March 31, 1997. The Auditor General's report was qualified because the accrual basis of accounting was not used, certain employee-related liabilities and costs were not recorded, certain program costs were not allocated to the correct departments, and all accountable entities were not consolidated.

The Auditor General's office performed the following additional work:

- Examination of processes followed and information gathered when reviewing post-secondary business plans
- Examination of systems used to assess the adequacy of capital planning at post-secondary institutions
- Reporting on results of certain key performance indicator data
- Examination of systems used to measure and report on the performance of certain programs and contracts
- Examination of the University of Alberta's Board governance system
- Completion of a year 2000 risk questionnaire

Internal auditors and auditors general departments (government auditors employed by the federal and provincial governments) perform a significant amount of financial auditing similar to that done by public accounting firms. In addition, public accounting firms assist the auditors general with audits of government units. The concepts and methodologies discussed throughout this book apply to audits by internal auditors and auditors general departments and to audits of government units by public accounting firms. The first part of this chapter describes the role of internal auditors with particular emphasis on financial auditing.

The next part of the chapter deals with operational auditing. In operational audits, the focus is on whether an organization's operating procedures are efficient and effective. Operational audits are in demand, and, while they are principally done by internal auditors and auditors general departments (where they are usually referred to as value-for-money or V-F-M audits), they also represent a growing segment of public accounting firms' activities. This portion of the chapter deals with differences between financial and operational auditing and provides an overview of performing these audits. A number of examples are provided to assist in understanding the nature of these engagements.

The last part of the chapter deals with comprehensive audits, the financial, compliance, and value-for-money audits conducted by the federal and provincial governments' auditors general departments. It describes the Public Sector Accounting Board (PSAB) and the public sector auditing standards issued by its predecessor, the Public Sector Accounting and Auditing Board (PSAAB). It also describes the CCAF-FCVI and the standards that that body has suggested for effectiveness reporting.

INTERNAL AUDITING

OBJECTIVE 25-1

Understand the role of internal auditors.

As discussed in Chapter 1, internal auditors are employed by companies to do both financial and operational auditing. Their role in auditing has increased dramatically in the past two decades, primarily because of the increased size and complexity of many corporations.

In financial auditing, internal auditors are responsible for evaluating whether their company's internal controls are designed and operate effectively and whether the financial statements are fairly presented. Because internal auditors spend all of their time with one company, their knowledge about the company's operations and internal controls is much greater than the external auditors' knowledge.

Guidelines for performing internal audits for companies are not as well defined as for external audits. This occurs because of the wide variety of internal audits. Based on user requirements, the audit purpose, audit methods, and audit reports must be customized. Management of different companies may have widely varying expectations of the type and extent of financial auditing to be done by internal auditors. For example, management of one company may decide that internal auditors should evaluate the internal controls and financial statements of every division annually, whereas others may decide that a five-year rotation is sufficient.

INSTITUTE OF INTERNAL AUDITORS

Internal auditors look to the Institute of Internal Auditors (IIA) for professional guidance. The IIA is an organization that functions for internal auditors much as the CICA does for CAs, the CGAAC for CGAs, and the SMAC for CMAs; it establishes ethical and practice standards, provides education, and encourages professionalism for its approximately 35,000 members. The IIA has played a major role in the increasing influence of internal auditing. For example, the IIA has established a highly regarded certification program resulting in the designation of Certified Internal Auditor (CIA) for those who meet the testing and experience requirements.

The IIA Practice Standards include five categories of guidance that encompass both financial and operational auditing: independence, professional proficiency, scope of work, performance of audit work, and management of the internal auditing department.

RELATIONSHIP OF INTERNAL AND EXTERNAL AUDITORS

There are both differences and similarities between the responsibilities and conduct of audits by internal and external auditors. The primary difference is to whom each party is responsible. The external auditor is responsible to financial statement users who rely on the auditor to add credibility to the statements. The internal auditor is responsible to management. Even with this important difference, there are many similarities between the two groups. Both must be competent as auditors and remain objective in performing their work and reporting their results. They both, for example, follow a similar methodology in performing their audits, including planning and performing tests of controls and substantive tests. Similarly, they both use the audit risk model and materiality in deciding the extent of their tests and evaluating results. Their decisions about materiality and risks may differ, however, because external users may have different needs from management's.

External auditors rely on internal auditors through the use of the audit risk model. Auditors significantly reduce control risk and thereby reduce substantive testing if internal auditors are effective. The fee reduction of the external auditor is typically substantial when there is a highly regarded internal audit function. External auditors typically consider internal auditors effective if they are independent of the operating units being evaluated, competent and well trained, and have performed relevant audit tests of the internal controls and financial statements.

Section 5050, "Using the Work of Internal Audit," permits the external auditor to use the internal auditor for direct assistance on the audit. This means that the external auditor is permitted to treat internal auditors much like his or her own audit staff. The incentive for management is a reduced audit fee, whereas the incentive for the public accounting firm is retaining the client. The risk to the external auditor is the lack of competent and independent performance by the internal auditors. Before using internal auditors, the external auditor must be confident of their competence, independence, and objectivity. In addition, external auditors typically reperform a sample of the internal auditor's work to make certain that it was done correctly.

OPERATIONAL AUDITING

Although *operational auditing* is generally understood to deal with efficiency and effectiveness, there is less agreement on the use of that term than one might expect. Many people prefer to use the terms "management auditing" or "performance auditing" instead of "operational auditing" to describe the review of organizations for efficiency and effectiveness. Those people typically describe operational auditing broadly, including evaluating internal controls and even testing those controls for effectiveness (tests of controls). Others do not distinguish among the terms "performance auditing," "management auditing," and "operational auditing."

We prefer to use the term "operational auditing" broadly, as long as the purpose of testing is to determine the effectiveness or efficiency of any part of an organization. Testing the effectiveness of internal controls by an internal auditor is therefore part of operational auditing if the purpose is to help an organization operate its business more effectively or efficiently. Similarly, the determination of whether a company has adequately trained assembly-line personnel is also part of operational auditing if the purpose is to determine whether the company is effectively and efficiently producing products.

DIFFERENCES BETWEEN OPERATIONAL (INTERNAL) AND FINANCIAL AUDITING

OBJECTIVE 25-2

Distinguish internal auditing from financial auditing.

Three major differences exist between internal/operational auditing and financial auditing: the purpose of the audit, the distribution of the reports, and the inclusion of nonfinancial areas in operational auditing.

Purpose of the audit The major distinction between financial and operational auditing is the purpose of the tests. Financial auditing emphasizes whether historical information was correctly recorded. Operational auditing emphasizes effectiveness and efficiency. The financial audit is oriented to the past, whereas an operational audit concerns operating performance for the future. An operational auditor, for example, may evaluate whether a type of new material is being purchased at the lowest cost to save money on future raw-material purchases.

Distribution of the reports For financial auditing, the report typically goes to many users of financial statements, such as shareholders and bankers; whereas operational auditing reports are intended primarily for management. As indicated in Chapter 2, well-defined wording is needed for financial auditing reports as a result of the widespread distribution of the reports. Because of the limited distribution of operational reports and the diverse nature of audits for efficiency and effectiveness, operational auditing reports vary considerably from audit to audit.

Inclusion of nonfinancial areas Operational audits cover any aspect of efficiency and effectiveness in an organization and can therefore involve a wide variety of activities. For example, evaluating the effectiveness of an advertising program or the efficiency of factory employees would be part of an operational audit. Financial audits are limited to matters that directly affect the fairness of financial statement presentations. Operational audits also differ from financial audits in that financial audits are done on an annual basis. Operational audits are done cyclically in that parts of the organization are audited each year and the entire organization is audited over a five- or six-year period.

EFFECTIVENESS VERSUS EFFICIENCY

Effectiveness refers to the accomplishment of objectives, whereas efficiency refers to the resources used to achieve those objectives. An example of effectiveness is the production of parts without defects. Efficiency concerns whether those parts are produced at minimum cost. Economy, which may be defined as acquiring goods or services of suitable quality at the best price, is often included with efficiency.

Before an operational audit for effectiveness can be performed, there must be specific criteria for what is meant by effectiveness. An example of an operational audit for effectiveness would be to assess whether the elevator maintenance department of a hotel chain has met its assigned objective of achieving elevator safety in the chain's many hotels. Before the operational auditor can reach a conclusion about the department's effectiveness, criteria for elevator safety must be set. For example, is the objective to see that all elevators in the chain's hotels are inspected at least once a year? Is the objective to ensure that no fatalities occurred due to elevator breakdowns, or that no breakdowns occurred?

EFFICIENCY

As with effectiveness, there must be defined criteria for what is meant by doing things more efficiently before operational auditing can be meaningful. It is often easier to set efficiency than effectiveness criteria if efficiency is defined as reducing cost without reducing effectiveness. For example, if two different production processes manufacture a product of identical quality, the process with the lower cost is considered more efficient.

Table 25-1 outlines several types of inefficiencies that frequently occur and often are uncovered through operational auditing.

TABLE 25-1

TYPES OF INEFFICIENCIES

TYPES OF INEFFICIENCY	EXAMPLE
• Acquisition of goods and services is excessively costly.	• Bids for purchases of materials are not required.
• Raw materials are not available for production when needed.	• An entire assembly line must be shut down because necessary materials were not ordered.
• There is duplication of effort by employees.	• Identical production records are kept by both the accounting and production departments because they are unaware of each other's activities.
• Work is done that serves no purpose.	• Copies of vendor's invoices and receiving reports are sent to the production department where they are filed without ever being used.
• There are too many employees.	• The office work could be done effectively with one less secretary.

RELATIONSHIP BETWEEN OPERATIONAL AUDITING AND INTERNAL CONTROLS

In Chapter 9, it was stated that management establishes internal controls to help it meet its own goals. Certainly, two important goals of all organizations are efficiency and effectiveness. The following four concerns in setting up good internal controls were identified and discussed in Chapter 9:

- To maintain reliable systems
- To safeguard assets including records
- To optimize the use of resources
- To prevent and detect error and fraud

Each of those four concerns can be part of operational auditing if the purpose is to achieve efficient and effective operations. For example, reliable cost accounting information is important to management in deciding such things as which products to continue and the selling price of products. Similarly, failure to safeguard assets such as accounts receivable files on a computer could result in the company being unable to collect money owing when it is due.

There are two significant differences in internal control evaluation and testing for financial and operational auditing: the purpose of the evaluation and testing of internal controls, and the normal scope of internal control evaluation.

The primary purpose of internal control evaluation for financial auditing is to determine the extent of substantive audit testing required. The purpose of operational auditing is to evaluate efficiency and effectiveness of internal control and make recommendations to management. Although control procedures might be evaluated in the same way for both financial and operational auditing, their purpose differs. To illustrate, an operational auditor might determine if internal verification procedures for duplicate sales invoices are effective to ensure that the company does not offend customers but also receives all money owed. A financial auditor often does the same internal control evaluation, but the primary purpose is to reduce confirmation of accounts receivable or other substantive procedures. A secondary purpose, however, of many financial audits is to make operational recommendations to management.

The scope of internal control evaluation for financial audits is restricted to matters affecting financial statement accuracy, whereas operational auditing concerns any control affecting efficiency or effectiveness. Therefore, for example, an operational audit could be concerned with policies and procedures established in the marketing department to determine the effectiveness of catalogues used to market products.

TYPES OF OPERATIONAL AUDITS

There are three broad categories of operational audits: functional, organizational, and special assignments. In each case, part of the audit is likely to concern evaluating internal controls for efficiency and effectiveness.

FUNCTIONAL AUDITS

Functions are a means of categorizing the activities of a business, such as the billing function or production function. There are many different ways to categorize and subdivide functions. For example, there is an accounting function, but there are also cash disbursement, cash receipt, and payroll disbursement functions. There is a payroll function, but there are also hiring, timekeeping, and payroll disbursement functions.

As the name implies, a functional audit deals with one or more functions in an organization. It could concern, for example, the payroll function for a division or for the company as a whole.

A functional audit has the advantage of permitting specialization by auditors. Certain auditors within an internal audit staff can develop considerable expertise in an area, such as production engineering. They can more efficiently spend all their time auditing in that area. A disadvantage of functional auditing is the failure to evaluate interrelated functions. The production engineering function, for example, interacts with manufacturing and other functions in an organization.

ORGANIZATIONAL AUDITS

An operational audit of an organization deals with an entire organizational unit, such as a department, branch, or subsidiary. The emphasis in an organizational audit is on how efficiently and effectively functions interact. The plan of organization and the methods to coordinate activities are especially important in this type of audit.

SPECIAL ASSIGNMENT AUDITS

Special operational auditing assignments arise at the request of management. There are a wide variety of such audits. Examples include determining the cause of an ineffective information system, investigating the possibility of fraud or other irregularities in a division, and making recommendations for reducing the cost of a manufactured product.

WHO PERFORMS OPERATIONAL AUDITS?

Operational audits are usually performed by one of three groups: internal auditors, government auditors, or public accounting firms.

Internal auditors are in such a unique position to perform operational audits that some people use internal auditing and operational auditing interchangeably. It is, however, inappropriate to conclude that all operational auditing is done by internal auditors or that internal auditors do only operational auditing. Many internal audit departments do both operational and financial audits as well as compliance audits. Often, operational and financial audits are done simultaneously. An advantage that internal auditors have in doing operational audits is that they spend all their time working for the company they are auditing. They thereby develop considerable knowledge about the company and its business, which is essential to effective operational auditing.

To maximize their effectiveness, the internal audit department staff should report to the audit committee of the board of directors, although in practice they often report to the president or a senior vice-president. In the latter case, they should also have access to and ongoing communications with the audit committee. This organizational structure helps internal auditors remain independent. For example, if internal auditors report to the controller, it is difficult for them to evaluate independently and make recommendations to senior management about inefficiencies in the controller's operations.

The Canadian and provincial auditors general also perform operational auditing, which is more commonly known as *value-for-money auditing* in the public sector, as part of comprehensive auditing. Discussion of operational auditing from their perspective will be discussed as part of the discussion of comprehensive auditing later in the chapter.

There are other auditors employed by governments such as Revenue Canada auditors and provincial tax auditors. However, the discussion in this chapter focuses on government auditors who do operational or value-for-money audits.

THE AUDITOR GENERAL'S OFFICE EXAMINES THE SYSTEMS DEVELOPMENT PROCESS

The federal government has undertaken to develop many new information systems. Systems under development involve budgets totalling *billions* of dollars. Every year, the federal Office of the Auditor General (OAG) examines some of these projects. Reports are printed as chapters in the annual *Report of the Auditor General of Canada to the House of Commons*.

Extracts from Chapter 23, December 1997, provide some insight into these audits. The Audit objective for this work was:

. . . to conduct risk assessments of three in-house development initiatives relative to best practices in management.

Sources for criteria were identified as coming from a Symposium on Best Practices, from industry best practices, and from Treasury Board policies and guidelines. The scope was specified as three in-house systems that, at the time of the audit, were the most significant in government and by their size also serviced Canadians directly, and an update review of eight other projects that had been examined in previous years.

The OAG considered project planning, project tracking, oversight, and quality assurance for each project. Weaknesses were found in all areas. The OAG presented its findings with management's response. A key flaw was performance measurement. All projects were late, had to

> **have additional funds added, or were reduced in scope for the same amount of funding.**
>
> **Ironically, the government does not always apply to itself the performance measures it demands of the [information systems] contractor.**
>
> Source: "Systems Under Development: Taking Charge," *Report of the Auditor General of Canada to the House of Commons*, Chapter 23, December 1997.

PUBLIC ACCOUNTING FIRMS

When public accounting firms do an audit of historical financial statements, part of the audit usually consists of identifying operational problems and making recommendations that may benefit the audit client. The recommendations can be made orally, but they are typically made by use of a *management letter*. Management letters were discussed in Chapter 21.

The background knowledge about a client's business that an external auditor must obtain in doing an audit often provides useful information for giving operational recommendations. For example, suppose the auditor determined that inventory turnover for a client slowed considerably during the current year. The auditor is likely to determine the cause of the reduction to evaluate the possibility of obsolete inventory that would misstate the financial statements. In determining the cause of the reduced inventory turnover, the auditor may identify operational causes, such as ineffective inventory acquisition policies, that can be brought to the attention of management. An auditor who has a broad business background and experience with similar businesses is more likely to be effective at providing clients with relevant operational recommendations than a person who lacks those qualities.

It is also common for a client to engage a public accounting firm to do operational auditing for one or more specific parts of its business. Usually, such an engagement would occur only if the company does not have an internal audit staff or the internal audit staff lacks expertise in a certain area. In most cases, a management advisory staff of the public accounting firm, rather than the auditing staff, performs these services. For example, a company can ask the public accounting firm to evaluate the efficiency and effectiveness of its computer systems.

> ## PUBLIC WORKS SELECTS PRICEWATERHOUSECOOPERS TO HELP OVERHAUL OPERATIONS
>
> **PricewaterhouseCoopers was awarded a contract, valued at $999,932, to conduct a review of "the use of human, financial and technological resources within the RCMP headquarters and across the country." The purpose of the project is to conduct a resource review of the past five years and make projections for the force's priorities and resources for the next three to five years. The consulting firm faces the challenge of finding "potential areas where efficiencies can be made and savings can occur" for the RCMP, which has approximately 19,500 employees. Consultants are given access to classified information to conduct the review and must have federal government security clearance to be part of the project.**
>
> Source: *The Globe and Mail*, March 15, 1999, p. B13.

INDEPENDENCE AND COMPETENCE OF OPERATIONAL AUDITORS

The two most important qualities for an operational auditor are *independence* and *competence*.

To whom the auditor reports is important to ensure that investigation and recommendations are made without bias. Independence is seldom a problem for public accounting firm auditors because they are not employed by the company being audited. As stated earlier, independence of internal auditors is enhanced by having the internal audit department report to the audit committee or president. Similarly, government auditors should report to a level above the operating departments. The Canadian Auditor General, for example, reports to an all-party committee of Parliament as a means of enhancing independence.

The responsibilities of operational auditors can also affect their independence. The auditor should not be responsible for performing operating functions in a company or for correcting deficiencies when ineffective or inefficient operations are found. For example, it would negatively affect their independence if auditors were responsible for designing an automated information system for acquisitions or for correcting it if deficiencies were found during an audit of the acquisitions system.

It is acceptable for auditors to recommend changes in operations, but operating personnel must have the authority to accept or reject the recommendations. If auditors had the authority to require implementation of their recommendations, they would actually have the responsibility for auditing their own work the next time an audit was conducted. Independence would therefore be reduced.

The Institute of Internal Auditors considers independence of internal auditors critical. It has established in its Statement of Responsibilities of Internal Auditing a special requirement for independence, as follows:

> Internal auditors should be independent of the activities they audit. Internal auditors are independent when they can carry out their work freely and objectively. Independence permits internal auditors to render the impartial and unbiased judgments essential to the proper conduct of audits. It is achieved through organizational status and objectivity.
>
> Organizational status should be sufficient to assure a broad range of audit coverage, and adequate consideration of and effective action on audit findings and recommendations.
>
> Objectivity requires that internal auditors have an independent mental attitude and an honest belief in their work product. Drafting procedures, designing, installing, and operating systems are not audit functions. Performing such activities is presumed to impair audit objectivity.

Competence is, of course, necessary to determine the cause of operational problems and to make appropriate recommendations. Competence is a major problem when operational auditing deals with wide-ranging operating problems. For example, imagine the difficulties of finding qualified internal auditors who can evaluate both the effectiveness of an advertising program and the efficiency of a production assembly process. The internal audit staff doing that type of operational auditing would presumably have to include some personnel with backgrounds in marketing and others with backgrounds in production.

CRITERIA FOR EVALUATING EFFICIENCY AND EFFECTIVENESS

OBJECTIVE 25-4

Plan and perform an operational audit.

A major difficulty found in operational auditing, as with assurance services discussed in Chapters 23 and 24, is determining specific criteria for evaluating whether operations have been efficient and effective. In auditing historical financial statements, GAAP are the broad criteria for evaluating fair presentation. Audit objectives are used to set more specific criteria in deciding whether GAAP have been followed. In operational auditing, no such well-defined criteria exist.

One approach to setting criteria for operational auditing is stating that the objectives are to determine whether some aspect of the entity could be made more effective or efficient and to recommend improvements. While perhaps adequate for experienced and well-trained auditors, this poorly defined approach would be difficult for most auditors to follow.

SPECIFIC CRITERIA

More specific criteria are usually desirable before operational auditing is started. For example, suppose you are doing an operational audit of the equipment layout in plants for a company. The following are some specific criteria, stated in the form of questions, that might be used to evaluate plant layouts:

- Were all plant layouts approved by home office engineering at the time of original design?
- Has home office engineering done a re-evaluation study of plant layout in the past five years?
- Is each piece of equipment operating at 60 percent of capacity or more for at least three months each year?
- Does the layout facilitate the movement of new materials to the production flow?
- Does the layout facilitate the production of finished goods?
- Does the layout facilitate the movement of finished goods to distribution centres?
- Does the plant layout effectively utilize existing equipment?
- Is the safety of employees endangered by the plant layout?

SOURCES OF CRITERIA

There are several sources that the operational auditor can utilize in developing specific evaluation criteria. These include the following:

Historical performance   A simple set of criteria can be based on actual results from prior periods (or audits). The idea behind using these criteria is to determine whether things have become better or worse in comparison. The advantage of these criteria is that they are easy to derive; however, they may not provide much insight into how well or poorly the audited entity is really doing.

Benchmarking   Most entities subject to an operational audit are not unique; there are many similar entities within the overall organization or outside it. In those cases, the performance data of comparable entities are an excellent source for developing criteria for benchmarking. For internal comparable entities, the data are usually readily available. When the comparable entities are outside the organization, they are often willing to make such information available. It is also often available through industry groups and governmental regulatory agencies.

Engineered standards   In many types of operational auditing engagements, it may be possible and appropriate to develop criteria based on engineered standards — for example, time and motion studies to determine production output rates. These criteria are often time-consuming and costly to develop as they require considerable expertise; however, they may be very effective in solving a major operational problem and well worth the cost. It is also possible that some standards can be developed by industry groups for use by all their members, thereby spreading the cost and reducing it for each participant. These groups may be within the industry of the subject organization or may be functional such as an application system's users' organization.

Published standards or criteria   As discussed in the previous chapter, there are ISO (International Organization for Standardization) standards for a variety of management processes, such as quality control management and environmental management. Published best practices for the development of automated information systems are available from the Software Engineering Institute (SEI) at Carnegie Mellon University, which was initially funded by the U.S. Department of Defence. Details are available at **www.sei.cmu.edu.**

Discussion and agreement   Sometimes objective criteria are difficult or costly to obtain, and criteria are developed through simple discussion and agreement. The parties involved in this process should include management of the entity to be audited, the operational auditor, and the entity or persons to whom the findings will be reported.

PHASES IN OPERATIONAL AUDITING

There are three phases in an operational audit: planning, evidence accumulation and evaluation, and reporting and follow-up.

PLANNING

The planning in an operational audit is similar to that discussed in earlier chapters for an audit of historical financial statements. Like audits of financial statements, the operational auditor must determine the scope of the engagement and communicate it to the organizational unit. It is also necessary to staff the engagement properly, obtain background information about the organizational unit, understand internal control, and decide on the appropriate evidence to accumulate.

The major difference between planning an operational audit and planning a financial audit is the extreme diversity in operational audits. Because of this diversity, it is often difficult to determine specific objectives of an operational audit. The objectives will be based on the criteria developed for the engagement. As discussed in the preceding sections, these will depend on the specific circumstances at hand. For example, the objectives for an operational audit of the effectiveness of internal controls over petty cash would be dramatically different from those of an operational audit of the efficiency of a research and development department.

Another difference is that staffing is often more complicated in an operational audit than in a financial audit. This again is because of the breadth of the engagements. Not only are the areas diverse — for example, production control, advertising, and strategy planning — but the objectives within those areas often require special technical skills. For example, the auditor may need an engineering background to evaluate performance on a major construction project.

Finally, it is important to spend more time with the interested parties reaching consensus on the terms of the engagement and the criteria for evaluation in an operational audit than in a financial audit. This was alluded to in the preceding section for criteria developed through discussion. Regardless of the source of the criteria for evaluation, it is essential that the auditee, the auditor, and the sponsor of the engagement (e.g., the audit committee) be in clear and complete agreement on the objectives and criteria involved. That agreement will facilitate effective and successful completion of the operational audit.

EVIDENCE ACCUMULATION AND EVALUATION

The seven types of evidence studied in Chapter 6 and used throughout the book are equally applicable for operational auditing. Because internal controls and operating procedures are a critical part of operational auditing, it is common to extensively use documentation, client inquiry, and observation. Confirmation and reperformance are used less extensively for most operational audits than for financial audits because accuracy is not the purpose of most operational audits.

To illustrate evidence accumulation in operational auditing, we return to the example discussed earlier about evaluating the safety of elevators for a chain of hotels. Assume that there is agreement that the objective is to determine whether an inspection is made annually of each elevator in every hotel in the chain by a competent inspector. To satisfy the completeness objective, the auditor would, for example, examine blueprints of the hotel buildings and elevator locations and trace them to the head office's master list to ensure that all elevators are included in the population. Additional tests on newly constructed hotels would be appropriate to assess the timeliness with which the central listing is updated.

Assuming that the head office list is determined to be complete, the auditor can select a sample of elevator locations and evidence can be collected as to the timing and frequency of inspections. The auditor may want to consider inherent risk by doing heavier sampling of older elevators with previous safety defects. The auditor may also want to examine evidence to determine whether the elevator inspectors were competent to evaluate elevator safety. The auditor may, for example, evaluate inspectors' qualifications by reviewing résumés, training programs, competency exams, and performance reports.

It is also likely that the auditor would want to reperform the inspection procedures for a sample of elevators to obtain evidence of inconsistencies in reported and actual conditions.

In the same manner as for financial audits, operational auditors must accumulate sufficient appropriate evidence to afford a reasonable basis for a conclusion about the objectives being tested. In the elevator example, the auditor must accumulate sufficient evidence about elevator safety inspections. After the evidence is accumulated, the auditor must decide whether it is reasonable to conclude that an inspection is made annually of each elevator in each hotel owned by the chain by a competent inspector.

REPORTING AND FOLLOW-UP

Two major differences between operational and financial auditing reports affect operational auditing reports. First, in operational audits, the report is usually sent only to management, with a copy to the unit being audited. The lack of third-party users reduces the need for standardized wording in operational auditing reports. Second, the diversity of operational audits requires a tailoring of each report to address the scope of the audit, findings, and recommendations. The report may include responses to the auditor's findings by the auditee.

The combination of these two factors results in major differences in operational auditing reports. Report writing often takes a significant amount of time to communicate audit findings and recommendations clearly.

Follow-up is important in operational auditing when recommendations are made to management. The purpose is to determine whether the recommended changes were made, and if not, why.

EXAMPLES OF OPERATIONAL AUDIT FINDINGS

Each issue of the *Internal Auditor*, a bimonthly publication of the Institute of Internal Auditors, includes several internal operational audit findings submitted by practising internal auditors. In reviewing a multitude of these reported findings, we concluded that almost all of them relate to efficiency rather than effectiveness. We believe the reason is that readers of the journal find efficiency findings more interesting reading than those related to effectiveness. If someone can state, for example, that an operational audit resulted in a savings of $68,000, it is likely to be more interesting than reporting on improved accuracy of financial reporting. The following examples from the *Internal Auditor* include two related to effectiveness and the rest to efficiency.

Acquisition Audits Save $150,000

Wanting to expand their share of the market, the company entered into agreements to acquire two smaller but similar companies. To help determine the fairness of the prices for the proposed purchases, the internal auditor performed several acquisition audits.

The internal auditor found one company's net worth overstated by approximately $50,000 owing to obsolete inventory, idle assets, and unrecorded liabilities. The internal auditor also found the company was committed to irrevocable lease agreements totalling $700,000 as well as purchase agreements amounting to $500,000. The audit's results caused management to reduce the purchase price by $50,000 and also revise its post-acquisition plans.

During the audit of another company's books, the internal auditor found unrecorded travel and entertainment reports, salespersons' commissions, and purchase invoices. This finding alone reduced the net worth of the company by about $100,000. The auditor also found an improper sales cutoff for the period which would cause a future overstatement of the company's net worth.

As a result of this audit, the purchase price was reduced for a savings of more than $100,000. The lack of controls which caused the overstatement of the company's net worth was corrected as a result of the internal auditor's recommendations.[1]

Use the Right Tool

The company leased 25 heavy-duty trucks for use by service employees who installed and repaired about 20,000 vending machines in a large metropolitan area. All of the trucks were equipped with hydraulic lift-gates for loading and unloading vending machines.

The internal auditor found that only a few of the trucks were actually delivering and picking up vending machines. The large majority of the trucks were used for service calls which consisted of on-the-scene repair of coin boxes or other simple adjustments not requiring the hydraulic lift-gates.

The auditor recommended most of the heavy-duty trucks be phased out and replaced by conventional light vans. Management agreed and the savings in lease rates and operating expenses were estimated at $25,000 a year.[2]

Dog-Gone Revenues

During a review of the county agency responsible for collecting dog-licensing fees, the auditor wondered whether a lot of dogs did not live very long or the dog owners were not renewing the annual dog licences as the law required. Fortunately for dog lovers, the auditor found the latter to be true. The auditor determined that the main reason for the nonrenewals was that no follow-up procedures existed. The county agency had never contacted owners about the nonrenewal of the dog licences.

The auditor knew that another county's dog-licensing agency mailed a reminder letter to dog owners when the licence was not renewed and over a third of the owners who received the letter paid the fee. The auditor recommended such a procedure be instituted, and, as a result, more than $40,000 in renewal fees were collected for an expenditure of less than $1,000.[3]

Lapping of Accounts Receivable

The company's treasurer saw the employee on a Saturday in Las Vegas and at work on Friday in New York and on Monday also. The employee worked late a few evenings each week and this was attributed to diligence. The employee never took a vacation, but claimed he needed extra money and took the vacation time as extra pay. The employee's duties were to open the mail, sort the cheques, count the cash, prepare the bank deposit, and post the accounts receivable ledger. Oh yes, the employee worked for a travel agency that received a great deal of cash from customers.

The perfect setup for lapping . . . as the auditor discovered.

After the Las Vegas incident, the company's treasurer thought it might be a good idea to have the auditor go over the books rather than wait for the year-end closing audit. Not that there was anything wrong, but seeing the employee in Las Vegas, well . . .

---

[1]From "Round Table," *Internal Auditor* by The Institute of Internal Auditors, Inc., 249 Maitland Avenue, Altamonte Springs, FL 32701. Reprinted with permission.

[2]Ibid.

[3]Ibid.

While reviewing deposit slips, the auditor found the details on 75 percent were different from what was recorded in cash receipts and posted to the accounts-receivable ledger. The auditor also determined from customers that cheques had not been credited on the recorded deposit date, but on a subsequent date. No doubt about it, the employee was manipulating the accounts receivable for personal gain, but by how much?

Fortunately for the auditor, the employee gave customers a receipt whenever cash was received and most of the customers had retained their receipts. The auditor secured some copies of these receipts and traced them to the deposit slips prepared on the same dates as the receipts. None of the slips agreed with the signed receipts. In fact, almost no cash was ever deposited. The amount of manipulation of the books was monumental — no wonder the employee worked nights and never had time for a vacation.

As we said, it was a perfect setup for lapping. No separation of duties, confirmation of accounts receivable, or internal controls. The auditor is still trying to determine the extent of loss.[4]

The following examples of value-for-money audits were extracted from the *1998 Annual Report of the Provincial Auditor of Ontario to the Legislative Assembly*, presented by Erik Peters in the fall of 1998. Twelve reports on value-for-money audits were completed, as well as a summary of a special report on the government's progress in dealing with the year 2000 issue. Electronic versions of the report are available at **www.gov.on.ca/opa**. Several departments were indicated as achieving their objectives and performing effectively. The following two situations provide examples where significant weaknesses were found:

Ministry of Natural Resources — Financial Controls Review

The Office of the Provincial Auditor (OPA) reviewed financial controls, systems, and procedures. The objectives stated were to "ensure that expenditures were properly authorized, processed and recorded, and that revenues were properly billed, collected and recorded." The auditors observed that the Ministry's accountable advance account had accumulated errors totalling $1.3 million. Poor controls over payroll resulted in employees being paid when they did not work and being paid incorrect termination amounts. There was also a concern that water power fees received during the 1997/98 fiscal year were appropriately collected.

Recommendations included: proper record keeping, investigation of errors accumulated over a five-year period, collection of employee advances, better payroll controls, and billing and collection processes to collect water power fees.

Ministry of the Solicitor General and Correctional Services — Review of Ontario Provincial Police

The OPA compared stated Ministry objectives with actual performance. It found that the OPP (Ontario Provincial Police) had not fully implemented community policing initiatives and needed additional methods to measure success in reducing road fatalities and personal injuries. It also found mismatches between hours worked and service levels. Five municipalities had not been billed for OPP services totalling $23 million for three years as of the end of 1997. Five others had been billed but had not paid for about $6.6 million of OPP services since 1993.

---

[4]Ibid.

The Public Sector Accounting Board (PSAB) was introduced in Chapter 1 as one of the three Canadian Institute of Chartered Accountants' standard-setting bodies; the other two are the Accounting Standards Board and the Assurance Standards Board. The PSAB is responsible for issuing accounting standards that contain recommendations dealing with accounting issues in the public sector. Prior to March 1999, this board was called the Public Sector Accounting and Auditing Board (PSAAB). However, effective March 1999, the Assurance Standards Board (ASB) assumed responsibility for public sector auditing, so PSAAB lost one of its As. At that time, the ASB's size and composition was expanded. Thus, over the next year or two, auditing recommendations in the *CICA Handbook* will be reorganized to effectively integrate public sector auditing.

Paragraph .03 of "Introduction to Public Sector Accounting and Auditing Recommendations" (effective February 1999) of the then *PSAAB Handbook* indicated that the public sector refers to "federal, provincial, territorial, and local governments, government organizations, organizations jointly owned by two or more governments, and school boards." Subsequent paragraphs defined government organizations and indicated that generally the Accounting Recommendations applied except to business-type organizations (e.g., the Manitoba Telephone System), which follow the *CICA Handbook*, and not-for-profit government organizations, which would follow the not-for-profit sections of the *CICA Handbook*. Paragraph .13 indicated that the Auditing Recommendations applied to all entities in the public sector.

As was pointed out in Chapter 1, under various legislation, the federal and provincial governments are required to have comprehensive audits of the many government departments for which they are responsible. In addition, as was mentioned in Chapter 1, federal Crown corporations are required to have both annual financial audits and special examinations (essentially value-for-money audits) performed on their operations and activities at least once every five years.

The CCAF-FCVI was also introduced in Chapter 1.[5] It conducts research into, publishes material about, brings together people interested in, and provides courses dealing with comprehensive auditing. The theme that runs through the reports of the Auditor General of Canada, Denis Desautels, and the provincial auditors general, through material developed and disseminated by the CCAF-FCVI and through the (former) PSAAB standards, is accountability. Accountability has been defined as ". . . an obligation on the part of an individual or group to reveal, to explain, and to justify the discharge of responsibilities [conferred on the individual or group] . . . ."[6] Comprehensive auditing, through its combination of financial audits, compliance audits, and value-for-money audits, helps assess whether accountability has been served in a more complete way than does a financial audit alone.

---

[5]The interested reader is directed to the CCAF-FCVI, whose offices are in Ottawa. The CCAF-FCVI has published and continues to publish a wealth of interesting material. Much of the material in this part of Chapter 25 is drawn from CCAF-FCVI material. Of particular interest is *Accountability, Performance Reporting, Comprehensive Audit — An Integrated Perspective* written by Guy Leclerc, W. David Moynagh, Jean-Pierre Boisclair, and Hugh R. Hanson and published by the CCAF-FCVI in 1996. It contains a thorough discussion of accountability, performance reporting, and comprehensive auditing theory and practice.

[6]Leclerc, Guy, W. David Moynagh, Jean-Pierre Boisclair, and Hugh R. Hanson, *Accountability, Performance Reporting, Comprehensive Audit — An Integrated Perspective*, Ottawa: CCAF-FCVI, 1996, p. 44.

ASB Public Sector Auditing Recommendation General Standards Section 5000, "Auditing in the Public Sector," provides a setting for the auditing recommendations that follow it. As was pointed out earlier, a comprehensive audit has three components. Section 5200 is entitled "Audit of Financial Statements in the Public Sector," Section 5300 is entitled "Auditing for Compliance with Legislative and Related Authorities," and Section 5400 is entitled "Value-for-Money Auditing Standards." They were developed to provide guidance with respect to the three kinds of audits.

Financial audits and compliance audits have a long history; auditors have been performing them for some time. Value-for-money audits are a newer concept, and it is probably for that reason that the ASB (previously issued by the former PSAAB) had issued a series of Public Sector Auditing Recommendation Interpretations and Applications: Section 6150 "Using the Work of Internal Audit," Section 6410 "Planning for Value-for-Money Audits," Section 6420 "Knowledge of the Audit Entity," and Section 6430 "Engaging and Using Specialists."

Public Sector Auditing Recommendation General Standards Sections 5200 and 5300 are similar to the auditing standards in the *CICA Handbook* and will not be discussed further. Section 5400 will be dealt with in some detail since there are fairly significant differences between a financial audit and a value-for-money audit. At the same time, there are many similarities between an operational audit, discussed in the first part of this chapter, and a value-for-money audit.

VALUE-FOR-MONEY
AUDITS

OBJECTIVE 25-6

Understand the ASB
public sector
recommendations
relating to a
value-for-money
audit.

There are two general standards; the first is of particular interest because it recognizes the diversity of backgrounds that a value-for-money audit team will require. It states in paragraph 5400.10:

> The person or persons carrying out the examination should possess or collectively possess the knowledge and competence necessary to fulfill the requirements of the particular audit.

The knowledge and competence requirements are broader than for a financial audit.

The second general standard for value-for-money audits appears in paragraph .14 and states the requirements with respect to due care and an objective state of mind.

There are three examination standards for value-for-money audits; the first and third are similar to the first and third examination standards of GAAS discussed in Chapter 1 of the text. The second examination standard is very different from the GAAS second examination standard.

Earlier in this chapter, criteria for evaluating efficiency (and economy) and effectiveness were discussed. Recall that determining appropriate criteria to evaluate efficiency and effectiveness is often difficult for operational auditors. As you might imagine, selecting appropriate criteria for a value-for-money audit is also difficult but necessary. Paragraph 5400.24 states:

> Criteria for evaluating the matters subject to audit should be identified and the auditor should assess their suitability in the circumstances.

The following six paragraphs in the Standard expand on paragraph 5400.24.

The reporting standards for value-for-money audits are not as specific as the reporting standards of GAAS for financial statement audits discussed in Chapter 2 because every value-for-money audit, like every operational audit, is different and the report must be tailored to the audit. Paragraph 5400.37 recommends that the auditor's report should:

- Describe the objectives and the scope of the audit including any limitations therein.
- State that the examination was performed in accordance with the standards recommended in [Section 5400] and accordingly included such tests and other procedures as the auditor considered necessary in the circumstances.
- Identify the criteria [the auditor used] and describe the findings which form the basis for the auditor's conclusion.
- State the auditor's conclusions.

The report will vary depending on the auditor's mandate which is likely to vary from one government department to another and even within single departments. Like an operational audit report, the report may include the auditor's recommendations and management's response to those recommendations.

There are several other points worth noting in Section 5400. The section describes the different skills needed for a value-for-money audit and suggests an audit team might include persons with such diverse skills as engineering, statistical analysis, human resource management, and economics. The auditor in charge must be skilled in value-for-money auditing and also be able to coordinate the activities of these disparate specialists.

The auditor is concerned with the *significance* rather than the materiality of deviations or problems discovered; significance has more of a qualitative connotation and is therefore more appropriate than materiality, which has more of a quantitative connotation. For example, an auditor doing a value-for-money audit of the department of Citizenship & Immigration Canada, which deals with refugees, would probably assess the average processing time for an application and have to determine whether variances from departmental guidelines discovered were significant enough to report.

EFFECTIVENESS

OBJECTIVE 25-7

Report on effectiveness.

The reports that the Auditor General of Canada and the provincial auditors general provide to their respective legislatures are of the form called "direct reporting." Direct reporting was discussed in Chapter 23 and 24 in the discussions about standards for assurance engagements. The form of report is similar to that provided to management on completion of a management audit. The report summarizes the auditor's findings with respect to an entity or portion of an entity that was audited. The report may or may not contain recommendations by the auditor and may or may not include comments from management responding to the auditor's findings and recommendations. The important point is that the report is prepared by the auditor, and the contents are therefore the auditor's representations; remember, the representations in financial statements are those of management and the auditor's role is to provide an opinion on those representations.

The CCAF-FCVI set an independent panel to study how effectiveness could best be audited and reported. The panel's report was published in 1987; it recommended that management issue a report in which they would make representations about effectiveness and that auditors provide opinions on those representations. The panel suggested 12 attributes of effectiveness on which management would make the representations in its report.

The panel indicated that it believed the 12 attributes were a unit and suggested that all 12 attributes should be considered by management in making its representations. Management need not give all 12 attributes equal weight but should consider all 12; management should provide an explanation with respect to any attribute that was not considered. The 12 attributes of effectiveness are:

- Management direction
- Relevance
- Appropriateness
- Achievement of intended results
- Acceptance
- Secondary impacts
- Costs and productivity
- Responsiveness
- Financial results

- Working environment
- Protection of assets
- Monitoring and reporting[7]

SUMMARY

The value-for-money component of comprehensive auditing is becoming increasingly important as federal, provincial, and municipal governments, school boards, hospitals, universities, and all other public sector organizations try to deal with declining revenues and increasing costs. Accountability to those who confer responsibility and funding must be provided.

ESSENTIAL TERMS

Compliance audit — an audit of an organization's activities which is performed to determine whether the organization is following specific procedures or rules set down by some higher authority (p. 801).

Comprehensive audit — an audit in the public sector consisting of three components: (1) financial statement audit; (2) compliance audit; and (3) value-for-money audit covering economy, efficiency, and effectiveness (p. 800).

Economy — the degree to which goods and services of suitable quality are acquired at the lowest price (p. 789).

Effectiveness — the degree to which the organization's objectives are achieved (p. 789).

Efficiency — the degree to which costs are reduced without reducing effectiveness (p. 789).

Functional audit — an operational audit that deals with one or more specific functions within an organization, such as the payroll function or the production engineering function (p. 791).

Institute of Internal Auditors (IIA) — an organization for internal auditors that establishes ethical and practice standards; provides education, a professional exam and a professional designation; and encourages professionalism for its members (p. 788).

Operational auditing — the review of an organization for efficiency and effectiveness. The terms *management audit-*

ing, *performance auditing*, and *operational auditing* are often used synonymously (p. 789).

Organizational audit — an operational audit that deals with an entire organizational unit, such as a department, branch, or subsidiary, to determine how efficiently and effectively functions interact (p. 791).

Public sector — federal, provincial, territorial, and local governments, government organizations, organizations jointly owned by two or more governments, and school boards (p. 800).

Public Sector Accounting Board (PSAB) — a committee of the CICA that has the responsibility for establishing accounting standards for entities in the public sector (p. 800).

Special assignment — a management request for an operational audit for a specific purpose, such as investigating the possibility of fraud in a division or making recommendations for reducing the cost of a manufactured product (p. 791).

Standards for the Practice of Internal Auditing — guidelines issued by the Institute of Internal Auditors, covering the activities and conduct of internal auditors (p. 788).

Value-for-money audit — a public sector audit that considers the economy, efficiency, and effectiveness with which an entity's operations are conducted; see also *operational auditing* (p. 801).

---

[7]The source of the material on effectiveness is *Effectiveness: Reporting and Auditing in the Public Sector*, Ottawa: Canadian Comprehensive Auditing Foundation, 1987. The complete study and a summary report of it are available from the CCAF-FCVI. See also Leclerc, Guy, W. David Moynagh, Jean-Pierre Boisclair, and Hugh R. Hanson, *Accountability, Performance Reporting, Comprehensive Audit — An Integrated Perspective*, Ottawa: CCAF-FCVI, 1996, pp. 138–144.

25-1 Explain the role of internal auditors for financial auditing. How is it similar to and different from the role of external auditors?

25-2 Explain the difference in the independence of internal auditors and external auditors in the audit of historical financial statements. How can internal auditors best achieve independence?

25-3 Describe what is meant by an "operational audit."

25-4 Identify the three major differences between financial and operational auditing.

25-5 Distinguish between efficiency and effectiveness in operational audits. State one example of an operational audit explaining efficiency and another explaining effectiveness.

25-6 Identify the four concerns that management has in establishing internal controls. Explain how each of those four concerns can be part of operational auditing.

25-7 Distinguish among the following types of operational audits: functional, organizational, and special assignment. State an example of each for a hospital.

25-8 Explain why many people think of internal auditors as the primary group responsible for conducting operational audits.

25-9 Explain the role of public accountants in operational auditing. How is this similar to and different from the role of internal auditors?

25-10 Under what circumstances are external auditors likely to be involved in operational auditing? Give one example of operational auditing by a public accounting firm.

25-11 Explain what is meant by the "criteria for evaluating efficiency and effectiveness." Provide five possible specific criteria for evaluating effectiveness of an automated information system for payroll.

25-12 Identify the three phases of an operational audit.

25-13 Explain how planning for operational auditing is similar to and different from financial auditing.

25-14 What are the major differences between reporting for operational auditing and financial auditing?

25-15 Explain why the Auditor General of Canada performs comprehensive audits rather than simply performing financial audits of the various government departments.

25-16 Describe what the term "value-for-money audit" means.

25-17 What does the term "accountability" mean in the context of comprehensive auditing?

25-18 Why are criteria so important that they are mentioned specifically in Public Sector Auditing Recommendation 5400? What does the term "criteria" mean in this context? Provide an example of a criterion that might be used by an auditor in auditing the passenger service of Via Rail.

25-19 Explain the difference between the direct reporting by the Auditor General and the reporting on financial statements.

The following questions are adapted from CPA, CIA, and CMA (U.S.) examinations.

25-20 The following questions deal with independence of auditors who do operational auditing. Choose the best response.

a. The operational auditor's independence is most likely to be compromised when the internal audit department is responsible directly to the
   (1) president.
   (2) vice-president of finance.
   (3) controller.
   (4) audit committee of the board of directors.

b. The independence of the internal audit department will most likely be assured if it reports to the
   (1) president.
   (2) vice-president of finance.
   (3) treasurer.
   (4) audit committee of the board of directors.

c. Which of the following may compromise the independence of an internal auditor?
   (1) Performing an audit where the auditor recently had operating responsibilities
   (2) Failing to review the auditor's report with the auditee prior to distribution
   (3) Reviewing automated systems prior to implementation

   (4) Following up on corrective action in response to audit findings

d. Internal auditors should be objective in performing audits. Which of the following situations violates standards concerning objectivity?
   (1) The auditor reviews a department in which the auditor has the responsibility for cosigning cheques.
   (2) The auditor who reviews accounts receivable worked in that department for three months as a trainee two years ago.
   (3) The auditor reviews a department that continues to use procedures recommended by that auditor when the department was established.
   (4) The auditor reviews the same department for two years in succession.

25-21 The following questions deal with operational auditing. Choose the best response.

a. Which of the following best describes the operational audit?
   (1) It requires constant review by internal auditors of the administrative controls as they relate to the operations of the company.
   (2) It attempts and is designed to verify the fair presentation of a company's results of operations.

(3) It concentrates on seeking out aspects of operations for which waste would be reduced by the introduction of controls.

(4) It concentrates on implementing financial and accounting controls in a newly organized company.

b. Complaints from the public were received about processing automobile licence applications in the provincial Ministry of Transportation. You were assigned by the provincial Auditor General's office to review this operation. Which of the following should be your first audit step?

(1) Discuss the nature of the complaints with several licensing clerks.

(2) Discuss the nature of the complaints with the deputy minister in charge of motor vehicles licensing.

(3) Send out questionnaires to recent licensees.

(4) Test the system by licensing a vehicle.

c. The first step an operational auditor should take in performing a management study to help the director of marketing determine the optimum allocation of the advertising budget for company products is to

(1) establish and discuss with the director the key objectives of the study.

(2) analyze prior years' advertising costs.

(3) hold discussions with media personnel.

(4) determine the amount of projected sales for the purpose of establishing the proposed sales budget.

d. A preliminary survey of the human resources in a data-processing function includes a review of personnel records and practices. When the audit objective is to ascertain the economy of operation of the data-processing function, the internal auditor would seek evidence with respect to

(1) training programs that are in conformity with company policies and procedures.

(2) backup procedures relative to absenteeism, disability, and retirement.

(3) adequacy of the company's information dissemination procedures regarding personnel policies.

(4) assignment of personnel to tasks for which their education and training are appropriate.

25-22 The following questions deal with internal auditing departments and their responsibilities. Choose the best response.

a. Which of the following is generally considered to be a major reason for establishing an internal auditing function?

(1) To ensure that operating activities comply with the policies, plans, and procedures established by management

(2) To safeguard resources entrusted to the organization

(3) To ensure the accuracy, reliability, and timeliness of financial and operating data used in management's decision making

(4) To relieve overburdened management of the responsibility for establishing effective internal control

(5) To assist members of the organization in the measurement and evaluation of the effectiveness of established internal controls

b. Which of the following is generally considered to be the primary purpose of an internal auditor's evaluation of the adequacy of internal control?

(1) To determine if internal control is functioning as intended by management

(2) To determine if internal controls provide reasonable assurance that the objectives and goals of the organization will be met in an efficient and economical manner

(3) To determine the extent of reliance that the internal auditor can place on internal controls in the process of evaluating the financial statements prepared by the organization

(4) To determine if all risks and exposures of the enterprise have been reduced or eliminated by internal controls

DISCUSSION QUESTIONS AND PROBLEMS

25-23 Mont Louis Hospital, which is affiliated with a leading university, has an extremely reputable research department that employs several renowned scientists. The research department operates on a project basis. The department consists of a pool of scientists and technicians who can be called on to participate in a given project. Assignments are made for the duration of the project, and a project manager is given responsibility for the work.

All major projects undertaken by the research department must be approved by the hospital's administrative board. Approval is obtained by submitting a proposal to the board outlining the project, the expected amount of time required to complete the work, and the anticipated benefits. The board also must be informed of major projects that are terminated because of potential failure or technological changes that have occurred since the time of project approval. An

overall review of the status of open projects is submitted to the board annually.

In many respects, profit-making techniques utilized by business firms are applied to the management of the research department. For example, the department conducts preliminary research work on potential major projects that it has selected prior to requesting the board to approve the project and commit large amounts of time and money. The department also assesses the potential for grants and future revenues of the project. Financial reports for the department and each project are prepared periodically and reviewed with the administrative board.

Over 75 percent of the cost of operating the department is for labour. The remaining costs are for materials utilized during research. Materials used for experimentation are purchased by the hospital's central purchasing department.

Once these materials are delivered, the research department is held accountable for their storage, their utilization, and the assignment of their costs to the projects.

In order to protect the hospital's right to discoveries made by the research department, staff members are required to sign waiver agreements at the time of hire and at certain intervals thereafter. The agreements relinquish the employees' rights to patent and royalty fees relating to hospital work.

Mont Louis's excellent reputation is due in part to the success of the research department. The research department has produced quality research in the health-care field and has always been able to generate revenues in excess of its costs. Mont Louis's administrative board believes that the hospital's continued reputation depends on a strong research department, and therefore, the board has requested that the university's internal auditors perform an operational audit of the department. As part of its request for the operational audit, the board has presented the following set of objectives that the internal audit is to achieve.

The operational audit to be conducted by the university's internal audit department should provide assurances that

- the research department has assessed the revenues and cost aspects of each project to confirm that the revenue potential is equal to or greater than estimated costs.
- appropriate controls exist to provide a means to measure how projects are progressing and to identify if corrective actions are required.
- financial reports prepared by the research department for presentation to the administrative board properly reflect all revenues (both endowment and royalty sources and appropriated funding) and all costs.

Required

a. Evaluate the objectives presented by the administrative board to the university's internal audit department in terms of their appropriateness as objectives for an operational audit. Discuss fully
   (1) the strengths of the objectives.
   (2) the modifications and/or additions needed to improve the set of objectives.

b. Outline, in general terms, the basic procedures that would be suitable for performing the audit of the research department.

c. Identify three documents that members of the university's internal auditing staff would be expected to review during the audit, and describe the purpose that the review of each document serves in carrying out the audit.

(CMA adapted)

25-24 Lajod Ltd. has an internal audit department consisting of a manager and three staff auditors. The manager of internal audit reports to the corporate controller. Copies of audit reports are routinely sent to the audit committee of the board of directors as well as to the corporate controller and the individual responsible for the area or activity being audited.

The manager of internal audit is aware that the external auditors have relied on the internal audit function to a sub-

stantial degree in the past. However, in recent months, the external auditors have suggested that there may be a problem related to objectivity of the internal audit function. This objectivity problem may result in more extensive testing and analysis by the external auditors.

The external auditors are concerned about the amount of nonaudit work performed by the internal audit department. The percentage of nonaudit work performed by the internal auditors in recent years has increased to about 25 percent of their total hours worked. A sample of five recent nonaudit activities are as follows:

1. One of the internal auditors assisted in the preparation of policy statements on internal control. These statements included such things as policies regarding sensitive payments and standards of internal controls.

2. The bank statements of the corporation are reconciled each month as a regular assignment for one of the internal auditors. The corporate controller believes that this strengthens internal controls because the internal auditor is not involved in the receipt and disbursement of cash.

3. The internal auditors are asked to review the budget data in every area each year for relevance and reasonableness before the budget is approved. In addition, an internal auditor examines the variances each month, along with the associated explanations. These variance analyses are prepared by the corporate controller's staff after consultation with the individuals involved.

4. One of the internal auditors has recently been involved in the design, installation, and initial operation of a new computer system. The auditor was primarily concerned with the design and implementation of internal accounting controls and the computer application controls for the new system. The auditor also conducted the testing of the controls during the test runs.

5. The internal auditors are frequently asked to make accounting entries for complex transactions before the transactions are recorded. The employees in the accounting department are not adequately trained to handle such transactions. In addition, this serves as a means of maintaining internal control over complex transactions.

The manager of internal audits has always made an effort to remain independent of the corporate controller's office and believes that the internal auditors are objective and independent in their audit and nonaudit activities.

Required

a. Define "objectivity" as it relates to the internal audit function.

b. For each of the five situations outlined, explain whether the objectivity of Lajod Ltd.'s internal audit department has been materially impaired. Consider each situation independently.

c. The manager of internal audit reports to the corporate controller.
   (1) Does this reporting relationship result in a problem of objectivity? Explain your answer.

(2) Would your answer to any of the five situations in requirement (b) above have changed if the manager of internal audit reported to the audit committee of the board of directors? Explain your answer.

(CMA adapted)

25-25 Van Staveren Corporation has an internal audit department operating out of the corporate headquarters. Various types of audit assignments are performed by the department for the eight divisions of the company.

The following findings resulted from recent audits of Van Staveren Corporation's Maritimes Division.

1. One of the departments in the division appeared to have an excessive turnover rate. Upon investigation, the personnel department seemed to be unable to find enough workers with the specified skills for this particular department. Some workers are trained on the job. The departmental supervisor is held accountable for labour efficiency variances but does not have qualified staff or sufficient time to train the workers properly. The supervisor holds individual workers responsible for meeting predetermined standards from the day they report to work. This has resulted in a rapid turnover of workers who are trainable but not yet able to meet standards.

2. The internal audit department recently participated in a computer feasibility study for this division. It advised and concurred on the purchase and installation of a specific computer system. While the system is up and operating, the results are less than desirable. Although the software and hardware meet the specifications of the feasibility study, there are several functions unique to this division that the system has been unable to accomplish. Linking of files has been a particular problem. For example, several vendors have been paid for materials not meeting company specifications. A revision of the existing software is probably not possible, and a permanent solution probably requires replacing the existing computer system with a new one.

3. One of the products manufactured by this division was recently redesigned to eliminate a potential safety defect. This defect was discovered after several users were injured. At present, there are no pending lawsuits because none of the injured parties have identified a defect in the product as a cause of their injury. There is insufficient data to determine whether the defect was a contributing factor.

The director of internal auditing and assistant controller is in charge of the Internal Audit Department and reports to the controller in corporate headquarters. Copies of internal audit reports are sent routinely to Van Staveren's board of directors.

Required

a. Explain the additional steps in terms of field work, preparation of recommendations, and operating management review that ordinarily should be taken by Van Staveren Corporation's internal auditors as a conse-

quence of the audit findings in the first situation (excessive turnover).

b. Discuss whether there are any objectivity problems with Van Staveren Corporation's internal audit department as revealed by the audit findings. Include in your discussion any recommendations to eliminate or reduce an objectivity problem, if one exists.

c. The internal audit department is part of the corporate controllership function and copies of the internal audit reports are sent to the board of directors.
(1) Evaluate the appropriateness of the location of the internal audit department within Van Staveren's organizational structure.
(2) Discuss who within Van Staveren Corporation should receive the reports of the internal audit department.

(CMA adapted)

25-26 Haskin Inc. was founded 40 years ago and now has several manufacturing plants in Central and Western Canada. The evaluation of proposed capital expenditures became increasingly difficult for management as the company became geographically dispersed and diversified its product line. Thus, the Capital Budgeting Group was organized in 1997 to review all capital expenditure proposals in excess of $50,000.

The Capital Budgeting Group conducts its annual planning and budget meeting each September for the upcoming calendar year. The group establishes a minimum return for investments (hurdle rate) and estimates a target level of capital expenditures for the next year based on the expected available funds. The group then reviews the capital expenditure proposals that have been submitted by the various operating segments. Proposals that meet either the return on investment criterion or a critical need criterion are approved to the extent of available funds.

The Capital Budgeting Group also meets monthly, as necessary, to consider any projects of a critical nature that were not expected or requested in the annual budget review. These monthly meetings allow the Capital Budgeting Group to make adjustments during the year as new developments occur.

Haskin's profits have been decreasing slightly for the past two years in spite of a small but steady sales growth, a sales growth that is expected to continue through 2000. As a result of the profit stagnation, top management is emphasizing cost control, and all aspects of Haskin's operations are being reviewed for cost reduction opportunities.

Haskin's internal audit department has become involved in the company-wide cost reduction effort. The department has already identified several areas where cost reductions could be realized and has made recommendations to implement the necessary procedures to effect the cost savings. Tom Watson, internal audit director, is now focusing on the activities of the Capital Budgeting Group in an attempt to determine the efficiency and effectiveness of the capital budgeting process.

In an attempt to gain a better understanding of the capital budgeting process, Watson decided to examine the history of one capital project in detail. A capital expenditure proposal of Haskin's Regina plant that was approved by the Capital Budgeting Group in 1999 was selected randomly from a population of all proposals approved by the group at its 1998 and 1999 annual planning and budget meetings.

The Regina proposal consisted of a request for five new machines to replace equipment that was 20 years old and for which preventive maintenance had become very expensive. Four of the machines were for replacement purposes, and the fifth was for planned growth in demand. Each of the four replacement machines was expected to result in annual maintenance cost savings of $10,000. The fifth machine was exactly like the other four and was expected to generate an annual contribution of $15,000 through increased output. Each machine cost $50,000 and had an estimated useful life of eight years.

Required

a. Identify and discuss the issues that Haskin Inc.'s internal audit department must address in its examination and evaluation of the Regina plant's 1999 capital expenditure project.

b. Recommend procedures to be used by Haskin's internal audit department in the audit review of the Regina plant's 1999 capital expenditure project.

(CMA adapted)

25-27 Lecimore Limited has a centralized purchasing department that is managed by Joan Jones. Jones has established policies and procedures to guide the clerical staff and purchasing agents in the day-to-day operation of the department. She is satisfied that these policies and procedures are in conformity with company objectives and believes there are no major problems in the regular operations of the purchasing department.

Lecimore's internal audit department was assigned to perform an operational audit of the purchasing function. Its first task was to review the specific policies and procedures established by Jones. The policies and procedures are as follows:

- All significant purchases are made on a competitive bid basis. The probability of timely delivery, reliability of vendor, and so forth, are taken into consideration on a subjective basis.
- Detailed specifications of the minimum acceptable quality for all goods purchased are provided to vendors.
- Vendors' adherence to the quality specifications is the responsibility of the materials manager of the inventory control department and not the purchasing department. The materials manager inspects the goods as they arrive to be sure that the quality meets the minimum standards and then sees that the goods are transferred from the receiving dock to the storeroom.

- All purchase requests are prepared by the materials manager based on the production schedule for a four-month period.

The internal audit staff then observed the operations of the purchasing function and gathered the following findings:

- One vendor provides 90 percent of a critical raw material. This vendor has a good delivery record and is very reliable. Furthermore, this vendor has been the low bidder over the past few years.
- As production plans change, rush and expedite orders are made by production directly to the purchasing department. Materials ordered for cancelled production runs are stored for future use. The costs of these special requests are borne by the purchasing department. Jones considers the additional costs associated with these special requests as "costs of being a good member of the corporate team."
- Materials to accomplish engineering changes are ordered by the purchasing department as soon as the changes are made by the engineering department. Jones is very proud of the quick response by the purchasing staff to product changes. Materials on hand are not reviewed before any orders are placed.
- Partial shipments and advance shipments (i.e., those received before the requested date of delivery) are accepted by the materials manager who notifies the purchasing department of the receipt. The purchasing department is responsible for follow-up on partial shipments. No action is taken to discourage advance shipments.

Required

Based on the purchasing department's policies and procedures and the findings of Lecimore's internal audit staff:

a. Identify weaknesses and/or inefficiencies in Lecimore Limited's purchasing function.

b. State the impact of the weakness on the operations of the purchasing function.

c. Make recommendations for those weaknesses/inefficiencies that you identify.

Use the following format in preparing your response.

WEAKNESSES/ INEFFICIENCIES	IMPLICATIONS	RECOMMENDATIONS

(CMA adapted)

25-28 Superior Ltd. manufactures automobile parts for sale to major Canadian automakers. Superior's internal audit staff is to review the internal controls over machinery and equipment and make recommendations for improvements where appropriate.

The internal auditors obtained the following information during the assignment.

- Requests for purchase of machinery and equipment are normally initiated by the supervisor in need of the asset. The supervisor discusses the proposed acquisition with the plant manager. A purchase requisition is submitted to the purchasing department when the plant manager is satisfied that the request is reasonable and if there is a remaining balance in the plant's share of the total corporate budget for capital acquisitions.
- Upon receiving a purchase requisition for machinery or equipment, the purchasing department manager looks through the records for an appropriate supplier. A formal purchase order is then completed and mailed. When the machine or equipment is received, it is immediately sent to the user department for installation. This allows the economic benefits from the acquisition to be realized at the earliest possible date.
- The property, plant, and equipment ledger control accounts are supported by lapsing schedules organized by year of acquisition. These lapsing schedules are used to compute amoritization as a unit for all assets of a given type that are acquired in the same year. Standard rates, amortization methods, and salvage values are used for each major type of capital asset. These rates, methods, and salvage values were set 10 years ago during the company's initial year of operation.
- When machinery or equipment is retired, the plant manager notifies the accounting department so that the appropriate entries can be made in the accounting records.
- There has been no reconciliation since the company began operations between the accounting records and the machinery and equipment on hand.

Required

Identify the internal control weaknesses and operational implications of those weaknesses, and recommend improvements that the internal audit staff of Superior Ltd. should include in its report regarding the internal controls employed for capital assets. Use the following format in preparing your answer.

WEAKNESSES	IMPLICATIONS	RECOMMEN-DATIONS

25-29 You noticed the following job advertisement that appeared in a recent edition of the *Capital City Journal:*

PROVINCIAL MINISTRY OF HEALTH

The Province funds 20 autonomously operated hospitals. The Ministry is currently involved in a project to improve hospital service and, at the same time, achieve cost control. In this regard, we are looking for a Coordinator of Hospital Comprehensive Audits (Coordinator) to introduce comprehensive auditing into the hospitals.

You, as Coordinator, would be responsible for coordinating and evaluating the comprehensive audits at the 20 hospitals and providing direction and guidance to the hospitals as necessary. You would report directly to the Deputy Minister of Health.

Qualifications

The successful candidate will have a professional accounting designation. The position demands initiative, self-confidence, superior communication and motivational skills, and the ability to sell ideas.

Apply in confidence to the address below. Submit a brief report, addressed to the Deputy Minister, discussing the role of comprehensive auditing in hospitals and how you would convince the executive directors of the individual hospitals of the benefits of comprehensive auditing.

The Ministry of Health is an equal opportunity employer.

> Deputy Minister
> Ministry of Health
> P. O. Box 007
> Capital City
> O0O 1L1

Required

Draft the report requested in the advertisement.

(CICA adapted)

INDEX